Financial Accounting

A DECISION-MAKING APPROACH

THOMAS E. KING
Southern Illinois University at Edwardsville

VALDEAN C. LEMBKE
The University of Iowa

JOHN H. SMITH
Northern Illinois University

JOHN WILEY & SONS, INC.

NEW YORK CHICHESTER WEINHEIM BRISBANE SINGAPORE TORONTO

ACQUISITIONS EDITOR	Mark Bonadeo
MARKETING MANAGER	Clancy Marshall
SENIOR PRODUCTION EDITORS	Kelly Tavares/Robin Factor
SENIOR DESIGNER	Harold Nolan
PHOTO DEPARTMENT MANAGER	Hilary Newman
PHOTO RESEARCHER	Teri Stratford
ILLUSTRATION COORDINATOR	Sandra Rigby
ART STUDIO	Illustrations updated by Matrix Art Services
COVER PHOTOGRAPH	© Chad Ehlers/Tony Stone Images, New York

This book was set in Times Roman by UG / GGS Information Services, Inc. and printed and bound by Von Hoffmann Press. The cover was printed by Phoenix Color.

This book is printed on acid free paper.

ISBN 0-471-32823-5

Printed in the United States of America

10 9 8 7 6 5 4 3 2 1

About the Authors

THOMAS E. KING, CPA, is Professor of Accounting in the School of Business at Southern Illinois University at Edwardsville, where he served as Chairman of the Accounting Department for seven years. He received his B.S. degree in accounting from California State University, Northridge, and holds an M.B.A. and Ph.D. from the University of California, Los Angeles. Professor King has a number of years of business and consulting experience, and he has been teaching for more than 20 years. He previously was on the faculty of The University of Iowa and has taught courses for the Illinois and Iowa CPA Societies, the Iowa Department of Revenue, the Institute of Internal Auditors, and a major international CPA firm. Professor King has published numerous articles in journals such as *The Accounting Review*, the *Journal of Accounting, Auditing, and Finance, Accounting Horizons*, the *Journal of Accountancy*, and *Financial Executive*. He also coauthored *Advanced Financial Accounting*, now in its fourth edition. Professor King recently completed his second term on the Board of Governors of the St. Louis Chapter of the Institute of Internal Auditors and is active in the Financial Executives Institute and the Institute of Management Accountants. In addition, he serves on the editorial boards of *Advances in Accounting* and *Advances in Accounting Education*. Professor King has taught financial and managerial accounting at all levels and has had a special interest in presenting accounting information so that it can be understood and used by non-accountants.

VALDEAN C. LEMBKE is Professor of Accounting in the College of Business Administration at The University of Iowa. He received his B.S. degree from Iowa State University and his MBA and Ph.D. from the University of Michigan. He has internal audit and public accounting experience. He has been active in the American Accounting Association, including service as President of the Midwest Region and book review editor for *Issues in Accounting Education*. Professor Lembke has been a faculty member at The University of Iowa for more than 25 years, where he was named the first recipient of the Gilbert Maynard Excellence in Accounting Instruction award. He has served two terms as department head and is currently head of the professional program in accounting. Professor Lembke has authored or coauthored articles in *The Accounting Review*, the *Journal of Accounting, Auditing, and Finance*, the *Journal of Accountancy*, and the *Internal Auditor*. He also coauthored an advanced financial accounting textbook with Richard Baker and Thomas King. His teaching has been in undergraduate and graduate financial accounting and governmental and not-for-profit accounting coursework, including responsibility for the introductory financial accounting course.

JOHN H. SMITH, CPA, is Professor of Accountancy, Emeritus, at Northern Illinois University in DeKalb, Illinois. He has served as Accounting Department Chairman at Northern Illinois University and at The University of Iowa. He has held visiting professorships at the University of Hawaii and has been a staff member in the Office of the Chief Accountant of The Securities and Exchange Commission. He also has experience with a major international public accounting firm. Professor Smith holds a Ph.D. from the University of Illinois and M.A. and B.B.A. degrees from the University of Missouri. He has published in numerous journals and has held offices in academic and professional accounting organizations. He also led the task force that organized the 150-hour education requirement in Illinois. He has taught introductory accounting and all levels of financial accounting, including financial accounting for non-accountants at the S.E.C and in numerous other programs. He has won awards for teaching excellence at both the undergraduate and M.B.A. levels. Teaching accounting to business managers has led to a lifelong interest in improving the instruction of accounting and is reflected in this textbook. Professor Smith believes that accounting should be a manager's best friend.

PHOTO CREDITS

Preface

Relevant and reliable information has become the key to success, and even survival, in today's rapidly changing business world. In the competitive world of business, the decision maker with the best information, and the best understanding of that information, is likely to be the winner. All students of business and management will ultimately use accounting information, and the better they understand it, the better they will be able to use it to make wise decisions.

Although they won't necessarily need the detailed knowledge that an accountant is expected to have, students must gain more than just a working knowledge of accounting terminology. They need to understand what the accounting numbers are telling them and how that relates to their decisions.

USING ACCOUNTING INFORMATION WISELY: THE GOALS OF THIS TEXT

Financial Accounting: A Decision-Making Approach has been designed to provide students with a general perspective and knowledge of accounting that will support real-world decision making. Specifically, this text will

- Help students understand how events are currently reported in financial statements and how specific items of reported financial information are used for business decisions.

- Provide the means for students to link their understanding of accounting to the requirements of the specific financial decisions for which the information will be used.

- Help students understand the elements that make up external accounting reports, how the information is selected and recorded, and how the accounting process affects the way the information can be used for decisions.

Financial decision makers who understand how the accounting process measures real-word events and accumulates, classifies, summarizes, and reports information about these events can use financial accounting information wisely.

THE FRAMEWORK FOR MAKING SUCCESSFUL BUSINESS DECISIONS: KEY FEATURES OF THIS TEXT

We view *Financial Accounting: A Decision-Making Approach* as reflecting an evolutionary rather than revolutionary change in the approach used to help students understand accounting. Therefore, we have maintained the traditional focus on understanding the elements of the financial statements. However, we do not concentrate on the mechanics of the accounting process. Instead, we have carefully crafted this text to teach students how to use accounting information for making decisions. Here are some highlights of the Second Edition:

DECISIONS LINKED TO FINANCIAL INFORMATION

Accounting comes alive when it is used rather than just studied. In each chapter after Chapter 1 (and excluding Chapter 7 on the accounting process), we have reinforced the link between business decisions and the need to understand accounting information. We begin each major topic with a feature new to the Second Edition called **Information for Decisions**, a summary of the accounting information that will be discussed and the types of decisions that business people make with that information. Several sample decision questions show students how financial decision makers benefit from understanding the material presented. This link between the topic and real decisions is continued into the end-of-chapter materials as well.

ABUNDANT REAL-WORLD EXAMPLES

Never before in history has understanding the details of financial reports been so important before making business decisions. In the Second Edition more financial statements from actual companies have been introduced early in the book (Chapters 1 and 2) so students can begin focusing on the types of accounting reports they will be studying throughout the course. And throughout the text, accounting concepts are supported by examples from the current financial reports of real companies.

UNDERSTANDING THE NEW INFORMATION AGE: GATEWAY, INC.

We have chosen Gateway, Inc.'s annual report to illustrate throughout the text how accounting information is used for decisions. Gateway is an excellent example of the new model of a flexible manufacturing company. For this type of company, the traditional measures of "return on investment" do not work very well and can be misleading. To understand Gateway, you must understand the detailed financial information it reports about its activities and its customer base.

THE ROLE OF CASH FLOWS IN THE DECISION-MAKING PROCESS

To allow discussion of the importance of cash flows in decision making early in the discussion of accounting, the chapter on cash flows has been moved from Chapter 4 in the First Edition to Chapter 3 in the Second Edition. In doing this, we have also streamlined the discussion of cash flows and deleted some peripheral topics. This earlier placement also facilitates comparisons when accrual accounting is discussed in detail in Chapter 4.

The time-value of money discussion has been consolidated in the second half of Chapter 3 and separated as Part II. Although we have introduced the time-value concepts in a very simple, understandable way and think that students need to understand the importance of the timing of cash flows in financial decisions early in the course, this arrangement of the chapter makes it possible to delay coverage of this topic until later in this course or to a subsequent course.

AN ACTIVE LEARNING ENVIRONMENT

Throughout the text, students are encouraged to read actively. One way this is done is by posing questions for students to think about before reading, such as in the **Information for Decisions** feature. In addition, **You Decide** situations in each chapter reinforce an understanding of how accounting information is used or encourage students to think beyond the specifics of the chapter presentation. The end-of-chapter materials are designed to support and reinforce both the decision-making focus of the book and the active learning environment.

A significant new feature in the Second Edition is the **Annual Report Project**, in which students select a company of interest to them and follow it throughout their study of accounting. By answering questions on the chapter topic with information about the company they have chosen, students learn to apply accounting to real situations.

ACCOUNTING PROCEDURES

What do introductory accounting students need to know about the procedural system that generates the information used for business decisions? Do they need to know about journal entries? This is a difficult question on which many instructors disagree. As the features of our text show, we believe that the first course in financial accounting should emphasize the use of accounting information for making wise decisions. However, as in any other technical field, understanding the outcome that is reported often requires some understanding of the process that generated that outcome.

Our solution is to avoid detailed discussions of accounting mechanics in the first six chapters. In this way, students can focus on the general meaning of the accounting information and how it is linked to financial decisions without becoming bogged down in mechanics. Chapter 7 then provides a concise description of the mechanics of the accounting process, illustrated with journal entries. This chapter is largely self-contained and could be omitted. However, we believe that the procedural material in Chapter 7 strengthens the student's appreciation of the information reported in financial statements.

Subsequent chapters explore each of the financial statement elements in more detail, again focusing on using the information, and do not depend on Chapter 7 or the use of journal entries. All discussions are presented in terms of financial statement effects, with a visual presentation of the financial statement effects accompanying the discussion. However, for those who wish to use them, journal entries are presented within these chapters, set off from the main presentation so not to intrude on the discussion. However, they are readily available for those instructors who choose to use them.

THE BOOK AT A GLANCE

ORGANIZATION

Several sections of the text were rearranged and shortened in the Second Edition to improve the flow of the discussion. For several topics, complex applications were moved to an appendix or, in some cases deleted, so that the main focus would remain on gaining a solid understanding of basic accounting.

The organization of the text provides flexibility in the choice of materials to be covered in a one-semester course, as follows:

Basic framework and key concepts, including cash flows	Chapters 1–3
Accrual accounting: reporting income and financial position	Chapters 4–6
The accounting process	Chapter 7
Financial statement elements	Chapters 8–13
Special topics	Chapters 14–16

We anticipate that most instructors will include Chapters 1 to 13 in a one-semester course. As mentioned previously, we discuss and illustrate the analysis of cash flows and the use of time value of money concepts in Part II of Chapter 3. These concepts are presented in the context of both business and personal decisions. Some faculty may prefer to cover this topic later in the course, and the organization of the text facilitates this choice. Chapter 7 is a relatively self-contained unit that provides coverage of the basic accounting process. Chapters 1–13 provide the basics of accounting and reporting. Chapters 14–16 cover selected topics in somewhat greater depth and may be used in total or in part, as time permits. Some instructors have used parts of these chapters in combination with earlier chapters. For example, the effects of the exchange of foreign currencies on accounts receivable, discussed in Chapter 16, may be covered with the material on accounts receivable in Chapter 8. Chapter 15 summarizes the financial ratios and techniques for analysis introduced in earlier chapters. Instructors may wish to use this part of Chapter 15 as a capstone for the course.

LEARNING AIDS IN THE SECOND EDITION

The learning aids featured in the First Edition have been continued in this edition. Users of the text liked the way these features helped students focus on the links between financial decisions and reported accounting information. In the Second Edition, several pedagogical improvements have been made to guide and support students in their study.

Where This Chapter Fits.   Each chapter begins with this new feature that places the chapter in the overall scheme of the book. Students see a brief review of the material from previous chapters, a quick overview of the chapter coverage, and a taste of what lies ahead.

The Personal View and The Business View.   Next, **The Personal View** helps the students to relate to the chapter material on a personal level, and **The Business View** illustrates an aspect of real-world organizational decision making that is relevant to the chapter coverage.

Information for Decisions.   New to the Second Edition, this important and unique feature begins the major topics of each chapter (excluding Chapters 1 and 7). It identifies the information to be discussed in the section and directly links this information to decisions by posing several questions that can be answered with the information. The direct link between accounting information and decision making is completed in the end-of-chapter materials, where students are asked to answer specific decision questions.

You Decide.   Throughout the chapters, these active learning scenarios present students with a variety of situations in which to either apply the concepts discussed or go beyond the discussion. Most of these thinking exercises do not have a single correct answer but rather challenge students to be creative in addressing issues or making decisions. They make excellent starting points for class discussion.

Company Financial Statements.   The financial statements of **Hewlett-Packard** are included in Chapter 1 to focus students on the importance of reported financial information. Many other examples of real-company financial statements are included throughout the text.

Updated in this edition, the **In Practice** feature offers many examples from companies' current financial reports to illustrate specific points and emphasize different aspects of financial reporting and the accounting process. Each example includes an *Analysis* section that helps students understand what lies beneath the reported numbers and ties the example to the concepts discussed in the chapter. Web addresses are included for all companies used in these illustrations and in examples throughout the text.

The full set of financial statements of **Gateway, Inc.**, along with other selected portions of Gateway's annual report, are included in an appendix to the text, and the individual financial statements are incorporated where relevant in selected chapters.

Our Video Store.   This hypothetical example used in the First Edition is continued and expanded in this edition. It begins in Chapter 1 and is used throughout the early chapters to illustrate basic accounting principles and to provide students with an intuitive understanding of the need for accounting information. Discussions related to this example are marked with a logo in the margin.

A Closer Look At.   The text is richly illustrated with numerous focused examples. The many hypothetical examples, highlighted in **A Closer Look At** boxes, are spread throughout the text to clarify the discussion and illustrate specific points in greater detail. The use of hypothetical examples permits students to concentrate on the specific point being discussed without the complication of other factors.

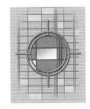

Financial Statement Effects.   In all hypothetical examples when an event or transaction would affect the financial statements, the effects are shown in the margin as increases or decreases in the balance sheet (assets, liabilities, and owners' equity) and income statement (revenue and expenses). This marginal notation provides the students with an easy way to see the link between financial transactions and financial statement reporting.

End-of-Chapter Assignments.   The end-of-chapter materials have been revised and significantly expanded. Many new exercises have been added to focus on mastering basic concepts and their application throughout the text, and the link between the end-of-chapter materials and the text discussion has been strengthened. These extensive materials contain a wide variety of assignments and are grouped as follows to facilitate selection:

- *Examining the Concepts.*   These questions review basic definitions, terminology, and concepts and how they relate to information in financial reports.

- *Understanding Accounting Information.*   These are exercises in which students apply the basic concepts developed in the chapter and relate the material to financial statement information. The first several exercises in each chapter are decision focused and linked to each of the major chapter headings and to the questions in the **Information for Decisions** that follow each chapter heading. Multiple-choice exercises and individual-issue exercises help students understand the nature of the accounting information discussed in the chapter before they proceed to use the information for decision making. The number of exercises in this section has been increased significantly in this edition to 35–40 per chapter.

- *Using Accounting for Decision Making.*   These problems provide an opportunity to deal with more complex issues and to apply accounting information to decision-making situations. A number of additional problems of this type have been added to this edition.

- *Expanding Your Horizons.*   A variety of case materials, special team projects, and library or Internet assignments (marked with a research icon) help build further understanding of the ways financial information is presented by different companies and the ways this information can be used in making decisions. Most chapters have an ethics case and cases using actual financial reports taken from the Internet or from companies' annual reports.

- *Internet Exercises.* Additional exercises can be found at **www.wiley.com/ college/king.**

- *Annual Report Project.* In this continuing project, students select a company of interest to them or one assigned by their instructor from the recommended list on the Web site and follow it throughout their study of accounting. At the end of each chapter, students learn to apply accounting to real situations by answering questions as they relate to the companies they have chosen.

Appendices. Selected chapters include appendices that contain topics that are less central to the study of accounting and that some, but not all, instructors may choose to cover. End-of-chapter materials relating to the chapter appendices are marked.

The financial statements and other excerpts from the annual report of Gateway, Inc., appear in Appendix A at the end of the book. Appendix B includes present value and future value tables.

Glossary. A comprehensive glossary is provided at the end of the text and includes all of the important terms highlighted in the book, as well as other terms that are useful in understanding accounting.

SUPPLEMENTS

We have worked with contributors to develop a complete set of valuable supplemental materials to assist students and instructors. Following is a description of each of the available supplements.

Web Site. Recognizing that the Internet is a viable resource for students and instructors, we have developed a Web site at **www.wiley.com/college/king** to provide a variety of additional resources, including Internet exercises on current topics. Because the financial statements of actual companies are used extensively in the text, instructors and students may also wish to look at the Web sites of those companies for updates and more information. The Web address is provided, where available, for all company examples used in the text.

Student Study Guide. We have developed a comprehensive student guide that is closely coordinated with the text materials. Each chapter begins with a summary of key points in the chapter. Demonstration problems follow the key points. Numerous fill-in-the-blanks, true-false, and multiple-choice questions, along with short exercises, help students gain a better understanding of key points. These are followed by one or more comprehensive problems that students can use for review. Solutions are provided for all questions, exercises, and problems.

WebCT. Available to adopters of *Financial Accounting*, WebCT is an integrated set of course management tools that enable instructors to easily design, develop, and manage Web-based and Web-enhanced courses. The Wiley *Financial Accounting* WebCT course is the WebCT shell, with all its course management features, filled with Wiley content; it is an on-line learning and resource guide for the student. This WebCT course allows the instructor to present all or part of a course on-line and helps the student organize the course material, understand key concepts, and access additional on-line resources and tools. Your Wiley WebCT course can be customized by the instructor. Contact your Wiley representative for more information.

Solutions Manual. A comprehensive solutions manual prepared by the authors provides solutions to all end-of-chapter assignments. In many cases, the solutions manual goes well beyond the minimum answer needed to respond adequately to the item assigned. Answers include computations and detailed explanations that facilitate instructor use and can assist students in gaining mastery of the materials if the manual is placed in the library or otherwise made available to students. Instructors can prepare transparencies directly from the solutions manual or may choose from the transparency package.

Test Bank and Computerized Test Bank. A comprehensive set of test items consisting of both conceptual and applied questions has been prepared on a chapter-by-chapter basis and is available in either a hard copy or computerized format. True-false, multiple choice, and fill-in-the-blanks questions are provided, along with a series of short problems and cases. Where appropriate, one or more comprehensive problems have been provided.

Instructor's Resource Guide. This guide provides a variety of support materials for the instructor such as providing a consistent and thorough discussion of points to be considered for each *You Decide* situation presented in the text. In addition, outlines for the organization of lectures and the presentation of chapter materials are provided. More important, suggestions are provided throughout for ways to use the text and to present class materials more effectively. Additional examples for use in class are provided, along with aids to assist in the discussion and evaluation of assignments.

Solutions Transparencies. A package of solutions for selected exercises, problems, and cases is available to adopters.

PowerPoint Slide Presentations. A special electronic presentation package has been prepared to facilitate classroom instruction. The package includes both outline materials from the chapters and specific examples of accounting and reporting procedures. Instructors with a full version of PowerPoint can modify the presentations to match their own particular teaching styles. These presentations are available for download at the Web site (**http://www.wiley.com/college/king**).

Nightly Business Report Video. This video contains a series of clips from the highly respected *Nightly Business Report* that have been selected for their applicability to financial accounting and for their reinforcement of key concepts in the text. Each of the segments is approximately 3 to 5 minutes long and can be used to introduce topics to the students, enhance lecture material, and provide real-world examples. An Instructor's Manual with suggestions for using the material accompanies the video.

ACKNOWLEDGMENTS

The development and completion of a project of this magnitude required the collaboration of many individuals and organizations, and we are very grateful to all who participated. The following individuals reviewed the text at various stages, and their creative suggestions and ideas significantly influenced the content, sequencing, and presentation of the current edition.

Reviewers for *Financial Accounting: A Decision-Making Approach***, First Edition**
Richard Anderson, *Stonehill College*
Nancy Bagranoff, *The American University*
Larry Bailey, *Rider University*
Angela Bell, *Jacksonville State University*
Maureen Crane, *California State University, Fresno*

Richard Cross, *Bentley College*
Dean Edmiston, *Emporia State University*
Anita Feller, *University of Illinois*
James Greenspan, *University of Cincinnati*
Philip Jagolinzer, *University of Southern Maine*
Edward Ketz, *Pennsylvania State University*
Philip Landers, *Pennsylvania College of Technology*

Linda Malgeri, *Kennesaw State College*
Robert Maust, *West Virginia University*
Mary Maury, *St. John's University*
David Plumlee, *University of Kansas*
Mary Ann Reynolds, *University of Puget Sound*
Ralph Rumble, *Kankakee Community College*
Douglas Sharp, *Wichita State University*
Joanne Sheridan, *Montana State University–Billings*
Philip Siegel, *University of Houston–Downtown*
Kathleen Simons, *Bryant College*
Anita Stellenwerf, *Ramapo College of New Jersey*
Katherene Terrell, *University of Central Oklahoma*
Mary Tharp, *Kirkwood Community College*
Dean Wallace, *Collin Country Community College*
Michael Welker, *Drexel University*
Tom White, *College of William and Mary*
Gail Wright, *Bryant College*

Reviewers for *Financial Accounting: A Decision-Making Approach*, Second Edition
James Bannister, *University of Hartford*
Nancy Boyd, *Middle Tennessee State University*
Ken M. Boze, *University of Alaska–Anchorage*
Thomas Buchman, *University of Washington*
Sandy Callaghan, *Texas Christian University*
Somnath Das, *University of Illinois at Chicago*

Allan Falcon, *Loyola Marymount University*
Gloria Grayless, *Sam Houston State University*
David Guenther, *University of Connecticut*
Susan A. Lynn, *University of Baltimore*
Kevin Misiewicz, *University of Notre Dame*
Debra A. McGilsky, *Central Michigan University*
Norlin Rueschhoff, *University of Notre Dame*
Shahrokh Saudagaran, *Santa Clara University*
Ragnor Seglund, *California State University, Sacramento*
Kenneth Shaw, *University of Maryland*
Kathleen Simons, *Bryant College*

Ancillary Authors and Contributors
Elsie Ameen, *Sam Houston State University*, Test Bank author
Denise English, *Boise State University*, PowerPoint author
Jessica Frazier, *Eastern Kentucky University*, Internet exercises and NBR Video preparer
Gloria Grayless, *Sam Houston State University*, Test Bank author
Alice Ketchand, *Sam Houston State University*, Test Bank author
Elizabeth Mauch, *Southern Illinois University*, Solutions Manual accuracy checker
Linda Sweeney, *Sam Houston State University*, Test Bank author

A special debt of gratitude goes to the staff at John Wiley & Sons, Inc., for their efforts on behalf of this project, and especially to Susan Elbe, Publisher; Mark Bonadeo, Acqusitions Editor; Julie Kerr, Associate Editor; Clancy Marshall, Marketing Manager; Kelly Tavares and Robin Factor, Senior Production Editors; Harry Nolan, Senior Designer; Hilary Newman, Photo Department Manager; Teri Stratford, Photo Researcher; Sandra Rigby, Illustrations Coordinator; Dana Bigelow, Editorial Assistant; Ilse Wolfe, Executive Marketing Manager; and Joanne White and Terry Ann Kremer, freelance Editors. The project was certainly a team effort, and we very much appreciate the considerable efforts of everyone involved.

Out greatest thanks are reserved for our wives who continued to provide support and encouragement over the past several years as we have worked on this project. To Robin, Lois, and Stephanie, we salute your patience, thoughtfulness, and endurance.

Thomas E. King
Valdean C. Lembke
John H. Smith

Table of Contents

CHAPTER 9 PREPAID EXPENSES AND INVENTORIES   328

CHAPTER 10 OPERATING ASSETS AND INTANGIBLES   366

SECOND EDITION

Financial Accounting

A DECISION-MAKING APPROACH

CHAPTER ONE

Decision Making and Information

WHERE THIS CHAPTER FITS

Chapter 1 introduces the process of decision making and how information is used for decision making. It explores decision making in the context of a market economy, and it introduces accounting by linking accounting information to the financial decisions that are made in a market economy.

LOOKING AHEAD

Chapter 2 continues with a discussion of how information is communicated in financial statements and the ways in which that information is used in making decisions. Subsequent chapters address the different areas of financial reporting in relation to specific information needs of decision makers.

Decisions, decisions, decisions! Life is full of decisions. What should I wear to class? Should I do my homework or go to the mall? Should I get a part-time job so I can afford a car? Should I go to graduate school, or is it not worth the cost? Should I enter the *Reader's Digest* Sweepstakes, or is it a waste of a good stamp? Boy, all of this thinking makes me hungry! Let's forget about making decisions and just chow down. Hmm, what am I going to eat—an apple or a Big Mac?

"When Harvey Harris started selling elaborate cut-rate personalized calendars in 1992, he anticipated strong demand. But not so strong that it would ruin him. In January, his Oklahoma City-based concern, Grandmother Calendar Co., went out of business. Mr. Harris blames the company's demise on an excess of success. 'I'm a salesman, and a good one, that started this company up and it exploded and just went crazy,' he told the Daily Oklahoman. . . . The hotter the item, the more quickly and deeply an inexperienced entrepreneur can get into trouble. . . . [Mr. Harris] said 'I'm not an accountant. I made mistakes and did not track receivables, payables, the funding. I should have made, well, better decisions.' "[1]

[1] Louise Lee, "A Company Failing From Too Much Success," *The Wall Street Journal*, March 17, 1995, p. Bl.

E veryone is a decision maker. In fact, people make hundreds of decisions every day. Many of these decisions can be made easily, while others require careful analysis. The decision to use an umbrella on a rainy day needs little consideration, but choosing a career may involve extensive thought. Furthermore, all of us not only make decisions, but we are continually affected by the results of our decisions (e.g., how much time we devote to studying) and also those of others (e.g., how much homework the professor assigns). Decisions are an important part of our lives, and a knowledge of the decision-making process can help us better understand how to approach choices.

Regardless of the complexity, all decisions require that some kind of information be used in making appropriate choices. Information may be obvious or quite subtle. It may be generated specifically for the decision or derived from past memory or intuition. This text focuses on one type of information that is used to make a variety of decisions: accounting information.

Accounting is often referred to as the "language of business" because it is so important in communicating the relevant knowledge decision makers need to make informed business choices. For example, bankers use accounting information when they make loan decisions, and stockbrokers use accounting information when they recommend investments.

Accounting information exists because it has value for making decisions. The focus of this book is on understanding accounting information so that you can use it to help make decisions. Because accounting and decision making are so intertwined, we'll start our study of accounting with a look at the decision-making process. Then, we'll look at the role that information, specifically accounting information, plays in decision making. After reading this chapter, you should be able to:

1. Understand and apply the steps of the decision-making process.

2. Indicate the major differences between a market economy and a planned economy, and explain the role that information plays in both.

3. Describe the different forms of business organization found in the United States, and explain the major advantages and disadvantages of each.

4. Describe the nature of accounting information and explain how it differs from other types of information.

5. Describe how each part of the accounting process results in useful information for decision makers.

THE DECISION-MAKING PROCESS

A **decision**, very simply, is a choice between two or more alternatives. We all are familiar with making decisions, but we seldom think much about the steps in the process of making these decisions. Let's take a closer look.

A FAMILIAR DECISION

To help understand the decision-making process, let's consider a familiar decision as an example—the purchase of a car—and think about the steps we go through in making the decision. Suppose you are about to buy a new car, and you have narrowed the choices to the Ford Mustang GT and the Dodge Stratus. The Stratus is well rated and provides comfortable and reliable transportation. The Mustang GT (V-8) is also fairly well rated but falls into the muscle-car class. Both cars are moderately priced, with the Mustang priced approximately $4,500 higher than the Stratus. Which car would you choose? Why? What factors would be important for you to consider? What information would you need to make your decision?

As an initial step in making your choice, think about those aspects of the car that are most important to you. Do you want a car that has a sporty appearance, extra seating capacity, fuel economy, low repair costs, or other features?

Once you have answered these questions, you have made a start in choosing a car. You have identified the attributes that you consider the most important. Now you need to gather information about these factors for both cars. A trip to the local library produces several sources of information: *Consumer Reports* and *The Consumer Guide Auto Series*, for example, provide descriptions, technical data, price and reliability information, repair costs, safety features and records, and insurance rates. In addition, when searching the Internet, you find a

Ford Mustang GT (left) and Dodge Stratus (right).

huge amount of valuable information about prices, features, and owners' experiences. Edmund's Web page (www.edmunds.com), a site that provides prices and vehicle information at no cost, is a good place to start.

Next you gather together all of the information from test drives, the Internet, reference books, and recommendations so you can compare the two cars. You might organize all this information as shown in Exhibit 1–1. However, this information, abundant as it may be, does not automatically result in a final decision. You rate the Mustang GT higher on sportiness, and you really enjoy driving it. However, the Stratus is roomier, more economical to operate, and costs considerably less. Therefore, you must determine which features

COMPARISON OF MUSTANG GT AND STRATUS

EXHIBIT 1-1

	Mustang GT	Stratus
Sportiness		
Test drive		
appearance	X	
handling	X	
Friends' opinions	X	
Parents' opinions		X
Safety		
Test drive		
handling	X	
Length	183 inches	186 inches
Weight	3,270 pounds	3,170 pounds
Air bags	standard	standard
Antilock brakes	optional	optional
Comfort		
Ride		X
Rear seat		X
Operating Costs		
Initial cost	$22,000	$17,500
Miles per gallon	17–24	20–29
Insurance	above average	average
Predicted reliability	much below average	average

X = preferred alternative

are most important to you. If driving a sporty car is of greatest importance, the Mustang GT is the obvious choice, and the higher operating costs are offset by the thrill of that powerful V-8 engine. Because this is a matter of personal preference, two different purchasers, looking at the same information, might make different choices. Information is crucial in making the decision, but so are individual preferences. Each person must determine which factors are important to the decision and how important each factor is in relation to the others.

STEPS TO A DECISION

Having looked at a common decision, let's take a closer look at the steps in the decision-making process, shown in Exhibit 1–2:

✔ 1. **Identify the goals.** The need for a decision must be identified. What are you trying to accomplish? Based on the goals, specific criteria for making the decision can be identified.

EXHIBIT 1-2 **STEPS IN THE DECISION-MAKING PROCESS**

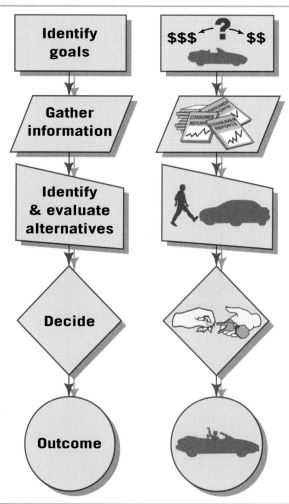

✔ 2. **Gather information.** Information can help change or reinforce the beliefs and expectations of the decision maker. Information helps the decision maker know what alternatives are available.

✔ 3. **Identify and evaluate alternatives.** Although many alternatives may exist, decision makers are limited to those of which they are aware and those they can discover through a reasonable expenditure of time and resources. Using information, decision makers can identify alternatives and the potential consequences of each.

✔ 4. **Choose a course of action.** In light of the potential consequences of each action, the decision maker chooses the course of action believed to be most likely to provide the greatest satisfaction, and then carries out the required action.

The choice and implementation of a course of action ultimately results in some outcome. This outcome may be different from the decision maker's expectations because of unanticipated events. This possibility adds uncertainty to the decision process. Outcomes are often evaluated in light of the identified goals so that corrective action can be taken when needed, and this begins a whole new round of decision making.

How does the car example fit into the decision-making framework? Think of each of the decision steps and how they relate to the decision to buy a car. You (the decision maker) have a goal to reach: to purchase a car that best satisfies your preferences. To reach this goal, you must make a choice (the decision) between two alternatives, the Mustang GT and the Stratus. You identify appropriate criteria relevant to the decision (sportiness, safety, reliability, comfort, and operating costs) based on your preferences. You gather information about the two alternatives and use that information to evaluate them. Then, based on what you have learned about the alternatives and how this relates to the criteria you established, you make a choice. The information you have gathered allows you to make an informed choice consistent with your goal.

All individuals are decision makers, and many decisions are the result of group efforts.

Finally, even though you have gathered extensive information to assist in your decision, there is much that you do not or cannot know. For example, the Stratus has a reasonably good repair record, but how do you know the particular car you buy will not be a lemon? Although information can help you understand decision alternatives and potential outcomes, it cannot guarantee the best decision will be made every time. An uncertain environment thus requires using both judgment and caution in the decision process.

DECISIONS IN A MARKET ECONOMY

In the United States, the decision of what car to purchase occurs in a **market economy**, where individuals and businesses are relatively free to make their own choices about how to earn money, what to purchase, what to produce, how much to produce, and what price to charge. This contrasts with a state-controlled or **planned economy**, where a central committee decides the types, quantities, and prices of products produced, and, consequently, products that consumers can purchase. One reason that planned economies, such as those of Cuba, North Korea, and the former Soviet Union, have been unsuccessful is that the central planners often lack sufficient information to make appropriate allocations of resources. For example, central planners might use society's resources for the production of hammers when people want shoes. In a market economy, by contrast, an increased demand for shoes drives up shoe prices, signaling shoe manufacturers that people want more shoes. Shoe manufacturers respond by increasing output to increase their profits. The market provides information, partly in the form of price changes, about what people want, thus allowing for an efficient allocation of society's resources.

Stock exchanges facilitate flows of capital and the exchange of ownership shares.

While making choices is the essence of a market economy, the market economy of the United States, like the market economies of many other countries, is not completely free. It is heavily regulated through state and federal laws and rules, and even through numerous international agreements. Many laws and regulations have been established to protect workers, investors, and consumers. These regulations are enforced by a number of government agencies, such as the Federal Trade Commission, the Federal Communications Commission, the Securities and Exchange Commission, and state public utilities commissions. Other market restrictions are introduced by agreements such as union contracts. Decision makers are free to make choices that further their goals and those of the organizations that employ them, but only within this regulatory framework.

CAPITAL MARKETS

One important element of a market economy is a functioning capital market. **Capital markets** provide for a flow of financial resources by channeling money away from those who do not expect to use it all for current purchases of goods and services to those who need the cash.

Think about how we often save cash now to purchase items later. We may save cash in a number of ways. For example, we might put money in a savings account at a bank. The bank lends that money to those needing to borrow. In this way, an organization might borrow money for its operations, while we are paid interest for the use of our money. We could also invest our money indirectly through mutual funds that pool the resources of many investors and provide professional management. This money is then channeled to organizations needing cash. Or, we can lend or invest our money directly by exchanging our cash for securities of organizations that need the money. **Securities** are financial instruments that represent either promises to pay (IOUs) or ownership rights. As in other markets, prices in the capital markets are determined by the supply of and demand for the items being exchanged—in this case, money and securities.

A key aspect of a market economy such as that in the United States is that individuals and organizations "carry out their consumption, saving, and investment decisions by allocating their present and expected cash resources."[2] Thus, an important focus is on information about the amount of cash held, how it is used, and what cash inflows and outflows are expected to occur in the future.

PROFESSIONAL MANAGEMENT

Most production and marketing of goods and services in the United States and other market-oriented countries are done through private enterprise. Organizations owned by individuals, rather than by the government, choose the activities in which they engage.

Many of these organizations employ professional managers to run them. Owners expect managers to protect and preserve the organization's resources and to use them as intended. However, managers are also typically expected to accomplish some goal or goals through the use of the resources. Examples of some goals of organizations are as follows:

Organization	Goal
Business enterprise	Earn a profit
Not-for-profit organization	Provide a needed service to society
Government	Provide for the health and welfare of the population

To accomplish set goals, managers must make decisions about the allocation of the resources under their control. Managers are then held accountable for their performance in achieving

[2] *Statement of Financial Accounting Concepts No. 1*, "Objectives of Financial Reporting by Business Enterprises," Financial Accounting Standards Board, 1978.

Professional managers make decisions about the allocation of resources entrusted to them.

the organization's goals. They are evaluated by other managers or by resource providers, such as owners, donors to not-for-profit organizations, and taxpayers. All of these individual managers and resource providers use information so they can make decisions regarding the resources under their control, decisions that will help them achieve their goals.

In Practice 1-1

LEVI STRAUSS & CO,

The chairman and chief executive officer of Levi Strauss & Co., Robert D. Haas, has a vision of what the corporation should be: an entity that will make profits and also be socially responsible, using the theme of "responsible commercial success."[3]

ANALYSIS

Management at Levi Strauss & Co. has a responsibility that it has defined as including social responsibility in addition to the responsibility to earn profits.

ORGANIZATIONS IN THE U.S. ECONOMY

Many different types of organizations operate within the U.S. economy. These organizations provide the food we eat, the clothes we wear, transportation, education, physical protection, and help in time of disaster. These organizations include the local bookstore, McDonald's, Amazon.com, General Motors, Bank of America, Safeway Supermarkets, Amtrak, The Red Cross, the city hospital, the federal government, your local government, and many thousands

[3] "Managing by Values," *BusinessWeek* (August 1, 1994), pp. 46–52.

of other organizations, large and small. Think for a moment of an organization on which you rely heavily and how your life would be different if it suddenly disappeared. Within this organization, who are some of the individuals using information and making decisions?

Business and Nonbusiness Entities.   Our economy includes both business and nonbusiness entities. Distinguishing between the two types of organizations is often important because of the difference in their goals and how they are operated and financed. In general, a **business enterprise** is established to sell goods and/or services to customers as a means of earning a profit for its owners. So long as the goods and services can be sold for an amount greater than the cost of producing and selling them, the business enterprise has an incentive to continue its existence.

A **nonbusiness entity** is established to provide a service, usually one that is viewed as advancing some social goal to some segment of society, and neither those who establish the entity nor those who provide resources expect to earn a profit from the entity's operation. Nonbusiness entities may be classified as *government entities* or *not-for-profit organizations*. Governmental entities at the local, state, and federal levels provide a vast number of services and social programs funded primarily through taxes (e.g., a state government, a school district) and sometimes through user fees (e.g., a water and sewer district). Not-for-profit organizations also engage in activities that are viewed as benefiting society, including religious, educational, and philanthropic work. The funding for not-for-profit organizations typically comes from voluntary donations.

Although these organizations do not exist to earn a profit, they nevertheless share some of the same concerns as business enterprises because they cannot continue to operate at a loss. In the long run, nonbusiness entities cannot continue to exist if they spend more than the resources they generate.

Forms of Business Organization.   Nearly all U.S. businesses are organized in one of three forms:

Sole proprietorship—an unincorporated business enterprise owned by a single individual. Examples include most auto repair shops, small cafes, and drinking establishments.

Partnership—an unincorporated association of two or more individuals conducting a business for profit. Examples include most law and accounting firms.

Corporation—a legal entity viewed under the law as an artificial person having many of the rights and obligations of a real person. Examples include most large national and international companies such as Motorola, Nike, and PepsiCo.

Exhibit 1–3 lists some of the important advantages and disadvantages of the different forms of business organization. One of the most important advantages and distinctions of the corporate form of organization is that corporations are separate legal entities. Legal separation provides **limited liability** to the owners. Only corporate assets are subject to the claims of the corporation's creditors, or those who have lent resources to the corporation. The **assets**, or items of value, of the owners are not usually subject to the claims of the corporation's creditors. With unincorporated businesses, however, the business and the owners are not legally separate. Therefore, if the business is unable to pay all of its debts, referred to as **liabilities**, the creditors may make claims against the personal assets of the owners.

In the United States, all three forms of organization are widely used. As Exhibit 1–4 shows, unincorporated businesses are far more numerous than corporations, but corporations account for the vast majority of business activity. Corporations have been able to grow very large because they are able to raise large amounts of money. Investors are willing to invest in corporations because they can become part owners of a business without having to risk any more of their personal assets than the amount invested. Further, investors need not actively participate in operating the business, but instead may hire profes-

| EXHIBIT 1-3 | **ADVANTAGES AND DISADVANTAGES OF DIFFERENT FORMS OF BUSINESS ORGANIZATION** |

Organizational Form	Advantages	Disadvantages
Sole proprietorship	Ease of formation Ease of dissolution Informality of structure Relative lack of regulation Allows full control of management	Unlimited liability Unsuited to multiple owners Ownership transfers relatively difficult Generally demands active participation Business tied to specific individual
Partnership	Ease of formation Ease of dissolution Informality of structure Relative lack of regulation Allows for multiple owners	Unlimited liability Unsuited to large number of owners Ownership transfers relatively difficult Each owner bound by partners' actions Often results in unwieldy management structure (too many bosses) Generally demands some level of participation Partnership ends with death, incompetency, or withdrawal of any partner
Corporation	Limited liability of owners Allows for many owners Allows for passive investment Relative ease of ownership transfers Relative permanence of entity Suited to raising large amounts of capital Suited to employment of professional management Convenient ownership structure (proportionate voting and sharing of profits and assets)	Individual owners may have little control over management Relatively heavily regulated Relative difficulty of formation Relative difficulty of dissolution

sional managers. Suppose you wanted to be in the automobile manufacturing business. Even if you were to gather together all of your friends and pool your resources, you would be unable to raise the money needed to start an automobile company. On the other hand, with a few hundred dollars you can own part of Ford or General Motors by buying an ownership interest in the form of shares of its **common stock**. Further, if you decide later that you would rather own an automobile than part of an automobile company, you could easily sell your ownership interest because there is an organized market for buying and selling shares of common stock.

IMPORTANCE OF ORGANIZATIONAL FORMS

EXHIBIT 1-4

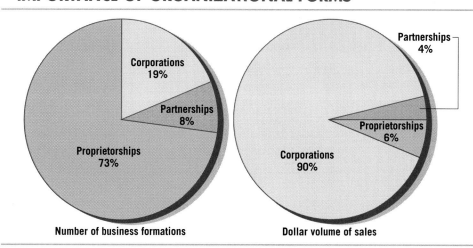

Number of business formations   Dollar volume of sales

Even with all the advantages of a corporation, when people first start a business, they often do not incorporate because of the legal procedures required. Proprietorships and partnerships can be organized relatively easily. Even with a partnership, however, all of the terms of the partnership should be carefully specified in a written agreement called the *articles of copartnership*. This agreement should specify, among other things, the rights and responsibilities of each partner, the way in which partnership profits and losses are to be divided, and how the partnership should be dissolved. Recall that with a partnership, all of the partners' personal assets are at risk. Unwritten informal agreements may be misunderstood and lead to difficulties.

Most businesses start small. For example, Henry Ford laid the foundation for an automotive empire by personally constructing a single automobile. As firms grow, however, money may be needed to hire more people, to invest in additional buildings and equipment, and to buy other goods and services. Most companies need large amounts of **capital**, or the money and other resources required to operate an enterprise. Capital is usually obtained by borrowing or by bringing additional owners into the business. For example, some companies "go public" by selling ownership shares to investors willing to provide resources.

The corporate form of organization is usually best for raising large amounts of ownership capital because of the ease of transferability of ownership and the advantage of limited liability. In addition, shares of stock conveniently designate an investor's ownership rights. Each share of stock provides a proportionate voting right, share of profits, and share of assets. If a company has 1,000 shares of common stock outstanding, and you own 100 of those shares, you are entitled to 10 percent of the profits and 10 percent of the assets (after liabilities are paid), and you hold 10 percent of the voting rights.

Because of the very clear advantages of the corporate form of organization, nearly all major business enterprises are incorporated. These large corporations, however, often have greater information requirements than other forms of business, for several reasons:

1. Because operations are frequently more complex, managers may need more information.

2. Because owners often are only indirectly involved in the operation of a corporation, they need to be informed regularly of the progress of the company so they can assess the status of their investments.

3. Because corporate business activity tends to have a greater effect on the economy and society than that of partnerships and sole proprietorships, regulatory agencies frequently impose extensive reporting requirements on organizations.

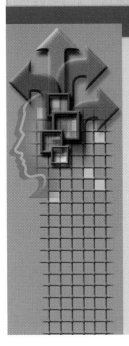

You Decide 1-1

IS A PARTNER REALLY A PARTNER?

Each summer, you and three of you high school friends have been selling ice cream and soft drinks at the park for the local baseball and soccer teams and their fans. You have not set up a formal business agreement, but next year you are going to have to put up more money for the permits, ice cream and drinks, and a new freezer. You think it would be a good idea to formalize the business arrangement. Also, because it is getting harder for all four of you to be actively involved, you want to look at several operating and financing options. You are considered the business expert and are asked to answer the following questions:

1. If you want to set up the least costly form of business, which would you recommend? Why?

2. If you want to protect yourselves from as much personal liability as possible, which form of business organization would you recommend? Why?

3. If one of you wants to contribute capital but is not going to be able to participate in operations, which form is best? Why?

4. If you want to sell the organization to other high school students next year, which form is best? Why?

THE ROLE OF INFORMATION IN DECISION MAKING

We have seen that information is a key element in the decision-making process. In a market economy, information helps decision makers make informed choices regarding the use of the resources under their control. When decision makers are able to make well-informed decisions, resources are used in a way that better meets the needs and goals of those within the market.

Let's look at an example that illustrates the types of decisions made in a market economy, and the kinds of information needed for those decisions. Suppose you notice that your neighborhood could really use a video rental store. You think this might be a prime opportunity to provide a service and to make some money at the same time. What would you need to know before entering the video rental business?

You conclude that the two most important questions are: "How much will it cost me to open a video rental store?" and "How much money will I make?" Let's look first at the costs involved. Obviously, the first thing you will need in the video rental business is videos. A visit to the Blockbuster Video store across town reveals that it carries thousands of titles, with multiple copies of the more popular videos. Competing with Blockbuster Video might be a bit ambitious, but fortunately Blockbuster is too far away to be convenient for people in your neighborhood.

Because of your limited resources, you decide to start small. You will have a few hundred specially selected movie titles and a few video games, with one or two copies of each. After reviewing local business directories at the library and searching the Internet, you find a number of video and game distributors. In general, you find that prices are about $20 for recent movie hits and $10 for older hits and classics. In addition, the video games cost about $20 each. After considerable thought, you decide the following mix of videos and games would satisfy the people in your neighborhood:

Recent hits	60 titles, 2 copies each @ $20	$2,400
Older movies	300 titles, 1 copy each @ $10	3,000
Video games	70 titles, 1 copy each @ $20	1,400
		$6,800

You find a small vacant store available in a shopping center near your home. Because a bookstore used to be located there, the shelves and lighting are already in place. You also hire an assistant to help you twenty hours each week so you can continue to go to school. You then estimate that your weekly costs, in addition to the purchase of videos, will be as follows:

Rent (including utilities)	$250
Assistant's salary and payroll taxes	150
Miscellaneous costs	50
Weekly costs	$450

So, in total, you will need about $6,800 to get started, plus $450 a week for operating costs.

OK, so how much will you make? First, you must find out whether people in your neighborhood will rent videos and games frequently. A brief door-to-door survey reveals that your neighbors are willing to rent movies and games regularly if they do not have to travel very far and the price is right. What about competition? The only movie theater is across town and charges $7 admission, plus a small fortune for popcorn, Junior Mints, and soft drinks. The only existing video rental store also is on the far side of town. Because your neighborhood is relatively small and somewhat out of town, cable TV is not available. Based on this information, you estimate that, after a few weeks to get established, you will have the following one-night rentals each week:

Monday through Thursday	50 recent hits @ $3	$150
	40 older movies @ $2	80
	5 video games @ $4	20
Friday through Sunday	100 recent hits @ $3	300
	170 older movies @ $2	340
	15 video games @ $4	60
Total weekly rentals		$950

Now let's compare your costs with how much you will take in from rentals:

Weekly rentals	$950
Weekly costs	450
Weekly difference	$500

This looks great, but where will you get the money to start? What about the money you have set aside for college next year? If you use that money now, how long will it take to make it back? Let's see: If you use $6,800 of your college money, and you clear $500 per week, you should be able to earn it all back in less than fourteen weeks ($6,800/$500). Although you would have to give up the 3 percent interest you currently are earning on the money you have set aside in a bank savings account, this venture seems profitable.

On the other hand, how do you measure the profit? Is the profit really $500 per week? What about the cost of the videocassettes and games? The videocassettes and games should each last about two years. Perhaps the cost should be spread over the period of time they are usable:

Weekly cost of cassettes and games = $6,800 ÷ 104 weeks = $65 per week

A more accurate estimate of the weekly income of the video rental venture might be:

Weekly rentals		$950
Less: Rent	$250	
Wages	150	
Other	50	
Cassette cost	65	
Total costs		515
Weekly profit		$435

Of course you would have to pay taxes on your profit. Figure about 15 percent for income taxes plus another 16 percent for self-employment tax. On the bright side, however, the actual cash produced weekly by this operation would exceed the $435 calculated profit because the $65 weekly cassette cost requires a cash outlay only at the beginning of the operation, and the amount shown as a weekly cost for cassettes does not actually use cash each week. Nevertheless, some cash would have to be set aside for new movies and games if you want to continue in business. People get tired of the same movies and games, so unless you want business to fall off, you need to buy new titles.

In thinking about this example, note that the decision to start this business, or any other, should be approached within the framework of the decision-making process, as discussed earlier. Information helps you understand the alternatives (start the video rental business or leave your money in the bank) and possible outcomes. Some of the information used in this example falls within the domain of accounting, such as the profitability information, while other important information, such as that used to assess demand and competition, is not accounting-based. As often is the case, some information used, such as the projected weekly rentals and the expected average lives of the videocassettes, is based on estimates.

In Practice 1-2

AN ENTREPRENEUR

As a freshman at Harvard University, Bill Haney noticed that most dormitory rooms had fireplaces but no firewood. So, he borrowed $1,000 to ship firewood to the school. His venture paid off in a $2,000 profit. For his next venture, he borrowed $10,000 and founded the company that eventually became Fuel Tech Inc. N.V. He sold out seven years later for $15 million. He then went on to form two more environmentally oriented companies.[4]

ANALYSIS

Haney's business, like most, started small and grew. Clearly his grew more than the average. Bill Haney is described as a skilled technology-spotter and deal maker. He also put together a staff of skilled business people who have a passion for what is being done in the company. These skills include the generation and use of financial information.

[4] "Firewood to Environmental Empire in 14 Years," *The New York Times* (June 26, 1994).

If your video store remains in operation for an extended period of time, the need for accounting information will become even more important. You will need information to continually assess the success of your operation, and you will need to file various types of tax returns. If the venture is especially successful, you may wish to expand, both in your current location and to other locations. This may require a loan from the local bank. Your local bankers, before agreeing to lend you money, will wish to see reports showing financial information about your store's resources and the results of its operations. They also will want to see your projections of the expected future profits of your expanded operations. If you are very successful, you might want to sell part ownership to others, but they also will want financial reports before investing their money. As you can see, accounting information is needed not only by you to make decisions about managing the venture, but also by those outside of the operation to make decisions relating to your venture.

THE NATURE OF ACCOUNTING INFORMATION

From the previous example, you can see that accounting information is one very important type of information used in making financial decisions. But exactly what is accounting information, and what makes it different from other kinds of information?

Accounting information can be distinguished from other types of information in three ways:

1. It is designed to be used in making financial decisions.
2. It is primarily quantitative and financial in nature.
3. It relates to a specific entity.

DECISION ORIENTED

Accounting information is aimed primarily at decision makers. Keep in mind that decisions relate only to the future. We can change the future through our choices, but try as we might, we can never change the past. Interestingly, though, most accounting information is historical information; that is, it tells us about the past. So, how does information about the past help us to make choices about the future? The answer is that the past often provides the key to relationships that will hold in the future. Understanding those relationships gives us insight into what might happen in the future. (See In Practice 1-3.)

QUANTITATIVE AND FINANCIAL NATURE

Both quantitative and nonquantitative types of information may be useful for making decisions. Accounting focuses on quantitative or numerical information. In most cases, accounting information is financial; that is, it is stated in terms of units of money. This does not imply that nonquantitative or nonfinancial information is not useful. It does mean that many decisions should not be made on the basis of accounting information alone. Quantitative and nonquantitative information frequently complement one another. In many cases, qualitative information may be more important than quantitative information. For example, reviewing the past profitability of a company's product line may be important when evaluating the company, but knowing the changing pattern of consumer preferences may be more important for forecasting future sales. The important point to remember is that decision makers are not restricted to a single type of information.

In Practice 1-3

YAHOO! INC.

For 1998, Yahoo! Inc. reported revenues of more than $203 million, up significantly from the year before. The company stated that the increase was "due primarily to the increasing number of advertisers purchasing space on the Company's online media properties as well as larger and longer-term purchases by certain advertisers." However, the company then went on to point out the following:

> *There can be no assurance that customers will continue to purchase advertising on the Company's Web pages, that advertisers will not make smaller and shorter term purchases, or that market prices for Web-based advertising will not decrease due to competitive or other factors. Additionally, while the Company has experienced strong revenue growth during the last three years, management does not believe that this level of revenue growth will be sustained in future periods.*

ANALYSIS

Both the earnings report and the accompanying warning relate to accounting information that is used by decision makers such as investors and creditors to make future decisions. Although the earnings information is historical, it helps decision makers understand relationships that are useful for projecting future occurrences. However, historical information must be interpreted in light of other current information that may indicate the need for modifying expectations based on the historical information. [www.yahoo.com]

ACCOUNTING ENTITY

When evaluating a particular company, you might want information about that company's operations and its products, the industry in which it operates, the economy, the overall political situation, and any number of other factors that relate to the decisions you are making. All of this information might be relevant, but only a portion of it is provided through the accounting process. Accounting develops information about an individual business. A business issues accounting reports that relate only to its own activities and position. The reports do not include information about other organizations.

In Practice 1-4

PHILIP MORRIS COMPANIES, INC.

Philip Morris Companies, Inc., in the annual financial report it issues to the public, presents information on the results of its activities for the year and its financial position at the end of the year. The report even includes a breakdown of its profits by different product line or type of operation, such as tobacco, food, and beer.

ANALYSIS

All of these operations are within the single reporting entity, and no information is provided about any other companies. [www.philipmorris. com]

INFORMATION AND THE ACCOUNTING PROCESS

We've talked about how accounting provides a specific type of information that helps decision makers in a market economy. But exactly what is accounting? **Accounting** can be defined as

> *the process of identifying, measuring, classifying and accumulating, summarizing, and communicating information about economic entities that is primarily quantitative and is useful to decision makers.*

A closer look at the accounting process provides a better understanding of the information it can provide.

IDENTIFICATION

Many aspects of an organization might be measured, but not everything about an organization can be reported. Accordingly, those attributes that are of the greatest interest and assistance to decision makers need to be identified. Because accounting is designed to provide information for financial decisions, only information relevant for those decisions should be included in accounting reports.

MEASUREMENT

Once the relevant aspects of an organization have been identified, they must be measured. This measurement requires the selection of an acceptable measurement method from among those that are available. (See You Decide 1-3.)

CLASSIFICATION AND ACCUMULATION

After relevant aspects of an organization have been identified and measured, the resulting information must be classified and accumulated to provide meaningful reports to decision makers. An effective accounting system provides for the accumulation of information by individual categories, such as sales, rent expense, cash, and equipment, that are of interest to decision makers. In the video store example, the categories rent, wages, and cassette cost were used. The accounting system can then easily provide specific information, such as the company's total sales for the period or the amount of cash on hand at the end of the year.

SUMMARIZATION

Suppose you were considering investing some spare cash in General Motors, and a crucial factor in your decision was the amount of sales the company had last year. How useful would the information be if General Motors provided you with a listing of each and every sale of automobiles, auto parts, and other products the company made last year? Even though all of the information relates only to the single category of sales, you still might conclude, after spending hours staring at a room filled with computer printouts, that in some cases less information is better. Overly detailed information might be costly to provide, but more importantly, it may be too overwhelming to be useful. Information appropriately summarized allows decision makers to focus on the factors and relationships that are important for their decisions.

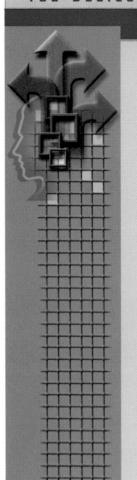

You Decide 1-2

MEASURING THE VALUE OF CALIFORNIA LAND

Warner Bros. Studios (www.wb.com) purchased land in California's San Fernando Valley many decades ago. Since then, the surrounding area has grown to a population of well over a million people, and the land has become extremely valuable. How should the land be valued in the company's accounting reports? Should the land be reported at its original cost to the company or at its current value? How would you determine the land's original cost? How would you determine its current value?

COMMUNICATION

No matter how good information is, it is useless unless it is provided to the appropriate decision makers in a timely manner and in a form that allows them to understand the meaning of the information and use it effectively. For example, financial reports that are overly complex and written in technical jargon may not be understood by the average reader. Because this is one of the most important aspects of the accounting process, we'll look more closely in the next section and next chapter at how accounting information is communicated and how it is used.

OBTAINING ACCOUNTING INFORMATION

How is accounting information about an organization provided to decision makers who are outside of that organization? Most external decision makers receive accounting information in the form of **financial statements,** which provide information about the operations, cash flows, and financial position of a specific organization. Two such financial statements of Hewlett-Packard Company (www.hp.com), a large corporation best known for its computer-related products, are presented in Exhibits 1–5 and 1–6. Hewlett-Packard's income statement (Exhibit 1–5) presents the results of the company's operations, reporting the amount of the company's sales (revenue), as well as its costs of operations (expenses). By comparing the company's sales with its operating costs for the year, the income statement provides a basis for evaluating the success of the company's activities. One measure of that success is the company's net income or net earnings, the excess of revenues over expenses. From the income statement in Exhibit 1–5, you can see that Hewlett-Packard reported net earnings of $2.945 billion in 1998. Hewlett-Packard's balance sheet (Exhibit 1–6) presents its financial position, reporting the things of value the company owns (its assets) and what it owes (its liabilities). The balance sheet also reports the owners' financial interest in the enterprise, $16.919 billion for Hewlett-Packard at October 31, 1998. The information in these financial statements is provided by the management of Hewlett-Packard and is based on accepted accounting methods.

These financial statements, along with two others, are normally provided to owners, creditors, and other interested parties in a comprehensive annual report distributed by the company. The **annual report** typically includes a great deal of information from management, including a description of the company, its products, and its operations, in addition to the four basic financial statements. It also includes notes to the financial statements and an auditor's report. As an illustration, a full set of financial statements for Gateway, Inc., a major computer company, is included in Appendix A, along with the accompanying notes, auditor's report, and some other elements of the annual report.

Annual reports are usually easy to obtain if the company's securities are traded in the capital markets. Generally, a phone call to the company's shareholder relations department will result in the company's annual report being mailed to you at no charge within a few days. If the company subscribes to an annual report service, ordering an annual report may

HEWLETT-PACKARD'S INCOME STATEMENT

EXHIBIT 1-5

CONSOLIDATED STATE OF EARNINGS			
For the years ended October 31 In millions except per share amounts	1998	1997	1996
Net revenue:			
Products	$40,105	$36,672	$33,114
Services	6,956	6,223	5,306
Total net revenue	47,061	42,895	38,420
Costs and expenses:			
Cost of products sold	27,477	24,217	22,013
Cost of services	4,595	4,102	3,486
Research and development	3,355	3,078	2,718
Selling, general and administrative	7,793	7,159	6,477
Total costs and expenses	43,220	38,556	34,694
Earnings from operations	3,841	4,339	3,726
Interest income and other, net	485	331	295
Interest expense	235	215	327
Earnings before taxes	4,091	4,455	3,694
Provision for taxes	1,146	1,336	1,108
Net earnings	$ 2,945	$ 3,119	$ 2,586
Net earnings per share:			
Basic	$ 2.85	$ 3.04	$ 2.54
Diluted	$ 2.77	$ 2.95	$ 2.46
Average shares used in computing basic net earnings per share	1,034	1,026	1,019
Average shares and equivalents used in computing diluted net earnings per share	1,072	1,057	1,052

| EXHIBIT 1-6 | **HEWLETT-PACKARD'S BALANCE SHEET** |

CONSOLIDATED BALANCE SHEET		
October 31		
In millions except par value and number of shares	**1998**	**1997**
Assets		
Current assets:		
Cash and cash equivalents	**$ 4,046**	$ 3,072
Short-term investments	**21**	1,497
Accounts receivable	**6,232**	6,142
Financing receivables	**1,520**	1,123
Inventory	**6,184**	6,763
Other current assets	**3,581**	2,350
Total current assets	**21,584**	20,947
Property, plant and equipment, net	**6,358**	6,312
Long-term investments and other assets	**5,731**	4,490
Total assets	**$33,673**	$31,749
Liabilities and shareholders' equity		
Current liabilities:		
Notes payable and short-term borrowings	**$ 1,245**	$ 1,226
Accounts payable	**3,203**	3,185
Employee compensation and benefits	**1,768**	1,723
Taxes on earnings	**2,796**	1,515
Deferred revenues	**1,453**	1,152
Other accrued liabilities	**3,008**	2,418
Total current liabilities	**13,473**	11,219
Long-term debt	**2,063**	3,158
Other liabilities	**1,218**	1,217
Commitments and contingencies		
Shareholders' equity:		
Preferred stock, $1 par value		
(authorized: 300,000,000 shares; issued: none)	—	—
Common stock and capital in excess of $0.01 par value		
(authorized: 4,800,000,000 shares; issued and outstanding:		
1,015,403,000 in 1998 and 1,041,042,000 in 1997)	**10**	1,187
Retained earnings	**16,909**	14,968
Total shareholders' equity	**16,919**	16,155
Total liabilities and shareholders' equity	**$33,673**	$31,749

be even more convenient. For example, *The Wall Street Journal*, in its "Money and Investing" section, indicates selected companies in its listings for which annual reports can be obtained quickly at no charge by calling a toll-free number. A similar service providing free annual reports for more than 3,600 companies is available online from The Public Register's Annual Report Service at www.prars.com. Another valuable free service available on the Internet is the Report Gallery (www.reportgallery.com). It includes annual reports that can be viewed or downloaded for almost 1,000 companies. It also provides direct access to many companies' home pages and provides other types of financial information.

In many cases, annual reports can be obtained or ordered over the Internet through a company's home page. Home page addresses are often based on the company's name (e.g., www.sears.com; www.motorola.com). Many companies include their annual reports on their home pages, and you can view or download the report directly.

Perhaps the most comprehensive source of accounting (and other) information about a company is from filings the company makes with the Securities and Exchange Commission (SEC), an agency of the federal government responsible for regulating information disclosures by companies with securities trading in the capital markets. All major companies, and many smaller ones, are required to file annual, quarterly, and many other reports with the SEC. All of these reports are available online within several days of filing through the SEC's Electronic Data Gathering, Analysis, and Retrieval System (EDGAR). On the SEC's home page (www.sec.gov), press the EDGAR button and type in the exact name of the company to have access to all of its SEC filings for the past several years.

Today, accounting information is easily accessed through the Internet and other more traditional sources. Keep in mind, however, that accounting information is only one type of information used in making financial decisions. Although the ready availability of information clearly is a boon to decision makers, information is not useful unless it is clearly understood. The chapters that follow aim at helping you understand the accounting information that you will be using to make decisions.

SUMMARY

Every individual is a decision maker. Whether a decision is simple or complex, the basic elements of the decision process are the same. A decision maker, attempting to achieve a particular goal, makes a choice between two or more alternatives, each of which leads to different outcomes or results and different levels of satisfaction. This choice always takes place in a world of uncertainty. Information is a key element in the decision process. It helps in formulating the beliefs and expectations that make up the decision maker's view of the world within which the decision is made.

Information is important to the efficient functioning of a market economy because it allows individual decision makers to make informed choices. A market economy is characterized by a relative freedom of choice on the part of individuals within the economy as to how they wish to allocate the resources under their control. Decision makers in a market economy need information to help them make choices about the allocation of their resources or those resources that have been entrusted to them by others. Those who entrust others to manage resources for them typically require information that reports on the performance of those resource managers.

A number of different types of organizations play major roles in the economy of the United States. Business enter-

prises, not-for-profit organizations, and government entities all are important. Businesses typically exist primarily to earn profits. The major forms of business organization in this country are sole proprietorship, partnership, and corporation. Corporations are most suited to growth and expansion because of the limited liability of owners and the ease of ownership transfer. Not-for-profit and local governmental entities do not have a profit motive, but rather exist to provide some service to society.

Regardless of the type of organization about which decisions are being made, information is crucial for those decisions. Accounting information is one type of information used by decision makers. It can be distinguished from other types of information in that it (1) is decision oriented, (2) is primarily quantitative and financial, and (3) relates to a specific entity. Accounting information results from the accounting process, which involves identifying and measuring attributes that are relevant for decision making; classifying, accumulating, and summarizing the resulting information; and communicating it to decision makers. Accounting information is most frequently provided to those decision makers outside of the reporting entity in the form of financial statements.

LIST OF IMPORTANT TERMS

accounting *(19)*
annual report *(21)*
assets *(11)*
business enterprise *(11)*
capital *(13)*
capital markets *(9)*

common stock *(12)*
corporation *(11)*
decision *(4)*
financial statements *(20)*
liabilities *(11)*
limited liability *(11)*

market economy *(8)*
nonbusiness entity *(11)*
partnership *(11)*
planned economy *(8)*
securities *(9)*
sole proprietorship *(11)*

EXAMINING THE CONCEPTS

Q1-1 Why is accounting often referred to as the language of business?

Q1-2 How do an individual's preferences affect the decisions she or he may make?

Q1-3 What are the steps involved in making a decision? Why is each of these steps necessary?

Q1-4 What role does information play in decision making?

Q1-5 You are considering purchasing a new television set. What information would you attempt to gather? What sources might you use?

Q1-6 Why might the outcome of a decision not be consistent with a decision maker's expectations? Give an example in which this has happened to you.

Q1-7 Describe the types of information that were helpful to you in choosing which college to attend. Did you receive any information about colleges that was not useful to you? If so, describe why it was not useful.

Q1-8 How might the speed with which information is provided to the decision maker affect its usefulness? Give an example.

Q1-9 How might the steps in the decision process be different in a market economy than in a planned economy?

Q1-10 What role do securities play in a market economy? How do they affect the decision-making process?

Q1-11 What are the stewardship responsibilities of professional managers in a market economy?

Q1-12 Why are not all of the activities of society carried on by business entities in a market economy?

Q1-13 Differentiate between a business entity and a not-for-profit entity.

Q1-14 What are the three major forms of business organization? Which form of organization is used most commonly?

Q1-15 What is the difference between a sole proprietorship and a partnership? From an owner's perspective, why is this important?

Q1-16 What characteristics of a corporation lead to the widespread use of this form of business organization?

Q1-17 How can accounting information be distinguished from other types of information?

Q1-18 In what ways do quantitative and nonquantitative information often complement one another in the decision-making process?

Q1-19 What is accounting? Describe the important aspects of the accounting process.

Q1-20 Who is responsible for generating the accounting information used by investors and creditors? In what ways do investors and creditors use accounting information?

Q1-21 In what ways does management use accounting information in making its decisions?

Q1-22 In what form does a business generally provide information to external decision makers?

UNDERSTANDING ACCOUNTING INFORMATION

E1-1 The Decision-Making Process Ralph was strolling down the street on his way back from class when he spotted a beautiful ring in the jewelry store window. He immediately went inside and purchased the ring and had it giftwrapped for his new girlfriend. That was the start of a bit of difficulty for Ralph. When he arrived home, a phone message informed him that his new girlfriend had just gotten engaged to another fellow and she was leaving school. When he took the ring out of the box to look at it, the setting fell out of the ring. A trip to the store proved even more frustrating. The manager pointed to the "all sales final" sign and said they would not take it back, and since they were closing the store they no longer had a repair department that could reset the stone. Ralph also learned that when he charged the ring to his credit card it had exceeded his credit limit, and within a few days he began to get threatening no-

tices and telephone calls from the credit card company. Unfortunately, he will not have any money to pay on his credit card bill until next term starts.

Four steps were presented in the decision model outlined in the chapter. How might these steps have been used by Ralph to attain a more favorable result?

E1-2 Decisions in a Market Economy

a. The Stringy Bagel Factory has experienced a tremendous increase in sales in its home town, and the owners are convinced their special recipe will be very profitable if they can attain national distribution. How might the owners get enough money to supplement their current resources so they can expand?

b. What would be the advantages and disadvantages of being organized as a proprietorship, partnership, or corporation?

E1-3 The Role of Information in Decision Making The Goodnews Bookstore purchases books from six different wholesalers. It classifies the books it purchases as business, religious, and general, and applies a different profit markup on each class of books. The accountant for the bookstore keeps track of the amount purchased from each wholesaler, credit terms offered by each wholesaler, total sales by each class of books, and the length of time the books are on display prior to sale. How might the accounting information be used in deciding which wholesalers to purchase books from and which books to stock? What additional information might also be useful in making the evaluation?

E1-4 The Nature of Accounting Information In which of the following cases will accounting information be important in helping the manager of Zuckermans Market make his decision? Explain why the information would or would not be important.

a. Determining the number of cases of fruit and cheese to stock before Christmas.
b. Deciding which wholesaler to use as a supplier of potatoes.
c. Selecting the theme to be placed in ads in the local newspaper.
d. Deciding who to hire for an entry-level position in the meat department.
e. Deciding whether to borrow money from a local bank or to borrow money from a large regional bank.
f. Estimating whether future consumption of beef and veal on a per capita basis is likely to increase or decrease.
g. Deciding whether to continue to rent or purchase the building currently being used for all operations.

E1-5 Information and the Accounting Process Stanwood Grain Supply Company purchases soybeans and corn from farmers in the Midwest and transports them by rail and barge to New Orleans for shipment overseas. It has approximately fifty locations that purchase and store grain.

a. What attributes of the soybeans currently held by Stanwood are measurable?
b. Why is classification and accumulation important in determining the amount to be reported by Stanwood as its grain on hand?
c. Why is summarization important in developing the financial statements for Stanwood?

E1-6 Obtaining Accounting Information Joyce has decided to go backpacking with a friend during spring break. After looking at the cost of hiking boots, tents, and other supplies, Joyce concluded companies that produce and market backpacking and sports equipment must be quite profitable. She has decided to do an analysis of a company that carries this type of equipment as a project for one of her courses.

a. Will the company's income statement or balance sheet provide Joyce with information about the profitability of the company she chooses?

b. How might she obtain a copy of the last annual report the company distributed to its shareholders?
c. If Joyce has delayed writing her report and needs the information immediately, what sources might she use to acquire the information needed?
d. What is EDGAR and why is it a useful source of information?

E1-7 Multiple Choice: The Decision Process Select the correct answer for each of the following:

1. The steps in the decision-making process include:
   a. Identifying and evaluating alternatives.
   b. Gathering information.
   c. Identifying the goal.
   d. All of the above.
2. In arriving at a decision, a business manager should:
   a. Gather only information that supports the beliefs of the decision maker.
   b. Be able to determine the outcome of the decision.
   c. Attempt to determine the potential consequences of each alternative course of action.
   d. Choose the course of action likely to be of the greatest direct personal benefit to the decision maker.
3. The information used in arriving at a decision should be:
   a. Pertinent to the decision being made.
   b. Complete and not summarized.
   c. Consistent with the biases of the information provider.
   d. Accurate regardless of the cost.
4. The decision process is useful to which of the following decision makers?
   a. Managers, but not investors.
   b. Investors, but not creditors.
   c. Creditors, but not managers.
   d. Both creditors and managers.

E1-8 Multiple Choice: Types of Organizations and Entities Select the correct answer for each of the following questions:

1. Which of the following activities is most likely to be operated as a sole proprietorship?
   a. A local motel.
   b. A regional public accounting firm.
   c. A large medical clinic.
   d. A public school district.
2. Which of the following best describes the attributes of a partnership?
   a. Limited ability to raise capital; unlimited personal liability of owners.
   b. Ability to raise large amounts of capital; limited personal liability of owners.
   c. Limited ability to raise capital; limited personal liability of owners.
   d. Ability to raise large amounts of capital; unlimited personal liability.
3. Which of the following best describes a large corporation?
   a. Run by owners; unlimited personal liability.
   b. Run by professional managers; limited personal liability.

c. Run by owners; limited personal liability.
d. Run by professional managers; unlimited personal liability.

4. Which of the following is true?
   a. Corporate shareholders are personally liable for the liabilities of the corporation if the company is unable to pay them.
   b. Partners are personally liable for the liabilities of the partnership if the partnership is unable to pay them.
   c. Normally, corporate shareholders can only sell their ownership interests when the corporation terminates.
   d. Partners can normally transfer their partnership interests with ease.

E1-9 Multiple Choice: Evaluating Information Select the correct answer for each of the following questions:

1. Your company is interested in purchasing a new laser printer. You have contacted several suppliers and received bids from them. Which of the following pieces of information is not likely to be useful in making this decision?
   a. The maintenance contract proposed by one supplier covers a shorter time period than the others.
   b. The actual payment price might vary under the proposal submitted by one of the suppliers.
   c. Your major competitor is a frequent customer of one of the suppliers.
   d. Only one of the brands appears to have the graphics capability you need.

2. A typical accounting system:
   a. Provides for the accumulation and summarization of information.
   b. Provides detailed data to investors and creditors.
   c. Instantly provides information to decision makers.
   d. Includes substantial amounts of nonquantitative information for use by individual decision makers.

3. Which information is not likely to be included in the information provided by management to creditors and investors?
   a. Information on the company's past operating results.
   b. Information on the resources currently held by the company.
   c. Information on the cash flows for the last period.
   d. Information on competitors' projected sales.

4. Which set of company policies and guidelines is not likely to have an impact on the decision as to which new color monitor for a microcomputer to purchase?
   a. Company policy with regard to the purchase of equipment with an expected life of more than ten years.
   b. Company policy with regard to the country of origin of purchased equipment.
   c. Company policy with regard to the acceptance of the lowest bid from qualified bidders.
   d. Company policy with regard to approval of purchases over $100.

5. Management is concerned with decisions about:
   a. Which types of financing to use.
   b. How to best use available resources.

c. Generating information about operating success and cash flows for use by investors and creditors.
d. All of the above.

E1-10 Making a Decision Describe an important decision that you made recently or that you are about to make. Identify the goal, the criteria bearing on the decision, the possible alternative choices, the factors important in choosing one alternative over the others, and the information relevant to the decision.

E1-11 Sales Decisions Next semester, one of your friends is planning to take the economics course in which you are enrolled this term and has asked if you would sell her the book you are using. What factors would you take into consideration before giving her an answer?

E1-12 Purchase Decisions Tom Blackman works in the accounting department of one of the large retail stores in town and has just completed an evaluation of microcomputers to decide which model the store should purchase. Tom is also giving serious consideration to purchasing a microcomputer for his own use at home. How might the steps used in the decision process be different between these two decisions?

E1-13 Information Used in Purchasing a Product Explain how information about each of the following may be useful to Marv Headwater in deciding whether to purchase or rent scuba gear and in selecting the best type of gear:

a. Depth of average dive.
b. Duration of average dive.
c. Number of times scuba gear is used per year.
d. Cost of scuba equipment.
e. Changes in technology of scuba equipment.
f. Cost of equipment purchased through catalog sales.
Name at least two other factors that Marv should consider before making a decision.

E1-14 Identifying and Evaluating Alternatives Pamela will graduate from high school at the end of the year and plans to be a computer science major in college. She has developed a list of the most important criteria in deciding which college to attend. Although each of the criteria may have substantial merit, discuss the pros and cons of each:

a. She does not wish to be more than 150 miles from home so she can return home on weekends.
b. Freshmen should not be required to live in the dorms.
c. Class size should not be greater than 20 students.
d. High school grade point average and standardized test scores should not be a major determinant in admission to the college or in acceptance as a computer science major.
e. Majors should be permitted to take a minimum of 60 semester hours of computer science courses as part of a 120-semester-hour program.

E1-15 Acquiring Information Billy Jarvis recently found a baseball card he received in a pack of bubble gum nearly twenty years ago. While reading a sports magazine, he saw an ad offering top prices for baseball cards. What information should Billy gather before offering the card for sale? How can he decide if the offer he receives is fair?

E1-16 The Decision Process Garwood Construction Company has just decided to purchase Amatron Electrical Supply Company. Garwood has been searching for the past two years to find a way of adding other product lines to its home development division. Garwood previously had given thought to acquiring a building materials supply company or a plumbing supply company. It also considered producing its own line of electrical fixtures for homes and businesses. In deciding to purchase Amatron, Garwood's president acquired information on housing starts in the southeastern part of the United States and the sales volume of electrical, plumbing, and building materials suppliers in each of the states in that area over the last decade. The company also evaluated the number of home mortgages taken out each year and the composition of family units purchasing new homes.

Identify the steps of the decision process presented in the chapter and determine where each of Garwood's actions fit into the process.

E1-17 Forms of Organization Indicate whether the following business entities are more likely to be established as a sole proprietorship (SP), partnership (P), or corporation (C):

a. Neighborhood barbershop.
b. Malls Throughout America Hairstyling Parlors.
c. Local law firm.
d. Barbara's Bakery.
e. Fred and Jane's Bowling Bonanza.
f. Interstate Moving Company.

E1-18 Factors Affecting Organizational Form Indicate whether each of the following is likely to be important (I) or unimportant (U) in deciding whether a new business should be established as a sole proprietorship, partnership, or corporation:

a. The number of individuals who will hold ownership.
b. The number of locations nationally and internationally where products will be manufactured.
c. The average age of the owners.
d. The average sale price per unit of products sold.
e. The need to generate a large amount of cash through external funding sources.
f. The protection of personal assets of owners from creditors.
g. The ability of owners to be able to continue to manage the company.
h. The number of days it is expected to take to collect payment from customers.

E1-19 Form of Organization Indicate whether the following criteria would favor using a proprietorship, partnership, or corporate form of organization:

a. JoAnn wishes to minimize the cost of starting a computer repair business.

b. Frank and Tom want to be sure their business activities are not disrupted if one of them dies or withdraws from the business.
c. Martha and Jean want to be sure they can continue to do all the purchasing for their bath accessories stores.
d. Dan wants to be subject to as little regulation as possible.
e. Ann and Sandra want to be able to sell ownership to a number of friends by the end of the first year of operations.
f. Bill and Peter aren't sure whether they want to keep their business as a single company or split it into two separate businesses once they have started to earn a profit.
g. Frieda is concerned about being personally liable for the debts of the business.

E1-20 Accounting Information Indicate whether the following information would be measured, classified, summarized, and communicated in the financial statements of Norbert Company:

a. Cost of land owned by the company.
b. Total dollar amount of sales to customers during the year.
c. Names of customers.
d. Results of a customer satisfaction survey.
e. Amounts owed to banks and other lenders.
f. Repair records of machines used in production.
g. Repair records of computer equipment manufactured and sold by the company.
h. Salary and wage costs for the year.
i. Cash balances on hand.
j. Cost of repairing machines used in production.
k. Names of company shareholders.

E1-21 Reporting Process Place the steps in the financial accounting reporting process given below in correct order:

a. Add together amounts assigned to each category of expense.
b. Determine the types of items that should be assigned to each expense category.
c. Report the total amounts assigned to each expense category to financial statement users.
d. Determine which expenses to report.
e. Assign the amounts paid to the correct expense categories.

E1-22 Steps of Reporting Process The financial reporting process includes five steps: (1) identify the factors to be reported, (2) measure those factors, (3) classify and accumulate information by individual categories, (4) summarize the information assigned to each category, and (5) communicate the information to financial statement users. Assign each of the following actions taken by Pleasant Corporation to the appropriate step of the reporting process:

a. Compute the total amounts spent on labor and materials during the period and combine these amounts to determine the total cost of products sold during the period.
b. Determine which types of labor and materials costs should be combined and reported as cost of goods sold.
c. Develop an income statement that includes cost of goods sold and give a copy to Ralph Schmudge, who owns the company.

d. Record the dollar amounts of all payments for labor and materials made during the period.

e. Assign payments made to employees and suppliers to appropriate expense categories.

E1-23 Operating Costs Early in 1999, the manager of Farnsworth Laundry Supply Company purchased enough detergent to meet its anticipated demand for three years. It also paid $60,000 in advance for a three-year lease on its storage facility. In 2000, Farnsworth reported sales of soap of $120,000, labor costs of $30,000, and $90,000 of profit. In computing its profit, has Farnsworth properly considered all of its costs of doing business? Explain what other costs should be considered and how they should be measured.

E1-24 Obtaining Accounting Information Information about an organization's operations and financial position can be found in its income statements and balance sheets. For each of the questions below, indicate whether you would expect to find the required information in the company's income statements, balance sheets, or another source.

a. Has the company earned more revenue this year than last year?

b. Is the company's net investment in property plant and equipment increasing?

c. Does the company have long-term debt? If so, has additional debt been issued during the past year?

d. What is the company's largest operating cost or expense? What percent is this cost or expense of total net revenue? Has the percent increased or decreased during the past three years?

e. How much income tax did the company pay during the last year?

f. If I hold 100 shares of the company's stock, did my earnings on each share increase or decrease this year?

g. How many people are employed by the company?

E1-25 Financial Statements You have obtained the following information about Zazz Company and wish to evaluate the success of its operations for the last year:

Tax expense	$ 9,000
Cost of products sold	85,000
Total net revenue	155,000
Interest expense	10,000
Interest and other income	6,000
Advertising expense	23,000
Other selling expense	8,000
Administrative expense	13,000

a. Organize the information into an income statement format and calculate Zazz's net income for the year.

b. If you believe a company's net income must be at least 10 percent of total net revenue to be successful, was Zazz successful?

E1-26 Building a Hospital Retirement City, Florida, is considering building a city-owned hospital with specialty care for the elderly. What information regarding the demand for patient care and the costs of providing hospital care should Retirement City consider before making a decision to move forward with this project?

USING ACCOUNTING FOR DECISION MAKING

P1-27 Rental Information In attempting to find housing for his first year of college, Kandwani read the listings of apartments available in the local newspaper. The first ad read as follows:

> *For Rent: Lovely apartment with refrigerator and stove, bath, excellent lighting; conveniently located; no pets; references required. Call 555-4490 after 7, evenings.*

a. How would you rate the information in this ad with regard to its usefulness in arriving at a decision? Indicate why.

b. List the additional information you would need to gather to make a judgment on whether or not to rent the apartment.

P1-28 Selecting Useful Information Different decisions often require different information about the same individual or business. Assume you work for a local savings and loan association and an individual enters and asks for an automobile loan. That afternoon the same individual calls and asks you out on a date.

a. List five items about the individual you think would be important in deciding on whether or not to approve an auto loan.

b. List five items about the individual you think would be important in deciding whether or not to go on a date with that person.

c. List three items you think would be important for both decisions.

P1-29 Choosing the Form of Organization Anna Garza just graduated from college and is planning to start her own business. Anna is trying to decide on the best form of business organization and is debating between setting up practice as a sole proprietor or establishing a corporate entity and serving as its president.

a. What advantage(s) would there be to operating as a sole proprietorship?

b. What advantage(s) would there be to operating as a corporation?

c. Which form of business organization, if any, would Anna's customers be likely to prefer? Why?

P1-30 Evaluating Operating Results Rita Janson has a significant ownership interest in three business enterprises. Five years ago, she and a friend borrowed several hundred thousand dollars and built a large bowling alley in a new mega-shopping mall. The business is run as a partnership and was quite profitable the first several years. This past year, however, it operated at a loss. Rita also holds 70 percent of the common stock of a medium-size corporation that produces plastic drain tile, and has a successful local beverage distributorship that she runs as a sole proprietorship.

a. From the viewpoint of the bank loan officer who is concerned about receiving the next annual payment on the loan associated with the bowling alley, tell what claim the bank has against:
   1. The assets of the bowling alley.
   2. The assets of the drain tile company.
   3. The assets of the beverage distributorship.
b. What other assets might the bank be able to claim if the loan associated with the bowling alley is not paid?
c. If you were preparing a listing of Rita Janson's assets and liabilities, would it be appropriate to include her portion of each of the assets and liabilities of the bowling alley? How would her ownership in the other two business entities be reported? In each case, explain how you reached your conclusion.

P1-31 Acquiring Information   The purchasing officer of Acme Finance Company was very concerned about the reliability of a piece of equipment it was about to purchase from Bumble Manufacturing Company. Before purchasing the equipment, the officer asked a number of questions about the frequency-of-repair record of the equipment, the length of time needed for repairs, whether the manufacturer did the repair work, and the average cost of repairs. In each case, the sales representative of Bumble Manufacturing responded that there were no more repair problems with this equipment than with any of the other models in their product line.

a. How would you evaluate the response by the sales representative?
b. How might Acme acquire additional information about the equipment?
c. How would Acme determine if the information provided by the sales representative was accurate?
d. How important would you consider the manufacturer's warranty to be in this case?

P1-32 Forming a Partnership   Three students attending Rockystone College have decided to start a summer lawn care service in their hometown rather than work at the local suds and burger places where they had worked the past two summers. They are planning to form a partnership. List those factors that might be of importance in determining how profits are to be shared.

P1-33 Evaluating Information   The head of the accounting department of Stanway Manufacturing has attempted to design a formal set of reports on the operations and activities of the company. At the end of each week, he now prepares an Excel spreadsheet analysis of company activities for the week and gives it to each department head and company officer. The three company officers started Stanway in 1963 just after they graduated from high school. All three have been involved heavily in the day-to-day business activities of Stanway and have not had time to take any business or computer courses. How might the backgrounds of the officers affect their views of the reports prepared by the accountant?

<hr>

EXPANDING YOUR HORIZONS

C1-34 Review of the Decision Process   Jocelyn Franklin has just graduated from college near the top of her class with a degree in management. Her grandfather is so proud of her that he rewards her with a cash gift of $100,000. Jocelyn is ambitious and is determined to succeed, but she quickly needs to make a decision. Although she has a number of good job opportunities, she has narrowed the alternatives under consideration to two. She has been offered a job as an assistant store manager at Worthington's World of Values (WWV), a local discount megastore, starting at $40,000 per year, with good opportunities for advancement. If she takes that job, she will put the $100,000 from her grandfather in the bank to earn 5 percent annual interest.

On the other hand, Jocelyn has always been somewhat of a free spirit, and a little risk has always been exciting to her. Also, she prefers to be her own boss. Her friend André Preneur started his own business several years ago. His business has been very successful, and he now is looking for an additional supplier of one of the elements of his product. If Jocelyn is interested, André will purchase all of the counter-hardened extrusalized bermits she can produce. The special machines needed to produce the bermits cost $50,000 each and are expected to last for 20 years. Not having established her credit, Jocelyn is unable to borrow money to purchase the machines, but she can use the $100,000 her grandfather gave her. If Jocelyn purchases 2 of the machines, she can produce 40,000 bermits per year, and André will purchase them for $5 each. Her cost for materials, employees, rent, utilities, repairs, and other items she figures will be about $95,000 per year, but she will not have to pay these costs until the cash starts rolling in from André. Of course, if André's business falls off, Jocelyn will be in big trouble unless she can find another customer, which would be difficult unless the economy was exceptionally strong.

Tired of living on a student's budget, Jocelyn decides she needs at least $45,000 a year before taxes to get her started living in the style to which she wants to become accustomed. Faced with an important decision, Jocelyn settles back to think this one over. She thinks back to one of her early management classes that taught her the structure of the decision process, and she begins to organize her thinking about the decision at hand.

a. Identify the primary alternatives available to Jocelyn.
b. From what you know about Jocelyn, construct her set of values and preferences related to the decision at hand and reasonable criteria for making the choice between Jocelyn's primary alternatives.
c. List the available information useful for the decision.
d. Identify the steps in the decision-making process that Jocelyn should take.
e. Given the information that is available, which alternative do you think Jocelyn will choose? Why?

C1-35   Making a Decision   Your parents are giving serious thought to purchasing a new wide-screen television set. When you called home last night to discuss your travel plans for semester break with them, they asked for your assistance in deciding which television set to purchase.

a. List those attributes you think are important in selecting a new television set.
b. From what sources might you gather relevant information about different models of televisions?
c. Once your parents have narrowed their choice down to three models, how might they find the lowest prices?

 C1-36   Choosing a Major   Well, here you are taking an introductory accounting course. You've thought about various majors, but have had some trouble deciding. Engineering just doesn't seem to be for you. And English? Give me a break! Business, on the other hand, does seem to offer some variety, and there are jobs. But, what area of business is for you? Accounting? Well, let's see what happens in this course. Finance? Marketing? Management? Management Information Systems? Obviously this is an important decision, so it deserves some real thought.

a. Identify two possible majors that might be of interest to you. They can be different areas of business or majors other than business.
b. Specify your goal structure or set of values and preferences relevant to your choice of major. In other words, specify the factors that are important to you in choosing a major and a possible career. Which of these factors are most important to you?
c. Develop decision criteria for making a choice of majors. The criteria should be derived from and consistent with the values you specified in (b), with the criteria weighted by the degree of importance you assigned to them.
d. Identify the sources from which you can acquire information relevant to your decision. Acquire the information you feel will be useful in making your decision.
e. List all of the information you have available about each of your specified alternatives that you think is relevant to your decision. If you are not sure about some of the no-

tions you have relating to the alternatives, list them anyway. Indicate how reliable you think each listed item is.
f. What factors over which you have no control may have an impact on the outcome of your decision? In other words, once you have made your decision and undertaken the chosen major, what factors may result in an outcome different from what you expect?
g. Make a choice between the alternatives you have listed. Justify your choice.

C1-37   Get a Job!   In college, you prepare yourself for a career—a lifetime of opportunities. While in college, however, students often must be employed to pay for living and college costs. List the decision criteria that you would use right now to select a job if you were seeking employment (or a change in employment) for the remainder of your time in college. Then, list the decision criteria you will use when you seek career employment for when you complete your degree. Compare the two lists. How are they similar? How are they different?

C1-38   Ethical Decisions   Federal prosecutors announced in July 1993 that Biopharmaceutics, Inc., had pleaded guilty to felony charges as a result of submitting false information in attempting to gain governmental approval to market various genetic drugs.

a. What factors may motivate a company to report information that it knows is unreliable or falsified?
b. How do you believe you would respond if your superior suggested that by making a few relatively minor changes in data you have generated from a series of tests that it would be possible to immediately gain approval for producing and selling a new product? Justify your anticipated response.

C1-39   Our Market Economy   A market economy thrives on the entrepreneurial spirit and the laws of supply and demand. Nowhere is this more evident than with ticket scalpers. They buy large quantities of tickets at box office prices and resell them at higher prices. The most profits are to be made when demand is the highest. For example, when the Atlanta Braves began postseason ticket sales in 1999, a line formed outside the stadium the night before. Ticket scalpers have been known to hire street people to stand in line all night to buy the maximum number of tickets so the scalpers have an ample supply for resale.

a. Is ticket scalping merely another form of the law of supply and demand? Is there anything unethical about scalping?
b. Who benefits from scalping?
c. Should scalping be prohibited or otherwise regulated?
d. What controls could a business put in place to deter scalping?
e. Suppose each ticket costs $30 at the box office and each purchaser in line can buy 12 tickets until all are sold. How will the scalper arrange to pay for the tickets so the individuals hired to stand in line do not leave with the money or the tickets?

 C1-40   The Restaurant Critic   Every time you visit a new restaurant, you serve as your own restaurant critic. You determine what you like and don't like about that establishment. Based on your experience, you then decide whether or not you will return to that restaurant.

Select a restaurant that you have never visited. Based on what is important to you, prepare a list of criteria for evaluating the restaurant. Have breakfast, lunch, or dinner at the restaurant. Using your list of criteria, determine whether you will continue dining at this establishment. Write a one-page restaurant critique explaining your decision criteria, your dining experience, and your decision regarding future visits to this restaurant.

 C1-41 Information and Decisions Look through several publications referred to as "the popular press," such as your local newspaper or a major news magazine such as *Time, Newsweek,* or *U.S. News and World Report.* Find an article that illustrates how information had an impact on an important decision by a local, regional, or federal government unit. The article should detail how specific information helped in making an informed decision or how misleading or sparse information led to making a bad decision. Write a brief memo of no more than half a page to your instructor reporting on the information and decision-making aspects of the article.

 C1-42 An Important Business Decision Look through several publications referred to as "the business press," such as the business section of a major city newspaper or a major business publication such as *The Wall Street Journal, BusinessWeek,* or *Forbes.* Find an article that illustrates how information had an impact on an important *business* decision. The article should detail how specific information helped in making an informed decision or how misleading or sparse information led to making a bad decision. Write a brief memo of no more than a page to your instructor reporting on the information and decision-making aspects of the article and indicating how the business and others were affected by the decision.

 C1-43 Acquiring Information from Reference Sources

a. Go to the library and look up AT&T in *Moody's Industrial Manual.*
   1. What was the original name of the company, and when was it established?
   2. What are AT&T's primary business activities?
   3. In 1996, what new name was given to AT&T Global Information Solutions, and what was AT&T's plan for the division?
   4. What amount of total revenue was reported for the most recent year?
b. Go to *Value Line Investment Survey* and look up AT&T.
   1. What is the timeliness rating given for AT&T? What does this mean?
   2. What is the safety rating given for AT&T? What does this mean?
   3. What amount is reported as total debt?

   4. How does the information in *Value Line* appear to differ from that presented in *Moody's Industrial Manual*?

 C1-44 Team Project: Business Information Organize in groups of three to five students. Pick any local business nearby, and list the types of information that you think are important to operating that business. Think of information used by those operating the business, as well as information the business must provide to others. Which of these types of information would you classify as accounting information and which are not accounting information? What is the source of each of these types of information? Set up an appointment to talk with the manager of the business, or if the business is large, with an accountant at the business. Review your list of information with the individual from the business and see if any crucial types of information are missing from your list.

 C1-45 Team Project: Starting a Business The Tuff N' Chewy Pizza chain has been growing by leaps and bounds since it was established by three members of the food and nutrition faculty at Foodstuff University. The primary selling point of the pizza is the exceptionally thick and succulent crust that keeps its flavor five times longer than other brands and takes much longer to chew. As a result, consumers can enjoy real pizza flavor while consuming fewer slices, thereby ingesting far fewer calories. Many repeat customers even order Tuff N' Chewy pizza with no toppings at all.

At present, the Tuff N' Chewy Pizza Company gives the right to operate a Tuff N' Chewy Pizza Palace for a franchise payment of $50,000 a year. For this payment, the operator, called a franchisee, receives (1) the right to sell pizza under the Tuff N' Chewy trade name and to use the Tuff N' Chewy special trademark, (2) the right to send three people each year to a special training program designed to teach participants how to operate a Tuff N' Chewy franchise efficiently, and (3) the special Tuff N' Chewy recipe and a year's supply of the two vital ingredients that give Tuff N' Chewy pizza its unique characteristics.

Assume your team is a group of friends who are interested in the possibility of opening a Tuff N' Chewy Pizza Palace near your campus. Prepare a report, written or oral, as designated by your instructor, that addresses the following issues:

a. Competition is an important factor in determining whether to start a business. Make a list of pizza places located within about one mile of your campus. How many other types of food places are located within that area? Make a list of the other types of food places and decide whether they are likely to compete for the same customers you would be likely to attract.
b. What additional information relating to costs would you need before deciding whether or not to enter the pizza business? Where would you go to gather each type of additional information?

c. What is the average price charged by your competition for a large, medium, and small pizza with cheese and one topping? How would you approach setting the price for Tuff N' Chewy pizza, assuming the company gives you that option?

Internet Exercises: Visit our Web site for additional exercises.

Annual Report Project Part 1

The purpose of this project is to provide you with the opportunity to apply what you learn about accounting by examining and analyzing the financial statements of a real company. As specific topics are discussed throughout the text, you can apply what you have learned to understanding the financial statements of the company you have chosen. Along with gaining a better understanding of the company you are analyzing, you will gain valuable insight into how accounting principles are applied in practice.

INSTRUCTIONS

1. Select a manufacturing or merchandising company (not a financial institution or service provider) that has securities (stocks or bonds) held by the public. Virtually all well-known companies have issued securities to the public. To be sure that the company you choose has publicly traded securities outstanding, look for your company's name in the security-price listings of *The Wall Street Journal* (Money & Investing section) or any major newspaper. Be sure to select a company based in the United States unless directed otherwise by your instructor. Some well-known foreign companies such as Toyota prepare financial statements for issuance in the United States, but the accounting principles and reporting practices are not always the same as for U.S. companies and, therefore, may not be consistent with what you are studying in the text. Alternatively, your instructor might provide a list of companies from which to choose.

2. Obtain a copy of the company's latest annual report. As discussed in the chapter, company annual reports (and filings with the U.S. Securities and Exchange Commission, such as proxy statements and Form 10-Ks) can generally be obtained by calling the shareholder relations department of the company. They also can often be obtained by downloading directly from the company's home page; sometimes a paper copy can be ordered directly from the home page. Annual reports for many companies also can be ordered free through

annual report services, such as those offered by *The Wall Street Journal* or found online at *www.prars.com*. Reports ordered through report services are generally received within a few days of ordering but can take several weeks.

The U.S. Securities and Exchange Commission's home page at *www.sec.gov* is one of the most comprehensive and immediately available sources of information about companies with publicly traded securities. Annual reports filed with the SEC are filed on Form 10-K and almost always include the company's financial statements and accompanying notes. However, the Form 10-K generally includes extensive amounts of information of which the financial statements represent just a small part.

Be sure that the annual report you obtain includes a full set of the company's financial statements and related notes. Some companies now issue summary annual reports that contain only condensed financial statements. Once you have obtained the annual report for the company you select, examine the report to make sure that it is not labeled "summary annual report" and that the financial statements are not labeled "condensed" financial statements. The annual report should also contain a full set of accompanying notes to the financial statements, usually averaging five to twenty pages in length. Summary annual reports usually omit the notes or include condensed notes averaging only one to three pages in length. If the company you choose prepares only a summary annual report for stockholders or presents condensed financial statements, you will also need to obtain the complete set of financial statements and notes, usually found in the company's proxy statement or Form 10-K filed with the SEC.

3. The annual report used, or a copy, must be submitted with each assignment unless your instructor indicates otherwise.

4. As part of your first assignment, you will be asked to look over the company's financial statements

and related notes, examine any other information you feel is appropriate, and decide whether you want to buy the company's stock or sell the stock short. Selling stock short involves selling at the current price shares you borrow but do not own. These shares must be replaced at a later time by buying them at the price current then. Thus, if you decide to buy the stock now, you would be expecting the price to increase so you could sell the shares later at a higher price. If you sell the stock short currently, you would be expecting the price of the shares to decrease, and you would purchase the shares later at a price lower than that at which you sold the shares. In a later part of the project, you will be given the opportunity to evaluate your investment decision.

5. Answer the questions asked in each part of this continuing project in this chapter and the chapters that follow. Provide specific sources and locations for each answer (e.g., annual report p. 25; note 3 to the financial statements; *The Wall Street Journal*, p. C5). Where computations are needed to answer a question, clearly present those computations.

6. All questions should be answered in a clear and concise manner, using proper grammar, spelling, and terminology.

QUESTIONS FOR PART I:

a. What is the name of the company you have chosen?

b. How would you describe the nature of your company's business? What products does your company sell?

c. What are some of the familiar company or brand names associated with your company?

d. In what city is your company headquartered?

e. In what geographic areas does your company conduct its operations?

f. What form of business organization (e.g., partnership, corporation) does your company use? Why do you think this form of organization is appropriate for your company?

g. What are the names of the financial statements included in your company's annual report?

h. What is the date of each of the financial statements presented by your company?

i. What is the current price of your company's stock (ownership shares)? Indicate the date of that price. Do not use the stock prices provided in the annual report because they are not current. Instead, find your company's listing in the security-price section of *The Wall Street Journal* or other major newspaper, or use the Internet.

j. What is the 52-week price range of your company's stock?

k. Look over your company's financial statements and any other information you may have available about this company. Based on this information and the current stock price, do you choose to (1) buy or (2) sell short this company's stock with the expectation of closing your investment position at the end of the project? Briefly indicate the primary reason or reasons for your choice. Because you are only beginning your study of accounting and you may currently have little knowledge of financial concepts, your decision to buy or sell short might be based primarily on your general knowledge of the company or on intuition.

ADDITIONAL ASSIGNMENT:

Obtain a recommendation or assessment relating to investing in your company's stock from a reputable investment service, such as the *Value Line Investment Survey,* that you find in the library or online.

CHAPTER TWO

Accounting in a Decision-Making Environment

REVIEW

Chapter 1 looked at decision making and included a brief discussion of the accounting process.

WHERE THIS CHAPTER FITS

The final step in the accounting process is communicating accounting information. In this chapter, we continue our look at the type of accounting information communicated through financial statements. This chapter explores who uses financial statements and accounting information, how the information is generated, and who provides and regulates that information.

LOOKING AHEAD

In Chapter 3, we will look more closely at cash flows, which are at the heart of financial decision making, and the type of accounting information presented with respect to cash flows.

I've been hearing that these Internet companies are really hot. That new online stock trading company, Trades-R-Us, is sure to be a winner. I bet if I invest in that company, I'll be rich in no time. But, how will I know when to sell? What if I lose my money? Then I won't be able to buy that new car or go on the vacation I planned. Maybe I should learn more about the company before I invest.

"All public offerings [of securities] start with hiring a securities attorney and accounting firm to prepare audited financial statements. . . . sources say it pays to use the best legal and accounting firms you can find."[1]

[1] *The Business Journal of Portland*, November 11, 1994.

I f you were considering investing in the Trades-R-Us Company, what would you want to know about that business before committing your hard-earned money? Obviously, you would want to know how the company will fare in the future. Unfortunately, only fortune tellers know the future, and even they apparently do not see sufficient detail to prosper. Even when the future becomes the present, without sufficient information, we may be unsure about what has happened.

What information do you think would be most helpful in making an investment decision? Think about it and list four or five items of information that you think would be available to you. Save your list and then compare it with what you learn about accounting over the next several weeks. See if you would change the list, and see if accounting provides you with all the information you need to make decisions about investing in a company. As a decision maker, you be the judge.

In this chapter we explore how accounting information is provided to decision makers. We also take a closer look at the decision makers who use accounting information, as well as the accountants who provide it.

Finally, we look at how the content of accounting reports is determined. After reading this chapter, you should be able to:

1. Identify the four basic financial statements and explain how the financial statements provide useful information to decision makers.

2. Identify how the relationships that exist among the financial statements serve to present a complete picture of a company's operations and financial position.

3. Understand the types of decisions that users of financial statements make based on accounting information.

4. Explain how accounting information systems help ensure useful information for decision makers.

5. Describe the different types of accounting activities and the role each plays in providing information for decision makers.

6. Describe the role of accounting rules or standards in ensuring useful information for decision makers.

7. Describe how the current social and economic environment influences the accounting profession.

THE BASIC FINANCIAL STATEMENTS

Information for Decisions

Investors, creditors, and others making financial decisions often rely on financial statements that contain information about the operations, cash flows, and financial position of an organization. Understanding why financial statements are provided and the information that can be found in each statement helps a potential investor, credi- tor, or other decision maker answer questions such as these: Do I want to invest in or provide money to this company? Has the company been profitable over a period of time? What items of value does the company own, and what claims are there against those items? Does the company generate enough cash to meet its obligations?

As we discussed in Chapter 1, the capital markets bring together potential suppliers of capital with businesses and others needing capital. Those potential suppliers of capital must decide to what extent they will provide capital to those wanting it. To make these decisions, suppliers of capital need information, and some of this information is often in the form of financial statements. Recall that **financial statements** are accounting-based presentations that provide information about the operations, cash flows, and financial position of a specific organization. Businesses, not-for-profit organizations, and governmental entities all issue financial statements. A full set of financial statements presents the results of an entity's operations for a period of time and the financial position of the entity at a specific point in time. How is this information useful to decision makers, and why do organizations provide it? Let's return to our example from Chapter 1.

Remember the video venture you started in Chapter 1? Guess what? It's a success! At least you think it is. Almost one month has gone by, and your estimates have worked out ex- actly. You might have rented more videos, but when you reached the number of weekly rentals you planned, you were so tired that you just shut down until the weekend. You seem to have made about a thousand dollars.

You think, though, that you can make a lot more money. However, that would mean working more and buying more videos. You could easily hire more help, and buying more videos is easy. On the other hand, you need all the money you are getting from the business to pay for school. But you have a friend who lives down the hall—maybe she would like to join your business as a partner.

When you asked her if she was interested, she started asking all sorts of pointed ques- tions. How much is already invested in the venture? What does the "company" own and how much does it owe? How profitable was the company last month, and what were the revenues and expenses? What would be her share of the profits? She was really interested in the com- pany's potential cash flow. She also started talking about income statements, balance sheets, and the like. Wow! You didn't know about any of that stuff. You just did a little planning, bought some videos, started renting them out, and it all seemed to work.

After thinking about it, though, you realize that no one is going to join you unless you can show what has happened so far. That, your friend explained, is what financial statements are for: to provide information that will answer decision makers' questions about an organi- zation. Convinced, you pull together receipts, bank records, and other scraps of paper. With a lot of help from her, you prepare a set of financial statements for the venture she is now call- ing Our Video Store. These statements appear in Exhibit 2–1.

FINANCIAL STATEMENTS FOR OUR VIDEO STORE

EXHIBIT 2-1

OUR VIDEO STORE
INCOME STATEMENT FOR THE FIRST MONTH OF OPERATION

Revenues:		
Video rentals	$3,480	
Game rentals	320	
Total revenues		$3,800
Expenses:		
Rent	$1,000	
Wages	600	
Cost of videos and games (allocated)	260	
Other	200	
Total expenses		2,060
Net income		$1,740

OUR VIDEO STORE
BALANCE SHEET
AS OF THE END OF THE FIRST MONTH OF OPERATION

Assets:	
Cash	$2,000
Videos and games ($6,800−$260)	6,540
Total assets	$8,540
Liabilities	$ - 0 -
Owner's equity	8,540
Total liabilities and owner's equity	$8,540

OUR VIDEO STORE
STATEMENT OF CASH FLOWS FOR THE FIRST MONTH OF OPERATION

Cash generated from operations:		
Video and game rentals		$3,800
Less cash expenses:		
Rent	$1,000	
Wages	600	
Other	200	
Total cash expenses		(1,800)
Total cash generated from operations		$2,000
Cash used in investing activities:		
Purchase of videos		(6,800)
Cash from financing activities:		
Investment by owner		6,800
Total cash generated		$2,000

OUR VIDEO STORE
STATEMENT OF CHANGES IN OWNERS' EQUITY
FOR THE FIRST MONTH OF OPERATION

Balance, beginning of month	$ - 0 -
Add: Investment by owner	6,800
Net income for first month	1,740
Balance, end of month	$8,540

The financial statements for Our Video store illustrate the four basic financial statements prepared by virtually all companies that need to raise capital:

- Income statement
- Statement of financial position (balance sheet)
- Statement of cash flows
- Statement of changes in owners' equity or statement of changes in retained earnings (retained earnings statement)

The financial statements of major corporations are similar to those of Our Video Store, except that they are more complex because the businesses and their transactions are more complex. The financial statements for Gateway, Inc., are shown in Exhibits 2–2, 2–3, 2–4, and 2–5. Those financial statements, along with notes to the financial statements and some other elements of Gateway's annual report, are also presented in Appendix A. The notes to the financial statements are important because they clarify some of the elements in the financial statements and provide additional information. The notes are considered to be an integral part of the statements. In some cases, the notes or additional disclosures can be quite lengthy. For example, Ralston Purina's additional disclosures several years ago added almost ninety pages to its annual report.

Because decision makers receive much of their information about businesses from financial statements, a thorough understanding of these statements is crucial. We'll take a brief look at the financial statements next, and then explore them in more detail in later chapters.

EXHIBIT 2-2   **GATEWAY'S INCOME STATEMENT**

CONSOLIDATED INCOME STATEMENTS FOR THE YEARS ENDED DECEMBER 31, 1996, 1997, AND 1998 (IN THOUSANDS, EXCEPT PER SHARE AMOUNTS)			
	1996	**1997**	**1998**
Net sales	$5,035,228	$6,293,680	$7,467,925
Cost of goods sold	4,099,073	5,217,239	5,921,651
Gross profit	936,155	1,076,441	1,546,274
Selling, general and administrative expenses	580,061	786,168	1,052,047
Nonrecurring expenses	—	113,842	—
Operating income	356,094	176,431	494,227
Other income, net	26,622	27,189	47,021
Income before income taxes	382,716	203,620	541,248
Provision for income taxes	132,037	93,823	194,849
Net income	$ 250,679	$ 109,797	$ 346,399
Net income per share:			
Basic	$1.64	$.71	$2.23
Diluted	$1.60	$.70	$2.18
Weighted average shares outstanding:			
Basic	152,745	153,840	155,542
Diluted	156,237	156,201	158,929

INCOME STATEMENT

Making a profit is a primary goal of businesses. Decision makers want to know about a business's success in achieving this goal. The **income statement** presents information about the firm's profitability for a period of time. For Our Video Store, the period is one month; for Gateway, the period is one year.

The income statement provides specific information on the individual elements that determine the firm's profit or income. **Revenues**, the amounts generated from the sale of a firm's products or services, increase income. **Expenses**, the costs the firm incurs in doing business, reduce income. The firm's **net income** is the difference between its revenues and expenses. The amount of detail provided for revenues and expenses varies by the size and complexity of the business and at the discretion of management. (See In Practice 2-1.) As can be seen from Exhibit 2–2, Gateway reports a relatively small number of items in its income statement, although it has more than $7 billion in sales. It also includes income statements for the two previous years so that comparisons can be made across years.

STATEMENT OF FINANCIAL POSITION

The **statement of financial position,** or **balance sheet,** lists all of a company's items of value, called **assets,** and the claims against those assets. Our Video Store has only two types of assets, cash and videos. Gateway has a much wider range of assets.

The claims against a company's assets are of two types, those of creditors, called **liabilities,** and those of owners, called **equities.** Our Video Store has paid cash for all of its purchases so far, but if money were borrowed to acquire more videos, a liability would be created. All major companies report a number of different types of liabilities, as can be seen in Gateway's balance sheet in Exhibit 2–3. Companies such as Gateway typically incur liabilities as a normal part of their operations. For example, they may purchase merchandise or equipment from suppliers on credit, giving rise to a liability (accounts payable), or they may

EXHIBIT 2-3 **GATEWAY'S BALANCE SHEET**

CONSOLIDATED BALANCE SHEETS		
DECEMBER 31, 1997 AND 1998		
(IN THOUSANDS, EXCEPT PER SHARE AMOUNTS)		
	1997	**1998**
ASSETS		
Current assets:		
Cash and cash equivalents	$ 593,601	$1,169,810
Marketable securities	38,648	158,657
Accounts receivable, net	510,679	558,851
Inventory	249,224	167,924
Other	152,531	172,944
Total current assets	1,544,683	2,228,186
Property, plant and equipment, net	376,467	530,988
Intangibles, net	82,590	65,944
Other assets	35,531	65,262
	$2,039,271	$2,890,380
LIABILITIES AND STOCKHOLDERS' EQUITY		
Current liabilities:		
Notes payable and current maturities of long-term obligations	$ 13,969	$ 11,415
Accounts payable	488,717	718,071
Accrued liabilities	271,250	415,265
Accrued royalties	159,418	167,873
Other current liabilities	70,552	117,050
Total current liabilities	1,003,906	1,429,674
Long-term obligations, net of current maturities	7,240	3,360
Warranty and other liabilities	98,081	112,971
Total liabilities	1,109,227	1,546,005
Commitments and Contingencies (Notes 3 and 4)		
Stockholders' equity:		
Preferred stock, $.01 par value, 5,000 shares authorized; none issued and outstanding	—	—
Class A common stock, nonvoting, $.01 par value, 1,000 shares authorized; none issued and outstanding	—	—
Common stock, $.01 par value, 220,000 shares authorized; 154,128 shares and 156,569 shares issued and outstanding, respectively	1,541	1,566
Additional paid-in capital	299,483	365,986
Retained earnings	634,509	980,908
Accumulated other comprehensive loss	(5,489)	(4,085)
Total stockholders' equity	930,044	1,344,375
	$2,039,271	$2,890,380

owe amounts at the end of the period for costs such as rent or wages (accrued liabilities). In addition, companies may borrow cash directly, giving rise to a liability for repaying the loan (notes payable or long-term debt). Although liabilities reflect creditors' claims against the assets, they also indicate one source of resources used to acquire the assets.

Owners' claims, or equities, are residual claims in that the claims of creditors have priority over those of owners. If a company goes out of business, owners get only the assets that are left after the creditors' claims are satisfied. In some cases, few or no assets may remain for owners. However, if a firm is successful, the owners' claims increase while those of creditors remain fixed. Because Our Video Store has been successful, the owner's equity at the end of the first month ($8,540) is greater than the amount originally invested ($6,800). Gateway's owners had an interest in their company that exceeded $1.3 billion at December 31, 1998, as reported in the balance sheet in Exhibit 2–3.

The balance sheet provides valuable information to decision makers. For example, it helps creditors decide if their claims will be satisfied in a timely manner. It lists the amount and types of assets currently available to satisfy those claims, and it helps creditors project the assets that will be available when future claims must be satisfied. The balance sheet is also used by owners in valuing their claims on the company's assets.

STATEMENT OF CASH FLOWS

Decision makers need to be able to assess the probability, amount, and timing of future cash flows. Any organization must generate enough cash to satisfy obligations that require outlays of cash, such as for payment of rent, wages, and loans. The **statement of cash flows** lists the types and amounts of cash received (inflows) and paid out (outflows) by the firm during a period of time. As can be seen from Gateway's cash flow statement in Exhibit 2–4, the cash flows are categorized as relating to operating activities, investing activities, and financing activities. This helps decision makers understand where the cash came from and where it went, and this, in turn, should help them be better able to assess future cash flows.

Looking at the financial statements for Our Video Store, why is the cash generated from operations ($2,000) not the same as net income ($1,740)? The difference is that, in computing net income, the cost of videos is spread over the periods they are being used, but all of the cash for their purchase was paid out at the time they were acquired. Because the computation of net income involves considerations other than cash flows, both an income statement and a statement of cash flows are needed. Being profitable does not always mean a company will have sufficient cash. It might, for example, use its cash to purchase goods to sell and equipment to use and may have no cash left to pay its other bills.

STATEMENT OF CHANGES IN OWNERS' EQUITY

While the balance sheet reports a company's financial position at a specific point in time, both the income statement and statement of cash flows provide information about how the company's financial position changed during a period of time. Each of the two statements provides just a part of the picture relating to the change. The remaining part of the picture is provided by the **statement of changes in owners' equity**, which describes the changes during the period in the specific elements making up the owners' interest in the business enterprise. In general, the elements of the owners' equity of a corporation relate to (1) direct investment by the owners (common stock and additional paid-in capital) and (2) earnings of the company reinvested in the business (retained earnings). As you can see from Exhibit 2–5, Gateway's statement of changes in owners' (stockholders') equity reports changes in several elements of equity for a three-year period. The statement explains how the stockholders' equity section of Gateway's balance sheet changed from period to period. Gateway did not issue any ownership shares during the periods included in the statement except to employees

EXHIBIT 2-4	**GATEWAY'S CASH FLOW STATEMENT**

CONSOLIDATED STATEMENTS OF CASH FLOWS			
FOR THE YEARS ENDED DECEMBER 31, 1996, 1997, AND 1998			
(IN THOUSANDS)			
	1996	1997	1998
Cash flows from operating activities:			
Net income	$250,679	$109,797	$ 346,399
Adjustments to reconcile net income to net cash			
provided by operating activities:			
Depreciation and amortization	61,763	86,774	105,524
Provision for uncollectible accounts receivable	20,832	5,688	3,991
Deferred income taxes	(13,395)	(63,247)	(58,425)
Other, net	1,986	42	770
Nonrecurring expenses	—	113,842	—
Changes in operating assets and liabilities:			
Accounts receivable	(66,052)	(41,950)	(52,164)
Inventory	(54,261)	59,486	81,300
Other assets	(13,311)	(54,513)	451
Accounts payable	176,724	66,253	228,921
Accrued liabilities	51,390	48,405	144,899
Accrued royalties	1,885	34,148	8,455
Other current liabilities	43,057	35,816	76,278
Warranty and other liabilities	22,699	42,256	21,252
Net cash provided by operating activities	483,996	442,797	907,651
Cash flows from investing activities:			
Capital expenditures	(143,746)	(175,656)	(235,377)
Purchases of available-for-sale securities	—	(49,619)	(168,965)
Proceeds from maturities or sales of			
available-for-sale securities	3,030	10,985	48,924
Acquisitions, net of cash acquired	—	(142,320)	—
Other, net	2,667	(4,055)	(992)
Net cash used in investing activities	(138,049)	(360,665)	(356,410)
Cash flows from financing activities:			
Proceeds from issuances of notes payable	10,000	10,000	—
Principal payments on long-term obligations			
and notes payable	(14,047)	(15,588)	(13,173)
Stock options exercised	9,520	5,741	36,159
Net cash provided by financing activities	5,473	153	22,986
Foreign exchange effect on cash and cash			
equivalents	(1,457)	(5,044)	1,982
Net increase in cash and cash equivalents	349,963	77,241	576,209
Cash and cash equivalents, beginning of year	166,397	516,360	593,601
Cash and cash equivalents, end of year	$516,360	$593,601	$1,169,810

and officers. As is common with technology-related companies, Gateway provides its employees the opportunity to acquire ownership shares in the company at reduced prices.

Gateway's net income, reported in its income statement, is also included in the statement of changes in stockholders' equity because the net income belongs to the owners and increases their interest in the enterprise. Therefore, Gateway's statement of changes in stockholders' equity reports an increase in retained earnings for the amount of net income earned.

GATEWAY'S STATEMENT OF CHANGES IN OWNERS' EQUITY — EXHIBIT 2-5

CONSOLIDATED STATEMENTS OF CHANGES IN STOCKHOLDERS' EQUITY AND COMPREHENSIVE INCOME
FOR THE YEARS ENDED DECEMBER 31, 1996, 1997, AND 1998
(IN THOUSANDS)

	Common Stock Shares	Amount	Additional Paid-in Capital	Retained Earnings	Accumulated Other Comprehensive Income (Loss)	Total
Balances at December 31, 1995	149,106	$1,492	$279,701	$274,033	$ 293	$ 555,519
Comprehensive income:						
Net income	—	—	—	250,679	—	250,679
Other comprehensive income:						
Foreign currency translation	—	—	—	—	225	225
Unrealized gain on available-for-sale securities	—	—	—	—	31	31
Comprehensive income						250,935
Stock issuances under employee plans, including tax benefit of $30,451	6,545	66	39,905	—	—	39,971
Stock retirement	(2,139)	(22)	(30,862)	—	—	(30,884)
Balances at December 31, 1996	153,512	1,536	288,744	524,712	549	815,541
Comprehensive income:						
Net income	—	—	—	109,797	—	109,797
Other comprehensive income:						
Foreign currency translation	—	—	—	—	(6,053)	(6,053)
Unrealized gain on available-for-sale securities	—	—	—	—	15	15
Comprehensive income						103,759
Stock issuances under employee plans, including tax benefit of $5,003	616	5	10,739	—	—	10,744
Balances at December 31, 1997	154,128	1,541	299,483	634,509	(5,489)	930,044
Comprehensive income:						
Net income	—	—	—	346,399	—	346,399
Other comprehensive income:						
Foreign currency translation	—	—	—	—	1,549	1,549
Unrealized loss on available-for-sale securities	—	—	—	—	(145)	(145)
Comprehensive income						347,803
Stock issuances under employee plans, including tax benefit of $29,769	2,423	24	65,904	—	—	65,928
Stock issued to officer	18	1	599	—	—	600
Balances at December 31, 1998	156,569	$1,566	$365,986	$980,908	$ (4,085)	$1,344,375

If some of the profits were distributed to the owners in cash, rather than being retained in the business, retained earnings would have been reduced by the amount distributed. Distributions of income to owners are called **dividends**. Gateway did not pay any dividends because management chose to reinvest the profits in the business to provide for future growth. Dividend information is important to owners and potential owners because it helps them assess anticipated future cash distributions.

A few companies present a statement of changes in retained earnings rather than a full statement of changes in stockholders' equity. These companies must then disclose changes in the other equity accounts in the notes to the financial statements. Unincorporated businesses, such as Our Video Store, typically include fewer elements in their statements of changes in owners' equity than corporations, as shown in Exhibit 2-1.

RELATIONSHIPS AMONG THE FINANCIAL STATEMENTS

The four basic financial statements for a business entity fit together to form a unified whole, with this relationship referred to as the articulation of the financial statements. Together, they provide decision makers with a complete picture of a company's operations and financial position. Further, the financial statements are interrelated in such a way that changes in the items shown in one statement usually affect one or more of the other statements. A knowledge of financial statement articulation is central to understanding the financial statements.

The financial statement elements related to financial position are tied together in a fundamental manner:

$$\text{Assets} = \text{Liabilities} + \text{Equity}$$

This relationship is referred to as the **accounting equation**. The amount of an entity's assets or resources must always equal the claims on those assets. The claims on the assets of a business entity are those of either the creditors (liabilities) or the owners (equity). The equity represents a residual claim in the sense that once all of the liabilities are satisfied, any remaining assets are claimed by the owners. This aspect of the relationship may be seen through a restatement of the accounting equation obtained by subtracting liabilities from both sides of the equation:

$$\text{Assets} - \text{Liabilities} = \text{Equity}$$

You have already seen the accounting equation at work in the balance sheet of Our Video Store:

$$\text{Assets} = \text{Liabilities} + \text{Equity}$$
$$8,540 = \quad -0- \quad + 8,540$$

The accounting equation is bound by all of the normal rules that apply to equations. For example, if an asset of Our Video Store increases, it must be accompanied by a corresponding decrease in another asset or by an increase in liabilities or equity. The accounting equation for Our Video Store would appear as follows if the store purchased $800 of videos for cash:

$$\text{Assets} \qquad\qquad = \text{Liabilities} + \text{Equity}$$
$$8,540 + 800 \text{ (videos)} - 800 \text{ (cash)} = \quad -0- \quad + 8,540$$

EXHIBIT 2-6	**RELATIONSHIPS AMONG THE FINANCIAL STATEMENTS**

Assets = Liabilities + Equity
Assets − Liabilities = Equity
Equity = Owners' Investments + Retained Earnings
Retained Earnings = Previously Undistributed Income + Net Income − Distributions
Net Income = Revenues − Expenses

If instead the videos were purchased on credit, the equation would be:

$$\text{Assets} = \text{Liabilities} + \text{Equity}$$
$$8{,}540 + 800 = 800 + 8{,}540$$

Assets, liabilities, and equity are all related to the other elements of the financial statements, as shown in Exhibit 2–6. They are changed by and are the cumulative result of the other elements. For example, an entity's change in equity during a period is equal to all investments made by owners during the period, plus the entity's net income for the period, minus all distributions made to owners during the period. Net income reflects the difference between revenues and expenses. Retained earnings is part of equity but does not come from the owners' investment; rather, it represents the amount of the enterprise's cumulative income not distributed to the owners.

You Decide 2-1

COMPARING FINANCIAL STATEMENTS

Compare the financial statements of Gateway (Exhibits 2–2 to 2–5) with those of Our Video Store (Exhibit 2–1). The basic form is the same, but the details are very different. What similarities and differences do you see? Why do you think the differences exist?

USERS OF ACCOUNTING INFORMATION

Information for Decisions

Financial statements must meet the information needs of many different types of users. Users of financial statements must understand for whom the financial statements are prepared and how the information in the statements addresses the needs of different users. This will allow decision makers to answer questions such as these: Is the information in the financial statements relevant to the types of decisions I need to make? What are the shortcomings of the financial statements for my types of decisions? For what other types of decisions might the financial statements be useful?

We have discussed how decision makers are provided with information about an entity through its financial statements. But who are these decision makers? In this section, we'll find out who uses the accounting information provided by businesses. These users are summarized in Exhibit 2–7.

Let's look once again at the financial statements for Our Video Store. Who might be interested in these statements and why?

| **EXHIBIT 2-7** | **USERS OF ACCOUNTING INFORMATION AND TYPES OF JUDGMENTS AND DECISIONS** |

Internal Users

Owners/managers
- Allocate resources
- Choose products and services
- Arrange staffing
- Arrange financing

Employees
- Assess employment prospects
- Negotiate wages and benefits

External Users

Owners (not actively involved)
- Decide future investment or disinvestment
- Select management representatives

Creditors
- Set lending practices
- Set collection practices

Vendors (suppliers)
- Sell products and services
- Extend credit

Public interest groups
- Review treatment of employees
- Determine exorbitant profits
- Address community concerns
- Address environmental and safety concerns

Regulators
- Restrict profits
- Set rates or prices
- Establish operating restrictions and conditions

Taxing authorities
- Assess taxes
- Establish compliance

INTERNAL USERS

First, you are certainly going to be interested in the financial statements of your company. You are the owner as well as the manager of the operation, and you can use accounting information to make critical decisions about various factors:

- Allocation of resources (hire an additional worker, purchase new or used videos)
- Methods of funding (use your own money only, borrow, take in a partner)
- Level of operations (stay open later at night, increase number of videos, open second store)
- Methods of operation (accept reservations, provide home delivery)
- Pricing (charge higher price on weekends and for new releases, number of nights for same price)

You are an internal user of accounting information, or someone within the business. Other internal users include your employees. They may use accounting information to do their jobs, assess security of their jobs, and determine the likelihood of salary increases. Accounting information used for decision making within an organization is referred to as **managerial accounting** information.

EXTERNAL USERS

Accounting information provided to external parties, such as creditors or prospective owners, is called **financial accounting** information. How is this information useful to external decision makers? Think about your friend who is considering becoming a partner in your business. She must decide if the **return on investment,** or her profit, is high enough to risk taking money out of a safe investment, such as an insured savings account. Our Video Store's financial statements can help her evaluate the risk by providing financial information about your video rental operation: the assets you currently are holding, what obligations you have, and how profitable the business has been to date. Further, she'll use the statements to see whether the business generates sufficient cash to make any distributions to her as one of the owners.

If you try to buy your next batch of videos on open account, which is an extension of credit for a short time, you will deal with another external decision maker. The supplier, referred to as a *vendor*, will need to decide whether to extend credit to you. The vendor may wish to see your financial statements or may check your credit rating with a credit agency. Credit agencies that rate the creditworthiness of large companies typically examine the financial statements of those companies.

Companies that issue securities to the public are required by securities laws and regulations to provide accounting information to the public. People can use this information to decide if purchasing a company's securities is a wise investment. Other companies, such as banks, insurance companies, brokerage firms, and utilities, are required to provide accounting information so regulators can determine if the companies are operating in accordance with certain restrictions.

Even if companies were not legally required to provide information to external parties, they would need to do so because these decision makers would be unlikely to provide resources without information. As with Our Video Store, resource providers must be able to assess the likelihood that they will benefit from agreements into which they enter. To make those assessments, they need information.

ACCOUNTING INFORMATION SYSTEMS AND DECISION MAKING

Information for Decisions

Organizations design their accounting information systems to prepare financial statements and to ensure the reliability of information. Understanding how a company's information system is organized helps decision makers answer questions such as these: Can I obtain more information than is provided by the general purpose financial statements? How do I know that the company's accounting system is providing accurate information?

To provide information needed by decision makers, organizations develop accounting information systems. These systems meet two needs of the organization. They produce useful accounting information for internal and external decision makers, and they facilitate internal control.

INTERNAL AND EXTERNAL ACCOUNTING REPORTS

In general, no restrictions are placed on the types of accounting reports that organizations use internally. Therefore, companies may design systems that provide whatever types of information internal decision makers need.

As we have seen, many different external groups are interested in an organization, and each group has its own goals and different decisions to make. Different types of decisions often require different types of information. Providing a unique set of information to each external decision maker, however, would be too expensive. Instead, most organizations issue a single set of financial statements designed to meet the needs of many different external decision makers. These financial statements are referred to as general purpose financial statements. Gateway's financial statements shown in Appendix A are general purpose financial statements, as are those of Our Video Store.

Some external decision makers have special needs. If those parties have sufficient power, they may force an organization to provide additional financial statements designed to meet specific needs, called special purpose financial statements. For example, if you were to ask a bank to lend you money for Our Video Store, the bankers might want additional information. You would have to provide that information if you wanted the loan.

INTERNAL CONTROL

Management is responsible for the entity's accounting system. A reliable accounting system not only ensures the accuracy of the accounting information, but also provides accounting safeguards for the entity's resources. This feature of accounting systems is referred to as **internal control**. The importance of good internal control can be seen in the results of a recent survey by a large international CPA firm; poor internal controls were cited as the explanation for almost 60 percent of frauds.[2] Strong internal control helps protect an organization's resources, and it results in greater reliability of information generated by the system.

Internal controls include all those policies and procedures designed to ensure that the goals of the organization will be achieved. Internal control, for example, works toward ensuring that the company's resources are adequately protected and efficiently used, the company is in compliance with the laws of the countries in which it operates, ethical standards are being followed in interactions with others, and financial statements are fairly presented.

ACCOUNTANTS: THE PROVIDERS OF FINANCIAL INFORMATION

Information for Decisions

Accountants provide, interpret, and verify financial information. Knowledge of the accountant's role in this process and how accountants are regulated helps financial statement users answer questions such as these: Who prepared and who is responsible for the information included in the financial statements I am using? What is the role of CPAs, and how does this affect the reliability of these financial statements? What do the different types of audit reports mean, and to what extent can I rely on them?

[2] KPMG, *1998 Fraud Survey*, p. 14.

Accounting information is crucial to both internal and external decision makers. The individuals who provide, verify, and interpret the accounting information are called accountants. There are many different types of accountants, in various types of organizations, performing numerous functions, as shown in Exhibit 2–8. Understanding the different roles played by accountants can help decision makers evaluate the usefulness of the information provided to them.

In Practice 2-2

DEL MONTE

Del Monte Foods Company closed one of its four Midwestern vegetable packing plants in 1993. In 1998, company management announced a four-year plan to consolidate its California manufacturing operation. Both decisions significantly reduced costs and allowed the company to better meet the competitive challenges of the market. The company's managers made the decisions that resulted in these increased efficiencies based on data provided by their accountants.

ANALYSIS

Information such as plant capacity, current operating volume, and costs of shipping products from various locations all would be helpful in determining which plants to continue operating. The accounting staff provides management with this information, plus much more. [www.delmonte.com]

THE WORLD OF ACCOUNTANTS

EXHIBIT 2-8

- *General accountant*—maintains the accounting information system, records information, and prepares internal accounting reports and external financial statements. As these accountants advance, they often are given titles such as chief accountant, controller, or chief financial officer (CFO).

- *Cost accountant*—maintains detailed records of the costs associated with the production of a company's products and provides cost information for both external and internal accounting reports. These accountants may carry titles such as plant accountant, production accountant, or division controller.

- *Tax accountant*—works with information relating to a company's tax liability within the context of the laws and regulations pertaining to income and other types of taxes; may be involved in planning to minimize taxes. These accountants are found in business enterprises or working for accounting firms providing services to numerous clients; tax accountants also are employed by taxing agencies.

- *Independent auditor*—examines the accounting information system and records of client organizations to verify that the financial statements are fairly presented.

- *Internal auditor*—examines the information system, records, and operations of the employing organization to help ensure the effectiveness and efficiency of operations and the integrity of the records.

- *Academic accountant*—teaches others to understand the body of accounting knowledge.

- *Consultant*—provides advice to managers relating to accounting, information systems, and other business matters. Although most consultants are not accountants, an accountant's experience often provides a broad knowledge of different aspects of the operations of many different types of entities.

ACCOUNTING REGULATION

If you were a banker deciding whether to make a loan to an organization, would you trust the financial statements presented by the owners or managers of that organization? How would you know the statements were accurate and not deceptive? The U.S. Securities and Exchange Commission (SEC), under the authority granted to it by Congress, has taken the position that when decisions involving significant personal wealth are made based on accounting information, that information should be regulated to protect citizens.

The regulation of accounting takes many forms and affects accountants and the public in a number of different respects. Some regulations relate to the education, qualifications, and behavior of accountants. Others deal with the information provided through the financial reporting process. Why is regulation needed? Regulation provides a basis for trust: the professional seems more trustworthy, and the information seems more reliable. Regulation, however, cannot ensure that information is used wisely and that good decisions necessarily result from its use.

REGULATION AND CERTIFICATION OF ACCOUNTANTS

Accountants serve the public in a variety of roles, such as tax advisors, consultants, and auditors. Some of these accountants serve as expert independent accountants who can express opinions on the fairness of entities' financial statements. Because of the crucial roles they play, these accountants are regulated and given the special designation of **Certified Public Accountant (CPA)**. CPA requirements are established by individual states. Certification for public accountants also is found in other countries, usually with the designation of either CPA or Chartered Accountant (CA). Requirements, however, differ markedly from country to country.

Other types of certification, which indicate special qualifications and expertise, are given by professional organizations and are not regulated by law. Two well-known designations are those of Certified Management Accountant (CMA) and Certified Internal Auditor (CIA). CMAs and CIAs do not offer their services directly to the public but provide accounting services within organizations.

Although certification cannot guarantee the abilities of an accountant, it does provide assurance that certain minimum levels of education, experience, and competency have been attained. Exhibit 2–9 provides information about the primary types of certification found in accounting.

EXHIBIT 2-9 **PROFESSIONAL ACCOUNTING CERTIFICATIONS**

	CPA	CMA	CIA
Governing body	States	Institute of Management Accountants	Institute of Internal Auditors
Approximate number certified	430,000	21,000	25,000
Approximate number sitting for exam annually	125,000	10,000	5,000
Education required	B or M	B	B
Experience required	0–3 years*	2 years	2 years

B = Bachelor's degree or the equivalent number of credit hours

M = Master's degree or 150 semester hours; required by most states

*Varies by state (or other jurisdiction)

THE ROLE OF AUDITORS

The role of the auditor is especially important because management prepares the financial statements, reporting on the results of its own activities. This is somewhat like your accounting professor letting you assign your own grade for the course. A question might arise, therefore, as to the reliability of the statements. Are such reports free from management's biases? Do the reports fairly represent the position and activities of the entity? If external decision makers think they cannot rely on the financial statements provided by management, those financial statements will no longer be useful.

The reliability of the financial statements can be increased when an independent third party, known as an **auditor**, examines the financial statements and expresses an opinion as to whether those statements were prepared using acceptable accounting and reporting practices and are fairly presented. A key aspect of the information contained in financial statements is that it is verifiable. Without an opinion by independent auditors, external decision makers might have no way of knowing whether the information in the financial statements will serve their purposes or only those of management.

Returning to Our Video Store, do these statements reflect a complete lack of management bias? What about videos that did not rent at all last month? You are certain they are good videos and have included them in the balance sheet among the store's assets. An independent auditor, however, might have a more objective viewpoint. Before providing an opinion that the financial statements are fairly presented, the independent auditor might require you to treat those videos as worthless and remove them from the balance sheet.

Financial Auditing.   The process of gathering information about an entity to help form an opinion on the fairness of its financial statements is known as the financial **audit**. The auditors examine the entity's records and review the accounting methods used to prepare the financial statements. The auditors normally select only a sample of the records to examine in detail because the benefits of a complete examination would ordinarily not justify the cost. Typical audit procedures include examining the entity's accounting procedures, tracing amounts in the financial statements to the accounting records and the supporting documents, contacting those owing money to the entity to confirm the amounts owed, and observing the existence of inventories and other assets.

Audits aim at confirming the overall fairness of the financial statements, but should also uncover major fraud or dishonesty. The existence of periodic audits undoubtedly deters those in the organization who might contemplate unlawful self-enrichment schemes at the entity's expense.

Audit Reports.   After performing a financial audit, an independent auditor issues an **audit report**. The report clearly indicates the auditor's responsibility and expresses an opinion about the fairness of the financial statements. Several types of opinions might be expressed by an auditor:

- **Unqualified opinion.** An unqualified or "clean" opinion indicates the auditor's belief that the financial statements are fairly presented. An example of an unqualified opinion using the standard format and wording is included immediately before Gateway's financial statements in Appendix A. Most large companies with publicly traded securities carefully prepare their statements so as to receive unqualified opinions. The government can limit the sale or trading of a company's securities if the company's financial statements do not receive an unqualified opinion.

- **Qualified opinion.** An exception to the standard unqualified opinion is issued if the auditor believes the financial statements overall are fairly presented but a specific item or set of items within the statements is not presented in conformity with accepted accounting practices or disclosure is inadequate. A qualification also might arise if the auditor's examination is restricted in some way. This type of opinion is appropriate when the exception is clearly identified and the remainder of the financial statements are judged to be fairly presented.

- **Adverse opinion.** An adverse opinion indicates that the financial statements are not fairly presented in accordance with accepted accounting practices. Adverse opinions are rarely seen because most entities amend their accounting and reporting practices to avoid them.

- **Disclaimer.** A disclaimer of opinion means the auditor has been unable to gather sufficient reliable data to form an opinion as to the fairness of the entity's financial statements. This situation might occur if the entity severely restricts the audit, the entity's accounting records are incomplete, or major uncertainties surround the entity's position, operations, or ability to continue in operation.

Assessing Internal Control. Auditors must normally assess internal control when conducting an audit. Feedback regarding weaknesses in internal control can help management make needed improvements. From an independent auditor's viewpoint, knowledge of an entity's internal control is essential for planning the audit. The stronger an entity's internal control, the more the auditor can rely on the accounting system to provide accurate information.

Internal Auditing. Many organizations employ internal auditors to examine the accounting systems, assess other aspects of internal control, and appraise operations. Internal auditors conduct audits to ensure the accuracy and reliability of an entity's financial statements and to evaluate the efficiency and effectiveness of the organization's operations.

In Practice 2-3

GEORGIA-PACIFIC CORPORATION

Georgia-Pacific Corporation evaluates its internal audit staff in part on the criterion of whether demonstrated cost savings from implemented audit recommendations exceed audit costs.

ANALYSIS

Since Georgia-Pacific employs internal auditors to improve the efficiency and effectiveness of its operations, it expects cost savings from the audit outcome. [www.gp.com]

SETTING STANDARDS FOR ACCOUNTING INFORMATION

Information for Decisions

Regulatory organizations set accounting standards for the preparation of financial statements. Knowing what regulatory organizations exist and what their responsibilities are helps financial statement users answer questions such as these: Who has the responsibility for initially deciding what is to be reported in the financial statements I am using? If the financial statements are representations of management, how much latitude does management have in deciding how to report this company's financial position and results of operations? To what extent are the accounting standards relating to the information in the financial statements enforceable by law?

Decision makers use financial statement information that is prepared and verified by accountants. But who determines what information will be reported? The answer is that management of the reporting entity chooses the specific information that is reported in financial statements. However, the reporting must conform to certain standards.

The broad set of accepted accounting practices that entities use to prepare their financial statements is referred to as **generally accepted accounting principles (GAAP)**. As implied by the term, these are accounting methods used in financial reporting that have gained widespread acceptance. In some cases, alternative methods are acceptable for reporting the same events or activities. A number of bodies, both governmental and professional, regulate the financial reporting process and the information that is included in financial statements provided to investors and the public.

THE STANDARD SETTING ORGANIZATIONS

The task of specifying GAAP in the United States has, for the most part, been a joint venture of the accounting profession and the U.S. Securities and Exchange Commission. Today, the primary organizations regulating financial reporting for businesses are the Securities and Exchange Commission and the Financial Accounting Standards Board.

The Securities and Exchange Commission (SEC).   Following the 1929 stock market crash and the Great Depression, the federal government passed the Securities Act of 1933 and the Securities Exchange Act of 1934, which regulate the initial issuance and subsequent trading of securities and provide for continued reporting by companies issuing securities. The legislation also established the **Securities and Exchange Commission (SEC)**. The SEC oversees the issuance and trading of securities of publicly held companies and has been given the authority to establish reporting and disclosure requirements for these companies. The SEC's rules and regulations are designed to ensure that investors have relevant and reliable information for their decisions.

Financial Accounting Standards Board (FASB).   Although the SEC is charged by law with ensuring full and fair disclosure by publicly held companies, the private sector has been permitted to take the lead in developing acceptable accounting principles, with the SEC acting in an oversight capacity. The private-sector body currently playing the most important role in developing accounting and reporting standards is the **Financial Accounting Standards Board (FASB)**. The FASB consists of seven members, all of whom are full-time and paid. It includes representatives from public accounting, industry, the securities field, and academia. The FASB issues pronouncements after a lengthy process of research, examination, public hearings, consultation with the SEC, and exposure drafts. In most cases, auditors are prohibited by their Code of Professional Conduct from issuing an opinion that financial statements are fairly presented if the statements depart from FASB standards.

PRACTICAL ASPECTS OF STANDARD SETTING

On the surface, the current structure for setting accounting and reporting standards seems straightforward. The SEC has the power by law to establish accounting and reporting requirements. However, the SEC has indicated that the private sector should take the lead in establishing such standards. It has stated that financial statements prepared in conformity with FASB pronouncements will be presumed to be in accordance with generally accepted accounting principles. Thus, the SEC effectively has provided the pronouncements of the FASB with the force of law.

A CLOSER LOOK AT

STANDARD SETTING: IS IT A RENTAL OF A SALE?

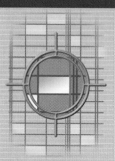

Suppose that over the weeks you have been operating Our Video Store, you have had a number of inquiries from people wanting to rent video players. One of your best customers, a marketing major, proposes that you sell video players to customers who might be interested. He proposes that you advertise a package plan under which a customer could pay a flat $30 every month and would be given use of a new video player for a year. In addition, the customer would receive two free video rentals each month. The customer could return the tape player at any time and make no further payments, or, if at the end of one year all payments had been made, the customer would own the video player. This plan should increase revenues by adding the video player rentals and also should help market your video rentals.

In checking around, you find that one of the large chains, Big Block Video, is doing the same thing. The controller at Big Block Video tells you that Big Block reports the total amount from the package plan, $15 million for the year, as rental revenue. However, Big Block's auditors, Peat Waterhouse & Co., are not sure this is appropriate because the arrangement seems more like a sale of the video player with payments made over time, an installment sale. They wonder if the portion of the monthly rental related to the video player should be reported as sales revenue separately from video rentals, with the cost of the video player to the company deducted. Maybe even a portion of the rental revenue should be treated as interest income if part of the rental is treated as a sale; in effect, the purchaser is borrowing the cost of the video player and paying for it over time. If part of the package is treated as an installment sale of the video player, Big Block's income could be significantly different.

Researchers in the national office of Peat Waterhouse cannot find any FASB or SEC rule that indicates how this type of transaction should be reported. They do find that several other companies are concerned with this same type of reporting problem, and they decide to take the issue to the FASB. In the meantime, the SEC indicates it will accept Big Block's financial statements as they are currently prepared. However, to protect investors, additional information must be provided to disclose the total costs and revenues associated with the package rentals, an estimate of the number of players rented during the year that actually will become sales, and the effect on reported revenue and income.

After studying the issue and holding public hearings, the FASB issues a new standard requiring sales of assets (e.g., video players) included in rental contracts to be treated as installment sales. Putting emphasis on the substance of the transaction over its form, the standard does not permit the total payment to be reported as rental revenue. The SEC then requires application of this new standard in all SEC filings.

THE CURRENT ENVIRONMENT OF ACCOUNTING

Information for Decisions

Economic and social factors often influence the development of financial reporting practices. When decision makers understand these influences, it can help them answer questions such as these: Can the accountants be blamed if I invest in this company and it fails? What effect will changes in the tax laws have on the company's financial statements? How can accounting help bring about quality-of-life improvements in areas such as health care and the environment?

Just as decisions exist in an uncertain environment, so does the accounting profession. A number of social and economic factors have affected the past development of accounting and no doubt will influence the future development of accounting. Dramatic events, such as the stock market crash in 1929, influence the way financial information is reported. The accounting profession must continue to grapple with the question of how to react to the social, political, and business evolution of the world in the new millennium. Let's look at a few of the more important current influences on accounting.

INCOME TAXATION

Income tax requirements have a pervasive effect throughout our economy. All businesses, as well as most individuals, are required to file income tax returns. Tax payments are often substantial. For many companies, federal and state (and foreign) income taxes tend to be one of the largest costs of doing business, often taking 40 percent of a company's income.

Tax rules are exceedingly complex and change frequently. Taxing agencies such as the Internal Revenue Service (IRS) audit companies to ensure compliance with tax laws and regulations. In fact, IRS agents have permanent offices at some large companies. Many decisions made by organizations have significant tax implications. Tax planning is an integral part of decision making in today's business world. Although general income measures for tax purposes are the same as for financial reporting, some specific details differ because tax laws are aimed at raising money for the government, as well as attempting to achieve a whole host of social goals, such as stimulating the economy. In some cases, tax laws have influenced financial reporting practices.

INTERNATIONAL ACCOUNTING

We now have a global economy. Many U.S. companies, not just the largest, conduct business in a number of countries, and many foreign companies do business in the United States. For example, Toyota and Mitsubishi operate factories in this country, and many other companies trade their securities in the U.S. capital markets. Every day we see and buy familiar products produced by foreign companies: food from Nestlé, electronics from Sony, gasoline from Shell, and cars from Honda. Similarly, U.S. products blanket the world. Airlines throughout the world fly Boeing 747s and 737s, Coca-Cola is everywhere, and the first Moscow McDonald's was mobbed by excited patrons. (See In Practice 2-4.)

As investment decisions are made and business is conducted across national boundaries, the need for information prepared on a common basis from country to country increases. The International Accounting Standards Committee has established a set of international accounting standards as a first step in this direction. Member countries, including the United States, have agreed to take steps to bring their national standards into agreement with international standards, but compliance so far has been limited. Nevertheless, international accounting standards are beginning to have a significant effect on U.S. accounting standards.

LITIGATION

The United States is a very litigious society. There are 307.4 lawyers in the United States for every 100,000 people—there are only 12.1 per 100,000 people in Japan. Annual lawsuit filings in the United States total in the millions.

Accountants are not exempt from the litigation trend. Large investment decisions are made using information contained in financial statements. When the results of those investments are not as anticipated, decision makers may claim the information in the finan-

In Practice 2-4

FLUOR CORPORATION

Fluor Corporation reported profits for its fiscal year ending October 31, 1998, of $235.3 million. Profits were up 61 percent from the preceding year even though revenues of more than $13 billion were down slightly. Fluor Corporation is an Irvine, California, engineering, construction, and mining company that has placed special emphasis on an aggressive overseas expansion and has been reporting record profits in recent years. *Engineering News-Record* magazine has generally ranked Fluor Daniel, a major subsidiary of Fluor Corporation, the number one engineering and construction company in the United States. Fluor's international business exceeded its domestic business for the first time in 1993.

ANALYSIS

The chief executive officer of Fluor has indicated that in recent years the company has found better growth opportunities in the international market than nationally. While the financial problems in the Asia Pacific region may cause Fluor to focus less on this area in the short-term, long-term this will continue to be a very important market. [www.fluor.com]

cial statements was misleading and blame accountants. In cases where a company has failed, the creditors and investors often bring suit against the outside auditors because the auditors are the only ones left with any money. This is called the "deep pockets" approach to liability.

Recent court cases have provided some relief for auditors, but the accounting profession continues to seek protection from the lawsuits that have already proved so costly to the medical profession. At the same time, the profession continues to examine its own practices to ensure that they are consistent with the needs of society and that the public understands the nature of the services provided.

ETHICAL CONSIDERATIONS

Law, medicine, and accounting are all considered ethical professions. Each field has a code of ethics, and penalties for violating the code of ethics may include loss of the license to practice. In addition, many companies and other organizations have developed their own ethics policies and codes of conduct for employees.

Ethical dilemmas sometimes arise, and their resolution may not be easy. In some ethical dilemmas, the right course of action is clear even though it may have a negative effect. In other cases, though, the issues may be so complex and conflicting that the right course of action is far from clear. Although no code of behavior can specify what is right in all situations, each individual develops a sense of morality and ethical behavior based on his or her upbringing, religion, or other beliefs and values. Each individual must reconcile those beliefs and values with the norms found within society and within the profession chosen.

In Practice 2-5

THE ETHICS OF PRICING

American Airlines President Robert Crandall once telephoned Howard Putnam, president of Braniff International Airlines. Both companies were suffering from money-losing competition on routes from their home base of Dallas. In the conversation, Crandall suggested that they both raise their fares 20 percent so they could increase profits. Putnam objected, arguing that they were not supposed to talk about pricing.[3]

ANALYSIS

The U.S. Justice Department agreed with Putnam. It alleged that Crandall's suggestion of a 20 percent fare increase amounted to an illegal attempt to monopolize airline routes, but settled the suit when Crandall agreed to avoid future fare discussions with competitors.

You Decide 2-2

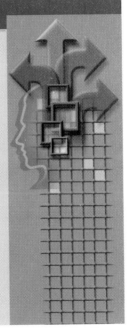

TOUGH CHOICES

Assume you manage a manufacturing company, Merrymen Products, and the independent auditors have just completed the audit of your company. The financial statements are ready to be issued, along with an unqualified opinion. The audit report is particularly important because Merrymen is counting on a sizable bank loan to expand its operating facilities. Approval of the loan depends on the audit report. Unfortunately, you have just learned from a confidential study by the company that high doses of the company's primary product caused cancer in laboratory rats. Obviously, the company's assets will be worth only a fraction of the reported amounts if the product has to be withdrawn from the market. If this information were made public, the banks would not approve the loan and the public would be afraid to purchase the product. The company would be doomed, many people would lose their jobs, perhaps including you, and the local economy would suffer serious harm. However, the results of the study are preliminary and are considered confidential. And, after all, this is only one study, and the results cannot be considered conclusive.

How would you handle this situation? What about the people who might suffer some type of harm (financial, emotional, or physical) because of your decision? What would you expect the auditors to do?

ACCOUNTING FOR SOCIETAL ISSUES

As the public has become more aware of problems facing society and the complexity of finding effective solutions, a greater emphasis has been placed on accountability. Accountability requires measures of costs and benefits, even though such measures are not always stated in terms of dollars and cents.

[3] From John R. Schermerhorn, *Management* (New York: John Wiley & Sons, 1999), p. 122.

Accountants play an important role in efforts to make informed decisions about social issues. Recent examples are the decisions to close military bases and to restructure the student loan program. In both cases, decision makers used information about the costs and benefits of the alternative courses of action considered. The U.S. Congress's General Accounting Office regularly examines and reports on the costs and benefits of many programs that have significant implications for society.

Accounting information is needed in many areas of social concern. However, two areas are expected to be of special importance over the next decade: health care and the environment.

Health Care Accounting. Government and the public continue to search for a solution to the problems of health care costs and quality. In finding a solution, an examination of costs and benefits associated with alternate types of care, coverage, and procedures is needed. New means of processing information related to health care services are needed so the health care system operates efficiently and administrative costs are reduced. More importantly, accounting must take the lead in developing and applying measures of productivity and societal and individual benefits and costs.

Environmental Accounting. We have not always been kind to the environment. Global warming, acid rain, water pollution, soil exhaustion and erosion, toxic wastes, and resource depletion all are issues of increasing concern to the government and the public. No one really knows how much damage we have done, nor do we know the cost of remedying the damage.

Environmental accounting is a relatively new area, and clearly one that presents many challenges. The issues are difficult, and costs and benefits are not always easy to measure. For example, a company that is severely polluting the air may be able to install the latest antipollution devices at a cost of, say, $400 million, a cost that may be measured relatively easily. What is the cost, however, if the company goes out of business because it is unable to conform to clean air standards? Many people lose their jobs, which affects the surrounding community businesses. How do you measure the true costs and benefits of preventing pollution? Clearly accountants have an important role to play in measuring costs and benefits of environmental efforts and alternative uses of natural resources.

SUMMARY

Organizations issue financial statements that provide information about their activities and financial position. Businesses include four basic financial statements in their reports:

* *Income statement*—reflects the results of operations for the current period and includes revenues from sales and services, expenses reflecting the cost of earning revenues, and the difference, net income

* *Balance sheet*—as of a specific point in time, lists the assets (things of value owned by the entity), liabilities (obligations), and equities (the owners' claims on the entity's assets)

* *Statement of changes in owners' equity*—reflects changes in the owners' financial interest in the enterprise resulting from additional investment or withdrawals during the period, current profits or losses, and distributions of income to the owners

* *Statement of cash flows*—details the specific types of cash inflows and outflows during the current period, classified as to those relating to operations, financing activities, and investing activities

Together the financial statements provide decision makers with a complete picture of an entity's operations and financial position. The statements are interrelated in such a way that changes in one statement often affect one or more of the other statements. The accounting equation, Assets = Liabilities + Equity, controls these interrelationships.

Users of financial statements include many interested parties: investors or owners, creditors, employees, vendors, customers, and regulatory bodies. Managers may use information contained in financial statements, but they rely more heavily on managerial accounting information for decision making.

Accountants serve many different roles in business and nonbusiness organizations. One role is to serve as an independent auditor. Independent auditors verify the financial statements issued by the management of an entity and issue opinions regarding whether the statements are fairly presented. Decision makers can thus place greater reliance on the financial statement information that management reports.

A number of bodies, including the Securities and Exchange Commission and the Financial Accounting Standards Board, regulate the practice of accounting and set standards that specify accounting principles and methods used in preparing financial statements. These regulations and standards help assure that accounting information will be useful to decision makers.

The accounting profession exists in a changing environment. More information is needed by society. Factors currently influencing accounting include income tax laws and regulations, the advent of the global economy, the dramatic rise in the number of lawsuits filed against accountants, an increasing awareness of ethical considerations, and an awareness of the role accounting can play in resolving social issues.

LIST OF IMPORTANT TERMS

accounting equation *(44)*

adverse opinion *(52)*

assets *(39)*

audit *(51)*

audit report *(51)*

auditor *(51)*

balance sheet *(39)*

Certified Public Accountant (CPA) *(50)*

disclaimer *(52)*

dividends *(43)*

equities *(39)*

expenses *(39)*

financial accounting *(47)*

Financial Accounting Standards Board (FASB) *(53)*

financial statements *(36)*

generally accepted accounting principles (GAAP) *(53)*

income statement *(39)*

internal control *(48)*

liabilities *(39)*

managerial accounting *(46)*

net income *(39)*

qualified opinion *(51)*

return on investment *(47)*

revenues *(39)*

Securities and Exchange Commission (SEC) *(53)*

statement of cash flows *(41)*

statement of changes in owners' equity *(41)*

statement of financial position *(39)*

unqualified opinion *(51)*

EXAMINING THE CONCEPTS

Q2-1   What are the four basic financial statements normally prepared by business entities?

Q2-2   What is an asset?

Q2-3   What is a liability?

Q2-4   How do the balance sheet and income statement differ? What is the purpose of each?

Q2-5   What information is presented in the statement of cash flows? Why is knowledge of cash flows important?

Q2-6   What are the elements of the accounting equation? How does the use of cash to acquire another asset affect the accounting equation? How does the use of cash to pay a liability affect the accounting equation?

Q2-7   Who are the primary users of financial statement information? In what ways do internal decision makers use accounting information?

Q2-8   Why do businesses spend time and money providing accounting information to external parties? In what ways do external decision makers use accounting information?

Q2-9   What is meant by the term *internal control?* Why is it important to have internal controls?

Q2-10   Why is the regulation of accountants and accounting information important for people making economic decisions?

Q2-11   What is the difference between a Certified Public Accountant, a Chartered Accountant, and a Certified Management Accountant? How does the work they do differ?

Q2-12   Why is the certification of accountants important?

Q2-13   What is the nature of the work done by external auditors? Why is it important to the functioning of securities markets?

Q2-14   What is an unqualified audit opinion? Why would most business entities want to receive an unqualified opinion on their financial statements?

Q2-15   What types of audit opinions might an auditor give other than an unqualified opinion? Why would a company not want to receive an opinion other than an unqualified opinion?

Q2-16 Why is having expertise in taxation an important part of the knowledge base for those who work in accounting? Do managers who are not accountants need some knowledge of taxes? Why?

Q2-17 What impact does the introduction of business activity across national borders have on reported financial information?

Q2-18 Why has the increase in litigation in our society affected the field of accounting?

Q2-19 Why is maintenance of a high ethical standard by accountants important?

Q2-20 How are accountants involved in identifying and finding solutions for societal problems?

Q2-21 What are the names of the primary standard-setting organizations in accounting? Which is a government agency and which is not? What is the primary mission of the Securities and Exchange Commission?

UNDERSTANDING ACCOUNTING INFORMATION

E2-1   The Basic Financial Statements

a. Most businesses prepare an income statement, balance sheet, statement of cash flows, and statement of changes in owners' equity. The members of your investment club have raised a number of questions about one of the stocks that was purchased last year. For each of the following, indicate which financial statement would contain the information needed.
   1. What was the revenue from the business's sales last year?
   2. Was the business profitable last year?
   3. Does the company have its own production facilities?
   4. What kind of claims are there against the company's assets?
   5. How much cash did the business generate last year?
   6. Have the business's profits been increasing or decreasing?
   7. What was the amount of dividends distributed to stockholders last year?
b. Who provides most of the accounting information to decision makers? How often is it provided?

E2-2   Users of Accounting Information   Select the financial statement user most likely to use accounting information in the manner indicated and explain why:

a. (owner or vendor) Determine the frequency with which dividends are paid.
b. (employee or creditor) Determine whether salary levels are comparable to other companies in the industry.
c. (regulator or creditor) Compare profit ratios to other companies to see if a company has excess earnings.
d. (taxing authority or employee) Determine whether the company has correctly computed sales tax withholdings.
e. (public interest group or manager) Estimate the cost of cleaning up waste materials being discharged into a local river.
f. (manager or owner) Establish the most efficient number of parts to ship to a major customer at one time.
g. (regulator or manager) Set the maximum amount of goods to be shipped without requiring prepayment.
h. (owner or employee) Evaluate whether to purchase additional shares of the company.

i. (regulator or vendor) Set limits on the amount of debt a public utility can issue.
j. (employee or manager) Choose which products to sell after a new labor contract has been negotiated.

E2-3   Accounting Information Systems and Decision Making

a. You are thinking of purchasing stock of The Sinfully Sweet Bakery Company, which produces the rolls that you have for breakfast every morning. You know they hire a number of bakers for their products each year and you will only invest if at least half of their bakers are women. Would you expect company management to know this information? Should you be able to get this information from the general purpose financial statements? Would you expect the bank that lends money to Sinfully Sweet to get this information if it thinks it is necessary in making its loan decision?
b. Different external groups interested in an organization have different goals and different decisions to make. Explain how businesses typically provide the information needed by financial statement users in an economical way.
c. Internal controls include those policies and procedures designed to ensure that the goals of the organization will be achieved. Identify at least two examples of goals that internal control may be used to achieve.

E2-4   Accountants: The Providers of Financial Information

a. Accountants have different roles in providing financial information to decision makers. Which type of accountant would an owner, investor, or creditor be most likely to hire to perform the role indicated?
   1. Develop a series of classes designed to help students pass the certified management accounting examination.
   2. Determine the amount of tax owed to Canadian taxing authorities for products exported to Canada in the past year.
   3. Verify the accuracy of a company's financial statements.
   4. Maintain detailed records of the costs associated with the production of a company's products.

5. Maintain the accounting information system, record information, and prepare financial reports and financial statements of a company.

6. Examine the information system of an organization to help ensure its effectiveness and efficiency.

7. Provide advice to managers relating to accounting information systems and other business matters.

b. You and your roommate are talking about choosing professional careers. Your roommate wants to be a CPA so she can be independent, but she cannot understand why CPAs are subject to regulation. Explain to her why CPAs are regulated.

c. An audit report that contains an unqualified opinion indicates the accountant's belief that the financial statements are fairly presented. If an auditor thinks that an unqualified opinion is inappropriate, what other types of opinions might be issued? For each type, describe why the auditor would not issue an unqualified opinion.

E2-5 Setting Standards for Accounting Information
Who is responsible for the following?

a. Preparing the financial statements using generally accepted accounting procedures.

b. Establishing rules and regulations to ensure investors have relevant and reliable information on which to base their decisions.

c. Developing financial accounting and reporting standards to be followed by publicly held companies, subject to oversight by the Securities and Exchange Commission.

d. Checking to be sure a company's financial statements follow reporting standards established by the Financial Accounting Standards Board before issuing an audit opinion.

e. Overseeing the issuance and trading of securities of publicly held companies.

E2-6 The Current Environment of Accounting

a. An article in your local newspaper tells you that a retail grocery business in your hometown has just declared bankruptcy. You are not surprised because your parents and others have said it was not a pleasant place to shop. The newspaper article also reports that the accountants who audited the business are being sued by the investors and creditors of the failed business.
   1. How might the auditors of a failed business be liable?
   2. What is the "deep pockets" approach to liability, and how does it involve the auditors?
   3. How can auditors best protect themselves from being found liable in such cases?

b. It is said that income tax laws are designed, in part, to raise money for government operations. What does "in part" mean? What other purposes might the income tax laws serve?

c. Health care and environmental concerns are two well-known current social issues. Describe how accounting information could be used to find or evaluate potential solutions to each of these concerns.

E2-7 Multiple Choice: Accounting Reports Select the correct answer for each of the following:

1. The set of basic financial statements for a business entity does not include the:
   a. Statement of financial position.
   b. Statement of cash flows.
   c. Statement of individual shareholder wealth.
   d. Statement of changes in owners' equity.

2. The income statement includes:
   a. Contributions from owners.
   b. Proceeds received from borrowing.
   c. Information on profits distributed to shareholders.
   d. Revenue generated from the sale of goods and services.

3. The statement of financial position (balance sheet) does not include:
   a. Revenues.
   b. Assets.
   c. Equities.
   d. Liabilities.

4. Assets reported by a corporation represent:
   a. The claims of owners on the company.
   b. Obligations and commitments to others.
   c. Items having value to the company.
   d. Resources expended during the current period.

E2-8 Multiple Choice: Use of Accounting Select the correct answer for each of the following:

1. The accounting equation:
   a. Is used to determine the amount of liabilities owed.
   b. Shows the claims on the entity's assets represented by creditors and owners.
   c. Shows the claims on the owners' equity represented by creditors.
   d. Is used to determine the amount of income earned during the most recent accounting period.

2. In the accounting equation, an increase in assets can be associated with:
   a. An increase in liabilities.
   b. A decrease in equities.
   c. A decrease in liabilities.
   d. An increase in equities.
   e. Both a and b.
   f. Both a and d.

3. Accounting information is used by managers to:
   a. Decide on the acquisition of new machinery and equipment.
   b. Evaluate the efficiency of operations.
   c. Calculate year-end bonuses.
   d. All of the above.

4. Accounting information is used by external decision makers to:
   a. Decide on the acquisition of new machinery and equipment.
   b. Estimate the amount of risk associated with investing in a company.

c. Estimate future demand for a company's products in new markets.

d. Determine the amount of advertising to be undertaken by the company.

E2-9   Multiple Choice: Auditing   Select the correct answer for each of the following:

1. An external auditor may issue which of the following opinions in connection with an examination of the financial statements of a client?
   a. Diminished responsibility opinion.
   b. Qualified opinion.
   c. Reserved opinion.
   d. Special services opinion.
2. In issuing an unqualified opinion, an auditor is stating that:
   a. The client's financial statements are fairly presented.
   b. There was not sufficient audit evidence to determine the status of the financial statements.
   c. The auditor was not qualified to conduct all phases of the audit.
   d. There may be certain circumstances under which it is not appropriate to use the financial statements as presented.
3. A significant area of responsibility for the internal auditor is:
   a. To ensure the reliability and accuracy of the financial statements.
   b. To assess the adequacy of internal controls.
   c. To evaluate the efficiency and effectiveness of operations.
   d. All of the above.
4. The Financial Accounting Standards Board:
   a. Establishes the detailed procedures external auditors must follow when carrying out audits.
   b. Establishes standards that internal auditors must follow in carrying out their responsibilities.
   c. Establishes accounting procedures for governmental entities.
   d. Establishes financial reporting standards for business entities.

E2-10   Accounting Reports   Briefly indicate the purpose of each of the following financial statements:

a. Statement of income.
b. Statement of financial position.
c. Statement of cash flows.
d. Statement of changes in owners' equity.

E2-11   Financial Statement Users   Select which of the following financial statement users would be most likely to use accounting information for the purposes indicated:

1. Managers.
2. Employees.
3. Investors.
4. Creditors.
5. Vendors.
6. Public interest groups.
7. Regulators.
8. Taxing authorities.
   a. _____ Estimate the impact of a change in property tax rates on total tax collections.
   b. _____ Evaluate a company's ability to pay dividends.
   c. _____ Determine whether to replace old equipment with new, more efficient equipment.
   d. _____ Evaluate the effects of proposed environmental protection laws on employment levels in the lumber industry.
   e. _____ Evaluate whether natural gas prices should be reduced because companies have been earning excess profits.
   f. _____ Estimate a company's ability to generate cash for future debt repayment.
   g. _____ Compare hourly wage rates to those of other companies to determine if employees are being underpaid.
   h. _____ Determine whether payment must be received before products are shipped to a customer.

E2-12   Accounting Specialization   Select which of the following types of accounting specialists would be most likely to perform each of the functions listed:

1. General accountant.
2. Cost accountant.
3. Tax accountant.
4. Independent auditor.
5. Internal auditor.
6. Academic accountant.
7. Consultant.
   a. _____ Provide instruction to those studying to become certified management accountants.
   b. _____ Prepare the financial statements for the company.
   c. _____ Express an opinion on the fairness of a company's financial statements.
   d. _____ Prepare international tax returns for the company.
   e. _____ Install a new inventory control system and train company employees (employed on a contractual basis).
   f. _____ Evaluate the efficiency of the company's procedures in handling accounts receivable.
   g. _____ Determine the cost of each of the inputs (such as raw materials and labor) used in producing a new product.

E2-13   Identification of Transactions   Indicate whether the following financial statement elements are reported in the balance sheet, income statement, or statement of changes in owners' equity:

a. Sales revenue.
b. Accrued liabilities.
c. Salary expense.
d. Merchandise for sale to customers.

e. Owners' investment.

f. Rent expense.

g. Retained earnings.

h. Interest expense on outstanding debt.

i. Net income.

j. Dividends paid to owners.

E2-14 Financial Statement Elements You have been asked by a friend with a new business to answer a few questions on financial reporting. Your friend has asked you to indicate whether each of the following items will be reported in the business's balance sheet (BS), income statement (IS), neither the balance sheet nor income statement (N), or both the balance sheet and income statement (B):

a. Revenues.

b. Liabilities.

c. Expenses.

d. Cash flows from financing activities.

e. Net income.

f. Retained earnings.

g. Equities.

h. Assets held by the business entity.

i. Earnings distributed to owners during the period.

j. Assets held by owners.

E2-15 Accounting Equation Balances Determine how each of the following transactions affects the accounting equation:

a. Merchandise for resale is purchased on credit.

b. A bank loan is repaid.

c. Owners invest cash.

d. Buildings are purchased with cash.

e. Land is sold for its original cost and cash is received.

f. Land is sold for more than its original cost and cash is received.

g. Wages earned by employees last year are now paid.

h. Dividends are paid to shareholders.

E2-16 The Accounting Equation For each of the following transactions, give the effect on each element of the accounting equation:

a. Issuance of stock for cash.

b. Payment of a debt.

c. Purchase of land for cash.

d. Purchase of equipment on credit.

e. Payment of cash to owners, reflecting a distribution of income.

f. Receipt of a loan from the bank.

E2-17 Applying the Accounting Equation Banker Company reported assets of $90,000, liabilities of $40,000, and owner's equity of $50,000 at January 1, 2001. During the year, Banker Company engaged in the following transactions:

a. Purchased land for $23,000 cash.

b. Purchased equipment costing $35,000 by signing a 3-month note payable.

c. Paid liabilities of $12,000.

d. Sold new shares of stock for $32,000 cash.

e. Borrowed $6,000 from a local bank on a 6-month note payable.

Compute the totals reported in each of the three major elements of the accounting equation following these transactions.

E2-18 Total Assets Tiz Corporation reported total liabilities of $108,000 and owners' equity of $65,000 on January 1. During the month of January, Tiz Corporation (a) acquired land with a value of $65,000 in exchange for an ownership interest in Tiz, (b) used $35,000 of cash to purchase additional land, (c) purchased $40,000 of merchandise on credit, and (d) paid creditors a total of $25,000. What amount of total assets did Tiz Corporation report on January 1 and January 31?

E2-19 Owners' Equity Mortin Company reported owners' equity of $450,000 at December 31. During December, Mortin's owners had invested an additional $90,000, dividends of $20,000 were paid to owners, and reported net income was $42,000.

a. What amount had Mortin Company reported as owners' equity at December 1?

b. If Mortin reported total assets of $979,000 at December 1, what amount of total liabilities did it report at December 1?

E2-20 Audit Opinions All Fluff Corporation has just been told that the external auditors would be issuing an adverse opinion as a result of their audit of the All Fluff financial statements.

a. When is an adverse opinion issued by a CPA?

b. Why would an audit firm be reluctant to issue an adverse opinion?

c. What is the likely response of the securities markets to an adverse opinion?

d. What is the likely response of the management of All Fluff Corporation to the auditors' indication that an adverse opinion will be issued?

E2-21 Unqualified Audit Opinion The following companies wish to receive an unqualified audit opinion so they can issue additional securities at advantageous rates. In discussing their status with the external auditor, the following situations came to light:

a. Tumble Company purchased $600,000 of merchandise for resale during the period and still owes the supplier $80,000 at year-end.

b. A lightning strike at the general headquarters of Fry Company deleted part of the memory in Fry's mainframe computer system and scrambled much of the remaining information. After approximately two weeks of audit work, the auditor concluded that it would be impossible to verify the accuracy of many of Fry's transactions during the current year.

c. An error was made in recording accounts receivable of Grove Company. Rather than reporting the correct balance of accounts receivable of $15,000 and total assets of $105,000, the balance sheet reports accounts receivable of $510,000 and total assets of $600,000.

d. Stopper Company reports merchandise on hand of $950,000 and total assets of $2,550,000. Although audit standards require auditors to verify the existence of the merchandise, the auditors of Stopper Company were, due to an airline strike, unable to travel to New Zealand to verify the existence of $400,000 of the merchandise. The auditors believe the company has good internal controls and the merchandise is correctly reported.

For each of these situations, determine which type of audit opinion the auditor would be expected to provide, and give justification for your answer.

E2-22 Authoritative Support While you are at lunch, the president of the company for which you work suggests recording as assets some items that you doubt can appropriately be treated as such. Which authoritative bodies might provide you with guidance as to whether you are correct? How might your external auditor be of assistance?

E2-23 Authoritative Support Determine whether the Securities and Exchange Commission (SEC) or Financial Accounting Standards Board (FASB) normally has responsibility for each of the following:

a. Establishing the conditions that must be met before research and development costs can be recorded as an asset.
b. Monitoring brokerage firms to be sure they follow appropriate procedures when trading securities.
c. Establishing accounting procedures to be used in determining the amount to be reported as pension costs.
d. Establishing the procedures to be followed in informing the public before a new bond issue is publicly traded.
e. Establishing the conditions under which a new and unusual form of sales agreement can be treated as a sale at the time it is signed.
f. Determining which financial statements must be prepared for filings under the 1934 Securities and Exchange Act.

E2-24 International Investments The officers of Broadale Corporation tentatively have decided to establish manufacturing facilities in Germany and Mexico. Are the accounting and financial reporting procedures used in these countries likely to be the same as those used in the United States? Are any attempts being made to standardize accounting standards?

E2-25 Ethical Considerations Certified public accountants are expected to maintain independence from their audit clients. Any action that might cause the CPA to compromise his or her judgment at some future date must be avoided. In which of the following situations would the auditor be judged as unethical by failing to maintain an appropriate degree of independence?

a. The auditor and several members of management go out to lunch on the last day of the audit and the company pays for the lunch.

b. The company has an extra pair of tickets to the first game of the national basketball league playoffs and gives them to the partner in charge of the audit.
c. The partner in charge of a bank audit finances a $400,000 home mortgage with the bank and receives a substantially lower interest rate than other customers.
d. The partner in charge of the audit of a local gasoline station purchases a lot of gas at the station and frequently has cars serviced there.
e. The auditor discovers that the company published inaccurate financial statements for the prior year and the auditor had failed to find the error during the course of the audit. The company wishes to issue new securities, and disclosing the mistake may make it difficult to do so. The auditor agrees with the company that it should ignore the error.
f. The auditor discovers that the company has taken questionable deductions in its tax returns for the prior year. The auditor notifies the company of this and does nothing more.

E2-26 Professional Standards Why are there requirements for those practicing law, medicine, and accounting to maintain high ethical standards? How do those who practice as professionals in these fields know whether they are operating at an acceptable ethical level?

E2-27 Income Statement Rork Corporation expected its net income for the month of August to be at least $4,500. During the month, Rork reported the following:

Wages and salaries earned by employees during the month	$ 6,400
Cost of telephone and electricity used	800
Cash sales to customers	8,500
Sales to customers on credit	14,000
Cost of merchandise sold	9,000
Monthly rent payment on machinery and equipment	2,000
Monthly rent payment on building	1,500

a. Prepare an income statement for the month of August.
b. Determine whether Rork Corporation was successful in meeting its projected level of net income for August.

E2-28 Balance Sheet Preparation Orange Company has goods held for sale to customers of $34,000, equipment that it purchased recently for $56,000, and cash of $3,800 in the bank. The company owes its employees $1,600 for wages and has a loan from the bank with a remaining balance of $8,000. Owners have an equity in the company of $84,200. The company has asked its bank for an additional loan, but the bank is reluctant to lend the company in total more than half of the amount of the company's owners' equity. Prepare a balance sheet for Orange Company and determine the maximum additional loan for which Orange might qualify.

E2-29 Preparing Basic Financial Statements You work part-time at a bank and have been given the following information by a local business that is seeking a loan:

Accounts payable to suppliers	$ 20,000
Accounts receivable from customers	82,000
Wages payable to employees	11,000
Additional paid-in capital from owners	60,000
Administrative expenses	35,000
Cash	12,000
Common stock outstanding	100,000
Cost of goods sold	320,000
General expenses	20,000
Interest income	10,000
Interest expense	15,000
Inventory	60,000
Long-term obligations (notes)	160,000
Property, plant, and equipment	346,000
Income tax expense	38,000
Retained earnings	149,000
Sales	550,000
Selling expenses	75,000

You are to organize the information into an income statement and a balance sheet for your supervisor.

E2-30 Analyzing Profitability The following information was included in the most recent president's letter to the stockholders of Westwind Company.

Westwind continues its record of successful operations with net income of $1,375,000 in 2001 on sales of $19,650,000. Sales in 2001 were 10 percent higher than last year and 15 percent higher than in 1999. Westwind also has continued to enlarge its operations. Total assets in 2001 were $22,750,000, a $5,000,000 increase from the previous year and an $11,000,000 increase from 1999. Westwind's net income in 2000 and 1999 was $1,300,000 and $1,380,000, respectively.

a. Prepare a table that shows sales, net income, and total assets of Westwind for each of the three years.
b. Compute Westwind's net income as a percent of sales and of total assets for each of the three years.
c. Do you agree with Westwind's president that operating results have improved over the three-year period? Explain.

E2-31 Financial Statement Classification Indicate whether each of the following items will be reported in the balance sheet (BS), income statement (IS), neither the balance sheet nor income statement (N), or both the balance sheet and income statement (B):

a. Cash.
b. Loans payable.
c. Interest income.
d. Income distributed to shareholders.
e. Salary expense.
f. Anticipated sales next period.
g. Common stock.
h. Payment to retire debt during the period.
i. Sales of goods and services.
j. Buildings and equipment.

USING ACCOUNTING FOR DECISION MAKING

P2-32 Analyzing Operations The Tasty-Baked Store sold goods to customers for $125,500 during the month of January. These goods originally had been purchased from Aunt Martha's Bakery by the Tasty-Baked Store for $71,000. In addition, the store paid rent of $3,200 and wages of $28,000. Prepare an income statement for the Tasty-Baked Store. Who made more from the store's operations during January—the owners or the employees? What actions might Tasty-Baked take to increase its profits during the next months?

P2-33 Audit Opinions The financial statements of Brown Corporation were issued several months ago and included an unqualified audit opinion from a major CPA firm. Three weeks later a newspaper article indicated that, prior to the end of the fiscal year, one of the officers was arrested for stealing several pieces of office equipment. Moreover, two checks the company had received prior to the end of the year bounced and were never collected.

a. What does an unqualified audit opinion indicate?
b. Why might the audit firm have been justified in issuing an unqualified opinion even if the auditors were aware that these events had occurred?
c. If the auditors had discovered these events prior to completing their audit work and had decided they could not issue an unqualified opinion, what other types of responses might they have given?
d. What effect is the issuance of an opinion other than an unqualified opinion likely to have on external decision makers?

P2-34 Selecting Reporting Procedures The president of Vainway Company thinks that the manner in which the company is currently recording certain of its assets is inconsistent with common logic and forces it to misrepresent the total amount of assets it actually holds. The president has already talked with the financial accountants in the company and with the external CPAs who do the annual audit for Vainway, but the president's suggestions have been rebuffed.

a. The financial statements ultimately are the responsibility of corporate management. Does this mean the president can use the methods he wants anyway?
b. What authoritative bodies are charged with determining appropriate accounting standards?
c. What factors might assure the president that the accountants are knowledgeable about currently acceptable accounting standards?
d. As a potential investor in Vainway, who would you prefer had the final say in the accounting methods to be used in preparing the company's financial statements: the president, who is most knowledgeable about the company, or the auditors, who purport to be independent? Why?

P2-35 Internal Controls The external auditor relies heavily on the internal controls maintained by those companies that it audits and may also rely on some of the work of the internal audit staffs of the companies.

a. What is meant by internal controls?
b. Why is heavy reliance placed on internal controls in determining audit procedures?
c. How might the existence of an internal audit staff in the company enter into the evaluation process used by the external auditor?
d. Is the external auditor likely to accept as accurate something the internal auditor indicates is properly stated? Why?

P2-36 Competitive Bidding For many decades, CPA firms did not directly compete with one another for audit clients on the basis of fees charged. Competitive bidding was considered unethical. Now, however, competitive bidding is a common practice. How might the change to competitive bidding for audit engagements affect the following?

a. The cost of having your company's financial statements audited.
b. The quality of audit work done.
c. The securities markets as a whole.

P2-37 Accounting Reports Crabtree Enterprises was established as a sole proprietorship with an investment from its owner. Even though the owner does all of the work for the business and does not draw a salary, the business was expected to operate at a loss during the first two years. However, the business was able to complete its second year of operations with a small profit. During the second year, Crabtree purchased, at a cost of $90,000, inventory to sell to customers. It received $120,000 when the inventory was sold during the year. At the end of the year, Crabtree purchased for cash $75,000 of additional inventory to sell to customers, but that inventory was not sold during the year. Crabtree currently leases a building and all of its equipment. It made

$25,000 in lease payments for the year. Also during the year, Crabtree purchased for $50,000 cash a piece of land on which it hopes to build a new facility. To pay for the land, Crabtree had to borrow $15,000 from the bank.

a. Prepare an income statement for Crabtree for its second year of operations.
b. Prepare a statement that shows Crabtree's cash inflows and cash outflows for the second year.
c. How can a company operate profitably for the year and yet have a negative cash flow (a net cash outflow)?
d. Do you think the company's profit for the year or its negative cash flow is a better indicator of its potential success? Explain.

P2-38 Cash Flow Analysis Gas'n'Goodies Corporation, an operator of several convenience stores, received cash of $103,200 from sales to customers during the period. In addition, an employee paid back a $500 loan from the company. Near the end of the period, the company sold an old display rack it no longer used for $100. Because of expansion plans, the company borrowed $50,000 from the bank. The company made payments of $42,000 for gas and $34,000 for merchandise during the period. In addition, $6,800 was paid for wages, $1,100 for utilities, and $2,000 for rent. The company paid $400 cash for a new sign and entered into a lease for a new location at a rent of $1,000 per month, starting next period.

a. Prepare a listing of the company's cash inflows and outflows. Present the cash flows in a way you feel would be useful. Justify your presentation.
b. As a decision maker, do you think the cash flow for Gas'n'Goodies this period is a good predictor of cash flows in future periods? Explain your answer.

P2-39 Financial Statement Evaluation You have been retained by the Headeddown Company to straighten out the company's accounting records. It seems that the company's trusted accountant for the past forty-two years, Prunella Drebits, has just run off with the new office boy, Freddy Fresh, on an extended around-the-world cruise. Unfortunately, in her rush, she seems to have misplaced the company's books. Now the bank is asking for the latest financial statements so it can determine whether to renew the company's loan. Luckily, you manage to find a listing of accounts and balances she left on the back of a travel brochure for Tahiti:

Cash on hand (in third desk drawer)	$ 120
Accounts receivable from customers	24,200
Sales to customers	71,500
Loan balance owed to Last National Bank	15,000
Wages owed to employees (not yet paid)	1,215
Cash in bank account	725
Wage expense	3,500
Interest income	515
Equipment	51,500
Goods held for sale to customers (Inventory)	15,750

Cost (to the company) of goods sold to customers	53,625
Rent expense	1,600
Interest expense	1,500
Loss from flood damage	4,024
Temporary investments	5,125
Income (dividend) distributions to owners	500

Because Prunella was always very meticulous, you feel certain the list is complete except for the amount of the owners' equity in the business. You know, however, that the owners'

equity is equal to the amount of the assets remaining after deducting the amount of the creditors' claims.

a. Using the information Prunella left behind, prepare a balance sheet and an income statement for the Headeddown Company. Is the company profitable?
b. How do the company's debts compare with the amount of the owners' equity? Why might a comparison of a company's debt with its owners' equity be useful?
c. The listing of accounts includes equipment. Do you think some or all of the cost of equipment used in operations should be included in the computation of income? Explain.

EXPANDING YOUR HORIZONS

C2-40 Costs and Benefits of a Decision Corrosion Chemical Company has been accused by some of its workers of discharging impurities into a local river. Corrosion representatives claim the company has tested the water repeatedly and the emissions from the plant are only occasionally above federally mandated levels. Moreover, a variety of fish are found in the river near the plant, and they have been found safe to eat. What are some of the potential costs and benefits of requiring Corrosion Chemical Company to install new equipment that might satisfy the workers' concerns? How might you measure the costs and benefits?

C2-41 Personal Decisions The decision-making process is not unique to business and not-for-profit organizations. As individuals, we often must go through the same basic process in our personal lives. During the last week of classes before spring break, you learn that your grandmother has fallen and fractured her hip. Your parents indicate she will be in the hospital for approximately three weeks and then discharged. Unfortunately, no close relatives live in the same area as your grandmother, and she will not be able to care for herself for several more months. Your parents have asked you to go to the community where your grandmother lives and see if you can select a nursing home where your grandmother can live until she is ready to resume living independently.

a. What information will you accumulate about care facilities in the community before making a choice?
b. How might you summarize the information you have obtained to make it more useful? How might you use summarized information from other sources?
c. Your grandmother has limited funds and has never thought of living in a care facility. While she seems mentally alert, she is somewhat easily confused by questions about her cash inflows and outflows and about her financial situation. What information will you communicate to her?
d. There may be some question as to who will be the decision maker in this case. If your grandmother makes choices, who should she consult before making a final decision?

C2-42 Ethics and the Global Economy Global Corporation has just learned that it was low bidder on a major contract to build a hospital complex in another country. Global also has learned that its bid is "more likely" to be accepted if it agrees to pay a 10 percent expediting fee to a local government official. The contract appears to be quite lucrative and could well lead to work in adjacent countries.

a. How should Global proceed?
b. If Global learns that this is the normal way of doing business in the country and that companies from Germany and France regularly pay such fees, should this affect Global's actions? Explain.

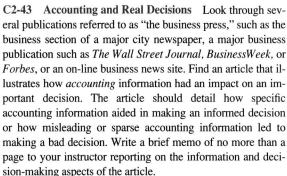 **C2-43 Accounting and Real Decisions** Look through several publications referred to as "the business press," such as the business section of a major city newspaper, a major business publication such as *The Wall Street Journal, BusinessWeek,* or *Forbes*, or an on-line business news site. Find an article that illustrates how *accounting* information had an impact on an important decision. The article should detail how specific accounting information aided in making an informed decision or how misleading or sparse accounting information led to making a bad decision. Write a brief memo of no more than a page to your instructor reporting on the information and decision-making aspects of the article.

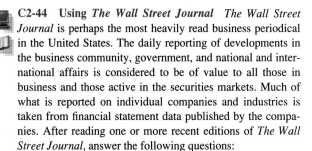 **C2-44 Using *The Wall Street Journal*** *The Wall Street Journal* is perhaps the most heavily read business periodical in the United States. The daily reporting of developments in the business community, government, and national and international affairs is considered to be of value to all those in business and those active in the securities markets. Much of what is reported on individual companies and industries is taken from financial statement data published by the companies. After reading one or more recent editions of *The Wall Street Journal,* answer the following questions:

a. Who is the publisher of *The Wall Street Journal*?
b. Each issue of *The Wall Street Journal* normally has three sections. Describe the type of information found in each of the three sections.

c. Which section of the paper contains the digests of recent earnings reports of individual companies?

d. Which section contains information on stock prices for companies listed on the New York Stock Exchange? What other stock listings are included?

e. What type of information is included in the "What's News—Business and Finance" column in the first section?

f. Is *The Wall Street Journal* online? If so, how can you access it?

C2-45 Team Project: What Does a CPA Do? Form teams as assigned by your instructor. Select a practicing CPA, CPA firm, or accounting firm in your area. Contact the individual or firm and ask for an appointment, explaining that you wish to discuss a school assignment. When keeping your appointment, make sure that you are on time, have a professional appearance (including professional attire), and maintain a professional demeanor. Prepare questions in advance, but at a minimum determine the following from the person with whom you meet:

a. What form of business organization is used? If other than a sole proprietorship, how many partners or owners are there? How many professional staff are there? How many offices are there?

b. What is the main type of work (e.g., tax, audits)?

c. What types of clients does the firm have?

d. Is there more work at a particular time of year? Why?

e. What type of education or training does the person with whom you are meeting have? What types of skills are particularly important?

C2-46 Team Project: Understanding Business Form teams as assigned by your instructor. Choose a business organization in your vicinity that has five or more employees. Call someone in authority at that organization, such as the owner, manager, or controller. Explain the nature of your project and ask to make an appointment to visit that person, or another person suggested by the person to whom you are speaking, at their place of business. Complete each of the following steps and incorporate all information gathered into a formal memo to your instructor:

a. Make sure you follow the appropriate etiquette for a professional visit, with special emphasis on appropriate behavior and dress.

b. Gather whatever general information you can about the organization from the library or your own knowledge or that of friends. What is the organization's primary product or service? About how long has the organization been in existence? Approximately how large is the organization, and how many locations does it have?

c. When you visit the organization, look around and observe as much as you can about the general environment and the activities. Write a description of what you see. Are the organization's primary activities conducted at that location?

d. Ask the person with whom you have an appointment at the organization the following:

1. What form of organization (proprietorship, partnership, corporation, or other) is used by the entity, and what are the primary considerations in using that form of organization?

2. Does the entity provide accounting or financial reports to any external parties? If so, what types of reports does it issue, and to whom?

3. Does the entity use the same accounting information for internal decision making that it provides to external parties? If not, how does the information used internally differ from information reported externally? If the entity does not report to any external parties, determine what types of accounting information and financial reports are used internally.

4. Ask one additional question from each member of your team about the entity, its operations, or its financial reporting system.

e. Prepare and send a thank-you letter to the person who helped you at the organization. Attach a copy of the letter to the memo you prepare for your instructor.

C2-47 What Does Big Blue Do? Gain access to the consolidated financial statements of IBM. These may be obtained from the company, through many libraries, or from the Internet or other electronic databases. Focus on IBM's income statement.

a. What does IBM call its income statement?

b. What are the primary lines of business from which IBM earns revenues?

c. Which line of business generated the most revenue in the latest year reported? In the year before?

d. Which line of business generated the greatest gross profit in the latest year reported? In the year before?

e. Do any lines of business seem to be showing exceptional strength in growth?

f. Do any lines of business seem to be declining?

g. Does the income statement provide any indication that IBM has been successful in controlling its costs? Explain.

www.wiley.com/college/king

Internet Exercises: Visit our Web site for additional exercises.

Annual Report Project Part 2

Refer to the Annual Report Project, Part 1, at the end of Chapter 1. Using the annual report of the company you have chosen, and any other available information, answer the following questions, providing sources and computations where appropriate.

a. Who (e.g., management, auditors, SEC) prepared your company's annual report? Does anything in the annual report indicate who has responsibility for the financial statements? Explain.

b. To what extent do you think your company's financial statements provide reliable information? What leads you to believe this?

c. What is the name of your company's independent audit firm?

d. What type of audit opinion did the independent auditors issue for your company? Indicate the general nature of special exceptions or other items, if any, disclosed in the report of the independent auditors.

e. In your opinion, have your company's operations been successful in recent years? What in the financial statements leads you to this conclusion?

CHAPTER THREE

Understanding Cash Flows

REVIEW

Chapters 1 and 2 discussed decision making, the role of accounting in a free-market economy, and the usefulness of the information presented in financial statements.

WHERE THIS CHAPTER FITS

This chapter continues the discussion of the importance of accounting information by looking at one of the most important elements of financial decision making—cash flows. It discusses why cash flows are so central to decision making, and the type of accounting information presented with respect to cash flows.

LOOKING AHEAD

Chapter 4 and those that follow focus in more detail on the accounting information that is presented in financial statements and how it is used for decision making.

"Let's see. I have 40 bucks until payday. I was going to get some new clothes, but then I won't have money for Saturday when I promised to take Jo to dinner and a movie. Maybe I could borrow the money for my date. Who would lend it to me? Jo? No, wait. That won't work. Let's start over again. Now if I skip my car payment, I'll have lots of money. But then . . ."

"'Like all businesses,' writes [Michael] Mauboussin [of Credit Suisse First Boston], 'Internet companies are valued on their ability to generate cash. If Internet companies have higher valuations than their offline counterparts, the market must believe that they have higher cash values.'"[1]

[1]Excerpts from Richard Young and Andrew Sawers, "Why E-Businesses Are Only Relatively Overvalued," *Financial Director* (August 1, 1999), p. 29.

C ash is a problem! What do you do with it when you have it, and how do you get it when you don't? College students, professors, business executives, and homemakers all have the same problem of finding enough cash when it is needed and using cash that is available efficiently and effectively. An individual's financial success, and often personal well-being, depends in part on the ability to manage cash. The same is true for all types of organizations. Just as individuals must plan their expenditures of cash to coincide with available cash balances, major corporations must pay careful attention to their cash inflows and outflows.

Part I of this chapter explores the different types of cash flows a business might have, some decisions regarding cash, some of the important aspects of accounting for and controlling cash, and why these factors are important for anyone evaluating a business. Part II focuses on the importance of the timing of cash flows for

decisions. When you are finished reading this chapter, you should be able to:

1. Describe the elements of cash flow and the importance of cash flow information.

2. Explain the importance of forecasting future cash flows.

3. Explain what is meant by the cash cycle and describe some important aspects of cash management.

4. Explain why internal control over cash is important and describe some aspects of good cash control.

5. Describe how cash flows are reported.

6. Demonstrate the effects of interest on cash flow and explain what is meant by the time value of money and why it is important.

7. Compute future values and present values of expected cash flows and use these computations for decision making.

In Practice 3-1

UNITED AIRLINES

UAL Corporation (United Airlines) had total cash, cash equivalents, and short-term investments amounting to $815 million at December 31, 1998. The company generated about $3.2 billion of cash from operations in 1998, but it also spent $2.8 billion on additions to property, plant, and equipment, UAL reported that in the current year it replaced thirty-nine aircraft and purchased two new additional aircraft, and it plans to retire and replace thirty-three aircraft in the near future. In addition, it spent more than $460 million to purchase shares of its own stock.

ANALYSIS

UAL had considerable cash and equivalents on hand and large cash inflows during the year. It made significant expenditures during the year and extensive commitments for future cash outflows. Given the huge amounts of cash and cash flows, cash management for UAL is extremely important. Financial statement users need to assess whether UAL will be able to meet its commitments for future expenditures of cash. [www.ual.com]

PART I

UNDERSTANDING CASH FLOWS

Information for Decisions

Successful organizations must generate sufficient cash to support their activities and make payments to investors and creditors. Information on cash inflows and outflows helps investors and creditors answer questions such as these: Will the company's existing sources of cash flows continue in the future? Can the timing and amounts of the company's cash flows be predicted? Do the company's cash flows differ substantially from similar companies or other types of entities?

Cash flows are simply receipts or payments of cash. Cash amounts coming in to an individual or organization are cash inflows. Payments made by the individual or organization to others are cash outflows. Cash inflows can occur regularly like a paycheck or infrequently like the cash from the sale of your CD player. Similarly, cash outflows may occur regularly like payment of your monthly phone bill or infrequently, such as for the purchase of a car.

Businesses also have different types of cash flows. Some cash flows relate to the business's primary operations, such as amounts collected from customers and amounts paid to suppliers. These cash flows are **operating cash flows.** Other cash flows, referred to as **investing cash flows**, have to do with the company's investment in the assets that it needs to operate, such as when the company purchases new equipment. A third type of cash flows, **financing cash flows,** have to do with getting the money needed for the enterprise's operating and investing activities. Financing cash flows include amounts borrowed from long-term creditors and cash distributions of profits to owners.

When assessing the cash flows of a business, five different aspects of the cash flows are important:

1. Reason: Where is the cash flow coming from (source) or where is it going (use), and why (purpose)?
2. Amount: How much is the cash inflow or outflow?
3. Frequency: Is the cash flow recurring?
4. Timing: When will the cash flow occur?
5. Impact: Will the cash flow affect some other cash flow?

Exhibit 3–1 illustrates a typical pattern of cash inflows and cash outflows for a business. Much of a business's cash inflow should come from its primary activities or central operations. When a business sells goods or services to customers, it generally receives cash or claims to cash (the customer's promise to pay), which it ultimately converts into cash.

A company's central operations may generate fairly constant cash flows throughout the year, or the level of operations and the resulting cash flows may change significantly over the period. Operations that follow a predictable pattern of change during the year are characteristic of a seasonal business and require special planning to ensure cash is available when needed. Farmers, for example, often arrange for bank loans to meet their seasonal cash needs.

For a company to generate cash inflows from its central operations, it typically must make cash payments to acquire the goods and services it needs to operate. Examples of such operating items include the following:

- Salaries of employees
- Goods purchased for resale to customers or to use in the production of the company's products
- Goods and services used in the operations, such as utilities, supplies, and advertising
- Interest payments on money borrowed

Some cash flows related to operations may be less predictable, such as the cash outflows related to major industrial accidents.

BUSINESS CASH FLOWS

EXHIBIT 3-1

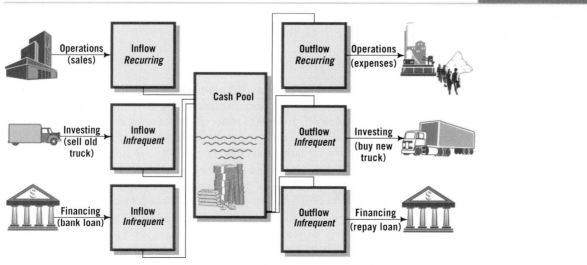

In addition, companies have cash flows outside of those directly associated with normal operations. Cash flows related to investing and financing activities are usually less frequent than those related to operations. For example, cash inflows may be generated from temporary investments or by selling some of the company's old equipment.

You Decide 3-1

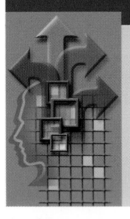

LET'S GO TO THE FOOTBALL GAME

Your brother works in the College Athletic Department, and he has a plan! The two of you will arrange bus trips to all of the away football games this fall. He figures you can get 50 students to go to each game, charge them $50 a person for the game, transportation, and refreshments, and make bundles of money. He can get tickets for $15 each, and he knows a bus driver who will take a group to each game for $300 round trip. It sounds great! After a few phone calls, you figure that you can provide box lunches on the bus for $4 per person and additional refreshments for $10 per person. You find that you can get 1,000 copies of a flyer for each trip printed for $50, and you guess there might be another $100 of miscellaneous costs per trip. Finally, you and your brother agree that if you cannot make at least $200 per trip each, it's not worth it. What do you think? Can you make a go of it?

ESTIMATION OF CASH FLOWS

Information for Decisions

An organization's ability to pay its debts as they come due and provide for its other needs depends on its ability to generate net cash inflows from operations and convert other assets to cash. Forecasts of future cash flows are crucial for management to operate the organization effectively and efficiently. Accounting information helps management in this regard, but it can also assist investors and creditors in answering questions such as these: Does the company exhibit the signs of a "cash-poor" company? What factors are important in determining the company's potential future cash inflows and outflows? Which cash flow attributes are of greatest importance in evaluating this company?

Cash management is important for businesses. They must have cash when needed, and they must make decisions about how to get cash and how to use it. An important part of cash management is the estimation of cash flows. Many of the factors management considers in estimating cash flows also are relevant for cash-flow estimates made by external decision makers, such as stockholders, creditors, and other suppliers of resources.

Estimates of the amounts and timing of future cash flows are called **cash forecasts**. All entities have to estimate future cash flows. They must time their cash inflows and outflows appropriately to ensure having enough cash when needed. Surprisingly, even very profitable companies have failed because they did not have sufficient cash to pay their debts on time. Although the companies were profitable, they might have been "cash poor" because the cash they should have had was still owed to them by their customers or had been used to purchase inventory and equipment.

An entity's ability to pay its debts when due is referred to as its **solvency**. An entity that is unable to pay its debts is said to be insolvent. The ability of an entity to have cash available, either by holding cash or by holding other assets that can easily be converted into cash, is referred to as **liquidity**. An entity with a high degree of liquidity is less likely to become insolvent than an entity that is not very liquid.

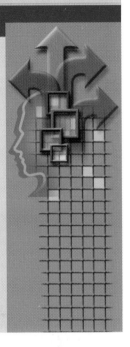

You Decide 3-2

CASH! WHO NEEDS IT, AND WHEN?

Refer to *You Decide 3–1*. You decide to take a group to one game to see what happens (your entrepreneurial spirit is marginal at best). Now the serious stuff:

- You need to buy the flyers for $50 and get them out two weeks before the game.
- You will require a $10 deposit from each participant one week before the game, with the balance to be paid at the start of the trip.
- The game tickets have to be purchased for $15 each a week before the game. The bus driver wants half the round-trip cost as a deposit one week before the trip, with the balance paid when you start.
- The box lunch and the refreshments will have to be bought the day before the trip at a cost of $14 per person.
- Finally and most importantly, you can put up cash of $125 to get started, and your brother can match it.

Is the $250 that you and your brother can invest, plus the deposit each rider makes one week before the game, going to be enough to cover the advance payments you have to make? Will you have to borrow money? How much? When?

FORECASTS OF CASH INFLOWS

Cash inflows may come from an entity's central activities or from other sources. Some are relatively easy to forecast because they are routine and recurring. Others are more difficult to forecast because they vary considerably from period to period or may be totally unexpected.

Revenue Forecasts.   Forecasts of cash inflows for businesses usually start with forecasts of revenues from sales of goods and services. We prepared a revenue forecast in Chapter 1 for Our Video Store, but most revenue forecasts are more complex. Although based on past experience, revenue forecasts also look to the future and, as pictured in Exhibit 3–2, consider factors such as trends in customer preferences, the state of the economy, cyclical and seasonal factors, competitor actions, and technological advances. In addition, the company may be able to affect sales through its advertising and its pricing strategy.

Cash Generated from Sales.   After a business forecasts its future revenues, it must forecast cash collections. Depending on the type of business, some sales result in immediate cash payments. In other cases, however, customers are granted credit and allowed to pay for their purchases at a later time. These sales are said to be made "on account." They provide the seller with **accounts receivable**, which are claims on the purchaser's cash because they reflect the purchaser's promise to pay. Thus, companies not only must forecast the timing and amount of sales, but they also must estimate how quickly the accounts receivable, the

| EXHIBIT 3-2 | **A REVENUE FORECAST** |

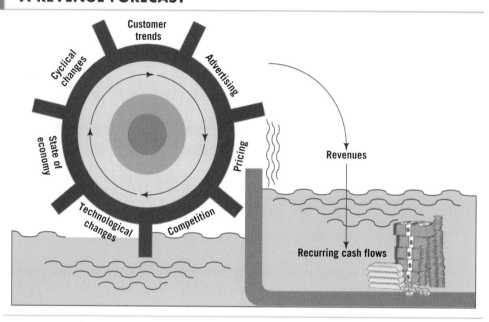

| EXHIBIT 3-3 | **TIMING CASH INFLOWS: CASH GENERATED FROM SALES** |

Activity	Sales		Cash Inflows
1. Cash Sale	$10,000		$10,000
2. Sale on Account	$10,000	Accounts Receivable $10,000	- 0 -
3. Sale on Account	$20,000	Accounts Receivable $10,000 20,000 $30,000	- 0 -
4. Collect one-half of sale in (2) above	. . . . . .	Accounts Receivable $ 5,000 20,000 $25,000	$ 5,000

Totals:

Sales	$40,000	
Accounts Receivable		$25,000
Cash Inflow		$15,000

amounts due from customers, will be collected. As shown in Exhibit 3–3, cash inflow is a function of sales and changes in the accounts receivable balance.

Some receivables may not be collected at all; not all customers pay their debts. If collection efforts fail, the unpaid receivables are treated as **uncollectible accounts** that will not provide cash inflows.

In Practice 3-2

THE MCGRAW-HILL COMPANIES, INC.

The McGraw·Hill Companies

The McGraw-Hill Companies, Inc., a diversified company with operations that include publishing, financial services, and broadcasting, in a recent annual report listed revenues of $3,534,095,000 and included the following information about its receivables:

Accounts receivable, end of year	$1,155,078,000
Allowance for doubtful accounts	182,629,000

The report also states the following:

Accounts receivable ... increased $113.4 million, or 10.9%, primarily as a result of increased revenues. The year-to-year increase was effectively controlled through timely collections. Number of days sales outstanding, a key indicator of collection efficiency, increased two days ... due to the increased sales in education markets where terms of sales are longer.

ANALYSIS

Note the large amount of cash tied up in receivables, an amount equal to 82 days of sales revenue. Think how much return The McGraw-Hill Companies could earn if the company actually had that amount of additional cash to invest. The McGraw-Hill Companies recognize the importance of getting cash out of receivables quickly and disclose that the company is paying particular attention to timely collections. However, the collection efficiency has decreased because of increased sales in a market where payment terms are longer than in other markets. The amount of accounts not expected to be collected is substantial and represents an important cost of giving credit to customers. [www.mcgraw-hill.com]

Nonrevenue Cash Inflows.   Cash inflows from sources other than normal revenues sometimes are difficult to forecast because they do not occur on a regular basis and may not be under management's control. For example, the timing of a cash inflow from the settlement of a lawsuit may depend on appeals and various other factors. In other cases, cash inflows may not be regularly recurring but are relatively easy to forecast because they are at least partially under the control of the entity. For example, a company may choose to sell some of the buildings and equipment it previously used in its operations. Because this sale is not a frequently recurring event, it results in a one-time cash inflow, but one the company can time (within limits) to serve its purposes.

Cash inflows from borrowings often are very important for companies. If, for example, a company forecasts that its cash outflows will exceed its cash inflows during the period, the company must either have sufficient cash on hand to meet the excess cash outflows or raise the cash in some way, such as by selling assets or borrowing.

In Practice 3-3

DEKALB GENETICS

DEKALB Genetics, a company that sells seed for crops such as corn, soybeans, and oats, included the following statement in its annual report: "DEKALB Genetics continues to cover its seasonal operating cash requirements with bank borrowings."

ANALYSIS

Accurate cash forecasting allows companies such as DEKALB Genetics to anticipate their cash requirements and arrange for loans when needed. [www.DEKALB.com]

FORECASTS OF CASH OUTFLOWS

Exhibit 3–4 illustrates a typical company's cash outflows. Most of a company's cash outflows are usually tied to the company's normal operations. Forecasting the normal recurring cash outflows related to operations requires an estimate of the company's level of operations and an understanding of its cost structure.

Cash Outflows and Cost Structure. Understanding an entity's operations helps provide an understanding of its cost structure. An entity's cost structure has to do with the way its costs are incurred in relation to other factors, such as the level of operations (e.g., how many units are

---

EXHIBIT 3-4 **BUSINESS CASH OUTFLOWS**

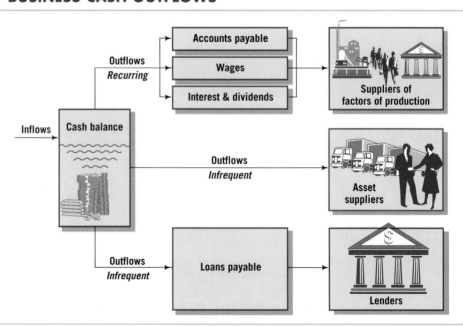

produced). Some costs do not, within limits, change with the level of operations; these costs are **fixed costs**. If a company pays a store manager a fixed salary of $75,000 per year regardless of the amount of the store's sales, that salary represents a fixed cost. Costs that change directly with the level of activity are **variable costs**. For example, if a company rents a truck and agrees to pay $1 per mile driven, that cost is a variable cost. Some costs do not fit neatly into one category, so the important issue is how a particular cost behaves and not what it is called.

Why should financial statement users understand the cost structure of businesses they are evaluating? Because they need to know how a company's costs will respond to market changes and management's actions. For example, decision makers need to know whether a company's costs would drop if its sales were to fall, or whether its costs would remain relatively constant.

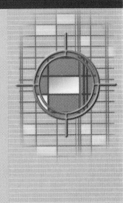

A CLOSER LOOK AT

ANALYZING COST STRUCTURE

Aardvark Airlines leases a DC-3 under a five-year lease for $10,000 per year and uses it for scheduled service between Booneytown and Swamp Creek. The airline incurs a cost for each one-way flight of $600 for fuel, the crew's wages, and landing fees. In addition, each passenger is provided with a deluxe gourmet meal and a beverage at a cost to the airline of $3 per passenger. What are the relevant cost characteristics for Aardvark Airlines? The $10,000 per year lease payment is a fixed cost because it will be incurred whether the airline makes many flights or no flights. The $600 cost of each flight for fuel, wages, and fees is fixed if the flight is made, but is avoided if the flight is canceled. The $3 food and beverage cost is variable with the number of passengers flown.

An analysis of Aardvark's cost structure indicates that, as long as a particular flight is to be made, each additional passenger provides the company with a cash inflow requiring very little additional cash outflow. On the other hand, a decline in the number of passengers on scheduled flights results in a decrease in cash inflows with almost no reduction in outflows.

Infrequently Recurring Cash Outflows. Cash outflows that do not recur frequently may be easy or difficult to forecast. The replacement of old equipment may not occur often, but it can usually be forecast well in advance. Bank loans may come due only once every few years, but the dates usually are known at the time the loans are made. On the other hand, some significant cash outflows may be impossible to predict because they are beyond a company's control and occur irregularly and infrequently. For example, uninsured losses, such as those resulting from floods and earthquakes, may be large in amount and impossible to forecast. Because companies are unable to predict such unexpected and sudden cash needs, they may protect themselves by keeping cash reserves on hand or by entering into credit arrangements with banks so that loans are available when needed.

IMPORTANCE OF DISTINGUISHING TYPES OF CASH FLOWS

Do decision makers care whether cash flows are recurring? Do they care about the source of cash inflows? Consider an example. Some years ago, MGM sold a large portion of its motion picture library, which had previously generated rental fees. It traded a stream of future cash receipts, the rentals, for a single current cash receipt. It was important for MGM's financial statement users to know the source of this large cash inflow to help them assess the future prospects of the company. They needed to know that the large cash inflow in one period was not from an activity that could be repeated, but in fact would reduce future cash generated from movie rentals because the movie library was reduced significantly.

Investors have lost millions of dollars because they did not understand differences in types of cash flows and incorrectly forecast future cash flows. For example, in a type of scam known as a Ponzi scheme, named after Charles Ponzi, a Boston swindler of the 1920s, individuals invest large sums of money on the promise of exceptionally high returns. After a few months, they start receiving large cash payments and are told these cash payments represent profits from their investments. Because of what the investors think are outstanding profits, they often invest more and encourage their friends to do the same. As more money pours in from additional investments, a portion is returned as "profits," prompting additional investments. In reality, the large "returns" investors receive on their investments are amounts drawn from earlier investments, other investors, and perhaps from borrowings.

In Practice 3-4

PRUDENTIAL-BACHE

One of the nation's largest brokerage firms, a unit of Prudential Insurance, agreed to settle, for hundreds of millions of dollars, charges of improperly selling partnership interests. Some of the firm's internal documents indicated that the firm "inflated payouts on some of its money-losing partnerships by distributing borrowed funds to investors."[2]

ANALYSIS

Investors thought they were receiving exceptional profits, when in fact the cash flows they were receiving were not from partnership operations. [www.prudential.com]

Understanding the nature of past and current cash flows is crucial for forecasting future cash flows. An understanding of the past, together with a knowledge of what will affect the relevant future, are the key elements in developing useful forecasts.

EVALUATING CASH MANAGEMENT

Information for Decisions

Management's effectiveness and efficiency in the use of cash is important to the success of an enterprise. In evaluating a company, investors and creditors must answer questions such as these: Does the company have sufficient cash on hand to meet its needs? Does it have too much cash on hand? Has the company made effective use of credit terms from suppliers and credit arrangements with lenders? Are the internal controls sufficient to ensure the safeguarding of cash?

---

[2]"Prudential Unit to Settle SEC Charges," *The Wall Street Journal* (September 30, 1993), p. C1.

Cash management is one of the most important, and often neglected, areas contributing to the success or failure of an organization. Cash is valuable to an organization, or an individual, because it can be used to buy items of value or invested to earn a return. An interesting property of cash is that, if invested properly, it can generate more cash over time. This characteristic is referred to as the *time value of money* and, because of its importance, is discussed in detail in Part II of this chapter.

Cash management is concerned with the way in which cash is employed within an organization. Good cash management results in the entity's cash being used effectively and efficiently in the attainment of the organization's objectives. Several important aspects of cash management are as follows:

1. Because of the time value of money, available cash always should be employed as fully as possible. The more liquid or the closer to cash an asset is, the less return it is likely to earn. In general, cash on hand earns no return, bank deposits and short-term investments earn a small return, intermediate-term investments earn a moderate return, and long-term investments earn a greater return.

2. Because there is a time value of money, cash generally should be obtained as quickly as possible and should not be paid out until necessary to do so.

3. Cash is a valuable commodity in universal demand and appropriate steps should be taken to safeguard it.

Assessing whether an enterprise is managing its cash effectively often begins with understanding its cash cycle.

THE CASH CYCLE

Businesses acquire resources and then use those resources to generate revenues, with the goal of making a profit. The period of time between the expenditure of cash to acquire resources and the receipt of cash from revenues generated is referred to as the **cash cycle** or the **operating cycle**. For example, the cash cycle of a typical merchandising firm, such as a department store, might appear as in Exhibit 3–5. The company invests cash in inventory, sells the goods to customers, and receives the customer's promise to pay. At some later time, the

THE CASH CYCLE

EXHIBIT 3-5

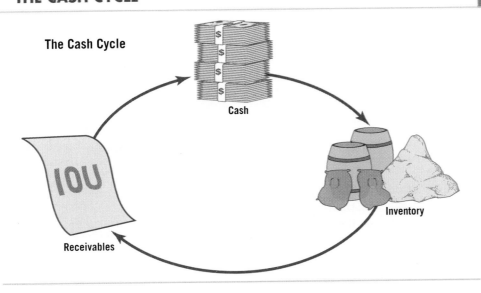

The Cash Cycle

Cash

Inventory

Receivables

customer pays what is owed, and the company receives cash. The operating cycle of a business selling to customers on credit and purchasing inventory to be paid for at a later date generally is longer than that of a business that uses cash for all transactions.

Why is the cash cycle important? Because of the time value of money, companies generally prefer to give up cash as slowly as possible and collect cash as quickly as possible. A company cannot earn interest on money that is tied up in inventory or receivables, so, all other things being equal, companies prefer to hold as little inventory as possible and to collect receivables as quickly as possible. The opportunity cost of having cash tied up in inventory and receivables is equal to what the company could have earned by employing the cash in its next best use.

Cash cycles may differ between industries because of the characteristics of the industries. For example, a company that develops property and builds and sells homes may take more than a year to recover its investment in land, wages, and building materials through the sale of the homes. A distillery that produces fine Tennessee whiskey may have a cycle of five or ten years, while a grocery store has a very short cycle because it sells its inventory quickly and usually for cash.

Within a particular industry, there may be differences in the length of the cash cycle because of operating policies of the companies involved. For example, two department stores may have different cycles because one sells on credit using bank credit cards (e.g., VISA or Mastercard) and is able to receive cash from the bank almost immediately, while the second sells on credit using its own credit card and is very liberal in its credit policies, allowing several payments to be missed before taking action to collect past due receivables. The first store would be expected to have a much shorter cash cycle than the second.

When a company is being evaluated, specific measures often are compared with those of other companies and with industry averages. The length of a company's cash cycle may be used to learn about its operating characteristics. Measures related to the cash cycle, such as how quickly inventory is sold or how fast receivables are collected, are indicators of performance. For example, as illustrated by The McGraw-Hill Companies' financial statement disclosures (In Practice 3-2) earlier in the chapter, many companies use the number of days' sales carried in receivables as a measure of collection efficiency.

However, an in-depth analysis of a company's performance involves more than an examination of a few summary measures. For example, one store may collect its cash faster by accepting bank credit cards but also incurs a fee imposed by the credit card companies, usually in the range of 2 to 5 percent of the amount charged. Another store may speed collection on its own credit card receivables through its credit policies, but may lose sales by not extending credit to some individuals. Summary measures and indicators are useful for decision making, but should not be used in isolation.

You Decide 3-3

WHERE'S THE CASH?

Glenn Corporation holds about $350,000 of inventory on average throughout the year and has an average balance of accounts receivable of about $45,000. If Glenn had excess cash, it could invest the money and earn a 10 percent return. Glenn has considered not offering credit to its customers any longer and has explored having inventory shipped directly from its suppliers to its customers, avoiding the need to carry inventory. If Glenn no longer offers credit to its customers, sales can be expected to decline slightly, resulting in lost profits on the forgone sales of about $10,000. What do you recommend to Glenn regarding continuing to offer credit and carry inventory? How much would be saved or lost under the new plan?

EFFICIENT EMPLOYMENT OF CASH

Cash is a valuable commodity; there is seldom enough to go around, and a price must be paid for not using it wisely. But what does it mean to use cash wisely?

As with other assets, cash should be employed fully in the attainment of the organization's objectives. The depression-era notion of keeping cash tucked safely away in a mattress to avoid bank failures is an example of poor cash management. Not only might the cash be lost to theft, fire, and flood, but cash differs from rabbits in that it will not multiply. Putting cash in a savings account, for example, not only protects it, but also makes it grow.

The first step in cash management is being aware of cash needs and expected cash flows. Accurate cash forecasts and the development of a cash budget provide the basis for good cash management. Given anticipated cash needs, only enough cash should be kept on hand to meet those needs and to provide some protection against the uncertainties of forecasts.

To avoid keeping money in checking accounts that bear little or no interest, organizations with large potential cash needs may keep excess cash invested in marketable securities that provide a return and can be quickly converted into cash. Many organizations have adopted a "zero-balance" policy of depositing just enough cash in checking accounts to cover checks written. Some organizations, and more than a few individuals, go a step further by "playing the float" on their checking accounts. Although technically illegal, they write checks for more than is in the account, knowing that checks will not be presented to the bank for payment for at least several days after they are mailed, as illustrated in Exhibit 3–6. Money to cover the checks is used in some other manner until the checks are expected to clear the bank. The cash is transferred in time to be available for payment.

There may be some question about the effectiveness of a company's cash management if the company keeps large amounts of cash on hand for extended periods of time. Although large amounts of cash may improve a company's liquidity and reduce the chances of insolvency, the company's efficiency may be impaired. If the cash is needed by the company, it normally should be invested in the operations; if the cash is not needed, it should be distributed to the owners so they can decide how it should be invested to maximize their return.

LIFE OF A CHECK

EXHIBIT 3-6

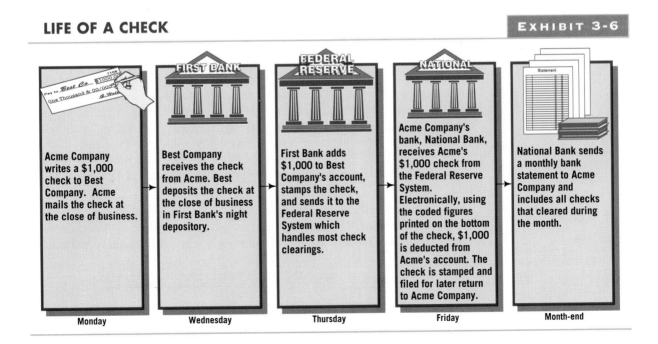

| FIRST BANK | FEDERAL RESERVE | NATIONAL | Statement |

Acme Company writes a $1,000 check to Best Company. Acme mails the check at the close of business.

Best Company receives the check from Acme. Best deposits the check at the close of business in First Bank's night depository.

First Bank adds $1,000 to Best Company's account, stamps the check, and sends it to the Federal Reserve System which handles most check clearings.

Acme Company's bank, National Bank, receives Acme's $1,000 check from the Federal Reserve System. Electronically, using the coded figures printed on the bottom of the check, $1,000 is deducted from Acme's account. The check is stamped and filed for later return to Acme Company.

National Bank sends a monthly bank statement to Acme Company and includes all checks that cleared during the month.

| **Monday** | **Wednesday** | **Thursday** | **Friday** | **Month-end** |

USE OF CREDIT

An essential part of good cash management is the careful use of credit. If a company purchases goods for $20,000 and has the choice of paying the $20,000 today or one month from today, the company should wait to pay because it could invest the money during the intervening time and earn a return. Of course, the company should not delay payment so long as to incur additional charges, tarnish its credit rating, or harm its relationship with suppliers.

Companies also may meet cash needs by borrowing rather than by keeping large amounts of cash on hand. If their cash needs are known, companies may borrow from the public by issuing short-term notes or IOUs, referred to as commercial paper. For unexpected cash needs that have the potential of being large in amount, a company may enter into an agreement with a financial institution to borrow cash whenever it is needed, up to some pre-approved limit. This type of borrowing arrangement is referred to as a line of credit. For example, AT&T disclosed in its annual report that it had received a credit commitment from a group of lenders making $5 billion available for general corporate purposes. While there normally is a small fee for maintaining a line of credit, the savings from not having large cash balances on hand to meet contingencies often is substantial.

INTERNAL CONTROL

While all of a company's assets need to be protected, the safeguarding of cash must be given special attention. Cash is easy to hide and convert to personal use. Specific control procedures are needed to ensure that cash is not stolen, lost, or used inappropriately. Further, the procedures must ensure that cash is reported correctly in financial statements.

All organizations should develop and enforce specific policies relating to the receipt, handling, and payment of cash, as well as the associated recordkeeping. Also, all cash-related functions should be supervised closely. Some general internal control procedures for cash are as follows:

1. Physical safeguards should be provided for cash. All cash receipts should be deposited in total in the bank at least daily. Cash on hand should be kept to a minimum, it should be under lock and key, and someone should be made directly responsible for it.

2. There should be a separation of duties relating to handling and accounting for cash. Those individuals preparing accounting records for cash should not have access to it. Those individuals involved with cash receipts should not be involved with cash payments. Personnel dealing with cash should be bonded.[3]

3. There should be appropriate documentation and authorization. All cash payments, with the possible exception of very small expenditures, should be made by check. Separate individuals should be responsible for authorizing, preparing, signing, and mailing the checks. Individuals responsible for cash receipts should list all receipts during the day, and a different individual should compare the total with the bank deposits for the day. Cash payments should never be made directly from cash receipts, and both should be accounted for separately.

4. All bank accounts should be compared periodically with the accounting records and any discrepancies explained. The document comparing bank balances as shown on bank statements with those recorded in the accounting records is called a **bank reconciliation**

---

[3]Bonding involves having an independent third party, usually a bonding company, agree to reimburse the company for losses incurred because of a bonded employee's dishonest acts. Bonding is important because bonding companies usually conduct background checks on individuals they bond.

and is discussed in detail in Appendix 3–1 of this chapter. The person responsible for reconciling the bank accounts with the accounting records should not be involved in handling or accounting for the cash.

5. Cash balances and the records pertaining to cash should be audited.

THE CASH FLOW STATEMENT

Information for Decisions

The cash flow statement is one of the four required financial statements and provides decision makers with information essential to the evaluation of the cash flows of an organization. A careful review of the cash flow statement makes it possible for investors and creditors to answer questions such as these: Are the major sources and uses of cash consistent with other companies in the industry? Do the company's operations generate sufficient cash to sustain the company on a long-run basis? What are the major uses of the company's cash, and what does this imply for future cash needs? Are the company's sources of cash sufficient to provide cash to pay off maturing debt and provide cash distributions to owners?

Investors and creditors are interested in assessing the amounts and likelihood of future cash flows they might receive from enterprises for which they provide financing. They want to know how much cash they will get back and when. The answer will depend on the future profits and cash flows of the enterprise. The ability of an enterprise to provide cash flows to its owners and creditors is closely related to its success in generating its own cash inflows and explains the need for a cash flow statement in addition to an income statement and balance sheet.

Because cash flows are so important to those analyzing businesses, the cash flow statement is required by generally accepted accounting principles. This statement provides a summary of all the entity's cash inflows and outflows during the period. To facilitate analysis, it classifies cash flows along the lines of an enterprise's major activities: operating, investing, and financing. In this way, decision makers can evaluate cash flows of a recurring nature separate from those not expected to recur frequently in the future, those related to the entity's central operations separate from those stemming from peripheral activities, and those that imply the likelihood of similar cash flows in the future separate from those that may result in the opposite cash flows. Exhibit 3–7 illustrates some of the types of cash flows related to operations, investing activities, and financing activities, and indicates whether each represents a source of cash (inflow) or use of cash (outflow).

The statement of cash flows for Our Video Store was developed in Chapter 2 and is presented in Exhibit 3–8. Storage Technology Corporation's statement of cash flows is shown in Exhibit 3–9. Storage Technology is a much larger and more complex enterprise than Our Video Store, and its cash flow statement is more complex. However, the two statements are quite similar. Both report the cash flows from operating activities, investing activities, and financing activities. In the operating section of their statements, both companies report the cash received from their customers and the cash paid to suppliers and employees. Storage Technology's statement is tied to the balance sheet by showing that the change in cash and cash equivalents during the period is equal to the change in cash and cash equivalents from the amount reported in last year's balance sheet to the amount reported in this year's balance sheet. Storage Technology reports cash and cash equivalents together, treating financial in-

EXHIBIT 3-7	**CASH FLOW SOURCES AND USES**

Nature of Activity	Type of Cash Flow	Source/Use
Operations	Collections from customers	Source
	Interest income	Source
	Payments to suppliers	Use
	Payment of wages	Use
	Payment of rent	Use
	Payment of interest	Use
Investing	Purchase of building	Use
	Purchase of equipment	Use
	Investment in securities	Use
	Sale of old equipment	Source
	Sale of investment securities	Source
Financing	Investment by owners	Source
	Loan from bank	Source
	Distribution of profits to owners	Use
	Repayment of loan	Use

struments maturing in three months or less from the date of purchase as equivalent to cash. The company also includes with its cash flow statement a reconciliation (not shown in Exhibit 3–9) of cash provided by operating activities with net income, so the cash flow statement is tied in with the income statement.

Organizations are permitted some latitude in how they present operating cash flows in the statement of cash flows. Thus, the operating section of the cash flow statement for many companies appears somewhat different than illustrated here, although the amount of cash generated from operations is unaffected by the statement format. Because of the importance and complexity of the cash flow statement, it will be discussed in greater depth in Chapter 13.

EXHIBIT 3-8	**OUR VIDEO STORE'S STATEMENT OF CASH FLOWS**

OUR VIDEO STORE		
STATEMENT OF CASH FLOWS FOR THE FIRST MONTH OF OPERATION		
Cash generated from operations:		
Video and game rentals		$ 3,800
Less cash expenses:		
Rent	$1,000	
Wages	600	
Other	200	
Total cash expenses		(1,800)
Total cash generated from operations		$ 2,000
Cash used in investing activities:		
Purchase of videos		(6,800)
Cash from financing activities:		
Investment by owner		6,800
Total cash generated		$ 2,000

STORAGE TECHNOLOGY'S STATEMENT OF CASH FLOWS

EXHIBIT 3-9

STORAGE TECHNOLOGY CORPORATION AND SUBSIDIARIES
CONSOLIDATED STATEMENT OF CASH FLOWS
(IN THOUSANDS OF DOLLARS)

	Year Ended		
	December 25, 1998	December 26, 1997	December 27, 1996
OPERATING ACTIVITIES			
Cash received from customers	$ 2,124,070	$ 2,110,587	$ 2,158,927
Cash paid to suppliers and employees	(1,926,451)	(1,615,636)	(1,662,990)
Interest received	15,274	29,103	26,448
Interest paid	(6,657)	(3,640)	(21,866)
Income taxes paid, net	(118,131)	(73,754)	(35,819)
Net cash provided by operating activities	88,105	446,660	464,700
INVESTING ACTIVITIES			
Short-term investments, net	77,275	(48,099)	(29,176)
Purchase of property, plant and equipment, net	(116,903)	(65,893)	(68,946)
Other assets, net	(21,008)	8,366	10,059
Net cash used in investing activities	(60,636)	(105,626)	(88,063)
FINANCING ACTIVITIES			
Repayments of nonrecourse borrowings and other debt, net	(4,936)	(5,245)	(100,036)
Repurchases of common stock	(359,395)	(484,996)	(195,498)
Proceeds from credit facilities, net	273,211		
Proceeds from employee stock plans	36,924	29,790	39,154
Net cash used in financing activities	(54,196)	(460,451)	(256,380)
Effect of exchange rate changes on cash	2,393	(12,665)	3,642
Increase (decrease) in cash and cash equivalents	(24,334)	(132,082)	123,899
Cash and cash equivalents—beginning of the year	256,319	388,401	264,502
Cash and cash equivalents—end of the year	$ 231,985	$ 256,319	$ 388,401

CASH FLOWS AND PERFORMANCE EVALUATION

Information for Decisions

Because a company's cash flows are vital to its success, investors and creditors use cash flow information, particularly that found in the statement of cash flows, in evaluating the company's viability and prospects for the future. Cash flow information can help financial statement users answer questions such as these: What do the company's cash flows imply for future cash flows and income? Do income and cash flow measures lead to the same assessments of the company's performance, and, if not, why not?

As discussed throughout this chapter, a company's cash flows play a crucial role in its success, and an evaluation of those cash flows is crucial for financial statement users when assessing a company's performance and its potential for the future. A company must sustain itself in the long run by generating positive cash from operations. Cash inflows from sales of operating or other assets not related to the company's central operations, as well as from borrowing, cannot recur indefinitely. Thus, cash generated from operations, rather than the total amount of cash generated during the period, is an important indicator of a company's success in the short run and may serve as a basis, with additional information, for forecasting future operating cash flows.

Other information about cash flows can also help in assessing a company's performance and potential for the future. For example, cash outflows for new plant and equipment indicate that the company is making efforts to maintain and perhaps expand its productive capacity. Cash outflows to repay debt imply that the company has improved its borrowing capacity and may be in a good position to borrow in the future, should the need arise. On the other hand, cash inflows from borrowing improve the company's cash position, but they also indicate that the company will have to make cash payments for interest and debt repayment in the future. Cash inflows from additional investment by owners indicate that the company has arranged long-term financing without the risk of having fixed debt payments to make. Cash payments representing distributions of profits to owners are of particular interest to owners and potential investors because investments are made with the expectation of ultimately receiving cash payments in return.

As useful as it is, cash flow information does not provide a complete picture; it reflects only one aspect of an organization's activities. For example, large infrequent cash flows, such as a cash inflow from a large loan or a large cash outflow for the purchase of new plant and equipment, may significantly affect cash flows in a single period, while the actual effect on the company's activities and performance occurs over a long period of time. Although focusing on cash generated from operations, rather than total cash flows, may help avoid the impact of large infrequent cash flows, it also does not provide a complete picture of performance. For example, credit sales would not be included in cash generated from operations if the accounts were not collected until the next period, and expenses would not be included if they were not paid in cash during the period. For most businesses, cash flow alone does not provide a reliable measure of operating success. Thus, decision makers rely not just on cash flow statements, but on other financial statements as well. In particular, the income statement reports on the success of a company's operations during a period.

PART II

DECISIONS AND THE TIMING OF CASH FLOWS

Information for Decisions

Evaluating the timing of cash receipts and payments is important in determining whether companies use their cash effectively. Timing is also central to assessing the value of cash flows occurring at different times and, accordingly, forms the basis for decisions relating to investing. Because of their importance, time-value-of-money concepts are included in the accounting procedures used to prepare financial statements. Decision makers need to understand how time-value-of-money concepts are incorporated in the financial statements and how these concepts relate to their financial decisions. Investors and creditors answer these types of questions using time-value concepts: Will the anticipated future cash flows associated with an investment adequately compensate for the dollar amount and length of the investment? Will the return on an investment exceed the cost of the capital invested?

We know that decision makers are interested in assessing future cash flows. We also know that the timing of cash flows is important because entities and individuals need to have sufficient cash inflows to meet anticipated cash outflows. However, the timing of cash flows is important for another reason as well.

If you had the choice of receiving a specific sum of money now or one year in the future, which would you choose? One important reason for getting the money quickly, even if it is not needed until some later time, is that the money can be used to earn more money. At the very least, money can be put in a savings account to earn interest; by the end of the year you will have more money than if you waited until the end of the year to be paid.

The ability to use cash to generate more cash over time is a very important aspect of managing cash. This is referred to as the **time value of money**. It is embodied in such sayings as "It takes money to make money" or "The rich get richer." For example, if you put money in a savings account, the bank can lend your money to someone else, and the bank charges the borrower for the use of the money. In turn, the bank pays you, at a lower rate, for the use of your money.

In Practice 3-5

FEDERAL EXPRESS

Federal Express Corporation reported $88 million of cash and short-term investments in its balance sheet at the end of its 1999 fiscal year. From its deposited cash and short-term investments, FedEx earned interest of approximately $4.5 million during the year.

ANALYSIS

Federal Express took advantage of the time value of money by investing its excess cash to earn a significant return. However, the company's interest income has decreased significantly over time as interest rates have fallen and the company has reinvested cash in its operations. [www.fedex.com]

The time value of money plays a central role in both personal and business decisions. In fact, the time value of money enters into nearly all financial decisions. Investors and creditors cannot make good financial decisions without considering the time value of money. Thus, understanding concepts related to the time value of money is essential for understanding many common decisions, as well as understanding the way in which business and other entities account for many types of transactions and events.

THE TIME-VALUE RATE

Interest reflects the cost of money. Just as someone might obtain the temporary use of property by renting it, money can be used temporarily by borrowing it. Interest is the "rent" paid for the temporary use of money. As with the price of other commodities, the price of money, or the interest rate, is determined by supply and demand, or how much money is available and how much is needed.

The interest rate that an entity is willing to incur indicates its time value of money, also referred to as its time preference for money. The more an entity values having cash currently rather than in the future, the higher the interest rate it is willing to pay. Companies need cash to invest in their business opportunities, and theoretically they will pay any interest rate up to the amount expected to be earned from those opportunities. Thus, the time value of money for an entity can be expressed as the highest rate it is willing to pay to acquire capital. In practice, this rate may be somewhat difficult to determine, but all major companies estimate their cost of capital because it is essential information for business decisions. The rate expressing the time value of money is also referred to as the **discount rate.**

DETERMINING FUTURE VALUES

Exhibit 3–10 shows how money grows when it earns interest. Let's look at this process in more detail.

Suppose that after allowing for your living expenses and the cost of school, you determine that you have $1,000 to set aside for a nice vacation after graduation. You find a local bank that pays 5 percent annual interest on savings accounts, and you open an account by depositing the entire $1,000. One year later, you check the balance in your account. The account balance includes your original $1,000 and the 5 percent interest you earned on that amount, as follows:

Original amount	$1,000
Interest earned for 1 year	
($1,000 × .05)	50
Total at end of 1 year	$1,050

This situation might be viewed as involving an immediate cash outflow of $1,000 and a cash inflow of $1,050 one year later. Using a time-line representation, it can be visualized as follows:

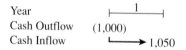

Year	1
Cash Outflow	(1,000)
Cash Inflow	1,050

EXHIBIT 3-10   **TIME TIME VALUE OF MONEY: MONEY GROWS THROUGH INTEREST**

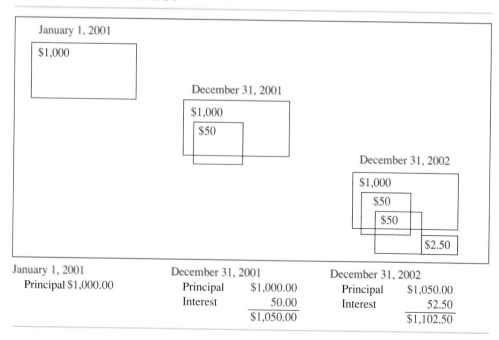

January 1, 2001	December 31, 2001		December 31, 2002	
Principal $1,000.00	Principal	$1,000.00	Principal	$1,050.00
	Interest	50.00	Interest	52.50
		$1,050.00		$1,102.50

The way in which a sum of money grows as it earns interest can be expressed using the following notation:

pv = a **present value** or current sum of money
fv = a **future value** or an amount at some time in the future
r = the relevant interest rate (or discount rate)
i = an amount of interest; equal to r times the amount on which interest is being earned
n = the number of periods during which an amount earns interest

In the savings account example, the balance of the savings account at the end of one year was determined as follows:

$$\$1,050 = \$1,000 + (\$1,000 \times .05)$$
$$\$1,050 = \$1,000 + \$50$$

where:

$$pv = \$1,000$$
$$r = 5\%$$
$$i = \$50$$
$$n = 1 \text{ year}$$

and fv is calculated as $1,050.

The balance at the end of one year is equal to the original amount plus 5 percent interest on the original amount. This can be generalized as follows:

$$fv = pv + i$$

With i equal to $(pv \times r)$, then:

$$fv = pv + (pv \times r)$$
$$fv = pv \times (1 + r)$$

Using the numbers from the savings account example:

$$fv = \$1,000 \times (1 + .05) = \$1,050$$

A CLOSER LOOK AT

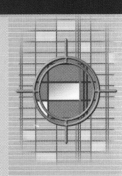

COMPUTING A FUTURE VALUE

Dan Wrigley invests $7,500 in a savings account for one year at 4 percent. How much does he have at the end of one year? At the end of two years?

Answer: The focus is on an amount in the future, a future value. At the end of one year, Dan will have his original investment plus the interest on that investment:

$$fv = pv\,(1 + r)$$
$$fv = \$7,500\,(1 + .04)$$
$$fv = \$7,500\,(1.04) = \underline{\$7,800}$$

At the end of two years, Dan will have the amount he had at the end of the first year plus the interest on that amount:

$$fv = \$7,800\,(1.04) = \underline{\$8,112}$$

To determine an amount at the end of the second year, all we have to do is multiply the amount at the end of the first year by $(1 + r)$:

$$fv = pv \, (1 + r)(1 + r)$$

Restated, this is:

$$fv = pv \, (1 + r)^2$$

For each additional year that the original amount and the earned interest remains in the savings account, it grows by r and is equal to the amount at the beginning of the year multiplied by $(1 + r)$. If the original amount earns interest for n periods, the future amount into which the original amount will grow is calculated as follows:

$$fv = pv \, (1 + r)^n$$

A CLOSER LOOK AT

FREQUENCY OF INTEREST COMPUTATION

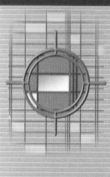

Jane Womack lends $2,000 to her friend Jake for five years. Jake agrees to pay interest of 6 percent per year. How much interest will Jake pay if the interest is calculated each year and added to the amount of the loan annually? How much interest will Jake pay if the interest is calculated only at the end of five years?

Answer: If the interest is calculated each year, the total due at the end of five years, a future value, is determined as follows:

$$fv = \$2,000 \, (1 + .06)(1 + .06)(1 + .06)(1 + .06)(1 + .06)$$
$$fv = \$2,000 \, (1 + .06)^5 = \$2,676$$

The amount of interest over the five-year period is equal to the total payment due at the end of five years minus the original loan:

$$i = \$2,676 - \$2,000 = \underline{\$676}$$

If interest is calculated only at the end of five years for the entire five-year period, the total amount of interest is determined as follows:

$$i = \$2,000 \times .06 \times 5 = \underline{\$600}$$

THE ROLE OF COMPOUNDING

In the example of Jane Womack, interest was calculated two different ways. First it was calculated each year and added to the amount of the loan, so that in subsequent years interest was calculated on the previously earned interest. The process of computing interest periodically and then computing interest in future periods on both the principal and the previously computed interest is called **compounding**. Interest computed in this manner is called **compound interest**. The second way in which interest was computed in the example was to calculate the interest for each year independent of the other years, basing the interest only on the original amount of the loan and not on other interest earned. Interest computed in this manner is referred to as **simple interest**. Note that compound interest is greater than simple interest because the compound interest includes interest on the interest.

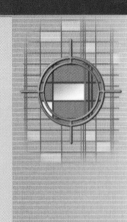

A CLOSER LOOK AT

THE EFFECTS OF COMPOUNDING

Darlene Fry has $10,000 to put in a savings account for twenty years. The Last National Bank of Amarillo advertises 10 percent interest compounded quarterly. Bigabucks Savings and Loan Association advertises 10.3 percent interest compounded annually. Which savings account provides Darlene with the better deal?

Answer: The solution involves finding a future value amount under two different approaches to computing interest. Quarterly compounding of 10 percent interest results in the following balance at the end of 20 years:

$$fv = \$100,000 \, (1 + .025)^{80} = \underline{\$72,096}$$

Annual compounding of 10.3 percent interest provides the following balance at the end of twenty years:

$$fv = \$10,000 \, (1 + .103)^{20} = \underline{\$71,041}$$

The account with the lower stated rate compounded more frequently is the better choice in this case. When interest is compounded more frequently than annually (e.g., monthly, quarterly), the annual interest rate is divided by the number of compounding periods within the year to determine the interest rate that applies to each compounding period. The Last National Bank has four compounding periods per year, with a quarterly interest rate of .025 and 80 quarterly periods in 20 years.

Interest is always stated on an annual basis unless indicated otherwise. However, the stated interest rate is not always the same as the effective rate. The **stated (nominal) rate** does not consider compounding, while the **effective rate** or **yield** takes into consideration the effects of compounding. In the example, the bank's stated rate is 10 percent, but the effective annual rate is 10.38 percent $[(1 + .025)^{4} - 1]$; the savings and loan association's stated and effective rates both are 10.3 percent. Truth-in-lending and truth-in-savings legislation requires the disclosure of effective rates in addition to stated rates in many situations. Under current regulations, the effective rate charged on loans and credit card balances is called the annual percentage rate (APR), and the effective rate earned on savings is called the annual percentage yield (APY).

DETERMINING PRESENT VALUES

As we have seen, we can determine the amount *fv* into which the current amount *pv* will grow, as follows:

$$fv = pv \, (1 + r)^{n}$$

Suppose, however, we know how much we need for some purpose in the future, and we want to know how much to set aside today to earn interest so we have the amount we need in the future. This type of problem is similar to the determination of future value amounts, except here we already know the future amount; instead we want to know the amount we need today, or the present value amount. Because we already know the relationship between present and future values, we can solve our problem for the present value by rearranging the equation:

$$fv = pv\ (1 + r)^n$$
$$pv = fv/(1 + r)^n$$

The process of determining a present value equivalent for some future amount is referred to as **discounting**.

A CLOSER LOOK AT

COMPUTING A PRESENT VALUE

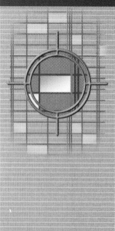

Hectre Gonzales needs $10,000 for a new car he wants to purchase in three years. If he puts the money in the bank now, he can earn 5 percent interest on it during the three-year period. How much must he deposit currently to have $10,000 at the end of three years?

Answer: What Hectre wants to know is how much to set aside today, a present value amount. The present value of $10,000 at 5 percent for three years is computed as follows:

$$pv = \$10,000/(1 + .05)^3 = \underline{\$8,638}$$

This can be seen through a time line of payments Hectre makes to and receives from his bank account, as follows:

Year	1	2	3
Cash Inflow			10,000
Cash Outflow (8,638)	←		

The answer can easily be checked by starting with the present value and working toward the future value:

$$\$8,638 \times 1.05 = \$9,070$$
$$\$9,070 \times 1.05 = \$9,524$$
$$\$9,524 \times 1.05 = \underline{\$10,000}$$

Present value concepts are at the heart of many business decisions and are widely used in determining much of the information included in financial reports. Most financial decisions are based on one important aspect of the time value of money: receiving a dollar today is better than receiving a dollar in the future because the dollar today can be invested to provide you with more than a dollar in the future. Similarly, the promise of a dollar in the future is worth less than a dollar today. You could invest some amount less than a dollar today and, with the interest earned, have a dollar in the future.

MULTIPLE PAYMENTS

In many situations, you might be interested in a series of cash payments rather than just a single payment. For example, instead of depositing just one payment in a savings account and letting it earn interest, you might wish to deposit $50 each week as you get your paycheck. Here, too, present value and future value concepts apply. After all, a series of payments is just a single payment made a number of times. Each single payment in the series can be treated individually, with the results summed. For example, a series of cash payments of $5,000 each, to be made at the end of each period for three periods, could be represented with the following time line:

Year   1   2   3
Cash Outflow   (5,000) (5,000) (5,000)

The future value of this stream of cash payments can be determined by computing the future value amount for each payment and summing the amounts. Similarly, the present value of this stream of payments can be determined by computing the present value amount for each payment and summing the amounts.

When all the payments in a series of cash flows are the same and are made at equal intervals, the stream of cash payments is called an **annuity**. Conceptually, annuities are no different than other streams of cash flows, but computations involving annuities can be simplified, as discussed later.

A CLOSER LOOK AT

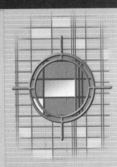

COMPUTATION OF THE FUTURE VALUE OF MULTIPLE PAYMENTS

Joe Dolan wants to buy a new car when his pickup truck wears out in about four years. He figures he can afford to set aside $4,000 at the end of each year for the next four years. How much will he have at the end of four years if he can earn 6 percent on his money?

Answer: Joe wants to know how much he will have 4 years in the future, a future value amount. This future value of an annuity can be determined by computing the future value of each individual payment and summing the results, as follows:

First payment	$4,000 \times (1.06)^3 =$	$ 4,764
Second payment	$4,000 \times (1.06)^2 =$	4,494
Third payment	$4,000 \times (1.06) =$	4,240
Fourth payment	$4,000 \times 1 \quad =$	4,000
Total		$17,498

This situation can be shown using a time line, as follows:

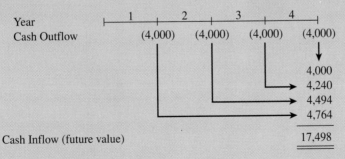

Year   1   2   3   4
Cash Outflow   (4,000) (4,000) (4,000) (4,000)
                                                 4,000
                                                 4,240
                                                 4,494
                                                 4,764

Cash Inflow (future value)   17,498

Because the deposits are put in the savings account at the end of each year rather than at the beginning, they do not earn interest for the year in which they are deposited. Therefore, the first payment earns interest only for three years, and the last payment, made at the end of the fourth year, does not earn any interest because all amounts are withdrawn at that time to purchase the car.

From the example you can see that each payment is treated individually and the results are summed to obtain the total future value amount. Similarly, a present value of a stream of cash flows can be determined by summing the present values of the individual cash flows.

A CLOSER LOOK AT

COMPUTATION OF THE PRESENT VALUE OF MULTIPLE PAYMENT

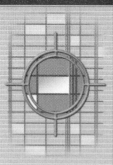

Irma Blough has just been accepted to the University of Tuleville, a prestigious private school. Her wealthy grandfather told her that if she were accepted, he would immediately write her a check to cover her four years of tuition, providing she would keep the money in a bank account and use the interest for tuition, also. Tuition payments are expected to remain constant at $10,000 each year. Her first tuition payment is due one year from today, with the remaining three payments due at one-year intervals. Today she will deposit the check from her grandfather in a savings account earning 4 percent interest, compounded annually. What should be the amount of the check from her grandfather?

Answer: Irma's grandfather needs to deposit an amount today. Therefore, he would compute a present value amount as follows:

First tuition payment	$10,000/(1.04) =	$ 9,615
Second tuition payment	$10,000/(1.04)^2 =	9,246
Third tuition payment	$10,000/(1.04)^3 =	8,890
Fourth tuition payment	$10,000/(1.04)^4 =	8,548
Total		$36,299

The payment to the bank account (outflow) and the payments received as withdrawals from the bank account (inflows) can be shown using a time line, as follows:

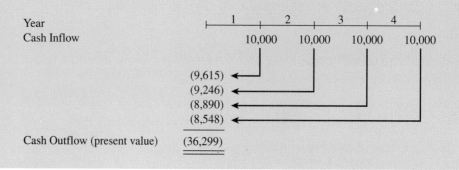

The approach illustrated applies equally well to situations involving unequal cash payments.

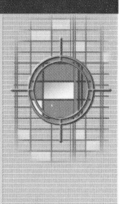

A CLOSER LOOK AT

STANDARD SETTING: IS IT A RENTAL OR A SALE?

If Irma Blough expected her tuition to increase at the rate of 10 percent per year instead of remaining constant, what should be the amount of the check her grandfather gives to her today?

Answer:

First tuition payment	$10,000/(1.04) =	$ 9,615
Second tuition payment	$11,000/(1.04)^2 =	10,170
Third tuition payment	$12,100/(1.04)^3 =	10,757
Fourth tuition payment	$13,310/(1.04)^4 =	11,377
Total		$41,919

USING PRESENT AND FUTURE VALUES

Present and future values are widely used in decision making. Keep in mind, however, that present and future value computations are based on information. The results of present value computations are only as reliable as the information used in the computations. The information needed for these computations includes the amount and timing of cash flows, as well as relevant interest rates. In many cases not all of this information is known, and estimates must be used.

Present and future value computations can be made using the formulas presented previously, but they can become rather cumbersome in complex situations. Fortunately, popular computer software and many calculators make these computations quickly and easily. In addition, tables are available to facilitate computations; Appendix B provides these four tables:

1. Future value of a single amount
2. Present value of a single amount
3. Future value of an annuity (multiple equal payments)
4. Present value of an annuity (multiple equal payments)

These tables simply summarize the computations used earlier and incorporate the results in tables. To use the tables, first determine which table is relevant. Are you trying to find:

A current amount (an amount today)?	Use a present value table.
An amount in the future?	Use a future value table.

Are you dealing with:

A single payment?	Use a single amount table.
Multiple equal payments?	Use an annuity table.

If you have unequal multiple payments, you must treat each one as a single payment and sum the results.

Once you have determined the appropriate table to use, find the factor in the table that corresponds to the applicable interest rate and number of periods or payments. Then, multiply that factor by the amount of the payment.

A CLOSER LOOK AT

USING THE TABLES: PRESENT VALUE OF A SINGLE AMOUNT

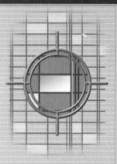

If you need $12,000 to go on a round-the-world cruise five years from now, how much would you have to deposit in the bank today at 4 percent interest to get the needed amount? You know the future amount that you need, but what you want to know is the amount to deposit currently, a present value amount. You could calculate the present value amount as follows:

$$pv = \$12,000/(1.04)^5$$

Dividing $12,000 by $(1.04)^5$ is the same as multiplying it by $1/(1.04)^5$, or .82193. Thus, the present value amount is computed as follows:

$$pv = \$12,000 \times [1/(1.04)^5]$$
$$pv = \$12,000 \times .82193 = \underline{\$9,863}$$

As an alternative, you could use the table for the present value of a single amount (Table 2 in Appendix B). Looking at the intersection of the 5-year row and the 4 percent column, you find a factor of .82193. Note that this factor is the same as the amount we computed previously:

$$[1/(1.04)^5] = .82193$$

By multiplying this factor times the future amount needed, the following present value amount is obtained:

$$\$12,000 \times .82193 = \underline{\$9,863}$$

A CLOSER LOOK AT

USING THE TABLES: FUTURE VALE OF A SINGLE AMOUNT

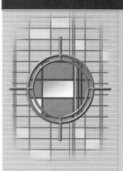

If you were to deposit $9,863 in the bank today so you could go on a round-the-world cruise five years from now, how much would you have in your account at the end of five years if the money earned 4 percent annual interest? In this case, you know the amount you have currently, but you want to know how much it will grow into in the future, a future value amount. This could be computed in the same way as before:

$$fv = \$9,863 \times (1.04)^5$$
$$fv = \$9,863 \times 1.21665$$
$$fv = \underline{\$12,000}$$

As an alternative, you could use the table for the future value of a single amount (Table 1 in Appendix B). From the intersection of the 4 percent column and the 5-year row, you would extract the factor 1.21665, which is equal to $(1.04)^5$, and compute the future value amount as follows:

$$\$9{,}863 \times 1.21665 = \underline{\$12{,}000}$$

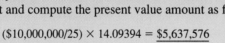

A CLOSER LOOK AT

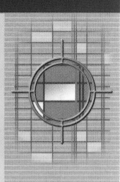

COMPUTATION OF THE FUTURE VALUE OF MULTIPLE PAYMENTS

Congratulations! You have just won the grand prize of $10 million in the National Publishers' sweepstakes. The money will be paid to you in equal annual installments over twenty-five years, starting one year from today. National Publishers will put sufficient money in a bank account to provide for payment of your prize. Let's figure out how much National Publishers must deposit today, a present value amount, if the bank guarantees 5 percent interest. Using the table for the present value of an annuity (Table 4 in Appendix B), the stream of cash payments National Publishers will make, we extract the factor for 25 payments at 5 percent and compute the present value amount as follows:

$$(\$10{,}000{,}000/25) \times 14.09394 = \underline{\$5{,}637{,}576}$$

A CLOSER LOOK AT

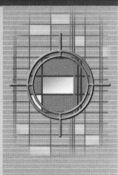

USING THE TABLES: EQUAL PAYMENTS PLUS A LUMP SUM

Whoops! On reading the fine print detailing the rules of the National Publishers' sweepstakes, you note that the $10 million prize is to be paid in equal annual installments of $200,000 for twenty-four years starting one year from today, with the balance of $5,200,000 paid at the end of the twenty-fifth year. Let's take a look at how much National Publishers must deposit today in a bank account earning 5 percent to make the required payments:

- Present value of an annuity of 24 payments of $200,000 each, discounted at 5 percent: $200,000 × 13.79864 = $2,759,728
- Present value of a single payment, discounted at 5 percent for 25 years: $5,200,000 × .29530 = $1,535,560
- Total present value: $2,759,728 + $1,535,560 = $4,295,288

Note in these last two examples the difference in the actual cost to the sweepstakes sponsor of delaying payment—the time value of money.

DECISIONS AND TIME VALUE OF MONEY

Time-value-of-money concepts allow us to determine relationships between cash flows occurring at different times. This ability is extremely important to anyone making financial decisions because investments typically involve giving up cash now to receive a greater amount of cash in the future. If you have extra cash now but will have a particular need for cash in the future, you can swap the cash you have now for cash in the future by entering into an exchange with someone who is willing to give up cash in the future to get cash now. The capital markets exist to facilitate this exchange of different cash flows.

An investor's purchase of stock involves sacrificing cash now in exchange for the possibility of greater future cash flows.

Managers within businesses almost always include time-value-of-money considerations in their analyses when making important investment decisions, such as major purchases of new plants and equipment. Similarly, external decision makers also consider the time value of money. Investors and creditors are interested in assessing the amounts, timing, and likelihood of future cash flows associated with the enterprise in which they might invest. They wish to know, if they provide cash to the enterprise, how much cash they will get back, and when. For example, an investor might acquire an ownership interest in a company by purchasing shares of the company's stock with the expectation that the company will pay a specific cash dividend (distribution of profits) each year. The investor might also expect the stock to increase in value so it ultimately can be sold at an amount higher than its purchase price. Thus, the investor would expect a stream of periodic future cash flows plus a large cash inflow at the time the investment is sold. The investor can determine, in part, whether the ownership interest provides a sufficient return on the original cost of the investment to justify investing by comparing the present value of the future cash flows with the initial cost of the investment.

A CLOSER LOOK AT

AN INDIVIDUAL INVESTMENT DECISION

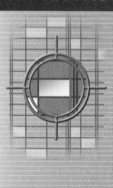

Jack Black is considering purchasing stock in Mammoth Enterprises for $10,000. He expects to receive dividends of $500 at the end of each year for three years and expects to sell the stock at the end of three years for $12,000. Jack is not willing to invest in a stock unless he can earn at least 10 percent annually. Should Jack invest in Mammoth stock?

Answer: The present value of the projected future cash flows is as follows:

$$pv = \$500/(1.10) + \$500/(1.10)^2 + \$12,500/(1.10)^3$$
$$= \$455 + \$413 + \$9,391 = \underline{\$10,259}$$

The present value of the future cash flows can then be compared with the initial cost of the investment:

Present value of future cash inflows	$10,259
Cost of investment (initial cash outflow)	10,000
Excess over cost of investment	$ 259

This analysis indicates that Jack should invest in Mammoth Enterprises if Jack's sole criterion is earning a 10 percent return on his investment. Once the projected future cash inflows are adjusted for Jack's 10 percent time value of money, they still exceed the initial cash outflow for the investment. By adjusting for the time value of money, the cash flows at different points in time can be compared. The excess of the present value of the projected future cash inflows over the initial cash outflow, a positive net present value, indicates that the investment is expected to earn a rate of return greater than 10 percent, Jack's minimum required return.

Because time-value-of-money concepts are central to financial decision making, special attention should be paid to the information needed to use these concepts successfully. In particular, the usefulness of time-value techniques depends on being able to accurately forecast future cash flows and determine the appropriate interest rate to use for discounting.

You Decide 3-4

TOUGH CHOICES

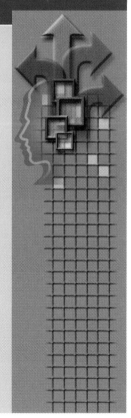

It looks like you are actually going to graduate. Your rich aunt is so thrilled that she wants to help you get a successful start in life. As a graduation gift she allows you to choose one of two alternatives:

1. You can have a two-thirds interest in and be a full-time manager of one of her businesses, a car wash, or

2. She will make you a gift of $200,000 with the stipulation that it must be invested in a portfolio of stocks and held for at least three years.

You analyze the two alternatives by first gathering additional information. You decide that you wouldn't want to be a car wash manager for very long and would sell the car wash at the end of three years. The car wash currently is appraised at a market value of $300,000, and you figure it probably can be sold for this amount after three years (and your share will be two-thirds). Your salary as manager of the car wash would be $45,000 per year. Based on stock market averages, the stock portfolio probably will grow at a little better than 10 percent a year and should be worth about $275,000 at the end of three years. If you do not work at the car wash, you can get a management trainee job on your own that will pay $25,000 a year.

Question: If you choose to become a management trainee and hold the stock portfolio, how much better or worse off would you expect to be financially at the end of three years as compared with choosing the other alternative? Assume your time value of money is 8 percent per year. What considerations might be relevant to this decision other than your financial well-being at the end of three years?

SUMMARY

Cash flows are extremely important for decision makers. To make good choices, decision makers must understand the cash flows related to their decisions. The important aspects of cash flows for decision making include the amount, timing, and source or use of cash inflows and outflows. Cash flows from infrequent or one-time activities affect decisions differently than regular cash flows from operations.

Good cash management involves understanding the effects of decisions on cash inflows and outflows and ensuring that cash is used effectively. Cash should always be employed or invested fully except for amounts needed on hand to facilitate transactions and provide a margin of safety against uncertainties. Judicious use of credit is a significant factor in good cash management.

The cash flow statement identifies cash flows by source or use and, therefore, helps in assessing the performance of an entity. The cash flow statement provides a summary of all of an entity's cash flows during a period and classifies those cash flows as being related to operations, investing activities, or financing activities. Information about past cash flows often is helpful in making forecasts of future cash flows.

Cash flow information is crucial for evaluating some aspects of the performance of a business. However, cash flow information does not provide a complete picture of a company's performance. Thus, external decision makers rely heavily on both the income statement and cash flow statement in assessing performance.

The timing of cash flows is especially important because there is a time value to money. Money can be invested over time so that it earns a return and grows in amount. Therefore, having a dollar today is usually preferable to receiving a dollar in the future. The time value of money plays a significant role in financial decisions.

LIST OF IMPORTANT TERMS

accounts receivable *(75)*

annuity *(95)*

bank reconciliation *(84)*

cash cycle *(81)*

cash flows *(72)*

cash forecasts *(74)*

compounding *(92)*

compound interest *(92)*

discounting *(94)*

discount rate *(90)*

effective rate *(93)*

financing cash flows *(72)*

fixed costs *(79)*

future value *(91)*

investing cash flows *(72)*

liquidity *(75)*

operating cash flows *(72)*

operating cycle *(81)*

present value *(91)*

simple interest *(92)*

solvency *(75)*

stated (nominal) rate *(93)*

time value of money *(89)*

uncollectible accounts *(77)*

variable costs *(79)*

yield *(93)*

APPENDIX 3-1

RECONCILIATION OF BANK ACCOUNTS

An important part of maintaining control over cash is preparation of periodic bank reconciliations. While routine, this procedure is important enough that managers as well as accountants need to be familiar with it. All organizations prepare bank reconciliations.

UNDERSTANDING A BANK RECONCILIATION

A bank reconciliation simply compares the balance of the bank account as shown on the statement sent periodically from the bank with the account's balance in the entity's accounting records or books. The comparison is made between the two balances at a specific point in time, such as at the close of business on the last day of the month. Because the balance shown on the company's books and that shown by the bank are for the same account, both the company and the bank might be expected to reflect the same balance. However, differences usually arise from delays in processing or accounting for certain items, mistakes, or other causes.

The following is a partial listing of the items that might cause differences between the bank balance and the balance in the accounting records:

- **Checks outstanding**. At the time an organization writes a check, it subtracts the amount of the check from the cash account in the accounting records. After a check is mailed, there is a time span of several days while the check moves through the mail, is processed by the payee (the person or organization to which the check is made payable), processed by the payee's bank and the banking system, delivered to the issuer's bank, and deducted from the issuer's account. Thus, the issuer's bank does not deduct the amount of the check from the account until sometime after the issuer deducts the amount in its accounting records. During this time before the check clears the bank, the bank will show a higher balance than the company's books.

- **Deposits in transit**. Because good internal control for cash involves depositing all cash receipts daily, many companies deposit all of the cash received during the day at the close of business. However, most banks close before most businesses do, so these deposits are placed in a night depository, a trap door at the bank through which deposits are made. Because the bank is closed, it does not officially receive the deposits until the next morning. The bank then records receipt of the deposit one day later than the depositor records the deposit. At the close of business after making such a deposit, the company's books reflect a higher balance than the bank's books.

- **Bank charges**. Banks often reduce customer accounts for certain bank charges, such as monthly service charges, check printing charges, and overdraft (checks written against insufficient funds) charges. A company may not be aware of the amount of these charges until receiving the bank statement. Because the company has not deducted the charges from its cash balance as the bank has, the bank statement will reflect a lower balance than shown on the company's books.

- **Automatic deposits or withdrawals**. In some cases, a bank may collect amounts due to a customer and automatically deposit them in the company's account. This results in a higher bank balance than that shown on the company's books. In other cases, a company may authorize the bank to make certain types of routine payments from its account each month, such as those to pay loan amounts due or utility bills. These payments result in the bank showing a lower balance for the company's account than shown on the company's books.

- **NSF checks**. Included in a company's deposits during the period might be some checks from its customers (or others) for which payment is refused by the issuer's bank because the issuer does not have sufficient funds (NSF) in its account. The checks are returned to the depositor and the amounts deducted from its account.

- **Errors**. Although infrequent, errors can occur on the part of either the bank or the company. For example, the bank might pay another customer's check from the company's account or neglect to record a deposit correctly. The company might fail to record a check written against its account or incorrectly record the amount by transposing two digits (e.g, record $167 as $176).

- **Fraud or misappropriation of funds**. Employee dishonesty resulting in the loss of cash by the firm may come to light by comparing recorded amounts on the company's books with those on the bank statements. Such dishonesty might appear through discrepancies in deposits and by uncovering altered or unrecorded checks. Good internal control requires the bank reconciliation to be prepared by people other than those handling cash or cash records.

The idea of a bank reconciliation is a simple one: Determine why there is a difference between the balance shown on the bank statement and the balance of the account shown in the company's books on that date. Once all reasons for the difference are identified and the bank account is reconciled, the company can decide how to deal with each difference:

1. Some differences require no action other than future monitoring because the differences are expected to resolve themselves. For example, checks outstanding at the end of one period should clear the bank by the end of the next period, eliminating this difference (although different checks will be outstanding at the end of each period). Deposits in transit at the end of one period should be received and recorded by the bank the next day, eliminating this difference.

2. Some differences require accounting treatment. Items correctly recorded by the bank but not recorded by the company, such as bank charges and automatic collections and payments, must be recorded by the company in its accounting records. Once these items are recorded by the company, the differences disappear.

3. Some differences require corrections to be made. If a company's books are in error, the books must be corrected. If the bank is responsible for an error, it must be notified and the situation monitored to assure corrective action is taken by the bank.

4. Some differences require other types of action to be taken. Repeated mistakes may indicate a need for change in the company's accounting system or its cash-handling procedures. An apparent misappropriation of funds would require further investigation and appropriate action to assure there would be no further occurrences. NSF checks require additional collection measures.

Although bank reconciliations tend to bring errors to light more frequently than they uncover dishonesty, knowledge that bank reconciliations are prepared on a regular basis serves as a deterrent to employees of questionable integrity.

PREPARATION OF A BANK RECONCILIATION

The key to preparing a bank reconciliation is understanding the nature of each item that might result in a difference between the bank statement and a company's books. The form of the reconciliation is unimportant because its goal is simply to identify all the various differences. The preparation of a bank reconciliation involves the following steps:

1. Carefully examine the bank statement to identify items such as bank charges, automatic collections and payments, and NSF checks.

2. Determine which checks have been issued and are still outstanding.

3. Determine the amount of any deposits in transit.

4. Determine the amount of any unexplained differences by comparing the balances of the bank account as listed on the bank statement and shown on the company's books and adjusting for the known differences.

5. Compare, if necessary, individual items on the bank statement with individual items from the company's books to reconcile any unexplained differences.

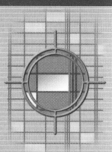

A CLOSER LOOK AT

A BANK RECONCILIATION

Laslow Corporation receives its monthly bank statement for its checking account, with a balance indicated of $27,622 as of July 31. The bank account balance listed in the company's books at that date is $29,325. By comparing the checks paid by the bank and deducted from the account with those listed on the company's books, Laslow's accountant determines that twelve checks, totalling $1,923, are outstanding at July 31. Deposits listed on the bank statement and those recorded on the company's books are as follows:

	Bank Statement	Books
July 1	$6,610	
July 10	4,500	$4,500
July 20	3,200	3,200
July 25	2,000	
July 31		5,100

The July 1 deposit shown on the bank statement had been recorded by the company on June 30. The July bank statement also showed a service fee of $18, a customer's check in the amount of $35 that had been returned NSF, a loan payment of $500 that was deducted automatically by the bank, and a $2,000 deposit from a note that was collected for Laslow by the bank. A $27 unexplained difference between the bank statement and the books is determined to be a check recording error by Laslow. Prepare a bank reconciliation for Laslow Corporation as of July 31 working toward a corrected balance.

Answer:

Laslow Corporation
Bank Reconciliation
July 31

Balance per bank	$27,622
Checks outstanding	− 1,923
Deposits in transit	+ 5,100
Correct balance	$30,799
Balance per books	$29,325
Bank service charge	− 18
Check returned NSF	− 35
Loan payment	− 500
Note collection deposited	+ 2,000
Check recording error	+ 27
Correct balance	$30,799

For each item identified as resulting in a difference between the bank statement and the books, a determination must be made as to whether the bank balance or the book balance is misstated. The item is then added to or subtracted from the misstated balance, as appropriate, to work toward a corrected balance.

Because bank reconciliations are concerned with finding differences between the bank and book balances, different forms of the reconciliation work equally well. Thus, the reconciliation could as easily have been prepared working from the balance per bank to the balance per books, rather than to a corrected balance, or from the balance per books to the balance per bank.

Overall, bank reconciliations are important vehicles for safeguarding cash and controlling the accuracy of cash records. Regardless of the level of sophistication of the accounting system, the bank reconciliation is an important element of control.

EXAMINING THE CONCEPTS

PART I

Q3-1   Why is information about past cash flows important?

Q3-2   Why is knowing the source of a cash inflow important?

Q3-3   What factors are important in evaluating cash flows?

Q3-4   Why is it important that an individual or a business entity be able to estimate the timing of cash inflows and outflows?

Q3-5   Transactions in one period often affect cash inflows or outflows in subsequent periods. Explain how a sale of goods at a profit today may affect the future cash flows of a retail establishment.

Q3-6   What is a cash forecast? Why is it important?

Q3-7   What factors must a company consider when forecasting the amount of cash generated by sales each period?

Q3-8   What does it mean when an entity is said to be insolvent? Why should insolvency be avoided?

Q3-9   What does the term *liquidity* mean? What are the advantages and disadvantages of a high level of liquidity?

Q3-10   What is the cash or operating cycle of a company? Why is it important for companies to minimize the length of the operating cycle?

Q3-11   Why should a company attempt to minimize the balance in its checking account? What are the dangers of doing so? What should a company do with money not kept in a checking account?

Q3-12   What is meant by *internal control*? Why is adequate internal control over cash especially important?

Q3-13   What are some of the important internal controls over cash?

Q3-14   Why is the cash flow statement included as one of the required financial statements under generally accepted accounting principles?

Q3-15   What are the major sections or classifications in the cash flow statement? Why are these categories used?

Q3-16   A company may feel it needs to maintain a large balance in a noninterest bearing checking account to meet sudden and unexpected needs for cash. What other approaches might a company use to deal with such contingencies?

Q3-17A   What is a bank reconciliation? Why should bank accounts be reconciled on a regular basis?

Q3-18A   What is a deposit in transit? How are deposits in transit treated in the bank reconciliation?

Q3-19A   What does it mean when a check is returned as NSF? How are NSF checks treated in the bank reconciliation?

Q3-20A   Give several examples of items that might come to light while doing a bank reconciliation that would cause a company to adjust its reported cash balance.

PART II

Q3-21   Why is the concept of the time value of money important in making investment decisions?

Q3-22   Why is the assumed earnings rate, or discount rate, important in determining the present value of future cash flows? What effect will changes in the rate have on the computed present value?

Q3-23   When is the concept of future value important? Explain how future value amounts are computed.

Q3-24   What is the meaning of compound interest? Why is compound interest important in valuing future cash flows?

Q3-25   What is an annuity? What factors must exist for a stream of cash payments to be defined as an annuity?

Q3-26   Assume you have a fixed amount deducted from your paycheck each month and invested in a money market savings account. What impact will an increase or a decrease in the interest rate earned on the savings have on the amount available to you after ten years? Explain why.

Q3-27   If you want to set aside today enough money to make your college tuition payments over the next several years, will the amount you have to set aside now be larger or smaller if the rate of interest you can earn increases from 4 percent to 6 percent? Explain why.

UNDERSTANDING ACCOUNTING INFORMATION

PART I

E3-1   Understanding Cash Flows

a. Archer Corporation is a ski manufacturer. Production takes place primarily in the months of January through March and shipments to customers are primarily in the months of July through September. Baker Corporation produces office supplies and has relatively constant sales throughout the year. Casper Corporation specializes in extinguishing fires in oil wells. How are the cash flow patterns of these companies likely to differ?

b. What types of activities may cause a company with sales that are relatively uniform throughout the year to report substantially different levels of cash inflows and outflows during some months of the year?

E3-2   Estimation of Cash Flows

a. What types of conditions may result in a company becoming "cash poor"? What steps could a company take to offset these conditions?

b. Cash flow forecasts usually begin with a forecast of cash receipts from revenues and cash payments of expenses
   1. Identify two or more factors that should be considered in making a revenue forecast.
   2. Explain why cash generated from sales may not be the same as sales reported for the period.
   3. Give an example of a regularly recurring cash inflow and an example of an infrequent or irregular cash inflow.

c. Explain briefly why a company may be maintaining a large cash reserve or may have borrowed money even though it has a positive cash flow from its operating activities.

E3-3   Evaluating Cash Management

a. You are thinking of investing in a company that reports its balance of cash and cash equivalents as almost 50 percent of total assets. Explain the effect this level of cash might have on the company's ability to do the following:
   1. Acquire operating assets for future growth
   2. Repay existing long-term debt
   3. Minimize the effects of seasonality or unexpected cash outflows
   4. Earn an above-average return for its investors

b. If you discover that a company spent $1,500,000 expanding its plant and equipment during the year, but its operations generated only $500,000 of cash, what would you look for as sources of cash for the additional amount spent?

c. Dogma Corporation received an adverse opinion on its audited financial statements from its external auditor due to "inadequate internal controls relating to cash." Give three examples of internal control procedures that are considered important related to the receipt, handling, and disbursement of cash.

E3-4   The Cash Flow Statement

a. A company's cash flow statement is classified by major categories of activities:
   1. Identify each of the three categories.
   2. For each category, identify at least one major source of cash, one major use of cash, and indicate whether the sources and uses you have identified would be considered regular and recurring or infrequent.

b. You are considering investing in a company. Which cash flow category or categories of the company's cash flow statement would be of greatest use in answering the following questions? Explain your choice in each case.
   1. Does it appear the company will be able to meet annual payment requirements on a new ten-year bank loan?
   2. Did the company sell additional stock during the period?
   3. Did the company purchase additional production equipment during the period? If so, how was the cash generated?
   4. Did the company sell off unused equipment during the period?
   5. Did cash on hand go up or down as a result of the company's operating activities in the period?

E3-5   Cash Flows and Performance Evaluation   Monster Motor Company reported net income of $370,000 and an increase in cash and cash equivalents of $560,000 in 2000. A total of $230,000 was reported as cash generated from operations in Monster's cash flow statement. You have been asked to provide assistance in interpreting the cash flows for 2000 and in preparing a cash flow projection for the company for 2001:

a. Why isn't the change in cash and cash equivalents for the year always a good predictor of cash generated by operations?

b. Assuming the level of sales in 2001 is the same as in 2000, would you expect an increase of $560,000 in cash and cash equivalents in 2001? Explain.

c. Why is cash generated from operations not always a good predictor of net income?

d. Assuming the level of sales in 2001 is the same as in 2000, what amount of net income would you expect Monster Motors to report for 2001? Explain why.

E3-6   Multiple Choice: Cash Flows   Select the best answer for each of the following:

1. Which of the following factors is (are) important in managing cash resources?
   a. Knowing the source of cash flows.
   b. Knowing when cash flows will occur.
   c. Knowing the amount of cash flows.
   d. All of the above.

2. A company is considered to be insolvent if:
   a. It is unable to sell all of its output in a given period.
   b. It is unable to pay its debts.
   c. It has more long-term debt than short-term debt.
   d. Its debt exceeds the amount of its stockholders' equity.
3. The cash or operating cycle refers to:
   a. The length of time that elapses between an outlay of cash for resources and the receipt of cash from the sale of goods or services.
   b. The length of time that elapses between the time an item is purchased and payment is made.
   c. The length of time it takes to collect receivables from customers who have been extended special credit terms.
   d. The length of time it takes to collect receivables from customers who have been extended normal terms.
4. Businesses generally prefer to collect money from customers quickly because:
   a. The longer an account is unpaid, the less is the likelihood of collecting it.
   b. Forecasting and managing cash flows is easier if cash is collected within a specified period of time.
   c. There is a time value of money.
   d. All of the above.

E3-7 **Multiple Choice: Evaluating Cash Flows** Select the best answer for each of the following:

1. An issuance of stock is reported in the cash flow statement as a part of:
   a. Cash flows from investing.
   b. Cash flows from financing.
   c. Cash flows from operations.
   d. Cash flows from unaffiliated parties.
2. The section dealing with cash flows from operations in the cash flow statement provides information on:
   a. Vehicles and equipment purchased during the period.
   b. Bank loans paid during the period.
   c. Payments to suppliers during the period.
   d. Contributions by owners during the period.
3. Good cash management practices include:
   a. Avoiding keeping any cash on hand because cash is a nonearning asset.
   b. Paying suppliers as quickly as possible to avoid keeping excess amounts of cash on hand.
   c. Waiting as long as possible to pay suppliers, even if they offer substantial cash discounts for early payment.
   d. Keeping only enough cash on hand to meet anticipated needs and to provide some protection against uncertainties.
4. Which of the following is not considered to be part of the internal control system over cash?
   a. Depositing all cash receipts in the bank on a daily basis.
   b. Investing all surplus cash receipts in short-term securities to earn an appropriate return.
   c. Making all payments by check.

d. Having separate individuals responsible for the receipt and disbursement of cash.

E3-8 **Cash from New Product Line** SnowFluff Corporation has produced and sold top-quality snowblowers for more than three decades. The company sells through exclusive dealerships, and its snowblowers have been the most expensive available. This line is quite profitable, but the company is interested in utilizing its productive capacity more fully and generating more profits. As a result, SnowFluff is giving serious thought to producing and selling four new inexpensive snowblower models. What factors does SnowFluff need to take into consideration in estimating the amount of cash it can generate under the expansion proposal?

E3-9 **Forecasting Cash Flows** Crown Company started business on January 1, 2001, and anticipated sales of $50,000, $100,000, $200,000 and $150,000, for the months of January, February, March, and April, respectively. Cash collections are expected to be 50 percent in the month of sale, 40 percent in the second month, and 10 percent in the third month. Inventory is purchased and paid for in the month of sale. Sale price is based on cost plus a 100 percent markup on the cost of inventory. Other operating costs for the four months are expected to be $24,000, $30,000, $40,000 and $50,000, respectively. Compute the amount of expected net cash flow for each of the periods. In which period is the largest cash flow expected to occur? Is the outcome consistent with your expectations based on total monthly sales? Explain your answer.

E3-10 **Cash Management** HID Company used nearly all its available cash to purchase additional operating assets and has been unable to pay its suppliers on a punctual basis during the last three months. In what way or ways has the management of HID made good use of its cash? In what way or ways has management's action not been wise?

E3-11 **Internal Control** Identify and describe five general internal control procedures for cash that a company might use. For each, indicate why the lack of a control procedure could result in poor cash management.

E3-12 **Evaluation of Internal Control** The controller of Plano Corporation is evaluating the cash control procedures used by its operating divisions. For each of the following situations, determine whether the procedure that is used represents strong or weak internal control over cash, and why:

a. Cash collected during the day in the Reno office is taken home each evening by the head cashier and deposited in the bank on her way to work in the morning.
b. Immediate cash payment is given to all drivers that deliver products to the Minneapolis office.
c. The checking account balance of the San Antonio office is reconciled each year on December 31 by the head of the cash receipts division. Monthly bank statements are checked on a random basis to see if they appear to be accurate.

d. The Des Moines office recently changed its procedures so that the person who receives cash payments from customers is not permitted to make cash payments to suppliers.

e. Clarence handles all the cash receipts in the Kalamazoo office and Irma handles all the payments. Because of the similarity in the work, they take over responsibility for the other person's job when that person is on vacation.

E3-13 Cash Flow Statement Lakeland Company reported the following cash receipts and payments during the year ended December 31, 2001:

Payments for inventory and supplies	$340,000
Receipts from sale of used equipment	68,000
Repayment of 5-year bank loan	90,000
Receipts from sales to customers	525,000
Purchase of land to build new production facilities	160,000
Payments of wages	115,000
Payment of interest on bank loan	6,000
Receipts from sale of long-term investments at book value	35,000
Receipts from issuing common stock	123,000

Prepare a statement of cash flows for the year 2001 for Lakeland Company.

E3-14 Reported Cash Flows Baker Corporation had the following cash receipts and payments during the month of September:

Cash received from customers	$690,000
Interest received on short-term investments	12,000
Sale of investments	70,000
Payment of bank loan	190,000
Payment of salaries and wages	400,000
Payment of utility bills	115,000
Payments to suppliers	90,000
Cash receipts from issuance of common stock	150,000
Cash purchase of building	330,000

Prepare a statement of cash flows for the month of September for Baker Corporation.

E3-15 Evaluation of Cash Flows The controller of Tigler Corporation is somewhat confused after looking at the cash flow statement for December. You are asked to provide at least two possible explanations for each of the following situations:

a. Cash generated from operations was negative, but the corporation had operated very profitably during December.

b. Cash collected from customers declined even though sales increased for the month.

c. Cash payments to suppliers declined even though purchases increased.

d. Although cash generated from operations reported in the cash flow statement was negative, the company reported a large profit when income was computed on a cash basis.

E3-16A Multiple Choice: Bank Reconciliations Select the best answer for each of the following:

1. Bank reconciliations are needed to:
   a. Be sure that all cash receipts are being used efficiently.
   b. Assist in determining if cash projections have been correct.
   c. Be sure products are not being sold below cost.
   d. Identify differences between the cash balances reported by the company and its bank.

2. An adjustment to a company's reported cash balance is needed if:
   a. Its bank has incorrectly recorded a check.
   b. A check has been written that has not yet been received by its bank.
   c. A notice of a bank service charge is received with its bank statement.
   d. There was a deposit in transit at the end of the period.

3. The cash balance your company reports should be increased if in doing the bank reconciliation you discover:
   a. A note receivable has been collected for you by the bank.
   b. Not all of the checks written this period have yet cleared the bank.
   c. A check from one of your customers has been returned for insufficient funds.
   d. A deposit in transit included in your bank reconciliation last period is shown by the bank as received at the beginning of this period.

4. When preparing a bank reconciliation, which of the following must be done to arrive at the correct cash balance?
   a. Checks outstanding must be deducted from the balance reported by the company.
   b. Deposits in transit must be deducted from the balance reported by the bank.
   c. Checks outstanding must be added to the balance reported by the bank.
   d. Deposits in transit must be added to the balance reported by the bank.

E3-17A Bank Reconciliation Horatio Galway is attempting to reconcile his checking account balance. Indicate whether each of the following items should be added (A) to his checking account balance, deducted (D) from his checking account balance, or ignored (I) by Horatio to get to a correct balance in his checkbook:

a. The bank indicates that two checks received by Horatio and deposited in his account had been returned as uncollectible.

b. A monthly service charge has been deducted from the account by the bank.

c. Two checks written by Horatio were paid by the bank; however, Horatio had forgotten to record them in his checkbook.

d. Cash payments received by Horatio the last day of the month and deposited that evening are not shown as deposits by the bank.

e. An automatic deduction for Horatio's electric bill was made by the bank. He had recorded the amount in his checkbook earlier this month.

f. A loan to Horatio from the bank matured during the month and was deducted by the bank from his checking account. Horatio had forgotten about the loan coming due.

g. An expense reimbursement check from Horatio's employer was deposited directly in his checking account during the month, but was not recorded by Horatio.

h. Deposits in transit at the end of last period are shown as having been received by the bank at the beginning of this period.

i. Five checks written by Horatio during the period have not yet cleared the bank.

E3-18A   Adjusting Reported Cash Balances   Maria Gallardo notices that the balance recorded in her checkbook is $820, which is $440 less than the balance shown on her bank statement. Examining the checks included with the bank statement, she sees that three checks she wrote totaling $412 have not yet cleared the bank. Also, she notices that a check that did clear was written for $86 but was mistakenly recorded in her checkbook as $68 dollars. In addition, a $10 check given to her by a coworker was returned for insufficient funds, and an automatic deposit for $60 was made to her account that she had not yet recorded. The bank also deducted a service charge, but the bank statement is smeared and she cannot determine the amount of the charge. Calculate the bank service charge.

E3-19A   Bank Reconciliation   The following data have been gathered for Trender Company:

a. The bank balance at August 31 was $3,000.

b. An electronic funds transfer of $550 for a monthly lease payment was received by the bank and deposited in Trender's account. Trender has not recorded the payment on its books.

c. The bank statement included two checks returned as NSF written by Posh Corporation for a total payment of $410 on its account.

d. Checks #400 and #407 for $600 and $190, respectively, were not included with the canceled checks included with the bank statement.

e. Trender Company incorrectly recorded check #413 at $75 rather than $750.

f. The August 31 deposit made by Trender in the amount of $650 did not appear on the bank statement.

g. A bank service charge of $30 was assessed against Trender Company by the bank on the NSF checks from Posh Corporation.

h. The bank mistakenly reduced the balance of Trender's account for a $380 check written by Trembler Company.

i. The balance in the cash account reported by Trender at August 31 was $3,805.

Prepare an August 31 bank reconciliation for Trender Company.

PART II

E3-20   Decisions and the Timing of Cash Flows

a. You are considering entering into the following transactions. In determining your course of action, should you use the formulation for the present value or future value of the cash flows in arriving at a decision?

1. You wish to know how much money you must deposit now to have $20,000 for a down payment on a house five years from now.

2. You have received an investment from your aunt that will pay you $30,000 per year for each of the next 10 years. You would like to pay off college debts and want to know how much a banker would give you if you sold the rights to the payments to the bank.

3. You just deposited $5,000 in a three-year certificate of deposit and wish to know how much you will receive when it matures.

4. You have a loan that matures in six years and will require a payment of $17,000 at maturity. How much money would you need to set aside today to have sufficient cash to make the payment when it comes due?

5. You wish to deposit enough money currently to receive cash payments of $35,000 per year for the next 15 years.

6. You wish to determine how much money you would have to deposit each year to accumulate $500,000 by the time you retire at age 62.

7. You wish to know how the monthly car payments are determined when you purchase a new Corvette with a down payment of $1,500.

8. You are unable to pay off a loan of $10,000 that matures next month and want to know how much you will have to pay if you delay payment by one year and the bank charges you the existing consumer loan interest rate plus a penalty of 5 percent.

b. The present value or future value of a cash flow is based on the amount of cash to be received or paid, the number of periods during which interest is earned, and the relevant interest rate. Under normal circumstances:

1. Will the present value increase or decrease when the interest rate is increased?

2. Will the future value increase or decrease when the interest rate is increased?

3. Will the present value increase or decrease when the future payment amount is decreased?

4. Will the future value increase or decrease when the amount deposited today is decreased?

5. Will the present value of a single future payment increase or decrease when the number of periods is decreased?

6. Will the future value increase or decrease when the number of periods is increased?

7. How will the present value be affected by substituting a series of equal payments (annuity) of $1,000 at the end of each of five years in place of a single payment of $5,000 at the end of five years?

E3-21 Multiple Choice: Present Values Select the correct answer for each of the following:

1. The time value of money concept refers to the notion that:
   a. When cash is received is not important, so long as it is collected.
   b. Cash received later is better than sooner.
   c. Cash paid out later is better than sooner.
   d. Cash paid out sooner is better than later.
2. Compound interest refers to:
   a. Interest earned during the first year the money is invested.
   b. A higher than normal rate of interest.
   c. Interest on two or more investments being received at the same time.
   d. Computing interest on principal plus previously earned interest.
3. Which of the following rates considers the compounding of interest?
   a. Effective interest rate.
   b. Stated interest rate.
   c. Nominal interest rate.
   d. All of the above.
4. The present value of a future cash payment:
   a. Is always greater than the actual amount of the payment.
   b. Is always smaller than the actual amount of the payment.
   c. Decreases if the time of payment is changed to be several years sooner.
   d. Increases if the time of payment is delayed several years.

E3-22 Multiple Choice: Present and Future Values Select the best answer for each of the following:

1. The present value of a future cash payment:
   a. Increases as the effective interest rate goes up.
   b. Decreases as the effective interest rate goes up.
   c. Is determined by using the nominal rate of interest.
   d. Is determined by using the stated rate of interest.
2. The future value of a cash payment:
   a. Represents the amount that must be deposited today to receive a desired amount at some later date.
   b. Generally is less than the amount that must be deposited today to receive a desired amount at some later date.
   c. Represents the amount that will be received today if the recipient agrees to pay a given amount at some later date.
   d. Represents the amount that will be available at some later date if a given amount is deposited today.
3. An annuity represents:
   a. A series of equal payments made at uniform intervals over a number of periods.
   b. A series of equal payments paid at differing intervals over a number of periods.
   c. Any series of payments over a number of periods.
   d. Any series of payments made at uniform intervals over a number of periods.

4. An investment of cash in a project is appropriate if:
   a. The present value of the expected cash receipts is greater than the required investment.
   b. The total of the expected cash receipts is greater than the required investment.
   c. The future value of the expected cash receipts is greater than the required investment.
   d. The present value of the expected cash receipts is greater than the future value of the expected cash receipts.

E3-23 Computing Future Cash Flows Planning for future expansion, Tom's Clothing Store has just deposited $10,000 in a savings account with an annual interest rate of 7 percent. What amount will be available if the money is withdrawn at the end of (a) one year, (b) two years, or (c) three years?

E3-24 Single Payment Ann has just agreed to pay $14,245 to another student at the end of three years in exchange for a cash payment today. If a 9 percent annual interest rate is used, what amount should the student be willing to give Ann at the time the agreement is signed?

E3-25 Present Values Sarah Trom has cash to invest and wishes to know how much she would have to pay presently to acquire each of the following investment alternatives. Compute the present value of each of the following single payments:

a. $20,000 received 10 years from now, discounted at 8 percent annually.
b. $30,000 received 15 years from now, discounted at 5 percent annually.
c. $100,000 received 20 years from now, discounted at 15 percent annually.
d. $80,000 received 30 years from now, discounted at 6 percent annually.
e. $50,000 received 6 years from now, discounted at 10 percent annually.

E3-26 Future Values Simple Enterprises wishes to know how much money it will receive upon expiration of the following investment alternatives. Compute the future value of the following single payments:

a. $60,000 invested for 10 years at an annual rate of 8 percent.
b. $20,000 invested for 17 years at an annual rate of 12 percent.
c. $70,000 invested for 8 years at an annual rate of 6 percent.
d. $300,000 invested for 25 years at an annual rate of 9 percent.
e. $100,000 invested for 6 years at an annual rate of 11 percent.

E3-27 Present Value of Annuity Payments Hertziger Corporation has agreed to make the following annual payments to Gonzo Company. Payments are made at the end of the year. Compute the present value of each of the following series of payments:

a. $30,000 paid annually for 12 years, with an annual interest rate of 8 percent.

b. $8,000 paid annually for 15 years, with an annual interest rate of 6 percent.

c. $40,000 paid annually for 25 years, with an annual interest rate of 12 percent.

d. $75,000 paid annually for 9 years, with an annual interest rate of 5 percent.

e. $25,000 paid annually for 20 years, with an annual interest rate of 4 percent.

E3-28 Future Value of Annuity Payments Blooper Corporation plans to make a deposit at the end of each year into its retirement fund. Compute the amount that will be available at the end of the contribution periods for each of the following:

a. $32,000 deposited annually for 8 years, with an annual interest rate of 11 percent.

b. $42,000 deposited annually for 8 years, with an annual interest rate of 8 percent.

c. $15,000 deposited annually for 14 years, with an annual interest rate of 15 percent.

d. $10,000 deposited annually for 19 years, with an annual interest rate of 6 percent

e. $45,000 deposited annually for 30 years, with an annual interest rate of 4 percent.

E3-29 Present Value of Monthly Payments Funkel Corporation has signed three separate agreements to make payments at the end of each month, as indicated below. Compute the present value of the following:

a. 36 monthly payments of $400 each, with an annual interest rate of 24 percent.

b. 24 monthly payments of $7,000 each, with an annual interest rate of 6 percent.

c. 14 monthly payments of $2,000 each, with an annual interest rate of 12 percent.

E3-30 Future Value of Monthly Payments Nifty Pearson is attempting to save money for college. He anticipates making the following monthly deposits in Eureka Investment Corporation. Compute the amount that Nifty will have available at the time he completes making payments if he makes the following payments at the end of each month:

a. $300 deposited monthly for 24 months, with an annual interest rate of 9 percent.

b. $275 deposited monthly for 36 months, with an annual interest rate of 18 percent.

c. $800 deposited monthly for 14 months, with an annual interest rate of 12 percent.

E3-31 Car Payment Wendy has decided to buy a new car. She is able to pay cash of $2,300 upon delivery of the car and finances the remainder on a 3-year contract with an annual interest rate of 12 percent and payments at the end of each month of $450.

a. Determine the amount that Wendy would have been required to pay if she had been able to make full cash payment for the car.

b. What is the total amount of interest Wendy will pay over the life of the financing contract?

E3-32 Equipment Purchase on Contract Johnson Products has elected to purchase equipment by signing a contract in which it will pay $4,500 at the end of each month for the next 2 years. Johnson Products is a relatively risky company and has been told it will have to pay an annual interest rate of 18 percent on the contract. Johnson Products plans to keep the asset for at least five years and wishes to record the asset at the present value of the cash payments. What amount should Johnson Products record?

E3-33 Computation of Annual Payments Bates Gas N'Goodies has decided to replace its existing car wash with a new brushless unit at a cost of $86,000. Bates wishes to make payments at the end of each year for the next 12 years and agrees to pay annual interest of 12 percent. What amount must Bates Gas N'Goodies pay each year?

E3-34 Comparison of Present Values Growl Company has elected to purchase additional vending machines and has discussed loan agreements with a vice-president of Friendly Bank. The banker has offered a choice of two loans: one alternative is to make payments of $20,000 per year for 20 years, including an 11 percent annual interest charge; the second alternative is to pay $17,000 per year for 15 years, including an annual interest charge of 8 percent. All payments are made at year-end. Which alternative would give Growl Company the largest amount of cash to use in purchasing machinery? Explain why.

E3-35 Comparison of Future Cash Availability Dolphin Corporation plans to make an annual cash deposit for 12 years in a medical health program for retired employees. It can deposit $60,000 at the end of each year in a very safe investment and earn a 6 percent return annually. As an alternative, it can deposit $52,000 at the end of each year in a riskier investment, but earn a 9 percent return.

a. Which investment will result in the largest cash balance at the end of 12 years, assuming the expected rate of return is earned each year?

b. What other factors should be taken into consideration in deciding which alternative to pursue?

E3-36 Multiple Payments Case Products just agreed to pay $1,500 at the end of each year for three years of insurance coverage on property it owns. What amount would Case be willing to pay immediately for the cost of the policy for all three years if its time value of money was 7 percent?

E3-37 Future Value of Deposits Tony's wealthy aunt has told his parents that each year at Christmas she will give them a check for $25,000 as a gift. They plan to put the money in an account to provide for their retirement. Assuming checks are received for 8 years, how much money will Tony's parents have available for their retirement immediately after the eighth payment if the amounts deposited earn 5 percent interest?

E3-38 Present Value of Retirement Benefits The first president and founder of Atwood Airlines retired three years ago and the company is paying her an annual retirement benefit of $60,000. The airline recently sold farmland adjacent to its landing strip and wishes to deposit enough money with a local bank to provide for the founder's retirement benefits of $60,000 per year for the next fifteen years. Payments are made at the end of the year.

a. If a minimum annual earnings rate of 4 percent is guaranteed by the bank, how much must be deposited currently to provide for the payments?

b. How much money must be deposited currently if the assumed earnings rate is 8 percent?

E3-39 Present Value of Future Payment Lucille will graduate from high school four years from now. Her parents have estimated that they will need $120,000 to cover the costs of her college education at that time. Assuming deposits earn 6 percent annual interest:

a. How much would Lucille's parents need to deposit immediately as a single payment to assure the required amount is available in four years?

b. How much would they need to deposit annually at the end of each of the next four years to assure the required amount is available?

c. Why must Lucille's parents contribute more total dollars under the second alternative?

E3-40 Price of Debt Hasis Corporation issues noninterest-bearing debt, called zero-coupon bonds, with a maturity value of $10,000,000 in five years. Hasis will make no interest payments on the debt, and a single payment of $10,000,000 will be paid when the debt matures in five years. Bedrock Financial Corporation is interested in purchasing all of the debt at the time of issue as an investment.

a. If Bedrock requires a 9 percent annual return on such investments, how much would the company be willing to pay for the entire issue?

b. If instead of noninterest-bearing debt Hasis issued 5 percent bonds that made cash interest payments of $500,000 at the end of each year for five years, with the full maturity value of the bonds due in five years, how much would Bedrock be willing to pay, again assuming it requires a 9 percent return?

E3-41 Length of Investment Pat Mance is going to invest $4,000 so she can buy a boat in the future. The boat is expected to cost $6,000. If Pat can earn 8 percent on her money, how long will it be before she has enough to buy the boat?

E3-42 Rate of Return Pete Nance is going to invest $4,000 so he can buy a boat in the future. The boat is expected to cost $6,000. If Pete wants to buy the boat in ten years, what is the minimum return he must earn on his investment to have sufficient money for the purchase?

USING ACCOUNTING FOR DECISION MAKING

PART I

P3-43 Evaluating Cash Flow Potential Aaron Stemper has just been given an opportunity to become a franchise owner for a new product line of Eze Breeze household cleaning products. As a major franchise owner, he would be given exclusive rights to sell Eze Breeze products in the state of Oregon and would go through an intensive two-week training program. Although the franchise would cost $75,000, Eze Breeze executives claim he will quickly recover his investment and make a substantial annual profit through the sale of cleaning products and by finding other franchisees in his territory. Aaron would receive $2,500 of the franchise payment made by each new franchise owner in the state of Oregon and would receive 5 percent of the sales price of all products sold by them.

a. What factors should Aaron consider in evaluating the potential associated with becoming a major franchise owner for Eze Breeze cleaning products?

b. Where might Aaron find information useful in arriving at a decision on whether to use his cash resources to purchase the franchise?

P3-44 Safeguarding Cash Receipts Herb Gardens, Inc., is a successful regional producer of herbs and spices. During the year just ended, the company estimates that it sold 9,000 pounds of herbs and spices at an average price of $26 a pound. Most of the herbs and spices are hung on drying racks in a large old barn to dry and for storage. When a customer comes in to purchase goods, the owners or one of the six employees goes out to the barn and brings in an appropriate amount of goods, gives it to the customer, and collects the cash for the sale. Written receipts are given to those who need them for tax purposes. During the summer, the owners try to have enough cash on hand to pay for supplies at the time they are delivered so that additional time does not need to be wasted making payments later or balancing the checkbook. In what ways might Herb Gardens, Inc., strengthen its internal control over cash and improve its overall cash management?

P3-45 Cash Receipts and Disbursements Allworth Corporation provided the following cash reconciliation for the month of April:

Balance at beginning of month	$ 32,000
Cash receipts:	
Collections from customers for	
sales in April	$ 440,000
Collections from customers for	
sales made in March	180,000
Sale of land	128,000
Proceeds from new bank loan	590,000
Total cash receipts	$1,338,000
Total cash available	$1,370,000
Cash payments:	
Purchase of inventory	
and supplies	$495,000
Payment of property taxes	82,000
Purchase of equipment	295,000
Retirement of common stock	194,000
Payment of wages	187,000
Payment of interest on	
bank loan	15,000
Total cash payments	(1,268,000)
Balance at end of month	$ 102,000

a. Prepare a statement of cash flows for the month of April.

b. Did Allworth have favorable or unfavorable cash flow from operations for the month of April?

c. Did Allworth have positive or negative cash flows from investing activities and financing activities for the month of April?

P3-46 Analysis of Cash Flow Statement   Buckle Corporation reported the following cash flows for the year 2000:

Buckle Corporation
Statement of Cash Flows
Year Ended December 31, 2000

Operating activities		
Cash received from customers		$ 800,000
Cash paid to suppliers	$500,000	
Cash paid for salaries and wages	190,000	(690,000)
		$ 110,000
Interest payments on bank loans		(43,000)
Cash generated from operations		$ 67,000
Investing activities		
Sale of land	$ 90,000	
Sale of buildings and equipment	310,000	
Purchase of new equipment	(40,000)	
Cash generated from		
investing activities		360,000
Financing activities		
Repayment of bank loans	$250,000	
Repurchase of common stock	100,000	
Dividends paid to shareholders	84,000	

Cash used in financing activities		(434,000)
Net reduction in cash		$ (7,000)
Cash balance at beginning of year		211,000
Cash balance at end of year		$ 204,000

a. Did Buckle Corporation increase or decrease its cash balance during the year? How much cash was generated from operations during the year?

b. Does Buckle Corporation appear to be expanding or contracting its operations? Explain your answer.

c. Should creditors be concerned that the total of dividends paid and common stock repurchased during the year was substantially greater than the cash generated by operations? Explain.

P3-47 Evaluating Alternative Cash Flows   Blaine recently completed his degree at Sun Tan College and TV Repair Center in San Diego. During his final semester, he won the national greased sand volleyball championship and received $75,000 in prize money. After paying off his college debts, Blaine had $50,000 to invest and talked with an investment counselor. The counselor suggested purchasing either the common stock of Ace Corporation or a 10-year certificate of deposit from a local bank. The common stock pays only a small dividend each year but is likely to increase in value as the company grows. The certificate of deposit pays 5 percent interest annually and can be cashed in at any time without penalty.

a. What factors might lead Blaine to purchase the stock?

b. What factors might lead Blaine to purchase the certificate of deposit?

c. If the certificate of deposit could not be cashed in until maturity, what factors might cause Blaine to purchase a five-year rather than a ten-year certificate of deposit even if he did not anticipate having a need for the money at the end of five years?

P3-48A Evaluating Reported Bank Balances   Bill just received his monthly bank statement for April and was irritated when he saw he had been charged $7 for a monthly bank service charge. The charge is only supposed to be made if his bank balance is less than $400, and Bill shows a balance of approximately $500. After comparing the bank statement and the amounts recorded in his checkbook, Bill found the following differences:

Balance per Bill's checkbook	$500.35
Balance per bank statement	355.30
Checks written by Bill that did not yet clear bank	
#332 to Midland Muffler Repair	165.22
#338 to Armstrong Apartments	420.03
#349 to Joe's Bar & Grill	34.10
Bank service charge	7.00
Automatic deduction for gas and electric bill	144.10

Auto-teller withdrawals not recorded by Bill:

April 4	100.00
April 19	30.00
April 27	70.00
Check from parents deposited on April 30 not recorded by bank	361.00
Automatic deduction for March phone bill	79.30
Bank credit to Bill's account for NSF fee improperly charged to Bill's account in March	25.00

Bill also discovered that he had recorded check #329 as $74.14; however, it had actually been written for $47.14

a. Prepare a bank reconciliation for Bill's checking account and determine the proper balance for his account.
b. Is it safe for Bill to write a check for $113.00 to purchase a new pair of air pump basketball shoes? Explain.
c. Was the bank charge correct, or should Bill object?

PART II

P3-49 Computing Loan Balances Andrew Floyd Webber lent money to a friend so he could purchase an old opera house. The loan required annual payments of $50,000 at year-end for 30 years and was based on an annual interest rate of 12 percent. At the end of ten years, Mr. Webber was offered an opportunity to sell the loan to another friend at a price that would provide an annual yield of 9 percent to the purchaser of the loan. Legal costs and fees for the transfer are to be paid by Mr. Webber and are estimated at $7,000.

a. What amount did Mr. Webber lend his friend?
b. At the end of ten years, what amount would Mr. Webber report as the balance in the loan receivable?
c. If the loan is sold for an amount that will allow the purchaser to earn a 9 percent annual return with twenty annual payments remaining, what amount should Mr. Webber receive?
d. How much of a gain or a loss on the sale of the loan should Mr. Webber report?
e. What factors other than the gain or loss on the sale should Mr. Webber consider before selling the loan?

P3-50 Using Present Values in Evaluating Loans Alabaster Corporation purchased a small office building, with a portion of the purchase price paid for through a 20-year mortgage loan of $200,000. The loan requires equal payments at the end of each year and carries a 10 percent annual interest rate. At the end of five years, Alabaster Corporation was approached by a local banker offering to refinance the remaining 15 years of the loan at an annual interest rate of 8 percent. The company would need to pay the banker $10,000 to cover all costs associated with the refinancing.

a. What is the amount of the annual payment on the original loan?

b. What is the amount of the unpaid loan at the end of five years?
c. If Alabaster Corporation enters into a new loan agreement at 8 percent and borrows enough to pay off the old mortgage plus the refinancing costs, what is the amount of the annual payment on the new loan?
d. By what amount would the annual payment change if Alabaster Corporation refinances? Should the company refinance?

P3-51 Present Value of Lottery Winnings The Sugar Maple Lottery run by the State of Maine just announced its new $5,000,000 grand prize contest. The winner will receive payments of $200,000 at the end of each year for twenty-five years. By law, the lottery must immediately deposit sufficient money with a local bank to provide for the payments. If the money deposited earns 10 percent interest compounded annually:

a. How much will the lottery need to deposit today to provide for the full amount of the payments?
b. If the lottery has sold only $3,900,000 of tickets by the time of the scheduled drawing, should officials proceed with the drawing or give refunds and cancel the drawing? Explain why.
c. Assume a winner has been selected and she proposes that the lottery distribute her winnings at the rate of $250,000 per year for twenty years. Should the lottery officials accept her proposal? Explain.

P3-52 Choosing among Loan Options Al Green is considering buying a car and financing it on a one-year basis. The dealer has offered Al a choice of paying $11,300 at the end of the year or making twelve monthly payments of $900 each, with the payments made at the end of the month. The dealer pointed out that Al can save $500 by using the monthly payment alternative. An 18 percent annual interest rate is being charged on car loans at the moment.

a. Is the dealer correct in saying that Al will save $500 under the 12-payment option?
b. Which of the two options should Al choose?
c. What amount will be saved by selecting the best option?

P3-53 Computing Interest on Bonds John invested surplus cash by paying $751.30 to purchase a series Z savings bond that pays no interest annually but matures at $1,000 in three years. The bondholder will earn 10 percent interest compounded annually.

a. What amount of interest will John's investment earn in each of the three years?
b. At the end of the second year, John needs cash and can either redeem his bond for $900 or can borrow $900 at a 12 percent annual rate. Which of the two options should he choose? Explain why.

P3-54 Valuing a Lease Contract Friendly Al's Auto Leasing Company purchases new and used cars and leases them to customers for periods of one to six years. Al just agreed to lease a used auto to Betty's Rent-A-Wreck for 25 months with a payment of $425 at the end of each month. The car is expected to be of no value at the end of the lease. Al is able to sell the lease to a local bank that charges an annual interest rate of 24 percent. His only cost in doing so is a $200 processing fee. Because of connections with an auto towing and repainting service, Al was able to acquire the car and deliver it to the lessee at a cost of $6,500.

a. What amount is the bank willing to pay Friendly Al's Auto Leasing for the lease contract?
b. Has Al made a profit or a loss on the combined transaction? How much?
c. At the end of the first four months, how much interest income will the bank have earned?

EXPANDING YOUR HORIZONS

PART I

C3-55 Analyzing Gateway, Inc., The financial statements of Gateway, Inc., presented in Appendix A include both a consolidated balance sheet and a consolidated statement of cash flows. By examining these two financial statements, answer the following questions:

a. What is the total of cash and cash equivalents reported by Gateway at December 31, 1998, in its balance sheet? Has this total increased or decreased from the prior year?
b. How does this total compare to net cash provided by operating activities, as reported in the statement of cash flows? What amount of cash and cash equivalents would Gateway have at the end of 1998 if it had retained all of the cash generated by operations in 1998?
c. What were the primary nonoperating uses of Gateway's cash during 1998?
d. Was Gateway able to pay for its capital expenditures during 1998 with the cash generated by operations?
e. In what ways can an analysis of the statement of cash flows help the decision maker in estimating the amounts and timing of future cash flows? How does the amount invested in property, plant, and equipment and Gateway's dividend policy impact its cash flows?

C3-56 Analyzing Storage Technology Corporation Looking at Storage Technology's Consolidated Statement of Cash Flows shown in Exhibit 3–9, did the company improve its liquidity during the latest year reported? Explain. Does the company seem to generate sufficient cash from its operations to remain solvent, or does it need to borrow extensively? What was the company's major use of cash in 1998? Why might the company choose this course of action?

C3-57 Evaluating the Timing of Cash Flows The manager of Champion Catering was quite excited when he learned that the cash flows for his business had more than doubled in November. Instead of the normal $5,000 positive cash flow per month, the cash flow for November was $12,400. To be sure there was not an error, he made up the following summary of cash receipts and disbursements for the month:

Collections on catering provided this month	$11,500
Collections on catering provided last month	3,200
Deposits for catering to be provided next month	3,400
Payments for salaries and catering supplies	4,500
Payment of building rent	1,200

He also noted that his new "Pay Ahead—Get A Discount" program had been very successful. He had no uncollected receivables from customers at the end of November and had received prepayment for catering to be provided at several Christmas parties. He remembered that one of his employees was on vacation over Thanksgiving and was not paid for the second half of the month. A total of $3,000 is owed to the employee for work in November.

The manager is hopeful that this upturn in cash flows will continue for the next several months so he can purchase his own building. Evaluate the November cash flow for Champion Catering and assess the likelihood of being able to sustain the good fortunes of November.

C3-58 Cash Management and Forecasting Falmouth Enterprises sells a popular household product to retailers and small service companies. The company has been having cash difficulties lately and is concerned about the cash position for the next month. As the assistant to the chief financial officer, you have been asked to prepare a cash forecast for the month of May. You gather the following information to assist you in preparing the forecast:

1. The company's sales forecast projects sales of 100,000 units at $12 each during May. This forecast reflects a significant increase in sales, a trend that is expected to continue over the next year.
2. Payments for all sales are due in 60 days, and virtually all customers wait until the due date to pay.
3. Sales for March were 60,000 units, and sales for April appear to be headed towards 75,000 units.
4. The sales price has not changed for almost a year.
5. Approximately 1 percent of all sales are never collected.
6. The company orders all of its product electronically, and receipt of the goods takes place within two days of plac-

ing orders. Therefore, the amount of inventory on hand at month-end always is negligible.

7. The company is billed at the end of each month for its purchases of product during the month. The company always pays immediately and receives a 2 percent discount on the purchase price of the product.

8. The company has been paying $6.75 per unit for its product until the beginning of April, when the price was raised to $7.00 per unit. In addition, the company must pay freight charges at the time of delivery of $.25 per unit (not discountable).

9. Labor payments for May are expected to total $250,000.

10. Cash payments for utility, rent, and other miscellaneous expenses are expected to be $131,000 for the month of May.

11. The cash balance at the end of April is expected to be $51,000.

12. Company policy dictates maintaining a cash balance of at least $50,000.

13. Any cash balances that exceed $50,000 at the beginning of the month and that are not expected to be needed during the next month are transferred to a savings account earning 5 percent annually.

14. Any expected cash shortfalls during the month are made up through borrowing. The company's only borrowing options are as follows:

   a. Borrow money for two months at a 12 percent annual rate, with no additional loan costs.

   b. Borrow money for one year at 8 percent interest, with a $500 loan arrangement fee, payable on receipt of the loan.

Required:

a. Prepare the cash forecast for May, showing separately all expected cash inflows and cash outflows. Neatly show all of your computations in separate supporting schedules.

b. If Falmouth Enterprises must resort to outside borrowing, which of the two available alternatives would you recommend? Why?

c. What steps might you recommend to your boss to improve the company's cash management practices? Support your recommendations.

C3-59 No Payments! No Interest! No Money Down!!! The ad screams out from the Sunday paper: BUY NOW AND PAY NOTHING UNTIL THE YEAR AFTER NEXT! NO INTEREST! Such promotional campaigns have appeared with increasing frequency in recent years, often offered by such major companies as Best Buy and Rhodes Furniture. They may offer 6 months or more of interest-free loans. For purchases made in November or December, they may offer 14 months with no payments or interest, thus permitting purchasers to defer any cash outlays until early in the year after next. However, if full payment is not made by the specified date, interest is typically due from the original date of purchase, often at 18 to 24 percent.

a. Why would a company be willing to allow customers to delay payment for 6 to 14 months and not charge interest?

b. If a company permits customers who purchase merchandise in December 2000 to defer payment until January 2002, how does the company pay its bills in the meantime? Do you think the retail company extends credit itself, or might it enter into some type of arrangement with a financial institution? What type of credit arrangement do you think might be used?

c. Best Buy Co. has a fiscal year ending at the end of February. Why would Best Buy be unlikely to make this type of offer near its year-end?

d. Assume you are a customer about to purchase $2,500 of furniture and can choose between purchasing it at either of two stores having special sales:

   Zippy Furniture Sales: 14 months with no payments or interest; if the full amount is not paid by the end of that time, interest must be paid from the date of purchase at a 24 percent annual rate.

   Zappy Home Interiors: All merchandise on sale for 20 percent off; cash must be paid at the time of purchase.

   Although you currently have the cash to make the purchase, you were hoping to invest that cash in the stock-market and earn a 12 percent annual return. Which alternative would you choose? Explain.

e Suppose you were choosing between the two alternatives, but you would not have the needed cash for 18 months. However, because of your excellent credit record you can get a bank loan whenever you need it at a 10 percent annual rate. What actions would you take? Why?

PART II

C3-60 Cash Management Chitonya Jackson is considering investing in the stock of Bradley Corporation. Looking at Bradley's balance sheet, Chitonya feels reassured that the company seems to face little risk of insolvency because it keeps large amounts of cash on hand. Further, the company has no long-term debt and little short-term debt. In fact, management's discussion accompanying the financial statements indicates that management does not believe in incurring debt and, therefore, does not borrow except in unusual cases and normally pays suppliers immediately upon being billed. Because of the large amount of liquid assets held by Bradley, the company is paying only 6 percent interest on the small amount of debt it currently owes. Chitonya also notices that the company's accounts receivable and inventory have been growing at the rate of about 20 percent per year, so the company has a large amount of current assets, an amount that is several times the amount of the company's total liabilities. The company's revenues and income both have been growing at about 10 percent each year, so the company not only appears safe, but seems to be very successful as well. Overall, the company seems to be earning annual profits averaging about 18 percent of stockholders' equity. However, Chitonya notices that the company's cash, while still exceeding the total of all liabilities, has been declining slightly each year.

Chitonya thinks that Bradley is a safe and potentially profitable investment for her, although she is not sure the company is run as efficiently as it should be. However, she decides that she probably will invest $10,000 in Bradley's stock if she is satisfied with the answers to a few questions. Help Chitonya with her decision by answering the following questions:

a. Does the fact that Bradley is holding a large amount of cash and other current assets mean that management is doing a good job? Explain in detail.

b. Do you think the company's policy of borrowing very little is a good policy? Explain.

c. If Bradley Corporation is so profitable, why is its cash declining slightly rather than growing? Describe several factors that might account for this phenomenon.

d. If the management of Bradley Corporation estimates that the company's stockholders individually can earn 10 percent returns on their money, what should management do with any excess cash on hand? Why? What should management do with the excess cash if it estimates the stockholders can earn 20 percent returns on their money elsewhere? Why?

e. Chitonya plans to invest $10,000 in Bradley's stock, which she expects to grow in value at the rate of 12 percent per year. She also expects the stock to pay her a cash dividend of $500 at the end of each year, which she will put in a savings account earning 5 percent annual interest. If Chitonya does invest the money in Bradley's stock and all her projections are realized, how much cash will she have at the end of 10 years if she sells the stock and withdraws all of her money from the savings account at that time?

C3-61 Planning for the Future Sam and Sheila Gimble are determined that their newborn son Junior will attend college. They expect the tuition for four years of college will be $64,000 at the time Junior is ready to attend. Having just received a small inheritance from Sheila's Aunt Tilley, they decide to set aside enough money in a savings account so they have the full amount of Junior's tuition when he turns eighteen.

a. Assuming the savings account pays 6 percent annual interest, how much should Sam and Sheila set aside on the day Junior is born so they have enough for his tuition on his eighteenth birthday?

b. Assuming the interest rate will be 4 percent for the first eight years and then 6 percent until Junior turns eighteen, how much should Sam and Sheila put in Junior's savings account?

c. Describe how your calculations would change if, instead of withdrawing all of the money on Junior's eighteenth birthday, $16,000 is to be withdrawn each year for four years starting on Junior's eighteenth birthday.

d. What timing of deposits and withdrawals would yield Junior the most money for college?

C3-62 Business for Sale! Glancing through *The Wall Street Journal* recently, you came across the following business opportunity:

Type of Business:	Monthly newsletter
Location:	Isle of Mancala
Market:	Local residents, upscale, approximately 1,200 subscribers
Population:	97,000 residents on the island
Overview:	Owned by an individual on the mainland who devotes part time to the newsletter. The newsletter employs an advertising manager who sells ads, and it contracts with freelance writers to write stories. The subscribers pay $34.95 annually. The newsletter has a renewal rate of 58% to 70%.
Price:	$150,000

Financial Information:

	1998	1999	2000
Gross revenue	$57,800	$86,400	$98,300
After-tax cash inflows	18,200	16,500	17,000

You have $150,000 to invest, and you wonder if this might not be a good business opportunity. Analyze this potential investment, and address the following issues:

a. You are dissatisfied with the current level of revenue. What can you do to improve the revenue stream?

b. After careful analysis and planning a few strategic changes, you determine the expected cash inflows (after taxes) for the business for the next five years should rise to the following:

2001	$30,000
2002	30,000
2003	45,000
2004	50,000
2005	60,000

If your cost of capital is 8 percent, determine whether this business is a good investment based on a present-value analysis.

c. What makes this firm vulnerable to competitors?

Internet Exercises: Visit our Web site for additional exercises.

Annual Report Project Part 3

Refer to the Annual Report Project, Part 1, at the end of Chapter 1. Using the annual report of the company you have chosen, and any other available information, answer the following questions, providing sources and computations where appropriate.

a. How does your company define cash equivalents?

b. How much cash and equivalents did your company have on hand at the end of the latest fiscal year? How does this compare with the previous year?

c. How much cash did your company generate from, or use in, its operations during its most recent fiscal year?

d. During the latest period reported, what was the cost (interest expense) to your company of using money borrowed from others?

CHAPTER FOUR

Accrual Accounting and Financial Reporting

Own a piece of The Tower: Wow! Stratosphere Corporation offered ownership units for $5 each to people wanting to invest in the 1,149 foot Stratosphere Tower on the Las Vegas Strip, the tallest observation tower in the country. They sent me lots of great information, but I couldn't figure out what it all meant. I really wanted to own a piece of The Tower, but I didn't do anything. Just as well, because the company didn't do very well. But now I have a second chance to buy, and at a lower price. If only I could figure out these financial statements . . .

"Above the Arctic Circle and half a mile down a Russian nickel mine, a young drill operator is wondering what it means to be a shareholder in Norilsk Nickel Inc. . . . He was supposed to have received shares in the newly privatized company months ago. But he and fellow workers have yet to see any. The stock hasn't paid dividends, either—and the company hasn't said whether or when it will. . . . Norilsk offers none of the statistics that any informed investor would routinely want. The company puts out no statements on earnings, revenue, debt or cash flow. . . . All of which leads dealers holding shares they don't quite own and can't quite sell to explain that Norilsk is a stock for sophisticated investors. [One trader] says the way to value Norilsk is simply as an attractive unknown, 'sort of like the Mona Lisa.'"[1]

[1]Excerpts from Claudia Rosett, "In Russia, Norilsk Poses Plenty of Risk for Its Shareholders," *The Wall Street Journal*, December 12, 1994, p. A1.

How would you decide if investing in the Stratosphere Tower would be profitable for you? What information would you need, and how would you use the information to make your decision? If you do buy a piece of The Tower, it will be because you expect to get a return for your investment.

Millions of people regularly invest or lend their money to others, but usually not without first obtaining information that allows them to assess the chances of getting it back and earning a return. The well-developed U.S. and international capital markets in which people invest and lend their money exist partly because investors and creditors are able to obtain reliable information that allows them to assess their alternatives. Much of this information becomes available through the financial reporting process.

But how do decision makers gain sufficient understanding of accounting and the financial reporting model so that financial statement information is useful to them? Should they memorize all of the accounting and reporting procedures? No, that would be virtually impossible, and even then, new reporting procedures arise every day. A better and simpler way to understand financial statements is to understand the basic accounting and financial reporting model.

For most of this chapter, we'll focus on the main aspects of the financial reporting model: the objectives of financial reporting, the qualities of accounting information, the basic concepts of financial accounting, and some important recognition and measurement attributes. By understanding the basic concepts of financial reporting, you will gain an appreciation of the strengths and weaknesses of financial statement information. After completing this chapter, you should be able to:

1. Understand the main objectives of financial reporting.
2. Describe the qualities of useful accounting information and explain why each is important.
3. Explain the basic concepts that underlie financial accounting, and briefly discuss the implications of each.
4. Describe the role of recognition and measurement in accounting, and how both impact financial statement information.
5. Relate the matching concept to accounting and the usefulness of accounting information.
6. Explain how a basic understanding of the financial reporting model is important to financial statement users.

EVALUATING FINANCIAL ACCOUNTING INFORMATION

Information for Decisions

Accounting information must be useful to decision makers. Financial accounting information is developed to meet specific objectives, and it has a number of qualities that affect its usefulness for decisions. Knowledge of these objectives and qualities can help a decision maker answer questions such as these: Will financial accounting information help me make the types of decisions I need to make? What strengths and weaknesses does the information have, and how might these affect my decisions? Can accounting information be used for comparison with similar information from other companies or different time periods?

The information that is provided through the financial reporting process is useful for making financial decisions, but it does not meet all needs. A knowledge of the objectives of financial reporting and the characteristics of financial accounting information is needed to help decision makers assess whether the information will be useful for their specific decisions.

OBJECTIVES OF FINANCIAL REPORTING

The financial reporting process aims mainly at providing information to investors and creditors who cannot obtain it directly from companies or other sources (as might a well-connected financial analyst, for example), but who are reasonably knowledgeable about business and who are willing to study the information. The objectives of financial reporting for businesses can be summarized as follows:[2]

- Meet the needs of investors and creditors (primary) and other external parties (secondary).
- Meet the needs of those unable to acquire information from other sources.
- Provide comprehensive information to informed and responsible users.
- Provide information to assess cash flows.
- Provide information about economic resources and claims to those resources.
- Provide information about periodic earnings.
- Provide information about management's performance.

You Decide 4-1

WHAT CAN YOU TELL YOUR PARTNER?

Remember when your potential partner in Our Video Store asked you for financial information about the operations (in Chapter 2)? Did she know about the objectives of financial reporting? Look at the list of financial objectives just provided. Prepare a set of questions that your new partner could have asked to get the information reflected in those objectives.

QUALITIES OF ACCOUNTING INFORMATION

Everyone agrees that information should be useful. But, what is meant by useful information, and what qualities make it useful? Accounting information is useful if it has the potential for making a difference in a decision. The qualities that make accounting information useful are shown in Exhibit 4–1. Let's look at the most important qualities more closely.

Relevance. First, the information must be **relevant.** It must pertain to the decision at hand by helping decision makers understand what has occurred in the past or assess what might happen in the future. Also, decision makers must receive the information when it is needed.

Say we are deciding about whether to invest in Tandy Corporation stock. Tandy owns the RadioShack stores. One thing we would want to know is what to expect from Ra-

---

[2]Paraphrased from *Statement of Financial Accounting Concepts No. 1*, "Objectives of Financial Reporting by Business Enterprises," Financial Accounting Standards Board, 1978.

EXHIBIT 4-1 # A HIERARCHY OF ACCOUNTING QUALITIES

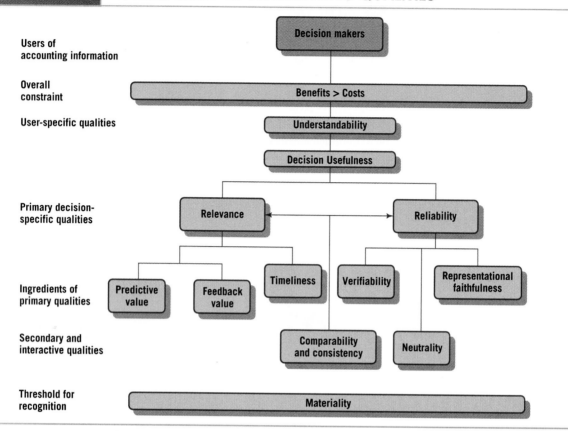

Source: Adapted from *Statement of Financial Accounting Concepts No. 2*, "Qualitative Characteristics of Accounting Information," Financial Accounting Standards Board, 1980.

dioShack sales. Exhibit 4–2 shows that RadioShack's sales mix, or the relative sales of each product, changed somewhat during the three-year period reported; sales from communications equipment and services increased while sales in most other categories decreased.

This information is certainly relevant to our decision. It helps us to understand the past and form expectations about future sales trends. The information also must be timely, how-

EXHIBIT 4-2 # RADIOSHACK SALES BY CATEGORY

Class of Products	Percent of Total Sales Year Ended December 31		
	1998	1997	1996
Electronic parts, accessories and specialty equipment	30.0%	31.5%	32.3%
Communications	28.5	27.5	24.4
Audio/Video	15.5	16.8	18.0
Personal electronics and seasonal	10.4	11.6	12.4
Personal computers and peripherals	9.1	9.4	10.4
Service and other (including prepaid wireless airtime)	6.5	3.2	2.5
	100.0	100.0	100.0

ever. If we were making the investment decision in 1999, the information would be considered timely. We still might use the information to help in making the decision today, but we would want more recent information as well.

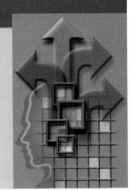

You Decide 4-2

CHANGES AT RADIOSHACK

Exhibit 4–2 shows information about the relative sales of RadioShack's products. A full page of narrative included in the report highlighted and explained the changes in the mix of RadioShack's sales over the past three years. If you were considering investing in Tandy's stock, would that information be useful to you? Why do you think RadioShack's sales mix is changing? If the telecommunications industry continues to evolve, of what relevance would this information be in forming your expectations about RadioShack?

Reliability. For information to be useful, decision makers must have confidence in it and be able to rely on it. To be **reliable**, information must reasonably reflect the real-world situations that it represents. Does the sales information shown in Exhibit 4–2 reflect what you have seen in RadioShack stores? What changes have you seen in the merchandise displayed at your local RadioShack over the past several years? What changes might you expect in the future?

The reliability of information also depends on its being free of bias. Bias results when reported information is consistently different from the reality it represents. Because Tandy and other companies must follow generally accepted accounting principles in preparing their financial statements, the extent to which management's biases can affect the financial statements is lessened.

Finally, information also must be **verifiable** to be reliable. Individuals other than those who developed the information initially, but having similar skills and training, must be able to reconstruct the information. Remember that the information reported in financial statements is presented by management but is verified by independent auditors. Statement users who have a copy of Tandy's full financial report can find the auditor's opinion immediately before the financial statements and, thus, are given a certain degree of assurance that they can rely on the financial statements.

Investors need relevant and reliable accounting information on which to base decisions about their nest eggs.

Understandability. Information cannot be useful if it cannot be understood. Financial statements are prepared under the assumption that users will have a general knowledge of business and a very basic knowledge of accounting, thus allowing them to analyze and interpret the information presented. Tandy's sales mix presentation seems to meet the criterion of **understandability**.

Comparability. For accounting information to be useful, it must be **comparable**. The information must be reported so that comparisons between similar entities can be made. Suppose, for example, you are comparing two automobiles. You find that one has a

250-horsepower engine and the other is red. While both power and color may be relevant factors, they cannot be meaningfully compared with one another. Financial information from different companies can best be compared when the companies follow the same accounting practices.

Consistency. An important characteristic of information over time is **consistency**, using the same accounting methods from period to period. The information decision makers receive is a result of both what happens to the entity and the accounting process used to gather and prepare the information:

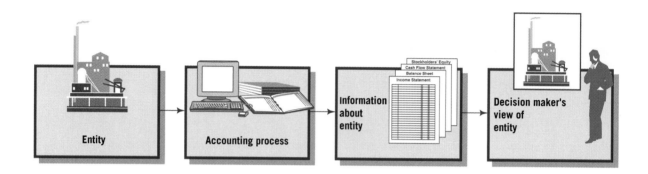

If the accounting process changes, the information, and thus the decision maker's view of the entity, may be distorted. For example, the method of classifying products used by RadioShack should remain constant from year to year, or any trend analysis could be misleading. If RadioShack reclassified some radios as toys, included in the personal electronics and seasonal category, the decline in the audio category may well reflect the accounting change rather than a real-world event. Only if the same accounting methods are used consistently over time can users rely on the information as being free from distortions introduced by accounting changes.

CONSTRAINTS ON ACCOUNTING INFORMATION

Although accounting information must have certain characteristics to be useful, the information is provided to decision makers within certain constraints. An overall constraint is that the benefits derived from accounting information should be greater than the cost to provide it. The question of whether specific information should be provided to users is not just a question of whether the information is useful, but whether it is useful enough that its benefits exceed its cost. Although the costs and benefits of accounting information often are difficult to measure, a cost–benefit comparison should be a part of all information choices. In many cases, as with the RadioShack sales information, management already has or should have the information, and only a small additional cost is incurred to publish it.

Another constraint in accounting, and one representing a practical application of the cost–benefit constraint, is that of **materiality**. Materiality has to do with whether information is important enough to influence a decision. If information does not have the potential for influencing a decision, it is immaterial. Immaterial items need not be disclosed separately in financial statements, and the accounting treatment of such items is of no concern. The idea of materiality is relative; an expenditure of $50,000 might be material for a small business, but not to General Motors. Further, too much detailed data might actually decrease the usefulness of information by resulting in "information overload."

HOW MATERIAL IS IT?

Look at the financial statements and accompanying notes of Gateway in Appendix A. Identify at least two types of financial information for which a great deal of detail is disclosed. Compare this with at least two types of information for which little or no detail is disclosed. For each comparison, why was one type of information considered material enough to disclose details, while the other type was not? What decisions might be affected by the detail of the information?

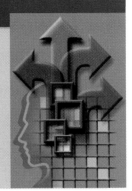

THE FINANCIAL ACCOUNTING INFORMATION MODEL

Information for Decisions

Financial statements are the end result of an accounting process that recognizes real-world events, records them, and reports them to financial statement users. An understanding of the accounting process and the elements of the financial statements will help statement users answer questions such as these: How does a company track real-world events to report them in the financial statements? What does each item reported in the financial statements tell me about the enterprise's financial position and changes in position? What do the financial statement elements tell me about the success of a company's operations? Where can I find additional explanations of the dollar amounts reported in the financial statements?

Accounting links real-world transactions and events with information reported in financial statements. Most of this information flows through an organized system of recording, classifying, accumulating, summarizing, and reporting. The elements of this system fit together as follows:

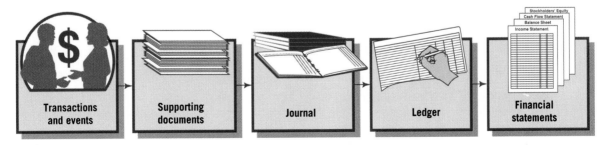

| Transactions and events | Supporting documents | Journal | Ledger | Financial statements |

Accountants recognize real-world events by recording or entering them in the financial records and ultimately reporting them in the financial statements.

FINANCIAL RECORDS

The financial records of an organization consist of the documents and other records held internally and used as a basis for preparing financial reports. These include:

- *Supporting Documents*—Almost every financial transaction is evidenced by some type of document, such as an invoice (bill) or remittance advice (document explaining an attached payment). These **supporting documents** serve as the basis for recording transactions in the accounting system, and they provide evidence of the transaction for future verification.

- *Records (Books) of Original Entry*—Financial transactions are first recorded by organizations in the **journal**, which provides a chronological history of an entity's activities. Although most companies now use computers rather than handwritten records, the term *books* is still widely used to refer to an organization's formal accounting records.

- *Accounts for Classification, Accumulation, and Summarization*—**Ledger accounts** are used to accumulate information about individual financial statement items. For example, RadioShack records all retail store sales by type of item sold; sales of cordless telephones are recorded in an account separate from sales of computers.

FINANCIAL STATEMENTS

The **financial statements** are the end result of the accounting process and reflect what has been recorded by the company in its financial records. Recall that the four basic financial statements are the:

- Statement of financial position (balance sheet)
- Income statement
- Statement of changes in owners' equity (or a retained earnings statement)
- Statement of cash flows

The elements reported in the financial statements are listed in Exhibit 4–3. Understanding the financial statement elements is crucial for using accounting information for decision making.

In addition to the basic financial statements, companies usually include the following in their financial reports:

- *Notes to Financial Statements*—The notes provide detailed information and additional explanations necessary to use the statements effectively, including a summary of the accounting methods used to prepare the statements.

- *Other Financial Information*—Additional information, summaries, or supplemental schedules are often included to make the financial statements more informative or to expand on them.

BASIC CONCEPTS OF FINANCIAL ACCOUNTING

Information for Decisions

A number of concepts underlie the financial accounting information model. An understanding of these concepts will help financial statement users make decisions by answering questions such as these: Are all the businesses controlled by this company included in the financial statements I am examining? Are the company's assets reported at the dollar amounts expected to be received from sale or liquidation? Does a company record its revenue when a customer places an order, when the order is paid for, or at some other time?

ELEMENTS OF THE FINANCIAL STATEMENTS

EXHIBIT 4-3

Elements Related to Financial Position

Assets—probable future economic benefits controlled by a particular entity as a result of past transactions or events.

Liabilities— probable future sacrifices of economic benefits arising from present obligations of a particular entity as a result of past transactions or events.

Equity—the residual interest in the assets of an entity that remains after deducting its liabilities; equal to *net assets* (assets minus liabilities).

Elements Related to Changes in Financial Position

Changes Resulting from Operations

Revenues—inflows of assets from delivering or producing goods, rendering services, or other activities that constitute the entity's ongoing major or central operations.

Expenses—outflows or using up of assets or incurrences of liabilities from delivering or producing goods, rendering services, or carrying out other activities that constitute the entity's ongoing major or central operations.

Gains—increases in equity (net assets) from peripheral or incidental transactions and events.

Losses—decreases in equity (net assets) from peripheral or incidental transactions and events.

Net Income—the change in the equity of a business enterprise during a period from transactions and other events and circumstances, excluding those related to prior periods and other than investments by or distributions to owners.

Changes Resulting from Transactions with Owners

Investments by Owners—increases in equity of a particular business enterprise resulting from transfers to it of something valuable to obtain or increase ownership interests in it.

Distributions to Owners—decreases in equity of a particular business enterprise resulting from transferring assets or incurring liabilities by the enterprise to owners.

Source: Definitions of all elements except net income are based on those in "Elements of Financial Statements," *Statement of Financial Accounting Concepts No. 6*, Financial Accounting Standards Board, 1985.

The financial accounting information model provides information to decision makers through an established set of accounting and reporting procedures. Underlying these procedures is a framework of basic concepts. While these concepts are theoretical in nature, they will help you understand and evaluate the information contained in financial statements. Let's look at how these concepts relate to the information reported by businesses, with In Practice 4-1 as an example.

THE ACCOUNTING ENTITY

From an accounting perspective, each business enterprise is considered to be a separate **accounting entity** for which financial statements are prepared. No other interests of the owners are reflected in the financial statements of the entity. As an illustration of the entity concept, you can see that the Morton entity (In Practice 4-1) has changed since 1989, both from a legal and an accounting perspective. The single entity Morton Thiokol became three entities: Morton International, Thiokol Corporation, and Autoliv AB. Then, in 1999, Morton International became part of another business enterprise when it was acquired by Rohm and Haas Company.

The accounting entity is not always the same as the legal entity. Although the corporate form of business organization results in a separate legal entity, unincorporated businesses (proprietorships and partnerships) are not legally separate from their owners. In some cases, the accounting entity will not include the entire legal entity, as with a partnership. In that case, financial statements are prepared only for the business enterprise and exclude the owners' other activities, assets, and liabilities. In other cases, the accounting entity sometimes in-

In Practice 4-1

MORTON INTERNATIONAL: WHO MAKES MORTON SALT?

In 1998, Morton International, Inc., reported total sales of $2,530,100,000. Sales from salt of all kinds totaled $793,186,000, or only about 31 percent of total sales. Obviously Morton International is more than a salt company. Sales of specialty chemicals of all kinds totaled $1,736,914,000 in 1998, or about 69 percent of total sales. Morton also reported that in the 1998 fiscal year, salt sales increased by 20 percent due to the impact of the acquisition of Salins du Midi, a French-based salt company. Excluding this acquisition, salt sales would have declined by 4 percent. Specialty chemical business grew by 3 percent.

ANALYSIS

Prior to 1989, the company was known as Morton Thiokol, Inc., and its business included salt, specialty chemicals, airbags, and aerospace. In 1989, the aerospace operations, including those related to the space shuttle, were placed in a separate company named Thiokol Corporation, with the ownership shares distributed to the owners of Morton. The name of the company encompassing the salt, specialty chemicals, and airbag operations was changed to Morton International, Inc. Both Morton International and Thiokol were owned by the same individuals immediately following the reorganization, but they were separate legal and accounting entities. In this realignment, the risky aerospace business was separated from the chemical and airbag operations. In 1998, Thiokol changed its name to Cordant Technologies.

In a 1997 reorganization, the airbag business was combined with Autoliv AB of Sweden in a new corporation, creating the largest automobile occupant-restraint company in the world. Morton International continued with the salt and specialty chemical business. In 1998, Morton acquired Salins du Midi, the largest independent salt company in Europe with its well recognized "LaBaleine" label. Morton International now says that it is focused exclusively on its core business, specialty chemicals and salt. Exhibit 4–4 shows the progression of Morton's reorganizations. In 1999, Morton was acquired by Rohm and Hass Company and is now operated as a wholly owned subsidiary. [www.morton.com] [www.thiokol.com]

cludes more than one legal entity, such as when a number of companies are all owned by the same corporation. In that case, a single set of financial statements is prepared for all the legal entities under common control, as if they formed a single company. These common situations are shown in Exhibit 4–5.

Now that Rohm and Haas owns all of Morton International's stock, Morton is a **subsidiary** and Rohm and Haas is its **parent company**. The financial statements of Rohm and Haas will be combined with the financial statements of all of its subsidiaries, including Morton, and a single set of **consolidated financial statements** will be issued that portrays all of the related companies as if they were a single entity.

Morton International provides an example of a company that chose to restructure the accounting entity to change the reported information. Because the riskier Thiokol was no longer part of the the same accounting entity as Morton, its debt was no longer shown on Morton's balance sheet, and changes in Thiokol's earnings had no effect on the reported earnings of Morton. Further, any potential liability resulting from lawsuits, such as those

REORGANIZATIONS OF MORTON

EXHIBIT 4-4

Before 1989	1990–1997	After 1997
Morton Thiokol	*Morton International*	*Morton International*
Aerospace	Salt	Salt
Salt	Inflatable restraints	Specialty chemicals
Inflatable restraints	Speciality chemicals	
Specialty chemicals		*Cordant Technologies*
	Thiokol Corporation	Aerospace
	Aerospace	
		Autoliv AB
		Automotive-occupant restraints

stemming from the 1986 Challenger space shuttle disaster, would not affect Morton or its financial statements. Thus, a change in the accounting entity can greatly alter the picture reflected in the financial statements.

OBJECTIVITY

In accounting terms, **objectivity** means that information appearing in financial statements should be reliable and subject to verification. Recall that, because financial statements are representations of management, the information contained in the statements must be subject to verification by parties other than management. Verification is why many entities value their assets based on **historical cost**. For example, a parcel of land purchased by a company twenty years ago for $100,000 might now be worth far more. However, the actual value cannot be verified until the company sells the land. Only when the land changes hands in an exchange transaction is the market price of the land established. This exchange price can be

THE ACCOUNTING ENTITY

EXHIBIT 4-5

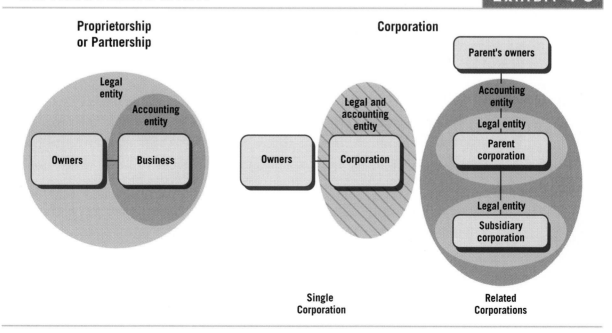

verified by examining the supporting documents. Thus, while management's estimate of the value of the land does not provide verifiable evidence, an exchange transaction does. As long as the land is held by the company, it is valued at its original cost, established in the exchange transaction when it was acquired.

The assets listed by Morton International in its annual report are mostly based on historical cost. Listed amounts reflect an objective and verifiable determination of what was paid for the assets, not the current market value.

THE GOING CONCERN

Financial statements are prepared under the assumption that the entity will continue to operate indefinitely. The **going-concern concept** assumes that the entity will stay in business at least long enough to meet its obligations and to use its assets in the intended manner. This assumption affects how an entity values its assets and liabilities. For example, Morton International's assets are not reported at the amount for which they could be sold because the company's intent is not to sell its assets but to use them in its operations. As long as the company is assumed to be a going concern, it will need to use its assets to continue in operation, and objectivity leads to the use of historical cost for valuing them.

In some cases, the going-concern assumption may not apply because there is evidence that a company will not continue operating. Then, the going-concern assumption might be dropped and assets and liabilities revalued to more relevant amounts, such as the amounts for which they could be sold.

PERIODICITY

If business ventures existed only for short time spans, there would be no need for the **periodicity** concept. People interested in the venture could simply wait until its operations were over and receive a full accounting. Most major companies, however, are expected to continue in operation indefinitely (the going-concern concept). Unfortunately, decision makers cannot wait until the life of the company is over to receive financial reports. They need to make decisions about that company while it is still operating. Thus, entities provide information periodically. Financial statements are prepared that show the results of the entity's activities for each period and its position at the end of the period. Companies typically issue full financial statements annually and summarized statements quarterly.

You Decide 4-4

WHY NOT A CALENDAR YEAR?

Morton International presents its financial statements for the fiscal year (twelve-month accounting period) ending June 30. The company's income statement and statement of cash flows are presented for the fiscal year just ended and the two previous years. Why would the company use a year ending June 30 instead of December 31? Why would the company report information for more than one year?

The need for periodic reports results in some uncertainty in the information reported. Because accounting principles often require allocations of amounts among past, present, and future periods, the operating results and financial position reported at any one point in time are tentative. For example, asset values and income reported by Morton International may need to be reconsidered if, for example, technological advances make its production equipment obsolete. The uncertainty of the amounts reported in the financial statements needs to be considered when making decisions.

DISCLOSURE

More detailed information, referred to as additional disclosures, usually accompanies the financial statements to assist statement users. For example, Tandy Corporation provided a three-year analysis of product sales mix for RadioShack in its annual report, and decision makers could use this information in projecting future sales.

The disclosure concept dictates that external accounting reports must include any additional information needed to make sure that the financial statements are not misleading. This concept places responsibility on management and the independent auditors to do more than simply follow established accounting and reporting requirements. For example, suppose a company issues financial statements for a calendar year. If a major earthquake occurs on January 5 of the following year and destroys all of the company's production facilities, the balance sheet prepared as of the previous December 31 is still correct as of December 31. However, unless informed otherwise, statement users will assume the company holds a similar collection of assets a week or a month later. Not disclosing the subsequent event would be misleading. Therefore, information about the earthquake and its consequences would have to be provided under the disclosure concept, even though the event occurred after the close of the fiscal year.

CONSERVATISM

Although **conservatism** is a concept that has never been well-defined, it has significantly influenced financial reporting. Conservatism helps to offset the natural optimism of management that might result in reporting an overly favorable picture of a firm's activities and financial position. The concept suggests that if an accountant is faced with having to assign one of two values to an asset and there is no other basis for measurement, the lower amount should be used. Similarly, for a liability or an expense or loss, the higher amount should be assigned. Another way to state conservatism is that if there is an expectation of a specific loss occurring in the future, the loss should be included in the reports even though it has not yet occurred. Gains, however, should never be reported until they occur. Recognize that undue conservatism introduces a bias in the financial statements. (See In Practice 4-2.)

One of the clearest examples of conservatism involves the valuation of inventory. Goods held for sale to customers are generally reported at the original cost or current market value, whichever is lower.

RECOGNITION AND MEASUREMENT

So far, our discussion of the financial reporting process has focused on what makes accounting information useful, and some of the concepts on which that information is based. But, what must actually occur for an event to be reported in the financial statements? The process

CHECKERS

Checkers Drive-In Restaurants, Inc., sells modular restaurant kits to franchisees. The company's rapid earnings growth came to a halt in 1994 when the company posted a $500,000 loss for the first half of the year compared with $7.8 million in profit for the first half of 1993. What happened?

ANALYSIS

When Checkers sold its modular restaurant kits to franchisees, it recorded the full sales price as revenue because the sales were completed, even though construction may not have been. This is an acceptable accounting practice, but it is considered aggressive rather than conservative accounting. When several franchises began to fail and some franchises under construction were not completed, sales of additional franchise kits stopped and profits turned to losses. A more conservative approach for Checkers would have been to wait until a restaurant started operating before recognizing the revenue from the sale.

In 1999, Checkers had ownership interests in 230 restaurants, and an additional 232 restaurants were operated by franchisees. During 1998, the number of franchised restaurants decreased by 5. In the year ending December 28, 1998, Checkers reported a net loss of $5.3 million following losses in 1995, 1996, and 1997. In August 1999, Checkers and Rally's Hamburgers, Inc., merged. [www.checkers.com]

relating to when and how real-world events are reported in the financial statements can be illustrated as follows:

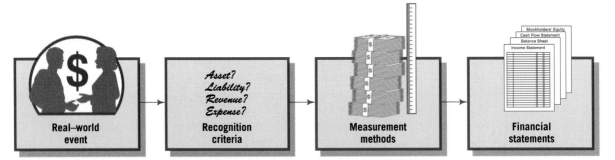

Recognition Criteria. The FASB has described **recognition** as the process of recording an item in the financial statements of an entity as an asset, liability, revenue, expense, or the like.[3] Recognition criteria determine when specific events or transactions are included in an entity's accounting records and ultimately are reported in the financial statements. Recognition criteria are linked to the characteristics of useful accounting information we discussed previously. An item should be recognized when it meets the definition of an element of the financial statements (see Exhibit 4–3), is relevant to a decision, and can be measured reliably.

So when should revenue from the sale of a company's products or services be included in the income statement? This question will be answered in more detail in the next chapter, but generally revenues are recognized when (1) they are earned and (2) an exchange takes

[3]*Statement of Financial Accounting Concepts No. 5*, "Recognition and Measurement in Financial Statements of Business Enterprises," Financial Accounting Standards Board, 1984, para. 6.

place. For most sales of goods, the sale (and delivery) of the goods to the customer is viewed as the last significant step in the earning process. The sale also reflects an exchange: the seller provides goods to the purchaser in exchange for cash or a claim to cash. A claim to cash normally is a promise from the purchaser to pay cash to the seller in the future. For example, when Morton sells a shipment of its salt to a food wholesaler on credit, it receives the purchaser's promise to pay, a claim to cash. Thus, once Morton sells and delivers salt to a customer, the conditions for reporting revenue from the sale have been met: the revenue has been earned, and Morton has exchanged the salt for the customer's promise to pay. Reporting the revenue from the sale is not delayed until the cash is collected.

When an exchange transaction occurs, the form of the company's assets changes significantly, and the event requires recognition in the accounts. Instead of holding salt, Morton now has a claim to cash that ultimately will be converted into cash. The exchange also is important because it provides a means of verifying the value of the transaction. The value placed on the sale by Morton is substantiated by the wholesaler's acceptance of the goods at that price. The supporting sales documents can be used at a later time to verify the amount of the revenue. Thus, the exchange provides verifiable evidence of the value of the transaction in accordance with the objectivity concept.

Measurement Methods.   Not all items included in the financial statements are measured or valued in the same way. Several different measurement methods, including historical cost and current market value, are used in accounting and are reflected in the financial statements. The particular method used to value each financial statement element depends on which provides the most relevant and reliable information. For example, the market value of land on which a company's building stands may be irrelevant because the land will not be sold. Because it is used in the company's operations and the purchase cost can be verified, the land is valued at historical cost. On the other hand, the best measurement method to use for land held as a short-term investment might be its market value because the land is expected to be sold shortly. Specific measurement methods will be discussed in detail throughout the following chapters.

MATCHING COSTS AND BENEFITS: THE HEART OF ACCRUAL ACCOUNTING

Information for Decisions

Accrual accounting is used by virtually all large companies because it reports revenues when they are earned rather than when cash is collected, and it reports expenses when the related benefits are received rather than when cash is paid out. Under this method, net income provides a measure of the success of a company's efforts and accomplishments, rather than just a measure of cash inflows and outflows. If financial statement users understand how a company determines which costs are to be recorded and how these costs are matched to revenues to determine the amount of net income reported, they can answer these questions: How successful was the company in generating benefits this period that exceeded the costs of getting those benefits, and what does this imply about the company's future? What costs already incurred by the company are expected to provide future benefits, and what types of benefits are expected to be generated by those costs?

The system of accounting that is generally accepted as providing the most useful information for decision making is referred to as **accrual accounting**. Under accrual accounting, the amount of revenues, expenses, and net income reported during a period is based on the recognition criteria and measurement methods that we just discussed, rather than simply reflecting the amount of cash inflows and outflows during the period. Accrual accounting takes the view that because a business exists to make a profit by obtaining benefits that exceed its costs, the best measure of its success is one that matches its costs and benefits. The **matching concept** thus plays a central role in determining the amount of expenses and net income to be reported within individual periods. It is, perhaps, the single most important concept for understanding the framework of generally accepted accounting principles.

THE MATCHING CONCEPT

Matching compares the costs of a business's activities with the benefits they provide. **Costs** are economic sacrifices. A business usually incurs costs with the expectation that the costs will provide benefits to the enterprise in current or future periods. Examples of costs and the associated benefits are as follows:

Costs	Benefits
cost of product sold	revenues
cost of money borrowed (interest)	use of money
cost of insurance	insurance protection
rent for office building	use of building
purchase price of equipment	use of equipment
salaries	employee labor

The actual process of matching involves the following:

1. Determining the amount of a specific cost incurred
2. Identifying the benefits expected from having incurred that cost
3. Determining when the benefits are received
4. Reporting the cost as an expense in the period in which the benefits are received

If the benefits are received in more than one period, a portion of the cost is allocated to each of the periods in proportion to the benefits received during that period.

The primary benefit a business expects to receive from its operations is revenue from the sale of its products or services. In the period in which revenues are reported in the income statement, the costs of generating those revenues are also reported. The costs are matched against the revenues, and the difference is the entity's income for the period. Expenses are costs that are included in the income statement because they provide benefits during the period.

A CLOSER LOOK AT

MATCHING COSTS WITH REVENUES

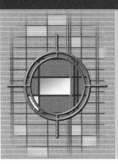

Suppose you decide to make a little extra money by selling compact discs to your friends and other students living nearby. Taking $1,000 you have saved, you purchase 200 CDs from a distributor, paying cash at the time of purchase. During the first month of your venture, you are too busy getting the business organized to sell any CDs. During the second month, you sell half of the CDs for cash of $800, and the remaining CDs are sold just before the end of the term for cash of $700. How would you compute net income under the matching concept?

Answer: Revenues are recognized at the time of the sales, and the cost of CDs sold is matched against the revenue recognized to compute income:

	Month			
	1	**2**	**3**	**Total**
Revenue	$ -0-	$800	$700	$1,500
Expenses	-0-	500	500	1,000
Net Income	$ -0-	$300	$200	$ 500

In the example, the success of your venture can be judged period by period by looking at the excess of benefits over costs. In the second month, the first month in which you actually engaged in your central activity of selling CDs, you sold for $800 CDs that cost you $500, thus earning an excess of revenues over costs of $300. In the third month, you sold for $700 CDs that cost you $500, earning net income of $200.

The matching concept applies to virtually all of the costs incurred by a business enterprise. Some other examples of matching are as follows:

Cost	Report as Expense
interest on 2-year bank loan	over the 2-year period of the loan
premium on 3-year insurance policy	over the 3-year period of coverage
cost of delivery truck	over estimated useful life of truck
commissions earned by sales staff	at time of sales

Thus, a company's income statement includes the revenue it earned during the period, as well as the various expenses incurred in producing that revenue and operating during the period.

Note that revenue and expense recognition are independent of when cash flows take place. Also note that the need for the matching concept grows out of the periodicity concept. Because of period-by-period reporting, accountants regard the matching concept as necessary to reflect the success or failure of the enterprise's activities during the period.

CLASSIFYING COSTS

Costs play a central role in the matching process. Accordingly, knowing how accountants classify and treat costs is important for understanding the information presented in financial statements. Accountants treat costs as being either unexpired or expired, as follows:

Unexpired costs—those costs expected to result in future benefits for the entity.

Expired costs—those costs not expected to result in future benefits for the entity.

The progression of a cost from unexpired to expired can be viewed as follows:

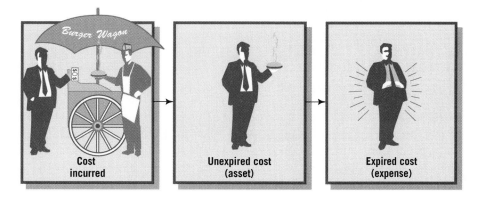

| Cost incurred | Unexpired cost (asset) | Expired cost (expense) |

If a company purchases equipment that is expected to run for ten years (a ten-year life), the cost is considered an unexpired cost because the benefits of the equipment will be received over future periods. Unexpired costs are reported on the balance sheet as assets. However, a portion of the cost of the equipment, referred to as **depreciation**, will expire each period. Thus, depreciation costs are reported in the income statement as expenses. This sequence of events can be viewed as follows:

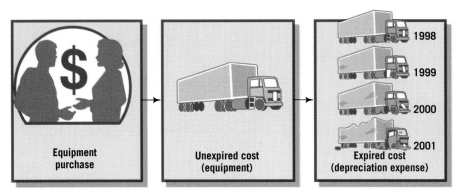

Unexpired costs, or assets, are viewed as having service potential, or the ability to provide future benefits. An unexpired cost expires as the service potential is used up. For example, if the equipment with a ten-year life is used for five years, half of its service potential has expired. Therefore, half the equipment's original cost would be treated as unexpired, an asset. The other half would be considered expired and would have been reported as an expense in the income statement over the first five years of the equipment's usage.

Expenses are expired costs. They are the costs associated with the current period's operations and expire as the benefits are received. As an example, suppose near the end of the year, a company purchases goods (inventory) for $10,000 to be resold to customers. As of the end of the year, the inventory is held by the company. The cost of that inventory is an unexpired cost, an asset, because it is expected to provide the company with a future benefit, sales revenue. When the inventory is sold during the next period for $14,000, the benefit is received and the cost of the inventory expires. The expired cost, or expense, is matched against the benefit by reporting both the sales revenue and the expense in the income statement. In this way, the success of the undertaking can be determined by calculating the difference ($4,000) between the revenue ($14,000) and the cost ($10,000).

If a cost expires without providing benefits, such as when inventory becomes worthless because of damage or obsolescence, it is immediately recognized as an expense. As a general rule, no cost should be reported as an asset unless it is expected to provide future benefits.

A CLOSER LOOK AT FINANCIAL STATEMENTS

Information for Decisions

To evaluate a business's financial statements, a decision maker must understand each of the elements reported. Understanding the elements and the meaning of the dollar amounts reported will help financial statement users answer questions such as the following: Is the company holding the appropri- ate collection of assets and is management employing the assets effectively and efficiently? Will the company be able to meet its obligations as they come due? How do the company's performance and financial position compare with previous years and with other companies in the same industry?

You should now have a general understanding of the financial reporting process. But, will this help you, a decision maker, evaluate financial statements? Let's look at the financial statements of Motorola, Inc., and discover just how important understanding the financial reporting process is to decision makers. Motorola (www.motorola.com) is a leading provider of wireless communications, semiconductors, and advanced electronic systems and services. Exhibit 4–6 contains Motorola's balance sheets as of December 31, 1998 and 1997. Exhibit 4–7 contains Motorola's statements of operations (income statements) for the years 1998, 1997, and 1996. Motorola also includes statements of stockholders' equity and statements of cash flows in its annual report.

Companies typically provide financial statement information for multiple years, as has Motorola. The information for prior years is provided so statement users are able to discern trends and compare the operations and financial position of one year with those of other years. Multiple-year statements are called **comparative financial statements.**

MOTOROLA BALANCE SHEETS

EXHIBIT 4-6

MOTOROLA, INC., AND SUBSIDIARIES
CONSOLIDATED BALANCE SHEETS

	December 31	
(In millions, except per share amounts)	1998	1997
ASSETS		
Current assets		
Cash and cash equivalents	$ 1,453	$ 1,445
Short-term investments	171	335
Accounts receivable, net	5,057	4,847
Inventories	3,745	4,096
Deferred income taxes	2,362	1,726
Other current assets	743	787
Total current assets	13,531	13,236
Property, plant and equipment, net	10,049	9,856
Other assets	5,148	4,186
TOTAL ASSETS	$28,728	$27,278
LIABILITIES AND STOCKHOLDERS' EQUITY		
Current liabilities		
Notes payable and current portion of long-term debt	$ 2,909	$ 1,282
Accounts payable	2,305	2,297
Accrued liabilities	6,226	5,476
Total current liabilities	11,440	9,055
Long-term debt	2,633	2,144
Deferred income taxes	1,188	1,522
Other liabilities	1,245	1,285
Stockholders' equity		
Preferred stock, $100 par value issuable in series	—	—
Authorized shares: 0.5 (none issued)		
Common stock, $3 par value	1,804	1,793
Authorized shares: 1998 and 1997, 1,400		
Issued and outstanding: 1998, 601.1; 1997, 597.4		
Additional paid-in capital	1,894	1,720
Retained earnings	8,254	9,504
Non-owner changes to equity	270	255
Total stockholders' equity	12,222	13,272
TOTAL LIABILITIES AND STOCKHOLDERS' EQUITY	$28,728	$27,278

EXHIBIT 4-7   MOTOROLA INCOME STATEMENTS

MOTOROLA, INC., AND SUBSIDIARIES
CONSOLIDATED STATEMENTS OF OPERATIONS

(In millions, except per share amounts)	Years Ended December 31		
	1998	**1997**	**1996**
NET SALES	**$29,398**	$29,794	$27,973
COSTS AND EXPENSES			
Manufacturing and other costs of sales	**20,886**	20,003	18,990
Selling, general and administrative expenses	**5,493**	5,188	4,715
Restructuring and other charges	**1,980**	327	—
Depreciation expense	**2,197**	2,329	2,308
Interest expense, net	**216**	131	185
TOTAL COSTS AND EXPENSES	**30,772**	27,978	26,198
EARNINGS (LOSS) BEFORE INCOME TAXES	**(1,374)**	1,816	1,775
INCOME TAX PROVISION (BENEFIT)	**(412)**	636	621
NET EARNINGS (LOSS)	**$ (962)**	$ 1,180	$ 1,154
BASIC EARNINGS (LOSS) PER COMMON SHARE	**$ (1.61)**	$ 1.98	$ 1.95
DILUTED EARNINGS (LOSS) PER COMMON SHARE	**$ (1.61)**	$ 1.94	$ 1.90
DILUTED WEIGHTED AVERAGE COMMON SHARES OUTSTANDING	**598.6**	612.2	609.0

Exhibit 4–8 briefly describes each of the items reported in Motorola's financial statements. Companies typically include a relatively small number of account titles or line-items in the financial statements. In reality, any large company has hundreds of accounts. To avoid undue complexity, however, many account balances are combined in preparing the financial statements. Although some information may be lost, the financial statements may actually be more useful by eliminating unnecessary detail.

BALANCE SHEET

Motorola's balance sheets, showing the company's financial position at the close of business on December 31, 1998 and 1997, include two main sections: (1) assets and (2) liabilities and stockholders' equity. The company's financial position at any point in time reflects the accounting equation; therefore, total assets equals the total of liabilities and stockholders' equity.

Most of the items in Motorola's balance sheets are typical of those appearing in the balance sheets of large companies. Some items, such as cash, inventories, and accounts payable, are largely self-explanatory. Others, such as additional paid-in capital, are less clear. We'll discuss each of the items in later chapters.

Motorola's balance sheets group assets and liabilities in subcategories. **Current assets** are expected to be sold, converted into cash, or consumed within a relatively short period of time, usually one year. **Current liabilities** are expected to be satisfied (paid) within a relatively short period of time, usually one year. Current liabilities are typically satisfied with current assets. Current assets and current liabilities are often evaluated and compared in assessing a company's ability to meet its short-term obligations.

The stockholders' equity section of the balance sheet provides information on the shares of stock outstanding and the amount of undistributed (retained) earnings. We'll explore the world of stocks in Chapter 12.

| EXHIBIT 4-8 | **SELECTED FINANCIAL STATEMENT ELEMENTS** |

Elements Included in the Balance Sheets

ASSETS

Cash	Currency, coins, checks, and liquid bank deposits
Cash equivalents	Short-term investments that can be quickly converted to cash
Short-term investments	Investments held as an alternative to cash but that cannot be converted to cash as quickly as cash equivalents, usually because of longer maturities
Accounts receivable, net	Amounts owed to the company by others, primarily arising from sales to customers on credit; after deducting an allowance for doubtful accounts
Allowance for doubtful accounts	The amount of accounts receivable not expected to be collected
Inventories	Goods held for sale to customers or materials used to produce goods for sale to customers
Deferred income taxes	Expected future income tax benefits
Other current assets	Assets expected to provide benefits to the company in the near future, such as expenses paid in advance
Property, plant and equipment, net	Total investment in facilities and properties used in the company's operations, less the portion of the original cost of buildings, machinery, and equipment deemed to have benefited the current and prior periods and recognized as expense in those periods

LIABILITIES

Notes payable	Amounts payable to banks and other creditors evidenced by a written document
Current portion of long-term debt	The amount of long-term debt due within the next year
Accounts payable	Amounts owed to suppliers for purchases on credit; also referred to as trade payables
Accrued liabilities	Amounts owed to others for expenses that have not yet been paid
Long-term debt	Amounts owed to others, not due within the next year
Deferred income taxes	Amounts that may be due for income taxes in future periods
Other liabilities	Other amounts owed, including estimated amounts for retirees' pension and health care benefits

STOCKHOLDERS' EQUITY

Preferred stock	An ownership interest with a limited claim on earnings and assets ahead of common shareholders
Common stock	The true residual ownership interest of the company
Additional paid-in capital	Amounts paid to the company at the time its common stock was issued that exceeded the par value (an arbitrary amount) of that stock
Retained earnings	Accumulated past earnings of the company not distributed to the owners as dividends

Elements Included in the Statements of Operations (Income Statements)

Net sales	Sales less sales returns and allowances; sales allowances reflect price reductions for substandard products or services
Cost of sales	The cost incurred to purchase or produce the products sold to customers during the period; also called cost of goods sold
Selling expenses	Sales commissions, advertising, and other costs associated with the sale of products and services
General and administrative expenses	Costs associated with operating the company as a whole, including salaries of top management, costs of headquarters operations, research and development costs, insurance, and other costs not specifically identified
Depreciation expense	The cost of long-lived assets allocated to the current period, other than amounts included in cost of sales
Interest expense (net)	The cost of borrowing money for the period, after deducting interest earned from investments
Income tax provision or benefit	Income taxes expensed during the period, whether payable currently or in the future, or the tax savings from reporting a loss
Net earnings	The earnings (income) generated from all sources for the accounting period; when expenses are greater than revenues, the company reports negative earnings, or a *loss*
Earnings per common share	The amount of net earnings allocated to each share of common stock outstanding; determined by dividing net earnings by the average number of common shares

INCOME STATEMENT

Motorola presents income statements for three years, a longer period of time than for its balance sheets. Trends in operations are difficult to discern from only two years' data. The income statements are for specific periods of time, one year each, where the balance sheets are as of an instant in time. The income statement reports, in summarized form and following accrual accounting concepts, revenues that are earned during the year. Motorola's revenues include sales of its products and services and interest income from its finance subsidiary, which finances sales to Motorola's customers. Expired costs and other expenses for the period are matched against revenue to arrive at net earnings (or loss). As a decision maker, you know that Motorola has not included any unearned revenue and that any costs that have expired during the year are reported as expenses in determining net income. Motorola has elected to use the term "statement of operations" rather than "income statement" in presenting its operating results, but this does not imply any differences in the purpose or content of the statements.

The statements of operations also show the amount of income earned per share of common stock. Earnings per share (EPS) information provides stockholders a way to assess the extent to which they share in the income of the company. Investors often use the company's earnings per share to assess the return on their investments. The amount of earnings per share must be presented for each year for which income is reported.

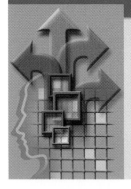

You Decide 4-5

GROWTH AT MOTOROLA

How would you characterize Motorola's growth? Is it positive or negative? Fast or slow? What information in its financial statements helps you make this determination? Is the information relevant, reliable, understandable? What effect does the going-concern concept have on your evaluation of the company?

SUMMARY

The financial reporting model provides a framework for understanding the information provided in financial statements. In general, financial statements help decision makers assess the activities and position of an entity. Further, they help decision makers form judgments about the entity's future activities and how the decision maker might be affected by those future activities. Accounting information, including that in financial statements, possesses certain qualities that add to its usefulness for making decisions. However, care must be taken to ensure that the benefits of providing accounting information are greater than its costs.

The financial reporting model starts with real-world events and records them in the financial records of the entity.

Ultimately, this recorded information is processed into financial statements issued to interested parties. The model specifies how transactions and events are recognized in an entity's records based on an interrelated set of definitions, basic concepts, recognition criteria, and measurement methods. This conceptual framework guides accountants in reporting transactions and events and helps financial statement users understand the meaning of the information included in the statements. The basic concepts of accounting include the accounting entity, objectivity, going-concern, periodicity, disclosure, and conservatism. The two most important concepts provide the basis for when to report revenues and expenses in the income statement. Revenues are generally reported in the period in which they are earned and an exchange takes place. Expenses are recognized based on the matching concept, under which expenses are reported in the income statement in the period in which the associated benefits are received by the enterprise. Expenses are deducted from the revenue produced, resulting in net income for the period.

LIST OF IMPORTANT TERMS

accounting entity *(129)*	depreciation *(138)*	parent company *(130)*
accrual accounting *(135)*	expired costs *(137)*	periodicity *(132)*
comparable *(125)*	financial statements *(128)*	recognition *(134)*
comparative financial statements *(139)*	going-concern concept *(132)*	relevant *(123)*
conservatism *(133)*	historical cost *(131)*	reliable *(125)*
consistency *(126)*	journal *(128)*	subsidiary *(130)*
consolidated financial statements *(130)*	ledger accounts *(128)*	supporting documents *(128)*
costs *(136)*	matching concept *(136)*	understandability *(125)*
current assets *(140)*	materiality *(126)*	unexpired costs *(137)*
current liabilities *(140)*	objectivity *(131)*	verifiable *(125)*

EXAMINING THE CONCEPTS

Q4-1 What qualities of accounting information make it useful?

Q4-2 What is meant by the relevance of accounting information?

Q4-3 What attributes must accounting information possess to be reliable?

Q4-4 Why is freedom from bias important for accounting information?

Q4-5 What does it mean for information to be verifiable? How might a lack of verifiability affect a decision maker's use of information?

Q4-6 What does comparability of information mean? Give an example of comparability.

Q4-7 What does it mean for accounting information to be consistent? Why is consistency important?

Q4-8 Why are financial statements often prepared for an accounting entity rather than a legal entity? When are the two not the same?

Q4-9 When is a company referred to as a parent company? Why would a parent company choose to include information on one or more subsidiaries in its financial statements?

Q4-10 Why does the objectivity concept often lead to the use of historical costs in valuing assets?

Q4-11 Why are exchange transactions important for accounting recognition? What role do exchange transactions play in verifying accounting information?

Q4-12 What is the going-concern concept and why is it important?

Q4-13 What is the periodicity concept? Why is it important for companies to provide periodic information?

Q4-14 What is meant by conservatism and why is it used in preparing financial statements?

Q4-15 What measures, other than historical cost, might be used in valuing assets for financial reporting purposes? Are these measures ever used?

Q4-16 How does the accrual accounting model differ from the cash flow model?

Q4-17 How does the matching concept affect the recognition of costs? Why is it used?

Q4-18 What steps are involved in the matching process? Give two examples of cases where the matching concept should be applied.

Q4-19 What is the difference between an unexpired cost and an expired cost? When does an unexpired cost expire? Give an example of each of the two types of costs.

Q4-20 What is meant by future service potential? What accounting treatment is accorded an asset when its future service potential expires?

Q4-21 When are assets classified as current assets in the balance sheet? Why is it important to know what portion of the assets is current?

Q4-22 When are liabilities classified as current liabilities? What assets are typically used to pay current liabilities?

UNDERSTANDING ACCOUNTING INFORMATION

E4-1 Evaluating Financial Accounting Information In its most recent income statement, the Electronic Shop reported the following information about its revenues for the past two years:

	2001	2000
Revenues:		
Computers and related equipment	$120,000	$200,000
Computer software	235,000	135,000
Repairs and service	85,000	45,000
Total revenue	$440,000	$380,000

a. You are considering investing in the Electronic Shop, but are concerned that several recent articles have indicated there may be a nationwide slowdown in sales of computers and related equipment. Does the information on the Electronic Shop's revenue for 2001 support or contradict the information provided in the articles?

b. What characteristics of accounting information should provide assurance to the financial statement reader that the revenue information provided by the Electronic Shop can be relied upon?

c. Would your ability to evaluate the Electronic Shop's revenues be changed if the company reported revenue in only two categories, as shown below? How?

	2001	2000
Sales of computers and computer software	$355,000	$335,000
Repairs and service	85,000	45,000
Total revenue	$440,000	$380,000

E4-2 The Financial Accounting Information Model Financial statements are the end result of the accounting process and reflect what has been recorded by a company in its financial records.

a. What role do supporting documents have in the accounting process? Give an example of a supporting document.

b. Why are gains and losses on peripheral or incidental transactions and events reported separately from revenues and expenses? How does this assist the financial statement reader?

c. Why are changes in financial position resulting from operations and those resulting from transactions with owners reported separately? How does this assist the financial statement reader?

E4-3 Basic Concepts of Financial Accounting

a. The Acme Trailer Company produces trailers in Indiana. Acme owns 100 percent of two of its suppliers, the Ace Wheel and Bearing Company and the Omega Wood Products Company. Which companies should be included in Acme's financial statements? Explain.

b. Aftel Company received an order for its products three months prior to the date of requested delivery. It produced the products two months before the delivery date. At the time the order was received, Aftel knew the sale price, and at the time it produced the products, it knew the cost of producing and shipping the products to the customer. When should revenue on the sale be recorded? What accounting concepts apply to the recognition of revenue?

c. Land held for future plant expansion was purchased some years ago and is worth a great deal more today than was paid at the time of purchase. Should the company's balance sheet report the higher amount? What accounting concepts apply to the valuation of the land?

d. What does it mean when a company is considered to be a going concern? Why might investors and creditors value the assets of a company differently if they conclude that a company is no longer a going concern?

E4-4 Matching Costs and Benefits: The Heart of Accrual Accounting Under accrual accounting, the matching concept plays a central role in determining the amount of expenses and net income to be reported in the financial statements within individual periods. Your assistance is needed in applying the matching concept for Mountain Supply Company. Mountain Supply Company paid $10,000 for a freezer to be used to store products that it sells to the public. The freezer is expected to last 10 years and have no value at the end of that period. At the end of the first year, Mountain Supply reported $1,000 of the cost of the freezer as an operating expense.

a. How did Mountain Supply determine that the $1,000 cost should be an expense in the first year? Where will this expense be reported in the financial statements?

b. What is the unexpired cost of the freezer at the end of the first year? Where will the unexpired cost be reported in the financial statements?

c. If at the end of the fifth year an electrical short ruins the freezer and it has to be discarded, how should Mountain Supply account for the remaining unexpired cost?

E4-5 A Closer Look at Financial Statements

a. While analyzing the financial statements of the Morris Company, you notice that a $50,000 note payable to the First National Bank was listed as a long-term debt last year but it is listed as a current liability this year.

1. What would cause Morris Company to report the note as a current liability?

2. If the note payable has a 6 percent annual interest rate and Morris Company reported total interest expense of $7,000 on all liabilites last year, how much would you expect to be reported as interest expense next year and in subsequent years?

b. The income statement for Morris Company includes both net income and an earnings per share amount. What information is provided in the earnings per share number that is not provided by net income?

c. How can an analysis of multiple-year financial statements provide an investor with additional insight into the desirability of investing in Morris Company?

E4-6 Multiple Choice: Financial Reports Select the correct answer for each of the following:

1. For accounting information to be useful, it must be:
   a. Relevant to a decision at hand.
   b. Reliable.
   c. Understandable.
   d. Prepared in a consistent manner from period to period.
   e. All of the above.

2. Accounting information is relevant if:
   a. It is timely.
   b. It helps the user understand and evaluate past actions and activities.
   c. It helps the user formulate assessments about what might happen in the future.
   d. All of the above.

3. The concept of consistency means:
   a. All companies should report events in the same way.
   b. A company should report similar events over time in the same way.
   c. A company should report dissimilar events in the same way.
   d. Different companies with dissimilar events should report them in the same way.
   e. Answers a and b.

4. Verifiability means:
   a. The numbers are correctly reported.
   b. The numbers are not biased in favor of management.
   c. Two companies with similar events will report them in the same way.
   d. Individuals with similar skills and training are able to reconstruct the information.
   e. All of the above.

E4-7 Multiple Choice: Financial Statement Concepts Select the correct answer for each of the following:

1. An accounting entity:
   a. Almost never consists of more than one legal entity.
   b. Is always the same as the legal entity.
   c. Is ignored if the business is run as a partnership and only financial statements for the partners are prepared.
   d. Frequently includes more than one legal entity.

2. One of the reasons historical costs are used in valuing assets for financial statement purposes is:
   a. They are more easily verified than current market values.
   b. Except in unusual cases, they generally represent the current market values of the assets at the time a balance sheet is prepared.
   c. They make the accounting process easier.
   d. Most companies do not wish to disclose the actual value of their assets.

3. Materiality means:
   a. An asset is of value to the company.
   b. Two competent individuals may interpret the results differently.
   c. An item of information is important enough to influence a decision.
   d. Two companies must report similar events in the same manner.
   e. All of the above.

4. The going-concern concept assumes:
   a. The company can sell its assets at the reported amounts.
   b. The company will continue in business for a period not in excess of ten years.
   c. The company will continue in business indefinitely.
   d. The company has sufficient cash reserves to support it into the indefinite future.

E4-8 Multiple Choice: Accounting Concepts Select the correct answer for each of the following:

1. The matching concept refers to:
   a. Adding together similar types of assets and liabilities when preparing a balance sheet.
   b. Including all the assets and liabilities in the balance sheet.
   c. Reporting costs in the income statement in the same period in which benefits obtained from those costs are reported.
   d. Adding together similar types of revenues and expenses when preparing the income statement.

2. Under the concept of conservatism:
   a. Assets are recorded as expenses at the time of purchase.
   b. Liabilities are not recognized until paid.
   c. The lowest possible value is always assigned to assets.
   d. When alternative valuations are possible, the lower value is assigned to an asset.

3. When preparing a balance sheet and faced with the choice of two different values to assign, the concept of conservatism could lead to:
   a. Assigning the lower value, both for assets and liabilities.
   b. Assigning the higher value, both for assets and liabilities.
   c. Assigning the higher value for assets and the lower value for liabilities.
   d. Assigning the lower value for assets and the higher value for liabilities.

4. In the balance sheet, the valuation of most assets is based on:
   a. Current cost.
   b. Historical cost.
   c. Net realizable value.
   d. Market value.

E4-9 Multiple Choice: Financial Reporting Select the correct answer for each of the following:

1. An asset is considered to be:
   a. An unexpired cost.
   b. An expired cost.

c. Something that will be sold for cash.

d. An anticipated future cash outflow.

2. Which of the following items should not appear in the income statement of Spartan Company?

a. Investment by owners.

b. Revenues.

c. Losses.

d. Expenses.

3. Which of the following is not an example of the matching concept?

a. Recording sales commission expense at the time of sale.

b. Recording rent expense each year during a five-year lease.

c. Recognizing income on the sale of inventory on credit at the time payment is received.

d. Recognizing cost of goods sold for the units of inventory sold during the period.

4. An accounting entity may consist of:

a. A single corporation.

b. Two or more corporations.

c. A partnership.

d. A sole proprietorship.

e. Any of the above.

E4-10 Accounting Equation Ballentine Company has assets of $1,000, liabilities of $300, and owners' equity of $700. Using the accounting equation, answer each of the following independent questions:

a. At what amount will liabilities be stated if total assets increase by $200 and owners' equity remains constant?

b. At what amount will owners' equity be stated if Ballentine pays off $150 of liabilities with cash?

c. At what amount will assets be stated if total liabilities increase to $525 and owners' equity remains constant?

d. At what amount will assets be stated if total liabilities decrease by $100 and owners' equity increases by $250?

e. What would be the impact on the accounting equation for Ballentine if the owners withdrew $550 cash?

E4-11 Changes in the Accounting Equation Toland Corporation reported owners' equity of $150,000 and liabilities of $250,000 on January 1, 2001. Using the accounting equation, answer each of the following independent questions:

a. If Toland issues additional common stock for $45,000 during 2001, what amount of total assets will be reported?

b. If Toland reports net income of $65,000 and distributions to owners of $17,000 during 2001, what amount of total assets will be reported at December 31, 2001?

c. If accounts payable in the amount of $69,000 are paid during the year and additional inventory is purchased on account for $45,000, what amount of total assets will be reported at December 31, 2001?

d. If owners' equity increases by $5,000 and total assets decrease by $17,000, what balance will be reported as liabilities?

e. If liabilities decrease by $15,000, net income of $35,000 is reported, and new shares are issued for $20,000, what amount of total assets will be reported at December 31, 2001?

E4-12 Changes in Balances For each of the following, indicate whether an increase or a decease is required:

a. An investment by owners is reported as _____ in cash and _____ in owners' equity.

b. Sale of land at a profit results in _____ in cash and _____ in land. The excess of the sale price over its cost will be reported as _____ in reported income.

c. A purchase of inventory on credit will result in _____ in inventory and _____ in accounts payable.

d. A distribution to owners in the form of a dividend results in _____ in cash and _____ in owners' equity.

e. When legal services are provided to a client by a law firm, the client must recognize _____ in an expense and _____ in accounts payable or _____ in cash.

E4-13 Financial Statement Effects Staple Company reports on a calendar-year basis. Determine which of its balance sheet and income statement accounts will be affected by the following transactions, and indicate whether the account balances will be increased or decreased:

a. Land previously purchased for $24,000 is sold for $30,000 cash.

b. New shares of common stock are issued for $70,000.

c. Inventory is sold on account for $50,000. The inventory had previously been purchased for $34,000.

d. A bank loan of $100,000 is taken out on December 31.

e. A three-year insurance policy is purchased for $45,000 on January 1. Insurance expense is recognized at year-end.

f. A patent with an expected life of 5 years was purchased for $80,000 on December 31 of the preceding year.

E4-14 Elements of Financial Statements Determine whether the following elements should appear in Champion Corporation's income statement, balance sheet, or neither.

a. Cash held at year-end.

b. Cost of inventory sold.

c. Amounts owed to suppliers.

d. Amounts received as advance payments from customers.

e. Earnings per share.

f. Cash held by Champion's shareholders.

g. Depreciation expense on property, plant, and equipment.

h. Property, plant, and equipment.

i. Unpaid income taxes.

j. Salary and wage expense for the year.

k. Cash payments for utilities used during the year.

l. Shares of common stock issued during the year.

E4-15 Analysis of Income Statement Items Jake Redding owns and operates a tire and auto repair shop named Jake's Jack 'em and Fix 'em Shop as a sole proprietorship. During the month, the following events occurred:

1. The shop charged customers $8,300 for repair work completed.

2. The total cost of parts used in repair work during the month was $2,700.
3. Jake earned $120 interest in his personal savings account.
4. Jake paid $600 for monthly rent on the repair shop and $150 for monthly rent for a small building behind the repair shop that he uses as living quarters.
5. Jake paid $250 for utilities for the month for the repair shop and $50 for utilities for his living quarters.
6. Jake paid his friend Clem $320 for helping him at the repair shop during the month and another $40 for painting his bedroom.
7. Other expenses related to operating the repair shop for the month totaled $1,400.
8. Jake incurred costs for food and other miscellaneous living expenses of $390.

Using the concepts discussed in this chapter, determine the amounts that would properly be reported in the income statement for Jake's Jack 'em and Fix 'em Shop. If an item is excluded, explain why.

E4-16 Recognition Criteria Under generally accepted accounting principles, revenue is included in the income statement in the period in which it is earned. For each of the following, determine the amount of revenue that should be reported by Gross Corporation during 2001, if any:

a. Cash sales totaled $500,000, and sales on account to customers totaled $350,000.
b. Payment of $120,000 was received on June 30, 2001, from a customer for monthly cleaning services to be provided over the next 24 months. Gross provided the services stipulated in the contract starting July 1, 2001.
c. Cleaning services provided to Lint Company in December 2001 were not billed to Lint until early January 2002. The amount billed in January was $7,000.
d. On December 1, 2001, Gross received $18,000 payment for cleaning services to be provided from January to June 2002.
e. Payment in the amount of $22,000 was received in January 2001 for cleaning services performed in 2000.

E4-17 Expired Costs Buck Company reported prepaid insurance in the amount of $48,000 at January 1, 2000. The policy provides coverage through June 2002.

a. What amount of expired cost should Buck Company report for the year ended December 31, 2000?
b. What amount of unexpired cost should Buck Company report at December 31, 2000?
c. What amount of expired cost should Buck Company report for the year ended December 31, 2001?
d. What amount of unexpired cost should Buck Company report at December 31, 2001?

E4-18 Matching Concept For each of the following independent cases, indicate how much of the cost should be recognized as expense in the months of October and November, applying the matching concept:

a. Employees work Monday through Friday and are paid on Monday for the previous week's work. The total payroll is $2,500 per week. October 31 falls on a Wednesday.
b. A new lease on buildings that are being rented goes into effect on November 1 and decreases the rent from $1,500 per month to $1,200. Rent for the next month is always prepaid on the last day of the current month.
c. The company borrowed money on October 1. The 45-day loan is to be repaid on November 15 along with $75 interest.
d. The company purchased a supply of solvents for $690 on October 1. The solvent is used in the company's operations and is expected to last until March 31 of the next year.

E4-19 Expense Recognition Computer Supply Company operates a number of large computer supply stores that sell all types of computer supplies and equipment at discount prices to individuals and small businesses. The company prepares financial statements at the end of each calender year. For each of the following, state the nature of the benefit you would expect the company to receive from incurring the cost, how much of the cost should be recognized as an expense in the current year, and how much should be recognized as an expense in the following year.

a. A two-year insurance policy is purchased for $12,000 on October 1 of the current year.
b. A two-year $8,000 loan with 9 percent annual interest is taken out on July 1 of the current year.
c. A payment of $9,000 is made March 31 as prepayment on a one-year lease for a storage facility. The lease starts April 1.
d. An information networking system costing $35,000 is put in service on July 1 of the current year. The system is expected to be used for five years.
e. During the current year, the company had goods available for sale to customers that cost a total of $836,000. Of that amount, goods costing $772,600 were sold for $815,750. The remaining goods were sold in the following year.

E4-20 Accounting Concepts For each of the assets listed below, indicate the amount at which the asset should be recorded in the balance sheet and which basic concepts or constraints lead to that valuation.

a. Land held as a future warehouse site was purchased for $90,000 three years ago, but has an appraised value of $150,000 at present.
b. Goods that cost $40,000 are held for sale to customers. Because of rain damage it appears the goods can be sold for no more than $25,000.
c. Goods that cost $80,000 are held for sale to customers. Because of unusually heavy demand and a national shortage, it would cost $110,000 to purchase the goods currently and the company should be able to sell the goods for at least $140,000.
d. Five special computer covers were purchased for $15 each. The covers are expected to last the life of the computers, estimated to be four years.

e. The company owns a warehouse in Italy that cost $1,750,000 to construct two years ago. The warehouse is no longer being used, and it is estimated that the company will only receive $800,000 when it is sold, even though it is still in good condition.

f. The company owns a warehouse in London that cost $1,750,000 to construct two years ago. Because of its specialized nature, it could be sold for only $1,000,000 today. The company has highly profitable operations in Great Britain and plans to continue to use the warehouse for at least 15 more years.

E4-21   Interest on a Bank Loan   Dorsal Company borrowed $100,000 from Kindly National Bank on a three-year note payable. The agreement requires no payment by Dorsal until the note matures. At that time, Dorsal must pay the $100,000 principal of the note and interest of $33,100. The interest payment is computed on the basis of 10 percent interest on the unpaid balance at the start of each year. What amount of interest expense should Dorsal Company report in its income statement for each of the three years?

E4-22   Computation of Income   Retail Corporation purchased inventory for $60,000 during 2000 and sold 70 percent of the inventory prior to the end of the year for $210,000. It paid salary and wages of $36,000 during 2000 and owed employees an additional $9,000 for work performed prior to the end of the year. On January 1, 2000, Retail Corporation paid $180,000 for a three-year lease on the building that it uses as its warehouse and sales facility. It also paid real estate and income taxes totaling $17,000 for the year. Compute Retail Corporation's net income for 2000.

E4-23   Income Determination   Packler Company has service revenues of $356,000 for the year, rent expense of $15,000, wage expense of $210,000, supplies expense of $6,000, and miscellaneous expenses of $45,000. In addition, the company uses equipment that was purchased two years ago at a cost of $56,000. The equipment is expected to have a total useful life of eight years. Compute Packler's net income for the year.

E4-24   Asset Valuation   Landon Corporation purchased a tract of land for $150,000 roughly twenty years ago and has now divided the land into two parcels. The company intends to sell one of the parcels and keep the other. Landon estimates it can sell the one parcel for $280,000. It already has a firm offer of $180,000 from a local business, and it has a tentative offer from the brother of the president of Landon Corporation for $325,000.

a. What accounting concepts and objectives might be used by the president of Landon in support of recognizing the value of the parcel at $280,000?

b. What accounting concepts and objectives might be used to argue against recognizing the proposed value?

c. Is it appropriate to revalue one of the parcels and not revalue the other?

d. At what amount should the parcels be valued?

E4-25   Recognizing Changes in Value   Two years ago, Atlas Card Company purchased a large, four-color printing press for $500,000 with the intent of using it for 7 years. Recently, the production manager just learned that replacing the press with a comparable new one would cost $800,000. On the other hand, if the company were to attempt selling the current machine, the production manager estimates it would receive $100,000. The manager also estimates the company can make $1,300,000 from selling materials produced on the press over the next 5 years.

a. What should be the value assigned to the press in Atlas Card's financial statements?

b. Under what conditions should the press be valued at $1,300,000?

c. Under what conditions should the press be valued at $800,000?

d. Under what conditions should the press be valued at $100,000?

E4-26   Analysis of Transactions   The accounting equation provides a convenient mechanism for showing the impact of various transactions and activities on the amounts reported as assets, liabilities, and owners' equity in the balance sheet. Ann and Greg Fenway run a small art gallery and custom framing business. How will the following transactions affect the amounts reported as assets, liabilities, and owners' equity in the balance sheet for their business?

a. The Fenways purchase 5 pictures for cash.

b. Framing materials are purchased on credit.

c. A loan from the bank is repaid (ignore interest).

d. A picture is sold for cash at an 80 percent profit.

e. A plaster statue falls from a shelf and is broken and discarded.

f. A receivable is collected on a major framing project completed last month for a local law office.

g. Payment is made for the framing materials previously purchased.

h. A cash withdrawal is made by Ann and Greg to meet living costs.

E4-27   Cash Held by Multiple Entities   McGregor Company holds 100 percent ownership of Lansing Company and Dubuque Company. At December 31, 2000, the individual companies reported cash on hand of $150,000, $90,000, and $40,000, respectively, and the owners of McGregor held cash of $70,000 in their personal accounts. Hometown Bank agreed to lend McGregor $240,000 and deposit the balance in McGregor's checking account any time McGregor made a request. On December 29, 2000, McGregor asked to have the money deposited, and the bank deposited it into McGregor's checking account on January 1, 2001.

a. What cash balance should be reported in McGregor's consolidated balance sheet at December 31, 2000?

b. In this situation, explain why the accounting entity includes or excludes McGregor Company, the owners of McGregor Company, Lansing Company, Dubuque Company, and Hometown Bank.

E4-28 Sales Between Related Entities McGregor Company holds 100 percent ownership of Lansing Company and Dubuque Company. During 2001, McGregor Company reported sales of $500,000, Lansing reported sales of $400,000, and Dubuque reported sales of $300,000. The operations of the three companies are highly integrated. One hundred percent of Dubuque's sales are to McGregor Company and 60 percent of Lansing's sales are to McGregor Company.

a. Why is it appropriate for McGregor to include the operations of Lansing Company and Dubuque Company when it prepares an income statement?

b. What amount of sales should it report in its 2001 consolidated income statement?

c. Why must the sales between McGregor Company and its subsidiaries be excluded from consolidated revenues?

E4-29 Conflict in Concepts The concepts of relevance and reliability sometimes conflict with one another, yet both are important in making accounting information useful.

a. Define relevance and reliability, and explain why they are important.

b. Explain how these two concepts might conflict in attempting to reach a judgment on the price to be paid for land that will be used for a new regional airport. The land under consideration is a short distance outside of town and was purchased by its current owner ten years ago as top quality agricultural land at $1,800 per acre. The land is expected to have a value in the range of $300,000 to $500,000 per acre once airport improvements have been added. Airport improvements are expected to cost between $250,000 and $400,000 per acre.

E4-30 Going-Concern Concept Fly-By-Day Airlines was established shortly after World War II to provide crop dusting and spraying services for local farmers on weekdays and pleasure flights for tourists on weekends. The company has never been more than marginally profitable; however, it has never missed a payroll and has always paid its bills on time. Although no formal agreement was ever established, the founder and former president of Fly-By-Day Airlines retired five years ago and is being paid an annual retirement benefit of $30,000. The outside auditors have approached the current president and proposed that a formal liability be established for the pension benefit. One of the members of the board of directors has questioned whether the liability should be shown in the balance sheet because she is not sure the company meets the going-concern assumption.

a. What is the going-concern concept? What factors should be considered in determining whether or not the company is a going concern?

b. What effect might violation of the going-concern assumption have on the financial statements of Fly-By-Day Airlines?

c. What effect might the going-concern assumption have on whether the company recognizes a liability for the future pension payments to the former president?

E4-31 Matching Concept Lester Brown opened a small plumbing repair business two years ago when he left his previous job. By electing to immediately take his accumulated retirement benefits from his former employer in cash, Lester was able to purchase a small lot on which he hopes to build a retail outlet sometime next year, purchase a new panel truck for the business, and prepay the health insurance costs for himself and his three employees for the next four years.

The concept of matching is important in determining the amount to be reported as periodic income.

a. Define matching and explain why it is important in the income determination process.

b. For each of Lester's three cash payments, determine how the matching concept should be applied.

E4-32 Conservatism A local disk jockey for FM radio station WFSS, while helping to clean the attic of a record store that was going out of business, found five unopened copies of what appeared to be the first album released by Billy Joel. She purchased the records for a total of $40. Later in the day, she sold one of the records to a friend who is a Billy Joel fanatic for $25. The following week she auctioned off one of the records on the air for $375 after announcing that all proceeds would go to a neighborhood well-baby clinic. If she were preparing financial statements in accordance with generally accepted accounting principles, the concept of conservatism might be relevant in assigning a value to the remaining three records, which she believes are worth a minimum of $750.

a. Define the concept of conservatism and explain why it is used in the financial reporting process.

b. In this situation, what different methods might be used to assign a value to the remaining records? At what amount would the records be valued under a strict interpretation of conservatism?

E4-33 Reporting Entity Amy and Brad Chen have been entrepreneurs for several decades and have established a relatively broad array of business holdings. Chen Enterprises is a corporation created some time ago. In addition to its primary business operation, the corporation holds all of the ownership of MidTown Corporation and is a one-third owner in a partnership that owns and operates a very successful small shopping mall. Last year, Amy started a travel agency that has its offices in the shopping mall and is operated by her as a sole proprietorship. Brad and Amy also have invested some of their personal savings in the stock of major corporations.

a. If financial statements are prepared for Chen Enterprises, which operations should be considered part of the relevant reporting entity?

b. If financial statements are prepared for Amy and Brad, how would the definition of the reporting entity change?

c. Why is it important to go beyond the definition of legal entity in establishing the reporting entity in this type of situation?

E4-34 International Businesses International Bearing Corporation incurs significant costs each year when it translates the financial statements of its international subsidiaries from foreign currency units to U.S. dollars and converts the statements from the foreign accounting procedures to those used in the United States.

a. Which accounting concept leads to foreign subsidiaries being included in parent company financial statements?
b. Which accounting concept results in the parent and subsidiary using similar accounting procedures for similar transactions?

c. Which accounting concept requires that, once a subsidiary's financial statements have been included in those of the parent, this practice will continue in the future?
d. Which accounting concept allows a foreign subsidiary's financial statements to be excluded from those of the U.S. parent under certain conditions?
e. During the period, the parent shipped a large quantity of its main product to one of its international subsidiaries, making a profit on the intercompany sale. The subsidiary is expected to resell the product to its customers, but has not yet done so. Which concepts require an adjustment to the financial statements to remove the profit recorded by the parent?

USING ACCOUNTING FOR DECISION MAKING

P4-35 Determining Balance Sheet Totals One of the owners of THE REALLY SINFUL COOKIE SHOP is considering selling his ownership and wishes to determine his equity in the cookie shop using good accounting principles. The owners know the following transactions have occurred since they started operations at the beginning of the year:

- $35,000 was borrowed from the bank to help get the business started, and $10,000 was repaid by year-end. In addition, the owners contributed $15,000 to get the business started.

- Ingredients costing $40,000 were purchased during the year, and 80 percent was used in goods baked during the year. All but $6,000 of the ingredients was paid for by the end of the year.

- Cookie ovens were rented during the year for $13,000. At year-end, an option to purchase the ovens was exercised, and $37,000 was paid to acquire ownership.

- Salaries of $20,000 were earned by employees during the year; all were paid except taxes of $3,000, which were withheld and will be forwarded to the proper agencies early next year.

- After collecting $86,000 for goods sold, the cash balance at the end of the year was $25,000, and net income of $21,000 was reported.

a. List each of the assets and liabilities of the bakery at the end of the year.
b. Compute the amount of the equity of the owners at year-end.
c. Prepare a simple balance sheet for the bakery at year-end.
d. For what amount should the owner be able to sell his 25-percent ownership interest?

P4-36 Applying Matching Concept Tom Driver decided to retire from stock car racing and invest all his winnings in a fish farm. He had majored in genetics in college and experimented with many different species of fish before coming up with a catfish that has the texture and taste of ocean trout. Moreover, contacts from his previous profession made it pos-

sible for him to acquire feed for his unique form of fish at very low prices. In December 2000, Tom decided to explore expansion possibilities. He talked with his banker about getting a loan and presented an income statement for 2000, based strictly on cash flows, as follows:

Cash collected from sale of Tom's		
Gourmet Fish		$510,000
Less: Feed purchases	$420,000	
Purchase of new fish tank	50,000	
Wage expense	75,000	545,000
Operating loss		$ (35,000)
Plus: Sale of land		100,000
Net income		$ 65,000

From discussions with Tom, the banker learned the following:

- $180,000 of the cash collected in 2000 was from shipments delivered prior to the start of the year. Payment for all the sales this year were collected prior to year-end.

- The feed can be stored indefinitely, and about half of 2000's purchases remain on hand at year-end.

- Two fish tanks were purchased in 1999 at a total cost of $100,000. These tanks, along with the one purchased at the beginning of 2000, were used all year. Each tank is expected to last five years.

- The land sold for $100,000 had been purchased in 1998 for $60,000.

Provide Tom and his banker with responses to each of the following:

a. Why is the matching concept important in this case?
b. What amount of revenue from the sale of merchandise should be included in 2000?
c. What amount of expense for fish food should be reported in 2000? How should the remainder of the food purchased be reported?

d. Should some amount for the fish tanks be included in computing income for 2000? How much?

e. What amount of gain on the sale of land should be included in income for 2000?

f. Should Tom stay in the fish business or go back to auto racing? What factors other than the income computations would be relevant to evaluating the potential future for Tom's fish farm?

P4-37 Accounting Concepts The principles of conservatism, matching, going concern, and revenue recognition are important concepts in determining the amounts to be included in financial statements prepared in accordance with generally accepted accounting principles. Each of the four situations outlined below illustrates at least one of these concepts. In each case, indicate which concept is most applicable and explain why it is important for decision makers. Describe why decision makers might find it useful.

a. Elkport Manufacturing is considering going out of business. Although it reports equipment at $275,000 on its balance sheet, it estimates that it would receive only $125,000 if it sells the equipment and would incur costs of $50,000 for removing the equipment and getting it ready for sale.

b. Candy Corporation produces premium chocolates at a cost of $15 per box and sells them for $25 per box. During the current month, Candy sold chocolates for $75,000 and incurred $60,000 of costs in producing inventory, some of which was not sold.

c. Allstar Oil Company recently discovered new oil reserves that should produce 100 million to 200 million barrels of oil. The current price of this grade of crude oil is $12 per barrel. The management of Allstar is confident it can sign a contract with a major oil distributer to sell the oil at $18 per barrel.

d. Kipper Computer Company has just signed a contract with a major retail company under which the retailer will purchase at least 5,000 computers from Kipper at a price that will guarantee Kipper a profit of $150 per computer. The computers will be delivered during the next two years, as instructed by the retailer.

P4-38 Operating Expenses Zorex Corporation recently sold one of its new BlunderBuss VII copy machines to Uptown Copy Center, Inc., and a second unit to Suburban Forms 4U. Uptown Copy is a high-volume operation located in the heart of the financial district; Suburban Forms is located in a small shopping center in a new residential area and does a great deal of custom work involving small, specialized jobs. The machines sold to the two companies are identical, and both companies paid the same purchase price of $18,500. Under generally accepted accounting principles, both of the copy centers must recognize as an expense each year an appropriate portion of the purchase price of their copy machines. You have an opportunity to compare the income statements of the two enterprises and note that the annual reported expense related to the original purchase price of the copy machines differs between the two companies.

The disclosure of accounting information is critical when outside parties attempt to evaluate and compare different enterprises. Keeping in mind the use of accounting information to evaluate and compare the two copy enterprises, answer the following questions:

a. What information about the BlunderBuss VII copy machines and the amounts reported as expense each period would you need to know to make an intelligent evaluation of the operation of the two copy centers? Indicate why you think the information would be important.

b. Which basic concept or concepts of accounting do you think are most important in determining the amount of the copy machine's original purchase price to report as expense each year? Explain.

c. Why might the two copy centers report different amounts annually as depreciation expense?

P4-39 Preparing Financial Statements The Historical Preservation Guild of the Town of Lower Switchback was created more than twenty years ago to help restore and preserve the hallowed history of the town. The guild was formed with hopes of restoring the town to its past glory. Five years ago, the guild was able to persuade Elmer Switch, the great grandson of the town's founder, to invest in their town. Elmer became a successful real estate developer after the family left Lower Switchback. Elmer formed a company, The Lower Switchback Corporation, to carry out the restoration. Many of the members of the guild and other town leaders invested in Elmer's new corporation. The corporation purchases property identified by the guild and, with the help of the guild, restores the buildings and lists them on the town's historical register. Each building is then sold to a new owner who is required to maintain the building in its original state and obtain approval from the guild for any significant change in its use. To date, the corporation has restored 10 buildings. Its work, along with the guild's restoration of the old courthouse, has had a significant impact on the town.

The purchase prices of the buildings acquired by the corporation have ranged from $275,000 to $410,000. The corporation spends between $150,000 and $250,000 on the restoration of each building. Much of the money needed to purchase and restore the buildings is borrowed from the Lower Switchback National Bank, a loyal supporter of the Historical Preservation Guild. To date, 8 of the 10 restored buildings have been sold and, in all cases, the buyer was able to obtain a bank loan and pay the corporation the full price.

a. Explain why the corporation needs financial statements.

b. Matching is an important part of the income measurement process for businesses. When the corporation undertakes the process of purchasing and restoring a building, how is the matching concept applied? What is the relevance for the management of the corporation? What is the relevance for the investors in the corporation?

c. Since each restoration project is unique, should the corporation prepare an income statement each year or for each project? Why?

d. How should the corporation value the two buildings that have not yet been sold?

EXPANDING YOUR HORIZONS

 C4-40 Obtaining Financial Information from the Library External decision makers have a number of sources of information available to them. A knowledge of the information available and how the various types of information differ from one another can be invaluable in selecting the information to be used for particular types of decisions.

a. Turn to the financial statements and other information from the annual report of Gateway, presented in Appendix A of this textbook. Look through the information to determine what is provided.
b. Go to your library and look up Gateway in *Moody's Industrial Manual* and compare the information provided by *Moody's* to that contained in the annual report in Appendix A. What information is included in the company's annual report that it is not included in *Moody's*? What information is provided in *Moody's* that is not provided in the annual report? Who might find the additional information contained in the annual report useful?
c. Look up Gateway's stock in the securities-price section of *The Wall Street Journal* or another newspaper that prints such information. What information is included there? Can that information also be found in the annual report or *Moody's*?
d. Look up the company in the *Value Line Investment Survey*. What information is included there? Can that information also be found in the annual report or *Moody's*? What information is provided by *Value Line* that is not provided in the annual report, *Moody's*, or *The Wall Street Journal*?
e. Briefly describe the differences in the nature of the information provided to decision makers in these four sources.

C4-41 Evaluating Transactions Misty Valley Estates is a real estate development company established nearly forty years ago when several thousand acres of land in California were purchased. Despite attempts to develop a wine-growing area, a commercial development park, a ski run, and several different residential areas, land sales have been slow. The owners of Misty Valley are relatively wealthy and are not under pressure to complete the development quickly. However, the owners would like to borrow money for other purposes and pledge some of the residential lots as collateral. A local banker has agreed to lend them 80 percent of the market value of the lots. The banker is aware of the following:

• The average cost of a lot at the time the land was purchased was $4,000.
• Four lots were sold two years ago for $16,000 each.
• Ten lots recently were purchased by a construction company at a price of $25,000 per lot. The company will start building as soon as houses are presold on the lots.
• Two lots were sold to the owner's son-in-law for potential future development purposes at $10,000 each.

• One lot recently was sold for $42,000 cash. Because the purchaser is considering moving to another state, he can request a refund if he does not start building a house on the lot by the end of the current year.
• A builder recently purchased for a total of $5,000 an option granting the right to buy 5 lots for $35,000 each. If the option is not exercised by the end of next year, it will expire and the $5,000 will not be refunded. If the option is exercised, the $5,000 will apply toward the total purchase price.
• A builder has reserved six lots on which to build custom homes. Although the builder has not purchased any of the lots, he has the right to purchase them at the average price paid for the last five comparable lots sold. The builder is delaying purchasing any lots until orders are received for homes.

The banker is aware of the importance of exchange transactions in valuing assets.

a. Which of the above activities qualify as exchange transactions? Explain your answer.
b. What market value do you think the banker should place on the lots? Why?

C4-42 Team Exercise: What to Report The audit of Belchfire Industries has just been completed, and for the first time in many years, the company will report a significant loss. Prior to the final preparation of the financial statements, the company's president and its chief financial officer meet with the auditor and propose a change to a different set of accounting methods. Using the proposed accounting methods, the company will show a small profit for the year. The president argues that the new methods better reflect the results of the company's operations than the current methods that have been used for many years. The chief financial officer isn't so sure that they do, but does like the bottom-line result. The auditor is convinced that the only reason for the change is to avoid reporting a loss. On the other hand, the proposed methods are considered acceptable to the accounting profession, and the change will be disclosed in the financial statements. The auditor is wavering because the president has threatened to find another auditor if agreement is not reached on the changes, and Belchfire is the audit firm's largest client. The audit manager's career would not seem terribly promising if the firm's largest client were lost. Nevertheless, the auditor feels the public might be misled by the change in accounting methods. Besides, the company would have to incur substantial additional audit fees if it changed auditors, and the financial statements would be delayed, not something the president wants.

Organize in teams of four or five people. One person play the role of the president, one play the chief financial officer, one play the auditor, and one or two play interested external parties (e.g., major stockholder, creditor). Present your position on the change in accounting methods and reasons supporting your position. Resolve the conflict and come to a solution.

C4-43 Business for Sale! Glancing through the local newspaper recently, you came across the following business opportunity:

Type of Business:	Monthly newsletter
Location:	Isle of Mancala
Market:	Local residents, upscale, approximately 1,200 subscribers
Population:	97,000 residents on the island
Overview:	Owned by an individual on the mainland who devotes part time to the newsletter. The newsletter employs an advertising manager who sells ads, and it contracts with freelance writers to write stories. The subscribers pay $34.95 annually. The newsletter has a renewal rate of 58% to 70%.
Price:	$150,000

Financial Information:

	1998	1999	2000
Gross revenue	$57,800	$86,400	$98,300
After-tax cash inflows	18,200	16,500	17,000

You have $150,000 to invest, and you wonder if this might not be a good business opportunity. Analyze this potential investment and address the following issues:

a. Comment on the qualitative characteristics of the information presented in the ad. Is the information
   (1) Relevant?
   (2) Reliable?
   (3) Understandable?
   (4) Consistent?
b. Can you determine from the information given what revenue recognition principles were applied?
c. Can you determine what expenses were matched with revenues?
d. What other information would you want so you could make an informed decision about this investment opportunity?

 C4-44 IBM's Financial Position Gain access to the consolidated financial statements of IBM. These may be obtained from the company, through many libraries, or from the Internet or other electronic databases. Focus on IBM's balance sheet.

a. Identify each of the items in the current asset section of the statement of financial position. As best you can, describe what each title means.
b. Look at the different lines of business indicated in IBM's statement of operations. To which lines of business do you think each of the current assets relates?
c. Does IBM have more or less debt than it did a year ago?
d. Would you judge IBM's overall financial position to be improving or deteriorating? Does IBM's statement of operations seem to support your view? Explain.

www.wiley.com/college/king

Internet Exercises: Visit our Web site for additional exercises.

Annual Report Project Part 4

Refer to the Annual Report Project, Part 1, at the end of Chapter 1. Using the annual report of the company you have chosen, and any other available information, answer the following questions, providing sources and computations where appropriate.

a. How many years' balance sheets are provided in your company's latest annual report? How many years' income statements are provided? How many years' cash flow statements are provided?

b. List the title or subject of each note to the financial statements of your company.

c. List four areas for which your company discloses accounting policy choices it has made. You need not state the specific accounting methods chosen.

d. Does your company have more than a single operating segment? If so, what are the different operating segments? What percentage of the company's revenues come from each operating segment? [*Note:* Information about operating segments is generally disclosed in one of the last notes to the financial statements. A few companies disclose segment information in management's discussion and analysis, usually appearing just before the financial statements in the annual report.]

e. Does your company operate outside of the United States? If so, for what specific geographic areas does your company list sales revenues?

CHAPTER FIVE

Understanding Income

REVIEW

Chapter 3 discussed the importance of cash flows for financial decision making and the type of accounting information presented with respect to cash flows. Chapter 4 examined the basic concepts that underlie the accrual accounting approach to measuring income and financial position under generally accepted accounting principles.

WHERE THIS CHAPTER FITS

This chapter builds on Chapters 3 and 4 by discussing how reported income is used for estimating future cash flows and making decisions. The chapter discusses the elements of income, the measurement of income using the accrual method, and the relationship between income and cash flows. The chapter concludes with a more detailed look at the elements of the income statement.

LOOKING AHEAD

Chapter 6 concentrates on another financial statement, the balance sheet, and discusses the importance of financial position.

Boy! I saw in the paper this morning that Bonanza Motors had income of more than a billion dollars last year. What I couldn't do with all that money! I wonder what they do with all that cash—or is it really cash? I get my paycheck every Friday and cash it on the way home. I wonder how Bonanza gets its income. Who cashes Bonanza's paycheck?

"Reading a statement of income is a lot like looking at a barometer to get a weather forecast. These reports can help [readers] determine if the [companies] are in the center of a financial storm, such as decreasing revenue, or are caught up in an industrywide tsunami."[1]

[1] Thomas Hoffman, "Statement of Income," *Computerworld* (June 14, 1999), p. 65.

Every day the financial press carries hundreds of stories about American businesses, what they are doing, and what is happening to them. While these stories may all deal with different aspects of business, the common thread tying them together is an emphasis on income. Whatever the subject of the story, readers want to know what the effect is on income. If an employee layoff is announced, the anticipated future cost savings are discussed. If the story reports the development of a new drug by a pharmaceutical company, invariably an estimate of the anticipated impact on company revenues and earnings is included.

Why is such an emphasis placed on income? Because reported income provides a measure of financial success and reflects the creation of wealth. Many of us value other things in life more highly than financial success and wealth, but no one can deny that having the money we need, or perhaps want, is important. A steady income allows us to reach our goals and to achieve a certain type of security and stability.

Whether good or bad, society focuses on the net income measure so much that the phrase "the bottom line," referring to the bottom line of the income statement, net income, has now come to mean *the key point* in a discussion. Health-care experts state that the bottom line is that health-care costs will rise 10 percent per year for the next five years. Sociologists tell us the bottom line is that we are losing the war on drugs. These statements emphasize the single most important aspect of the discussion. In financial reporting, the aspect usually considered most important is net income.

Determining business income is complex, and many accounting decisions are made before arriving at the "bottom line." This chapter will help you develop an understanding of business income and improve your ability to use reported income to make financial decisions. When you have completed the chapter you should be able to:

1. Discuss what income is and explain its importance for forecasting.

2. Understand how income recognition is accomplished in accrual accounting through revenue realization and expense matching.

3. Explain the difference between cash flow and accrual-basis income, and analyze the relationship between the two measures of business activity.

4. Describe the elements normally included in income and reported in the income statement, and discuss who uses the information and how.

THE NATURE OF INCOME

Information for Decisions

The income statement provides summary measures of the results of a company's activities for a given period of time. Understanding a company's reported income helps financial statement users answer questions such as these: Has this company been successful in its operations? Which income items are most relevant for my projections of future income and cash flows?

Net income represents the change in owners' equity during a period, excluding the effects of any additional investments or withdrawals by the owners. It is computed as the difference between revenues and expenses.

If a company's activities during a period are successful, positive net income will be reported, and the owners' equity of the company will increase. The company's **net assets**, or assets minus liabilities, will also increase because the accounting equation, discussed in Chapter 2, ensures that assets minus liabilities always equals owners' equity. If a company's activities are not successful, the company will report negative net income, referred to as a **net loss**, and its net assets and owner's equity will decrease. Sometimes other terms, such as *net earnings* or *profit*, are used in place of the term *net income*.

Income is earned continuously by an entity but is measured for a particular period, such as a year or month. Even though the activities producing the income may be ongoing, measurements are made periodically so that decision makers will have timely information.

THE INCOME STATEMENT

The **income statement** reports the results of a company's activities for a specified period of time. It identifies the major sources of the company's income and the different costs incurred in running the business. The final result of all of the firm's activities during the period is

EXHIBIT 5-1	THE PROCTER & GAMBLE COMPANY INCOME STATEMENT

CONSOLIDATED STATEMENTS OF EARNINGS

Amounts in Millions Except Per Share Amounts	Years Ended June 30		
	1998	1997	1996
Net Sales	**$37,154**	$35,764	$35,284
Cost of products sold	**21,064**	20,510	20,938
Marketing, research, and administrative expenses	**10,035**	9,766	9,531
Operating Income	**6,055**	5,488	4,815
Interest expense	**548**	457	484
Other income, net	**201**	218	338
Earnings Before Income Taxes	**5,708**	5,249	4,669
Income taxes	**1,928**	1,834	1,623
Net Earnings	**$ 3,780**	$ 3,415	$ 3,046
Basic Net Earnings Per Common Share	**$2.74**	$2.43	$2.14
Diluted Net Earnings Per Common Share	**$2.56**	$2.28	$2.01

summarized in the bottom line of the income statement, net income. The income statement for Procter & Gamble (www.pg.com) is fairly typical of a manufacturing company's income statement and is shown in Exhibit 5–1.

Although not all of an entity's activities and events during the period appear in the income statement, the items that are included are taken directly from the accounting records of the company. The company's many revenue and expense items are summarized into a relatively few categories and then reported in the income statement. Any event not recognized in the accounts of the entity cannot appear in the income statement.

OPERATING AND NONOPERATING INCOME

The income statement shows the dollar amount of sales of the company's products or services during the period, listed as revenues, sales, or sales revenue. Many companies use the term *net sales* to indicate the amount of sales revenue earned after deducting sales returns and allowances. The statement also shows the cost of goods and services used up by the company during the period in producing revenues, listed as expenses. Revenues and expenses are usually related to the company's central operations, its primary reason for being.

The income statement also may report a number of items that are included in the computation of net income for the period that are not directly related to the company's principal operations. For example, a manufacturing company might report interest income from temporarily investing excess cash, or it might report a major fire loss in a particular year. To help financial statement users distinguish between items directly related to normal ongoing operations and those not directly related to operations and not regularly recurring, income statements often provide a subtotal, labeled *operating income*, obtained by deducting operating expenses from revenues, followed by a section titled *nonoperating income and expenses*. Decision makers typically place greater emphasis on operating rather than nonoperating items when projecting future income and cash flows.

THE IMPORTANCE OF INCOME

Information for Decisions

Investors increase their wealth by earning income on their investments. Often the success of their decisions, and of the businesses they are evaluating, is judged by the amount of income earned. Investors and creditors need to understand the importance of income to answer questions such as these: Can I expect this company to prosper in the future? What levels of cash flows with respect to this company can be expected in the future?

To understand why income is important, think about why individuals who own resources allow others to use those resources. They do it with the expectation that they will get back the value of their resources plus some extra amount for allowing others to use those resources. In other words, they do it to increase their wealth by earning income. When you put money in a savings account, you do it to earn interest. You want to increase the amount of cash you have so you can later purchase things you need or want.

The success of a person's decisions and efforts is often judged by the amount of income earned. Similarly, the success of a business is judged by its income. Income is important because it provides additional resources that can be used to reach goals. Decision makers use income-related information to help assess a company's projected earnings, anticipated cash flows, and value.

A MEASURE OF CONTRIBUTION TO SOCIETY

By examining income statement information, decision makers can evaluate the degree to which a company's contributions to society are valued. If the company is well managed and provides something of value to society, it will be rewarded with profits. For example, a company that takes raw materials such as steel, aluminum, plastic, and glass and, using labor, technology, and machinery, efficiently transforms the raw materials into automobiles, provides something society wants and will make a profit. If, however, the company operates inefficiently and wastes society's resources because, for example, it uses outdated technology, it may suffer losses. A company's income serves as a measure of whether the company plays a valuable role in society and, therefore, is likely to prosper.

A BASIS FOR FORECASTING CASH FLOWS

For a company to remain in business, it must generate sufficient cash to acquire resources on a continuing basis and purchase new assets as existing ones are sold, used up, become obsolete, or cease functioning efficiently. Sufficient cash also must be generated to reward owners so they remain interested in continuing the enterprise. Income is an important factor in the overall financial picture of a business because it normally is, and should be, the primary source of cash for a company. (See In Practice 5-1.)

In Practice 5-1

POSITRON CORP.

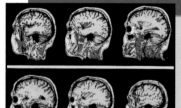

The following report from *The Wall Street Journal* makes clear the connection between income and cash:

> "Positron Corp., Houston, said it is running short of cash and will need either a cash infusion or a jump in sales to keep operating beyond Dec. 31. . . . The company attributed its cash shortage to an inability to sell imaging systems in large enough quantities to be profitable."[2]

ANALYSIS

Although Positron was able to keep operating temporarily by borrowing, its financial condition continued to deteriorate. By early 1999, with its short-term obligations fifty times the amount of its cash and receivables, it seemed to be facing bankruptcy or being taken over by another company. Shortly thereafter, however, the company seemed to be moving toward profitability. Sales must be Positron's primary continuing source of cash or the company has no long-run future.

[2] "Shortage of Cash Threatens Ability to Keep Operating," *The Wall Street Journal* (November 16, 1995), p. B9.

Because reported income is useful for forecasting future cash flows, investors place heavy emphasis on income when choosing from among investment alternatives. Ventures reporting very little income are likely, in the long-run, to generate little or no cash flow to their investors, while those reporting substantial income are more likely to provide significant cash flows to investors.

Beyond just knowing the amount of an entity's income, an understanding of how income is computed and reported is important in assessing the cash flow potential of a business. Often, the bottom line is not a sufficient basis on which to make a decision, and knowing the elements that contributed to the income reported by a business is important. Unexpected, unusual, and nonrecurring events do occur, and investors who rely solely on the amount of reported earnings to measure success may incorrectly assess future earnings potential and likely cash returns.

You Decide 5-1

DOES THE TYPE OF INCOME MAKE A DIFFERENCE?

Suppose you are deciding whether to invest in Company A or Company B, both of which report the same net income. Further analysis discloses that almost all of the income of Company A last year came from regular business operations, while nearly all of Company B's income was from a one-time sale of a factory building no longer used. In which company would you invest? Which type of income would be most likely to continue in the future and to result in steady cash flows to investors? Explain your answers.

THE CONNECTION BETWEEN THE PAST AND THE FUTURE

People make decisions about the future, not the past. Yet, much of the information used for those decisions is about the past. Financial statement users analyze information relating to current and past income so they may better understand the important relationships surrounding a business's operations. Such an understanding can help decision makers better forecast future earnings and cash flows. Knowing a company's reported income for last year does not automatically provide a good estimate of next year's income or cash distributions to owners, but it does provide one input for forming judgments about the future.

INCOME STATEMENT USERS

Many different types of decision makers rely on financial statements, as discussed in Chapter 2. Exhibit 5–2 lists some of the different types of users of income statement information and identifies some examples of how the information might be useful for their decisions. Although income statement information is only one of many types of information used by decision makers, there is no doubt about its importance.

EXHIBIT 5-2 USES AND USERS OF INCOME STATEMENT INFORMATION

INTERNAL USERS:

Owners/Managers
- Evaluate success in meeting established goals
- Compute bonus or other contingent compensation
- Project future cash distributions
- Determine success in achieving operating efficiencies
- Assess success in generating recurring operating income
- Manage effects of reported income on taxes and regulation
- Assess success of previous actions
- Identify areas for potential cost-cutting or productivity gains

Employees and Labor Unions
- Assess stability of employment opportunities
- Determine effects of increased pension, health-care, and other benefit costs
- Support collective bargaining negotiations
- Compute profit-sharing amounts

EXTERNAL USERS:

Owners/Investors
- Evaluate success in meeting investment goals
- Project future cash distributions
- Evaluate performance of management
- Assess long-run profit potential
- Compare performance with other companies in industry
- Identify areas for potential cost-cutting or productivity gains through comparisons with other companies and other periods

Creditors
- Assess the adequacy of income to cover interest cost
- Evaluate the potential for long-run profitability to provide adequate cash to retire debt
- Determine whether provisions of debt-related agreements have been met

Vendors
- Assess stability of company as customer
- Evaluate credit-worthiness
- Project future purchases

Taxing Agencies, Regulators, and Public Interest Groups
- Evaluate relationship between taxable income and income reported on income statement
- Assess fairness of overall return to owners
- Evaluate legitimacy and fairness of sources of income
- Evaluate reasonableness of specific expense categories

COMPONENTS OF INCOME

Information for Decisions

A company's income is the result of a number of different elements. Decision makers need to know how each of these elements affects net income, how these elements are reported in the financial statements, and which elements are critical for particular decisions so questions such as the following can be answered: Is the company's level of business increasing or decreasing? Is the company's revenue enough higher than the cost of inventory sold to cover other expenses and pay a return to me? Can I be sure that the company's profit does not result just from the sale of its operating assets or other resources needed for future operations?

A number of different elements are included in the computation of an entity's net income. The most important categories are revenues and expenses. In very simple situations, net income is computed as the difference between revenues and expenses. Computed income is always reported in the income statement for a specific period of time, such as one year.

REVENUES

Revenues are generated from an entity's ongoing central operations. Revenues represent increases in an enterprise's assets from selling goods and services.

Because the main reason that business enterprises exist is to sell products and services to customers for a profit, the following apply with respect to revenues:

1. Any sales or transfers within the company do not generate revenues; only sales to outsiders generate revenues.

2. Income from activities that are peripheral to the business's central operations is not included in revenues.

Many large companies are organized into departments or divisions, and they often transfer goods or services from one division to another. For example, a computer manufacturer may produce circuit boards, some of which are sold directly to customers and some of which are transferred to another department for inclusion in computers manufactured by the company. The amount of circuit board sales to outsiders would be recognized as revenue, while the transfers to the other department would not. The other department would recognize revenues when it sold the computers it produced. Because the business enterprise as a whole is viewed as the accounting entity, only sales to parties outside of the entity may be reported as revenues in the company's income statement.

Income may come from a number of sources, but revenues result only from the company's primary activities. The sale of a retail company's products to a customer gives rise to revenue, but the sale of an old delivery truck does not because the company is not in the business of selling old delivery trucks. Because financial statement users forecast future revenues, income, and cash flows based on past revenues and earnings, reporting irregularly or infrequently occurring items in the same manner as those related to normal operations could prove misleading. (See In Practice 5-2.)

In Practice 5-2

AMERITECH

Ameritech's income statement included revenues of $15.998 billion from its primary operations, including local phone service and directory activities. In addition, the company reported other income of $390 million, consisting largely of income from investments in foreign telecommunications companies and gains on sales of investments in telecommunications companies.

ANALYSIS

The other income sources were not considered part of the company's central operations and, therefore, were not included in revenues even though they were included in the computation of the company's net income. [www.ameritech.com]

EXPENSES

Expenses reflect the cost of goods and services used up during the period in conducting the company's central operations. They arise when assets are consumed or liabilities are incurred, and they represent expired costs, costs that have no service potential for the future. Expenses reduce net income.

Businesses incur many different types of operating costs. Typical costs include, among others, those incurred for labor, raw materials, goods purchased for resale to customers, supplies, equipment, buildings, and income taxes. Ultimately, these costs are reported as expenses in the income statement as they are matched against revenues to compute net income.

Merchandising firms, such as Wal-Mart, purchase goods from their suppliers and resell those goods to their customers. Manufacturing firms, such as Ford Motor Company, purchase raw materials and parts from their suppliers and fashion the raw materials and parts together to produce a finished product. For both types of companies, the largest and most important expense item is usually the cost to the company of purchasing or manufacturing the goods or products it sells. This amount normally is disclosed as a separate item in the income statement labeled **cost of goods sold** or **cost of sales**. Ralston Purina Company (www.ralston.com) reports *Cost of product sold* equal to almost 50 percent of net sales, which is about 57 percent of its total expenses.

Service organizations, such as Andersen Consulting, rather than selling a product, provide some service to customers (often referred to as clients) for a fee. For these types of enterprises, wage and employee benefits expense typically is the largest single expense item. Ameritech Corporation, for example, reported labor expenses, including pensions and other employee benefits, of more than $4 billion in 1998. These expenses were the largest single operating expense item for the year, accounting for about one-third of total operating expenses.

GAINS AND LOSSES

Gains and losses typically occur relatively infrequently and arise from events not directly associated with the entity's ongoing central operations. Gains increase net income and losses decrease net income.

A CLOSER LOOK AT

GAINS AND LOSSES

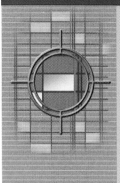

A manufacturing company owns an old warehouse it no longer uses, and the warehouse has a book value of $400,000. The **book value** or **carrying amount** of an item is the amount at which it is shown in the accounting records, or on the books. If the warehouse is uninsured and is completely destroyed by fire, the company would record a loss equal to the book value of the asset destroyed, $400,000. Obviously the destruction of the warehouse by a fire is not an event central to the operations of the company. Similarly, if the company had sold the warehouse (prior to the fire) for $500,000, it would recognize a $100,000 gain equal to the difference between the selling price of the warehouse and its book value. Although the company might sell unused or old assets from time to time, it is not in that business.

NONOPERATING INCOME AND EXPENSES

Items classified as other income and expenses stem from activities that are incidental to the primary focus of the business. Examples include interest income from temporary investments and rental income from leasing an unused portion of the company's factory. Other expenses might include interest expense and costs of reorganizing a struggling company.

MEASUREMENT OF INCOME

Information for Decisions

A number of different methods of measuring income exist. Financial statement users need to understand the methods that are used to measure income in practice so they can answer questions such as these: Does the company's reported income provide me with useful information for assessing the company's future prospects? Is the company's reported income comparable with that reported by other companies?

We have seen that decision makers rely on net income for assessing success and forecasting future earnings and cash flows. So, how do you measure income? Does everyone measure income in the same way? Is the net income figure from one company's income statement comparable to the net income figure from another company's income statement? Unfortunately, income measurement is a complex issue. (See In Practice 5-3.)

In Practice 5-3

THE WALT DISNEY COMPANY

In 1992, The Walt Disney Company opened its Euro Disney theme park near Paris, France. Euro Disney reported operating losses after it was opened. However, because of the financing agreement between Disney and Euro Disney and the financial reporting procedures used, Disney was able to report income from its investment in Euro Disney in 1990 and 1991, even before the theme park opened, and again in 1992 after the park operated at a loss.

ANALYSIS

Because of the complexity of some income measurement and recognition methods, a careful analysis of the methods being employed is essential. The methods are disclosed in the notes to the financial statements. [www.disney.com]

General rules exist for the recognition and measurement of income, but the rules are sufficiently flexible that the income numbers reported by different companies are not all comparable. Two primary methods of measuring and reporting income are found in practice, both

| EXHIBIT 5-3 | **CASH-BASIS VS. ACCRUAL-BASIS RECOGNITION** |

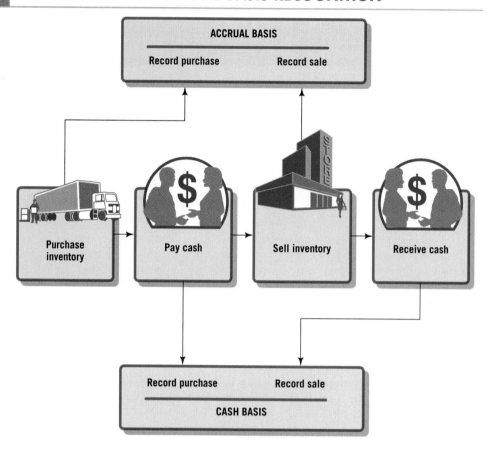

of which were illustrated briefly in Chapter 1. The cash basis for income recognition is based on the amounts and timing of cash inflows and outflows. The accrual basis of accounting is based on a series of recognition and measurement rules and places much less emphasis on the timing of cash flows. Exhibit 5–3 contrasts the two methods for a purchase and sale of inventory. The accrual basis is required to be used for financial statements prepared in accordance with generally accepted accounting principles.

INCOME RECOGNITION ON THE CASH BASIS

Information for Decisions

With the cash basis of accounting, cash receipts are treated as revenues and cash disbursements are treated as expenses. When decisions are based on cash-basis financial statements, investors and creditors need to be able to answer questions such as these: Why is the cash basis of accounting being used? Do cash-basis financial statements provide an appropriate basis for assessing this company?

Although not considered generally accepted for financial reporting, the cash basis of income measurement is widely used by individuals and small businesses that do not need audited financial statements prepared in accordance with generally accepted accounting principles. Under the cash basis, cash inflows (receipts) are generally treated as revenues and cash outflows (disbursements) as expenses. Cash-basis income is the difference between cash receipts and disbursements. Investments by and distributions to owners are never included in the computation of income.

The primary advantage of using cash receipts and disbursements as a measure of income is the simplicity of the system. Cash-basis income can be computed quickly by deducting total cash disbursements from total cash receipts. Income can be more objectively determined under the cash basis than under accrual accounting.

A simple listing of cash receipts and payments may be sufficient to provide an accurate picture of the activities of businesses that conduct virtually all of their transactions for cash and do not hold assets beyond the end of the period. For example, the vendor who hawks hot dogs in the stands at baseball games may operate entirely on a cash basis. The vendor may pay the concessionaire cash for a steaming tray of Old Barnyard Hot Dogs and sell them to hungry fans at a price set by the concessionaire. Each trip into the stadium is a new business venture, with the success of the venture known immediately. Determining income for the day is a simple matter in this setting. The change in the amount of cash in the vendor's pocket between the beginning and end of the game provides a quick measure of income.

The cash-basis method generally proves adequate in simple situations. As the business activity becomes more complex, however, use of this method may result in reported information that is inaccurate and perhaps misleading.

CASH-BASIS REVENUE RECOGNITION

In simple cases, the receipt of cash occurs at completion of the sales process and removes any uncertainty as to the amount to be received from the sale. However, cash is often not received by the seller at the time of delivery of goods or services. Instead, a sale may take place at one point in time, with cash received at some other time. Three alternatives with respect to the timing of a sale and the receipt of cash from the sale are as follows:

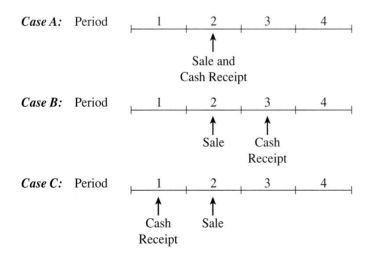

Case A is the simplest situation, one in which the sale and cash collection take place at the same time, as with the hot dog vendor.

Case B illustrates the most common type of sale between commercial entities. A sale is made on credit, with the cash payment made a few weeks following the sale. When Kmart takes delivery of a shipment of Tide laundry detergent, the receiving clerk on the loading dock does not hand the truck driver cash for the shipment. Instead, Kmart has agreed to send a check to Procter & Gamble, the maker of Tide, within a few weeks. Should P&G recognize the revenue from the sale at the time of delivery, the time the cash is received, or at some other time? If P&G were using cash-basis accounting (which it does not), the revenue would be recognized when the check was received from Kmart.

Case C portrays a situation in which the seller receives the cash before delivering the goods or service. For example, when Trans World Airlines sells for $960 a fully refundable ticket for travel to Hawaii five months later, the cash is received by TWA long before the travel actually takes place. If TWA were using cash-basis accounting, the revenue from the sale would be recognized when the cash was received. Suppose the traveler decided not to go and asked for a refund of the cash paid?

CASH-BASIS EXPENSE RECOGNITION

When income is computed on a cash basis, cash outflows are treated as expenses in the period in which payment is made. Total expenses for the period are easy to determine using the cash basis because they equal total cash payments, excluding cash distributions to owners. A cash payment represents the final step in acquiring goods and services from others and removes any uncertainty regarding the cost.

INCOME RECOGNITION USING THE ACCRUAL METHOD

Information for Decisions

All major companies use accrual accounting to match costs incurred with the associated benefits received to determine net income. Decision makers need to understand how reported income statement numbers reflect accrual-basis revenue recognition rules and the matching concept to answer questions such as these: Have the company's operating efforts during the period been successful? Does the company's net income reflect all of the company's sales during the current period, even though the balance sheet indicates that amounts are still owed to the company for some sales? Have all of the company's costs of making the current period's sales been deducted from income in the current period?

The accrual basis of accounting is used by all businesses that prepare financial statements in accordance with generally accepted accounting principles. While the cash basis emphasizes cash inflows and outflows as a basis for revenue and expense recognition, the accrual basis does not. Under accrual-basis accounting, the timing of cash flows is relatively unimportant for determining when to recognize revenues and expenses. Revenue and expense recognition may occur before, at the time of, or after the associated cash flow takes place, depending on the circumstances.

THE MATCHING PROCESS

One of the key concepts that differentiates the cash basis from the accrual basis is the matching concept. The central focus of accrual accounting is matching costs and benefits so financial statement users can see the direct period-by-period results of an entity's activities. The matching process involves determining in which period specific benefits are received by the enterprise and then recognizing in that period both the benefits and the costs incurred to get the benefits. This allows a comparison between costs and benefits so financial statement users can assess how successful the company has been in incurring costs that generate benefits in excess of those costs.

Most business activities are aimed at acquiring one particular benefit, sales revenue. Therefore, much of accrual accounting involves determining when to recognize revenue and what costs are associated with the revenue recognized during the period.

ACCRUAL-BASIS REVENUE RECOGNITION

In general, accrual accounting recognizes revenues when they are realized and earned. **Realization** is the process of converting noncash assets into cash or claims to cash. For revenues to be recognized, two conditions ordinarily must be met:

1. An exchange must take place.
2. The earning process must be substantially complete.

In a typical sales transaction, a seller provides a product or service to a purchaser in exchange for cash or for the purchaser's promise to pay a specific amount of cash in the future. The exchange provides evidence that two independent parties, the seller and purchaser, have agreed on a value for the transaction, and this exchange amount provides objective evidence for recognition in the accounts.

Not only must an exchange take place for revenue to be recognized, but the revenue also must be earned. In determining when revenues are earned, a "critical-events" approach is typically used. The earning process is considered substantially complete once the critical event in the earning process has taken place.

What is the critical event? That depends on the situation. The critical event is the event, or events, most crucial for earning the right to cash. For example, if you manufacture shoes, you might be able to produce millions of pairs of shoes, but you are not successful unless someone buys the shoes; the critical event is the sale or exchange transaction. Thus, if revenue is earned from the sale of a product, the sale is normally considered the critical event, and the earning process is considered complete at the time the goods are delivered to the customer. When the local J. C. Penney store sells you a pair of shoes, the earning process is complete once you give the sales clerk cash or sign a charge-card slip and the sales clerk gives you the shoes.

If revenues are earned by providing a service, the earning process is usually considered substantially complete once the service has been provided and the revenues are billable. When the accounting firm of Deloitte & Touche completes an audit, it has the right to bill the client, and the revenue has been earned.

If revenues are earned by allowing others to use the company's assets, revenues are earned as those assets are made available to the other party after that party has agreed to pay for their use. For example, if a real estate management company rents a building to another company for $25,000 per year on a three-year lease, the real estate company would recognize $25,000 rental revenue each year regardless of whether the rent was paid in cash annually, all in advance, or all at the end. Similarly, banks lending money recognize interest revenue over the time the money lent is used by the borrower.

Note that revenue is recognized under accrual accounting whether cash is received immediately or not. The timing of revenue recognition is based on the recognition criteria rather than the timing of the cash inflow. In most cases, collection of cash once the purchaser has promised to pay is not considered to be a critical event in the earning process. Before extending credit, a seller normally evaluates the creditworthiness of the purchaser and concludes that payment is likely. Some purchasers ultimately might fail to pay, but special procedures discussed in Chapter 8 are used to account for this possibility.

ACCRUAL-BASIS EXPENSE RECOGNITION

Expenses are generally recognized under accrual accounting based on the matching concept. For each cost that an enterprise incurs in connection with its operations, the following determinations must be made:

1. What benefit will be received from having incurred the cost?
2. When will the benefit be received?

The cost is reported as an expense (an expired cost) in the period in which the associated benefit is received by the entity. If the benefit is received in more than one period, the cost is allocated to each of the periods in which a benefit is received, and an expense is recognized each period roughly in proportion to the benefits received.

A CLOSER LOOK AT

MATCHING COSTS AND BENEFITS

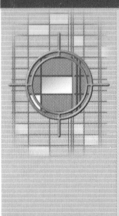

Ajax Corporation purchases a truck for $50,000 to use for deliveries of merchandise to its customers. The truck is expected to last for 200,000 miles and then will be scrapped. It is purchased at the end of 1999 but is not used until the following year. In 2000, the truck is driven 20,000 miles, and during 2001 it is driven 30,000 miles. What is the benefit to be received from incurring the $50,000 cost? The expected benefit is the use of the truck to deliver merchandise. What amount of depreciation expense associated with the truck should be recognized in 1999, 2000, and 2001? Because the truck was not used in 1999, no benefit was received from it and no expense should be recognized. In 2000 and 2001, expense would be recognized in proportion to the benefits received; that is, expense would be computed based on the usage of the truck during each year in relation to the total service potential of the truck:

$$2000: (20{,}000 \text{ miles} \div 200{,}000 \text{ miles}) \times \$50{,}000 = \$5{,}000$$
$$2001: (30{,}000 \text{ miles} \div 200{,}000 \text{ miles}) \times \$50{,}000 = \underline{\underline{\$7{,}500}}$$

The primary purpose for operating a business is to generate revenue and related profits. Therefore, matching most often involves tying costs to associated revenues so that both can be included in the computation of income for the same period.

A CLOSER LOOK AT

MATCHING COSTS WITH REVENUES

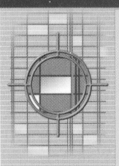

Benlow Company purchases inventory in 2000 for $70,000 cash and sells half of it on account (credit is extended) during 2001 for $50,000. In addition, the company pays a salesperson a 5 percent commission on the 2001 sale. How much expense should be recognized in 2001? The $35,000 ($70,000 ÷ 2) of inventory sold in 2001 produced a benefit in that year and should be expensed. In addition, the sales commission is a cost associated with producing the sale. Therefore, cost of goods sold expense of $35,000 and sales commission expense of $2,500 ($50,000 × .05) would be recognized in 2001 and matched against the sales revenue of $50,000, resulting in income of $12,500.

As in the case of revenue recognition, a cash flow does not necessarily occur at the time an expense is recognized under the accrual model. Some expenses are recognized before the cash payments are made and others are recognized after the cash payment is made. In the Benlow Company example, inventory was purchased in 2000 and a cash outflow occurred at that time. However, no expense was recognized then for the inventory cost. Only when some of the inventory was sold in 2001 was expense (cost of goods sold) recognized, even though no cash outflow for the inventory occurred during that year.

Some costs provide benefits other than revenues. However, these costs are still matched with the benefits they produce. A typical example is the purchase of a three-year insurance policy with all premiums paid in advance. The benefit received is insurance protection, and it is received over a three-year period. Accordingly, the premium is recognized as an expense over the three-year period during which the insurance coverage is received.

RECOGNITION OF GAINS AND LOSSES

Under accrual accounting, gains are generally recognized when realized, largely in the same manner as revenues. The treatment of losses, on the other hand, is more conservative. Losses are sometimes recognized before there is objective evidence that they have occurred. Losses are recognized when both of the following two conditions exist:

1. It is probable that an asset has been impaired or a liability incurred.
2. The amount of the loss can be reasonably estimated.

SUMMARY OF ACCRUAL-BASIS RECOGNITION RULES

Exhibit 5–4 summarizes the accrual-basis recognition criteria for revenues, expenses, gains, and losses. Note that the criteria listed are general in nature and, although they apply in most cases, there are some exceptions.

GENERAL ACCRUAL-BASIS RECOGNITION CRITERIA   EXHIBIT 5-4

Revenues
  Recognized when realized and earned, meaning both of the following conditions are met:
    1. An exchange has taken place.
    2. The earning process is substantially complete.

Application to:
  Sales of goods: when the goods are delivered to the customer and the customer agrees to pay
  Sales of services: when, after the customer has agreed to pay for specified services, the services have been provided to the customer and the amounts are billable
  Allowing others to use assets: as time passes, during which the assets are available for the use of another party after that party has contracted to pay for their use

Expenses
  Recognized through the matching process by recognizing the expense in the same period as the associated revenue or other associated benefit

Gains
  Recognized when realized

Losses
  Recognized when (1) it is probable that an asset has been impaired or a liability incurred and (2) the amount can be estimated

RELATIONSHIP BETWEEN INCOME AND CASH FLOWS

Information for Decisions

Net income reported on an accrual basis can be a better predictor of future cash flows than the company's current cash flows. Financial statement users who understand the relationship between income and cash flows can use this information to their advantage and answer questions such as these: What are the major factors that cause a difference between the company's net income and its net cash flow, and how should these differences affect my assessment of future cash flows? What does the company's net income imply about future cash flows?

In general, a close association between income and cash flows exists over the long run. Revenues generate cash inflows, while expenses generate cash outflows. If revenues exceed expenses, income results, and ultimately net cash flows can be expected to be positive.

Although these relationships exist, differences are found in the timing of when revenues and expenses are recognized using the accrual method and when the associated cash flows occur. Accounting recognizes changes in cash when cash flows actually occur. Revenues and expenses, on the other hand, are recognized using the accrual method based on the specific recognition criteria previously discussed. The key point to remember is that revenue and expense recognition is generally not determined by when the related cash flows occur.

Over a long enough period of time, the differences between cash flow and income disappear, but because businesses report periodically, substantial differences often exist between accrual-basis and cash-basis income. These differences could significantly affect decisions made using the reported information.

USEFULNESS OF ALTERNATIVE INCOME FIGURES

As we have seen, cash-basis accounting is simple and, therefore, is generally less costly and requires less expertise to apply. In some very simple cases, as with the hot dog vendor, cash-basis income provides an accurate measure of the results of enterprise activity. Many business situations are much more complex, however, and cash inflows are not always associated so directly with efforts and accomplishments. Several examples may be helpful in examining the usefulness of cash-basis and accrual-basis measures of income, as presented in You Decide 5-2, 5-3, and 5-4.

The usefulness of the alternative income figures should be judged based on how well they capture what has occurred during each of the periods and the extent to which each is helpful in projecting future earnings and cash flows.

CASH FLOWS OR ACCRUAL-BASIS INCOME?

Recall that an important objective of financial reporting is to assist financial statement users in assessing future cash flows. But, if cash flows are so important and net income often differs from cash flow, why bother computing net income? A significant amount of research in the fields of accounting and finance has focused on the usefulness of different types of in-

CASH-BASIS VERSUS ACCRUAL-BASIS INCOME MEASURES

The Allen Shoe Store started business in March. During the month, the store purchased $10,000 of shoes, but had no sales. During April, the store sold for $8,000 half of the shoes purchased in March; no additional shoes were purchased in March; no additional shoes were purchased in April. During May, the store sold for $8,000 the remaining shoes purchased in March and also purchased an additional $12,000 of shoes. All purchases and sales were for cash. The activities can be pictured in the following timeline:

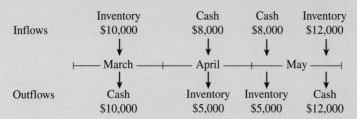

	Inventory $10,000	Cash $8,000	Cash $8,000	Inventory $12,000
Inflows	↓	↓	↓	↓
	├── March ──┼── April ──┼── May ──┤			
Outflows	↓	↓	↓	↓
	Cash $10,000	Inventory $5,000	Inventory $5,000	Cash $12,000

Income (loss) computed on a cash basis is the difference between the cash inflows and the cash outflows for each of the months, as follows:

$$\text{March: } \$0 - \$10,000 = \underline{\underline{\$(10,000)}}$$
$$\text{April: } \$8,000 - \$0 = \underline{\underline{\$\ \ 8,000}}$$
$$\text{May: } \$8,000 - \$12,000 = \underline{\underline{\$\ \ (4,000)}}$$

Income on an accrual basis is computed as the difference between Allen's revenues and expenses. In March, no sales take place, so no revenue is recognized. Because no benefit is received during the period, no expense is recognized. In April, revenue of $8,000 is recognized, and the cost associated with the sales is the cost of the inventory sold, $5,000; this amount is expensed during the period. In May, revenue of $8,000 and expense of $5,000 are recognized, as in April. Accrual-basis net income for the three months is summarized as follows:

$$\text{March: } \$0 - \$0 = \underline{\underline{\$\ \ \ \ 0}}$$
$$\text{April: } \ \ \$8,000 - \$5,000 = \underline{\underline{\$3,000}}$$
$$\text{May: } \ \ \ \$8,000 - \$5,000 = \underline{\underline{\$3,000}}$$

Compare the income computed under the cash basis with that computed under the accrual method and think about which set of income numbers would be more useful to you if you were thinking of investing in the Allen Shoe Store. Which income figures provide the more accurate and useful portrayal of the store's activities for the three-month period? Which do you think would be most useful for projecting future earnings and cash flows?

formation for predicting future cash flows. This research indicates that accrual-basis net income predicts future cash flows better than information about current cash flows. The matching process used in computing accrual-basis net income removes much of the random impact reflected in cash flows of highly variable factors such as major purchases of plant and equipment and early or late payments of receivables and liabilities. Net income results

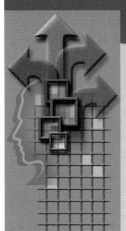

You Decide 5-3

CASH-BASIS VERSUS ACCRUAL-BASIS INCOME MEASURES

Peppy Puppy Magazine, a new publication, accepts subscriptions only on a calendar-year basis. The company, at a cost of $4,000, advertises on television during the first several days of each year, and takes orders over the phone. All subscriptions start with the January issue. All orders are paid within a few days, and the company pays cash for all costs it incurs. The company starts business by offering a special three-year subscription for only $60, payable in advance. At the beginning of the first year of business, 1,000 subscriptions are sold at the special price. In each of the next two years, 2,000 one-year subscriptions are sold for $25 each. Each subscription costs the company $15 per year for printing and mailing. The company's activities can be pictured in the following timeline:

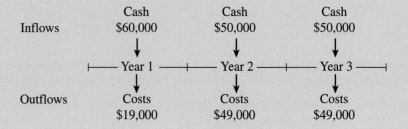

	Cash	Cash	Cash
Inflows	$60,000	$50,000	$50,000
	Year 1	Year 2	Year 3
Outflows	Costs	Costs	Costs
	$19,000	$49,000	$49,000

Income computed on a cash basis is as follows for each of the years:

Year 1: $60,000 − ($15 × 1,000) − $4,000 = $41,000
Year 2: $50,000 − ($15 × 3,000) − $4,000 = $ 1,000
Year 3: $50,000 − ($15 × 3,000) − $4,000 = $ 1,000

Net income using the accrual method would have been computed as follows:

Year 1: ($60,000 ÷ 3) − ($15 × 1,000) − $4,000   = $ 1,000
Year 2: [($60,000 ÷ 3) + $50,000] − ($15 × 3,000) − $4,000 = $21,000
Year 3: [($60,000 ÷ 3) + $50,000] − ($15 × 3,000) − $4,000 = $21,000

Which set of income figures best portrays the company's activities, its efforts and accomplishments for each period, and the way in which income is earned over time? Explain. How might one set of numbers be better for decision making than the other?

in a more direct matching of efforts and accomplishments, the foundation for generating future cash flows.

Although accrual-basis income may provide better forecasts of future cash flows, current cash flow information is also useful to financial statement users in understanding a company's operations. For this reason, companies are required to provide both income and cash flow statements.

MORE ON CASH-BASIS AND ACCRUAL-BASIS MEASURES

Index Corporation leases a small building for its new sales office. The company signs a three-year lease, and pays rent in advance of $75,000 for the full three-year period. Excluding the cost of the lease, the company earns income of $60,000 each year from this sales office. All of the company's transactions are for cash. The company's activities for this sales office can be pictured in the following timeline:

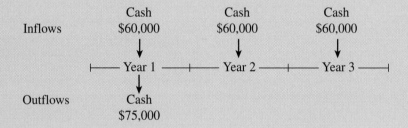

Inflows
Cash $60,000   Cash $60,000   Cash $60,000

├── Year 1 ──┼── Year 2 ──┼── Year 3 ──┤

Outflows
Cash $75,000

Income computed on a cash basis is as follows for each of the years:

Year 1: $60,000 − $75,000 = $(15,000)
Year 2: $60,000 − $0 = $ 60,000
Year 3: $60,000 − $0 = $ 60,000

Income computed using the accrual method is as follows:

Year 1: $60,000 − ($75,000 ÷ 3) = $35,000
Year 2: $60,000 − ($75,000 ÷ 3) = $35,000
Year 3: $60,000 − ($75,000 ÷ 3) = $35,000

Which set of income numbers do you think is most useful for decision making? For example, if you were assessing the future potential for this sales office after the first year, what would each of the two sets of numbers suggest for the future? Explain.

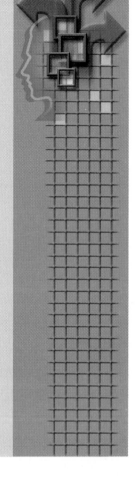

REPORTING INCOME STATEMENT ELEMENTS

Information for Decisions

The income statements of most companies use a similar format and include similar terminology. Knowledge about the form of the statement and its terminology will help investors and creditors effectively use the income statement for decisions and help answer questions such as these: What sources of income are most important to the com-pany's success? Is the company's operating income comparable with other companies in the same industry? Given my ownership interest, what is my share of the company's income? Which items included in the company's income this period can be expected to occur again in the future?

The form of the income statement is not entirely specified by authoritative requirements, but most companies prepare income statements that follow a general pattern. Some companies minimize the number of individual items shown in the income statement, while others provide much more detail. The income statement for Our Video Store, shown in Exhibit 2–1, includes revenues from two types of rentals and lists several expenses. Because the business is not incorporated, neither income taxes nor earnings per share are reported. A simplified corporate income statement might appear as follows:

MODEL COMPANY		
INCOME STATEMENT		
FOR THE YEAR ENDED DECEMBER 31, 2001		
Revenues		$1,000,000
Operating expenses:		
Cost of goods sold	$470,000	
Selling expenses	150,000	
General and administrative expenses	110,000	
Miscellaneous expenses	35,000	
Total operating expenses		(765,000)
Operating income		$ 235,000
Nonoperating income and gains		23,000
Nonoperating expenses and losses		(8,000)
Income before income taxes		$ 250,000
Income tax expense		(100,000)
Net income		$ 150,000
Earnings per common share		$1.50

REVENUES

Revenues result from the primary activities of the business enterprise. If a company is involved in a variety of activities, the revenues derived from each of the major activities should be disclosed separately, either in the income statement or in a separate presentation, to help financial statement readers better understand the operations of the company. For example, Deere & Company (www.deere.com), a major producer of farm and lawn and garden equipment, also has financial and health services divisions. Deere & Company provides a breakdown of revenues in its income statement to show separately those derived from equipment sales, finance and interest income, and insurance and health premium income. Because information provided

You Decide 5-5

THE IMPACT OF REVENUE CHANGES

UAL Corporation (United Airlines) (www.ual.com) reports revenues in three categories: Passenger, $15,342,000,000; Cargo, $892,000,000; and Other Operating Revenues, $1,144,000,000. Which would be more significant to UAL, and to you as a decision maker: a 10 percent decrease in cargo shipments resulting from the loss of a government contract, or a 5 percent decline in passenger revenue from the loss of gate space at New York's Kennedy Airport? Explain.

about revenues varies considerably among companies, financial statement users should be sure they understand a company's various revenue sources when assessing the company's future. (See You Decide 5-5.)

Some companies report sales revenues net, while others report gross sales and show a deduction to arrive at net sales, as follows:

Sales revenue	$78,654,000
Less returns and allowances	(602,000)
Net Sales	$78,052,000

The term *net* means after deductions, while the term *gross* means before deductions. Some companies permit purchased goods to be returned for a refund under certain conditions, and some companies may give customers allowances if goods or services are in some way unsatisfactory. The amount of **sales returns and allowances** during the period is deducted from sales revenue, resulting in net sales. If the amount of returns and allowances is significant, it should be disclosed. A large amount of returns and allowances may indicate problems, such as overly aggressive sales personnel or inadequate quality control procedures.

OPERATING EXPENSES

Operating expenses include those costs associated with supporting the central activities of the company. For a manufacturing or merchandising company, the largest operating expense is typically the cost of the inventory sold during the period, while for a service company, the largest single cost may be salaries and associated benefits.

Companies usually have many different operating expenses, perhaps fifty or a hundred different kinds. To avoid undue complexity in the income statement, most companies combine various expenses into several major categories. For example, UAL Corporation's income statement lists ten categories of operating expenses.

Cost of Goods Sold. For many companies, the cost of products sold exceeds all of the other operating expenses combined. This expense includes those materials, labor, and other costs associated with manufacturing or purchasing products that have been sold during the period and the revenue from which is included in revenues. For example, a producer of breakfast cereals would include, for all products sold during the period, the cost of corn, wheat, rice, sugar, and other ingredients, together with the cost of production labor, packaging, and other production costs, in the reported cost of goods sold.

For manufacturing and merchandising companies, cost of goods sold is such an important item that it is often shown separate from other expenses, as follows:

Sales revenue	$45,389,000
Cost of goods sold	26,885,000
Gross profit	$18,504,000

Other operating expenses are shown following gross profit. The term **gross profit** or **gross margin** simply refers to net sales minus cost of goods sold. Because the profits of a manufacturing or merchandising company come from the sale of the company's products, gross profit is an important figure for assessing the company's current operations and its future. If, for example, a company's gross profit as a percentage of sales is low compared with other companies in the industry, it might indicate the company is operating inefficiently or its products have an inferior reputation. Similarly, a declining gross profit over time would not bode well for the company's future.

An income statement that reports cost of goods sold separately and shows a gross profit figure is called a multistep income statement. An income statement that shows cost of goods sold with the other operating expenses—and, accordingly, does not include a gross profit figure—is called a single-step income statement. Unlike in decades past, many companies today are engaged in a number of different types of operations, often including the sale of both goods and services. For these types of enterprises, called conglomerates, single-step income statements may be best because cost of goods sold may relate to only a portion of the revenues reported and the gross profit figure may be meaningless.

Marketing, Advertising, and Promotional Expenses.   Selling or marketing expenses are found in the income statements of most companies. Businesses often need well-trained sales staffs to sell their products or services, and incur costs for sales salaries and commissions, as well as training and travel costs and the costs of operating sales offices.

Also, companies attempt to influence people to purchase their goods and services by providing them with selected information in the form of advertisements. As we watch endless T.V. commercials or listen to the latest attempt at a memorable soft drink jingle, we are receiving a message that may or may not be useful for our decisions and may or may not influence us. In addition, companies attempt other types of promotions to try to get us to purchase what they are selling. Does anyone not know about the sweepstakes promoted by Ed McMahon? Mr. McMahon, of course, does not work for free, and the sweepstakes prizes, although having a present value far below the total value advertised, are substantial. All of these costs are reported as advertising and promotional expenses and often constitute a significant portion of total operating expenses.

The amount and type of advertising and promotional activities may differ from company to company and industry to industry. Nevertheless, all companies must promote their products or services in some way, and the cost of doing so often is important information for financial statement users.

General and Administrative Expenses.   Many companies incur considerable costs in the overall operation of the business. These costs might include salaries and benefits for the corporate management and office staff, utility expenses, insurance expense, legal and accounting fees, the cost associated with operating the corporate headquarters, and costs of new product development.

Interest Expense.   Most major corporations have borrowed and currently owe significant amounts of money. For example, long-term debt of about $1.8 billion has financed nearly one-third of the total assets of Ralston Purina Company. The cost of borrowing, interest expense, often is an important factor in the profitability of a company. Interest on long-term debt is essentially a fixed cost that does not change with the level of operations, and financial statement users are concerned with the amount of operating profits that must be generated to ensure coverage of interest. As an example, TWA had such a large amount of debt and related interest expense before entering its first bankruptcy that the company had virtually no chance of being profitable, regardless of the success of its operations. Some companies classify interest expense as a nonoperating item.

Other Operating Income and Expenses.   Other operating income and expenses arise from a number of sources. Examples include gains and losses related to sales of assets or to foreign currency changes, environmental costs, and litigation settlements.

OPERATING INCOME

Operating income is computed as the difference between revenues and operating expenses and represents the income earned from the central operations of the business. Operating income is expected to be the mainstay of the enterprise. It provides the incentive for owners to continue as suppliers of capital and, therefore, represents one of the most important pieces of information used in evaluating future prospects.

Comparisons of operating income over time for a particular company or comparisons to operating incomes of other companies in relation to their revenues can reveal whether earnings are improving or declining and how efficiently the company is operated relative to other companies. However, there is not complete uniformity in the items included in or excluded from operating income, so caution should be exercised when making comparisons across companies. For example, Ralston Purina includes investment income in the computation of operating income where many companies would report this as a nonoperating item. Further, not all companies separately identify operating income, so detailed analysis of the income statement is especially important.

GAINS, LOSSES, AND NONOPERATING ITEMS

A variety of items are unrelated or only partially related to the normal operating activities of a business, yet they are part of the overall activities of the company and must be included in the computation of net income. **Gains** are increases in net assets resulting from peripheral activities or incidental events, and **losses** are decreases in net assets resulting from peripheral activities or incidental events. Examples include a gain on the sale of old equipment no longer used in operations and an uninsured loss from an earthquake. Other nonoperating items might include costs of reorganizing the company or costs related to other unusual events.

INCOME TAX EXPENSE

Income tax expense reflects the amount of federal, state, local, and foreign taxes the company expects to pay based on its income. This amount is often quite significant, draining off perhaps one-third of a company's pretax profits, as with Procter & Gamble, or even more. Because of its significance, income tax expense is of concern to financial statement users and is reported separately. Some companies label this item "Provision for Income Taxes."

Tax laws are exceedingly complex. Many special tax provisions often make a company's income tax expense difficult to estimate based simply on a knowledge of the company's pretax income and current tax rates. Therefore, companies are required to provide a detailed description of the computation of income tax expense in the notes to the financial statements.

NET INCOME

Net income or net earnings is the "bottom line" of the income statement. Net income is an all-inclusive figure. It includes everything that affects the wealth of the business, with the exception of additional investments by owners, distributions to owners, and a few special items.

The amount reported as net income represents a return to the owners for investing in the company. Often a portion of the reported net income is distributed to owners in the form of dividends. The portion of the earnings not distributed to owners is added to the owners' equity or retained earnings balance in the balance sheet. Companies seldom pay out all of their net income as cash dividends because they often need to conserve cash for reinvestment in additional assets and operations.

Not all of the dividend payments necessarily go to the true residual owners of the corporation, the common shareholders. In some cases another class of stock, preferred stock, might be outstanding. **Preferred stock** represents a special ownership interest with rights specified by the agreement between the preferred stockholders and the corporation. Preferred stockholders usually have preference over common shareholders in receiving dividend distributions and distributions of assets if the corporation is liquidated. Preferred stock usually has a fixed dividend rate, but the right to vote is typically withheld. Because preferred dividends normally must be paid before dividends can be paid to common shareholders, preferred dividends are deducted when determining the income remaining for common shareholders. Note, however, that dividends, whether common or preferred, are not expenses, but distributions of income.

EARNINGS PER SHARE

Earnings per share (EPS) is the most commonly quoted measure of operating success. Investors rely heavily on EPS information in determining how much to pay for a company's stock. Net income alone may not be a sufficient measure of operating success because it fails to consider the effects of the number of owners who share in the income available to common shareholders.

A CLOSER LOOK AT

EARNINGS PER SHARE

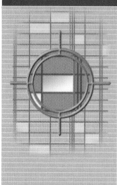

Sandy Barcon owns 100 shares of Blue Company's common stock and 100 shares of Orange Company's common stock. Blue has a total of 10,000 shares of common stock outstanding, and Orange has 25,000 shares outstanding. Both companies report net income of $100,000 for the year. What is Sandy's share of the income of each of the two companies?

	Blue	Orange
Net income	$100,000	$100,000
Number of common shares	÷ 10,000	÷ 25,000
Earnings per common share	$ 10	$ 4
Shares held by Sandy	× 100	× 100
Sandy's share of income	$ 1,000	$ 400

By considering the number of shares outstanding, the EPS number provides a clearer picture of the extent to which each share of stock participates in the earnings of the company and the extent to which it may be expected to share in future profits and cash flows. The magnitude of the difference in EPS between Blue and Orange suggests a significantly higher future cash return from owning a share of Blue stock. Accordingly, Blue's stock could be expected to sell at a higher price per share than Orange's stock.

In its simplest form, EPS is computed by dividing net income by the weighted average number of shares of common stock outstanding during the period. If the company has preferred stock outstanding, preferred dividends must be deducted before computing EPS. This complex topic is discussed in more detail in Chapter 14.

ADDITIONAL ELEMENTS OF THE INCOME STATEMENT

In addition to the major elements typically found in the income statement, several special items may appear on an irregular basis. To alert financial statement users to the inclusion of these items in income, they are separately disclosed in the income statement if the amounts are material. Exhibit 5–5 illustrates how a complex income statement that includes all of the special items might appear.

BUSINESS ENTERPRISE OPERATING STATEMENT

EXHIBIT 5-5

MODEL COMPANY
INCOME STATEMENT
FOR THE YEAR ENDED DECEMBER 31, 2001

Revenues	$1,000,000
Operating expenses	(765,000)
Operating income	$ 235,000
Other income and gains	23,000
Other expenses and losses	(8,000)
Income from continuing operations before income taxes	$ 250,000
Income tax expense	(100,000)
Income from continuing operations	$ 150,000
Loss from discontinued operations	(85,000)
Income before extraordinary loss and cumulative adjustment	$ 65,000
Extraordinary loss	(50,000)
Income before cumulative adjustment	$ 15,000
Cumulative adjustment from change in accounting principle	25,000
Net income	$ 40,000

Earnings Per Share:	
Income from continuing operations	$1.50
Income before extraordinary loss and cumulative adjustment	.65
Income before cumulative adjustment	.15
Net income	.40

Three types of special items are classified separately in the income statement: (1) income and losses from discontinued operations, (2) extraordinary gains and losses, and (3) cumulative adjustments from changes in accounting principles. All these items must be reported "net of taxes." This means that the income tax effect of each of these items must be included in the reported amount for the item rather than being included in reported income tax expense. For example, if a company with a 40 percent tax rate reported operating income before taxes of $100,000 and a $50,000 extraordinary gain on an insurance settlement, the bottom portion of its income statement would appear as follows:

Operating income before income taxes	$100,000
Income tax expense (40 percent)	(40,000)
Income before extraordinary gain	$60,000
Extraordinary gain (net of $20,000 taxes)	30,000
Net income	$ 90,000

Discontinued Operations. A dynamic business environment means companies must constantly change if they are to remain competitive. In some cases, a company may discontinue a major product line or dispose of an operating division that has become unprofitable or no longer fits into the company's overall strategic plan.

A decision to eliminate a major product line or operating division has greater potential impact on the future operating capability of a company than does the sale of individual assets. For that reason, a gain or loss on the disposal of an operating segment must be shown separately in the income statement, along with any income earned by that segment from the beginning of the reporting period until the time of disposal.

Extraordinary Items. Events that are (1) unusual in nature and (2) not expected to recur in the foreseeable future are called **extraordinary items**. Gains and losses arising from extraordinary items must be reported separately in the income statement if they are material in amount. An example of an extraordinary loss would be an uninsured flood loss in a region where floods seldom occur.

Why does anyone care if an item is classified as extraordinary? Extraordinary events are considered anomalies and should not be considered as part of the recurring earnings of the company. Separate classification of such items allows financial statement users to focus on recurring earnings when assessing enterprise performance and attempting to project future earnings and cash flows.

Changes in Accounting Principles. Although consistency dictates that the accounting methods used by a company should remain constant from period to period, changes in circumstances sometimes lead to changes in accounting principles. In most cases, a change from one acceptable accounting principle to another is done through a "catch-up" adjustment so that subsequent financial statements are the same as if the company had always used the new principle. This *cumulative adjustment from a change in accounting principle* is reported at the bottom of the income statement immediately before net income.

These changes in accounting principles are included in the computation of net income, but they do not arise from operations. In fact, they are simply "paper events" resulting from a decision to change the way in which real events are given recognition in the accounts. To avoid distortions of income projections that might result if these adjustments were included in the income figures on which forecasts are based, cumulative adjustments must be classified separately, with an explanation provided in the notes.

ADDITIONAL DISCLOSURES

Companies provide considerable additional income-related information in their annual reports beyond the income statement itself. Although not required, most major companies include in their annual reports financial summaries that include selected income statement information for some number of periods, such as five or ten years, for comparative purposes. These summaries typically include net sales, gross margin, operating income, net income, and earnings per share. They may also include other items such as interest expense and income taxes.

The notes to the financial statements also provide additional income statement information, depending on the type of entity and the detail in the income statement. Common items found in the notes include the following:

- A summary of significant accounting policies
- The amount of repairs and maintenance expense
- The amount spent for research and development
- An explanation of the computation of income tax expense
- A detailing of significant debt terms and debt maturities
- Information related to the cost of retirement plans and other postretirement benefits
- Sales, income, and assets of different operating and geographic segments of the enterprise
- Computation of earnings per share
- The effects of recent authoritative accounting pronouncements

REPORTING COMPREHENSIVE INCOME

Information for Decisions

Some events affect the well-being of a business but are not directly related to normal operations. Accounting rules require that certain of these items be excluded from net income and be reported separately so their effects on the enterprise's current performance and financial position can be considered by financial statement users. Understanding these items can help decision makers answer questions such as the following: To what extent did the company become better or worse off during the period by holding (and not selling) investments in securities? To what extent was the company's position with respect to its foreign subsidiaries affected by changes in the rate at which foreign currencies can be exchanged for U.S. dollars?

A few events that affect the well-being of the business enterprise in the long run are not as closely tied to management's decisions during the period as those transactions and events reported in the income statement. These items are not included in the computation of net income. Instead, they are included in a new measure of performance called **comprehensive income**.

Comprehensive income includes all changes in owners' equity during the period except capital transactions (investments by and distributions to owners). Comprehensive income is equal to net income plus other comprehensive income. Other comprehensive income includes the following three elements:

* Unrealized gains and losses from holding (rather than selling) certain types of investments (see Chapter 8)
* Gains and losses from translating foreign-currency financial statements of foreign subsidiaries into U.S. dollars (see Chapter 16)
* Special adjustments relating to pensions

Companies may report other comprehensive income elements in any one of three ways:

* In a combined statement of income and comprehensive income, following net income
* In a separate statement of comprehensive income, starting with net income
* Separately within the statement of changes in stockholders' equity

Most companies report other comprehensive income in the statement of changes in stockholders' equity. This alternative downplays other comprehensive income, consistent with the views of most corporate chief financial officers that this information is not very useful. However, the FASB may eliminate this alternative in the future. Few companies present a combined statement of income and comprehensive income to avoid confusing readers as to which measure of performance is primary.

The computation of net income is unaffected by the rules governing comprehensive income, and net income is expected to continue as the primary performance measure. The cumulative effect of other comprehensive income from the current and all prior periods is reported in the balance sheet in a special stockholders' equity account in a manner similar to the way in which the effects of net income for the current and past periods are accumulated in Retained Earnings.

In Practice 5-4

MAYTAG'S COMPREHENSIVE INCOME

Maytag Corporation's financial statements include a separate statement of comprehensive income, with comparative statements included for the three years ending December 31, 1998 (in thousands):

CONSOLIDATED STATEMENTS OF COMPREHENSIVE INCOME

	Year Ended December 31		
	1998	**1997**	**1996**
Net income	$280,610	$180,290	$136,429
Other comprehensive income items, net of income taxes:			
Unrealized losses on securities	(1,257)	(3,605)	
Minimum pension liability adjustment		107	5,549
Foreign currency translation	(2,929)	(445)	585
Total other comprehensive income	(4,186)	(3,943)	6,134
Comprehensive income	$276,424	$176,347	$142,563

In addition, in its December 31, 1998, balance sheet, Maytag reports a negative Accumulated Other Comprehensive Income balance of $15 million.

ANALYSIS

Maytag has experienced all three types of other comprehensive income over the three-year period reported. The company uses a clear, straightforward presentation of comprehensive income by providing a separate statement of comprehensive income. The negative balance sheet amount, Accumulated Other Comprehensive Income, reflects a cumulative decrease in stockholders' equity up to the end of the current year. As can be seen from the statement of other comprehensive income, approximately $8 million of that amount occurred in the past two years. [www.maytag.com]

SUMMARY

Income is the incentive for businesses to exist. It attracts investors to risk their money with the expectation of getting back their investments, with a return on the investment in addition. Income is a measure of the extent to which society values what it is that a business entity does. If the enterprise does something society values, the enterprise will prosper; otherwise, the enterprise will incur losses and will ultimately cease to exist.

Businesses report the results of their operations periodically so interested parties can use the information to make decisions about the future. In particular, information about past income may be useful for forecasting future earnings and cash flows. Many different groups use income information, but primary among them are investors and creditors.

In a simple situation, net income is the excess of revenues and gains over expenses and losses. Revenues derive from the sale of an enterprise's goods and services through its central operations. Revenues are usually recognized when they are realized and earned, which is when (1) an exchange has occurred in which the seller receives cash or a claim to cash and (2) the earning process has been completed. Expenses reflect the cost of goods and services used up in the production of revenues and are recognized when the related revenues or other benefits are recognized. Gains and losses derive from activities and events that are peripheral or unrelated to the central operations of the enterprise. They often are not included in operating income, although they are included in the net income of the entity.

Some small businesses recognize income on a cash basis, treating cash inflows as revenues and cash outflows as expenses. Because the cash basis fails to match efforts and accomplishments by period, the cash basis is not generally accepted. The accrual basis of measuring income matches costs with the benefits they produce, reporting both in the same period. This approach is considered more useful for assessing the results of an enterprise's activities and as a basis for forecasting future earnings and cash flows.

The income statement reports on a business's productive activities for a period of time. While the bottom line, or net income, is important, a complete analysis of the items within the statement must be made for a thorough under-standing of the enterprise. In particular, comparisons with other enterprises and across time may be especially useful. The amount of earnings per share of common stock is a figure that receives particular attention from investors and financial analysts.

Some items reported by businesses affect the overall well-being of the company but are excluded from net income. Several such items are reported as elements of other comprehensive income and, together with net income, result in total comprehensive income.

LIST OF IMPORTANT TERMS

book value *(162)*	gains *(177)*	net income *(156)*
carrying amount *(162)*	gross margin *(175)*	net loss *(156)*
comprehensive income *(181)*	gross profit *(175)*	preferred stock *(177)*
cost of goods sold *(162)*	income statement *(156)*	realization *(167)*
cost of sales *(162)*	losses *(177)*	sales returns and allowances *(175)*
extraordinary items *(180)*	net assets *(156)*	

EXAMINING THE CONCEPTS

Q5-1   Why do investors place a great deal of emphasis on reported net income?

Q5-2   How is net income defined?

Q5-3   What parties other than shareholders use income statement information in arriving at economic decisions?

Q5-4   In what ways does corporate management use income statement data?

Q5-5   In what ways can employees find income statement data useful?

Q5-6   In what ways may taxing and regulatory authorities find income statement data useful?

Q5-7   Why should an investor not rely solely on the amount of reported net income or loss for the current period in arriving at a decision on whether or not to purchase the stock of a particular company?

Q5-8   When is the term *cost of goods sold* used in the income statement and what does it mean?

Q5-9   What are the primary advantages and disadvantages of recording revenue on a cash basis?

Q5-10   What are the primary advantages and disadvantages of recording expenses on a cash basis?

Q5-11   Using the accrual basis of accounting, when is revenue recognized?

Q5-12   Using the accrual basis of accounting, when are expenses recognized?

Q5-13   Why is it generally considered inappropriate to recognize revenue at the point of production for most products? For what type(s) of business operations might it be appropriate to recognize income at the time of production?

Q5-14   When are losses recognized for financial reporting purposes?

Q5-15   When are gains generally recognized? Why are different standards used in the recognition of gains and losses?

Q5-16   What factors may cause the cash generated from operations to be substantially greater than the amount of reported operating income?

Q5-17   Most of Stone Jewelry's sales are on the store's charge cards and are collected evenly over 120 days. If about 80 percent of the store's sales are in November and December, in which months will reported revenue be greatest under cash-basis accounting and under accrual accounting?

Q5-18   When do sales returns and allowances arise? How are they reported in the financial statements?

Q5-19   What is gross profit, and how is it computed? Why is it important?

Q5-20   What types of expenses are normally classified as general and administrative expenses in the income statement?

Q5-21 How is operating income measured, and why is it important to decision makers?

Q5-22 In what way do preferred shareholders participate in the distribution of dividends and in the distribution of assets if the corporation is liquidated?

Q5-23 Why is a provision for income taxes typically included in the income statement of a business entity?

Q5-24 How is earnings per share calculated? Why is earnings per share considered useful?

Q5-25 What events are reported as discontinued operations, and why are they reported separately?

Q5-26 What events are reported as extraordinary items, and why are they reported separately?

Q5-27 When are cumulative adjustments reported in the income statement, and what does the amount reported represent?

Q5-28 Distinguish between a sales return and a sales allowance. How are these items included in the income statement?

Q5-29 Why is earnings available to common shareholders used in place of net income in computing earnings per share?

UNDERSTANDING ACCOUNTING INFORMATION

E5-1 **The Nature of Income** Acme Company prepared the following income statement for the year 2000:

Acme Company
Income Statement
Year Ended December 31, 2000

Net Sales	$44,545
Cost of products sold	(30,734)
Marketing, administrative and other	
operating expenses	(10,743)
Operating income	$ 3,068
Interest expense	(599)
Other income, net	410
Earnings before income taxes	$ 2,879
Income taxes	(466)
Net earnings	$ 2,413

Use the income statement of Acme Company and your knowledge of income reporting to answer each of the following:

a. What was the change in owners' equity during the period excluding the effects of any additional investments or withdrawals by the owners?

b. Over what period was Acme's income measured?

c. What was the major source of Acme's income?

d. What costs did Acme incur in running the business?

e. What item or items were included in the income statement that were not directly related to Acme's operating activities for the period?

E5-2 **The Importance of Income**

a. The success of a company's efforts is often judged by the amount of income it earns.

1. How does the fact that a company manufactures television sets and generates a profit from its operations indicate society values its activities?

2. How is reported income used in forecasting future cash flows?

3. Should investors rely primarily on the amount reported as net income in assessing a company's future earnings potential and cash flows? What effect will an unexpected or unusual event have on these assessments?

b. You are considering buying an insurance agency and have received the following information on two agencies operating in your city:

	Agency A	Agency B
Total revenue for the year	$100,000	$125,000
Total operating expenses for the year	60,000	88,000
Nonoperating income and expense	-0-	-0-
Net income	$ 40,000	$ 37,000
Total number of insurance policies sold	1,000	1,250

Which agency seems to be the more efficiently operated? Explain why.

E5-3 **Components of Income**

a. For each of the following, indicate whether the item would be classified as an operating revenue, operating expense, gain or loss, nonoperating income, nonoperating expense, or not included in the computation of net income:

1. Sale of products to other divisions within the company.

2. Sale of products to parties outside the company.

3. Cost of goods sold.

4. Income taxes.

5. Labor costs.

6. Pension costs.

7. The amount received in excess of the carrying amount of land that is sold.

8. Interest income from temporary investments.

9. The cost of reorganizing a struggling company.

b. Indicate which of the items above you would consider important in developing a forecast of a company's future net income and cash flows. If you are not sure if a component should be included, indicate the reason for your uncertainty.

E5-4   Measurement of Income   You are planning to invest in either Company A or Company C. In making your decision, you want to project future income and future cash flows for each company. The following information was made available by the companies:

Company A
Income Statement
Year Ended December 31, 2000

Revenues	$15,000
Costs and expenses	(10,000)
Operating income	$ 5,000
Gain from sale of building	10,000
Interest income from temporary investment	2,000
Net Income	$17,000

Company C
Income Statement
Year Ended December 31, 2000

Cash receipts:	
Collected from sales	$18,000
Sale of building	45,000
Interest income	1,000
Total receipts	$64,000
Cash payments:	
Costs and expenses paid	$ 8,000
Purchase of delivery trucks	30,000
Distribution to owners	5,000
Total payments	($43,000)
Net cash flow	$21,000

Company A has measured income on the accrual basis, while Company C has measured income using cash receipts and disbursements. Identify and describe the differences in the measures used by the two companies and indicate how these differences will affect your comparison of the companies.

E5-5   Income Recognition on the Cash Basis

a. Although the cash basis of income measurement is not generally accepted for financial reporting purposes, it is often used. Indicate the reasons why a company or an individual may use cash basis income measurement and reporting.

b. Jim Golden regularly builds and sells custom-made furniture. Some customers pay cash for the furniture at the time they place the order, other customers pay cash when the furniture is delivered, and still others pay for the furniture 30 days after delivery. If Jim uses the cash basis for income recognition, when will he recognize revenue from the sale of furniture?

E5-6   Income Recognition Using the Accrual Method

a. When are revenues recognized under the accrual accounting model? What conditions must be met?

b. Use the matching concept to determine the amount of expense or other items to be recognized in the income statement of the current year for each of the following:

1. The Morales Company purchases a delivery truck for $40,000 at the beginning of the year and expects to use the truck for 5 years. Repairs and operating costs during the first year are $4,700.

2. Takayama Company received $25,000 from the sale of a building that originally cost $100,000 and had a carrying value of $60,000 at the time of sale.

3. Lucinda Company purchased inventory costing $48,000 last year and $30,000 this year. A total of three-fourths of the inventory purchased last year was sold during that year. The remaining one-fourth was sold this year, along with one-half of the inventory purchased this year. What amount of cost of goods sold should be recognized in each of the years?

4. Tasis Company borrowed $50,000 on July 1 of the current year. The amount of the note and all accumulated interest are to be repaid in 18 months, assuming an annual interest rate of 8 percent. What amount of interest expense should to be recognized for the current year?

E5-7   Relationship Between Income and Cash Flows   In each of the following cases, indicate whether reported income on the accrual basis will be greater than or less than the reported net cash flow.

a. The company purchases buildings and equipment for cash.

b. Money borrowed in the prior year is repaid this year.

c. The company is short of cash and delays payment on many of its current expenses.

d. The company makes a major effort to collect its outstanding receivables, and the amount of customer's receivables outstanding is reduced by 50 percent.

e. A supplier goes into bankruptcy and the company purchases enough inventory to meet its production needs for the next two years.

E5-8   Reporting Income Statement Elements

a. Gross profit as a percentage of Orion Company's sales has declined from 20 percent to 15 percent over the past three years. Has cost of goods sold been increasing or decreasing relative to sales during these years? Explain.

b. Reclassify the expenses of Company B so the operating incomes of Company A and Company B may be compared. After the reclassification, determine which company has the highest operating income as a percentage of sales.

Company A
Income Statement
Year Ended December 31, 2000

Revenues		$1,000,000
Cost of goods sold		(600,000)
Gross profit		$ 400,000
Selling & administrative expenses		(100,000)
Operating Income		$ 300,000
Other income and expense:		
Interest income	$ 20,000	
Income tax expense	(150,000)	
Other gains & losses	(30,000)	(160,000)
Net Income		$ 140,000

Company B
Income Statement
Year Ended December 31, 2000

Revenues	$2,500,000
Cost of goods sold	(1,300,000)
Selling and administrative expenses	(550,000)
Interest expense	(25,000)
Other losses	(50,000)
Income tax expense	(200,000)
Special provision for reorganization	(35,000)
Net Income	$ 340,000

E5-9   Reporting   Comprehensive   Income   Gladbrook Corporation reported income from operations of $500,000 and net income of $240,000 for 2000. In addition to its income statement, Gladbrook reported a statement of other comprehensive income, as follows:

Gladbrook Corporation
Statement of Other Comprehensive Income
For the Year Ended December 31, 2000

Net income	$240,000
Gain on holding certain marketable securities	88,000
Comprehensive income	$328,000

Gladbrook Corporation is accumulating money for a major expansion in its facilities and in January 2000 invested $600,000 in marketable securities, which increased in value to $688,000 at December 31, 2000. Because the securities have not been sold and the gain is unrealized, the $88,000 increase is not included in net income. Gladbrook paid no dividends in 2000.

a. By what amount will retained earnings increase in 2000?

b. By what amount will Gladbrook's reported net assets increase in 2000?

c. As a potential investor, does the disclosure of comprehensive income provide useful information? Explain.

d. Would your response to part c change if the value of the securities declined in 2001 and Gladbrook were to sell them for $580,000? Explain why.

E5-10   Multiple Choice: Using Income Data   Select the correct answer for each of the following:

1. An income statement provides information on:
   a. Cash receipts and disbursements for the period.
   b. The amount of money contributed to the business entity by shareholders during the period.
   c. The amount of money contributed to the business entity by creditors during the period.
   d. The operating results for the business entity during the period.

2. Shareholders often find income statement information useful in:
   a. Developing estimates of future cash flows from the business entity.
   b. Developing estimates of the value of long-term assets held by the business entity.
   c. Determining the amount of long-term debt and new equity securities that have been sold during the period.
   d. All of the above.

3. Income statement information often is useful to:
   a. Individual investors.
   b. Creditors and suppliers.
   c. Labor unions.
   d. All of the above.

4. Corporate management focuses on net income:
   a. As a primary basis for deciding when to sell long-term assets.
   b. As an important measure of the operating success for the current period.
   c. As a way of determining how much cash was generated from operations during the period.
   d. As a way of determining how much cash was generated from the sale of stock and long-term liabilities during the period.

5. Income statement data is especially useful in:
   a. Determining trends in profitability from period to period.
   b. Comparing the profitability of similar companies.
   c. Deciding whether to discontinue operations in an operating division.
   d. All of the above.

E5-11   Multiple Choice: Income Statement Amounts Select the correct answer for each of the following:

1. Under generally accepted accounting principles, revenue normally includes:
   a. Cash and receivables generated from the sale of goods and services.

b. The amount of cash generated from the sale of long-term assets.

c. Increases in the value of long-term assets and decreases in the value of long-term liabilities.

d. Increases in the value of inventory produced during the period.

2. A gain is recorded when:

a. Inventory held for resale is sold at more than its carrying amount.

b. Inventory held for resale is sold for less than its carrying amount.

c. Land is sold for more than its carrying amount.

d. Land is sold for less than its carrying amount.

3. Cost of goods sold normally includes:

a. The cost of raw materials included in products sold.

b. The cost of labor used to produce goods currently held in inventory.

c. The cost of production equipment purchased during the period.

d. All of the above.

4. Other expenses reported in the income statement should include:

a. The cost of materials used in the production process.

b. Interest expense on bank loans.

c. The purchase price of land acquired during the period to be used as a future building site.

d. The cost of labor used in the production process.

E5-12 Multiple Choice: Cash Versus Accrual Income Select the best answer for each of the following:

1. When cash-basis income measurement is used:

a. Income nearly always will be greater than income reported on an accrual basis.

b. Income nearly always will be less than income reported on an accrual basis.

c. Actual cash receipts and cash payments serve as a basis for determining the amount of income to be reported.

d. Actual cash receipts and cash payments are adjusted to match the cash flows with the timing of the underlying economic events.

2. The cash basis of income measurement is most likely to be appropriate for:

a. A small company that sells on credit and pays for everything with cash.

b. A major corporation with a great deal of cash coming in and going out each day.

c. A middle-sized company that leases all facilities and equipment annually and sells only for cash.

d. A small video rental store that has just purchased a large number of new video tapes.

3. The cash basis of income measurement:

a. Does not recognize insurance expense in the current period if a three-year policy was purchased in the prior period.

b. Recognizes revenue at the time the product is delivered to the customer.

c. Recognizes the cost of producing the product as an expense at the time the cash payment is received from the sale of the product.

d. All of the above.

4. The accrual basis of income measurement:

a. Recognizes revenue at the time cash payment is received from selling a product to a customer.

b. Recognizes revenue in the period in which a product is produced.

c. Recognizes the cost of producing a product as an expense in the period in which the product is produced.

d. Recognizes the cost of producing a product as an expense in the period in which the product is sold.

5. The matching concept means that:

a. The full cost of a noncurrent asset is matched against revenue in the period in which the asset is purchased.

b. A proportionate share of the cost of a long-lived asset is matched against revenue in the periods in which the asset is used.

c. The cost of producing a product is treated as an expense in the period in which the product is produced.

d. The cost of producing a product is treated as an expense in the period in which the product is made available for sale.

E5-13 Multiple Choice: Reporting Income Select the best answer for each of the following:

1. Which of the following is not reported in the income statement?

a. Cash received from operations.

b. Dividend income from investments.

c. Provision for income taxes.

d. Cost of goods sold.

2. Net sales are derived by deducting from gross sales:

a. The cost of all items sold this period.

b. Interest expense and other financing costs.

c. Sales returns and allowances.

d. Manufacturing costs not included in cost of goods sold.

3. A cumulative adjustment is reported in an income statement when:

a. A highly unusual event occurs and a gain or loss results.

b. A long-lived asset is sold and a gain or loss results.

c. A major segment of the business is sold and a gain or loss results.

d. A change in accounting principle occurs.

4. An extraordinary item is reported in the income statement when:

a. An unusual and infrequent event occurs.

b. A major segment of a business is sold.

c. A significant price reduction is given to a customer as a result of shipping the wrong product.

d. A warehouse is sold at a significant loss.

5. In computing earnings per share:

a. Net income is divided by the total number of shares of common and preferred stock actually outstanding.

b. Net income is reduced by the amount of dividends paid to common shareholders before it is divided by the weighted average number of common shares outstanding.

c. Net income is reduced by the amount of dividends paid to preferred shareholders before it is divided by the weighted average number of preferred shares outstanding.

d. Net income is reduced by the amount of dividends paid to preferred shareholders before it is divided by the weighted average number of common shares outstanding.

E5-14 Income Statement Effects Explain how each of the following individual transactions affects (increases, decreases, or does not affect) the amount of net income Southwest Company would report under generally accepted accounting principles; if income is unaffected, explain why:

a. Products are sold for $55,000.
b. The cost of materials used in producing the products sold is $25,000.
c. The cost of labor used to produce the products sold is $12,000.
d. Cash collected on accounts receivable from the prior year is $15,000.
e. Land costing $8,000 is purchased.
f. Equipment with a carrying amount of $7,200 is sold for $6,300.
g. Property taxes amounting to $8,700 are paid.
h. Dividends of $1,700 on investments in other companies are received, and dividends of $7,500 are paid by Southwest Company.

E5-15 Income Statement Items Explain how each of the following individual transactions affects (increases, decreases, or does not affect) the reported accrual-basis net income of Central Corporation. If income is unaffected, explain why:

a. Payments of $35,000 are made on accounts payable.
b. Inventory costing $75,000 is purchased and all but $8,000 of it is sold during the period for $32,000.
c. Land previously purchased for $84,000 is sold for $97,000.
d. A change of accounting methods results in an upward cumulative adjustment of $6,300.
e. Utility bills totaling $4,100 are received during the period, but remain unpaid at the end of the period.
f. Total credit sales for the period are $285,000. At the end of the period, $82,000 is uncollected. All accounts receivable are expected to be collected.
g. Additional shares of common stock are sold by Central Corporation for $325,000.

E5-16 Basic Income Statement Copper Corporation recorded sales of $720,000 during 2000. Operating costs for the year included cost of goods sold of $550,000, salaries and wages of $90,000, and other operating costs of $42,000. Copper Corporation also received dividend income of $15,000 and miscellaneous income of $19,000. During 2000, Copper recorded interest expense of $31,000 and income tax expense of $16,000. You have been asked by the vice president of finance to prepare an income statement in good form.

E5-17 Computing Income Cyril's Bowling Lanes recorded the following revenues and expenses for the month of September:

Receipts from bowling	$75,000
Receipts from locker rentals	1,200
Receipts from shoe rentals	2,800
Salary expense	43,000
Repairs on lanes and equipment	19,000
Cleaning supplies and materials	400
Gain on sale of used bowling balls	650
Building rental expense for September	5,000

The local banker wishes to have an income statement for the month of September prepared before approving renewal of a loan to Cyril. Cyril has requested your assistance in preparing an income statement in good form.

E5-18 Income Statement During April, Totz Company sold for $875,000 merchandise for which it had paid $612,000. The company paid wages of $106,000 during the month, all related to work performed during April, and owed an additional $3,000 of wages at the end of the month. The company's rent is $1,500 per month. April's rent was paid at the end of March, and May's rent will be paid on the first of May. Aside from wages, the company's only liability is a $10,000 six-month, 12 percent note to the bank, which was issued on January 17, with the interest paid at the end of each calendar month. Other expenses totaled $45,000 for the month. Prepare a formal income statement for April for Totz Company in accordance with generally accepted accounting principles.

E5-19 Comparative Income Computations Broadhurst Corporation had cash sales of $175,000 during the month of January. On credit sales in January, $120,000 was collected prior to the end of the month, and $40,000 remains to be collected in February. Also in January, $65,000 was collected on accounts receivable held at January 1. If total expenses for January were $264,000, what amount of net income will Broadhurst Corporation report for January using each of the following:

a. A cash basis of income measurement?
b. An accrual basis of income measurement?

E5-20 Cash and Accrual Basis During July, Tamblyn Corporation paid $25,000 for July's heat, light, and power and $200,000 for materials and supplies. All but $30,000 of the materials and supplies were used during the month. Total payments for salaries and wages for the month were $70,000. Additional salaries of $15,000 for the last four working days of July have not yet been paid at the end of July. If all sales are made on a cash basis and sales revenue for Tamblyn was

$350,000, what amount of net income will Tamblyn report for July using each of the following:

a. A cash basis of income measurement?
b. An accrual basis of income measurement?

E5-21 Accounting Classifications Janet Gomez is attempting to evaluate the desirability of investing some of her savings in Stanway Enterprises. Stanway Enterprises is a regional food wholesaler and has provided her with a list of its transactions during the last accounting period. She has sought your help in determining whether some of the transactions included on the list should be classified under accrual accounting as revenues (R), gains (G), expenses (E), losses (L), or items that should not appear in the income statement (O):

a. Sales of meat products for cash.
b. Sales of vegetables on credit, with cash to be collected early in the next period.
c. Cost of meat products sold during the period.
d. Cost of vegetables sold during the period.
e. Cost of frozen juice products to be sold next period.
f. Total sales price of unused delivery vehicles.
g. Excess of the selling price of land sold during the period over its cost.
h. Uninsured cost of building repairs necessitated by fire damage that occurred during the period.
i. Cost of new delivery equipment purchased during the period.

E5-22 Income Statement Strain Manufacturing produces specialized exercise equipment for professional athletes. At the end of 2000, the head of marketing for Strain was given a printout with the following amounts:

Sales of exercise equipment	$530,000
Gain on sale of investments	20,000
Cost of products sold	300,000
Salaries and wages	70,000
Shipping costs	45,000
Property tax expense	23,000
Depreciation expense	20,000
Interest expense	18,000
Income tax expense	24,000

The head of marketing for Strain does not have a background in finance or accounting and needs to have an income statement prepared. You are asked to prepare an income statement for Strain Manufacturing for 2000.

E5-23 Retail Income Statement Tonya's Diveshop had the following cash receipts and payments during July:

Sale of diving equipment	$100,000
Purchase of diving equipment for sale	90,000
Salary and wage payments	18,000
Receipts from apartment rentals	8,000
Heat, light, and power used in July	3,200
Summer advertising campaign	4,200

A review of the supporting documents indicates the following:

a. Customers must pay for all diving equipment on a same-day-as-purchase basis.
b. One-third of the diving equipment purchased in July is still on hand at July 31 and is expected to be sold in August at normal prices.
c. Salaries and wages are paid in full on the last day of the month.
d. The building the store is located in is owned by Tonya and has five large apartments on the upper floors. Rent of $1,600 covering the months of July and August was collected in advance on July 1 on each of the apartments.
e. Depreciation of $2,500 per month on the building is considered appropriate.

Prepare an income statement for Tonya's Diveshop for July in accordance with generally accepted accounting principles.

E5-24 Gross Profit Computations Compute the missing figure in each of the following independent cases:

	Sales Revenue	Sales Returns	Sales Allowances	Cost of Goods Sold	Gross Profit
a.	$340,000	$10,000	$15,000	$230,000	$_____
b.	_____	1,000	9,000	70,000	13,000
c.	215,000	21,000	4,000	_____	36,000
d.	541,000	_____	7,000	316,000	214,000

E5-25 Gross Profit Cogburn Corporation recorded sales of $800,000 during 2000. Cogburn had sales returns of $45,000 and gave special sales allowances of $19,000 for late delivery of products due to a strike by its delivery personnel. Cogburn took delivery of $527,000 of inventory during the year. It reported inventory of $107,000 at January 1 and $88,000 at December 31. Prepare the gross profit section of Cogburn's income statement for 2000.

E5-26 Gross Profit Computation Thunder Company reported inventory of $36,000 at January 1 and $47,000 at December 31. A total of $208,000 of inventory was purchased during the year. Sales returns of $14,000 were experienced on total sales of $341,000. Special sales allowances of $9,000 were given to long-standing customers. Compute gross profit for Thunder Company for the year.

E5-27 Computation of Net Sales and Gross Profit Lamb Company reported the following summary data for the year ended December 31, 2000:

Cash sales	$333,000
Collections on accounts receivable	441,000
Accounts receivable, January 1	174,000
Accounts receivable, December 31	162,000
Cost of goods sold	416,000

a. Compute the amount of sales on account during 2000.

b. Compute the amount of total sales for 2000.

c. Compute the amount to be reported as gross profit for 2000.

E5-28   Computation of Gross Sales   Rollman Corporation reported the following data for the year ended December 31, 2000:

Accounts receivable, January 1	$ 65,000
Accounts receivable, December 31	84,000
Cash collected from customers	188,000

a. Compute the amount reported as total sales by Rollman Corporation for 2000.

b. What effect do sales returns and allowance have on net sales and accounts receivable?

c. What amount of total sales did Rollman record during 2000 if it had $11,000 of sales returns and allowances?

E5-29   Income Computations   Compute the missing figure in each of the following independent cases:

	Revenues	Expenses	Gains	Losses	Net Income
a.	$35,000	$17,000	$3,000	$ 0	$_____
b.	50,000	34,000	7,000	12,000	_____
c.	_____	6,000	500	1,000	8,700
d.	82,500	_____	1,700	2,500	18,800

E5-30   Income Statement Preparation   Bill Braddock started a small business in 1999 with rented equipment and soon found that his business was booming. After a successful 1999, Bill decided to invest additional money so the company could purchase equipment and additional inventory. Selected account balances for the Braddock Corporation at the end of 2000 are as follows:

Cash on hand	$ 4,500
Cash in the bank	51,200
Accounts receivable	161,700
Inventory	388,900
Equipment	620,000
Cost of goods sold	964,300
Rent expense	56,000
Wage expense	412,000
Utilities expense	131,000
Miscellaneous expense	53,700
Accounts payable	147,500
Taxes payable	3,600
Notes payable (11 percent)	25,000
Capital stock	700,000
Sales revenue	1,790,400
Income tax expense	22,300

All of Braddock's equipment was purchased on July 1, 2000, and is expected to have a ten-year life with no residual value. The note payable to the bank was taken out on December 31, 1999, and is due on June 30, 2001. Braddock has not recorded any interest on the note because no principal or interest payments are due until the note matures. Braddock also has left unrecorded $1,500 of wages that will be paid to employees in 2001 for work performed in 2000. The recorded rent expense includes $4,000 rent that has been prepaid for 2001. Now Bill wants to know how his company is doing.

a. Prepare a formal income statement for Braddock for 2000 in accordance with generally accepted accounting principles.

b. How does Braddock Corporation seem to be doing? Explain.

E5-31   Other Income Items   Compute the missing figure in each of the following independent cases:

	Gross Profit	Other Income (Expense)	Extraordinary Gain (Loss)	Net Income
a.	$204,000	$(9,000)	$17,000	$_____
b.	94,000	16,000	_____	78,000
c.	_____	(11,000)	41,000	160,000
d.	630,000	_____	(70,000)	578,000

E5-32   Owners' Equity   Compute the missing figure in each of the following independent cases:

	Beginning Owners' Equity	Net Income	Additional Investments	Distri- butions	Ending Owners' Equity
a.	$118,000	$23,000	$20,000	$15,000	$_____
b.	751,000	84,000	10,000	95,000	_____
c.	_____	50,000	2,000	10,000	329,000
d.	420,000	_____	25,500	12,000	452,800
e.	500,000	_____	32,000	10,000	515,000

E5-33   Unusual Events   During November, Stable Trucking Corporation reported a gain of $45,000 as a result of changing from one generally acceptable accounting principle to another. Also during November, Stable Trucking reported a loss of $38,000 as a result of an accident in which a nearly new cement transport truck was destroyed.

a. The president of Stable Trucking thinks the $45,000 gain should be reported as a cumulative adjustment somewhere in the income statement. When are cumulative adjustments reported? Does this change qualify as a cumulative adjustment? Explain.

b. The president also thinks the $38,000 loss on the accident should be reported as an extraordinary item. When are extraordinary items reported? Does this accident qualify as an extraordinary item? Explain.

E5-34 Earnings Per Share Gonzalez Enterprises reported net income of $360,000 for the current period. Gonzalez Enterprises is a broadly held company with 30,000 shares of common stock outstanding. What amount of earnings per share will Gonzalez Enterprises report? How can a shareholder determine whether the amount reported this year is good news or bad news?

E5-35 Earnings Per Share with Additional Stock Issued
Barton Company reported net income of $84,000 and $92,000 in 1999 and 2000, respectively. On January 1, 1999, Barton had 10,000 shares of common stock outstanding, and on January 1, 2000, it issued an additional 10,000 shares.

a. What was the weighted average number of common shares outstanding in each of the years?
b. Compute earnings per share for 1999.
c. Compute earnings per share for 2000.

E5-36 Earnings Per Share with Preferred Stock Kurt Corporation issued 50,000 shares of common stock and 30,000 shares of preferred stock on January 1, 1996. On January 1, 2000, it issued an additional 20,000 shares of common stock. The preferred stock has an annual dividend rate of $4 per share. If Kurt Corporation reported net income of $426,000 for 2000, compute the following:

a. The weighted average number of common shares outstanding during 2000.
b. Earnings per share for 2000.

E5-37 Other Income Statement Elements Prowell Company reported the following income statement elements for the year ended December 31, 2000:

Gross profit	$420,000
Interest income from investments	32,000
Loss on sale of discontinued operations	71,000
Extraordinary gain on insurance settlement	14,000
Cumulative adjustment for change in depreciation methods (loss)	21,000
Income tax expense	87,000

Prowell Company had 40,000 shares of common stock outstanding on January 1, 2000, and that number did not change during the year.

a. Compute Prowell's net income for 2000.
b. Compute Prowell's earnings per share for 2000.

E5-38 Complex Income Statement Waldo Company reported the following income statement elements for the year 2001:

Sales	$639,000
Cost of goods sold	428,000
Extraordinary loss on flood (net of tax)	27,000
Gain on sale of operating division (net of tax)	52,000
Loss on sale of used equipment	8,000
Other operating expenses	63,000
Income tax expense	31,000

Prepare an income statement for Waldo Company for 2001.

E5-39 Recognizing Changes in Asset Values Al and Jana Bushweiler purchased Acme Cleaning Supplies, Inc., approximately nine years ago. The previous owners had planned to expand the operations from a small midwestern business to a national supply chain and, just before Al and Jana purchased the company, acquired property in Florida, California, and Oregon. Although the property has not yet been used for expansion purposes, the value of the property in all three states has increased substantially since Al and Jana acquired Acme. In preparing the financial statements for Acme Cleaning Supplies for the current period, Al and Jana plan to report the current values of the property in the balance sheet and show the full amount of the increase as "other income" in the income statement for this year.

a. How is land and other property normally valued for financial statement purposes?
b. When is an increase in the value of property included in the income statement?
c. When is a decrease in the value of property included in the income statement?
d. If a CPA is hired to audit the financial statements of Acme Cleaning Supplies, how is the auditor likely to react to the proposal?

E5-40 Income Recognition on a Cash Basis

a. For each of the following, indicate whether it would normally be appropriate or inappropriate for a company to recognize income measured on the cash basis. Explain your answer.
   1. Financial statements are prepared for an individual or small business.
   2. Financial statements are to be prepared in accordance with generally accepted accounting principles.
   3. Sales are made on a "cash only" basis.
   4. Payments for parts and labor are made as work progresses. Final products require three years to complete.
b. There are three alternative possibilities with respect to the timing of the receipt of cash from a sale. Identify the three alternative possibilities and the alternative under which cash-basis income is appropriate.

E5-41 Cash-Basis Income During the month of March, Dallway Corporation received $400,000 of inventory, and it paid suppliers $205,000 for inventory received and sold in February and $195,000 for inventory received in March. The total cost of inventory sold during the month of March was $500,000. Sales of $690,000 were reported in March, with collections from customers totaling $335,000 from March sales and $80,000 from February sales.

a. If Dallway had no other cash receipts or payments during March, compute the amount reported as net income using the cash basis.

b. How well does cash-basis income appear to represent the results of operations for Dallway Corporation for March?

E5-42 **Evaluation of Cash-Basis Net Income** Toz Company reports sales revenue and operating expenses on a cash basis. How will each of the following affect the accuracy with which cash-basis net income reports the monthly operating results of Toz?

a. A building used as a warehouse is purchased for $350,000 rather than continuing to pay monthly rent for its use.
b. All of the materials needed for production for the year are purchased in early January because prices are at a low at that time of year. Under normal circumstances, materials are purchased monthly.
c. At present, payment from customers is received within 30 days of the time the product is shipped. Toz is considering requiring customers to make payment by wire transfer on the day the order is shipped.
d. Income taxes have been paid annually in February. Toz is considering making monthly payments.
e. Employees currently are paid on the 10th of the month for work done in the previous month. The company is considering changing its procedures so that it can make payment on the last day of the month for work done that month.

E5-43 **Conversion from Cash to Accrual** Tucker Corporation had the following cash receipts and payments in the month of November:

Cash received from customers	$364,000
Cash paid to suppliers	185,000
Wages and salaries paid	90,000
Cash received from sale of vehicles	28,500
Payment of liability insurance policy	30,000
Payment of estimated income taxes	37,000

In reviewing its accounting records for November, the chief accountant found the following:

1. Cash received from customers during November included collections of $26,000 from sales in October. Sales totaling $47,000 made on account during November will be collected in December.
2. Cash payments to suppliers in November included $21,000 for merchandise purchased in November but unsold at the end of the month. Payments to suppliers in October included $17,000 for merchandise sold in November.
3. Wage and salary payments made in November included payment of $9,000 for wages earned by employees in October. Unpaid wages earned by employees at the end of November were $13,000.
4. Vehicles sold in November had a carrying value of $16,500 on Tucker's books at the time of sale.
5. A 12-month liability insurance policy was paid in advance on November 1. Tucker had no insurance coverage prior to November 1.

Prepare an accrual-basis income statement for November for Tucker Corporation.

E5-44 **Earnings Per Share—Two Classes of Stock** El Paso Corporation reported net income of $80,000 for the year 2001. El Paso Corporation has 20,000 shares of common stock and 5,000 shares of preferred stock outstanding. The preferred stock, which cannot be converted into common stock, pays an annual dividend of $3 per share.

a. What amount of earnings per share would El Paso report if there were no preferred stock outstanding?
b. What amount of earnings per share will El Paso report for 2001?
c. What will be the effect on reported earnings per share if a dividend of $1 per share is paid on the common stock of El Paso Corporation in 2001? Explain your answer.

USING ACCOUNTING FOR DECISION MAKING

P5-45 **Evaluating Income** A friend of yours has a copy of Goody Corporation's financial statements for 2000, and the following comparative income statement information is included:

	2000	1999
Revenue	$800,000	$600,000
Cost of goods sold and other		
operating expenses	(400,000)	(420,000)
Operating income	$400,000	$180,000
Other income	250,000	60,000
Income before taxes	$650,000	$240,000
Income taxes	(260,000)	96,000
Net income	$390,000	$336,000

Although your friend was told by a relative about the wonderful prospects for Goody Corporation's future sales and the way management has taken control of the company, your friend is skeptical and would like your opinion. Goody Corporation is a small company, and its financial statements are not audited. Which income statement items would you like to explore in more detail? Explain why.

P5-46 **Determining Sales Revenue** The management of Brainway Corporation reported sales revenue of $655,000 for the month of September. Sales revenue consists of the following:

1. A total of $420,000 was received from customers who came to the store and made immediate payment; they took their purchases with them.

2. An additional $65,000 of products were sold to customers with established credit who came to the store and picked up their purchases, but have not yet paid for their purchases.
3. Advance payments of $80,000 were received from customers who ordered products that Brainway will deliver during October.
4. Orders for $90,000 of sales were received prior to the end of September. The goods were prepared for shipping, but were not yet sent.

Assuming income is measured on an accrual-accounting basis:

a. Explain why or why not each item listed is appropriately included in Brainway's sales revenue for September.
b. Compute the total revenue that should be reported for September.
c. Which of the items listed above would be reported in the same period under both cash-basis and accrual-basis accounting?
d. Why is focusing on the completion of the earning process rather than the receipt of cash important for the recognition of revenue? Why does accrual-basis revenue recognition provide more useful information for external decision makers?

P5-47   Income Statement Preparation   At the request of its local bank, Spotfree Cleaners is attempting to prepare an income statement for 2000 using correct financial reporting methods. The following list of transactions was developed by carefully examining the company records and looking at a variety of receipts and vouchers:

1. Cash received from customers totaled $397,000. Of this total, $42,000 represented payments on commercial work that had been completed and billed in 1999. At the end of 2000, $23,000 of additional billings had been mailed, but payment had not yet been received.
2. Salary expense is recorded at the time of payment. To date, salary payments of $115,000 have been made during 2000. An additional $9,000 of salary was earned by employees between the date of the last payment and the end of the year.
3. Cleaning solvent costing $45,000 was received and paid for in 1999 but was used in 2000. Cleaning solvent costing $75,000 was purchased during 2000. A total of 80 percent of this solvent was used up before the end of the year.
4. On January 1, 2000, $48,000 was paid for professional liability insurance to cover a three-year period beginning with the date of payment.
5. The company borrowed $100,000 from a local bank at the beginning of 1999. At the end of 2000, Spotfree Cleaners repaid the loan and $12,000 of interest for the two-year period.
6. The company decided to initiate a new advertising campaign focusing on college students and paid $8,000 for ads to be run in the local campus newspaper during the last four weeks of 2000 and the first four weeks of 2001.

Spotfree Cleaners is requesting an additional bank loan, and, as their bank loan officer, you have been trying to make sense out of their income information.

a. For each income or expense item listed, determine the amount that should be reported in 2000. Explain your treatment of each item.
b. Prepare an income statement for Spotfree Cleaners for 2000.
c. Based on the limited information available, what is your assessment of Spotfree's ability to repay the loan?

P5-48   Evaluating Income   Barbara Farzner has received financial statements from Green Corporation and Wilke Company and is attempting to determine which of the companies would be a better investment. The 2000 income statements of the two companies are as follows:

Income Statement Item	Green Corporation	Wilke Company
Revenue from sale of product	$520,000	$550,000
Investment income	80,000	150,000
Total revenue	$600,000	$700,000
Cost of products sold	$400,000	$350,000
Advertising expense	250,000	30,000
Other expenses	50,000	20,000
Total operating costs	$700,000	$400,000
Operating income	($100,000)	$300,000
Gain on sale of land	200,000	
Loss on sale of investments		(160,000)
Cumulative adjustment from change in accounting principle		(200,000)
Net income	$100,000	($ 60,000)

Although Green Corporation reports the higher net income, Barbara is concerned about the significance of several of the income statement amounts and seeks your advice:

a. Is operating income or net income a better indicator to use when evaluating companies? Explain.
b. Are the sale of land by Green and the sale of investments by Wilke likely to be recurring or infrequent? What impact is the sale of land likely to have on Green's income next year? What impact is the sale of investments likely to have on Wilke's income next year?
c. What is meant by a cumulative adjustment from a change in accounting principle? Will the deduction be repeated next year?
d. On the basis of the income statement data presented, in which company would you advise Barbara to invest? Explain why.

P5-49   Income Statement Recognition   During 2000, the following events occurred that affected Northeastern Fisheries, Yarmouth, Maine:

1. Products costing $300,000 were sold for $450,000 cash.
2. A building with a book value of $285,000 was destroyed by fire. Insurance proceeds were $244,000.
3. The Great Lakes Canning Division was sold for a gain of $372,000. Great Lakes Canning provided approximately 40 percent of Northeastern's total revenue in the prior year.

4. A change in accounting principle resulted in a $68,000 reduction of the carrying value of inventory, with a corresponding decrease in income.
5. A meteorite struck one of the fishing boats as the boat was coming back into port and caused damage of $97,000.
6. The president of Northeastern Fisheries fell while he was walking on the dock and required medical assistance of $12,000.

Income statements typically classify the effects of different types of events and transactions separately. Assume that you are acquiring information about Northeastern Fisheries because you might be interested in buying stock in the company.

a. For each of the events listed, explain how it should be reported in Northeastern's 2000 income statement.
b. Why are the income statement effects of discontinued operations, extraordinary gains and losses, and accounting changes not included as part of operating income?
c. If the gain on the disposal of the Great Lakes Canning Division was included in operating income and not separately disclosed, how might you, as a potential investor, be misled?

P5-50 Earnings Per Share After finally paying off your car, you have saved enough money to take the plunge in the stock market. You have been particularly interested in two companies, but only have enough money to invest in one. In trying to make a choice between them, you have paid special attention to income, and have focused on the growth in income over the past several years. Dawn Company reported net income of $4 million five years ago, and it now reports net income of $10 million. That looks great, but Boomer Company's net income has grown from $3 million to $16 million during the same period. Of course, that latest income figure includes an extraordinary gain of $4 million, but still, that's pretty impressive growth. The other good thing about Boomer is that it has virtually no debt, financing all of its growth from operations and by issuing stock. Boomer now has 6 million shares outstanding, having issued about 2.5 million during the past five years. Dawn's shares outstanding have remained constant at 4 million.

a. How would you analyze the earnings growth of Dawn and Boomer? What income numbers would you use, and what role would earnings per share play?
b. Discuss how the growth of the two companies compares. Based on an analysis of earnings, do you judge one of the companies as being better than the other for a potential stock investment? Explain.
c. List at least two pieces of information in addition to earnings data that you would find crucial in making your investment decision. Explain why.

P5-51 Cash Basis Net Income Temple Corporation reported the following cash receipts and payments during 2000:

Collection on accounts receivable:	
From sales in current year	$340,000
From sales in prior year	50,000
Cash sales	240,000
Payments for salaries and wages	180,000
Payment received for issuing additional common stock to shareholders	100,000
Utility bills paid	60,000
Payments to suppliers on accounts payable:	
From purchases in current year	190,000
From purchases in prior year	80,000
Payments to suppliers on cash purchases	27,000
Sale of used equipment	15,000
Purchase of new delivery truck	30,000

a. Assuming Temple Corporation uses the cash basis in reporting income, compute net income for the year 2000.
b. Which cash receipts and payments do not appear to represent income or expenses associated with the results of Temple Corporation's activities during 2000?

P5-52 Cash Flow as a Measure of Income Stone City Weavers reported the following net income for the month of July, computed on a cash basis:

Sales		$48,000
Less: Cost of goods sold	$ 7,000	
Salaries and wages	34,000	
Rent	2,000	(43,000)
Net Income		$ 5,000

Stone City Weavers produces high-quality birch-bark baskets. Sales are made on a cash basis only to tourists who visit the workshop. Due to the unusual nature of the baskets and the high-quality workmanship, all baskets are sold on the day they are completed. Raw materials for the baskets are purchased monthly with immediate payment made. All employees are paid for work performed during the month on the last day of the month. Rent on the building is paid on the first day of the month.

a. Does cash-basis income for Stone City appear to accurately reflect its operations?
b. Would a change in sales approach to distribution through a national catalog that features high-quality merchandise affect the accuracy of cash flow as a measure of monthly income? In what way?
c. The owners of Stone City are considering adopting a profit-sharing plan for their employees. The company has reported net income in excess of $100,000 each year for the last six years. Under the proposed plan, employees would receive 25 percent of all company profits in excess of $50,000 per year. What effect would the adoption of such a plan have on the accuracy of reported net income on a cash basis?

P5-53 Income Generation Nordic Enterprises manufactures snowmobiles and recreational equipment and has reported the following revenues and expenses in 2000:

Equipment sales	$ 7,000,000
Cost of parts and equipment sold	4,600,000
Wages and salaries	1,300,000
Sales of replacement parts	1,200,000

Revenue from labor charges for	
repair work	800,000
Income tax expense	775,000
Shipping and delivery costs	750,000
Property taxes	112,000
Interest expense on mortgage	
payable	103,000
Interest income on investments	88,000

a. Prepare a 2000 multistep income statement for Nordic Enterprises.

b. In 1999, Nordic Enterprises reported net income of $1,150,000 and earned an 18 percent return on total revenue (net income divided by total revenue). The goal for 2000 was to earn income in excess of $1,300,000 and earn a 20 percent return on total revenue. What amounts were reported? Did Nordic attain its goals in 2000?

c. In setting its goals for net income and return on sales for future periods, what types of factors should Nordic take into consideration?

P5-54 Income Statement Preparation and Analysis Tensel Corporation markets high-quality grinding tools. During 2000, Tensel Corporation recorded the following:

1. Total sales revenue was $578,000.
2. Inventory purchases were $345,000.
3. In addition to selling all of the inventory purchased during 2000, inventory was reduced from $120,000 at January 1, 2000, to $75,000 at December 31, 2000.
4. Wage and salaries expense was $100,000.
5. Dividend income on investments was $26,000.
6. Interest expense on bank loans was $35,000.

7. The company decided to sell the cars driven by sales personnel and lease all automobiles. The cars sold had a book value of $85,000 and were sold for $165,000.
8. As a result of a change in accounting procedures, the book value of certain depreciable assets as of January 1, 2000, was increased from $220,000 to $255,000, with an accompanying $35,000 cumulative adjustment (increase) to income for 2000.
9. Using the new accounting procedures, depreciation expense on equipment used for delivery during 2000 was $40,000.
10. Sales returns and allowances for 2000 were $12,000.
11. The company paid a special $9,000 bonus to the company president on December 20, 2000.
12. On December 30, 2000, the board of directors declared and paid a dividend on common stock in the amount of $50,000.
13. Income tax expense for 2000 was computed to be $30,000.

Using this information, do the following:

a. Prepare an income statement for Tensel Corporation for 2000.

b. Compute the return on total sales (net income divided by sales revenue) for 2000. The company has a goal of earning a 20 percent return on total sales. Did Tensel Corporation meet its goal in 2000?

c. Determine what factors in addition to the sale of products were important in generating Tensel's reported net income for 2000. Does it appear likely that Tensel will meet its goal in 2001? Describe the factors you consider important in answering.

EXPANDING YOUR HORIZONS

C5-55 Accrual-Basis Income Sport Company has been expanding rapidly over the past five years. Because it is privately owned and has not needed to borrow any large sums of money, Sport has prepared its financial statements on a cash basis. It is now considering selling some of its shares to outside investors and needs to prepare accrual-based financial statements. The 2000 income statement for Sport company prepared on a cash basis resulted in reported net income of $185,000, consisting of the following amounts:

Collections from customers	$400,000
Payments to suppliers	250,000
Wage and salary payments	90,000
Income tax payments	30,000
Sale of land	220,000
Purchase of equipment	65,000

Had Sport used accrual accounting, its balance sheet accounts would have included the following:

	Jan. 1	Dec. 31
Accounts receivable	$ 40,000	$75,000
Inventory	100,000	70,000
Wages and salaries payable	15,000	20,000
Income taxes payable	10,000	32,000

The equipment purchased by Sport Company was delivered and payment made on December 31, 2000. Sport also sold the land on that date. The land had been purchased for $235,000 several years earlier. An analysis of fixed assets indicates that Sport Company would have recorded $24,000 of depreciation expense for 2000 on an accrual-accounting basis. Also during 2000, Sport Company was forced to scrap

$46,000 of equipment that was destroyed when an earthen dam built in 1946 collapsed and water entered the plant. Fortunately, the equipment was insured, and Sport Company has reached an agreement with the insurance company. Payment of $90,000 will be received in January 2001.

a. Prepare an income statement for Sport Company for 2000 on an accrual-accounting basis.
b. What are the major changes in net income computed under the accrual basis?
c. Is cash-basis income a good measure of Sport's operations for 2000? Explain.
d. A potential investor in Sport Company is a friend; would you recommend she invest in the company? Explain.

C5-56 Analyzing Gateway, Inc. Examine the Consolidated Income Statements of Gateway, Inc., in Appendix A and answer the following questions:

a. What was the percentage change in net sales in the two most recent years?
b. What was the percentage change in cost of goods sold in the two most recent years? Did cost of goods sold increase more rapidly or less rapidly than net sales during the past two years?
c. What was the percentage change in earnings before income taxes during the past two years? Have earnings increased more rapidly or less rapidly than net sales?
d. What was the percentage change in basic earnings per share during the past two years? Has earnings per share increased more rapidly or less rapidly than net sales?
e. Would you consider purchasing shares of Gateway if you had money available for investment? What other information about Gateway might you wish to collect before purchasing Gateway shares?

C5-57 Revenue Recognition Methods Following are excerpts from the footnote disclosures of two companies, both in the business of transporting passengers:

American Airlines
Passenger ticket sales are initially recorded as a current liability. Revenue derived from the sale is recognized at the time transportation is provided.

Carnival Cruise Lines
Customer cruise deposits, which represent unearned revenue, are included in the balance sheet when received and are recognized as cruise revenue upon completion of voyages with durations of ten days or less and on a pro rata basis computed using the number of days completed for voyages in excess of ten days. Revenues from tour and related services are recognized at the time the related service is performed.

---

a. Explain the revenue recognition issues faced by airlines. What method does American Airlines use in recognizing revenues? How does American Airlines treat amounts received from the sale of tickets prior to recognizing revenue? How would you justify this treatment?
b. Explain the revenue recognition issues faced by cruise lines. What method(s) does Carnival use in recognizing revenues? How does Carnival treat amounts received for cruises prior to recognizing revenue? How would you justify this treatment?
c. Would it be appropriate for Carnival to recognize revenue at the beginning of each trip when the ship sails? Explain.

C5-58 The American Dream Pilgrim Corporation offers the American dream to people wanting to "get away from it all." Pilgrim purchases unspoiled woodland and farmland plots in parcels of 200 to 300 acres. The company divides the parcels into 15-acre plots and resells them as building lots for vacation homes. Although the lots are unimproved, they are quite marketable because they are usually within a two-hour drive of a major metropolitan area. Each lot sells for $22,500. In 2000, Pilgrim sold 1,600 plots. Approximately 20 percent of Pilgrim's customers pay cash for their purchases. The remainder of the sales are on contract under the terms of which the customer makes a 15 percent down payment and signs a 10-year note with Pilgrim. The interest rate on these notes currently is 12 percent, figured on the balance of the note outstanding during the year. Buyers pay the interest and one-tenth of the principal at the end of each year (December 31) for 10 years. Assume (for simplicity) that customers pay a full year's interest in the year land is purchased on contract. The cost of the land sold in 2000 was $15 million, and Pilgrim held $7 million of land that had not yet been sold at the end of 2000. Pilgrim started business on December 31, 1999, by issuing stock for $6.4 million.

a. How do you think Pilgrim should record revenues from the sale of land? Explain your method for recognizing revenues and your reasons for choosing that method.
b. Based on the revenue recognition method you chose in part a, prepare an accrual-basis income statement for 2000. All of Pilgrim's expenses other than the cost of land sold total $820,800.
c. Prepare a schedule showing Pilgrim's cash inflows, outflows, and changes in its cash balance for 2000. All of Pilgrim's land purchases and other expenses are paid in cash.
d. Evaluate Pilgrim's cash position at the end of 2000.
e. What revenue recognition approaches might Pilgrim have adopted other than the one you recommended in part a? How would you characterize those methods, and the one you chose in part a, from aggressive to conservative? What problems do you see with the other methods?

C5-59 Evaluating Income Buzzer Corporation reported the following operating income and net income amounts:

	Income from Continuing Operations	**Net Income**
1997	$ 380,000	$ 450,000
1998	400,000	400,000
1999	(285,000)	(375,000)
2000	160,000	190,000

The income from continuing operations reported by Buzzer includes operating income and other income and expenses. Included in the 1999 loss from continuing operations was a $150,000 write down for an anticipated loss on inventory. Although inventory prices had not dropped, the emergence of new products on the market increased the possibility that the resale value of the inventory would decline. All of the inventory held at the end of 1999 was sold in 2000 at normal profit margins.

Included in 1997 net income was a $70,000 gain on bond retirement, which under generally accepted accounting principles must be reported as an extraordinary item. A $90,000 charge for overtime worked by employees in 1998, but recorded as an expense and paid in 1999, also was treated as an extraordinary item. A change in accounting principle in 2000 increased income by $30,000. Because Buzzer had excess cash on hand on January 1, 1999, it paid $72,000 for three years' equipment rental and recorded rent expense for the full amount. Income from continuing operations for 2000 also included a $14,000 gain on the sale of land to another company.

Upon receiving a copy of the reported operating results of the company for the four-year period, one of the new members of the board of directors of Buzzer Corporation demanded that the company recompute reported income for 1999 and 2000. He was especially concerned that the management of Buzzer used an approach called the "big bath," under which companies write off excessive amounts to expense in years when they will already be reporting a loss. This then makes reported operating results in subsequent years appear more favorable than they should.

a. What amounts should Buzzer Corporation have reported as income from continuing operations and net income for each of the four years? Were Buzzer's operations profitable in 2000? Explain.

b. Would you agree that the big bath approach was used by the management of Buzzer Corporation? Explain.

c. How would it be possible for management to adjust the amounts spent for other items such as advertising and publicity to shift reported income from one period to another? In general, would this seem to be a wise strategy for management to pursue? Why?

d. Would the use of cash-basis net income rather than the accrual basis used by Buzzer Corporation increase or decrease the possibility of management being able to influence the amount of income reported in a particular period? Explain.

C5-60 Earnings Per Share Starburst Corporation reported net income of $300,000 for the year 2000. On December 31, 1999, Starburst had 75,000 shares of common stock outstanding. On January 1, 2000, Starburst sold an additional 25,000 shares of common stock and 10,000 shares of preferred stock. The preferred stock pays an annual total dividend of $60,000. A dividend of 60 cents per share currently is being paid on common shares, and is likely to continue at that level for the next five years.

a. Compute earnings per common share for 2000.

b. Suppose the preferred stock (known as convertible preferred) had a feature allowing stockholders to convert the preferred stock into a total of 50,000 shares of common stock at their option. Even though the preferred shares have not been converted into common stock by the end of 2000, why would a common shareholder be concerned about possible future conversion?

Internet Exercises: Visit our Web site for additional exercises.

Annual Report Project Part 5

Refer to the Annual Report Project, Part 1, at the end of Chapter 1. Using the annual report of the company you have chosen, and any other available information, answer the following questions, providing sources and computations where appropriate.

a. How has your company's sales revenue changed over the past three years?

b. How has your company's cost of goods sold changed over the past three years?

c. Assess the trend in your company's gross profit (gross margin) over the current and preceding two years.

d. Assess the trend in your company's earnings per share over the current and preceding two years

e. Reported income tax expense is approximately what percentage of your company's income before taxes?

f. What percentage of the company's income was distributed to owners during the most recent fiscal year?

g. Did your company report any elements of other comprehensive income during the latest annual reporting period? If so, in which financial statement did the company report other comprehensive income?

Understanding
Financial Position

REVIEW

Previous chapters have established the basic concepts of financial reporting. We have looked at both cash flows and income, and how they are reported in the financial statements.

WHERE THIS CHAPTER FITS

This chapter focuses on financial position and how it is reported in the balance sheet. The chapter establishes the basic principles of accounting for assets, liabilities, and owners' equity, and explores how the items reported in the balance sheet can be used in making decisions.

LOOKING AHEAD

Later chapters continue the discussion with an in-depth examination of individual financial statement elements. But before that, Chapter 7 examines the process by which information reported in financial statements is generated.

I know roughly how much income I earn from my part-time job, and I know how much cash I spend each week for rent, food, clothes, and stuff. But I wonder how much I'm worth. I read that Bill Gates at Microsoft is worth more than $80 billion. Let's see: I have $462 in the bank, my six-year-old car (is that an asset or liability?), and my CD collection. But I owe plenty on my student loans, and I won't even count my credit card 'cause that's not due for two weeks yet. Grandma says I'm worth my weight in gold, but I don't think so.

The stock of Oxford Health Plans lost 62 percent of its value in one day. "How could analysts have known Oxford was heading for trouble? Well, they could have read the balance sheets. Indeed, even as Oxford reported quarter after quarter of increased earnings, its premiums receivable were growing almost as fast, meaning that it wasn't collecting payments ... At the same time, its medical costs payable actually decreased ... which meant that either all those new members weren't using any medical services or that Oxford somehow wasn't logging their bills."[1]

[1]Amy Virshup and Walecia Konrad, "Bad Medicine," *Smart Money* (January 1998), p. 112.

A lthough cash flows and income represent the results of activities during a period of time, decision makers are often interested in a company's financial position at a specific point in time. What is owned? What is owed? Does the financial position provide a sound footing for meeting future goals?

Decision makers look at the balance sheet, or statement of financial position, for a listing of a business's assets, liabilities, and equities so they can form a picture of where the business stands and how it is situated for the future. The balance sheet provides a snapshot of the enterprise at an instant in time, with the resources and obligations that provide the foundation for that business's activities in the future.

Cash flows, income, and financial position provide the basis for analyzing a company's past success and po-

tential for the future. Having already examined the importance of understanding cash flows and income for making decisions about an enterprise, the next step is to examine the balance sheet. In this chapter, we discuss assets, liabilities, and equities, and how the relationships among financial statement items can be used in making decisions about an entity. Particularly important is that cash flows, income, and financial position should not be viewed as being independent of one another. Rather, each affects the others, and careful attention should be paid to the interrelationships. After completing this chapter, you should be able to:

1. Explain the purpose of a balance sheet and identify the kind of decisions for which it provides useful information.

2. Describe the items you would expect to find in a balance sheet and how they might help decision makers.

3. Distinguish between the current and noncurrent balance sheet classifications, and describe how this distinction is important for decision making.

4. Describe what owners' equity indicates about the entity's financing.

5. Describe the different methods used to value assets and liabilities and explain their relevance for decision making.

6. Explain key relationships important for analyzing a company's financial position.

UNDERSTANDING BALANCE SHEETS

Information for Decisions

A balance sheet provides a picture of a company's financial position at a specific date in accordance with certain rules and traditions. By understanding the balance sheet, decision makers can answer a number of questions about a company, such as these: Does the fiscal year chosen by the company make a difference in the picture of financial position that I get from the company's balance sheet? Will the categories in the balance sheet of the company I am evaluating be comparable with those in the balance sheets of other companies that I might want to evaluate?

The balance sheet lists a company's assets, liabilities, and equities, the things of value the company owns or controls and the specific types of claims against it. Although a balance sheet provides a picture of a company's financial condition at a specific point in time, businesses are complex, and capturing a complete and accurate portrayal of a company's financial position in a single snapshot is not easy. The FASB, SEC, IRS, and tradition all affect what is included in this picture. Rules based on general principles define how each asset, liability, and equity account is classified, valued, and reported so that companies' financial statements are reasonably comparable.

Exhibit 6–1 shows the consolidated balance sheets of GTE Corporation (www.gte.com), a leading telecommunications provider, as of December 31, 1998 and 1997. As is traditional, and required by SEC regulations, GTE presents comparative statements for the current and previous year. So decision makers will not be bogged down with excessive detail, amounts are reported in millions of dollars, and many individual accounts are combined and reported in a limited number of categories. Even though companies maintain detailed records of individual assets and liabilities for control and operating purposes, external decision makers do not need such detailed information. In the case of GTE, all of more than $43 billion of assets is reported in just eleven groups.

Although the balance sheet answers many questions, it may also generate additional ones that must be answered for a more complete analysis. The notes accompanying the financial statements answer some of these questions. For example, note 9 to GTE's financial statements lists the company's short-term and long-term debt by type and states the amount of long-term debt repayments due during the next five years.

The picture of GTE's financial position provided in its balance sheet is useful for many types of decisions. Without a further understanding of the balance sheet, however, that picture may look a little fuzzy. This chapter will help clear up the picture.

GTE'S BALANCE SHEETS

EXHIBIT 6-1

CONSOLIDATED BALANCE SHEETS
GTE CORPORATION AND SUBSIDIARIES

	December 31,	
(Dollars in Millions)	**1998**	**1997**
Assets		
Current Assets		
Cash and cash equivalents	$ 467	$ 551
Receivables, less allowances of $395 and $333	4,785	4,782
Inventories and supplies	668	846
Deferred income tax benefits	167	51
Net assets held for sale	274	—
Other	420	307
Total current assets	6,781	6,537
Property, plant and equipment, net (including $1,600 held for sale at December 31, 1998, see Note 11)	24,866	24,080
Prepaid pension costs	4,927	4,361
Franchises, goodwill and other intangibles	3,144	3,232
Investments in unconsolidated companies	2,210	2,335
Other assets	1,687	1,597
Total assets	$43,615	$42,142
Liabilities and Shareholders' Equity		
Current Liabilities		
Short-term obligations, including current maturities	$ 4,148	$ 3,398
Accounts payable and accrued expenses	4,138	4,672
Taxes payable	1,071	771
Dividends payable	470	466
Other	528	534
Total current liabilities	10,355	9,841
Long-term debt	15,418	14,494
Employee benefit plans	4,404	4,756
Deferred income taxes	1,948	1,782
Minority interests	1,984	2,253
Other liabilities	740	978
Total liabilities	34,849	34,104
Shareholders' Equity		
Common stock—991,374,778 and 984,252,887 shares issued	50	49
Additional paid-in capital	7,884	7,560
Retained earnings	2,740	2,372
Accumulated other comprehensive loss	(375)	(243)
Guaranteed ESOP obligations	(509)	(550)
Treasury stock—23,377,388 and 26,253,088 shares, at cost	(1,024)	(1,150)
Total shareholders' equity	8,766	8,038
Total liabilities and shareholders' equity	$43,615	$42,142

You Decide 6-1

GTE'S BALANCE SHEET

Look at GTE's comparative balance sheets and see what you can tell about the company. How does GTE's cash and cash equivalents balance in 1998 compare to its current liabilities total? How do you suppose the company will pay its current liabilities? Did GTE invest in property, plant, and equipment in 1998? Did GTE borrow money in 1998? How do you know?

FISCAL YEAR

While income, cash flows, and changes in stockholders' equity are all reported for a period of time, the balance sheet reports the company's financial position at a single point in time, the end of the company's fiscal year. The **fiscal year** is the annual period over which the company's operating results and activities are reported. As do most companies, GTE has chosen to use the calendar year, ending on December 31, as its fiscal year. However, companies may select any year-end as long as the reporting period is approximately a year in length and is used consistently.

Often a company selects a fiscal year that corresponds to a particular point in its annual business cycle. Typical of retail companies, for example, Wal-Mart Stores, Inc., uses January 31 as the end of its fiscal year. Retail stores often reach a low point in their operations and in their inventory holdings after the holiday selling season and the January clearance sales. This low point may be a good time to "close the books" and take a "snapshot" of where the company stands before it starts the next cycle.

In Practice 6-1

TOYS "R" US AND SUBSIDIARIES

The notes to the financial statements of Toys "R" Us include the following description of the company's fiscal year:

The Company's fiscal year ends on the Saturday nearest to January 31. References to 1997, 1996, and 1995 are for the 52 weeks ended January 31, 1998, and February 1, 1997, and for the 53 weeks ended February 3, 1996, respectively.

ANALYSIS

Usually Toys "R" Us, Inc., uses a 52-week year (364 days). Thus, its year-end varies from January 28 to February 3. The major selling season for toy stores is the December holiday period, and sales returns are usually completed by the end of January. Because each fiscal year has 52 weeks (1995 was an exception), the company is able to make week-to-week comparisons, and annual comparisons are based on a uniform number of days. [www.toysrus.com]

BALANCE SHEET FORM AND CLASSIFICATION

Given that a balance sheet is simply a listing of asset, liability, and owners' equity balances as of a specific point in time, it might seem not to make any difference what form is used in presenting this listing or how the items in the statement are classified. In fact, the form is considered rather important. Why? For balance sheet information to be useful, decision makers must be able to analyze and compare it to some standard, past information, information about other companies, or industry averages. Comparisons of financial position would be very difficult, even impossible, without some agreement about what should be reported in the balance sheet and how it should be reported.

To facilitate its use, information is usually classified or grouped within the balance sheet. For example, rather than a random listing of account balances, all assets are grouped together, as are all liabilities. Within these categories, various subgroupings are usually provided to further facilitate the use of the information. Our Video Store's balance sheet, shown in Exhibit 2–1, is too simple to include detailed categories because the business has very few different types of assets and no liabilities. Exhibit 6–2, on the other hand, illustrates a classified corporate balance sheet for a company with a much greater range of assets and liabilities. Let's look next at the different balance sheet classifications, starting with assets.

BUSINESS ENTERPRISE BALANCE SHEET   EXHIBIT 6-2

MODEL COMPANY
BALANCE SHEET
DECEMBER 31, 2001

Assets			Liabilities		
Current assets:			Current liabilities:		
Cash	$ 67,200		Accounts payable	$ 351,400	
Marketable securities	322,000		Wages payable	1,800	
Accounts receivable	118,700		Interest payable	9,200	
Inventory	512,100		Rent payable	2,000	
Prepaid expenses	2,300	$1,022,300	Unearned revenue	8,500	$ 372,900
Investments:			Long-term liabilities:		
Securities	920,000		Notes payable	160,000	
Real estate	140,000	1,060,000	Bonds payable	1,000,000	
			Premium on bonds	4,000	
Property, plant, and equipment:			Pension obligation	117,000	
Land	185,000		Deferred taxes	346,000	1,627,000
Buildings and equipment	9,109,000				
Less accumulated depreciation	(2,820,000)	6,474,000	Total liabilities		$1,999,900
			Stockholders' equity		
Intangible assets:			Common stock, $1 par	$1,000,000	
Patents	210,000		Additional paid-in		
Copyrights	44,500	254,500	capital	2,250,000	
			Retained earnings	3,560,900	6,810,900
			Total liabilities and		
Total assets		$8,810,800	stockholders' equity		$8,810,800

ASSETS

Assets are expected to provide future economic benefits to an entity. Knowing what benefits to expect from assets, how the assets are classified, and which assets are in each classification can help financial statement users answer questions such as these: Is this company fully and efficiently using its assets to generate a return for investors like me? Does the company have other types of assets that can provide a margin of safety if the company runs short of cash? Will the company have to sell operating assets to raise cash to pay maturing debt? Why does only one of the two companies I am evaluating list intangible assets in its balance sheet when I know they both have valuable names and reputations?

Recall that assets are things of value owned or controlled by the entity. More precisely, **assets** are

> *probable future economic benefits obtained or controlled by a particular entity as a result of past transactions or events.*[2]

An asset has value to the entity in that it is expected to provide economic benefits that accrue to the entity in the future. The benefits are at least partially controlled by the entity, and the ability to get the benefits was obtained through a past transaction.

The air we breathe is not an asset in the accounting sense because, while it does provide benefits (life), we cannot control it to the exclusion of others. Similarly, employees of a company are, from an accounting perspective, not considered assets because no entity can force individuals to provide their services, even when a contract has been signed (although the company can sue for damages if an individual breaches an employment contract). And, if a company were negotiating to buy a parcel of land, the land would not be counted among the company's assets until actually purchased because the land is not controlled by the company and has not yet been obtained through a past transaction.

The expected benefits from assets might come in different ways. Some assets are sold or used up in producing revenues. Others provide protection from loss or the ability to avoid a cost in the future. Understanding the benefits expected from specific assets can provide decision makers with a better understanding of a company's financial position and its activities.

ASSETS AND DECISION MAKING

A look at the asset section of the balance sheet provides important information about a company's operations and its ability to meet its obligations. Large amounts of cash and other liquid assets indicate the company is in a good position to pay debts. However, these assets tend to earn little or no return, and a very liquid position may indicate that management has given up some profitability for safety. In some cases, an exceptionally liquid position could mean that the enterprise lacks profitable opportunities for reinvestment, casting doubt on its long-term prospects.

Large amounts of plant and equipment indicate that a heavy investment, requiring substantial financing, is needed for this type of enterprise. Reinvestment in new plant and equipment will be needed as the old wears out or becomes obsolete. Accordingly, the enterprise's

[2]*Statement of Financial Accounting Concepts No. 6,* "Elements of Financial Statements," Financial Accounting Standards Board, 1985.

income and cash flow must be examined to ensure that replacement of the company's asset base, and, hence, continued operation, is possible.

Financial statement users also need to analyze the amounts and types of assets to determine whether cash will be available to pay debts as they come due. In addition, comparison of income with the amount of assets indicates how efficiently the assets are being employed.

HOW ASSETS ARE CLASSIFIED

Most balance sheets report assets classified by group. An important balance sheet distinction is between current and noncurrent assets. **Current assets** are cash and those assets expected to be sold, converted into cash, or consumed within one year or the operating cycle of the firm, whichever is longer. The operating cycle of the firm is the average length of time needed for a company to complete one full set of transactions; that is, the time to go from cash to inventory (if any), to receivables, and then back to cash. Operating cycles vary from a few weeks for many merchandising companies, to months for many manufacturing companies, to years for some construction companies.

Those assets that are not classified as current are **noncurrent assets,** also referred to as long-lived assets. They are usually classified on the balance sheet in a number of categories, such as investments, plant and equipment, and intangible assets.

Companies may present assets in a way that focuses attention on specific aspects of their financial position and helps meet the information needs of decision makers. Most companies list assets in their balance sheets in the general order of liquidity. Because current assets are the most liquid, they are usually listed first, with intangible assets listed last. On the other hand, some utilities report their property, plant, and equipment before current assets because of the importance of these assets in their operations and for rate-setting decisions.

In Practice 6-2

LACLEDE GAS COMPANY

The balance sheet of Laclede Gas Company, a St. Louis-based utility, reports the following categories, in order:

> Assets
>> Utility Plant
>> Other Property and Investments
>> Current Assets
>> Deferred Charges
> Capitalization and Liabilities
>> Capitalization
>> Current Liabilities
>> Deferred Credits and Other Liabilities

ANALYSIS

The ordering of the balance sheet categories is much different from that of GTE, shown in Exhibit 6–1, reflecting a difference in the priority for decision makers. Rather than listing current assets first, Laclede emphasizes its utility plant. In the capitalization category, Laclede includes both stock and long-term debt, with the common stockholders' equity reported first. This ordering reflects the importance of permanent financing for the types of assets held by a utility. [www.lacledegas.com]

Current and noncurrent assets differ from one another in the length of time held and the role they play in an enterprise's activities. Accordingly, decision makers use the information about each differently in analyzing an enterprise. Let's look next at some of the individual types of assets and how financial statement information about them may be useful for decision making.

You Decide 6-2

HOW MANY ASSETS ARE ENOUGH?

USS Company		UMC Company	
Assets	$15,000	Assets	$1,500,000
Liabilities	2,000	Liabilities	500,000
Owners' Equity	13,000	Owners' Equity	1,000,000
Revenue	$1,000,000	Revenue	$1,000,000

USS Company and UMC Company have very different balance sheets, yet they both generated the same amount of revenue. What different types of businesses might have this much difference in their balance sheets? What differences would you expect in the income statements?

CURRENT ASSETS

Current assets are generally not expected to be held individually in their current form for very long. Cash will be disbursed, receivables collected, inventory sold, and others consumed. The most frequently reported current assets include:

Cash and cash equivalents—coins and currency on hand, bank deposits in checking and savings accounts, and very short-term, near-cash securities, such as U.S. Treasury bills.

The amount of cash on hand indicates a company's ability to pay debts that will soon mature. Too much cash, however, may signal that resources are being used inefficiently because cash and cash equivalents earn little or no return.

Marketable securities—short-term investments in stocks, bonds, and other securities that have a ready market value and can be sold quickly at an established price.

The money invested in marketable securities is intended to be available to meet needs as they arise, yet it earns a higher return than keeping the money in cash or cash equivalents. Because the return on these assets is relatively low, the balance should be no larger than needed to meet anticipated needs and provide for unexpected events.

Accounts receivable—amounts due from customers arising in the regular course of business; accordingly, a type of trade receivable.

Although not yet cash, these assets will turn into cash as they are collected and will provide cash to meet operating needs. Accounts receivable typically do not earn interest, and too large a balance in receivables may indicate management inefficiency, poor credit policies, and possible collection difficulties.

Inventory—merchandise or products held for sale to customers or to produce goods for sale to customers.

Ultimately, the sale of inventory is expected to generate cash, which then can be used to meet operating needs and provide a return to owners. However, the collection of cash from the sale of inventory will be some time in the future, awaiting the sale of the inventory and the collection of resulting receivables. Money tied up in inventories does not earn a direct return until the inventory is sold. Thus, companies try to minimize inventory levels, consistent with efficient operations. Too much money in inventories may indicate management inefficiency, unanticipated declines in sales, or possibly obsolete inventory. Too little inventory can cost the company through lost and delayed sales, referred to as stock-out costs.

Prepaid expenses—amounts paid in advance for operating expenses, such as insurance and rent, that will benefit future periods.

Although typically small in amount, prepaid expenses allow the company to receive benefits in the future while avoiding the related cash outflows in the periods benefited.

Other current assets—items that will result in cash inflows or other benefits and meet the definition of a current asset.

Examples include nontrade receivables, such as those from employees or for tax refunds, and deposits made to suppliers. If material in amount, these items must be analyzed individually to determine their future impact on the entity.

INVESTMENTS

The **investments** category includes long-term holdings of stocks, bonds, and notes of other companies, securities issued by governments, and real estate and other items held for investment, rather than operating purposes. By including items in the investment category rather than as current assets, management has indicated its intention not to sell them in the near future. Nevertheless, investments do represent a potential source of cash if needed. Not all investments are readily marketable, however, and buyers for some may be found only at greatly reduced prices. Accordingly, decision makers must carefully analyze the investments category to determine to what extent the items included can be converted to cash if necessary.

Also, a company's current cash flow may be affected differently by different investments. For example, an investment in corporate bonds may provide periodic cash inflows in the form of interest payments, while an investment in real estate may result in periodic cash outflows (e.g., for property taxes) and provide a single cash inflow only when sold.

In Practice 6-3

GENERAL ELECTRIC AND KIDDER, PEABODY

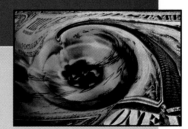

A few years ago, General Electric acquired nearly all of the common stock of Kidder, Peabody, Inc., a large brokerage firm. After stunning losses at Kidder, G. E. felt compelled to pump hundreds of millions of dollars into the brokerage firm to keep it afloat. G. E. eventually sold what parts of Kidder it could, and suffered large losses.

ANALYSIS

Although G. E. had no legal obligation to transfer money to Kidder, management wanted desperately to keep its subsidiary afloat. G. E. had purchased Kidder's stock with the intention of making profits, but the investment actually became a major drag on G. E.'s earnings. [www.ge.com]

In some cases, one company may acquire the common stock of another to exert control or influence over the other company. Special reporting rules apply to such investments, and additional disclosures are normally required. Major investments of this type should be examined for the possible effects of these intercorporate relationships. These relationships may provide special benefits for the investing company, but also may result in unanticipated pitfalls. (See In Practice 6-3.)

The investments category for financial institutions, such as insurance companies and banks, is more significant than for manufacturing or merchandising companies. For example, the investments category accounts for more than 50 percent of the assets of Berkshire Hathaway, a diversified insurance company, while less than 5 percent of Minnesota Mining and Manufacturing Company's (3M) assets are in the investments category. Financial institutions derive a significant portion of their income from investments.

PROPERTY, PLANT, AND EQUIPMENT

Most companies use a number of long-lived assets in their operations. These assets are usually classified as **property, plant, and equipment** and are sometimes called **fixed assets**. These long-lived assets are expected to provide benefits over a number of future years. These assets are also **tangible assets**, meaning they have a physical presence—they can be seen and touched. Assets in this category include only operating items, such as land, buildings, production equipment, delivery trucks, office furniture, and computers.

Property, plant, and equipment have value to a company because they are essential elements in the company's operations. Although a company might be able to sell these items for

In Practice 6-4

ABBOTT LABORATORIES AND SUBSIDIARIES

The following information is included in Abbott Laboratories' consolidated balance sheet (amounts in thousands of dollars):

Property and Equipment, at Cost:	
Land	152,791
Buildings	1,746,772
Equipment	6,486,512
Construction in progress	404,082
	8,790,157
Less: accumulated depreciation and amortization	4,220,466
Net Property and Equipment	4,569,691

ANALYSIS

The difference between the balance sheets of GTE (Exhibit 6–1) and Abbott Laboratories is not in the number of accounts they use to keep track of noncurrent assets, but in the amount of detail they choose to report. Note that Abbott reports separately in the balance sheet the amount of accumulated depreciation related to property and equipment, but GTE reports only a single figure for property, plant, and equipment net of (after deducting) the accumulated depreciation. GTE's accumulated depreciation is reported in the notes. [www.abbott.com]

cash, they are not held for that purpose. They are intended to be used in the company's operations and to generate cash only indirectly through revenues from the sale of the company's products and services. If a company were to sell its operating assets, it could not continue operating unless those assets were replaced.

Most companies list only one or two types of property, plant, and equipment in the balance sheet even though they obviously hold many different kinds. Gateway, Inc., (Appendix A) shows only a single line-item for property, plant, and equipment in its balance sheet. In the notes to the financial statements (Note 10), Gateway lists eight types of items under property, plant, and equipment. Although the company has separate accounting records for each long-lived asset it owns, that information is not considered necessary for external financial statement users.

The amount of asset cost that has been allocated to expense since the buildings, machinery, and equipment were acquired is shown in the notes as a deduction for accumulated depreciation and amortization. Companies keep track of the cumulative amount of fixed-asset cost that has expired and been allocated to expense in a separate **contra-asset account**. This account is deducted from the asset cost for financial reporting. (See In Practice 6-4.)

INTANGIBLE ASSETS

Noncurrent assets that lack physical existence and are not included in the investment category are called **intangible assets.** By and large, intangible assets consist of rights, such as the following:

Patent—the exclusive right to use an idea or invention for twenty years.

Copyright—the exclusive right to a literary, musical, or artistic work for the life of the creator plus fifty years.

Tradename—an exclusive name or phrase for an entity, product, or service; protected while in constant use.

Trademark—an exclusive symbol or logo; protected while in constant use.

Franchise—an exclusive right (usually within a limited area) to sell a product or service and/or use certain identifiers (tradenames, trademarks) and ideas.

License—a right to operate in a certain locality or to use a specific idea or technology.

Examples of valuable intangible assets include the Pepsi name, the Pillsbury Doughboy, the local McDonald's franchise, and the permission given by your local government to a cable TV company to serve your area.

Although the main attribute that sets an intangible asset apart from other noncurrent assets is that it lacks physical existence, that attribute should be of little importance. What makes any asset valuable is not whether you can see and touch it, but whether it is expected to provide future benefits. McDonald's franchises sell for a small fortune because McDonald's restaurants are virtually certain to make profits. Other intangibles are expected to contribute future revenues over and above what a company could generate without the intangible.

Because intangibles lack physical existence, they have always been viewed suspiciously by accountants and the investment community. The value is often difficult to determine, and many companies resist reporting detailed information about them because they sometimes represent secrets. Some companies, including Motorola and Toys "R" Us, lump intangible assets in with assets such as long-term prepayments in a category labeled "Other Assets."

In general, intangible assets are recorded only if purchased from another party. As with other assets, their costs are matched against benefits provided by expensing them over the useful lives of the assets, a process referred to as **amortization**. The resulting amortization expense is reported in the income statement and is analogous to the depreciation expense of tangible fixed assets. Traditionally, amortization is deducted directly from intangible assets rather than being accumulated in a contra-asset account, as with depreciation. Intangible assets are then reported in the balance sheet net of amortization. Because accountants tend to be especially conservative in valuing intangible assets, financial statement users often must use additional information to assess whether the amounts assigned to intangibles are meaningful.

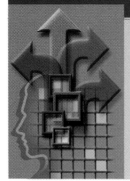

You Decide 6-3

COCA-COLA'S SECRET FORMULA

The amount of property, plant, and equipment listed in Coca-Cola's balance sheet is $5,771,000,000. The secret formulas for some of its soft drinks have been written down to virtually nothing. Which do you feel are more valuable, the tangible operating assets or the secret formulas? Explain. Why do you think Coke decided to keep its original formula a secret rather than acquiring patent protection? [www.coke.com]

LIABILITIES

Information for Decisions

Liabilities are obligations that will be satisfied in the future, usually through the use of assets. Liabilities provide one means by which an entity finances its activities. Knowing the types of obligations a company has and when they must be satisfied helps decision makers answer questions such as these: How risky is the company I want to invest in given the combination of debt and equity that it uses to finance its operations? If the company is planning to make major purchases of assets for expansion, will its current debt position permit borrowing additional money? When assessing next year's cash flow, which liabilities will have to be paid? As a creditor, how can I be assured that the company's assets will be used to pay the amounts owed to me?

The liabilities reported in an entity's balance sheet are obligations of the entity that will have to be satisfied in the future. Specifically, **liabilities** are defined as

> *probable future sacrifices of economic benefits arising from present obligations of a particular entity to transfer assets or provide services to other entities in the future as a result of past transactions or events.[3]*

Loans from banks and amounts owed to employees for past services are reported as liabilities because the entity has a present obligation to make economic sacrifices in the future because of past transactions. On the other hand, if a company expects to purchase a parcel of land

[3]*Statement of Financial Accounting Concepts No. 6,* "Elements of Financial Statements," Financial Accounting Standards Board, 1985.

within the next few weeks in exchange for its note payable due in three years, no liability would be reported now. Although the company expects to make a future sacrifice, it currently has no obligation to do so because the purchase transaction has not yet occurred.

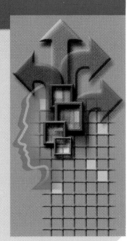

You Decide 6-4

AN OBLIGATION FROM SELF-INSURANCE?

While examining the financial statements of Conflagration Chemical Company, you notice a liability labeled "Self-Insurance Obligation." A note to the statements explains that the company dropped its fire and casualty insurance a few years ago and now pays for all such losses directly. Conflagration's management figures that it has a major casualty loss once every several years and that the losses average out to about $5 million a year. Therefore, it started charging $5 million to self-insurance expense each year and recognizing an equal amount in a self-insurance liability account. Fortunately, the company has experienced no losses for a number of years now, and its recorded liability stands at $40 million. Does this item meet the accounting definition of a liability? Should it be reported as a liability in the balance sheet? Should some other type of disclosure be made? If you were thinking of investing in this company's stock, how would you view the self-insurance liability in your investment decision?

LIABILITIES AND DECISION MAKING

Examining liabilities helps decision makers assess the extent to which the asset acquisitions and activities of the entity have been financed by borrowing. Financing with debt is often viewed as riskier for a business than issuing stock because the amount borrowed must be repaid at a specific time, and periodic interest payments must usually be made. However, liabilities are an important source of financing. The assets and services purchased with borrowed money are expected to generate earnings that, in turn, are used to repay the liability and provide an investment return to the shareholders.

Liabilities also tell decision makers about creditors' claims against an entity's assets. If a company encounters financial difficulty and liquidates, creditors must normally be paid in full before payment can be made to the owners. Comparing the amount of debt to total assets helps in determining the degree of safety for the creditors and the likelihood of payment for owners. Generally, the balance sheet and related notes disclose the amount of each type of debt, the type of claim on company assets debtholders have, and the maturity date of the debt. This information helps decision makers project the amounts needed to make debt payments, assess the possibility of an entity being unable to pay its debts when they come due, and determine which groups of resource providers are most likely to have their claims met. (See In Practice 6-5.)

HOW LIABILITIES ARE CLASSIFIED

Liabilities are listed in the balance sheet roughly in the order in which they are expected to come due. Liabilities typically fall into two major categories. **Current liabilities** are obligations expected to be satisfied within one year or the operating cycle of the enterprise, whichever is longer, using current assets or by incurring other current liabilities. Current liabilities gener-

In Practice 6-5

GATEWAY, INC.

The liabilities section of Gateway's consolidated balance sheet (Appendix A) includes seven categories of liabilities rather than listing each specific debt. Notes 2 and 3 accompanying the financial statements describe the company's financing arrangements and provide more detailed information about the company's long-term debt and amounts due during the next five years, including some lease commitments not reported in the balance sheet as liabilities.

ANALYSIS

Financial statement users do not need to know the identity of each creditor; the important considerations involve the amount, type, and maturity dates of debt. Knowledge of the required future cash payments over the next several years is particularly important when analyzing a company's ability to pay, especially when some commitments, such as Gateway's operating lease commitments (Note 3), are not listed as liabilities on the balance sheet. [www.gateway.com]

ally arise from the normal operations of the entity. **Long-term liabilities** are those obligations related to the entity's overall financing and are due in the more distant future.

CURRENT LIABILITIES

Being closely related to day-to-day operations, individual current liabilities come and go. Companies purchase inventory or services on credit, giving rise to **accounts payable,** and typically pay the accounts within thirty to sixty days. Another current liability, wages payable, arises from companies using the services of their employees and not paying for a few days or weeks. As some current liabilities are paid, new ones arise to take their place. Thus, current liabilities continually turn over, but a balance always remains.

Most current liabilities do not provide a claim against any specific assets, but rather are expected to be paid from the cash generated from current operations. For example, accounts payable and current notes payable are "trade payables" in that they reflect amounts due to suppliers for purchases of inventory and other items for normal company operations. Similarly, accrued liabilities (also called accrued expenses) reflect amounts due for expenses that grow over time, such as rent and interest. The balances of current payables can be expected to grow as the company's operations grow, but disproportionately large growth in these amounts might indicate that bills are not being paid on time, which, in turn, might be a sign of financial difficulty. Continued late payment or nonpayment could lead to a loss of suppliers. Wages due to employees may be included in accrued liabilities or reported separately. The balance of this item is typically small, and an inordinate amount might indicate that payrolls are not being met, a sign of extreme financial distress.

Income taxes payable reflects the amount of income taxes determined, or estimated, to be due in the near future. The amount should usually be small because companies are required to make estimated tax payments throughout the year. A large balance might indicate required payments are not being made, which could lead to penalties and may be a sign of financial difficulties.

Another current liability, unearned revenues, reflects amounts collected in advance for products, services, or resources the company is required to provide to others in the future. For example, a company selling maintenance service agreements might collect the full contract price in advance, but cannot recognize the revenue until the specified services are provided. In the meantime, the company reports its obligation to provide the future services as a current liability. However, this liability differs from other current liabilities in that it is not an obligation to make a direct cash payment, but rather an obligation to perform in some manner. But, such performance may require a significant expenditure of cash. Therefore, a large balance in this account indicates that the company has a significant obligation for future performance that will require the sacrifice of resources without related cash inflows (already received).

Other current liabilities may represent obligations to repay direct cash loans. Notes payable to banks, when included in the current category, reflect short-term operating loans. The description "to banks" distinguishes these notes from trade payables. These types of loans may provide a relatively inexpensive means of meeting seasonal needs for cash. Current maturities of long-term debt reflect the portion of the company's debt financing that must be paid off in the near future. These amounts are often substantial, and decision makers need to assess whether the company has sufficient liquid resources to meet these obligations.

LONG-TERM LIABILITIES

Long-term liabilities are those debts not due within the current year or operating cycle, or that will be paid with assets other than current assets. Many different long-term liabilities might be reported, but the most important include notes and bonds payable, obligations for pensions and other postretirement benefits, and deferred income taxes.

Notes payable include a large number of different types of borrowings evidenced by formal written documents. A **bond** is a common type of note payable that usually includes a more formal borrowing agreement, referred to as the **bond indenture**. Bonds may be of longer duration, usually over five years, and they often are for larger amounts than obligations labeled notes payable. Companies also must report liabilities for the present value of pension and other benefits, such as health insurance, to be paid to retired employees in the future based on their service to date. Given longer life expectancies and increasing health-care costs, these obligations may be especially significant and could impose severe burdens on companies in the future. Deferred income taxes indicate a possible obligation for the future payment of income taxes that have been postponed because some items are recognized at different times for financial reporting and income tax reporting. Each of these items will be discussed in more detail in later chapters.

STRENGTH OF CREDITOR CLAIMS

An important aspect of all long-term borrowings is the strength of the creditors' claim on assets because not all creditors have the same type of claim. Some debt is backed by collateral in that it provides creditors with a first claim on a specific asset or group of assets; specific assets can be taken directly by the lender if the borrower is unable to pay. As individuals, we give creditors a direct claim on our automobiles when we borrow money to buy them. Most people who own homes borrow the original purchase price and give the lenders a direct claim on their homes, referred to as a mortgage. Creditors with debt backed by collateral have a better chance of collecting what is owed them than other creditors in the event the debtor company fails. Collateral arrangements, if significant, are disclosed in the notes to the financial statements. Assets commonly used as collateral include accounts receivable, inventory, land and buildings, and equipment. For example, many railroads issue equipment trust notes to purchase rail cars; these notes payable use the rail cars as collateral, with title to the cars held in trust until the notes are paid. Debt backed by collateral is referred to as **secured debt**, while bonds backed only by a company's promise to pay are called **debentures**.

Other terms of borrowing agreements may also affect the chances of particular creditors collecting what is due them if the company incurs financial difficulties. For example, some debt, referred to as *senior debt*, is given preference over others, referred to as *subordinated*. Unsecured creditors with no special preferences are considered general creditors and, in a liquidation, share whatever assets remain after secured and senior creditors are paid.

A CLOSER LOOK AT

DEBT PREFERENCES

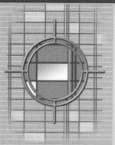

Bardon Company can no longer meet its debts as they mature. Thus, management decides to liquidate the company. When it ceases operations, it has the following debt outstanding:

Accounts payable	$ 350,000
Equipment trust notes	2,400,000
First mortgage bonds	15,000,000
Senior unsecured notes	10,000,000
Subordinated debentures	25,000,000
	$52,750,000

The company's assets have fair values, as follows:

Cash	$ 200,000
Accounts receivable	3,500,000
Inventory	8,400,000
Furniture and fixtures	750,000
Equipment (collateral for equipment trust notes)	1,500,000
Land and buildings (collateral for first mortgage bonds)	29,000,000
	$43,350,000

If the company receives cash equal to the fair values of its assets when it liquidates, the following amounts will be paid on the debts:

Equipment trust notes (value of collateral)	$ 1,500,000
First mortgage bonds	15,000,000
Senior unsecured notes	10,000,000
	$26,500,000

Cash remaining after payment of secured and senior debt is:

Cash available from sale of assets	$43,350,000
Cash paid from sale of assets	(26,500,000)
Cash remaining for general claims	$16,850,000

Remaining claims of general creditors:

Accounts payable	$ 350,000
Equipment trust notes (excess over value of collateral)	900,000
Subordinated debentures	25,000,000
	$26,250,000

The remaining claims will be settled for about 64 cents on the dollar ($16,850,000 ÷ $26,250,000), shared equally among remaining creditors.

OWNERS' EQUITY

Information for Decisions

Owners' equity is the owners' investment in an entity and indicates the owners' claim on the entity's assets. It is the residual amount of an entity's assets after the claims of the creditors are satisfied. Investors and creditors need to know about owners' equity to be able to answer questions such as these: Are the owners financially committed to this company in that they have a significant investment in it? If I invest in this company, to what extent will I share in the profits and be able to influence management? To what extent can I expect the company to finance its future growth through money earned from its operations?

Owners' equity represents the dollar value of the owners' investment in company assets. It is the amount invested by owners plus their share of company earnings not distributed to them. This amount can also be viewed as the owners' claim against the assets. The owners' equity of corporations is referred to as stockholders' equity.

Owners' equity reflects the residual interest in company assets. This means that whatever assets are left after paying creditors go to the owners. The amount of owners' equity may be particularly important for those analyzing a company's financial statements because it provides one indication of the owners' commitment to the enterprise. It also reflects the margin of safety for creditors because assets must be used to meet creditors' claims before they can be distributed to owners.

Under generally accepted accounting principles, all companies are required to report changes in owners' equity for the period. Although a few companies present a statement of changes in retained earnings in their annual reports, with other changes in stockholders' equity shown in the notes to the financial statements, most companies present a statement of changes in stockholders' equity that details changes in all equity elements, including retained earnings. Corporate stockholders' equity includes two major categories, contributed capital and retained earnings. Exhibit 6–3 shows Gateway's statement of changes in stockholders' equity.

CONTRIBUTED CAPITAL

Contributed capital is the owners' direct investment in the business; it is the amount of initial and subsequent financing provided by the owners through asset (usually cash) transfers into the company. The ownership of corporations is evidenced by shares of **capital stock**. Capital is contributed to the corporation when investors purchase capital stock directly from the corporation.

Large corporations sometimes issue two types of capital stock, preferred and common. **Preferred stock** gives shareholders certain preferences over common shareholders, such as the right to share in corporate profits before profits can be distributed to common shareholders and the right to receive assets in a liquidation before common shareholders. **Common stock** provides shareholders with a true residual interest in the corporation, with all profits and assets remaining after meeting the claims of creditors and preferred shareholders going to the common stockholders. Usually, only the common stockholders have the right to vote on corporate matters.

Shares of capital stock are often assigned an arbitrary dollar amount called the *par value* or *stated value*. This amount is typically unrelated to the actual value of the shares and has only very limited meaning, as we will discuss in Chapter 12. The issue price of capital stock

| EXHIBIT 6-3 | GATEWAY'S STATEMENT OF CHANGES IN OWNERS' EQUITY |

CONSOLIDATED STATEMENTS OF CHANGES IN STOCKHOLDERS' EQUITY AND COMPREHENSIVE INCOME
FOR THE YEARS ENDED DECEMBER 31, 1996, 1997, AND 1998
(IN THOUSANDS)

	Common Stock		Additional Paid-in Capital	Retained Earnings	Accumulated Other Comprehensive Income (Loss)	Total
	Shares	Amount				
Balances at December 31, 1995	149,106	$1,492	$279,701	$274,033	$ 293	$ 555,519
Comprehensive income:						
Net income	—	—	—	250,679	—	250,679
Other comprehensive income:						
Foreign currency translation	—	—	—	—	225	225
Unrealized gain on available-						
for-sale securities	—	—	—	—	31	31
Comprehensive income						250,935
Stock issuances under employee						
plans, including tax benefit						
of $30,451	6,545	66	39,905	—	—	39,971
Stock retirement	(2,139)	(22)	(30,862)	—	—	(30,884)
Balances at December 31, 1996	153,512	1,536	288,744	524,712	549	815,541
Comprehensive income:						
Net income	—	—	—	109,797	—	109,797
Other comprehensive income:						
Foreign currency translation	—	—	—	—	(6,053)	(6,053)
Unrealized gain on available-						
for-sale securities	—	—	—	—	15	15
Comprehensive income						103,759
Stock issuances under employee						
plans, including tax benefit						
of $5,003	616	5	10,739	—	—	10,744
Balances at December 31, 1997	154,128	1,541	299,483	634,509	(5,489)	930,044
Comprehensive income:						
Net income	—	—	—	346,399	—	346,399
Other comprehensive income:						
Foreign currency translation	—	—	—	—	1,549	1,549
Unrealized loss on available-						
for-sale securities	—	—	—	—	(145)	(145)
Comprehensive income						347,803
Stock issuances under employee						
plans, including tax benefit						
of $29,769	2,423	24	65,904	—	—	65,928
Stock issued to officer	18	1	599	—	—	600
Balances at December 31, 1998	156,569	$1,566	$365,986	$980,908	$ (4,085)	$1,344,375

almost always equals or exceeds the par or stated value, and the excess amount is reported as **additional paid-in capital**.

When viewing a company's balance sheet, the amounts reported for capital stock and additional paid-in capital together indicate the amount of owners' direct investment in the enterprise, or the total contributed capital. The contributed capital portion of stockholders' equity is considered the most permanent type of financing.

RETAINED EARNINGS

The amount reported by a corporation as **retained earnings** reflects its accumulated undistributed income. This amount accrues to the owners of the corporation, but has not yet been distributed to them. Reported retained earnings may be useful for external decision makers because it indicates the extent to which a company has been able to finance its growth internally through its profitable operations.

THE VALUATION OF BALANCE SHEET ELEMENTS

Information for Decisions

All balance sheet elements are assigned dollar amounts or values. Historical cost or value is the dollar amount recorded in the original transactions when an asset is acquired or liability incurred. However, other valuation methods are also used in some cases to report balance sheet elements. Understanding balance sheet valuations, how they are determined, and when they are used will help decision makers answer questions such as these: How is my cash flow forecast affected by the allocation of asset costs? How much cash will be realized from receivables so that it will be available to pay current liabilities? Have any of the company's assets held for sale declined in value?

Understanding the various financial statement elements and the way in which they are classified is an important first step in being able to use accounting information for decision making. The next step is to understand what the numbers assigned to these elements mean.

Valuation is the process of assigning dollar amounts or values to the individual financial statement elements. The original dollar amount recorded in a transaction is referred to as historical cost for assets or historical value for liabilities and equities. However, as shown in Exhibit 6–4, historical cost or value is only one of several valuation bases used in accounting. Other valuation methods are used when accountants believe, consistent with the information evaluation criteria discussed in Chapter 4, that the resulting information will be more useful to financial statement users. Let's take a closer look at some of the different valuation bases.

HISTORICAL COST

Historical cost has been one of the most stable conventions in accounting. It certainly meets many of the criteria for evaluating accounting information. Historical cost information helps decision makers understand what has occurred, and it is understandable, reliable, verifiable, consistent, and, in most cases, unbiased. Historical cost information is also timely because it can be reported immediately.

Interestingly, only a relatively small number of items are reported on the balance sheet at their unadjusted historical values. Land is usually valued at its historical cost, many liabilities are reported at their historical values, and contributed capital is shown at its historical value. However, the values assigned to most other elements are adjusted in some way. For example, the amount reported for accounts receivable is adjusted for possible uncollectible

EXHIBIT 6-4	ALTERNATIVE VALUATION BASES	

Valuation Method	Definition	Examples of Financial Statement Use
Historical cost or value	Price paid or received in the original exchange	Inventory Land Short-term payables Capital stock
Unallocated historical cost	Cost not yet matched to the benefits that will be generated	Buildings Equipment Prepaid expenses Intangible assets
Fair value	Current market price or estimated worth for buying or selling	Investments in securities Inventory (if below cost)
Net realizable value	Estimated amount collectible, or selling price less selling costs	Accounts receivable Inventory (if below cost and above fair value)
Present value	Discounted present value of future cash receipts or disbursements	Long-term debt (when issued) Leased assets (when acquired)

accounts, inventory is adjusted for material declines in value, and the cost of equipment is allocated over its expected life for a proper matching.

Although historical cost plays an important role in accounting, it does not always provide the most useful number to report in financial statements. For example, we know that when a company buys inventory, it records the original cost of the units purchased. What happens if, before the inventory is sold, its value drops so much that it can be sold only below cost? Would management, investors, and creditors want to know about this? The obvious answer is *yes*. Continuing to report the inventory at historical cost would hide the decrease in value, hampering the ability of financial statement users to forecast accurately cash flows relating to the sale of the inventory. Thus, historical cost information may not always be the most relevant available, nor does it always score well in "predictive value." Accordingly, other valuations have been used in accounting to improve the usefulness of reported information.

ALLOCATED HISTORICAL COST

Under the matching concept, costs incurred are matched with the benefits they provide. Some assets benefit more than one period, and, accordingly, a portion of the cost is recognized as an expense in each period benefited. The carrying amount, or **book value**, of the asset at any point in time is the remaining unallocated cost of the asset, and this is the amount reported in the balance sheet. This remaining unallocated cost is the portion of the cost that is expected to provide future benefits and will be allocated to future periods. As an example, assets that are used or consumed in the operations of an enterprise and that benefit more than one period, such as buildings, equipment, intangible assets, and prepaid expenses, are valued based on the allocation of historical cost.

Valuing assets at *unallocated* historical cost is still a valuation based on historical cost, even though the amount reported is different from the original cost. The resulting valuation does not necessarily bear any relationship to the current market value of the asset.

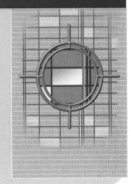

A CLOSER LOOK AT

REPORTING UNALLOCATED HISTORICAL COST

A machine is purchased for $25,000. The machine is expected to have a useful life of five years, with no residual value at the end of that time. If an equal amount of cost is charged to expense each year, the annual depreciation expense is $5,000 ($25,000 ÷ 5 years). At the end of three years, a total of $15,000 ($5,000 × 3 years) of the original cost will have been charged to expense, and the remaining unallocated historical cost will be $10,000. This amount will be reported in the balance sheet at the end of three years as follows:

Machinery	$25,000
Less accumulated depreciation	(15,000)
Book value of machinery	$10,000

FAIR VALUE

For some types of items, primarily those that will or might be sold, fair value is considered to be more relevant than historical cost. The fair value of an asset is the amount for which it could be bought or sold if there were a willing seller or purchaser. The fair value of an asset might be its market value if an active market exists. The fair value of a liability is the current amount that would have to be paid to liquidate it or to persuade someone to take over (assume) the obligation. Many types of investments are reported at fair value because they are expected to be sold, or at least might be sold, to raise cash.

NET REALIZABLE VALUE

Some assets are valued at their net realizable values, or the amount of cash into which an asset could be converted, after deducting any costs of conversion. The most important asset valued at net realizable value is usually accounts receivable. The balance sheet lists the full amount owed to the company by its customers, less a deduction for the amount expected not to be collected. This net amount provides the best estimate of the expected cash inflow to the company. For example, Gateway lists accounts receivable of $559 million, net of the allowance for uncollectibles.

PRESENT VALUE

Many decisions are based in part on the present value of future cash receipts and disbursements. The present value concepts discussed in Chapter 3 permit comparisons of streams of cash flows for which the timing and amounts of the cash flows differ. These concepts are extremely useful for decision making, and some balance sheet items are valued at amounts based on present values. For example, the historical cost of assets acquired by making cash payments in installments over time is the present value of the future cash payments. While the valuation basis is historical cost, that cost is computed as a present value amount. Similarly, many liabilities, such as lease and pension obligations, are recorded initially based on present value computations.

You Decide 6-5

GATEWAY'S VALUATION METHODS

Look at each of the assets and liabilities in Gateway's balance sheet shown in Appendix A. What valuation basis is used for each of Gateway's assets and liabilities? How can you determine the valuation basis? Are there any assets or liabilities in Gateway's balance sheet that you think would be better valued using a method different from the one used? Explain.

BALANCE SHEET ANALYSIS

Information for Decisions

The goal of accounting is to provide useful information in the reports to financial statement users. When users understand the information, it will help them make comparisons, evaluations, and interpretations by answering questions such as these: How does the financial position of this company compare to the industry average and to its top competitor? If the market for the company's products declines and it cannot sell its inventory at a normal price, will it have enough cash to pay current liabilities on a timely basis without borrowing? Will this company be able to meet all of its long-term debt obligations? Given the extent to which this company is leveraged, is it too risky an investment for me?

Accounting information systems provide important information for making financial decisions. The preparation of financial reports is not the goal of accounting. Rather, the goal is to ensure that financial statements and other accounting reports provide useful information to help managers, investors, creditors, and others make informed decisions. The structure of the balance sheet and the use of generally accepted accounting principles help facilitate the comparison, evaluation, and interpretation of balance sheet information when assessing an entity's financial position.

Financial statement information tends to be most useful when it is used comparatively. It might be used in comparison with the same data from other companies or industry averages to assess one company's position and activities against those of others. Similarly, information might be compared with that of other periods to discern trends. Frequently, financial statement amounts are compared with other financial statement amounts, and the resulting ratios are used as key indicators of performance and position, often in comparison with those of other companies or time periods.

INDICATORS OF LIQUIDITY

Liquidity refers to an entity's ability to have cash available quickly. A high degree of liquidity permits the payment of debts as they come due and allows the entity to deal with unexpected situations. Short-term creditors are particularly concerned with liquidity because they expect to be paid in the near future. However, all decision makers must consider an entity's liquidity because a lack of liquidity not only may mean debts will not be paid on time, but opportunities may be missed, assets might have to be sold at panic (low) prices, or hurried and costly borrowings might have to be arranged. The three most common indicators of liquidity are the amount of working capital, the current ratio, and the quick ratio.

Working Capital.   The difference between an entity's current assets and its current liabilities is referred to as its **working capital.** In other words, if a company used its current assets to pay off all its current liabilities, how much would it have left? This comparison is a reasonable one because current liabilities are generally expected to be paid using current assets. The greater an entity's working capital, the greater is its liquidity. Higher liquidity means lower risk. However, liquid assets typically earn a lower return than other assets, so staying liquid generally means that some income is sacrificed for safety.

Looking at Gateway's balance sheet in Appendix A, you can see that Gateway's current assets and liabilities are as follows (in millions):

	1998	1997
Current assets	$2,228	$1,545
Current liabilities	1,430	1,004

Based on these numbers, working capital can be computed for both years as shown in Exhibit 6–5. As you can see, Gateway's working capital increased by $257 million during 1998. Thus, the company has a greater margin of safety in meeting its current obligations as they come due.

Current Ratio.   Like the amount of working capital, the **current ratio**, or working capital ratio, is also an indicator based on the relationship between current assets and liabilities. However, this measure of liquidity is the ratio of current assets to current liabilities and indicates an entity's ability to pay current liabilities in the normal course of business operations. The current ratio assumes that existing inventories will be sold and net accounts receivable collected, thereby generating cash to be used to pay current liabilities. A high current ratio indicates good liquidity and that current debts can be paid. A low current ratio is a warning that liquidity may be inadequate to pay current liabilities as they come due.

Gateway's current ratios are computed in Exhibit 6–5. Although Gateway's current assets increased by $683 million, its current ratio remained virtually unchanged.

Many lenders look for a current ratio of about 2 to 1 to indicate sufficient liquidity. However, what constitutes a satisfactory current ratio depends on the type of company and

GATEWAY'S WORKING CAPITAL AND LIQUIDITY RATIOS   EXHIBIT 6-5

Working capital:
  1998 $2,228 − $1,430 = $798
  1997 $1,545 − $1,004 = $541

Current ratio:
  1998 $2,228 ÷ $1,430 = 1.56
  1997 $1,545 ÷ $1,004 = 1.54

Quick ratio:
  1998 $1,887 ÷ $1,430 = 1.32
  1997 $1,143 ÷ $1,004 = 1.14

the composition of the current assets and liabilities. Gateway's current ratio is lower than that of many other manufacturing firms, but this does not indicate a lack of liquidity. In this case, a relatively low current ratio indicates operating efficiency because of the small amount of inventory Gateway carries. Companies with very high current ratios could have too many dollars in low-earning current assets, indicating management inefficiency.

In Practice 6-6

RYDER SYSTEM, INC.

Ryder System, Inc., a freight-hauling and diversified transportation services company, reported current assets of $1,162,000,000 and current liabilities of $1,195,000,000 on September 30, 1998. The company's current ratio was less than 1.0.

ANALYSIS

Trucking companies have little or no inventory and low receivables because most freight receivables must be paid within a few days. Therefore, a trucking company's current ratio can be expected to be much lower than that of a manufacturing or merchandising company. [www.ryder.com]

Quick Ratio. The **quick ratio**, or acid-test ratio, is a more stringent measure of liquidity than the current ratio because it focuses on cash and other items that can be quickly converted into cash, such as short-term investments in marketable securities and accounts receivable. The quick ratio compares the amount of these quick assets to total current liabilities. Inventories are not included in quick assets because they must be sold and the resulting receivables collected before the cash is in hand. Prepaid expenses are excluded because they do not generate cash to pay debts.

Many lenders look for a quick ratio of about 1 to 1, but, as with the current ratio, a satisfactory level depends on the specific company and the composition of its assets. Gateway's quick ratio indicates more than adequate liquidity and may be a better indicator for this type of company because of its unusually small amount of inventory.

OTHER INDICATORS

Indicators related to aspects of an entity's financial position other than liquidity are also available. For example, financial statement users are also interested in an entity's **solvency**, its ability to pay debts as they come due. Solvency and liquidity are related, but are not the same. Solvency has to do with all types of debt, both short-term and long-term. For example, a company might not be very liquid, yet still be able to pay its debts as they mature if the debts are not due for a number of years and the company is very profitable. Related measures deal with the degree of **leverage**, or the extent to which an entity has financed its assets through borrowing. One example is the ratio of long-term debt to total assets.

In many cases, the most useful indicators are developed by comparing information from the balance sheet and the income statement. We will discuss many of these indicators in later chapters. However, as useful as all of these summary measures are when analyzing a company's financial statements, they are no substitute for understanding the individual numbers in the statements and the information found in the accompanying notes.

SUMMARY

The balance sheet indicates the financial position of an entity at a particular point in time. It includes three types of elements: assets, liabilities, and owners' equity. Assets are probable future economic benefits controlled by the entity as a result of past transactions. Liabilities are present obligations for probable future sacrifices resulting from past transactions. Owners' equity reflects the owners' interests in the entity and is the residual difference between assets and liabilities.

These three types of elements are usually reflected in the balance sheet's major classifications. The asset category on the balance sheet is typically subdivided into current assets, investments, plant and equipment, and intangible assets. Current assets are those expected to be sold, converted into cash, or consumed within one year or the operating cycle of the firm, whichever is longer. Liabilities are usually classified in the balance sheet as current and long-term. Current liabilities are obligations expected to be satisfied within one year or the operating cycle of the enterprise, whichever is longer, using current assets or by incurring other current liabilities. The owners' equity section of a corporate balance sheet includes two major elements: contributed capital, the amount of the owners' direct investment in the company, and retained earnings, the amount of the company's accumulated past profits that have not been distributed to owners. The balance sheet

form and categories are relatively standardized to facilitate use and comparison, but variations are found because different types of information may be more important for different types of enterprises.

Several different methods are used in determining the numbers assigned to the various balance sheet elements, a process referred to as valuation. Historical cost, unallocated historical cost, fair value, net realizable value, and present value are all used in valuing balance sheet elements, depending on the type of element and how the information is expected to be used. Valuations based on historical amounts, including allocations of those amounts, are found most frequently.

For decision makers to understand an entity, they often look to the information presented in financial statements. The analysis of financial statements is often most useful when information is compared across companies or time periods. Financial statement users are often interested in a company's liquidity, solvency, and leverage. Three common indicators of liquidity are the amount of working capital, the current ratio, and the quick ratio. Although there are a number of indicators of various aspects of a company's financial position, summary measures should not be viewed as a substitute for an in-depth analysis of the individual financial statement elements and related notes.

LIST OF IMPORTANT TERMS

accounts payable   (212)

accounts receivable   (206)

additional paid-in capital   (216)

amortization   (209)

assets   (204)

bond   (213)

bond indenture   (213)

book value   (218)

capital stock   (215)

cash and cash equivalents   (206)

common stock   (215)

contra-asset account   (209)

contributed capital   (215)

current assets   (205)

current liabilities   (211)

current ratio   (221)

debentures   (213)

fiscal year   (202)

fixed assets   (208)

intangible assets   (209)

inventory   (206)

investments   (207)

leverage   (222)

liabilities   (210)

long-term liabilities   (212)

marketable securities   (206)

noncurrent assets   (205)

notes payable   (213)

preferred stock   (215)

prepaid expenses   (207)

property, plant, and equipment   (208)

quick ratio   (222)

retained earnings   (217)

secured debt   (213)

solvency   (222)

tangible assets   (208)

working capital   (221)

EXAMINING THE CONCEPTS

Q6-1   What is an asset? Why is a precise definition of an asset important?

Q6-2   What is a liability? List three liabilities.

Q6-3   What determines if an asset is classified as current or noncurrent? Why is this distinction important?

Q6-4   Why would a supplier ask to look at the balance sheet of a new customer before extending credit? Which elements of the balance sheet would the supplier be most likely to examine?

Q6-5 Why are the amounts reported in the balance sheet often rounded to thousands or even hundreds of thousands? Does this make it difficult to make comparisons?

Q6-6 Why do some companies choose a fiscal year that is different from the calendar year?

Q6-7 Why would a banker look at a company's balance sheet before agreeing to lend it money for ten years? What elements of the balance sheet would the banker be likely to examine?

Q6-8 Bullwhip Corporation carries large inventory balances because it takes a very long time to produce its products and it must be able to make immediate delivery when an order is received. Because of its importance, should inventory be listed as the first item in the current asset section? Indicate why or why not.

Q6-9 Assets are expected to provide a company with economic benefits. An agreement giving a company the exclusive right to use a brand name may provide economic benefits. Would you classify it as an asset? Why? If yes, at what amount would you report it in the balance sheet?

Q6-10 What is the operating cycle, and what effect does it have on the classification of assets and liabilities in the balance sheet?

Q6-11 What assets are reported as investments? In what types of companies would you expect to find a large balance reported as investments? In what companies would you expect the investment balance to be relatively small?

Q6-12 Obsolete Steel Corporation invested large sums of money in production facilities approximately thirty years ago, but shows only a relatively small dollar amount for property, plant, and equipment on its current balance sheet. Has it made an error in preparing the balance sheet? Explain your answer.

Q6-13 What does it mean for an asset to be used as collateral? What types of assets are typically used as collateral, and why?

Q6-14 Your company owns nearly 1,000 acres across the road from the site where a new amusement park, Alligator

Acres, is supposed to be built, and your cousin Vinny says the land is worth forty times what you paid for it. At what amount is the land reported on your company's balance sheet? If your company were borrowing money from the bank and needed to use the land as collateral, do you expect the bank would assign a value to the land based on the reported amount, Vinny's estimate, or some other amount? Explain.

Q6-15 If a company's stockholders' equity is made up of 90 percent retained earnings, does it mean the shareholders have provided most of the net assets used by the company? Explain.

Q6-16 How is the amount of working capital determined? When is this number particularly useful?

Q6-17 Historical cost is used in valuing many of the elements of the balance sheet. Why is historical cost used rather than current market values for plant and equipment? Do the same arguments hold for marketable securities? Explain.

Q6-18 When might a decision maker wish to know the net realizable value of inventory? What basis normally is used in valuing inventory?

Q6-19 What information is obtained from the quick ratio? Which financial statement users are most likely to be interested in using the quick ratio to reach a decision?

Q6-20 Why is an examination of trends useful when analyzing a company? Give two examples for which the analysis of trends might be useful in reaching a decision about a company. Indicate the specific information to which you are referring and the type of decision that might be helped.

Q6-21 What is meant by the solvency of a company? What indicator might cause you to believe the solvency of a company has declined?

Q6-22 Tomorrow, you are scheduled to talk with your banker about renewing a loan to your company. Which balance sheet ratios is the banker likely to ask you to provide? Why?

Q6-23 What impact does the format of the balance sheet and classification of balance sheet items have on the effectiveness of comparative analysis between companies?

UNDERSTANDING ACCOUNTING INFORMATION

E6-1 **Understanding Balance Sheets**

a. Tarn Company has chosen a fiscal year that ends at October 31. Would you expect Tarn Company to report higher or lower current assets and current liabilities on that date than a company of similar size that uses a December 31 fiscal year-end? Explain your answer.

b. You are considering whether to extend credit to Extra Company and note that Extra's current liabilities are much higher this year than last year. The major cause appears to be a note payable for $150,000 that was included in long-term debt last year and is now reported as a current liability. Has Extra made a mistake in classifying this note?

Can a company simply list a note payable wherever it wants? Explain why the note may have been reclassified.

E6-2 Assets Balance sheet assets are classified by group to facilitate analysis and decision making. In each of the following situations, indicate which balance sheet asset classification would contain the information needed, and list the assets that normally would be included in the classification:

a. You wish to determine the amount of assets that are expected to be available to pay the debts that will be due within one year.
b. When comparing two companies, you wish to determine which one has invested the larger amount in operating assets.
c. You wish to determine the amount of assets the company has that can be used for a major expansion to take place two years from now.
d. You wish to determine the amount the company paid to purchase the brand name of a product line from another company.

E6-3 Liabilities

a. When you borrow money from a bank to purchase a car, the loan agreement gives the bank the right to repossess the car if you fail to make the required payments. What does it mean when a company issues secured debt to acquire operating assets? How does the claim of a secured bondholder differ from that of someone who purchases a debenture?
b. You have been contacted by one of your customers, Bark Company, and asked to increase its line of credit with your company. Bark forwarded the following information to you:

	Year 2000	**Year 1999**
Total sales	$1,500,000	$1,200,000
Accounts payable	700,000	300,000
Long-term debt	1,000,000	500,000
Owners' equity	300,000	300,000
Total assets	2,000,000	1,100,000

Would you recommend extending additional credit to Bark Company? Explain your answer.

E6-4 Owners' Equity Although bondholders have a priority claim to the assets of a company, the rate of interest paid to the bondholders is typically greater than the dividend rate paid to common shareholders. For example, the dividend rate on AT&T's common stock recently was 2.2 percent while the interest rate on its bonds that mature in 3 years was approximately 5.2 percent. Explain this difference by comparing the nature of bonds payable and common stock.

E6-5 The Valuation of Balance Sheet Elements

a. The balance sheet of Model Company is presented in Exhibit 6–2. For each of the assets and liabilities listed in

Model Company's balance sheet, indicate whether they are valued at historical cost, unallocated historical cost, fair value, net realizable value, or present value for financial reporting purposes.
b. What is the cash flow effect of allocating a portion of the historical cost of equipment to expense each year?

E6-6 Balance Sheet Analysis The balance sheets of Company A and Company B are presented below:

Company A
Balance Sheet
Year ended December 31, 2000

Assets:	
Cash	$ 20,000
Accounts receivable	100,000
Inventory	200,000
Long-term investments	150,000
Plant and equipment	800,000
Total	$1,270,000

Liabilities & Owners' Equity	
Accounts payable	$ 120,000
Short-term notes	60,000
Long-term notes	500,000
Capital stock	500,000
Retained earnings	90,000
Total	$1,270,000

Company B
Balance Sheet
Year ended December 31, 2000

Assets:	
Cash	$ 40,000
Accounts receivable	120,000
Inventory	300,000
Long-term investments	50,000
Plant and equipment	1,000,000
Total	$1,510,000

Liabilities & Owners' Equity	
Accounts payable	$ 100,000
Short-term notes	50,000
Long-term notes	950,000
Capital stock	300,000
Retained earnings	110,000
Total	$1,510,000

You have been asked to evaluate the comparative liquidity and leverage positions of the two companies:

a. For the liquidity comparison, compute the working capital, current ratio, and quick ratio for each company. Which company is more liquid?

b. For the leverage comparison, compute the ratio of long-term debt to total assets for each company. Which company is more highly leveraged?

E6-7 Multiple Choice: Balance Sheet Classification Select the correct answer for each of the following:

1. Which of the following elements normally is not included in working capital?
   a. Accounts receivable.
   b. Bonds payable.
   c. Taxes payable.
   d. Inventory.
2. Which of the following is not included in property, plant, and equipment?
   a. Delivery trucks.
   b. Blast furnaces.
   c. Prepaid insurance.
   d. General headquarters.
3. Which of the following is a noncurrent asset?
   a. Land.
   b. Inventory.
   c. Prepaid insurance.
   d. All of the above.
4. Which of the following is an intangible asset?
   a. Trademarks.
   b. Copyrights.
   c. Patents.
   d. All of the above.
5. Property, plant, and equipment:
   a. Is always considered to be a current asset.
   b. Consists primarily of intangible assets.
   c. Is deducted from current liabilities in computing working capital.
   d. Is reported net of accumulated depreciation by many companies.

E6-8 Multiple Choice: Analyzing the Balance Sheet Select the correct answer for each of the following:

1. Which of the following will lead to an increase in working capital?
   1. Receipt of payment on accounts receivable.
   b. Payment of accounts payable.
   c. Issuance of stock for cash.
   d. Purchase of land for cash.
2. Which of the following would Gettings Company consider to be a cash equivalent?
   a. Land with an established cash value equal to its carrying value.
   b. A one-month CD at Crawdad Savings and Loan.
   c. A thirty-day note payable to Cummings Corporation.
   d. Prepaid insurance.
3. Care must be taken in analyzing balance sheet information because:
   a. Many assets are reported at historical cost, which does not necessarily reflect the prices at which they could be sold.

b. Equity balances are stated at historical cost and assets are stated at market value.
   c. Liabilities are stated at historical cost and equity balances are stated at market value.
   d. None of the above.
4. Total assets reported on the balance sheet at year-end:
   a. Include intangible assets that have been purchased.
   b. Include property, plant, and equipment net of accumulated depreciation.
   c. Include both a and b.
   d. Include neither a nor b.
5. Generally the balance sheet and related notes disclose information about liabilities and claims on company assets. A secured debt might be labeled:
   a. Subordinated debenture bonds.
   b. Accounts payable.
   c. Equipment trust certificates.
   d. Any of the above.
6. Each of the following is considered a part of contributed capital except:
   a. Par value of preferred stock.
   b. Additional paid-in capital.
   c. Retained earnings.
   d. Par value of common stock.

E6-9 Multiple Choice: Ratio Analysis Select the correct answer for each of the following:

1. Ratio analysis is helpful in analyzing a company's balance sheet because:
   a. The absolute balance sheet amounts are not always accurate.
   b. It facilitates comparisons between companies of different size.
   c. The way in which individual companies value their assets and liabilities becomes less important with ratios.
   d. Ratio analysis compensates for differences between companies in the way they classify their assets and liabilities for reporting purposes.
2. The current ratio is computed by:
   a. Dividing total current assets by total current liabilities.
   b. Dividing current assets by total assets.
   c. Dividing working capital by current assets.
   d. Dividing working capital by current liabilities.
3. The liquidity of a company is reflected in its:
   a. Current ratio.
   b. Net income.
   c. Total assets.
   d. All of the above.
4. Which of the following is a misclassification that would increase the current ratio?
   a. Current maturities of long-term debt are classified as current liabilities.
   b. Prepaid expenses are included in accounts receivable.
   c. Unearned revenues are not recognized as liabilities.
   d. A six-month note payable to the bank is included in trade accounts payable.

E6-10 Classification of Balance Sheet Elements For each item listed, indicate whether it is a current asset, investment, fixed asset, intangible asset, current liability, long-term liability, or component of stockholders' equity:

1. Accounts receivable.
2. Notes receivable from customers due in normal trade terms.
3. Patent.
4. Inventory held for sale to customers.
5. Inventory of cleaning supplies to be used internally.
6. Wages payable.
7. Retained earnings.
8. Merchandise inventory held pending return to supplier.
9. Shares of stock of an affiliated company held for long-term appreciation.
10. Additional paid-in capital.
11. Bonds payable due in five years.
12. Note receivable from company vice president.
13. Amounts payable to employees' union for dues withheld from salaries.
14. Amounts paid out in advance for future periods' rent.
15. Accounts payable.
16. Note receivable from customer due in five years.

E6-11 Elements of the Balance Sheet For each item listed, indicate whether it qualifies as an element of the balance sheet and why, and, if it does, how it would be classified:

1. Coca-Cola's secret formula for its classic soft drink.
2. The creative personnel employed by The Walt Disney Company.
3. A company's commitment to its employees to treat them in a fair and equitable manner.
4. A fifteen-year-old machine that is still operating even though it was expected to last only ten years.
5. The cost of expected future warranty claims on equipment sold during the past several years with the company's five-year guarantee.
6. Inventory that is now out of style, but can still be sold for 60 percent of its original selling price.
7. A common herb that grows wild throughout much of the United States and, according to the company's marketing efforts, cures baldness.

E6-12 Balance Sheet Classification Horn Publishing Corporation wishes to prepare a classified balance sheet. During the past two weeks, Horn was involved in the following transactions that have not been recorded:

1. Inventory costing $800 was sold on account for $1,000.
2. A total of $5,000 was borrowed from a local bank on a five-year note payable.
3. Cash of $4,500 was received from annual renewals of magazine subscriptions.
4. Employees earned wages of $600 and were paid immediately.
5. A patent costing $17,000 was purchased.
6. Payment of $1,800 was made for a three-year insurance policy.

You have been asked to analyze each transaction and:

a. Indicate which balance sheet element(s) will be changed and whether the reported balance(s) will increase or decrease when the transactions are recorded.
b. Indicate whether each of the elements affected is a current or noncurrent asset, current or noncurrent liability, owners' equity item, or none of the above.

E6-13 Property, Plant, and Equipment An increasing number of companies report property, plant, and equipment net of (after deducting) accumulated depreciation in the balance sheet. Under generally accepted accounting principles, companies must report both historical cost and the amount of accumulated depreciation.

a. When only the net balance is reported, are total balance sheet assets and liabilities understated, overstated, or correctly stated? Explain.
b. Where can the historical cost and accumulated depreciation amounts be found when fixed assets are reported net?
c. Two companies, New Corporation (organized in 1998) and Old Corporation (organized in 1979), both use large amounts of equipment with very long lives (25 years or more). Both report identical amounts of net property, plant, and equipment. Which company most likely paid the larger amount for its fixed assets? Which company's fixed assets are most likely to be reported closest to their fair values in balance sheets prepared at December 31, 2000? For both answers, explain why.

E6-14 Intangible Assets Pineway Manufacturing Company reports both equipment and patents in its balance sheet.

a. Explain how the dollar amount for each asset is determined.
b. If both assets were purchased three years ago for $10,000 each and had estimated useful lives of ten years, what amounts would be reported in the balance sheet at the end of the current period? Explain.
c. Financial analysts sometimes ignore intangible assets in analyzing financial statements. Do you think this is appropriate? Explain.

E6-15 Classified Balance Sheet The balance sheet of Profit Corporation included the following amounts:

Property, plant, and equipment (net)	$400,000
Retained earnings	170,000
Wages payable	70,000
Patents	50,000
Accounts payable	150,000
Common stock	30,000
Accounts receivable	100,000
Bonds payable	300,000
Inventory	130,000
Cash and cash equivalents	40,000

a. Prepare a classified balance sheet for Profit Corporation.

b. Determine the amount of working capital. Does Profit appear to have the capability to pay its bills? Explain.

E6-16 Classification of Balance Sheet Items Assign each of the items given below to the proper balance sheet classification, if appropriate:

1. Note payable due in twenty-six months.
2. Computer purchased for office use.
3. Unpaid wages.
4. Magazine subscriptions sold in advance.
5. Estimated taxes related to sales of next period.
6. Exercise bikes purchased for resale.
7. Trademark.
8. Shares of preferred stock outstanding.
9. Ninety-day certificate of deposit.
10. Undistributed profits from last period.
11. Cash estimated to be received on sales of next period.
12. Delivery truck.
13. Insurance premium paid in advance.
14. Taxes withheld from employees' pay.
15. Amounts not yet collected from sales of inventory.

The following balance sheet classifications should be used:

CA = Current asset
PPE = Property, plant, and equipment
IA = Intangible asset
CL = Current liability
LTL = Long-term liability
OE = Owners' equity
NA = Not a balance sheet item

E6-17 Balance Sheet Preparation The following balance sheet amounts were reported by Sparce Company at December 31, 2000:

Accounts payable	$ 98,000
Common stock	20,000
Prepaid insurance	12,000
Accumulated depreciation	120,000
Wages payable	34,000
Cash	40,000
Retained earnings	261,000
Accounts receivable	121,000
Buildings and equipment	470,000
Notes payable (long-term)	180,000
Inventory	70,000

Prepare a classified balance sheet for Sparce Company.

E6-18 Balance Sheet Accounts Portley Company reported the following balance sheet amounts at December 31, 2000:

Preferred stock	$ 50,000
Taxes payable	54,000

Investment in T Company stock	27,000
Additional paid-in capital	80,000
Inventory	52,000
Accounts payable	24,000
Cash	7,000
Accumulated depreciation	76,000
Retained earnings	62,000
Land	12,000
Bonds payable	120,000
Accounts receivable	43,000
Buildings and equipment	351,000
Common stock	40,000
Prepaid rent	14,000

Prepare a classified balance sheet for Portley Company at December 31, 2000.

E6-19 Balance Sheet Preparation Luis Baldazar incorporated a business on January 3, 2000. The following is a summary of the business's transactions during 2000.

1. On January 3, Luis transferred cash of $100,000 from his personal checking account into the business checking account. In exchange, the business issued 10,000 shares of $1-par common stock to Luis.
2. On January 3, Luis signed a three-year lease agreement for a building and paid $42,000 to cover the rent for the entire three-year period.
3. On January 3, Luis purchased equipment for $25,000 and signed a four-year, 10 percent note payable for the full amount. All interest is paid at the end of each year, and the full principal is due at the maturity of the note. The equipment has a ten-year life and no expected residual value.
4. During the year, the business had sales, all on credit, of $680,000 and collected $636,000. All remaining accounts are expected to be collected.
5. During the year, the business incurred total expenses of $512,000. All were paid in cash except for depreciation, wages of $1,500 still owed, and $41,000 owed to suppliers at year-end. The appropriate amount of rent expense was included in the total.
6. Because of the business's success, Luis declared and paid himself a dividend of $20,000.

Based on the information given, prepare a classified balance sheet as of December 31, 2000.

E6-20 Using Ratios The following amounts were reported by Liquid Corporation in its most recent balance sheet:

Cash	$ 30,000
Accounts receivable	75,000
Savings deposits	10,000
Inventory	220,000
Prepaid insurance	30,000
Accounts payable	55,000
Wages payable	20,000
Income taxes payable	25,000

| Sales taxes payable | 4,000 |
| Short-term notes payable | 60,000 |

a. Calculate the quick ratio and the current ratio for Liquid Corporation.
b. Based on a review of other companies in the industry, the management of Liquid Corporation thinks it should maintain a quick ratio of 1 or more and a current ratio of 2 or more. The ratios at the end of the prior year were 1.2 and 1.8, respectively. How successful has the company been in achieving the desired results this period?
c. How could the company improve its current position?

E6-21 Current Asset Transactions Invincible Corporation was started January 1, and had the following transactions in January 2001:

1. A total of 7,000 shares of stock was issued for $9 per share.
2. Inventory costing $79,000 was purchased on account.
3. On January 31, $7,000 was paid for an insurance policy for the next 12 months.
4. Payments of $46,000 were made to vendors for past inventory purchases.
5. Inventory costing $60,000 was sold on account for $106,000.
6. Payments of $29,000 were received from customers before the end of the month.
7. Land was purchased for $9,500. Its value at the end of January is $12,500.

Prepare the current assets section of the January 31, 2001, balance sheet for Invincible Corporation.

E6-22 Ratio Analysis The following amounts were reported in Monte Company's balance sheet:

Cash	$ 70,000
Marketable securities	50,000
Accounts receivable (net)	81,000
Inventory	108,000
Prepaid insurance	22,000
Land	15,000
Buildings and equipment (net)	130,000
Total	$476,000
Accounts payable	$ 57,000
Wages payable	12,000
Taxes payable	31,000
Common stock	90,000
Retained earnings	286,000
Total	$476,000

a. What is the amount of Monte's working capital?
b. What is Monte's quick ratio?
c. What is Monte's current ratio?

E6-23 Working Capital and Liquidity The following balance sheet accounts and amounts are found at year-end on the books of Thorson Products Corporation:

Buildings and equipment	$230,000
Bonds payable	125,000
Accumulated depreciation	90,000
Inventory	80,000
Additional paid-in capital	70,000
Accounts receivable	62,000
Retained earnings	60,000
Capital stock	50,000
Land	45,000
Accounts payable	47,000
Cash	44,000
Trademarks	35,000
Unearned service revenue	26,000
Wages payable	20,000
Taxes payable	16,000
Prepaid insurance	5,000
Tax refund receivable	3,000

a. Prepare a classified balance sheet in good form.
b. Compute the amount of Thorson's working capital.
c. At the beginning of the current period, Thorson reported total current assets of $120,000 and current liabilities of $55,000. Compute the current ratios for Thorson at the beginning and end of the period. Has the current ratio improved or declined during the period?
d. At the beginning of the current period, working capital was $65,000. Has Thorson's working capital position and its overall liquidity improved or declined during the year?
e. How might Thorson evaluate whether or not its working capital position and overall liquidity are adequate?

E6-24 Balance Sheet Preparation Sam has asked his uncle to renew the loan he made to Sam's Bar and Grill. Dear old Uncle, however, has said that Sam must provide him with a balance sheet for the business prepared as of the end of the current calendar year in accordance with generally accepted accounting principles before he will consider the request. The following pieces of information have been provided to you by Sam, who is fearful that he will be unable to continue in business unless the loan is renewed:

a. Several years ago, Sam's Bar and Grill borrowed $60,000 from Sam's uncle. Interest of $3,500 is paid at the end of each year; however, the payment for the current year will not be made until early next year.
b. At the end of the current year, Sam has on hand beer that cost $4,500 and soda that cost $1,700. Sam still owes $1,500 for the beer and $700 for the soda.
c. As a promotional gimmick, the bar sold 1,000 coupon books to customers. Each book sold for $15 and entitled the holder to 25 glasses of beer, which normally sell for $1 each. All coupons are expected to be used. By the end of the current year, half of the coupons have been used.

d. Unpaid wages at the end of the current year total $23,000.

e. Sam's Bar and Grill exercised the purchase clause in its lease agreement for furniture and equipment and paid $85,000 at the end of the current year to buy these items.

f. Halfway through the current year, Sam's Bar and Grill paid Nofault Insurance Company $21,000 for three years' liability coverage to comply with the dram law insurance requirements for the State of Tennessee, coverage to start on that date.

g. The cash balance on hand at the end of the year is $14,000.

Prepare a balance sheet for Sam's Bar and Grill as of the end of the current year. Based on the balance sheet data, do you think Uncle is likely to renew the loan? Why?

E6-25 Operating Cycle Toni Company manufactures sophisticated power-generation control systems, each taking approximately two years to complete. Because the sales price of these systems is quite high, purchasers are extended credit for 180 days from delivery. Over the years, Toni has accumulated a sizable retained earnings balance. All of Toni's other account balances are as follows (in thousands):

Cash	$ 28
Notes receivable from customers (92-day average maturity)	1,200
Note receivable from Oregon Power Company (due in 2 years)	410
Note receivable from Toni's president (due in 5 years	100
Parts inventory (expected to be used on systems that will be sold in approximately 2.5 years)	299
Inventory in process (1.5-year average expected delivery date)	3,400
Completed inventory (awaiting delivery)	2,100
Prepaid insurance (covering next 2 years)	88
Accounts payable (58-day average due date)	650
Salaries payable	41
Bank loan payable (due in 18 months)	250
First mortgage note payable ($400 due in 16 months; remainder due in 5-year intervals thereafter)	2,400
Common stock	1,000

a. Prepare a classified balance sheet for Toni Company in good form.

b. Inot Company is a manufacturing company selling small replacement parts to power companies. The parts take about three days to manufacture, and they are sold to customers with payments due in 30 days. Which items in Toni's balance sheet would you expect to be classified differently if they were in Inot's balance sheet? Why?

E6-26 Using Ratio Analysis Solvent Company's current assets and current liabilities at December 31, 2001, consisted of the following:

Cash	$ 27,000
Accounts receivable (net)	93,000
Inventory	?
Prepaid insurance	16,000
Accounts payable	52,000
Wages payable	6,000
Taxes payable	22,000

a. Solvent reported a current ratio of 4 to 1 at December 31, 2001. What was the total amount of current assets reported at that date?

b. What was Solvent's working capital balance at December 31, 2001?

c. What was Solvent's quick ratio at December 31, 2001?

d. What was the inventory balance at December 31, 2001?

E6-27 Intangible Assets Determine the balance sheet amounts to be reported by Wisp Corporation at December 31, 2000, for each of the following:

a. A copyright is purchased for $60,000 on January 1, 2000, and is expected to benefit a 15-year period.

b. A trademark was acquired on January 1, 1996, for a total price of $36,000. The trademark will expire at December 31, 2004.

c. On January 1, 1999, Wisp paid $50,000 for an exclusive franchise to sell "slick stuff" wax products in the state of Maine for the next 4 years.

d. Wisp purchased patents for a new production process. The patents cost $130,000. They have a legal life of 20 years from the date of purchase, July 1, 1998, but are expected to provide benefits for only 10 years.

E6-28 Asset Valuation The following assets were held by Quagmire Corporation at December 31, 2000:

Asset	Date Acquired	Expected Life	Cost	Fair Value
Accounts receivable	Dec. 1–31, 2000	n/a	$230,000	$210,000
Inventory	Jan. 1, 2000	n/a	150,000	162,000
Buildings and equipment	Jan. 1, 1990	30 years	600,000	370,000
Patent	Jan. 1, 1997	8 years	32,000	27,000
Marketable securities	Jan. 1, 2000	n/a	22,000	19,000
Prepaid insurance	Jan. 1, 1997	5 years	20,000	5,000

Determine the amount to be reported for each asset in Quagmire's balance sheet at December 31, 2000.

E6-29 Reported Assets Shakeup Corporation reported the following assets and values at December 31, 2000:

Asset	Acquisition Price	Carrying (Book) Value	Net Realizable Value
Accounts receivable	$230,000	$230,000	$215,000
Inventory	420,000	420,000	406,000
Prepaid insurance	24,000	16,000	5,000
Building and equipment	400,000	320,000	350,000
Land	80,000	80,000	88,000

a. At what amount should Shakeup Corporation report each asset if it is planning to remain in business for the next twenty years?

b. At what amount should Shakeup Corporation report each asset if it is planning to discontinue its business on January 2, 2001, and liquidate its assets?

E6-30 Asset Valuation Tardy Brewing Company is preparing its balance sheet at year-end and needs guidelines on how a variety of its assets should be valued. For each of the items listed, indicate the valuation process normally used and the potential impact on financial statement analysis if an alternative measure is used:

	Book Value	Fair Value	Present Value
a. Cash	$45,000	$45,000	$45,000
b. Accounts receivable	30,000	28,000	28,000
c. Inventory A	12,000	32,000	32,000
d. Inventory B	9,000	8,000	7,500
e. Machinery	65,000	83,000	94,000
f. Patents	18,000	24,000	29,000

E6-31 Liability and Equity Valuations The owner of Montana Manufacturing is in the process of preparing a balance sheet at year-end and needs guidance on valuing liability and equity items for financial reporting purposes. For each of the items listed, indicate the valuation process normally used and the potential impact on financial statement analysis if an alternative measure is used:

	Book Value	Fair Value	Present Value
a. Wages payable	$ 9,000	$ 9,000	$ 9,000
b. Bonds payable	75,000	73,000	74,000
c. Common stock outstanding	4,000	45,000	50,000
d. Retained earnings	60,000	0	0
e. Deferred income taxes	15,000	0	1,000

E6-32 Unrecorded Transactions Wisper Corporation discovered at the end of the year that it had failed to record several transactions or activities. Those specifically identified were:

1. Inventory purchased on account for $35,000.
2. Payment on accounts payable of $25,000.
3. Depreciation expense of $10,000.
4. Wages of $8,000 earned by employees since the last payroll payment.
5. Issuance of a $5,000 long-term note payable for cash.

If Wisper Corporation reports total current assets of $240,000 and current liabilities of $140,000 prior to correcting its omissions, determine what amounts should be reported for each of the following:

a. Current assets.
b. Current liabilities.
c. Working capital.
d. Current ratio.

E6-33 Determining Reported Amounts Partial balance sheet data for Bell Corporation at August 28, 2000, were as follows:

Bell Corporation
Balance Sheet
August 28, 2001

Cash		$ 65,000
Accounts receivable		94,000
Inventory		?
Buildings and equipment	$425,000	
Less accumulated depreciation	?	255,000
Total		$?
Accounts payable		$ 51,000
Wages payable		19,000
Notes payable		200,000
Common stock ($2 par value)		18,000
Additional paid-in capital		45,000
Retained earnings		?
Total		$537,000

a. What is the amount of total assets at August 28, 2001?

b. Bell reported inventory of $177,000 at the beginning of the period, purchased inventory costing $303,000 during the period, and sold inventory that had cost $357,000. What is the amount of inventory at August 28, 2001?

c. What is the balance in accumulated depreciation at August 28, 2001?

d. If wages payable increased by $2,500 during the period, what was the balance at the start of the period?

e. Bell had 8,000 shares of common stock outstanding and additional paid-in capital of $23,000 at the beginning of the period. How many additional shares were issued during the period?

f. What was the price per share received by Bell Corporation for the shares issued?

g. What is the balance in retained earnings at August 28, 2001?

USING ACCOUNTING FOR DECISION MAKING

P6-34 Financial Statement Preparation Montage Company reported the following income statement and balance sheet amounts at December 31, 2000:

Sales	$635,000
Salary and wages payable	21,000
Prepaid insurance	16,000
Depreciation expense	25,000
Preferred stock	50,000
Salary and wage expense	140,000
Accounts payable	76,000
Land	74,000
Federal income tax expense	90,000
Accumulated depreciation	160,000
Common stock	100,000
Accounts receivable (net)	132,000
Notes payable (due January 1, 2005)	195,000
Cost of goods sold	310,000
Cash	80,000
Buildings and equipment	440,000
Inventory	90,000
Retained earnings, January 1, 2000	160,000

a. Prepare an income statement for Montage Company for 2000.
b. Compute the balance in retained earnings at December 31, 2000.
c. Prepare a classified balance sheet at December 31, 2000.

P6-35 Accounting Equation Noylot Corporation reported the following balance sheet amounts at December 1, 2001:

Noylot Corporation
Balance Sheet
December 1, 2001

Cash		$ 73,000
Accounts receivable (net)		136,000
Inventory		108,000
Prepaid insurance		20,000
Land		40,000
Buildings and equipment	$410,000	
Less accumulated depreciation	(170,000)	240,000
Total assets		$617,000
Accounts payable		$ 43,000
Wages payable		21,000
Bonds payable		250,000
Common stock		25,000
Additional paid-in capital		20,000
Retained earnings		258,000
Total liabilities and owners' equity		$617,000

Noylot Corporation had the following transactions during December 2001:

1. Inventory costing $34,000 was purchased on account.
2. Depreciation expense of $21,000 was recorded.
3. Wages payable of $16,000 were paid.
4. Accounts receivable in the amount of $65,000 were collected.
5. A total of 2,000 new shares of common stock was issued at $12 each. The stock has a par value of $5 per share.
6. Prepaid insurance of $2,000 expired during December.
7. Salary and wage expenses of $15,000 were paid in cash during December.
8. Inventory that cost $40,000 was sold on credit for $70,000.

a. Analyze the effects of each transaction on the accounting equation (A = L + SE) for Noylot Corporation.
b. Prepare a classified balance sheet at December 31, 2001, that incorporates the effects of the above transactions.

P6-36 Comparative Analysis Chan Corporation is interested in evaluating its assets and liabilities to see if it is operating effectively and efficiently. It is planning to make comparisons of its amounts to:

a. Budgeted amounts.
b. Industry averages.
c. Last year's amounts.
d. Amounts from similar companies.

Assume that Chan Corporation will use only one of the listed amounts. For each one, indicate the advantages and disadvantages of using that comparison and give your recommendation as to which one should be chosen.

P6-37 Valuation of Balance Sheet Elements Bland Corporation has applied to your bank for a large long-term loan. In carefully reviewing the balance sheet and other information, you note the following:

1. The unadjusted historical cost of equipment is $600,000 and accumulated depreciation is $380,000. The estimated cost of replacing the assets with new pieces of equipment is $850,000. The cost of buying comparable used equipment is $180,000.
2. The carrying value of inventory is $210,000. The cost of producing the entire amount currently would be $230,000, and the estimated sales price under normal conditions would be approximately $350,000, but only $250,000 if liquidated quickly.
3. Ten-year bonds payable were issued at par value of $500,000 two years ago. Interest rates have risen since then, and the bonds are now trading at $450,000.

What values should be used for financial reporting purposes? Indicate what values are the most useful for your loan decision under each of the following situations, and explain why:

a. The company is profitable and plans to operate in a manner similar to its current mission into the foreseeable future.
b. The company has been experiencing losses recently, and its future is uncertain without some major changes.
c. The company is very profitable, and it is planning to re-place some of its production equipment at the end of the year with new units.

P6-38 Balance Sheet Classification At the end of his first year of working as the financial vice president of Astor Company, Paul Reed is perplexed by some of the de-cisions that must be made in preparing a balance sheet for the company, a major retailer. Because he knows you cur-rently are taking an accounting course, he would like you to assist him by (a) determining which of the following should be reported as current assets and liabilities and (b) determining the impact an improper classification is likely to have if an investor uses the reported amounts to analyze Astor's balance sheet:

1. The company has bonds with an $800,000 par value out-standing. One-fourth is due and payable at the end of each of the next four years. Because they are long-term bonds, Paul plans to list them as a long-term liability.
2. Just prior to the end of the current period, Astor Company paid $500,000 for exclusive rights to a trademark devel-oped by the son of Astor's president, I. M. Dunn. Because the trademark is being used on inventory items that are available for sale, it is listed as a current asset and should have value for the next four years.
3. Also included in current assets is a $50,000 payment made at year-end to prepay an insurance policy for the next two years.
4. The company has a fleet of delivery vans and will trade in several 12-year-old vans and purchase new units during the next year. Mr. Reed believes the vans should be classi-fied as current assets because they will be sold within the next year.

P6-39 International Companies Sanchez Bearing Com-pany produces and markets bearings that are lightweight and have a very high heat tolerance. Sanchez's balance sheet in-cludes the assets and liabilities of its foreign subsidiaries, which are located in five different countries. In preparing the balance sheet for Sanchez, assets and liabilities located in dif-ferent countries are combined. What difficulties might arise from the combination for:

a. The classification of balance sheet items?
b. The valuation of assets and liabilities?
c. Analyzing the current ratio and working capital?
d. Making comparisons to other bearing manufacturers?

P6-40 Analyis of Assets You have money to invest, and a friend suggested that you consider Galena Ski Products

common stock. Because you may need to sell the stock within the next two years to pay for college expenses, you start your analysis of the company data by computing (1) working capital, (2) the current ratio, and (3) the quick ratio. Galena's balance sheet is as follows:

Current Assets	
Cash and cash equivalents	$218,000
Inventory	320,000
Other current assets	32,000
Noncurrent Assets	
Buildings and equipment	300,000
Land	16,000
Other	25,000
Total	$911,000
Current Liabilities	$165,000
Long-Term Debt	400,000
Common Stock	150,000
Retained Earnings	196,000
Total	$911,000

a. What amount of working capital currently is maintained? Would you recommend the company maintain that level? Explain why.
b. Your preference is to have a quick ratio of at least .80 and a current ratio of at least 2.0. How do the existing ratios compare with your criteria? Using these two ratios, how would you evaluate the company's current asset position?
c. The company sells only on a cash basis currently and had sales of $700,000 this past year. How would you expect a change from cash to credit sales to affect the balance sheet ratios?
d. Galena's balance sheet is presented just before the start of shipments for its fall and winter season. How would your evaluation change if these balances existed in late Febru-ary following completion of its primary business for the skiing season?

P6-41 Financial Statement Presentation and Analysis Paperweights, Inc., is doing a thriving business and is about to declare an extra cash dividend at year-end as a result of its strong earnings report for the year. The balance sheet for Pa-perweights is as follows:

Cash	$ 25,000
Accounts receivable (net of accounts	
payable of $190,000)	130,000
Inventory (at selling price)	160,000
Prepaid insurance	20,000
Buildings and equipment	350,000
Land	40,000
Goodwill	225,000
Total	$950,000

Wages payable	$ 55,000
Taxes payable	30,000
Long-term bonds payable	500,000
Accumulated depreciation	120,000
Capital stock	80,000
Retained earnings	100,000
Adjustment for increase in inventory value	65,000
Total	$950,000

I. M. Gullable, president of Paperweights, Inc., is very proud of the 4.1 current ratio and reported net working capital of $235,000. He also is proud of the long-term debt to total asset ratio of only 53 percent. During the annual audit, the auditor has raised concerns about whether or not the financial statements are correctly prepared. For example, the auditor noted that Goodwill had been recorded to reflect the estimated value of increased business stemming from Mr. Gullable's various charitable and civic activities and contributions. Assuming generally accepted accounting procedures are used:

a. What is the correct amount of working capital?
b. What is the correct amount of current assets and current liabilities? What is the correct current ratio?
c. What is the proper total of noncurrent assets? How does the total compare with the amount reported by the company?
d. Do the corrected amounts confirm Mr. Gullable's analysis and assessment of the company's safety? Explain.

P6-42 Creditors' Claims Celin Company's balance sheet at December 31, 2001, appeared as follows:

Cash	$ 12,000
Accounts receivable (net of $11,000 bad debt allowance)	120,000
Inventory	180,000
Prepaid insurance	30,000
Buildings and equipment (net)	480,000
Land	25,000
Secret product formulas	200,000
Goodwill	300,000
Total	$1,347,000
Accounts payable	$ 55,000
Taxes payable	10,000
First mortgage note	300,000
Secured note payable	200,000
Senior unsecured notes	230,000
Subordinated debentures	200,000
Capital stock	75,000
Additional paid-in capital	150,000
Retained earnings	127,000
Total	$1,347,000

Celin Company has just approached the bank for which you work as a loan officer to seek additional financing. Celin has not been profitable recently, but it expects its current cost-cutting program to return the company to profitability. The company's collections of accounts receivable have been slow, and the company is afraid it may run out of cash while it is working on improving its working capital management.

The company wants to borrow $200,000 for equipment repairs and to improve liquidity. It is willing to give the bank a secondary claim on its receivables and inventory as collateral for the loan, but the holder of the secured note payable has first claim on the receivables and inventory and must be paid before any amounts from these assets could go to the bank. You would like to help Celin because the bank already holds $100,000 of the company's senior unsecured notes. The senior unsecured notes must be paid in full before any amounts are paid to holders of the subordinated debentures and other unsecured creditors.

After reviewing the balance sheet, you have some concerns about the company's assets. First, you know the goodwill would be worthless if the company were liquidated, and probably is worthless even if the company continues operating. The secret product formulas do not seem to have helped business much, so their value is questionable. The land has been appraised at $40,000, and the buildings and equipment have been appraised at $400,000 if sold. Another bank holds the first mortgage note on the building and land, giving it first claim. The other assets seem fairly valued.

a. If you do not approve Celin's loan and the company is liquidated, which creditors will be paid, and how much? Prepare a listing. How much, if anything, will the bank lose? Which creditors do you think would be most against liquidating the company? Why? What would the stockholders get if the company were liquidated?
b. Are there any assets that are troublesome to you when trying to value them? Explain why. What assumptions did you make about the value of the different assets when estimating how much each creditor would get?
c. Suppose you approve the $200,000 loan to Celin. If the company uses $150,000 to repair equipment, increasing the equipment's liquidation value by $30,000, and holds the other $50,000 in marketable securities, how much can the bank expect to lose if Celin is liquidated? Show how assets would be apportioned to different claimants.
d. Based on the information given, would you approve the loan knowing that Celin probably would liquidate without it and had a reasonable chance of survival with it? Explain your decision.

EXPANDING YOUR HORIZONS

C6-43 The Ethics of Measurement The Baker Corporation obtained most of the financing for its recent expansion by borrowing from the local bank. The bank loan is payable over ten years, and, because the bank was concerned that Baker might not maintain sufficient liquidity to meet current obligations, one of the loan provisions is that Baker must maintain a current ratio of at least 2 to 1. If the ratio falls below this level, the bank loan immediately becomes due. The ratio is to be measured on the last day of each month. On February 28, 2001, the current ratio falls short (current assets of $720,000 and current liabilities of $370,000). The next day, Mary, the president, is told that Baker Corporation may be in violation of the loan provisions. She angrily calls Tom, the financial vice president, into her office and demands to know what he is going to do about this. Tom is desperate, and the only alternative he can think of is to suggest writing checks for a total of $20,000 to pay accounts payable and backdate them to February 28.

Can this strategy work? What are the implications of backdating the checks? Will the financial statements then be misstated? Discuss the ethical implications of such an approach.

C6-44 Team Assignment: Analyzing Financial Position Using a listing of companies provided by your instructor or other listings you have available:

a. Select two companies that are in different types of businesses (e.g., a retail enterprise and a manufacturing company).
b. Find the companies' financial statements in the most recent issue of *Moody's Industrial Manual* or in an electronic database. Become familiar with the financial statements for the two companies.
c. Acquire an actual annual report for both of the companies. (Many large companies have toll-free phone numbers for ordering free annual reports or provide for ordering by e-mail. Many companies include their annual reports on their Web pages, but make sure you obtain a full annual report.) Review the form in which the balance sheet is presented in the annual report and compare it to the information presented in *Moody's Industrial Manual*.
d. Calculate the current ratio and ratio of long-term debt to total assets from *Moody's* data and from the annual reports for both companies. Do you get the same numbers based on both sources?
e. Compare the financial positions of the two companies as a team. What differences do you see in their financial positions? Evaluate the differences as to whether they occur because the companies are in different industries or because one has a stronger financial position than the other.
f. For one of the companies, as a team, review the discussion of operations by management and the footnotes to the financial statements presented in the annual report and look at the ratios you have calculated. Reach a team consensus as to the strength of the company's financial position. Describe the factors that led to your conclusion.

C6-45 Analyzing the Numbers The following ratios and other information are based on a company's comparative financial statements for a two-year period:

	Year 1	Year 2
Current ratio	1.74	1.28
Quick ratio	.89	.44
Debt-to-assets ratio	.60	.88
Debt-to-equity ratio	1.52	7.33
Earnings per share	1.65	.51
Gross profit percentage	37%	35%
Total assets	$1,825,109	$6,258,089
Current assets	$1,302,206	$3,105,439

a. What is the amount of current liabilities at the end of Year 2?
b. What is the amount of total debt at the end of Year 2?
c. What is total equity at the end of Year 2?
d. Do you think this company is a merchandising or manufacturing company, a financial institution, or a service organization? Why?
e. If the company has 58,905,230 shares of common stock outstanding for all of Year 2 and has issued no other stock, what is its net income for Year 2?
f. Based on the information available, what is your assessment of the company's liquidity? Explain. Given the limited information, what is your assessment of the company's overall financial position? Explain.
g. What changes do you see between Year 1 and Year 2 that appear particularly significant? What explanation might there be for these changes?

C6-46 Evaluating Dayton Hudson's Financial Position Following are the comparative balance sheets (next page) and footnote disclosure relating to accounts receivable for Dayton Hudson Corporation:

Retained Securitized Receivables

The fair value of the retained securitized receivables was lower than the aggregate receivables value by $126 million and $119 million at year-end 1997 (January 31, 1998) and 1996 (February 1, 1997), respectively, due to our estimates of ultimate collectibility.

The securitization of accounts receivable permits the company to borrow against the balance of accounts receivable.

a. Is the company's liquidity position better or worse at January 31, 1998, as compared with February 1, 1997? Explain.
b. What is the amount owed to Dayton Hudson by its customers at January 31, 1998? How much of that amount does the company expect to receive?

c. What is the total original historical cost of property and equipment in service (use) at January 31, 1998?

d. What is the total net book value of property and equipment in service (use) at January 31, 1998?

e. How much of the long-term debt does the company expect to pay off in the next year?

f. How many classes of stock does the company have outstanding?

g. Has the company generally been profitable or unprofitable since its inception? How do you know?

DAYTON HUDSON CORPORATION		
CONSOLIDATED STATEMENTS OF FINANCIAL POSITION		
(Millions of Dollars)	**January 31, 1998**	**February 1, 1997**
ASSETS		
Current Assets		
Cash and cash equivalents	$ 211	$ 201
Retained securitized receivables	1,555	1,720
Merchandise inventories	3,251	3,031
Other	544	488
Total Current Assets	5,561	5,440
Property and Equipment		
Land	1,712	1,557
Buildings and improvements	6,497	5,943
Fixtures and equipment	2,915	2,652
Construction-in-progress	389	317
Accumulated depreciation	(3,388)	(3,002)
Net Property and Equipment	8,125	7,467
Other	505	482
Total Assets	$14,191	$13,389
LIABILITIES AND COMMON		
SHAREHOLDERS' INVESTMENT		
Current Liabilities		
Accounts payable	$ 2,727	$ 2,528
Accrued liabilities	1,346	1,168
Income taxes payable	210	182
Current portion of long-term debt and notes payable	273	233
Total Current Liabilities	4,556	4,111
Long-Term Debt	4,425	4,808
Deferred Income Taxes and Other	720	630
Convertible Preferred Stock, Net	30	50
Shareholders' Investment		
Convertible preferred stock	280	271
Common stock	73	72
Additional paid-in capital	196	146
Retained earnings	3,930	3,348
Loan to ESOP	(19)	(47)
Total Shareholders' Investment	4,460	3,790
Total Liabilities & Shareholders' Investment	$14,191	$13,389

C6-47 How R Us Doing? Examine the comparative income statements and balance sheets of Toys "R" Us, Inc., and answer the following questions:

a. Based on the income statements, what is your assessment of this company's performance? Explain.

b. Based on the balance sheets, what is your assessment of this company's leverage and solvency? Explain. Has the company's solvency changed significantly?

c. What is your assessment of this company's liquidity? Support your view by presenting common indicators of liquidity. Has the company's liquidity changed significantly?

d. What is your conclusion regarding this company's performance and financial position? Explain.

TOYS "R" US, INC. AND SUBSIDIARIES
CONSOLIDATED STATEMENTS OF EARNINGS

	Year Ended		
(In millions except per share data)	**January 31, 1998**	**February 1, 1997**	**February 3, 1996**
Net Sales	$11,038	$9,932	$9,427
Cost of sales	7,710	6,892	6,592
Gross Profit	**3,328**	3,040	2,835
Selling, advertising, general and administrative expenses	2,231	2,020	1,894
Depreciation, amortization and asset write-offs	253	206	192
Other charges	—	60	397
Total Operating Expenses	**2,484**	2,286	2,483
Operating Income	844	754	352
Interest expense	85	98	103
Interest and other income	(13)	(17)	(17)
Interest Expense, Net	**72**	81	86
Earnings Before Income Taxes	772	673	266
Income Taxes	282	246	118
Net Earnings	$ 490	$ 427	$ 148
Basic Earnings Per Share	$ 1.72	$ 1.56	$ 0.54
Diluted Earnings Per Share	$ 1.70	$ 1.54	$ 0.53

TOYS "R" US, INC. AND SUBSIDIARIES
CONSOLIDATED BALANCE SHEETS

(In millions)	January 31, 1998	February 1, 1997
ASSETS		
Current Assets:		
Cash and cash equivalents	$ 214	$ 761
Accounts and other receivables	175	142
Merchandise inventories	2,464	2,215
Prepaid expenses and other current assets	51	42
Total Current Assets	2,904	3,160
Property and Equipment:		
Real estate, net	2,435	2,411
Other, net	1,777	1,636
Total Property and Equipment	4,212	4,047
Goodwill, net	356	365
Other Assets	491	451
	$7,963	$8,023
LIABILITIES AND STOCKHOLDERS' EQUITY		
Current Liabilities:		
Short-term borrowings	$ 134	$ 304
Accounts payable	1,280	1,346
Accrued expenses and other current liabilities	680	720
Income taxes payable	231	171
Total Current Liabilities	2,325	2,541
Long-Term Debt	851	909
Deferred Income Taxes	219	222
Other Liabilities	140	160
Stockholders' Equity:		
Common stock	30	30
Additional paid-in capital	467	489
Retained earnings	4,610	4,120
Foreign currency translation adjustments	(122)	(60)
Treasury shares, at cost	(557)	(388)
Total Stockholders' Equity	4,428	4,191
	$7,963	$8,023

Internet Exercises: Visit our Web site for additional exercises.

Annual Report Project Part 6

Refer to the Annual Report Project, Part 1, at the end of Chapter 1. Using the annual report of the company you have chosen, and any other available information, answer the following questions, providing sources and computations where appropriate.

a. What is the amount of total assets held by your company?

b. During the latest year, did the proportion of current assets (as compared with total assets) change? Explain.

c. By what amount did working capital increase or decrease during the past year?

d. Assess your company's liquidity.

e. Based on the balance sheet, how would you characterize the growth of your company during the past year? Did it (1) not grow, (2) grow at a slow or moderate rate, or (3) expand rapidly? Explain.

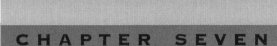

CHAPTER SEVEN

The Accounting Process

REVIEW

In Chapters 1 through 6, we established the basic concepts of financial reporting and the principles on which the information reported in financial statements is based.

WHERE THIS CHAPTER FITS

In this chapter we look at the process that generates the information reported in financial statements. This process captures real-world events in words and numbers and reports them to decision makers through the financial statements.

LOOKING AHEAD

In the following chapters, we will again focus on the financial statements by looking at the meaning of individual elements.

If accounting is the language of business, then do I have to be able to record and decipher journal entries and ledger postings to be able to figure out what is going on? Is learning accounting like learning a foreign language, where you must be able to conjugate the verbs and construct sentences properly? Or, is it like driving a car, where you don't really need to know much about how the motor works—you just put in some gas and it does what you want it to do?

"As financially strapped Washington, D.C., begs for a congressional bailout amid charges of bookkeeping gimmicks, auditors for the district blame the huge budget shortfall on the city. . . . Audits recommended hundreds of improvements in the district's financial reporting procedures, which, if implemented, could have averted the city's financial plight. . . . The auditors suggested measures for strengthening internal financial controls for the district . . . The district's outdated financial management system impedes the ability of district officials to make informed decisions . . . [C&L audit partner Peter Nunn said] 'the district has no systems by which necessary financial information is routinely gathered, analyzed and incorporated into financial statements.'"[1]

[1] Excerpts from "Financial Woes Mount for Washington, D.C.," *Public Accounting Report*, February 28, 1995, p. 1.

Just as you don't need to know how a car is made or how its engine works to drive it, you don't need to know all the details of how accounting information is processed to use it. On the other hand, understanding a little about your car's engine may help you decide if "that funny noise" is a serious problem that needs immediate repair or just a rattle that can be safely ignored. Similarly, knowing some of the details of the accounting process will improve your understanding of accounting information and help you make better decisions.

The financial accounting information reported about any organization depends on that entity's accounting system. Understanding the entity's system, with its strengths and weaknesses, helps you understand the information you use in making your decisions.

This chapter provides you with a general understanding of the workings of an accounting system and a greater knowledge of the factors underlying the accounting information that appears in financial statements. As a decision maker, you will be better able to use accounting information effectively if you understand the choices that are made in generating and presenting that information. Once you finish this chapter, you should be able to:

1. State how the accounting system relates to the accounting process and how it is designed to provide useful information to decision makers.

2. Describe how the accounting equation is useful in understanding and communicating the effects of different transactions and events.

3. Explain how ledger accounts are used to process information about transactions and events to facilitate financial decisions.

4. Discuss the benefits of the double-entry bookkeeping system for financial statement users.

5. Differentiate between permanent and temporary accounts and explain how the differences in these accounts relate to the types of decisions financial statement users make.

6. Describe the role that each of the accounting cycle steps plays in providing useful information for decision makers.

7. Explain how end-of-period adjustments help ensure that financial statements are fairly presented and describe typical types of adjustments.

ACCOUNTING SYSTEMS

Every organization must have an accounting system to generate information needed by decision makers. As we discussed in Chapter 2, the design and operation of an accounting system must consider the anticipated users of the information and the types of decisions they are expected to make. The size, complexity, and type of entity all influence the kinds of decisions that need to be made and, therefore, the way in which information is accumulated and reported in the financial statements.

In Practice 7-1

THE VILLAGE OF HAMEL AND RALSTON PURINA

The village of Hamel, Illinois, a small town with total revenues of about $385,000, reports to the penny the compensation paid to each individual employee and all amounts exceeding $1,000 paid to individual vendors, a total of 129 separate line-items. In contrast, Ralston Purina, a company with revenues of almost $5 billion, reports only five expense categories, and rounds all amounts to $100,000.

ANALYSIS

Local governments must typically publish an exact listing of all expenditures over a certain amount for taxpayers' review. In contrast, a large corporation with many complicated transactions may publish reports with many items combined and amounts rounded off. Because the information needs differ in these two cases, so does the form of the information reported. [www.ralston.com]

Most entities have an accounting procedures manual that specifies the policies and procedures to be followed in accumulating information within the accounting system. This manual details what events are to be recorded in the accounts and when and how the information is to be classified and accumulated. The way information is accumulated is based on the accounting equation.

THE ACCOUNTING EQUATION: THE BASIS FOR USEFUL INFORMATION

As we discussed in Chapters 2 and 4, the financial statements are articulated, meaning they are interrelated to form an overall picture of an entity's activities and position. The relationships are based on the accounting equation:

$$\text{assets} = \text{liabilities} + \text{equity}$$

This equation can be expanded by detailing the individual asset, liability, and equity elements. For example, the accounting equation for a small store might appear as follows:

ASSETS			=	LIABILITIES		+	EQUITY	
cash +	accounts receivable	+ inventory =		accounts payable	+ other payables	+	capital stock	+ retained earnings

In fact, all of the store's financial transactions can be seen in terms of the accounting equation. Exhibit 7–1 illustrates a series of transactions for the store and shows the effects on the store's accounting equation.

Because the accounting equation must always balance, each transaction or event must have at least two effects. For instance, when the store purchases inventory for cash, one asset (inventory) increases while another asset (cash) decreases by an equal amount. In some cases, as Exhibit 7–1 shows, a transaction might have more than two effects. When the store sells inventory for more than its cost, inventory is reduced by the cost of the inventory sold ($2,500), the accounts receivable balance is increased by the sales price of the inventory ($4,000), and, because profits accrue to the owners, retained earnings is increased for the amount of the profit ($1,500). Thus, the left side of the equation increases by $1,500, reflecting the increase in total assets, while the other side of the equation increases by an equal amount, reflecting the owners' increased claim on the assets.

USING LEDGER ACCOUNTS FOR ACCUMULATION AND ANALYSIS

We know that decision makers are interested in the individual elements of financial statements. For instance, a creditor evaluating a company's ability to repay a short-term loan considers the amount of cash the company holds, its current receivables, and its current payables. Simply knowing the amount of the company's total assets and total liabilities would not allow the decision maker to focus on relevant factors. Because decision makers need detailed information, and the type of information needed varies from one decision maker to the next, an accounting system must be designed to accumulate and communicate information about individual financial statement items.

Information about individual financial statement elements is accumulated in **ledger accounts**. Each entity maintains its own list and description of the individual accounts that it

EXHIBIT 7-1 THE EFFECT OF TRANSACTIONS ON THE ACCOUNTING EQUATION

	Cash	+	Accounts Receivable	+	Inventory	=	Accounts Payable	+	Other Payables	+	Capital Stock	+	Retained Earnings
Initial balances prior to start of business	$ -0-	+	$ -0-	+	$ -0-	=	$ -0-	+	$ -0-	+	$ -0-	+	$ -0-
Owners invest $10,000 by having store issue capital stock	+10,000										+10,000		
Store purchases inventory for $2,000 cash	− 2,000				+2,000								
Store purchases inventory for $5,000 on account					+5,000		+5,000						
Store pays $1,000 on account	− 1,000						− 1,000						
Store sells on credit for $4,000 inventory that had cost $2,500			+4,000		−2,500								+1,500
Customers pay $800 on account	+ 800		− 800										
Miscellaneous expenses are recognized but not paid									+ 900				− 900
Store pays $500 dividend to owners	− 500												− 500
Ending balances	$ 7,300	+	$3,200	+	$4,500	=	$4,000	+	$900	+	$10,000	+	$100

uses, referred to as the **chart of accounts**. Each account is typically assigned both a title and a number. Let's look more closely at how information is accumulated in ledger accounts.

HOW LEDGER ACCOUNTS WORK

Information for an individual asset, liability, or owners' equity item is accumulated in an account, which can be represented for a simple handwritten system as follows:

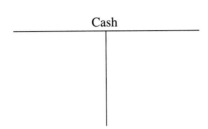

Cash

Not surprisingly, this form of a ledger account is referred to as a **T-account**. Most companies now accumulate information electronically, but we'll use T-accounts to show how information flows through the accounting system and to show the relationship between the accounts and financial statements.

In Practice 7-2

COMPUTERIZED ACCOUNTING SYSTEMS

Computerized accounting systems are within the reach of even small companies through the use of accounting software packages. Such programs are available from a number of manufacturers. Two of the most widely used are Great Plains Accounting and Peachtree. Data can be input using a personal computer, and, based on the company's needs, the software automatically accumulate's the information. Financial reports can then be generated at any time.

ANALYSIS

The same principles guide the recording and accumulation of information in a computerized accounting system as in a handwritten system. However, the information can be processed more efficiently and often used more effectively with a computerized system.

A T-account is used for each asset, liability, and owners' equity element. A T-account reflects increases, decreases, and a running total for a particular item. All amounts that increase an account balance are placed on one side, while all decreases are shown on the other side. With cash, for example, all increases are shown on the left and all decreases on the right. The amount of cash on hand at any point in time is determined by adding up each side of the account and subtracting one total from the other.

A CLOSER LOOK AT

T-ACCOUNTS

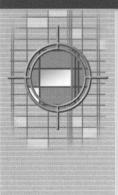

Barker Corporation started the month with a cash balance of $25,000. During the month, Barker received cash inflows of $3,000, $41,000, and $16,000. Barker also made cash payments of $58,000 and $12,000. Barker's cash T-account reflects a $15,000 balance at the end of the month and appears as follows:

Cash	
(increases)	(decreases)
bal. 25,000	
3,000	58,000
41,000	12,000
16,000	
bal. 15,000	

T-ACCOUNTS AND THE ACCOUNTING EQUATION

Each element of the balance sheet is included in the accounting equation, and a T-account can be used for each one. For example, the accounting equation for a very simple company, along with the associated T-accounts, appears as in Exhibit 7–2.

Because assets are on the left side of the accounting equation, their normal balances are placed on the left side of the T-accounts. In this simple scheme, increases in assets are placed on the left side of the T-account and decreases are placed on the right side. Conversely, the normal balances for items on the right side of the accounting equation, liabilities and equities, are found on the right side of the T-accounts. Increases in those items are placed on the right side of the T-account and decreases on the left. Using T-accounts and thinking of the accounting equation, with assets on the left and liabilities and equities on the right, can help you visualize the effect of different events on the financial statement elements.

You Decide 7-1

COMPUTERIZED SYSTEMS AND THE ACCOUNTING EQUATION

Computers store accounting information as magnetic charges, with no left or right side as in a T-account. Changes to stored information are made through electronic impulses. Do the differences between computerized and handwritten accounting systems affect the relationships in the accounting equation? Explain. In what ways might computerized systems affect the information provided to decision makers, as compared with handwritten systems?

T-ACCOUNTS AND THE ACCOUNTING EQUATION

EXHIBIT 7-2

ASSETS		LIABILITIES	OWNERS' EQUITY	
Cash	Inventory	Accounts Payable	Common Stock	Retained Earnings
12,000	+ 28,000	= 7,000	+ 30,000	+ 3,000

DEBITS AND CREDITS

Every profession develops specialized terminology useful for communicating in precise terms. Two terms that are important in accounting are *debit* and *credit*. For handwritten systems, the term **debit** (abbreviated *dr.*—don't ask why) traditionally means (1) the left side of an account, (2) an entry or amount on the left side, or (3) the act of making an entry to the left side of an account. Similarly, **credit** (abbreviated *cr.*) refers to (1) the right side of an account, (2) an entry or amount on the right side, or (3) the act of making an entry to the right side of an account.

By looking at the accounting equation and the T-accounts for each item within the equation, you can see that a debit entry, or one to the left side of a T-account, increases the balance of an asset account. Similarly, a credit, or an entry to the right side of a T-account, increases the balance of a liability or owners' equity account. Conversely, a debit decreases the balance of a liability or owners' equity account, while a credit decreases the balance of an asset account. These effects can be viewed as follows:

Assets		Liabilities and Owners' Equity	
(debit) increase	(credit) decrease	(debit) decrease	(credit) increase

Although T-accounts help us see how the accounting process works, we know that most companies accumulate accounting information using computerized systems. With these systems, right and left become meaningless because the "accounts" within a computer do not have right and left sides. Instead, the terms *debit* and *credit* reflect the following changes in an account:

Debits (dr.)
- increase assets
- decrease liabilities
- decrease equities

Credits (cr.)
- decrease assets
- increase liabilities
- increase equities

Continuing to visualize the accounting equation and T-accounts, however, can help you better understand the effects of transactions on financial statements.

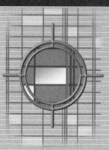

A CLOSER LOOK AT

THE EFFECT OF TRANSACTIONS ON T-ACCOUNTS

The Carbon Company began by issuing common stock for $80,000 cash. It purchased a small building for $90,000 by paying $25,000 cash and borrowing the remaining amount from the bank. Carbon then purchased $18,000 of inventory on credit. Because Carbon is just starting in business, all of its accounts start with zero balances. Amounts are added and subtracted as follows:

	Account and Effect	**Dr.**	**Cr.**
(1) Stock issuance:	Cash (increase)	80,000	
	Common Stock (increase)		80,000
(2) Building purchase:	Buildings (increase)	90,000	
	Cash (decrease)		25,000
	Loan Payable (increase)		65,000
(3) Inventory purchase:	Inventory (increase)	18,000	
	Accounts Payable (increase)		18,000

After entering the appropriate debit or credit amounts for each account, Carbon's ledger accounts appear as follows:

Assets						=	Liabilities				+	Owners' Equity	
Cash	+	Inventory	+	Buildings		=	Accounts Payable	+	Loans Payable		+	Common Stock	
debit	credit	debit	credit	debit	credit		debit	credit	debit	credit		debit	credit
80,000	25,000	18,000		90,000				18,000		65,000			80,000
55,000		18,000		90,000				18,000		65,000			80,000

DOUBLE-ENTRY BOOKKEEPING: ONE ASPECT OF RELIABILITY

Double-entry bookkeeping is an ingenious system developed more than five hundred years ago to record business transactions in a way that keeps track of the effects of each transaction, facilitates preparation of financial statements, and provides for a regular check on the proper functioning of the process. The double-entry system is used throughout the world.

The double-entry system is based on the accounting equation. Thus, each recorded event or transaction must have at least two effects, as summarized in Exhibit 7–3.

Because the accounting equation always holds, a built-in check feature of double-entry accounting is that the debits must always equal the credits. This is true for each individual transaction recorded in the accounts, and, in addition, the sum of all debit account balances must equal the sum of all credit account balances. If debits and credits are not equal, an error has been made.

A double-entry system is important for decision makers, who must consider the multiple aspects of each transaction. In addition, the required equality of debits and credits helps ensure that information is processed accurately and completely by the system, increasing the reliability of the resulting information.

THE EFFECTS OF TRANSACTIONS IN DOUBLE-ENTRY BOOKKEEPING

EXHIBIT 7-3

If . . .	Then One or More of the Following Must Occur
An asset increases	• Another asset decreases • A liability increases • Equity increases
An asset decreases	• Another asset increases • A liability decreases • Equity decreases
A liability increases	• Another liability decreases • Equity decreases • An asset increases
A liability decreases	• Another liability increases • Equity increases • An asset decreases
An ownership claim increases	• Another ownership claim decreases • A liability decreases • An asset increases
An ownership claim decreases	• Another ownership claim increases • A liability increases • An asset decreases

USING LEDGER ACCOUNTS TO CLASSIFY INFORMATION

After accounting information is originally entered in the accounting records through double-entry accounting, the double-entry system continues in ledger accounts where the information is accumulated and further classified before it is used to prepare financial statements. However, two types of accounts are used, one for accumulating information on a continuing basis and the other for accumulating information period by period.

TWO TYPES OF ACCOUNTS: AN IMPORTANT DISTINCTION

Accounting records of all entities contain two major types of accounts, classified according to how the information the account contains is used for decision making. The types of accounts and the financial statements in which they appear are summarized in Exhibit 7–4. **Permanent accounts** are reported in the balance sheet and relate to the financial position of the entity. The balances of these accounts are maintained on a continual basis and carry over from one period to the next. For instance, those evaluating the creditworthiness of a company might wish to know its cash balance and the balance that is owed to creditors. The cash account and the accounts payable account maintain continuous balances of these amounts, and the balances are carried over from one period to the next.

    Temporary accounts are reported in a company's income statement or retained earnings statement and relate to activities during a period. These accounts have balances

| EXHIBIT 7-4 | **TYPES OF ACCOUNTS** | | | |

TYPES OF ACCOUNTS

Type of Account	Statement Element	Normal Balance	Reported On
Permanent	Assets	Debit	Balance sheet
	Liabilities	Credit	Balance sheet
	Owners' equity	Credit	Balance sheet
Temporary (All are equity accounts and are closed to Retained Earnings)	Revenues	Credit	Income statement
	Expenses	Debit	Income statement
	Gains	Credit	Income statement
	Losses	Debit	Income statement
	Dividends	Debit	Retained earnings statement

that are carried only for one period of time. Although the account itself might continue for the entire life of the entity, the balance relates only to a specific period. For example, a financial statement user might want to assess a company's sales revenue for the past year—a specific period of time—and compare this revenue to selling expenses for the same period of time.

All temporary accounts are equity accounts because they ultimately affect retained earnings. Revenues increase net income and, consequently, owners' equity, while expenses decrease net income and owners' equity. Distributions of income, or dividends, do not affect net income but do reduce owners' equity.

At the end of each period, the balances of all temporary accounts are transferred to Retained Earnings, a permanent account. This is done so owners' equity is correctly stated at the end of the period, and so all temporary accounts start the next period with zero balances for the accumulation of information during that period. Owners' equity, or, more specifically, retained earnings, ties the income statement, retained earnings statement, and balance sheet together. We will see how in the next section.

You Decide 7-2

ANALYZING REVENUES

You are currently analyzing the operations of two companies, with the possibility of investing in one of the two. In assessing the potential for future sales, you examine the sales revenues reported by the two companies. You learn that Olde Tyme Corporation has had total sales revenues since it started in 1946 of $42,569,074,541. On the other hand, Upstart Company has had total revenues since it started in 1995 of $136,485,220. Based on this information, can you tell which company seems to have the better prospects? Explain. Suppose you also learn that Olde Tyme's revenues last year were $2,569,291,000 and $1,331,584,000 this year, while Upstart's revenues were $32,456,000 last year and $65,711,000 this year. What does this indicate about the two companies? Which information is more useful: the cumulative information or the year-by-year information? Why?

THE ACCOUNTING EQUATION EXPANDED

Because elements of owners' equity are crucial to understanding a company's activities, let's expand the accounting equation to look at owners' equity more closely:

Assets = Liabilities + Owners' Equity

Assets = Liabilities + Capital Stock + Retained Earnings

Assets = Liabilities + Capital Stock + Beginning Retained Earnings + Revenues
     − Expenses − Dividends

This last form of the accounting equation shows the temporary accounts contained within retained earnings. Keep in mind the following:

Retained Earnings at the beginning of the period
+ Net Income (which equals revenues minus expenses)
− Dividends
= Retained Earnings at the end of the period

This simple formulation ties together the income statement (revenues, expenses, net income), retained earnings statement (net income, dividends, retained earnings), and balance sheet (retained earnings).

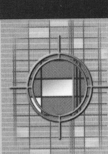

A CLOSER LOOK AT

AN EXPANDED ACCOUNTING EQUATION

The Lane Corporation began by issuing common stock for $80,000 cash. Lane then purchased $18,000 of inventory on credit and paid rent of $1,000. It sold half its inventory for $15,000 cash. With all of Lane's ledger accounts starting with zero balances, amounts are added and subtracted as follows:

	Account and Effect	Dr.	Cr.
(1) Stock issuance	Cash (increase)	80,000	
	Common Stock (increase)		80,000
(2) Inventory purchase	Inventory (increase)	18,000	
	Accounts Payable (increase)		18,000
(3) Rent payment	Rent Expense (increase)	1,000	
	Cash (decrease)		1,000
(4) Inventory sale	Cash (increase)	15,000	
	Sales Revenue (increase)		15,000
	Cost of Goods Sold (increase)	9,000	
	Inventory (decrease)		9,000

After entering the appropriate debit or credit amounts for each account, Lane's T-accounts appear as follows:

Cash		+	Inventory		=	Accounts Payable		+	Common Stock		+	Rated Earnings		+	Revenues		−	Expenses	
debit	credit		debit	credit		debit	credit		debit	credit		debit	credit		debit	credit		debit	credit
80,000	1,000		18,000	9,000			18,000			80,000						15,000		1,000	
15,000																15,000		9,000	
			9,000				18,000			80,000									
94,000																		10,000	

You should note several points from the example. First, because revenues increase owners' equity, the normal balance of a revenue account is a credit. On the other hand, expenses reduce owners' equity, and the normal balance of an expense ledger account is a debit rather than the normal credit balance found in other equity accounts. If the total of the expenses is subtracted from the total of the revenues, the resulting number is the company's net income of $5,000.

Second, remember that decision makers are interested in revenues and expenses for specific periods of time. Therefore, revenues and expenses are accumulated only for one period. At the end of the period, the balances of these temporary accounts are removed and transferred to retained earnings, as follows:

Account and Effect	**Dr.**	**Cr.**
Revenues (decrease)	15,000	
Retained Earnings (increase)		15,000
Retained Earnings (decrease)	10,000	
Expenses (decrease)		10,000

The revenue, expense, and retained earnings accounts appear as follows after transferring the revenue and expense balances:

Retained Earnings		Revenues		Expenses	
debt	credit	debt	credit	debt	credit
			15,000	1,000	
				9,000	
10,000	15,000 ← 15,000				10,000
	5,000		-0-	-0-	

The transfer leaves the revenue and expense accounts with zero balances so they may be used to accumulate information for the next period. In this example, the balance in the retained earnings account is equal to the net income to date because no distributions of income to owners have been made.

Third, notice the two different aspects of the sale transaction. The first is the inflow of cash, with the source of this cash being the sale. Accordingly, cash, an asset, is increased, and an equity account, revenues, is increased as well. At the same time, inventory is transferred to the customer. The cost of this inventory expires because it can no longer provide a future benefit to Lane. Therefore, the cost of the inventory sold is transferred from an unexpired cost (asset) account to an expired cost (expense) account. This treatment matches costs (cost of goods sold) with revenues so the income statement reflects Lane's net income for the period.

Also, recognize that for illustration purposes we've only used one revenue account and one expense account. In practice, companies may use dozens of revenue accounts and even hundreds of expense accounts. Although many separate classifications may be needed for internal decision making, a number of these items are combined in the financial statements because external decision makers do not need the detail that internal managers typically do.

Finally, notice that amounts were placed directly in T-accounts in this simple example. In actuality, the accounting process consists of a number of steps, as discussed in the next section.

OVERVIEW OF THE ACCOUNTING CYCLE

So far, we've looked at only one part of the accounting process: accumulating and classifying information. Now, we'll expand our discussion to explore the entire series of steps needed to record, accumulate, process, and report financial information, referred to as the

accounting cycle. Being familiar with the accounting cycle can help you better understand how the numbers in the financial statements are generated. This, in turn, will help you understand the strengths and limitations of the information for decision making.

The accounting cycle begins with the first transactions of a new accounting period and ends with the preparation of financial statements. The steps in the accounting cycle, summarized in Exhibit 7–5, are as follows:

1. *Occurrence of transaction:* An event requiring accounting recognition is identified based on the recognition criteria mentioned in Chapter 4. The events or transactions are evidenced by source documents such as sales receipts, cash register tapes, and invoices.

2. *Analysis of transaction:* Based on source documents or other evidence, the transaction or event is classified and measured so we know which accounts are affected and by what amount.

3. *Recording of transaction:* After the transaction or event has been identified, classified, and measured, it is recorded in a **journal**. This step is often referred to as *entering* or *journalizing* the transaction in the books of original entry. The journal provides a chronological record of an entity's activities and is the only place where each individual transaction is recorded in its entirety. The journal entry normally includes the date, titles and numbers of the accounts affected, and the specific debit or credit dollar amount. For example, an entry to record the receipt of cash from a customer on account might appear as follows:

			Amounts	
Date	Acct. #	Account Titles	Dr.	Cr.
11/22/2001	110	Cash	5,600	
	120	Accounts Receivable		5,600

All accounts debited are listed first and on the left. All credits are listed next and on the right. This handwritten notation, called the *general journal entry form*, is rarely used today because most records are computerized and entries are recorded as account increases or decreases. However, we will use this format for illustration purposes because it allows us to see precisely the effects of various events on the elements in the financial statements.

4. *Posting to ledger accounts:* Each amount in the journal is transferred to the appropriate ledger account, a process referred to as *posting*. All the ledger accounts for an entity are maintained together in the **general ledger**. In the ledger, amounts are accumulated by individual item or financial statement element. Where the journal lets us view one transaction at a time in its entirety, ledger accounts help us analyze how events have affected specific financial statement elements. Although posting in handwritten systems is done after entering information in the journal, computerized systems post at the same time entries are made.

5. *Preparation of trial balance:* A **trial balance** is simply a listing of the balances of all ledger accounts. A trial balance provides one check on the accuracy of the recording and posting processes by making sure the sum of the debit balances equals the sum of the credit balances. Also, the trial balance can be used in determining whether balances are fairly stated or need to be adjusted. Although the first four steps in the accounting cycle occur throughout the accounting period, preparation of a trial balance and all subsequent steps are part of the process of preparing financial statements and usually occur only at the end of the period.

| EXHIBIT 7-5 | **THE ACCOUNTING CYCLE** |

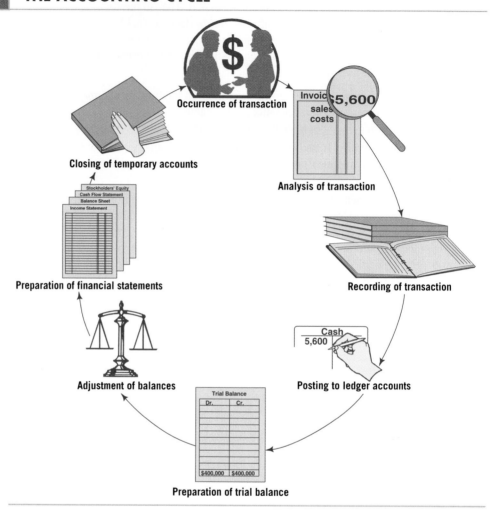

6. ***Adjustment of balances:*** All account balances must be examined prior to the preparation of financial statements to determine if they are appropriate under generally accepted accounting principles. If balances are not fairly stated, they are changed to the appropriate amounts with **adjusting entries**. As with other entries, adjusting entries are made in the journal and then posted to ledger accounts. After adjusting entries are made, an adjusted trial balance is prepared.

7. ***Preparation of financial statements:*** Financial statements are prepared using the account balances listed in the adjusted trial balance. To avoid excessive detail in the financial statements, similar accounts are often combined.

8. ***Closing of temporary accounts:*** The balances of temporary accounts must be transferred, or closed out, and left with zero balances at the end of the period so the accounts may be used again the next period. Remember that the balances of these accounts are closed to retained earnings because all temporary accounts relate either to income earned or dividends distributed during the period. The entries to transfer the balances of temporary accounts to retained earnings are called **closing entries.** They are made in the journal and posted to ledger accounts, leaving all temporary accounts with zero balances. A post-closing trial balance is then usually prepared to check that the accounting equation is still in balance and to show the beginning balances for the next period.

ADJUSTMENTS: THE MATCHING CONCEPT AT WORK

Without the sixth step in the accounting cycle, making adjustments, revenues and expenses might not be reported in the proper periods. Because such information could prove misleading to decision makers, adjusting entries are crucial to ensuring useful accounting information. In fact, proper adjusting entries are one of the main aspects of an accrual accounting system, and they reflect some of the basic accounting concepts we discussed in Chapter 4, such as matching and revenue recognition. Let's take a closer look at adjustments to find out why they are so vital to the accounting process.

In general, end-of-period adjustments are needed because recording all events that affect a company when they occur is not cost-effective. A sale of inventory and the purchase of a building are discrete events that can easily be recorded in the accounts at the time they occur. On the other hand, if a bank lends money to a customer, the bank earns interest on that loan every day, even every second, that the customer has use of the bank's money. Obviously, recording the bank's interest income as each penny is earned on each loan outstanding is a needless and time-consuming task. The cost of generating such information exceeds any benefits to be obtained from it. As a result, the bank may delay recording the interest earned until the information is to be reported. If reporting occurs at the end of the month, the bank must adjust all of its accounts at that time so the reported information is up to date.

To determine the adjusting entries that need to be made, accountants examine all account balances and ask two questions with respect to each account:

1. What is the current balance reflected in the account?

2. What is the correct balance that should be reflected in that account under generally accepted accounting principles?

The accountant then makes an adjusting entry to bring the account balance from what it is to what it should be. In the following sections, we'll explore typical types of adjustments that should be made prior to preparing financial statements.

ACCRUED INCOME

Income should be included in the income statement in the period in which it is earned. Any income that has been earned during the period but has not been recorded should be recorded at the end of the period.

Some types of income grow over time rather than being realized at a single point in time. This type of income is said to **accrue**. One example of **accrued income** is the interest you earn on a certificate of deposit that has not yet matured. Another example is uncollected rental income. If you rent property to someone else for $3,000 per month, and at year-end you have not yet collected the December rent, you would make the following adjusting entry on your books:

	Dr.	Cr.
Rent Receivable	3,000	
Rental Income		3,000

Income Statement Effects	
Income	+ 3,000
Net Income	+ 3,000
Balance Sheet Effects	
Assets	+ 3,000
Owners' Equity	+ 3,000

This entry shows that you have a claim for $3,000, which is an asset reported on the balance sheet, and that you have earned that amount of income during the month.

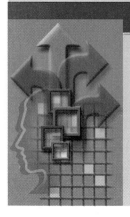

You Decide 7-3

RECOGNIZING ACCRUED INCOME

Which financial statements are affected by the adjusting entry to record accrued rent? Will this be true for all adjusting entries? Explain how the financial statements being tied together (articulated) relates to what is portrayed in the financial statements.

ACCRUED EXPENSES

The matching concept requires expenses (expired costs) to be reported in the period in which the related benefits are received, regardless of when the associated cash flows take place. On the other hand, accounting systems are designed so that journal entries are triggered by cash flows and other specific events, but not just by the passage of time. Therefore, for a proper matching, some expenses need special treatment because cash will not be disbursed until after benefits are received.

Expenses that grow over time and are paid after the related benefits are received are called **accrued expenses**. For example, suppose a company pays employees every Friday and has a weekly payroll of $50,000. Because the company's fiscal year ends on Wednesday this year, the employees earn three days' wages in the current fiscal year. However, they are paid those wages, plus wages for two days of the next year, on the first Friday of the new fiscal year. The wages for the first three days of the week in which the fiscal year ends must be recognized in the current year, even though the cash is not paid until next year. The following adjusting entry is made at the end of the fiscal year to recognize the accrued wages ($50,000 × 3/5):

Income Statement Effects	
Expense	+ 30,000
Net Income	− 30,000

Balance Sheet Effects	
Liabilities	+ 30,000
Owners' Equity	− 30,000

	Dr.	Cr.
Wage Expense	30,000	
Wages Payable		30,000

The adjusting entry ensures the following:

* All wage expense incurred by the company during the current period is reported in the current period's income statement.

* The company's obligation to pay those wages in the future is reported as a liability in the balance sheet.

UNEARNED INCOME

Sometimes a company may receive cash payment for income it has not yet earned. When this occurs, the company should recognize **unearned income**, a liability reflecting the company's obligation to provide something to the payer in the future. For example, a company leasing a building to another company may receive a rent payment in advance. The rent should be reported as income, however, only in the period to which the rental payment applies. In the meantime, the lessor must report as a liability, Unearned Rent, its obligation to make the building available to the lessee in the future. Once the rental income is earned, an adjusting entry is made to recognize the income and reduce the liability.

In Practice 7-3

TIME WARNER, INC.

Time Warner reports the unearned portion of subscriptions of $741,000,000 in its December 31, 1998, balance sheet.

ANALYSIS

The balance sheet liability reflects the company's obligation to provide magazines in the future to subscribers who have already paid for their subscriptions. The company will have to incur future costs to provide these subscriptions, but it has already received the cash generated from these subscriptions. The income will not be recognized until it is earned by providing the magazines. [www.timewarner.com]

PREPAID EXPENSES

Frequently, some types of operating costs are paid in advance of the period(s) in which they provide benefits. Common examples of these costs, referred to as **prepaid expenses,** include rent and insurance premiums paid in advance. Prepaid expenses are assets because they are costs that are expected to provide future benefits. As the company receives the benefits from having incurred these costs, adjusting entries are needed to transfer amounts from the unexpired cost category (prepaid expense) to the expired cost category (expense) so income reported for each period reflects a matching of costs and benefits.

A CLOSER LOOK AT

PREPAID EXPENSES

Benelier Corporation paid a one-year insurance premium of $2,400 at the beginning of its fiscal year. The full amount was recorded as an asset, Prepaid Insurance. When preparing quarterly financial statements three months later, the following adjusting entry is needed:

Insurance Expense	600	
Prepaid Insurance		600

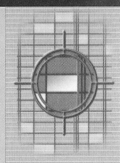

This entry recognizes expense ($2,400 × 3/12) for the portion of the total insurance cost that expired during the first 3 months of the year, and it reduces the Prepaid Insurance asset account so that only the cost relating to future insurance protection remains.

Income Statement Effects	
Expense	+ 600
Net Income	− 600
Balance Sheet Effects	
Assets	− 600
Owners' Equity	− 600

DEPRECIATION OF ASSETS

Companies purchase long-lived operating assets, such as buildings and equipment, to be used in generating revenues over a number of periods. Therefore, to report income properly under the matching concept, a portion of the cost of these assets must be charged to expense in each of the periods benefiting from their use. As the service potential of these assets is used up, a portion of the cost is transferred from the unexpired cost category (asset) to the expired cost category (expense). The portion of the cost of these assets recognized in each period benefited is called *depreciation expense*. If, for example, a company purchased a building for $250,000, and that building was expected to benefit the company over a period of twenty-five years, the company would record $10,000 of depreciation expense each year with the following adjusting entry:

Income Statement Effects	
Expense	+ 10,000
Net Income	− 10,000
Balance Sheet Effects	
Assets	− 10,000
Owners' Equity	− 10,000

	Dr.	Cr.
Depreciation Expense	10,000	
Accumulated Depreciation		10,000

The Accumulated Depreciation account is a negative, or **contra-asset account**, shown as a reduction of the Building account in the balance sheet.

A FINAL WORD ABOUT ADJUSTMENTS

The fact that an entity's books are not completely correct during much of the accounting period does not usually cause any problems because information needs to be current and correct only at the time it is used. Accordingly, adjustments must be made anytime financial statements or other accounting reports are prepared.

You Decide 7-4

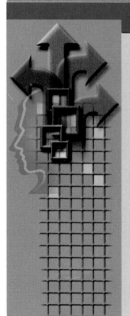

COMPUTING INCOME

Robert Company calculated net income of $106,000 for the current year. When examining its books, however, the company's auditors discovered the following:

1. The company properly recorded the purchase of equipment at the beginning of the year for $100,000, but made no further entries with respect to the equipment even though it was used for the entire year. The equipment has an expected life of 5 years.

2. The company had purchased and paid $27,000 for a three-year insurance policy at the beginning of the previous year. The policy was correctly recorded when purchased, but no further entries have been made with respect to the insurance.

3. The company received a $42,000 cash payment at the beginning of the current year. This amount represents full payment for a two-year service contract under which the company provides specified technical services to the customer during the current year and next year. The full $42,000 was recognized as service income when the payment was received.

Do you think Robert's net income is correctly stated as calculated? If not, what amount of income do you think should be reported? Explain. Are there any items on Robert's balance sheet that you think may be stated incorrectly? Why?

Individual adjustments that involve income or an expense on one side and either an asset or liability on the other provide an excellent demonstration of how the financial statements are articulated. For example, if a company increases its income by, say, earning interest, its assets increase. If a company decreases its income by incurring, say, rent expense, its assets decrease or its liabilities increase. Thus, adjusting entries are crucial to fairly presenting both financial position and the results of operations.

COMPREHENSIVE ILLUSTRATION OF THE ACCOUNTING CYCLE

Now that you have a basic understanding of accounting systems and procedures, let's take another look at Our Video Store. By now, your operation has been very successful, and your new partner, Maria, thinks it's time to expand your business. Maria finds a better location for the store, with more room. At her suggestion, you sell your original business, with the videos, to Vinny (of Vinny's Videos), and you and Maria incorporate a new business with the two of you as stockholders. She sets up an accounting system so you know how the new business is doing and because she thinks your new company will want to borrow money soon to expand even further. She has big plans!

CLASSIFICATION AND ORIGINAL ENTRIES

Let's follow the new Our Video Store during its first month of operation in the new location. We'll accumulate information about each transaction and event and consider the impact. After processing the information, we'll report on the store's activities through a set of financial statements.

Maria sets up Our Video Store's chart of accounts, shown in Exhibit 7–6. The events occurring in June, the new store's first month of business, are classified and recorded as follows:

June 1: You and Maria each contribute $20,000 cash to start the new business. You immediately hire an attorney to establish Our Video Store as a corporation. The corporation then issues you and Maria each a 1,000-share certificate of stock to acknowledge your ownership.

Analysis   The contribution by the owners in exchange for stock is classified separately from other sources of assets. This entry shows how much money has been placed "at risk" in the company by the owners.

Classification & Entry

			Dr.	Cr.
(1)	110	Cash	40,000	
	510	Capital Stock		40,000

Income Statement Effects	
Net Income	0
Balance Sheet Effects	
Assets	+ 40,000
Owners' Equity	+ 40,000

Discussion   The corporate form of business organization is indicated by the use of a capital stock account, but the identity of individual stockholders is not disclosed. The names of the stockholders are kept in the company files to determine who has voting rights on corporate issues and who is to receive dividends.

EXHIBIT 7-6 — OUR VIDEO STORE'S CHART OF ACCOUNTS

110 Cash	510 Capital Stock
120 Accounts Receivable	530 Retained Earnings
130 Video Inventory	550 Other Equity
140 Supplies on Hand	
150 Other Current Assets	710 Video Rental Revenue
	750 Other Operating Revenue
210 Land	
220 Shelves & Fixtures	810 Salary and Wage Expense
225 Office Equipment	815 Outside Labor Expense
230 Accumulated Depreciation	820 Rent Expense
250 Other Long-term Assets	830 Supplies Expense
	840 Utilities Expense
310 Accounts Payable	850 Legal Expense
320 Notes Payable	860 Depreciation Expense
351 Wages Payable	
360 Interest Payable	910 Interest Income
	920 Interest Expense
410 Secured Note Payable	950 Other Income/Expense
450 Other Long-term Debt	

June 1: Our Video Store makes a $3,000 advance rental payment for the month of June for a large store located in a busy strip mall.

Analysis The payment of cash for the use of retail space is an exchange of an asset for the use of someone else's resources. Rent expense for the month must be included in the June income statement.

Classification & Entry

Income Statement Effects						Dr.	Cr.
Expense	+ 3,000						
Net Income	− 3,000	(2)	820	Rent Expense		3,000	
Balance Sheet Effects			110	Cash			3,000
Assets	− 3,000						
Owners' Equity	− 3,000						

Discussion Comparing revenue generated to rent and other expenses allows information users to determine how successful Our Video Store was in covering its operating expenses in June.

June 1: Acme Supply delivers and installs shelves and fixtures, expected to last ten years, and a computer system, expected to be useful for five years. Acme Supply provides an invoice, shown in Exhibit 7–7, indicating that the cost of the shelves and fixtures is $15,000 and the cost of the computer system is $5,000. The corporation makes a 10 percent cash down payment. The balance must be paid in fifteen days to avoid a 1 percent late payment charge.

Analysis A purchase of shelves and fixtures and the computer equipment is an acquisition of operating assets to be used in generating revenues over a number of years.

Classification & Entry

Income Statement Effects						Dr.	Cr.
Net Income	0	(3)	220	Shelves & Fixtures		15,000	
Balance Sheet Effects			225	Office Equipment		5,000	
Assets	+ 20,000		110	Cash			2,000
Assets	− 2,000		310	Accounts Payable			18,000
Liabilities	+ 18,000						

AN INVOICE

EXHIBIT 7-7

ACME SUPPLY COMPANY
1825 YORK ROAD
TOWSON, MARYLAND 21204

Invoice

Date: June 1, 2001

Sold to: Our Video Store

Shelves and Fixtures	$12,000
Labor, Installation	3,000
Computer System and Setup	5,000
Total Charge	$20,000
Received on account	$ 2,000
Balance due by June 16	18,000

THANK YOU FOR YOUR BUSINESS

A 1 percent late charge is added to all amounts past due

Discussion   The dollar amount of the assets purchased is recorded and will be included in the financial statements. In addition, Our Video Store will maintain detailed records of these assets and their location so their existence, condition, and use can be checked periodically. External decision makers, however, are generally interested only in the total dollar amounts invested in these assets and any amounts owed to others.

June 1:   Our Video Store purchases 1,000 videos from Videotastic Distributors, having negotiated an average price of $25 each. Because of your previous dealings with the distributor, you are granted credit for thirty days. These videos are expected to have useful lives of five years.

Analysis   The purchase of the videos provides the corporation's major operating asset, its inventory of videos. Although you have not generated any cash from operations yet, you have thirty days to pay for the videos.

Classification & Entry

			Dr.	Cr.
(4)	130	Video Inventory	25,000	
	310	Accounts Payable		25,000

Income Statement Effects	
Net Income	0
Balance Sheet Effects	
Assets	+ 25,000
Liabilities	+ 25,000

Discussion   The video inventory is different from normal merchandise inventory because it will not be sold. Instead, it will be used in operations over a number of periods. Therefore, its cost will have to be allocated to those periods to match against the rental revenue generated.

June 1:   Maria negotiates a three-year $26,000 loan from the Next-to-Last National Bank and signs a promissory note, shown in Exhibit 7–8. The new videos and computer are used as collateral for the note. The note carries 9 percent annual interest. Both the interest and principal are payable in full in three years.

| **EXHIBIT 7-8** | **A PROMISSORY NOTE** |

Next-to-Last National Bank
Promissory Note

For value received, the undersigned agree this __first__ day of __June__ in the year 20 __01__, to pay to the Next-to-Last National Bank the sum of __$26,000__, with interest accrued from date at the rate of __9__ percent per annum, all amounts to become due and payable on __June 1, 2004__ at Baltimore, Maryland.

Security Interest: This loan is secured by __the entire inventory of videocassettes owned by Our Video Store and by the computer and peripheral equipment owned by Our Video Store.__ In the event of a default on this note, the title and possession of the named property will be transferred to the Next-to-Last National Bank.

In the event payments on this note are not timely made, borrowers agree to pay all costs of collection and reasonable legal fees.

Signed for __Our Video Store,__

_____
(Signature of Authorized Officer)

_____

Analysis   Cash is received by incurring an obligation for future cash payments. The title of account 410, Secured Note Payable, indicates that specific assets are pledged as collateral for payment of the note and can be claimed by the bank if the note and interest are not paid in accordance with the terms of the agreement.

Income Statement Effects	
Net Income	0

Balance Sheet Effects	
Assets	+ 26,000
Liabilities	+ 26,000

Classification & Entry

			Dr.	Cr.
(5)	110	Cash	26,000	
	410	Secured Note Payable		26,000

Discussion   A large portion of Our Video Store's assets have come from borrowing, and creditors have a considerable claim on those assets. Because the business has an obligation to satisfy these claims in the future, a portion of future cash inflows must be used to repay the loans and interest. Decision makers will want to know about Our Video Store's obligation for future cash outflows. In addition to reporting the dollar amount of the liability, the maturity date and interest rate should be reported. Usually the name of the bank or other lender is not reported.

June 3:   Our Video Store purchases office supplies and other promotional materials from Supplies Unlimited for $1,500, with payment due in thirty days.

Analysis   Our Video Store has acquired assets that it will consume as part of its operations and has incurred a short-term obligation.

Income Statement Effects	
Net Income	0

Balance Sheet Effects	
Assets	+ 1,500
Liabilities	+ 1,500

Classification & Entry

			Dr.	Cr.
(6)	140	Supplies on Hand	1,500	
	310	Accounts Payable		1,500

Discussion   Financial statements report only the total dollar amounts for supplies and current debt. However, Our Video Store's management needs to maintain records of the kinds of supplies purchased so it can determine how much is used, what they were used for, and when to reorder. It also must keep sufficient records to determine which suppliers must be paid and how much, and when payments are due.

June 3: After interviews with the three top candidates, you hire Dana to work full-time in the store and to do the bookkeeping. Dana's salary will be $1,500 per month, paid at the beginning of the month following the month worked. Dana starts work immediately and will be paid June's salary in full on July 1.

Analysis Because Dana has provided no benefits to Our Video Store at the time of hiring, and the corporation, therefore, has no obligation to pay a salary until it is earned, no entry is recorded at the time of hiring. Dana's salary will be recorded as an adjusting entry at the end of each month to recognize the cost of work performed during that month. The cash payment will be recorded at the beginning of the following month.

Income Statement Effects	
Net Income	0
Balance Sheet Effects	
Assets	0
Liabilities	0
Owners' Equity	0

Classification & Entry

    (7)   No entry at the time of hiring

Discussion Dana's salary will be reported as an operating expense in the income statement and matched against operating revenue each month. It is a fixed operating expense that must be covered regardless of sales. Records on each employee that detail such information as wages and fringe benefits paid and taxes withheld must be maintained, but these details are not reported in the financial statements.

June 5: Our Video Store transfers some old home movies onto videotape for a customer and bills the customer for ten hours of work at $50 per hour ($500).

Analysis Our Video Store earns its first operating revenue, which will be included in the operating results reported for the month of June. Because no cash is collected, a receivable is recorded, with the source of the receivable being revenue.

Income Statement Effects	
Revenue	+ 500
Net Income	+ 500
Balance Sheet Effects	
Assets	+ 500
Owners' Equity	+ 500

Classification & Entry

			Dr.	Cr.
(8)	120	Accounts Receivable	500	
	750	Other Operating Revenue		500

Discussion Because Our Video Store uses accrual accounting, revenue is recognized when it is earned, and a current asset is established to recognize the claim against the customer. External decision makers may want to evaluate the corporation's receivables to determine when cash is likely to be collected and how the timing of expected cash inflows coincides with expected cash outflows. Details of receivables, including clients' names, addresses, and due dates of the accounts, will be maintained by Our Video Store to facilitate collection but are not included in the financial statements.

June 12: A check for $18,000 is written to Acme Supply for full payment of the account arising from purchase of the shelves, fixtures, and computer system.

Analysis Our Video Store has used some of its available cash to pay a short-term obligation.

Classification & Entry

Income Statement Effects	
Net Income	0
Balance Sheet Effects	
Assets	− 18,000
Liabilities	− 18,000

			Dr.	Cr.
(9)	310	Accounts Payable	18,000	
	110	Cash		18,000

Discussion Transactions (5) and (9) reflect the change in the nature of Our Video Store's debt. Because the source of funding for the assets changes from a short-term account payable to a long-term note due in three years, the risks to investors and creditors changes. While Our Video Store must earn enough to repay the note plus interest in three years, the pressure to make a large cash payment this year is removed. Long-term operating assets are generally best financed through investments from owners or through long-term borrowing so the debt repayment period is similar to the earning period of the assets purchased.

June 29: Our Video Store's customer pays for the services billed on June 5.

Analysis One current asset, accounts receivable, is converted to another, cash.

Classification & Entry

			Dr.	Cr.
(10)	110	Cash	500	
	120	Accounts Receivable		500

Income Statement Effects
Net Income 0

Balance Sheet Effects
Assets + 500
Assets − 500

Discussion Although total assets remain the same, the type of asset held changes. All uncertainty about collection of the account is eliminated. Liquidity is improved because more cash is available to pay expenses, reduce liabilities, and distribute to investors.

June 29: A $400 bill for services provided in June is received from Our Video Store's attorney and is immediately paid.

Analysis Legal services are a necessary expense for most businesses. In this case, the bill is for routine services, and is viewed as a normal cost of doing business in June. Therefore, the cost is matched against revenues earned during the month and is reported in June's income statement.

Classification & Entry

			Dr.	Cr.
(11)	850	Legal Expense	400	
	110	Cash		400

Income Statement Effects
Expenses + 400
Net Income − 400

Balance Sheet Effects
Assets − 400
Owners' Equity − 400

Discussion Legal expenses are usually not separately reported in the financial statements because the amounts are not material. Instead, they may be combined with other expenses in the income statement and reported as administrative expenses. For internal decision making, however, Our Video Store decides to keep track of legal expenses to maintain control over them.

June 30: Our Video Store totals its video rental revenues for June. A total of $17,150 has been received.

Analysis The video rental revenues reflect the benefits from Our Video Store's primary activity and provide a significant inflow of cash.

Classification & Entry

			Dr.	Cr.
(12)	110	Cash	17,150	
	710	Video Rental Revenue		17,150

Income Statement Effects
Revenue + 17,150
Net Income + 17,150

Balance Sheet Effects
Assets + 17,150
Owners' Equity + 17,150

Discussion Our Video Store's computer system actually enters revenues directly from the cash register each time a rental is made. Here, this summary entry is presented for illustrative purposes only. Video Rental Revenue as a source of cash is particularly important because the business will ultimately succeed or fail based on this activity.

June 30: In accordance with your agreement with Maria, you and Maria each receive a salary of $2,000 per month.

Analysis The payment to you and Maria represents an outflow of cash and an expense to the store.

Classification & Entry

			Dr.	Cr.
(13)	810	Salary and Wage Expense	4,000	
	110	Cash		4,000

Income Statement Effects
Expenses + 4,000
Net Income − 4,000

Balance Sheet Effects
Assets − 4,000
Owners' Equity − 4,000

Discussion Salaries and wages are the major operating expense of service companies like Our Video Store and must be matched with revenues earned to evaluate the store's success in its first month of operations.

END-OF-PERIOD ADJUSTMENTS

At the end of June, Maria reminds Dana that adjustments are needed to ensure that all revenues earned during the period are reported and that all expenses incurred in generating the revenues are recognized for a proper matching. Our Video Store must make the following adjustments:

June 30: Dana's $1,500 salary is recorded.

Analysis   Because the store received the benefit of Dana's labor during June, the salary is an operating expense for the month and is recorded at month-end even though the cash is not paid until next month. The store's obligation to pay is also recorded.

Classification & Entry

			Dr.	Cr.
(14)	810	Salary and Wage Expense	1,500	
	351	Wages Payable		1,500

Income Statement Effects	
Expenses	+ 1,500
Net Income	− 1,500
Balance Sheet Effects	
Liabilities	+ 1,500
Owners' Equity	− 1,500

Discussion   Salary and Wage Expense is increased and matched against revenues recorded in June. The Wages Payable account is a current liability. When the cash is disbursed to Dana in July, the store's obligation will be satisfied, and the liability account Wages Payable will be reduced (debited), with a corresponding decrease (credit) to Cash.

June 30: Bills totaling $450 for telephone and other utilities for the month of June are received on June 30. Payment will be made in July.

Analysis   These costs represent expenses of doing business in June. The store has an obligation to pay for the services received.

Classification & Entry

			Dr.	Cr.
(15)	840	Utilities Expense	450	
	310	Accounts Payable		450

Income Statement Effects	
Expenses	+ 450
Net Income	− 450
Balance Sheet Effects	
Liabilities	+ 450
Owners' Equity	− 450

Discussion   Matching requires the cost of the month's utilities to be reported in June rather than in July when the bills are paid. If no adjusting entry were made, the store's utility expense for June would not be fairly stated in the financial statements.

June 30: Our Video Store records interest accrued on its bank loan.

Analysis   The $26,000 note given to the bank on June 1 accrues interest at a 9 percent annual rate. At the end of June, Our Video Store owes the bank $195 ($26,000 × .09 × 1/12) for interest, in addition to the $26,000 loan.

Classification & Entry

			Dr.	Cr.
(16)	920	Interest Expense	195	
	360	Interest Payable		195

Income Statement Effects	
Expenses	+ 195
Net Income	− 195
Balance Sheet Effects	
Liabilities	+ 195
Owners' Equity	− 195

Discussion   Interest is a charge for the use of money over time. Interest expense is matched to a particular time period during which the benefit, the use of the borrowed money, is received. The interest is a fixed obligation and accrues regardless of the amount of the store's sales or other activities. The expense must be included in June's income statement to provide a fair picture of the cost of borrowed money used in the business, and the liability must be reflected in the balance sheet. Interest expense is traditionally shown as a separate item in the income statement.

June 30:   Dana estimates that approximately 80 percent of the supplies purchased early in June remain on hand at the end of the month.

Analysis   Approximately 20 percent of the supplies ($1,500 × .20) were used during June, and their cost must be taken out of the asset account and charged to expense.

Classification & Entry

Income Statement Effects

Expenses	+ 300
Net Income	− 300

Balance Sheet Effects

Assets	− 300
Owners' Equity	− 300

			Dr.	Cr.
(17)	830	Supplies Expense	300	
	140	Supplies on Hand		300

Discussion   This adjustment matches the cost of supplies used with the revenue generated in June. Or, as an alternative, the store could have recorded an expense each time any supplies, such as a pencil or pad of paper, were used. However, such detailed accounting would be costly and would not increase the usefulness of reported information.

June 30:   Depreciation of the videos and computer equipment for one month is determined to be $500 based on expected five-year lives. Depreciation of the shelves and fixtures is determined to be $125 based on a ten-year life.

Analysis   A portion of the cost of the long-lived assets must be allocated to the current period. If the assets are viewed as benefiting all periods equally, their cost might be spread evenly over their estimated lives:

Videos and computer	$30,000 ÷ 60 months = $500
Shelves and fixtures	$15,000 ÷ 120 months = $125

Income Statement Effects

Expenses	+ 625
Net Income	− 625

Balance Sheet Effects

Assets	− 625
Owners' Equity	− 625

The reduction in the future service potential of the assets also must be reported.

Classification & Entry

			Dr.	Cr.
(18)	860	Depreciation Expense	625	
	230	Accumulated Depreciation		625

Discussion   The number of years of potential use of operating assets is limited. As the assets are used, an operating expense is matched against the revenue earned for the period. An Accumulated Depreciation account is used to report the cumulative amount of the asset's cost that has been charged to expense since the asset was acquired. Accumulated Depreciation is included in the balance sheet as an offset against the original cost of the asset.

ACCUMULATION AND SUMMARIZATION

The information included in Our Video Store's journal entries is accumulated by transferring or posting the amounts to ledger accounts. Each entry provides the name and number of the ledger account to which the dollar amount indicated is posted, and each entry makes clear whether the item is posted to the ledger account as a debit or credit. The individual ledger accounts for the store, shown in T-account form after posting, are presented in Exhibit 7–9. Although not illustrated in the exhibit, the date of the entry and a posting reference to the original journal entry are typically recorded in the ledger accounts as well. These provide an audit trail so a transaction can be traced back from the ledger to the journal and from the journal back to the source documents.

For Our Video Store, we've done the posting at the end of the process, after making adjusting entries. Typically, posting is done more frequently. In automated systems it normally occurs at the same time journal entries are made.

OUR VIDEO STORE'S GENERAL LEDGER AT JUNE 30, 2001   EXHIBIT 7-9

#110 Cash			
(1)	40,000	(2)	3,000
(5)	26,000	(3)	2,000
(10)	500	(9)	18,000
(12)	17,150	(11)	400
		(13)	4,000

#120 Accounts Receivable			
(8)	500	(10)	500

#130 Video Inventory	
(4)	25,000

#140 Supplies on Hand			
(6)	1,500	(17)	300

#220 Shelves and Fixtures	
(3)	15,000

#225 Office Equipment	
(5)	5,000

#230 Accumulated Depreciation			
		(18)	625

#310 Accounts Payable			
(9)	18,000	(3)	18,000
		(4)	25,000
		(6)	1,500
		(15)	450

#351 Wages Payable			
		(14)	1,500

#360 Interest Payable			
		(16)	195

#410 Secured Note Payable			
		(5)	26,000

#510 Capital Stock			
		(1)	40,000

#710 Video Rental Revenue			
		(12)	17,150

#750 Other Operating Revenue			
		(8)	500

#810 Salary & Wage Expense	
(13)	4,000
(14)	1,500

#820 Rent Expense	
(2)	3,000

#830 Supplies Expense	
(17)	300

#840 Utilities Expense	
(15)	450

#850 Legal Expense	
(11)	400

#860 Depreciation Expense	
(18)	625

#920 Interest Expense	
(16)	195

PREPARATION OF FINANCIAL STATEMENTS

The culmination of the accounting process is the preparation of financial statements to provide information to decision makers. Financial statements are usually prepared from the company's adjusted trial balance, which is illustrated in Exhibit 7–10. This trial balance is simply a listing of the account balances taken from the general ledger. The income statement, statement of changes in owners' equity, and balance sheet for Our Video Store are shown in Exhibit 7–11. The cash flow statement is not prepared directly from the trial balance and is not illustrated here; cash flow statements are discussed in Chapter 13.

One last step in the accounting process is that Our Video Store's temporary accounts must be closed. Although not illustrated here, a Retained Earnings account would be created and the balances of all of the temporary accounts transferred to it. This is normally done after the preparation of financial statements.

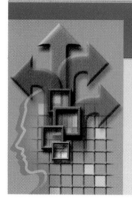

You Decide 7-5

USING OUR VIDEO STORE'S FINANCIAL STATEMENTS

Examine the financial statements for Our Video Store for the month of June. Would this information help someone decide whether to invest in the store? Lend it money? Sell it supplies on account? Work for it? Explain. What additional accounting information might help in making these decisions? What nonaccounting information might be useful?

EXHIBIT 7-10 **OUR VIDEO STORE'S TRIAL BALANCE**

OUR VIDEO STORE ADJUSTED TRIAL BALANCE JUNE 30, 2001	Account Debit	Balance Credit
#110 Cash	$ 56,250	
#120 Accounts Receivable	0	
#130 Video Inventory	25,000	
#140 Supplies on Hand	1,200	
#220 Shelves & Fixtures	15,000	
#225 Office Equipment	5,000	
#230 Accumulated Depreciation		$ 625
#310 Accounts Payable		26,950
#351 Wages Payable		1,500
#360 Interest Payable		195
#410 Secured Note Payable		26,000
#510 Capital Stock		40,000
#710 Video Rental Revenue		17,150
#750 Other Operating Revenue		500
#810 Salary & Wage Expense	5,500	
#820 Rent Expense	3,000	
#830 Supplies Expense	300	
#840 Utilities Expense	450	
#850 Legal Expense	400	
#860 Depreciation Expense	625	
#920 Interest Expense	195	
Totals	$112,920	$112,920

OUR VIDEO STORE'S FINANCIAL STATEMENTS

EXHIBIT 7-11

OUR VIDEO STORE
INCOME STATEMENT
MONTH OF JUNE, 2001

Revenue		
Video Rental	$17,150	
Other Operating Revenues	500	
		$ 17,650
Operating Expenses		
Salary and Wages	$ 5,500	
Rent	3,000	
Utilities	450	
Depreciation	625	
Supplies	300	
Interest	195	
Other	400	
		10,470
Net Income		$ 7,180

OUR VIDEO STORE
CHANGES IN OWNERS' EQUITY
MONTH OF JUNE, 2001

Capital Stock		
Balance June 1	$ -0-	
Issued during June	40,000	
		$ 40,000
Retained Earnings		
Balance June 1	$ -0-	
Net Income, June 2001	7,180	7,180
Total Owners' Equity, June 30		$ 47,180

OUR VIDEO STORE
BALANCE SHEET
JUNE 30, 2001

ASSETS		
Current Assets		
Cash	$56,250	
Supplies on Hand	1,200	
		$ 57,450
Fixed Assets		
Office Equipment	$ 5,000	
Shelves and Fixtures	15,000	
Video Inventory	25,000	
Less Accumulated Depreciation	(625)	
		44,375
Total Assets		$101,825

(continued)

EXHIBIT 7-11 **OUR VIDEO STORE'S FINANCIAL STATEMENTS (CONT.)**

OUR VIDEO STORE		
BALANCE SHEET		
JUNE 30, 2001		

LIABILITIES AND OWNERS' EQUITY			
Liabilities:			
Current Liabilities			
Accounts Payable	$26,950		
Wages Payable	1,500		
Interest Payable	195		
		$28,645	
Long-term Debt			
Secured Note Payable		26,000	
Total Liabilities			$ 54,645
Owners' Equity:			
Capital Stock	$40,000		
Retained Earnings	7,180		
Total Owners' Equity			47,180
Total Liabilities and Owners' Equity			$101,825

SUMMARY

The accounting information system is designed to provide useful information for those making decisions about an entity. Each system should be designed by considering the specific decisions for which it will provide information. Understanding the accounting system can help financial statement users understand the information and help them make better decisions.

The accounting process uses ledger accounts, represented in this chapter by T-accounts, to accumulate financial information about economic events and transactions. Although T-accounts have generally been replaced by computerized ledger accounts in practice, they can help illustrate the effects of various events and transactions on the financial statement elements.

Two terms ingrained in accounting are *debit* and *credit*. Debit has traditionally referred to the left side of a T-account or journal entry, but more generally means a positive asset balance, an increase (or the act of making an increase) in an asset balance, or a decrease (or the act of making a decrease) in a liability or equity balance. Credit has traditionally referred to the right side of a T-account or journal entry, but more generally means a positive liability or equity balance, an increase (or the act of making an increase) in a liability or equity balance, or a decrease (or the act of making a decrease) in an asset balance.

Accounting records economic events using a double-entry system. The double-entry system is a natural outgrowth of every transaction having at least two effects and is consistent with the accounting equation. In addition, the double-entry system provides built-in checks on accuracy. By using the double-entry system to examine the effects of transactions on elements of the accounting equation, you can gain a better understanding of the information included in financial statements.

Accounting systems include two types of accounts: permanent and temporary. The balances of permanent accounts carry over from one period to the next and provide information about balance sheet elements at a specific point in time. The balances of permanent accounts are reported in the balance sheet. Temporary accounts, which are types of equity accounts, reflect events that have occurred only during a single period. For some financial statement elements, decision makers are interested in a period-by-period analysis. The balances of temporary accounts are reported in the income statement, except for dividends declared which are reported in the retained earnings statement. The balances of all temporary accounts are closed to retained earnings at the end of each period so retained earnings is correctly stated and so the temporary accounts can be used to accumulate information for the next period.

The accounting cycle is the set of steps used to accumulate the information reported in financial statements. Based on source documents, key information about events and transactions is recorded in the accounts. Once transactions have been classified, they are chronologically entered in the journal. The journal provides a history of the entity's activities and is the only place an individual transaction can be seen in its entirety. The information from these entries is then separated by type and accumulated in individual ledger accounts. At the end of each period, account balances are adjusted if needed to bring them into accordance with the revenue recognition and matching concepts. Financial statements are then prepared to report the information contained in the accounting system to decision makers. Finally, temporary accounts are closed.

LIST OF IMPORTANT TERMS

accounting cycle *(253)*

accrue *(255)*

accrued expenses *(256)*

accrued income *(255)*

adjusting entries *(254)*

chart of accounts *(245)*

closing entries *(254)*

contra-asset account *(258)*

credit *(247)*

debit *(247)*

double-entry bookkeeping *(248)*

general ledger *(253)*

journal *(253)*

ledger accounts *(243)*

permanent accounts *(249)*

prepaid expenses *(257)*

T-account *(245)*

temporary accounts *(249)*

trial balance *(253)*

unearned income *(256)*

EXAMINING THE CONCEPTS

Q7-1 If you do not intend to become an accounting major and all you want is to be able to read and use accounting reports, why should you know something about the accounting system?

Q7-2 Is the expression "assets on the left, liabilities and equity on the right" correct? How is it related to the balance sheet? How is it related to the accounting equation?

Q7-3 How would balance sheet accounts be affected if an expense was erroneously recorded for $11,000 rather than the correct amount of $8,000?

Q7-4 Claims against assets are on the right side of the accounting equation. Will they normally have a debit or credit balance?

Q7-5 What is a ledger account, and what is its purpose? How does the T-account format differ from the way transactions are recorded in a computer system?

Q7-6 In normal business practice, balance sheet accounts contain both increases and decreases, while many income statement accounts contain only increases. Why?

Q7-7 Express the term *debit cash* in another way so that it will be more meaningful to someone who has not studied accounting.

Q7-8 Explain why double entry in accounting is comparable to maintaining equality of an equation in mathematics.

Q7-9 Will the double-entry system be used in a computerized accounting system that does not record changes in account balances as debits and credits? Explain.

Q7-10 When you purchase an item for cash in a retail store, you receive a copy of the sales receipt. How does the retail store provide documentation for its records? When and how would you expect this transaction to be entered into the store's accounting system?

Q7-11 Why would you expect companies to record transactions as quickly as possible? What information about transactions typically is recorded?

Q7-12 Why are income statement accounts considered to be temporary accounts?

Q7-13 Accounts payable normally are paid in a relatively short period of time. Why is Accounts Payable considered to be a permanent account?

Q7-14 In what way is a trial balance in the accounting system similar to the table of contents in a textbook?

Q7-15 If an accounting information system records increases to assets and expenses as positive numbers and increases to liabilities and revenues as negative numbers, will the total of all accounts on the trial balance be positive or negative? Explain your answer.

Q7-16 If a company fails to make an adjusting entry needed to properly state the account balances at the end of the period, will the trial balance be in balance?

Q7-17 Why do companies generally have an accounting procedures manual with a chart of accounts included? Would you expect your university to have one? Why?

Q7-18 When does the matching concept for revenues and expenses result in a liability being recorded? Give an example.

Q7-19 Give an example of an adjusting entry needed to meet the financial reporting concept of matching.

Q7-20 Why are adjusting entries important when financial statements are going to be prepared? What is their purpose?

Q7-21 You have been given an income statement that was prepared without adjusting entries to use in your decision whether to invest in the Black Company. Why would you be concerned about accrued expenses not yet recorded?

Q7-22 Decision makers are interested in revenue and expense for specific periods of time. Generally, companies report quarterly and annually. Some companies seem to need monthly, weekly, or even daily revenue and expense reports. Why?

Q7-23 When a company records a purchase of office supplies as an asset at the time of purchase, an adjusting entry will be needed at year-end to record an expense for those supplies used. If, on the other hand, a company records office supplies as an expense at the time of purchase, what type of adjustment will be needed at year-end? Explain.

Q7-24 A company has long-term notes payable outstanding that were issued ten years ago. They are classified as long-term liabilities. These notes are due in the middle of the next year. Other than interest, will any adjustments be needed to properly report these notes payable?

Q7-25 What role do closing entries play in the accounting cycle?

Q7-26 Given that the same temporary accounts are seen period after period, in what way are they temporary? In which financial statement(s) do temporary accounts appear?

UNDERSTANDING ACCOUNTING INFORMATION

E7-1 Accounting Systems Neither Dowl Manufacturing nor Ed's Plumbing and Heating mention in their financial statements that they have an accounting procedures manual. Dowl sells fabricated steel products nationally. Ed's plumbing is owned by Ed and his brother and operates locally.

a. Is it safe to assume that neither company has an accounting procedures manual?
b. Which company is likely to have the greater need for an accounting procedures manual? Explain why.
c. What assurances do financial statement users receive if they know a company has an accounting procedures manual and the company follows the policies and procedures that are specified?

E7-2 The Accounting Equation: The Basis for Useful Information Tang Industries reported a 100 percent increase in owners' equity and a 70 percent increase in total assets during the year. The balance sheet prepared by Tang at January 1 showed owners' equity of $40,000 and total assets of $100,000.

a. Did Tang's liabilities increase or decrease during the year? By what amount?
b. How would information about the change in individual owners' equity accounts assist an investor in evaluating the profitability of Tang for the year?

c. How would detailed information about the change in the individual asset and liability accounts assist an investor in evaluating the financial position of the company at December 31?

E7-3 Using Ledger Accounts for Accumulation and Analysis The owner of Dozee Corporation sometimes fails to record an account payable or a reduction in cash when purchases are made. At the start of each month, it typically takes several days to compile the information needed to prepare Dozee's financial statements for the preceding month. With some frequency, the accounts don't balance and an owner's "fudge factor" has to be added or deducted in order to get the balance sheet to balance.

a. How would the use of double-entry bookkeeping improve the accuracy of Dozee's financial statements?
b. How would the use of ledger accounts improve the accuracy of Dozee's accounting system?
c. In what way would the value of the ledger accounts be diminished if the assistant bookkeeper entered amounts in the correct ledger accounts, but became confused and randomly entered the amounts as debits or credits?

E7-4 Using Ledger Accounts to Classify Information The owners' equity of Blowen Company at January 1 consisted of $300,000 of common stock outstanding and

$520,000 of retained earnings. Assuming no dividends were paid, explain what additional event or events must have occurred for each of the following:

a. Retained earnings increased by $75,000. Expenses for the year were $610,000.
b. Retained earnings increased by $120,000. Revenues for the year were $940,000.
c. Retained earnings decreased by $45,000. Expenses for the year were $480,000.
d. Owners' equity increased by $120,000. Revenues for the year were $220,000 and expenses were $190,000.
e. Owners' equity increased by $230,000. Revenues for the year were $750,000. Additional stock was issued for $325,000.

E7-5 Overview of the Accounting Cycle Fargus Corporation has established a seven-step sequence in the accounting cycle for its payroll department; however, the steps were scrambled the last time they were printed out. You have been asked to place the steps in the proper sequence.

1. Close out the balance in each of the payroll expense accounts at the end of the period.
2. Record the amount paid as an expense and a reduction in cash.
3. Determine which payroll expense account will be increased by each payment.
4. Prepare a listing of all account balances.
5. Receive payroll documents showing the amount paid to each employee.
6. Deduct payroll expense as an operating cost in the income statement for the month of January.
7. Add the amounts assigned to each of the payroll expense accounts to the existing balances in those accounts.

E7-6 Adjustments: The Matching Concept at Work Faulty Corporation reported net income of $350,000 for the year, but failed to take into consideration four adjustments the assistant bookkeeper thought should be included:

1. Equipment with an expected economic life of five years was purchased on January 1 for $180,000. No depreciation was recorded for the period.
2. A three-year insurance policy was purchased on January 1 for $30,000. The full amount is reported as prepaid insurance at December 31.
3. Repair work costing $26,000 was done on Faulty's computer equipment in early December, but no expense was recorded because the bill has not been paid.
4. Faulty Corporation provided professional services for customers in the amount of $85,000 in late December, but nothing has been recorded because the bills will not be sent out until the second week of January.

a. For each of the above, determine which accounts should be adjusted and the amount of the adjustment.
b. Determine the effect of the required adjustments on total assets and total liabilities reported at the end of the year and reported net income for the year.

E7-7 Multiple Choice: Accounting Systems Select the correct answer for each of the following:

1. Which of the following events would not be considered an accounting transaction to be entered into the accounting system?
   a. Payment of fees to a marketing consultant.
   b. Purchase of advertising for a new product.
   c. Sales of a new product during the first month on the market.
   d. Tabulation of the results of a customer satisfaction survey.
2. Which of the following events is recorded in the accounts?
   a. Obtaining a building permit on land purchased two years ago for expansion purposes.
   b. Paying the contractor for building the factory for which the permit was obtained.
   c. Hiring workers for the new factory building.
   d. Deciding to go to double production shifts at the new factory.
3. Which of the following is not true of an accounting system?
   a. Information to be recorded in the system is taken from source documents.
   b. Classification of transactions is necessary before they can be entered into the system's accounts.
   c. Ledger accounts are used to accumulate information about individual financial statement elements.
   d. The number of ledger accounts used by a company will be the same as the number of accounts appearing in the annual financial statements.
4. Adjusting entries at the end of an accounting period might be recorded for all but:
   a. An estimated additional liability.
   b. An estimated expense.
   c. An estimated increase in the fair value of equipment.
   d. Revenue earned but not yet billed to customers.
5. The accounting cycle is:
   a. The sequence of procedures used by a business to process economic information and to produce financial statements.
   b. The length of time it takes to complete a set of financial statements after the books are closed.
   c. A process that begins with adjusting entries and ends with the preparation of financial statements.
   d. The length of time it takes to make payment after a bill is received from a supplier.

E7-8 Multiple Choice: Information Accumulation and Analysis Select the correct answer for each of the following:

1. The year-end balance sheet of Orange Company reported assets of $10,000, liabilities of $3,000, and equity of $7,000. The income statement for the year reported revenue of $9,000 and expenses of $6,000. Which of the following statements is correct?

a. The accounting equation is out of balance because total equity and net income are not the same.
b. Net income for the year was $7,000.
c. Cash generated during the period was $7,000.
d. The balance in equity at the beginning of the period was $4,000.

2. During 2001, the total assets of the AIT company increased by $350,000. The increase could have resulted from:
a. A decrease in liabilities of $700,000 and an increase in equity of $350,000.
b. Net income of $350,000.
c. A decrease in liabilities of $350,000 and net income of $350,000.
d. Collecting $350,000 of accounts receivable.

3. The primary function of an account in the accounting system is to:
a. Identify the type of organization.
b. Determine at what point a transaction should be recorded.
c. Accumulate accounting information.
d. Store accounting transactions until they are classified.

4. Which of the following is an important factor in the choice of individual accounts used by a company?
a. The type of information needed by decision makers.
b. The number and types of products sold.
c. The decision to form a corporation rather than a partnership.
d. All of the above.

5. Debits and credits are:
a. Used only for adjusting entries.
b. Used to indicate whether an account balance is increased or decreased.
c. Needed to determine which accounts are used to record transactions.
d. All of the above.

E7-9   Multiple Choice: Classifying Information   Select the correct answer for each of the following:

1. The three primary functions of debits and credits in an accounting system are:
a. To serve as labels for the left and right sides of T-accounts, to describe increases and decreases in accounts, and to permit the use of bookkeeping on a cash basis.
b. To serve as labels for the left and right sides of the T-accounts, to indicate in which financial statement an account will be reported, and to identify the normal balance in each account.
c. To indicate in which financial statement an account will be reported, to describe increases and decreases in accounts, and to identify the normal balance in each account.
d. To serve as labels for the left and right sides of the T-accounts, to describe increases and decreases in accounts, and to identify the normal balance in each account.

2. Which of the following transactions correctly maintains equality in the accounting equation?
a. To record the collection of cash from a previous sale, Cash is increased and the Accounts Receivable account is increased by $8,000.
b. To record the payment of a note to the bank, Notes Payable is decreased and Cash in Bank is increased by $3,500.
c. To record the purchase of a new piece of equipment, Equipment is increased and Cash in Bank is decreased by $23,000.
d. To record the payment of salaries to workers, Salaries Expense is increased and Cash in Bank is increased $6,500.

3. Financial statement articulation is illustrated:
a. When an increase in revenue reported in the income statement results in an increase in the net assets reported on the balance sheet.
b. When total revenue in the income statement equals the amount of cash reported on the balance sheet.
c. When expenses incurred and paid are included as liabilities on the balance sheet.
d. When an increase in an expense reported in the income statement results in a decrease in a liability reported on the balance sheet.

4. When accounting information is accumulated in individual accounts, a chart of accounts is:
a. Limited to those accounts that will appear in the balance sheet.
b. A listing of each account that will be used to accumulate information.
c. Changed each year by a company as a function of the success or failure of the previous year's operations.
d. Used to determine whether a debit or credit balance will appear in each of the accounts at the end of the accounting period.

5. Balance sheet accounts are:
a. Temporary accounts.
b. Permanent accounts.
c. Adjusting accounts.
d. Debit-balance accounts only.

E7-10   Multiple Choice: Adjustments   Select the correct answer for each of the following:

1. Paying insurance bills in advance gives rise to:
a. Unearned income.
b. Accrued income.
c. Accrued expense.
d. Prepaid expense.

2. The concept of matching often requires the use of adjusting entries. An example of matching is:
a. Recording a prepaid expense when an accrued expense is recorded.
b. Recording a prepaid expense when accrued income is recorded.

c. Recording a current liability when accrued income is recorded.

d. Recording a current asset when accrued income is recorded.

3. In December 2001, The Carm Property Management company received the January 2002 rent payments from one-third of its renters and recorded the payments as income. If Carm prepares financial statements on December 31, 2001, an adjustment will be necessary to recognize:

   a. Unearned income.

   b. Accrued income.

   c. Accrued expense.

   d. Prepaid expense.

4. When a company owns an interest-bearing certificate of deposit issued by a bank, interest often is not paid until the certificate of deposit matures. If a five-year certificate of deposit is purchased on January 1, 2001, the company will make an adjusting entry at December 31, 2001. The bank also will make an adjusting entry. The entries will be:

   a. Unearned income for the company and accrued expense for the bank.

   b. Accrued income for the company and prepaid expense for the bank.

   c. Accrued income for the company and accrued expense for the bank.

   d. Unearned income for the company and prepaid expense for the bank.

5. Adjusting entries may be required at the end of the year to make sure that the accounting concept of matching is met. Which of the following would be most likely to require an adjusting entry?

   a. A new union contract has been approved that will increase wage expense by 25 percent next year.

   b. Wages earned by office employees at the end of this year are paid on the fifteenth day of the following month.

   c. Company sales in December of this year were 10 percent less than sales for the same month last year.

   d. Orders for $35,000 of goods were received from customers in December and will be shipped early next year.

E7-11 Review of the Accounting Cycle Screen Corporation reported the following adjusted trial balance amounts at December 31:

Cash	$ 50,000	
Accounts receivable	160,000	
Inventory	220,000	
Buildings and equipment (net)	300,000	
Accounts payable		$100,000
Notes payable		300,000
Common stock		200,000
Retained earnings		90,000
Sales revenue		225,000
Salary and wage expense	75,000	
Depreciation expense	15,000	
Other operating expenses	95,000	
Total	$915,000	$915,000

a. Where are the adjusted trial balance totals found?

b. Which of the accounts presented in the trial balance represent permanent accounts? Which represent temporary accounts?

c. What amount of net income did Screen Corporation earn for the year?

d. If a trial balance were to be prepared at the start of business on January 1 of next year, determine the balance that would be reported in the trial balance for:

   1. Cash.

   2. Salary and wage expense.

   3. Retained earnings. (Note that this amount is not reported in the December 31 trial balance.)

E7-12 Realization The realization concept requires that income be recorded when it is realized, not when cash is received. Assume you invest $8,000 in a 5 percent, twelve-month certificate of deposit on September 1, 2000.

a. How much interest will be earned for the entire term of the certificate of deposit?

b. When will this interest normally be paid?

c. How much interest will be earned as of December 31, 2000?

d. What accounts will be adjusted and how much will they be increased or decreased in the accounting period ending December 31, 2000?

E7-13 Accounting Cycle For each of the following steps in the accounting cycle, (1) describe the step and its purpose; (2) indicate the step in the cycle that precedes it (or the activity, if it is the first step); and (3) indicate the step in the cycle that follows it:

a. Adjustment of balances.

b. Recording of transactions.

c. Posting to ledger accounts.

d. Preparation of trial balance.

E7-14 Accounting Cycle Place the steps of the accounting cycle in the correct sequence:

1. Adjust balances reported in trial balance.
2. Analyze transaction to see which accounts are affected.
3. Post amounts to ledger accounts.
4. Prepare financial statements.
5. Identify the events or transactions to be recorded.
6. Close the temporary accounts.
7. Prepare a trial balance.
8. Record transactions in journal.

E7-15 Account Classifications For each of the following, indicate whether the account is classified as an (A) asset, (L) liability, or (SE) stockholders' equity item and whether the account balance has been increased or decreased by the activity:

a. Debit accounts receivable.
b. Debit bonds payable.
c. Credit buildings and equipment.
d. Debit retained earnings.
e. Credit cash.
f. Credit wages payable.
g. Debit common stock.
h. Credit retained earnings.
i. Debit land.
j. Debit accounts payable.

E7-16 Permanent versus Temporary Accounts For each of the following, indicate whether the account is classified as a permanent or temporary account:

a. Capital Stock.
b. Prepaid Insurance.
c. Wage Expense.
d. Retained Earnings.
e. Cost of Goods Sold.
f. Unearned Rent Income.
g. Gain on Sale of Land.
h. Accumulated Depreciation.
i. Notes Payable.
j. Sales Revenue.

E7-17 Changes in Account Balances The balances in two accounts are affected by each of the following transactions. For each transaction, indicate (1) the accounts in which the transactions are recorded, (2) whether the balances increase or decrease, and (3) whether the accounts are debited or credited when the transaction is recorded:

a. Accounts receivable of $45,000 are collected.
b. A two-year insurance policy is purchased for $30,000.
c. Depreciation expense of $11,000 is recorded.
d. Capital stock is issued for $95,000.
e. Sales of $320,000 are made on account.
f. Payment for engineering services of $25,000 is received in advance.
g. Inventory costing $260,000 is purchased on account.

E7-18 Impact of Debits and Credits Indicate whether the account balance for each of the following accounts will be increased or decreased by the action taken:

a. Sales Revenue is credited.
b. Depreciation Expense is debited.
c. Accumulated Depreciation is credited.
d. Accounts Receivable is credited.
e. Land is debited.
f. Wages Payable is debited.
g. Capital Stock is credited.
h. Unearned Revenue is debited.
i. Prepaid Insurance is credited.
j. Accounts Payable is credited.

E7-19 Net Income Determination For each of the following, indicate whether net income will be (I) increased, (D) decreased, or (U) unaffected:

a. Debit salary expense.
b. Credit sales revenue.
c. Debit land.
d. Debit cost of inventory sold.
e. Credit investment income.
f. Credit common stock.
g. Debit insurance expense.
h. Debit rent revenue.

E7-20 Accrual Accounting Branwit Company uses accrual accounting and recorded a number of journal entries in 2000. For each transaction shown below (a) give the other account that was debited or credited in the journal entry, (b) indicate whether a debit or credit was made to the other account, and (c) indicate whether the other account was increased or decreased by the transaction.

1. Accounts receivable is decreased by $4,000.
2. Accounts payable is decreased by $12,000.
3. Wages payable is increased by $5,000.
4. Depreciation expense is increased by $30,000.
5. Capital stock is increased by $70,000.
6. Supplies on hand is decreased by $2,500.
7. Inventory is increased by $28,000.
8. Prepaid insurance is decreased by $3,500.
9. Prepaid insurance is increased by $8,000.
10. Rent receivable is increased by $21,000.

E7-21 Use of Trial Balance Amounts The account balances of Sound Corporation at March 31 were as follows:

	March 31 Debit	Credit
Cash	$ 125,000	
Accounts Receivable	201,000	
Inventory	170,000	
Prepaid Insurance	3,000	
Land	21,000	
Buildings and Equipment	360,000	
Cost of Goods Sold	290,000	
Wage Expense	85,000	
Depreciation Expense	12,000	
Insurance Expense	2,000	
Sales		$ 470,000
Accumulated Depreciation		140,000
Accounts Payable		180,000
Notes Payable		200,000
Capital Stock		150,000
Retained Earnings, March 1		129,000
Total	$1,269,000	$1,269,000

a. Prepare an income statement for the month of March for Sound Corporation.
b. Prepare a balance sheet for Sound Corporation at March 31.

E7-22   Using the Trial Balance   A printout of the account balances of Miller Wholesale Furniture at December 31, 2001, appeared as follows:

Cash	$ 16,000	
Accounts receivable	12,000	
Buildings and equipment	80,000	
Cost of goods sold	100,000	
Wage expense	55,000	
Depreciation expense	10,000	
Other expenses	15,000	
Sales		$200,000
Accumulated depreciation		25,000
Accounts payable		7,000
Wages payable		4,000
Bank loans (5 year)		15,000
Capital stock		25,000
Retained earnings		
(Jan. 1, 2001)		12,000
	$288,000	$288,000

Required:
a. Prepare an income statement for Miller Wholesale Furniture for 2001.
b. Prepare Miller's balance sheet as of December 31, 2001.

E7-23   Debits and Credits   You have learned that debits increase assets and credits increase liabilities. Why does a bank debit your account when it reduces your account balance (your cash asset) and issue a credit when it increases your bank account balance?

E7-24   Double Entry   Use of the double-entry system can assist decision makers in a number of ways. Explain how the double-entry system can help provide the following:

a. Assurance that all assets acquired by the business have been recorded.
b. Knowledge of the sources of the money used in the business.
c. Information on the debts owed.
d. Information on the total sales for the period.

E7-25   Articulated Financial Statements   When recording the sale of inventory, the asset account Inventory is reduced and an expense account, Cost of Goods Sold, is increased. Is it always true that when an asset account is reduced an expense is increased? Explain.

E7-26   Documentation   During the past week, you have probably made a number of purchases. Each of these purchases was an exchange transaction, with revenue to the seller and either an asset received or an expense to you. What documentation was used by the sellers to record the transactions? List at least three such transactions and the documentation.

E7-27   Using Accounting Information   The following accounts are taken from the income statement of a small manufacturing company. Using the principles of realization and matching, for each account give an example of an adjustment that might be needed to accomplish the proper realization and matching.

a. Interest Income.
b. Supplies Expense.
c. Wages and Salaries Expense.
d. Insurance Expense.

E7-28   Recording Transactions   Prepare entries in general journal form to record each of the following transactions for Soullard Company:

a. The company issues capital stock for $100,000.
b. A three-year lease is signed on a building, and Soullard pays $24,000 rent in advance.
c. Equipment is purchased on credit for $18,000.
d. Inventory is purchased on credit for $67,000.
e. The company receives a $50,000 loan from the Quicksand Savings Bank.
f. The company sells inventory for $12,400 cash and $35,200 on credit.
g. Soullard pays $20,000 on account.
h. Accounts from customers in the amount of $22,500 are collected.
i. A bill for $620 is received from the local gas and electric company.
j. A full-time sales associate is hired at a salary of $1,500 per month.
k. A piece of the company's equipment is repaired at a cost of $330, the full amount paid in cash.
l. The company earns $25 interest on the money it has in the bank.
m. The sales associate's monthly salary is paid.
n. Depreciation expense of $800 is recorded.
o. Interest accrued (but unpaid) on the loan is $3,000.

E7-29   Using T-Accounts   Brandy Company reported the following account balances at January 1:

Cash	$15,000
Accounts Receivable	48,000
Inventory	35,000
Accounts Payable	21,000

During the month of January, Brandy Company had the following transactions:

1. Inventory costing $160,000 was purchased on account.
2. Inventory that had cost $150,000 was sold for $230,000.
3. Payments of $182,000 were received on accounts receivable.
4. Payments of $154,000 were made on accounts payable.

a. Prepare the journal entries for Brandy Company for January.
b. Prepare T-accounts for each of the balance sheet and income statement accounts included in the above entries,

enter the beginning balances (where appropriate), enter the amounts recorded during January, and determine the balances at January 31.

E7-30 Adjusting Entries Stall Personnel Services had the following transactions during the month of March:

1. Insurance premiums in the amount of $28,800 were paid on March 1. The policies provide coverage through the month of February of the following year.
2. Income taxes for the month of February in the amount of $20,000 were paid on March 5. Income computed before income tax for the month of March was $80,000. Stall Personnel Services has a federal income tax rate of 32 percent. Tax expense for the month of March is not yet recorded.
3. A total of $124,000 was paid on March 20 and recorded as salary and wage expense. Salaries and wages earned by employees during March were $160,000.
4. Payment of $60,000 for legal services to be performed in March and April was received in advance and credited to unearned service revenue. A total of 30 percent of the services was performed during the month of March.

a. Prepare the journal entries recorded by Stall Personnel Services during the month of March.
b. Prepare the adjusting entries needed at March 31.

E7-31 Adjusting Entries Bali Company reports on a calendar-year basis. During 2000, the company engaged in the following transactions:

1. A two-year insurance policy was purchased on May 1, and the full premium of $5,400 for the two years was prepaid.
2. A four-year lease, effective October 1, was signed on equipment, and $18,000 was paid for the first year's rent.
3. Payment for new service contracts in the amount of $72,000 was received on July 31. Bali will provide the purchased services evenly over a one-year period beginning August 1.
4. On December 1, Bali borrowed $250,000 from Great Nation Bank on a five-year, 9 percent note. Interest is paid annually on November 30.

a. Record each of the listed transactions on the books of Bali Company in general journal form.
b. Record in general journal form any adjusting entries needed by Bali at the end of 2000.

E7-32 The Accounting Cycle Bonart Service Corporation prepares financial statements monthly. The company started business in May with the issuance for cash of $250,000 of common stock. Also in May, the company signed a four-year lease on a building (effective June 1), prepaying the first year's rent of $24,000. Bonart also pur-

chased equipment, which was delivered on May 31, for $30,000 cash; the equipment is expected to have a five-year life, with no residual value. Bonart's operations commenced on June 1, and the following transactions occurred during June:

1. On June 1, Bonart borrowed $40,000 from Louie's Bank on a six-month note at 9 percent annual interest.
2. Supplies were purchased on account for $61,300.
3. The company billed customers $59,000 for services performed.
4. The company paid $32,000 of amounts owed to suppliers.
5. The company collected $27,400 on account.
6. Bonart billed customers $18,600 for services performed.
7. Wages of $41,000 were paid.
8. Utility bills of $910 were received.
9. Repair bills of $620 related to water damage from a leaky pipe were received and paid.
10. Cash of $9,000 was received for services to be provided in July.

At the end of June, Bonart owed employees wages of $2,100 and had $44,600 of supplies remaining on hand.

a. Record each of the listed transactions for June on the books of Bonart Service Corporation in general journal form.
b. Set up the appropriate ledger accounts (T-accounts) and enter any beginning (June 1) balances.
c. Post each of the journal entries to ledger accounts.
d. Record in general journal form any adjusting entries needed by Bonart at the end of June and post them to ledger accounts.
e. Prepare a trial balance for Bonart at the end of June, and make sure it balances.
f. Prepare Bonart's June income statement and a balance sheet as of June 30.

E7-33 Computing Revenues and Expenses For each of the following, determine which income statement account would be used to report the revenue or expense for September and the amount that would be reported:

a. Wages payable were $52,000 at September 1 and $47,000 at September 30. Employees were paid $198,000 during the month.
b. Inventory costing $350,000 was purchased during September. Inventory of $97,000 and $113,000 was reported at September 1 and September 30, respectively.
c. Accounts receivable of $183,000 and $195,000 were reported at September 1 and September 30, respectively. A total of $306,000 was collected on accounts receivable during the month.
d. Income taxes in the amount of $135,000 were paid during September. The balance of income taxes payable at September 30 was $69,000. The amount payable at September 1 was $58,000.

E7-34 Determining Income The Alto Company prepared an income statement for its bank in support of its request to renew a loan that comes due January 3, 2002. The reported net income for 2001 was $54,500. However, Alto did not make any adjusting entries for the following:

1. In January 2001, Alto recorded as prepaid insurance the $15,000 cost of a three-year liability insurance policy covering its store operations.
2. On January 2, 2001, Alto borrowed $100,000 from the bank for 12 months at 9 percent interest. No interest expense entries have been made.
3. The bank loan was used to purchase three new delivery trucks in January 2001 for a total cost of $100,000. The trucks are expected to last five years. While the purchase was correctly recorded, no further entries were made relating to these trucks.

Required:
a. What is the correct net income for Alto Company for 2001?
b. The banker has informed Alto that it must have 2001 earnings of at least $20,000 for the loan to be renewed for an additional year. Does Alto qualify?

E7-35 Recording Salary Expense Grover Company reported wages payable of $45,000 at November 1. During the month of November, additional wages of $290,000 were earned by employees and a total of $275,000 was paid to employees. The payment by Grover was recorded with the following journal entry:

Wages Payable	45,000	
Wage Expense	230,000	
Cash		275,000

a. If Grover records no other entries relating to wage expense or wages payable during November, will reported net income for November be understated or overstated? By what amount?
b. What adjusting entry must Grover Company record on November 30 to correct the account balances?

E7-36 Recording Insurance Expense Eld Company reported prepaid insurance of $40,000 on January 1 on a flood insurance policy that provides coverage until August 31. Because of increased claims due to substantial flooding problems in the area, the twelve-month premium paid on September 1 was increased to $84,000 and was recorded by Eld as follows:

Insurance Expense	84,000	
Cash		84,000

No other entries relating to insurance expense were recorded during the year.

a. What amount of insurance expense should Eld Company report for the year?
b. If no adjusting entry is made at year-end, what will be the effect on reported net income and balance sheet accounts?
c. Give the adjusting entry Eld Company must record at December 31 to ensure the appropriate amounts are reported.

E7-37 Understanding the Trial Balance Recently a banker proposed a loan-review policy that included examining the company's account balances. The banker making the proposal argued that accountants hide things on the financial statements, so the banker wanted the trial balances for this year and for last year, with the balances of all of the individual accounts shown, rather than the summarized information reported in the financial statements. What are the advantages and disadvantages of using trial balances instead of financial statements?

E7-38 Recognition of Income *Gentlemen's Computer Quarterly* magazine expects to put out its first regular issue in January of next year. It is now soliciting subscriptions by mailing out a sample preliminary issue with information about how to subscribe. The quarterly has budgeted the following subscriptions, all paid in advance:

> *50,000 three-year subscriptions at $100 each.*
> *80,000 two-year subscriptions at $80 each.*
> *20,000 one-year subscriptions at $50 each.*

a. How much cash will *Gentlemen's Computer Quarterly* receive from subscriptions in the first year? How much revenue will be reported in the first year?
b. If the same number of subscriptions are sold in the second year of operations, how much cash will be received and how much revenue will be reported in the second year?

USING ACCOUNTING FOR DECISION MAKING

P7-39 Classifying Information When a company makes a sale on account, the accounts receivable account is increased with a debit and the sales revenue account is increased with a credit. Most companies keep more detailed records about sales than is contained in this entry. As one who uses accounting information to make decisions, what additional information would you like to have? Consider, for example, what the manager of a department store would need to know.

P7-40 Classifying Information

The accounting process is similar for all companies; however, the individual accounts a company selects to classify transactions reflect the kind of information needed to make decisions about its specific business operations. For each of the following types of businesses, identify a revenue account and an expense account that would be important in their recordkeeping systems. For each account, explain how the information will improve a decision.

a. A law firm that does legal work and tax work.
b. A vending machine service company.
c. A local restaurant.
d. A book publisher.

P7-41 Matching

A local pizza delivery truck driver has been offered the opportunity to buy her own delivery truck and deliver pizza at a higher commission than the one received when using the company truck. She knows that the cost of her truck has to be included in deciding whether it would be best to own her own truck. She puts together the following information:

Cost of delivery truck, fully equipped	$20,000
Average life of delivery trucks	5 years
Average commission and tips for each delivery with a company truck	$3.00
Average commission and tips for each delivery with a privately owned truck	$5.00
Average number of deliveries per week	100

a. Explain briefly how the cost of the truck can be matched to her future revenue from deliveries.
b. Prepare a simple schedule that illustrates this matching.
c. Would this matching be done at the end of a month or year as an adjustment or recorded as a daily expense of operations? Explain.

P7-42 Chart of Accounts

Your uncle is planning to set up a small, part-time business developing landscape plans for new homes. He expects to get customers from referrals by two local nurseries. He wants to keep records for his landscape business separate from his personal affairs. Recommend a chart of accounts for him. Use no more than ten balance sheet accounts and no more than ten income statement accounts. Assume that paper and supplies are to be used, but no purchases of equipment, buildings, land, or other major assets are expected. Part-time help may have to be hired.

P7-43 Accounting Transactions

For each of the following transactions:

a. Identify a decision by a manager, investor, or creditor that could be influenced by information about the transaction.
b. Analyze the transaction and indicate the accounts that should be used and the dollar amount that should be recorded.
c. Identify the financial statement disclosures that would be made.

Transactions:

1. Merchandise is sold on account for $3,500, the cash to be collected in thirty days.
2. Inventory of $17,350 is purchased on account and is to be paid for in fifteen days.
3. The company takes in a new partner who invests $150,000 cash in the business.
4. The company borrows $250,000 on a three-year note from the local bank. Interest at 10 percent annually is to be paid at the end of each quarter.
5. The customer in the first transaction pays the account in full.

P7-44 Recording and Reporting Transactions

Brown Company reported the following account balances at January 1:

Cash	$ 58,800	
Accounts Receivable	77,000	
Prepaid Insurance	1,200	
Buildings and Equipment	150,000	
Accumulated Depreciation		$ 24,000
Accounts Payable		23,000
Wages Payable		10,000
Common Stock		100,000
Retained Earnings		130,000
Total	$287,000	$287,000

The following transactions or adjustments to account balances were recorded during January:

1. Professional services were provided and billed to clients in the amount of $220,000.
2. Wages payable at January 1 were paid.
3. Additional wages of $110,000 were earned by employees.
4. Cash of $205,000 was collected on account.
5. Equipment costing $40,000 was purchased for cash.
6. A total of $96,000 of wages earned in January was paid.
7. Payment of $13,000 was made on accounts payable.
8. Insurance in the amount of $300 expired in January.
9. Depreciation in the amount of $6,000 was recorded.

a. Record the journal entry for each of the transactions and adjustments.

b. Create the appropriate general ledger T-accounts and post the beginning balances and journal entries to the T-accounts.

c. Prepare an adjusted trial balance at January 31.

d. Prepare an income statement and statement of changes in owners' equity for the month of January and a balance sheet as of January 31.

P7-45 Comprehensive Problem Pamper Lawn Service is started on March 1, 2000. It established the following chart of accounts for its accounting system:

No.	Account Title
110	Cash
120	Accounts Receivable
130	Fertilizer and Chemical Inventory
140	Prepaid Insurance
240	Truck and Tanks
250	Accumulated Depreciation
310	Accounts Payable
320	Unearned Revenue
330	Wages Payable
510	Capital Stock
520	Retained Earnings
610	Service Revenue
700	Depreciation Expense
710	Attorney Fees
720	Advertising Expense
730	Fuel Expense
740	Insurance Expense
750	Wage Expense
760	Fertilizer and Chemical Expense

a. Record in general journal form entries for each of the following transactions and adjustments. Service Revenue is recorded as services are provided.

1. Capital stock is issued for $40,000 on March 1. A total of $30,000 is spent immediately to purchase a used lawn-service truck and fertilizer tank.

2. In March, a bill for $200 is received from an attorney for drawing up the incorporation papers and helping apply for licenses. The bill is not paid immediately.

3. In March, $400 is paid to the local newspaper to run a series of ads promoting Pamper Lawn Service and offering a discount for early sign-up.

4. In April, $300 is paid for another series of newspaper ads.

5. In April, a $50 deposit is received from each of 100 customers who contracted for services for the summer. These deposits are considered to be payment for the initial inspection and the first month of treatment. Inspections and the first month of treatment are scheduled for April and May. After the first month, routine monthly treatments are $40 per month.

6. A payment of $1,200 is made for insurance coverage on equipment and business liability.

7. On April 15, a shipment of fertilizer and chemicals is received, along with a bill for $5,000.

8. Twenty customers from (5) above receive their lawn inspection and first monthly treatment in April.

9. The remainder of the customers in (5) receive their inspection and first treatment in May. The initial twenty are billed an additional $40 for a second treatment in May.

10. In June, 100 customers are billed $40 each for the lawn treatment.

11. In June, $3,000 is received from customers in payment for their lawn services previously billed.

12. $3,500 is paid on account to the supplier of fertilizer and chemicals.

13. Wages of $2,600 are paid to employees.

14. On June 28, a bill for $500 for fuel used in the company truck is received and immediately paid.

15. Depreciation expense for the four-month period is based on expected lives of ten years for the truck and fertilizer tank.

16. A total of 60 percent of the fertilizer and chemicals received in April is used during the period ended June 30.

17. The insurance policy covers a twelve-month period beginning March 1.

18. Wages owed to employees for work completed prior to the end of June are $600. Payment will be made in July.

b. Create the appropriate general ledger T-accounts and post the entries to the T-accounts.

c. Prepare an adjusted trial balance as of June 30.

d. Prepare an income statement and statement of changes in owners' equity for Pamper Lawn Service for the four-month period ending June 30, 2000, and a balance sheet as of June 30.

e. On June 30, 2000, the owners of the Pamper Lawn Service receive an offer to buy the business, including all customer contracts, equipment, and supplies as of July 1, 2000, for a price of $50,000. The owners agree that they do not have the time to expand the business beyond the current 100 customers, but they can keep operating at the current level. The buyers plan to expand the operations. Should the owners sell? Why or why not?

EXPANDING YOUR HORIZONS

C7-46 Charting the Accounts Following is information taken from the chart of accounts and the adjusted trial balance of Global Computers, Inc., as of December 31, 2000:

1000	Cash	$ 14,850
1100	Accounts receivable	141,600
1110	Allowance for uncollectible accounts	11,400
1200	Notes receivable	6,000
1300	Software inventory	12,580
1310	Hardware inventory	43,400
1320	Replacement parts inventory	2,640
1400	Prepaid insurance	1,800
1500	Computer software	3,200
1505	Amortization of software (expense)	-0-
1600	Computer hardware	16,000
1620	Accumulated depreciation, hardware	-0-
1700	Office furniture	15,000
1701	Accumulated depreciation, office furniture	3,000
1800	Office building	80,000
1810	Accumulated depreciation, office building	30,000
1900	Land	40,000
2000	Accounts payable	104,400
2150	Federal withholding taxes payable	5,325
2250	State withholding taxes payable	887
2400	FICA (Social Security taxes) payable	4,525
2401	Unemployment taxes payable	290
2454	Health insurance payable	1,800
2600	Notes payable	4,000
2601	Mortgage payable	93,000
2700	Common stock	10,000
2800	Additional paid-in capital	30,000
2900	Retained earnings (beginning)	46,914
3000	Hardware sales, in-state	417,000
3100	Software sales, in-state	118,078
3200	Service revenue, in-state	64,700
3300	Sales, out-of-state	93,400
3400	Other income	720
6000	Cost of software sold	98,300
6100	Cost of hardware sold	311,480
6200	Cost of repair parts	27,300
6300	Salary and wage expense	115,274

6401	FICA (Social Security taxes) expense	18,096
6402	Unemployment tax expense	1,736
6403	Health insurance expense	7,200
6500	Materials and supplies expense	1,800
6510	Advertising expense	6,000
6520	Bad debt (uncollectible accounts) expense	15,400
6530	Car and truck expense	11,680
6540	Sales commissions	9,740
6550	Amortization expense	-0-
6560	Depreciation expense	7,000
6600	Freight expense on goods shipped	1,400
6610	Insurance expense	800
6620	Legal and professional fees expense	900
6630	Office expense	1,650
6640	Utility expense	5,880
6650	Other expenses	700
6700	Interest expense	7,800
6800	Tax expense	4,045
6900	Dividends	8,188

Analyze this company's chart of accounts and recommend any changes you think would improve it.

C7-47 Financial Statements—Putting It All Together

a. Using the chart of accounts and adjusted trial balance information from C7-46, prepare an adjusted trial balance for Global Computers, Inc., as of December 31, 2000.
b. Prepare Global's 2000 income statement.
c. Prepare Global's balance sheet as of December 31, 2000.
d. After Global's financial statements are prepared, you realize that management forgot to make adjusting entries for the following items:

* Depreciation of $2,000 was not recorded on computer hardware.

* Salaries of $4,000 were not recorded at year-end.

How will these errors affect the 2000 financial statements?

C7-48 A Look in the Books Early in February, you decide to take a closer look at the computerized accounting records of your employer, United Sales Corporation. In particular, you are interested in cash receipts and expenditures, and you decide to focus on the cash and accounts receivable ledger accounts. Accordingly, you print out the January account histories for those two ledger accounts, with the following results:

02-09-2000			PAGE 1
09:26:40AM	ACCOUNT HISTORY		
	1000 CASH		
	01-01-2000 THROUGH 01-31-2000		

Date	Description	Debits	Credits
01-01-00	Beginning balance	14,850.00	
01-02-00	Pay on acct: Banco Sales		3,000.00
01-03-00	Receive on account: Dover Mfg	10,000.00	
01-05-00	Pay federal withholding tax		5,325.00
01-10-00	Pay on acct: Realtime Co		2,900.00
01-11-00	Receive on acct: Farrow Corp	20,000.00	
01-15-00	Pay federal taxes		5,702.00
01-16-00	Issue stock	2,600.00	
01-17-00	Payroll		2,100.00
01-19-00	Receive on acct: Axel	6,000.00	
01-21-00	Pay on acct: Verlin Supply		9,500.00
01-22-00	Deposit: cash sales	9,000.00	
01-22-00	Pay on acct: Newtech		23,800.00
01-24-00	Pay repair invoice: Ronland	1,200.00	
01-25-00	Issue stock	14,000.00	
01-25-00	Pay health insur: BCC		1,800.00
01-26-00	Pay freight invoice: Yellow		650.00
01-27-00	Pay supplies invoice: Supplymart		250.00
01-29-00	Pay on acct: Virginia Supply Co		2,250.00
01-30-00	Receive on acct: Eggers	8,200.00	
01-31-00	Payroll		2,300.00
01-31-00	Ending balance	26,273.00	

02-09-2000			PAGE 2
09:26:44AM	ACCOUNT HISTORY		
	1100 ACCT REC		
	01-01-2000 THROUGH 01-31-2000		

Date	Description	Debits	Credits
01-01-00	Beginning balance	94,600.00	
01-03-00	Received on acct: Dover Mfg		10,000.00
01-05-00	Sale on account: Eggers	8,200.00	
01-08-00	Sale on account: Darnell	21,340.00	
01-09-00	Sale on account: Baker Transp	4,930.00	
01-11-00	Received on acct: Farrow Corp		20,000.00
01-12-00	Sales return: Baker Transp		1,200.00
01-14-00	Sale on account: Versatile Prod	9,700.00	
01-16-00	Sale on account: Baker Transp	820.00	
01-19-00	Received on acct: Axel		6,000.00
01-20-00	Sale on account: Basslin Elec	26,450.00	
01-29-00	Sale on account: Green Grp	21,300.00	
01-30-00	Received on acct: Eggers		8,200.00
01-31-00	Sale on account: Basslin Elec	3,930.00	
01-31-00	Ending balance	145,870.00	

Based on the information available in these two account printouts, answer the following questions:

a. What is the amount of net sales revenue that United Sales Corporation should recognize for January?

b. How much cash did United Sales collect on account in January? Was that the only cash received from customers during the month? Explain.

c. Compare the beginning and ending balances of the Accounts Receivable account. Is there anything here that might lead you to be concerned? If so, why? Give one possible reason for the increase in the balance that might be favorable for the company and one possible reason that might be unfavorable.

C7-49   Team Project: Classifying Information   Each morning you stop and talk to the owner of a convenience store that is on your way to campus (and has good coffee and donuts). This morning the topic of the store's income came up, and the manager tells you that yesterday a sales representative tried to sell her a new cash register system that would record sales for up to twenty-five individual product lines. You think "Ah ha! Account classification—I know something about that." The manager says she now keeps track of sales for gasoline separate from all other convenience items and she doesn't know why she would want more information on other products. The store carries a variety of products; among them are magazines, dairy products, pop and beer, grocery items, and, of course, coffee and donuts. You don't agree with her. You think perhaps additional information could be useful.

a. Form teams, as indicated by your instructor. As a group, identify the different categories of sales that would be useful to the manager of a convenience store of this type and write a short memo on why you think her decisions could be improved with the additional information.

b. Earlier in the week the store manager had talked about the need to expand the store. She knows that the margin on the sale of convenience items is greater than on the sale of gasoline, so she wants to expand the store space. Visit at least one convenience store and identify the major product lines carried. See if you can find out what product lines have the best profit margins and include this information in your analysis. Draw up a proposal using the information from part a that will help her decide which product lines to expand.

C7-50   Ethics or Measurement?   The Charger Company distributes automobile replacement parts to repair shops. Paul Charger, the owner and a close friend, wants to expand the business and is applying for a bank loan to purchase a new delivery truck. He will also hire one new driver. Paul plans to ask for a loan of $40,000, and he will buy a truck at a cost of $60,000. The bank told Paul that he needs a projected income statement that will show the outcome of the expansion pro-

posal. Paul has asked you to help. He gives you the following draft of an annual income statement projection for the expanded business:

Estimated new revenue		$200,000
Estimated costs of parts		140,000
Gross margin		$ 60,000
New driver salary	$25,000	
Gas, oil, parking	20,000	45,000
Net income for new truck		$ 15,000

Paul says the cash-flow projection looks good. He can make the principal and interest payments on the loan, which will be $10,000 in the first year, and he will still make a little income. The bank should be happy because he will be profitable and he can repay the loan.

You are not so sure. When you look at Paul's projected income statement, there is no depreciation expense on the new delivery truck, no interest expense for the bank loan, no insurance expense, and no expense for general office supplies. You know that Paul will need insurance and that he will use more office supplies. When you ask Paul about these items, he tells you that he does not take depreciation expense because when the truck is worn out he will replace it the same way he is buying this new truck. There is no insurance expense because he bought a three-year policy two years ago and paid for all of it at that time. It will cover the new truck. Also, he "got a deal" on office supplies and he bought enough to last several years. You obtain additional information from Paul and prepare the following projected annual income statement for his expansion:

Estimated new revenue		$200,000
Estimated costs of parts		140,000
Gross margin		$ 60,000
New driver salary	$25,000	
Gas, oil, parking	20,000	
Depreciation expense on new truck	8,000	
Interest on new loan (10%)	4,000	
Insurance (⅓)	2,500	
Office supplies	1,500	61,000
Net loss		($ 1,000)

You run through a brief explanation of matching and adjusting entries for Paul. He says you may be right, but he didn't include those items the last time he got a loan, and he won't take your income statement to the bank because this time they won't give him a loan if he projects a loss. Who is right, you or Paul? What should you do now? What would you expect the banker to do in this case? Is Paul's action unethical?

Internet Exercises: Visit our Web site for additional exercises.

Annual Report Project Part 7

Refer to the Annual Report Project, Part 1, at the end of Chapter 1. Using the annual report of the company you have chosen, and any other available information, answer the following questions, providing sources and computations where appropriate.

a. Compare the financial statements of your company with those of Our Video Store presented in the text. How would the chart of accounts for the two companies be likely to differ?

b. Indicate two unrelated items in the financial statements of your company that were affected by the company's end-of-period adjustments.

c. Indicate an item in your company's income statement or balance sheet that is a summarized total for which the specific components are detailed in the notes to the financial statements.

CHAPTER EIGHT

Cash, Receivables, and Investments

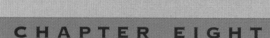

REVIEW

Chapter 7 introduced the process by which the information reported in the financial statements is generated.

WHERE THIS CHAPTER FITS

This chapter begins an in-depth examination of the individual elements that are reported in the financial statements, beginning with cash, receivables, and investments. The concepts emphasized in reporting these assets differ from those used in reporting other types of assets. Reporting for cash, receivables, and investments focuses on available or realizable amounts and on present values.

LOOKING AHEAD

Chapters 9 and 10 discuss other types of assets and focus on the matching concept.

Well, my tuition for this year is due, and I need to come up with the monthly payment for that car I just bought. Fortunately, I'm rolling in dough. Let's see. I have that certificate of deposit Aunt Jane gave me when I graduated from high school. But that doesn't mature for two years. Well, OK. I have that bond that Uncle Harry left me. Oh, swell! I'll be an old geezer, at least 40, by the time that thing comes due. What about my stock in the Big Bonanza Gold Mine? Uh ... I guess that's not worth much since they struck water in the mine and their idea of a desert beach resort fell through. Well, let's see; I have about $3 in my pocket, and ... oh yeah, a coupon for a free super jumbo drink if I buy a triple cheese burger.

What to look for in a promising company, from an interview with "Wall Street Wizard" Peter Lynch: "Its annual report. Take a look at its balance sheet. Look at cash and marketable securities to see what its cash position is, compared with its long-term debt. In a company that's doing well, cash should be increasing relative to debt."[1]

[1] *Modern Maturity* (January–February 1995), p. 60.

I ndividuals, businesses, and other entities all have cash needs. As we discussed in Chapter 3, some of these cash needs are known in advance, while others arise unexpectedly. Being able to meet obligations in a timely manner and take advantage of opportunities as they arise is a key aspect of success and often requires timely access to cash. Accordingly, the management of cash and those assets related to cash is important.

Financial statements provide important information about a company's liquidity, solvency, and operating efficiency. Cash and near-cash resources are critical to a company's ability to acquire labor, inventory, and operating assets and to pay obligations. Having inadequate near-cash resources is a sign of financial weakness. On the other hand, excessive cash and near-cash assets, or an improper mix of these assets, is a sign of poor management.

In this chapter we begin an in-depth exploration of assets and liabilities by looking at cash and those assets that are closely related to cash. Because these assets play an important role in the functioning of any entity, decision makers must understand how to analyze them. After completing this chapter, you should be able to:

1. Describe the types of items labeled in financial statements as cash, receivables, and investments, and explain how they differ from other types of assets.

2. Identify the methods normally used to value cash, receivables, and investments, and explain how these valuations are related to decisions that financial statement users make.

3. Explain how information about cash, receivables, and investments is captured in the financial statements and how this information is related to decisions that financial statement users make.

4. Identify and explain how changes in receivables and investments affect reported income.

5. Discuss the cash-flow implications of receivables and investments.

CASH, RECEIVABLES, AND INVESTMENTS: CHARACTERISTICS AND VALUATION

Information for Decisions

Information about a company's cash, receivables, and investments, including how they are valued in the financial statements, is essential in assessing a company's ability to continue in operation and to prosper. With this information, investors and creditors can begin to understand how the company manages these resources and answer questions such as the following: Will the company have sufficient cash to meet its normal operating needs and satisfy its obligations as they come due? Does the company have sufficient cash or near-cash assets to take advantage of favorable opportunities when they arise and protect against unfavorable situations that might occur unexpectedly?

Many types of assets are needed to accomplish the goals of an entity. Although they are all used together in the entity's activities, assets often differ from one another in their essential characteristics. Because of this, information about different assets may be used differently by decision makers. As a result, accounting and reporting practices differ across assets.

Several characteristics of cash, receivables, and investments distinguish these assets from others. Cash, receivables, and many types of investments are the most liquid of all assets. Cash is generally available for expenditure, receivables are usually collected fairly quickly to provide operating cash, and investments may result in cash inflows from their sale or maturity. Contrast this with equipment, for example, that is used to produce inventory. The equipment does not generate cash until the inventory it produces is sold and the resulting receivables are collected.

Cash, receivables, and investments are usually stated (or denominated) in terms of a fixed number of dollars or other currency units. For example, an account receivable and a certificate of deposit (CD) both represent claims that are fixed in dollar amount. If you sell to a customer on credit and the customer's account has a balance of $500, the customer owes you $500; if you own a $1,000 CD, the bank owes you $1,000 (plus interest). However, some near-cash assets and investments are not denominated in terms of a fixed number of dollars. The dollar value of these assets can change over time. For example, the asset value represented by an investment in shares of common stock changes with the stock price. The primary assets we'll discuss in this chapter, and how they are denominated, are listed in Exhibit 8–1.

Another characteristic of cash, near-cash assets, and investments is that they generally lack physical existence. Although a stack of dollar bills does have physical existence, most of a company's cash is held in bank accounts and is evidenced only by a statement from the

TYPES OF FINANCIAL ASSETS AND INVESTMENTS

EXHIBIT 8-1

Fixed in Dollar Amount	Not Fixed in Dollar Amount
Cash (U.S. dollars)	Cash held in foreign currencies
Accounts receivable	Investment in stock
Notes receivable	Investment in bonds (to be held for sale)
Certificates of deposit	Investment in precious metal
Investment in bonds (to be held to maturity)	Investment in land
	Other investments

bank. Similarly, receivables and most investments are evidenced only by a piece of paper that represents a claim on the assets of others, and the asset itself cannot be seen or touched. A few investments are actually in the form of tangible assets, such as investments in land or precious metals. From an accounting and decision-making viewpoint, however, the important characteristic is not whether an asset has physical existence, but whether it has value.

Because most financial assets and investments are ultimately expected to be exchanged for cash, they are valued in the balance sheet at an amount that provides an indication of the cash expected to be received. Common financial assets and investments are valued as follows:

Asset	Valuation Basis
Cash	Denominated amount
Accounts receivable	Net realizable value (legal claim less the amount expected to be uncollectible)
Notes receivable, long-term	Present value, adjusted over time to maturity value
Marketable securities held for trading or possible sale	Market value
Certain other investments held for trading or possible sale	Estimated fair value (when market value is not determinable)
Investments in debt securities expected to be held to maturity	Cost, adjusted over time to maturity value

The amount assigned to each asset is meant to provide the most useful indication of the expected cash receipts, depending on the timing of the expected conversion to cash.

You Decide 8-1

ALTERNATIVE VALUATION METHODS

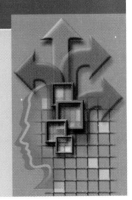

Assume that two companies both invest in identical ten-year bonds. The price paid by both companies is $1,000 per bond, and the bonds pay $1,000 each at maturity and 8 percent annual interest until maturity. One company is certain that it will hold the bond until maturity, but the other company intends to sell the bond whenever it needs the cash. After three years, the market value of the bonds falls to $950 because of a steep increase in general interest rates. In the balance sheet prepared at the end of the third year, one company reports its investment in bonds at $1,000 per bond, while the other company reports its investment at $950 per bond. From the point of view of a potential stockholder in the company, which investment value is more useful? Explain.

Now let's look at the specific valuation and reporting requirements for individual financial assets and see how these requirements aim at providing useful information for decision makers.

REPORTING CASH

Information for Decisions

Cash is the most liquid of all assets and the only one that represents a universally accepted means of exchange. Information about cash and cash equivalents helps decision makers understand how a company uses its cash and assists in answering questions such as these: Does the company have sufficient cash on hand to meet normal operating needs and provide a margin of safety against the unexpected? Are there any restrictions on cash that might prevent the company from spending it as needed? Is the company reducing its profitability by the amount of cash it holds?

Under current financial reporting practices in the United States, financial statements reflect the use of a single measuring unit, the dollar. Because it serves as a basis for valuing all elements in the financial statements, cash is generally the easiest asset to value and report. Cash is simply reported as the amount owned at the close of business on the balance sheet date.

Cash includes coins and currency on hand and amounts currently available on deposit in banks. The key to reporting items as cash is that they are currently available for the company's use. Accordingly, amounts in checking and savings accounts are classified as cash. Checks and money orders on hand are also classified as cash. On the other hand, amounts in restricted accounts, such as money market funds and certificates of deposit, are classified as temporary or long-term investments, depending on the length of the restriction, because they may not be immediately available for use or a penalty may have to be paid for immediate use. In some cases, a fine line separates cash from temporary investments, such as the difference in treatment between bank checking accounts and money market funds with check-writing privileges.

Many companies avoid making these fine distinctions by using a single classification on the balance sheet titled "Cash and Cash Equivalents," where cash equivalents are defined to include marketable securities of no longer than three months duration. The rationale is that these securities can be sold at any time because of a ready market, and even if they are not sold, they will mature at a known amount within a very short time. Financial statement readers, however, should examine the notes to the financial statements to determine what types of securities are included as cash equivalents, if disclosed, because some near-cash items might be riskier than they appear. For example, some money market funds that had been viewed as being nearly as safe as bank deposits suffered major losses a few years ago by investing in risky financial instruments called derivatives.

RESTRICTED CASH

From a financial statement user's perspective, the important point with cash is how much is available to pay obligations and meet the other needs of the enterprise. Therefore, any restrictions on the use of the company's cash must be examined to determine how they affect cash availability.

For example, under some lending arrangements, banks require borrowers to maintain specified deposits in checking or savings accounts or certificates of deposit with the banks. These deposits are referred to as *compensating balances* and often are significant in amount. Because the borrower does not have use of the money, the balances should be separately disclosed to alert financial statement users.

Companies sometimes restrict cash for internal management purposes. A company, for example, might accumulate money for the construction of a new plant. These restrictions are not legally binding and can be removed at management's discretion. Nevertheless, because management intends that the restricted cash not be available for general use, amounts of cash so restricted should be separately disclosed.

FOREIGN CURRENCY DEPOSITS

Many companies doing business in foreign countries hold cash deposits in those countries. In cases where the deposits are denominated in the local currency units, they must be translated into U.S. dollars using the exchange rates as of the balance sheet date for inclusion in the company's financial statements. As can be seen in Exhibit 8–2, if a company held a bank account in France with a balance of 100,000 euros on the balance sheet date, and the exchange rate on that date was $.90 = 1 euro, the amount of cash reported in the company's U.S. balance sheet as being on deposit in the foreign bank would be $90,000 (100,000 × $.90). If material, the amount of cash denominated in foreign currency units should be segregated from domestic deposits in the balance sheet or disclosed in the notes. Because foreign currency deposits are often riskier than U.S. dollar deposits due to fluctuations in exchange rates and possible exchange restrictions, financial statement users need information about an entity's exposure to foreign currency risk. For example, U.S. investors and companies with investments and bank deposits in Brazil suffered significant losses when the Brazilian real declined in value in 1999.

TRANSLATING FOREIGN CURRENCY

EXHIBIT 8-2

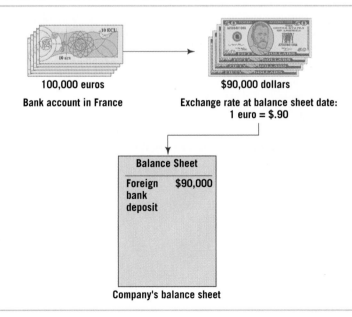

100,000 euros
Bank account in France

$90,000 dollars
Exchange rate at balance sheet date:
1 euro = $.90

Balance Sheet

Foreign bank deposit	$90,000

Company's balance sheet

REPORTING ACCOUNTS RECEIVABLE

Information for Decisions

Amounts receivable from customers arising from normal business activities represent the major recurring source of cash for most companies. Financial statements report information about the amount of accounts receivable, the amount of cash expected to be collected, and the timing of the collection. Decision makers need to understand how this information is reported so they can answer questions such as these: Will the accounts receivable provide adequate liquidity by generating sufficient cash to pay maturing obligations? How does the efficiency with which this company handles and collects its accounts receivable compare with other companies in the industry and with last year? Does the level of credit losses indicate any problems?

Accounts receivable reflect amounts due from customers, arising in the normal course of business. Traditionally, they have been considered customers' unwritten promises to pay, but today most accounts receivable are evidenced by some written document. For example, if you purchase an item from a store using a credit card, you will sign a charge slip that provides evidence of your purchase on credit.

Financial statement readers pay special attention to accounts receivable because, for most entities, the cash to support continued operations comes through their receivables. An assessment of the amount of receivables to be collected and the timing of those collections is crucial for decision making.

In Practice 8-1

FLUOR CORPORATION'S RECEIVABLES

Fluor Corporation reported total accounts and notes receivable of $959,416,000 for the fiscal year ended October 31, 1998. Fluor also reported a current asset of $596,983,000 for contract work in progress and a current liability of $546,816,000 for advance billings on contracts.

ANALYSIS

Goods and services normally must be delivered to customers before revenue is recognized and accounts receivable are recorded. However, engineering, construction, and mining companies such as Fluor sometimes recognize revenue on work not yet billed. Notes to Fluor's financial statements provide the following description:

> *Revenues recognized in excess of amounts billed are classified as current assets under contract work in progress. Amounts billed to clients in excess of revenues recognized to date are classified as current liabilities under advance billings on contracts. The company anticipates that substantially all incurred costs associated with contract work in progress at October 31, 1998, will be billed and collected in 1999.*

All of these accounts must be considered when evaluating the anticipated cash flows from revenues and receivables. [www.fluor.com]

THE COSTS OF EXTENDING CREDIT

Most businesses extend credit to some or all of their customers for a number of reasons. For example, some businesses may not want their sales or delivery employees handling cash because the opportunities for misdirecting the cash may be too great. The primary reason for selling on credit, however, is that it increases sales. Managers of retail stores know that customers purchase more if they do not have to pay immediately with cash. Further, customers have come to expect credit, and companies not offering it may find themselves at a competitive disadvantage, losing customers to businesses that do.

Although companies may find it advantageous to offer credit, there are also associated costs. Some companies that wish to offer credit accept bank credit cards, such as VISA or Mastercard, that provide for payment from the bank to the merchant within a few days after the sale. These merchants are relieved of the other costs of credit, but must pay the credit card companies amounts typically ranging from 2 to 5 percent of the credit sales.

Companies that extend credit and carry accounts themselves incur a number of costs associated with the credit function. For example, they often establish credit departments to investigate the creditworthiness of applicants, and they have to pay fees to companies that provide credit reports. Additional recordkeeping is also needed when sales are made on account. One of the most significant costs of offering credit is that the cash from sales is not received for some period of time, usually thirty to ninety days. This cash cannot be reinvested in operations until it is received. Companies with large amounts in receivables incur significant opportunity costs equal to the lost return that would have been earned if cash had been collected immediately.

Accounts Receivable Efficiency.   One indicator of the efficiency with which a company handles and collects its accounts receivable is **accounts receivable turnover.** This measure is computed by dividing net sales (sales from normal operations, less any returns and allowances) by accounts receivable. The average accounts receivable balance should be used, if available, but otherwise the reported amount in the balance sheet is used. If, for example, a company reported net sales revenue of $4,000,000 and had accounts receivable of $500,000, its accounts receivable turnover can be computed as follows:

$$\text{Accounts receivable turnover} = \frac{\text{Net sales revenue}}{\text{Accounts receivable}} = \frac{\$4,000,000}{\$500,000} = 8.0$$

The higher the turnover, the quicker cash is collected and the shorter the time the use of the cash is foregone.

Other costs of offering credit are incurred when customers do not pay on time. Not only is cash unavailable for a longer time, but costly collection steps often must be taken. If an account is never collected, the company incurs another cost in that it loses the amount of the sale. The amount of credit losses, or bad debt expense, as a percentage of sales (or specifically credit sales) provides an indication of the effectiveness of a company's sales and credit policies.

Speeding Cash Collections.   Many companies give customers an incentive to pay for purchases quickly, for several reasons:

· The sooner a company collects cash, the sooner the cash can be invested to earn a return.

· The longer an account remains unpaid, the less likely it is to be collected.

· Cash forecasting and cash management both are made easier if cash is collected from customers within a specified time.

To speed collection, some companies, such as credit card companies and utilities, add penalties or interest to balances not paid by a specified date. Other businesses offer their commercial customers **cash discounts** for paying within a specified time. For example, many companies offer cash discounts of 2 percent of the sale amount if the full amount less the discount is paid within ten days of the billing date; otherwise the full amount, not allowing for any discount, is due within thirty days. These terms are expressed as "2/10, net 30." If the terms are "1/20, net 60," this indicates that a 1 percent discount is allowed if the bill is paid within twenty days, or the full amount must be paid within sixty days. Terms of "net 30" mean that no discount is allowed, and the full amount is due in thirty days.

A CLOSER LOOK AT

COMPUTING CASH DISCOUNTS

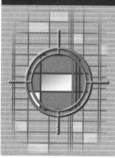

Baker Corporation sold $3,000 of lumber to Happy Home Builders, with terms of 2/10, net 30. The bill for the lumber was dated June 2. If Happy Home Builders paid the bill on June 12, it would pay $3,000 less the 2 percent discount of $60 ($3,000 × .02), or a net amount of $2,940. On the other hand, if the bill was not paid until July 1, the full $3,000 would have to be paid.

Terms of 2/10, net 30 lead most customers to pay within the discount period because of the additional cost they otherwise would incur. If customers did not pay within the discount period, they would have the use of the money, in effect borrowing it, for an additional twenty days (30 minus 10). However, paying 2 percent for twenty days' use of money is equivalent to an annual interest rate of more than 37 percent. In the example of Baker Corporation, the customer chooses between paying $2,940 by the tenth day and $3,000 by the thirtieth day. In effect, $60 interest is paid for borrowing $2,940 for twenty days. The annual rate of interest can be computed as follows:

Cost of borrowing for 20 days	$ 60
Amount borrowed for 20 days	÷2,940
20-day interest rate	.0204
Annualized 20-day interest rate	
.0204 × (365/20) =	.3723

An annual interest rate of 37 percent is extremely high; similar bank loans carry interest of 8 to 15 percent. Accordingly, most customers able to pay their accounts normally pay within the discount period when faced with terms of 2/10, net 30. Even if a customer is temporarily short of cash, borrowing the money from the bank and paying the account within the discount period almost always is less costly than losing the discount. Companies that do not pay within the discount period when faced with terms such as 2/10, net 30 are generally in serious financial difficulty and are unable to pay (or borrow), or they are poorly managed.

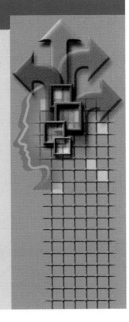

GETTING CUSTOMERS TO PAY

This school year you have been working part-time for a company that sells sunglasses to convenience stores in your area. You have been requiring cash on delivery (COD) from the customers when you deliver the glasses and put them in the delivery racks. To meet competition, your company regularly gives customers 10 percent off the wholesale price. Your boss now wants to offer customers a choice of purchase plans. She thinks these options will "get the jump on competition" and lead to a significant increase in sales. She plans to give customers the following choices:

1. COD—10 percent off the listed price, as is currently done
2. Pay in 30 days—5 percent off the listed price
3. Pay in 60 days—pay list price

You anticipate that all of your customers will pay their bills and that your company will have to pay 12 percent annual interest on the operating cash that it has to borrow to finance any accounts receivable balance. Do you think the plan is a good one? Why? If total monthly sales are $50,000, prepare an analysis of cash flows, including the cost of money, to show your boss how well each option will work.

RECOGNITION AND VALUATION OF ACCOUNTS RECEIVABLE

Accounts receivable arise at the time a sale is made on credit and given accounting recognition. As we discussed in Chapter 5, sales are usually recognized based on the realization concept. Accordingly, sales are recognized when (1) an exchange takes place and (2) the earning process is substantially complete. The exchange price agreed to by both seller and purchaser provides the basis for valuing the sale.

ACCOUNTS RECEIVABLE

Bassler Company sells electrical equipment to a customer for $1,000 on account. The sale is recognized in the accounting system by a $1,000 increase in accounts receivable and a $1,000 increase in sales. Current assets in the balance sheet and total revenue in the income statement are both increased by $1,000.

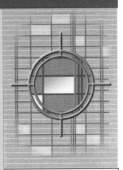

Journal Entry

Accounts Receivable	1,000	
Sales Revenue		1,000

Income Statement Effects	
Revenue	+ 1,000
Net Income	+ 1,000
Balance Sheet Effects	
Assets	+ 1,000
Owners' Equity	+ 1,000

Accounts receivable are initially recorded at the amount of the associated sale, and they are carried in the accounting records at that amount until they are partially or completely paid by the customer. If all customers paid their accounts, no other adjustments would be needed. Unfortunately, some customers do not keep their promises to pay, and their accounts are never collected. The expense of uncollectible accounts is an ordinary cost of doing business. Because this cost directly affects cash inflows, information needs to be provided in the financial statements to help users assess the extent to which cash inflows from receivables will be reduced by uncollectible accounts. Therefore, accounts receivable are reported in the balance sheet at the actual amount of cash expected to be collected, a valuation method referred to as **net realizable value**. Reporting for uncollectible accounts affects both the computation of a company's income and the way in which receivables are valued on the balance sheet.

In Practice 8-2

SBC'S UNCOLLECTIBLE ACCOUNTS

SBC Communications reports in the current asset section of its 1998 balance sheet both the amount of accounts receivable it expects to collect and the amount it expects not to collect, as follows (dollars in millions):

Accounts receivable—net of allowance for uncollectibles of $472 $5,790

ANALYSIS

The type of presentation used by SBC permits financial statement users to assess the amount of cash expected to be collected by SBC through normal operations and provides information helpful in evaluating SBC's credit and collection policies. [www.sbc.com]

ACCOUNTING FOR UNCOLLECTIBLE ACCOUNTS

Sales on account are made with the expectation that cash will ultimately be collected. Accordingly, sales are recognized under accrual accounting when they occur, rather than when the cash is collected. However, if the cash is never collected, the cost of the uncollected account must be recognized. This cost is reflected as **bad debt expense** and reported as a normal operating expense in the income statement. The timing of bad debt recognition affects both the computation of income and the valuation of receivables.

The difficulty that arises in accounting for bad debts is that accounts are often not determined to be uncollectible until some period after the one in which the revenue is recognized. Suppose, for example, that among the credit sales in one period is a $5,000 account that, after extensive collection efforts, is determined to be uncollectible in the next period:

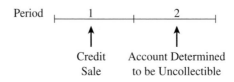

Rather than waiting to recognize the expense until the account is determined to be uncollectible, an alternative is to anticipate in the first period the uncollectibility of the account and recognize the expense in the same period as the revenue. In this way, the cost of not collecting the account is pulled back into the period in which the revenue giving rise to the account has been recognized, and the cost and revenue are matched:

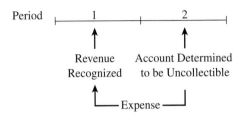

This approach not only provides a more useful comparison of costs and benefits, but it also ensures a more useful accounts receivable balance for decision makers who will use the information to forecast short-term cash inflows. To avoid indicating the expectation of receiving a cash inflow equal to the full receivable balance, the financial statements indicate the probable impairment of the receivable.

In this case, the reported receivable is reduced, but not directly. The legal claim against the customer still exists and is treated as an asset. However, a valuation account is used to revalue the reported amount to the amount expected to be collected, the net realizable value. A **valuation account** is an account that changes the reported amount of a financial statement element by being added to or subtracted from the other balance. In this case, a valuation account called **Allowance for Uncollectible Accounts** is subtracted from the balance of Accounts Receivable reported in the balance sheet. If, for example, a company was owed $5,000 by customers but expected to be unable to collect $1,000 of that amount, its accounts receivable would be reported as follows in its balance sheet:

Accounts Receivable	$5,000
Less Allowance for Uncollectible Accounts	(1,000)
Net Realizable Value of Receivables	$4,000

Because this valuation account reduces an asset balance, it is referred to as a **contra-asset account** and has a balance opposite that of the asset. Once the allowance account is deducted from Accounts Receivable, the resulting amount provides an estimate of the cash expected to be collected from the receivables.

Recognition of bad debt expense and adjustment of the allowance for uncollectible accounts occur at the same time because asset valuation and income recognition are related. The company's income is reduced because of the cost associated with an uncollectible account, and this is reflected in the reduced valuation of accounts receivable. Periodically, companies estimate the cost of uncollectible accounts for the period and adjust their books by recording Bad Debt Expense and increasing the balance in the Allowance for Uncollectible Accounts. This procedure reduces both income and assets. This approach to reporting uncollectible accounts is called the **allowance method**. Because this method is consistent with the matching concept, it is the only generally accepted method of reporting uncollectible accounts.

Estimating Bad Debts and Uncollectible Accounts.   The goal of the allowance method for reporting uncollectible accounts is to match the cost of bad debts with the revenue that originally gave rise to the uncollectible accounts. The only way to recognize in the current period a cost to be incurred in the future is to estimate the amount of that future cost.

You Decide 8-3

RECOGNITION OF BAD DEBT EXPENSE

Grove Enterprises does not know in advance which of its accounts receivable will go bad in the future. Therefore, the company waits until an account is known to be bad before recognizing the bad debt expense, an approach referred to as the direct write-off method. Should Grove continue to use this method? What impact does this choice of methods have on reported income and on the balance sheet? From a potential investor's viewpoint, does this approach provide the most useful information for decisions? Explain.

So, at the end of each accounting period, companies make estimates on which to base their recognition of bad debts and value their receivables. Most companies use estimates based on past experience or industry averages, adjusted for changes in economic conditions. An adjusting entry is then made to record bad debt expense and increase the allowance for uncollectibles. Because the adjusting entry is based on an estimate, decision makers need to keep in mind the tentative nature of reported income and the net balance of accounts receivable.

Making the Necessary Estimates.   Two alternative approaches are used in estimating the amount of uncollectible receivables. Using an income statement approach, an estimate of the income statement account Bad Debt Expense is based on a percentage of the period's total sales or credit sales, another income statement account. The amount estimated is reported as Bad Debt Expense in the income statement, and the same amount is added to the Allowance for Uncollectible Accounts in the balance sheet.

A CLOSER LOOK AT

USING PERCENTAGE OF SALES TO ESTIMATE UNCOLLECTIBLES

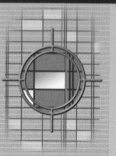

Ajax Company has Accounts Receivable of $1,605,000 and a prior balance in its Allowance for Uncollectible Accounts of $1,200. Total sales on account for the year were $12,354,000. Based on past experience, Ajax has found that approximately 1 percent of its sales are never collected. Accordingly, Ajax reports in its income statement Bad Debt Expense for the period equal to 1 percent of its sales, or $123,540. In addition, that amount is added to the $1,200 prior balance of the Allowance for Uncollectible Accounts, resulting in a new balance in the allowance of $124,740. Thus, the balance sheet reports the following:

Income Statement Effects	
Expenses	+ 123,540
Net Income	− 123,540
Balance Sheet Effects	
Assets	− 123,540
Owners' Equity	− 123,540

Accounts Receivable	$1,605,000
Less Allowance for Uncollectible Accounts	(124,740)
Net Receivables	$1,480,260

Adjusting Journal Entry
Bad Debt Expense   123,540
    Allowance for Uncollectible Accounts   123,540

Because Bad Debt Expense is a temporary account and its balance is closed out at the end of each period, it has a zero balance until the adjusting entry is made. The allowance account, however, is a permanent account, and its balance carries over from period to period. The balance of the allowance account is increased by the adjusting entry made at the end of the period to record bad debts and is decreased when individual accounts are determined to be bad and are written off, as discussed in the next section.

The balance sheet approach is an alternative that focuses on estimating the balance that should be in one balance sheet account, the Allowance for Uncollectible Accounts, based on the balance in another balance sheet account, Accounts Receivable, at the balance sheet date. Some companies apply a percentage estimate to ending receivables to estimate the balance of the allowance account. Others attempt to increase the accuracy of their estimates by analyzing their receivables by the age of the accounts. Accounts that are long overdue have a lower likelihood of being collected than those that are current. Estimating the Allowance for Uncollectible Accounts by applying a different percentage to each age category of receivables is referred to as **aging of accounts**.

A CLOSER LOOK AT

AGING OF ACCOUNTS TO ESTIMATE UNCOLLECTIBLES

Ajacks Company classifies its accounts receivable into categories by age and, based on its past experience, applies a different percentage estimate of uncollectibles to each category. Its aging schedule appears as follows:

	Accounts	**Percentage**	**Estimated Uncollectible**
Current	$1,193,400	02	$23,868
Up to 90 days past due	328,500	10	32,850
More than 90 days past due	83,100	30	24,930
Total	$1,605,000		$81,648

Based on its estimate of uncollectibles, Ajacks should report its Accounts Receivable and the related Allowance for Uncollectible Accounts in its balance sheet as follows:

Accounts Receivable	$1,605,000
Less Allowance for Uncollectible Accounts	(81,648)
	$1,523,352

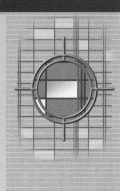

Income Statement Effects	
Expenses	+ 80,448
Net Income	− 80,448

Balance Sheet Effects	
Assets	− 80,448
Owners' Equity	− 80,448

This presentation reflects both the legal claim of Ajacks and the actual amount it expects to collect, the net realizable value of the receivables. Because the prior balance of the Allowance for Uncollectible Accounts was $1,200, the increase needed to bring the balance to $81,648 is the difference of $80,448. This increase, $80,448, is reported in the income statement as Bad Debt Expense.

Adjusting Journal Entry

Bad Debt Expense	80,448	
Allowance for Uncollectible Accounts		80,448

Writing Off Uncollectible Accounts.   When management adjusts its books at the end of the period to record bad debt expense, it knows, based on past experience, that some of its accounts will go bad. It does not know, however, which ones will go bad. What happens when management determines that a specific account is not going to be collected? It must then "write off" that specific account. If the account is no longer expected to provide a benefit to the company in the form of a future cash inflow, it can no longer be considered an asset. Therefore, the Accounts Receivable balance must be reduced by the amount of that account determined to be uncollectible.

But what is the other side of the entry that is made to reduce Accounts Receivable? Should an expense be recognized for the amount of the uncollectible account when it is written off? No! That would be double counting. Remember that at the end of each period, the company makes an adjusting entry anticipating that some accounts will go bad. In the adjusting entry, the company recognizes the estimated expense and establishes a contra-asset account to allow for the uncollectible accounts. Thus, when a specific account is determined to be uncollectible, the company has already allowed for it. Accordingly, when a specific account is pulled out of Accounts Receivable because it has gone bad, an equal amount is also removed from the allowance account. You can think of that amount of the allowance as no longer being needed because the anticipated event for which an allowance is made, an account going bad, has occurred. Because the asset is reduced directly by the write-off, that portion of the contra-asset no longer is needed.

A CLOSER LOOK AT

WRITING OFF UNCOLLECTIBLE ACCOUNTS

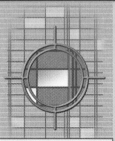

Several months into its fiscal year, Balsam Company determines that seven accounts totaling $45,635 will not be collected. It therefore writes off the bad accounts by reducing both the asset account Accounts Receivable and the contra-asset account Allowance for Uncollectible Accounts by $45,635. Because both the asset and the related contra-asset account are reduced by the same amount, the net amount of accounts receivable reported in the balance sheet remains unchanged. Income is also not affected by the write-off of individual accounts because the expense of uncollectible accounts is recorded as an adjustment at the end of each period.

Income Statement Effects	
Expenses	0
Net Income	0
Balance Sheet Effects	
Assets	− 45,635
Assets	+ 45,635
Owners' Equity	0

Journal Entry

Allowance for Uncollectible Accounts	45,635	
Accounts Receivable		45,635

SUMMARIZING UNCOLLECTIBLE ACCOUNTS

The key to understanding how the Bad Debt Expense reported in the income statement is computed and how the contra-asset Allowance for Uncollectible Accounts in the balance sheet is determined is remembering the importance of the matching concept. Revenue recognized at the time of a sale on credit is a benefit, and one of the costs of generating that revenue is the cost of accounts ultimately not collected. To provide a proper matching of costs and benefits, the future cost associated with currently held accounts going bad must be estimated and recognized in the same period as the revenue. These estimates are made at the end of the period, prior to the preparation of financial statements. When individual accounts are actually determined to be uncollectible, they are written off the books, and the allowance established in anticipation of such write-offs is reduced accordingly.

Both the adjustment recording the estimated bad debt expense and anticipated uncollectibles and the write-off of bad accounts are important elements in the process of accounting for bad debts. A comparison of the two is as follows:

	Adjustment to Record Bad Debts	**Write-off of Bad Accounts**
Nature of Entry	Adjusting Entry	Entry to Record Event
When Recorded	End of Period	When Account Determined Uncollectible
Accounts Affected	Bad Debt Expense (+) Allowance for Uncollectible Accounts (+)	Allowance for Uncollectible Accounts (−) Accounts Receivable (−)
Effect on Income	Decreases	None
Effect on Total Assets	Decreases	None
Level of Analysis	Total Accounts Receivable	Individual Accounts

The adjusting entry that matches the costs and benefits is the more important of the two entries for estimating future cash flows. It is the one that affects both income and total assets. The write-off entry only offsets the uncollectible account against a portion of the allowance account, having no effect on income, net receivables, or total assets. In effect, it only gives final recognition to something that was already anticipated in the accounts.

A CLOSER LOOK AT

REVIEW OF ACCOUNTING FOR BAD DEBTS

Dallon Company makes all of its sales on credit. At the end of 2001, Dallon reported in its balance sheet Accounts Receivable of $110,000 and an Allowance for Uncollectible Accounts of $5,800. During 2002, Dallon records sales of $841,300 and collections of $790,700 on account. During the year, the company examines its past due accounts and writes off $3,800 of accounts as uncollectible. At the end of the year, based on its past experience, Dallon estimates bad debts at 1 percent of its sales and records bad debt expense of $8,413 ($841,300 × .01). Thus, Dallon's 2002 income statement includes $8,413 of bad debt expense, and its balance sheet presents its trade receivables as follows:

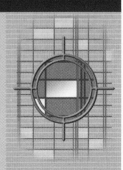

Accounts Receivable	$156,800
Less Allowance for Uncollectible Accounts	(10,413)
	$146,387

The Accounts Receivable balance at December 31, 2002, is equal to the balance at the end of 2001 ($110,000) plus new receivables arising from sales during the year ($841,300) minus collections on account ($790,700) and accounts written off during the period ($3,800). The Allowance balance at the end of the year is equal to the balance at the end of last year ($5,800) less accounts written off during the current year ($3,800), with the estimate of bad debts ($8,413) added at the end of the year.

Income Statement Effects	
Revenue	+841,300
Expense	+ 8,413
Net Income	+832,887
Balance Sheet Effects	
Assets	+841,300
Assets	+790,700
Assets	−790,700
Assets	− 3,800
Assets	+ 3,800
Assets	− 8,413
Owners' Equity	+832,887

Journal Entries

Accounts Receivable	841,300	
Sales Revenue		841,300
Cash	790,700	
Accounts Receivable		790,700
Allowance for Uncollectible Accounts	3,800	
Accounts Receivable		3,800
Bad Debt Expense	8,413	
Allowance for Uncollectible Accounts		8,413

T-Accounts

Accounts Receivable			Allowance for Uncollectible Accounts	
bal. 110,000				5,800 bal.
841,300				
	790,700		3,800	
	3,800			8,413
bal. 156,800				10,413 bal.

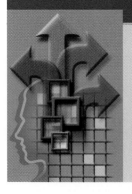

You Decide 8-4

UNCOLLECTIBLE ACCOUNTS

Zollars Corporation initially based its estimate of bad debts on an industry average of 1 percent of sales. After six years of operation, however, management has noticed that, while its sales have been increasing at about 8 percent each year, its receivables have grown at about 12 percent per year. Further, its Allowance for Uncollectible Accounts seems unusually high. Does Zollars have a problem? What are some explanations for these occurrences? Suggest possible actions that might be taken from both a management and an accounting perspective.

TIMING OF CASH COLLECTIONS FROM ACCOUNTS RECEIVABLE

Financial statement readers have an interest in knowing whether a company's cash inflows will meet cash outflow requirements. In particular, they want to know whether normal cash inflows from operations will provide the cash needed to meet operating obligations as they come due, and the financial statements should provide that information.

Most accounts receivable are classified as current assets. Remember, current assets include those expected to be converted into cash within one year or the operating cycle of the firm, whichever is longer. For many types of companies, such as merchandising and manufacturing companies, receivables are collected in thirty to sixty days. However, some companies, such as construction companies, have operating cycles exceeding a year. In such cases, the collection period for their trade receivables may considerably exceed the time in which their normal operating costs must be paid. Although classifying receivables as current assets provides some indication of the timing of cash flows, a closer examination is warranted.

Sometimes companies make special arrangements to allow customers to pay their accounts over longer periods than normal. This may occur, for example, when the customer's purchase is especially large. In this case, the customer may sign a note providing for payment over several periods. Because the credit is extended for a longer period, the receivable has to be classified as noncurrent if it is not due within one year or the normal operating cycle.

FINANCING THROUGH RECEIVABLES

In some cases, cash inflows from receivables can be speeded up by either selling the receivables or borrowing against them. If accounts have been used as collateral for a loan, a liability such as Notes Payable will be listed in the balance sheet. However, the balance sheet itself may not give any clue to the terms of the financing, so the notes to the financial statements should always be examined carefully. Accounts that have been sold are removed from the balance sheet and a gain or loss on the sale recognized in the income statement. The sale of receivables may be with or without recourse. *Recourse* means the lender can require the transferror of the account to pay if the debtor does not. Any liability under recourse agreements should be indicated in the notes.

Understanding a company's cash-flow situation with respect to receivables requires careful analysis. In some cases, companies routinely finance using their receivables. In other cases, the assignment or sale of receivables is a sign of trouble. Remember that normal cash inflows from trade receivables are used to meet operating needs. If the cash inflow cycle is interrupted by selling the receivables or by using the cash inflows to pay nontrade debt, cash may not be available to meet other needs. In addition, the outright sale of receivables is usually an expensive means of financing and may be used because credit is not available from more desirable sources. Also keep in mind that a company that has sold its receivables may have a significant liability for payment if the sale was made with recourse.

NOTES AND OTHER RECEIVABLES

Information for Decisions

Companies sometimes have receivables other than accounts receivable. In some cases, these receivables may be evidenced by notes from customers, or the receivables may be from parties other than customers. Financial statement users need to understand these receivables so they can answer questions such as these: Will the reported receivables be collected in the current year so the proceeds will be available for expenditure? Why does the company have receivables other than those arising in the normal course of business? Is the company earning interest on these receivables?

Sometimes a company will sell on credit and have the customer sign a formal note for the amount due. These written promises to pay are called **notes receivable**. Typically, the notes are for a longer duration than accounts receivable and earn a stated rate of interest. Notes not designated otherwise (e.g., Notes Receivable from Officers) are assumed to be from customers. The source of a receivable may have a bearing on its collectibility and also may shed light on the nature of some of management's business practices.

INTEREST-BEARING NOTES

Most notes bear interest that is explicitly stated and are referred to as **interest-bearing notes**. Interest is accrued on these notes at the end of each period. Thus, the financial statements reflect the amount of interest earned during the period and the total amount due to the company. Payments made on the note are applied first toward the accrued interest and then toward payment of principal. Remember that when interest rates are quoted, they relate to an annual period unless otherwise indicated.

A CLOSER LOOK AT

INTEREST-BEARING NOTES

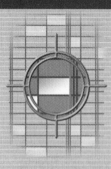

On July 1, 2001, Tolivar Corporation sells $10,000 of merchandise to Sam's Surplus Store in exchange for a 2-year note bearing interest at 10 percent. A $4,000 payment is due on June 30, 2002, with the balance due on June 30, 2003. Tolivar prepares financial statements on a fiscal year ending June 30. An interest-computation table for the 2-year life of the note is as follows:

Year	Balance	Rate	Interest	Total	Payment Interest	Principal
First	$10,000	.10	$1,000	$4,000	$1,000	$3,000
Second	7,000	.10	700	7,700	700	7,000

Tolivar recognizes income from two sources. Sales revenue is recognized all in the first year, at the time of sale. Interest income is earned over the two-year term of the note as the customer uses Tolivar's money. The cash payments are applied first to pay the interest that Tolivar has earned to the date of the payment, with the remainder of the payment used to pay principal. Interest in the second year is less than in the first because the amount of the loan is reduced at the end of the first year.

Income Statement Effects, Fiscal Year	
2002 Revenue	+ 10,000
Interest Inc. +	1,000
Net Income +	11,000
2003 Revenue	0
Interest Inc. +	700
Net Income +	700

Balance Sheet Effects, June 30	
2002 Assets	+ 10,000
Assets	+ 4,000
Assets	− 3,000
Owners' Equity	+ 11,000
2003 Assets	+ 7,700
Assets	− 7,000
Owners' Equity	+ 700

Journal Entries

July 1, 2001

Notes Receivable	10,000	
Sales Revenue		10,000

June 30, 2002

Cash	4,000	
Interest Income		1,000
Notes Receivable		3,000

June 30, 2003

Cash	7,700	
Interest Income		700
Notes Receivable		7,000

NONINTEREST-BEARING NOTES

In some cases, sales are made in exchange for so-called **noninterest-bearing notes.** These notes do not have an explicitly stated interest rate, but because money is not free, interest is included implicitly in the amount of the note. If the note is other than a trade note due in less than one year, the **implicit interest** must be recognized.

The **face amount** of the note is the amount that must be paid when it matures. The difference between the note's maturity value and its present value is interest that is earned over the life of the note. Typically, the note is recorded at its face amount, with the unearned interest shown as a contra-asset account, Discount on Notes Receivable. Because the interest is implicit in the face amount of the note, but has not yet been earned, the contra-asset account is used to deduct the unearned interest from the face amount of the note in the balance sheet to report the net amount due at that date. As the interest is earned, it is recognized as income and the carrying value of the note is increased by reducing the discount.

A CLOSER LOOK AT

STANDARD SETTING: IS IT A RENTAL OR A SALE?

On January 2, 2000, Bolivar Corporation, a company operating on a calendar year, sells merchandise to Sam's Surplus Store in exchange for a 2-year noninterest-bearing note with a maturity value of $10,000. The full payment of $10,000 is due on December 31, 2001. A normal interest rate for this type of note is 10 percent. The present value of the $10,000 cash payment (adjusted for rounding) is $8,265 [$10,000 × 1/(1.10)^2]. At the end of both periods, the implicit interest earned is added to the balance receivable. An interest-computation table is as follows:

Beginning Balance	Rate	Interest	Ending Balance
$8,265	.10	$826	$ 9,091
9,091	.10	909	10,000

The sales revenue is equal to the present value of the future cash payment, $8,265, and is earned at the time of the sale. The interest is earned over the 2-year term of the note. The note is reported in Bolivar's balance sheet at December 31, 2000, as follows:

Note Receivable	$10,000
Less Discount	(909)
Net Receivable	$ 9,091

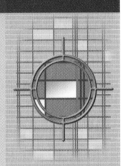

Income Statement Effects		
2000 Revenue	+	8,265
Interest Inc.	+	826
Net Income	+	9,091
2001 Revenue		0
Interest Inc.	+	909
Net Income	+	909

Balance Sheet Effects		
2000 Assets	+	8,265
Assets	+	826
Owners' Equity	+	9,091
2001 Assets	+	909
Assets	+	10,000
Assets	−	10,000
Owners' Equity	+	909

Journal Entries

January 2, 2000

Notes Receivable	10,000	
Discount on Notes Receivable		1,735
Sales Revenue		8,265

December 31, 2000

Discount on Notes Receivable	826	
Interest Income		826

December 31, 2001

Discount on Notes Receivable	909	
Interest Income		909
Cash	10,000	
Notes Receivable		10,000

You can see in the example that as the unearned interest is earned, income is recognized and the discount is reduced. Because the discount is a contra-asset account, reducing the discount increases the reported amount of the note. Had the implicit interest not been given explicit recognition in the accounts, the following reporting errors would have occurred:

1. Sales revenue would have been overstated in 2000 because it would have included the unearned interest.

2. The net amount of the note would have been overstated because the face amount includes interest that is not yet earned or due prior to December 31, 2001.

3. Interest income would have been understated in 2000 and 2001 because all of the interest would have been recognized in 2000 as sales revenue.

Recognizing implicit interest is an example of how accounting attempts to present economic reality by emphasizing substance over form. Although the note is a noninterest-bearing note in form, the reality is that all long-term borrowings include interest, whether it is explicitly stated or not. These accounting procedures better inform financial statement users of the source of a company's income, whether it is from selling goods and services or lending money, and the period in which it is earned.

OTHER RECEIVABLES

Companies may have receivables other than trade receivables listed in their balance sheets, including the following:

* Loans to owners, officers, or employees
* Loans to related companies
* Interest earned but not yet collected or dividends on investments held that are declared but not yet collected
* Receivables relating to claims against others, such as tax refunds or insurance claims
* Deposits to be refunded or applied against purchases

These receivables must be shown separately from trade receivables and given appropriate descriptive titles. Any receivables not meeting the definition of a current asset are classified as noncurrent in either the Investments or Other Assets category. Loans to others are typically treated in the same manner as notes receivable, while the other receivables are usually reported at the amount expected to be received or applied against future purchases.

INVESTMENTS

Information for Decisions

Some companies hold assets that are not used in the companies' central operations but from which they hope to profit. These assets are generally reported in the balance sheet as investments, and investors and creditors can use the information reported to answer questions such as these: Why is the company accumulating investments instead of distributing more cash to its owners? What is the expected timing of the conversion to cash of the different types of investments reported, and how will these investments affect the company's ability to meet current obligations? To what extent does the company gain the ability to influence or control other companies through its investments?

In one sense, every asset on a company's balance sheet other than cash might be considered an investment. Companies invest in plant, equipment, inventories, and other assets to operate a business and earn a profit. Accountants, however, make a distinction between operating assets and those acquired for a purpose unrelated, or only indirectly related, to the enterprise's main business.

Many entities have significant amounts of money in investments. They may acquire investments for a number of reasons, including to:

* Earn a return on cash needed in the future but not immediately

* Take advantage of a potentially profitable situation

* Control another enterprise

* Influence another enterprise, such as ensuring a potential supply of raw materials

In Practice 8-3

ARCHER DANIELS MIDLAND COMPANY'S INVESTMENTS

The balance sheet of Archer Daniels Midland (ADM) at June 30, 1998, included substantial investments in marketable securities:

Cash and cash equivalents	$ 346,325,000
Marketable securities	379,169,000
Long-term marketable securities	1,168,380,000
Total cash and marketable securities	$ 1,893,874,000
All other assets (combined)	11,939,660,000
Total assets	$13,833,534,000

ANALYSIS

Manufacturing companies are normally expected to carry major amounts of inventory, plant, and equipment. They are not expected to have substantial balances in cash and marketable securities. However, ADM, a major processor of agricultural products, has experienced significant growth and has spent approximately $4.5 billion during the past five years for construction of new plants, expansions of existing plants, and acquisitions. During 1998, the Company's cash and marketable securities, net of short-term debt, decreased $762 million, reflecting the company's additional investment in property, plant, and equipment during the year. [www.admworld.com]

Typical investments include debt securities, equity securities, and real estate. Debt securities represent legal claims to collect a determinable amount from another party at a determinable future time. Equity securities represent ownership claims on other entities, including common stock, preferred stock, and options that permit the holders to buy or sell shares of stock at a fixed price. Real estate investments include land and buildings not used in the company's central operations. Let's look at these investments more closely to understand how information about them is useful to decision makers.

INVESTMENTS IN SECURITIES

All investments are recorded initially at the acquisition cost, which includes any brokerage commissions and transfer fees. However, the type of security and the purpose for which it has been acquired will affect the way in which it is reported in subsequent periods. Two companies may report different carrying values and different amounts of income from investments in identical securities. Thus, investors must be very careful in analyzing and comparing companies that have substantial amounts of investments.

Investments in debt securities, and in equity securities with reasonably determinable fair values, must be grouped into three categories:[2]

1. Held-to-maturity securities—debt securities for which the reporting entity has the intent and ability to hold them to maturity.

2. Trading securities—debt and equity securities acquired and held for the purpose of selling them in the near term.

3. Available-for-sale securities—debt and equity securities not classified in either of the other two categories.

Exhibit 8–3 summarizes the financial reporting for the three categories of investment securities.

Held-to-Maturity Securities.   This category includes only bonds and other debt securities. They are reported at *amortized cost* in either the current asset section or investments section of the balance sheet, as appropriate. Valuing the securities at amortized cost means that any difference between the original purchase price and the maturity value of the security must be allocated or amortized over the time the security is held. (Amortization of bond discount and premium is discussed in Chapter 11.) The important point to note with respect to held-to-maturity securities is that they are not revalued to market value while they are held.

Trading Securities.   At the other end of the spectrum from held-to-maturity securities are those investments acquired to gain short-term profits. Financial institutions are the primary companies in the business of trading securities. Other businesses, however, may also occasionally purchase securities with an eye toward short-term gains. This category includes any debt or equity security held for trading if its fair value can be reasonably determined.

All trading securities are reported at their fair (or market) values. Changes in values give rise to gains and losses. As long as the securities continue to be held, the gains and losses are considered to be unrealized, but they are recognized in income, nevertheless. At the end of each reporting period, the individual securities held in the trading portfolio are revalued to fair value at the balance sheet date.

Available-for-Sale Securities.   For most companies that are not in the business of trading securities, the majority of their securities held as investments are classified as available-for-sale. Placing a security in this category indicates that the security may be sold if additional

EXHIBIT 8-3	**REPORTING INVESTMENTS IN SECURITIES**	
Investment Category	**Balance Sheet Valuation**	**Recognition of Unrealized Gain or Loss**
Held to maturity	Amortized cost	Not recognized
Trading	Fair or market value	Reported in net income
Available for sale	Fair or market value	Reported in other comprehensive income

[2] *Statement of Financial Accounting Standards No 115*, "Accounting for Certain Investments in Debt and Equity Securities," Financial Accounting Standards Board, 1993.

cash is needed or if market conditions favor sale. Placing securities in this category gives companies the flexibility to use investments in the most advantageous way without being locked into a particular course of action.

Securities classified as available-for-sale are reported as current or noncurrent assets, as appropriate, and the carrying value of each group of securities (current and noncurrent) is adjusted to fair value at the end of each period. Changes in value during the period, or unrealized gains and losses, are not reported in net income. Instead, these unrealized gains and losses are reported as an element of other comprehensive income. As discussed in Chapter 5, other comprehensive income for the period is reported after net income in a combined statement of income and comprehensive income, in a separate statement of comprehensive income, or in the statement of stockholders' equity. Accumulated unrealized gains and losses (of the current and prior periods) from available-for-sale securities are reported separately in the stockholders' equity section of the balance sheet.

In Practice 8-4

MERCANTILE BANCORPORATION'S INVESTMENTS

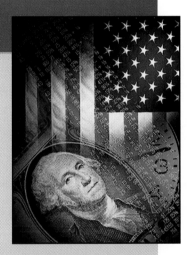

Mercantile Bancorporation reported investments in securities in its balance sheet as follows (amounts in thousands):

Investments in debt and equity securities:	1998	1997	1996
Trading	$ 126,540	$ 70,536	$ 31,361
Available-for-sale (Amortized cost of $9,185,770, $4,139,525 and $4,731,005)	9,246,790	8,059,066	4,741,677
Held-to-maturity (Estimated fair value of $99,336, $341,954 and $661,632)	97,607	335,279	656,721

In its income statement, Mercantile reported the following 1998 income related to its investments in securities:

Interest Income
Investments in debt and equity securities:

Trading	$ 8,821
Taxable	558,635
Tax-exempt	23,230

Other Income

Securities gains	$ 15,435

ANALYSIS

Mercantile Bancorporation held securities in all three reporting categories. The company also reported $14 million of other comprehensive income, net of taxes, from gains and losses on available-for-sale securities, and a $41 million "Accumulated other comprehensive income" account in the Stockholders' Equity section of its balance sheet. Mercantile is one of the relatively few companies presenting a separate statement of comprehensive income. Mercantile recently merged with Firstar Corporation. [www.mercantile.com]

Other Securities.   Two types of investments in equity securities do not fall within any of the three categories listed previously. These special investment situations are as follows:

1. *Investments conveying control*—These investments involve a significant portion, usually a majority, of another company's common stock. The Investment in Common Stock account is eliminated and the financial statements of the companies are combined. Consolidated financial statements are issued reporting the companies as if they were a single company.

2. *Investments conveying significant influence*—These investments typically involve 20 to 50 percent of a company's common stock. They are reported in the balance sheet using what is called the "equity method" under which the investor's share of the investee's profit or loss is recognized by the investor when that profit or loss is recognized by the investee; the carrying amount of the investment is adjusted to reflect the investor's changing equity in the investee.

An important point to note about these investments is that they may be less marketable than other types of securities and, therefore, less liquid.

INVESTMENTS OTHER THAN SECURITIES

Although not common, companies may invest in assets other than securities, such as real estate or collectibles. For example, some companies have acquired valuable art collections. Such assets are typically less liquid than marketable securities, and values for them are often difficult to determine. Generally, these assets are reported at original cost unless evidence of a material impairment of value exists. An exception is that buildings held as investments and rented to others are generally depreciated, even when their values might be increasing.

IMPAIRMENT OF VALUE

A material decline in the value of any investment must be recognized if the decline is judged to be other than temporary. A loss is recognized in the income statement, and the investment is written down to the new lower value, which then becomes its new initial carrying amount for purposes of future accounting. Trading securities are accorded this treatment as a matter of practice. However, this treatment also applies to all other investments if they suffer a material decline, other than one expected to be temporary, regardless of the type of investment, the method used to account for it, and its classification. This practice aims at preventing failing investments being reported at inflated values.

CASH-FLOW IMPLICATIONS

Information for Decisions

Receivables and investments generate cash inflows when they are collected or sold, and they may provide cash from interest, dividends, rents, or other periodic payments. Financial statement users need to understand the degree of liquidity provided by the different types of assets so they can answer questions such as these: Will the company's receivables provide sufficient cash to sustain normal operations? What portion of the company's cash inflows are from investments as compared with cash inflows from its central operations? How will the company's receivables and investments affect its ability and need to borrow?

EXHIBIT 8-4 **DISCLOSURE OF RECEIVABLES BY DEERE & COMPANY**

DEERE & COMPANY
CONSOLIDATED BALANCE SHEET

	Consolidated (Deere & Company and Consolidated Subsidiaries)	
	October 31	
(In millions of dollars except per share amounts) ASSETS	1998	1997
Cash and short-term investments	$ 309.7	$ 330.0
Cash deposited with unconsolidated subsidiaries		
Cash and cash equivalents	309.7	330.0
Marketable securities	867.3	819.6
Receivables from unconsolidated subsidiaries and affiliates	36.2	14.6
Trade accounts and notes receivable-net	4,059.2	3,333.8
Financing receivables-net	6,332.7	6,404.7
Other receivables	536.8	412.7
Equipment on operating leases-net	1,209.2	774.6
Inventories	1,286.7	1,072.7
Property and equipment-net	1,700.3	1,524.1
Investments in unconsolidated subsidiaries and affiliates	172.0	149.9
Intangible assets-net	217.6	157.8
Prepaid pension costs	674.3	592.9
Other assets	109.7	107.2
Deferred income taxes	396.3	543.6
Deferred charges	93.5	81.6
Total	$18,001.5	$16,319.8

Notes to Financial Statements:
TRADE ACCOUNTS AND NOTES RECEIVABLE
Trade accounts and notes receivable at October 31 consisted of the following in millions of dollars:

	1998	1997
Trade accounts and notes:		
Agricultural	$2,756	$2,137
Construction	322	388
Commercial and consumer	784	624
Total	3,862	3,149
Other receivables	228	220
Total	4,090	3,369
Less allowance for doubtful receivables	31	35
Trade accounts and notes receivable-net	$4,059	$3,334

FINANCING RECEIVABLES
Financing receivables at October 31 consisted of the following in millions of dollars:

	1998	1997
Retail notes:		
Equipment:		
Agricultural	$3,030	$3,412
Construction	953	877
Commercial and consumer	351	282
Recreational products	1,044	1,606
Total	5,378	6,177
Revolving change accounts	764	630
Financing leases	387	331
Wholesale notes	894	653
Total financing receivables	7,423	7,791
Less:		
Unearned finance income:		
Equipment notes	590	654
Recreational product notes	360	590
Financing leases	50	48
Total	1,000	1,292
Allowance for doubtful receivables	90	94
Financing receivables-net	$6,333	$6,405

Financing receivable installments, including unearned finance income, at October 31 are scheduled as follows in millions of dollars:

	1998	1997
Due in months:		
0–12	$2,954	$2,765
13–24	1,585	1,685
25–36	1,100	1,186
37–48	722	782
49–60	451	471
Thereafter	611	902
Total	$7,423	$7,791

An analysis of the allowance for doubtful credit receivables follows in millions of dollars:

	1998	1997	1996
Balance, beginning of the year	$94	$93	$88
Provision charged to operations	50	38	43
Amounts written off	(36)	(31)	(32)
Transfers related to retail note sales	(18)	(6)	(6)
Balance, end of the year	$90	$94	$93

OTHER RECEIVABLES
Other receivables at October 31 consisted of the following in millions of dollars:

	1998	1997
Insurance and health care premiums receivable	$ 94	$ 90
Reinsurance receivables	94	91
Receivables relating to asset backed securitizations	162	165
Taxes receivable	129	2
Other	58	65
Other receivables	$537	$413

Because receivables and investments are closely related to potential future cash flows, they should be given careful consideration when assessing the liquidity and solvency of the entity. Many of these assets generate cash inflows during the time they are being held. Notes receivable and investments in bonds, for example, typically generate cash interest receipts, and investments in stocks generate inflows from dividends. Further, and often of greater importance, the assets themselves may be exchanged for cash in the future. Receivables are collected, and short-term investments in debt securities mature. Other investments, particularly those that are readily marketable, can be exchanged for cash whenever the need arises.

Looking beyond the body of the balance sheet itself is important in assessing the adequacy of the timing of cash flows. The notes to the statements should be examined for additional information on the liquidity and maturity of various investments and for the timing of cash needs related to the maturity of debt. For example, Exhibit 8–4 illustrates the type of additional disclosures that help decision makers assess future cash flows. Not only does Deere & Company's balance sheet indicate the major classes of receivables, but extensive notes to the financial statements provide a more detailed description of the receivables and provide information on maturities and uncollectibles. Keep in mind that a company's cash, receivables, and investments provide it with flexibility, while nonliquid assets, such as plant and equipment, cannot easily be used to meet unexpected cash needs except under extreme circumstances.

SUMMARY

Cash, receivables, and investments provide an entity with liquidity, solvency, and flexibility. Investments may include financial investments, such as certificates of deposit, stocks, and bonds, or nonfinancial assets such as real estate and art.

Cash is the most liquid of all assets, but it earns no return. Organizations must hold some cash to meet daily operating needs and for unexpected occurrences, but flexibility can be maintained and profitability improved by investing most cash in short-term investments. When assessing an organization's ability to meet cash-flow requirements, financial statement classifications and disclosures should be examined for restrictions on cash and for the liquidity of investments.

Accounts receivable are amounts owed to an organization by its customers and typically provide the primary source of cash for ongoing operations. Accounts receivable are reported in the balance sheet at net realizable value so financial statement users can assess expected cash inflows. The full amount owed to the organization is reported, with the amount expected to be uncollectible deducted through an allowance account. The amount of uncollectible accounts is estimated before specific accounts are actually determined to be uncollectible so that the cost of bad debts can be reported in the same period as the sales giving rise to the uncollectible accounts. This provides a proper matching of costs and revenues, and reports the receivables at the amount expected to be collected.

Sometimes businesses make sales in exchange for notes from their customers promising to pay in the future. In most cases, the notes include interest explicitly or implicitly. In either case, the interest earned must be recognized over the term of the note, and the income from financing the sale must be separated from the sales revenue so that decision makers can distinguish the sources of income.

Investments in securities are classified so statement users can evaluate why the securities are being held and to what extent they contribute to liquidity. Most securities held as investments are classified as (1) held-to-maturity securities, (2) trading securities, or (3) available-for-sale securities, depending on the holder's intent. Securities in the latter two categories are valued at fair value. Only debt securities are classified as held to maturity, and they are reported at cost, with any discount or premium amortized to maturity. Investments in assets other than securities usually are valued at cost. Any investment that suffers a material decline in value that is other than temporary is written down to its fair value and a loss is recognized.

LIST OF IMPORTANT TERMS

accounts receivable *(292)*

accounts receivable turnover *(293)*

aging of accounts *(299)*

allowance for uncollectible accounts *(297)*

allowance method *(297)*

bad debt expense *(296)*

cash discounts *(294)*

contra-asset account *(297)*

face amount *(305)*

implicit interest *(305)*

interest-bearing notes *(304)*

net realizable value *(296)*

noninterest-bearing notes *(304)*

notes receivable *(303)*

valuation account *(297)*

EXAMINING THE CONCEPTS

Q8-1 What are the characteristics of an asset classified as a financial asset? What assets typically are classified as financial assets?

Q8-2 Why is knowledge of the anticipated holding period important in judging the value of a financial asset?

Q8-3 How does the concept of liquidity relate to financial assets? Which types of financial assets are regarded as highly liquid? Which financial assets are regarded as illiquid?

Q8-4 What assets are included in the cash balance reported in the balance sheet? Why might it be argued that a company does not know its exact cash balance at any given point in time?

Q8-5 What is a compensating balance? Why do they arise? Why should financial statement users be aware of them?

Q8-6 How is the amount reported as accounts receivable determined? Why is the net amount reported as accounts receivable often less than the total of all amounts owed to the company by customers?

Q8-7 Why is establishing an allowance for uncollectible accounts important? Why does a company not simply write off accounts not expected to be collected, rather than establishing an allowance?

Q8-8 Compare the direct write-off and allowance methods of accounting for bad debts. Which is the more appropriate method? Explain.

Q8-9 How is the amount of bad debt expense estimated for a period? Why might an aging of accounts analysis at the end of the period be important?

Q8-10 Why might a company sell its accounts receivables?

Q8-11 When is a trade (or customer) note receivable used? How does a trade note receivable differ from an account receivable?

Q8-12 What is meant by a noninterest-bearing note receivable? How are such notes valued when received in payment for sales?

Q8-13 How is interest income on a noninterest-bearing note receivable determined? What inaccuracies in the financial statements will occur if no implicit interest is recognized?

Q8-14 How should loans to corporate officers or employees be reported?

Q8-15 What types of securities may be classified as held-to-maturity? How does this category differ from those classified as trading securities?

Q8-16 Distinguish between the procedures used in valuing securities classified as trading versus those classified as available-for-sale for purposes of (1) computing income for the period and (2) balance sheet presentation.

Q8-17 How is the increase or decrease in the value of a stock investment treated for financial reporting purposes when the securities are classified as trading?

Q8-18 How is the increase or decrease in the value of a stock investment treated for financial reporting purposes when the securities are classified as available-for-sale?

Q8-19 When is an investment in common stock not included in any of the categories of trading, available-for-sale, or held-to-maturity?

Q8-20 What does it mean to have an impairment of value of an investment? How should an impairment of value be treated for financial reporting purposes?

Q8-21 Why would a company consider investing in the common stock of another company to control or significantly influence the other company? Do you know of any such examples today?

UNDERSTANDING ACCOUNTING INFORMATION

E8-1   Cash, Receivables, and Investments: Characteristics and Valuation The financial statements of Stern Corporation appear to include some assets valued at the amounts paid to acquire them, some valued at amounts less than was paid to acquire them, and others valued at more than was paid to acquire them.

a. Why is it considered appropriate to report accounts receivable at less than the full amount owed to the company by those who have purchased on account?
b. Why is it considered appropriate to report an investment in marketable securities being held for potential immediate sale at its current market price rather than the amount paid?
c. Why is it considered appropriate to revalue financial assets such as accounts receivable and marketable securities but not considered appropriate to revalue nonfinancial assets such as buildings and equipment?

E8-2   Reporting Cash Worldcorp Manufacturing has production sites around the world. In its financial statements, the reported cash balance includes amounts on deposit in a variety of places with some balances designated for specific purposes. How might knowledge of the information presented in each of the independent situations listed below assist an investor in evaluating the liquidity position of Worldcorp Manufacturing?

a. Nearly all cash held in U.S. banks is in the form of compensating balances.
b. A significant part of the cash balance is held in Mexican pesos even though the Mexican government has been seriously discussing devaluing the peso.
c. The company reports virtually no cash, but has a significant amount classified as cash equivalents.
d. Cash constitutes a very large portion of current assets even though the company has no plans to purchase additional assets or declare a major dividend in the near future.

E8-3   Reporting Accounts Receivable Turbo Manufacturing reported sales on account of $3,000,000 and bad debt expense of $40,000 for the current year. Adams Department Stores reported sales on account of $2,600,000 and bad debt expense of $57,000. Jacks Land Development Corporation reported sales on account of $2,000,000 and bad debt expense of $90,000.

a. What factors might cause the ratio of bad debt expense to total sales to be quite different in these three companies?
b. Does the fact that Jacks Land Development has the highest estimated loss from bad debts mean that it is the least desirable investment alternative among the three companies? Explain.
c. How may the accounts receivable turnover ratio affect the accuracy in estimating the bad debt percentage?

E8-4   Notes and Other Receivables AB Company and RT Company both received notes of $10,000 from customers on the same date with the same maturity dates. However, the note receivable recorded by AB Company was interest bearing and the note recorded by RT Company was noninterest bearing.

a. Which of the companies will report the greater carrying value for its note receivable at the date the note is accepted? Explain why.
b. Which company will receive the greater cash flow over the life of the note receivable? Explain.
c. If the stated interest rate on AB's note is the same as the implicit interest rate used in valuing RT's note, which company will report the greater amount of interest income in the first year? Explain.

E8-5   Investments Tim Lane is confused when the financial statements of one of the companies he is attempting to analyze reports three different classes of investments (trading securities, available-for-sale securities, and held-to-maturity securities) and appears to account for each of them differently.

a. In what way does managerial intent differ between securities placed in the three categories?
b. In what way does the balance sheet presentation of the investment differ between securities placed in the three categories?
c. In what way does the recognition of income on changes in the market value of the securities differ between securities placed in the three categories?

E8-6   Cash Flow Implications What should be the effect of each of the following situations on the evaluation of Gray Company's financial assets?

a. A significant part of the current receivables is from a single customer that has a strong credit rating and a record of prompt payment.
b. A significant part of the current receivables is from a single customer that has a spotty payment record and relatively poor credit rating.
c. A significant portion of Gray's cash is on deposit in European banks.
d. A significant portion of total financial assets is invested in marketable securities that have declined in value since the time of purchase.
e. Accounts receivable are reported at the total amount receivable. Accounts receivable are reduced and bad debt expense recorded when it is established that an account cannot be collected.
f. A noninterest-bearing note receivable due in 5 years is included in financial assets at its face amount.

E8-7   Multiple Choice: Reporting Financial Assets Select the correct answer for each of the following:

1. Which of the following would not be considered a financial asset?
   a. Certificate of deposit.
   b. Investment in marketable securities.
   c. Accounts receivable.
   d. Investment in equipment.
2. In general, financial assets:
   a. Are nearly always valued at the amount paid to acquire them.
   b. Can be readily converted into cash.
   c. Include all current assets except for prepaid insurance.
   d. Represent a tangible asset that will be used in producing goods and services in the next accounting period.
3. The cash balance reported in the balance sheet normally will not include:
   a. Small amounts of cash (petty cash) kept on hand in the office.
   b. Checks received from customers and deposited in the bank.
   c. Money orders.
   d. Temporary investments due in one year.
4. Knowledge of financial assets is important in determining if a company:
   a. Has the ability to pay existing liabilities.
   b. Has the ability to issue additional debt.
   c. Has too much stock outstanding.
   d. Has been profitable during the last accounting period.

E8-8   Multiple Choice: Valuation of Accounts Receivable   Select the correct answer for each of the following:

1. A company records an account receivable:
   a. Each time an exchange transaction occurs.
   b. Each time a cash sale is made.
   c. When another company extends credit to it.
   d. When an exchange has taken place, the earning process is complete, and payment has not yet been received.
2. Bad debt expense represents:
   a. That portion of this period's sales on account not likely to be collected.
   b. That portion of the balance in accounts receivable at the end of the period not likely to be collected.
   c. The amount of accounts receivable written off as uncollectible during the current period.
   d. The total of those accounts receivable written off during the period and the amount judged to be uncollectible at the beginning of the period.
3. The allowance for uncollectible accounts is:
   a. Increased when an account receivable is collected.
   b. Decreased when an account receivable is collected.
   c. Increased when an account receivable is written off.
   d. Decreased when an account receivable is written off.
4. In reporting accounts receivable in the balance sheet:
   a. An aging schedule is used to determine which accounts should be written off prior to preparing the balance sheet totals.
   b. The allowance for uncollectible accounts is deducted from accounts receivable.
   c. The direct write-off method is used to determine the appropriate balance in the allowance for uncollectible accounts at year-end.
   d. Only those accounts likely to be collected before the beginning of the next period should be included in the accounts receivable.

E8-9   Multiple Choice: Reporting for Notes Receivable   Select the best answer for each of the following:

1. Interest-bearing notes receivable are likely to be received from:
   a. Customers who appear to be unable to pay for products purchased.
   b. Customers who have a temporary cash-flow problem.
   c. Customers with excess cash.
   d. Customers who make frequent purchases.
2. When a noninterest-bearing note receivable is accepted at the time of a sale:
   a. The sale is recorded then for the amount to be collected when the note matures.
   b. The sale is not recorded until the proceeds of the note are collected.
   c. A discount on notes receivable is recorded for the amount of the unearned implicit interest on the note.
   d. A discount on notes receivable is recorded for the excess of the total cash payment to be received over the original cost of the products sold.
3. The implicit interest on a noninterest-bearing note receivable:
   a. Represents the extra payment to be made by the customer for delaying the payment of cash until a future time.
   b. Represents the annual cash payment received from the customer until the note matures.
   c. Represents the interest rate the company would need to pay if it borrowed money from the bank.
   d. Represents the interest rate the company would earn if it invested the cash in the customer's stock.
4. At the end of the accounting period, implicit interest is recorded on a noninterest-bearing note:
   a. In an amount equal to the interest payment received during the current period.
   b. As a reduction in the carrying value of the note receivable.
   c. To recognize interest earned on the note during the current period.
   d. To adjust the sales price of the products exchanged for the note receivable.

E8-10   Multiple Choice: Reporting for Investments   Select the best answer for each of the following:

1. Cash normally is used to purchase short-term investments as a means of:
   a. Earning a higher return than would be earned by investing in plant and equipment.

b. Obtaining control of another company.

c. Earning a higher return than would be earned by holding excess cash.

d. Participating in the higher returns found in the stock market.

2. Investments in securities classified as held-to-maturity:

a. May be either stock or debt securities.

b. May be debt securities only.

c. Should always be recorded at maturity value at the time of purchase.

d. Should always be reported at original cost.

3. For an investment in common stock classified as a trading security:

a. An unrealized gain is included in income if the value of the security increases during the period.

b. An unrealized loss is included in income if the value of the security decreases during the period.

c. Dividend income is recorded for dividends received during the period.

d. All of the above.

4. For an investment in common stock classified as available-for-sale:

a. An unrealized gain is included in income if the value of the security increases during the period.

b. An unrealized gain is included in other comprehensive income if the value of the security increases during the period.

c. Dividend income for dividends declared and received during the period is deferred and recognized at the time of sale.

d. Both a and c are correct.

E8-11 Determining Cash Balances Murphy Corporation will be needing a substantial amount of cash to pay off a note receivable that is maturing early in 2001. On December 31, 2000, the controller of Murphy Corporation made a list of cash balances and expected cash flows and has asked you for assistance in computing the amount to be reported as cash in the company's balance sheet at December 31, 2000. The following items were listed:

Cash in Neighborhood Bank	$203,000
Certificate of deposit maturing Jan. 21, 2001	65,000
Balance in savings account at Local Savings & Loan	27,000
Rent payment to be received Jan. 4, 2001	10,000
Checks received Dec. 28, 2000, and deposited in Neighborhood Bank on Jan. 2, 2001	31,000
Notification from Neighborhood Bank received on Jan. 3, 2001, that payment on a note receivable from a customer had been received and deposited in account on Dec. 29, 2000	18,000
Investment in U.S. Treasury bills maturing Jan. 2, 2001	40,000

Bank service charges deducted from checking account in December 2000, not recorded by Murphy Corporation	400
Collection of accounts receivable made on Jan. 3, 2001	140,000
German marks (DM) on deposit at branch operation in Germany (exchange rate at Dec. 31, 2000, 1 DM = .66 U.S. dollars)	200,000 DM

The president of Murphy Corporation had promised the board of directors that the company would have at least $240,000 of cash on hand by the end of 2000.

a. Determine the balance of cash and cash equivalents that Murphy Corporation should report in its balance sheet at December 31, 2000.

b. Did the president reach the goal?

E8-12 Compensating Balances A note to the financial statements of Special Company indicates that $75,000 of the balance reported as Cash and Cash Equivalents in the December 31, 2001, balance sheet must remain on deposit in accordance with an agreement with the bank. Special Company has a considerable amount of borrowings from the bank and has agreed to keep a minimum of that amount on deposit at all times.

a. Special Company apparently has cash that it is unable to use. Why would Special enter into an agreement of this type?

b. How should the $75,000 be reported in Special's balance sheet?

c. One of the employees has suggested that the $75,000 should be deducted from the amount borrowed and the net liability reported as notes payable. Would such a treatment be appropriate? Explain.

E8-13 Cash Flows and Valuing Foreign Deposits Blankman Corporation has operations in a number of foreign countries. The corporate controller has included in the cash balance what she believes to be appropriate amounts by translating each foreign currency balance into U.S. dollars using current exchange rates. However, the president of finance is concerned about misleading investors by reporting amounts that may never be brought back to the United States as currency. He is especially concerned about three foreign currency totals:

1. A balance of 600,000 currency units from the country of Innstable. The current government is unlikely to remain in power after the next election and, at present, foreign companies are not permitted to transfer currency out of the country.

2. A balance of 1,500,000 currency units from the country of Inncrease. Prices have been increasing within the country at a rate much faster than in the United States, and there are fears the currency may eventually be devalued and will be worth far fewer U.S. dollars.

3. A balance of 800,000 currency units from the country of Outflow. The country has had a serious trade deficit for the past 5 years and within the next decade may have trouble making payments on amounts borrowed from international banks.

  a. What factors should Blankman Corporation consider in deciding whether or not each of these balances is to be included as cash in the corporate balance sheet?

  b. Which, if any, of the balances should be included as cash in Blankman's balance sheet? Explain.

  c. Which, if any, of the balances would you expect to be disclosed in notes? Explain.

E8-14 Evaluation of Allowance for Uncollectibles Talvez Company started business on January 3, 2001. The company made credit sales of $800,000 during 2001 and received payments of $410,000 prior to the end of the year. It also wrote off as uncollectible $7,000 of its receivables when it learned the customer filed for bankruptcy. Other than the entry to write off the $7,000 of receivables, Talvez Company has made no entries relating to bad debt expense for the period. The industry average for bad debt expense for companies similar to Talvez Company is 2 percent of credit sales. If Talvez Company uses the allowance method of accounting for bad debts and adopts the industry percentage in estimating bad debt expense for 2001:

a. What should be the balance reported in the Allowance for Uncollectible Accounts at December 31, 2001?

b. What Accounts Receivable balance would be reported in the balance sheet at December 31, 2001?

c. Evaluate the reasonableness of the balance in the Allowance for Uncollectibles at December 31, 2001.

E8-15 Reporting Accounts Receivable Nomad Corporation reported credit sales of $435,000 in 2001 and collected $350,000 prior to year-end. Bad debt expense equal to 2 percent of credit sales was recorded during 2001. A total of $7,100 of accounts receivable was written off as uncollectible during the year.

a. What amount of bad debt expense should be recorded for 2001?

b. If the January 1 balance in accounts receivable was $69,000, what is the balance in accounts receivable at December 31, 2001?

c. If Nomad reported a balance of $900 in its allowance for uncollectible accounts at January 1, what is the balance at December 31?

E8-16 Collection of Accounts Receivable Qeff Company reported the following amounts in its December 31, 2000, trial balance:

Cash Sales	$142,000
Credit Sales	?
Accounts Receivable	
January 1	407,000
December 31	?

Allowance for Uncollectible Accounts	
January 1	28,000
December 31	38,980
Bad Debt Expense	43,080

Qeff Company uses the allowance method for reporting uncollectible accounts and estimates that 6 percent of its credit sales will be uncollectible.

a. Determine the amount of credit sales in 2000.

b. Determine the amount of accounts receivable written off as uncollectible during 2000.

c. Assuming $831,000 of accounts receivable was collected in 2000, determine the balance in accounts receivable at December 31, 2000.

E8-17 Accounting for Receivables Whipple Corporation reported accounts receivable and an allowance for uncollectible accounts of $179,000 and $7,500, respectively, at January 1. The following transactions and adjustments to account balances were recorded during the year:

  1. Cash sales and credit sales were $235,000 and $820,000, respectively, for the year.

  2. Bad debt expense was recorded at 4 percent of credit sales.

  3. Payments of $762,000 on accounts receivable were received.

  4. A total of $29,600 of accounts receivable was written off as uncollectible during the year.

  5. Corporate management reviewed the accounts receivable balances at the end of the year and decided the balance in the allowance for uncollectible accounts at year-end should be $14,200.

a. Prepare the journal entries recorded by Whipple Corporation for each of the above items.

b. What is the net amount of accounts receivable reported at year-end by Whipple Corporation?

E8-18 Matching Credit Sales and Bad Debts Gunderson Corporation was started on January 1, 2001, and reported the following year-end balances in accounts receivable, credit sales, and write-offs of accounts receivable during 2001 and 2002:

	Accounts Receivable December 31	Credit Sales	Amounts Written Off as Uncollectible During the Year
2001	$105,000	$410,000	$ 5,400
2002	180,000	630,000	26,700

Gunderson Corporation writes off bad accounts receivable as they are determined to be uncollectible. Thus, it reported bad expense of $5,400 and $26,700 in 2001 and 2002, respectively. Management of Gunderson believes the company will experience a 4 percent bad-debt rate each year.

a. What amount of bad debt expense would Gunderson have reported if it had used the allowance method for each year?

b. What balance in the allowance for uncollectible accounts would Gunderson have reported at year-end for each year if the allowance method had been used?

c. Determine the amount of understatement or overstatement of net income for each of the years as a result of using the direct write-off method.

E8-19 Computing Bad Debt Expense AK Company reported an allowance for uncollectible accounts receivable of $16,200 at January 1 and $19,500 at December 31. If a total of $42,600 of accounts receivable was written off as uncollectible during the year and the company estimated bad debt expense at 3 percent of credit sales:

a. What was bad debt expense for the year?

b. What were total credit sales for the year?

E8-20 Bad Debt Expense Crocket Corporation prepared the following aging schedule of its accounts receivable at December 31, 2000:

Number of Days Outstanding	Amount	Estimated Uncollectible Percentage
0–20	$540,000	2
21–40	180,000	3
41–60	90,000	4
61–80	60,000	5
Over 80	70,000	7

Crocket reported sales on account of $2,600,000 during 2000 and wrote off $37,600 of accounts receivable as uncollectible for the year. Accounts receivable at January 1, 2000, was $895,000 and the allowance for uncollectible accounts was $41,200.

a. Compute the required balance in the allowance for uncollectible accounts at December 31, 2000.

b. Compute the amount that Crocket Corporation must record as bad debt expense for 2000 to bring the balance in the allowance for uncollectible accounts to the required level.

c. Compute the balance in accounts receivable at December 31, 2000.

d. Compute the amount of money received as payment on accounts receivable during 2000.

E8-21 Balance in Allowance for Uncollectible Accounts Groth Company reported the following ledger account balances at December 31, 2000.

Accounts Receivable

Bal. 1/1	120,000	(2)	580,000
(1)	630,000	(3)	15,750
Bal. 12/31	154,250		

Allowance for Uncollectibles

(3)	15,750	Bal. 1/1	6,300
Bal. 12/31	9,450		

Bad debt expense for 2000 has not been recorded. The management of Groth Company estimates that a balance of $9,600 is needed in the allowance for uncollectible accounts at December 31, 2000.

a. What amount of credit sales was reported for 2000?

b. What amount of cash payment was received from customers in 2000?

c. What amount of accounts receivable was written off as uncollectible in 2000?

d. What amount must Groth Company record as bad debt expense for 2000?

E8-22 Aging Accounts Receivable Denver Company sells products primarily to small hardware supply companies. At December 31, 2001, the total accounts receivable balance for Denver Company was $750,000 and an allowance for uncollectibles of $27,000 was on its books. An analysis of accounts receivable at December 31, 2001, disclosed the following:

Receivable Amount	Number of Days Outstanding	Estimated Percent That Will Be Collected
$400,000	Less than 20	98%
200,000	21–40 days	95
120,000	41–60 days	90
30,000	More than 60	70

a. If the estimated percentages are correct, is the allowance for uncollectibles for Denver Company appropriate? What adjustment, if any, should be made to the allowance?

b. Assume that the management of Denver Company has concluded that the amount of uncollectibles is too high. What actions might be taken to reduce the amount of uncollectibles? What additional effects might these actions have?

E8-23 Aging Accounts Super Products Corporation had a balance in its accounts receivable account at December 31, 2000, of $120,000 and a $4,000 balance in its allowance for uncollectible accounts. During 2001, the company sold equipment on credit in the amount of $820,000. Total cash collections during 2001 were $790,000. The company also determined that $5,000 of accounts would not be collected, and it wrote them off. At the end of 2001, Super Products prepared the following aging schedule:

Length of Time Outstanding	Accounts Receivable Balance	Estimated Uncollectible Percentage
Less than 30 days	$80,000	1
31 to 60 days	30,000	3
61 to 90 days	20,000	8
More than 90 days	15,000	10

When you receive this information, you are asked to:

a. Identify the accounts and the amounts that would be used by Super Products during 2001 to record its credit sales.
b. Present the journal entry to record collection of the payments received.
c. Identify the effects of writing off the $5,000 of bad accounts during 2001.
d. Compute the proper balance that should be reported in the allowance for uncollectible accounts at December 31, 2001, using the aging schedule. Also, show how the accounts would be adjusted to recognize bad debt expense for 2001.

E8-24   Note Receivable from Sale of Product   Ply Company sold inventory on January 1, 2000, for $300,000 and accepted a 3-year note bearing a 6 percent interest rate. Interest is paid annually on December 31. Give the journal entries to record the following:

a. Sale of inventory.
b. Receipt of interest at December 31, 2000 and 2001.
c. Receipt of interest and payment of the note on December 31, 2002.

E8-25   Exchange Resulting in Note Receivable   Bonnet Corporation exchanged land for a 4-year $250,000 note receivable bearing an annual interest rate of 6 percent. Payments of $70,000 are to be received by Bonnet at December 31 of each of the first 3 years. Payment at the end of the fourth year is to include the unpaid balance of the note receivable plus interest for the fourth year.

a. Compute the amount Bonnet Corporation should report as interest income in each of the years and the balance of the note receivable at December 31 each year.
b. What is the total amount recorded as interest income over the 4-year period?
c. What is the total amount of cash received by Bonnet during the fourth year?

E8-26   Income from Note Receivable   On January 1, 2000, Ester Corporation loaned $161,986 to Topper Company on a 4-year note receivable with a 9 percent annual interest rate. Topper agreed to pay Ester Corporation $50,000 on December 31 each year.

a. Compute the amount of interest income recorded by Ester Corporation in each of the 4 years and the balance of the note receivable at December 31 each year.

b. What is the total amount recorded as interest income over the 4-year period?
c. If Ester Corporation had an opportunity to sell the note receivable to a bank for $85,000 on January 1, 2002, would it report a gain or loss on the sale? What amount would be reported?

E8-27   Financing Sale to Customer   Crazy Hal's Furniture Warehouse submitted the low bid to provide office furniture for a new building. Under the terms offered, the buyer signed a 2-year noninterest-bearing note on January 1, 2000, that requires the buyer to pay Crazy Hal's Furniture Warehouse $200,000 on December 31, 2001. Both parties agree that a 10 percent rate of interest on such notes is appropriate. The present value of the $200,000 payment at January 1, 2000 is $165,290.

a. What amount should Crazy Hal's Furniture Warehouse record as sales revenue on January 1, 2000?
b. What amount of discount on notes receivable should be recorded on January 1, 2000?
c. What amount of interest income should be reported by Crazy Hal's Furniture Warehouse in 2000 and 2001?

E8-28   Sale of Land on Noninterest Bearing Note   Farmland Corporation sold 80 acres of land to Bigtime Developers, January 1, 2000, on a noninterest-bearing note with a maturity date of December 31, 2006, and a maturity amount of $1,000,000. A 9 percent return in the form of interest is considered appropriate on the loan. The present value of the $1,000,000 payment at January 1, 2000, was $547,030. On December 31, 2000, Farmland recorded interest income as follows:

| Interest Receivable | 90,000 | |
| Interest Income | | 90,000 |

a. At what amount should Farmland record the sale of land on January 1, 2000?
b. What amount of discount on notes receivable would Bigtime record on January 1, 2000?
c. Is the interest income recorded by Farmland Corporation at December 31, 2000, correct? If not, what amount should have been recorded?
d. What amount of interest income should Farmland record at December 31, 2001?

E8-29   Computing Cash Discount   Pearson Corporation purchased equipment on account on July 1, with terms 3/10, net 30. Payment of $795,400 was made on July 9.

a. What was the gross amount of the purchase?
b. How much money was saved by paying within the discount period?

E8-30   Cash Discounts   Tandem Corporation receives a bill from Burl Company for $6,500. The terms of the invoice are 4/10, net 60. The invoice is dated April 30 and states that

1 percent interest per month will be charged starting 60 days after the date of billing if the bill has not been paid.

a. If Tandem pays the bill by May 8, how much must it pay?
b. If Tandem pays the bill on June 7, how much must it pay?
c. If Tandem pays the bill on July 29, how much must it pay?

E8-31 Multiple Cash Discounts For each of the following, determine the amount that must be paid by Hanover Corporation:

	Date of Purchase	Amount of Purchase	Purchase Terms	Date of Payment
a.	January 1	$ 50,000	2/10, net 30	January 9
b.	March 28	24,000	2/10, net 30	April 9
c.	June 26	120,000	5/15, net 40	July 6
d.	August 9	80,000	5/15, net 60	August 20
e.	October 27	60,000	10/5, net 25	October 31
f.	November 1	200,000	15/20, net 30	December 27

E8-32 Cash Discounts versus Notes Receivable Both Torn Building Materials and Grim Steel Products make a majority of their sales to companies that build office buildings. The companies typically do not receive payment on sales for at least 6 months from the date of billing and have adopted different pricing and cash collection strategies. Torn prices its products at a higher dollar amount and grants a substantial cash discount if payment is received within 90 days. Grim prices its products at a lower dollar amount, but requires customers to sign a note receivable and began paying interest for any days the payment is delayed beyond 90 days. On January 1, 2000, the companies purchased products for $400,000 and sold them to customers on the same day. Torn sold its products for $500,000 and offered a cash discount of 6/90, net 180. Grim sold its products for $460,000, but with a requirement that if the sale price is not paid within 90 days the customer must sign a note payable with an annual interest rate of 16 percent.

a. If both companies collect their receivables on March 28, 2000, which company would receive the larger payment? By what amount?
b. If both companies collect their receivables on June 30, 2000, which company would receive the larger payment? By what amount?
c. If both companies collect their receivables on December 31, 2000, which company would receive the larger payment? By what amount?

E8-33 Investing in Trading Securities Modar Company purchased 200 common shares each of Otter, Plain, and Tarm companies on January 1, 2001, at a cost of $100, $40, and $70 per share, respectively. On December 31, 2001, the market values of the shares were $110, $35, and $58, respectively, and Modar Company considers the shares to be part of its trading portfolio.

a. At what amount will the investments be reported in Modar's balance sheet at December 31, 2001?
b. Will any other balance sheet or income statement accounts be affected by the accounting treatment of these securities? If so, which accounts, and what will be the effect?

E8-34 Earnings from Trading Securities During 2000, Pilser Company received dividends of $1,200, $1,600, and $300, respectively, from its investment in the common shares of Ace, Day, and Ming companies. The shares of these companies are included in Pilser's trading securities portfolio. If Pilser Company reported income from operations of $170,000 and an unrealized gain on trading securities of $4,000 in 2000:

a. What amount of net income will Pilser Company report for 2000?
b. If Pilser's total investment in the three companies at January 1, 2000, was $150,000, did it meet its goal of earning a 10 percent return on trading securities during 2000?

E8-35 Investing in Available-for-Sale Securities Security Corporation purchased 200 shares of the preferred stock of Brown Company for $70 each on January 7, 2001. It also purchased 100 shares of Blue Corporation common shares for $30 per share on that date. At December 31, 2001, the shares of Brown preferred were selling at $74 and the common shares of Blue were selling at $14. Security Corporation considers the shares to be part of its available-for-sale securities portfolio.

a. At what amount will the investments be reported in the December 31, 2001, balance sheet?
b. Will any other balance sheet or income statement accounts be affected by the accounting treatment of these securities? If so, which accounts, and what will be the effect?

E8-36 Earnings from Available-for-Sale Securities Butter Company holds 4,000 shares of common stock of Zoltar Corporation and 7,000 shares of preferred stock of Rant Company. During 2000, Butter Company received dividends of $4 per share from Zoltar Corporation and $6 per share from Rant Company. Due to a decline in the stock market, the market price of the shares held by Butter decreased from $300,000 on January 1 to $276,000 on December 31, 2000. Both securities are carried in Butter's available-for-sale investment portfolio.

a. If Butter reports income from operations of $245,000 for 2000, what amount of net income will it report for the year?
b. If Butter wishes to earn a 15 percent return on its stock investment, has it accomplished its goal in 2000?

E8-37 Financing with Accounts Receivable Each of the following excerpts are taken from the notes to the financial statements of companies providing additional information about their financial assets and their financing policies. For each one, state:

a. Whether the information indicates that borrowing has taken place.
b. Who is responsible for collecting the company's accounts receivable.
c. What happens if the accounts receivable in question are not paid by the customers.

Company A: The company has borrowed money from the Flush Bank, giving it a security interest in accounts receivable in general.

Company B: The company has sold with recourse the receivables from two government agencies.

Company C: The company has sold a portion of its accounts receivable for cash, without recourse. During the current year, $231,000 of receivables were sold and, during the previous year, $103,000 of receivables were sold.

E8-38 Investment in Bonds On January 11, 2000, Flank Corporation invested $700,000 of cash held for future investment in 5-year bonds issued by Tuna Corporation. The bonds pay 7 percent interest annually. Flank plans to hold the bonds until they mature.

a. If interest rates increase during 2000 and the market price of the bonds declines to $674,000 by December 31, why is it not necessary for Flank Corporation to adjust the bonds to current market price at December 31, 2000?
b. What action relating to financial reporting, if any, should Flank take if the market value of the bonds declines to $635,000 in December 2000 as a result of an announcement by Tuna Corporation that reduced profits may require the company to cease operations?

E8-39 Noninterest-Bearing Note Receivable On January 1, 2001, Amherst Corporation sold equipment to South Company for $18,040. In payment, Amherst agreed to accept a 3-year note that called for payments of $7,000 to be received annually beginning on December 31, 2001. Amherst considers an 8 percent rate of interest on such notes to be appropriate.

a. Compute the interest income to be recorded in each of the 3-years by Amherst Corporation and the balance of the note receivable at the end of each year.
b. Why does the amount of interest income decline each period?

E8-40 Noninterest-Bearing Note On January 1, 2001, Stone Manufacturing accepted a 3-year noninterest-bearing note in the amount of $20,000 in exchange for machinery with a market value of $15,876. The note, which matures on December 31, 2003, provides an 8 percent return in the form of interest to Stone Manufacturing.

a. Compute the interest income to be recorded in each of the 3 years by Stone Manufacturing and the balance of the note receivable at the end of each year.
b. Why does the amount of interest income increase each period?
c. If Stone Manufacturing were to sell the note receivable at December 31, 2001, and the purchaser was willing to accept an 8 percent return, what would be the selling price of the note?

USING ACCOUNTING FOR DECISION MAKING

P8-41 Uncollectible Accounts Town Company is involved in the manufacture and sale of toys. At the end of 2000, Town's balance sheet reported total accounts receivable of $223,000 and an allowance for uncollectible accounts of $21,000. During 2001, the following events occurred:

1. Credit sales in the amount of $1,600,000 were made.
2. Collections of $1,550,000 were received.
3. Town recorded bad debt expense for 2001 as 2 percent of credit sales.
4. Customers with total payables of $19,000 to Town were declared bankrupt, and those accounts receivable were written off.

As director of finance of Town, you have been asked by a member of the executive committee to:

a. Analyze the above activities by giving the journal entries to be recorded by Town for each of the transactions.
b. Illustrate Town's balance sheet disclosure of accounts receivable at December 31, 2001.

c. Evaluate the adequacy of Town's allowance for uncollectible accounts at December 31, 2001.

P8-42 Determining Bad Debt Expense On December 31, 2001, Bethel Manufacturing had accounts receivable of $180,000 and determined a need for an allowance for uncollectible accounts in the amount of $35,000. During 2002, Bethel made sales of $980,000 and collected $1,000,000 of receivables. Also during 2002, Bethel was forced to write off as uncollectible $19,000 of its receivables from 2001 and $41,000 of its 2002 sales. At December 31, 2002, Bethel concluded that it needed an allowance for uncollectibles of $26,000, all of which applies to accounts receivables recorded in 2002.

a. Would you expect Bethel Manufacturing to report bad debt expense for 2002? If not, why not? If reported, in what amount?
b. Prepare an analysis of Accounts Receivable and the Allowance for Uncollectible Accounts for 2002.

c. In 2001, bad debt expense was 6 percent of credit sales. The management of Bethel Manufacturing budgeted a 4 percent bad debt expense in 2002. Was the company successful in its efforts to reduce bad debt losses in 2002?

P8-43 Income Recognition with Noninterest-Bearing Notes On December 31, 2000, Video Systems, Inc., completed installing an instant video and surround-sound speaker system at a new arena football league stadium. Video System's cost of installation was $350,000, and the agreed upon price was $600,000. However, the owners of the stadium are short of cash, and some accommodation might be needed for Video Systems to receive payment. I. M. Sharp, one of the owners of the stadium, is sure it will become profitable with the help of the new video system. He has proposed that Video Systems accept as full payment a 5-year noninterest-bearing note for the $600,000 price. Video Systems can earn an 8 percent return on money it has to invest. The present value of the note at December 31, 2000, is $408,348. As the controller of Video, you are asked to provide answers to the following questions regarding the sale on credit:

a. Assuming Video Systems recognizes sales revenue on completing the system installation, what amount of revenue should be recognized on December 31, 2000?
b. If Video Systems had no other video installations during 2000, what amount of net income would the company report for the year?
c. What amount of interest income should Video Systems recognize in 2000 and each of the following 5 years?
d. The sales manager of Video Systems thinks that the full $250,000 ($600,000 − $350,000) of profit should be reported in 2000, since that is when the entire installation process was completed. Explain why it is not appropriate to do so under generally accepted accounting principles.
e. After your analysis, would you recommend that Video Systems undertake an identical project next period, providing the same financing terms? Explain.

P8-44 Direct Write-off of Accounts Receivable Folley Corporation records uncollectible accounts receivable as bad debt expense at the time it is learned they cannot be collected. Folley Corporation started business on January 1, 2000, and had credit sales of $180,000 in 2000, $135,000 of which was collected by year-end, and $3,000 of which was written off as uncollectible.

Credit sales in 2001 were $320,000 and cash collections from 2001 sales were $175,000. In addition, Folley collected $34,500 of receivables from 2000, and the remainder of 2000 receivables were written off as bad debt expense.

a. Compute Folley's net income for 2000 and 2001, assuming operating expenses (excluding bad debt expense) of $40,000 and $90,000, respectively.
b. Evaluate the accuracy of the amounts reported as net income for each of the years by comparing them to a more

acceptable treatment of bad debts. If you were evaluating the company's operations as a potential investor, which method of accounting for uncollectible accounts would you prefer the company to use? Explain.

P8-45 Analyzing the Allowance for Uncollectibles Cranberry Products, Ltd., reported the following account balances at January 1, 2000, and December 31, 2000, respectively:

Item	January 1, 2000	December 31, 2000
Sales		$850,000
Accounts receivable	$140,000	90,000
Allowance for uncollectibles	15,000	19,300
Bad debt expense		25,500

All of Cranberry Products, Ltd., sales are made on credit. The company uses the allowance method of accounting for bad debts.

a. Prepare an analysis of the allowance for uncollectibles account for 2000. Based on the information given, what amount of accounts receivable was determined to be uncollectible in 2000 and written off?
b. Give the journal entry for:
   1. Sales for 2000.
   2. Recording of bad debt expense for 2000.
   3. The write-off of uncollectible accounts receivable for 2000.
   4. The receipt of cash from collection of accounts receivable for 2000.
c. Evaluate the adequacy of the Allowance for Uncollectibles at December 31, 2000.
d. In the event a review by management concluded that the balance in the Allowance for Uncollectibles at December 31, 2000, should be $9,300, what entry would be needed to adjust the account balances to the appropriate totals?

P8-46 Evaluating Accounts Receivable Balances Ready Manufacturing made credit sales of $650,000 during the 12-month period ending June 30, 2000. At June 30, the company prepared the following aging schedule:

Receivable Amount	Number of Days Outstanding	Estimated Percent That Will Be Collected
$170,000	Less than 30	95%
60,000	31–60	92
40,000	61–90	90
80,000	More than 90	75

The Allowance for Uncollectibles on the company's books at June 30 is $13,000. Assuming the estimated percentages used for aging are considered correct:

a. What adjustment, if any, is needed to bring the allowance for uncollectibles to the desired level? Give the journal entry needed to accomplish the desired change.

b. The sales manager of Ready Manufacturing feels the company would increase sales if it extended its normal collection cycle by 30 days and sold on terms of 2/10, n/60 rather than its existing terms of 2/10, n/30. Should the president accept or reject the recommendation? Why? What factors should be considered?

c. What suggestions would you make with regard to the management of accounts receivable by Ready Manufacturing?

P8-47 Maintaining Control of Accounts Receivable
The vice president of finance of K. Boom Chemical Company became concerned upon discovery that $76,000 of accounts receivable had been written off as uncollectible during the fiscal year ended May 31, 2000, and that an allowance for uncollectibles in the amount of $48,000 was needed to cover expected losses on accounts receivable at year-end. The manager of the accounts receivable department explained that the company had not previously done an aging schedule for its accounts receivable and that when one was done, the allowance for uncollectibles was much too small and an adjustment was needed.

The following journal entries were recorded to establish bad debt expense at 4 percent of the $400,000 of credit sales and to record the write-off of accounts receivable during the year:

Bad Debt Expense	16,000	
Allowance for Uncollectibles		16,000
Allowance for Uncollectibles	76,000	
Accounts Receivable		76,000

An additional entry to adjust bad debt expense and the Allowance for Uncollectibles at the end of the year was made as follows:

Bad Debt Expense	108,000	
Allowance for Uncollectibles		108,000

In early June, a number of irate customers called, saying they had been told they must pay in advance for all purchases from K. Boom Chemical because of failure to pay past bills. The customers claimed to have paid in full. The company also noticed that the manager of the accounts receivable department had not been to work for nearly 2 weeks and there was no answer on his home phone.

a. What was the ratio of bad debt expense to sales for 2000 for K. Boom Chemical? Is the vice president right to be concerned?

b. What action by the manager of accounts receivable might explain the apparent problem with accounts receivable?

c. Assume that a search of the accounts receivable written off as bad debts indicated that an initial bill and one follow-up bill had been sent. No further efforts had been made to collect from customers. What other actions might a company take to avoid such large bad debt losses?

d. If the company unexpectedly recovered $25,000 of receivables that had been written off earlier in the year, how should the company account for the recovery?

P8-48 Evaluating Cash Discounts The sales representative of Paper Corporation has just left your office. Although you have done business with Paper Corporation for many years, you think it might be better to purchase supplies from Discount Office Supplies. You normally purchase $80,000 of supplies per month from Paper Corporation, but Discount Office Supplies has offered identical merchandise for $78,000. A small inconvenience will be associated with purchasing from Discount Office Supplies in that a cashier's check for the full amount of the purchase must be given to the delivery person when the goods are received. Paper Corporation permits payment on a 2/10, net 30 basis.

a. Which supplier should be used? Explain.

b. Would your decision change if Paper Corporation offered terms of 3/10, net 20? Explain.

P8-49 Trading Securities Bark Company invested in the following securities:

Date of Purchase	Name of Company	Amount Paid	Market Price Dec. 31, 2000	Market Price Dec. 31, 2001
Feb., 2000	Short	$80,000	$70,000	$72,000
Mar., 2000	Long	45,000	40,000	56,000
Jun., 2000	Medium	22,000	32,000	25,000

All of the securities are common stock and all are considered to be trading securities by Bark Company. Bark Company received no dividends from its investments in 2000; however, dividends of $7,000, $1,000, and $1,400 were received from Short, Long, and Medium, respectively, during 2001.

The chair of the executive committee of Bark Company decides she needs more information to determine whether or not the company should continue to invest excess cash in this manner. You are asked to:

a. Compute the amount of net income reported each year, assuming Bark Company reported operating earnings (excluding income from investments) of $90,000 in 2000 and $110,000 in 2001.

b. Explain why taking into consideration both the dividends received and the change in market value is important in evaluating the performance of equity securities classified as trading securities.

P8-50   Valuation of Securities   Portal Company had excess cash and invested in the following securities:

1. 300 shares of Diamond Company were purchased for $60 each. A dividend of $4 per share was received and the market price per share was $82 at year-end. The shares were classified as available-for-sale securities.
2. 150 shares of Emerald Company were purchased for $100 each. A dividend of $5 per share was received and the market price was $130 per share at year-end. The shares were classified as trading securities.

3. 400 shares of Ruby Company were purchased for $20 per share and classified as available-for-sale securities. No dividends were received during the year. The market price at year-end was $25 per share.
4. 1,000 shares of Sapphire Company were purchased for $15 per share and classified as trading securities. Dividends of $2.50 per share were received during the year. The year-end market price was $12 per share.

a. What amount of dividend income will be reported by Portal for the year?
b. What is the total dollar value of investments in securities to be reported by Portal in its year-end balance sheet?
c. What is the net unrealized gain or loss on investments to be reported in Portal's income statement for the year?
d. What will be the amount of the total increase in owners' equity resulting from Portal's ownership of the four securities? Show computations.

EXPANDING YOUR HORIZONS

C8-51   Analyzing Gateway   Using the information in Gateway's annual report shown in Appendix A, answer each of the following:

a. Is it possible to determine the amount of cash on hand and in the bank from the balance sheet data?
b. What types of assets does Gateway classify as cash equivalents? What is the longest acceptable date to maturity for investments classified as cash equivalents?
c. What was the total amount of financial assets reported for 1998? Did the amount reported increase or decrease from 1997? By what amount?
d. What was the total amount of cash and cash equivalents generated from operations in 1998? Did the amount increase or decrease over 1997?
e. Was the net increase in cash and cash equivalents during 1998 more than or less than the net cash and cash equivalents reported as provided by operations? What specific activities other than operations either generated additional cash or used cash during 1998?
f. Compare accounts receivable at the end of 1997 and 1998. Was there an increase or decrease? What was the amount?
g. Did the net amount reported as accounts receivable increase or decrease as a percent of sales and total assets in 1998 over 1997? Are these changes desirable or undesirable? Explain why.

C8-52   Managing Financial Assets   Snappy Biscuit Company reported the following financial assets in its balance sheets at December 31, 2001 and 2002:

	12/31/02	12/31/01
Cash	$ 22,000	$ 75,000
Cash Equivalents	120,000	50,000
Accounts Receivable	450,000	270,000
Less: Allowance for Uncollectibles	(125,000)	(12,000)
Notes Receivable	380,000	190,000
Investment in Trading Securities	60,000	150,000
Total	$907,000	$723,000

After reviewing the reported results, you are asked to respond to the following policy questions by the management of Snappy Biscuit Company:

a. During 2002, the company adopted a policy of investing all cash not expected to be needed within four working days. As a result, the reported cash balance has declined substantially and the controller has sometimes had to delay making payment on accounts payable because there was not enough cash in the checking account to cover checks that needed to be written that day. Evaluate the desirability of this policy.
b. Snappy has adopted a new compensation policy for sales representatives under which sales personnel are compensated based primarily on sales. The company is very pleased because sales increased from $750,000 to $1,650,000 during 2002. How would you evaluate the re-

sults of its change in policy? What negative effects might the policy have?

c. Because some of its customers have had trouble paying for their purchases promptly, Snappy adopted a policy in early 2002 of converting accounts receivable into notes receivable, with an annual interest rate of 5 percent, and allowing the companies to take advantage of their sales discounts. Snappy's normal terms of sale are 2/10, n/30. Evaluate the results of Snappy's policy.

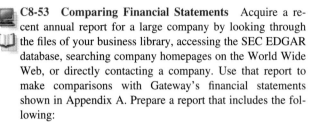 **C8-53 Comparing Financial Statements** Acquire a recent annual report for a large company by looking through the files of your business library, accessing the SEC EDGAR database, searching company homepages on the World Wide Web, or directly contacting a company. Use that report to make comparisons with Gateway's financial statements shown in Appendix A. Prepare a report that includes the following:

a. Compare the number of different types of financial assets reported in the balance sheets of the companies and the way in which they have been summarized and described.

b. Compare the amount of financial assets reported by each company. Which of the two companies has the greater amount of financial assets reported?

c. Review the notes to the financial statements of the companies. Do they have similar or different supplemental information on financial assets in their notes? Which company's disclosure do you feel is most useful? Explain why.

d. Go to your library and select a company listed in *Moody's Industrial Manual*. Compare the amount of information and the form of disclosure about financial assets for the company from *Moody's* with that presented in the financial statements of the other two companies. Which company's information do you find to be the most useful? Explain why. When would the information contained in *Moody's* be more useful than that contained in the financial statements?

C8-54 Quaker Oats—The Positive Side of Negative Cash Selected account balances reported in the balance sheet of Quaker Oats are as follows (in millions of dollars):

	1998	**1997**
Cash and cash equivalents	326.6	84.2
Accounts payable	168.4	191.3
Total current assets	1,115.0	1,133.0
Total current liabilities	1,009.1	945.7

A footnote disclosure from the annual report describes the accounting for cash and cash equivalents:

Cash and Cash Equivalents—Cash equivalents are composed of all highly liquid investments with an original

maturity of three months or less. As a result of the Company's cash management system, checks issued but not presented to the banks for payment may create negative book cash balances. Such negative balances are included in trade accounts payable and totaled $40.8 million and $45.1 million as of December 31, 1998 and 1997, respectively.

Based on the information presented, answer the following questions:

a. The balance sheets indicated that Quaker Oats had positive cash balances, yet the footnote disclosures indicated negative cash balances. How can this be?

b. Explain in general terms the company's cash management system as it relates to payments and the issuance of checks. Why does this lead to the confusion surrounding whether cash balances are positive or negative? (*Hint*: Draw a time line of events relating to the payment of invoices received and indicate the accounting entries the company makes at different points along the line.)

c. If the checks not yet presented to the banks for payment had not been reclassified as accounts payable, what cash balances would Quaker Oats have shown in its balance sheets? How would the amount of working capital reported each year have been different? How would the current ratios have been different each year?

d. Is the company's reporting approach reasonable given the nature of its cash management system? Explain.

C8-55 Sprint's Uncollectibles The following selected information is taken from the financial statements of Sprint Corporation (in millions of dollars):

	1998	**1997**	**1996**
Accounts Receivable (net)	2,384.3	2,495.6	2,343.6
Allowance for Doubtful Accounts	174.8	146.7	117.4
Accounts Written Off	339.4	363.6	255.4
Uncollectible Accounts Expense	364.9	388.9	248.5
Net Operating Revenues	16,016.9	14,873.9	13,887.5

Based on the information from Sprint's financial statements, answer the following questions:

a. What percentage of total accounts receivable is considered uncollectible in each of the three years presented?

b. What percentage of sales is bad debt expense in each of the three years presented?

c. Did Sprint's collection of accounts receivable improve over the 3-year period? Explain.

d. The cloning of cellular phones currently is a serious problem. Cloning involves copying access/billing codes from cellular phones belonging to others. Cellular phone companies typically absorb charges for unauthorized calls on cellular phones, amounts involving many millions of dollars. If cloning continues to be a problem as cellular business grows, how would this affect the financial statements of a company like Sprint?

C8-56 Team Project: Analyzing Financial Statements Acquire the financial statements of a large manufacturing company, such as General Motors, a large electric or gas utility company, such as Duke Energy Corporation or Ameren Corporation (previously Union Electric Company), and a large bank, such as Wells Fargo & Company. Prepare a short report in which you include the following:

a. Do an in-depth analysis of the cash and other financial asset balances held by each company. Be sure to review the balance sheet accounts and all related footnotes.
b. Look at the cash flow statements to see if you can determine the major sources of cash inflows and outflows during the past year. Did the companies borrow money during the year? Did they issue stock?
c. Make a list comparing the operating characteristics of the companies that might affect the amount of financial assets they would have on hand. For example, which of the three businesses would be likely to have the most dependable and predictable cash inflows and outflows? Which of the companies would realize most of its profits from holding financial assets?
d. Compare the cash and financial asset balances and inflows and outflows of the companies for the last 2 years. Are the balances reported consistent with the expectations you developed in the preceding step? Review the management discussion that precedes the financial statements to see if you are able to find explanations for any situations that are not consistent with your expectations.
e. Analyze the bad debt expense reported by each of the companies during the last 2 years. Are there major differences between the companies? Are these differences in the amounts reported consistent with your list of operating characteristics? Explain why any differences may have occurred.

C8-57 Accounting and Ethical Behavior The Santos Company pays its sales representatives a commission on each sale. The rate of commission is in accordance with the following schedule:

Sales Level	Commission Rates	Maximum Commission
$1 to $1,000,000	1% on all sales	$ 10,000
to $5,000,000	1.5% on all sales	75,000
to $10,000,000	2% on all sales	200,000
over $10,000,000	4% on all sales	None, minimum 400,000

Sales representatives occasionally reach the $5 million sales level. Until this year, no one has ever reached the $10 million level. Barbara Barnes is about to close a $2 million deal that would increase her sales total for the year to just over $10 million. Not only will it be the biggest order she has ever taken, she will get a commission of 4 percent ($80,000) on the $2 million sale. Also, even more significantly, all her commissions for the year will be paid at the 4 percent level, an increase of $160,000 in commissions on her prior sales [$8,000,000 × (.04 − .02)].

There is just one small problem. Barbara is not sure the customer wants all $2 million of the order, and she is not sure it will be able to pay for the order if its business does not increase. She knows that the customer would much rather contract for a sale of only $1 million. But, on the other hand, it might really need all $2 million, and the extra $160,000 of commission would get Barbara the house she would like to buy. Santos has a fairly liberal return policy, and her customer could just return some of the merchandise next year if it bought too much. Maybe if it returned just a little each month, that wouldn't look too bad. Also, Santos's credit manager relies a lot on the sales representatives when granting credit, and if Barbara says the customer is acceptable, the credit will probably be granted. The company also wants the sales revenue. What should Barbara do? What should Santos do?

Internet Exercises: Visit our Web site for additional exercises.

Annual Report Project Part 8

Refer to the Annual Report Project, Part 1, at the end of Chapter 1. Using the annual report of the company you have chosen, and any other available information, answer the following questions, providing sources and computations where appropriate.

a. What is the amount of your company's allowance for uncollectible accounts, if disclosed? Has that amount changed in relation to total accounts receivable over the past year?

b. Based on ending accounts receivable, assess your company's accounts receivable turnover as compared with last year.

c. Does your company report any receivables other than normal trade receivables from customers? If so, describe those receivables.

d. Does your company hold any investments other than short-term marketable securities classified as cash equivalents? If so, describe these investments and how income (including gains and losses) from these investments is reported.

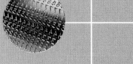

CHAPTER NINE

Prepaid Expenses and Inventories

REVIEW

Chapters 4 and 6 introduced the basic principles of accounting for and reporting assets. Chapter 8 provided more detail about the principles and rules that apply to financial assets and investments.

WHERE THIS CHAPTER FITS

This chapter continues the discussion by focusing on current nonfinancial assets. For these assets, determining cost and then matching that cost with the benefits provided are the key concepts on which financial reporting is based.

LOOKING AHEAD

Chapter 10 completes the examination of assets by discussing operating assets.

I was going to have someone special over for dinner the other night—fix one of my gourmet creations, something exotic. But, when I went to the cupboard, the shelves were bare. I had forgotten that I didn't buy any food the past two weeks because I was low on money, and I didn't want the stuff to sit around getting stale, anyway. Then I went to the store, and I couldn't find any of the special stuff I needed. Seemed like they were out of everything. I don't understand why the stores can't keep their shelves filled all the time. They should buy extra inventory so they never run out.

"Day Runner [North America's top maker of address books and organizers] said . . . it lost $5.2 million . . . in the three months ended June 30 . . . as several major U.S. customers tightened their inventories and cut back orders. The company said it restated results for the first three quarters because of accounting errors that resulted in overstated inventory and understated costs of goods sold."[1]

[1] "Day Runner Ready to Answer Acquisition Bids," *Los Angeles Times* (September 1, 1999), Part C, p 3.

I ndividuals depend on nonfinancial assets, such as their homes, appliances, cars, computers, and even their groceries, to lead happy and productive lives. Similarly, businesses, such as manufacturers and merchandisers, need buildings in which to operate, merchandise to sell, equipment to produce and deliver the merchandise, furniture for their employees, fixtures for displaying goods, and patents to protect their ideas. Although service companies and financial institutions depend less heavily on nonfinancial assets, even they need buildings, equipment, furniture, fixtures, and supplies.

In this chapter, we continue our examination of assets by dealing with nonfinancial assets. We focus on the importance of the matching concept in the treatment of these assets and discuss valuation in relation to the information needs of decision makers. We then discuss two types of nonfinancial assets, prepaid expenses and inventories, in more depth, with the other nonfinancial assets discussed in Chapter 10. After completing this chapter, you should be able to:

1. Describe the role that nonfinancial assets held by businesses play in operations.

2. Identify the different methods used to value nonfinancial assets, and describe how the different methods relate to the types of decisions made.

3. Explain how the matching concept is applied to accounting and reporting for nonfinancial assets, and why this is important for decision making.

4. Describe prepaid expenses and how they relate to decision making.

5. Describe the methods used to value and account for inventories, and explain how they help decision makers better assess a company's activities and financial position.

NONFINANCIAL ASSETS AND THEIR VALUATION

Information for Decisions

Nonfinancial assets are the earning assets of a business. Information about these assets helps investors and creditors assess a company's earning capacity and future potential. Financial statement information can help answer questions such as these: What amount of nonfinancial assets does the company hold, and what do the assigned dollar amounts imply about those assets? Which of the assets are to be sold or used in the ordinary course of business within the next operating cycle? Are the company's assets invested in a profitable manner? Are sufficient assets available for creditors in the event of a loan default?

Nonfinancial assets are either held for sale to others in the normal course of business or they are used in the company's operations. Nonfinancial assets include all assets except cash, receivables, and investments.

Most nonfinancial assets are tangible, meaning they have physical existence, but some are intangible, such as rights that are purchased. Nonfinancial assets are sold, consumed, or used in operations. They may be classified as either current or noncurrent, depending on whether they are expected to be sold or consumed within one year or the operating cycle of the business, whichever is longer. Typical nonfinancial assets are as follows:

Current assets:	Prepaid expenses, inventory
Noncurrent assets:	Land, buildings, equipment, furniture and fixtures, intangibles

Nonfinancial assets are typically valued in the balance sheet based on historical cost. If, when a cost is initially incurred, it is expected to provide future benefits, it is **capitalized**, or recorded as an asset. Any cost that is not expected to provide future benefits cannot be capitalized and must be expensed or written off as a loss. Because nonfinancial assets are expected to provide future benefits, the cost is capitalized when the assets are acquired.

After acquisition, some nonfinancial assets continue to be valued at original cost, while the valuation of others might change, depending on the information considered most useful for decision makers. Typical bases for valuing nonfinancial assets in the balance sheet are as follows:

Asset	Valuation Basis
Prepaid expenses	Cost not yet allocated
Inventory	Cost or market value, whichever is lower
Tangible operating assets:	
Land	Cost
Buildings	Cost not yet allocated
Equipment	Cost not yet allocated
Furniture and fixtures	Cost not yet allocated
Intangibles:	
Research and development costs (not treated as an asset)	None (cost is expensed as incurred)
Other intangibles	Cost not yet allocated

For most nonfinancial assets, valuation is based on cost. However, the specific valuation method will depend on the nature of the asset and its intended use.

SEARS, ROEBUCK AND CO.

In its 1993 annual report, Sears included the following note about the valuation of its real estate:

Real estate
Operating properties are carried at cost net of accumulated depreciation. Properties are carried at the lower of cost or net realizable value when the Company no longer plans to retain the properties.

ANALYSIS

Sears reorganized its merchandising business in 1992 and planned to sell some of its real estate. Because real estate was being held for sale rather than for use, the market value became relevant. It then was valued like inventory rather than as property in use. The intended use of an asset influences which valuation method provides the most useful information for decision makers. [www.sears.com]

REPORTING NONFINANCIAL ASSETS: THE MATCHING CONCEPT APPLIED

Information for Decisions

Under the matching process, costs that are expected to provide future benefits are reported as assets in the balance sheet. Those costs are then transferred from the balance sheet to the income statement and are reported as expenses in the period in which the associated benefits are received. A knowledge of financial reporting practices regarding nonfinancial assets will help financial statement users answer questions such as these: How have the company's asset values and income been affected by the company's treatment of costs, and what effect will this have on future income? How does the company treat finance charges associated with borrowing money to acquire nonfinancial assets, and what is the effect on current and future income? Are the company's income and cash flows both affected in the same manner by expenses associated with nonfinancial assets?

Nonfinancial assets are recorded at historical cost when acquired. After acquisition, the initial cost of a nonfinancial asset is matched with the benefits it provides. Before a matching can take place, however, the first step is to determine what amounts should be included in the initial cost.

DETERMINING COST

The key to understanding what is included in the cost of an asset is identifying those costs a company must incur to acquire the asset and get it in the location and condition so the company can do with the asset what it intends. Only costs that are necessary to get the desired benefits from the asset are recorded as the asset's cost. With that in mind, the following items may be relevant in determining the total cost of an asset:

- *Invoice price*—the amount billed to the purchaser; this usually is the starting point for determining cost.
- *Discounts*—reductions in the amount that must be paid to acquire an asset; cost, therefore, is based on the amount that has to be paid after subtracting discounts.
- *Freight*—shipping charges the purchaser must pay to get an asset to where it is wanted.
- *Manufacturing costs*—the costs of producing inventory or changing its form.
- *Preparation costs*—the costs of getting an asset ready to use or sell, such as the cost of packaging inventory or readying a machine or building for use.
- *Transfer costs*—costs associated with conveying legal possession, including transfer taxes, filing fees, and legal fees.

Finance charges associated with borrowing money to acquire an asset represent a cost of borrowing money rather than a cost that must be incurred to acquire an asset (because the asset could be acquired for cash). Therefore, they are not included in the cost of the asset for most asset acquisitions.

A CLOSER LOOK AT

DETERMINING COST

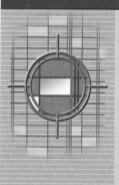

Butler Company purchases equipment with a list price of $459,500, but receives a trade discount of $50,000. The company pays all shipping charges, totaling $2,000. A special crew is hired from the labor hall at a cost of $1,800 to move the equipment into the appropriate place in the factory, and preparation and testing of the machine cost another $800. The recorded cost of the equipment is determined as follows:

List price	$459,500
Less trade discount	(50,000)
Invoice price	$409,500
Shipping	2,000
Installation and preparation ($1,800 + $800)	2,600
Recorded cost of equipment	$414,100

The cost of all nonfinancial assets is determined in the same way, although the specific elements included in cost may vary for different types of assets. Because no cost can be capitalized unless it is expected to provide a future benefit, the asset costs reported in a company's balance sheet indicate that those assets are expected to provide future benefits at least equal to the amounts reported.

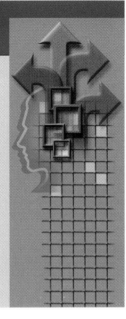

IS IT COST, IS IT EXPENSE, OR IS IT JUST PLAIN FUN?

Your company is considering buying a printing press to produce your own direct-mail advertising. While on vacation in Europe, you see a new, efficient printing press that would be perfect for your company. You bring a description back with you and, after several phone calls, decide to buy the machine. To help your accountant determine the cost of the printing press, you prepare the following summary:

Invoice price (in dollars)	$80,000
Discount from invoice for cash payment	10%
Shipping costs from Germany	9,000
Cost of converting dollars to German marks	200
Your European vacation costs	7,500
Costs to bolt press to floor and adjust	6,000
Fees for registering a foreign purchase	300

What cost should be recorded for the printing press? Explain.

MATCHING COSTS AND BENEFITS

After a nonfinancial asset has been recorded in the accounts, what happens to its cost? Once recorded, the cost is treated in accordance with the matching concept. The cost of the asset must be matched against the benefits it provides. Thus, as shown in Exhibit 9–1, the entire process of accounting for nonfinancial assets is one of recording the original cost as an asset, and then recognizing the expired cost as an expense in the income statement in the period or periods in which it provides benefits.

The matching process is the same for all nonfinancial assets, although the specific accounting procedures and financial statement presentations may vary for different types. For example, inventory is reported in the balance sheet until it provides a benefit at the time it is sold. Then it is reported in the income statement as an expense; the cost of the inventory (cost of goods sold) is matched with the benefit, sales revenue. Similarly, the cost of a delivery truck is reported in the balance sheet as an asset, but as the company benefits from its use, a portion of the cost is reported as an expense (depreciation) in the income statement in each period in which the truck is used. For a proper matching of costs and benefits, the original cost of the asset, the type of benefits expected to be provided, and the period or periods in which the benefits are expected to be received all must be identified. This matching process facilitates decision making by providing a comparison of costs and resulting benefits.

Let's now look at how the valuation and matching concepts discussed are applied to individual assets, starting with prepaid expenses and inventories. As you examine individual types of assets in this chapter and Chapter 10, focus on the similarities in the way initial asset valuations are determined and asset costs are matched against benefits.

EXHIBIT 9-1	**ALLOCATING COSTS: THE MATCHING PROCESS**	
Transaction	**Balance Sheet Effect**	**Income Statement Effect**
1. Inventory		
Purchase inventory on account	Increase inventory Increase accounts payable	
Sell inventory on account	Increase accounts receivable Decrease inventory	Increase sales Increase cost of goods sold
2. Prepaid Insurance		
Purchase insurance	Increase prepaid insurance Decrease cash	
Insurance coverage for period	Decrease prepaid insurance	Increase insurance expense
3. Equipment		
Purchase equipment	Increase equipment Decrease cash	
Use equipment during period	Increase accumulated depreciation	Increase depreciation expense

PREPAID EXPENSES AND SUPPLIES

Information for Decisions

Expenses that are paid in advance are not reported as expenses in the income statement in the current period. Rather, they will be reported as expenses in later periods when they provide benefits. Investors and creditors should be aware of the effect of prepayments so they can answer questions such as these: Did the level of prepayments change this year, and, if so, what effect does it have on net income and cash flows? What effect does a large, unusual prepayment have on the company's net income and cash flow for the current and future periods? Can the company reduce prepaid expenses to improve cash flows?

Prepaid expenses are future operating costs that have already been paid. Although the cash payment has already been made, the benefits will be received in future periods. The most common examples are payments made in advance for rent and insurance. Because the cash payment entitles the company to receive some benefit in the future, an asset is reported for the amount of the prepayment, the cost of the future benefit. As the benefit is received and the future service potential of the cost expires, the cost is transferred from being treated as an asset (unexpired cost) in the balance sheet to being reported as an expense (expired cost) in the income statement. This provides decision makers with a picture of the firm's income-producing activities based on a matching of costs and benefits rather than when the cash is paid.

A CLOSER LOOK AT

ACCOUNTING FOR PREPAID EXPENSES

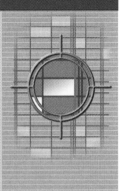

Bullen Company operates on a calendar-year basis. On December 1, 2000, the company enters into a one-year rental agreement for a storage facility and agrees to pay the full rent of $12,000 immediately. Although one month of the agreement falls within the current year, eleven months fall in the next fiscal year. Accordingly, one-twelfth of the $12,000 rental cost should be recognized as an expense in 2000, with the remainder recognized in 2001. Bullen records $12,000 of prepaid rent, a current asset, when the cash payment is made. At the end of 2000, the company recognizes the expiration of one-twelfth of the prepaid rent by taking $1,000 out of the Prepaid Rent account and putting it in the Rent Expense account. By doing this, the company reports rent expense of $1,000 for 2000 and prepaid rent as an $11,000 asset at year-end. During 2001, the remaining $11,000 of prepaid rent expires by providing its remaining benefits during the year, and it is reported as rent expense in the 2001 income statement. In summary, the following amounts are reported in the financial statements for 2000 and 2001:

Income Statement Effects		
2000 Expenses	+	1,000
Net Income	−	1,000
2001 Expenses	+	11,000
Net Income	−	11,000

Balance Sheet Effects		
2000 Assets	+	12,000
Assets	−	12,000
Assets	−	1,000
Owners Equity	−	1,000
2001 Assets	−	11,000
Owners' Equity	−	11,000

Balance Sheet		**Income Statement**	
December 31, 2000		2000	
Assets:		Expenses:	
Prepaid rent	$11,000	Rent expense	$1,000
December 31, 2001		2001	
Assets:		Expenses:	
Prepaid rent	-0-	Rent expense	$11,000

Journal Entry: December 1, 2000

Prepaid Rent	12,000	
Cash		12,000

Adjusting Entry: December 31, 2000

Rent Expense	1,000	
Prepaid Rent		1,000

Adjusting Entry: December 31, 2001

Rent Expense	11,000	
Prepaid Rent		11,000

Prepaid expenses are usually classified as current assets and involve payments relating to relatively short periods of time. Prepayments that do not meet the criteria for classification as current should be classified as other assets or deferred charges. The **deferred charges** category on the balance sheet might include long-term prepayments and other balance sheet items with debit balances that do not fit neatly in other categories.

Prepaid expenses are usually small in amount and, accordingly, have little effect on decisions. However, sometimes prepayments may be substantial, and these can be important because they reflect cash amounts that will not have to be paid in the future. Thus, they have a direct bearing on assessments of future cash outflows. In most cases, large prepayments are classified as deferred charges because they relate to more than one period.

Prepaid expenses are valued at historical cost at acquisition, as are other purchases. Because the cost is amortized, or allocated to the periods benefiting from it, the amount reported on the balance sheet is the unamortized or unallocated cost.

In Practice 9-2

INTERNATIONAL BUSINESS MACHINES CORPORATION (IBM)

IBM reports the following prepaid expenses in 1998 and 1997 as one item of total current assets:

(in millions)	1998	1997
Prepaid expenses and other current assets	$4,611	$3,900

These amounts are 11 percent and 10 percent of total current assets.

ANALYSIS

On IBM's balance sheets, the amount of prepaid expenses and other current assets is larger than two other items reported as current assets. Marketable securities is one of the smaller items, $393 million in 1998 and $447 million in 1997. However, while footnotes report details about the types of marketable securities held and their valuation, no such information is provided for prepaid expenses. Why? Apparently, the definition and content of the prepaid expense account is clear and understandable without additional disclosure. [www.ibm.com]

You Decide 9-2

HOW MUCH INSURANCE SHOULD YOU BUY?

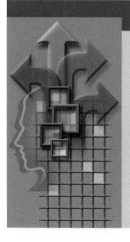

You have been assigned the responsibility of selecting an insurance company to write the product liability insurance policy for your company. You have found two companies that will sell you a policy. One, Ace Insurance, offers a three-year policy for $100,000 per year, with all $300,000 payable in advance. The other, Boca Insurance, offers a similar three-year policy for $115,000 per year, payable at the beginning of each of the three years. You present both offers to your manager and recommend Ace. Your manager says "No! The company's income is down this year so we can't have $300,000 of insurance expense. We will have to choose Boca and report just $115,000 of insurance expense this year." How much expense will be shown in the first year income statement under each policy? How can you convince your manager to choose Ace? What considerations are relevant?

Note that the amount reported in the balance sheet for prepaid expenses does not necessarily indicate that cash in that amount can be generated by liquidating the asset. In fact, many prepaid expenses will fetch little or nothing in a liquidation. Consistent with the going-concern assumption, prepaid expenses are valued at historical cost not yet allocated because they are expected to be used up in operations rather than being sold. Thus, the valuation indicates the cost of services and rights acquired that will not require the use of cash in the future.

For office supplies and other goods that are consumed in normal operations, the accounting treatment is virtually identical to that given prepaid expenses. And, as with prepaid expenses, the dollar amounts are typically small.

INVENTORIES

Information for Decisions

Merchandising and manufacturing companies exist to sell their inventories at a profit. Financial statement users need to know how a company values its inventory and how it assigns inventory costs so they can answer questions such as these: Are the company's inventory levels appropriate for its anticipated operations? How do the company's inventory levels and turnover compare with those of other companies in the industry and with those of last year? How is income of the current and future periods affected by the methods the company uses to account for its inventory? How do the company's inventory accounting methods affect the quality of its earnings and comparability with other companies? Did the company manufacture or purchase more inventory than it could sell this year?

Inventories are one of the most important assets of merchandising and manufacturing companies. These types of companies exist to sell their goods and typically need to carry inventories to operate effectively. For example, if goods are immediately available to customers, there is less likelihood of customers purchasing from competitors or substituting other products. And, for some types of companies, such as retail stores, displaying more merchandise leads to "impulse buying," with customers seeing and purchasing items they might not otherwise buy.

From a manufacturing viewpoint, large production runs or purchases of materials might lead to economies of scale resulting in lower costs. Further, maintaining inventories of materials needed for production can often prevent shutdowns when supplies are interrupted. For example, strikes by coal miners and automotive parts production workers have threatened serious production disruptions for their companies' customers. Sometimes large inventory holdings can be used to reduce the effects of expected future price increases, such as when the price of paper doubled in 1994.

On the other hand, carrying large amounts of inventory is expensive. Cash used to buy inventory cannot be invested elsewhere to earn a return. Companies also incur other carrying costs for inventory, such as the cost of insurance, storage, and security. Further, carrying large amounts of inventories can lead to significant inventory shrinkage from obsolescence, deterioration, and theft. Accordingly, as reflected in Exhibit 9–2, companies must balance the costs of carrying inventory against the costs of not having inventory when needed.

To reduce inventory carrying costs, many companies have taken steps to reduce their inventory levels. For example, many companies now use just-in-time inventory methods, tak-

EXHIBIT 9-2 **BALANCING INVENTORY CARRYING COSTS AGAINST LOST SALES**

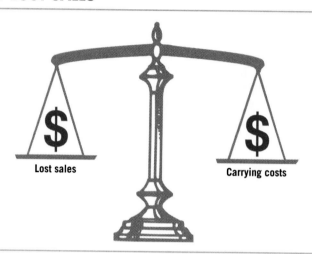

Lost sales   Carrying costs

ing delivery of inventories almost at the moment they are needed. While cost-efficient, the dangers of such an approach became evident following a major earthquake in Kobe, Japan. Kobe is the home of many just-in-time suppliers, and numerous industries, such as automobile manufacturers, faced immediate supply shortages following the earthquake. Other companies eliminate inventories altogether by simply taking orders and having shipments made directly from suppliers to customers.

INVENTORY EVALUATION MEASURES

When analyzing the efficiency of a company, an important factor is whether it carries an appropriate amount of inventory. Of course, the amount of inventory may vary with the size and type of a company's operations. Some types of inventories can be expected to be sold or "turned over" more quickly than others. For example, fresh produce must be sold faster than automobiles or clothing. **Inventory turnover** is one indicator of a company's efficiency with respect to inventory and is computed by dividing the cost of goods sold expense reported in the income statement by the inventory amount reported in the company's balance sheet.[2] If, for example, a company reported cost of goods sold of $3 million and held inventory of $1 million, its inventory turnover can be computed as follows:

$$\text{Inventory Turnover} = \frac{\text{Cost of Goods Sold}}{\text{Inventory Balance}} = \frac{\$3,000,000}{\$1,000,000} = 3.0$$

In effect, the company sells its entire inventory three times during the year. This figure can be compared with those of other companies in the same industry or with industry averages. A company with a low turnover in relation to similar companies, or in comparison with prior years, may have poor inventory management practices or large amounts of obsolete or damaged goods.

[2] Because inventories held at year-end may not be representative of a company's normal inventory levels during the year, turnover should be computed using average inventory levels throughout the year. However, this information may not be available to financial statement users except through company filings with the SEC.

In Practice 9-3

ALBERTO-CULVER'S INVENTORY TURNOVER

For 1997, Alberto-Culver Company and Subsidiaries reported sales of $1,775,258,000, an increase of $184,849,000, or more than 11 percent, over 1996. Costs of products sold increased by $75,336,000 to $880,416,000, an increase of just over 9 percent. Inventory on hand increased by $55,343,000, over 19 percent, and inventory turnover, based on ending inventory, decreased from 2.79 to 2.56.

ANALYSIS

Even though sales increased more than 11 percent at Alberto-Culver, the inventory on hand increased proportionally even more, and inventory efficiency was a little lower in 1997. Several years before, the company had introduced a new inventory management system for its Sally Beauty Company subsidiary, and inventory turnover had increased somewhat. The turnover drop in 1997, however, exceeded gains in the previous few years. [www.alberto-culver.com]

Another measure related to inventory that often signals important information to financial statement users is the gross profit percentage. As we discussed in Chapter 5, a company's gross profit, or gross margin, is equal to its sales revenue minus its cost of goods sold. For manufacturing and merchandising companies, the gross profit may make the difference between success and failure. If the selling price of a company's product is too low given its cost, or, conversely, if the cost of the company's inventory is too high given the price for which it can be sold, the gross profit may be too small to cover other costs the company incurs. This will significantly affect the profit or loss recognized by the company. Thus, for many companies, the relationship between sales revenue and cost of goods sold is crucial. So that comparisons with other companies in the same industry, but of different size, can be made, this relationship is often measured as a percentage. The **gross profit percentage** (gross margin percentage) is computed as the gross profit (margin) divided by net sales revenue. If, for example, a company reported net sales of $5,000,000 and cost of goods sold of $3,000,000, its gross profit would be $2,000,000 ($5,000,000 − $3,000,000). The gross profit percentage can be computed as follows:

$$\text{Gross Profit Percentage} = \frac{\text{Gross Profit}}{\text{Net Sales}} = \frac{\$2,000,000}{\$5,000,000} = 40 \text{ percent}$$

This percentage can be compared with the gross profit percentage from previous years or for other companies in the same industry. A low gross profit percentage could indicate that the company's profit margins are being "squeezed" by the competition or that the company is operating inefficiently in purchasing or manufacturing its inventory. On the other hand, a high gross profit percentage could indicate that the company holds some special advantage that attracts customers to pay a higher price for the company's product, or that the company is especially efficient in purchasing or manufacturing its inventory.

VALUATION OF INVENTORIES

For merchandising companies, inventory is, perhaps, the most important asset because the enterprise's existence depends on selling that merchandise. Therefore, the valuation of that inventory is important to investors, creditors, and other decision makers. If inventory is over-valued, future revenues may be impaired and inventory values may never be realized in a liquidation.

Consistent with the valuation of other nonfinancial assets, inventory is generally valued initially at its cost. As the matching concept is applied, this cost is matched with the benefits it provides by recognizing sales revenue and the related cost of goods sold in the income statement in the same period. Valuation issues that arise with respect to inventories have to do with determining the cost of inventory and whether, under certain conditions, valuation methods other than cost provide better information for decision makers.

In Practice 9-4

LESLIE FAY

The audit committee of Leslie Fay Co.'s board of directors found widespread fraud at the troubled apparel maker, according to its report:

> To boost sales and lower costs, the report claims, midlevel company officials forged inventory tags, ignored expected inventory shrinkage, multiplied the value of items in inventory, improperly inflated sales and made up phantom inventory.[3]

ANALYSIS

Because of irregularities in accounting for inventory, Leslie Fay appeared to be doing much better than it was. Much of what was reported was, in fact, untrue, and the company was actually in serious financial difficulty. Leslie Fay subsequently declared bankruptcy. In accordance with the company's reorganization plan, Leslie Fay's previous stockholders' equity has been extinguished. [www.leslie-fay.com]

Determining Cost.   As with all nonfinancial assets, the inventory amount reported on the balance sheet includes all costs incurred by the company to acquire that inventory. Thus, any shipping charges borne by the company to get the inventory initially, referred to as **freight-in**, and, once it is owned, any costs of transferring it from one company location to another are considered costs of the inventory. Similarly, any costs of preparing the goods for sale, such as packaging, are costs assigned to the inventory.

If inventory is acquired on credit and interest charges are incurred, the interest is typically viewed as a cost of borrowing money, rather than a cost of the inventory. The interest is expensed during the periods the company has the use of the money, providing a matching of costs (interest) and benefits (use of the money). An exception to this treatment occurs for companies that construct inventories as individual projects rather than manufacturing inventories on a repetitive basis in large quantities. For example, a shipbuilding company may have an inventory of several partially completed ships. When construction takes an extended period of time to complete, the interest cost of borrowed money, if material, is added to the other costs of construction. Only interest costs incurred during the construction period can be included in the cost.

[3] Lee Burton, "Audit Report Details Fraud at Leslie Fay," *The Wall Street Journal* (March 28, 1995), p. B1.

Lower of Cost or Market.   After acquisition, if the market value of inventory held drops below its cost, the inventory reported in the balance sheet at the end of the period usually is reduced to the lower market value. This approach to the valuation of inventories is referred to as the **lower-of-cost-or-market rule**. Why is this rule applied to inventories and not to, say, equipment? The reason is that inventory is held to be sold, so market values are relevant to decision makers; equipment is held to be used internally and not sold, so market values are viewed as less relevant. Recall from Chapter 8 that a similar distinction is made for investments: those that might be sold are valued at market value, while those to be held to maturity are valued based on cost.

Why are inventories valued at market value only when that value is lower than cost? The reason is that, because the company is in business to sell its inventory, the cost of inventory sold needs to be matched with revenues so financial statement users can assess the company's success in making profits through inventory sales. The use of a lower market value is a conservative approach used only when inventory appears to have lost some of its ability to provide future benefits. By reducing the inventory to a lower market value and recognizing a loss, decision makers are not misled into believing the company will receive more when the inventory is sold than is likely.

The specific procedures for applying the lower-of-cost-or-market rule are complex. As an overview, market value is based on the cost of replacing the inventory, referred to as **replacement cost**. However, inventory is never valued at an amount greater than its anticipated selling price, or **realizable value**, so the resulting market valuation is neither too high nor too conservative. If the market value, determined based on replacement cost and realizable value, is below historical cost, the inventory is revalued downward and reported at the lower market value in the balance sheet, and a loss is recognized in the income statement.

Inventory valuation policies must be disclosed by companies, either in the body of the financial statements or in the accompanying notes. A typical disclosure is the following from Gateway's notes to the financial statements:

> *Inventory . . . is valued at the lower of first in, first out (FIFO) cost or market.*

A CLOSER LOOK AT

VALUING INVENTORIES AT LOWER OF COST OR MARKET

Dempster Company holds inventory originally purchased for $287,500. At the end of the fiscal year, Dempster determines that the current replacement cost of the inventory is only $210,000. Under the lower-of-cost-or-market rule, the company must write down the inventory to its new market value and recognize a loss for the $77,500 decline. Thus, a $77,500 loss is recognized in the income statement for the year, and the inventory is reported at $210,000 in the year-end balance sheet.

Journal Entry

Loss on Decline in Value of Inventory	77,500	
Inventory		77,500

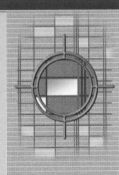

Income Statement Effects	
Loss	+ 77,500
Net Income	− 77,500
Balance Sheet Effects	
Assets	− 77,500
Owners' Equity	− 77,500

Inventory may be valued at lower-of-cost-or-market based on individual units of inventory, different categories of inventory, or the inventory as a whole. If the valuation is based on the inventory as a whole, increases in the market value of some types of inventory may hide declines in other types. Also, a write-down of inventory may not always be obvious from the income statement because some companies include the losses in cost of goods sold or other expense categories. However, disclosures in the balance sheet or related notes will indicate if the inventory is valued at an amount materially below its cost.

In Practice 9-5

INVENTORY WRITE-DOWNS AT DELL COMPUTER

The following excerpt is from the notes to the financial statements of Dell Computer Corporation:

During the first half of 1994, the Company also recorded $29.3 million of other costs, consisting mostly of inventory writedowns and related costs. These charges arose from the Company's determination that certain products and inventory were excess or obsolete because the products were scheduled to be replaced with newer products or because the Company otherwise had lowered its estimates of expected demand...

ANALYSIS

Rapidly changing technology in the computer business left Dell holding inventory with a value well below its historical cost. The inventory was written down and a loss recognized because the inventory was expected to provide much reduced future benefits. This write-down illustrates the risk of carrying inventories in an industry with rapidly changing technology. After the write-down of obsolete inventory, Dell was able to increase its inventory turnover significantly to 11.8 in 1996, 28 in 1997, and 52 in 1998. [www.dell.com]

Market Values. In a few cases, inventories are valued at market value, regardless of whether the market value is above or below original cost. In these cases, market value is based on anticipated selling price. Market value is used only when a reliable market value exists and all units of inventory are basically the same. Such conditions are typically found only with commodities, such as wheat and corn, and precious metals, such as gold and silver. When analyzing financial statements, an examination of the inventory valuation method used is important because not all companies value similar inventories using the same method. Keep in mind also that market values may change frequently, so dramatic swings in inventory values might occur for companies valuing inventories at market value. (See You Decide 9-3.)

ASSIGNING COSTS TO INVENTORY

We have seen the importance of cost for valuing most inventories, but a practical problem that arises is how to assign costs to units or groups of inventory. This issue is important because the assignment of cost affects both the amount reported in the income statement as Cost of Goods Sold and the amount reported in the balance sheet as Inventory. Two primary approaches are used to assign costs to inventory: specific identification and cost flow assumptions.

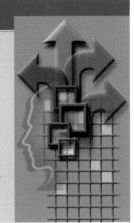

IS THE MARKET UP OR DOWN?

During 2000, Ace Material Processing Company purchased 100,000 tons of a new mineral, X-Base, at a cost of $1,000 a ton. The mineral will be used to manufacture a new insulating material to replace asbestos. At the end of 2000, the market for this material had not developed, and the price of X-Base dropped to $600 a ton. Ace's marketing department still predicts that the market will develop in the next year or two and that the value of X-Base will again be at least $1,000 a ton. What dollar value should be used to report the X-Base inventory in the 2000 financial statements to provide the most useful information for decision makers? If prices increase in 2001, how would you report the X-Base inventory at the end of that year? Should any gain or loss be reported? Explain how your approach provides the most useful information for decision makers.

Specific Identification. In many cases, the actual cost of specific units of inventory can be readily identified, such as when the company's inventory consists of a relatively small number of high value units. For example, automobile dealerships and jewelry stores keep track of the cost of individual units of inventory. Keeping track of the specific cost of individual units of inventory is referred to as **specific identification**. This method of tracking the costs of units of inventory is becoming more widespread since the adoption of bar-code labels on many products and the use of electronic scanners.

Cost Flow Assumptions. The specific identification method works for many types of inventories, but how do you suppose a company could keep track of the cost of individual units of inventory if it sold heating oil from a large holding tank, with the company purchasing different amounts at different prices and adding them to the tank? Or suppose a company sold finished lumber, with identical pieces of lumber purchased at different times at different prices and added to the stacks held in the lumber yard. Should a tag be placed on each 2 × 4 and plywood sheet with its cost so the accountants can charge the correct amount to expense when the lumber is sold? In this case, the cost of tagging all of the lumber would exceed the value of the resulting information.

Where a company's inventory consists of a large number of similar, relatively small-value items, **cost flow assumptions** are used to assign costs to inventory, with these assigned costs used for reporting the cost of goods sold during the period and the cost of inventory remaining on hand. Generally accepted accounting principles permit companies to make assumptions about how inventory costs flow through the accounts from inventory to cost of goods sold expense. The most common cost flow assumptions are:

- **Average cost:** the costs of different purchases are averaged together, using a weighted average based on the number of units purchased at each price, to determine an average cost per unit; this average cost is assigned to all units in inventory and as the cost of units sold.

- **First-in, first-out (FIFO):** the costs of the first units purchased are assigned to the first units sold (cost of goods sold), while the costs of units purchased later are assigned to the units remaining in inventory.

- **Last-in, first-out (LIFO):** the costs of the units purchased most recently are assigned to the first units sold (cost of goods sold), while the costs of units purchased earlier are assigned to the units left in inventory.

A CLOSER LOOK AT

INVENTORY COST FLOW ASSUMPTIONS

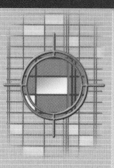

Marsh Enterprises makes the following purchases of inventory during the year:

First Purchase	1,000 units @ $4.00 =	$ 4,000
Second Purchase	3,000 units @ $4.20 =	$12,600
Third Purchase	2,000 units @ $4.60 =	$ 9,200
Total	6,000 units	$25,800

A total of 4,500 units are sold during the year, leaving 1,500 units in inventory at the end of the year. Under three different inventory cost flow assumptions, the dollar amounts assigned to Inventory in the year-end balance sheet and to Cost of Goods Sold in the income statement for the year are computed as follows:

Average Cost
$25,800/6,000 units = $4.30 per unit

Cost of Goods Sold:	4,500 units @ $4.30 =		$19,350
Inventory:	1,500 units @ $4.30 =		$ 6,450
	6,000 units		$25,800

First-in, First-out

Cost of Goods Sold:	1,000 units @ $4.00 =	$ 4,000	
	3,000 units @ $4.20 =	$12,600	
	500 units @ $4.60 =	$ 2,300	
			$18,900
Inventory:	1,500 units @ $4.60 =		$ 6,900
	6,000 units		$25,800

Last-in, First-out

Cost of Goods Sold:	2,000 units @ $4.60 =	$ 9,200	
	2,500 units @ $4.20 =	$10,500	
			$19,700
Inventory:	500 units @ $4.20 =	$ 2,100	
	1,000 units @ $4.00 =	$ 4,000	
			$ 6,100
	6,000 units		$25,800

Under each cost flow assumption, the total cost is the same. The difference between the cost flow assumptions is in how the total cost of $25,800 is allocated between the units sold and the units remaining in inventory at the end of the period. Because the cost of goods sold expense is different under each of the methods, Marsh's reported income will depend on the method selected.

The cost flow assumption chosen does not necessarily reflect the actual physical flow of inventory. The assumption chosen simply reflects a means of assigning costs to units of inventory. Some companies may attempt to choose a cost flow assumption that reflects the physical flow of inventory, but others do not. Some companies, for example, choose LIFO because they argue that it most closely matches current costs (the latest costs incurred) with current revenues, while FIFO matches old costs (the first costs incurred) with current revenues. Supporters of LIFO argue that it provides a better measure of current income. However, the main reason that LIFO is used is because it often results in lower income taxes and the Internal Revenue Service requires that if it is used for tax purposes it must be used for financial reporting also.

The Effects of Cost Flow Assumptions.   Why should financial statement users care which cost flow assumption is used? From the previous example you can see that the choice of methods affects the amount reported as cost of goods sold, which, in turn, affects net income. Because the financial statements are interrelated, the amount reported for inventory in the balance sheet is also affected. Assuming that prices *rise* over time, the effects of the different cost flow assumptions are as follows:

- FIFO costing results in the lowest reported cost of goods sold, highest net income, and highest reported inventory.

- LIFO costing results in the highest reported cost of goods sold, lowest net income, and lowest reported inventory.

- Average costing results in cost of goods sold, net income, and inventory amounts falling between those reported under FIFO and LIFO.

If prices are falling instead, a situation that is unusual but does occur with some items, the effects of FIFO and LIFO are reversed. If prices do not change over time, the method used does not really matter.

In Practice 9-6

GENERAL MILLS'S INVENTORY

General Mills's May 31, 1998, balance sheet reported inventory of $389.7 million, 10 percent of its total assets. A note to the balance sheet included the following information:

The components of inventories are as follows (in millions):

Raw materials, work in process and supplies	$ 83.3
Finished goods	262.5
Grain	83.0
Reserve for LIFO valuation method	(39.1)
Total inventories	$389.7

ANALYSIS

In addition to listing the types of inventory, the note discloses that inventories of $221.4 million were valued at LIFO. General Mills uses a contra-asset account referred to as a LIFO reserve to revalue inventories from FIFO to LIFO. From this account, the difference between the two methods can be seen to be $39.1 million. [www.generalmills.com]

Although FIFO generally results in higher income and asset amounts than LIFO, does that mean a company is better off using FIFO? No, because the transactions are the same, regardless of the method used to account for them. Therefore, financial statement users must be careful when evaluating companies, and especially when making comparisons between companies, to consider the accounting methods used. A company might actually be better off using LIFO, even though FIFO leads to a higher reported net income. If LIFO is used for tax purposes (and therefore is required for financial reporting), the company's income taxes will be lowered, assuming rising prices, because LIFO will lead to lower taxable income than FIFO. Lower taxes result in real cash savings, at least temporarily.

LIFO also leads to lower asset valuations than FIFO in a time of rising prices because the amounts included in inventory are the first costs incurred. This conservative valuation means that the ultimate selling price of the inventory is likely to be higher in relation to its reported inventory valuation under LIFO. Another way of thinking about the effect of these methods on financial statements is that if in a time of rising prices two companies appeared identical, but one used FIFO and the other used LIFO, the LIFO firm probably would be the better choice. All other things equal, LIFO would result in the more conservative income figure and inventory valuation, and produce a tax savings.

Thus, when decision makers evaluate a company, they should consider not just its earnings, but also the **quality of earnings**. That is, decision makers should examine the extent to which a company's accounting methods are aggressive or conservative. Aggressive methods result in higher reported income and assets, while conservative methods result in lower reported income and asset amounts. Because alternative acceptable accounting methods exist in a number of areas, management can influence reported amounts by the choice of accounting methods. Accordingly, an understanding of a company's accounting methods is crucial for evaluation, especially when comparisons are made with other companies that may use different accounting methods.

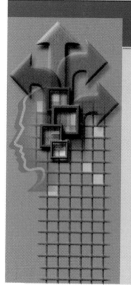

You Decide 9-4

I LIKE LIFO, BUT WHAT HAPPENED TO CURRENT ASSETS?

You have been looking at the potential tax savings from using LIFO for valuing inventories. The cost of your inventory has been increasing regularly, and you could deduct the higher recent costs of inventory on the tax return if you used LIFO. When you propose the switch to the company financial vice president, she tells you to check the effect on the current ratio. You remember that because of the borrowing agreement with the bank, the company has to maintain a current ratio of at least two to one. You have gathered the following information:

Current assets (FIFO inventory)	$3,350,000
Current liabilities	1,600,000
Reduction in inventory from switching to LIFO	200,000

Should your company adopt LIFO? Do you think you can "sell" the bank on LIFO? What arguments would you use?

ACCOUNTING FOR INVENTORY TRANSACTIONS

Inventory transactions include the purchase of inventory and its sale. When inventory is sold, revenue is recognized from the sale, and the cost of the inventory sold is recognized as an expense for a proper matching. The cost of the inventory, previously reported as an asset, is viewed as expiring because it provides benefits at the time of the sale, but will provide no additional benefits in the future.

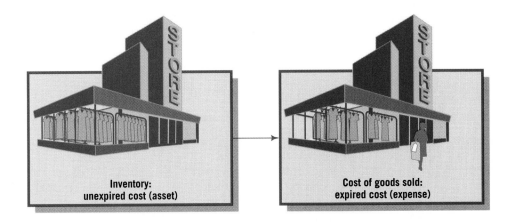

Inventory: unexpired cost (asset)

Cost of goods sold: expired cost (expense)

The way in which the cost of inventory moves through the asset stage to the expense stage reflects the way in which inventory moves through a business enterprise. All inventory available for sale during the period must come from one of two places: It must be on hand at the beginning of the period, or it must be purchased during the period. All inventory available for sale must go to one of two places: It must be on hand at the end of the period, or it must be sold (assuming none is stolen or destroyed). This inventory movement can be depicted as follows:

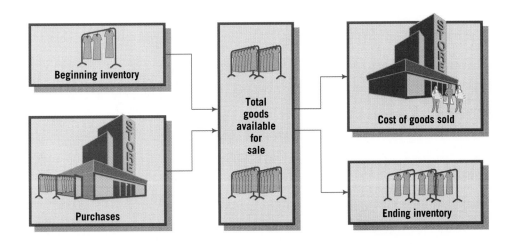

Beginning inventory

Purchases

Total goods available for sale

Cost of goods sold

Ending inventory

Similarly, from an accounting perspective, the cost of the goods available for sale during the period is the sum of the beginning inventory cost and the cost of goods purchased (or manufactured) during the period. This cost is then assigned either to the inventory units sold during the period or the units remaining on hand at the end of the period. The cost of those goods sold during the period is expensed, while the cost of the inventory remaining on hand is reported as an asset.

Two different types of inventory systems are found in practice for determining the amount of cost to be assigned to the goods sold and those still on hand: *perpetual* and *periodic*. Let's look at these two types of inventory systems and see why most companies have been switching to perpetual systems.

Perpetual Inventory Systems. With a **perpetual inventory system**, the company keeps track of the cost of all purchases and sales of inventory. Therefore, the amount of inventory on hand at any point in time can be determined through the accounting records. When merchandise is purchased, the Inventory account is increased by the cost of the goods purchased.

When merchandise is sold, the Inventory account is reduced by the cost of the goods sold, and that amount is transferred to an expense account.

A CLOSER LOOK AT

INVENTORY TRANSACTION

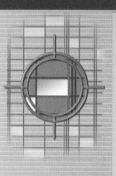

Xavier Company (a) purchases on credit inventory for $98,000 plus $2,000 of freight charges. Shortly afterward, the company (b) sells 40 percent of the inventory for $65,000. Xavier uses a perpetual inventory system and records the purchase of the inventory by increasing its Inventory account and its Accounts Payable by $100,000 in total. The later sale of the inventory is recorded with a $65,000 increase in Accounts Receivable (or Cash) and Sales Revenue. Under a perpetual inventory system, Xavier must also record at the time of the sale the decrease in the company's inventory and the expense associated with the sale. When the inventory is sold, the cost of that inventory expires. It no longer will provide future benefits to Xavier because it provides the benefits currently. Therefore, the $40,000 cost of the inventory sold must be transferred from an asset account (Inventory) to an expense account (Cost of Goods Sold). Xavier's income statement reflects the sale as follows:

Sales revenue	$65,000
Cost of goods sold	40,000
Gross profit	$25,000

Journal Entries

Purchase

Inventory	100,000	
Accounts Payable		100,000

Sale

Accounts Receivable	65,000	
Sales Revenue		65,000
Cost of Goods Sold	40,000	
Inventory		40,000

Income Statement Effects

(b) Sales	+	65,000
Expenses	+	40,000
Net Income	+	25,000

Balance Sheet Effects

(a) Assets	+	100,000
Liabilities	+	100,000
(b) Assets	+	65,000
Assets	−	40,000
Owners'		
Equity	+	25,000

Many companies previously found perpetual inventory systems too expensive because of the need to account for each inventory transaction. However, the widespread use of electronic tracking systems, such as grocery and department store bar-code scanners, has made perpetual tracking of inventory affordable and has helped improve inventory management. (See You Decide 9-5.) Even when a company keeps track of its inventory on a perpetual basis, though, it still must physically count the inventory periodically, usually once each year, as a check on the accuracy of the accounting numbers.

Periodic Inventory Systems.   The second type of inventory system, referred to as a **periodic inventory system**, keeps track of inventory purchases but not the cost of inventory sold. Under this type of system, all purchases of inventory are recorded in a separate account. The inventory on hand at the end of the period is determined through a physical count be-

You Decide 9-5

WHAT DO YOU WANT TO KNOW ABOUT INVENTORY?

Recently you noticed that your favorite candy bar supplier, the local convenience store, had installed a barcode scanner and now scans all merchandise to record the sale. You ask the manager if the system was costly, and she acknowledges that it was. Then she listed numerous time-saving advantages, as well as the advantage of being able to reorder items more quickly. In fact, she says that if the store runs out of your candy bars, she can order more in the evening and they will be delivered the next morning. How would this system save the manager's time? How can inventory needs be determined and supplied so quickly? How might the system lead to cost savings?

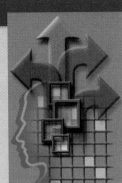

cause the accounting records do not contain this information. With no perpetual record of the cost of the goods sold during the period, this amount must be computed as follows:

$$
\begin{array}{l}
\quad \text{Beginning Inventory} \\
+\ \underline{\text{Purchases of Inventory}} \\
=\ \text{Total Goods Available for Sale} \\
-\ \underline{\text{Ending Inventory}} \\
=\ \text{Cost of Goods Sold}
\end{array}
$$

Adjusting entries are made at the end of the period to record the cost of the goods sold during the period and to adjust the inventory balance from the beginning amount to the ending amount.

Several aspects of periodic inventory systems make them less desirable than perpetual systems. First, the accounting records do not indicate the inventory on hand or the cost of goods sold until the end of the period when the physical count is made. Second, the accounting system does not provide an independent check on the amount of inventory that should be on hand at the end of the period. The physical count tells how much inventory is on hand, but not how much should be there. What if the count is wrong? How do we know if inventory has been destroyed or stolen? For example, one company that manufactures small electronics parts did not know it had a severe employee theft problem until the auditors noticed that the gross margin was a much smaller percentage of sales than for other companies in the industry. With a perpetual system, the problem would have come to light much sooner through the system's accounting control.

Inventory Errors. Because inventory is such a crucial item for merchandising and manufacturing companies, inventory errors can be especially significant when analyzing a company's financial statements. Inventory errors can affect both the income statement and balance sheet, and the errors can extend over more than one year. A number of common inventory errors are as follows:

* Counting the same inventory units twice because of poor controls
* Failing to record a purchase made near the end of the year until the following year

Keeping track of inventory is important for both accurate financial reporting and efficient operations.

- Overlooking inventory in the physical count, possibly because it is being stored in a different warehouse, in transit from the manufacturer, or held by another party (a consignee) attempting to sell it for a commission
- Counting inventory on hand that belongs to others, such as inventory held (on consignment) to sell on commission
- Assigning the wrong cost to units of inventory
- Including damaged or obsolete inventory as if it were first-rate merchandise
- Including nonexistent inventory, such as oil thought to be in underground storage but that has been removed

Companies with a material amount of inventory must establish good internal control procedures to be sure that inventory is accurately counted, properly valued, and correctly recorded. Inventory accuracy is also tested by the external auditors as part of the annual audit examination.

MANUFACTURING INVENTORIES

The types of inventories held depend on the type of company. Merchandising companies purchase goods in one market (e.g., wholesale) and sell the goods in another market (e.g., retail). They do not change the basic form of the goods, although they may make minor changes, such as in the packaging. Manufacturing firms, on the other hand, take raw materials or partially completed components and fashion them into products that are sold to customers.

In Practice 9-7

SEARS, ROEBUCK AND TENNECO, INC

Sears, Roebuck, a major retailer, reports inventory in its balance sheet as follows:

Merchandise inventory	$5,044,000,000

Tenneco, Inc., a major manufacturer, reports inventory in a note to its balance sheet in the following manner:

Finished goods	$467,000,000
Work-in-process	100,000,000
Raw materials	265,000,000
Materials and supplies	118,000,000
	$950,000,000

ANALYSIS

Although Sears carries a large dollar amount of a wide variety of merchandise, all of it is considered to be finished goods awaiting sale and is reported in a single category. Tenneco, however, changes raw materials into goods that it sells to its customers and reports inventory in several stages of completion. [www.sears.com] [www.tenneco.com]

A merchandising firm, while it may sell many different products, holds only one major category of inventory, finished goods ready to be sold to customers. A manufacturing firm, however, holds several major categories of inventory:

- **Raw materials**—the basic inputs to the manufacturing process from which the company's products are made
- **Work-in-process**—units of product that have been started in the manufacturing process but have not yet been completed
- **Finished goods**—units of the completed product ready to be sold to customers

With a manufacturing operation, all costs of manufacturing the company's product are included in the cost of the inventory. These costs include the costs of the raw materials, the labor needed for production, and the cost of equipment used in production. In addition, many other costs are typically incurred in production that may be less direct, such as rent or depreciation of the factory building, supplies, utilities, and factory labor not directly working on production, such as maintenance crews and factory administrators.

All costs directly or indirectly related to production are considered part of the cost of the inventory manufactured. These costs are viewed, in effect, as attaching to individual units of inventory as those units are produced. The flow of costs through a manufacturing cycle can be represented as in Exhibit 9–3. All manufacturing costs are ultimately assigned to units of inventory, and those costs are expensed as cost of goods sold when the inventory is sold.

In addition to questions relating to inventories in general, decision makers may be interested in the relationship between the three types of manufacturing inventories. For example, a high level of finished goods inventory in relation to the other two categories might indicate that goods are being produced but not sold. A very low level of raw materials might indicate exceptionally good inventory management, or could mean the company is susceptible to production disruptions if raw material shipments are halted.

ACCUMULATING COSTS IN A MANUFACTURING OPERATION EXHIBIT 9-3

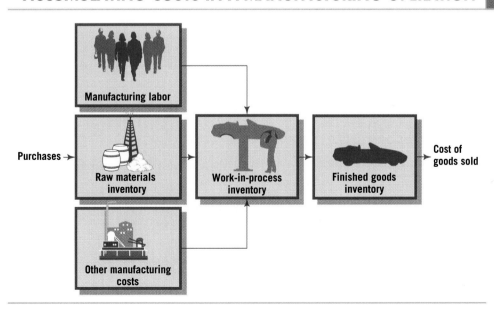

SUMMARY

Nonfinancial assets are either held for sale to others in the normal course of business or used in the company's operations. They include all assets except cash, claims on others, and investments. Nonfinancial assets can be tangible or intangible, and they are classified as either current or noncurrent, based on whether they are expected to be sold or consumed within one year or the operating cycle of the business, whichever is longer. Current nonfinancial assets include prepaid expenses and inventories.

All nonfinancial assets are recorded initially at cost. The historical cost of a nonfinancial asset includes all costs that have to be incurred to acquire the asset and get it in the location and condition so the entity can do with it what it intends. Once the cost of the asset is recorded, that cost, or an appropriate portion, is expensed and matched with the benefits provided by the asset.

Inventory costs that can be identified with specific units are charged to Cost of Goods Sold when those units are sold. Because assignment of cost to specific units is difficult for many types of inventory, assumptions about inventory cost flows are often made. Common assumptions include averaging all costs, assuming the first costs incurred are related to the earliest units sold (FIFO), and assuming the last costs incurred are related to the earliest units sold (LIFO). Because inventories are to be sold, market values are more relevant than for operating assets. Therefore, if the market value of inventory falls below its historical cost, it is usually written down to the lower marker value under the lower-of-cost-or-market rule.

Perpetual inventory systems are used by an increasing number of companies as improved technology makes their use feasible. These systems keep track of inventory on hand and the cost of goods sold during the period. Perpetual systems provide greater accounting control over inventories and facilitate better inventory management than periodic systems. Under periodic inventory systems, the amount of inventory on hand at any point in time is determined through a physical count because the system does not track increases and decreases in inventory.

Manufacturing companies produce goods for sale from raw materials and other components. They typically hold three types of inventories, reflecting different stages of completion: raw materials, work in process, and finished goods. All costs of manufacturing inventory are assigned to units of inventory and are expensed only when the units are sold.

Because of the importance of nonfinancial assets, proper asset management is crucial to success. Asset management may be assessed in a number of ways, but the level of inventories and the speed with which they are "turned over" or sold in relation to other companies in the industry are particularly important. Because inventories are costly to hold, companies must balance inventory carrying costs against the cost of lost sales and production disruptions.

LIST OF IMPORTANT TERMS

average cost *(343)*
capitalized *(330)*
cost flow assumptions *(343)*
deferred charges *(335)*
finished goods *(351)*
first-in, first-out (FIFO) *(343)*
freight-in *(340)*

gross profit percentage *(339)*
inventory turnover *(338)*
last-in, first-out (LIFO) *(343)*
lower-of-cost-or-market rule *(341)*
periodic inventory system *(348)*
perpetual inventory system *(347)*

quality of earnings *(346)*
raw materials *(351)*
realizable value *(341)*
replacement cost *(341)*
specific identification *(343)*
work-in-process *(351)*

EXAMINING THE CONCEPTS

Q9-1 How are nonfinancial assets differentiated from financial assets? Why is this distinction important?

Q9-2 Which, if any, nonfinancial assets typically are classified as current assets? How important are these assets in the operation of a manufacturing or merchandising company? Explain.

Q9-3 Which nonfinancial assets are classified as noncurrent? Of these assets, which generally are most important in a manufacturing setting? Which would be most important to a software development company? In both cases, explain why.

Q9-4 What valuation basis is used for reporting depreciable and amortizable assets?

Q9-5 Why are prepaid expenses considered assets? Why are they normally classified as current assets?

Q9-6 How does a prepaid expense differ from other types of current and noncurrent assets?

Q9-7 Explain the importance of inventory turnover in evaluating the operating results of a (a) manufacturing company, (b) retail chain, and (c) law firm.

Q9-8 What are the major categories of inventory in a manufacturing company? Why is it important to distinguish the different categories?

Q9-9 How are inventories normally valued? What costs are included in inventory? Explain why the costs of ordering inventory generally are not included in the cost of inventory.

Q9-10 What is the lower-of-cost-or-market rule in valuing inventory? Why is this procedure used for inventories?

Q9-11 When are inventories reported at market value? What conditions must exist for inventory to be reported at market value?

Q9-12 When would an enterprise be likely to use specific identification in assigning inventory costs? When would it be unlikely to do so?

Q9-13 What effect has the use of optical scanning and barcode labels had on the use of specific identification for assigning costs to inventory?

Q9-14 What does it mean to value inventory on a first-in, first-out basis? Which purchases are included in ending inventory using FIFO?

Q9-15 What does it mean to value inventory on a last-in, first-out basis? Which purchases are included in ending inventory using LIFO?

Q9-16 In a period of rapidly increasing prices, is the amount reported on the balance sheet under LIFO or FIFO likely to provide the best estimate of the current cost of replacing inventory sold? Explain why.

Q9-17 When cost flow assumptions such as LIFO and FIFO are used rather than assigning the specific costs of individual units of inventory to those units, how is the accuracy of the financial statements affected? What concepts of accounting are relevant when assessing whether cost flow assumptions are reasonable substitutes for specific identification?

Q9-18 Distinguish between perpetual and periodic inventory systems.

Q9-19 Is a perpetual or a periodic inventory system likely to provide the most current information on the number of units available for sale at any point in time? Explain.

Q9-20 At what point in time is cost of goods sold recognized under a perpetual inventory system?

Q9-21 Will a perpetual or a periodic inventory system lead to the greatest amount of cost of goods sold reported in a period? Explain.

Q9-22 How is cost of goods sold computed using a periodic inventory system? Why must the inventory balances at both the beginning and end of the period be included in the computation?

Q9-23 What are the advantages of a perpetual inventory system over a periodic system? What disadvantages might a perpetual inventory system have?

Q9-24 Most companies count their inventory at least once each year. What kinds of errors could be made during this count? What effect would each of these errors have on the accuracy of the balance sheet and the income statement?

Q9-25 When is it appropriate to include depreciation costs for buildings and equipment as part of the cost of inventory? When is it inappropriate?

Q9-26 Under what conditions should interest cost be included in the cost of an asset? Slow Corp. purchased inventory three years ago, and the inventory has yet to be sold. Should interest and other carrying costs of the inventory be included in the cost of the inventory? Explain.

Q9-27 Indicate how raw materials inventory, work-in-process inventory, and finished goods inventory differ from one another.

UNDERSTANDING ACCOUNTING INFORMATION

E9-1 **Nonfinancial Assets and Their Valuation**

a. The balance sheet of Tools, Inc., lists the following nonfinancial assets. Indicate which of these assets you would expect to be sold or consumed within the next fiscal year and which assets you would expect to be consumed over longer periods of time.
1. Prepaid expenses.
2. Inventory.
3. Buildings.
4. Equipment.
5. Furniture.
6. Intangibles.

b. Your former college roommate is planning to open a convenience store next to campus and is planning to spend a total of $135,000 to start the business. Indicate which of the following costs would be expected to provide future benefits and would be capitalized and recorded as an asset, and which costs would not be expected to provide future benefits and must be expensed in the year they are incurred:
1. Furniture and fixtures.
2. Insurance on the store and inventory.
3. Land.
4. Merchandise inventory.
5. Salaries.

6. Store building.
7. Utilities.

E9-2 Reporting Nonfinancial Assets: The Matching Concept Applied

a. The New Idea Company incurred a number of costs during 1999 in acquiring inventory, preparing it for sale, and contacting potential buyers. For each of the following, indicate whether the cost(s) should be recorded as a part of the total cost of inventory or immediately charged to expense.

List price of inventory purchased	$158,000
Trade discounts on inventory purchased	(46,000)
Shipping costs for inventory purchased	15,000
Advertising for the sale of inventory	25,000
Interest costs on money borrowed to buy inventory	8,000
Costs to prepare the inventory for sale	5,000
Customs fees for inventory purchased overseas	2,000
Travel costs to visit new inventory suppliers	15,000

b. An appropriate portion of the cost of a nonfinancial asset such as equipment or a building is matched against revenue in the periods in which the benefits are received. For each of the following, assume a company purchases equipment to produce products that will be sold in future periods:
1. What costs are capitalized as part of the cost of the equipment?
2. How will the cost of the equipment be matched to the benefits it provides in future periods? What portion of the cost should be reported as an expense each period?
3. When deciding how profitable the company has been in a single year, why is it important that the cost of using the equipment be considered?

E9-3 Prepaid Expenses and Supplies

a. You are comparing the reported income and cash flow of two companies. Company A lists a $50,000 prepaid expense in its balance sheet for an insurance policy on its buildings and equipment. In a footnote, Company A indicates that the policy is for two years, and one year has expired. Company B does not report any prepaid insurance in its balance sheet. Company A reports $50,000 of insurance expense in its income statement for this year and Company B reports insurance expense of $55,000.
1. In comparing the two companies, what effect will the prepaid expense have on the cash flow and current assets reported by Company A compared to Company B?
2. What amount should Company A report as insurance expense in the next year? What amount will Company B report?

b. The bank you work for is considering lending money to a local bakery. In its loan application, the bakery listed the following amounts for cash on hand, accounts receivable, finished goods inventory, and prepaid expenses:

Cash on hand	$ 500
Accounts receivable	1,500
Finished goods inventory	8,500
Prepaid expenses	2,000
Total	$12,500

In the event of liquidation, what amounts are likely to be generated from the disposition of each of the assets?

E9-4 Inventories

a. Your bank is considering making an operating loan to the Voss Company to finance its inventory purchases, and you have been assigned the task of evaluating the Voss Company's inventory levels. You have collected the following information:

	Voss Company		Industry Averages	
	2001	2000	2001	2000
Inventory as a percent of assets	25%	23%	19%	20%
Inventory turnover	10	17	15	14

What is your evaluation of Voss Company's inventory levels?

b. In comparing the income statements of two companies you are considering for an investment, you note that Company A uses LIFO to value its ending inventory, while Company B uses FIFO. Total sales for the two companies are approximately equal for the current year. Inventory prices have been rising.
1. What effect will the choice of inventory method have on reported income of the two companies?
2. What effect will the choice of inventory method have on reported cash flows of the two companies?
3. Under what conditions might Company B be expected to report a "Loss on Decline in Value of Inventory?"

c. The total inventory of Gumbad Manufacturing Company increased by 20 percent from last year. When you review the balance sheets and related footnotes for the last two years, you find the following information on Gumbad's inventories:

	2001	2000
Finished goods	$183,000	$120,000
Work-in-process	28,000	40,000
Raw materials	89,000	90,000
Total	$300,000	$250,000

What would you conclude about the increase in Gumbad's inventory balances? Why might you be concerned about investing in this company?

E9-5 Multiple Choice: Asset Valuation Select the correct answer for each of the following:

1. Which of the following is likely to be reported at lower of cost or market?
   a. Supplies inventory.
   b. Finished goods inventory.
   c. Prepaid expenses.
   d. All of the above.
2. Which of the following is reported at an amount based on historical cost?
   a. Prepaid expenses.
   b. Equipment.
   c. Land.
   d. All of the above.
3. Inventory might be valued at:
   a. Cost.
   b. Replacement cost.
   c. Realizable value.
   d. Any of the above.
4. Tangible operating assets with limited lives normally are valued at:
   a. Cost not yet allocated to periodic expense.
   b. The amount paid originally.
   c. Current market value.
   d. Lower of cost or market.
5. The amount recorded as the cost of equipment should include:
   a. Costs of shipping in the equipment.
   b. Installation and preparation costs.
   c. Reductions for trade discounts.
   d. All of the above.

E9-6 Multiple Choice: Assigning Costs to Inventory Select the correct answer for each of the following:

1. A company with a small number of very expensive inventory items may find which of the following inventory costing methods most useful?
   a. First-in, first-out.
   b. Last-in, first-out.
   c. Average cost.
   d. Specific identification.
2. A chemical company running a continuous blending process would probably use which of the following inventory costing systems?
   a. First-in, first-out.
   b. Last-in, first-out.
   c. Average cost.
   d. Specific identification.
3. The inventory costing method likely to result in the highest reported net income in a period of rising prices is:
   a. First-in, first-out.
   b. Last-in, first-out.
   c. Average cost.
   d. Specific identification.
4. The inventory costing method likely to result in the highest reported cost of goods sold in a period of declining prices is:

   a. First-in, first-out.
   b. Last-in, first-out.
   c. Average cost.
   d. Specific identification.

E9-7 Multiple Choice: Accounting for Inventory Transactions Select the best answer for each of the following:

1. Companies using a periodic inventory system:
   a. Normally have small inventory balances.
   b. Do not require immediate information on inventory balances on hand.
   c. Keep track of inventory costs by using the most recent purchase prices.
   d. Keep track of cost of goods sold by recording the cost of inventory sold as each sale occurs.
2. A perpetual inventory system:
   a. Records the cost of goods sold at the end of the period in which the inventory is sold.
   b. Records purchases at the end of the period.
   c. Requires knowing ending inventory totals before cost of goods sold can be calculated.
   d. Facilitates the calculation of inventory losses from theft, spoilage, and other types of shrinkage.
3. In computing cost of goods sold with a periodic inventory system:
   a. Ending inventory and purchases are added to beginning inventory.
   b. Beginning inventory is added to goods available for sale.
   c. Purchases are deducted from beginning inventory plus ending inventory.
   d. Ending inventory is deducted from total goods available for sale.
4. With a periodic inventory system, cost of goods sold will be overstated if:
   a. Ending inventory is understated.
   b. Obsolete inventory is improperly included in ending inventory.
   c. Nonexistent inventory is included in ending inventory.
   d. Beginning inventory is understated.

E9-8 Matching Process Determine whether the items presented below describe the matching process associated with accounting for one or more of the following: (1) prepaid expense, (2) inventory, (3) depreciable assets, or (4) none of the above:

a. Recorded as expense when purchased
b. Recorded as expense as used in production
c. Recorded as cost of goods sold at the time of sale
d. Allocated to expense uniformly over time
e. Reported as a current asset
f. Reported as an operating asset
g. Characterized as a financial asset
h. Valued at lower-of-cost-or-market

E9-9 Prepaid Insurance Special Corp. paid $12,000 for a 5-year insurance policy covering all losses from business interruption resulting from fire, wind, or other casualties. Payment on the policy was made on April 1, 2000, with coverage beginning immediately.

a. Prepare a schedule showing the amount of insurance expense to be reported in each of the years covered by the policy and the balance sheet amounts relating to insurance that should be reported each period.
b. At December 31, 2000, should a portion of the amount paid for insurance be reported as a noncurrent asset? Explain your answer.
c. Present the journal entries to be recorded by Special Corp. in 2000 and 2001 related to the insurance policy.

E9-10 **Prepaid Expenses** Sunrise Company reported Prepaid Rent of $11,000 and Supplies Inventory of $2,900 on December 31, 2000. During 2001, Sunrise purchased supplies costing $5,000 and had supplies on hand at December 31, 2001, of $3,100. It also prepaid additional rent of $30,000 during 2001 and had an ending Prepaid Rent balance of $15,000. The Cash balance at January 1, 2001, was $43,000.

a. Prepare T-accounts for Supplies Inventory, Supplies Expense, and Cash, and post the 2001 beginning balances and transactions to the accounts.
b. Prepare T-accounts for Prepaid Rent and Rent Expense, and post the 2001 beginning balances and transactions to the accounts using the same cash account as in part a.
c. Prepare journal entries to record the purchase of supplies and prepayment of rent and journal entries to record supplies expense and rent expense for 2001.

E9-11 **Prepaid Advertising** Sloan Ornament Company produces ornaments for Christmas trees. In January of the current year, Sloan's marketing department hired a new advertising agency and prepaid $240,000 in advertising costs for the year. Because of the seasonality of Sloan's sales, all its ads are run in magazines in the months of September (40 percent of the total), October (40 percent of the total), and November (20 percent of the total). Although some sales occur in September and October, a majority of the sales occur in the months of November and December.

a. What arguments can be made in favor of reporting the full $240,000 as advertising expense at the time payment is made? At the time the ads are run? At the time increased sales occur?
b. Give the amount that should be reported as advertising expense for each month of the current year under the preferred alternative.
c. What other factors might be taken into consideration in determining when advertising expense should be recognized?

E9-12 **Rent Paid Annually** Dither Company rents a warehouse and pays the rent annually on June 1. The company provided the following information at the end of the current year:

Prepaid rent, January 1	$2,000
Prepaid rent, December 31	2,250
Rent expense for year	5,150

a. What amount did Dither Company pay on June 1? Give the journal entry for the payment.
b. What was the monthly rent expense in January?
c. What was the monthly rent expense in December?

E9-13 **Unrecorded Prepayment** Cather Corporation pays the annual premium on its liability insurance policy on April 1 each year and recognizes the full amount as expense. The amount paid last year was $18,000. Due to increased claims against the company, the premium paid in the current year was raised to $31,200. It has been suggested that the company's accounting treatment of the payments is not in accordance with generally accepted accounting principles.

a. What amount should Cather Corporation report as insurance expense for the current calendar year?
b. What amount would the company report as prepaid insurance at the end of the current year under its existing procedures? What amount should it report?
c. What would be the effect on reported net income for the current year if generally accepted accounting procedures were followed?

E9-14 **Legal Services** Shaky Company has been threatened with a major lawsuit by one of its former customers. In preparation for any potential suit, Shaky Company gave a $150,000 retainer to the law firm of Gotcha and Thensome for legal services for the next three years.

a. Is the $150,000 payment an asset or an expense to Shaky Company? Explain.
b. If the law firm does no work for Shaky in the first year, should any legal expenses be recognized for the first year? Explain.
c. If a prepaid legal services account is established, where should the account be reported in the balance sheet?
d. Would the payment of the retainer qualify as a deferred charge? Explain.

E9-15 **Inventory Costs** Marymount Company purchased inventory for $132,000 on April 1, 2000. The seller paid freight charges of $7,500 and sent Marymount Corporation a bill for $139,500. The terms of payment allowed a 12 percent quantity discount on the cost of the inventory (excluding freight). Marymount paid for the inventory on May 10, 2000, and treated the discount as a reduction of its inventory cost. On June 15, Marymount sold 50 percent of the inventory for $86,500 cash.

a. Compute the carrying value of the inventory on May 10, 2000.
b. Compute Marymount's June 15 cost of goods sold.

E9-16 Determining Cost of Goods Sold Fast Company reported an inventory turnover ratio of 15.6 for the year based on average inventory. It had $240,000 of inventory at the beginning of the year and $200,000 at the end of the year.

a. What amount was reported as cost of goods sold for the year?
b. What amount of inventory was purchased during the year?

E9-17 Gross Profit Rinser Corporation reported total sales of $540,000 for the current period. Rinser had $95,000 of inventory on hand at the start of the period and $125,000 at the end of the period. A total of $360,000 of inventory was purchased by Rinser during the period.

a. Compute the gross profit on Rinser's sales.
b. Compute the gross profit percentage on Rinser's sales.

E9-18 Computation of Beginning Inventory Sorter Company recorded the following journal entries during 2001:

Inventory	483,000	
Cash		483,000
Cost of Goods Sold	508,000	
Inventory		508,000

If the inventory reported at December 31, 2001, was $41,000, what was the balance in inventory reported by Sorter Company at January 1, 2001?

E9-19 Income Statement Belware Company reported the following account balances at December 31, 2000:

Inventory, January 1, 2000	$ 16,000
Sales	623,000
Salaries and wage expense	97,000
Depreciation expense	40,000
Inventory purchased in 2000	371,000
Utilities expense	28,000
Interest expense	23,000
Inventory, December 31, 2000	38,000

Prepare an income statement for Belware Company for 2000 that includes a computation of cost of goods sold.

E9-20 Gross Profit Zone Company sells radar ranges purchased from suppliers in Europe. Zone incurred the following costs associated with acquiring and selling inventory in 2000:

Invoice price of radar ranges purchased	$420,000
Cost of uncrating and checking inventory	190,000
Freight costs for inventory purchased	70,000
Costs of advertising in local newspapers	40,000
Quantity discount granted by suppliers	60,000

During the year, Zone purchased 5,000 radar ranges, and it sold 3,600 of them for $210 each. Compute the gross profit on Zone Company's sales for 2000.

E9-21 Inventory Turnover Lower Company and Master Corporation reported the following information for the current year:

	Lower Company	Master Corporation
Beginning inventory	$ 60,000	$ 400,000
Ending inventory	100,000	100,000
Inventory purchased	300,000	1,400,000

a. Explain why companies that use specific identification in assigning costs to inventory and cost of goods sold may be expected to have a lower inventory turnover ratio than companies using FIFO, LIFO, or average cost.
b. Compute the inventory turnover ratios for Lower Company and Master Corporation (*Note:* cost of goods sold must be computed first).

E9-22 Inventory Turnover Ratios The inventory turnover ratios for Ronto Manufacturing, Star Jewelers, and Kelty Food Marts, are 4.5, 1.2, and 12.3, respectively.

a. How is the inventory turnover ratio calculated? What information is provided by this ratio?
b. How is inventory turnover evaluated? Is the company with the highest turnover ratio operated the most efficiently? Explain your answer.
c. Evaluate the turnover ratios for the three enterprises. Are the differences in ratios consistent with what you would expect? Explain.
d. What other ratios would you examine to assess operating efficiency for the companies?

E9-23 Lower of Cost or Market Brandise Company manufactures electric motors for use in household appliances. At the end of the year, Brandise held 200 motors that it had produced for a company that is now out of business. The cost of producing each of the motors was $78. Brandise believes that it can sell the motors for $85 each, but selling and delivery costs will be $11 per unit. New efficiencies introduced into Brandise's production process permit the company to produce the motors now at a cost of $58 each.

a. What arguments can be made for valuing the motors at cost?
b. What arguments can be made for valuing the motors at net realizable value?
c. What arguments can be made for valuing the motors at replacement cost?
d. What value should be placed on the motors for financial reporting purposes? Explain why.

E9-24 Lower-of-Cost-or-Market Glenn Corporation recognized a $17,000 loss on the decline in value of its inventory at December 31, 2001. During 2001, Glenn Corporation purchased inventory costing $374,000 and recorded cost of goods sold at $412,000. Glenn had reported inventory of $94,000 at December 31, 2000.

a. What was the carrying value of Glenn's inventory prior to recognizing the loss?

b. What was the carrying value of Glenn's inventory after recognizing the loss?

c. If Glenn Corporation had failed to recognize the loss at December 31, 2001:

1. Would its inventory be understated or overstated at December 31, 2001?

2. Would its net income for 2001 be understated or overstated?

3. And the inventory on hand at December 31, 2001, is sold in 2002, would net income for 2002 be understated or overstated?

E9-25 Inventory Write-down Belt Company reported inventory of $34,000 on October 1, 2001, and purchased $174,000 of inventory on account during the month. Cost of goods sold for October was $153,000. In preparing adjusting entries at October 31, 2001, the company learned that the current replacement cost of its inventory was $46,000. Give the journal entry to record the inventory adjustment at October 31, 2001.

E9-26 Inventory Valuation Import Co. purchases handmade clocks from around the world for sale in the United States. According to its records, Import Co. had the following purchases and sales of clocks in 2001:

Clock No.	Date Purchased		Amount Paid	Date Sold		Sale Price
423	January	22	$1,500	March	8	$3,200
424	February	9	6,000			
425	June	6	2,500	June	16	4,900
426	June	6	3,000	August	9	4,800
427	September	27	2,000			
428	December	8	1,200	December	27	1,800

Import Co. has used average cost in computing its cost of goods sold and inventory balances, but is thinking of changing to specific identification.

a. Compare the dollar amounts that would be reported as cost of goods sold and ending inventory under average cost and specific identification.

b. What conditions generally must exist for specific identification to be used? Explain why.

c. Which of the two methods best represents the operating results for Import Co.? Explain your answer.

E9-27 FIFO Inventory Totals Rust Company made the following inventory purchases during the month of April:

April 6	70 units @ $15 each	
April 14	50 units @ $16 each	
April 28	45 units @ $20 each	

Rust had 20 units of inventory on hand at April 1 at a cost of $12 each. Ending inventory reported by Rust at April 30 was $1,220 using a FIFO cost flow assumption.

a. How many units of inventory did Rust Company have on hand at April 30?

b. How many units of inventory did Rust Company sell in April?

c. What was the cost of goods sold reported by Rust Company in its April income statement?

E9-28 LIFO Inventory Totals Trevor Company made the following inventory purchases during the month of July:

July 1	40 units @ $35 each	
July 21	70 units @ $40 each	
July 26	60 units @ $38 each	

Trevor Company had 10 units of inventory on hand at July 1 at a cost of $30 each. At July 31, Trevor recorded cost of goods sold of $4,880 using a LIFO cost flow assumption.

a. How many units of inventory did Trevor Company sell in July?

b. How many units of inventory did Trevor Company have on hand at July 31?

c. What was the dollar amount reported as ending inventory at July 31?

E9-29 Inventory Cost Flows—FIFO Crossties Company uses the FIFO cost flow assumption to determine its cost of goods sold. During the first quarter of 2001, Crossties accumulated the following inventory information:

	Units	Total Cost
January 1 (beginning inventory)	1,000	$25,000
February 15 (purchase)	2,000	54,000
March 1 (purchase)	1,500	42,000
March 30 (purchase)	1,000	30,000

March 31 inventory was 1,200 units, and sales revenue for the quarter was $250,000.

a. What is the balance in inventory at the end of the first quarter of 2001?

b. What is the cost of goods sold for the first quarter?

c. Compute the gross profit for the first quarter.

d. Compute the inventory turnover for the first quarter.

E9-30 Inventory Cost Flows—LIFO Growtop Company increased the balance of its inventory of rooftop miniature greenhouses from 200 units at a total cost of $30,000 on April 1 to 250 units on April 30. Since inventory costs also have been increasing, Growtop management is worried about whether it is maintaining a reasonable gross profit percentage. Growtop uses the LIFO inventory cost flow assumption for its greenhouses. You are given the following information about purchases and sales in April:

Purchases	Units	Unit Cost
April 5	250	$160
April 12	100	170
April 24	300	180

Sales revenue for April was $200,000.

a. Compute the amount to be reported as inventory at April 30.
b. Compute Growtop's cost of goods sold and gross profit for April.
c. Compute the gross profit percentage and inventory turnover for April.

E9-31 Inventory Cost Flows—Average Cost On January 1, 2001, the Pocket Phone Corporation had 1,500 cell phones in inventory at an average cost of $27. During 2001, total sales of phones was $210,000 and the ending inventory on December 31 was 1,000 units. Purchases during 2001 were:

Purchases	Units	Unit Cost
1st quarter	1,000	$28.00
2nd quarter	1,200	30.00
3rd quarter	800	32.50

Using the average cost flow assumption:

a. What was the cost of Pocket Phone's ending inventory?
b. Compute the cost of goods sold and gross profit for 2001.
c. Compute the gross profit percentage and the inventory turnover for 2001.

E9-32 Inventory Cost Flow Assumptions The Comfort Zone Bed Company started its business on January 1, 2000, with an inventory of 40 beds purchased for $80 each. During the first six months of operations Comfort Zone sold 130 beds for $120 each. Comfort Zone is interested in obtaining a bank loan to expand its operations. The bank wants information on Comfort Zone's sales, inventory balances, and gross profit before approving the loan. Comfort Zone has 50 beds on hand at June 30 and reports its inventory costs have been declining. The company provides the following information about inventory purchases during the first six months of operations:

Purchases:			
	April 12	50 beds	$75.00
	May 24	50 beds	70.00
	June 15	40 beds	65.00

a. Comfort Zone has not chosen an inventory cost flow assumption for its operations. To help it make a choice, determine the following information using FIFO, LIFO, and average inventory cost flow assumptions.
  1. The inventory balance at June 30.
  2. Cost of goods sold and gross profit for the six-month period.
  3. Gross profit percentage and inventory turnover for the six-month period.
b. Which inventory cost flow assumption would be the most positive for obtaining the bank loan? Are there any disadvantages to its use?

E9-33 Choice of Inventory Costing Methods Best Co. recorded the following inventory transactions during 2001:

	Number of Units	Unit Purchase Price	Unit Sale Price
Inventory balance			
January 1, 2001	75	$5	
Purchase	150	$6	
Sale	100		$15
Purchase	50	$8	
Purchase	80	$7	
Sale	160		$16

a. Calculate cost of goods sold and gross profit for Best Co. for 2001 assuming Best uses a first-in, first-out cost-flow assumption.
b. Calculate cost of goods sold and gross profit for Best Co. for 2001 assuming Best uses a last-in, first-out cost-flow assumption.
c. Which of the two methods provides the most conservative estimate of the carrying value of inventory? Which provides the best estimate of the current cost of replacing the inventory? Explain your answers.
d. Which method provides the most conservative estimate of reported income? Under what circumstances would the opposite be true?

E9-34 Perpetual Inventory System On January 10, Pastel Corp. purchased inventory for $240,000 and paid freight charges of $30,000 to acquire 9,000 units of inventory. On January 18, Pastel sold on credit 4,000 units of the inventory at $45 each. Payment of $100,000 was received on account on January 26. Pastel uses a perpetual inventory system.

a. Present Pastel's journal entries to record these transactions in January.
b. Compute the amount of gross profit on sales for January.

E9-35 Periodic and Perpetual Inventory Systems On November 1, Howard Retailers had in inventory 1,000 toasters that had been purchased for $6 each. On November 10, Howard Retailers purchased 10,000 new toasters costing $85,000 and paid freight charges of $7,000. Howard Retailers sold 800 toasters between November 1 and November 10, and another 7,700 were sold during the remainder of the month. The toasters sell for $14 each.

a. Assume Howard Retailers uses a perpetual inventory system, keeping track of its cost of goods sold at the time of each transaction. Show the computation of gross profit for Howard Retailers for November if the company costs its inventory using (1) LIFO; (2) FIFO.

b. Assume Howard Retailers uses a periodic inventory system, computing its cost of goods sold only at the end of the month. Show the computation of gross profit for Howard Retailers for November if the company costs its inventory using (1) LIFO; (2) FIFO.

E9-36 Inventcry Transactions Martie Company had a beginning inventory of 100 units with a cost of $17 each. During May, the company engaged in the following transactions:

May 1	Purchased 1,000 units of inventory at a list price of $19 each; because of a special promotion, Martie is given a special 10 percent quantity discount and payment terms of net 30.
5	Paid freight charges of $2,000 on the May 1 purchase.
7	Sold 500 units for $25 each, with terms of net eom (end of month).
9	Paid for the May 1 purchase.
10	Purchased 200 units of inventory for $20 each, freight included; terms: net 30.
15	Sold 100 units for cash of $25 each.
19	Purchased 800 units of inventory for $22 each, freight included; terms: net 30.
25	Sold 1,200 units for $30 each on account; terms: net 30.
30	Purchased 200 units of inventory for $23 each, with terms of net 30; freight charges of $400 will be due in 5 days.

Martie Company uses a perpetual inventory system, computing its cost of goods sold for each sale and its new inventory balance after each inventory transaction. The company assigns inventory costs on a FIFO basis.

a. Prepare a schedule showing the computation of Martie's cost of goods sold for May.

b. Prepare a schedule showing the composition of Martie's inventory at the end of May.

c. If Martie assigned inventory costs on a LIFO basis rather than FIFO, compute the company's cost of goods sold and ending inventory for May.

d. If Martie assigned inventory costs on a moving-average basis, recomputing the average cost of its inventory after each purchase, compute the company's cost of goods sold and ending inventory for May.

E9-37 Recording Inventory Transactions Prepare journal entries to record all of the transactions listed in E9-36.

Assume Martie Company uses a perpetual inventory system and assigns inventory costs on a FIFO basis.

E9-38 Inventory Revaluation Kim Corporation carries a number of different types of widgets. At the end of 2000, the chief financial officer of Kim Corporation noted that the international price of widgets had been dropping appreciably. Widgets currently on hand that had been purchased in July 2000 for $9 per unit could be replaced at the end of December for $6 per unit.

a. If Kim Corporation has 3,000 widgets on hand at December 31, 2000, at what dollar amount should inventory be reported? Is any other information needed to determine the year-end reporting amount? Explain.

b. Why is the decline in the replacement price of widgets relevant in this situation?

c. Which accounting concept(s) are relevant in deciding the dollar amount of inventory to be reported? Explain why these concepts are important.

E9-39 Lower of Cost or Market Taylor Department Stores has just finished counting its inventory at the end of the year. After carefully compiling the results and gathering other data, the company controller reported the following information with regard to the four inventory groups held by Taylor:

Inventory Group	Purchase Price	Market Value
Women's Apparel	$350,000	$460,000
Men's Apparel	250,000	315,000
Appliances	600,000	540,000
Toys	290,000	270,000

a. Why is inventory typically valued at the lower of its cost or market value?

b. For each of the individual inventory categories listed, what dollar amount do you think would provide the most useful information to decision makers if reported in Taylor's balance sheet? Why?

c. In a retail environment, what might cause the estimated net sales price of inventory to be lower than its cost?

d. If Taylor were to write down the carrying amount of its inventory, what effect would this have on its financial statements? Specifically, which accounts would be affected?

e. Would the amount of Taylor's inventory write-down be different if the year-end valuations were based on the inventory as a whole rather than individual categories of inventory? Explain. Which approach do you think provides more useful information for decision makers?

E9-40 Alternative Inventory Systems Uppercut Corporation purchases boxing gloves and markets them to local YMCAs and gymnasiums. Uppercut had on hand at the beginning of April an inventory of 50 units, previously purchased for $31 each. Transactions in April were as follows:

April 1 Purchased 400 units of inventory at $30 each, on account.
 5 Paid $400 freight charge on April 1 purchase.
 8 Sold 150 units at $50 each, on account.
 9 Paid for inventory purchased on April 1.
 20 Received payment for 100 units sold on April 8.

a. Prepare journal entries to record the transactions for April, assuming the company uses a perpetual inventory system. What is the dollar amount of inventory shown on Uppercut's books at the end of April?
b. A physical count of Uppercut's inventory at the end of April reveals an ending inventory of 280 units costed at $31 each. Compute the company's cost of goods sold for April assuming it uses a periodic inventory system.
c. What reasons might explain the discrepancy in the ending inventory balance between parts a and b? How would the discrepancy be treated in Uppercut's accounting records if the company were using a perpetual inventory system?

E9-41 Manufacturing Inventories Oddsen Ends Manufacturing Company started business at the end of May by renting a factory building for $3,000 per month and renting all of its equipment for $7,000 per month. The company also purchased $15,000 of raw materials. During June, its first month of operations, Oddsen Ends used $9,000 of raw materials to produce its product and paid production workers $20,000. Utility costs for the factory were $2,500 for June. During June, the company produced a total of 2,000 units of finished product and sold 800 units for $75 each. No work was in process at the end of the period. The company paid outside sales representatives a 12 percent commission on each unit sold. Administrative costs for the company as a whole totaled $14,500 for June.

a. Compute the dollar amount of raw materials inventory and finished goods inventory on hand at the end of June.
b. Prepare an income statement for June for Oddsen Ends.

E9-42 Inventory Turnover Field Company reported total inventory at January 1 and December 31, 2000, of $200,000 and $160,000, respectively. Cost of goods sold for 2000 was $470,000. Field's nearest competitor reported inventories of $350,000 and $400,000 at January 1 and December 31, 2000, respectively, and reported cost of goods sold of $900,000 for 2000. Total 2000 sales for Field Company and its competitor were $600,000 and $1,250,000, respectively.

a. Compute the inventory turnover ratios for the two companies for 2000.
b. Compute the gross profit percentage (gross profit divided by sales) for the two companies for 2000.
c. On the basis of inventory turnover, which company is superior?
d. On the basis of gross profit percentage, which company is superior?
e. Which company would you recommend as best managed? Indicate why.

USING ACCOUNTING FOR DECISION MAKING

P9-43 Perpetual Inventory Methods Clifton Enterprises uses a perpetual inventory system under which inventory costs and cost of goods sold are recomputed after each inventory transaction. During March, the company engaged in the following transactions:

Mar. 1 Inventory on hand: 10 units @ $6.00 each.
 5 Purchased 15 units @ $8.00 each.
 9 Purchased 12 units @ $8.50 each.
 16 Sold 23 units @ $12.00 each.
 22 Sold 10 units @ $13.00 each.
 26 Purchased 35 units @ $9.00 each.
 31 Sold 19 units @ $14.00 each.

The company vice president does not understand the effects of different inventory costing methods and has asked that you provide computations showing:

a. Ending inventory at March 31, and cost of goods sold for March, assuming the inventory costing method used is:
 1. FIFO.
 2. LIFO.
 3. Moving average (average inventory cost calculated after each purchase).

b. The cash savings or additional payment related to income taxes in March if Clifton Enterprises switches from FIFO to LIFO at March 1. Clifton's current income tax rate is 30 percent.
c. President I. M. Simple is reluctant to switch from FIFO to LIFO for fear of obsolescence from keeping old inventory on hand while selling the latest units purchased. Are the president's concerns valid? Explain.

P9-44 Inventory Valuation Turnbell Manufacturing held no inventory at the beginning of March. Inventory purchases by the company during March were as follows:

March 7 Purchased 8,000 units @ $25.00 each
 14 Purchased 4,000 units @ $20.00 each
 23 Purchased 12,000 units @ $15.00 each
 28 Purchased 6,000 units @ $17.50 each
  30,000 units

Turnbell uses a periodic inventory system. At the end of March, the company had 10,000 units of inventory on hand.

a. Compute cost of goods sold for March using an average cost flow assumption.

b. Compute cost of goods sold for March using a first-in, first-out cost flow assumption.

c. Compute cost of goods sold for March using a last-in, first-out cost flow assumption.

d. Which inventory cost flow assumption results in the greatest net income for March? Which results in the smallest?

e. Which inventory cost flow assumption results in the largest inventory balance at March 31? Which results in the smallest balance?

f. If Turnbell was not restricted to using the same inventory costing method for both income tax and financial reporting, which methods should it use? Explain why.

P9-45 Cost of Goods Manufactured and Sold Torid Manufacturing Company produces heating equipment that is used by other companies in their manufacturing operations. Torid's accounting department provided the following cost information for 2001:

Inventory Type	Inventory Balances	
	Jan. 1, 2001	Dec. 31, 2001
Finished goods	$310,000	$490,000
Work-in-process	280,000	70,000
Raw materials	320,000	285,000
Production supplies	75,000	30,000
Total	$985,000	$875,000

Payroll records showed that labor costs related to manufacturing were $430,000 in 2001. Raw materials in the amount of $850,000 and supplies totaling $140,000 were purchased during the year. Other manufacturing costs totaled $125,000 for the year.

a. Why are labor and supplies costs included along with the cost of raw materials in computing the cost of finished goods inventory produced during the period?

b. Determine the amount reported as cost of goods sold for 2001.

c. How can information on raw materials and work-in-process inventories assist in your evaluation of the operations of Torid Manufacturing for 2001? What factors might be associated with a significant increase in the raw materials inventory?

P9-46 Manufacturing Inventories Bronze Manufacturing developed patents on several information transmission relays and has been producing and selling the relays for the past six years. At the end of 2000, Bronze reported the following inventory balances:

Finished goods	$450,000
Work-in-process	140,000
Raw materials	225,000
Production supplies	85,000
Total	$900,000

It takes Bronze approximately seven working days to complete the relays from the time they are put into production. For the year 2000, Bronze Manufacturing reported sales of $1,400,000, with 65 percent of the sales occurring in the third quarter of the year. Total cost of goods sold for 2000, was $720,000.

a. What is the difference between raw materials inventory and the production supplies inventory? What dangers are there in having excess raw materials inventory?

b. What amount of Bronze's inventory is available for shipment on December 31, 2000?

c. What dangers are there in having excess finished goods inventory?

d. What factors should be examined in judging the adequacy of the finished goods inventory at December 31, 2000? Does Bronze appear to have an appropriate amount of finished goods inventory on hand at December 31, 2000? Explain your answer.

P9-47 Financial Reporting Measures Tripod Industries uses the last-in, first-out inventory costing method in accounting for its purchases of cameras and film. On September 1, Tripod had 300 packages of professional-quality film on hand at a cost of $10 per package. Purchases and sales in September were:

Sept.	1	Purchased 200 packages @ $12 each
	9	Sold 350 packages @ $20 each
	10	Purchased 400 packages @ $9 each
	14	Sold 200 packages @ $18 each
	20	Sold 150 packages @ $22 each
	28	Purchased 250 packages @ $15 each

a. Compute cost of goods sold and ending inventory for September if Tripod uses a periodic inventory system.

b. By what amount would cost of goods sold have been more or less if Tripod had used the first-in, first-out method of costing its inventory?

c. The controller of Tripod is interested in computing cost of goods sold and inventory balances on a more frequent basis as a means of improving the information available for decision making. Assuming Tripod costs its inventory on a LIFO basis using a perpetual inventory system, compute cost of goods sold and ending inventory for September.

d. Compare the results from using last-in, first-out for the period overall in part a and those using perpetual computations in part c. What is the amount of the change? What causes this difference? Which method more accurately measures operating results? Should an external decision maker care whether a company uses a perpetual or periodic inventory system? Explain.

P9-48 Inventory Controls Highland Manufacturing produces overhead conveyer systems and has in inventory at any given time more than $2,000,000 of equipment ready for delivery. Highland stores its inventory in a covered and fenced yard with no other security systems. Soundbox Stereo Corporation produces stereo systems for owner installation in automobiles and normally has $600,000 of completed stereo systems in inventory. Soundbox stores its inventory in buildings that are locked at night and have elaborate alarm systems. In addition, employees are required to wear company uniforms while at work and must change to street clothes before leaving work.

a. What factors may dictate the need for different security and control systems for the protection of inventory in the two companies? Why does Soundbox feel the need to lock its building and have an alarm system while Highland does not? Why does Soundbox require its employees to wear company uniforms at work and change into street clothes before leaving?

b. Both companies also receive large amounts of direct cash payments from customers. What controls should the companies have in place to ensure that cash is not stolen?

c. How does the use of a perpetual inventory system assist companies in determining whether inventory theft has occurred?

EXPANDING YOUR HORIZONS

C9-49 Analyzing Gateway The Gateway financial statements and accompanying notes included in Appendix A provide information that can be used in responding to the following:

a. What amount of inventory is reported in the most recent consolidated balance sheet? What proportion of current assets and total assets does inventory make up? Did inventory increase or decrease in 1998? By what amount?

b. What amount of cost of goods sold was reported for 1998? Compute the gross profit percentage for 1998 and the prior two years. Has the gross profit percentage remained relatively stable over this period, or has there been substantial change from year to year?

c. Inventory turnover is often calculated using average inventory for the year rather than the year-end balance. Compute Gateway's inventory turnover for 1998 using its average inventory balance. Using only the inventory balance at year end, what was Gateway's inventory turnover for 1998? Is the turnover based on the average inventory balance greatly different from turnover based on the year-end balance? Is the difference enough to affect an investor or creditor's decisions? Explain.

d. What proportion of Gateway's inventory at December 31, 1998, is in the form of components and subassemblies versus finished goods? Why does Gateway not report any raw materials inventory?

e. If Gateway's goals include keeping inventory levels no higher than 10 percent of current assets and attaining a gross profit percentage of at least 25 percent, was the company successful in 1998? How else might you assess Gateway's inventory levels, inventory turnover, and gross profit percentage?

C9-50 Inventory Problems for General Mills General Mills's 1994 annual report cited "disappointing" financial results. The poor results were believed to be the result of two major problems in the cereal segment of the business: promotional activities and inventories. The following is an excerpt from the 1994 annual report:

The second major problem affecting Big G cereals and 1994 results was the improper substitution of an unregistered pesticide during the year by a licensed independent contractor who treated part of the company's raw oat supply. While the substitution did not present any consumer health hazard, it did represent a regulatory violation. We voluntarily halted shipments of affected oat-containing products and did not seek permission to ship affected inventories because the process required to secure regulatory approval proved so lengthy, it would exceed the product age limits we employ to ensure freshness in the market. Production and shipment of our oat cereals was interrupted for a month-long period in June and July. By late July, the company resumed full production and shipment of oat-containing products.

a. What effect might General Mills's inventory problem have had on its income statement?

b. What effect might the inventory problem have had on General Mills's balance sheet?

c. How would you account for this inventory problem?

C9-51 Analysis of ADM Archer Daniels Midland Company (ADM) is in the business of procuring, transporting, storing, processing, and merchandising agricultural commodities. The company reported record-high sales and cost of products sold in 1998. Selected financial statement information from ADM's 1998 annual report is as follows (in thousands of dollars):

	1998	1997
Net sales and other operating income	$16,108,630	$13,853,262
Cost of products sold and other operating costs	(14,727,670)	(12,552,718)
Gross profit	$ 1,380,960	$ 1,300,544
Inventories, January 1	$ 2,094,092	$ 1,790,636
Inventories, December 31	2,562,650	2,094,092

Based on ADM's financial statement information, respond to each of the following questions:

a. What was the percent increase in sales for 1998?

b. What was the dollar increase in inventory during 1998? If inventory had increased the same percent as sales, what would the dollar increase have been?

c. What was the percent increase in inventory during 1998? Did ADM satisfactorily control its inventory level during 1998? Explain.

d. If a company's sales volume increases significantly, would you expect its inventory turnover to increase or decrease? Explain. Did ADM's inventory turnover improve from 1997 to 1998?

 C9-52 Team Project: Analyzing Financial Statements
Acquire the financial statements of a large manufacturing company, such as General Motors, a large electric or gas utility company, such as Duke Energy Corporation or Ameren Corporation (previously Union Electric Company), and a large bank, such as Wells Fargo & Company. For each company, examine the balance sheet, income statement, statement of cash flows, and notes to the financial statements. Prepare a short report in which you include the following:

a. Compute the proportion of total assets represented by inventory and property, plant, and equipment. Which company has the greatest percentage of each of these two asset categories? Explain how these percentages are related to the type of company.

b. Which companies have inventories? What methods are used in valuing and accounting for the inventories? Did any of the companies change inventory methods during the year? If so, evaluate the rationale given for the change.

c. For the manufacturing company, what was the total cost of goods sold for the most recent period? What was the amount of gross margin? What was the gross margin percentage? What was the inventory turnover ratio for the most recent period?

d. Can amounts comparable to those computed for the manufacturing company be computed for the utility company? If not, what profitability or efficiency ratios can be substituted?

e. How would you determine if the measures computed in parts c and d are reasonable? From a library or database find appropriate data to use for comparative purposes. Include in your report why your comparisons are appropriate, and discuss how the companies you have chosen have performed in relation to your comparative data.

C9-53 Inventory Decisions During 2000, the management of Getz Furniture Manufacturing Company decided that too much money was tied up in inventory. Most of Getz's furniture is manufactured based on advance orders, and the amount of raw materials and other supplies needed can be determined in advance. A corporate program was started early in 2001 to coordinate the sales staff, production schedulers, suppliers, and shipping companies to reduce the need for keeping large amounts of inventory on hand by having it delivered to the manufacturing plant no sooner than two days

before it is to be used. Shipments to customers are to be made within one week of completion of the furniture. Now, at the end of 2001 you are evaluating Getz to decide whether the program was successful and whether there were any unexpected costs. If the program worked, you are going to try it in your company. You have gathered the following information from Getz's financial statements.

	2000	2001
Inventory:		
Raw materials	$ 435,000	$ 400,000
Work-in-process	85,000	185,000
Finished goods	365,000	35,000
Total	$ 885,000	$ 620,000
Sales	3,355,000	3,000,000
Cost of goods sold	2,355,000	2,250,000

a. Will you recommend a similar program for your company? Why or why not? In your analysis, consider at a minimum the inventory turnover in total and for each type of inventory, gross margin percentages, and total sales.

b. If Getz had reported that its volume of sales remained at 2000 levels in 2001 and that raw materials purchases declined almost 20 percent, would your recommendation change? Explain.

C9-54 Ethics and the Valuation of Inventory Your company manufactures a line of processed snack foods using a soybean base with a low fat content. The line was very popular until recent publicity that emphasized that the product is very high in salt and contains numerous chemical preservatives. Now, you have inventory on hand that will be hard to sell. The inventory originally cost $3,500,000. Its wholesale selling price prior to the publicity had been $7,000,000. The sales division has presented the following alternative proposals to the executive committee of which you are a member:

Proposal 1: Offer the product at deep discounts to the regular customers. If the discount is large enough, all the inventory will probably be sold. The expected selling price for the total inventory under these conditions is estimated to be about $2,000,000.

Proposal 2: Market the product in third-world counties as a nutritious soybean-based food. Marketing costs will probably be $1,000,000, but the entire inventory could be sold at regular list price of $7,000,000. Nutrition disclosure requirements are virtually nonexistent in most of these countries.

As a member of the executive committee, address each of the following issues:

a. Do any accounting entries need to be made to reflect the inventory problems?

b. Which proposal would you favor? Would you suggest any other alternatives?

c. What type of financial disclosure would you expect your company to make if financial statements were prepared prior to the selection of an alternative for disposing of the inventory?

Internet Exercises: Visit our Web site for additional exercises.

Annual Report Project Part 9

Refer to the Annual Report Project, Part 1, at the end of Chapter 1. Using the annual report of the company you have chosen, and any other available information, answer the following questions, providing sources and computations where appropriate.

a. Does your company disclose, either in the balance sheet or accompanying notes, any prepaid expenses? If so, what is the amount and nature of those prepaid expenses?

b. Does your company manufacture the inventory it sells, or does it just buy and resell inventory?

c. What inventory valuation and costing methods does the company use?

d. Inventory represents what percentage of current assets for your company? What percentage of total assets? Did these percentages change significantly during the latest reporting period?

e. Based on ending inventory, assess the company's inventory turnover compared with last year.

f. Does your company disclose, either in the balance sheet or accompanying notes, different categories of inventory? If so, what are they?

g. Did your company have any special write-offs or write-downs of inventories during the most recent reporting period? If so, describe them.

CHAPTER TEN

Operating Assets and Intangibles

REVIEW

Chapter 9 presented the basic concepts of accounting and reporting for nonfinancial assets and focused on prepaid expenses and inventory.

WHERE THIS CHAPTER FITS

This chapter continues the discussion of nonfinancial assets by focusing on operating and intangible assets. As with prepaid expenses and inventories, the determination of cost and the matching of that cost with the benefits provided are the key concepts on which financial reporting of operating and intangible assets is based. This chapter concludes the discussion of assets by looking at some aspects of asset financing.

LOOKING AHEAD

The next two chapters complete the discussion of the financial statement elements. Chapter 11 examines liabilities, and Chapter 12 focuses on the components of owners' equity.

My friend wants to sell me his old car, but I really had my heart set on buying a brand new one. He says that new cars are a waste of money. He told me a new car depreciates $2,000 just driving it off the showroom floor. Why, at that rate, it will probably be worthless by the time I get it home. What is depreciation, anyway?

"Conventional wisdom is that capitalizing [research and development] spending . . . is aggressive [accounting] because there is no way of knowing if the spending will ever pay off. But you can say the same thing for most capital spending on plant and equipment. In the 1970s, the U.S. steel industry poured tens of billions into new equipment that became obsolete almost as soon as it was installed. Yet the steel companies were showing healthy profits and the new plants were carried as assets, though they turned out to be worthless."[1]

[1] Bernard Condon, "Gaps in GAAP," *Forbes* (January 25, 1999), p. 78.

The acquisition of long-lived assets, such as houses and cars, is an important step for individuals. Similarly, businesses often invest huge sums of money in plant, equipment, and other long-lived assets, and a company's success, or even its survival, may depend on the efficiency with which these assets are used.

Nearly all large companies, as well as many small ones, have at least some investment in long-lived assets. For manufacturing firms, that investment tends to be large and especially significant for the success of the enterprise. Thus, decision makers examining a company's financial statements must pay particular attention to the amount of a company's long-lived assets, when and how those assets will be replaced, how they are financed, and how efficiently they are used.

The purpose of this chapter is to continue our discussion of nonfinancial assets by focusing on long-lived assets. The principles of accounting and reporting for long-lived nonfinancial assets are the same as for current nonfinancial assets. Specifically, the major accounting issues involve determining asset cost and allocating that cost, through the matching process, to the periods benefiting from the use of the asset. When you have completed this chapter, you should be able to:

1. Describe long-lived nonfinancial assets and their importance for decision making.

2. Describe the valuation methods used for long-lived nonfinancial assets both at acquisition and after acquisition, and explain how these methods facilitate decision making.

3. Explain how intangible assets differ from tangible assets; describe the similarities and differences in accounting and reporting for tangible and intangible assets, and describe how they might affect decision making.

4. Define key ratios and indicators for financial analysis related to long-lived nonfinancial assets, and use these ratios and indicators to understand a company's activities and financial position.

5. Describe the different means of financing asset acquisitions, and indicate the important considerations for decision making relating to financing asset acquisitions and reporting for them.

UNDERSTANDING OPERATING ASSETS

Information for Decisions

To be successful, companies must use their operating assets effectively and efficiently. Financial statement information about operating assets can be used to answer questions such as these: How does the rate of return earned on the company's assets compare with last year and with other companies in the industry? Does the company have considerable money tied up in operating assets, and what does this mean for future capital requirements? Is the company's collection of operating assets appropriate for its operations? Is the operating asset base expanding or contracting?

The main assets used in a company's central activities may be viewed as operating assets, but are usually labeled *fixed assets* or *property, plant, and equipment*. The important characteristics of these assets are that they are used in operations rather than held for sale to customers, they are tangible in that they have physical existence, and they are long-lived in that they are expected to last beyond a single period or operating cycle.

For merchandising companies, operating assets may include land on which buildings and parking lots are constructed, buildings, furniture and fixtures for offices and sales outlets, moving equipment (e.g., forklifts), and delivery equipment. For manufacturing enterprises, operating assets also include production equipment and other production-related items such as tools. Thus, both types of companies almost always have a significant amount of operating assets.

In Practice 10-1

MCDONALD'S CORPORATION

In 1998, McDonald's reported total assets worldwide of $19.8 billion. Of this total, net property and equipment was reported (in millions) as:

Property and equipment, at cost	$21,758.0
Accumulated depreciation and amortization	(5,716.4)
Net property and equipment	$16,041.6

ANALYSIS

More than 80 percent of McDonald's total assets are in operating property and equipment. In a footnote, McDonald's states that these assets are depreciated over three to twelve years for equipment and up to forty years for buildings. Depreciation and amortization in 1998, reflecting the cost of using these assets, was $881.1 million. [www.mcdonalds.com]

Because operating assets may be costly, an evaluation of the company often focuses on whether these assets are being used efficiently and profitably. For example, a commonly used measure of profitability is return on assets. **Return on assets** is typically measured by dividing net income for the year by either the average balance of operating assets or the average amount of total assets on hand during the period.[2] If, for example, a company reported net income of $1,500,000 and had total assets of $10,000,000, the return on assets would be:

$$\text{Return on Assets} = \frac{\text{Net Income}}{\text{Average Total Assets}} = \frac{\$1,500,000}{\$10,000,000} = .15 \text{ or } 15\%$$

If investments in a company's assets provide a lower return than for other companies in the same industry, the company may be operating inefficiently. Similarly, if the percentage return is less than might be earned by investing the shareholders' money in other alternatives, the company may be in the wrong business, or perhaps should not be in business at all. On the other hand, a high return on assets relative to other investment alternatives might signal a good use of investment capital.

Some companies separate the return on assets calculation into two separate components that contribute to return on assets:

$$\frac{\text{Net Income}}{\text{Sales}} \times \frac{\text{Sales}}{\text{Average Total Assets}} = \frac{\text{Net Income}}{\text{Average Total Assets}}$$

The first component, net income divided by sales, is referred to as the **margin on sales**, or the profit margin. It indicates the portion of sales remaining as profit after expenses. The second component, sales divided by average total assets, is referred to as the **asset turnover**. This is a measure of the extent to which sales are generated, based on the assets held, and is an indication of the effectiveness with which assets are used. A similar measure is the **fixed asset turnover**, equal to sales revenues divided by average fixed assets. For example, the fixed asset turnover for Procter & Gamble, which reported revenues of $37,154 million and had average fixed assets of $11,778 million, would be calculated as follows:

$$\text{Fixed Asset Turnover} = \frac{\text{Sales}}{\text{Average Fixed Assets}} = \frac{\$37,154 \text{ million}}{\$11,778 \text{ million}} = 3.15$$

The higher the turnover, the more efficient the enterprise is in generating revenues using its current investment in property, plant, and equipment.

Large investments in operating assets usually mean large expenditures will be needed in the future for maintenance, repairs, and replacement. Accordingly, a company should be generating enough income and cash so that it is able to make the expenditures necessary to maintain its operating asset base. Further, the company may be required under asset acquisition arrangements, such as leases or installment purchases, to make fixed payments over time. Failure to make such payments might result in the loss of operating assets. The amount of Accumulated Depreciation reported in relation to the reported cost of depreciable assets may be important because it provides some indication of the age of the assets and to what extent their service potential has expired.

Because operating assets are so crucial to the continuing activities of manufacturing and merchandising companies, any major changes in the levels of these assets should be examined. Large increases indicate an expectation for increased activity in the future, but also typically require additional future resources. Large decreases may indicate a serious decline in the current or expected future activity level, or may indicate the company is having difficulty financing its current asset base.

---

[2] This computation of return on assets is often used because of its simplicity. A better formulation is obtained by adding back the after-tax effect of interest expense to net income before dividing by average total assets.

In Practice 10-2

MORRISON KNUDSEN

The construction firm of Morrison Knudsen Corp., best known for building Hoover Dam many decades ago, attempted in the 1980s and 1990s to become a major provider of rail transportation systems and equipment. The company's efforts were so costly that it began selling off plant and equipment to generate needed cash. Ultimately, it found that it no longer owned many of the assets it needed to operate and had to lease them from others.

ANALYSIS

Poor operating results were hidden by gains on sales of operating assets until the company no longer had assets it could sell. Then it did not own the assets it needed for operations and had to enter into costly lease agreements to continue operating. A careful analysis of the company's financial statements, focusing on long-lived assets and the sources of income and cash flows, should have provided signs of the company's distress. (Subsequently, Morrison Knudsen reorganized and merged with Washington Construction. In 1998, the company reported that it was essentially debt-free.) [www.mk.com]

ACCOUNTING AND REPORTING FOR OPERATING ASSETS

Information for Decisions

To help in the evaluation of the success of a company's operations, accrual accounting matches the costs of assets used against the benefits generated. When assessing the role of operating assets in a company's success, financial statement users need to be able to answer questions such as these: What costs have been included in the amounts reported as operating assets, and how are similar costs treated by other companies in the industry? How are the costs of operating assets matched with the benefits provided? What effect does this matching have on the income of each period in which the operating assets are used?

As with other nonfinancial assets, operating asset values are based on cost. Market values are typically not relevant because the assets are meant to be used in the company's operations, not sold. Rather, the relevant concept with operating assets is matching. Financial statement users can best assess the success of a company's operations if the costs of using assets are matched with the revenues produced, reporting both the costs and revenues in the income statement in the same period. Therefore, the cost of assets such as buildings and equipment must be matched with the benefits received from using those assets. This is done by reporting a portion of the cost of the assets as expense in each period benefited:

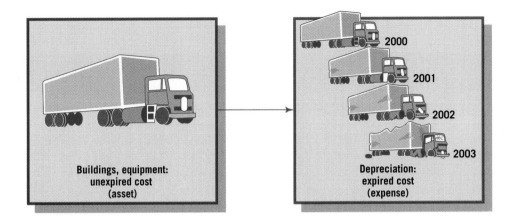

Land held as an operating asset is usually reported at its cost as long as it is held. Land has an unlimited life, and its original cost is expected to be recovered if the land is ever sold. Therefore, its cost need not be matched against benefits because it is not expected to expire.

Let's look next at the two main issues relating to accounting for operating assets: determining cost and the matching of costs and benefits.

DETERMINING COST

As with inventory, the amount reported on the balance sheet for operating assets includes all costs necessarily incurred by the company to acquire those assets. Thus, any shipping charges borne by the company, as well as any transfer costs, such as legal fees, become part of the cost of operating assets acquired. Any costs of preparing operating assets for their intended use also become part of the cost of those assets. For example, if a company purchased land with the intention of using it as a parking lot, the cost of demolishing an existing building on the land would be treated as part of the cost of the land.

Remember that when nonfinancial assets are acquired on credit and interest charges are incurred, the interest is typically viewed as a cost of borrowing money rather than a cost of the asset. However, when operating assets are constructed over an extended period of time rather than being purchased ready-to-use, the cost (interest) of money borrowed during the construction period is viewed as a cost of acquiring the asset. Therefore, that interest becomes part of the cost of the asset. Once the asset is ready to be put into use, no further interest may be added to the cost.

MATCHING THE COST OF OPERATING ASSETS

Virtually all operating assets with the exception of land have lives that are limited by wear and tear, deterioration, and obsolescence. When assets are no longer useful to the company, they are usually sold or scrapped. The proceeds received when an asset is sold or scrapped, referred to as **salvage value**, are usually much less than the original purchase price. The company, therefore, incurs a net cost of using the asset equal to the difference between the original cost of the asset and its salvage value. This net cost, or depreciable base, must be recognized by the company as an operating expense over the useful life of the asset. In the next section, we'll discuss how depreciation matches an asset's cost against the benefits provided from using the asset.

ALLOCATING THE COST OF OPERATING ASSETS

Information for Decisions

For those companies with a substantial investment in operating assets, the allocated portion of the cost of those assets matched against income in the current period (depreciation expense) and prior periods (accumulated depreciation) can significantly affect reported income and financial position. An analysis of the financial statements can help answer questions such as these: To what extent would the reported income of the company have been different if different depreciation methods had been employed, and how will the company's depreciation policies affect income in future periods? How do the company's depreciation policies compare with other companies in the industry? To what extent has the service potential of the company's operating assets been used up, indicating the possibility of major expenditures for replacement in the near future?

The allocation of the cost of a tangible operating asset to the periods benefiting from its use is referred to as **depreciation**. Accounting depreciation is different from the popular notion that depreciation is a reduction in current market value. The accounting concept of depreciation reflects only an allocation of cost and does not involve an attempt to revalue assets to market value.

As the service potential of an operating asset is used up, its cost is transferred from the asset account to an expense account, Depreciation Expense, so the cost is recognized in the same period as the benefit. The asset account is not reduced directly, however, so that financial statement users can continue to see the original cost of operating assets. Instead, a contra-asset account, **Accumulated Depreciation**, is used. The amounts of the asset cost that have expired over time are accumulated in this contra-asset account, and the balance of this account is deducted from the asset account in the balance sheet. Keep in mind that Depreciation Expense is a temporary account reported in the income statement and is closed at the end of each period, while Accumulated Depreciation is a permanent balance sheet account carried over from period to period as long as the asset is owned.

The **book value** of an asset is the amount at which the asset is reported in the financial statements. For limited-life operating assets, the book value is equal to the original cost of the asset minus the accumulated depreciation to date. Book value does not necessarily provide an indication of the fair value of the asset.

A CLOSER LOOK AT

DEPRECIATION

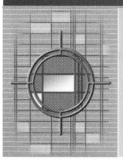

Speedy Parcel Service purchases a delivery truck for $25,000. The truck is expected to last for ten years, after which time it will have no value. If the truck provides Speedy with roughly equal benefits each year, Speedy will recognize $2,500 ($25,000 ÷ 10 years) of depreciation expense each year in its income statement. The amount of the accumulated depreciation, reported as a contra-asset in the balance sheet, will grow by $2,500 each year. At the end of the third year, the truck will be reported in the balance sheet as follows:

Equipment	$25,000
Less Accumulated Depreciation	(7,500)
Book Value	$17,500

By the end of ten years, the full cost of the asset will have expired and been allocated to expense over the ten-year period.

Annual Adjusting Entry

| Depreciation Expense | 2,500 | |
| Accumulated Depreciation | | 2,500 |

Income Statement Effects	
Expenses	+ 2,500
Net Income	− 2,500
Balance Sheet Effects	
Assets	− 2,500
Owners' Equity	− 2,500

Because depreciation reflects an attempt to match costs and benefits, the amount of cost charged to expense each year should be roughly proportional to the amount of benefit received from the asset. If an equal amount of benefit is expected to be received each year, an equal amount of depreciation expense should be recognized each year. If, on the other hand, an asset is expected to provide decreasing benefits as time passes, the depreciation expense should be allocated more heavily to the early years. Accordingly, a number of different depreciation methods are used in practice and are considered generally accepted. To simplify recordkeeping, many companies depreciate assets in categories or groups, using an average life rather than as individual assets. The depreciation methods most commonly used for financial reporting are straight-line and declining-balance, both based on the passage of time, and activity-based depreciation, based on usage.

STRAIGHT-LINE DEPRECIATION

The example of Speedy's delivery truck given earlier used **straight-line depreciation**. An equal amount of cost is allocated to each period benefited and is reported as Depreciation Expense in the income statement. This method is appropriate when the asset provides approximately equal benefits each period; that is, the asset's service potential expires evenly over time. For example, the building housing a company's sales offices might be viewed as benefiting equally each period during its life. The depreciation expense per period is equal to the asset's depreciable base, the cost minus expected salvage value, divided by its expected useful life to the company.

DECLINING-BALANCE DEPRECIATION

Many assets are expected to provide more net benefits in their early years, as compared with later in their lives. Some types of equipment, for example, may be more efficient when new, have less downtime, and cost less for repairs and maintenance. A depreciation method that allocates more cost to early years and less to later years is referred to as **accelerated depreciation**. One type of accelerated depreciation is the declining-balance method. Using **declining-balance depreciation**, a constant percentage is applied each year to the decreasing book value (cost minus accumulated depreciation) of the asset. Thus, the amount of depreciation is less each year as the book value decreases.

What percentage is used in declining-balance depreciation? That depends on how fast the asset is to be depreciated. The larger the percentage, the faster the asset is depreciated. The two most commonly used percentages for financial reporting are 200 percent and 150 percent because these percentages are accepted for tax reporting. The percentage chosen is multiplied times the straight-line rate and then applied to the book value of the asset. For example, if an asset has a ten-year life, it is depreciated at 10 percent per year (1 ÷ 10) using the straight-line method. Using 200 percent of the straight-line rate, commonly called **double-declining-balance depreciation**, the percentage applied to the asset's book value each year is 20 percent (.10 × 2.00). If 150 percent declining-balance depreciation is used for the same asset, the appropriate rate is 15 percent (.10 × 1.50).

In Practice 10-3

LA-Z-BOY INCORPORATED

In its fiscal 1998 year-end balance sheet, La-Z-Boy Incorporated includes the following information about its property, plant, and equipment:

Items capitalized, including significant betterments to existing facilities, are recorded at cost. Depreciation is computed using primarily accelerated methods over the estimated useful lives of the assets.

Note 4 to the financial statements provides the following presentation with respect to the company's property, plant, and equipment:

(Amounts in Thousands)	Life in Years	Depreciation Method	4/25/98	4/26/97
Land and land improvements	0–20	150%DB	$ 12,937	$ 11,296
Buildings and building fixtures	15–30	150%DB	116,145	110,875
Machinery and equipment	10	200%DB	114,502	107,316
Network and production tracking systems	5–10	SL	2,407	1,873
Transportation equipment	5	SL	15,606	14,974
Information systems	3–5	150–200%DB	20,738	16,295
Other	3–10	Various	18,048	14,186
			300,383	276,815
Less: accumulated depreciation....................			178,621	162,157
Property, plant and equipment, net			$121,762	$114,658

DB = Declining Balance   SL = Straight Line

ANALYSIS

La-Z-Boy provides a more detailed listing of property, plant, and equipment than most companies. The company is using both accelerated and straight-line depreciation, with declining-balance depreciation applied using two different write-off percentages. More than half of the cost of the company's property, plant, and equipment has been expensed to date. [www.lazboy.com]

Keep in mind that the appropriate percentage is applied to the asset's book value and not to its depreciable base, as with other depreciation methods. Salvage value is ignored when using declining-balance depreciation. Therefore, this method leads to a book value at the end of the asset's useful life that is not necessarily the anticipated salvage value unless, as is often done, the company switches to straight-line toward the end of the asset's life.

ACTIVITY-BASED DEPRECIATION

Depreciation might be based on usage rather than the passage of time. The **service-hours method of depreciation** bases the computation of depreciation expense on the ratio of the number of hours the asset was used during the period to the total number of hours expected in its service life. For example, if a machine is expected to operate a total of 20,000 hours during its life and it operates 4,000 hours during the current period, the amount of depreciation expense is calculated by multiplying the depreciable base by $4,000 \div 20,000$, or 0.2. The **units-of-production method of depreciation** is similar in that it is based on the number of units produced by an asset during the current period as a percent of the total expected production from the asset over its life.

EVALUATING DEPRECIATION METHODS

Given the different depreciation methods that are acceptable, which method should a company use? Remember that depreciation is a means of matching the cost of an asset purchased at one point in time with benefits provided by that asset over a number of periods so financial statement users can see the relationship between an enterprise's efforts and accomplishments. Accordingly, a company should choose depreciation methods that best match the depreciation expense with the benefits received. (See In Practice 10-4.) To understand better the alternative methods companies might use, let's look at some of the similarities and differences in the common depreciation methods.

A CLOSER LOOK AT

ALTERNATIVE DEPRECIATION METHODS

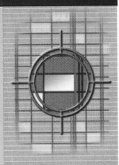

Dukes Corporation purchases a delivery van for $20,000. The van is expected to last five years and travel 100,000 miles during that time. Afterward, it is expected to be sold for about $2,000. After being placed in service, the van is driven 15,000 miles in the first year, 25,000 miles in each of the next three years, and 10,000 miles in the last year. Depreciation expense for each of the five years of the van's life is computed as follows under the three common depreciation methods:

Straight-line
  ($20,000 − $2,000)/5 years = $3,600 per year
  Total: $3,600 × 5 years = $18,000

Yr 2 Income Statement Effects	
Expenses	+ 3,600
Net Income	− 3,600
Yr 2 Balance Sheet Effects	
Assets	− 3,600
Owners' Equity	− 3,600

Double-declining-balance

Year 1	$(2.00 \times .20) \times (\$20,000) =$		$ 8,000
2	$(2.00 \times .20) \times (\$20,000 - \$8,000) =$		4,800
3	$(2.00 \times .20) \times (\$20,000 - \$12,800) =$		2,880
4	$(2.00 \times .20) \times (\$20,000 - \$15,680) =$		1,728
5	Depreciate down to salvage value		592
Total			$18,000

Activity-based

Year 1	$(15,000/100,000) \times (\$20,000 - \$2,000) =$		$ 2,700
2	$(25,000/100,000) \times (\$20,000 - \$2,000) =$		4,500
3	$(25,000/100,000) \times (\$20,000 - \$2,000) =$		4,500
4	$(25,000/100,000) \times (\$20,000 - \$2,000) =$		4,500
5	$(10,000/100,000) \times (\$20,000 - \$2,000) =$		1,800
Total			$18,000

Yr 2 Income Statement Effects

Expenses	+ 4,800
Net Income	− 4,800

Yr 2 Balance Sheet Effects

Assets	− 4,800
Owners' Equity	− 4,800

Yr 2 Income Statement Effects

Expenses	+ 4,500
Net Income	− 4,500

Yr 2 Balance Sheet Effects

Assets	− 4,500
Owners' Equity	− 4,500

Each of these three depreciation methods results in a different amount of annual depreciation expense. One method results in the same expense each year, one results in more depreciation during the early years and less later in the asset's life, and one varies based on asset usage. However, all of the methods attempt to allocate the company's cost of the asset over the periods benefited from the asset's use so the financial statements reflect a matching of costs and benefits in the computation of net income. No asset should be depreciated below its estimated salvage value.

Sometimes matching is not the only consideration in the choice of depreciation methods. For example, some companies choose straight-line because it is easy to compute. Others may choose straight-line or declining-balance because they also use it for tax purposes,

In Practice 10-4

NIKE, INC.

Nike reported property, plant, and equipment of $1,819.6 million and $1,425.8 million in 1998 and 1997, less accumulated depreciation of $666.5 million and $503.4 million, respectively. Footnote 1 to its financial statements indicated that property, plant, and equipment are recorded at cost. Depreciation for financial reporting purposes is determined on a straight-line basis for buildings and principally on a declining-balance basis for machinery and equipment, based on estimated useful lives ranging from two to forty years.

ANALYSIS

Nike's financial statements demonstrate that different depreciation methods may be used by the same company for different classes of assets. Like many manufacturers, Nike views the cost of using specialized assets as being higher in the earlier years of the asset lives. [www.nike.com]

and recordkeeping is reduced by using a single method for both. Thus, decision makers should be aware that a company's income may not always be based on an ideal matching of costs and benefits.

For mature companies that have reached a stable state where they are neither growing nor shrinking, the choice of depreciation methods may have little effect on the financial statements. Because in the long-run all depreciation methods allocate the same cost against income, the difference is in the amount allocated to each period. Thus, the real differences appear with companies that are growing rapidly and acquiring large amounts of new plant and equipment. For these companies, the use of accelerated depreciation may significantly reduce reported income in early years, but decision makers should remember that lower depreciation charges in later years will favorably affect income at that time.

You Decide 10-1

DECELERATED DEPRECIATION?

Swinging Lifestyles, Inc., recently opened a new apartment complex of three hundred small furnished apartments aimed at young singles. The apartment complex includes tennis courts, a swimming pool, and a recreation room. Because the complex is so large, it will take several years before it is fully occupied. The company will charge low rents initially to attract tenants. Therefore, revenues are expected to be low during the first few years, gradually increasing. In addition, advertising and sales expenses will be high in the early years, as will interest on the money borrowed to build the complex. Because more benefits are expected to be received by the company in later years than in the first few, the company develops a depreciation method that expenses less depreciation in early years than in later years. Is the company justified in adopting such a depreciation method? Explain. Would such a method provide the most useful view of the company's operations?

DEPRECIATION AND INCOME TAXES

An important aspect of depreciation is that it reduces income taxes. While all necessary business expenses are deductible in determining taxable income and, therefore, reduce taxes, depreciation results in a tax saving without a concurrent cash outflow for the expense. Although cash may have been expended originally to acquire the asset, depreciation is expensed after acquisition without requiring additional cash outlays. When the depreciation expense is recognized for tax purposes, however, it reduces income taxes, resulting in the reduction of a cash outflow. Depreciation, therefore, is said to provide a "tax shield." In general, companies prefer to use accelerated depreciation for tax purposes because they get the tax savings sooner rather than later.

With a few exceptions, depreciation for federal tax reporting is based on a **Modified Accelerated Cost Recovery System (MACRS)**. Under this system, the depreciation periods for different categories of assets are specified in the tax code, and they generally are shorter than actual lives. In addition, salvage value is ignored in computing depreciation. Depending on the category, either double-declining-balance or 150-percent-declining-balance depreciation must be used, with a switch to straight-line in the year in which declining-balance becomes less. For assets in the longest-life categories, straight-line depreciation is used throughout.

Federal income tax law does not have the same objectives as financial reporting. In the area of depreciation, the tax law aims at encouraging investment in productive assets and at narrowing areas of judgment in computing depreciation. Companies are permitted to use one depreciation method for tax purposes and another for financial reporting. The method used for financial reporting should provide a proper matching of costs and benefits.

DEPRECIATION OF MANUFACTURING ASSETS

Recall from our discussion of manufacturing inventories in Chapter 9 that all costs of producing inventory become part of the cost of the goods produced and are assigned to the individual units of inventory. When depreciable assets, such as factory buildings and equipment, are used in the manufacture of inventory, the depreciation of those assets is considered a cost of producing the inventory. Accordingly, the depreciation is assigned to the units of inventory produced rather than being expensed directly. The depreciation then becomes part of Cost of Goods Sold when the inventory is sold. Thus, any depreciation expense reported in the income statements of manufacturing companies relates only to non-production assets such as office buildings, office equipment, and delivery equipment. No depreciation expense related to manufacturing assets is reported directly because it is included in Cost of Goods Sold.

A CLOSER LOOK AT

DEPRECIATION EXPENSE

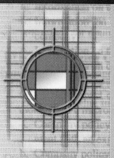

The Crumble Cookie Company produces cookies it sells retail at its outlet store, located in the same building as its ovens, and wholesale to local restaurants and convenience stores. Joe Crumble, the founder, and his son Tom deliver cookies to the local stores with their chocolate delivery truck. Crumble's $120,000 of depreciation expense for the period is included in several categories, as follows:

Cost of Goods Sold	$500,000 ($90,000 is depreciation on the mixers, ovens, and part of the building)
Selling Expense	$150,000 ($20,000 is depreciation on the chocolate delivery truck and part of the building)
Administrative Expenses	$50,000 ($10,000 is depreciation on office equipment and part of the building)

Like most companies, Crumble allocates depreciation expense to several categories in the income statement based on how the underlying assets are used.

DEPLETION: MATCHING THE COSTS OF NATURAL RESOURCES

Some companies develop holdings of natural resources, such as gas and oil, iron ore, coal, and timber. The resources are extracted or separated from the land and then sold, or converted into other forms, which are then sold. In effect, the company acquires an operating asset, resource-bearing land. It extracts and perhaps refines or modifies the resources, which are considered inventory, and then sells those resources. The process of accounting for the development and sale of natural resources is virtually identical to that of any manufacturing operation.

Resource-bearing land is acquired at a cost that includes the value of anticipated recoverable resources contained on the property. The value of that land is typically lower once the resources are removed, similar to the salvage value of depreciable assets. Thus, as with any other limited-life operating asset, the net cost to the company of using the asset is matched with the benefits provided. Included in the asset's net cost, in addition to acquisition costs, should be the costs of developing the property for removal of the resources and any costs of restoring the property after removal, such as reclamation costs following strip mining.

The cost of the developed property minus the residual value after considering restoration costs is allocated to units of the natural resources and is considered part of the cost of those resources. This cost is referred to as **depletion** and is similar to depreciation on manufacturing equipment. As with depreciable assets used in manufacturing, the depletion cost becomes part of the cost of the inventory produced. Extraction costs are also added to the cost of the inventory. The cost flows for the extraction and sale of natural resources can be pictured as follows:

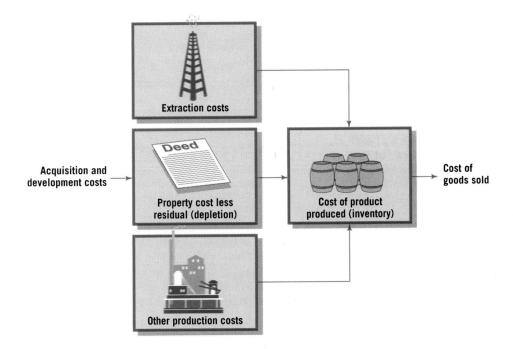

Depletion costs are allocated on a units-of-production basis. The total cost to be allocated is divided by the number of units of resources (e.g., barrels of oil, tons of coal) expected to be extracted from the property to determine a depletion cost per unit. Then, that amount is assigned to each unit of the resource extracted.

A CLOSER LOOK AT

ASSIGNING DEPLETION COSTS

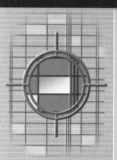

Grimy Coal Company purchases land containing coal deposits for $2,500,000 and spends an additional $800,000 for roads and removal of trees and surface soil. The company estimates that 1,000,000 tons of coal can be extracted from the property. The land is expected to be sold for about $100,000 after the coal deposits are removed. During the first year of operation, 500,000 tons of coal are extracted, and 400,000 tons are sold for $8.00 per ton. Additional extraction and production costs total $1,000,000 during the year. Depletion costs and the costs assigned to each ton of coal produced are computed as follows:

Depletion base = $2,500,000 + $800,000 − $100,000 = $3,200,000

Depletion cost per unit = $3,200,000 ÷ 1,000,000 tons = $3.20/ton

Other production costs per unit = $1,000,000 ÷ 500,000 tons = $2.00/ton

Total production cost per unit = $3.20 + $2.00 = $5.20/ton

Total cost of units produced during year = $5.20 × 500,000 = $2,600,000

Total cost of units sold during year = $5.20 × 400,000 = $2,080,000

Total depletion taken during year = $3.20 × 500,000 = $1,600,000

Grimy's financial statements for the year would include the following elements:

Income Statement

Sales Revenue ($8 × 400,000 tons)	$3,200,000
Cost of Goods Sold ($5.20 × 400,000 tons)	2,080,000

Balance Sheet

Current Assets:

Coal Inventory ($5.20 × 100,000 tons)	$ 520,000

Property, Plant, and Equipment:

Land with Coal Deposits (at cost of $3,300,000, less accumulated depletion of $1,600,000)	$1,700,000

Depletion does not appear in the income statement as a separate expense item. Instead, it is included in the cost of the resources sold during the period. This treatment permits decision makers to assess the success of a company's activities by comparing the total cost of the goods sold during the period with the revenues generated from selling those goods.

DISPOSALS AND IMPAIRMENTS OF OPERATING ASSETS

As we have seen, some or all of the cost of most operating assets is allocated, through depreciation or depletion, to the periods in which benefits are received from using those assets. Once specific operating assets are no longer needed, they are usually sold or scrapped. When this occurs, a gain or loss is recognized for the difference between the proceeds received, if any, and the book value (cost minus accumulated depreciation or depletion) of the asset. Although gains and losses on the disposal of assets are included in reported net income, the main focus when analyzing a company's financial statements should be on its recurring operating income.

A CLOSER LOOK AT

STANDARD SETTING: IS IT A RENTAL OR A SALE?

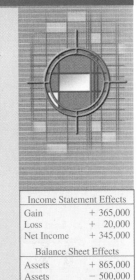

Ballard Company sells an unused parcel of land for $865,000. The land had originally cost the company $500,000, so a gain of $365,000 is recognized on the sale. The company also scraps old equipment that had cost $630,000; accumulated depreciation to the date of disposal is $610,000, giving the equipment a book value of $20,000. The cost of disposing of the equipment is equal to the proceeds received from a scrap metal dealer. Accordingly, the loss on disposal is equal to the equipment's book value. Although the gain and loss together increase net income by $345,000, operating income is not affected because the disposals are peripheral activities.

Journal Entries

Cash	865,000	
Land		500,000
Gain on Sale of Land		365,000
Loss on Disposal of Equipment	20,000	
Accumulated Depreciation	610,000	
Equipment		630,000

Income Statement Effects	
Gain	+ 365,000
Loss	+ 20,000
Net Income	+ 345,000

Balance Sheet Effects	
Assets	+ 865,000
Assets	− 500,000
Assets	− 630,000
Assets	+ 610,000
Owner's Equity	+ 365,000
Owner's Equity	− 20,000

Assets Held for Disposal.   Assets that are no longer used and are being held for disposal are written down to net realizable value (expected sales proceeds minus costs of disposal) if less than book value. Market values become relevant because the assets are expected to be sold. The assets are not depreciated because they are no longer being used and are not providing benefits against which to match costs. If the assets being held for disposal are held more than one period, they must be revalued to net realizable value at the end of each period and a gain or loss on the revaluation reported in the income statement. They may not be valued at an amount higher than the remaining unamortized cost when taken out of service.

Typically, assets held for disposal are relatively minor in amount and are not a factor in analyzing a company. However, large amounts of such assets may indicate that the company is reorganizing or significantly reducing its operating capacity. If these assets are held for a long period of time, especially if they are repeatedly revalued downward, this may be a sign that the company is unable to realize the anticipated proceeds on sale and could have implications for the value of similar assets currently in use.

Impairment of Assets.   Sometimes the value of an operating asset currently in use becomes impaired. This means that the expected future net cash flows from using the asset and ultimately selling it are less than its current book value. Such an asset must be revalued to its lower fair value, and an impairment loss must be recognized in the income statement. Significant impairment losses on operating assets do not bode well for the enterprise because they may indicate that future cash flows from operating activities are expected to be less than previously anticipated.

INTANGIBLE ASSETS

Information for Decisions

Intangible assets may often be vital to a company's success. Financial statement users need to pay special attention to intangible assets because the characteristics and value of these assets is often less clear than those of other operating assets. The financial statements help answer questions such as these: What types of intangible assets are owned, and to what extent are these intangibles expected to provide future benefits? Will they have any value if the company is liquidated? Does the company have any other valuable intangibles that are not reported because of special accounting rules? To what extent are the company's income and cash flow affected by the write-off of intangibles during the period?

The value of any asset comes from its ability to provide benefits to the enterprise. Although lacking the physical existence of operating assets, intangible assets may be among the most valuable assets held by an enterprise. Patents and copyrights protect ideas and intellectual property that may be the basis for the company's profitability, or even its existence. Franchises permit many companies to take advantage of well-known names and proven formulas for success, while licenses may allow companies to use special production technology not available to others. In some cases, the bulk of a company's value may be related to its intangibles. For example, when Abbott Laboratories purchased MediSense, Inc., a manufacturer of blood self-testing products, nearly all of the $867 million purchase price was allocated to intangibles.

The value of intangible assets often tends to be less obvious than for tangible assets. Some intangibles cannot be sold, while the value of others may be questionable. For example, a company going out of business may be able to sell its factory building, but the value of its patents may be doubtful, given that they apparently provided little advantage to the company. Thus, intangibles deserve special scrutiny when evaluating a company's financial statements.

In general, accounting for intangible assets is the same as for other long-lived assets. When purchased, they are recorded at cost, and that cost is subsequently matched with the benefits provided. The accounting for purchased intangibles that confer rights is straightforward, but several other intangibles deserve special attention.

INTANGIBLE ASSETS THAT CONFER RIGHTS

Most intangible assets confer an exclusive right, such as the right to use a name or symbol, intellectual property, idea, formula, or process. Although these assets are rights rather than physical assets, the normal principles of accounting still apply. Each asset is recorded initially at the cost to acquire that asset. As with other assets, any cost necessary to acquire the asset is included in the asset's recorded cost. With a patent, for example, all costs of drafting the patent document, patent registration fees, and legal costs of registering the patent are included in the recorded cost of the patent.

Once the cost of an intangible asset is recorded, it is matched with the benefits provided, just as is done with other assets. Accordingly, the cost is allocated to the periods benefiting from the intangible. Allocating the cost of an intangible to the periods benefiting from its use is referred to as **amortization** and is similar to depreciation for tangible operating assets. All intangible assets must be amortized over their useful economic lives, but authoritative standards prohibit amortizing over a period longer than forty years. A few intangibles, such as some franchises, have unlimited legal lives, but they also must be amortized over forty years, or a shorter period if the franchise is expected to lose its value before then. Intangibles are typically amortized on a straight-line basis, and the asset is reduced directly rather than through a contra-asset account.

Remember that intangibles are reported at unamortized cost, not at current market value. Because many financial statement users are skeptical of the value of intangibles assets, they frequently subtract the reported amounts from total assets before computing ratios such as debt to assets.

You Decide 10-2

WHEN IS A PATENT A BENEFIT?

At the beginning of 2001, Delson Corporation purchased a patent for a new product for $510,000. The patent provides legal protection for twenty years, but the new product is expected to produce revenues for only about five years until it becomes obsolete. Delson expects to earn about $300,000 from the patented product in each of the next five years. How much of the cost of the patent would you expense in 2001 and subsequent years? Explain how your approach is more useful for decision making than possible alternatives.

RESEARCH AND DEVELOPMENT COSTS

Costs incurred to discover new knowledge and develop new products or improve existing products are called **research and development costs**. These costs are incurred because they are expected to provide future benefits. Therefore, these costs could be considered assets to be capitalized and then amortized over the periods benefited. The FASB, however, because of the uncertainty of realizing the future benefits, requires all research and development costs to be expensed as incurred. Capitalizing such costs is not acceptable.

The FASB requires disclosure of the amount of expenditures for research and development during the period. For some types of companies, these costs are extremely significant, both in terms of magnitude and the future viability of the company. Many companies, such as pharmaceutical companies and genetic engineering companies, survive only through the success of their research efforts. Thus, a company that skimps on research and development expenditures may increase its income in the short term but severely limit its future. Because research and development costs must be expensed as incurred, decision makers must keep in mind that companies will report lower income currently if they want to increase future income through the development of new products and processes.

A CLOSER LOOK AT

ACCOUNTING FOR INTANGIBLE ASSETS

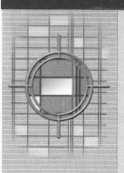

During 1999, Kelly Company undertakes a crash program to develop a new drug to relieve headaches from too much studying. During the year, the company spends $1,358,000 developing the new drug. Because of the uncertainty surrounding whether such research and development efforts will be successful, current accounting standards require that the entire $1,358,000 of research and development costs be expensed in the year incurred. Early in 2000, Kelly Company completes development of its new product, called Head-Ez, and the company secures a patent for it. The $82,000 total cost of the patent includes fees for the patent registration, attorney, technical writer, and consulting chemist, but excludes any research and development costs. The new drug is expected to sell well among college students and to be a huge money maker over the next few years, starting immediately. After about 5 years, however, new drugs are expected to make Head-Ez obsolete. Therefore, the $82,000 cost of the patent is capitalized as an asset, and this cost is then amortized at $16,400 ($82,000 ÷ 5) per year over the 5-year period during which the company is expected to receive benefits from it. By the end of 5 years, the $82,000 cost of the patent will have been completely written off to expense, and the asset will no longer remain on the company's balance sheet.

The amount of research and development costs expensed each period in the income statement will indicate to readers the company's commitment to developing future products. The book value of the patent reported in the balance sheet indicates the existence of a right expected to provide future benefits, but gives little clue as to its value.

Income Statement Effects	
1999 Expenses	+1,358,000
Net Income	−1,358,000
2000 Expenses	+ 16,400
Net Income	− 16,400

Balance Sheet Effects	
1999 Assets	− 1,358,000
Owners' Equity	− 1,358,000
2000 Assets	+ 82,000
Assets	− 82,000
Assets	− 16,400
Owners' Equity	− 16,400

Journal Entries

As Costs Are Incurred

Research and Development Expenses	1,358,000	
Cash		1,358,000
Patents	82,000	
Cash		82,000

At End of Each Year for Five Years

Patent Amortization Expense	16,400	
Patents		16,400

GOODWILL

The most peculiar intangible asset of all is called goodwill. Both the definition and nature of goodwill are elusive, but we do have a means of measuring it, or at least measuring something we call goodwill.

Goodwill is the combination of all those factors that make the value of an ongoing business higher than the value of the individual assets held by the business. It includes nonspecific factors such as superior location, reputation, and management. Goodwill is that intangible that allows an ongoing business to earn a higher return than could be earned by the other assets individually.

SUN MICROSYSTEMS

In April 1996, Sun Microsystems, Inc., purchased the assets and liabilities of Integrated Micro Products for approximately $105,700,000. The excess of the purchase price over the estimated fair value of the net tangible assets acquired was allocated to various intangibles, primarily purchased research and development and goodwill. The $43,000,000 of purchased in-process research and development was written off against income immediately; the goodwill and other intangible assets are being amortized over periods ranging from two to five years.

ANALYSIS

In the technology business, much of the value of a company is often related to the value of its patents, ideas, and creative work force, rather than its inventory, plant, and equipment. The in-process research and development purchased by Sun Microsystems was a valuable part of the acquired company, but under current accounting rules, research and development costs cannot be capitalized as an asset. However, the cost assigned to the goodwill and other intangibles was capitalized and is being amortized over future periods. The short amortization periods may reflect rapidly changing technology in the industry, or may be due to excessive conservatism.
[www.sun.com]

Goodwill is recorded only when one company purchases another in a business combination. The amount paid for goodwill is measured as the difference between the total price paid for the acquired business as a whole and the fair value of its individual identifiable assets less its liabilities acquired. For example, if one company purchases another for $10,000,000 and the fair value of the purchased company's assets less liabilities totals $8,000,000, the amount of goodwill recorded in the business combination is $2,000,000. Once recorded, the goodwill is amortized over the period of time benefiting from the excess earning power acquired, but not to exceed forty years.

THE BURLINGTON NORTHERN AND THE SANTA FE

In 1994, both the Union Pacific and Burlington Northern Railroads attempted to acquire the Santa Fe Railroad and began bidding against one another for Santa Fe's stock. The bidding started at $14 per share and finally concluded in 1995 at about $20 per share after Union Pacific withdrew. In this business combination, as in many, the final purchase price was considerably higher than the initial offer. What factors do you suppose led to the higher purchase price? Do you think that all of the additional price is for excess earnings (goodwill)? How do you suppose the additional purchase price will be reflected in the financial statements?

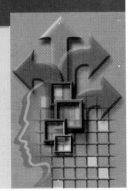

Clearly the essence of a successful company is in putting together a collection of assets and liabilities that provide a greater return working together than separately. Nevertheless, the purchase of a business for an amount in excess of the fair value of its assets and liabilities certainly does not guarantee future earnings. Thus, many people have difficulty viewing goodwill as an asset. Further, this asset cannot be sold separately from the business and is worth nothing in a liquidation.

NONFINANCIAL ASSET DISCLOSURES

Information for Decisions

The notes provide relevant information about nonfinancial assets in addition to what is included in the body of the financial statements. These disclosures help answer questions such as the following: Have the company's operating assets been used as collateral for loans? What are the useful lives of the company's long-lived assets? Do the financial statements reflect aggressive or conservative depreciation methods?

In addition to the numbers reported in the financial statements, the valuation basis for each type of nonfinancial asset must be disclosed. The disclosures must also indicate the methods of amortizing the cost of limited-life assets and the amortization periods.

Of particular importance are required disclosures about creditors' claims on assets, including details of asset financing arrangements and required future cash payments. Some assets may be used as collateral for borrowings unrelated to their acquisition. In any case, specific creditor claims on particular assets must be disclosed. Decision makers need to know under what conditions others might claim an entity's assets. Such claims might affect a company's ability to continue operating, and will certainly affect the distribution of assets if a company ceases operations.

In Practice 10-6

TRANS WORLD AIRLINES

TWA reports a large dollar amount of aircraft in its balance sheet, with aircraft obviously being the most important single type of asset held. However, many of those aircraft are leased, and when TWA defaulted on lease payments, the lessors threatened to repossess the aircraft, presenting a significant obstacle to continued operations.

ANALYSIS

The details of creditors' claims are found in the notes to the financial statements and, together with TWA's cash-flow problems indicated in its statement of cash flows, alerted financial statement users to the riskiness of TWA's position. [www.twa.com]

FINANCING ASSET ACQUISITIONS

Information for Decisions

Because operating assets are often very costly, how asset acquisitions are financed may determine whether certain assets are acquired, and the type of financing may significantly affect profitability. Financial statement information can help decision makers answer questions such as these: What type of financing (e.g., borrowing, leasing, internal reinvesting) has the company used to acquire its operating assets, and how does this compare with how other companies in the industry are financing their operating assets? What is the effect of the financing on current and future income and cash flows? If the company does not meet all of the terms of the financing agreements, what effect will this have on assets available for future operations or for distributions to other creditors and to owners?

When an airline takes delivery of ten new aircraft or a bank acquires a new office building for its headquarters, the companies do not simply hand over the hundreds of millions of dollars from cash on hand. If companies are operating efficiently, they seldom have such large amounts of cash available. Instead, most companies finance major asset acquisitions through some type of borrowing arrangement.

Companies might issue bonds and use the proceeds to acquire a number of different assets. In other cases, such as with real-estate purchases, the financing is tied to the specific acquisition, and the property is used as collateral for the loan. Sometimes, as is common with aircraft, the assets are not purchased at all, but are leased. When you fly on a Boeing 747, you might think the airline owns the plane, but it might actually be leased from an aircraft leasing company, or even the manufacturer. An aircraft leasing company might have a better credit rating than the airlines and be able to raise money at less cost. This allows the leasing company to borrow money, buy the aircraft, lease them to an airline at a lower cost than if the airline borrowed directly, and still make a profit. Aside from the lower financing costs, the airline may see little difference in owning or leasing the aircraft.

In substance, there may be little difference between the various types of financing arrangements, except in two areas: tax benefits and security for the loan. Taking maximum advantage of tax planning may benefit all parties involved (except the tax collectors). For example, an airline expected to have weak profits over the next few years might lease aircraft so the benefits of the deduction for accelerated depreciation can be taken by the leasing company and shared with the airline through lower lease payments.

Lenders obviously prefer their loans to be as secure as possible. Therefore, they often require that they or a trustee hold title to the assets being purchased with the borrowed money, or they may require a direct legal claim against the property. A lease allows the lender, or *lessor*, to hold title to the leased property while the borrower, or *lessee*, has the benefit of its use. If lease payments are not made, the lessor already has title to the leased property and only needs to take physical possession. Similarly, lenders to the purchaser of an office building will hold a mortgage on the building, giving the lenders the right to foreclose and take possession of the building if the borrower defaults. However, simply having collateral under a financing arrangement does not guarantee that the lender will not suffer a loss. If the value of the collateral falls below the remaining amount owed by the borrower, the balance of the lender's claim is unsecured.

THE SEARS TOWER BURIED BY DEBT

In 1994, the tallest building in the world, the 110-story Sears Tower in Chicago, was losing $40 million a year because of falling rents and a 45 percent vacancy rate. Even Sears Merchandise Group had moved to the suburbs. The building's value was perhaps as little as half of its $850 million mortgage. Sears considered simply walking away from the building, leaving it to the lenders.[3]

ANALYSIS

Sears ultimately decided not to "walk away" from its mortgage obligation on the Sears Tower, but the lenders made concessions because of that possibility. Sears no longer owns the Sears Tower, and it recognized a gain of $195 million on being released from the mortgage. The lenders made concessions because they would have suffered a huge loss if Sears had walked away, given that the value of the collateral had declined below the remaining amount of the loan. Under the lending arrangement, known as a purchase-money mortgage, the lenders had no claim on the other assets of Sears. [www.sears.com]

Differences in the substance of various types of financing arrangements are often more legalistic than economic. Accordingly, the accounting for different types of long-term financing arrangements, such as borrowing and leasing, tends to be similar.

BORROWING TO PURCHASE ASSETS

Accounting for purchases through borrowing involves distinguishing the cost of borrowing from the cost of the assets purchased and then treating each of the costs separately. The cost of the assets purchased must be recognized over the periods of their use through depreciation, while the cost of money borrowed is recognized as interest expense over the time during which the money is used.

LEASING ASSETS

Many organizations obtain the use of assets by leasing them from others. In some cases, no long-term commitment is made with respect to the assets, and such leases are referred to as **operating leases**. In other cases, most of the risks and rewards of ownership are transferred from the lessor to the lessee, and these leases are called **capital leases**. The distinction between these two types of leases is very important for decision makers because the lessee makes significant noncancelable commitments for future cash payments under a capital lease.

Capital Leases: A Transfer of Risks and Rewards. Capital leases are long-term arrangements that transfer the risks and rewards of ownership—and in some cases, transfer actual ownership. Thus, this type of lease is a means of financing the acquisition of an asset to be used on a long-term basis and serves as a substitute financing arrangement for borrowing. In

[3] Based on a report by *Crain's Chicago Business* (January 17, 1994).

many capital leases, the substance of the lease is nearly the same as borrowing the money and purchasing the asset.

Except for the terminology, accounting for capital leases is virtually identical to accounting for an installment purchase of an asset. The leased asset is recorded at the present value of the cash payments, both current and future, to be made under the lease, and a lease liability is recorded for the present value of all future cash payments under the lease. Any portion of the liability meeting the conditions for a current liability is classified as such, with the remainder classified as a long-term liability. Interest expense is calculated on the liability using the same rate used to compute the present value of the lease payments. An illustration of accounting for asset financing through both borrowing and leasing is presented in Appendix 10–1.

Because cash payments relating to leases are generally fixed in amount, must be made at specific times, and often are quite significant, decision makers are particularly interested in assessing an entity's lease commitments and whether the entity's resources will be sufficient to meet scheduled payments. Accordingly, specific lease disclosures are required in the financial statements or related notes. For example, future required lease payments must be disclosed in total and for each of the next five years. Also, the total minimum payments to be received from noncancelable sublease agreements must be disclosed.

Operating Leases: A More Flexible Commitment. Operating leases are widely used as a means of acquiring the temporary use of assets. Because the rewards and risks of ownership do not transfer, the leased property remains on the lessor's books. The lessee does not record either an asset or liability under an operating lease except for any rent that is prepaid or accrued at the end of the period. Rent expense is simply recognized in accordance with the provisions of the lease agreement. For example, if a company leased a truck for $2,000 a month for six months, it would report equipment rental expense of $12,000.

Financial statement disclosures relating to operating leases must include a general description of the lease arrangements, the amount of rental expense for each period reported, and amounts received from subleasing to others. For operating leases with more than one year remaining, the future required rental payments must be disclosed in total and for each of the next five years, and minimum rentals to be received from noncancelable subleases must be disclosed. As with capital leases, these disclosures help decision makers assess the entity's ability to meet its lease obligations. These disclosures are particularly important for operating leases because no capitalized lease liability is reflected in the balance sheet for these types of leases.

SUMMARY

Noncurrent nonfinancial assets are used in the company's operations. They can be tangible or intangible. Because the value to the company is in their use rather than their marketability, market values are generally less relevant to decision makers than the matching of their costs with benefits generated.

Nonfinancial assets are recorded initially at cost. The historical cost of a nonfinancial asset includes all costs that must be incurred to acquire the asset and get it in the location and condition so the entity can do with it what it intends. Once the cost of the asset is recorded, that cost, or an appropriate portion, is expensed and matched with the benefits provided by the asset, as follows:

* Limited-life operating assets: Through depreciation, over the periods in which the asset is used and provides benefits.

* Resource-bearing land: Through depletion, over the periods in which resources are separated from the land and sold.

* Intangible assets: Through amortization, over the periods in which the asset provides benefits, not to exceed forty years.

The cost of tangible operating assets is matched by recognizing depreciation expense each period, roughly in proportion to the benefits received from the asset. Common depreciation methods include straight-line, which assigns an equal amount of cost to each period during which the asset is used, declining-balance, which assigns more depreciation to early years and decreasing amounts to later years, and activity-based methods, which compute depreciation based on actual asset usage.

Depreciation computed on production assets is assigned to the units of inventory produced as part of their cost. The depletion cost of resource-bearing land is computed using an activity-based method, referred to as the units-of-production method, and is assigned as part of the cost of the resources produced.

Intangible assets lack physical existence, but the expectation of future benefits, not physical existence, is the important aspect in defining an asset. The cost of an intangible is allocated over its useful life, usually on a straight-line basis. Special rules relating to intangibles require expensing re-search and development costs as incurred, permit recording the cost of goodwill only when it is purchased in a business combination, and prohibit amortizing any intangible over a period greater than forty years.

When evaluating the efficiency with which operating assets are used, return on assets, or net income divided by total assets, is especially important. Also, the relationship between debt and assets is important in determining whether the assets provide sufficient security for lenders and which lenders have claims on specific assets.

LIST OF IMPORTANT TERMS

accelerated depreciation   *(373)*

accumulated depreciation   *(372)*

amortization   *(383)*

asset turnover   *(369)*

book value   *(372)*

capital leases   *(388)*

declining-balance depreciation   *(373)*

depletion   *(379)*

depreciation   *(372)*

double-declining-balance depreciation *(374)*

fixed asset turnover   *(369)*

goodwill   *(384)*

margin on sales   *(369)*

Modified Accelerated Cost Recovery System (MACRS)   *(377)*

operating leases   *(388)*

research and development costs   *(383)*

return on assets   *(369)*

salvage value   *(371)*

service-hours method of depreciation *(375)*

straight-line depreciation   *(373)*

units-of-production method of depreciation   *(375)*

APPENDIX 10-1

A CLOSER LOOK AT FINANCING ASSET ACQUISITIONS

To illustrate asset financing through both borrowing and leasing, assume that Telecomp Corporation decides to acquire a large computer. The equipment is expected to have a useful life of three years and no salvage value. Telecomp uses straight-line depreciation and prepares financial statements on a calendar-year basis.

Telecomp needs to finance the computer acquisition and identifies two alternatives:

1. ***Borrowing:*** Telecomp will purchase the computer from the manufacturer, Digi-Log Computers. Digi-Log will finance the purchase by accepting Telecomp's noninterest-bearing note for $329,004. Telecomp will pay three annual installments of $109,668 each, with the first payment due at the time the computer is delivered on December 31, 2000. The current interest rate for this type of note is 10 percent.

2. ***Leasing:*** Friendly Finance Corporation will purchase the computer from Digi-Log for $300,000 and lease it to Telecomp under a three-year noncancelable lease agreement. Telecomp will pay Friendly three annual installments of $109,668 each, with the first payment due at the beginning of the lease term, December 31, 2000. The lease payments include 10 percent interest. Title to the equipment will pass to the lessee at the end of the lease term. From an accounting perspective, this is a capital lease.

Under either arrangement, Telecomp's liability upon entering into the agreement is equal to the present value of the future payments to be made. The present value of the three payments at 10 percent is $300,000, equal to the value of the equipment at acquisition. In either case, the cost of the asset to Telecomp is equal to the present value of the cash payments to be made, $300,000.

Because a payment of $109,668 is made at the date of acquisition, the total of the remaining payments is $219,336 ($109,668 × 2). The reported liability immediately after making the first payment is $190,332, equal to the initial present value of all future payments less the first payment (300,000 − $109,668). The difference between the total of the two remaining payments ($219,336) and the present value of those payments ($190,332) is the interest relating to future periods ($29,004).

Annual interest is computed on the book value of the liability at the beginning of the year, with the book value equal to the stated amount less the discount. Implicit interest recognized by Telecomp each year is as follows:

	(a) Book Value of Liability January 1	(b) Interest Expense (a × .10)	December 31		
			(c) Liability Before Payment (a + b)	(d) Payment	(e) Liability After Payment (c − d)
Year					
2000			$300,000	$109,668	$190,332
2001	$190,332	$19,034	209,366	109,668	99,698
2002	99,698	9,970	109,668	109,668	-0-
2003	-0-	-0-			

Telecomp's financial reporting for the two alternative methods of asset financing in its December 31, 2000 and 2001, balance sheets and its 2001 income statement is as follows:

Purchase and Borrow		**Capital Lease**	
2000			
Balance Sheet—December 31			
Assets:		Assets:	
Equipment	$300,000	Equipment Under Capital Lease	$300,000
Liabilities:		Liabilities:	
Notes Payable	$190,332	Capital Lease Obligation	$190,332
2001			
Income Statement			
Depreciation Expense	$100,000	Depreciation Expense	$100,000
Interest Expense	19,034	Interest Expense	19,034
Balance Sheet—December 31			
Assets:		Assets:	
Equipment	$300,000	Equipment Under Capital Lease	$300,000
Accumulated Depreciation	(100,000)	Accumulated Depreciation	(100,000)
	200,000		200,000
Liabilities:		Liabilities:	
Notes payable	$ 99,698	Capital Lease Obligation	$ 99,698

Under both alternatives, the equipment is recorded at the $300,000 present value of the cash payments to be made. The cost is depreciated over the three-year life of the equipment. The liability reported in the December 31, 2000, balance sheet is equal to the $300,000 present value of the total cash payments to be made under the lease, less the initial payment of

$109,668. Because a payment is made on the liability at the end of 2001, the liability at the beginning of 2002 is less than at the beginning of 2001, and, accordingly, the interest for 2002 is less. The liability is paid off by the end of 2002, so no interest is recognized in 2003.

EXAMINING THE CONCEPTS

Q10-1 Distinguish between the terms *fixed assets, property, plant & equipment,* and *noncurrent assets.*

Q10-2 For what types of companies would fixed assets be expected to be very important? For what types of companies would fixed assets be expected to be relatively unimportant?

Q10-3 How is the return on assets ratio computed? What information does the ratio provide?

Q10-4 How is the asset turnover ratio computed? Why would a decision maker be interested in this ratio?

Q10-5 How is the margin on sales ratio computed? What information does it provide? How might there be a trade-off between the margin on sales ratio and the asset turnover ratio?

Q10-6 In general terms, what is the total amount recorded as the cost of an operating asset purchased? List some of the elements that might be included in the recorded cost of a purchased operating asset.

Q10-7 If a company purchases an asset on credit, paying the current market rate of interest, explain how the recorded cost of the asset will compare with the amount that would have been recorded if the company had paid cash.

Q10-8 How does a company account for the cost of an operating asset subsequent to acquisition? What basic accounting concept is most important in accounting for the costs of operating assets subsequent to acquisition? Explain.

Q10-9 What is depreciation? How is it related to the matching concept?

Q10-10 Explain how depreciation and amortization are related.

Q10-11 What is meant by the salvage value of an asset? How is salvage value used in accounting for depreciable assets?

Q10-12 What is accelerated depreciation? Give an example of an accelerated depreciation method. How does accelerated depreciation differ from straight-line depreciation?

Q10-13 What is activity-based depreciation? How does activity-based depreciation differ from declining-balance depreciation? For what type of assets is activity-based depreciation most likely to be used?

Q10-14 What role does a change in the fair value of a depreciable asset normally play in determining depreciation expense for the year? Discuss why this is the case.

Q10-15 Which depreciation method normally results in the largest amount of depreciation expense being recorded in the first year of asset ownership? Which method normally results in the largest amount of depreciation being recorded in the last year of ownership?

Q10-16 At what stage in a company's life will the choice of depreciation method make the greatest difference? Explain why.

Q10-17 What is book value? How is the book value of a depreciable asset determined? How is the book value of an intangible asset determined?

Q10-18 Why do most companies use accelerated depreciation for tax purposes? Does this mean that they should also use accelerated depreciation for financial reporting purposes? Explain.

Q10-19 What is the Modified Accelerated Cost Recovery System? When is depreciation computed using this method? How does this method differ from straight-line depreciation?

Q10-20 From an accounting perspective, what is depletion? How is the amount of depletion normally computed? At what point is depletion recognized as an expense?

Q10-21 What does it mean for the value of an asset to be impaired? What factors might lead to an impairment of value? How, if at all, is the impairment of an asset recognized for financial reporting purposes?

Q10-22 What difficulties often are associated with determining the amount of amortization to be recognized on intangible assets?

Q10-23 If equal amounts are paid for a depreciable and an amortizable asset, how will the amounts reported in the balance sheet at the end of the second year of ownership differ for the two assets?

Q10-24 How are research and development costs normally treated for financial reporting purposes? Explain why.

Q10-25 What is goodwill? When and how is goodwill recognized for financial reporting purposes? When, if ever, is goodwill recognized as an expense?

Q10-26 What reasons might a company have for leasing rather than purchasing assets?

Q10-27 How is the substance of an operating lease different from that of a capital lease? Which type of lease is most similar to purchasing an asset?

Q10-28 What amount(s) are recognized as expense each period under an operating lease?

Q10-29 What balance sheet elements are different when a lease is treated as a capital lease rather than an operating lease? Why might a company wish to record a lease as an operating lease rather than a capital lease?

Q10-30 In general, when should a lease be capitalized?

UNDERSTANDING ACCOUNTING INFORMATION

E10-1 Understanding Operating Assets You have been asked to evaluate two companies and have acquired the following information:

	Company B	Company L
Total sales for 2001	$900,000	$400,000
Net income	85,000	60,000
Fixed assets	150,000	250,000
Total assets	600,000	300,000

a. Compute the fixed asset turnover ratios (sales/fixed assets) and total asset turnover ratios (sales/total assets) for the companies. Which company appears to be the more desirable investment on the basis of these ratios?
b. Compute the margin on sales ratio (net income/sales) and return on total assets ratio (net income/total assets) for the two companies. Which company appears to be the more desirable investment on the basis of these ratios?
c. What factors may make it possible for Company B to have a smaller investment in fixed assets and still report more than double the sales of Company L?
d. Although Company B reports greater net income than Company L, explain why it may be desirable to invest in Company L rather than Company B.

E10-2 Accounting and Reporting for Operating Assets
Panther Chemical Company is considering building a new chemical plant and is negotiating with Sundrenched Orchards Corporation to purchase the land it needs for the new facility.

a. Chemical plants are Panther's major asset, and the land and trees are Sundrenched's major assets. Why must Panther Chemical report a significant amount of depreciation expense on its plants each period while Sundrenched does not report any depreciation on its land?
b. Why might it be argued that Panther Chemical should reduce the carrying value of the land on which its chemical plants are built through annual charges to expense, while Sundrenched has no need to do so?
c. If Panther purchases land from Sundrenched, what should it do with the costs of removing the orange and persimmon trees and filling the irrigation ditches, since they have nothing to do with actually building a chemical plant?
d. Panther Chemical expects its equipment to last for 20 years. Sundrenched Orchards expects its fruit trees to bear fruit for 15 years. While Panther depreciates less than the full cost of equipment over 20 years, Sundrenched expenses more than the cost of planting and caring for the trees until they bear fruit over the 15-year period. Why might the two companies use different procedures in determining the depreciable base for their assets?

E10-3 Allocating the Cost of Operating Assets Brunwist, Inc., a holding company with operating divisions in significantly different types of businesses, is reviewing the depreciation methods used by its divisions. The company controller has recommended to the president that all divisions classify their assets into one of four categories, based on the asset type. The controller has suggested they be classified as buildings, production equipment, office equipment, or other. For each category, all divisions would use straight-line depreciation over the same number of years and would assume no salvage value.

a. How might the adoption of uniform depreciation methods across all divisions provide useful information to financial statement users?
b. How might the adoption of uniform depreciation methods across all divisions provide financial statement users with misleading information?
c. Some of Brunwist's operating divisions currently use straight-line depreciation and some use double-declining-balance depreciation. Under what conditions would straight-line depreciation provide useful information on the cost of using depreciable assets? Under what conditions would an accelerated depreciation method such as double-declining-balance provide more useful information?
d. Why should the company consider using something other than straight-line depreciation for federal income tax reporting purposes? What is the advantage in doing so?

E10-4 Intangible Assets Scenter Company is considering purchasing the net assets of Ripple Corporation. Ripple's reported net assets are as follows:

Current Assets	$ 15,000,000
Fixed Assets (net)	315,000,000
Intangible Assets	270,000,000
Total Assets	$600,000,000
Total Liabilities	(200,000,000)
Net Assets	$400,000,000

Ripple's fixed assets are depreciated on a straight-line basis over 15 years with no estimated salvage value. The intangible assets reported by Ripple consist of patent rights with an expected life of 5 years and goodwill that is expected to be of benefit during the next 10 years.

a. How must intangible assets be reported for financial reporting purposes? In Ripple's income statement, is depreciation expense on its tangible assets or amortization of its intangible assets likely to be greater? Explain.

b. In evaluating how much it should be willing to pay for Ripple, what value should Scenter place on Ripple's fixed assets? What value should it place on the patent rights held by Ripple?

c. How did the goodwill reported by Ripple arise? If goodwill is not an identifiable asset that can be sold, why is it recorded?

d. How will Scenter determine the amount of goodwill to be recorded when it purchases Ripple's net assets? Will the amount of goodwill recorded by Scenter be equal to the amount of goodwill currently reported by Ripple? Explain.

E10-5   Nonfinancial Asset Disclosures   You are considering investing in Solid Corporation. The company was established 3 years ago and its sales and net income have expanded very rapidly. Solid Corporation reports current assets of $350,000 and current liabilities of $290,000 at December 31, 2001. Its noncurrent assets consist of $80,000 invested in equipment and patent rights of $220,000. A review of the notes to the financial statements reveals the following:

a. Solid Corporation borrowed $300,000 from the bank on December 29, 2001, and used the cash to purchase the equipment and patent rights from Tamlet Company.

b. Solid Corporation rents its primary production facility and equipment from Friendly Corporation. Rent is paid annually on March 1.

What additional information about Solid Corporation's nonfinancial assets would you look for in the notes to Solid's financial statements before making a judgment on the risk associated with investing in the company?

E10-6   Financing Asset Acquisitions   Amber Corporation wishes to acquire a fleet of new delivery trucks. Amber must choose between a leasing agreement that will be classified as an operating lease and borrowing the money on a long-term note and purchasing the assets. Under which alternative or alternatives will the following be reported?

a. Interest expense.
b. Equipment rental expense.
c. Depreciation expense.
d. Equipment.
e. Notes payable.

E10-7   Multiple Choice: Accounting for Tangible Assets
Select the correct answer for each of the following.

1. Straight-line depreciation is used for reporting purposes by many companies because:
   a. It is always the best measure of the assets used up in the production process during the period.

b. It represents a systematic allocation of the cost of assets equally over the periods used.

c. Tax laws require use of straight-line depreciation for most tangible assets.

d. Noncurrent assets are used up so quickly that it makes little difference which depreciation method is used.

e. None of the above.

2. K Corp. recently purchased a new robotics production system to produce computer chips. The field is changing rapidly and new production processes are being developed each year. The company should use which of the following methods of treating asset costs?
   a. Straight-line depreciation.
   b. Accelerated depreciation.
   c. Permanent capitalization of all costs with no depreciation.
   d. Record the full cost of the assets as an expense in the year of purchase.
   e. None of the above.

3. Ace Bearing Co. has been depreciating delivery equipment on a straight-line basis on its tax return. If it begins to use an accelerated method on the tax return for newly acquired equipment:
   a. The depreciation expense listed on the tax return will increase but taxes paid will not change.
   b. The salvage value will have to be set at a higher level for the new equipment.
   c. Ace can continue to use straight-line depreciation for its financial statements.
   d. Ace will be in violation of generally accepted accounting principles because the use of two different depreciation methods by the same company is not permitted.

4. An asset's depreciable base:
   a. Is assumed to be zero in computing depreciation expense under double-declining-balance depreciation.
   b. Is computed by deducting the estimated salvage value from the cost of the asset.
   c. Is computed by deducting the estimated salvage value of the asset from the balance in accumulated depreciation.
   d. None of the above.

E10-8   Multiple Choice: Noncurrent Assets   Select the correct answer for each of the following.

1. Companies often are reluctant to record the costs of intangible assets as assets because:
   a. Outlays for intangible assets typically provide nothing of value to the company.
   b. Intangibles seldom have a useful life of more than one year.
   c. Management and investors generally are more skeptical of the value of assets that cannot be seen and touched.
   d. Intangible assets are already incorporated in the market price of the stock and to record them separately would involve double counting.

2. Which of the following is characteristic of depreciable assets?

a. The market value of the assets at the time of purchase typically is greater than the amount paid to acquire them.

b. The price at which the company could resell the assets immediately after their purchase typically is less than the amount paid.

c. The amount of depreciation expense recorded during the period is intended to represent the decline in the market value of the asset during the period.

d. Most depreciable assets increase in value over time.

e. None of the above.

3. Operating assets include:

a. Land and inventory.

b. Buildings and accounts receivable.

c. Land and equipment.

d. Furniture and accounts payable.

e. Both a and c.

4. When operating assets are no longer needed and are held for disposal:

a. The book value should be written down to the net realizable value.

b. The difference between the original purchase price and the expected disposal value should be recorded as a gain or loss.

c. The amount recorded as depreciation expense should be no more than the change in the net realizable value of the asset during the period.

d. The book value of the assets should be reduced to zero because it may not be possible to sell the assets to another company.

5. Goodwill is valued at:

a. The difference between the price paid for an ongoing business and the fair value of the identifiable assets acquired less liabilities assumed.

b. The difference between the fair value of the identifiable assets acquired and the liabilities assumed.

c. The total amount of cash paid out to acquire another company.

d. The total amount of cash paid out to acquire another company, less the value of the identifiable assets acquired.

E10-9   Multiple Choice: Valuing Noncurrent Assets Select the correct answer for each of the following.

1. The cost of a newly purchased truck subject to rapid obsolescence should be allocated to:

a. Depletion expense in the year of acquisition.

b. Depletion expense over a relatively short number of periods.

c. Amortization expense over a relatively short number of periods.

d. Depreciation expense using accelerated depreciation.

2. Which of the following is an example of accelerated depreciation?

a. Double-declining-balance depreciation.

b. Activity-based depreciation.

c. Straight-line depreciation.

d. Inverse-balance depreciation.

e. Both a and b.

3. From an accounting perspective, depletion represents:

a. The cost of using buildings and equipment.

b. The cost of using land.

c. The using up of natural resources.

d. The using up of all of the available inventory in one period.

4. When an asset is acquired, its recorded cost:

a. Includes interest whenever the purchase price is borrowed.

b. Is the list price, ignoring all discounts and price reductions.

c. Includes all costs necessary to acquire the asset and get it in the condition and location such that the company can do with it what it intends.

d. All of the above.

E10-10   Multiple Choice: Leases   Select the correct answer for each of the following.

1. A lease is considered a capital lease if:

a. The lease is less than one year in length.

b. The risks and rewards of ownership are transferred to the lessee.

c. The risks and rewards of ownership remain with the lessor.

d. The lease requires variable payments based on the amount the asset is used each period.

2. Under an operating lease on equipment, the lessee's annual lease payment is recorded as:

a. An expense.

b. A reduction of the liability for lease payments.

c. An adjustment to the leased equipment account.

d. An adjustment to the accumulated depreciation account.

3. Depreciation expense is recorded by the company (lessee) that has leased an asset:

a. Under both operating and capital leases.

b. Under operating leases but not under capital leases.

c. Under capital leases but not under operating leases.

d. Only if legal title is transferred to the lessee.

4. Interest expense is recorded under:

a. Operating leases.

b. Capital leases.

c. Both capital and operating leases.

d. Neither capital nor operating leases.

E10-11   Determining Asset Cost   Growth Company decided to expand its production facilities by adding an addition to its factory and acquiring additional equipment. The following occurred during the year:

| January | 4 | Equipment with a list price of $80,000 was received. |
| | 9 | Construction of the new addition to the main building was started. |

24 A bill in the amount of $2,700 was received for transporting the equipment (received on January 4) to Growth Company.

27 Architect's fees of $3,400 were paid for the preliminary design of the addition to the building.

February 3 Payment was made for the equipment and transportation. A 10 percent trade discount on the cost of the equipment was received.

March 9 Payment was made to the construction company in the amount of $235,000 following completion of the addition to the building.

14 Work crews installed the equipment and were paid $800.

15 A special ad was run in a local paper at a cost of $140 informing residents that the company would begin interviewing for new employees in two weeks.

24 A party costing $450 was held to celebrate completion of the new addition.

April 7 Testing of the new equipment was completed and it was placed in service. Total testing costs were $900.

a. Determine the costs that should be included as costs of the assets by Growth Company in the buildings account and in the equipment account.
b. What should be done with any costs not included?
c. List two additional costs that might have been incurred and included in the costs of the assets in connection with the expansion of facilities by Growth Company.

E10-12 Determining Asset Cost Welborne Corporation incurred the following costs of opening a new production area in its main factory building:

May 7 Paid $120,000 for removal of old structures to accommodate new production area.

10 Paid $220,000 for restructuring and finishing new production area.

15 Paid $80,000 for cement foundation for placement of new machinery.

20 Received new production equipment with an invoice price of $450,000. A business discount of 10 percent was applied to the gross purchase price.

27 Paid freight on equipment of $35,000.

29 Paid invoice for equipment.

30 Cost of installing equipment was $14,000.

June 2 Paid president's salary of $10,000 for June.

7 Received refund of $8,000 on cement work for equipment foundation.

9 Paid excise taxes on equipment of $19,000.

a. Compute the amount that should be included as equipment cost.

b. What treatment should be accorded those costs not included in the equipment cost?
c. How should depreciation on the equipment be reported in Welborne's income statement?
d. If Welborne had borrowed money to pay for the equipment, how should the interest on the amount borrowed be reported?

E10-13 Asset Similarity Kline Corporation rents a delivery truck on January 1, 2001, for one year, paying the rent of $6,000 in advance. On the same day, Kline purchases and installs a refrigeration unit on the truck at a cost of $30,000. The truck is expected to be rented each year for 5 years, and the refrigeration unit is expected to have a life of 5 years.

a. What assets and amounts would be reported in the balance sheet on January 1, 2001, and how would they be classified? What expenses would be reported in the income statement for 2001 and 2002? Explain how the assets are similar to and different from each other.
b. Is management more efficiently using its assets in either case? Explain.

E10-14 Depreciation Expense Polar Corporation purchased a building with an expected useful life of 30 years for $300,000 on January 1, 2000. The building is expected to have a residual value of $60,000.

a. Give the journal entries that would be made by Polar to record the purchase of the building in 2000 and depreciation expense for 2000 and 2001 assuming straight-line depreciation is used.
b. Give the journal entries that would be made by Polar to record the purchase of the building in 2000 and depreciation expense for 2000 and 2001 assuming double-declining-balance depreciation is used.

E10-15 Depreciation Methods Early in 2000, Cycle Corporation paid $180,000 to purchase equipment with an expected life of 4 years. Estimated salvage value of the equipment is $10,000. The machine is expected to be used a total of 18,000 hours, as follows: 2000 3,200; 2001 4,800; 2002 5,600; and 2003 4,400.

The controller of Cycle Corporation has requested your assistance in determining the annual depreciation expense and the balance in accumulated depreciation at the end of each of the years using the following depreciation methods:

a. Straight-line
b. Double-declining-balance
c. Activity-based

E10-16 Depreciation of Equipment Fiddle Company purchased equipment for $270,000. Fiddle expects to use the equipment for six years and to be able to sell it for $30,000 at the end of that period. If Fiddle uses straight-line depreciation:

a. Compute the amount to be reported as to depreciation expense each year, the accumulated depreciation at the end of each year, and the book value at the end of each year.
b. If Fiddle sells the equipment for $48,000 at the end of year five, will it report a gain or loss on the sale? What amount of gain or loss will be reported?

E10-17 Straight-line Depreciation Terrace Corporation purchased used bulldozers and other earth-moving equipment with an expected useful life of five years for $1,200,000. Terrace expects to be able to sell the equipment for $250,000 at the end of five years. Assuming Terrace uses straight-line depreciation:

a. What amount of depreciation expense will be reported each year?

b. What amount will be reported as accumulated depreciation at the end of each year?

c. What amount will be reported as the book value of the earth-moving equipment at the end of each year?

d. What amount of gain or loss will be reported by Terrace Corporation if the equipment is sold for $293,000 at the end of the fifth year?

E10-18 Double-Declining-Balance Depreciation Todd Company purchased a building with an expected life of twenty years by issuing common stock with a par value of $600,000 and a market value of $3,000,000. Todd Company expects to be able to sell the building for $500,000 at the end of 20 years. Assuming Todd Company uses double-declining-balance depreciation, compute following:

a. The amount reported as depreciation expense each year for the first five years.

b. The amount reported as accumulated depreciation at the end of each of the first five years.

c. The amount reported as book value at the end of each of the first five years.

d. The amount of gain or loss that Todd Company would report if it sold the building for $1,650,000 at the end of the fifth year of ownership.

E10-19 Accelerated Depreciation Amalgamated Health Spas purchased treadmills and other exercise equipment for $800,000. The equipment is expected to be used for eight years and is depreciated using double-declining-balance depreciation. Amalgamated expects to be able to sell the equipment for $85,000 at the end of eight years. Compute the amount to be:

a. Reported as depreciation expense each year.

b. Reported as accumulated depreciation at the end of each year.

c. Reported as book value of equipment at the end of each year.

d. Reported as a gain or loss at the end of year 8 if the equipment is sold for $95,000.

E10-20 Activity-Based Depreciation Row Manufacturing purchased production equipment for $450,000, which it expects to use for a total of 8,000 hours during the next five years. It expects to be able to sell the equipment as scrap for $30,000 at the end of five years. Row uses the equipment for 2,400, 1,600, 2,200, 1,000, and 800 hours during the five years, respectively. Assuming Row uses activity-based depreciation, compute the following:

a. Depreciation expense for each year.

b. Accumulated depreciation at the end of each year.

c. Book value of the equipment at the end of each year.

E10-21 Activity-Based Depreciation Extruded Molding Company uses special molds in producing high-quality window awnings. Each mold can be used to produce 3,000 awnings before it must be scrapped. Extruded Molding purchased a new mold for $129,000 and produced 400, 600, 900, 300, and 500 awnings, respectively, during the first five years of operation. Assuming Extruded Molding uses activity-based depreciation:

a. Compute the amount to be reported as depreciation expense for each of the five years.

b. Compute the amount to be reported as accumulated depreciation at the end of each of the five years.

c. Compute the amount reported as the book value of the mold at the end of each of the five years.

E10-22 Determining Tax Savings The president of Southeast Company anticipates rapid expansion in business in each of the next several years and is interested in reducing tax payments in 2000 and 2001 as much as possible. Southeast is currently using straight-line depreciation for both financial reporting and tax purposes. At the beginning of 2000, Southeast holds depreciable assets that cost $900,000 and have an expected salvage value of $60,000. The average life of the assets is expected to be six years from January 1, 2000. Southeast's income tax rate is 40 percent.

In 2000 and 2001, Southeast projects that it will report sales of $1,400,000 and $1,700,000, and expenses other than depreciation and income tax of $800,000 and $1,000,000, respectively.

a. Compute the amount of expected net income for 2000 and 2001 using straight-line depreciation.

b. Compute the amount of expected net income for 2000 and 2001 using double-declining-balance depreciation.

c. If Southeast were to use double-declining-balance rather than straight-line depreciation for income tax purposes, what amount of cash savings would it expect to realize in each of the two years?

d. Would Southeast be wise to use double-declining-balance depreciation for tax purposes if there was a chance that it would report an operating loss in one or both of the years? Explain.

E10-23 Depletion Oozzy Oil Company paid $35,000,000 to acquire an oil well containing an estimated 7 million barrels of crude oil. Oozzy immediately invested an additional $1,400,000 preparing the well for production. During the first four years of production, Oozzy pumped and sold 1,200,000, 1,600,000, 1,500,000, and 1,300,000 barrels of oil from the well. Compute the following:

a. Amount of depletion to be recorded in each of the four years.

b. Amount of accumulated depletion at the end of each of the four years.

c. Book value of Oozzy's investment in the oil well at the end of each of the four years.

E10-24 Depletion Amounts Salty Corporation purchased a salt mine in lower Michigan for $90,000,000. Salty expects to recover 2 million tons of salt from the mine. Because of its location, Salty expects to pay $8,000,000 to refill the mine once production is completed, and has agreed to sell the land to a local community college for $1,600,000. During the first four years of operations, Salty produced 40,000, 120,000, 300,000, and 180,000 tons of salt, respectively. Determine the amount of:

a. Depletion for each of the four years.
b. Accumulated depletion at the end of each of the four years.
c. Book value of the mine at the end of each of the four years based on its initial payment of $90,000,000.

E10-25 Sale of Asset On January 1, 1999, Timmins Company paid $400,000 to purchase equipment with an expected life of five years and no estimated salvage value. Due to a major flood, Timmins Company was forced to sell the equipment for $210,000 on December 31, 2000.

a. What amount of gain or loss would be recorded when the equipment is sold if Timmins uses straight-line depreciation?
b. Prepare the journal entry to record the sale, assuming Timmins uses straight-line depreciation.
c. What amount of gain or loss would be recorded when the equipment is sold if Timmins uses double-declining-balance depreciation?
d. Prepare the journal entry to record the sale, assuming Timmins uses double-declining-balance depreciation.

E10-26 Sale of Depreciable Asset Sunsweet Corporation purchased a building on January 1, 1991, for $900,000. It sold the building on January 1, 2000, and made the following journal entry:

Cash	495,000	
Loss on Sale of Building	27,000	
Accumulated Depreciation	378,000	
Building		900,000

Sunsweet used straight-line depreciation and an expected life of 20 years in depreciating the asset.

a. What was the annual depreciation expense reported by Sunsweet?
b. What was the estimated salvage value used in recording the annual depreciation?
c. If Sunsweet reported net income of $270,000 prior to considering the effects of the sale of the building, what amount will it report as net income for the year 2000?
d. Give the journal entry that would have been recorded by Sunsweet if it had sold the building for $531,000 on January 1, 2000.

E10-27 Depletion Costs Diggers, Inc., opened a new strip coal mine in early 2001. The company incurred the following costs during the year:

Payment for rights to coal	$650,000
Cost of removing and storing top soil	70,000
Legal fees for land purchase	20,000
Costs of removing coal this period	80,000
Property taxes on land for current year	8,000
Other operating costs	33,000

The company anticipates selling 100,000 tons of coal from the mine over its life. The expected cost of restoring the property following closing of the mine is $210,000. Following restoration of the land once the mine closes, it will be donated to the county to be used as a recreation area. A total of 20,000 tons of coal was removed from the mine in 2001 and 15,000 tons were sold at an average price of $20 per ton.

a. Compute the amount of depletion for 2001.
b. When the company records depletion for 2001, what accounts will be affected, and by what amounts?
c. At what amount will the land be reported in the company's balance sheet at the end of 2001?
d. At what amount will coal inventory be reported in the balance sheet at the end of 2001?
e. Compute 2001 net income for Diggers, Inc.

E10-28 Goodwill Bristol Company recently purchased General Enterprises to expand its dealer network to the west coast. Just before the acquisition, the following dollar amounts were reported by the two companies:

	Bristol Company	General Enterprises
Book value of total assets	$700,000	$380,000
Fair value of total assets	980,000	540,000
Book value of total liabilities	300,000	130,000
Fair value of total liabilities	270,000	150,000
Book value of stockholders' equity	400,000	250,000
Market value of common stock outstanding	900,000	430,000

After the acquisition, General's assets and liabilities were transferred to Bristol and recorded on Bristol's books. Bristol issued new preferred shares with a market value of $450,000 and par value of $350,000 in making the purchase.

a. What was the fair value of the net assets of General Enterprises when the company was acquired by Bristol? Why was the market price of General's stock more than the fair value of its net assets?
b. Why would Bristol pay more than the current market price of General's stock to make the acquisition?
c. What amount of goodwill would be reported by Bristol at the time of the purchase? What other accounts would be

affected on Bristol's books by the acquisition and by what amounts?

d. How must Bristol treat the goodwill for financial reporting purposes at the time of the acquisition and in subsequent years?

E10-29 Amortizing Goodwill Barley Brewery purchased the assets of Fox Grain Company for $950,000. Just prior to the purchase, Fox used its available cash to pay off all its liabilities. The book value of Fox's assets at the date of purchase by Barley was $600,000 and their estimated fair value was $750,000.

a. What amount will be reported by Barley Brewing as goodwill immediately following the purchase?

b. If the goodwill is expected to be amortized on a straight-line basis over 10 years, what impact will the amortization of the goodwill have on the reported net income of Barley Brewery in the second year of ownership?

E10-30 Amortization of Intangibles At January 1, 2001, Film Corporation reported the following balance sheet amounts:

Cash and receivables		$170,000
Inventory		100,000
Buildings and equipment	$300,000	
Less: Accumulated depreciation	(100,000)	200,000
Patents		70,000
Goodwill		40,000
Total assets		$580,000
Accounts payable		$190,000
Bonds payable		200,000
Common stock, $10 par value		50,000
Retained earnings		140,000
Total liabilities and owners'		
equity		$580,000

Buildings and equipment have been depreciated for four years on a straight-line basis and have no estimated salvage value. Patents have 10 years of remaining life and goodwill has been amortized for 2 years of its expected 10-year life. During 2001, Film Corporation spent $80,000 for research and development activities on a new production process that Film Corporation thinks will result in substantial cost savings over the next 10 years.

What dollar amount of expense should be reported in the 2001 income statement for each of the following?

a. Depreciation.

b. Amortization of patents.

c. Amortization of goodwill.

d. Research and development costs.

E10-31 Amortization of Intangibles Vinay Company purchases several intangible assets, as follows:

Asset	Cost
Patent	$ 50,000
Copyright	200,000
License	920,000

In addition to the purchase cost of each asset, legal fees associated with the acquisition of the license are $44,000. Although the patent has a legal life of 20 years, technological changes are expected to render it worthless after about 5 years. The copyright is good for another 20 years, but nearly all of the related sales are expected to occur during the next 4 years. The license is good in perpetuity, and sales under the license are expected to continue at the same level for many decades.

a. Compute the annual amortization, if any, for each of Vinay's intangible assets.

b. Show the presentation of the Intangible Asset section of Vinay's balance sheet prepared at the end of the third year after acquisition of the intangible assets.

E10-32 Research and Development Health Resources is involved in a large number of research projects in the health care industry. It has just completed a major breakthrough in developing a cure for male-pattern baldness. The cost of developing the initial product, laboratory testing, and testing on a representative group of adult males was $1,500,000.

a. How must Health Resources report the research and development costs associated with its new product?

b. As Health Resources completed development of its new product, it learned that a major competitor, Top Sciences had developed a product that keeps hair from turning gray. Top Sciences offered to sell its patent to Health Resources for $2 million. If Health Resources were to purchase the patent from Top Sciences, how would it record the purchase?

c. Evaluate the inconsistencies, if any, in the accounting treatment for the two products.

E10-33 Return on Assets On January 1, 1997, Johnson Corporation invested $800,000 in equipment with an expected useful life of twenty years and an anticipated residual value of $50,000. In 2000, Johnson reported sales of $1,100,000 and operating costs other than depreciation of $900,000. At December 31, 2000, Johnson held $100,000 of assets in addition to its equipment.

a. Assuming Johnson uses straight-line depreciation, what amount of net income will it report for 2000? What will be the return on assets for 2000 using total assets reported at December 31, 2000?

b. Assuming Johnson uses double-declining-balance depreciation, what amount of net income will it report for 2000? What will be the return on assets for 2000 using total assets reported at December 31, 2000?

c. For what type of asset would it be most appropriate to use double-declining-balance depreciation?

E10-34 Flint Company Ratios Flint Company reported the following account balances in its financial statements at December 31, 2001:

	Dec. 31, 2001	Jan. 1, 2001
Current assets	$200,000	$180,000
Fixed assets	600,000	520,000
Total liabilities	250,000	250,000
Owners' equity	550,000	450,000
Total sales for 2001		$900,000
Cost of goods sold for 2001		720,000
Net income for 2001		70,000

Compute the following:

a. Gross margin.
b. Gross margin percentage.
c. Return on assets.
d. Fixed asset turnover ratio.

E10-35 Change of Depreciation Methods Rustic Corporation purchased operating assets with an expected useful life of five years. The company paid $310,000 for the assets. At the end of the second year of operations, the carrying value (book value) of the assets was $202,000 using straight-line depreciation.

a. What, if any, is the estimated salvage value of the assets?
b. If Rustic sold the assets at the end of the second year for $225,000, what gain or loss would be recorded on the sale? Give the journal entry to record the sale.
c. What would the carrying value of the assets have been at the end of the second year if Rustic had used double-declining-balance rather than straight-line depreciation?
d. If the federal income tax rate is 30 percent, what amount of cash savings (loss) would Rustic have realized if it had used double-declining-balance depreciation for tax purposes rather than straight-line for the first two years of ownership?

E10-36 Operating Lease Boulder Dash Corporation leases automobiles from Zippo Leasing for use by its sales personnel. The leased vehicles are used for two years and then returned to Zippo Leasing. All maintenance and repair is done by Zippo. Boulder Dash makes a deposit of $5,000 at the beginning of the lease on each car and pays monthly rentals of $400 per car. The cars cost Zippo approximately $16,000 each. The deposit is refunded when the car is returned. Boulder Dash pays for all gas and annual registration fees. Boulder Dash currently has 22 cars under lease from Zippo.

a. Is the lease an operating lease or a capital lease? Explain why.
b. What amount of expense related to the lease will Boulder Dash record for the current year?
c. How is the $5,000 deposit per car reported by Boulder Dash?

E10-37 Operating Lease On January 1, 2000, Timber Corporation agreed to lease a new logging truck for three years at a cost of $30,000 per year, with payment to be made at the end of each year. Timber Corporation has determined the present value of the three payments, discounted at 8 percent, is equal to $77,313. Because the lease is for only three years and the expected economic life of the truck is 10 years, the lease is considered to be an operating lease.

a. What amount of lease expense will Timber Corporation report each period?
b. How will the lease be reflected in the accounting equation for Timber Corporation on January 1, 2000, if at all?
c. How would the effect on the accounting equation change if the lease were considered to be a capital lease?

E10-38 Capital Lease On January 1, 2000, Whitter Corporation leased a small warehouse and agreed to pay $18,878 at the end of each of 20 years. The lease is considered to be a capital lease. The lease payments include 7 percent interest and have a present value of $200,000, which equals the purchase price of the warehouse.

a. What effect will the signing of the lease have on the accounting equation of Whitter Corporation?
b. What amount of interest expense will Whitter Corporation report for the year 2000?
c. What amount of depreciation expense will Whitter Corporation report for the year 2000 if straight-line depreciation is used?
d. Will Whitter's net income for 2000 be increased or decreased as a result of recording the lease as a capital lease rather than an operating lease? By what amount?

E10-39A Financing Noncurrent Assets Bates Corporation is interested in adding to its production facilities and has identified two major routes to follow. Under the first alternative. Bates would acquire the use of additional building space by signing a seven-year lease, which would be treated as an operating lease. Bates Corporation would make annual payments of $298,036 at the end of each year. An implicit interest rate of 9 percent is included in the lease computations. Under the second alternative, Bates would purchase a building for $1,500,000 by borrowing that amount on a 7-year note requiring equal payments of $298,036 at the end of each year for 7 years. For depreciation purposes, the building has an expected life of twenty-five years and residual value of $300.000. Straight-line depreciation would be used.

a. Prepare a schedule showing the computation of interest expense over the 7-year term of the note if the second alternative is chosen and the note includes 9 percent implicit interest.
b. Determine the annual cost of the additional facilities in years 1 through 3 under the two alternatives.
c. Which alternative should Bates select? Explain why.

E10-40A Capital Lease Speedy Bus Service experienced a major increase in ridership in the last three months of 1999. On January 1, 2000, Speedy entered into an agreement to lease four new buses from Transport Leasing Company.

Speedy provides all maintenance and repairs on the buses. The lease agreement on each bus requires Speedy to pay $12,000 on January 1, 2000, followed by fifteen annual payments of $12,000 each, beginning with December 31, 2000. At the end of the lease term, title to the buses transfers to Speedy. The buses have a useful life of 20 years and are depreciated on a straight-line basis with no anticipated salvage value. The lease is structured with a 10 percent interest rate.

a. Is the agreement a capital or operating lease? Explain your answer.
b. Assuming Speedy records the leases on the four buses as capital leases, compute the present value of the lease payments.
c. Present the amounts related to the lease that would appear in the income statements and balance sheets of Speedy Bus Service for the years 2000 and 2001.

E10-41A Operating versus Capital Lease On January 1, 2001, Phillips Company signed an agreement to lease new machinery. The lease requires a payment of $50,000 on January 1, 2001, and on January 1 of each of the next four years (a total of five payments). The lease payments include 6 percent interest and have a present value of $223,255 at January 1, 2001. Machinery is depreciated on a straight-line basis. Determine the amounts that will be reported in the 2001 income statement and balance sheet as of December 31, 2001, for each of the following, assuming the lease is treated as (1) an operating lease; (2) capital lease:

	Operating Lease	Capital Lease
Rent Expense	a.	f.
Machinery Under Capital Lease	b.	g.
Depreciation Expense	c.	h.
Interest Expense	d.	i.
Accumulated Depreciation	e.	j.

USING ACCOUNTING FOR DECISION MAKING

P10-42 Profitability Measures In 2002, Cidad Corporation reported net income of $600,000 on total sales of $4,800,000. Total assets were $3,000,000 at January 1, 2002, and $3,300,000 at December 31, 2002. Cidad is considering purchasing $1,700,000 of additional assets. With the additional investment, Cidad estimates its asset turnover rate will increase to 1.6 and the return on assets will be 23.1 percent.

a. Compute the return on assets earned by Cidad Corporation for 2002.
b. Compute the (1) margin on the sales and (2) asset turnover ratio for 2002.
c. If Cidad had purchased the new assets on January 1, 2002, how much would sales and net income have increased?
d. Should Cidad expand? Explain your answer.

P10-43 Disposal of an Asset J. Electronics purchased a warehouse on January 1, 1992, for $950,000. At the time of purchase, J. Electronics anticipated the warehouse would be used to facilitate its expanded product line. The warehouse is being depreciated over 20 years and is expected to have a resale value of $50,000 at the end of that period. The company uses straight-line depreciation. On January 1, 2002, J. Electronics concluded that the warehouse would no longer be used and should be sold for its book value. At the end of 2002, the warehouse still had not been sold and its net realizable value was estimated to be only $300,000.

a. Compute the book value of the warehouse at January 1, 2002.
b. What amount of depreciation should be recorded in 2002?
c. If during 2003 J. Electronics sells the warehouse for $400,000, what accounts would be affected and by what amount?

d. During 2002, the financial vice president expressed concern that, if J. Electronics put the building up for sale, the company might have to report a loss for the year. Not wanting to reduce 2002 earnings any further, the vice president suggested continuing to treat the warehouse as an operating asset. How would the financial statements be different if the warehouse were treated as an operating asset during 2002? From a stockholder's perspective, do you believe the treatment makes any difference? Explain.

P10-44 Asset Acquisitions String Music Co. decided to expand its product line to include banjos and harmonicas. Rather than establish its own production facility, String Music Co. purchased the net assets of Discord Corporation for $360,000. Before making the purchase, String Music had appraisals made of Discord's operating assets and business operations. The appraisals were as follows:

Land	$ 40,000
Building	240,000
Production Equipment	100,000
Office Equipment and Materials	70,000

The appraisers also provided the following estimates of the remaining economic lives of these assets: buildings, 30 years; production equipment, 10 years; office equipment, 14 years; and goodwill or other intangible assets, 15 years. As part of the purchase agreement, String Music also agreed to take responsibility for $150,000 of debt on the machinery and equipment.

The financial vice president of String Music Co. was in charge of the acquisition and thought String Music would get quite a bargain by paying $360,000. The replacement cost for a new building was estimated at $375,000, the cost of buying new production and office equipment would be $250,000, and he estimates that it would take another $200,000 beyond the cost of the assets to develop customer contacts and gain an acceptable level of product recognition. This is a total of $825,000. The financial vice president therefore favors recording the assets at $825,000.

a. Is it appropriate to recognize all, or any part, of the $825,000 total suggested by the financial vice president? Explain.
b. If String Music pays $360,000 cash to acquire Discord, determine the amount it should assign to each of the assets and prepare the entry needed to record the purchase.
c. Assuming Discord reports sales of $400,000 and cost of inventory sold of $280,000 in the period following the acquisition, what amount of income will the purchase of Discord add to the earnings reported by String for the year?
d. String earns a gross margin of 45 percent on sales by its other operating divisions and a 10 percent return on total assets. How does the acquisition of Discord compare?

P10-45 Depreciation Methods Weiskoff and Associates recently completed construction of a new office building in downtown Eastwik. The land on which the building was constructed was purchased for $120,000, and $15,000 was spent to have an existing building removed. Legal fees were $22,000 for the transfer of title to the land. Architect fees on the new building were $80,000. Payment of $620,000 was made to the contractor upon completion of the building. A parking lot was built on the property at a cost of $70,000. Sidewalks, lighting, and landscaping cost a total of $35,000. A fence around the parking lot was added at a cost of $15,000. The building has an estimated useful life of 40 years, and land improvements are expected to be of benefit for 8 years.

a. Determine the amounts that should be reported as the cost of (1) land, (2) buildings, and (3) land improvements.
b. The company has decided to use straight-line depreciation for financial reporting purposes and double-declining-balance depreciation for tax purposes. Compute the depreciation both for financial reporting and tax reporting for the second year of ownership.
c. Assuming a 40 percent federal income tax rate, what amount of cash did the company save in tax payments during the second year by using double-declining-balance depreciation for tax purposes?
d. Weiskoff and Associates received an offer from an investor at the end of the second year of ownership who was willing to pay $935,000 for the property. What amount of gain or loss would be recorded on the sale? What factors should Weiskoff consider before selling?

P10-46 Recognizing Intangible Assets Lazar Corporation was organized on January 1, 2001, and immediately issued 30,000 shares of $10 par value common stock and 40,000 shares of $5 par value preferred stock at par value. Total cash received for the shares was $500,000. The first act of the com-

pany once it started operations was to purchase the rights to a self-cleaning car wax. The total payment for exclusive production rights for 5 years was $280,000. During the next 5 months, Lazar Corporation spent $110,000 on research and development on a special chrome polish that would instantly remove rust spots from automotive chrome. Although patent clearance has not been received, Lazar plans to market the chrome cleaner as a companion product to the car wax. To immediately produce both products, Lazar obtained a bank loan of $150,000, and paid $213,000 for the assets and liabilities of Slippery Wax Company. At that time, Slippery Wax held assets with a fair value of $350,000 and liabilities of $220,000.

a. Which, if any, of the costs incurred by Lazar Company qualify as research and development costs? How are these costs to be accounted for?
b. When is goodwill recognized? Should Lazar Corporation recognize any goodwill? How should Lazar account for goodwill?
c. Which, if any, of the costs qualify for capitalization as other intangible assets? What amounts should be capitalized? How are these costs to be accounted for?
d. Prepare a balance sheet for Lazar Corporation following completion of its acquisition of Slippery Wax Company.
e. If Lazar Corporation were to come to the bank where you were employed as a loan officer and apply for an additional loan of $50,000, what factors would you look at in determining whether to grant the loan?

P10-47 Analysis of Asset Position The 2001 consolidated balance sheet of Worldwide Parcel Delivery Corporation contained the following assets:

Current assets:	
Cash	$ 55,063,000
Short-term investments	10,109,000
Accounts receivable (allowance for doubtful accounts of $2,846,000)	150,969,000
Other current assets	3,224,000
Total current assets	$219,365,000
Investment in unconsolidated affiliates	7,595,000
Property, plant, and equipment (less accumulated depreciation of $34,096,000)	27,323,000
Deposits and other assets	4,604,000
Goodwill (less accumulated amortization of $4,674,000)	37,331,000
Total assets	$296,218,000

Worldwide Parcel Delivery Corporation is involved in international airfreight and seafreight shipping and delivery activities.

a. Is it logical for a company with nearly $300,000,000 of assets to report no inventory balance? Explain.
b. Do you think it is unusual for a company to report goodwill in excess of its investment in net plant and equipment? What portion of the total do each of these assets make up? How would the balance in goodwill have been derived? In evaluating Worldwide Parcel Delivery to as-

sess the desirability of purchasing some of its bonds, how would you treat goodwill?

c. Worldwide Parcel Delivery reports current liabilities of $138,547,000 and long-term debt of $78,464,000 at December 31, 2001. How would you assess the riskiness of this company?

P10-48A Lease Versus Purchase Starburst Brewery must replace some of its old equipment with new stainless-steel equipment to avoid losing its license. The controller is unsure whether to purchase new equipment with borrowed money or to lease the equipment. If purchased, on January 1, 2002, the equipment will cost $500,000 and have an estimated useful life of 20 years and no salvage value. Local Bank is willing to take a $500,000, 10-year, 12 percent note with interest-only payments to be made at the end of each year. Out-of-Town Leasing is willing to lease the equipment to Starburst for 9 years, with an option to purchase at the end

of the lease. The following payment schedule would be required, providing Out-of-Town with a 12 percent return:

January 1, 2002	$90,000 upon signing lease
December 31, 2002 to 2009	$90,000 per year
December 31, 2010	$75,000 purchase option

Starburst anticipates that it would exercise the purchase option because the option price is well below what the fair value of the equipment is expected to be at that date.

a. Compute the present value of the future cash outflows under both arrangements.
b. State what amounts would appear in Starburst's 2002 income statement and balance sheet under both alternatives.
c. Which of the two financing alternatives should be selected? Why? Explain what factors other than cash payments directly related to financing might be important to the decision.

EXPANDING YOUR HORIZONS

C10-49 Analysis of Gateway, Inc. The Gateway financial statements and accompanying notes included in Appendix A can be used in analyzing purchases and sales of property, plant, and equipment.

a. What was the increase in net property, plant and equipment in 1998?
b. At December 31, 1997 and 1998, what were the individual components of property, plant and equipment, and what was the dollar amount of each? What was the amount of increase in total investment in property, plant and equipment in 1998?
c. What amount was reported in the cash flow statement as net investment in property, plant and equipment in 1998? Does this amount agree with the increase in total property, plant and equipment calculated in part b? What is the amount of the difference? What factors might cause this difference?
d. What was the amount of increase in accumulated depreciation and amortization in 1998? Depreciation and amortization expense for the year reported in the statements of cash flows was $105,524,000. Is the increase in accumulated depreciation and amortization equal to depreciation and amortization expense for the year? What is the amount of the difference? What factors might cause this difference?

C10-50 Property and Equipment of Toys "R" Us Toys "R" Us lists the following property and equipment in its balance sheet (in millions of dollars):

	1/30/99	1/31/98
Property and Equipment:		
Real Estate, net	$2,354	$2,435
Other, net	1,872	1,777

The footnote disclosure in the company's annual report explains the accounting methods for property and equipment, as follows:

Property and Equipment
Property and equipment are recorded at cost. Depreciation and amortization are provided using the straight-line method over the estimated useful lives of the assets or, where applicable, the terms of the respective leases, whichever is shorter.

The company's 10-K filing with the SEC discloses the following additional information about property and equipment (in millions of dollars):

	Useful Life, Yrs.	1999	1998
Land		$ 829	$ 817
Buildings	45–50	1,842	1,849
Furniture and equipment	5–20	1,861	1,711
Leaseholds and leasehold improvements	$12\frac{1}{2}$–35	1,213	1,158
Construction in process		42	46
Leased property under capital lease		27	29
Total		$5,814	$5,610
Less accumulated depreciation and amortization		(1,588)	(1,398)
Property and equipment, net		$4,226	$4,212

From the information presented, answer the following questions:

a. What depreciation method is Toys "R" Us using?

b. What is the historical cost of the land? Of the buildings?

c. Depreciation, amortization, and asset write-offs were $255 million in 1999. If there were no disposals of property and equipment during the year, what amount of these assets were acquired during the period?

d. Which items are depreciated and which items are amortized?

C10-51 Asset Changes at Hewlett–Packard Company

The following information is taken from Hewlett–Packard Company's annual report and its 10-K filing with the SEC (in millions of dollars):

	1998	**1997**
Land	$ 450	$ 468
Buildings & Leasehold Improvements	4,997	4,672
Machinery & Equipment	7,123	6,636
Accumulated Depreciation	6,212	5,464

The following additional information regarding 1998 is also presented:

- Depreciation and amortization expense was $1,869.

- New investment in property, plant, and equipment was $1,997.

Based on the information provided, answer the following questions:

a. Which financial statement will provide information regarding depreciation and amortization expense?

b. Which financial statement will provide information regarding new investments in property, plant, and equipment?

c. Which financial statement will provide information about accumulated depreciation?

d. What was the historical cost of the fixed assets that were disposed of during 1998?

e. What was the book value of the fixed assets that were disposed of during 1998?

C10-52 America Online: Creating Intangible Assets

The following appeared in a *Newsweek* article about America Online under the subtitle "How creative accounting makes AOL look great":

One of AOL's hidden assets is the brilliant accounting decision it made to treat its marketing and R&D costs as capital items rather than expenses . . . In July, AOL began charging off marketing expenses over two years, up from about 15 months. Had the new policy been in effect in fiscal 1995, AOL would have reported operating profits of about $50 million rather than $23 million.

Why change to 24 months from 15? [AOL's chief financial officer Lenert] Leader said it's because the average life of an AOL account has climbed to 41 months from 25 months in 1992. How many AOL customers have been around for 41 months? Almost none, as Leader concedes. That's understandable, considering

that AOL has added virtually all its customers in the past 36 months. Leader says the 41-month average life number comes from projections.[4]

Forbes reports that AOL has run promotional campaigns costing more than $40 per new subscriber and that the average subscriber pays approximately $15.50 per month, including online time.[5] Other recent news reports have indicated that online services such as AOL might have trouble competing in the future with services providing low cost access to the Internet.

a. Should AOL capitalize as assets its promotional and marketing costs or should these costs be expensed as incurred?

b. If promotional and marketing costs were to be capitalized, over what period of time should they be amortized?

c. Should the accounting treatment of marketing costs for an on-line service such as AOL be different from that of advertising costs for major softdrink or tobacco brands? Explain.

C10-53 Team Project: Analyzing Financial Statements

Acquire the financial statements of a large manufacturing company, such as General Motors, a large electric or gas utility, such as Duke Energy Corporation or Ameren Corporation (formerly Union Electric Company), and a large bank, such as Wells Fargo & Company. For each company, examine the balance sheet, income statement, statement of cash flows, and footnotes to the financial statements. Prepare a short report in which you include the following:

a. Which companies have substantial investments in property, plant, and equipment? Is the type of fixed assets held the same for all three companies? Explain.

b. Do any of the companies have intangible assets? Describe the nature of those assets, if any.

c. Analyze the change in property, plant, and equipment during the most recent year. Review the discussion by management regarding the operating results and activities for the period and evaluate the reasons given for any major acquisitions or dispositions of assets.

d. What depreciation methods are used? Is the same method used for all assets? Is the same depreciable life used for all assets? If not, give the major classes and lives used. Do the companies use the same depreciation methods for financial reporting and tax purposes? How do you know?

C10-54 Analysis of Fedders Corporation

The following financial statement information was reported in the 1998 annual report of Fedders Corporation:

	1998	**1997**
Inventory	$ 52,261,000	$ 62,887,000
Total Current Assets	167,977,000	195,327,000
Net Property, Plant, and Equipment	56,318,000	63,994,000

[4]Allan Sloan, "Online's Bottom Line," *Newsweek* (October 30, 1995, p. 66.

[5] Gary Samuels, "What Profits?" *Forbes* (October 24, 1994), p. 74.

Goodwill	55,159,000	56,858,000
Total assets	304,629,000	329,014,000
Total current liabilities	74,341,000	53,591,000
Total long-term debt and other long-term liabilities	120,859,000	124,696,000
Total stockholders' equity	104,792,000	145,687,000
Net income	2,992,000	18,764,000

Fedders sales are concentrated in room air conditioners and dehumidifiers. Sales are made directly to dealers and through private-label arrangements with dealers and distributors.

a. What factor or factors most likely led to the $7,676,000 reduction in property, plant, and equipment?

b. According to the information in the annual report, a significant portion of the reduction in inventory was not directly related to the reduction of property, plant, and equipment. What factors are most likely to have led to a reduction of inventories?

c. Given that the company's net income has declined to $2,992,000 in 1998 from $18,764,000 in 1997, is it appropriate to continue to report goodwill in the balance sheet? Explain.

d. Compute Fedders return on equity, current ratio, and long-term debt and other liabilities to total assets ratio. What is your evaluation of Fedders performance for 1997 and 1998 and its financial position at year-end in 1998?

C10-55 A Company in Transition The Wright Company wants to raise money to finance the reorganization of its operations, and the company is seeking new investors. You have received a copy of Wright's financial statements. From these statements and other sources, you have gathered the following information about the company:

	2001	2000
Sales Revenue	$2,550,000	$1,950,000
Net Income	255,000	195,000
Total Assets	3,650,000	2,450,000

1. In January 2001 Wright borrowed money for the purchase of a small company to acquire its warehousing facilities. The total purchase price was $1,000,000 and was allocated $50,000 to the building and $950,000 to goodwill. The building is being depreciated over 20 years, and the goodwill is being amortized over 40 years.

2. In January 2002 Wright made the decision to discontinue its manufacturing operations and to contract out all the manufacturing of its products. Wright will distribute products under its own label, as before. This change has been under consideration for several years, and the new warehouse was purchased to facilitate this process. Wright plans to dispose of its old manufacturing plant and anticipates a significant loss from the disposal. The loss will be recorded in 2002 when the closing takes place.

3. Wright's employees rearranged the shelving in the new warehouse and took special training classes for the warehouse operations before it opened in March 2001. These costs of $50,000 were added to the cost of the building, as was the $8,000 cost of fire insurance for the first year.

Prepare an analysis of Wright Company to help you decide whether you would be interested in investing in the company. In your analysis, be sure to consider the company's return on sales and on assets in 2000 and 2001. Do you agree with the company's accounting treatments for the warehouse cost and the loss from closing the old manufacturing plant? Will Wright's accounting affect the quality of your return measures and your evaluation of the company? Does the fact that it will not be producing its own products raise any ethical issues?

Internet Exercises: Visit our Web site for additional exercises.

Annual Report Project Part 10

Refer to the Annual Report Project, Part 1, at the end of Chapter 1. Using the annual report of the company you have chosen, and any other available information, answer the following questions, providing sources and computations where appropriate.

a. What depreciation and amortization methods does the company use, and over what periods of time does it depreciate and amortize its fixed assets?

b. Has the amount of the company's plant and equipment increased or decreased? How would you characterize these changes (e.g., normal growth, major expansion)? Explain.

c. How did acquisitions or disposals of plant and equipment affect the company's cash flows? Explain.

d. Does the company lease a significant amount of its property, plant, and equipment? How do you know?

e. Based on the company's accumulated depreciation, would you judge the plant and equipment to be relatively new or relatively old? Explain.

CHAPTER ELEVEN

Reporting Liabilities

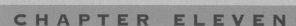

REVIEW

Chapter 6 discussed the basic aspects of reporting for assets, liabilities, and equity. Chapters 8, 9, and 10 provided more depth with respect to assets.

WHERE THIS CHAPTER FITS

This chapter discusses the different types of liabilities, their special characteristics, and how they are reported.

LOOKING AHEAD

The next chapter looks at the accounting and reporting aspects of owners' equity.

Let's see now. I owe money to the bank. The bank owes its depositors. We all owe money to the government. And the government owes more than all of us together will ever be able to pay. Wouldn't we all be better off if nobody ever borrowed anything?

The city of San Antonio seems unlikely to pay for a new arena for the San Antonio Spurs even though the promoters point out that the city would be at no risk because it could default on the debt and the financing firm would have to take over the arena. "City officials were not comforted. Even if the city was able to escape its liability by defaulting, it's hardly a good way of doing business. It can hurt bond ratings and lead to higher interest rates."[1]

[1] Rick Casey, "'New' Arena Idea Pitched Since '88," *San Antonio Express-News* (August 30, 1999).

Debt is an important part of life. Few people would own homes or cars without being able to borrow. And on the other side, what would savers do if there were no borrowers willing to pay for the use of money?

Individuals and businesses owe more than $14 trillion. Why does all of this debt exist? We all know that some individuals spend more than they earn. Similarly some businesses have experienced financial difficulties and have had to borrow to continue operating.

Although debt is often viewed negatively, it serves an important function in our society. Examples of beneficial uses of debt include:

* An individual with a steady income may purchase a home by borrowing most of the purchase price. Few people have the entire purchase price at the time they purchase a home, and borrowing allows people to acquire a valuable asset and pay for it over the time they use it.

* A new business has made a technological breakthrough, but lacks sufficient money to put its new product into production. A loan will allow the company to produce and sell its product and, if it is successful, to prosper. At the same time, society will benefit from the new product.

Because of the widespread use of debt, an understanding of liabilities and a knowledge of the financial reporting practices related to debt are crucial in being able to analyze an organization. This chapter discusses the types of debt that businesses use to finance their activities and the basic concepts relevant to reporting liabilities in financial statements. After reading this chapter, you should be able to:

1. Describe the types of liabilities reported by businesses and the types of transactions that give rise to each.

2. Explain how classifying liabilities as current or noncurrent is important for decision making.

3. Explain when liabilities are reported, and describe the valuation basis for different types of debt reported in financial statements.

4. Discuss why decision makers analyze an entity's operating liabilities.

5. Explain the role of leverage, and describe the aspects of long-term financing that are important for decision making.

6. Indicate the special reporting problems associated with postretirement benefits, income taxes, and "off-balance sheet financing," and explain why these items are important for assessing a company's future income, cash flows, and financial position.

7. Define key ratios for financial analysis involving liabilities and explain how they are used in decision making.

UNDERSTANDING LIABILITIES

Information for Decisions

Companies report their obligations to creditors in the financial statements as liabilities. By understanding the different types of liabilities reported, financial statement users can better understand a company's financial position and its activities that gave rise to the liabilities. They can answer questions such as these: Are short-term liabilities substantial enough to cause a liquidity problem in the near future? Does the company seem to be incurring liabilities over and above those necessary for day-to-day operations and for long-term financing of the organization? Why?

A liability is an obligation to transfer an economic benefit to another party in the future. The transfer may involve giving up an asset or providing a service to the other party. To be reported, the obligation must presently exist and must have arisen because of a transaction or event that has already occurred.

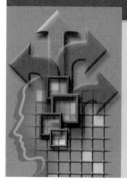

You Decide 11-1

WHERE DID THAT LIABILITY COME FROM?

Medical Appliance Development Corporation has just developed a new product that it expects to market within the next few months. Because all of its products are used in high-risk surgical procedures, the company has already experienced a large number of product liability suits related to its other products. Anticipating a number of such suits related to its new product, the company estimates that it will eventually settle the suits on its new product for approximately $23 million. Should the company record a liability for the anticipated amount of legal settlements associated with its new product?

TYPES AND CLASSIFICATION OF LIABILITIES

The assets of businesses are financed in two ways: by owners and by creditors. Liabilities reflect the financing by creditors and also represent the creditors' claim on the assets. Businesses incur many different types of liabilities, most of which are of the following types:

1. Those arising from day-to-day operations

2. Those related to the long-term financing of the organization

3. Special or unusual types of liabilities

Viewing liabilities in this way can help you better understand a company's financial position and its activities. As discussed in Chapter 6, however, the actual balance sheet classification of liabilities is somewhat different. Liabilities are typically reported in the balance sheet as either current or long-term. The distinction relates to when and how the obligation must be satisfied. Current liabilities are those expected to be liquidated within one year or the operating cycle, whichever is longer, using current assets. All other liabilities are classified as long-term.

The distinction between current and long-term liabilities in the balance sheet helps decision makers assess the likelihood that a company will be able to meet its obligations as they come due. By comparing current assets with current liabilities, decision makers can evaluate whether those resources will be sufficient to satisfy maturing obligations or whether other sources will have to be found.

LIABILITIES AND DECISIONS

Unlike equity, liabilities typically involved fixed commitments of resources, with little flexibility in timing. When an interest payment comes due or a loan matures, it must be paid. These aspects of liabilities are important in how decision makers view debt.

Considerations relating to debt are important for all types of decision makers. Management attempts to use debt in such a way that the debt benefits the company's profits and does not lead to cash shortages or the inability to meet obligations when they come due. Management's choices relating to alternative ways of financing operations can significantly affect the company's profitability and financial position. Investors must evaluate management's ability to effectively use alternative financing methods to increase the return to owners, avoid default, and have cash remaining after satisfying creditors. Of course, creditors want to be sure that they will be repaid in a timely manner. When focusing on liabilities, investors and creditors want information about an entity's liquidity, solvency, and even its long-term viability.

The financial statements provide a wealth of information about liabilities. In addition, the notes relating to all aspects of debt are usually quite extensive, providing valuable information about types and terms of debt, maturities, and collateral. The detailed information available in the financial statements and notes is essential to understanding how liabilities will affect the entity's future.

VALUATION OF LIABILITIES

Information for Decisions

Liabilities are generally reported at amounts based on their valuations as determined by the transactions that gave rise to those obligations. For long-term liabilities, these amounts are usually based on the present value of future cash payments. These valuations permit users of financial statements to assess the current equivalent amount of an obligation, the effective liability, even though the obligation need not be satisfied until some future time. Understanding how liabilities are valued permits financial statement users to answer questions such as these: If all obligations had to be satisfied today, would the entity's resources be sufficient? To what extent will the values assigned to the liabilities change before they must be satisfied by the entity, and what are the implications for the entity's ability to satisfy those obligations?

Most obligations arise when an organization receives cash, goods, resources, or services from others in an exchange transaction. In accordance with the objectivity concept, the values of the obligations are established at the time of the exchange. Because most obligations are ultimately expected to involve an outflow of cash, either directly or indirectly, the valuation is often based on present value concepts. The valuation bases at the date of recording for some common liabilities are as follows:

Liability	Valuation Basis
Trade payables (current)	Amount owed
Accrued expenses	Amount owed
Income taxes payable	Amount owed
Unearned revenues	Amount received
Estimated liabilities	Estimated amount of required payments
Loans, notes, or bonds payable	Present value of future payments
Lease obligations	Present value of future payments
Obligations for postretirement benefits	Present value of estimated benefits
Deferred income taxes	Amount of possible future payments
Contingent liabilities	Estimated amount of probable payments

While present value serves as the primary basis for valuing liabilities, other bases are used for some liabilities because the amounts do not differ materially from present value or because of the specific type of the liability. We'll discuss valuation in more detail as we next examine the different types of liabilities more closely.

LIABILITIES ARISING FROM DAY-TO-DAY OPERATIONS

Information for Decisions

Because most commercial transactions are on credit, entities incur obligations on a day-to-day basis as a normal part of their operations. Understanding these obligations, how they are valued in the financial statements, and how they are to be satisfied helps financial statement users evaluate a company's operations and answer questions such as these: Can the entity sustain itself by generating enough resources from normal operations to satisfy operating liabilities? Is the company in danger of harming its credit rating because current obligations are not being paid on time? How will the company's future income and cash flows be affected by the company's reported liability for unearned revenue? What is the nature of estimated liabilities reported by the company, and how confident can I be in those estimates?

Entities of all types incur numerous liabilities in their normal operations. They purchase goods and services on credit and expect to pay off these obligations within a few weeks. They use the labor of their employees and incur an obligation to make payment on the next scheduled payday. They incur costs for utilities, and have an obligation to pay the bills for the services within a specified time. Nearly all of these operating liabilities are expected to be paid within a short time, usually within sixty days.

Virtually all operating liabilities are classified as current liabilities because they are expected to be paid within one year or the operating cycle of the entity, whichever is longer, and are satisfied using current assets. A few operating liabilities, such as warranty obligations or occasional trade notes for periods longer than customary, are classified as long-term liabilities.

ANALYZING OPERATING LIABILITIES

As a financial statement user, why would you care whether liabilities were related to day-to-day operations or to something else? Debt is debt, right?

Actually, knowing the type of debt is important for several reasons. First, debt used to finance current operations must usually be repaid within a short time. Accordingly, the company must have sufficient resources on hand or coming in soon to make timely repayments. Second, if the company is to sustain its operations, the cash for short-term repayments should be generated from current operations. Although there are certainly exceptions, especially with a rapidly growing company, a company that is unable to meet its obligations arising from operations with cash generated from those operations eventually might be unable to continue. Also, the amount of operating liabilities might indicate whether the company has been paying its bills on time. Failure to pay bills promptly might be costly for the company (and its shareholders), result in future operating disruptions if vendors discontinue supplying goods and services, and indicate financial difficulty.

You Decide 11-2

ARE THE BILLS BEING PAID?

In looking at Drummond Company's financial statements, you notice that the company has accounts payable at year-end of $22,678,000. Its total operating expenses for the year, excluding wages, depreciation, and interest, were $53,444,000. Drummond is in the business of packaging frozen and other food products for institutions and restaurants. Does the amount of accounts payable at year-end seem unusually high, low, or about right? Explain. Based on this information, what else might you want to know if you were considering investing in Drummond's 90-day notes?

VALUING OPERATING LIABILITIES

Although liabilities are usually valued based on the present value of required future cash payments, operating liabilities generally are not. Because most operating liabilities will be paid within a very short time, the differences in the resulting information do not justify the detailed recordkeeping that would be required to figure interest on such short-term obligations.

Operating liabilities also include unearned revenues, which arise when a company collects in advance amounts for goods or services to be provided in the future. Examples include retainer fees received by lawyers in advance of the services provided and prepaid subscriptions for magazines. When a company receives payment for revenues it will earn in the future, it must reflect a liability for its obligation to provide the goods or services purchased by the customer. This liability, Unearned Revenues, does not indicate an amount of cash the company is obligated to pay in the future. Instead, it reflects the value of the goods or services to be provided. This value was agreed on in an exchange transaction between the purchaser and seller and provides an objective historical valuation for the liability. As the revenue is earned by the seller over time, the Unearned Revenue account is reduced and revenue is recognized.

ACCOUNTING FOR OPERATING LIABILITIES

Liabilities are recognized when an obligation is incurred. This may happen with a specific transaction, such as the purchase of inventory, or with the passage of time, such as with the accrual of rent. Remember that, given the dual nature of transactions, the entity is also affected in another way when a liability arises. Typically, the incurrence of a liability means the entity has incurred a cost. This cost might be an unexpired cost requiring recognition of an asset, as with the purchase of inventory on account, or it might be an expired cost requiring recognition of an expense, as when commissions are owed to the sales force.

A CLOSER LOOK AT

ACCOUNTING FOR OPERATING LIABILITIES

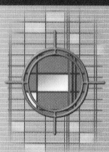

Babbitt Company incurs numerous obligations in its normal operations, with the following corresponding effects on its financial statements:

1. Babbitt purchases inventory on account for $3,000.

   An asset account, Inventory, increases, as does the liability Accounts Payable.

2. A utility bill for $1,250 is received.

   Because Babbitt has already used the services provided by the utility, an expense increases along with Babbitt's liability to pay the bill.

3. Babbitt pays the amounts due for both the inventory purchased and the utility bill.

   When Babbitt makes payment, both its cash and its obligation to make future payments decrease.

4. Inventory is purchased for $25,000; because of the large amount, the supplier takes in exchange Babbitt's one-year note payable.

   Babbitt's inventory increases, as does its liability Notes Payable, evidenced by the formal note given to the supplier.

5. $6,000 is received in advance for services to be provided in the future.

   Babbitt's cash increases, but so does the liability Unearned Service Revenue because Babbitt has accepted the obligation to provide services in the future.

6. At year-end, Babbitt adjusts its accounts to reflect earning $2,000 of service revenue that had been collected in advance, $800 of interest owed, and $1,400 of wages owed.

   Babbitt provides sufficient services to earn and recognize $2,000 of the service revenue collected in advance, thus reducing its obligation (Unearned Service Revenue) to provide those services in the future. Also, Babbitt recognizes the expense associated with using the inventory supplier's money (Interest Expense) and the associated obligation to pay that amount in the future (Interest Payable). Similarly, the cost of the labor used is recognized (Wage Expense), as is the obligation to make payment in the future (Wages Payable).

Journal Entries

1.	Inventory	3,000	
	Accounts Payable		3,000
2.	Utility Expense	1,250	
	Accounts Payable		1,250
3.	Accounts Payable	4,250	
	Cash		4,250
4.	Inventory	25,000	
	Notes Payable		25,000
5.	Cash	6,000	
	Unearned Service Revenue		6,000

Year-end Adjusting Entries

6.	Unearned Service Revenue	2,000	
	Service Revenue		2,000
7.	Interest Expense	800	
	Interest Payable		800
8.	Wage Expense	1,400	
	Wages Payable		1,400

Income Statement Effects

(2)	Expenses	+	1,250
	Net Income	−	1,250
(6)	Revenues	+	2,000
	Net Income	+	2,000
(7)	Expenses	+	800
	Net Income	−	800
(8)	Expenses	+	1,400
	Net Income	−	1,400

Balance Sheet Effects

(1)	Assets	+	3,000
	Liabilities	+	3,000
(2)	Liabilities	+	1,250
	Owners' Equity	−	1,250
(3)	Assets	−	4,250
	Liabilities	−	4,250
(4)	Assets	+	25,000
	Liabilities	+	25,000
(5)	Assets	+	6,000
	Liabilities	+	6,000
(6)	Liabilities	−	2,000
	Owners' Equity	+	2,000
(7)	Liabilities	+	800
	Owners' Equity	−	800
(8)	Liabilities	+	1,400
	Owners' Equity	−	1,400

ESTIMATED LIABILITIES

A liability must be recognized whenever an obligation is incurred, but what happens if the amount is uncertain? If the entity has incurred an obligation, the financial statements must reflect a liability. Therefore, liability amounts that are uncertain must be estimated.

Examples of estimated liabilities include income taxes payable, premium obligations, and warranty obligations. The exact amount of income taxes may not be known at the time financial statements are prepared because complex issues may not yet be resolved. However, reasonable estimates can be made.

Premium obligations arise when companies, such as cereal manufacturers, offer future gifts related to customer purchases. The costs of providing the premiums are viewed as a cost of generating the sales and, therefore, must be matched with those sales. However, because the number of gift redemptions will not be known until the future, the cost of providing premiums must be estimated. Both an expense and liability are recognized in the period in which the sales take place.

A CLOSER LOOK AT

ESTIMATING PREMIUM OBLIGATIONS

The Soggy Cereal Company undertakes a special promotion to boost sales of its premier product, Double Sweetened Coco-Lumps. For each customer mailing in five special box-tops from Coco-Lumps, Soggy will send a stuffed replica of the famous cartoon character, Rolly Rhino. The stuffed animals are made in China, and the importer will mail them directly to each person Soggy specifies for a total cost of $2.00 each. Soggy sells 300,000

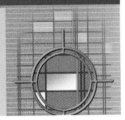

boxes of the cereal with special boxtops during the year, and it expects about 20 percent of the boxtops will be redeemed. Soggy estimates its premium cost as follows:

Estimated animals to be awarded: $(300,000 \times .20)/5 = 12,000$

Expected cost based on current sales: $\$2 \times 12,000 = \$24,000$

For the current year, Soggy reports in its income statement the $24,000 premium expense associated with this period's sales. Thus, the expense of the promotion is matched with the sales generated from the promotion by including the expense in the current income statement even though the cash will not be paid until the following year. A $24,000 liability is reported in the year-end balance sheet for the expected cost of the promotion based on sales to date.

In the next year when Soggy pays a $1,000 bill from the importer for the first batch of 500 stuffed rhinos shipped, no expense is recognized because the expense has already been recognized in the period in which the cereal sales occurred. Instead, the liability is reduced because it is partially satisfied.

Income Statement Effects		
Yr.1 Expenses	+ 24,000	
Net Income	− 24,000	
Yr.2 Expenses	0	
Net Income	0	
Balance Sheet Effects		
Yr.1 Liabilities	+ 24,000	
Owners'		
Equity	− 24,000	
Yr.2 Assets	− 1,000	
Liabilities	− 1,000	

Adjusting Entry, Year 1
Premium Expense 24,000
    Estimated Premium Liability 24,000

Journal Entry, Year 2
Estimated Premium Liability 1,000
    Cash 1,000

In Practice 11-1

MAYTAG'S WARRANTIES

Maytag Corporation, a major appliance manufacturer, reported more than $46 million as a liability for warranties in its 1998 financial statements. The company's summary of significant accounting policies states the following:

Revenue Recognition and Product Warranty Costs: Revenue from sales of products is generally recognized upon shipment to customers. Estimated product warranty costs are recorded at the time of sale and periodically adjusted to reflect actual experience.

ANALYSIS

Although the Maytag repairman in the advertisements may claim to be lonely, he must receive at least some attention, with this amount estimated for future warranty claims. In reality, this estimated liability for warranty claims covers a large number of products sold by Maytag under several different brand names, including Maytag, Jenn-Air, Hoover, and Magic Chef. This estimated liability for warranty claims is just over 1 percent of Maytag's $4 billion of reported sales for the year. [www.maytag.com]

Warranties are offered by many manufacturers of consumer products such as appliances, and these warranties result in warranty costs in the future. For example, if the manufacturer of a washing machine gives a three-year warranty on parts and labor to persuade people to buy the product, the costs associated with this warranty are viewed as being related to the sales of the washing machines. Accordingly, an estimated expense is matched with current revenues, and a liability is reported for the company's obligation to repair or replace in the future products sold currently. (See In Practice 11-1.) Warranty obligations are classified as current or long-term, based on the normal criteria for classifying liabilities.

Accounting for warranty costs is the same as accounting for premiums. However, warranty costs are often more substantial than premium costs and may extend over a longer period of time. Manufacturer's warranties sometimes have the potential for resulting in significant costs beyond the estimated amounts reported. For example, a major product defect could result in substantial unanticipated outlays. Therefore, decision makers need to evaluate a company's warranties and the potential risks associated with them.

LIABILITIES RELATED TO LONG-TERM FINANCING

Information for Decisions

Long-term financing with liabilities usually involves a formal written agreement with creditors, and it typically requires fixed payments of interest and principal. Because of the importance of long-term financing, financial statements include detailed information about long-term debt that is crucial for understanding an entity's financial position and assessing its future viability. The information in financial statements and related notes helps decision makers answer questions such as these: Has this company financed its operations in the best manner to increase return to the owners while still avoiding undue risk? To what extent will my claim on the income and assets of the company be protected in the future? What burden does the long-term debt place on the income and cash flows of the company, and how does this affect the riskiness of investing in this company? Although the entity currently is solvent, will it have sufficient resources to meet future maturities of long-term debt? If the entity does not meet all of its obligations, which assets might be lost to the entity, and how will this affect future operations?

Although short-term financing often plays an important role, organizations also need the stability of long-term financing. Because businesses usually expect to continue operating indefinitely, they need sources of financing that do not need to be renewed frequently. Without long-term financing, organizations would be reluctant to commit to acquiring long-lived assets or undertaking projects such as research and development that were not expected to provide a return in the near future.

As we discussed in Chapter 6, long-term borrowing usually involves entering into a formal written agreement with creditors. The financial instrument providing evidence of this agreement is called a note or a bond. The agreement between lender and borrower contains detailed provisions relating to interest, principal repayment, collateral, reporting to the lender(s), default, restrictions on the borrower, and other matters.

You Decide 11-3

WHY TAKE A CHANCE ON DEBT?

Our Video Store has been profitable and experienced exceptional growth, but has been unable to keep sufficient videos in stock. Your distributor has offered to sell you 400 used videos for $4,500. Although used, the videos should last for a year, and because they are popular ones, you know you could rent them for at least $10,000 during that year. A small problem—all of your money has gone for tuition and payments on a new car. Maybe you should borrow the money from your parents' neighbor, Mr. Worthington McValt, III. He has offered to lend you the money, although the interest rate is now up to 12 percent. Should you borrow the money? What are the pros and cons of taking the loan and buying the videos?

THE USE OF LEVERAGE

Using debt for long-term financing is referred to as **leverage**. Why might a business use debt rather than equity for long-term financing? First, the current owners might not want to share their profits and control with new owners. Second, the appropriate use of debt can increase the profits that accrue to the owners. Also, the cost of using debt is partially subsidized by the government in that interest is tax deductible.

A CLOSER LOOK AT

THE USE OF LEVERAGE

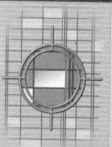

Balaban Enterprises currently has no long-term debt and is financed totally through 10,000 shares of stock outstanding. The company estimates that it can double its sales if it can raise $300,000 for new plant and equipment. The company determines that it can either issue (1) $300,000 of debt bearing 10 percent interest or (2) 5,000 additional shares of stock for $60 per share.

The company projects its net income and earnings per share of stock for different possible sales levels under each of the two alternatives. The projections are as follows (amounts in thousands of dollars, except per-share figures) and assume fixed expenses of $10,000, other expenses equal to 70 percent of sales, and taxes of 40 percent of income before taxes:

Issue Bonds:

	Current	Issue Debt			
Revenue	200	400	500	200	100
Fixed Expenses	(10)	(10)	(10)	(10)	(10)
Other Expenses	(140)	(280)	(350)	(140)	(70)
Interest		(30)	(30)	(30)	(30)
Income before Taxes	50	80	110	20	(10)
Income Taxes	(20)	(32)	(44)	(8)	4
Net Income	30	48	66	12	(6)
Earnings Per Share	3.00	4.80	6.60	1.20	(.60)

Issue Stock:

	Current	Issue Stock			
Revenue	200	400	500	200	100
Fixed Expenses	(10)	(10)	(10)	(10)	(10)
Other Expenses	(140)	(280)	(350)	(140)	(70)
Income before Taxes	50	110	140	50	20
Income Taxes	(20)	(44)	(56)	(20)	(8)
Net Income	30	66	84	30	12
Earnings Per Share	3.00	4.40	5.60	2.00	.80

The first column under both alternatives indicates Balaban's current situation. As revenues increase, the debt alternative is more profitable, based on the earnings accruing to each share of stock, than issuing more stock. At lower revenue levels, however, the interest on the debt must still be paid, and income is reduced accordingly. Thus, debt may increase profitability, but also increases risk.

Using debt may prove risky for a company and its owners. Debt typically involves fixed payments, both interest and principal, that must be made regardless of the company's earnings. Financing through equity does not necessarily require fixed payments to the owners, and stock typically does not have to be paid off at a fixed date. Another disadvantage of debt is that it tends to become more costly the more it is used. Companies with a high amount of debt in relation to equity have less of a margin of safety to protect the creditors. Examine, for example, the following balance sheets:

	Company A	Company B
Assets	$100,000	$100,000
Liabilities	$ 20,000	$ 60,000
Owners' Equity	80,000	40,000
Liabilities and Equity	$100,000	$100,000

Company A's ratio of debt to equity is 2 to 8, or 25 percent. This provides a large margin for the owners to absorb any losses before the company's assets are insufficient to pay creditors. Company B, on the other hand, has a debt-to-equity ratio of 6 to 4, or 150 percent. Although this may be a satisfactory relationship between debt and equity for some companies, the creditors are provided less of a margin of safety by the owners' capital.

LONG-TERM DEBT AND INTEREST RATES

As we discussed previously, long-term liabilities are generally valued at the present value of the future cash payments expected to be made. Two different interest rates play an important role in valuing bonds and other types of long-term debt.

The **nominal interest rate**, or **stated rate,** is the contractual rate of interest to be paid by a debt instrument. This rate is used to compute cash interest payments by applying the nominal rate to the face or par value of the instrument. The **face amount** or **par value** of a debt instrument is the principal amount that must be paid at maturity. Most corporate bonds pay interest every six months. As an example, if a company issues bonds with a face or maturity value of $1,000,000 and a stated interest rate of 8 percent, and if the bonds pay interest every six months, the cash interest payment made twice each year is ($1,000,000 × .08)/2 = $40,000.

However, the real interest rate on a debt instrument, referred to as the **effective rate** or **yield,** may be different from the stated interest rate and reflects the market rate of interest for the instrument on the date the yield is computed. This rate is used to discount the bond's future cash payments to a present value amount that becomes the bond's price. Most corporate bonds are issued at par value, and, therefore, the yield and stated rates are the same. If, however, a bond is issued at a price other than par, the stated rate and yield will differ because the amount borrowed is different from the amount to be repaid. Bonds might be issued at a price other than par because of a change in the market rate of interest just before the bonds were issued. Thus, the stated interest rate for the bonds would differ from what other similar securities were yielding in the capital markets, and the price of the bonds would be adjusted to yield the market rate of interest.

A CLOSER LOOK AT

STATED AND EFFECTIVE INTEREST RATES

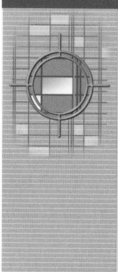

Baylor Corporation borrows $10,000 by issuing a $10,000 note due in one year with 10 percent interest. The stated rate of 10 percent is used to compute the $1,000 of interest accumulated at the end of one year ($10,000 × .10). The effective interest rate can be computed in this case by dividing the interest payment by the amount borrowed:

$$\$1,000 \div \$10,000 = 10 \text{ percent}$$

At the same time, Boiler Company, with a credit rating identical to that of Baylor, issues a one-year, 8 percent, $10,000 note. Given that similar securities are yielding 10 percent in the market, lenders are only willing to pay the present value of the note and its stated interest, discounted at the market rate of interest:

$$(\$10,000 \times 1.08) \div 1.10 = \$9,818$$

At this price, the bond will yield the market rate of interest because the return to the lender includes both the cash interest payment ($800) and the additional amount paid at maturity over the amount borrowed ($10,000 − $9,818):

$$[(\$10,000 \times .08) + (\$10,000 - \$9,818)] \div \$9,818 = 10 \text{ percent}$$

A number of factors determine a bond's effective interest rate, including market rates of interest, the riskiness of the debt, the length of its maturity, and whether the bond is callable or has call protection. A bond is **callable** if the issuer can, at its option, retire the bond at a stated price prior to maturity. A call feature is desirable from an issuer's perspective, but undesirable for bondholders because if market interest rates go down, an issuer may call its bonds and issue bonds with a lower rate to replace them.

Evaluating the Riskiness of Long-Term Debt. The perceived riskiness of debt has a major impact on the effective interest rate that a borrower must pay on its long-term debt. Riskiness is judged, in part, based on the overall creditworthiness of the organization, including its past credit history and its future prospects. Another factor is the amount of debt outstanding in relation to the company's equity or total assets. Also, the amount of cash interest payments required in relation to the company's income or cash flows generated by operations is an important indicator of the risk of failing to make interest payments. Further, debt with longer maturities is generally considered riskier than shorter-term debt and typically carries a higher interest rate.

As we discussed in Chapter 6, the seniority of debt and whether it is secured by collateral are both very important in determining the riskiness of debt. The type of collateral also is important in assessing how secure creditor claims are. Special titles listed in the balance sheet, such as "First Mortgage Bonds," and descriptions in the notes indicate the collateral arrangements.

In Practice 11-2

STRATOSPHERE'S ZOMBIE BONDS

A 1995 report from *The Wall Street Journal* included the following:

> "'Zombie bond' is the term coined by Salomon Brothers to describe some highly speculative bonds, once mistaken for dead, that have run up in recent weeks on fervent hopes that heaven and the Federal Reserve will bring the economy down gently. . . . Stratosphere Gaming, a tall, needle-tower casino project preparing to raise money, is getting wary attention from some investors now. 'First-mortgage bonds in Las Vegas have generally been good bets,' says Van Kampen's Mr. Mathews . . ."[2]

ANALYSIS

Stratosphere Gaming was and is a very speculative company. Its first-mortgage bonds were backed by properties in Las Vegas, but the amount of collateral was insufficient to fully protect the bondholders. Unfortunately, Stratosphere fell on hard times and was reorganized in 1998. All ownership interests were canceled, and 2,030,000 shares of new common stock were issued in exchange for the secured portion (direct claim on specific properties) of the First Mortgage Notes, approximately $120 million. The $104 million unsecured portion of the First Mortgage Notes (general claim on the properties after direct claims on specific properties were met) and all general unsecured claims were settled by a cash payment of a few cents on the dollar.

Collateral obviously provides an advantage to creditors because they can claim the proceeds from selling specific assets before the claims of other creditors are satisfied. However, if the collateral is insufficient to satisfy the claims of the secured creditors, their remaining claims are included with those of unsecured creditors. Numerous purchasers of debt securities have suffered substantial losses in recent years because they did not understand the underlying collateral. In some cases, the unsecured debt of a creditworthy firm may be less risky than the secured debt of a less creditworthy firm.

The riskiness of many bonds is evaluated by bond-rating services such as Moody's Investors Service and Standard and Poor's. These services provide summary ratings, described in Exhibit 11–1, that are widely used by investors. Differences in ratings often mean substantial differences in the yields required for entities to sell their bonds. For example, Moody's Investors Service lowered Nissan Motor Company's debt rating on its senior unsecured debt in 1999 from Baa3 to Ba1. Moody's was concerned that Nissan would have difficulty paying down its debt of 4.3 trillion yen ($36 billion) following DaimlerChrysler's decision to aban-

---

[2]Excerpts from Linda Sandler, "'Zombie Bonds' are Displaying Signs of Life, But They Could Pose Grave Risks for Investors," *The Wall Street Journal* (February 27, 1995), p. C2.

EXHIBIT 11-1	**BOND RATING DESCRIPTIONS**		
	Quality	**Moody's**	**Standard & Poor's**
	Highest Quality	Aaa, Aa, A	AAA, AA, A
	Medium Quality	Baa	BBB
	Speculative	Ba, B	BB, B
	Poor Quality	Caa, Ca, C	CCC, CC, C
	Questionable Value (in default or default imminent)		D

don its plan to acquire an ownership interest in Nissan. This placed the debt in a category referred to by investors and traders as *junk bonds* because such bonds involve significant risk. Lenders typically require a high yield in return for accepting such high risk, meaning Nissan's cost of raising additional capital is expected to be high.

Valuing Long-Term Liabilities. Long-term debt is valued initially at the present value of expected future cash payments. The future cash payments are discounted at the market rate of interest for similar obligations at the date the liability arises. Whether the future cash payments are called *interest* or *principal* is not important for pricing a bond. Only the amount and timing of the payments, and the market rate of interest, are needed to compute the price. Some bonds, called zero-coupon bonds, pay no cash interest. The price of these bonds is simply the present value of the maturity value. For interest-bearing debt, the price is equal to the present value of the maturity value plus the present value of the cash interest payments.

A CLOSER LOOK AT

PRICING INTEREST-BEARING DEBT

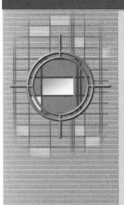

Gorman Corporation issues $500,000 of three-year debentures[3] with a stated interest rate of 10 percent, interest payable annually at year-end. The current market rate for similarly rated securities is 12 percent. The issue price of the bonds is determined from the present values of the maturity value and cash interest payments, as follows:

Interest payments:	3 payments of ($500,000 × .10) = $50,000 each
Maturity payment:	$500,000

Present value at 12 percent:[4]

Interest payments (3) = $50,000 × 2.40183 =	$120,092
Maturity payment = $500,000 × .71178 =	355,890
Bond issue price	$475,982

In this example, the stated interest rate on the bond is less than the market rate of interest. Accordingly, investors are not willing to pay par value for the bond because they can receive a better rate elsewhere. Thus, the price of the bond is reduced until the yield is equal to

[3]Bond maturities are usually five years or longer; a shorter life is used in this example for simplicity.

[4]Present value factors are from the present value tables in Appendix B.

the market rate. The difference between the par value or face amount of the bond and the issue price is referred to as a **bond discount**, equal to $24,018 in this example. The bond discount is a **contra-liability** or bond valuation account and is deducted from the face amount of the bonds when reporting the liability in the balance sheet:

Bonds payable	$500,000
Less discount	(24,018)
	$475,982

Thus, the balance sheet reports the net amount, or **book value**, of the liability, sometimes referred to as the *effective liability*. The maturity value of the bonds is also disclosed in the balance sheet or the accompanying notes so financial statement users know how much the company will ultimately have to pay to settle the obligation.

If the market rate of interest is less than the stated interest rate on bonds when they are issued, the bonds will sell above par. This difference is referred to as a **bond premium**. Like the discount, the bond premium is a bond valuation account, but is reported as an addition to the par value of the bonds in the balance sheet. Because this valuation account is added, it is referred to as an adjunct account.

Bonds that are issued to the public usually trade in the financial markets after issuance. The price of a bond will change in the market as changes occur in all of the factors that led to its initial price. These price changes are not reflected in the financial statements of the issuer, but are of obvious interest to investors. Prices after issue are determined in the same way as at the time of issue in that they reflect the present value of the future cash payments, discounted at the current market rate of interest. These prices are published daily, so you can look in *The Wall Street Journal*, for example, to find the price of a bond that is publicly traded. Exhibit 11–2 shows daily quotations of bond prices as a percentage of par value. Because bond prices are quoted as a percentage of par and most bonds are issued in $1,000 denominations, a $1,000 bond would sell for $990 if priced at 99 and for $1,020 if priced at 102.

Discount and Premium: An Adjustment to Interest.   As we have seen, a bond discount or premium arises because the stated interest rate on a bond is different from the market rate of interest. Therefore, the price of the bond must be adjusted so the bond yields the market rate. Whenever the issue price of a bond is different from the maturity value, the discount or premium reflects a difference in the cost of borrowing. That is, the company borrows one amount and pays back a different amount, with the difference increasing or decreasing the company's borrowing cost. Accordingly, accounting treats the discount or premium as an adjustment of the reported bond interest expense. The discount or premium is spread, or amortized, over the life of the bond as an adjustment to the interest expense recognized each period. Thus, reported interest expense for interest-bearing bonds has two components, the cash payment and the amortization of the discount or premium.

Generally accepted accounting principles require the amortization of bond discount or premium using the *effective-interest method*, which combines the cash interest payment and amortization of the discount or premium in a way that results in reported interest expense being equal to the effective interest rate times the book value of the bonds. This method is illustrated in Appendix 11–1. Another method, the *straight-line method*, may be used when it does not provide significantly different results from the effective-interest method, and that approach is illustrated here because of its simplicity. The straight-line method amortizes an equal amount of bond discount or premium as an adjustment of interest expense in each period the bonds are outstanding. Amortization of bond discount increases interest expense above the amount of the cash interest payment because the company will have to pay back more than it borrowed. Amortization of bond premium reduces interest expense because the company will pay back less than it borrowed.

EXHIBIT 11-2 PRICES FOR BONDS TRADED ON THE NEW YORK EXCHANGE

CORPORATION BONDS
Volume, $12,667,000

Bonds	Cur Yld.	Vol.	Close	Net Chg.
AES Cp 8s8	8.7	30	91½	− ½
AMR 9s16	8.7	10	103½	− 1⅜
ATT 5⅛01	5.2	10	98	...
ATT 7⅛02	7.1	50	99⅞	− ⅛
ATT 6¾04	6.9	55	98	− ¼
ATT 7s05	7.1	5	98⅝	− ⅜
ATT 8.2s05	8.2	57	100½	+ ¼
ATT 7½06	7.5	105	99½	− 1½
ATT 7¾07	7.5	12	102⅝	...
ATT 6s09	6.7	48	89	− ¼
ATT 8⅛22	8.1	131	99⅞	− ⅜
ATT 8⅛24	8.2	62	99⅝	...
ATT 8.35s25	8.0	8	103⅞	...
ATT 8⅝31	8.5	445	101⅞	− ⅝
Aames 10½02	11.7	140	90	+ 13
Alza 5s06	cv	4	112½	+ 2¼
Alza zr14	...	2	52½	...
ARetire 5¾02	cv	25	67⅛	+ ⅛
Amresco 10s03	16.3	95	61⅜	+ ⅞
Amresco 10s04	16.8	15	59½	− ⅛
Apache 9¼02	9.0	10	103	− ⅛
Argosy 13¼04	12.4	15	107	...
AutDt zr12	...	45	135¼	+ 4¼
BellPa 7⅛12	7.6	24	93¾	− ¼
BellsoT 6¼03	6.4	20	97⅛	...
BellsoT 6⅜04	6.6	10	96⅛	− ⅞
BellsoT 7s05	7.1	50	98⅞	− 1⅜
BellsoT 6½05	6.7	10	97	+ ¼
BellsoT 5⅞09	6.6	30	88⅝	+ ⅛
BellsoT 8¼32	8.3	79	99¾	− ⅛
BellsoT 7⅞32	8.1	22	97⅛	+ ⅝
BellsoT 7½33	8.1	113	92¾	+ ¼
BellsoT 6¾33	8.2	180	82⅝	− 1
BellsoT 7⅝35	8.1	5	94⅝	+ ⅛
BethSt 8.45s05	8.9	25	94½	+ ⅜
Bevrly 9s06	9.5	100	94¼	+ ¼
Bluegrn 8¼12	cv	10	77	+ 2
Bordn 8⅜16	10.4	143	80¾	+ ¾
BosCelts 6s38	11.2	35	53¾	+ ⅜
BrnSh 9½06	9.8	65	97	− ½
BurN 8.15s20N	8.5	6	96	− 9
BurNo 3.20s45	7.6	20	41⅞	...
ChaseM 6½09	7.1	3	92	− 1⅜
ChiqBr 10s09	13.0	15	76⅞	+ 1⅞
vjClardg 11¾02f	...	2	58	− 1
Coastl 10¾00	10.4	20	100	− 3⅜

Bonds	Cur Yld.	Vol.	Close	Net Chg.
Hollgnr 9¼07	9.6	90	96¼	− ½
Hollngr 9¼06	9.5	9	97¼	+ ⅛
Honywll zr01	...	35	89⅛	+ ¾
Honywll zr09	...	15	45½	− 1¼
HuntPly 11¾04	11.9	5	98½	+ 1½
IBM 6⅜00	6.4	32	99 9/16	− ¼
IBM 7¼02	7.2	24	100⅜	+ ¼
IBM 7½13	7.6	160	99	+ ¼
IBM 8⅜19	7.9	21	106½	+ ¼
IBM 6½28	7.5	55	86¾	+ 1
KCS En 8⅞08f	...	69	35¼	+ 3⅛
KaufB 9⅜03	9.5	16	99	...
KaufB 7¾04	8.1	35	95¼	+ ¾
KaufB 9⅝06	9.4	6	102⅞	+ 1⅝
KentE 4½04	cv	25	81½	− 1
KerrM 7½14	cv	9	95	− ½
LibPrp 8s01	cv	40	120½	+ 1¼
Loews 3⅛07	cv	12	82⅛	+ ⅛
LglsLt 8.2s23	8.4	1	98	...
LouN 2⅞03	3.3	86	87	− 3
Lucent 6.9s01	6.9	115	100½	+ ½
MBNA 8.28s26	9.4	10	88¼	+ ¼
MSC Sf 7⅞04	cv	75	87	− 1⅞
Mascotch 03	cv	100	75	− ½
McDnl 8 11	8.1	20	110	− 1
Medtrst 7½01	cv	80	90	+ 3⅛
MPac 4¼05	5.2	3	82	− 1⅛
Moran 8¾08f	cv	51	94	− 1
Motrla zr09	...	20	257	− 6
NatData 5s03	cv	25	90⅞	− ⅛
NtEdu 6½11	cv	20	87	+ 2½
NRurU 5¾08	6.9	5	84	− 4
NETelTel 6⅛06	6.7	30	91¼	− 1¼
NETelTel 6⅜08	7.0	1	91⅜	+ ⅜
NETelTel 6⅞23	8.0	20	86½	...
NETelTel 7⅞29	7.9	50	100	− 1½
NYTel 4⅞06	5.7	10	86	− ⅞
NYTel 6s07	6.6	5	91	− 1⅜
NYTel 7⅝23	8.0	1	95⅜	...
NYTel 6.70s23	7.9	50	85	...
NYTel 7s33	8.0	50	88	− ⅞
Noram 6s12	cv	15	83½	− 2½
OcciP 10⅛01	9.7	50	104⅜	+ 1⅝
OffDep zr07	...	10	63	+ 3
OffDep zr08	...	920	68¼	+ 1
OreStl 11s03	10.8	29	102¼	− ⅝
ParkElc 5½06	cv	99	83⅛	− 1⅛
ParkerD 5½04	cv	39	71¾	+ 1

Source: *The Wall Street Journal*

A CLOSER LOOK AT

BOND DISCOUNT AND INTEREST EXPENSE

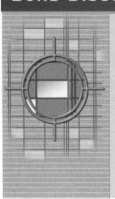

Gorman Corporation issues $500,000 of 3-year debentures with a stated interest rate of 10 percent, interest payable at the end of each year. Because the current market rate for similarly rated securities is 12 percent, the issue price of the bonds is $475,982, computed as the present value of the future interest and principal payments discounted for 3 years at the 12 percent market rate of interest.

Although the $50,000 cash interest paid at the end of each year is equal to the stated rate of 10 percent times the face amount of the bonds ($500,000), the reported interest expense for each year is equal to the cash interest payment plus a proportionate share of the $24,018 discount. The reported interest expense and discount amortization for each year are shown in Exhibit 11–3.

INTEREST EXPENSE AND AMORTIZATION OF BOND DISCOUNT

EXHIBIT 11-3

$500,000 par value bonds with 3-year maturity; 10% stated interest rate, 12% yield:

Year	Beginning Book Value	Interest Expense	Cash Interest	Bond Discount ⅓ Amortized In Period	Bond Discount Remaining Balance	Ending Book Value
					$24,018	$475,982
1	$475,982	$58,006	$50,000	$8,006	16,012	483,988
2	483,988	58,006	50,000	8,006	8,006	491,994
3	491,994	58,006	50,000	8,006	—	500,000

From Exhibit 11–3 you can see that one-third of the bond discount is amortized each year for the three-year life of the bonds. This amortization is then added to the amount of the cash interest payment to determine the total reported interest expense for the period. The cash interest payments on bonds are usually the same each period, and the reported interest expense will also be the same each year when straight-line amortization is used.

As the discount is amortized each year, it becomes smaller, leading to an increase in the book value of the bonds. In the example, the amount of the bonds reported in Gorman's balance sheet at the end of the second year is calculated as follows:

Bonds payable	$500,000
Less discount	(8,006)
Book value	$491,994

By the time the bonds mature, the discount is completely amortized, and the book value of the bonds is equal to their maturity value of $500,000.

When bonds are issued at a premium, the premium must be amortized each period in the same manner as the discount. The amortization of bond premium, however, has the opposite effect on reported interest expense compared with bond discount. The amortization of premium results in reported interest expense being less than the cash interest payment. Interest cost is reduced because the amount paid back to bondholders at bond maturity is less than the proceeds received at issue.

A CLOSER LOOK AT

INTEREST EXPENSE AND BOND PREMIUM

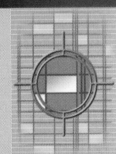

Gorman Corporation issues $500,000 of three-year debentures with a stated interest rate of 10 percent, interest payable at the end of each year. Because the current market rate for similarly rated securities is 8 percent, the issue price of the bonds is $525,770, computed as the present value at 8 percent of the future bond payments, as follows:

Interest payments (3) = $50,000 × 2.57710 =	$128,855	
Maturity payment = $500,000 × .79383 =	396,915	
Bond issue price	$525,770	

The $50,000 cash interest paid at the end of each year is equal to the stated rate of 10 percent times the face amount of the bonds ($500,000). The reported interest expense for each year is equal to the cash interest less the portion of the $25,770 premium amortized each year. The reported interest expense and premium amortization for each period are shown in Exhibit 11–4.

EXHIBIT 11-4 **INTEREST EXPENSE AND AMORTIZATION OF BOND PREMIUM**

$500,000 par value bonds with 3-year maturity; 10% stated interest rate, 8% yield:

Year	Beginning Book Value	Interest Expense	Cash Interest	Bond Discount ⅓ Amortized In Period	Remaining Balance	Ending Book Value
					$25,770	$525,770
1	$525,770	$41,410	$50,000	$8,590	17,180	517,180
2	517,180	41,410	50,000	8,590	8,590	508,590
3	508,590	41,410	50,000	8,590	—	500,000

FREQUENCY OF INTEREST PAYMENTS

For simplicity, the illustrations of the computation of bond interest assumed that the Gorman Corporation bonds paid interest once each year. However, some interest-bearing bonds may pay interest more frequently. Some bonds pay interest quarterly, and others pay monthly. Most corporate bonds pay interest twice each year. Because interest rates are quoted on an annual basis, computations for bonds paying interest more frequently must be adjusted. If, for example, Gorman issued three-year debentures with a stated interest rate of 10 percent, interest payable every six months, and the bonds were issued to yield 12 percent compounded twice annually, the bonds would make cash interest payments of $25,000 ($500,000 × .10/2) twice each year. The issue price of the bonds would be computed as the present value of the future bond payments, discounted at 6 percent per six-month interest-payment period for six interest-payment periods (3 years):

Interest payments (6) = $25,000 × 4.91732 = $122,933
Maturity payment = $500,000 × .70496 = 352,480
Bond issue price $475,413

Interest expense for each six-month interest-payment period would be computed by amortizing the bond discount over six, six-month periods. Gorman's interest expense for each six-month interest-payment period using straight-line amortization would be $29,098 [$25,000 + ($24,587 ÷ 6)].

RETIREMENT OF DEBT

When debt matures, the carrying amount or book value of the debt is typically equal to its maturity value, and no gain or loss is recognized on retirement. Cash and bonds are both reduced by the same amount.

However, if bonds are called or purchased and retired prior to maturity, the book value might differ from the amount paid to acquire the bonds. This difference is recognized as a gain or loss on retirement of the bonds. These gains and losses, if material, are classified as extraordinary items and are reported in a separate section of the income statement. Extraordinary items, discussed in detail in Chapter 14, are unusual in nature and recur infrequently. They are reported separately so financial statement users do not give undue weight to items not expected to be a significant part of an enterprise's future.

ACCOUNTING FOR LONG-TERM DEBT

We can see the accounting treatment of long-term debt by revisiting the Gorman Corporation example presented previously. While the example illustrates the treatment of bonds, notes and other types of long-term debt are accounted for in largely the same manner.

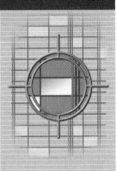

A CLOSER LOOK AT

ACCOUNTING FOR LONG-TERM DEBT

Gorman Corporation issues $500,000 of 3-year debentures with a stated interest rate of 10 percent, interest payable at the end of each year. The bonds are issued to yield 12 percent, and, accordingly, the issue price is $475,982. The interest and amortization of bond discount were shown in Exhibit 11–3. In accordance with the provisions of the bond indenture, Gorman calls the entire issue of bonds at the end of the second year and retires them for $490,000.

The effects of the various bond transactions on Gorman's financial statements are as follows:

(a) Bond Issuance

Cash is increased by the $475,982 issue price and liabilities are increased by an equal amount. The book value of the bonds, or the *effective liability*, on the date of issue is equal to the $500,000 maturity (par or face) value of the bonds less the $24,018 discount. The bonds are recorded by Gorman at par value, with the discount recorded in a separate contra-liability account.

(b) First Interest Payment

Gorman pays $50,000 of cash interest, thus decreasing cash. Interest expense, however, is $58,006 (see Exhibit 11–3). The difference between the cash interest paid and the interest expense reported in the income statement results from the $8,006 amortization of the bond discount. Because the bond discount is a contra-liability account, the decrease in the bond discount increases the book value of the bonds, and liabilities in total, by $8,006.

(c) Second Interest Payment

Gorman pays $50,000 of cash interest, thus decreasing cash. As in the first year, interest expense is $58,006, and the book value of the bonds increases by the $8,006 amortization of the bond discount.

(d) Bond Call and Retirement

When Gorman retires the bonds immediately after the second interest payment, the book value of the bonds is as follows:

Bonds payable	$500,000
Less discount	(8,006)
Book value	$491,994

The gain on bond retirement is $1,994, computed as the excess of the $491,994 book value over the $490,000 cost to Gorman to retire the bonds. Cash is reduced by the $490,000 cost to retire the bonds, and both the bond account and the related discount are eliminated, resulting in a $491,994 reduction in liabilities. Thus, assets decrease $490,000, liabilities decrease $491,994, and equity increases $1,994.

Income Statement Effects		
(b) Expenses	+	58,006
Net Income	−	58,006
(c) Expenses	+	58,006
Net Income	−	58,006
(d) Gain	+	1,994
Net Income	+	1,994

Balance Sheet Effects		
(a) Assets	+	475,982
Liabilities	+	475,982
(b) Assets	−	50,000
Liabilities	+	8,006
Owners'		
Equity	−	58,006
(c) Assets	−	50,000
Liabilities	+	8,006
Owners'		
Equity	−	58,006
(d) Assets	−	490,000
Liabilities	−	491,994
Owners'		
Equity	+	1,994

Journal Entries

(a) Bond Issuance

Cash	475,982	
Discount on Bonds Payable	24,018	
Bonds Payable		500,000

(b) First Interest Payment

Interest Expense	58,006	
Discount on Bonds Payable		8,006
Cash		50,000

(c) Second Interest Payment

Interest Expense	58,006	
Discount on Bonds Payable		8,006
Cash		50,000

(d) Bond Call and Retirement

Bonds Payable	500,000	
Discount on Bonds Payable		8,006
Cash		490,000
Gain on Bond Retirement		1,994

CURRENT MATURITIES OF LONG-TERM DEBT

Some bonds mature all at one time and are referred to as **term bonds**. Other bonds mature in installments and are called **serial bonds**. Regardless of how bond maturities are structured, sufficient resources must be available to meet maturing debt. So financial statement users can better assess an entity's ability to satisfy maturing obligations, long-term debt that will come due within the current year or operating cycle, whichever is longer, must be classified as a current liability. Thus, if some or all of a company's long-term debt will mature soon, it is moved, along with any associated discount or premium, from the noncurrent to the current category in the balance sheet.

An exception is permitted if the debt will not be satisfied with current assets. This might occur, for example, if the debt were to be retired using assets previously set aside in a bond sinking fund, reported in the (noncurrent) investments category. Another exception is for maturing debt that will be refinanced on a long-term basis under an existing noncancelable agreement.

CONVERTIBLE BONDS

Some bonds, called **convertible bonds**, can be exchanged for common stock at the option of the bondholder. The bond indenture specifies the rate at which the bonds may be exchanged for common stock and the time period for exchanges. Such bonds may be desirable for bondholders because the holder has the security of a fixed interest payment and maturity value if held to maturity, but can also share in the growth of the company by exchanging the bond for stock prior to maturity if the company's stock does well. From the company's viewpoint, it can offer bonds with a lower effective interest rate because convertibility acts as a "sweetener," and it will never have to pay off the bonds if they are converted. Most convertible bonds are callable and tend to be lower rated bonds that otherwise would carry high interest rates.

Convertible bonds present special problems because of the uncertainty of whether they will remain as debt or become common stock. This is particularly important to current and potential common stockholders because holders of convertible bonds will begin to share in the company's income in a different way if the bonds are converted. They no longer will receive fixed interest payments, but instead will share proportionately in all residual earnings. This may result in less income accruing to each share of common stock, an effect called **dilution of earnings per share**.

In general, convertible bonds are accounted for in the same way as if they were not convertible. However, the terms of each convertible bond issue must be disclosed. If convertible bonds are converted, the bond accounts are removed and the book value transferred to the common stock and additional paid-in capital accounts.

A CLOSER LOOK AT

THE CONVERSION OF BONDS

Bilbo Company has $1,000,000 of 12 percent convertible debentures outstanding. The bonds have been outstanding for several years, and the remaining amount of unamortized premium on the bonds is $40,000. During the year, the bonds are called, and all of them are converted into 100,000 shares of Bilbo's $5-par common stock. The total $1,040,000 book value of the bonds becomes the book value of the common shares issued. Because the shares have a par value of $5 each, the common stock account increases by $500,000 ($5 × 100,000), and the remainder ($540,000) is added to additional paid-in capital.

Once conversion takes place, interest is no longer paid on the bonds, increasing the company's income. However, that income will now have to be spread over 100,000 more shares.

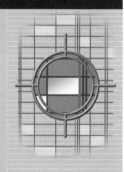

Journal Entry

Bonds Payable	1,000,000	
Premium on Bonds Payable	40,000	
Common Stock		500,000
Additional Paid-in Capital		540,000

Income Statement Effects	
Net Income	0
Balance Sheet Effects	
Liabilities	− 1,040,000
Owners'	
Equity	+ 1,040,000

In Practice 11-3

LONG-TERM DEBT DISCLOSURES OF MAY DEPARTMENT STORES

The May Department Stores Company included the following disclosure relating to long-term debt in the notes to its financial statements:

> The annual maturities of long-term debt, including sinking fund requirements, are $98 million, $260 million, $86 million, $270 million, and $134 million for 1999 through 2003.
>
> The fair value of long-term debt (excluding capital lease obligations) was approximately $4.5 billion and $4.2 billion at January 30, 1999, and January 31, 1998, respectively. The fair value was determined using borrowing rates for debt instruments with similar terms and maturities.

ANALYSIS

Financial statement users can compare the resources needed to retire long-term debt over the next five years with the resources May has available and the cash it generates. Also, readers can see the effect changing interest rates have had on May's outstanding debt by comparing the fair values with the amounts reported in the balance sheet. [www.maycompany.com]

ADDITIONAL DISCLOSURES

Because of the importance to decision makers of any information that will help them assess future cash flows, companies must provide additional disclosures regarding long-term debt and other obligations. All debt maturities and required sinking fund payments for each of the next five years must be disclosed. In addition, disclosures must include required payments for redemption of stock and for required purchases of goods and services (unconditional purchase obligations) for each of the next five years. Also, information about the fair value at the balance sheet date of a company's financial instruments, both assets and liabilities, must be disclosed. (See In Practice 11-3.)

SPECIAL LIABILITIES AND OBLIGATIONS

Information for Decisions

Companies often report obligations for future payments that are incurred by other than borrowing or from purchasing on credit. These obligations can be quite large and may require a significant use of resources in the future. Understanding these liabilities and how they are reported helps decision makers understand an entity's commitments for future expenditures of resources and answer questions such as these: To what extent will the company need resources to meet potential obligations disclosed in the notes to the financial statements but not reported as liabilities in the balance sheet? Will the company have sufficient resources to meet its pension commitments to retiring employees in the future? To what extent will changes in future health care costs affect the cost of the company's obligation to provide health insurance to its retirees?

Many entities incur one or more special types of liabilities that do not arise from direct borrowing, but nevertheless may involve significant obligations. These include contingent liabilities, pensions and other postretirement benefits, and deferred income taxes.

CONTINGENT LIABILITIES

A **contingent liability** is one about which there is uncertainty as to whether an obligation actually exists. However, do not confuse a contingent liability with an estimated liability, which clearly exists but is uncertain in amount. Examples of contingent liabilities might include:

- A customer falls while on the company's premises, is severely injured, and indicates the possibility of legal action.
- One of the company's suppliers borrows money to acquire machinery needed to produce parts for the company, and the company guarantees to pay off the loan if the supplier defaults.

In neither case does a certain obligation to sacrifice resources in the future exist. The issue is when should a possible, but not definite, liability be recognized or disclosed.

Three different levels of likelihood with the appropriate degree of disclosure are as follows:

1. *Probable:* If an event has occurred and it is probable that the event has given rise to a liability that can be reasonably estimated, the liability and associated loss should be recognized in the financial statements.

2. *Reasonably possible:* If an event has occurred that may have given rise to a liability, but the likelihood is less than probable, the possible liability and loss should be disclosed in the notes to the financial statements.

3. *Remote:* If an event has occurred that may, but is unlikely to, give rise to a liability, it need not be disclosed unless disclosure is customary for that type of item.

As you can see, accountants must exercise judgment in determining the appropriate treatment for a contingent liability. When evaluating an entity's potential exposure to liability, you should always examine the notes to the financial statements carefully for descriptions of contingent liabilities. Loan guarantees are routinely disclosed because of past custom, even when the chances of loss are remote. Even though a remote possibility, loan guarantees can prove a significant drain on an entity's resources if the unexpected occurs.

In Practice 11-4

MAY'S LOAN GUARANTEE

The following was included in the notes to the financial statements of The May Department Stores Company:

In connection with a 1986 real estate transaction, the company sold $165 million of notes received from the sale of real estate and became contingently liable for up to $42 million of the purchaser's debt in the event of default. The fair value of this guarantee is not significant.

ANALYSIS

Even if the chance of default is remote, loan guarantees have customarily been disclosed. While the amount of the loan is substantial, the fair value of the guarantee is considered insignificant because of the low probability of default. [www.maycompany.com]

OTHER LIABILITIES

For many companies, liabilities other than those resulting from direct borrowing may significantly affect a company's financial statements and potentially affect future cash flows. Of greatest importance for many companies are (1) the costs of providing pension and other benefits for retired employees and (2) income taxes that may involve payments that are different than the tax expense reported in the income statement. Notes to the financial statements of most companies contain additional disclosures about these obligations so users can better assess the effects on the company's income and cash flows.

Pensions and Other Postretirement Benefits.   Many companies agree to provide pensions and health care benefits to their retirees. Often the costs of providing these benefits are substantial, and, thus, a significant obligation is incurred by the employer. In theory, the accounting treatment of these items is straightforward. The cost of benefits to be provided to current employees after they retire should be matched with the benefits the company gains from the employees' current service. In other words, the costs of future pension and other postretirement benefits should be treated as additional compensation expense during the time the employees work for the company.

A company's pension expense can be determined easily if its only obligation is to make specified contributions to a pension fund—its expense is equal to the required contribution. This *defined-contribution* type of plan is typical of those included in many union contracts.

With a second type of pension plan, the company agrees to provide specified pension benefits to retirees. Under this *defined-benefit* type of plan, the benefits to be provided to retirees are based on a formula that typically includes such factors as salary and length of service. The company must incur whatever costs are required to provide those benefits. Because those costs will not be known until the current employees retire, the current additional compensation expense is more difficult to determine than when the contribution is defined. For the company to compute its current pension expense, it must estimate the pension benefits that it will provide to future retirees based on their current period's service and considering such factors as expected average retirement age and life expectancy. Because the pension benefits are generally not provided until many years in the future, the company recognizes as a current expense the present value of the employees' expected future pension benefits arising from their current employment. Any difference between the current pension expense and the amount of cash and investments that the company sets aside in a pension fund must be reported on the balance sheet as a pension liability.

In general, accounting for other postretirement benefits follows the same approach as for pensions. Health care benefits are the primary postretirement benefit other than pensions and present special problems because of the difficulty of estimating future health care costs. Because many companies have agreed to provide generous health care benefits to retirees, the liabilities recognized in their balance sheets are often large. Investors and creditors should be aware that these obligations may require substantial cash outflows in the future.

In Practice 11-5

OTHER POSTRETIREMENT BENEFITS DISCLOSURES FOR SBC

SBC Communications, Inc., provides medical, dental, and life insurance benefits to substantially all of its retired employees. In the notes to its financial statements, SBC discloses that its postretirement benefit cost (excluding pensions) for 1998 was $380 million. It also discloses that in making its cost estimates it has assumed the "medical cost trend rate in 1999 is 7.0%, decreasing linearly to 5.5% in 2002 . . . [and the] dental cost trend rate in 1999 is 5.75%, reducing to 5.0% in 2002." SBC also discloses the other assumptions used in its estimates.

ANALYSIS

Numerous assumptions are made in computing SBC's postretirement benefit cost. To help financial statement users understand the impact of these assumptions, SBC states that raising the annual medical and dental cost trend rates by one percentage point increases its related obligation as of December 31, 1998, by $488 million, and it indicates the estimated effects of a decrease as well. [www.sbc.com]

Deferred Income Taxes.   Companies often adopt one accounting method for financial reporting to provide a fair presentation and a different method for tax reporting to reduce or defer tax payments. The tax law permits tax reporting to differ from generally accepted accounting principles in a number of areas. For example, interest income from municipal bonds is income from a financial-reporting perspective but is usually exempt from federal income taxes.

Some differences between financial reporting and tax reporting occur because a particular item is included in the income statement and tax return in different periods. These temporary differences include the use of accelerated depreciation for tax purposes and straight-line depreciation for financial reporting, and recognizing income based on cash collection for tax purposes and when earned for financial reporting.

When temporary differences exist, current accounting standards require that income tax expense be computed as the amount of taxes that must be paid currently plus the future amounts that may have to be paid when the temporary differences reverse. The portion of the current expense to be paid later is reported as a liability in the balance sheet, **deferred income taxes**. For example, if Griffin Company had a 40 percent tax rate, its income statement reported income before taxes of $100,000 using straight-line depreciation, and its tax return reported taxable income of $80,000 based on the use of accelerated depreciation, Griffin would pay income taxes of $32,000 ($80,000 × .40). However, the company's income tax expense reported in its income statement would be $40,000 [32,000 + ($20,000 × .4)], and the $8,000 difference would be reported as a deferred tax liability in the balance sheet.

Sometimes the opposite occurs and a company's taxable income is greater than its income reported in its income statement because of a temporary difference. This situation usually occurs not because of the company's choice but because the tax law and current accounting standards require different treatments. This situation may give rise to a deferred tax asset, indicating that the company expects future tax benefits when reversal occurs.

Deferred taxes do not have the same characteristics as other assets and liabilities because they result from accounting practices rather than actual transactions. For example, they do not arise from direct borrowings, and they do not represent legal claims or obligations. Further, deferred tax assets and liabilities seldom shrink because new temporary differences continually arise. Because actual cash flows for payment of deferred tax liabilities and from collection of deferred tax assets are uncertain, or even unlikely, many financial analysts ignore deferred taxes on the balance sheet. For instance, analysts seldom include the deferred tax liability when computing a company's ratio of debt to equity. On the other hand, a large deferred tax liability may indicate a company's use of tax planning techniques to reduce current cash outflows; this is a sign of good management and directly affects the value of the company.

Because of the significance and complexity of income taxes, companies are required to provide extensive information about their income tax expense and payments in the financial statements and notes. Decision makers need to analyze the information reported about income taxes in the financial statements and related disclosures to assess the implications for future income and cash flows.

OFF-BALANCE-SHEET OBLIGATIONS AND COMMITMENTS

In the past, organizations have often incurred obligations or made commitments that have not been reported as liabilities in their balance sheets. Over the years, accounting standards have gradually changed to require most of these to be reported or disclosed. Nevertheless, managers continually find new ways to finance activities, and the accounting for new types of financing arrangements and other commitments may not always be clear. Accordingly, examining the notes to the financial statements, and other sources of information, for clues about financial arrangements and commitments is important. These might include loan guarantees, sales of assets with payment or performance requirements, financial instruments that may include commitments not reflected in their recorded amounts, asset purchase contracts, and other types of agreements requiring performance by the company.

ANALYZING LIABILITIES

Information for Decisions

A company must be able to pay its liabilities to survive. Investors and creditors can use their knowledge of how liabilities are reported in financial statements to evaluate a company's liquidity and solvency and answer questions such as these: Will the company have enough re- sources to pay the current liabilities as they come due? Over the long run, will this company generate sufficient income and cash flows to make its interest and debt payments in a timely manner? How much margin of safety is provided to creditors?

As discussed throughout the chapter, knowing the amounts and timing of an entity's obligations and commitments is crucial for knowing whether the entity will survive or fail. A number of summary measures are used in evaluating a company's debt position. As with all summary measures, however, they do not tell the whole story. They are useful for quick impressions, but are not a substitute for in-depth analysis.

Comparisons of current assets and current liabilities are important because current liabilities will require resource expenditures in the near future, and these generally will come from current assets. As we discussed in earlier chapters, the amount of working capital (current assets minus current liabilities) on hand, the current ratio (current assets

In Practice 11-6

THE FINANCING OF CANANDAIGUA BRANDS, INC.

Canandaigua Brands, Inc., is the United States' second largest maker of wine, with such well known labels as Almaden, Inglenook, and Paul Mason. In 1995, analysts were con- cerned because the company's long-term debt of $247 million was 44 percent of total capital, among the highest in the industry.[5] Although the company's cash flow was high enough to allow it to service its debt, there was concern that the industry might not re- main stable and Canandaigua might have difficulty meeting its fixed debt payments.

ANALYSIS

For the wine industry, a 44 percent ratio of long-term debt to total capital is high and could make it difficult for the company to meet fixed interest and principal payments in a downturn. In more stable industries, such as utilities, this ratio of debt to total capital may not be unusual. Fortunately for Canandaigua, the wine business has remained strong. The company has been able to meet all of its fixed payments, and it has expanded. By 1998, Canandaigua's long-term debt, excluding current maturities, was $309 million, but it was only 34 percent of total capital. [www.canandaiguabrands.com]

[5]Willy Stern, "Bottom Fishing in an Empty Pond," *Financial World* (March 14, 1995), pp. 40–41.

divided by current liabilities), and the quick ratio (cash, marketable securities, and current receivables divided by current liabilities) all provide summary measures of a company's liquidity.

A measure of solvency is provided by the **debt-to-equity ratio.** This ratio is widely used and is usually computed as total long-term debt (not including deferred taxes) divided by stockholders' equity. Other variations also are used, such as the ratio of long-term debt to total capital (long-term debt and stockholders' equity) or the ratio of long-term debt to total assets. Which ratio is used is not important, as long as the comparisons to other companies, other years, or industry averages are consistent. All of these ratios indicate the portion of the company's financing that comes from long-term creditors. (See In Practice 11-6.)

Other measures indicating a company's ability to service its debt by making required interest and principal payments are important. For example, the **number of times interest is earned,** usually computed as operating income (before deducting interest expense) divided by interest on long-term debt, indicates the extent to which recurring operations cover the required interest payments and provide a margin of safety. A similar ratio compares operating cash flow to debt payments and indicates the margin of safety with which the cash generated from operations meets interest and principal payments on long-term debt.

In Practice 11-7

BUMBLE BEE TUNA: SWIMMING AGAINST A TIDE OF DEBT

In 1989, Unicord PCL, Thailand's largest tuna processor, acquired Bumble Bee Seafoods, Inc., a major U.S. canned seafood producer. By 1995, "the five-year struggle to pay for the U.S. tuna concern ha[d] left Unicord . . . swimming in red ink."[6] Because of Bumble Bee's losses and interest payments stemming from the acquisition, Unicord was unable to meet its debt payments, and the debt had to be restructured in 1991. In July 1997, Bumble Bee was acquired by International Home Foods, Inc., for approximately $163 million in cash.

ANALYSIS

Many acquisitions of other companies are financed with debt. Often the price paid, and the debt incurred, is too high for the income and cash flows of the company acquired. Unicord was never able to make the acquisition of Bumble Bee successful because of the large amount of debt issued to acquire Bumble Bee. In the discussion of Bumble Bee's purchase from Unicord in International's 1997 financial statements, the company stated that Bumble Bee Seafoods had been highly leveraged and had capital constraints that limited its ability to acquire raw materials and most effectively market its products. To facilitate the purchase of the Bumble Bee business by International free and clear of existing liens, Bumble Bee Seafoods filed for bankruptcy prior to the acquisition. Interestingly, International borrowed approximately $110 million of the purchase price to acquire Bumble Bee. [www.bumblebee.com]

---

[6]Paul M. Sherer, "Thai Tuna Processor Finds Bumble Bee a Costly Catch," *The Wall Street Journal* (March 28, 1995), p. B4.

SUMMARY

Debt is an important part of the way our economy expands, the way we improve our standard of living, and the way that businesses finance their operations. It is, therefore, important to have an understanding of liabilities and a knowledge of financial reporting practices related to debt to evaluate whether debt has been used wisely. Liabilities are a source of assets for an organization, and they may be generated by day-to-day operations, such as with trade accounts payable, or through long-term financing, as with bonds. Liabilities are reported on the balance sheet as either current or long-term so that both the timing and the amount of the repayment can be identified.

Liabilities are normally valued at the date of the transaction that created the liability. The value is based on the present value of future cash payments, although the actual amount to be paid is used as the value for most current liabilities. An estimate of future payments is used to value some contingencies, such as warranty obligations. The price at which long-term debt is issued is determined by the present value of both the stream of interest payments and the principal repayment at maturity. When long-term debt is issued at an amount different than its face value, giving rise to a discount or premium, the liability is reported at its maturity value, adjusted for the unamortized discount or premium.

The reported interest expense is adjusted to include amortization of the discount or premium. Long-term debt maturing within one year is classified as a current liability.

Some special liabilities are based on estimates and are valued at the present value of those estimates. These include pension obligations and obligations for other postretirement benefits. The reporting of contingent liabilities is based on estimates relating both to probability of occurrence and amount. Deferred income taxes arise because of differences as to when amounts are reported for financial reporting and tax purposes.

An appropriate use of debt can increase the return to owners. On the other hand, debt usually has fixed interest and maturity payment requirements that make it a more risky means of financing than owners' equity. An understanding of debt and its requirements can be used to assess the degree of leverage and risk.

A number of comparisons, such as the amount of debt to equity, are useful in assessing a company's debt load. Similarly, the extent to which a company has sufficient income and cash flows to cover its interest payments with a margin of safety indicates the degree to which the company is subject to risk from unexpected downturns in business.

LIST OF IMPORTANT TERMS

bond discount *(421)*

bond premium *(421)*

book value *(421)*

callable *(418)*

contingent liability *(428)*

contra-liability *(421)*

convertible bonds *(426)*

debt-to-equity ratio *(433)*

deferred income taxes *(431)*

dilution of earnings per share *(426)*

effective rate *(417)*

face amount *(417)*

leverage *(416)*

nominal interest rate *(417)*

number of times interest is earned *(433)*

par value *(417)*

serial bonds *(426)*

stated rate *(417)*

term bonds *(426)*

yield *(417)*

APPENDIX 11-1

INTEREST EXPENSE AND THE EFFECTIVE-INTEREST METHOD

As we saw in the chapter, reported interest expense is computed by combining the periodic cash interest payment and the amortization of any discount or premium. For simplicity, the *straight-line method* of amortization was illustrated in the chapter. However, generally accepted accounting principles require the use of the *effective-interest method* of amortization if it produces results significantly different from straight-line amortization. The effective-interest method is required because it provides a better measure of the actual borrowing cost to the company than does the straight-line method. For example, if a company issues bonds to yield 12 percent, the company's cost of borrowing is 12 percent, and the effective-interest method results in reported interest expense each period equal to 12 percent of the effective bond liability. With the straight-line method illustrated in the chapter, the dollar amount of reported interest is the same each period, but the interest percentage (interest expense divided by the effective bond liability) changes and is not equal to the bond's original effective interest rate.

Using the effective-interest method, bond interest expense for the period is computed by multiplying the bond's effective interest rate (yield), determined at the date of issue, times the effective liability or the bond's book value (par value minus any discount or plus any premium) at the beginning of the period. The difference between the computed interest expense and the cash interest payment is the amortization of the discount or premium. As the discount or premium is amortized, it decreases, thus changing the book value of the bonds. Because each period's interest expense is based on the book value of the bonds at the beginning of the period, the dollar amount of the expense is different each period, but the percentage rate remains the same.

A CLOSER LOOK AT

EFFECTIVE-INTEREST AMORTIZATION

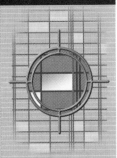

Gorman Corporation issues $500,000 of 3-year debentures at two different times. Both bond issues have a stated interest rate of 10 percent, with interest payable at the end of each year. The bonds are issued as follows:

1. Issued for $475,982 when the market rate for similarly rated securities is 12 percent.

2. Issued for $525,770 when the market rate for similarly rated securities is 8 percent.

Although the $50,000 cash interest paid at the end of each year is equal to the stated rate of 10 percent times the face amount of the bonds, the reported interest expense for each year is equal to the effective rate times the book value of the bonds at the beginning of the year. For the first bond issue, the interest expense is equal to the 12 percent effective rate times the book value of the bonds; the reported expense and resulting discount amortization are shown in Exhibit 11–5. For the second bond issue, the interest expense is equal to the 8 percent effective rate times the book value of the bonds; the reported expense and resulting premium amortization are shown in Exhibit 11–6. Note that, for the first bond issue, the interest expense increases each period as the effective liability increases. For the second bond issue, the interest expense decreases each period as the effective liability decreases.

EXHIBIT 11-5   EFFECTIVE-INTEREST AMORTIZATION OF BOND DISCOUNT

$500,000 par value bonds with 3-year maturity; 10% stated interest rate, 12% yield:

Year	Beginning Book Value	Interest Expense (Book Value × .12)	Cash Interest	Bond Discount Amortized In Period	Bond Discount Remaining Balance	Ending Book Value
					$24,018	$475,982
1	$475,982	$57,118	$50,000	$7,118	16,900	483,100
2	483,100	57,972	50,000	7,972	8,928	491,072
3	491,072	58,928*	50,000	8,928	—	500,000

*Adjusted for the effects of rounding

EXHIBIT 11-6 EFFECTIVE-INTEREST AMORTIZATION OF BOND PREMIUM

$500,000 par value bonds with 3-year maturity; 10% stated interest rate, 8% yield:

Year	Beginning Book Value	Interest Expense (Book Value × .08)	Cash Interest	Bond Discount Amortized In Period	Bond Discount Remaining Balance	Ending Book Value
					$25,770	$525,770
1	$525,770	$42,062	$50,000	$7,938	17,832	517,832
2	517,832	41,427	50,000	8,573	9,259	509,259
3	509,259	40,741	50,000	9,259	—	500,000

EXAMINING THE CONCEPTS

Q11-1 What is a liability? Are liabilities always certain in amount?

Q11-2 How do the responsibilities of a company differ with regard to debt versus common stock?

Q11-3 Which liabilities are classified as current? Why is this distinction important?

Q11-4 Which liabilities are valued at the present value of future payments rather than the amounts actually owed?

Q11-5 What events typically must occur for a liability to be recognized?

Q11-6 When are the estimated costs of warranties recorded? What procedures generally must be used in estimating the amount of the liability to be recorded for future warranty costs?

Q11-7 What information typically is included in the formal written agreement between the lender and borrower?

Q11-8 What does it mean when a company is said to have a high degree of leverage? What is the advantage to the company of using leverage?

Q11-9 What is the nominal interest rate on a debt obligation? How does it differ from the effective interest rate? Can an obligation have both? Explain.

Q11-10 Under what conditions will a debt instrument be sold at a premium? When is a debt instrument sold at a discount? What is accomplished by adjusting the sale price of the debt instrument?

Q11-11 How is a bond premium or discount reported in the balance sheet? What happens to a reported bond premium or discount over time? Why?

Q11-12 What is meant when a bond is callable? Would the company selling the bond or the purchaser prefer to have a call feature? Explain. When is a bond likely to be called?

Q11-13 How is a gain or loss on the retirement of bonds computed? How is such a gain or loss reported? Will a gain or loss on the retirement of bonds most likely occur at maturity of the bonds or prior to maturity? Explain.

Q11-14 What does it mean when a bond is secured by collateral? How important is this feature in deciding which debt instrument to purchase as an investment?

Q11-15 What is a zero-coupon or noninterest-bearing bond?

Q11-16 What is the difference between a term bond and a serial bond? Which type of bond is most desirable if there is concern about the ability of a company to pay off the bonds? Explain why.

Q11-17 When might a company not report the current maturities of long-term debt as a current liability?

Q11-18 What is a contingent liability? Under what circumstances are a loss and a liability related to a contingency reported in the financial statements? When is footnote disclosure of a contingent liability considered sufficient?

Q11-19 What is meant by a postretirement benefit? When must the costs of these benefits be recognized?

Q11-20 What impact does the recording of postretirement benefits have on the financial statements? What types of companies are most likely to be significantly affected by the recognition of postretirement benefits?

Q11-21 Distinguish between a defined benefit and a defined contribution retirement plan. What factors must be taken into consideration in recognizing pension expense in a defined benefit plan?

Q11-22 When is a difference between income reported for financial reporting and tax purposes a permanent difference? When is such a difference referred to as a temporary difference?

Q11-23 When must deferred income taxes be reported? Give an example of a situation in which deferred income taxes must be recognized.

Q11-24 Explain why deferred income taxes are recorded when accelerated depreciation is used for tax purposes and straight-line depreciation is used for financial reporting purposes. Which accounting concept(s) would be violated if deferred taxes were not recorded?

Q11-25 What is meant by off-balance-sheet financing? Why might the existence of off-balance-sheet financing be of concern to an investor?

Q11-26 What is the debt-to-equity ratio? How is it computed? How does it help financial statement users assess a company's position?

Q11-27 How is the times-interest-earned ratio calculated? What does this ratio indicate? Which financial statement users might be particularly interested in this ratio?

UNDERSTANDING ACCOUNTING INFORMATION

E11-1 Understanding Liabilities Auburn Corporation has experienced rapid growth in its current assets and property, plant, and equipment as a result of increased sales.

a. Is Auburn's growth in inventories likely to be financed by current or long-term liabilities? Explain.
b. Is Auburn's growth in property, plant, and equipment likely to be financed by current or long-term liabilities? Explain.
c. Although Auburn's total liabilities do not seem excessive, nearly all of them are in the form of current liabilities. What cash flows should be used to repay current liabilities? What might cause an investor to conclude that a disproportionate amount of liabilities is in the form of current liabilities?
d. Auburn's controller has suggested that its liabilities should be classified as current or long-term based on whether the money received was used to acquire current or long-term assets. In what way might an investor be misled if this approach is adopted?

E11-2 Valuation of Liabilities An investor is attempting to determine how quickly Fozzel Corporation must pay the following liabilities:

Noninterest-bearing note payable (5-year)
Income taxes payable (current)
Accounts payable
Lease obligations payable (10-year)
Unearned revenue
Wages payable
Deferred income taxes

a. Which of the above will require the use of cash currently on hand?
b. Which of the above will require the use of cash generated in future periods?
c. Which of the above is likely to be satisfied using something other than cash?

d. Which of the above will require total cash payments in excess of the amount recorded as a liability at the time the liability is recorded?

E11-3 Liabilities Arising from Day-To-Day Operations Dazee Corporation has not made year-end adjustments to recognize liabilities associated with the following:

1. The payroll system was changed during the year. All employees are now paid on the 20th of the month for work to that date rather than the last day of the month.
2. Dazee borrowed $500,000 on April 1 and will pay interest and principal on the note next April.
3. Near the end of the year, several large customers prepaid services that will be provided during the following year. The payments were treated as service revenue at the time they were received.
4. The company introduced a new product line during the year and offered customers free repair or replacement for 5 years if the product fails to operate as advertised.

a. What effect would taking each of the above situations into consideration have on Dazee's reported liabilities?
b. What effect would taking each of the above situations into consideration have on Dazee's reported net income for the current year?

E11-4 Liabilities Related to Long-Term Financing Makemore Corporation is quite profitable at present and anticipates substantially increased sales during the next decade. The company wishes to evaluate several alternative ways of acquiring the cash needed to expand its production facilities to meet the increased demand.

a. Why might it be desirable to issue additional long-term debt rather than common stock?
b. If Makemore issues additional long-term debt and the market rate of interest is 8 percent, what effect would issuing bonds with a stated interest rate of 7 percent have on the amount of cash received at the time the bonds are issued? Explain.

c. Makemore issued long-term bonds 2 years ago. The amount of interest expense recorded annually is less than the amount of interest actually paid on the bonds. What conditions would lead to this situation?

d. The controller suggests that one way of avoiding paying more than 7 percent interest is to issue convertible bonds. Why might the company be able to avoid paying a higher interest rate by issuing convertible bonds? What risk is associated with issuing convertible bonds?

E11-5 Special Liabilities Lanway's most recent financial statements have a note that states "the company is involved in legal proceedings resulting from a lawsuit filed against the company for failure to provide adequate financial counseling for employees who have retired under the new company retirement program. The plaintiffs are seeking a judgment of $800,000 against the company. The management of Lanway feels the suit is without merit and will eventually be dismissed."

a. Why is a situation such as this considered to be a contingent liability?

b. Does the fact that Lanway reported this in its notes rather than as a liability in its balance sheet mean the company will not be held liable? Explain.

c. What will be the financial statement effects if, at the time the suit is brought to trial, the management of Lanway concludes the company is likely to be found liable for damages of $350,000?

E11-6 Analyzing Liabilities Using financial statement data published by Farnsworth Company, an investment analyst computed the following ratios:

	2000	1999	1998	1997
Debt-to-equity ratio	1.39	1.43	1.03	.95
Times interest earned	18.20	16.90	27.60	30.40
Earnings per share	$8.95	$8.60	$6.30	$5.95

Answer each of the following and explain your answer:

a. Is Farnsworth Company relying more heavily or less heavily on debt financing in 2000 than it had previously?

b. From the viewpoint of its bondholders, has Farnsworth's ability to make the interest payments on its debt increased or decreased?

c. Should Farnsworth's bondholders be concerned about the company's ability to continue making its interest payments if its operating earnings decline?

d. Have the common shareholders benefited from the apparent increase in debt?

E11-7 Multiple Choice: Reporting Liabilities Select the correct answer for each of the following:

1. At the time they are recorded, most noncurrent liabilities normally are valued at:
   a. The present value of future cash payments.
   b. Lower-of-cost-or-market.

c. Market value.
d. The amount that must be paid.

2. Current liabilities are likely to arise from:
   a. Purchase of inventory and operating supplies.
   b. Receipt of advance payment for services to be rendered.
   c. Accrued interest on long-term loans.
   d. All of the above.

3. An example of an estimated liability is:
   a. Interest payable on bonds.
   b. Wages payable.
   c. Allowance for uncollectibles.
   d. Product warranties obligation.

4. What is an advantage of issuing long-term debt rather than common stock in raising capital?
   a. Interest payments are tax deductible and dividends are not.
   b. The par value of a bond is tax deductible and the par value of stock is not.
   c. Failure to make an interest payment will not reduce the market price of stock as much as failure to make a dividend payment.
   d. While the number of shares of stock a company can issue is limited, the number of bonds that can be sold is unlimited.

5. A number of operating liabilities may be recorded at the end of the year and are usually reported in the financial statements as "accrued liabilities." Which of the following would normally be included in accrued liabilities?
   a. Depreciation for the year.
   b. Insurance premiums paid in advance.
   c. Unpaid salaries.
   d. Estimated allowance for doubtful accounts.

E11-8 Multiple Choice: Noncurrent Liabilities Select the correct answer for each of the following:

1. The amount of the cash interest payment on a long-term bond is determined by:
   a. Issue price times the effective interest rate.
   b. Issue price times the nominal interest rate.
   c. Par value times the effective interest rate.
   d. Par value times the nominal interest rate.

2. When bonds are sold at a premium:
   a. Interest expense is greater than the interest payment.
   b. Interest expense is the same as the interest payment.
   c. Interest expense is less than the interest payment.
   d. Interest expense is unaffected by the existence of a bond premium.

3. A bond sells at a discount when:
   a. Bond rating services rate the bond as risky compared to other bonds sold at the same time.
   b. The nominal interest rate is less than the stated interest rate.
   c. The effective interest rate is greater than the stated interest rate.
   d. The effective interest rate is less than the stated interest rate.

4. Bonds issued with a call provision are:
  a. Convertible into common or preferred stock on a specified date.
  b. Subject to retirement by the issuer at any time after the call date.
  c. Almost always sold at a premium because of the value of the call provision to the purchasers.
  d. Reported as current liabilities because they may be called in the current year.

E11-9 Multiple Choice: Other Liabilities Select the correct answer for each of the following:

1. An example of a contingent liability is:
  a. Unearned subscription revenue.
  b. Bond premium.
  c. Wages payable.
  d. Potential future payment on a pending breach of contract lawsuit.
2. Deferred income tax does not need to be recorded when:
  a. Temporary differences will reverse within 5 years.
  b. The company does not know when the temporary difference will reverse.
  c. The future repayment of taxes is sufficiently far off that the present value of the payment approaches zero.
  d. Accelerated depreciation is used for both financial reporting and tax purposes.
3. A liability for deferred income taxes should be recorded when:
  a. Revenue included in income for financial reporting purposes will be taxed at a later time.
  b. Revenue included in income for financial reporting purposes is exempt from income tax.
  c. Straight-line depreciation is used for both financial reporting and tax purposes.
  d. Income taxes are paid in advance to avoid interest charges and late fees.
4. Under a defined-benefit pension plan:
  a. The employer agrees to make a specified contribution each period; the benefits received by the retiree are specified.
  b. The employer agrees to make a specified contribution each period; the benefits received by the retiree may vary.
  c. The employer's contribution may vary; the benefits received by the retiree are specified.
  d. The employer's contribution may vary; the benefits received by the retiree may vary.

E11-10 Financial Statement Effects of Liabilities Fiber Company was involved in a number of transactions during the month of August. For each of the following, list the balance sheet and income statement accounts affected, indicate whether the account balances are increased or decreased, and indicate the amount of the change:

a. Supplies costing $900 were purchased on account.
b. Building rent for the months of September and October in the amount of $4,000 was received in advance.

c. Wages of $2,500 were earned by employees after the last payroll payment in August.
d. Bonds with a par value of $400,000 were issued for $425,000 at the end of August.
e. A loan of $75,000 was repaid to a local bank along with interest for the month of August in the amount of $560.

E11-11 Current Liabilities Rubin Corporation operates on a calendar-year basis. At December 1, 2001, Rubin reported the following current liabilities:

Accounts payable	$53,700
Lease payable on building	24,000
Unearned income on repair services	8,000
Estimated warranty claims payable	38,000

During December 2001, the following events occurred:

1. Rubin purchased equipment at a cost of $36,000 on account, payable January 15, 2002. A bill for freight charges of $4,000 was received and must be paid by January 7, 2002.
2. Rubin purchased inventory for $87,500 on account.
3. Rubin made payments of $82,000 on account.
4. Rubin borrowed $60,000 from a local bank on December 1 at 8 percent annual interest. Principal and interest are due 6 months from the date of the loan.
5. Rubin owed 1 month's payment on the building it leases at the beginning of December and failed to make any payments during the month. The building lease has 3 years remaining and equal monthly payments are required.
6. Rubin earned one-half of the income for repair services that had been prepaid by customers on November 30.
7. Rubin's products are sold with a 4-year warranty. The company records its warranty expense for the year in the month of December and estimates warranty expense for 2001 to be $19,000. During December, Rubin paid $3,200 in warranty claims.
8. Employees of the company are paid a total of $1,650 per day. Two work days elapsed between the last payday and the end of the fiscal year.

Rubin has $300,000 par value 10 percent bonds outstanding. The bonds were issued October 1, 1992, at par and mature on October 1, 2002. Interest is paid semiannually at April 1 and October 1.

a. Prepare the current liability section of Rubin's balance sheet at December 31, 2001.
b. Explain your treatment of the bonds outstanding.

E11-12 Premium Liability The Pur-Shuger Cereal Company ran a special promotion during 2001 in which it offered purchasers of its cereal the opportunity to obtain 10 different mega-monsters. For 5 boxtops, a customer could obtain, free of charge, models of any of the famous mega-monster cartoon characters, from the lovable Manny Mangler to the ferocious Challenger of Doom. Pur-Shuger contracts with Shoddy Premium Company to ship the models at a cost of $3 each. During 2001, Pur-Shuger sold 600,000 boxes of cereal, and it expects 20 percent of the boxtops to be redeemed for models. During the year, Pur-Shuger had Shoddy Premium ship 14,500 of the models based on redemptions of boxtops.

a. What amount of premium expense should Pur-Shuger report in 2001 in connection with the premium offer?
b. What amount of premium liability should Pur-Shuger report in its balance sheet prepared at the end of 2001?
c. Each box of Pur-Shuger's cereal sells for $4.50 and costs the company $2.00 to manufacture, package, and distribute. If the premium offer increased sales of the cereal from 550,000 boxes to 600,000, was it worthwhile? Explain.

E11-13 Liability for Warranties Hardboard Treadmill Company provides a 60-day free parts and labor warranty plan for all treadmills sold. In addition, all parts but the walking tread are guaranteed for 1 year and replaced free of charge if the repair work is done by a factory-approved repair shop. Hardboard normally must repair 4 percent of the units sold within the 60-day period at an average cost of $172 per unit, and 15 percent of the units require replacement parts within the 1-year warranty at an average cost of $120 per unit. During 2002, Hardboard sold 40,000 treadmills at an average price of $1,500 per unit and provided warranty service costing $627,000 on treadmills sold in 2002.

a. What dollar amount of estimated warranty expense should Hardboard record in 2002?
b. What dollar amount of liability for warranty costs on treadmills sold in 2002 should Hardboard report at December 31, 2002?
c. After the year-end liability was established using the above information, Hardboard learned the average cost of replacement parts for the 2,600 units repaired under the 1-year warranty in the current year averaged $190 per unit rather than $120. If $190 per unit is used in estimating the liability on the remaining units, what adjustment should be made to the warranty liability at the end of the current period?

E11-14 Liability for Premiums As a promotion for its new line of Zappo nonalkaline batteries, American Battery Company offered a free glow-in-the-dark key holder. Customers must submit 4 special proof-of-purchase seals from packages of Zappo batteries and pay 50 cents for shipping and handling. American Battery sold 600,000 packages of batteries with the special proof-of-purchase seals during the current period and believes 35 percent of the proof-of-purchase seals will be returned for the free prize. The cost of purchasing the key holders and shipping them to customers is $1.30 per unit. A total of 36,000 key holders were shipped to customers in the current period.

a. What amount of premium expense should American Battery record for the current period?
b. How many proofs of purchase are likely to be received in the following period?

c. What amount of liability for premiums should American Battery report at the end of the period?

E11-15 Bond Issued at a Premium Lan Corporation issues $600,000 of 20-year bonds with a stated interest rate of 8 percent on January 1. The bonds pay interest annually on December 31. The current market rate for similarly rated securities at the time of issue is 6 percent. What is the issue price of the bonds?

E11-16 Bond Issued at a Discount Parsel Company issues $350,000 of 12-year bonds with a stated interest rate of 5 percent on January 1. The bonds pay interest annually on December 31. The current market rate for similarly rated securities at the time of issue is 6 percent. What is the issue price of the bonds?

E11-17 Valuation of Bonds Hadley Cycle Corporation has plans for a major plant expansion and needs to raise additional capital to pay for the construction. Hadley is considering selling 12-year, 10 percent first mortgage bonds with a par value of $600,000. The bonds will pay interest twice each year.

a. Compute the amount of cash Hadley will receive if the bonds are sold at an effective interest rate of:
   1. 10 percent.
   2. 8 percent.
   3. 12 percent.
b. Prepare the journal entry Hadley would record at the time of sale under each of the three alternative yields.

E11-18 Amortization of Bond Premium On January 1, Bold Corporation issues $600,000 of 4-year bonds with a stated interest rate of 9 percent. Interest is payable at the end of each year. The issue price is $628,000. Assuming straight-line amortization of the bond premium is used in computing interest expense:

a. What amount of interest expense will Bold report annually?
b. Prepare a bond interest and amortization table for the life of the bonds, as illustrated in Exhibit 11–4.
c. What is the book value of the bonds at the end of the second year?

E11-19 Amortization of Bond Discount Todd Corporation issued $400,000 of 4-year bonds with a stated interest rate of 7 percent. Interest is payable at the end of each year. The bonds were issued on January 1 and $382,000 was received. Assuming straight-line amortization of the bond discount is used in computing interest expense:

a. What amount of interest expense will Todd Corporation report annually?
b. Prepare a bond interest and amortization table for the life of the bonds, as illustrated in Exhibit 11–3.
c. What is the book value of the bonds at the end of the second year?

E11-20 Bond Issued at a Premium On January 1, Emperor Corporation issued $400,000 of 16-year bonds with a stated interest rate of 5 percent. Interest is paid at the end of each year. The current market rate for similarly rated bonds at the time of issue was 4 percent and Emperor received $446,610 when the bonds were issued. Assuming straight-line amortization of the bond premium is used in computing interest expense:

a. What amount of interest expense will Emperor report annually?

b. Prepare a bond interest and amortization table for the first 5 years the bonds are outstanding, as illustrated in Exhibit 11–4.

c. What is the book value of the bonds at the end of the fifth year?

E11-21   Bond Issued at a Discount   Bell Corporation issued a 5-year bond with a par value of $700,000 for $624,302 on January 1. The bond had a stated interest rate of 9 percent. The current market rate for similarly rated bonds was 12 percent at the time of issue. Assuming the bond pays interest annually on December 31, and straight-line amortization of the bond discount is used in computing interest expense:

a. What amount of interest expense will Bell report annually?

b. Prepare a bond interest and amortization table for the life of the bonds, as illustrated in Exhibit 11–3.

c. What is the book value of the bonds at the end of the fourth year?

E11-22   Bond Premium with Interest Paid Semiannually   Apple Corporation issued $200,000 of 3-year bonds with a stated interest rate of 12 percent on January 1. Interest is paid every 6 months. The current market rate for similarly rated bonds at the time of issue was 10 percent, and Apple received $210,152 for the bonds. Assuming straight-line amortization of the bond premium is used in computing interest expense:

a. What amount of interest expense will Apple report for each semiannual interest-payment period?

b. Prepare a bond interest and amortization table for the life of the bonds, as illustrated in Exhibit 11–4.

E11-23   Bond Discount with Interest Paid Semiannually   On January 1, Pear Corporation received $474,624 when it issued $500,000 of 3-year bonds with a stated interest rate of 8 percent. Interest is paid every 6 months. The current market rate for similarly rated bonds at the time of issue was 10 percent. Assuming straight-line amortization of the bond premium is used in computing interest expense:

a. What amount of interest expense will Pear report for each semiannual interest-payment period?

b. Prepare a bond interest and amortization table for the life of the bonds, as illustrated in Exhibit 11–3.

E11-24   Bond Retirement   Goldman Corporation received $445,974 when it issued $400,000 of 8-year 10 percent bonds on January 1, 2002. The bonds pay interest at the end of each year. The market rate of interest for similar secu-rities at the time of issue was 8 percent. Assuming Goldman uses straight-line amortization of the bond discount:

a. What is the carrying value of the bond liability at December 31, 2004?

b. If Goldman Corporation decides to reacquire the bonds at December 31, 2004, for $425,000, would it report a gain or a loss? What amount would be reported?

c. Why might Goldman Corporation wish to retire the bonds?

E11-25   Repurchase of Bonds Outstanding   Trendy Corporation recently generated a substantial amount of cash from the sale of an operating division and wishes to use some of the money to reduce its long-term debt. It has decided to retire $600,000 of bonds that were issued at a discount and have a current book value of $576,000. A recent increase in interest rates has driven the current market price of the bonds down, and Trendy can purchase the bonds for $569,000 in the open market.

a. If the bonds are retired at par value, what amount of gain or loss on bond retirement will be reported?

b. If the bonds are purchased in the open market and retired, what amount of gain or loss on bond retirement will be reported?

c. If the current market price of the bonds were $608,000 and Trendy purchased the bonds in the open market, what amount of gain or loss would be reported?

d. If the bonds are not retired, should Trendy adjust the carrying value of the bonds to $569,000? Explain.

e. If the bonds are selling in the open market at $608,000, should the management of Trendy wait until the bonds are selling at a discount before it retires the bonds? Explain.

E11-26   Bond Conversion   On December 31, Denic Corporation had $2,000,000 of 9 percent convertible bonds outstanding that will mature in 5 years. The book value of the bonds was $1,990,000 on December 31, and the discount is amortized on a straight-line basis. The bonds were called on December 31, and immediately after the interest payment, the entire issue was converted into 20,000 shares of common stock. Denic's common stock had paid an annual dividend of $4 per share for each of the past 5 years. The company's income tax rate was 30 percent.

a. On an annual basis, by how much will Denic's net income be different after the bond conversion?

b. By how much will Denic's debt change as a result of the bond conversion? By how much will Denic's stockholders' equity change as a result of the conversion?

E11-27   Using Deferred Taxes   Noble Company recently purchased additional buildings and equipment. Because it wishes to retain as much of its cash as possible for expansion, Noble is considering using accelerated depreciation on the newly acquired assets for income tax purposes to reduce the amount of taxes paid. The company plans to continue to use straight-line depreciation for financial reporting and has been told there is a possibility that this strategy could result in a large liability for deferred federal income taxes being reported on its balance sheet.

a. In what way can this strategy result in a tax savings during the early years of ownership?
b. Why is there likely to be a liability for deferred income taxes reported on Noble's balance sheet if it adopts this approach?
c. If Noble continues to expand, why may it not have to pay off the liability for deferred income taxes in the near future?

E11-28 Deferred Taxes Manson Company purchased equipment for $1,000,000 on January 1, 2001. The equipment is expected to last for 10 years and have no salvage value at that time. Manson Company uses straight-line depreciation for financial reporting purposes and double-declining-balance depreciation for tax purposes. Manson has a 30 percent income tax rate and income before depreciation and taxes of $620,000 for 2001.

a. What amount of depreciation expense will Manson Company report in its income statement for 2001? What amount of net income will Manson report for 2001?
b. What amount of income tax will Manson Company pay for 2001?
c. What amount of deferred income taxes will Manson report in its balance sheet at December 31, 2001?

E11-29 Contingent Liabilities Determine whether each of the following is or is not a contingent liability and give the basis for your decision. For those that are contingent liabilities, explain how they should be reported.

a. Current maturities of long-term debt.
b. Guarantee of a contract by a subsidiary to purchase supplies at a fixed price over the next 3 years.
c. Estimated income taxes payable.
d. Estimated future warranty payments.
e. Threat of a lawsuit against a grocery store by customer who claims the products emit radiation and are unsafe to eat.
f. Failure to make payments to the company pension plan for the past 2 years.
g. Allowance for doubtful accounts.

E11-30 Analyzing Company Liabilities Powder Corporation has been expanding rapidly and has issued additional debt each year for the last 10 years. The company has disclosed the following financial information:

	2000	1999	1998	1997
Operating income	$200,000	$160,000	$110,000	$ 80,000
Net income	206,000	185,000	115,000	76,000
Interest expense	28,000	15,000	7,200	4,000
Total long-term debt outstanding	350,000	187,500	90,000	50,000
Total owners' equity	600,000	400,000	200,000	120,000
Number of common shares outstanding	150,000	150,000	100,000	100,000

a. Has Powder's debt-to-equity ratio increased or decreased over the 4-year period?
b. Has Powder's times interest earned ratio increased or decreased over the 4-year period?
c. Has Powder's earnings per share increased or decreased over the 4-year period?
d. From the viewpoint of the bondholders, has the company become a more secure investment or more risky? Explain why.
e. From the viewpoint of the shareholders, has the company become a more desirable investment or a less desirable investment? Explain why.

E11-31A Bond Issued at a Premium On January 1, Emperor Corporation issued $400,000 of 16-year bonds with a stated interest rate of 5 percent. Interest is paid at the end of each year. The current market rate for similarly rated bonds at the time of issue was 4 percent and Emperor received $446,610 when the bonds were issued. Assuming the effective-interest method of amortization is used in computing interest expense:

a. What amount of interest expense will Emperor report for the first year?
b. Prepare a bond interest and amortization table for the first four years the bonds are outstanding, as illustrated in Exhibit 11–6.
c. What is the book value of the bonds at the end of the fourth year?

E11-32A Bond Issued at a Discount Bell Corporation issues a 5-year bond with a par value of $700,000 and a stated interest rate of 9 percent for $624,302. The current market rate for similarly rated bonds is 12 percent at the time of issue. Assuming the bonds are issued on January 1, pay interest annually on December 31, and the effective-interest method of amortization is used in computing interest expense:

a. What amount of interest expense will Bell report for the first year?
b. Prepare a bond interest and amortization table for the life of the bonds, as illustrated in Exhibit 11–5.
c. What is the book value of the bonds at the end of the second year?

E11-33A Amortization of Bond Premium On January 1, Good Corporation issues $800,000 par value bonds with a 4-year maturity; 9 percent stated interest rate; and an effective rate 8 percent. Interest is paid annually on December 31. Assuming the effective-interest method of amortization is used in computing interest expense:

a. Compute the amount Good Corporation will receive at the time the bonds are issued.
b. What amount of interest expense will Good report for the first year?
c. What amount of interest expense will Good report for the second year?
d. Prepare a bond interest and amortization table for the life of the bonds, as illustrated in Exhibit 11–6.

E11-34A Amortization of Bond Discount On January 1, Zond Corporation issues $600,000 par value bonds with a 4-year maturity; 6 percent stated interest rate; and an effective interest rate of 8 percent. Interest is paid annually on December 31. Assuming the effective-interest method of amortization is used in computing interest expense:

a. Compute the amount Zond Corporation will receive at the time the bonds are issued.
b. What amount of interest expense will Zond report for the first year?
c. What amount of interest expense will Zond report for the second year?
d. Prepare a bond interest and amortization table for the life of the bonds, as illustrated in Exhibit 11–5.

E11-35A Bond Premium with Interest Paid Semiannually Apple Corporation issues $200,000 of 3-year bonds with a stated interest rate of 12 percent. Interest is paid every 6 months. The current market rate for similarly rated bonds at the time of issue is 10 percent and Apple receives $210,152 for the bonds. Assuming the bonds are issued on January 1 and the effective-interest method of amortization is used in computing interest expense:

a. What amount of interest expense will Apple report for the first 6 months?
b. What amount of interest expense will Apple report for the second 6 month interest-payment period?
c. Prepare a bond interest and amortization table for the life of the bonds, as illustrated in Exhibit 11–6.

E11-36A Bond Discount with Interest Paid Semiannually Pear Corporation receives $474,624 when it issues $500,000 of 3-year bonds with a stated interest rate of 8 percent. Interest is paid every 6 months. The current market rate for similarly rated bonds at the time of issue is 10 percent. Assuming the bonds are issued on January 1 and the effective-interest method of amortization is used in computing interest expense:

a. What amount of interest expense will Pear report for the first 6 months?
b. What amount of interest expense will Pear report for the second interest-payment period?
c. Prepare a bond interest and amortization table for the life of the bonds, as illustrated in Exhibit 11–5.

E11-37A Bond Issue Price Merst Company issues $300,000 par value bonds with a stated interest rate of 10 percent and an effective interest rate of 12 percent on January 1, 2001. The bonds mature on January 1, 2011 and pay interest semiannually. Merst uses the effective-interest method of amortization in computing interest expense.

a. Compute the issue price of the bonds.
b. What amount of interest will Merst pay at June 30, 2001? What amount of interest expense will it record at June 30, 2001?
c. What amount of interest will Merst pay at December 31, 2001? What amount of interest expense will it record for the 6-month period ending December 31, 2001?
d. What will the book value of the bonds be at December 31, 2001?
e. Give the dollar amounts reported in Merst's balance sheet at December 31, 2001.

USING ACCOUNTING FOR DECISION MAKING

P11-38 Evaluating Liabilities Broader Company reported the following summarized balance sheet amounts at December 31, 2001:

Current Assets	$350,000
Buildings and Equipment (net)	500,000
Land	70,000
Goodwill	60,000
Total Assets	$980,000
Current Liabilities	$150,000
Bonds Payable	600,000
Deferred Income Tax	90,000
Common Stock, par value	100,000
Retained Earnings	40,000
Total Liabilities and Owners' Equity	$980,000

Broader reported operating income of $340,000 and net income of $298,000 for 2001. The 6 percent bonds outstanding were issued at par value in 1998.

a. Compute the current ratio.
b. Compute the debt-to-equity ratio.
c. Compute the number of times interest is earned ratio for 2001.
d. Why might an investor consider Broader's bonds risky?
e. Why might an investor consider Broader's bonds reasonably safe?

P11-39 Does a Receivable or Liability Exist? Motif Company entered into an agreement with Joe Putz in March 2000 in which Joe agreed to pay Motif $350,000 to develop a prototype of a self-washing window suitable for installation in homes. Joe gave $300,000 to Motif when the agreement was signed and promised to give the remaining $50,000 on

June 30, 2001, if the prototype was developed by that date. The agreement states that if Motif fails to deliver the prototype by June 30, 2001, it will return $200,000 to Joe within 60 days. Motif Corporation included an account receivable of $50,000 from Joe in its balance sheet at December 31, 2000.

a. What factors should be considered in determining whether Motif has an account receivable of $50,000 or a liability of $200,000 at December 31, 2000?

b. If at December 31, 2000, Motif concludes that it will be unable to meet the deadline, must a liability be reported at December 31, 2000? Explain.

c. If Motif concludes a liability must be reported at December 31, 2000, should the liability be classified as a current or long-term liability? Explain.

P11-40   EPS and Convertible Bonds   Deal Corporation reported net income of $360,000 for 2001. Deal had 50,000 shares of common stock outstanding during the year and issued convertible bonds with a par value of $400,000 and an annual interest rate of 10 percent on January 1, 2001. The bonds may be converted by the bondholders to 8,000 shares of common stock at any time. The effects of federal and state income taxes may be ignored.

a. What amount of earnings per share will Deal Corporation report for 2001 if the possible conversion of the bonds into common stock is ignored?

b. Would Deal's earnings per share for 2001 increase or decrease if the bonds were converted to common stock on January 2, 2001? By what amount?

c. If the carrying value of the bond liability on Deal's books at January 2 was greater than $400,000 and the bonds were converted to common stock on that day, would the difference between the carrying value and maturity value of the bonds be included as a gain or loss in the income statement for the period or would some other treatment be appropriate? Explain.

P11-41   Use of Leverage   Solid Corporation has operated for 30 years and has done so with very little debt. The last bond issue was retired in 1996, 5 years ahead of schedule. The company needs to expand and is planning to issue 10,000 additional shares of common stock at $25 per share. Another option would be to issue $250,000 of 20-year, 10 percent bonds.

Solid Corporation reported net income for the current year of $70,000 and currently has 40,000 shares of common stock outstanding. The company estimates that by investing in additional equipment and replacing some existing equipment, income before interest and taxes can be increased by $50,000 per year. The company's effective income tax rate is 40 percent.

a. What would be the expected increase in net income under each of the two financing alternatives?

b. What amount would be reported as earnings per share before the purchase of new equipment? What would be the estimated earnings per share under each of the financing

alternatives? Should Solid Corporation purchase the equipment? If so, which financing alternative should be used? Explain.

c. Would your answer be the same if expected earnings before interest and tax increased by $20,000, rather than $50,000? Explain.

P11-42   Bond Financing Alternatives   You are working for Short Company, which is expanding rapidly and anticipates having cash flow shortages for the next several years. You are considering using one of three alternative debt proposals for financing the company's expansion: (1) issue bonds with a $1,000,000 par value and a 6 percent stated rate, paying interest annually, due in 20 years; (2) issue bonds with a par value of $800,000 and a stated rate of 8 percent, paying interest annually, due in 10 years; and (3) issue bonds with a par value of $2,800,000 and a zero stated rate, due in 15 years. The company's general cost of borrowing on a long-term basis is estimated at 10 percent.

a. Calculate the issue price of each of the bonds. Which of the alternatives will result in the largest amount of cash proceeds?

b. If the company decides to issue the bond that generates the most cash at the time of issuance, show how the bond would be reported in Short's balance sheet immediately after issuance.

c. Compute the interest expense that Short would report for the first and second years on the three different bond issues if it uses the straight-line method of amortizing bond discount.

d. What factors other than the amount of cash to be received at the time of issuance should Short Company consider in deciding which of the three bonds to issue?

P11-43   Bond Issued at Discount   On January 1, 2002, Albany Corporation receives $438,000 when it issues bonds with a par value of $450,000 and a stated interest rate of 7 percent. The bonds mature on December 31, 2005, and interest is paid annually on December 31. Albany Corporation uses straight-line amortization of bond discounts and premiums.

a. What amount of interest payment will Albany make on December 31, 2002?

b. What amount of interest expense will Albany record on December 31, 2002?

c. Give the balance sheet presentation of the bond liability at December 31, 2002.

d. Give the journal entries recorded by Albany Corporation during 2002 and 2003.

P11-44   Bond Issued at Premium   Gigantic Enterprises issues bonds with a par value of $700,000 on January 1, 2001, and receives $724,000. The stated interest rate on the bonds is 10 percent and interest is paid annually on December 31. The bonds mature on December 31, 2006. Gigantic uses straight-line amortization of bond discounts and premiums.

a. What amount of interest payment will Gigantic make on December 31, 2001?

b. What amount of interest expense will Gigantic record on December 31, 2001?

c. Give the balance sheet presentation of the bond liability at December 31, 2001.

d. Give the journal entries recorded by Gigantic Enterprises during 2001 and 2002.

P11-45   Interest Expense   Huff Corporation issues 12-year 9 percent bonds with a par value of $150,000 on January 1, 2001. Interest is paid semiannually on June 30 and December 31. Huff Corporation uses straight-line amortization of bond premiums or discounts in computing interest expense.

a. If the bonds are issued at par value, give the journal entries for 2001 and 2002.

b. If the bonds are issued at 106, give the journal entries for 2001 and 2002.

c. If the bonds are issued at 98, give the journal entries for 2001 and 2002.

d. Why must amortization of the premium or discount be included in the computation of annual interest expense?

P11-46   Zero-Coupon Bonds   Coal Corporation is considering alternatives to provide funding for the future expansion of its mining activities. Management is concerned, however, that the company might have trouble meeting interest payments on additional debt until the new mining activities start producing revenues in several years. The controller of Coal Corporation has suggested that the company issue $500,000 of 10-year zero-coupon bonds. The effective annual interest rate for Coal Corporation is 12 percent.

a. Determine the issue price of the bonds and show how the bonds would be reported in Coal's balance sheet immediately after issuance.

b. The president of Coal Corporation was astonished to learn that the company would receive more money if it sold $350,000 of 12 percent, 10-year bonds. Explain why this is true. How much would the company receive if the market rate of interest is 12 percent?

c. Why might it be more desirable for Coal Corporation to issue $500,000 of zero-coupon bonds rather than $350,000 of interest-bearing bonds?

P11-47   Bond Retirement   Banner Company has bonds outstanding with a par value of $200,000 and a carrying value of $211,154 at July 1, 2002. The bonds can be called at 102 any time after January 1, 2002. The 5-year bonds have a stated rate of 14 percent and were issued on January 1, 2001, to yield 12 percent. Interest is paid semiannually.

a. If the bonds are retired at July 1, 2002, what amount of gain or loss will Banner report?

b. What factors should Banner Company take into consideration before deciding to retire the bonds?

c. If the market price of the bonds at July 1, 2002, was $198,000 and Banner Company wished to retire the bonds, should Banner exercise the call feature? Explain.

P11-48   Deferred Income Taxes Payable   Astro Corporation purchased a building for $800,000 on January 1, 2000, and recorded straight-line depreciation on the building for financial reporting purposes, using a 20-year life and no estimated salvage value. Astro uses double-declining-balance depreciation for tax purposes and has a 40 percent tax rate. Astro reported income before depreciation and income taxes of $230,000 for 2000.

a. Compute the amount of income tax expense Astro will report for 2000 in its income statement.

b. Compute the amount of income taxes Astro must pay in 2000.

c. What amount of deferred income taxes will Astro report at December 31, 2000?

d. What is the advantage of using accelerated depreciation if Astro must pay higher taxes in the later years of the life of the building and eventually reduce the balance in the deferred income tax account to zero?

P11-49   Recognition of Pension Liability   Dependable Products Corporation has a defined-benefit pension plan that provides a payment of $1,000 per month to each retiree who worked for Dependable Products for more that 10 years prior to retirement.

a. What is meant by a defined-benefit pension plan?

b. Why is it considered inappropriate to treat the amounts paid to retirees as compensation expense at the time of payment?

c. How should Dependable Products determine the amount to be recorded as pension expense for the current period?

d. List four factors that would be important in determining the amount of pension expense to record.

P11-50   Recognition of Postretirement Benefits   Post Corporation provides health care and dental insurance coverage for its retired employees. Post currently has 5,000 employees. It estimates each employee will live for 20 years after retirement and that it will cost $4,000 per year to provide health care benefits for each retiree.

a. What is the total dollar amount per employee that Post expects to pay for postretirement benefits following the employee's retirement?

b. Post Corporation wishes to include the cost of future benefits earned by employees in the current period as operating costs of the current period. Why is it not considered appropriate to wait until the employee retires and report the amount paid each period as compensation expense?

c. How should Post Corporation determine the amount to report as health care expense for the current period?

P11-51   Use of Leverage   Sarasota Enterprises has 50,000 shares of common stock outstanding and expects to report income before taxes of $51,000 in each of the next few years. The company reported the following summarized balance sheet amounts at December 31, 2000:

Current Assets	$ 40,000
Depreciable Assets (net)	450,000
Intangible Assets	80,000
Total Assets	$570,000
Current Liabilities	$ 30,000
Noncurrent Liabilities	200,000
Common Stock	150,000
Retained Earnings	190,000
Total Liabilities and Equities	$570,000

To increase future income, Sarasota will need $300,000 of additional capital to expand its motel facilities. If it carries out the proposed expansion, it expects income before taxes and interest to increase to about $95,000 per year.

Sarasota must choose whether to issue bonds or shares of preferred or common stock to finance the expansion. The company's income tax rate is 30 percent. If 20-year bonds are issued, they must yield 8 percent annually. If the company raises the $300,000 through the sale of preferred stock, 10,000 shares must be sold with a $3 per share annual dividend. A total of 8,000 shares of common stock must be sold to raise $300,000.

a. Under which financing alternative will the largest net income be reported?

b. Under which financing alternative will the largest income available to common shareholders be reported?

c. Under which financing alternative will the largest earnings per common share be reported?

d. What impact would the issuance of bonds have on debt-to-equity and debt-to-asset ratios?

e. What impact would each of the financing alternatives have on return on total equity (net income divided by total stockholders' equity) and the return on common equity (income available to common shareholders divided by common shareholders' equity)?

f. Does the proposed expansion appear to be justified? Explain. If the expansion is justified, which financing alternative would you favor if you were a major common shareholder? Why?

P11-52A **Effective-Interest Amortization of Bond Premium** On January 1, 2002, Pollard Corporation issued $250,000 of 4-year bonds with a stated interest rate of 6 percent. Interest is paid annually on December 31. The current market rate for similarly rated bonds at the time of issue was 5 percent, and Pollard received $258,864 when the bonds were issued. Assuming the effective-interest method is used in recording interest expense:

a. Prepare a bond interest and amortization table for the life of the bonds.

b. Give the journal entry recorded by Pollard at the time the bonds were issued.

c. Give the journal entries recorded by Pollard over the life of the bonds.

d. Give the balance sheet presentation of the bond liability at December 31, 2002.

P11-53A **Effective-Interest Amortization of Bond Discount** On January 1, 2001, Toll Corporation received $241,336 when it issued a 4-year bond with a par value of $250,000 and a stated interest rate of 5 percent. The current market rate for similarly rated bonds was 6 percent at the time of issue. Assuming the bond pays interest annually on December 31, and the effective-interest method is used in recording interest expense:

a. Prepare a bond interest and amortization table for the life of the bonds.

b. Give the journal entry recorded by Toll at the time the bonds were issued.

c. Give the journal entries recorded by Toll over the life of the bonds.

d. Give the balance sheet presentation of the bond liability at December 31, 2002.

P11-54A **Semiannual Payments and Bond Premium** On January 1, 2001, Franklin Corporation issued $500,000 par value, 15-year bonds with a 14 percent stated interest rate and an effective interest rate of 12 percent. Interest is paid semiannually on June 30 and December 31. Franklin Corporation uses the effective-interest method in recording interest expense.

a. Compute the amount Franklin Corporation received when the bonds were issued.

b. Prepare a bond interest and amortization table for 2001 and 2002.

c. Prepare the journal entry recorded by Franklin Corporation when the bonds were issued.

d. Prepare the journal entries to record the interest payments for 2001 and 2002.

P11-55A **Semiannual Payments and Bond Discount** On January 1, 2002, Playday Corporation issued $600,000 par value, 12-year bonds with a 16 percent stated interest rate and an effective interest rate of 18 percent. Interest is paid semiannually on June 30 and December 31. Playday Corporation uses the effective-interest method in recording interest expense.

a. Compute the amount Playday Corporation received when the bonds were issued.

b. Prepare a bond interest and amortization table for 2002 and 2003.

c. Prepare the journal entry recorded by Playday Corporation when the bonds were issued.

d. Prepare the journal entries to record the interest payments for 2002 and 2003.

P11-56A **Bond Financing Alternatives** You are working for Blower Corporation, which is considering issuing bonds so that it can purchase new production equipment. The company has talked with two financial institutions and is looking at two different debt proposals. Under the first alternative, the company would issue $500,000 par value, 15-year bonds with a 20 percent stated interest rate. The second alternative is to issue $800,000 par value, 10-year bonds with a stated interest rate of 10 percent. Both issues pay interest annually on December 31. The effective interest rate for Blower is 12 percent. Blower uses the effective-interest method in recording interest expense. The bonds will be issued on January 1, 2002.

a. Compute the amount of cash that would be received under each alternative.

b. If Blower is interested in selecting the alternative that results in receiving the larger amount of cash when the bonds are issued, which alternative should be chosen?

c. Compute the amount to be recorded as interest expense for 2002 under each alternative.

d. If Blower is interested in selecting the alternative with the lower amount reported as interest expense in 2002, which alternative should be chosen? Explain.

e. If Blower is interested in selecting the alternative with the lower annual interest payment, which alternative should be chosen? Explain.

P11-57A Selection of Payment Form Jane Keen decided on January 1, 2001, to purchase a new car as a reward for graduating from college and accepting a job. The car dealer has offered to sell her the model she likes most for payments of $650 at the end of each month for 48 months based on an annual interest rate of 18 percent. However, Jane may be able to pay cash to purchase the car. On January 1, 2001, she received a $20,000 par value bond from her grandmother. The bond matures in 12 years and pays interest of 10 percent annually at December 31. The market rate of interest for similar bonds on January 1, 2001, is 8 percent. Interest computations on the car loan and bond require use of the effective-interest method.

a. If Jane wishes to pay cash for the car, how much would she have to pay on January 1, 2001?

b. If Jane wishes to sell the bond on January 1, 2001, how much cash would she receive?

c. How much additional cash would Jane have to contribute, or how much cash would she have left if she sold the bond and paid for the car in cash?

d. What other options might Jane consider?

EXPANDING YOUR HORIZONS

C11-58 Analysis of Promotional Activities A special promotional program established by Hoover Europe, a subsidiary of Maytag Corporation, offered free airline flights within Europe for qualified buyers of Hoover products during the period August 1992 to January 1993. Based on the expected cost of the program, Hoover Europe recorded $12.2 million of selling and general and administrative costs in 1992 related to the program and established an estimated liability. Unfortunately, the program was structured such that customers could obtain free flights worth more than the selling prices of the Hoover products they purchased, and the public quickly took advantage of the promotional offer. In 1993, Hoover recognized promotional costs of $10.4 million for the program as a part of selling and general and administrative costs and a special $50 million expense to cover the additional unexpected cost of the program, raising the total expense recognized in 1993 for the program to $60.4 million. The financial statements of Hoover Europe are consolidated with other units of Maytag Corporation for financial reporting purposes. For the year 1993, Maytag Corporation reported net income of $51.2 million on total sales of $2,987 million.

a. What was the total cost of the program before taxes for Maytag?

b. What was the reduction in reported net income (after considering income taxes) for Maytag for 1993? Assume that the effective tax rate for Hoover Europe was 20 percent.

c. What actions might Hoover Europe have considered once it realized that the free-flight program was improperly designed? What are some of the potential costs of taking these actions?

d. What factors should be considered in establishing such a program? What role should the accountant have in establishing promotional campaigns?

e. Maytag treated the $50 million as a special expense. Should it have reported the additional cost as an extraordinary item? Explain.

C11-59 Decision Case: Improving Debt Ratings Williams Company has decided to issue bonds to raise cash needed for new equipment purchases. Company officials have met with representatives of the well-known investment banking firm Giltman Socks and have roughed out a preliminary description of the terms of the bond issue. The plan is to issue $100 million of subordinated debentures due in 20 years. Because the bonds are expected to be rated Baa by *Moody's* (See Exhibit 11–1), Giltman Socks has estimated the bonds will need to yield 10 percent to entice investors to purchase them. Managers at Williams are concerned about the high interest payments and the burden the interest will place on future cash flows. They wonder if steps couldn't be taken to improve the rating by Moody's. They estimate that the yield could be cut by 1 percentage point for each step upwards in the ratings. Outline steps that might be taken to improve the way in which the Williams Company bonds might be viewed by the bond raters and the market.

C11-60 Team Project: Analyzing Financial Statements Acquire the financial statements of a large manufacturing company, such as General Motors, a large electric or gas utility company, such as Duke Energy Corporation or Ameren Corporation (previously Union Electric Company), and a large bank, such as Wells Fargo & Company. For each company, examine the balance sheet, income statement, statement of cash flows, and footnotes to the financial statements. Prepare a short report in which you include the following:

a. Compute the proportion of total assets financed by noncurrent liabilities for each company. Which company has financed the largest portion of its total assets with noncurrent liabilities? Are the differences in percentages consistent with the operating characteristics of the three companies? Explain whether or not the results are consistent with your expectations. If not, attempt to find the reason for the difference.

b. Compute the ratio of noncurrent liabilities to total equity and to current liabilities for each company. Do the companies appear to be highly leveraged? Explain.

c. Compare the ratios computed in parts a and b with the ratios of another company in each of the same industries. How do the proportions of noncurrent liabilities for your three original companies compare with those of the three new companies selected? Do these comparisons lead you to change the judgments you made in parts a and b? Explain. Be sure to identify the other companies in your report.

d. Analyze the change in long-term debt during the past year for each of your three companies. Examine the beginning and ending balance sheet totals, any issuances or retirements of long-term debt reported in the cash flow statement, and the information presented in the footnotes. Are you able to account for the amount of change during the period? If not, what other reclassifications or activities may have occurred?

C11-61 The Ethics of Investing State pension plans have become a major force in the capital markets, with huge amounts of money to invest for pensions to be paid to retirees from state employment. The well being of state retirees, and sometimes the well being of state taxpayers, may depend on returns generated by the pension fund investments. State employees in Michigan participate in a pension plan managed by the Public Workers Pension Fund. This pension fund has invested almost $400 million of pension fund money in tobacco company stocks. At the same time, the state actively encourages citizens to stop smoking and spends almost $6 million in taxpayer money on anti-smoking campaigns and to curtail the smuggling of cigarettes into the state. The state treasurer has indicated that it is his responsibility to invest pension fund money in a way that maximizes the return, but some believe that investing taxpayer money in tobacco stocks in unethical. Similar concerns sometimes are raised regarding investments in companies with nuclear power plants and those considered to be heavy polluters or cruel to animals.

a. Discuss the ethics of investing taxpayer money in tobacco stocks or in the stocks of other companies about which social concerns have been raised. Consider the points of view of taxpayers, retirees, and other citizens.

b. Does your position on the ethics of investing depend on whether the pension plan is a defined-contribution plan or a defined-benefit plan? Explain.

C11-62 Ethics and Decisions The Road Masher Tire Company manufactures high-speed specialty tires for passenger cars. At the beginning of this year, it began selling a new tire under the brand name "The Racer." The tire has been popular, and 100,000 tires have been installed this year. In addition, another 100,000 tires have been sold to dealers. Now, as a member of Road Masher's executive committee, you are faced with a serious problem. Production testing has discovered that in cold weather, when the tire is operated at high speeds before it has been warmed up by lower-speed driving, the tread comes off. In fact, with a cold tire, the tread will always come off at speeds in excess of 90 mph. All previous testing had been done in Florida, and the defect was not anticipated. The defect has now been corrected, and there will be no problems with the tires shipped next year.

Road Masher recorded revenue of $20 million on the sale of Racer tires this year. Based on past experience, warranty expense and an estimated liability of 2 percent of sales ($400,000) was recorded. The executive committee has received the following reports and recommendations about the problem:

a. The production staff recommends announcing a 100 percent recall of all 200,000 tires and replacing them, at no charge, with tires of the corrected design.

b. The marketing department recommends replacing the 100,000 tires still in the hands of dealers as quickly as possible but not announcing it as a recall. News of a recall could have a significant adverse effect on sales for several years.

c. The legal department reports that the company could be subject to a number of costly lawsuits for failed tires that result in accidents. The loss of one such lawsuit would cause many more suits to be filed. The legal staff makes no recommendation, but warns of the potential liability.

d. The accounting department reports that:
   1. A recall of all 200,000 tires will cost about $10 million for replacement tires, plus about $500,000 for costs related to the replacement.
   2. Replacing the tires in the hands of dealers will cost about $5 million for the tires, plus about $100,000 for related costs.
   3. If the replacement is to take place, a more accurate estimate of the costs should be prepared and additional expense and a liability recorded immediately. This will result in an operating loss for the year.
   4. If replacement does not take place, warranty expense and the estimated liability for this year should be increased to match the new predicted failure rate. Also, whether the tires are replaced or not, the company should disclose the contingent liability for possible losses from failed tires.

As a member of the Executive Committee, what do you recommend? What part of your answer is based on financial issues and what part is based on ethical business issues? What part of your answer is based on what is best for society, what is best for the company, and what is best for you (given that a significant portion of your compensation is based on the company's reported net income)?

Internet Exercises: Visit our Web site for additional exercises.

Annual Report Project Part 11

Refer to the Annual Report Project, Part 1, at the end of Chapter 1. Using the annual report of the company you have chosen, and any other available information, answer the following questions, providing sources and computations where appropriate.

a. To what extent has your company employed leverage? Discuss.

b. Assess the company's solvency and the degree of safety afforded creditors.

c. Does the company use the same or different accounting methods for tax purposes as compared with financial reporting? How do you know? How has this affected the company's balance sheet?

d. Has your company disclosed any contingencies? If so, what is the nature of these contingencies, and what impact do you think they will have on your company's future? Explain.

CHAPTER TWELVE

Reporting Ownership Interests

REVIEW

Chapters 8, 9, and 10 discussed accounting and reporting concepts related to assets, while Chapter 11 discussed liabilities.

WHERE THIS CHAPTER FITS

This chapter focuses on the third element of the accounting equation, owners' equity. It considers the various elements of owners' equity and discusses what financial statement information relating to owners' equity can tell decision makers.

LOOKING AHEAD

Chapter 13 revisits the use of cash flow information for decision making and looks more closely at the cash flow statement.

My aunt gave me 25 shares of stock for my last birthday, and the annual report for the company just came in the mail. I have been trying to figure out which part of the company is mine. The stockholders' equity section of its balance sheet lists a lot of things. Do I own part of all of those things? What is additional paid-in capital? Does that mean my aunt paid more for the stock than it was worth? Maybe if I understood these stockholders' equity items I would have a better feel for what it means to be an owner of a large corporation.

"Kmart has determined that if Wall Street won't support its stock, the company will do so itself—to the tune of $1 billion. Stung by a stagnating stock price . . . Kmart['s] chairman . . . announced . . . recently that the corporation will buy back up to $1 billion of its common stock . . . to enhance shareholder value."[1]

[1]Laura Liebeck, "Kmart Set to Reacquire Stock," *Discount Store News* (June 7, 1999), p. 5.

We know that businesses own assets so they can operate. Sometimes they acquire those assets by borrowing money, as we discussed in Chapter 11. Other times, however, the money to acquire assets and operate a business comes from owners. If the enterprise is small, it might be owned by just one person or a small group of individuals. Large companies, however, need large amounts of capital, and they may be owned by many investors. With a large company, each owner may have just a small interest in the company, but together, thousands of investors provide the needed capital. What might owners or potential owners want to know about their equity in a business?

Information about owners' investment and their claims can be found in the financial statements. It can help investors judge whether the company is making good use of invested capital and assess the timing and probability of future cash flows. In this chapter, we'll examine the information relating to owners' equity that is provided in financial statements, and we'll evaluate how

that information can be used by decision makers. After reading this chapter, you should be able to:

1. Distinguish different types of ownership interests and explain why these differences and the distinction between debt and equity are important to decision makers.

2. Describe the different types of stockholders' equity elements and explain how disclosure of these elements assists decision making.

3. Describe the different types of distributions to owners and explain why this information is important for decision makers.

4. Explain the purpose of the statement of stockholders' equity.

5. Discuss the summary measures related to stockholders' equity that are useful for decision making.

6. Describe what information about ownership interests can be found in the financial statements of unincorporated businesses and to what degree that information is useful for decisions.

UNDERSTANDING OWNERS' EQUITY

Information for Decisions

The amount of owners' equity reported in the balance sheet reflects the claim of owners on the assets of the company. This claim differs greatly from the claim of creditors. Understanding owners' claims and the distinction between owners' and creditors' claims can help answer questions such as these: How large a margin of safety is provided by the owners' equity of this company, and to what extent can I expect to recoup my investment if the company is liquidated? Where does my claim on the assets of the company rank in relation to the claims of others? In what way will future profits be shared among different ownership groups? What demands do various creditor and ownership groups place on the company's cash?

The **owners' equity** of a business reflects the owners' interest in that business and their claim on the assets. It represents the amount of the owners' direct investment in the business, together with the accumulated profits of the business that have been reinvested rather than being distributed to the owners. Both liabilities and owners' equity represent claims on the assets of a business. However, creditors' claims have priority over those of owners, and owners' equity is the residual amount remaining after deducting the creditors' claims on the assets. For corporations, owners' equity is referred to as **stockholders' equity**.

The claims of creditors on the assets of a business are for fixed or determinable amounts to be paid at specified times. In contrast, a business has no obligation to pay any specific amount to owners except in the event the business is liquidated. Even then, owners receive only what is left, if anything, after all creditor claims are satisfied.

Owners of a business are typically viewed as having a voice in the management of the business, and they share in the profits of the enterprise, if any. However, not all ownership interests have the same ability to influence management, and different ownership interests may share in profits differently. Thus, understanding the different types of ownership interests is important.

The distinction between debt and equity is important for at least two reasons. First, interest on debt is an expense and reduces income. Payments to owners are not expenses, but are

You Decide 12-1

IS IT DEBT OR EQUITY?

Lowndes Corporation raises additional capital by issuing $5 million of redeemable preferred stock. This stock pays a fixed 6 percent dividend, and holders will receive $100 per share if the corporation is liquidated. Although holders of this stock have preference over common stockholders in having their claims satisfied, the creditors have preference over them. Holders of the redeemable preferred do not have the right to vote in corporate matters unless their dividend is not paid, in which case they gain the right to vote on an equal footing with common shareholders. The corporation may retire the stock at any time starting five years from issue, and it must retire the stock no later than twenty years from the date of issue. Would you view this stock as debt or equity? Explain your position.

considered distributions of income. They do not reduce reported net income, only the amount of income retained in the entity. Second, debt financing is considered riskier than equity financing because interest and principal payments must be made at specific times. Thus, the balance sheet classification of a financing instrument can affect how risky a company appears. (See You Decide 12-1.)

STOCKHOLDERS' EQUITY: THE ELEMENTS OF CORPORATE OWNERSHIP

Information for Decisions

The reported stockholders' equity of a corporation includes information about the original investment of its stockholders and the accumulated profits that have not been distributed as dividends. Decision makers can use this information to determine how a company has financed the assets it owns and how its income has been allocated. This in- formation can help answer questions such as these: Are there any ownership claims on the company's income that must be satisfied before mine? If I invest in this company, to what extent will I be able to influence management? If the company is forced to liquidate, what claim on the assets will my ownership interest provide?

A number of different elements might appear in the stockholders' equity section of a corporation's balance sheet. These elements include (1) capital stock, (2) additional paid-in capital, (3) retained earnings, and (4) other items. The amounts reported in the capital stock accounts and in additional paid-in capital together are referred to as **contributed capital.**

CAPITAL STOCK

All owners of a corporation hold shares of **capital stock,** which represent their ownership interests. The specific rights of an owner depend on the type of stock held and the terms of the stock agreement.

Types of Capital Stock.   There are two major classes of capital stock, common and preferred. **Common stock** represents the true residual ownership interest of a corporation. Common stockholders get whatever assets are left in a liquidation after all other claims are satisfied. Similarly, all profits and losses of the corporation accrue to the common shareholders after the profit claims of others are satisfied. Some companies issue only common stock, which then might simply be called capital stock.

Common shareholders have the right to participate in the selection of management by voting for the corporation's board of directors. In addition, other important matters, such as the authorization of additional shares of stock, are voted on by common shareholders. To avoid having their interests in an enterprise diluted by the issuance of additional shares of stock, common shareholders have the right, referred to as the *preemptive right,* to purchase a proportionate amount of additional issuances of common stock before nonshareholders. However, many corporations withhold the preemptive right because of the complexities of applying it for some stock issuances.

Infrequently, some companies issue more than one class of common stock. A company might issue, for example, Class A and Class B common stock. In some cases, one class might be more like preferred stock, and in other cases, the two classes of stock might be identical except that one has the right to vote and the other does not, or transferability of one is restricted, or they share in earnings differently. For example, General Motors, Ralston Purina, USX, and U.S. West all have two or more classes of common stock outstanding tied to different areas of their operations. The existence of more than one class of common stock is a signal to closely examine the financial statement notes to determine the specific features of each.

Preferred stock differs from common stock in a number of ways, depending on the terms of the stock issue. Preferred stock usually has a stated dividend rate. This means that the company, while having no legal obligation to do so, is expected to pay a specific dividend each year. This dividend must be paid before any dividends are paid to the common stockholders. Further, if a company liquidates, all preferred shareholders must be paid the liquidation value of their stock before any amounts are distributed to common shareholders. Of course, all creditors' claims must be satisfied before preferred shareholders are paid. In nearly all cases, the right to vote is withheld from preferred shareholders.

Preferred stock is usually callable, meaning that the corporation may, at its option, purchase the stock back from stockholders at a set price. Thus, if the company no longer needs the financing provided by the preferred stock, or if the company is able to finance in a less costly manner, it might retire some or all of its preferred stock.

Exhibit 12–1 summarizes the characteristics of debt, preferred stock, and common stock, highlighting their differences. Debt presents the least risk to investors, but also usually provides the lowest return. Common stock involves the greatest risk, but also has the potential for the highest returns. Preferred stock falls between debt and common stock, both in terms of risk and potential return. Because preferred stock does not reflect a true residual ownership interest and often has features normally associated with debt, its nature is not clear-cut. Most preferred stock is reported in the owners' equity section of the balance sheet, but the terms of the stock should be examined closely to determine its characteristics.

In addition to shares of capital stock, some companies issue **stock options.** These options give the holder the right to purchase shares of stock at a specified *exercise price*. Sometimes these rights are represented by formal financial instruments referred to as **stock warrants**. Even if the exercise price of a stock option is higher than the current market price of the underlying stock, the option has value as long as its expiration date is sometime in the future. The holder of the option hopes that the stock price will rise above the exercise price before the option expires. Stock options often are issued as additional compensation to the officers or employees of a company, giving them an added interest in seeing the company prosper. Stock options are not always reported on the balance sheet, so a careful examination of the notes is needed to determine how many additional common shares might be issued if the options are exercised.

Analyzing Capital Stock.   When examining a company, decision makers typically want to assess the amount, timing, and likelihood of returns and the possibility of a loss of capital. Accordingly, decision makers look to the financial statements and the accompanying notes to evaluate each security the company has outstanding.

Capital stock is usually reported in the financial statements at its par or stated value. A stock's **par value** is an arbitrary amount assigned to each share of stock and provides no indication of the stock's actual value. Par value is only significant in that it indicates the amount that must be paid in to the corporation for the shares to be "fully paid." Shares issued at more than par value are issued at a **premium,** while shares issued at less than par value are issued at a **discount.**

If original purchasers of common stock buy at a discount, they may be held liable for the difference between what they pay and the par value of the stock if the corporation is liquidated and the assets are not sufficient to meet the liabilities. To avoid such liability, and because of state laws, most par-value common stock issued today is assigned a low par value, such as $1 or 50¢. Most states now prohibit the issuance of common stock at a discount.

TYPICAL CHARACTERISTICS OF DEBT, PREFERRED STOCK, AND COMMON STOCK

EXHIBIT 12-1

	Debt	**Preferred Stock**	**Common Stock**
Description	Debt reflects a legal obligation to pay a specific amount at a determinable future time.	Preferred stock reflects a claim for a specific amount that must be paid only if the company is liquidated or the stock is retired.	Common stock represents a claim on all assets remaining after other claims are satisfied.
Interest/Dividend amount and status	Interest is fixed or determinable in amount and becomes a legal obligation as it accrues.	Dividends usually are fixed in amount but become a legal obligation only after declared by the board of directors.	Dividends, if any, are paid at the discretion of the board of directors and become a legal obligation after declaration.
Tax status	Interest is tax-deductible by the company.	Dividends are not tax-deductible.	Dividends are not tax-deductible.
Profit sharing	Creditors do not share in profits.	Preferred stockholders usually share in profits only to the extent of the stated dividend.	All profits and losses accrue to common shareholders after payment of preferred dividends.
Claim priority	Creditors' claims have preference over all stockholders' claims.	Preferred stockholders' claims have preference over those of common stockholders but are subordinated to those of creditors.	Common stockholders' claims are subordinated to those of creditors and preferred stockholders.
Voting rights	Creditors do not have the right to vote.	Preferred stockholders usually do not have the right to vote because it is withheld by agreement.	Common stockholders usually hold sole voting rights.
Transferrability	Debt may or may not be transferrable.	Preferred stock is usually transferrable.	Common stock is usually transferrable.
Preemptive rights	Creditors have no rights relating to the acquisition of stock or additional debt instruments.	Preferred stockholders do not have the right to purchase newly issued shares of stock before nonowners.	Common stockholders have the right to purchase newly issued shares of common stock before nonowners unless the right is withheld.
Callability	Debt may be callable.	Preferred stock is usually callable	Common stock is not callable.

To protect creditors and others, most states have specific laws defining the amount of stockholders' equity that must be maintained in the corporation and not distributed to shareholders, referred to as **legal capital.** In most states, legal capital is equal to the par value of the common shares issued. If, for example, a company issued 1 million shares of $1 par common stock for $20 per share, the balance sheet would report common stock of $1 million. The other $19 per share paid by those acquiring the stock would be reported in the balance sheet as additional paid-in capital or premium on common stock.

Some companies issue common stock without a par value, referred to as *no-par stock.* This stock may have an arbitrary amount assigned to it as the **stated value,** which may then be considered the legal capital, and is the amount reported for common stock. Some common stock might have neither a par value nor a stated value, and is **true no-par stock.** For this type of stock, the full issue price of the stock may be considered legal capital, depending on state law, and is the amount reported for common stock. Because different states define legal capital differently, the concept is only of limited importance to decision makers.

Preferred stock is usually issued with a par value, which often is close to the actual issue price, and is the amount reported in the stockholders' equity section of the balance sheet. Because preferred stock has certain preferences over common stock, it usually appears before common stock in the balance sheet. Companies often receive authorization to issue preferred stock in the event management decides additional financing is needed, but many of these companies never issue the stock.

In addition to the amounts assigned to different classes of stock, the following are disclosed in the body of the balance sheet:

- The par or stated value per share
- The number of shares authorized—the number of shares that the stockholders and the state of incorporation have agreed may be issued
- The number of shares issued—the number of shares actually sold
- The number of shares outstanding—the number of shares currently held by stockholders; this number could be less than the number of shares issued if the corporation has repurchased and is holding some of its shares

In Practice 12-1

LUCENT TECHNOLOGIES INC.

Lucent Technologies is a relatively new company formed in 1996 from the systems and technology units that were formerly part of AT&T Corp., including the research and development capabilities of Bell Laboratories. The company is one of the world's leading designers, developers, and manufacturers of communications systems, software, and products. The Stockholders' Equity section of the company's 1998 balance sheet includes the following:

	(Dollars in Millions)
Preferred stock—par value $1 per share	
Authorized 250,000,000 shares	
Issued and outstanding shares: none	$ —
Common stock—par value $.01 per share	
Authorized shares: 3,000,000,000	
Issued and outstanding shares:	
1,316,394,169 at September 30, 1998	13
Additional paid-in capital	4,485
Retained earnings	1,364

ANALYSIS

The company has not issued any preferred stock, but it can if management chooses to do so. In addition, it can issue many more common shares than it has issued so far. The common stock was assigned a nominal par value of $.01 per share and was issued at an amount above the par value, as indicated by the additional paid-in capital. The company has been operating profitably and has not distributed all of its profits to stockholders, as indicated by the retained earnings balance. Thus, Lucent has flexibility for future financing and dividends. [www.lucent.com]

The number of shares authorized is important because, when compared with the number issued, it indicates the ability to obtain additional financing through further issuances of stock. The number of shares issued and outstanding indicates to investors the extent to which the company's profits must be shared with other stockholders; the more shares outstanding, the smaller the profits that accrue to each share. On the other hand, a large number of shares outstanding usually means a ready market exists for the transfer of shares.

ADDITIONAL PAID-IN CAPITAL

Additional paid-in capital is a stockholders' equity category that includes capital paid into or contributed to the corporation over and above the par or stated value of the capital stock. On original issue, the portion of the stock price that is not reported in the capital stock account is reported as additional paid-in or contributed capital.

Additional paid-in capital may come from other sources, as well. As a basic rule, an ownership transaction can never give rise to a gain or loss, regardless of the circumstances, and it can never directly affect reported income. For example, a company retiring some of its stock for less than the original issue price would report the difference as additional paid-in capital.

RETAINED EARNINGS

A corporation's accumulated profits that have not been distributed to owners are reported in the stockholders' equity section of the balance sheet as retained earnings. If retained earnings is negative, the balance is an accumulated deficit. Because distributions to owners are made from current and past profits, the amount of retained earnings is important for financial statement users. A small retained earnings balance may limit the company's ability to pay future dividends and may indicate that the company's reinvestment prospects are not favorable.

Although the balance sheet reports the amount of retained earnings at the end of the period, a company's retained earnings statement or its statement of changes in stockholders' equity provides additional information by detailing the items that affected retained earnings during the period. Of course, the two most important items affecting retained earnings are the current income or loss and distributions of income to owners. Recall that at the end of an accounting period, a company's temporary accounts are closed to retained earnings. These temporary accounts include all revenue and expense accounts, which combine to result in the company's net income for the period. Thus, net income increases retained earnings, and a net loss decreases retained earnings. Another temporary account that is closed is the dividends declared account. This account is a temporary account, but is not included in the computation of net income. It is closed to retained earnings directly, reducing the balance of that account. Thus, Lucent Technologies reported the changes in its retained earnings as follows:

Balance at beginning of period	$ 595 (in millions)
Net income	970
Dividends declared	(201)
BALANCE AT THE END OF PERIOD	$1,364

The ending amount is then reported as retained earnings in the balance sheet.

Bond indentures, other contractual arrangements, and state laws sometimes place potential restrictions on retained earnings or the payment of dividends. Typically, these provisions have to do with assuring that creditors' claims are met before cash is distributed to owners. Restrictions on retained earnings and dividends are usually disclosed in notes to the financial statements.

OTHER STOCKHOLDERS' EQUITY ELEMENTS

Although capital stock and retained earnings appear in the balance sheets of all for-profit corporations, several other equity items are also sometimes included. For example, we saw in Chapter 8 that the FASB requires investments in available-for-sale securities to be revalued to market value periodically. Rather than including the unrealized gains and losses on revaluation in net income, however, companies must report them as an element of other comprehensive income. The cumulative amount of other comprehensive income for the current and prior years is reported in the stockholders' equity section of the balance sheet. A similar treatment is accorded certain types of adjustments resulting from foreign currency fluctuations, as we will discuss in Chapter 16. Other items may relate to some forms of employee compensation, such as employee stock ownership plans (ESOPs). These additional elements are generally described in the notes to the financial statements, although the description may be complex and difficult to decipher.

ACCOUNTING FOR CAPITAL STOCK

Information for Decisions

Information about the issue, reacquisition, and retirement of capital stock is reported by corporations in accordance with state laws and other regulations. By understanding how this information is reported, financial statement users can evaluate changes in ownership interests and answer questions such as these: How will my share of the company's earnings be affected by additional stock issued during the year? How will the company satisfy the need for additional shares of stock if the employees exercise all of their stock options? Does the company have sufficient flexibility if it wishes to issue additional shares of stock quickly?

Accounting and reporting for stockholders' equity has evolved from various state laws, pronouncements of authoritative bodies, and convention. We have seen that the capital stock account reflects the par or stated value of the shares issued, retained earnings shows the cumulative past profits of the company not distributed to owners, and additional paid-in capital arises from the issuance of capital stock in excess of its par or stated value or from other sources of capital contributed to the company. To better understand the information in the stockholders' equity section of the balance sheet, let's look at each of the elements in more detail, starting with capital stock.

ISSUANCE OF STOCK

When stock is issued for cash, the company's cash increases by the amount of the issue proceeds, less any costs of issuance. The capital stock account increases by the total par or stated value of the shares issued, and additional paid-in capital increases by the excess of the issue price over the par or stated value, less the costs of issue. If the stock issued is true no-par stock, all of the proceeds, less issue costs, are reported in the capital stock account, and no additional paid-in capital from the issue is reported.

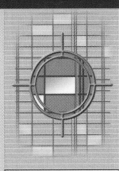

A CLOSER LOOK AT

ISSUING CAPITAL STOCK

Zambor Corporation's initial charter authorizes the issuance of 5,000,000 shares of $5-par common stock. The company issues 1,000,000 shares of its common stock for $20 per share. Stock registration fees and fees charged by an investment banking firm for marketing the issue total $2,000,000. Zambor's cash increases by $18,000,000 [($20 × 1,000,000) − $2,000,000], and the following is reported in the stockholders' equity section of its balance sheet:

Common stock ($5 par; 5,000,000 shares authorized;
   1,000,000 shares issued and outstanding) $ 5,000,000
Additional Paid-in Capital   13,000,000

If the stock had been true no-par stock, the full $18,000,000 would have been reported in the capital stock account.

Balance Sheet Effects	
Assets	+ 18,000,000
Owners'	
Equity	+ 18,000,000

Preferred stock is reported in the same way as common stock, but it usually is listed first in the stockholders' equity section of the balance sheet. If stock is issued for an asset other than cash, both the asset received and the stock issued are recorded at the value of the asset received or the value of the stock issued, whichever is more clearly determinable.

RETIREMENT OF STOCK

Companies may retire outstanding shares of their stock for a number of reasons. For example, a company may no longer need the financing provided by a preferred stock issue, and the entire issue may be called. In other cases, a company may have excess cash and use it to boost the value of its common stock by buying back and retiring some of the shares, thus giving each remaining share a larger portion of the enterprise. In any case, when a corporation retires shares of its stock, the capital stock account is reduced by the amount originally recorded in the account for those shares, usually the par or stated value. Amounts paid to retire the shares over and above the par or stated value are deducted from additional paid-in capital. If additional paid-in capital is insufficient, retained earnings is reduced. The reduction in retained earnings is considered a distribution of past earnings to retiring stockholders.

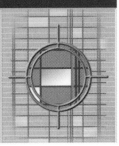

A CLOSER LOOK AT

STOCK RETIREMENT

The capital stock reported in Zambor Corporation's balance sheet appears as follows:

Common Stock ($5 par; 5,000,000 shares authorized;
   1,000,000 shares issued and outstanding) $ 5,000,000
Additional Paid-in Capital   13,000,000

Balance Sheet Effects	
Assets	− 6,000,000
Owners' Equity	− 6,000,000

A number of years after original issue, Zambor purchases 200,000 of its common shares in the open market for $30 per share, a total of $6,000,000, and retires the shares. The total par value of its shares outstanding is reduced by $1,000,000 ($5 × 200,000). The remaining $5,000,000 [($30 − $5) × 200,000] paid to retire the shares is deducted from additional paid-in capital, leaving Zambor with the following reported capital stock:

Common Stock ($5 par; 5,000,000 shares authorized; 800,000 shares issued and outstanding)	$4,000,000
Additional Paid-in Capital	8,000,000

While the number of shares issued and outstanding decreases by the number of shares retired, the original authorization remains unchanged.

TREASURY STOCK TRANSACTIONS

When a company reacquires its own shares, management may want to use those shares again in the future. Therefore, instead of retiring and canceling the shares, management might hold them in its treasury until needed. Shares of a company's own stock held by the company are referred to as **treasury stock**. These shares are reported as issued, but are not outstanding. The cost incurred by the company to acquire treasury stock is usually reported at the bottom of the stockholders' equity section of the balance sheet as a reduction in stockholders' equity.

When treasury shares are resold, the cost of the shares is removed from the company's books and the proceeds received are recorded. What happens if the shares are sold for more or less than their cost? Does the company recognized a gain or loss? No. Remember that gains and losses are never recognized on capital transactions. Instead, the difference between the sale price and the cost of the treasury shares changes additional paid-in capital. If the shares are sold for more than the cost to reacquire them, the difference is added to additional paid-in capital. If the shares are sold for less than their cost, the difference reduces aditional paid-in capital, or retained earnings if additional paid-in capital is insufficient.

In Practice 12-2

SBC'S TREASURY STOCK

SBC Communications reports 7,000,000,000 shares authorized of its $1 par common stock, with 1,984,141,868 shares issued as of December 31, 1998. Next to the last item reported in SBC's shareowners' equity is a deduction for $882 million, the cost of the 28,217,018 common shares held in its treasury.

ANALYSIS

SBC's treasury stock is considered issued but is not outstanding, and, accordingly, shareholders' equity, and the margin of safety it provides, is reduced. However, the treasury shares provide flexibility because they are available to be resold at any time or used for other purposes, such as business combinations or employee compensation. [www.sbc.com]

Although treasury stock reduces owners' equity, it gives the company flexibility because the shares can be resold, allowing the company to raise additional cash quickly. Treasury shares also can be used for other purposes, such as acquiring another business. The number of treasury shares held should be evaluated in light of the company's needs for additional shares. For example, stock options issued to employees might require a large number of shares if exercised.

OTHER CONTRIBUTED CAPITAL

Although contributed capital comes most frequently from the issuance of capital stock, it also may come from other sources. We have seen, for example, that stock retirements may result in some of the capital originally contributed being left in the corporation when stockholders give up their ownership interests. We have seen, too, that treasury stock transactions may affect additional paid-in capital. Additional contributed capital also may arise if, for example, a company has stock options outstanding that are reported in the stockholders' equity section of its balance sheet, and those stock options expire without being exercised, the amount assigned to those options is reclassified as additional contributed capital.

ACCOUNTING FOR DIVIDENDS

Information for Decisions

Dividends are distributions of profits to owners (stockholders) of the business. Examining a company's dividend history and management's discussion of dividend policy can help investors address questions such as these: Can I expect to receive regular cash flows from this company in the form of dividends? What are the prospects for this company reducing or eliminating its dividend? If the company is not currently paying a dividend, is it because the company is in financial difficulty or because it has such profitable opportunities for future growth that it needs to reinvest all earnings? How might the company's future dividends affect the price of my stock?

Investors purchase a company's stock because they expect to receive future cash flows from the investment, either through the sale of the stock or in the form of cash distributions from the company. Dividends are distributions of corporate earnings and reduce retained earnings.[2] The payment or issuance of dividends normally requires (1) sufficient retained earnings and (2) a declaration by the company's board of directors. Some states permit the payment of dividends out of the current year's earnings even if the retained earnings balance is insufficient. Distributions are usually made in cash, but also might be made using other assets or the company's own stock.

CASH DIVIDENDS

Dividends may be paid at any time during the year, but companies that pay dividends usually do so quarterly. Companies wishing to pay cash dividends must plan carefully to have suffi-

---

[2]Some dividends represent a return of capital rather than a distribution of income and are referred to as *liquidating dividends*. These types of dividends occur infrequently in relation to distributions of income.

cient cash on hand to make the payments. The process of distributing a cash dividend to shareholders is illustrated in Exhibit 12–2. Important dates relating to dividend distributions are as follows:

- **Declaration date**—the date the company's board of directors takes a formal action and declares a dividend. Once a dividend is declared, the company is legally obligated to pay the dividend. The dividend is recorded on the books of the company at the time of declaration by reducing retained earnings through the use of the temporary account "Dividends Declared." A current liability is established for the amount to be paid. The declaration always specifies the stock on which the dividend is declared, the amount of the dividend per share, the date on which the list of owners receiving the dividend will be compiled, and the date of payment.

- **Ex-dividend date**—the date the stock trades without the right to the latest dividend. Because several days are required to complete the processing of ownership transfers, the ex-dividend date usually falls about three days before the list of stockholders is prepared for dividend distribution. The company does nothing on this date, but it is important to those contemplating the sale or purchase of the stock. Published stock price reports typically note (usually with an X) when a stock is selling ex-dividend.

- **Record date**—the date on which the corporation compiles, from its stockholder records at that date, a list of those who will receive the latest dividend.

- **Payment date**—the date on which dividend checks are issued to the stockholders of record on the record date. Payment is usually made one to two months after declaration.

Preferred stocks typically have a fixed dividend, stated as a dollar amount per share or as a percentage of the par value. For example, a 10 percent preferred stock with a par value of $100 would be expected to pay a dividend of $10 per year. However, the company has no legal obligation to pay a dividend until a declaration is made by the board of directors. The board may choose to pass (not pay) the preferred dividend, but then no dividend may be paid to common shareholders either. With *cumulative preferred stock,* no future common dividends may be declared until all passed preferred dividends are paid. The cumulative feature is sometimes withheld from preferred stockholders, and then passed dividends from prior years are lost. Dividends that have not been declared on cumulative preferred stock are said to be "in arrears" and must be disclosed in the notes to the financial statements. Having dividends in arrears is usually a sign of financial distress, and common stockholders certainly need to assess their chances for future dividends.

A few preferred stocks not only have a fixed dividend rate, but they also share earnings distributions in some manner with common shareholders. This type of stock is called *participating preferred stock.* Examining the financial statements and related notes is extremely important to determine how income is distributed because participation features can significantly affect the amount of income available for the different classes of owners.

EXHIBIT 12-2 **DISTRIBUTION OF A CASH DIVIDEND**

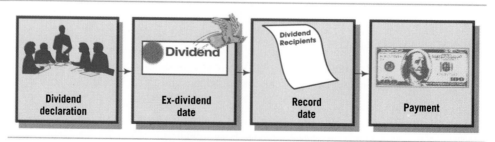

Common dividends are not fixed in amount and may be declared for any legal amount the board of directors chooses. Many companies have established dividend policies under which they declare dividends every quarter and attempt never to pay a lower dividend than in the previous quarter.

In Practice 12-3

IBM AND DIVIDENDS

"Many shareholders attending IBM's annual meeting . . . groaned when they heard that the board had voted not to raise the quarterly dividend even though profits . . . had surged. . . . Big Blue's chairman, Louis Gerstner, tried to console investors by pointing out that IBM's stock price doubled in two years to over $90. . . . Gerstner's argument certainly makes sense from a total-return standpoint—and it's one that a number of corporations are making. Dividends are taxed like ordinary income. For many investors, the levy on capital gains not only is lower but doesn't have to be paid until stocks are sold. . . . Instead of adding to dividend payouts, many corporations have chosen to use their increased cash flow to reduce debt, repair tattered balance sheets, upgrade machinery, or simply add to retained earnings for that next rainy day. Many have also embarked on massive stock-repurchase programs to enhance shareholder value."[3]

ANALYSIS

Many shareholders had expected IBM to increase its dividend because of increased earnings. They were disappointed because they were expecting an increase in current cash flows from their stock. Shareholders could increase their current cash flows, but they would have to sell some of their stock to do so. On the other hand, the tax treatment of stock sales is typically more favorable than that of dividends. IBM, and many other corporations, are using cash internally that might otherwise be used for current dividends, with the expectation that stockholders will benefit in the long-run. [www.ibm.com]

Some companies do not pay cash dividends, usually because they are doing very well or very poorly. Companies that are expanding and increasing profits rapidly, called growth companies, often prefer to reinvest earnings and preserve their cash for internal use. Companies that are in financial difficulty often do not have sufficient cash to pay dividends and may need to preserve their cash just to survive. The ability of a company to pay cash dividends currently or in the future is an important consideration in valuing a company because cash flows are important to investors. One measure that is used over time to indicate a company's inclination toward paying dividends is the **dividend payout,** equal to dividends as a percentage of net income. Another measure of importance to investors who desire current cash inflows is the **dividend yield,** which is equal to the annual dividend divided by the stock's price per share.

[3]Excerpts from Jack Egan, "Does Stinginess Pay Dividends?" *U.S. News & World Report* (May 22, 1995), p. 69.

In Practice 12-4

AMEREN'S DIVIDEND POLICY AND PAYOUT

Ameren Corporation is a holding company that was created in December 1997 to combine Union Electric Company, Missouri's largest electric utility, and CIPSCO Incorporated (Central Illinois Public Service Company). The combined dividends of Union Electric and Central Illinois Public Service in 1997 totaled 99 percent of their 1997 combined net income, and 1998 dividends of the combined company totaled 90 percent of Ameren's 1998 net income. However, dividends were less than 50 percent of the net cash provided from operations. In its annual report, Ameren stated the following:

The Board of Directors does not set specific targets or payout parameters for dividend payments; however, the Board considers various issues including the Company's historic earnings and cash flow; projected earnings, cash flow and potential cash flow requirements; dividend payout rates at other utilities; return on investments with similar risk characteristics; and overall business considerations.

ANALYSIS

As with many utilities, Ameren pays out a high percentage of its income as dividends. Although the company states that it does not set specific targets for dividends, the predecessor company, Union Electric, had established a clear pattern of increasing its common dividend each year for many years. However, recent pressure on earnings has made continuing the rate of increase difficult. Investors could be very disappointed if Ameren were not to resume Union Electric's rate of dividend growth, and particularly if the company were to reduce its dividends. [www.ameren.com]

STOCK DIVIDENDS AND SPLITS

Corporations sometimes declare dividends on their common stock payable in shares of the same stock. These dividends are called **stock dividends.** Whether these dividends represent distributions of earnings, and whether stockholders receive anything of value with a stock dividend, is subject to debate.

Stock dividends are proportional distributions of additional shares, with no additional resources being received by the company. For example, if a company had 1,000,000 shares of common stock outstanding and declared a 10 percent stock dividend, it would issue 100,000 shares of common stock as a dividend, resulting in 1,100,000 total shares outstanding. If an owner held 10,000 shares prior to the dividend, that owner would receive 1,000 additional shares as a dividend, resulting in total holdings of 11,000 shares. However, that individual's ownership was 1 percent before the dividend and 1 percent after the dividend. If the owner has the same percentage ownership before and after the dividend, and the total value of the company has not changed, can the stockholder have received anything of value?

When a stock dividend is declared, the issuer usually recognizes it at the fair value of the shares issued, and this amount is reported as a deduction in the retained earnings statement. This amount of retained earnings is transferred to contributed capital, resulting in a permanent reinvestment of past earnings. The issuance of stock is recorded as if the dividend had been paid in cash and all stockholders used the cash to purchase additional shares.

A CLOSER LOOK AT

STOCK DIVIDENDS

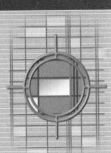

Fallbrook's stockholders' equity appears as follows:

Common Stock ($5 par; 5,000,000 shares authorized;	
1,000,000 shares issued and outstanding)	$ 5,000,000
Additional Paid-in Capital	13,000,000
Retained Earnings	9,000,000
Total	$27,000,000

The company declares a 5 percent stock dividend. On the date of declaration, its stock is selling for $30 per share. Thus, the company issues 50,000 (1,000,000 × .05) additional shares with a total value of $1,500,000 ($30 × 50,000). After distribution of the stock dividend, Fallbrook's stockholders' equity appears as follows:

Common Stock ($5 par; 5,000,000 shares authorized;	
1,050,000 shares issued and outstanding)	$ 5,250,000
Additional Paid-in Capital	14,250,000
Retained Earnings	7,500,000
Total	$27,000,000

The common stock account increased by the $250,000 par value of the 50,000 shares issued, and additional paid-in capital increased by the $1,250,000 [($30 − $5) × 50,000] excess of the fair value over the par value of the shares. Retained earnings decreased by the amount of the dividend, which was equal to the $1,500,000 value of the shares issued. The balances of individual stockholders' equity accounts changed, but total stockholders' equity remained the same. The effect of a stock dividend is to reduce the amount of retained earnings available for future dividends and to increase contributed capital.

Stock dividends are presumed to make stockholders feel as if they have gotten something, even though it is only paper. Management may use stock dividends to give something to stockholders while preserving the company's cash. Also, there is some evidence that management may use stock dividends as an indication of good news for the future of the company.

A **stock split** occurs when all of a company's common stock is replaced with some multiple of the shares previously outstanding, usually with a commensurate reduction in the par value. In a 2-for-1 split, for example, two shares are issued for each share previously outstanding, and the par value of each share is cut in half. Thus, the total par value of the shares outstanding remains the same; twice as many shares as before, each with half the par value, are outstanding following the split. Stock splits differ from stock dividends in that no amount of retained earnings is transferred to the capital stock accounts. All stockholders' equity accounts maintain the same balances after a stock split.

The rationale for stock splits is generally that shares of publicly traded stock receive wider distribution if they sell within a particular price range, say $5 to $99. At higher prices, individuals may be less inclined to buy shares. Doubling or tripling the number of shares outstanding, with a proportionate drop in the ownership interest represented by each share, reduces the price per share proportionally. Similarly, shares selling for very low prices are often considered speculative, and companies with low-price shares may undertake "reverse splits" to reduce the number of shares outstanding and increase the price per share. Realistically, the effect of a stock split on the distribution of a company's stock is probably marginal, given the large number of shares traded by institutions.

Following a stock dividend or stock split, comparative financial information relating to periods prior to the dividend or split is adjusted for the differing number of shares. Per-share information is restated as if the stock dividend or split had occurred prior to the earliest period reported.

A CLOSER LOOK AT

RESTATEMENT FOLLOWING A STOCK SPLIT

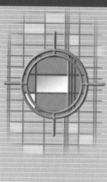

Ralph Company reported earnings per common share for 1999 and 2000 of $4.00 and $4.50, respectively. On January 2, 2001, Ralph effected a 2-for-1 stock split. Based on the new number of shares outstanding, Ralph reports earnings of $3.00 per share for 2001. In a comparative presentation, Ralph would restate the earnings-per-share figures for 1999 and 2000 to give effect to the stock split, as follows:

1999	2000	2001
$2.00	$2.25	$3.00

The stock split results in no change of economic substance. Although twice as many shares are outstanding following the split, each share exerts a claim only half as great as before the split. Restating the prior per-share figures allows financial statement users to examine trends based on consistent information.

ACCOUNTING FOR STOCKHOLDERS' EQUITY ILLUSTRATED

So that you clearly understand how the numbers reported in the stockholders' equity section of the balance sheet arise and what they mean, let's take a closer look at the effects of some common equity transactions on the accounts and trace them through to the financial statements:

2000

(1) January 2: Microtech, a new company, is incorporated and authorized to issue 2,000,000 shares of $1 par common stock. The company sells 500,000 shares to the public through an underwriter, the investment banking firm of Silverman, Sacks, Inc. The underwriter sells the shares to the public and keeps as its fee the difference between what the shares are sold for and the agreed remittance of $5,000,000, or $10 per share, to Microtech.

Balance Sheet Effects	
Assets	+ 5,000,000
Owners'	
Equity	+ 5,000,000

Financial Statement Effects The company's cash increases by $5,000,000, as does its stockholders' equity. The $500,000 ($1 × 500,000 shares) par value of the common stock issued is reported as Common Stock in the company's balance sheet, and the $4,500,000 of issue proceeds in excess of the par value is reported as Additional Paid-in Capital.

Analysis Ownership interests are sold to the public. Legal capital, reflected in the Common Stock account, is equal to the par value of $1 per share. Common Stock and Additional Paid-in Capital both are considered contributed capital accounts and together reflect the owners' direct capital investment in Microtech through the purchase of its stock.

(2) June 30: The common shareholders of Microtech authorize the issuance of 100,000 shares of $25 par preferred stock. No shares are issued.

Financial Statement Effects The financial statements are unaffected by the authorization of shares of stock, except that the number of shares authorized must be disclosed in the balance sheet or related notes.

Analysis Because no shares are issued, the accounts are not affected. The management of Microtech now has the flexibility to raise additional capital when needed and when market conditions are favorable.

---

(3) December 31: For the year, Microtech recognizes revenues of $850,000 and expenses of $530,000. It closes the temporary accounts to Retained Earnings.

Financial Statement Effects As Microtech recognizes revenues throughout the year, its net assets and revenues increase, thus increasing income. As expenses are recognized, the company's liabilities increase or its net assets decrease and expenses increase, thus decreasing income. Because the company is profitable, its owners' equity increases by the $320,000 amount of its net income, the difference between its revenue and expenses; that increase is reflected in Retained Earnings when the temporary revenue and expense accounts are closed into that account.

Income Statement Effects	
Revenues	+ 850,000
Expenses	+ 530,000
Net Income	+ 320,000

Balance Sheet Effects	
Net Assets	+ 850,000
Net Assets	− 530,000
Owners' Equity	+ 320,000

Analysis The difference between Microtech's revenues and expenses represents net income for the year of $320,000. Because there was no balance in Retained Earnings at the beginning of the period and no dividends were declared during the period, the ending balance of Retained Earnings is equal to the net income. The stockholders' equity section of Microtech's balance sheet at year-end appears in Exhibit 12–3.

---

(4) March 1: Microtech declares and issues a 2 percent stock dividend. Microtech's stock is trading at $12 a share.

Financial Statement Effects Retained Earnings is reduced by the $120,000 ($12 × 10,000 shares) amount of the stock dividend, which is the fair value of the stock issued. However, contributed capital is increased by the same amount. Thus, total stockholders' equity in the balance sheet remains unchanged. The $120,000 added to contributed capital is divided between Common Stock, which is increased by the $10,000 par value of the dividend shares issued, and Additional Paid-in Capital. The amount of the stock dividend is reported as a reduction in Retained Earnings in the statement of changes in stockholders' equity.

Balance Sheet Effects	
Owners' Equity	− 120,000
Owners' Equity	+ 120,000

Analysis Microtech issues 10,000 shares of stock as a 2 percent proportionate distribution to the current holders of the company's 500,000 shares. The $12 per share fair value of the stock is moved from Retained Earnings to the contributed capital accounts Common Stock and Additional Paid-in Capital, resulting in a permanent capitalization of retained earnings.

MICROTECH'S STOCKHOLDERS' EQUITY, DECEMBER 31, 2000 EXHIBIT 12-3

MICROTECH CORPORATION
STATEMENT OF FINANCIAL POSITION
DECEMBER 31, 2000

Stockholders' Equity:	
Preferred stock ($25 par; 100,000 shares authorized, no shares issued)	
Common stock ($1 par; 2,000,000 shares authorized, 500,000 shares issued and outstanding)	$ 500,000
Additional paid-in capital—Common	4,500,000
Retained earnings	320,000
Total stockholders' equity	$5,320,000

(5) May 10: Microtech purchases 20,000 shares of its common stock in the market for $11 per share and holds the shares in its treasury.

Balance Sheet Effects	
Assets	− 220,000
Owners' Equity	− 220,000

Financial Statement Effects   Microtech's cash and stockholders' equity both decrease by the $220,000 cost of the treasury stock acquired. Treasury Stock is reported in Microtech's balance sheet as a deduction from stockholders' equity, and the number of shares reported as outstanding decreases by 20,000.

Analysis   Because the shares of stock that are reacquired are not canceled, Common Stock is not reduced. However, total stockholders' equity is reduced by the amount Microtech pays to reacquire its shares, thus decreasing the margin of safety afforded creditors.

(6) July 7: Microtech resells 12,000 shares of its treasury stock for $13 per share.

Balance Sheet Effects	
Assets	+ 156,000
Owners' Equity	+ 156,000

Financial Statement Effects   Microtech's cash and stockholders' equity both increase by the $156,000 ($13 × 12,000 shares) received from the resale of the treasury shares. The increase in stockholders' equity results from the decrease in the Treasury Stock account, a negative stockholders' equity element, for the original $132,000 ($11 × 12,000 shares) cost of the treasury stock when repurchased. Also, Additional Paid-in Capital is increased by the $2 per share excess of the stock's sale price over its cost, a total of $24,000.

Analysis   The $11 cost of the 12,000 treasury shares sold is removed from the Treasury Stock account. Because the transaction is viewed as a capital transaction with owners, no gain or loss can be recognized. The $2 excess of the sale price over the cost of the shares is considered additional capital contributed to the company.

(7) November 15: Microtech splits its stock 2 for 1 and reduces the par value of each share to $.50.

Balance Sheet Effects	
Owners' Equity	− 510,000
Owners' Equity	+ 510,000

Financial Statement Effects   The financial statements are essentially unaffected. The $1 par common stock is replaced with twice as many shares of $.50 par stock, resulting in the Common Stock balance remaining at $510,000.

Analysis   In the 2-for-1 split, Microtech's 510,000 shares of common stock are exchanged for 1,020,000. The par value of each new share is half the old par value, resulting in the same total par value for the shares reported as issued. Because the dollar amount of the common stock does not change, Microtech need only note the split in the accounting records with a memo, or it can make a formal entry to reflect the replacement of the $1 par stock with $.50 par stock. Subsequent to the split, prior-period financial statements must be restated as if the split had occurred prior to the earliest period reported so that a consistent picture is presented from period to period.

(8) November 20: Microtech's board of directors declares a cash dividend of $.10 per common share, payable December 28, to shareholders of record December 10.

Balance Sheet Effects	
Liabilities	+ 100,400
Owners' Equity	− 100,400

Financial Statement Effects   With the declaration (but not payment) of a dividend, Microtech's stockholders' equity decreases and its liabilities increase by the amount of the dividend, $100,400 ($.10 × 1,004,000 shares). Retained Earnings decreases, usually through a temporary Cash Dividends Declared account that is used to keep track of dividends during the period and is closed into Retained Earnings at the end of the period. Thus, Retained Earnings decreases and a liability, Dividends Payable, increases by $100,400.

Analysis   The total number of common shares outstanding is 1,004,000 because 1,020,000 shares have been issued but 16,000 (8,000 × 2) are still in the treasury. Microtech's total cash dividend at $.10 per share is $100,400. Once the board of directors declares a cash dividend, the company has a legal obligation to pay it. Hence, a current liability is established until payment is made. The important event with regard to cash dividends is the declaration rather than the payment. The declaration has the effect of reducing Retained Earnings and establishing a liability.

(9) December 28:   The cash dividend previously declared is paid.

Financial Statement Effects   When the dividend is paid, both cash and liabilities are reduced.

Analysis   The obligation to pay the dividend, established at the date the dividend was declared, is eliminated by the payment of cash.

Balance Sheet Effects	
Assets	− 100,400
Liabilities	− 100,400

(10) December 31:   For the year, Microtech recognizes revenues of $994,000 and expenses of $640,000. It closes the temporary accounts to Retained Earnings.

Financial Statement Effects   As Microtech recognizes revenues throughout the year, its net assets and revenues increase, thus increasing income. As expenses are recognized, the company's liabilities increase or its net assets decrease and expenses increase, thus decreasing income. Because the company is profitable, its owners' equity increases by the $354,000 amount of its net income, the difference between its revenue and expenses; this increase is reflected in Retained Earnings when the temporary revenue and expense accounts are closed into that account. Closing the temporary dividend accounts, Cash Dividends Declared (#8) and Stock Dividends Declared (#4), reduces Retained Earnings by $100,400 and $120,000, respectively. The dividends represent distributions of income and do not affect the computation of net income. Thus, the net change in Retained Earnings resulting from income and the distribution of a portion of that income is $133,600 ($354,000 − $100,400 − $120,000).

Analysis   The company is in business to earn a profit and provide a return to the owners. The amount of the company's profit that is not distributed to the owners increases their investment in the business. The Retained Earnings balance reflects all past undistributed profits of the company and indicates the amount of the company's capital coming from the owners' reinvestment of their profits. Microtech's statement of changes in retained earnings for 2001 and the stockholders' equity section of its balance sheet at December 31, 2001, are shown in Exhibit 12–4.

Income Statement Effects	
Revenues	+ 994,000
Expenses	+ 640,000
Net Income	+ 354,000

Balance Sheet Effects	
Net Assets	+ 994,000
Net Assets	− 640,000
Owners' Equity	+ 354,000

Journal Entries, 2000

January 2
(1)	Cash		5,000,000	
		Common Stock—$1.00 par value		500,000
		Additional Paid-in Capital—Common		4,500,000

June 30
(2)   No entry at time of authorization

December 31
(3)	Assets		850,000	
		Revenues		850,000
	Expenses		530,000	
		Liabilities or Assets		530,000
	Revenues		850,000	
		Expenses		530,000
		Retained Earnings		320,000

EXHIBIT 12-4 **MICROTECH'S CHANGES IN RETAINED EARNINGS FOR 2001 AND STOCKHOLDERS' EQUITY AT DECEMBER 31, 2001**

MICROTECH CORPORATION STATEMENT OF CHANGES IN RETAINED EARNINGS 2001	
Retained earnings, January 1	$ 320,000
Net income	354,000
Less:	
Cash dividends declared	(100,400)
Stock dividends declared	(120,000)
Retained earnings, December 31	$ 453,600

MICROTECH CORPORATION STATEMENT OF FINANCIAL POSITION DECEMBER 31, 2001	
Stockholders' Equity:	
Preferred stock ($25 par; 100,000 shares authorized, no shares issued)	
Common stock ($.50 par; 2,000,000 shares authorized, 1,020,000 shares issued; 1,004,000 shares outstanding)	$ 510,000
Additional paid-in capital—Common	4,610,000
Additional paid-in capital—Treasury Stock	24,000
Retained earnings	453,600
	$5,597,600
Less treasury stock (16,000 shares, at cost)	(88,000)
Total stockholders' equity	$5,509,600

Journal Entries, 2001

March 1

(4)	Stock Dividends Declared	120,000	
	Common Stock—$1.00 par value		10,000
	Additional Paid-in Capital—Common		110,000

May 10

(5)	Treasury Stock	220,000	
	Cash		220,000

July 7

(6)	Cash	156,000	
	Treasury Stock		132,000
	Additional Paid-in Capital—Treasury Stock		24,000

November 15

(7)	Common Stock—$1.00 par value	510,000	
	Common Stock—$.50 par value		510,000

November 20

(8)	Cash Dividends Declared	100,400	
	Dividends Payable		100,400

December 28

(9)	Dividends Payable	100,400	
	Cash		100,400

December 31

(10)	Assets	994,000	
	Revenues		994,000
	Expenses	640,000	
	Liabilities or Assets		640,000
	Revenues	994,000	
	Expenses		640,000
	Retained Earnings		354,000
	Retained Earnings	220,400	
	Cash Dividends Declared		100,400
	Stock Dividends Declared		120,000

THE STATEMENT OF STOCKHOLDERS' EQUITY

Information for Decisions

The statement of changes in stockholders' equity reports any change in a corporation's stockholders' equity accounts. Owners and potential owners might examine this statement to answer questions such as these: How did the dividends declared during the period compare with earnings? To what extent did the claims of different classes of owners on the company's assets change during the period?

Companies are required to disclose the changes in their stockholders' equity accounts that occur during the period. Some companies report a statement of changes in retained earnings as a basic financial statement and changes in the other stockholders' equity accounts in notes to the financial statements. Most companies, however, include all changes in stockholders' equity in the same financial statement, the **statement of stockholders' equity.**

A statement of stockholders' equity simply shows how each of the beginning balances of a company's stockholders' equity accounts changed to become the ending balances. For example, the comparative Consolidated Statements of Stockholders' Equity for Emerson Electric Co., shown in Exhibit 12–5, include the information reported in a retained earnings statement, as well as changes detailed for all other stockholders' equity accounts. Because stockholders' equity is an important source of financing for the corporation, and because different elements of stockholders' equity reflect different types of claims, an understanding of changes in stockholders' equity is important for anyone attempting to analyze a company.

EXHIBIT 12-5 **EMERSON ELECTRIC'S STATEMENT OF STOCKHOLDERS' EQUITY**

CONSOLIDATED STATEMENTS OF STOCKHOLDERS' EQUITY
EMERSON ELECTRIC CO. AND SUBSIDIARIES
YEARS ENDED SEPTEMBER 30
(DOLLARS IN MILLIONS EXCEPT PER SHARE AMOUNTS)

	1998	1997	1996
Common stock	$ 238.3	$ 238.3	$ 238.3
Additional paid-in capital			
Beginning balance	3.3	12.3	15.0
Stock plans	(43.4)	(2.8)	.1
Treasury stock issued for acquisitions and other	68.0	(6.2)	(2.8)
Ending balance	27.9	3.3	12.3
Retained earnings			
Beginning balance	6,348.9	5,707.7	5,128.3
Net earnings	1,228.6	1,121.9	1,018.5
Cash dividends (per share: 1998, $1.18;			
1997, $1.08; 1996, $.98)	(521.0)	(480.7)	(439.1)
Ending balance	7,056.5	6,348.9	5,707.7
Cumulative translation adjustments			
Beginning balance	(205.9)	(29.2)	17.0
Translation adjustments	(30.3)	(176.7)	(46.2)
Ending balance	(236.2)	(205.9)	(29.2)
Treasury stock			
Beginning balance	(963.9)	(575.7)	(527.8)
Acquired	(498.4)	(427.2)	(99.5)
Issued under stock plans	108.5	18.3	14.2
Issued for acquisitions and other	70.6	20.7	37.4
Ending balance	(1,283.2)	(963.9)	(575.7)
Total stockholders' equity	$5,803.3	$5,420.7	$5,353.4

ANALYZING STOCKHOLDERS' EQUITY

Information for Decisions

Reported stockholders' equity can provide important information to owners or those considering becoming owners. This information can help them assess risk and project the future cash flows they can expect from their investment. It can help answer questions such as these: To what extent will the company's income be available to pay dividends on the common stock, and how likely is the company to maintain or increase its common dividend? If the company is forced to liquidate, what claims do the various classes of owners have on the assets?

When analyzing a company, decision makers examine the financing of the enterprise to assess the claims on future cash flows and profits, as well as the degree of risk associated with the enterprise. Let's look more closely at how decision makers evaluate a company's margin of safety and profitability by using information found in the stockholders' equity section of the balance sheet.

MARGIN OF SAFETY

As we discussed in Chapter 11, the relationship between debt and equity is important when evaluating the protection for creditors provided by owners' equity. We discussed the debt-to-equity ratio, a widely used indicator that compares the amount of resources obtained through debt and through equity. This comparison indicates the margin of safety for creditors, as well as the ability of the company to raise additional capital through debt financing. In general, the greater a company's owners' equity, the greater its ability to borrow.

Within stockholders' equity, the common stockholders' equity can be viewed as providing a margin of safety for the preferred stockholders, if any. The claims of the preferred shareholders must be met before those of the common shareholders. The claims of the preferred shareholders always include the stated preferred dividends for the current year. In addition, if the preferred stock is cumulative, the preferred shareholders are entitled to unpaid dividends of past years before common stockholders receive payment. In a liquidation, preferred shareholders receive a stated liquidation value per share, or the par value if no liquidation value is stated, plus any dividends to which they are entitled. However, they receive these amounts only if sufficient assets remain after the claims of creditors have been satisfied.

Common shareholders receive whatever assets are left after the claims of creditors and preferred shareholders have been satisfied. When looking at a balance sheet, most or all of the stockholders' equity amounts other than the amount in the preferred stock account can usually be viewed as accruing to the common shareholders, as long as preferred dividends to date have been paid.

The existence of outstanding preferred stock may have a significant effect on cash flows because preferred stock carries a fixed dividend that must be paid each period in cash. Technically, the dividend does not have to be paid unless declared by the board of directors, but passing a preferred dividend is usually viewed as a sign of severe financial difficulty. A commonly used measure related to the safety of the preferred dividend is **times preferred dividends earned:**

$$\text{Times Preferred Dividends Earned} = \text{Net Income} \div \text{Preferred Dividend}$$

PROFITABILITY

An important indicator of a company's profitability is return on invested capital. Recall that one measure of return on investment is the return on total invested capital, both debt and equity. Based on the accounting equation, return on debt plus equity is the same as return on total assets:

$$\text{Return on Total Assets} = \text{Net Income} \div \text{Total Assets}$$

In many cases, however, owners and potential owners want to know how efficiently owners' capital is being employed. This might be measured by looking at the return that accrues directly to the owners. **Return on owners' equity** is calculated as follows:

$$\text{Return on Owners' Equity} = \text{Net Income} \div \text{Owners' Equity}$$

Because owners' equity is equal to assets minus liabilities, referred to as *net assets*, this ratio is also called **return on net assets:**

$$\text{Return on Net Assets} = \text{Net Income} \div \text{Net Assets}$$

The return on owners' equity or net assets may indicate, among other things, how successful management is in using debt to increase the return to owners. As we discussed in Chapter 11, the proper use of debt can increase the return to owners, and ultimately the ability to provide a satisfactory return to owners determines whether a business is successful.

In Practice 12-5

MEAD CORPORATION

In the years immediately before Steve Mason became CEO of Mead Corporation, a large papermaker based in Dayton, Ohio, the company's performance was not good, reports *Financial World*[4] Its return on equity dropped from 16 percent to 5 percent, and debt to capital rose from 36 percent to 47 percent, increasing interest expense at the worst possible time.

ANALYSIS

Two signs of this company's distress can be seen in its return on equity, which decreased dramatically, and the increase in its borrowing relative to equity. Although borrowing can often increase the return to stockholders, it also presents risk because fixed payments must be made. A higher proportion of debt financing usually increases the cost of capital. Although Mead's performance improved temporarily after Mason became CEO, more recently its earnings per share dropped from $3.17 in 1995 to $1.14 in 1998, and its return on equity dropped once again to about 5 percent. Mason retired on October 31, 1997. [www.mead.com]

If a company has preferred stock outstanding, common shareholders may be particularly interested in the **return on common equity:**

$$\text{Return on Common Equity} = \frac{\text{Net Income} - \text{Preferred Dividends}}{\text{Stockholders' Equity} - \text{Preferred Claims}}$$

With the common shareholders viewed as the true residual owners of the business enterprise, this indicator reflects the return to them in relation to their investment.

You Decide 2-2

WHICH RETURN ON INVESTMENT IS BETTER?

Ajax and Bjax Companies both operate in the same industry and are similar in most respects, although Bjax has more debt outstanding than Ajax. Over the past three years, Ajax's return on total assets has averaged 16 percent and its return on stockholders' equity has averaged 14 percent. Bjax, on the other hand, has averaged a 12 percent return on total assets and an 18 percent return on stockholders' equity. All other things equal, which company do you think has demonstrated better performance? Explain. If you were to invest money in one of these companies, which would it be? Why? Would your view differ depending on whether you were a creditor or owner? Explain. Do the returns for one company suggest anything about the adequacy of the performance of the other company? Explain.

[4]Gregory E. David, "A Machine Called Chief," *Financial World* (March 14, 1995), p. 42.

OWNERS' EQUITY FOR UNINCORPORATED BUSINESSES

Information for Decisions

When reporting owners' equity, unincorporated businesses usually report only the owners' net capital after profits have been added and distributions have been deducted. Financial statement users need to be aware of this difference from corporations so they can use the information to answer questions such as these: Which partners have made a significant financial commitment to the partnership? To what extent does the amount of owners' equity provide protection to the creditors?

The owners' equity of unincorporated businesses is generally less complicated than that of corporations. Each owner is assigned a capital account that reflects that owner's original and subsequent investment, share of cumulative profits, and any withdrawals. The cumulative result of all capital transactions relating to a particular owner is reflected in that owner's capital account.

The balance sheet of a sole proprietorship reports a single owner's equity account, usually titled "Owner's Capital." A partnership balance sheet reports a separate capital account for each partner if the partnership is relatively small. For businesses with many partners, the capital of the partners is generally reported as a combined amount.

Within a partnership, profits and losses must be accounted for and allocated to the individual partners in accordance with the partnership agreement. Profits and losses can be distributed in any way the partners choose, except that no partner can be excluded from the sharing. If the partnership agreement is silent on the way in which profits and losses are to be shared, they will be shared equally among all partners. If the agreement specifies the profit-sharing ratio but makes no provisions for losses, then losses will be shared in the same way as profits. Some profit-sharing schemes may call profit allocations "salary" or "interest on investment," but regardless of the label applied, the allotments reflect allocations of partnership profits.

Allocating profits to partners increases the partners' capital accounts, and allocating losses decreases the capital accounts. Simply allocating profits to partners does not result in cash distributions. However, partners often have *drawing rights*, permitting them to withdraw cash or other assets from the partnership, and partners' drawings must be accounted for as reductions in their capital accounts. A statement of changes in partners' capital serves the same purpose as a statement of stockholders' equity for a corporation.

A CLOSER LOOK AT

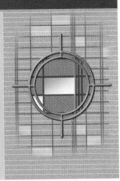

CHANGES IN PARTNERS' CAPITAL

The XYZ Partnership reports capital balances for its three partners at the end of 1999, as follows:

Xenda	$120,000
Yolanda	60,000
Zelda	20,000
Total Capital	$200,000

The partnership agreement provides that profits will be allocated 50 percent to Xenda and 25 percent each to Yolanda and Zelda.

For 2000, the partnership had revenues of $900,000 and expenses of $500,000. Also, Yolanda withdrew cash of $12,000 during the period.

Profits for the XYZ Partnership are allocated to the partners at the end of 2000, as follows:

Xenda	$400,000 × .50 = $200,000
Yolanda	$400,000 × .25 = 100,000
Zelda	$400,000 × .25 = 100,000
	$400,000

Changes in partners' capital accounts during 2000 appear as follows:

	Xenda	**Yolanda**	**Zelda**
Beginning balance	$120,000	$ 60,000	$ 20,000
Share of net income	200,000	100,000	100,000
Withdrawals		(12,000)	
Ending balance	$320,000	$148,000	$120,000

An important point to note about proprietorships and partnerships is that cash and other assets can often be withdrawn with relative ease, and withdrawals do not require the type of formal action needed within a corporation. This may result in less control over cash and other assets. Also, because of the unlimited liability of the owners of unincorporated businesses, their personal assets are subject to the claims of business creditors if business assets are insufficient. Accordingly, creditors and others attempting to evaluate unincorporated businesses often require personal financial statements of the owners, which we discuss in Chapter 15, in addition to financial statement of the businesses.

SUMMARY

Owners' equity represents the capital contributed to a business by the owners and also reflects their claim on the assets of the company. An examination of owners' equity is important because elements of equity arise from different sources and may represent claims of differing types and priorities.

The stockholders' equity section of a corporation's balance sheet includes one or more capital stock accounts, additional contributed capital, retained earnings, and other items. One type of capital stock is preferred stock, which includes a fixed dividend rate, has preference in liquidation and the payment of dividends over common stock, and typically does not have voting rights. Common stock represents the true residual ownership interest of a corporation. Common shareholders are entitled to all profits and assets remaining after the claims of creditors and preferred shareholders are satisfied. Common stockholders normally have the right to vote. The stock does not carry a fixed dividend rate; dividends are declared at the discretion of the board of directors.

The capital stock accounts reflect the par or stated value of the stock. Amounts in excess of the par or stated value paid into the company for the stock are reported as additional paid-in capital. For true no-par stock, the full proceeds of the stock issue are reflected in the capital stock account. The amount reported in the capital stock account usually represents the legal capital of the corporation, which is not subject to distribution to shareholders. When a company repurchases its own stock and does not cancel the shares, it usually reports the cost of the treasury stock as a deduction from stockholders' equity.

Retained earnings represents the accumulated past profits of the corporation not distributed to stockholders. Net income increases retained earnings, and distributions of income, or dividends, reduce retained earnings. Because dividends are usually declared from retained earnings, the amount of retained earnings is one indicator of a company's ability to declare dividends. The company has no obligation to pay dividends until they are declared by the board of directors.

Sometimes companies distribute stock dividends by making proportionate distributions of shares to stockholders. Although the stockholders then own more shares of stock, their ownership interests relative to other shareholders do not change. Stock dividends represent a permanent capitalization of retained earnings in that the amount of the dividend is transferred from retained earnings to the capital stock and additional paid-in capital accounts. Stock splits occur when a company issues some multiple of the common shares already outstanding and reduces the par or stated value of the shares proportionately. Stock splits do not affect any of the accounts or the owners' relative ownership interests.

When analyzing a company, financial statement users are interested in the relationship between different sources of capital because the different means of financing make different claims on future cash flows and carry different degrees of risk. Two measures frequently used that both deal with the relationship between debt and owners' equity are the debt-to-equity ratio and the ratio of debt to total capital. In addition, measures of the efficiency with which capital is employed by the enterprise include the return on total capital (or assets) and the return on owners' equity.

The owners' equity of an unincorporated business is usually reflected in a single capital account for each owner, unless the number of owners is large. This single account reflects the owner's initial and subsequent investments, share of profits, and distributions.

LIST OF IMPORTANT TERMS

additional paid-in capital *(457)*

capital stock *(453)*

common stock *(453)*

contributed capital *(453)*

declaration date *(462)*

discount *(454)*

dividend payout *(463)*

dividend yield *(463)*

ex-dividend date *(462)*

legal capital *(455)*

owners' equity *(452)*

par value *(454)*

payment date *(462)*

preferred stock *(454)*

premium *(454)*

record date *(462)*

return on common equity *(474)*

return on net assets *(473)*

return on owners' equity *(473)*

stated value *(455)*

statement of stockholders' equity *(471)*

stock dividends *(464)*

stockholders' equity *(452)*

stock options *(454)*

stock split *(465)*

stock warrants *(454)*

times preferred dividends earned *(473)*

treasury stock *(460)*

true no-par stock *(455)*

EXAMINING THE CONCEPTS

Q12-1 What is owners' equity? Which decision makers may find information about owners' equity most useful? Explain why.

Q12-2 What types of claims do owners have on the assets of a business enterprise?

Q12-3 Do different owners of a corporation have different types of claims? Explain.

Q12-4 Describe the different equity securities that a corporation might issue.

Q12-5 Who are the true residual owners of a corporation? Explain what is meant by residual ownership.

Q12-6 A common notion in finance is that rewards and risks go together. Explain how this idea applies to the different groups having a claim on the assets of a corporation.

Q12-7 How would you distinguish between debt and equity? What are the major characteristics of debt, and what are the major characteristics of equity?

Q12-8 In what sense is preferred stock preferred?

Q12-9 In what ways is preferred stock similar to debt? How does it differ from debt?

Q12-10 If a company has more than a single class of stock outstanding, what factors should a potential investor take into consideration before purchasing one of the classes of stock?

Q12-11 Distinguish between the number of shares of capital stock authorized, issued, and outstanding. How can a company have more shares issued than outstanding?

Q12-12 Why would a company have more shares of stock authorized for issuance than it intends to issue?

Q12-13 What is the par value of a share of capital stock? What does it mean? How does par value differ from stated value? Does stock always have a par or stated value? Would you be willing to invest in shares of stock that were selling for more than par value? Explain.

Q12-14 Why is common stock seldom issued at a discount?

Q12-15 Describe the various potential sources of a corporation's additional paid-in or contributed capital. Who "owns" the additional paid-in capital? Explain.

Q12-16 What is retained earnings? What does the reported retained earnings balance tell financial statement readers?

Q12-17 What are dividends? What types of dividends might a company pay?

Q12-18 Dividends and interest expense both decrease owners' equity. Is a dividend an expense? Explain. What are the similarities and differences between interest expense and dividends?

Q12-19 What elements normally are needed before a corporation can pay a cash dividend?

Q12-20 What dates relating to dividends are important from the corporation's perspective and from the investor's perspective?

Q12-21 Do stock dividends have value? Explain. What effect does a stock dividend have on a company's balance sheet? What effect does a cash dividend have on a company's balance sheet?

Q12-22 How does a stock split differ from a stock dividend? What additional value does a stockholder receive when a company splits its stock? Why might a company split its stock?

Q12-23 If a company has a large unrestricted retained earnings balance, does this mean it could immediately declare and pay a large cash dividend? Explain.

Q12-24 What is treasury stock, and how is it reported? Why would a company have treasury stock?

Q12-25 Why do many analysts pay close attention to a company's debt-to-equity ratio? Which is more favorable, a high or low one?

Q12-26 Why is "times preferred dividends earned" a useful indicator? Why do analysts typically not compute "times common dividends earned"?

Q12-27 What is meant by "return on investment"? Can return on investment be measured in different ways? Explain.

Q12-28 Given that creditors' claims have preference over those of stockholders, does the stockholders' equity section of the balance sheet have any relevance for creditors? Explain.

Q12-29 Describe the owners' equity section of the balance sheet for a sole proprietorship and a partnership. How are undistributed earnings of these entities reported?

UNDERSTANDING ACCOUNTING INFORMATION

E12-1 **Understanding Owners' Equity** Jope Company and Zent Corporation have identical assets, but different approaches in the way in which they have financed their assets. Summarized balance sheets are as follows:

	Jope	Zent
Cash	$ 200,000	$ 200,000
Accounts receivable	500,000	500,000
Buildings and equipment (net)	1,400,000	1,400,000
Total assets	$2,100,000	$2,100,000
Accounts payable	$ 80,000	$ 450,000
Wages payable	120,000	150,000
Bonds payable	200,000	1,000,000
Common stock	350,000	150,000
Retained earnings	1,350,000	350,000
Total liabilities and owners' equity	$2,100,000	$2,100,000

a. What is the advantage to Jope's bondholders of having a majority of its assets financed through owners' equity?
b. What is the advantage to Jope's common shareholders of having a majority of its assets financed through owners' equity?

c. What is the advantage to Zent's common shareholders of having a greater portion of its assets financed through bonds?

E12-2 **Stockholders' Equity: The Elements of Corporate Ownership** Quick Company reported the following stockholders' equity balances at December 31:

Preferred stock ($15 par; 12,000 shares issued and outstanding)	$ 180,000
Common stock ($4 par; 400,000 shares authorized;105,000 shares issued and outstanding)	420,000
Additional paid-in capital	310,000
Retained earnings	640,000
Total stockholders' equity	$1,550,000

a. If Quick Company wishes to issue an additional 20,000 shares of common stock, which shareholders have the right to purchase a proportionate share of the new shares issued? Why is this right important?
b. Which shareholders have a priority claim on dividend payments and on assets distributed if the company is liquidated? Why is priority given to some shareholders and not to others?

c. What is the source of additional paid-in capital? Is additional paid-in capital or retained earnings a better indicator of past operating success? Explain.

d. Why might Quick Company report lower net income per year than Slow Company and yet report a larger balance in retained earnings?

E12-3 Accounting for Capital Stock Allstar Corporation reported the following stockholders' equity balances at December 31:

Common stock ($10 par; 50,000 shares authorized; 30,000 shares issued; 24,000 shares outstanding)	$ 300,000
Additional paid-in capital	240,000
Retained earnings	720,000
Total	$1,260,000
Less: Treasury stock (6,000 shares, at cost)	(312,000)
Total stockholders' equity	$ 948,000

a. Were Allstar's shares issued at par value or some other amount? What was the average amount received per share?

b. Why is there a maximum number of shares that can be issued without receiving shareholder approval? How many additional shares could be issued by Allstar before receiving shareholder approval?

c. What effect, if any, would the issuance of 5,000 additional shares of common stock at $64 per share have on the amount reported as additional paid-in capital? Retained earnings?

d. Why are treasury shares reported as a deduction from stockholders' equity rather than a liability?

e. If the treasury shares were retired, what would be the effect on the stockholders' equity accounts?

E12-4 Accounting for Dividends The stockholders' equity sections of the balance sheets of Freemont Corporation and Tufler Corporation contained the following:

	Freemont	Tufler
Common stock, $10 par value	$ 500,000	$ 200,000
Preferred stock, $25 par value		600,000
Additional paid-in capital	300,000	
Retained earnings	400,000	400,000
Total stockholders' equity	$1,200,000	$1,200,000

The preferred stock of Tufler has an 8 percent dividend rate and is cumulative with respect to dividends.

a. Both companies are considering forgoing dividends for the next 3 years to save cash for expansion. Will such a plan raise difficulties for either company? Explain why or why not.

b. If both companies pay a dividend of $70,000, why might the common shareholders of Tufler receive no dividend?

c. If Tufler pays a dividend of $70,000 each year, what portion of the dividend will go to the preferred shareholders? To the common shareholders?

d. If preferred shareholders virtually always have a priority claim over common shareholders with respect to dividends, what is the advantage to common shareholders of having preferred stock outstanding?

E12-5 The Statement of Stockholders' Equity Absolt Corporation reported the following information in its statement of stockholders' equity for the year ended December 31, 2001.

	Year Ended December 31	
	2001	**2000**
Common stock ($30 par value)		
Beginning balance	$240,000	$150,000
Shares issued	60,000	90,000
Ending balance	$300,000	$240,000
Additional paid-in capital		
Beginning balance	$ 96,000	$ 96,000
Shares issued	34,000	—
Ending balance	$130,000	$ 96,000
Retained earnings		
Beginning balance	$490,000	$520,000
Net income (loss)	85,000	(30,000)
Cash dividends paid	(40,000)	—
Ending balance	$535,000	$490,000
Total stockholders' equity	$965,000	$826,000

a. In what ways can the statement of stockholders' equity help investors analyze changes in the ownership claims of Absolt shareholders?

b. Absolt's total stockholders' equity at January 1, 2000, was $766,000 and has increased by $199,000 between January 1, 2000, and December 31, 2001. Has the 26 percent increase been primarily attributable to operating results or other factors? What has been the major source of increase?

c. Absolt sold 3,000 shares of common stock in 2000 and 2,000 shares in 2001. Did investors appear to have placed a higher or lower value on the stock in 2001 than in 2000? How do you know?

d. If Absolt had repurchased 1,000 shares of common stock for $42 per share, what amount would be reported as total stockholders' equity in Absolt's balance sheet at December 31, 2001?

E12-6 Analyzing Stockholders' Equity Mercy Company and Nulty Corporation have equal amounts of preferred stock outstanding and each pays a preferred dividend of $20,000 annually. Using data from the most recent annual reports, the following ratios were calculated:

	Mercy Company	Nulty Corporation
Times preferred dividends earned	4.00	3.00
Return on total assets	10.0%	15.0%
Return on owners' equity	13.3%	20.0%
Return on common equity	15.0%	40.0%

a. Should an investor look for a company with a high or low times preferred dividends earned ratio? Explain.

b. Should an investor look for a return on owners' equity that is greater than or less than the return on total assets? Explain.

c. Should an investor look for a return on common equity that is greater than or less than the return on owners' equity? Explain.

d. Based on the information presented above, would you expect Mercy Company or Nulty Corporation to be the more desirable investment for someone wishing to invest in common stock? Explain.

e. If Mercy Corporation reported net income of $80,000 and Nulty Corporation reported net income of $60,000, how is it possible for Nulty Corporation to have a greater return on total assets?

E12-7 Owners' Equity for Unincorporated Businesses The balance sheet of E&C Partnership contained the following items:

Cash	$ 20,000
Accounts receivable	60,000
Buildings & equipment (net)	330,000
Total assets	$410,000
Accounts payable	$200,000
Partnership capital	
Emmet Jones	138,000
Clayton Jones	72,000
Total liabilities & equity	$410,000

The changes in partnership capital accounts for the year were as follows:

	Emmet Jones	Clayton Jones	Total
Beginning balance	$124,000	$106,000	$230,000
Share of net income	24,000	16,000	40,000
Withdrawals	(10,000)	(50,000)	(60,000)
Ending balance	$138,000	$ 72,000	$210,000

a. The partnership agreement specifies that 60 percent of net income is to be allocated to Emmet Jones and 40 percent to Clayton Jones. Why is it important to specify the income sharing ratio in the partnership agreement?

b. Why may creditors lend money to the partnership even if it does not appear to have a significant amount of assets that could be used for repayment?

c. How does the claim of the creditors of E&C Partnership differ from claims of a corporation's creditors?

d. What amount of the liabilities of the partnership might Emmet Jones be required to pay in the event the partnership encounters financial difficulties?

E12-8 Multiple Choice: Elements of Equity Select the correct answer for each of the following:

1. Which of the following is not an element of owners' equity?
   a. Capital stock.
   b. Creditors' capital.
   c. Additional paid-in capital.
   d. Retained earnings.

2. Preferred stock:
   a. Must be paid dividends before interest is paid to bondholders.
   b. Usually has the right to vote along with common stockholders.
   c. Usually has preference over common stock in receiving dividends.
   d. All of the above.

3. The true residual ownership of a corporation is found in the company's:
   a. Preferred stock.
   b. Common stock.
   c. Treasury stock.
   d. Authorized stock.

4. All business corporations have:
   a. Stock options.
   b. Preferred stock.
   c. Common stock.
   d. All of the above.

5. Additional paid-in capital includes:
   a. Amounts paid to the corporation in excess of the market value of its stock.
   b. Gains on the issuance of capital stock.
   c. Gains on the retirement of capital stock.
   d. Amounts paid to the corporation in excess of the par or stated value of its stock.

E12-9 Multiple Choice: Capital Stock Select the correct answer for each of the following:

1. Which of the following terms is not associated with corporate stock?
   a. Debentures.
   b. Options.
   c. Preferred.
   d. Treasury.

2. A stock issue carries a fixed dividend rate, has a fixed liquidation value, and gains the right to vote if its dividend is not paid when scheduled. This stock is probably labeled:
   a. Preferred.
   b. Common.

c. Treasury.

d. Callable.

3. A common stockholder shares in the profits of the corporation:

a. On a proportionate basis with all other common shareholders.

b. After the claims of creditors have been met.

c. After claims of the preferred shareholders have been met.

d. All of the above.

4. Which of the following statements about capital stock is true?

a. The right to vote can never be withheld by the corporation from any class of capital stock.

b. Common stock does not have a fixed dividend and sometimes pays no dividend at all.

c. Preferred stock usually has a fixed dividend and never shares in profits beyond that amount.

d. Once a share of common stock is issued, it must remain outstanding until the company is liquidated.

E12-10 Multiple Choice: Capital Stock Select the correct answer for each of the following:

1. Which of the following statements about capital stock is true?

a. A company is prohibited by law from repurchasing its own stock unless it retires the entire issue and cancels the shares.

b. Common stock is typically callable, while preferred stock is not.

c. Preferred stock is not considered to represent the true residual ownership interest of a corporation.

d. Both a and b are correct.

2. The capital stock account in the balance sheet includes:

a. The par or stated value of the shares issued.

b. The dates at which the shares were issued.

c. The names of all major shareholders.

d. The mandatory dividend rate for common shares.

3. Treasury stock:

a. Is usually reported as a deduction from total stockholders' equity.

b. Is usually reported at cost.

c. Reflects a reduction in the margin of safety afforded creditors.

d. All of the above.

4. When a corporation retires capital stock and pays less than the amount for which it was issued, the difference is reported as:

a. Additional paid-in capital.

b. A gain on the retirement of stock.

c. A special increase in retained earnings.

d. None of the above.

5. When a company issues capital stock with a par or stated value, which accounts are usually affected?

a. Only the capital stock account.

b. The capital stock account and additional paid-in capital.

c. The capital stock account and retained earnings.

d. The capital stock account and a gain on the issuance of capital stock.

E12-11 Multiple Choice: Retained Earnings Select the correct answer for each of the following:

1. The balance in the retained earnings account reflects the:

a. Amount of cash available to be distributed to owners.

b. Total margin of safety available to protect the claims of the creditors.

c. Total amount of the corporation's earnings from its inception.

d. Accumulated undistributed earnings of the corporation.

2. The current retained earnings balance of a company is important to investors because it:

a. Is one factor in the company's ability to pay dividends.

b. Indicates whether the company is profitable currently.

c. Is an important indicator of the company's liquidity.

d. All of the above.

3. Which of the following statements about dividends is true?

a. Dividends accrue in the same way that interest does.

b. Common stock typically receives a dividend equal to the amount paid to preferred shareholders, but preferred stock must be paid first.

c. Cash dividend disbursements occur on the ex-dividend date.

d. Dividends may be paid only after a dividend declaration by the board of directors.

4. Stock dividends:

a. Are proportional distributions of additional shares of stock to current shareholders with no change in an individual stockholder's ownership percentage.

b. Are valuable because they increase an individual stockholder's ownership proportion.

c. Reduce corporate assets.

d. Increase total stockholders' equity.

5. Which of the following statements is true?

a. Dividends and interest are both expenses related to corporate financing.

b. The retained earnings statement reports dividends declared, as well as all nonoperating gains and losses.

c. Once a cash dividend is declared, the corporation has a liability payable to its stockholders until the dividend is paid.

d. Stock dividends on common stock do not affect retained earnings.

E12-12 Computing Owners' Capital The Bar-Clay Partnership, with two partners, has assets of $650,000 and liabilities of $455,000. Two-thirds of the partnership's capital is that of Joe Bar. What is the amount that should be reported in Phil Clay's capital account?

E12-13   Changes in Owners' Capital   At the beginning of the year, the owners' capital of the Hot-Rod Company, a partnership, was allocated as follows:

Capital, Hilda Hot	$470,000
Capital, Irma Rod	240,000
Total	$710,000

Net income is allocated to the two partners by first crediting their capital accounts for 10 percent of their beginning capital balances and then splitting all remaining profits evenly between the two partners. Hot-Rod's net income for the current year was $268,000. During the year, Hilda invested an additional $200,000 in the partnership, while Irma withdrew cash of $78,000.

a. Prepare a statement showing the changes in the individual partners' capital balances during the year.
b. Should the partnership agreement specify how much cash or other assets may be withdrawn during the period by the individual partners, or would this be too restrictive? Explain.

E12-14   Determining Equity Balances   The stockholders' equity section of Tab Company's balance sheet appears as follows:

Preferred stock ($5 par; 500,000	
shares authorized, none issued)	$?
Common stock ($1 par; 2,000,000	
shares authorized, 800,000	
issued and outstanding)	800,000
Additional paid-in capital	2,200,000
Retained earnings	?
Less treasury stock	?
Total stockholders' equity	$3,650,000

Required:

a. At what average price per share was Tab's common stock issued?
b. What dollar amount should be reported for:
    1. Preferred Stock?
    2. Retained Earnings?
    3. Treasury Stock?

E12-15   Issuance of Capital Stock   Lopez Electronics was established on May 30, with authorization to issue 500,000 shares of $10-par capital stock. Shortly thereafter, the company issued 100,000 shares of stock for $25 per share and a month later issued another 50,000 shares for $30 per share. During the remainder of the year, the company incurred a net loss of $275,000 from its operations. Prepare the stockholders' equity section of the balance sheet for Lopez Electronics as of the end of the year.

E12-16   Equity Transactions   Explain how and by what amount each of the following transactions affects individual stockholders' equity accounts of Kline Company and total stockholders' equity.

a. Kline Company authorizes the issuance of 200,000 shares of $2-par common stock and 100,000 shares of $50-par, 8 percent preferred stock.
b. 120,000 shares of common stock are issued for $15 per share.
c. 40,000 shares of preferred stock are issued for $52 per share.
d. Kline reports net income of $480,000.
e. The full annual dividend on the preferred stock is declared and paid.
f. A dividend of $1.00 per share is declared on the common stock, but is not yet paid.
g. A 5 percent stock dividend is declared on the common stock and distributed. On the date of declaration, the market price of the stock is $18 per share.
h. When the common stock price dips to $14 per share, Kline purchases 20,000 shares in the market and holds the shares in its treasury.

E12-17   Treasury Stock   Putman Corporation has 400,000 shares of $10-par value common stock authorized. At January 1, 2000, the stockholders' equity section of its balance sheet consisted of the following:

Common stock	$ 700,000
Additional paid-in capital	140,000
Retained earnings	790,000
Total	$1,630,000

During 2000, Putman was involved in the following transactions:

1. An additional 50,000 shares of stock were sold at $27 each.
2. A total of 15,000 shares were repurchased at $43 per share.
3. 7,000 treasury shares were sold for $56 each.
4. An additional 2,000 treasury shares were sold for $40 each.
5. A cash dividend of $1.50 per share was declared and paid.
6. Net income for 2000 was $340,000.

Required:

a. Present the journal entries to record transactions 1 through 5.
b. Prepare the stockholders' equity section of Putman's balance sheet at December 31, 2000.

E12-18   Stock Issuance and Retirement   On December 31, 1999, the stockholders' equity section of Ortegren Corporation's balance sheet appears as follows:

Preferred stock (8 percent, $100 par)	$ 1,000,000
Common stock ($1 par)	500,000
Additional paid-in capital	8,320,000
Retained earnings	5,438,000
Total stockholders' equity	$15,258,000

The following occur during 2000:

1. Ortegren issues 40,000 additional shares of common stock for $35 per share.
2. The company declares and pays the dividend for the first half of the year on its preferred stock.
3. Immediately after declaring the preferred dividend for the first half of the year, the company retires the entire issue of preferred stock by paying cash of $103 per share.
4. The company earns net income of $966,000 for 2000.

Required:

a. Prepare a formal statement of changes in stockholders' equity for 2000 showing the changes in each of the individual equity accounts.
b. Give possible reasons as to why Ortegren might change its equity financing by eliminating preferred stock and issuing more common.

E12-19 Payment of Dividends Allstar Corporation reported the following stockholders' equity balances at December 31:

Common stock ($10 par; 50,000 shares authorized; 30,000 shares issued; 24,000 shares outstanding)	$ 300,000
Additional paid-in capital	240,000
Retained earnings	720,000
Total	$1,260,000
Less: Treasury stock (6,000 shares, at cost)	(312,000)
Total stockholders' equity	$ 948,000

a. What effect do treasury shares have on the amount of dividends paid? If Allstar were to pay a dividend of $2 per share, what would be the total amount of the dividend payment?
b. What would be the balance in each of the stockholders' equity accounts following the payment of the dividend?
c. How does Allstar's payment of dividends affect the balances in additional paid-in capital and retained earnings?

E12-20 Issuing Preferred Stock Bell Company issued 5,000 shares of 8 percent, $15 par value, Class A preferred stock on January 1, 1996, for $15 per share and 25,000 shares of 10 percent, $20 par value, Class B preferred stock on July 15, 1996, for $20 per share.

a. What amount of dividends must Bell declare if it wishes to distribute a dividend of $100,000 to its common shareholders at December 31, 2000?

b. If Bell has not paid a dividend since December 1997, and both issues of preferred stock are cumulative with respect to dividends, what amount of dividend must Bell declare at December 31, 2000, if it wishes to pay a dividend of $100,000 to its common shareholders?
c. If Bell has not paid a dividend since December 1997, and both issues of preferred stock are noncumulative with respect to dividends, what amount of dividend must Bell declare at December 31, 2000, if it wishes to pay a dividend of $100,000 to the common shareholders?
d. Why would the common shareholders be motivated to have preferred stock outstanding if the preferred stock routinely receives a larger dividend than the common stock?

E12-21 Accounting for Common Stock Tranquil Corporation has a total of 400,000 shares of $6 par value common stock authorized. A total of 150,000 shares were issued on January 1, 1998, for $23 per share. In October 1999 the company repurchased 7,000 shares of common stock at $42 per share. During June 2000, a total of 3,000 shares of the treasury stock were sold for $48 per share. Tranquil reported net income of $628,000 for 2000 and paid a dividend of $3 per share during December 2000. The retained earnings balance at January 1, 2000, was $580,000.

a. How many common shares were outstanding at December 31, 2000?
b. What was the total dollar amount of the dividend paid?
c. Prepare the stockholders' equity section of Tranquil's balance sheet at December 31, 2000.

E12-22 Cash and Stock Dividends Ballet Company reported the following stockholders' equity balances at December 31, 2000:

Common stock ($10 par; 90,000 shares authorized; 40,000 shares issued; 25,000 shares outstanding)	$ 400,000
Additional paid-in capital	260,000
Retained earnings	595,000
Total	$1,255,000
Less: Treasury stock (15,000 shares, at cost)	(345,000)
Total stockholders' equity	$ 910,000

Immediately after the balance sheet was prepared, Ballet Company declared a cash dividend of $2 per share, followed by a 6 percent stock dividend. Ballet's common stock was selling at $28 per share on December 31, 2000.

a. What was the amount of the cash dividend paid by Ballet?
b. What was the number of shares issued in the stock dividend?
c. What was the amount of the increase in the total par value of shares outstanding as a result of the cash and stock dividends?

d. What was the amount of the increase in additional paid-in capital as a result of the cash and stock dividends?

e. What was the decrease in retained earnings as a result of the cash and stock dividends?

f. What was the change in total stockholders' equity as a result of the cash and stock dividends?

E12-23   Cash Dividends   Steeple Company paid total cash dividends of $212,000 in 2001 after forgoing dividend payments in 1999 and 2000. The company authorized 25,000 shares of $20-par value 8 percent cumulative preferred stock on January 1, 1996, and immediately issued some of the shares at par value. Steeple also issued 40,000 shares of its $6-par value common stock on that date. If the cash dividend paid to common shareholders in 2001 was $3.50 per share, how many preferred shares were outstanding during 2001?

E12-24   Stock Split   Blend Corporation issued 25,000 shares of $6-par value common stock at $18 per share on January 1, 1996. A total of 100,000 shares was authorized for issuance. In the period between January 1, 1996, and December 31, 1999, Blend reported net income of $640,000 and paid cash dividends of $300,000. Net income for 2000 was $175,000. Blend Corporation declared and immediately distributed a 3-for-1 stock split in November 2000. A cash dividend of $1.20 on each new share was declared in early December 2000 and paid prior to December 31. Prepare the stockholders' equity section of Blend's balance sheet at December 31, 2000.

E12-25   Expiration of Stock Options   Alberts Corporation issues stock options to its employees as additional compensation. Under generally accepted accounting principles, the options are valued at $500,000. The company recognizes additional compensation expense of $500,000, and the options are reported at that amount in the stockholders' equity section of the balance sheet as Stock Options Outstanding. The options give employees the right to buy Albert's common stock at $50 per share for the next 3 years. Unfortunately for the employees, the stock price falls, and none of the options is exercised.

Because the stock options have expired, they no longer are outstanding and can no longer be reported as stock options in Albert's balance sheet. How should the $500,000 assigned to the stock options be reported subsequent to expiration? Would the company recognize a gain because the $500,000 assigned to the options is kept by the company? What treatment would you recommend? Explain.

E12-26   Income and Retained Earnings Statements   The following are selected account balances from Shandel Company's trial balance on December 31, 2000.

Revenues	$1,372,000
Cost of goods sold	666,500
Wage expense	243,700
Depreciation expense	135,000

Miscellaneous expense	117,500
Interest expense	17,000
Preferred dividends declared	51,000
Common dividends declared	100,000
Retained earnings, January 1, 2000	3,050,000

Prepare a 2000 income statement and retained earnings statement in good form for Shandel Company. Based on this information, how likely does the continuation of Shandel's common dividend appear to be? Explain.

E12-27   Dividends   You have been considering buying some common shares of Basler Freight. Basler has 500,000 shares of common stock outstanding. The company has been through difficult times, but now is doing better. Your main concern is whether you will receive cash dividends. In addition to the common shares, the company has 10,000 shares of 10 percent, $10-par Class A preferred stock outstanding, which is noncumulative and nonparticipating. The company also has 25,000 shares of 6 percent, $100-par Class B preferred stock outstanding. This stock is nonparticipating, but is cumulative. The normal dividend has been paid on both classes of stock until last year, when no dividends were paid. This year, however, Basler is doing exceptionally well and is expecting net income of $1,800,000. The company has not yet declared its annual dividends but has indicated that it plans to pay total dividends equal to 40 percent of net income. If you immediately buy 1,000 shares of Basler common stock in the stock market:

a. What amount of common dividend would you expect to receive?

b. What amount of common dividend would you expect to receive if the Class B preferred stock were noncumulative?

E12-28   Ability to Pay Preferred Dividends   Nort Corporation reported the following information in its financial statements:

	2001	2000
Net income	$ 95,000	$ 64,000
Preferred dividends paid	14,000	11,200
Balance sheet totals, December 31		
Total assets	900,000	819,000
Total liabilities	300,000	300,000
Preferred stock outstanding		
($10 par value)	200,000	160,000
Common stock outstanding		
($5 par value)	100,000	100,000
Retained earnings	300,000	259,000

a. What was the times preferred dividends earned ratio for each of the 2 years? Has the change between years been favorable or unfavorable?

b. Is this ratio of greater importance to creditors or common shareholders? Explain.

c. If this ratio had fallen to .75 in 2001, would Nort still be able to pay dividends? Why might it choose to not do so?

E12-29 Analysis of Profitability Nort Corporation reported the following information in its financial statements:

	2001	2000
Net income	$ 95,000	$ 64,000
Preferred dividends paid	14,000	11,200
Balance sheet totals, December 31		
Total assets	900,000	819,000
Total liabilities	300,000	300,000
Preferred stock outstanding		
($10 par value)	200,000	160,000
Common stock outstanding		
($5 par value)	100,000	100,000
Retained Earnings	300,000	259,000

a. What was the return on total assets for each of the 2 years?
b. What was the return on owners' equity for each of the 2 years?
c. What was the return on common equity for each of the 2 years?
d. Have the financial position and operating results of Nort Corporation for 2001 improved over 2000 or worsened? On what do you base your answer?
e. If the computed return on common equity had been less than the return on owners' equity, would it be more desirable to hold an investment in Nort's preferred stock or common stock? Explain.

E12-30 Analysis of Stockholders' Equity The stockholders' equity section of the balance sheet of Purity Company at December 31, 2000, contained the following balances:

Preferred stock ($10 par; 8% dividend rate; 100,000 shares authorized; 45,000 shares issued and outstanding)	$ 450,000
Common stock ($20 par; 50,000 shares authorized; 30,000 shares issued; 24,000 shares outstanding)	600,000
Additional paid-in capital	360,000
Retained earnings	870,000
Total	$2,280,000
Less: Treasury stock (6,000 shares, at cost)	(204,000)
Total stockholders' equity	$2,076,000

a. What was the average price received for the shares of common stock issued?
b. What was the average price paid for the treasury stock purchased?

c. If Purity pays a dividend of $1.75 per share to the common shareholders, what is the total amount of the dividend that must be declared?
d. What effect would the sale of 2,500 treasury shares at $41 per share have on the reported stockholders' equity balances? What effect would it have on the total amount of the dividend payment if the sale occurred prior to the dividend declaration?

E12-31 Analysis of Stock Dividend The stockholders' equity section of the balance sheet of Tropic Company at December 31, 2000, contained the following balances:

Preferred stock ($8 par; 8% dividend rate; 60,000 shares authorized; 40,000 shares issued and outstanding)	$ 320,000
Common stock ($10 par; 100,000 shares authorized; 60,000 shares issued and outstanding)	600,000
Additional paid-in capital	290,000
Retained earnings	750,000
Total	$1,960,000

If Tropic declares a 5 percent stock dividend when the common shares are trading at $58 each:

a. What number of additional shares will be distributed?
b. What effect will the stock dividend have on the par value per share of Tropic's common stock?
c. What stockholders' equity account balances will be increased or decreased? By what amounts?
d. What effect will the stock dividend have on the book value per share of Tropic's common stock?

E12-32 Comparative Dividend Information In evaluating companies for possible investment alternatives, Sarah acquired the following data on Buggy Whip Corporation and Ace Computer Company:

	Buggy Whip	Ace Computer
Net income for current period	$120,000	$100,000
Dividends paid in current period	86,000	15,000
Market price of shares	35	45
Book value per share	30	16
Par value per share	7	2
Total number of shares outstanding	20,000	10,000

a. What amount of dividends per share was received by current shareholders of each company?
b. What was the dividend payout ratio for each company?
c. What was the dividend yield for each company?
d. Are the dividend payout and dividend yield ratios of Buggy Whip Corporation and Ace Computer Company

consistent with expectations for companies in a mature industry or a rapidly growing industry? Explain.

E12-33 Shareholder Claims Tronic Corporation has financed its operations through a combination of debt and equity financing. The company's liabilities and stockholders' equity accounts are as follows:

Accounts payable and accrued expenses	$ 389,600
Short-term bank notes	500,000
Mortgage payable	1,300,000
Debentures	5,000,000
$100-par preferred stock, class A	10,000,000
$25-par preferred stock, class B	20,000,000
$10-par common stock	40,000,000
Additional paid-in capital from the issuance of $100 preferred stock	1,500,000
Additional paid-in capital from the issuance of $25 preferred stock	1,900,000
Additional paid-in capital from the issuance of $10 common stock	20,700,000
Additional paid-in capital from the expiration of stock options	100,000
Retained earnings (deficit)	(4,650,000)
Treasury stock (500,000 shares, at cost)	(9,000,000)

Tronic Corporation has very poor prospects for the future and has been unable to meet its obligations as they come due. Accordingly, the board of directors has decided to liquidate the company. The stated liquidation value of the Class B preferred stock is $28 per share. The Class A preferred stock has no stated liquidation value, and shareholder claims will be equal to the par value. The preferred stocks are noncumulative and nonparticipating. If Tronic has total assets worth approximately $50,000,000 in liquidation:

a. What amount would you expect to be available to meet the claims of the common shareholders? Prepare a schedule to support your answer.
b. How much would shareholders be likely to receive for each share of common stock held?

E12-34 Changes in Stockholders' Equity The stockholders' equity accounts of Astor Corporation at December 31, 2000 and 2001 appear as follows:

	2000	**2001**
Common stock	$ 200,000	$ 200,000
Additional paid-in capital	535,000	620,000
Retained earnings	470,000	580,000
	$1,205,000	$1,400,000
Less treasury stock	(175,000)	(35,000)
Total stockholders' equity	$1,030,000	$1,365,000

Astor declared and paid a $50,000 cash dividend during 2001. What do you think caused the changes in reported stockholders' equity accounts? Compute the amount of each of the items resulting in change.

E12-35 Stockholders' Equity and Dividends Atlantic Trading Company operates on a calendar-year basis. At the start of the year, it had 480,000 shares of $5 par common stock issued, with 480,000 shares outstanding. A total of 1,000,000 shares of common stock is authorized. The company had originally issued its common stock for $20 per share. In addition, Atlantic has 100,000 shares of $100-par, 8 percent preferred stock authorized, issued, and outstanding. The shares were issued several years ago at $102 per share. In February, the company declared a 10 percent stock dividend on the common stock when the price of the stock was $30 per share. On December 1, the board of directors declared the normal annual dividend on the preferred stock, payable on December 31, to stockholders of record December 16. On December 1, the board of directors also declared a cash dividend of $1 per share on the common stock, payable next January 5 to stockholders of record December 27. At the end of last year, Atlantic had reported retained earnings of $4,993,655. Atlantic computes its current year's net income as $1,531,760.

a. Prepare the stockholders' equity section of Atlantic's balance sheet as of the end of the year.
b. On December 26, Peter Li purchases 1,000 shares of Atlantic's common stock in the open market. What is the amount of the cash dividend that Peter will receive from those shares on January 5? Explain your answer.

USING ACCOUNTING FOR DECISION MAKING

P12-36 Stockholders' Equity Transactions The following events and transactions occurred with respect to Wilma Corporation:

2001

1. Wilma Corporation became chartered on January 1, 2001, and was authorized to issue 20,000 shares of common stock with a stated value of $1 and 1,000 shares of $100-par, 7 percent preferred stock. It immediately issued 8,000 common shares at a price of $15.
2. A large plot of land and a building were acquired by issuing 1,500 shares of common stock in exchange. At the time of the exchange, the common stock was selling for $22 per share.

3. The company reacquired 1,000 shares of its common stock for $20 per share to be used for employee compensation and future acquisitions.
4. Half of the treasury shares were resold for $28 per share.
5. The remaining treasury shares were sold for $19 per share.

2002

6. On January 1, 2002, Wilma issued 1,000 shares of preferred stock for $101 per share.
7. Wilma declared and distributed a 10 percent stock dividend on its common stock. On the date of declaration of the stock dividend, Wilma's common stock was selling for $21 per share.
8. Wilma declared and paid quarterly dividends on the preferred stock for the first 9 months of 2002. The last quarterly preferred dividend of the year was declared but will not be paid until the first week of 2003.

Wilma reported net income of $31,200 for 2001 and $54,500 for 2002. To examine the changes in Wilma's stockholders' equity, do the following:

a. Present journal entries to record each of Wilma's transactions listed for 2001 and 2002.
b. Prepare Wilma's statement of changes in stockholders' equity for 2002.
c. Present the stockholders' equity section of Wilma's balance sheet on December 31, 2002.
d. Answer the following questions:
   1. From the stockholders' equity section of the balance sheet, does it appear that Wilma's operations are successful? Explain.
   2. Are there any indications in the stockholders' equity section of the balance sheet that the payment of cash dividends to common stockholders might be warranted? Explain. Why might Wilma not want to pay cash dividends on common stock in the near future?
   3. What is likely to happen to the additional paid-in capital currently reported in Wilma's balance sheet over the next several years? What will happen to these amounts if Wilma liquidates?

P12-37 Determining Equity Balances Gabriel Company is just completing its second year of operations, expecting to report net income of $430,000. This amount is double its earnings in its first year of operations, and near the end of the second year, the company declared its first cash common dividend of $1 per share. The company started by authorizing 500,000 shares of $5-stated value common stock and issuing 100,000 of those shares for $16 per share. Since then, no additional common shares have been sold; however, a 10 percent stock dividend was declared and distributed at the end of its first year when the stock price was $19 per share. At the beginning of the second year, Gabriel repurchased 3,000 shares of its common stock for $20 per share, but a short time later resold 1,000 of those shares for $25 per share. The company also issued

at par all shares authorized of its 10 percent, $10-par preferred stock at the beginning of the second year. All normal dividends were paid on the preferred stock for the second year, an amount totaling $200,000.

a. Prepare the stockholders' equity section of Gabriel's balance sheet at the end of the company's second year of operations.
b. For the second year, compute the times-preferred-dividends-earned ratio. What does this measure indicate about the safety of the company's preferred dividend? What about implications for future common dividends?

P12-38 Stock Dividends and Splits The stockholders' equity section of Biff Corporation's balance sheet appears as follows on December 31, 2000:

Common stock ($10 par value; 1,000,000 shares authorized, 100,000 issued and outstanding)	$1,000,000
Additional paid-in capital	1,500,000
Retained earnings	2,345,000
Total stockholders' equity	$4,845,000

Near the beginning of 2001, Biff declares and distributes a 10 percent stock dividend. At the date of declaration, Biff's stock is selling for $89 per share. By the end of October, the price of Biff's common stock rises to $104 per share. Biff's board of directors decides to split the stock 4 for 1, with a commensurate reduction in the par value. Late in December, the board declares a cash dividend on the common stock of $1 per share, payable early in January 2002. In past years, the dividend generally had been about $3 per share.

a. Prepare the stockholders' equity section of Biff's balance sheet as of December 31, 2001.
b. What effect has each of the dividends had on the individual stockholders' equity accounts of Biff and on Biff's total stockholders' equity?
c. What reasons might a company have for declaring a stock dividend? What is your assessment of these reasons?
d. What reasons might a company have for splitting its stock? What is your assessment of these reasons?
e. If you were one of Biff's common stockholders, would you be happy or unhappy with the stock dividend and split? Why? How do you feel about the reduction in the cash dividend from $3 to $1? Explain.

P12-39 Retained Earnings and Dividends You recently have been considering investing in some of Costigan Company's common stock. The company has been pretty profitable over the years, and prospects for the future look good. However, the company recently has had to make heavy expenditures for new plant and equipment. The company's summarized balance sheet at the end of 2001 is as follows:

Cash	$ 50,000
Other current assets	943,000
Plant & equipment (net)	8,279,000
Total	$9,272,000
Current liabilities	$ 588,000
Long-term debt	2,500,000
Common stock	4,000,000
Retained earnings	2,184,000
Total	$9,272,000

The company has 200,000 shares of stock outstanding, and its earnings per share has increased by at least 10 percent in each of the last 10 years. In several recent years, earnings per share increased by more than 15 percent. Given the company's earnings and the amount of its retained earnings, you judge that it could easily pay cash dividends of $2 or $3 per share and hardly make a dent in retained earnings.

a. Evaluate the prospects of your receiving a cash dividend from Costigan during the next year if you were to purchase its stock.
b. Evaluate your prospects for receiving cash dividends from Costigan during the next 5 years if you were to purchase its stock.
c. Suppose Costigan borrowed cash of $2 million on a 5-year bank loan to provide working capital and additional operating flexibility. While no collateral would be required, the loan would stipulate that no dividends be paid in any year in which the ratio of long-term debt to equity was greater than 2 to 3. Evaluate your prospects for receiving cash dividends from Costigan in the short term and during the next 5 years if Costigan were to enter into the bank loan agreement.

P12-40 Treasury Stock and Total Equity The liability and stockholders' equity sections of Lovata Corporation's balance sheet appear as follows:

Current liabilities		$ 82,000
Long-term debt		4,500,000
Total liabilities		$4,582,000
Common stock ($10 par)	$1,000,000	
Additional paid-in capital	3,000,000	
Retained earnings	1,200,000	
Total equity		5,200,000
Total liabilities and equity		$9,782,000

Lovata typically pays out 60 percent of its net income in dividends, a policy that it has followed for several decades and that stockholders have come to rely on. The company expects to earn $710,000 this year. Lovata has always

made payments on its debt in a timely manner, but the company's debt covenants specify that the debt is in technical default if the company's ratio of total debt to equity exceeds 1 to 1.

During the past year, Lovata issued stock options to its employees as additional compensation. Because the exercise price of the options was equal to the market price of the stock on the date of grant, no value was assigned to the options. The company expects that most of the options will be exercised within the next 2 years and wants to have shares available when that happens. The company also wants shares of its stock available for a future business combination it is considering. Accordingly, the company is considering buying back 20,000 of its shares in the open market. The stock currently is selling for $50 per share.

As the company's newest financial analyst, you have been asked to evaluate the plan to repurchase company shares. Write a memo to the chief financial officer evaluating the desirability of issuing new shares versus purchasing treasury stock and make a recommendation as to how the company should proceed. Illustrate in your memo how the stockholders' equity section of Lovata's balance sheet would appear under the two different alternatives.

P12-41 Return on Investment Danley Corporation's balance sheet appears as follows:

Cash	$ 160,000
Other current assets	842,000
Plant & equipment (net)	8,841,000
Total	$9,843,000
Current liabilities	$ 512,000
Long-term debt	2,500,000
Preferred stock	2,000,000
Common stock	1,000,000
Additional paid-in capital	1,500,000
Retained earnings	2,331,000
Total	$9,843,000

For the year just ended, Danley reported net income of $728,000. During the year, the company declared and paid preferred dividends of $160,000 and common dividends of $300,000.

a. Compute the following for Danley:
  1. Return on assets.
  2. Return on long-term capital (long-term debt and stockholders' equity).
  3. Return on stockholders' equity.
  4. Return on common equity.
b. If the company's interest expense related to its long-term debt was $120,000 for the year, after taxes, and the long-term debt could have been replaced with $2,500,000 of common stock, what would the return on common equity have been for the year without debt financing? What does

this imply about the desirability of this company using long-term debt? Will this always be true? Explain.

c. Suppose the company had issued the bonds shown in its balance sheet, but had issued an additional $2,000,000 of

common stock rather than the preferred stock. What would the return on common equity have been? What does this imply about the desirability of this company using preferred stock?

C12-42 Issuance of Multiple Securities Garbanzo Corporation issues 100,000 shares of $100-par preferred stock for $107 per share. With each share purchased, 1 stock warrant is included. Holders of warrants can purchase 1 share of Garbanzo's common stock for $10 and 2 warrants at any time during the next 5 years. Based on the dividend yield of the preferred stock, its limited call protection, and other features, the underwriters estimate that the preferred stock would sell for $101 per share without the warrants. They are unable to estimate directly the value of the warrants.

a. Because the stock warrants are, in effect, being sold along with the preferred stock, a portion of the issue price will have to be allocated to the warrants, and the warrants will be reported as a separate item in the stockholders' equity section of Garbanzo's balance sheet. How much of the issue proceeds do you think should be assigned to Preferred Stock, Additional Paid-in Capital, and Stock Warrants Outstanding in Garbanzo's balance sheet? Explain.

b. Why would Garbanzo give the stock warrants to purchasers of its preferred stock? What are the advantages to Garbanzo? What disadvantages might there be?

C12-43 Analyzing IBM's Stockholders' Equity The following information is taken from the financial statements of IBM Corporation for the year ended December 31, 1998, (amounts are in millions, except for number of shares outstanding):

Preferred stock, par value $.01 per share	$ 247
Shares authorized: 150,000,000	
Shares issued: 2,546,011	
Common stock, par value $.50 per share	10,121
Shares authorized: 1,875,000,000	
Shares issued: 926,869,052	
Retained earnings	10,141
Treasury stock, at cost (962,146 shares)	(133)
Employee benefits trust (10,000,000 shares)	(1,854)
Accumulated gains and losses not	
affecting retained earnings	911
Total stockholders' equity	$19,433
Total liabilities and stockholders' equity	$86,100
Net income applicable to common shareholders	$ 6,308

a. What is the average issue price per share of the preferred stock?

b. What is the total par value of the common shares issued?

c. What is the average price at which the common stock was issued?

d. What is the average price paid to acquire the treasury shares held at December 31, 1998?

e. What is the number of common shares outstanding at December 31, 1998?

f. If IBM repurchases an additional $5.0 billion of its own common stock at an average price of $100 per share:

1. What is the number of shares outstanding after the treasury stock purchase?

2. What is the earnings per share after the treasury stock purchase?

C12-44 Changes in ADM's Stockholders' Equity The following information is taken from Archer Daniels Midland Company's statement of stockholders' equity (in thousands):

	Common Stock	
	Shares	**Amount**
Balance, June 30, 1997	557,874	$4,192,321
5% stock dividend	28,534	473,948
Treasury stock purchases	(3,767)	(81,154)
Common stock issued in purchase	13,953	298,244
Other	2,627	53,290
Balance, June 30, 1998	599,221	$4,936,649

In the company's annual report, the footnote disclosure relating to stockholders' equity states:

The company has authorized 800 million shares of common stock and 500,000 shares of preferred stock, both without par value. No preferred stock has been issued. At June 30, 1998 and 1997, the Company had approximately 5.9 million and 20.7 million common shares, respectively, in treasury. Treasury stock is recorded at cost, $102 million at June 30, 1998, as a reduction of common stock.

Based on ADM's financial statement information, answer the following questions:

a. What was the total number of shares of common stock outstanding at June 30, 1998?

b. What was the total number of shares of common stock that had been issued as of June 30, 1998?

c. On average, what was the price paid per share of treasury stock purchased during the year ended June 30, 1998?

d. Did the number of treasury shares held by ADM increase or decrease during the year ended June 30, 1998? By what amount?

e. What number of shares of treasury stock apparently were sold in the year ended June 30, 1998?

f. What effect did the stock dividend have on ADM's retained earnings? On its total stockholders' equity?

C12-45   Decision Case: Keep that Dividend! You've just been promoted to chief financial officer of Humongous Company. Boy, all those accounting and finance courses sure paid off. Trouble is, the company's not doing all that great. Year-end is rolling around, and the company's going to report a loss, again. The immediate problem is that the company has paid an annual dividend every year since 1908, but this year the dividend is questionable. Great, you finally get the job you've been after, and now you won't be able to pay a dividend. The company even paid dividends during the Great Depression of the 1930s. And now, you're going to break a 90-year streak. You've got to do something. Let's evaluate the alternatives. You could borrow the money for the dividend, and that would at least give you until this time next year to get things under control. Of course, borrowing could be expensive. Or, you remember reading about companies that distributed some of their inventories as dividends. You remember that one was a distillery, and some folks didn't like the idea of whiskey as a dividend. But hey! You could give something from your health food division—who could quarrel with that? What about a coupon for 1 package of Twiggy Burgers for each share of stock? Of course, you're not sure what that pension fund holding 100,000 shares of your stock will do with all those Twiggy Burgers, but it's something to think about. What other alternatives might there be? Write a formal memo to your board of directors addressing the dividend question.

a. Identify the alternative courses of action that you have as CFO with respect to the current dividend.

b. Identify the consequences, along with the advantages and disadvantages of each alternative, and state any additional information you might need to make a decision regarding the dividend.

c. Recognizing that you might not have all of the information you would like for making the decision, indicate which alternative you would choose with respect to the dividend and why.

C12-46   Researching Owners' Claims Using the SEC EDGAR database, company home pages on the World Wide Web, or other sources, find at least 4 companies that have preferred stock outstanding and answer the following:

a. Before you found 4 companies with preferred stock outstanding, how many companies did you find with preferred stock authorized but not outstanding? Why do you suppose the stock has been authorized if it is not issued?

b. How many issues of preferred stock did you find that were labeled as "redeemable" preferred stock? If you did not

find any, search until you do. How is the redeemable preferred stock classified in the balance sheet?

c. Look at the description of the redeemable preferred stock and the related notes and determine if the company is obligated to redeem the preferred stock or simply has the option to redeem (or call) it. Does the company's obligation seem related to the classification of the stock?

d. Find 2 companies that have had stock splits. Note the details of the splits, including the change in the number of shares and any change in par or stated value of the shares.

e. Find 2 companies that have reacquired some of their own common stock. Note how the stock is reported in the balance sheet. See if you can find why the companies reacquired their shares and how they intend to use them.

 C12-47   Team Assignment: Investing in Stock Form teams and identify 1 company of interest for each member of the team. Using the annual report for each company, or other sources of information, answer the following:

a. What is the amount of dividends paid by the company over the past 2 years? How frequently are dividends paid? What is the dividend payout? If the company is not currently paying a dividend on its common stock, has it before, and why is it not now paying?

b. How has the company's stock price changed over the past 2 years? (This information should be in the annual report, or can be obtained from *Value Line, The Wall Street Journal,* or various investment advisory services.)

c. What is the company's dividend yield? What stock price should you use to compute the dividend yield? Come to agreement among team members so the data are consistent for all companies studied.

d. If your team was actually an investment club and you were going to purchase the stock of one of the companies you studied, in which one would you invest your hard-earned money? What factors do you consider important in making your choice? Why are these important to you?

C12-48   Ethics and Financing The Allgood Corporation has been operating a refuse collection business for the past 5 years. The operations have not been profitable, and the interest on the bonds originally issued to finance acquisition of trucks and other equipment was not paid this year. Allgood has not paid any dividends to common stockholders since its formation.

Allgood management has been working on strategies for the company that will improve profits and improve cash flows so that interest and dividends can be paid. The only prospect seems to be to buy property to be used as a landfill. This kind of purchase would reduce or eliminate Allgood's biggest expense, landfill fees paid to outside companies. The problem is, how is Allgood going to raise the necessary capital to acquire the land, estimated to cost $5 million?

Allgood's legal advisors say that under the terms of the existing long-term debt, the company cannot issue any additional long-term debt as long as interest is unpaid. The investment experts that handled the initial stock offering say that it will not be possible to issue any additional common stock at this time because neither interest nor dividends were paid this year.

Finally, after much discussion, Allgood's director of finance proposes that Allgood issue preferred stock. The meeting is adjourned until the director of finance can check to see if preferred stock can be issued. At the next meeting the director reports that an insurance company may be willing to buy the preferred stock if the following conditions are met:

1. The stock must have preference as to dividends, and the dividends must be declared even when Allgood reports a loss and does not pay bond interest.
2. The dividend rate must be 2 percent over the current interest rate on bonds, and the dividends must be cumulative.

3. The preferred stock must have preference in liquidation, and it must be called at 100 percent of par in 5 years.
4. The preferred stock does not need to be voting or participatory.

In the discussion of the proposed terms you are asked to provide answers to the following questions:

a. What are the advantages and disadvantages to Allgood of issuing the proposed stock?
b. Is there anything illegal about issuing stock with the proposed provisions?
c. Will this issue be considered debt or equity? If issued, how would you report it in the financial statements?
d. Is it ethical to issue securities that may violate debt agreements? How would you handle this situation?

Internet Exercises: Visit our Web site for additional exercises.

Annual Report Project Part 12

Refer to the Annual Report Project, Part 1, at the end of Chapter 1. Using the annual report of the company you have chosen, and any other available information, answer the following questions, providing sources and computations where appropriate.

a. What classes of capital stock, and how many shares of each, does your company have authorized, issued, and outstanding?

b. Does the company hold any treasury shares? If so, is there any indication of the possible reasons for holding the treasury shares (e.g., for outstanding stock options, business combinations)?

c. Based on cash dividends declared during the latest year reported, what was your company's dividend payout?

d. Did your company issue or reacquire any of its own stock during the latest reporting period?

e. Assess your company's prospects for future dividends.

The Cash Flow Statement and Decisions

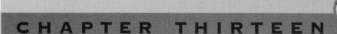

REVIEW

Previous chapters examined the information provided by the income statement, balance sheet, and statement of changes in owners' equity. In addition, a brief introduction to the cash flow statement was provided in Chapters 2 and 3.

WHERE THIS CHAPTER FITS

This chapter examines the cash flow statement in depth and focuses on how the information provided by this important statement is used for financial decisions.

LOOKING AHEAD

Chapters 14 and 15 complete an in-depth look at the financial statements and how the information provided is useful for decision making.

Why am I always broke? My job pays a decent salary, but somehow I never have cash when I need it. I get paid on the first of the month, but most of that goes for rent and food. My car payment is due on the tenth, but I don't get paid again until the fifteenth. Once I make my car payment and pay the late charges, I've used up most of that paycheck. Then come the credit card bills. Luckily, I can just make the minimum payments and let the rest go, although the interest charges are starting to be almost as much as my purchases. Maybe I need to figure out where all of my money goes.

The German company Siemens is a $60 billion conglomerate that manufactures everything from power stations to semiconductors. The company is known for its expert cash management and earns as much from interest income as from manufacturing. It is sometimes regarded as "a bank with an electronics department attached." "[T]he company usually has the cashflow to fund even the largest investments, such as this year's $1.5 billion acquisition of Westinghouse."[1]

[1]Laura Covill, "Siemens The Financial Engineer," *Euromoney* (August 1998), p. 65.

Individuals make personal decisions based in part on the amount of cash they have and their expectations about future cash flows. Similarly, current cash balances and forecasts of future cash flows are at the heart of many business decisions. Managers, investors, and creditors all need information about cash and cash flows so they can make decisions.

An important source of information about an organization's cash flows is the statement of cash flows. This statement, one of the four basic financial statements, provides information about the amounts and types of an entity's cash flows during the period. The purpose of this chapter is to examine the type of information provided in this statement and see how it is used in decision making. After completing this chapter, you should be able to:

1. Describe the type of information included in a cash flow statement, how it is organized, and how it is useful for decision making.

2. Describe the different types of cash flows that are important for decision makers and how these cash flows are reported.

3. Explain the cash flow effects of common types of transactions and describe how they are reported in the cash flow statement.

4. Explain how decision makers analyze cash sources and uses listed in the cash flow statement, and describe ratios often used in analyzing cash flows.

UNDERSTANDING THE STATEMENT OF CASH FLOWS

Information for Decisions

The statement of cash flows reports sources and uses of cash for an entity. This information is used by decision makers when assessing the adequacy of an entity's cash for future needs and in projecting future cash inflows and outflows. It helps financial statement users answer questions such as these: Is the company generating enough cash from normal operations to continue operating and to make required payments to creditors? Will the company generate sufficient cash for future expansion? Is the company generating sufficient cash to pay future dividends?

A **statement of cash flows** is required by generally accepted accounting principles to be included in a complete set of financial statements. A cash flow statement must be included for each year for which an income or operating statement is included. Thus, the annual reports of most organizations include cash flow statements for either two or three years for comparative purposes.

The purpose of the cash flow statement is to report how an organization generated and used its cash. Knowing where the cash comes from is important in projecting whether cash will be generated from those sources in the future. Knowing where the cash goes is important in assessing the organization's future cash needs. When presenting cash flow statements, most companies combine cash and cash equivalents because short-term investments classified as cash equivalents are used primarily as a substitute for cash.

Exhibit 13–1 shows the Consolidated Statement of Cash Flows of The May Department Stores Company, which is typical of those of major corporations. May Company reports earnings for three years and does the same for cash flows. The statements report all of the different sources and uses of cash during each of the three years and show the total change in cash and cash equivalents. Each item in May Company's cash flow statements reflects a summary of specific transactions. The organization of the statement of cash flows is standardized to facilitate understanding the organization's cash flows.

ORGANIZATION OF THE STATEMENT OF CASH FLOWS

The statement of cash flows, as you can see from May Company's, is divided into three categories: operating, investing, and financing. By categorizing the entity's cash flows in this way, the statement helps decision makers better understand how the company generates and uses its cash. This is important so that decision makers can better project future cash flows. Some of the different types of cash flows that a business might have are listed in Exhibit 13–2.

Cash flows from operations are generated from the organization's normal activities. These cash flows are generally routine and recurring. They are particularly important because most organizations must be capable of generating positive cash flows from operations over the long run to remain viable. (See In Practice 13-1.) Is May Company, for example, successful in generating cash from its operations?

Cash flows related to investing reflect how an organization's cash is used to provide future benefits, such as through the purchase of new plant and equipment, and investing in securities. For example, to what extent has May Company been making capital expenditures to acquire property and equipment and to expand?

MAY COMPANY'S CONSOLIDATED STATEMENT OF CASH FLOWS

EXHIBIT 13-1

CONSOLIDATED STATEMENT OF CASH FLOWS			
(dollars in millions)	1998	1997	1996
Operating activities:			
Net earnings	$ 849	$ 775	$ 755
Adjustments for noncash items included in earnings:			
Depreciation and amortization	439	412	374
Deferred income taxes	48	58	45
Deferred and unearned compensation	5	8	10
Working capital changes*	158	265	142
Other assets and liabilities, net	6	8	(43)
Total operating activities	1,505	1,526	1,283
Investing activities:			
Capital expenditures	(630)	(496)	(632)
Dispositions of property and equipment	44	33	29
Acquisition	(302)	—	—
Cash used in discontinued operation	—	—	(24)
Total investing activities	(888)	(463)	(627)
Financing activities:			
Issuances of long-term debt	350	—	800
Repayments of long-term debt	(221)	(340)	(388)
Purchases of common stock	(589)	(394)	(869)
Issuances of common stock	64	65	49
Dividend payments	(308)	(297)	(305)
Total financing activities	(704)	(966)	(713)
Increase (decrease) in cash and cash equivalents	(87)	97	(57)
Cash and cash equivalents, beginning of year	199	102	159
Cash and cash equivalents, end of year	$ 112	$ 199	$ 102
*Working capital changes comprise:			
Accounts receivable, net	$ 20	$ 262	$ 139
Merchandise inventories	(176)	(53)	(211)
Other current assets	12	46	45
Accounts payable	176	(30)	180
Accrued expenses	89	26	(20)
Income taxes payable	37	14	9
Net decrease in working capital	$ 158	$ 265	$ 142
Cash paid during the year:			
Interest	$ 297	$ 319	$ 288
Income taxes	411	355	380

Cash flows related to financing reflect amounts received by borrowing or from issuing stock, as well as payments made to retire debt, repurchase stock, and provide dividends to owners. For example, did May Company increase its financing through debt and equity?

One additional category occasionally included in the statement of cash flows relates to significant noncash activities. These are activities related to investing or financing, but that do not generate or use cash. For example, a company might have convertible bonds outstanding; the conversion of these bonds into common stock is an important change in financing but does not affect cash. Gateway has chosen to report noncash investing and financing activities in Note 11 to its financial statements rather than in its cash flow statement, as shown in Appendix A.

| EXHIBIT 13-2 | **SOME OF THE DIFFERENT TYPES OF CASH FLOWS** |

Cash Flows Related to Operating Activities:

- Cash receipts and collections from sales of goods and services
- Cash receipts from earnings on investments in securities (interest and dividends)
- Payments to suppliers
- Payments to employees
- Payments for interest
- Payments for taxes

Cash Flows Related to Investing Activities:

- Cash receipts from the sale of securities of other companies
- Cash receipts from sales of productive assets
- Payments for the purchase of securities of other companies
- Payments at the time of purchase for the acquisition of productive assets

Cash Flows Related to Financing Activities:

- Proceeds from issuing capital stock or other equity securities
- Proceeds from issuing debt securities or obtaining loans (other than trade credit)
- Payments for reacquisition of capital stock or other equity securities of the entity
- Payments for the retirement of debt securities (excluding interest)
- Payments of principal on loans (other than trade payables)
- Payments of dividends

In Practice 13-1

TIME WARNER

In its 1998 financial statements, Time Warner reported its fourth straight net loss applicable to common shares (after paying preferred stock dividends), a loss of $372 million. In management's discussion and analysis, various statements refer to expansion plans, and the company paid $155 million in dividends on common stock. In addition, the company reported cash outflows for capital expenditures, investments, and acquisitions of $671 million. Even though Time Warner reported a net loss applicable to common shares, the consolidated statement of cash flows showed cash generated from operations of almost $2 billion.

ANALYSIS

Although the company reported a loss applicable to common shares in 1998, it still generated significant cash inflows from operations and has for a number of years. Financing dividends and capital expenditures from operating cash inflows, therefore, appears feasible. [www.timewarner.com]

How Much Cash Flow Do You Need?

You have always wanted to be a part of some exciting business venture that might make you rich. Now you have the chance. The supervisor from your job has offered you the chance to invest $2,000 in a young software company he owns. You have the $2,000, and you were really interested until he said that, even though the company generates a lot of cash, he doesn't plan to pay any dividends for at least five years. At the end of five years he promises that your investment will be "worth a lot." If you could get cash flow information for last year and projections for the next five years, what would you look for to help you decide whether to invest $2,000?

TYING TOGETHER ACTIVITIES AND FINANCIAL STATEMENTS

Businesses engage in three main types of activities: operations, investing, and financing. Their regular operations represent their reason for being, why they exist. A certain amount of investment in assets is usually necessary for an enterprise to operate, and financing is necessary to have resources to invest and to be able to operate. Some aspects of these activities are reflected in the balance sheet, income statement, and statement of changes in stockholders' equity. The statement of cash flows, however, ties together all of these activities and the three other financial statements by reporting the effects of an entity's operating, investing, and financing activities on the cash balance. More specifically, the cash flow statement reflects the changes in the balances of all balance sheet items during the period. All changes are reported in terms of their effects on cash, or they are reported as noncash activities. In addition, the income or operating statement is tied to the cash flow statement because operations represent an important source (or use) of cash, and the statement of changes in stockholders' equity is tied in because dividends and other changes in equity are important elements related to financing. Looking at May Company's statement of cash flows in Exhibit 13–1, you can see that all of the items deal with income, dividends, or changes in balance sheet accounts.

Let's look at each major type of cash flow and see what it includes and what it tells us that is useful for decision making.

OPERATING CASH FLOWS

Information for Decisions

Cash provided or used by operations reflects the effect of an entity's main activities. Understanding operating cash flows, along with related adjustments, permits decision makers to better anticipate future recurring cash flows and answer questions such as these: Will this company be able to finance its future expansion internally without having to borrow or issue additional stock? How secure is the company's dividend when considered in relation to the cash generated from the company's operations? When a stockbroker tells me the company being recommended had a net loss but generated a great deal of cash from depreciation, should I buy the stock hoping the company will depreciate more in the future? What are the implications of a company's cash from operations coming largely from an increase in trade payables?

The operating section of the cash flow statement is most important because it deals with the cash generated or used by the entity's primary activities. These activities, and the related cash flows, are recurring. The cash flow statement reports past cash flows, but the same or similar activities and cash flows can be expected to occur in the future. If an organization cannot sustain itself over the long run with the cash generated from operations, it cannot survive.

Most companies present the operating section of the cash flow statement using an **indirect approach** under which they start with accrual-basis net income and adjust that figure to obtain the cash generated or used by operations. Although accrual-basis income is regarded as the best measure of operating success, it does not tell us the amount of cash flows from operating and must be adjusted for all items that affect income and cash differently. Thus, this section of the cash flow statement includes the following adjustments to net income to determine the cash generated or used by operations:

1. Expenses that reduced net income this period but did not use cash must be added back.
2. Cash payments made this period for expenses of other periods must be deducted.
3. Revenues that did not result in cash inflows during the current period must be deducted.
4. Cash collections for revenues earned in other periods must be added.
5. Items reported in the income statement but not directly related to normal operations must be removed.

Let's consider a few of the more common adjustments to net income needed to convert to a cash basis.

DEPRECIATION AND AMORTIZATION

Under accrual accounting, income is reduced for the cost of an operating asset's service potential used up during the period. As we have seen earlier, depreciation, or the amount of cost recognized during the period under the matching concept, is an allocation of the original cost of the asset. The depreciation expense recognized during a period is not a cash expense; it does not result in a decrease in the cash balance. Cash was reduced initially when the asset was first acquired. The expense is simply an accountant's allocation of a cost incurred previously. Therefore, while income for the period is decreased by the amount of the depreciation expense, cash is not. The difference in timing between the cash outflow for the purchase of a fixed asset and the related income effects can be shown as follows:

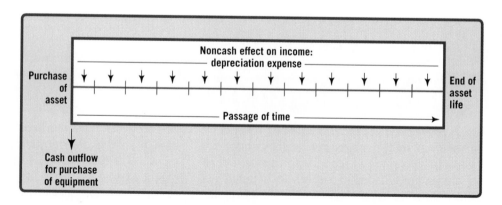

If we are interested in the amount of cash generated by a company's operations, then we need to add back the amount of depreciation expense to the company's net income. In other words, if all other revenues and expenses were cash items, net income would understate cash generated by the amount of the depreciation expense.

Because depreciation is added back to net income to get the cash generated from operations, financial analysts sometimes mistakenly refer to depreciation as a source of cash. But this is silly because firms cannot generate cash just by depreciating. If depreciation were a source of cash, a change to a more rapid depreciation method would cause the cash balance to go up. But, that will not happen. The addition of depreciation in the cash flow statement is simply a way of adding back an amount that was deducted from income but did not use cash. Depreciation is neither a source nor a use of cash.

In Practice 13-2

CASH GENERATED FROM OPERATIONS AT SONY COMPORATION

In fiscal 1999, Sony Corporation reported (in yen) net income of ¥179,004 million. However, net cash provided by operating activities was ¥663,267 million. Cash generated from operations was much higher than income because income had been reduced by depreciation and amortization expense of ¥307,173 million, a noncash expense. Also, the company reduced its receivables and merchandise inventory, freeing up additional cash, although this was partially offset by an increase in film inventories.

ANALYSIS

By reporting net income in the cash flow statement, Sony allows readers to reconcile cash generated from operations with the income reported in the income statement. Adjustments for depreciation, changes in receivables and inventories, and other items permit decision makers to see how the company's income translates into cash flows. [www.sony.com]

Some analysts also believe that, because depreciation is deducted from income but does not use cash, this creates a "reserve" for replacing assets when they are worn out or obsolete. This reasoning is faulty, however, because it assumes that the new assets will cost exactly the same as the old and that cash equal to the depreciation is set aside for replacement. In actuality, both assumptions are usually incorrect.

The amortization of intangible assets and the depletion of natural resources also result in noncash expenses. As with depreciation, these expenses are deducted to get net income, but do not use cash. Therefore, they are added back to net income to get the amount of cash generated from operations.

CHANGES IN DEFERRED INCOME TAXES

As we discussed in Chapter 11, companies must report income tax expense on an accrual basis by matching tax expense to reported income. If temporary differences exist between the income reported in the income statement and that reported on the tax return, a deferred tax liability or asset is affected. In addition, the tax expense reported in the income statement is different from cash tax payments. Therefore, the cash flow statement must report an adjustment to bring net income to the amount of cash generated from operations. May Company's cash flow statement, shown in Exhibit 13–1, reflects a $48 million positive adjustment from an increase in deferred income taxes, while Gateway's cash flow statement in Appendix A reports a negative deferred tax adjustment of more than $58 million for 1998.

AMORTIZATION OF DEBT DISCOUNT AND PREMIUM

As we saw in Chapter 11, debt discount arises when debt is issued for less than its maturity value. Because the debt ultimately must be repaid at maturity value, the actual (effective) interest costs are higher than the current cash interest payments. A portion of the discount is charged to interest expense each period under accrual accounting. However, the amount of discount expensed each period represents a noncash charge against income. When will cash actually be paid? When the debt matures, its maturity value will be paid in cash. The difference in timing between the cash flows and expense recognition can be shown as follows:

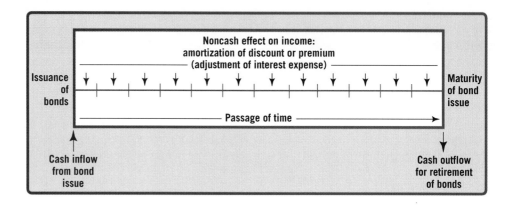

Because the company's interest expense contains a noncash portion, the net income figure must be adjusted to arrive at the cash generated from operations. Thus, when interest expense has been increased by the amortization of bond discount, an amount must be added to net income in the cash flow statement to determine the amount of cash generated from operations. If interest expense has been decreased by the amortization of bond premium, an amount must be deducted from net income in the cash flow statement to arrive at cash generated from operations.

GAINS AND LOSSES

Companies often include in their income statements gains and losses that are not directly related to their regular operations. For example, companies often report gains and losses from disposing of investments or fixed assets, and from retiring debt. Because these gains and losses are not related to regular operations, they must be eliminated from the operating section of the cash flow statement. Gains must be deducted from net income in the operating section of the cash flow statement to arrive at cash generated from operations, and losses must be added back. The cash effects of the transactions giving rise to the gains and losses are reported in the investing or financing sections of the cash flow statement.

CHANGES IN CURRENT ASSETS AND LIABILITIES

Current assets and current liabilities are important in the operations of a company and facilitate the flow of resources through the operating cycle. We discussed the operating or cash cycle in Chapter 3 and how changes in receivables, inventories, payables, and other current accounts can affect the amount of cash received. Because current assets and liabilities play such an important role in the way that cash moves through the operating cycle, changes in these items must be considered in determining the cash generated from operations. For example, sales increase income, but if the sales are on credit and the receivables are not immediately collected, no cash is generated. Thus, the cash generated from operations during the period can be determined only after adjusting net income for the change in receivables during the period: if receivables increase, less cash is collected than if receivables decrease.

Similarly, if a company does not pay its bills as quickly as in the past, and payables increase, less cash is used in operations. Because the expenses reduce income even though the cash has not been paid, the cash flow statement reports an adjustment added to net income in the cash flow statement to reflect more cash being generated from operations. A decrease in trade payables would indicate that more cash was being used to pay off bills and less was generated by operations. This would call for a negative adjustment to be reflected in the cash flow statement. Changes in current liabilities not directly related to sales or normal operating expenses, such as short-term bank loans or dividends payable, are reported in the financing section of the cash flow statement.

Exhibit 13–3 identifies the adjustments related to changes in current assets and liabilities that would be made to net income to arrive at cash generated from operations. The direction of adjustments for changes in all current assets is the same, and that for current liabilities is the opposite. Keep in mind that the purpose of these adjustments in the cash flow statement is to convert accrual-basis net income to cash generated from operations.

May Company, in the operating section of its cash flow statement, indicates the net effect of working capital changes on cash from operations. It details the individual working capital changes at the bottom of the statement. Gateway, on the other hand, details the adjustments for individual working capital items within the operating section of the statement.

ADJUSTMENTS RELATED TO CHANGES IN CURRENT ASSETS AND CURRENT LIABILITIES TO COMPUTE CASH FLOWS GENERATED FROM OPERATIONS

EXHIBIT 13-3

Current Assets

Accounts Receivable:
    Increases—subtract from net income to get operating cash flow
    Decreases—add to net income to get operating cash flow

Inventory:
    Increases—subtract from net income to get operating cash flow
    Decreases—add to net income to get operating cash flow

Other Current Assets (e.g., prepaid expenses):
    Increases—subtract from net income to get operating cash flow
    Decreases—add to net income to get operating cash flow

Current Liabilities

Accounts and Trade Notes Payable:
    Increases—add to net income to get operating cash flow
    Decreases—subtract from net income to get operating cash flow

Other Liabilities (e.g., accruals), excluding nontrade payables:
    Increases—add to net income to get operating cash flow
    Decreases—subtract from net income to get operating cash flow

A CLOSER LOOK AT

NET CASH PROVIDED BY OPERATION

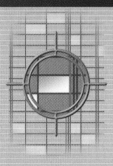

In 2001, Atkins Corporation reported net income of $275,000 and net cash provided by operations of $414,000 as follows:

Net cash provided by operations:		
Net income		$275,000
Add (deduct) noncash items		
Depreciation	$115,000	
Net increase in deferred income taxes	32,000	
Amortization of debt premium	(3,000)	
Unearned royalties	10,000	154,000
Add (deduct) changes in current assets and liabilities		
Accounts receivable increase	$ (30,000)	
Inventory decrease	8,000	
Accounts payable increase	39,000	
Short-term trade notes payable decrease	(32,000)	(15,000)
Net cash provided by operations		$414,000

The first two noncash adjustments reflect expenses that reduced net income but did not use cash. The third item, amortization of bond premium, reflects an expense reduction that did not affect cash, and the fourth item, unearned royalty income, is added back because cash was received but the item was not included in income. In the second section, decreases in current assets and increases in current liabilities increase the cash flow, and increases in current assets and decreases in current liabilities reduce cash flow.

ASSESSING CASH FLOWS FROM OPERATIONS

Why do companies report detailed information about operating cash flow? Why not just report the total? The answer is that, while the total operating cash flow is important, providing the details allows decision makers to develop a better understanding of a company's cash situation and, in turn, make better projections of future cash flows.

Starting the operating section of the cash flow statement with net income provides a comparison between accrual-basis income and cash flows and ties the cash flow statement to the income statement. Reporting individual adjustments allows decision makers to see precisely how a company's operations generate cash and why cash might be more or less than expected based on reported income.

The individual adjustments might show that cash is reduced because receivables and inventories are building, or perhaps that cash flow is increased through increases in payables. For example, Kellwood Company's fiscal 1998 net income was $42.7 million, but operating activities used $75.2 million of cash. An examination of individual adjustments in the cash flow statement showed that during the year receivables had increased by $48.5 million, inventory had increased by $75.5 million, and accounts payable had decreased by $14.4 million, all having a significant negative effect on the cash flows from operations.

By examining the elements of the operating section of the cash flow statement, decision makers might be able to identify cash, receivables, and inventory management problems that could ultimately affect liquidity. Or, they might be able to spot an impending credit crisis by determining that cash flow is being maintained by not paying bills. Whatever this section of the statement shows, the key is understanding the relationships between cash and the elements reported, and using that information to project future cash flows.

You Decide 13-2

HOW MUCH CASH DOES IT TAKE TO DELIVER FISH?

The Lewers Company is starting a fried fish delivery service to local restaurants. Lewers buys fish in bulk, cooks it, and delivers it to local restaurants. Joe Lewers figures that he will have a low overhead operation. He will do the deliveries and hire only one employee, the cook. The fish will be bought on credit, with payment due in ten days, and Joe will give his customers thirty days to pay him. Because it will be a credit operation, Joe figures he won't need much money. He figures all he will have to use cash for is gas and repairs on the van he will use for delivery. Do you think Joe can make a go of it? What would be the elements of Joe's cash flow statement for the first month? Would you lend Joe money to help his business grow? Explain.

INVESTING CASH FLOWS

Information for Decisions

The investing activities section of the cash flow statement reports the cash flow effect of purchases and sales of operating assets and other investments. Because investing activities are critical to a company's success or failure, decision makers need to evaluate investing cash flows to answer questions such as these: To what extent is the company investing in new plant and equipment needed for future operations? Is the company expanding its operations through the purchase of new plant and equipment or by investing in other companies? To what extent has the company generated cash by selling off fixed assets and investments?

Organizations usually must invest cash so they can conduct the operating activities needed to attain their goals. Thus, an understanding of an organization's investing activities is important for anyone analyzing the organization. Cash flows related to the investing activities of a business typically involve either operating assets (property, plant, and equipment) or investments in other companies. Cash outflows for operating assets are usually quite large for companies that are replacing assets or expanding. Cash inflows can be generated from selling operating assets no longer needed. Cash outflows for investments in stock often involve the acquisition of a controlling interest in other companies, referred to as affiliates. Sales of investments usually result in cash inflows.

Analyzing the investing activities section of the cash flow statement can tell decision makers whether a company is expanding or contracting its operating capacity, and how. Is the company expanding by acquiring new plant and equipment, or by investing in affiliated companies? Is the company generating a major portion of its cash inflows by selling off its productive assets, and can such cash inflows be sustained? Answers to these types of questions are crucial to understanding a company's future prospects and projecting future cash flows.

Examining the cash expended for plant and equipment in comparison with the amount of depreciation expense and the amount of plant and equipment reported in the balance sheet can provide some idea of the rate of growth or contraction. For example, as can be seen in Appendix A, Gateway made capital expenditures of about $235 million during 1998. This is significant when compared with its property, plant, and equipment base (net) at the beginning of the year (1997 balance sheet) of about $376 million and the increase in accumulated depreciation of about $76 million (Note 10 to the financial statements). Although Gateway's fixed asset base is small as compared to other types of manufacturing firms, the information from its financial statements indicates that those assets are relatively young, being only 30 percent depreciated, and that the company appears to be expanding, not just maintaining, its productive capacity. Gateway's comparative cash flow statements reflect capital expenditures that increased significantly each year. This implies that Gateway's management anticipates major future sales growth.

You Decide 13-3

HOW ARE ASSET ACQUISITIONS FINANCED?

From looking at Gateway's cash flow statement in Appendix A, can you tell how Gateway financed its capital expenditures? Where did Gateway get the cash to purchase new plant and equipment? Was the source the same for each of the three years reported? Where did May Company (Exhibit 13–1) get the cash for its capital expenditures? Do you view favorably the means of financing new plant and equipment used by these two companies? Explain.

FINANCING CASH FLOWS

Information for Decisions

The financing section of the cash flow statement provides information about cash provided by the suppliers of the company's capital, both creditors and owners, as well as cash paid to the suppliers of capital. Decision makers use this information to evaluate changes in financing and answer questions such as these: Has the riskiness of the company changed because of a shift in the mix of debt and equity financing? To what extent did dividends draw away cash that was needed to acquire new plant and equipment? How much of the company's additional financing during the period came from short-term sources in relation to long-term sources of capital?

As we have seen, much of an existing company's financing may come from operations. However, many companies, especially new ones and those that are expanding rapidly, need to rely on other sources to provide a stable financing base. As we discussed in Chapters 11 and 12, this type of financing comes either through borrowing or by selling ownership interests. The financing section of the cash flow statement reports on the cash effects of (1) borrowing (other than trade payables), (2) repaying debt, (3) issuing stock, (4) repurchasing stock, and (5) paying dividends.

In Practice 13-3

EMERSON ELECTRIC CO.

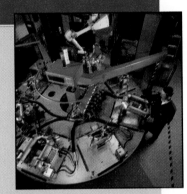

Emerson Electric invested almost $1.1 billion in fiscal 1998 and $860.6 million in 1997 in new plant and equipment and the net purchases of other businesses. Its financing activities for the fiscal years ended September 30, 1998 and 1997, are reported in its Consolidated Statements of Cash Flows as follows:

| | (in millions of dollars) | |
	1998	**1997**
Net increase in short-term borrowing	145.4	321.8
Proceeds from long-term debt	452.0	5.8
Principal payments on long-term debt	(132.5)	(13.1)
Net purchases of treasury stock	(499.4)	(376.6)
Dividends paid	(521.0)	(480.7)
Net cash used in financing activities	(555.5)	(542.8)

ANALYSIS

Considering the extent to which Emerson made cash investments in plant and equipment and used cash to reduce its debt, purchase treasury stock, and pay dividends, the company's operations must have generated significant amounts of cash. In fact, Emerson did generate more than $1.6 billion in cash from operations in fiscal 1998 and almost $1.5 billion in 1997. [www.emersonelectric.com]

CHANGES IN DEBT AND CAPITAL STOCK

Changes in debt reported in the statement of cash flows are simple and straightforward: increases in debt generate cash, and decreases use cash for repayments. Changes in nontrade notes payable, including commercial paper (short-term negotiable notes), and bonds payable are included in this section of the cash flow statement. Decision makers are often especially interested in the financing employed by companies because debt must be repaid and also usually requires periodic interest payments. The issuance of stock, on the other hand, results in earnings being shared by more owners and may result in pressure to use cash to pay dividends.

May Company's cash flow statement in Exhibit 13–1 shows that the company generated so much cash from operations that it actually reduced its reliance on external financing. In addition to paying dividends to its stockholders, the company paid off almost as much long-term debt as it issued during the period, and it reacquired more than half a billion dollars of its own stock. Gateway (Appendix A) paid off more debt than it issued, and its small amount of additional financing came from its employees exercising their stock options.

In Practice 13-4

HOW CALDOR CUT FINANCING COSTS AND WENT BROKE

Caldor Corp., a Norwalk, Connecticut, discounter, was profitable, having earned $3.3 million in the latest quarter, following a net income of $44 million in its latest fiscal year. And, it was in the midst of a major expansion and remodeling. However, the company entered bankruptcy in September 1995 after its factors (lenders) stopped providing the cash needed to finance its inventory. What happened? The company could have issued long-term debt or equity, but found that short-term financing from banks and trade creditors was much cheaper:

> *"If you took the time to look at their annual report," says one factor who did, "you would see the fixed assets going up, the working capital going down." . . . This factor adds: "They were expanding using working capital"—which, of course, is supposed to be used for short-term liquidity.*[2]

ANALYSIS

In Caldor's case, using trade credit and other short-term financing was cheaper than using long-term debt or equity financing. However, short-term financing, by definition, is not permanent and can quickly evaporate. Caldor's short-term creditors suddenly refused to renew the credit and, by that time, Caldor was no longer able to refinance on a long-term basis. By looking at Caldor's cash flow statement, the company's approach to financing its expansion should have been obvious.

PAYMENT OF CASH DIVIDENDS

Owners of a corporation expect a return on their investments. One way they receive a return on their stock investments is through corporate distributions of income to the owners, or dividends. Cash dividends paid during the period are reported in the financing section of the cash flow statement because they reflect a payment to one group of capital suppliers, and, therefore, are related to financing. Perhaps reflecting an inconsistency, interest expense—the return paid to suppliers of debt financing—is not reported in the financing section of the cash flow statement; it is included in the net income amount reported in the operating section of the statement.

Decision makers are often interested in the portion of the cash generated from operations that is used to pay dividends. Although the declaration of dividends is not required, many companies have established dividend policies that place great pressure on management to continue dividend payment trends. Thus, cash generated from operations should, at least in the long run, be sufficient to provide for dividends, as well as the replacement of assets.

From Exhibit 13–1, you can see that May Company pays significant dividends, totaling about 36 percent of net income. May Company is a relatively mature company and pays out a large portion of its income in dividends. Gateway, on the other hand, is a relatively young and rapidly growing company. It pays no dividends, reinvesting all of its earnings for future growth.

[2]Excerpts from Roger Lowenstein, "Lenders' Stampede Tramples Caldor," *The Wall Street Journal* (October 26, 1995), C1.

REPORTING CHANGES IN FINANCIAL POSITION

Information for Decisions

Decision makers analyze changes in financial position as a way of projecting future directions for a company's operations. The statement of cash flows explains balance sheet changes from one period to the next and can help answer questions such as these: Has the company's management taken proper advantage of changing interest rates by substituting debt with a different maturity for debt outstanding? Do the reported changes in plant and equipment include both increases and decreases that partially offset? Why did intangible assets reported in the balance sheet decrease from last year to this year?

The statement of cash flows provides vital information about an organizations's cash inflows and outflows, but it also does more. It bridges the gap between one balance sheet and the next. Decision makers want to know how an organization's financial position has changed during the reporting period, and the cash flow statement provides an explanation. Decision makers can look at this year's balance sheet, compare it with last year's, and see the changes. But what brought about those changes? Why did plant and equipment go up and investments go down? Why did short-term debt decrease and long-term debt increase? Decision makers can trace through the changes in financial position with the statement of cash flows.

The income statement provides part of the explanation as to why financial position changed during the year. The statement of changes in stockholders' equity provides an additional part of the answer. But, only the cash flow statement provides a comprehensive look at the changes in financial position during the period. A closer look at some common transactions can help you better understand how the cash flow statement reports cash flows and reflects all changes in financial position.

IDENTIFYING CASH EFFECTS

In many cases, the cash effects of a change in financial position can be determined easily. If, for example, the balance of the land account increases by $100,000 during the year, and only one transaction has occurred involving land, this would seem to indicate that land was purchased for $100,000; land increases and cash decreases by $100,000. However, suppose the company both bought and sold land during the period. Or, suppose the land was purchased in exchange for a long-term note. The cash effects of changes in financial position are not always as simple as they seem. Therefore, accountants must be careful to explain the changes in a company's financial position and the effects on cash so decision makers can understand what has occurred.

Changes in a particular account that involve both increases and decreases normally must be reported separately. For example, an increase in land during the period might involve both a sale of land and a purchase of land, and the two must be reported separately. In addition, the gain or loss on the sale of land is included in net income and, therefore, must be removed from the operating section of the cash flow statement because it does not relate to operations and does not have a cash effect separate from the sales price of the land.

A CLOSER LOOK AT

INCREASES AND DECREASES WITH GAINS OR LOSSES

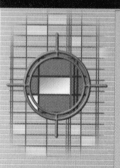

Bradley Company's land account increases $100,000 during the year. The company also reports a $10,000 gain on the sale of land in its income statement. The land account on the company's books appears as follows:

Land

1/1 Balance	350,000		
9/20 Purchase	140,000	7/15 Sale	40,000
12/31 Balance	450,000		

Thus, Bradley has sold one parcel of land for $50,000, its original cost of $40,000 plus the gain of $10,000, and purchased another parcel for $140,000. The statement of cash flows reports an adjustment of $10,000 deducted from net income in the operating section to remove the gain from operations and to avoid counting that $10,000 twice. The full $50,000 sales amount of the land is reported in the investing section of the statement as a cash inflow from the sale of land. In addition, the purchase of land for $140,000 is reported in the investing section, but as a cash outflow.

Increases and decreases in other assets or liabilities also must generally be dealt with separately. For example, from Exhibit 13–1, you can see that May Company reports in the financing section of its cash flow statement proceeds from issuance of debt separately from repayments of debt. In addition, the complications of depreciation and amortization must be dealt with when considering changes in limited-life assets.

A CLOSER LOOK AT

DEPRECIABLE ASSETS AND CASH FLOWS

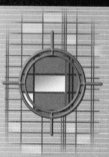

Robin Corporation sells equipment during the year at a loss of $2,000 and also purchases equipment for $100,000. On the company's books, the Equipment and related Accumulated Depreciation accounts appear as follows for the year:

Equipment

1/1 Balance	275,000		
9/30 Purchase	100,000	1/5 Sale	50,000
12/31 Balance	325,000		

Accumulated Depreciation—Equipment

		1/1 Balance	125,000
1/5 Asset Sale	30,000	12/31 Expense	40,000
		12/31 Balance	135,000

When recorded on Robin's books, the sale of equipment increases cash by $18,000, reduces equipment by the original cost of $50,000 and accumulated depreciation $30,000, and leads to a $2,000 loss on the sale, as follows:

Cash		$18,000
Less book value of equipment:		
Original cost	$ 50,000	
Accumulated depreciation	(30,000)	
Book value		20,000
Loss on sale		$ 2,000

The investing section of Robin's cash flow statement includes the following:

Cash provided by (used in) investing activities:	
Sale of equipment	$ 18,000
Purchase of equipment	(100,000)

The cash provided by the sale is equal to the $20,000 book value of the equipment sold (cost of $50,000, less accumulated depreciation of $30,000) minus the $2,000 loss. In the operating section of the statement, the $2,000 loss is eliminated through an adjustment adding it to net income because it is not related to operations and because the total cash effect of the sale is reported in the investing section. The amount of depreciation expense for the year, $40,000, is added to net income in the operating section of the statement because it had been deducted to arrive at net income but did not use cash.

SUPPLEMENTAL CASH FLOW INFORMATION

Some changes in financial position do not affect cash directly, yet they reflect important investing or financing activities of which decision makers should be aware. Because these activities do not provide or use cash, they are not reported in the operating, investing, or financing sections of the cash flow statement. However, authoritative standards do require that they be disclosed. In addition, companies are required to disclose cash payments made for income taxes and interest because of the importance of these two items.

These supplemental disclosures are made in a variety of ways, although the standards encourage that these disclosures be made on the face of the cash flow statement. (See In Practice 13-5.) Some companies include a separate section at the bottom of the cash flow statement for supplemental disclosures, as can be seen in Exhibit 13–1 for May Company's interest and income taxes. Others include the supplemental information in a note to the cash flow statement or in the notes to the financial statements in general.

ALTERNATIVE REPORTING APPROACHES

Nearly all companies, including May Company and Gateway, use what is referred to as an indirect approach to reporting cash flows. The operating section of the cash flow statement starts with net income and then presents adjustments to reach the amount of cash provided by operations. The advantage of this approach is that it reconciles the cash provided by operations with the income reported in the income statement and clearly presents the differences. The disadvantage is that financial statement users may have difficulty understanding the adjustments, and this leads to misunderstandings, such as referring to the "cash provided by depreciation."

In Practice 13-5

LUCENT TECHNOLOGIES AND PIZZA INN, INC.

Lucent Technologies includes the following information on the fifth page of its Notes to Consolidated Financial Statements:

SUPPLEMENTAL CASH FLOW INFORMATION (dollars in millions)

	Year Ended September 30 (Twelve Months)		Nine Months Ended September 30,
	1998	1997	1996
Interest payments, net of amounts capitalized	$ 319	$ 307	$209
Income tax payments	$ 714	$ 781	$142
ACQUISITIONS OF BUSINESSES			
Fair value of assets acquired	$2,341	$1,812	$527
Less: Fair value of liabilities assumed	$ 994	$ 244	$293
Acquisitions of businesses	$1,347	$1,568	$234

Pizza Inn includes the following presentation at the end of its Consolidated Statements of Cash Flows:

SUPPLEMENTAL DISCLOSURES OF CASH FLOW INFORMATION
(In Thousands)

	Year Ended		
	June 28, 1998	June 29, 1997	June 30, 1996
CASH PAYMENTS FOR:			
Interest	$526	$612	$880
Income taxes	160	150	110
NONCASH FINANCING AND INVESTING ACTIVITIES:			
Capital lease obligations incurred	$ —	$ —	$477

ANALYSIS

Although these two companies disclose the supplemental cash flow information in different locations, and some companies use different formats, all companies disclose the required information in their financial reports so that it is easily accessible. [www.lucent.com]

The FASB has recommended that companies present the cash flow statement using a format referred to as the **direct approach,** which focuses on cash flows directly rather than starting with net income and adjusting for noncash items. Under this approach, the operating section of the cash flow statement reports cash received from customers, cash interest or dividends received from investments, and cash received from other income sources, as well as cash payments made to suppliers and employees, and cash paid for interest and for taxes. Noncash revenues and expenses, as well as all nonoperating gains and losses, are not included because they have no direct cash flow effects. This direct approach is generally considered to be more understandable than the indirect approach, but a separate reconciliation with net income is needed. The investing and financing sections of the statement are the same under both approaches.

Both the direct and indirect approaches arrive at the same cash from operations, but the direct method focuses on the cash flows, while the indirect method focuses on net income and adjusting it to arrive at the net cash flow from operations. Although the indirect method allows users to tie the cash flow statement to the other financial statements more easily, the direct method provides a more intuitive presentation.

A CLOSER LOOK AT

ALTERNATIVE APPROACHES TO THE CASH FLOW STATEMENT

Ritts Company's comparative year-end balance sheet amounts are as follows:

	2001	2000	Increase (Decrease)
Cash	$ 3,400	$ 2,200	$ 1,200
Accounts receivable	24,000	25,500	(1,500)
Inventory	67,800	53,100	14,700
Land	55,000	41,400	13,600
Buildings and equipment	221,100	138,400	82,700
Accumulated depreciation	(36,100)	(20,500)	(15,600)
Patents	40,000	45,000	(5,000)
Total assets	$375,200	$285,100	$90,100
Accounts payable and accruals	$ 2,100	$ 1,400	$ 700
Taxes payable	1,200	700	500
Long-term debt	150,000	100,000	50,000
Capital stock	50,000	40,000	10,000
Additional paid-in capital	88,800	71,300	17,500
Retained earnings	83,100	71,700	11,400
Total liabilities and equity	$375,200	$285,100	$90,100

The following is the company's income statement for 2001:

Revenues	$ 565,000
Cost of goods sold	(323,000)
Gross margin	$ 242,000
Other income: gain on sale of land	3,000
Expenses:	
General operating expenses	(152,700)
Depreciation and amortization	(20,600)
Interest expense	(8,200)
Income taxes	(19,100)
Net income	$ 44,400

Ritts sold land during the year for $9,500 and purchased land for $20,100. The company did not sell any buildings, equipment, or patents. Ritts paid cash dividends of $33,000 during the year, and its interest expense was all paid in cash. From its financial statements and other information, Ritts prepares the cash flow statement shown in Exhibit 13–4, using the indirect approach. The cash expended for new buildings and equipment is determined from the increase in the balance sheet account, and the amortization of the patents is determined from the decrease in the Patents account.

If Ritts had used the direct approach to preparing its cash flow statement, the operating section of the statement would appear as in Exhibit 13–5. The rest of the statement would be the same as under the indirect approach. The cash collected from customers is determined by adding the decrease in accounts receivable to the sales revenue reported in the income statement. The cash paid to suppliers is computed by summing the cost of goods sold and operating expenses in the income statement, adding the increase in inventory, and subtracting the increase in accounts payable and accruals. The cash paid for interest is taken from the income statement, and the cash paid for income taxes is computed by subtracting the increase in taxes payable from the income taxes reported in the income statement.

EXHIBIT 13-4   **STATEMENT OF CASH FLOWS—INDIRECT METHOD**

RITTS COMPANY		
STATEMENT OF CASH FLOWS		
FOR THE YEAR 2001		
Cash Flows from Operations:		
Net income		$ 44,400
Adjustments:		
Depreciation and amortization of patents		20,600
Gain on sale of land		(3,000)
Decrease in accounts receivable		1,500
Increase in inventory		(14,700)
Increase in accounts payable and accruals		700
Increase in taxes payable		500
Cash provided by operations		$ 50,000
Cash Flows from Investing Activities:		
Sale of land	$ 9,500	
Purchase of land	(20,100)	
Purchase of buildings and equipment	(82,700)	
Cash flows used in investing activities		(93,300)
Cash Flows from Financing Activities:		
Issuance of long-term debt	$ 50,000	
Issuance of capital stock	27,500	
Dividends paid	(33,000)	
Cash provided by financing activities		44,500
Increase in cash		$ 1,200
Beginning cash balance		2,200
Ending cash balance		$ 3,400
Supplemental Information		
Cash payments for:		
Interest	$ 8,200	
Income taxes	18,600	

OPERATING SECTION OF STATEMENT OF CASH FLOWS— DIRECT METHOD

EXHIBIT 13-5

RITTS COMPANY	
STATEMENT OF CASH FLOWS	
FOR THE YEAR 2001	

Cash Flows from Operations:	
Cash collections from customers	$ 566,500[a]
Payments to suppliers	(489,700)[b]
Interest	(8,200)
Income taxes	(18,600)[c]
Cash provided by operations	$ 50,000

[a]$565,000 + $1,500

[b]($323,000 + $152,700) + ($14,700 − $700)

[c]$19,100 − $500

EVALUATING CASH FLOW INFORMATION

Information for Decisions

Cash flow information is often best used in comparison with other information over several time periods. This type of evaluation can help financial statement users answer questions such as these: Even though total cash flow is adequate, what is the relative reliability of each source of cash, and how does this compare to industry standards? Will this company generate enough cash flow per share to be able to continue its dividend payments? To what extent do the operations of the company generate available cash after maintaining the company's productive capacity?

Throughout this chapter we have seen that the information reported in the cash flow statement helps decision makers better understand an organization's activities. As with other accounting information, data about cash flows are generally most useful when used in comparison with other information. Some comparisons are made within the cash flow statement itself. For example, we saw that comparing the cash generated by operations with the cash used in investing activities is a good indication of how a company finances its growth and whether that growth can be sustained.

In some cases, decision makers may wish to determine the primary sources of cash for an organization. One way of looking at this information is to accumulate all of the organization's sources (not uses) of cash from the cash flow statement and determine the percentage contribution by each. For example, using the cash flow statement in Exhibit 13–4, Ritts Company's sources of cash can be analyzed as follows:

	Amount	Percent
Sources of Cash:		
Income before gain and after adjustment for depreciation and amortization: $44,400 + $20,600 − $3,000	$ 62,000	41.3%
Net increases in current liabilities	1,200	0.8%
Sale of assets	9,500	6.3%
Issuance of long-term debt	50,000	33.3%
Issuance of capital stock	27,500	18.3%
Total cash flow inflows	$150,200	100.0%

This analysis provides an overview of all of the sources that an organization is relying on for cash. These sources can then be considered for their reliability and durability. This type of analysis also can be useful in comparison with other companies in the same industry or the same company in prior years.

As we saw in earlier chapters, ratios are useful when analyzing a company's financial position and activities because they provide standardized comparisons. Although any ratios that a decision maker may find useful can be constructed, several are commonly used.

CASH FLOW MEASURES RELATED TO RETURN

Perhaps the most commonly used ratio relating to cash flows is operating cash flow per share, usually referred to simply as cash flow per share. For many years, the accounting profession discouraged reporting this number because it detracted from accrual-basis income and earnings per share. However, this measure is viewed as particularly useful in assessing a company's ability to pay dividends and, over time, as an indication of how successful a company's operations are. **Cash flow per share** is computed as follows:

$$\text{Cash flow per share} = \frac{\text{(Net cash provided by operations} - \text{Dividends on prefered stock)}}{\text{Common shares outstanding}}$$

Gateway does not report its cash flow per share, but based on its reported operating cash flows and the average number of common shares outstanding [from Note 1(n) to its financial statements], its cash flow per share for each of the three years for which its cash flow statement is shown in Appendix A is as follows:

1998	**1997**	**1996**
$\dfrac{\$907,651}{155,542} = \$5.84$	$\dfrac{\$442,797}{153,840} = \$2.88$	$\dfrac{\$483,996}{152,745} = \$3.17$

Gateway has no preferred stock outstanding, so no preferred dividend is deducted from cash flow. The number of common shares used in the computations is the same as that used to compute earnings per share.

As a potential investor, what does this ratio tell you? You can see that the cash flow generated by Gateway's operations is significant and, after dropping slightly in 1997, increased dramatically in 1998. This bodes well for the future of the company, indicating a significant capacity for internal financing of future growth. Further, although Gateway does not currently pay dividends, its cash flow per share indicates a growing potential for such payments in the future.

Another cash measure of return is the ratio of **cash flow to total assets.** This ratio is computed as follows:

$$\text{Cash flow to total assets} = \frac{\text{Cash flow from operations}}{\text{Average total assets}}$$

For Gateway, the ratio of cash flow to total assets in 1998 is:

$$\frac{\$907,651}{(\$2,039,271 + \$2,890,380)/2} = .368$$

The amount of average total assets is computed by summing total assets at the end of 1997 and 1998, and then dividing by 2. In effect, the ratio of cash flow to total assets provides a measure of cash return on the investment in assets and can be used over time as a measure of profitability. However, this measure tends to be more volatile than accrual-based return on assets.

One other measure that is often discussed by financial analysts is **free cash flow.** This measure indicates the amount of cash that is generated by operations after maintaining productive capacity. Free cash flow is measured as follows:

$$\text{Free cash flow} = \begin{pmatrix} \text{Cash generated} \\ \text{from} \\ \text{operations} \end{pmatrix} - \begin{pmatrix} \text{Cash invested} \\ \text{to maintain} \\ \text{capacity} \end{pmatrix}$$

The resulting figure provides a measure of the cash flows that can be used for expansion, paying off debt, retiring stock, or paying dividends to owners. Unfortunately, most companies do not report investments to maintain capacity separate from expansion investments. Therefore, some estimate must be made of the portion of investment representing a maintenance of the status quo. Many times, however, the entire amount of cash invested in operating capacity is deducted, thus understating the free cash flow.

CASH FLOW MEASURES RELATED TO SAFETY

Measures of cash flow related to safety typically have to do with how cash flows from operations compare with some required or anticipated payment. One such measure is the ratio of **dividends to operating cash flow,** which compares cash provided by operations with the current dividend to stockholders. For Gateway, the ratio is not meaningful because Gateway does not pay dividends. For May Company, based on Exhibit 13–1, this ratio is calculated as follows:

1998	**1997**	**1996**
$\dfrac{\$308}{\$1,505} = .205$	$\dfrac{\$297}{\$1,526} = .195$	$\dfrac{\$305}{\$1,283} = .238$

With May Company's dividend payments equal to about 20 percent of cash generated from operations, a reasonable margin of safety for the dividend is provided. In addition, some margin is provided for internal financing. However, a significant asset replacement or expansion could strain internal financing and require additional long-term financing.

In Practice 13-6

SARA LEE CORPORATION

In 1998, Sara Lee reported a net loss of $523 million. Yet, the company paid cash dividends to common shareholders of $358 million to continue its policy of paying regular cash dividends. Where did Sara Lee get the money to pay cash dividends? Its cash flow from operating activities in 1998 was $1.935 billion. Many of its 1998 expenses did not use cash, including $618 million of depreciation and amortization and, the main reason for its net loss, a restructuring charge of more than $2 billion.

ANALYSIS

The company's ratio of common stock dividends to operating cash flow was:

$$\frac{\$358 \text{ million}}{\$1,935 \text{ million}} = .185$$

This ratio indicates the high margin of safety reflected in Sara Lee's dividend policy.
[www.saralee.com]

Another measure of safety is the ratio of **cash flow to current maturities of debt.** This ratio indicates a company's ability to generate enough cash from its operations to repay debt commitments that mature in the near future, excluding normal trade payables. The ratio is calculated as follows:

$$\text{Cash flow to maturing debt} = \frac{\text{Cash provided by operations}}{\text{Debt maturing currently}}$$

Gateway's ratios are as follows:

1998	**1997**
$\dfrac{\$907,651}{\$11,415} = 79.5$	$\dfrac{\$442,797}{\$13,969} = 31.7$

These ratios are very high, indicating Gateway's ability to easily meet its current maturities of debt. The reasons that Gateway has such unusually high ratios of cash flow to current maturities of debt reflect the characteristics of Gateway's operations. First, Gateway's operations generate a very large cash inflow. Second, Gateway has little long-term debt, and, even though the majority of it will be coming due shortly, the amount is small.

A similar safety measure is the ratio of **cash flow to total debt.** This ratio takes a longer-run view by comparing current cash flow from operations with total liabilities. The higher the ratio, the better a company's debt-paying ability and the better the safety margin for creditors and stockholders. Gateway's ratios of cash flow to total debt are as follows:

1998	**1997**
$\dfrac{\$907,651}{\$1,546,005} = .587$	$\dfrac{\$442,797}{\$1,109,227} = .399$

The ratio of cash flow to total debt is a stringent safety measure related to cash flows. Gateway's ratios are very good because of its high cash flows from operations and the small amount of long-term debt.

SUMMARY

Much of current financial reporting is designed to project future cash flows. Accrual accounting, revenue and expense recognition principles, and valuation principles are all designed to assist in this projection. Accrual-basis income is considered useful for projecting both future income and cash flows. However, the statement of cash flows looks at current cash flows more directly, and information about cash flows is also considered useful by decision makers in projecting future cash flows. Decision makers use cash flow information to assess whether an organization will be able to meet its obligations in a timely manner, continue in business, have the means to expand, and provide cash distributions to the owners.

The cash flow statement reports how an organization's activities affected cash during the period, and it discloses significant noncash investing and financing activities. The statement reports sources and uses of cash in three main sections, reflecting the primary types of enterprise activities: operating activities, investing activities, and financing activities.

The major recurring source of cash for a business should be its operations. If a company cannot consistently generate cash from its operations over the long run, it eventually must stop operating. Most companies use an indirect approach to reporting cash from operations, starting with accrual-basis income and adjusting that amount to reflect cash generated from operations. While these adjustments may appear in the statement as if they are sources of cash, they are not; they are simply adjustments needed to determine the cash generated because some items affect net income and cash differently.

Cash flows related to investing activities are concerned primarily with the replacement and expansion of operating capacity, as well as the disposal of assets no longer used. This section of the cash flow statement is important because it indicates the company's commitment to maintaining and expanding its capacity.

Cash flows related to financing activities indicate to what extent a company has increased its cash or financed its investments through external sources. It also reports reductions in outside financing by using cash to retire debt or reacquire stock. Further, this section shows how much cash has been returned to owners through dividend distributions.

The analysis of a company's cash flow statement and related ratios is a key part of making decisions about the company. Useful comparisons relating to cash flows tend to focus on cash flows from operations and to compare these cash flows with current or expected future cash needs.

LIST OF IMPORTANT TERMS

cash flow per share *(514)*

cash flow to current maturities of debt *(516)*

cash flow to total assets *(514)*

cash flow to total debt *(516)*

cash flows from operations *(494)*

cash flows related to financing *(495)*

cash flows related to investing *(494)*

direct approach *(510)*

dividends to operating cash flow *(515)*

free cash flow *(515)*

indirect approach *(498)*

statement of cash flows *(494)*

EXAMINING THE CONCEPTS

Q13-1 The cash flow statement is one of four basic financial statements. What are the other three statements?

Q13-2 What is the purpose of the cash flow statement?

Q13-3 What are the three major sections of a cash flow statement? Give an example of an item that would be reported in each.

Q13-4 How can you tell whether a company is expanding or contracting by reading its cash flow statement?

Q13-5 Explain what is meant by the statement that managing a company's cash flow is, in part, a balancing of profitability and liquidity.

Q13-6 Identify at least three alternative uses of a company's cash generated from operations.

Q13-7 How does the statement of cash flows tie together the other three financial statements? Why is a full set of financial statements needed to understand a company's financial position and changes in that position?

Q13-8 When preparing the cash flow statement by the indirect method, why does net income need to be adjusted to arrive at operating cash flows?

Q13-9 Is depreciation a source of cash from operations? Explain.

Q13-10 If depreciation does not use cash, how is the cash outflow used to acquire depreciable assets reported?

Q13-11 Identify three expenses that do not involve cash outflows during the period the expenses are recognized. For each, explain why no cash flow occurs in the period in which the expense is recognized.

Q13-12 Explain how a company can increase its sales and, in the same year, experience a decrease in cash generated by operations.

Q13-13 Where in the statement of cash flows is a loss from the sale of equipment reported? Explain why this is done.

Q13-14 Under normal circumstances, when a company increases its accounts receivable balance from the previous year, it also increases its current assets, working capital, and current ratio. Does it also increase its cash inflows? If so, how and when is the cash inflow increased?

Q13-15 If a company reported only the total cash flows from operations without all of the confusing adjustments, identify at least one important piece of information that would be lost. What decision might this missing information affect?

Q13-16 What are the two main investing cash flows for most companies? List two others.

Q13-17 What is the possible significance of a company generating most of its cash from investing activities? What effect could this information have on an investor's or creditor's decisions about the company?

Q13-18 Companies often choose between issuing bonds and common stock when they need additional capital. How does the way in which interest payments on the debt are reported in the cash flow statement differ from the reporting of dividends paid on stock?

Q13-19 If a company obtains needed cash through financing activities rather than operations, does this mean the company is in financial difficulty? Explain.

Q13-20 Why might a company borrow short-term to repay long-term debt? Given that the short-term debt will need to be "rolled over," do you think such a company expects interest rates to be going up or going down in the future?

Q13-21 Why is the ratio of cash dividends paid to operating cash flow of interest to investors? To managers?

Q13-22 Johnson Company recently sold a building at a loss. How will the company report the transaction in the cash flow statement if it uses the indirect approach of presenting its statement?

Q13-23 What supplemental cash flow information must be reported? How would the exchange of outstanding bonds for common stock in a conversion be reported?

Q13-24 Companies are required to disclose the cash payments made for income taxes and interest. Why are these two items singled out? In what two ways do companies most often report these items?

Q13-25 If you are concerned that a company has reported positive cash flows by slowing its payments on current liabilities and by issuing additional long-term debt, what factors might you examine? Explain.

Q13-26 Compare cash flow per share and earnings per share. Would you expect one to be higher than the other? Why?

Q13-27 Explain how the ratio of a company's cash flows from operations to current maturities of its debt provides information about the safety of an investor's holdings in that company. Does the ratio of cash flow to total debt provide the same information? Explain.

UNDERSTANDING ACCOUNTING INFORMATION

E13-1 Understanding the Statement of Cash Flows Sorter Company reported the following summarized cash flows for the current year:

Cash flows from operations	$ 600,000
Cash flows from investing activities	(700,000)
Cash flows from financing activities	200,000
Net cash flows	$ 100,000
Beginning cash balance	70,000
Ending cash balance	$ 170,000

a. Does Sorter Company appear to be in a favorable position to pay a cash dividend of $130,000 at year-end?
b. Why are operating cash flows critical in evaluating Sorter's ability to pay future cash dividends?
c. If an investor wishes to determine if Sorter Company has generated cash by issuing additional stock, which portion of the cash flow statement would provide the information?
d. Is it possible for a company such as Sorter to report a positive cash flow for the period even though it has a negative cash flow from operations? Explain.

E13-2 Operating Cash Flows Moret Company's cash flow statement for the current year contained the following information on cash flows provided by operations:

Net income		$ 57,000
Depreciation and amortization	$ 42,000	
Increase in accounts receivable	(15,000)	
Decrease in inventory	7,000	
Increase in accounts payable	12,000	46,000
Cash provided by operations		$103,000

a. Why must noncash expenses such as depreciation be added to net income in computing the cash provided by operations?
b. If Moret Company had reported depreciation expense of $62,000 rather than $42,000, what impact would this change have on cash provided by operations for the year? Which of the above totals would change? By what amounts?
c. In what way does an increase in accounts payable represent a cash savings?
d. Why is the computation used above in determining Moret's cash provided by operations described as the indirect method?

E13-3 Investing Cash Flows Rigor Company reported the following net cash flow from investing activities in its cash flow statement:

Sale of equipment	$ 40,000
Sale of land	160,000
Purchase of Starback Corporation bonds	(350,000)
Cash used in investing activities	$(150,000)

a. If Rigor Company is expanding, would the cash flows from investing activities be expected to be positive or negative? Explain why.
b. Does Rigor Company appear to be expanding or contracting its operations? How do you know?
c. Is it possible to determine if a gain or loss was recorded on the sale of equipment by looking at the cash flow statement? Where would this amount be disclosed?
d. Does the $40,000 reported from the sale of equipment represent the cash received or the carrying value of the equipment at the time of sale?

e. In light of Rigor's cash flows from investing activities, would you expect Rigor to be generating cash flows from financing activities? Explain.

E13-4 Financing Cash Flows The cash flow from financing activities reported by Bobble Corporation included the following:

Issuance of preferred stock	$ 150,000
Issuance of common stock	720,000
Retirement of bonds payable	(210,000)
Dividends paid	(35,000)
Cash provided by financing activities	$ 625,000

a. Are the financing activities reported by Bobble consistent with a company that is expanding or contracting? Explain.
b. Which of the financing activities reported for the current year are not likely to occur on an annual basis?
c. If Bobble is operating profitably, is more of the $625,000 of cash provided by financing activities likely to be used on operating activities or investing activities?
d. Why are dividends excluded from the income statement but included in the statement of cash flows?

E13-5 Reporting Changes in Financial Position

a. Why does the change in cash balance reported in the cash flow statement typically differ from the change in retained earnings reported in the statement of changes in stockholders' equity?
b. What are the major sources of cash typically used to purchase long-term assets?
c. What are the major sources of cash typically used to retire short-term debt? Long-term debt?
d. Which section(s) of the cash flow statement is (are) reported differently if the direct method is used in preparing the cash flow statement?
e. Are total cash flows for the period computed using the direct method generally larger than, less than, or equal to cash flows computed using the indirect method? Explain.

E13-6 Evaluating Cash Flow Information An analysis of financial statement data for Grapp Company and Stomp Corporation resulted in the following ratio information:

	Grapp	Stomp
Earnings per share	$2.50	$1.20
Cash flow per share from operations	3.00	1.25
Cash flow to total assets	.20	.05

a. What is likely to cause the amount reported as cash flow per share to be greater than the amount reported as earnings per share?

b. Is the amount reported as earnings per share or cash flow per share more likely to be affected by a delay in paying suppliers? Explain.
c. Which of the two companies appears to be in a better position to pay a cash dividend at the end of the current accounting period? Explain.
d. Why is the ratio of cash flow to total assets computed using the cash flow from operations rather than the cash flow from all sources? How might use of the net cash flows from all sources mislead investors?
e. Which of the two companies appears to be in a better position to replace its operating assets? Explain.

E13-7 Multiple Choice: The Statement of Cash Flows
Select the correct answer for each of the following:

1. The cash flows from operations section of the statement of cash flows prepared using the indirect approach includes:
   a. Net income on an accrual basis.
   b. Adjustments for noncash expenses.
   c. Adjustments to remove gains and losses on the sale of noncurrent assets.
   d. All of the above.
2. Which of the following has the effect of increasing cash flows?
   a. Accounts receivable increases more than inventory increases.
   b. Accounts receivable increases less than inventory increases.
   c. Accounts receivable and inventory both decrease.
   d. Accounts receivable and inventory both increase.
3. The statement of cash flows ties together the other financial statements by:
   a. Reporting the adjustments necessary to reconcile net income and cash generated by operations.
   b. Reporting all changes in the balance sheet in terms of their effects on cash.
   c. Separating cash flow activities into operating, investing, and financing.
   d. All of the above.
4. The statement of cash flows is divided into three main categories. These categories are:
   a. Operating, investing, and cash collections.
   b. Operating, marketing, and investing.
   c. Cash outflows, cash inflows, and noncash activities.
   d. Operating, investing, and financing.
5. Which of the following describes the content of the categories of the statement of cash flows?
   a. Cash flows from operations are routine in nature and usually are expected to be repetitive.
   b. Cash flows related to investing reflect the use of cash for the purchase of new plant and equipment.
   c. Cash flows from financing reflect amounts received by borrowing or from issuing stock.
   d. All of the above.

E13-8 Multiple Choice: Operating Cash Flows Select the correct answer for each of the following:

1. Which of the following is added to net income in deriving cash flows generated from operations when using the indirect method?
   a. Increases in accounts receivable.
   b. Increases in accounts payable.
   c. Decreases in accounts payable.
   d. None of the above.

2. Which of the following is deducted from net income in deriving cash flows generated from operations when using the indirect method?
   a. Increases in accounts receivable and increases in inventory.
   b. Increases in accounts payable and decreases in inventory.
   c. Decreases in accounts receivable and decreases in inventory.
   d. All of the above.

3. Expenses that reduce net income in the current period but do not use cash are added back to determine cash generated by operations for the period. They include:
   a. Cost of goods sold.
   b. Interest expense on short-term bank loans.
   c. Amortization of intangible assets.
   d. Amortization of premium on bonds payable.

4. Which of the following decisions are likely to be influenced as much or more by cash flows from operations than by reported net income?
   a. Whether the company will have to enter the capital markets to finance its planned expansions.
   b. Whether the new product line added this year is profitable enough to improve the overall gross margin.
   c. Whether the company should reduce its investment in inventory in accordance with its plans for a just-in-time inventory management system.
   d. Whether the company would improve its liquidity by changing to an accelerated depreciation method for financial reporting.

5. Which of the following items reported in the operating section of the statement of cash flows might indicate a potential liquidity problem?
   a. Positive cash flow appears to have been maintained by increasing accounts payable.
   b. Cash inflows seem to be lower in the current year because of an increase in accounts receivable and inventory.
   c. Prepaid expenses have not decreased in the current year.
   d. Both (a) and (b) are correct.

E13-9 Multiple Choice: Cash Flows Select the correct answer for each of the following:

1. If a company is expanding, purchases of operating assets normally:
   a. Are treated as a deduction from depreciation expense in determining the change in cash flow from operations.
   b. Will be larger than the cash generated from issuing additional bonds or stocks.
   c. Will be larger than the depreciation expense adjustment to operating cash flows.
   d. All of the above.

2. Free cash flow is a measure of:
   a. The amount of cash that is generated by operations after maintaining productive capacity.
   b. The cash flow that is left after paying off debt.
   c. The cash flow used to retire stock and pay dividends.
   d. The ratio of cash flow to total assets.

3. The financing section of the statement of cash flows reports:
   a. The amount of cash made available by recording depreciation expense for the year.
   b. The cash effects of borrowing, repaying debt, issuing stock, repurchasing stock, and paying dividends.
   c. The amount of cash used to increase operating assets or long-term investments.
   d. The cash used to pay interest on long-term debt and dividends on outstanding stock.

4. The payment of cash dividends is:
   a. Limited to free cash flow.
   b. Limited to cash flow generated from operations.
   c. Reported in the financing section of the cash flow statement.
   d. Limited to the cash flow from operations, less any cash used to purchase investments.

5. The statement of cash flows presents a comprehensive look at the changes in financial position beyond the information reported in the balance sheet when:
   a. Property, plant, and equipment is both purchased and sold during the period.
   b. Long-term debt is retired and new debt is issued.
   c. Intangible assets are increased by the purchase of trademarks and copyrights and decreased by annual amortization.
   d. All of the above.

E13-10 Tying Together Activities and Financial Statements

a. Which part of the cash flow statement is most directly linked to the income statement?

b. Which part of the cash flow statement is most directly linked with an increase in noncurrent assets?

c. Which part of the cash flow statement is most directly linked to an increase in long-term liabilities?

d. Which part of the cash flow statement is most directly linked to the distribution of net income in the form of cash dividends?

e. Which section of the cash flow statement should investors examine if they wish to predict a company's ability to pay future dividends?

f. Which section of the cash flow statement should investors examine if they wish to predict a company's ability to pay off existing long-term debt?

E13-11 Statement Classification Indicate whether the (1) operating, (2) investing, or (3) financing section of the statement of cash flows is most likely to contain the information needed to answer the following questions. If the information is in more than one section, so indicate. If information from other financial statements is needed, so indicate.

a. Will there be enough cash to pay the accounts payable when they are due?
b. Are there unpaid wages, and will cash be available to make the payments?
c. Will there be enough cash to pay off the long-term debt when it is due without additional borrowing?
d. Does the company consistently generate enough cash to pay dividends?
e. How dependable are the company's sources of cash?
f. Has the company expanded in the past year and, if so, how was the expansion financed?
g. Does the company have sufficient cash inflows to make required interest payments?
h. Is the amount of cash generated through operating activities greater than the amount reported as net income?
i. Are receivables being collected on a timely basis?
j. How are the cash flows affected by unusual transactions or events such as losses from restructuring or write-offs of obsolete production facilities?
k. Were any bonds converted into common stock during the period?

E13-12 Classification of Activities Indicate whether each of the following items should be classified as an operating, investing, or financing activity when reported in the statement of cash flows, classified in some other way, or excluded from the statement:

a. Payment of cash dividends on common stock.
b. Borrowing cash by issuing a long-term note.
c. Sale of a warehouse at book value.
d. Purchase of common stock of an affiliated company to obtain control of its operations.
e. Interest payments on an outstanding long-term note.
f. Collection of accounts receivable.
g. Purchase of treasury stock.
h. Conversion of outstanding bonds to shares of common stock.
i. Declaration (but not payment) of dividends on preferred stock.
j. Acquisition of land in exchange for common stock.
k. Purchase of operating equipment.

E13-13 Sources of Cash Flows The Expando Company plans to invest approximately $500,000 each year for the next 3 years to expand its operations into a neighboring state. Net income for the last 3 years, most recent first, has been $225,000, $223,000 and $224,000, respectively. Cash generated by operations for each of the last 3 years has been $420,000, $410,000, and $398,000, respectively. Much of the difference between net income and cash flow from operations each year is due to depreciation expense.

a. Is it possible for Expando Company to fund its expansion from operating cash flows? What other uses may have to be made of the cash generated from operations? Will it help to increase depreciation? Explain.
b. Identify the alternative sources of cash that Expando should consider for its expansion.
c. Expando's management says that the expansion is needed because sales in the neighboring state have increased by $1,000,000 in the past 2 years. This, in turn, caused an increase in accounts receivable of $150,000 and inventory of $100,000. What effect has this had on cash generated by operations?

E13-14 Cash Flows from Operations You have been given the following information from the Albert Park Company. From the information, prepare a schedule that shows cash flows from operations using the indirect approach.

Net income	$775,000
Accounts receivable increase	163,000
Inventory decrease	187,000
Prepaid expense increase	12,000
Accounts payable increase	79,000
Depreciation expense	365,000
Amortization of goodwill	120,000
Decrease in deferred tax liability	185,000

E13-15 Cash Receipts and Payments Lazard Company had sales of $783,400 for the year. The company reported accounts receivable of $87,500 at the end of last year and $77,600 at the end of this year. Lazard's cost of goods sold this year was $510,000. In last year's balance sheet, Lazard reported inventory of $131,000 and accounts payable of $53,700. In this year's balance sheet, Lazard reported inventory of $142,600 and accounts payable of $55,900.

a. How much cash did Lazard collect from customers during the year?
b. How much cash did Lazard pay to suppliers for inventory during the year?

E13-16 Sale of Depreciable Assets Linwood Corporation purchased equipment for $300,000 on January 1, 1994, and used straight-line depreciation over a 10-year life. Estimated scrap value was $20,000. If Linwood sold the equipment for $88,000 on December 31, 2000, give the dollar amounts that would be reported in the cash flows from operations section and the investing section of Linwood's 2000 cash flow statement and state whether they would be added or deducted.

E13-17 Increases and Decreases in Operating Cash Flows Indicate whether each of the following items would be added to Melody Corporation's net income, deducted from net income, or have no effect in deriving cash provided by operations using the indirect method:

a. An increase of $6,000 in prepaid insurance.

b. A reduction of $21,000 in wages payable.

c. A purchase of land for $134,000.

d. A purchase of inventory for $49,000 on credit on December 31.

e. A transfer of $40,000 from the checking account to a money market account.

f. An $8,000 loss on the retirement of long-term bonds.

g. A purchase of $72,000 of treasury stock.

h. A sale of buildings for $320,000. The net book value at the time of sale is $274,000.

i. A receipt of $75,000 from the maturity of a 30-day certificate of deposit.

Melody Corporation includes cash and cash equivalents in its cash balance. Cash equivalents include all highly liquid investments purchased with an original maturity of 3 months or less.

E13-18 Operating Cash Flows Davis Enterprises reported net income for the year of $324,000 and paid cash dividends of $40,000. Included in net income was interest expense of $3,500, wage expense of $112,000, depreciation expense of $68,000, and cost of goods sold of $667,000. The company's income also included a loss of $7,000 on the sale of land and a gain of $10,000 on the sale of investments. During the year, the company's inventory increased $4,500, its accounts receivable increased $15,000, and its accounts payable decreased $7,200. The company's net income had been reduced by income taxes of $85,000. The balance of income taxes payable at the end of the year was $6,000 less than at the beginning of the year. Compute the amount of cash Davis Enterprises generated from its operations.

E13-19 Adjusting Operating Cash Flows Greenbow reported cash provided by operations of $175,000 and an increase in its cash balance from $90,000 to $210,000 during the year. In reviewing Greenbow's financial statements you discover the following:

1. Payments to suppliers were reduced by $200,000 for the current year as the result of a one-time saving from adopting a new inventory control system.

2. A major customer was forced to delay payment of $310,000 from November until January due to a strike by its employees. The customer is expected to resume paying promptly for all purchases starting in January.

3. Greenbow did not pay a dividend to its preferred shareholders during the current year. The preferred stock is cumulative and pays an annual dividend of $30,000. Greenbow plans to pay a dividend of $80,000 to its common shareholders next year.

4. Greenbow decided to change the depreciable lives of its long-term assets from 15 years to 20 years at the start of the year. The annual reduction in depreciation expense is expected to be $82,000.

a. What effect did each of these have on Greenbow's cash flow from operations or other cash flows reported in the cash flow statement in the current period?

b. What would you project Greenbow's cash generated from operations to be for next year if all other operating results are same as this year?

E13-20 Direct and Indirect Approaches Jalleen Associates started business on February 4, 2000. During its first year of operations, the company had sales of $445,600 and cost of goods sold of $284,000. At the end of the year, customers still owed Jalleen $17,000. The company reported wage expense of $85,000 for the year, including $3,000 of wages not yet paid at year-end. The company held inventory of $12,000 at the end of the year and owed $4,500 to suppliers. Jalleen recognized a total of $21,000 of depreciation expense for the year. All of the company's other expenses of $29,400 were paid in cash, except for $1,300 still owed at year-end.

a. Present the operating section of Jalleen's cash flow statement using the indirect approach.

b. Present the operating section of Jalleen's cash flow statement using the direct approach.

E13-21 Cash Flow Statement During 2001, the London Prime Company reported net income of $5,000,000 and paid dividends of $3,000,000. The company had no sales of property, plant, and equipment during the year. Use the following information for the London Prime Company to prepare a statement of cash flows for the year ended December 31, 2001, using the indirect approach:

London Prime Company
Balance Sheets, December 31

	2001	2000
Cash	$ 200,000	$ 180,000
Accounts receivable	580,000	510,000
Inventory	1,020,000	970,000
Prepaid expenses	50,000	70,000
Property, plant, & equipment	30,000,000	25,000,000
Less accumulated depreciation	(15,000,000)	(12,000,000)
Goodwill (net)	9,000,000	10,000,000
Total assets	$ 25,850,000	$ 24,730,000
Accounts payable	$ 300,000	$ 340,000
Income taxes payable	450,000	290,000
Long-term debt	9,000,000	10,000,000
Common stock	8,000,000	8,000,000
Retained earnings	8,100,000	6,100,000
Total liabilities and owners' equity	$ 25,850,000	$ 24,730,000

E13-22 Identifying Cash Flows Classify each of the following transactions or activities as increasing, decreasing, or having no effect on cash flows:

a. Selling merchandise on account.

b. Amortizing purchased trademarks.

c. Paying accounts payable.

d. Borrowing on a long-term note payable.

e. Prepaying premiums on a 3-year insurance policy.

f. Collecting accounts receivable.

g. Writing off a bad account to the allowance for uncollectibles.

h. Estimating and recording warranty expense and a liability account for expected future warranty costs.

i. Purchasing new factory equipment.

j. Declaring a dividend.

k. Paying a dividend previously declared.

l. Paying interest on bonds previously sold at a discount.

E13-23 Cash Flow Statement for Carey Corporation
Carey Corporation wishes to prepare a statement of cash flows for 2001. Carey had cash on hand of $58,000 on January 1, 2001. During the year, Carey reported the following:

1. Sales of $620,000.
2. Sale of investments for $135,000 (including a gain of $7,000).
3. Cost of goods sold of $450,000.
4. Purchase of treasury stock of $52,000.
5. Salaries and wage expense of $80,000.
6. Payment of $60,000 to retire bonds.
7. Purchase of land for $71,000.
8. Depreciation expense of $24,000.
9. Payment of dividends of $30,000.
10. Tax expense of $10,000.
11. Other expense of $20,000.

Carey Corporation also reported the following changes in current assets and liabilities during 2001:

12. Accounts receivables increased from $45,000 to $53,000.
13. Inventory decreased from $87,000 to $83,000.
14. Wages payable increased from $9,000 to $15,000.
15. Accounts payable decreased from $36,000 to $31,000.
16. Taxes payable increased from $6,000 to $7,500.

a. Compute net income for 2001 for Carey Corporation.

b. Prepare a statement of cash flows for 2001 for Carey Corporation.

E13-24 Operating Cash Flows—Indirect Method Mellon Company reported sales and expenses as follows for the month of March:

Sales	$95,000
Cost of goods sold	30,000
Depreciation expense	11,000
Utility expense	9,000
Wage expense	14,000
Amortization of goodwill	3,000

The following balances in current assets and liabilities were reported at the dates indicated:

	March 1	March 31
Accounts receivable	$40,000	$33,000
Inventory	55,000	72,000
Accounts payable to suppliers	24,000	28,000
Wages payable	20,000	18,500

a. Compute the amount reported as net income by Mellon Company for the month of March.

b. Present the cash flow from the operations section of Mellon's statement of cash flows using the indirect approach.

E13-25 Operating Cash Flows—Direct Method Using the information provided in E13-24, prepare the cash flow from operations section of Mellon's statement of cash flows using the direct method.

E13-26 Preparing a Cash Flow Statement Manchester Corporation reported the following transactions and changes in account balances during the year ended December 31, 2000:

Increase in:	
Accounts payable	$ 40,000
Inventory	55,000
Interest receivable	1,800
Decrease in:	
Accounts receivable	75,000
Wages payable	22,000
Depreciation expense	64,000
Loss on sale of investments ($55,000 carrying	
value at time of sale)	12,000
Purchase of new equipment	168,000
Purchase of treasury stock	90,000
Issuance of preferred stock	70,000
Dividends paid	85,000

Net income for 2000 was $160,000. The cash balance at January 1, 2000, was $34,900. Prepare a cash flow statement for the year 2000 for Manchester Corporation.

E13-27 Financial Statement Balances Provide correct answers for the following:

a. Snorkel Company reported cash receipts of $128,000 from the sale of land in the Cash Flow from Investing Activities section of its cash flow statement. It also reported a deduction of $23,000 from net income for a gain on the sale of land in the Cash Flow from Operations section of the cash flow statement. What was the carrying value of the land on Snorkel's books at the time of sale?

b. Turnbuckle Corporation reported cash provided by financing activities of $34,000, cash used in investing activities of $87,000, cash provided by operations of $135,000, a direct exchange of preferred stock with a fair value of $190,000 for land to be used for expansion, and an ending cash balance of $113,000. What was the cash balance at the beginning of the year?

c. Sulter Company reported cash provided by operations of $185,000. Adjustments to net income consisted of an increase in accounts receivable of $39,000, an increase in accounts payable of $27,000, a loss on sale of land of $13,000, depreciation of $22,000, and a decrease in taxes payable of $42,000. What amount did Sulter report as net income for the year?

E13-28 Analysis of Cash Flows Gerrard Company reported the following cash flows for the year ending December 31:

Cash flows from operations:		
Cash receipts from sales of		
product		$1,300,000
Cash payments to suppliers		(720,000)
Cash payments to employees		(410,000)
Cash payments to others		(120,000)
Cash provided by operations		$ 50,000
Cash flows from investing		
activities:		
Sale of investments	$ 600,000	
Purchase of equipment	(1,000,000)	
Cash used in investing		
activities		(400,000)
Cash flows from financing		
activities:		
Issuance of capital stock		380,000
Increase in cash		$ 30,000
Beginning cash balance		10,000
Ending cash balance		$ 40,000

Explain your answer to each of the following:

a. Is the presentation of Gerrard's cash flows from operations based on the direct or indirect method?

b. Is Gerrard in a good position to pay a cash dividend in the near future?

c. Is Gerrard expanding or contracting its operations?

d. Has Gerrard financed its purchase of new assets by borrowing additional money or by other means? What has been its primary sources of cash during the current year?

P13-29 Evaluation of Cash Flow Information An analysis of the financial statement data of Brown Company and Amber Company resulted in the following ratio information:

	Brown	**Amber**
Earnings per share	$4.00	$8.00
Dividends per share	1.50	3.00
Cash flow per share	5.00	7.50
Cash flow to total assets	.125	.125
Cash flow to total debt	.50	.20

Brown Company and Amber Company each have 20,000 shares of common stock outstanding.

a. Compute the amount of cash provided by operations for each company. Which company has the larger dollar amount of cash provided by operations?

b. Compute the amount of total assets reported by each company. Which company has the larger amount of total assets?

c. Which company has the larger amount of debt outstanding? What amounts are reported by each company?

E13-30 Computation of Cash Flows In preparing the cash flows from operations section of its statement of cash flows, Lester Corporation reported the following:

Net income		$188,000
Adjustments:		
Depreciation and amortization	$ 36,000	
Increase in accounts receivable	(44,000)	
Increase in inventory	(17,000)	
Decrease in accounts payable		
to suppliers	(24,000)	
Increase in interest payable	13,000	
Decrease in income taxes payable	(9,000)	(45,000)
Cash provided by operations		$143,000

In its income statement for the year, Lester Corporation reported sales of $980,000, cost of goods sold of $579,000, depreciation expense of $36,000, interest expense of $37,000, and income tax expense of $140,000.

a. What amount of cash did Lester Corporation receive from customers for the year?

b. What amount did Lester Corporation pay to its suppliers for the year?

c. What amount of interest payments did Lester Corporation make to its bondholders for the year?

d. What amount of income tax did Lester Corporation pay for the year?

e. Prepare the cash flows from operations section of Lester Corporation's statement of cash flows using the direct method.

E13-31 Analyzing Transactions For each of the following items, (1) identify the accounts affected and give the amounts by which they would be increased or decreased, (2) state the amount of any cash flow and whether cash is increased or decreased, and (3) identify how they would be reported in the statement of cash flows:

a. A depreciable asset is sold for $80,000. The asset originally cost $175,000, and the accumulated depreciation is $120,000.

b. A depreciable asset is purchased for $383,000. A cash payment of $83,000 is made, and the remainder is paid with a long-term note of $300,000.

c. Interest of 8 percent is paid on bonds that were originally issued at a $150,000 discount from their par value of $1,000,000. A total of $13,000 of the discount was amortized this year.

d. Goodwill of $630,000 from the purchase of a business was recorded several years ago. The goodwill is amortized over a 20-year period at the rate of $31,500 per year.

e. Income tax expense for the year is $1,300,000. The tax payment during the year was $1,150,000 because a portion of the revenue received will not be recognized on the tax return until next year.

E13-32 Cash Flow Statement Powell Corporation reported the following abbreviated balance sheet and income statement information:

Powell Corporation
Income Statement
Year Ended December 31, 2001

Sales		$ 400,000
Cost of goods sold		(180,000)
Gross profit		$ 220,000
Supplies expense	$25,000	
Depreciation expense	40,000	
Wages and salaries	90,000	
Interest expense	18,000	(173,000)
		$ 47,000
Other income		14,000
Net income		$ 61,000

Powell Corporation
Balance Sheets, December 31

	2001	2000
Cash	$ 11,000	$ 60,000
Accounts receivable	100,000	120,000
Inventory	320,000	260,000
Buildings & equipment (net)	400,000	350,000
Total assets	$831,000	$790,000
Accounts payable	$ 80,000	$ 90,000
Wages and salaries payable	25,000	20,000
Bonds payable	300,000	350,000
Common stock	170,000	100,000
Retained earnings	256,000	230,000
Total liabilities and equities	$831,000	$790,000

a. Prepare a cash flow statement for Powell Corporation for the year ended December 31, 2001.

b. Did working capital change by the same amount as cash generated by operations? Should these two be the same? Explain.

E13-33 Determining Cash Flows Dolores Company had a $261,800 cash balance at the beginning of 2000. The com-

pany reported net income of $388,900 for 2000. Included in the company's income statement was depreciation expense of $67,000, interest expense of $31,600, and income tax expense of $102,000. The following also occurred during 2000:

* Accounts receivable increased by $13,000.
* Inventory decreased by $7,000.
* Accounts payable increased by $3,500.
* Wages payable decreased by $1,300.
* Income taxes payable increased by $3,100, and the deferred tax liability increased by $12,000.
* The patent account increased by $27,400. One patent was purchased during the year for $31,200.
* The plant and equipment account increased by $465,000. One piece of equipment was sold during the year for $22,000. It originally had cost $51,000 and had a $17,000 book value at the time of sale.
* Dolores declared and paid cash dividends of $52,000 during 2000.
* The company repurchased shares of its common stock during the year for $44,000 and held them in its treasury.
* The company issued $100,000 of bonds during the year at 99. The amount of the discount amortized during 2000 was $200.

To help the management of Dolores Company better understand its sources and uses of cash, do the following:

1. Compute the cash generated from operations.
2. Compute the cash flow related to investing activities.
3. Compute the cash flow related to financing activities.
4. Prepare a cash flow statement for Dolores for 2000 in good form.

E13-34 Analysis of Cash Flows As a part of your evaluation of the return available from Mori Company, you decide to analyze its cash flows. You collect the following information:

Cash from operations for 2001	$ 600,000
Total assets, December 31, 2001	4,000,000
Total assets, December 31, 2000	3,600,000
Earnings per share	4.00
Net income	400,000
Preferred stock	-0-
Depreciation expense	300,000

The management of Mori Company states that depreciation expense is a fair measure of the expenditures needed to maintain operating capacity.

a. Using the information provided, compute the ratios of cash flow per share, cash flow to total assets, and free cash flow.

b. What information does each of these ratios provide?

c. How would you arrive at an evaluation of whether these ratios are satisfactory?

E13-35 Safety of Cash Flows When you review your results in E13-34, you realize that you should have looked at the safety of cash flows, also. You request and receive the following additional data so you can calculate additional ratios:

Cash dividends per share of common stock for 2001	$ 2.00
Current maturities of long-term debt	150,000
Total current liabilities	600,000
Total long-term debt	1,800,000

Required:

a. Calculate the ratio of dividends to operating cash flow, cash flow to maturing debt, and cash flow to total debt.
b. What additional information is provided by these ratios?
c. What is your evaluation of Mori Company? Does the company appear to be in a strong position or to be headed for future difficulties in meeting its cash flow commitments? Explain.

USING ACCOUNTING FOR DECISION MAKING

P13-36 Identifying Cash Flow Information Your consulting team is preparing a report about the operations of the Tower Company as a part of an overall evaluation to determine whether to help Tower obtain financing for a major project. You are trying to anticipate as many questions as possible that might come up in the next team meeting. Where would you look in Tower's financial statements or notes to answer the following questions?

a. Will Tower be able to pay off current maturities of long-term debt without additional borrowing?
b. Is the company retaining operating cash by delaying payment to its suppliers?
c. As sales increase, the accounts receivable and inventory balances will probably increase. Will Tower have to use the proceeds of the new financing to cover its operating cash needs?
d. If operating cash needs increase, will dividends have to be reduced?
e. To what extent is net income a reasonable forecast of the cash generated from operations by Tower?

P13-37 Further Cash Flow Analysis The team meeting about Tower Company that you prepared for in P13–36 went very well. You were well prepared, so much so that the team gave you another list of questions to answer. These look harder, but you remember that all the financial statements report on operating, investing, and financing activities, and the cash flow statement helps tie them all together. Again, where would you look in Tower's financial statements or notes to answer the following questions?

a. Over the past 2 years, has Tower been investing enough in operating assets to maintain operating capacity?
b. Does Tower have any long-term lease commitments and, if so, how much are the required annual payments on these leases?
c. Has Tower changed the ratio of debt to equity over the past 2 years? In other words, has Tower issued proportionally more debt than stock?

d. Has the company reported any major unusual transactions or events that have affected reported net income? What effect, if any, has this had on cash flows?
e. Are there significant unfunded pension or other post-employment benefit obligations? If so, when will they require cash payments?
f. Tower reports a deferred tax liability in the most recent financial report. When will this liability have to be paid? How much cash will be involved?

P13-38 Cash Flows at Disney The following cash flows were reported by The Walt Disney Company and Subsidiaries for 1998 (stated in millions):

Net Income	$1,850
Items Not Requiring Cash Outlays:	
Amortization of film and television costs	2,514
Depreciation	809
Amortization of intangible assets	431
Other	(75)
Changes In:	
Receivables	(664)
Inventories	(46)
Other assets	179
Accounts and taxes payable and accrued liabilities	218
Film and television costs—television broadcast rights	(447)
Deferred income taxes	346
	3,265
Cash Provided by Operations	5,115
Investing Activities:	
Film and television costs	(3,335)
Investments in theme parks, resorts, and other property	(2,314)
Acquisitions	(213)
Proceeds from sales of marketable securities and other investments	238
Purchase of marketable securities	(13)
Investment in and loan to E! Entertainment	(28)
	(5,665)

Financing Activities:	
Borrowings	1,830
Reduction of borrowings	(1,212)
Repurchases of common stock	(30)
Dividends	(412)
Exercise of stock options and other	184
	360
Decrease in Cash and Cash Equivalents	(190)
Cash and Cash Equivalents, Beginning of Year	317
Cash and Cash Equivalents, End of Year	$ 127

a. Did Disney's cash position increase or decrease during 1998? By what amount?

b. Is Disney's reported net income a good measure of total cash provided by operations in 1998? What proportion of total cash provided by operations does it represent?

c. What proportion of the adjustments to net income used in computing cash provided by operations is represented by depreciation and amortization?

d. Did Disney's additional investment in film and television and theme parks, resorts, and other property exceed depreciation and amortization for the year? By what amount?

e. What portion of the amount invested in film and television and theme parks, resorts, and other property was generated by issuing new long-term debt and common stock?

f. How does the information on cash provided (used) by investing activities and financing activities help investors to evaluate a company such as Disney?

P13-39 Cash Flow Statement for Dwight Company
Dwight Company paid dividends of $20,000 during 2002. Prepare a statement of cash flows for Dwight Company for 2002 based on the following balance sheet and income statement information:

DWIGHT COMPANY	
INCOME STATEMENT	
YEAR ENDED DECEMBER 31, 2002	
Sales		$ 840,000
Cost of goods sold		(490,000)
Gross profit		$350,000
Salary expense	$175,000	
Depreciation expense	35,000	
Rent expense	16,000	
Utilities expense	74,000	
Interest expense	18,000	
Total other expenses		(318,000)
Net income		$ 32,000

DWIGHT COMPANY		
BALANCE SHEETS		
DECEMBER 31, 2001 AND 2002		
	2002	**2001**
Cash	$ 28,000	$ 35,000
Accounts receivable	97,000	87,000
Merchandise inventory	120,000	132,000
Supplies	15,000	10,000
Buildings and equipment	510,000	410,000
Accumulated depreciation	(195,000)	(160,000)
Total assets	$ 575,000	$ 514,000
Accounts payable	$ 35,000	$ 41,000
Wages payable	21,000	39,000
Utilities payable	7,000	4,000
Bonds payable	240,000	200,000
Common stock	110,000	80,000
Retained earnings	162,000	150,000
Total liabilities and owners' equity	$ 575,000	$ 514,000

P13-40 Examining Best Buy The following are the cash flow statement and balance sheets of Best Buy Co., Inc. De-termine what amounts should appear in Best Buy's cash flow statement in the places marked by the letters A through I.

BEST BUY CO., INC.	
CONSOLIDATED STATEMENT OF CASH FLOWS	
FOR THE FISCAL YEAR ENDED FEBRUARY 2, 1998	
(STATED IN THOUSANDS)	
Operating Activities	
Net earnings	$ A
Charges to earnings not affecting cash:	
Depreciation and amortization	68,330
Other	3,254
	$166,037
Changes in operating assets and liabilities:	
Receivables	B
Merchandise inventories	C
Prepaid taxes and expenses	4,657
Accounts payable	D
Other liabilities	68,103
Income taxes	33,759
Deferred revenue	(24,603)
Total cash provided by operating activities	$542,388
Investing Activities	
Additions to property and equipment	$ (72,063)
Decrease in recoverable costs from developed properties	45,270
Decrease in other assets	4,494
Total cash used in investing activities	$ E
Financing Activities	
Decrease in obligations under financing arrangements	$ F
Long-term debt borrowings	10,000
Long-term debt payments	(22,694)
Common stock issued	14,869
Total cash used in financing activities	$ G
Increase in Cash and Cash Equivalents	$ 430,319
Cash and Cash Equivalents at Beginning of Period	H
Cash and Cash Equivalents at End of Period	$ I

BEST BUY CO., INC.		
CONSOLIDATED BALANCE SHEETS		
(STATED IN THOUSANDS)		

Assets	February 28, 1998	March 1, 1997
Current Assets		
Cash and cash equivalents	$ 520,127	$ 89,808
Receivables	95,702	79,581
Recoverable costs from developed properties	8,215	53,485
Merchandise inventories	1,060,788	1,132,059
Refundable and deferred income taxes	16,650	25,560
Prepaid expenses	8,795	4,542
Total current assets	$1,710,277	$1,385,035
Property and Equipment		
Land and buildings	$ 19,977	$ 18,000
Leasehold improvements	160,202	148,168
Furniture, fixtures and equipment	372,314	324,333
Property under capital leases	29,079	29,326
	$ 581,572	$ 519,827
Less accumulated depreciation and amortization	248,648	188,194
Net property and equipment	$ 332,924	$ 331,633
Other Assets	13,145	17,639
Total Assets	$2,056,346	$1,734,307

Liabilities and Shareholders' Equity		
Current Liabilities		
Accounts payable	$ 727,087	$ 487,802
Obligations under financing arrangements	35,565	127,510
Accrued salaries and related expenses	48,772	33,663
Accrued liabilities	163,744	122,611
Income taxes payable	24,608	
Deferred service plan revenue	18,975	24,602
Current portion of long-term debt	14,925	21,391
Total current liabilities	$1,033,676	$ 817,579
Deferred Income Taxes	7,095	3,578
Deferred Revenue and Other Liabilities	17,578	28,210
Long-Term Debt	210,397	216,625
Convertible Preferred Securities of Subsidiary	229,854	230,000
Shareholders' Equity		
Preferred stock, $1.00 par value: Authorized—		
400,000 shares; Issued and outstanding—none		
Common stock, $.10 par value: Authorized—		
120,000,000 shares; Issued and outstanding—		
89,252,000 and 86,574,000 shares, respectively	4,463	4,329
Additional paid-in capital	266,144	241,300
Retained earnings	287,139	192,686
Total shareholders' equity	$ 557,746	$ 438,315
Total Liabilities and Shareholders' Equity	$2,056,346	$1,734,307

P13-41 Analyzing a Cash Flow Statement The 2000 financial statements of White Company included the cash flow statement shown below.

a. Prepare an analysis of White Company's 2000 cash flow statement showing the total sources of cash and the percentage of cash coming from each.
b. Prepare an analysis of White's 2000 cash flow statement showing the uses of White's cash and the percentage going to each use.
c. Did White Company increase or decrease its current assets other than cash in 2000? Is this change consistent with an increase or a decrease in sales during the period? Explain.

Has White Company become more or less risky during 2000 from an investor's viewpoint? Explain why.

d. Does White appear to be expanding or contracting its operations? How can you tell? What other financial statement information might you examine to determine if White is expanding? Does White appear able to maintain its productive capacity without additional financing? Explain.

P13-42 Using Cash Flow Information The operating section of Jelic Custom Manufacturing Company's cash flow statement is shown at the bottom of the page.

WHITE COMPANY CASH FLOW STATEMENT YEAR ENDING DECEMBER 31, 2000		
Cash flows from operations:		
Net income		$ 444,000
Adjustment for depreciation		230,000
Adjustment for gain on sale of operating assets		(14,000)
Adjustment for change in current assets other than cash		(120,000)
Adjustment for change in current liabilities		80,000
Cash provided by operations		$ 620,000
Cash flows from investing activities:		
Purchase of operating assets	$(1,200,000)	
Sale of operating assets	300,000	
Cash used in investing activities		(900,000)
Cash flows from financing activities:		
Issuance of capital stock	$ 2,000,000	
Retirement of bonds	(1,300,000)	
Dividends paid	(250,000)	
Cash provided by financing activities		450,000
Increase in cash		$ 170,000

JELIC CUSTOM MANUFACTURING COMPANY STATEMENT OF CASH FLOWS FOR THE YEAR 2000		
Cash Flows from Operations:		
Net income		$ 732,000
Adjustments:		
Depreciation expense		320,000
Amortization of bond discount		27,000
Gain on sale of investments		(80,000)
Change in current items:		
Accounts receivable	$(260,000)	
Inventory	(20,000)	
Prepaid expenses	5,000	
Accounts payable	95,000	
Trade notes payable	2,000	(178,000)
Cash Provided by Operations		$ 821,000
Cash Balance, January 1		176,000
Cash Balance, December 31		$ 997,000

Using this information, answer the following questions. If a question cannot be answered from the information given, indicate why.

a. Have accounts receivable increased or decreased this year?

b. If Jelic has had only a single bond issue outstanding during the year, are those bonds reported at an amount above or below par value in the company's year-end balance sheet? How do you know?

c. Does the company appear to be more or less inclined to prepay expenses than in the past? Does this help or hurt its cash position? Explain.

d. Has inventory increased or decreased this year? Explain why this affects cash.

e. Compared with last year, does the company seem to be relying more or less heavily on trade credit to finance its activities?

f. Has depreciation expense increased from last year?

g. If you were a potential creditor of Jelic, do you see any warning signs in the cash flow statement that you would want to investigate further before lending the company money? Explain.

h. Jelic has $2,000,000 of bonds maturing on January 12, 2002. Jelic does not have a bond sinking fund established to pay off the bonds. Do you think Jelic will be able to meet its obligation to pay off the bonds without additional long-term financing? Discuss.

P13-43 Identifying Information You have been provided with limited summary information from the Wright Equipment Company. For each of the following questions, indicate what additional information you would need to answer the questions. Also, identify the financial statement or note where you would expect to find the information needed.

Cash flows provided by operations	$1,550,000
Cash flows used in investing activities	2,730,000
Cash flows provided by financing activities	1,200,000
Increase in cash	20,000

Questions:

a. What proportion of the cash flows from operations was provided by delaying payments on trade accounts payable?

b. What percentage of cash needs were provided by issuing debt?

c. Is cash flow per share high enough to assure the safety of cash dividends?

d. Has total cash flow increased this year?

e. What is the cash return on assets (operating cash flow to total assets) for the company?

f. Does cash flow from operations provide sufficient cash to maintain assets?

g. Do operating cash flows provide a reasonable margin of safety for payment of cash dividends?

h. Is the company generating enough cash from operations to repay debt commitments that mature in the near future? Is cash generated from operations enough to pay normal trade payables on a timely basis?

i. How does the ratio of cash flow to total debt compare to last year?

j. Are deferred taxes increasing? What does this mean for cash flows provided by operations?

k. What are the requirements for interest payments this year? Were operating cash flows sufficient to cover these payments?

EXPANDING YOUR HORIZONS

C13-44 Caterpillar's Condensed Statement of Cash Flow
Caterpillar published a condensed statement of cash flow containing the following information (stated in millions):

	1997	1996
Profit after Tax	$1,665	$1,361
Depreciation and amortization	738	696
Changes in working capital—		
excluding cash and debt	(552)	(696)
Capital expenditures—excluding		
equipment leased to others	(824)	(506)
Expenditures for equipment leased		
to others, net of disposals	(144)	(130)
Dividends paid	(338)	(289)
Net Free Cash Flow	**$ 545**	**$ 436**
Other significant cash flow items:		
Treasury shares purchased	(706)	(303)
Net increase in long-term finance		
receivables	(501)	(314)
Net increase in debt	1,109	1,059
Investments and acquisitions	(59)	(612)
Prefunding of employee benefit plans	(200)	(200)
Other	(383)	(217)
Change in Cash and Short-Term		
Investments	**$ (195)**	**$ (151)**

Based on the information presented in the condensed cash flow statement:

a. What appears to be the amount of cash provided by operations?

b. What appears to be the amount of cash provided (used) in investing activities (assuming the Prefunding of Employee Benefit Plans is a financing activity and Other is primarily investing activity)?

c. What appears to be the amount of cash provided (used) in financing activities (assuming the Prefunding of Employee Benefit Plans is a financing activity and Other is primarily investing activity)?

d. In what ways does the presentation of Caterpillar's cash flow statement differ from the presentation in the chapter?

e. Evaluate the usefulness of Caterpillar's condensed cash flow statement in comparison to Gateway's cash flow statement shown in Appendix A.

C13-45 Evaluating Cash Flows of Dell Computer and Gateway   Cash flow statements and selected balance sheet data are presented for Dell Computer Corporation and Gateway, Inc., as follows:

DELL COMPUTER CORPORATION CONSOLIDATED CASH FLOW STATEMENTS FOR THE YEARS ENDED FEBRUARY 1, 1998, AND JANUARY 29, 1999 (IN MILLIONS)		
	Jan. 29, 1999	**Feb. 1, 1998**
Cash flows from operating activities:		
Net income	$ 1,460	$ 944
Adjustments to reconcile net income to net cash provided by operating activities:		
Depreciation and amortization	103	67
Tax benefits of employee stock plans	444	164
Other	11	24
Changes in:		
Operating working capital	367	365
Non-current assets and liabilities	51	28
Net cash provided by operating activities	$ 2,436	$ 1,592
Cash flows from investing activities:		
Marketable securities:		
Purchases	$(16,459)	$(12,305)
Maturities and sales	15,341	12,017
Capital expenditures	(296)	(187)
Net cash used in investing activities	$ (1,414)	$ (475)
Cash flows from financing activities:		
Purchase of common stock	$ (1,518)	$ (1,023)
Issuance of common stock under employee plans	212	88
Proceeds from issuance of long-term debt, net of issuance costs	494	
Cash received from sale of equity options and other		37
Net cash used in financing activities	$ (812)	$ (898)
Effect of exchange rate changes on cash	$ (10)	$ (14)
Net increase in cash	$ 200	$ 205
Cash at beginning of period	320	115
Cash at end of period	$ 520	$ 320

GATEWAY, INC. CONSOLIDATED CASH FLOW STATEMENTS FOR THE YEARS ENDED DECEMBER 31, 1997 AND 1998 (IN THOUSANDS)		
	1998	**1997**
Cash flows from operating activities:		
Net income	$ 346,399	$ 109,797
Adjustments to reconcile net income to net cash provided by operating activities:		
Depreciation and amortization	105,524	86,774
Provision for uncollectible accounts receivable	3,991	5,688
Deferred income taxes	(58,425)	(63,247)
Other, net	770	42
Nonrecurring expenses	—	113,842
Changes in operating assets and liabilities:		
Accounts receivable	(52,164)	(41,950)
Inventory	81,300	59,486
Other assets	451	(54,513)
Accounts payable	228,921	66,253
Accrued liabilities	144,899	48,405
Accrued royalties	8,455	34,148
Other current liabilities	76,278	35,816
Warranty and other liabilities	21,252	42,256
Net cash provided by operating activities	907,651	442,797
Cash flows from investing activities:		
Capital expenditures	(235,377)	(175,656)
Purchases of available-for-sale securities	(168,965)	(49,619)
Proceeds from maturities or sales of available-for-sale securities	48,924	10,985
Acquisitions, net of cash acquired	—	(142,320)
Other, net	(992)	(4,055)
Net cash used in investing activities	(356,410)	(360,665)
Cash flows from financing activities:		
Proceeds from issuances of notes payable	—	10,000
Principal payments on long-term obligations and notes payable	(13,173)	(15,588)
Stock options exercised	36,159	5,741
Net cash provided by financing activities	22,986	153
Foreign exchange effect on cash and cash equivalents	1,982	(5,044)
Net increase in cash and cash equivalents	576,209	77,241
Cash and cash equivalents, beginning of year	593,601	516,360
Cash and cash equivalents, end of year	$1,169,810	$ 593,601

	OTHER FINANCIAL INFORMATION			
	DELL COMPUTER CORPORATION AND GATEWAY, INC.			
	Dell Computer (in millions)		Gateway (In thousands)	
Fiscal year ending	Jan. 29 1999	Feb. 1 1998	Dec. 31 1998	Dec. 31 1997
Current assets	$6,339	$3,912	$2,228,186	$1,544,683
Total assets	6,877	4,268	2,890,380	2,039,271
Current liabilities	3,695	2,697	1,429,674	1,003,906
Long-term liabilities	861	278	116,331	105,321
Stockholders' equity	2,321	1,293	1,344,375	930,044
Weighted average shares outstanding				
Basic	2,531	2,631	155,542	153,840
Diluted	2,772	2,952	158,929	156,201

Prepare an analysis of Dell and Gateway and report on their strengths and weaknesses. The following ratios or amounts should be computed and used in your analysis:

a. Earnings per share, basic
b. Earnings per share, diluted
c. Cash flow per share (based on weighted average basic shares outstanding)
d. Cash flow to total assets (based on total assets at year-end)
e. Free cash
f. Cash flow to total debt
g. Purchases of long-term assets to total assets
h. Long-term debt issued to total long-term debt
i. Total debt to total assets
j. Working capital
k. Current (working capital) ratio

 C13-46 Assessing Solvency Select two companies in the same industry, such as General Motors and Ford, and analyze their statements of cash flows for the most recent 2 years. Use annual reports available in your library or from electronic databases such as the SEC EDGAR database, company homepages on the World Wide Web, or Internet news sources. Calculate appropriate ratios and use the notes or management discussion and analysis to explain any unusual items. Assess the ability of the companies to meet current obligations and their capacity to meet additional debt servicing requirements (payments of interest and principal) if the companies were to issue new debt. To what extent are the companies able to finance possible expansion internally without having to resort to external financing?

C13-47 Ethics, Responsibility, and Reporting As senior personnel officer of the World Time Corporation, this has not been one of your best days. World Time specializes in the manufacture, assembly, and distribution of international communication equipment. Competition from electronic communication through Internet and other direct electronic transfers has made the past several years very difficult for World Time. In fact, World Time will have a serious cash shortage next year if no additional cash sources are found. The banks have already indicated that they will not lend World Time any more money. One of the reasons for the cash shortage is that World Time is diversifying by publishing international electronic mail directories, and the initial investments will use all the available cash. If this conversion of the business is successful, the company hopes to survive the changes in international communication.

What does all this have to do with personnel? The manufacturing work force has been reduced significantly in recent years, although it has been handled well through natural attrition and contract buy-outs. Now, however, one of the senior financial officers has suggested that the anticipated cash shortage next year could be made up by pulling some cash out of the pension fund set up for employees. The pension fund is held for World Time by a pension trustee. Because of higher-than-expected earnings on investments and the contract buy-outs of some senior employees, the trust fund assets exceed the current pension liability by about $15 million. This is more than the projected $6 million cash shortage predicted for next year. The company attorney has given an opinion that using the excess cash from the pension fund is legal as long as World Time meets the actuarial requirements of the plan. You argue that it is not right and it will cause real morale problems in a work force that is already concerned about future job security. The company accountant says that the source of cash will have to be reported in the cash flow statement, although it probably can be buried by showing it as a negative adjustment, along with all the others that appear there, to cash flows from operations.

a. Should World Time use this source of cash?
b. Is the accountant correct in "hiding" the source by treating it as an adjustment to operating cash flows?
c. Would your answer to part a depend on how certain you were that World Time could recover and be successful as a publisher of international electronic mail directories? Explain.

Internet Exercises: Visit our Web site for additional exercises.

Annual Report Project Part 13

Refer to the Annual Report Project, Part 1, at the end of Chapter 1. Using the annual report of the company you have chosen, and any other available information, answer the following questions, providing sources and computations where appropriate.

a. What have been the primary sources of the company's cash inflows during the period?

b. What have been the major uses of the company's cash during the period?

c. Was depreciation a major source of cash for your company? Explain.

d. How much were your company's cash payments for interest and income taxes?

e. Discuss the adequacy of the cash generated from your company's operations.

f. Did your company report any significant investing or financing transactions that did not affect cash? If so, describe those transactions.

CHAPTER FOURTEEN

Special Income Reporting Considerations

REVIEW

To this point, the basic concepts of financial accounting and reporting have been discussed and applied to understanding the items reported in the four basic financial statements. The discussion has focused on the individual financial statement elements and what they mean for decision making.

WHERE THIS CHAPTER FITS

This chapter revisits the topic of income. Although revenue and expense recognition and measurement have been considered throughout earlier chapters, we now look at these issues in more depth and consider several special topics related to income.

LOOKING AHEAD

The next chapter examines some additional issues related to financial reporting and analysis that help make the financial statements more useful to decision makers.

I got this invitation in the mail to apply for that new Spendabundle Charge Card everybody's getting. I want to get the application in as soon as possible, but it asks for my monthly income. I'm not sure what to put down. I know to include the $400 I get from my part-time job each month, but what about the money Dad pays me for helping him now and then with his business? What about that $500 I made last summer selling the vegetables I grew? Oh yeah, and what about the money I got from cleaning up and selling that old bike I bought at the police auction? Then there's the money I won at the school raffle—is that income? What *is* my monthly income?

"In fiscal 1991 alone, Intelligent Electronics had received from its vendors $32.4 million to pay for various marketing activities but had spent only one-third as much on such programs . . . That left IE with a windfall of $19.3 million, an amount equal to half of the company's operating income of $38.5 million that year.

It appeared that key suppliers, among them Apple Computer Inc., International Business Machines Corp. and Hewlett-Packard Co., didn't know that they were paying a big premium for marketing. Nor did most investors have any idea that, in an industry with razor-thin profit margins, Intelligent Electronics was making its own bottom line considerably firmer by profiting in this way."[1]

[1]Raju Narisetti, "Intelligent Electronics Made Much of Its Profit at Suppliers' Expense," *The Wall Street Journal* (December 6, 1994), p. A1.

Many decisions are based on income. Whether the Spendabundle Charge Card Company is evaluating your application for a credit card with a $2,000 credit limit or LaSalle National Bank is evaluating a major corporation's request to extend a $200 million line of credit, income affects the decision. Accordingly, the way in which income is reported is important because it will affect the picture that decision makers see.

To make good decisions about a business, financial statement users must understand the amount and source of a company's income, whether that income is expected to continue in the future, and the anticipated effects on cash flows. Not all income is the same, and the source and type of income can significantly affect assessments of future earnings and cash inflows. In the case of Intelligent Electronics, at the time the nation's largest computer reseller (and now a subsidiary of Xerox), most investors apparently thought the company's profits came primarily from selling computers, when in fact half came from a questionable business activity that might end at any time.

Although we discussed the basic concepts related to income in Chapter 5, this chapter focuses on some specific aspects and special problems of income measurement and reporting. After reading this chapter, you should be able to:

1. Describe the basic concepts that determine income recognition under generally accepted accounting principles and indicate when and how different elements of income are reported.

2. Explain the distinction between income from a company's central operations and that arising from peripheral activities or other events, why the distinction is important, and how it is reflected in financial statements.

3. Describe the conditions under which departures from the basic concepts of income and expense recognition occur, how these situations are treated, and how they might be justified.

4. Describe the special reporting treatment given to discontinued operations, extraordinary gains and losses, unusual gains and losses, accounting changes, and corrections of prior period profits, and explain why this special treatment provides more useful information to decision makers.

5. Explain the general approach to computing earnings per share and describe how convertible securities affect earnings allocations.

When decision makers understand the types of income reported in the income statement, they can better understand a company's activities and make better assessments of future earnings and cash flows.

RECOGNIZING INCOME: A KEY TO DECISION MAKING

Information for Decisions

Special circumstances and events may require special accounting procedures and reporting practices. Decision makers need to understand these special cases and the effect on reported income so, when making future projections, they can answer questions such as these: How have the company's reporting practices been adapted to the the company's operations? Having seen that the company's income has been significantly affected by a special event in the current period, what effect will that have on income and cash flows in future periods?

In Chapter 5, we discussed how the income reported by a business provides a key to understanding the entity's activities. This, in turn, helps decision makers assess the entity's future, including forecasting future income and cash flows.

Remember that income reported under generally accepted accounting principles is based on accrual accounting. Revenues are recognized when they are earned and, because of the objectivity concept, after an exchange has taken place. Expenses are recognized under the matching concept in the period in which the benefits they provide are received by the enterprise.

Although many of an enterprise's activities are routine and similar to one another, some may be unusual and occur less frequently. For example, Exhibit 14–1 lists a number of income elements. The frequency with which these items occur differs greatly, as does their relationship to the entity's main activities. The reporting of these and other items in the financial statements must be informative enough to permit decision makers to assess how often such activities or events are likely to occur in the future and the extent to which they will affect the enterprise.

Some types of revenues and expenses, because of their special nature, are recognized using procedures other than the normal recognition criteria. Other times, infrequent or un-

REPORTING SELECTED INCOME STATEMENT ELEMENTS   EXHIBIT 14-1

Source of Income Effect	Frequency and Type of Effect	Reporting Treatment
Sale of primary products	Recurring, from central operations	Element in income from continuing operations, before taxes
Sale of other products	Recurring, from central operations	Element in income from continuing operations, before taxes
Interest income from temporary investments	Recurring, from peripheral activity	Element in income from continuing operations, before taxes
Unusual gain or loss (e.g., from sale of previously used equipment)	Sporadically recurring, peripheral activity	Element in income from continuing operations, before taxes
Discontinued operations (e.g., sale of a major product-line division)	Infrequently recurring, peripheral activity	Separate section of income statement, net of taxes
Extraordinary gain or loss (e.g., major earthquake damage to facilities)	Infrequently recurring, nonoperating event	Separate section of income statement, net of taxes
Accounting changes: Change in principle	Infrequently recurring, accounting adjustment	Cumulative adjustment in separate section of income statement, net of tax effect
Special change in principle	Infrequently recurring, accounting adjustment	Cumulative adjustment in retained earnings statement, net of tax effect; restatement of prior financial statements
Change in estimate	Sporadically recurring, accounting adjustment	New estimate used from beginning of current year
Change in entity	Sporadically recurring, accounting adjustment	Restatement of prior financial statements
Prior-period adjustment	Infrequently recurring, accounting adjustment	Cumulative adjustment in retained earnings statement, net of tax effect; restatement of prior financial statements

usual events might affect the current period's income but may or may not have a significant impact on future income and cash flows. An understanding of these special reporting issues and the potential impact on reported financial information is important in the decision-making process. In particular, financial statement users need to focus on (1) how fairly the reported information represents the economic substance of the underlying transactions or events, (2) the extent to which the events are related to the central operations of the entity, and (3) the frequency with which the events are expected to recur.

SPECIAL INCOME RECOGNITION ISSUES

Information for Decisions

When a company's income measurement is not based on the realization and matching concepts, financial statement users need to be able to understand why and how the special measurement methods are used so they can answer questions such as these: Do the accounting methods used by the company result in reliable information? Do the methods used provide a better representation of the company's operations? To what extent are the financial statements of this company comparable with those of other companies in the same industry and with those of companies in other industries?

The methods that a company uses to account for its revenues and expenses can significantly affect its reported income. Therefore, understanding the recognition methods used is important when analyzing a company's financial statements. Although most income and expense recognition methods are based on the realization and matching concepts, special situations sometimes lead to departures from these concepts. Usually, these departures are acceptable only under specified conditions. In this section, we discuss two special cases: recognizing income on long-term contracts and from the production of precious metals and commodities.

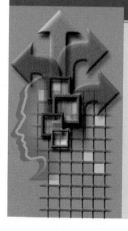

You Decide 14-1

A BETTER MEASURE OF PERIODIC INCOME?

Behemoth Construction Company undertakes major projects such as the construction of dams and bridges. Because each project is large and complex, the company only undertakes a single project at a time. On January 2, 2000, Behemoth began construction of a new dam for the Washington–Alameda Water Authority (WAWA), a project expected to take four years. The company is concerned that not recognizing any income until the project is completed and then recognizing the full amount in one year will provide a misleading picture of the company's activities. After all, the project is about 30 percent complete at the end of 2000, so it doesn't seem right to report no income for the year. In early 2001, you are considering investing in Behemoth. How might income be measured so that it would provide the most useful indication of Behemoth's activities for your investment decision?

LONG-TERM CONTRACTS

Many companies contract to undertake large projects that may take several years to complete. One approach to accounting for the income from such projects, consistent with the realization concept, is called the **completed-contract method.** Under this method, income is recognized only in the period in which the contract is completed and the project is accepted by the customer. Until then, costs incurred under the contract are treated as unexpired costs and reported as inventory. Once the contract is completed, all the income is recognized, and the costs are matched against the income. This approach is exactly the same as that used by any manufacturing firm to account for manufacturing costs and sales.

Would this method provide the most useful measure of income and a realistic portrayal of the company's activities for Behemoth Construction Company in You Decide 14–1? Many would argue that it would not because the income-producing activities take place over several periods, while all the income is recognized in one. With most manufacturing operations, the sale of the product is the critical event in the earning process; a company can manufacture as much of a product as it wishes, but income cannot be realized until the product is sold. With a long-term construction contract, however, the sale takes place at the time the contract is signed, and production (construction) is the critical event. If the contractor completes construction in accordance with the contract, the contractor then has a legally enforceable claim against the customer.

To avoid a misleading picture of a company's activities that might result from using the completed-contract method, another method is often used to account for long-term contracts. Under the **percentage-of-completion method** income is recognized as the project under contract progresses. The amount of profit recognized each period is based on estimates of the total expected profit on the contract and the portion of the contract completed, less any profits recognized in previous periods.

A CLOSER LOOK AT

ACCOUNTING FOR LONG-TERM CONTRACTS

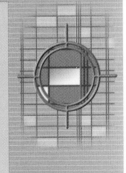

The Bilgeworks Shipyard enters into a contract with Zeon Petroleum Company to construct a tanker for a total price of $200 million. Bilgeworks estimates construction will take three years, and the total profit is estimated at $40 million. At the end of the first year, Bilgeworks estimates that construction is about 20 percent complete. By the end of the second year, Bilgeworks estimates construction is 75 percent complete. However, much of the progress during the second year was made by paying workers overtime, thus lowering the expected profit on the contract to $36 million. Bilgeworks completes the contract in the third year for a total profit of $37 million. Income is recognized in each of the three years under the two methods of accounting for the contract, as follows:

Completed-contract method:
Year 1   −0−
Year 2   −0−
Year 3: $37,000,000 × 1.00 = $37,000,000
Percentage-of-completion method:
Year 1 $40,000,000 × .20 = $8,000,000
Year 2   ($36,000,000 × .75) − $8,000,000 = $19,000,000
Year 3: $37,000,000 − ($8,000,000 + $19,000,000) = $10,000,000

Under the percentage-of-completion method, income is recognized in the first year based on the estimated percentage of completion and the estimated total profit on the project. In the second year, income is recognized based on the new estimate of total profit times the estimated percentage of completion to date, including the work of both the first and second years; this provides the amount of profit that should be recognized in the first two years. From this amount, the profit recognized in the first year is subtracted, and the remaining amount is recognized in the second year. Thus, the change in the estimated total profit on the contract is included in the second year's profit. In the final year, all profit not recognized previously is recognized.

The same amount of income is recognized by the two accounting methods over the life of a project. The difference is in the amount recognized each year. Although the percentage-of-completion method represents a departure from the realization concept, it is used by companies in many different types of businesses, as illustrated in Exhibit 14–2. It is generally accepted because it provides a better measure of periodic income when reliable estimates can be made of the total revenue (usually specified in the contract), expected costs, and the percentage of completion at the end of each period. (See In Practice 14-1.)

PRECIOUS METALS AND COMMODITIES

Although the percentage-of-completion method recognizes income from long-term contracts during production, income from precious metals and commodities is often recognized at the completion of production but prior to sale. Because no exchange has taken place, this approach also represents a departure from the realization concept.

Following the banking collapse of the 1930s, gold prices were fixed by the federal government and all gold not used in specific products was required to be sold to the government. With the assurance of immediate sale at a predetermined price, gold-mining companies began recording inventory at market price and recognizing income (market price less pro-

---

EXHIBIT 14-2 **SELECTED COMPANIES USING PERCENTAGE-OF-COMPLETION ACCOUNTING**

Company	Business
Fluor Corporation	Heavy construction, construction management, and consulting
LaBarge, Inc.	Electronic device design and manufacturing
The Boeing Company	Aircraft and aerospace manufacturing
Morrison Knudsen Corporation	Design, engineering, construction, and construction management
SofTech, Inc.	Computer software development and consulting
Todd Shipyards Corp.	Ship construction

ENVIRONMENTAL ELEMENTS CORP.'S LONG-TERM CONTRACTS

Environmental Elements Corp., a New York Stock Exchange company based in Baltimore, includes the following in its disclosure of significant accounting policies:

Long-Term Contracts

The Company records sales from long-term contracts using the percentage-of-completion method. Under this method, the Company recognizes as sales that portion of the total contract price which the cost of work completed bears to the estimated total cost of the work covered by the contract. Because contracts may extend over more than one fiscal period, revisions of cost and profit estimates are made periodically and are reflected in the accounting period in which they are determined. If the estimate of total costs on a contract indicates a loss, the total anticipated loss is recognized immediately.

ANALYSIS

Environmental Elements Corp. determines the percentage of completion by comparing costs incurred to date with the total cost expected to be incurred under the contract. As required, estimated losses are recognized immediately.

---

duction costs) as gold was produced. Although gold prices are now determined in international markets and vary considerably over time, many gold-mining companies continue to recognize income as gold is produced.

Income from other precious metals and from agricultural commodities is also often recognized on completion of production and the inventories valued at market value or net realizable value (selling price less remaining costs). These exceptions to the realization concept are usually acceptable only in situations where both of the following conditions are met:

1. All units of the product are the same.
2. There is an objectively determinable market price for the product.

For example, one bushel of a specific type of wheat is virtually identical to all other bushels of that type of wheat, and, because the market for wheat is almost purely competitive, the market price for wheat is objectively determinable. Whether or not a producer sells at a specific point in time, the price at which the wheat could have been sold can be verified even without an exchange occurring. Unlike with other products, the critical event in earning income from precious metals and commodities is producing the product rather than selling it because once it is produced, all of it can be sold at the current market price.

Because not all companies selling precious metals and commodities use market values, investors must exercise caution when making comparisons. Disclosure of the measurement methods used is included in the notes to the financial statements.

In Practice 14-2

PRECIOUS METALS AND CHICKENS

The Newmont Gold Company includes the following disclosure about inventories in its summary of significant accounting policies:

> *Ore and in-process inventories and materials and supplies are stated at the lower of average cost or net realizable value. Precious metals are stated at market value.*

Gold Kist Inc., an agricultural cooperative, includes the following statements about its inventories in its summary of accounting policies:

> *Inventories of marketable products consist primarily of dressed and further processed poultry. These inventories are stated, principally, on the basis of selling prices less estimated brokerage, freight, and certain other selling costs where applicable (estimated net realizable value).*

ANALYSIS

As with a number of mining companies, Newmont values its inventory of precious metals at market value and recognizes income (or a loss) when the inventory is written up (or down). Some companies, such as Echo Bay Mines, use the lower of cost or net realizable value rather than market value for their inventories of precious metals. Gold Kist follows the practice of valuing its agricultural commodities at selling price less remaining costs. While some companies follow this practice, others use cost instead. [www.newmont.com] [www.goldkist.com]

SPECIAL SALES CONSIDERATIONS

Information for Decisions

Different types of sales agreements, and related financing arrangements, may lead to terms that raise questions about when sales take place. Notes to the financial statements generally indicate a company's revenue-recognition methods. This information may be helpful in projecting future sales and answering questions such as these: Is the company's sales revenue accurately reported, given that the company has a liberal return policy? What sort of arrangement does the company have with its customers if the customers are unable to sell goods purchased from this company, and how might that arrangement affect future income?

As we discussed in Chapter 5, most sales involve the simple exchange of a product or service for cash or a receivable. However, a company's sales should be examined for any unusual terms or provisions. Sales involving complex financing arrangements and extended collection periods often lead to the greatest problems.

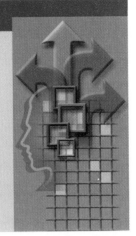

WHO LOSES?

Having just moved into your new third-floor apartment, you purchase a dishwasher at the local department store and put the full purchase price on your store charge card. To save additional costs, you decide to haul the dishwasher home and install it yourself. Getting that dishwasher up to the third floor isn't easy, but luckily you have an outside staircase straight to the top. You're just about to the top step when: "Whoa! Where did that cat come from? Look out below!" Wow, what a mess that dishwasher turns into when it tumbles down all those stairs! Clearly a total loss. Looking at the sales slip in your pocket to remind yourself how much you lost, you see that it says that title to all merchandise remains with the store until the account is fully paid. What luck! The store still owns the dishwasher and you don't have to pay for it. Or do you? Has the sale really taken place even though the store still has title to the demolished dishwasher?

Knowing when a sale is actually final is important because the timing of sales might significantly affect a company's reported income for the period. Companies have been known, for example, to ship extra merchandise at the end of the period to increase reported sales for the period, even though the merchandise will eventually be returned. This type of "window dressing" makes reported results look better than the economic reality. To preserve the reliability of reported information, a number of practices and rules have evolved regarding when companies may report sales.

TRANSFER OF TITLE

The transfer of title from one party to another is normally interpreted to mean that a sale has taken place. In general, title to property passes from the seller to the purchaser when the purchaser takes delivery of the property and agrees to pay for it. If the seller and purchaser are nearby, the delivery time is usually minimal. Suppose, however, that the seller is located in Pittsburgh and the purchaser is in Los Angeles, and at the end of the seller's fiscal year, the merchandise is on a truck passing through Las Vegas. Has delivery been made? Has a sale taken place? Well, that depends on the terms of the sale, as illustrated in Exhibit 14–3.

If the sale was made "f.o.b destination," delivery has not been made and the sale has not yet been finalized. F.o.b stands for **free on board,** which means that the seller has paid the freight charges to the point indicated. For goods shipped f.o.b. destination, the title to the goods remains with the seller until they reach their destination, and shipping charges are borne by the seller. If goods are shipped f.o.b. shipping point, title transfers to the purchaser when the goods are shipped, and the purchaser pays the shipping charges.

FINANCING ARRANGEMENTS

Sometimes sales of property on credit include financing arrangements under which title does not pass directly to the purchaser at the time of delivery. For example, a seller may hold title to property until the purchase price is paid. In other cases, a third party such as a bank or insurance company may lend the purchase price to the purchaser and require title to the pur-

| EXHIBIT 14-3 | **DETERMINING THE POINT OF SALE** |

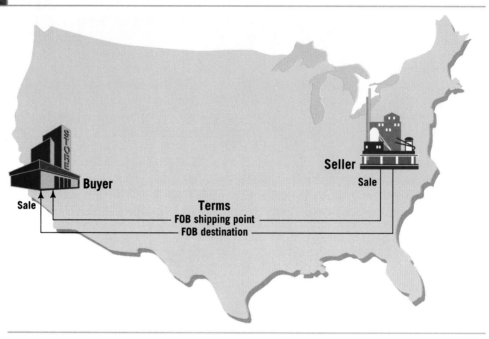

chased property as collateral for the loan. The key to analyzing financing arrangements is to separate the legal and economic aspects. Regardless of who legally holds title, the economic substance of this type of arrangement is that the seller has made a sale, the purchaser has acquired an asset and incurred a liability to pay for it, and the financing party has paid out cash and received the purchaser's promise to pay.

Regardless of who holds title to property, a sale usually occurs when the risk of owning the property shifts from the seller to the purchaser. The test is: "Who loses if the asset is destroyed?" Usually, the purchaser or holder of the asset, rather than the holder of the title, will sustain the loss. An understanding of the substance of a company's sales transactions can often be found by examining the notes to the financial statements.

SALES WITH THE RIGHT OF RETURN

If you purchased a small microwave oven from Wal-Mart, but decided that it did not suit your needs, Wal-Mart would take back the oven and refund your purchase price. From an accounting perspective, the company's sales would be reduced. Anytime a sale takes place, then, how can a company that permits returns be certain that the sale is actually final? Well, it can't, but for most companies, sales returns are a relatively small percentage of total sales. If sales returns and allowances are significant, however, the amounts should be disclosed in the financial statements or notes so that financial statement readers are made aware that a problem exists.

Specific rules have been established for recognizing sales when the right of return exists. These rules keep overly optimistic managers from prematurely recognizing sales or unscrupulous managers from inflating reported sales through sham transactions. The key to determining whether a sale is really a sale is found by looking at the economic substance of the transaction. Transactions that do not involve the transfer of the rewards and risks of ownership from the seller to the purchaser are not sales.

INTEL'S REVENUE RECOGNITION

In a note to its financial statements, Intel Corporation states:

> *Certain of Intel's sales are made to distributors under agreements allowing price protection and/or right of return on merchandise unsold by the distributors. Because of frequent sales price reductions and rapid technological obsolescence in the industry, Intel defers recognition of such sales until the merchandise is sold by the distributors.*

ANALYSIS

Under the terms of the sales to distributors, the sales are not final until the distributors resell the merchandise to their customers. Intel's accounting favors the substance of the transactions over their form. The actual shift of the rewards and risks of ownership does not occur until the sale is made by the distributor. [www.intel.com]

INVENTORY ON CONSIGNMENT

Companies sometimes transfer merchandise to other parties who hold it and attempt to sell it. The other parties, referred to as consignees, are paid a commission on the sales. This type of arrangement is referred to as selling on **consignment.** Here, the company owning the inventory, the consignor, does not recognize a sale until the inventory is actually sold by the consignee. Until then, no sale has actually occurred, even though the goods have been transferred to another party. The consignee holds the goods but does not own them.

Until the time of sale, the consignor reports the inventory in its balance sheet and the consignee does not. When the consignee sells the goods, the consignor recognizes sales revenue and commission expense, while the consignee recognizes commission income. Participation in consignment arrangements, if significant, is normally disclosed in the notes.

SPECIAL INCOME EVENTS

Information for Decisions

Financial statements report income items differently based on whether those items are frequently recurring and how central they are to the company's operations. This type of reporting aides financial statement users in distinguishing among elements that have different implications for the company's future. It helps decision makers answer questions such as these: Although the company reported a loss for the current period, to what extent can the factors that led to the loss be expected to affect income and cash flows in future periods? To what extent will the discontinuance of a segment reported in this year's income statement affect future income? How will income reported in future periods be affected by the change in accounting principle that resulted in an adjustment to the current period's income?

In addition to special rules relating to revenue recognition, income might also be affected by a number of special adjustments and events. Not all events should be viewed in the same way when decision makers make judgments about a company's future performance. One way in which financial statements assist readers in evaluating an entity is by separating the results of nonrecurring and noncentral activities or events from the results of the entity's ongoing central operations. Exhibit 14–1, shown previously, lists a number of different types of items and describes how they are reported. Different types of items are reported differently in the financial statements so decision makers are better able to assess trends and the importance of events for the future.

In Practice 14-4

LEVITZ FURNITURE, INCORPORATED

Levitz Furniture reported both extraordinary items and a change in accounting principle in its 1994 income statement, shown in Exhibit 14–4. In the notes to its financial statements, Levitz disclosed that all of the extraordinary loss in 1993 was from the early retirement of debt. In 1994, the company had an extraordinary loss on the early retirement of debt and an extraordinary gain from the insurance settlement resulting from Hurricane Andrew's destruction of its South Miami warehouse-showroom. The company's change in accounting principle resulted from changing the way it applies the LIFO method of inventory costing.

ANALYSIS

Levitz's losses from the early retirement of debt are required to be reported as extraordinary even though they may recur frequently. Hurricane Andrew was considered extraordinary, even for South Florida, because of its magnitude. The company also changed the method of computing its inventory cost and cost of goods sold. Both the extraordinary items and the effect of the accounting change are reported net of taxes, with the tax effects disclosed. The company also provided information to show the effect of the accounting change on current income and what the income and per share amounts would have been in past years if the new accounting method had always been used. [www.levitz.com]

DISCONTINUED OPERATIONS

Many enterprises engage in a number of different lines of business, with each line comprised of a group of related products or services. If a company decides to dispose of one of these business segments, it must follow special procedures to report its discontinued operations so that financial statement users can focus on the company's continuing operations.

The special reporting procedures apply only to the disposal of a segment that represents an entire line of business. The effects of the **discontinued operations** and their disposal are reported in a separate section of the income statement below Income from Continuing Operations. The effects of the discontinued operations are reported net of taxes, with the reported amounts already reduced for their tax effects.

As you can see from H&R Block's presentation (In Practice 14-5), the disposal of a segment of a company's operations may have two aspects that are separately reported. First, the company may have continued operating the discontinued segment pending disposal. The

INCOME STATEMENT PRESENTATION OF SPECIAL ITEMS

EXHIBIT 14-4

LEVITZ FURNITURE INCORPORATED
CONSOLIDATED STATEMENTS OF OPERATIONS
(TOP PORTION OMITTED; DOLLARS IN THOUSANDS, EXCEPT SHARE DATA)

| | Years Ended March 31 | |
	1993	1994
Income (Loss) before Income Taxes	$ (1,662)	$ 24,425
Income Tax Expense:		
Effect of change in tax law	—	1,447
Other current and deferred taxes	2,039	5,581
Total Income Tax Expense	2,039	7,028
Net Income (Loss) before Extraordinary Items and Cumulative Effect of Change in Accounting Principle	(3,701)	17,397
Extraordinary Items, Net of Tax Benefit of $636 in 1993 and $10,847 in 1994	(1,707)	(29,505)
Cumulative Effect of Change in Accounting Principle, Net of Tax Expense of $1,761	—	2,744
Net Loss	(5,408)	(9,364)
Preferred Dividends	(14,019)	(4,983)
Net Loss Available to Common Stockholders	$(19,427)	$(14,347)
Loss Per Common Share:		
Income (loss) before extraordinary items and cumulative effect of change in accounting principle	$ (1.27)	$ 0.48
Extraordinary items	(0.12)	(1.15)
Cumulative effect of change in accounting principle	—	0.11
Net Loss Available to Common Stockholders	$ (1.39)	$ (0.56)

profit or loss from operating that segment, net of taxes, is reported separate from the company's continuing operations because the company's future income will not include effects of the discontinued segment. Second, the gain or loss on the actual disposal of the segment is reported, also net of taxes.

EXTRAORDINARY GAINS AND LOSSES

As we mentioned in Chapter 5, some events that affect a company's income are so unusual that they must be called to the attention of financial statement users. Those that are both (1) unusual, in that they are unrelated to the company's normal operations, and (2) not expected to recur in the foreseeable future are considered extraordinary events. Material gains and losses from extraordinary events are classified separately in the income statement as **extraordinary gains and losses.** They are reported in the income statement, net of taxes, below the effects of discontinued operations.

Determining whether an item is extraordinary or not requires judgment on the part of management and accountants. Because different companies operate in different environments, an extraordinary event for one may not be considered as such by another. However, because extraordinary items are not related to normal operations, they never include such things as losses on receivables or inventory (unless resulting from an extraordinary event, such as a meteor smashing into a warehouse filled with inventory), gains and losses from the disposal of operating assets, and gains and losses from foreign currency fluctuations or revaluations. Fur-

In Practice 14-5

H&R BLOCK'S DISPOSAL OF A SEGMENT

H&R BLOCK

In 1994, H&R Block, Inc., the well-known income-tax preparation firm, disposed of its wholly owned subsidiary, Interim Services, Inc. The bottom portion of its income statement appeared as follows (in thousands):

	1994	1993
Earnings from Continuing Operations before Taxes	$283,184	$275,894
Taxes on earnings	119,189	104,877
Net Earnings from Continuing Operations	163,995	171,017
Net earnings from discontinued operations (less applicable taxes of $8,706 and $9,688)	9,268	9,688
Net gain on sale of discontinued operations (less applicable taxes of $16,711)	27,265	—
Net Earnings	$200,528	$180,705

ANALYSIS

The earnings of the discontinued segment are segregated in the income statement in the current year and in all previous years reported so that decision makers do not associate them with continuing operations. In the current year, the gain on the sale of the segment is reported. Amounts are reported net of taxes, with the tax effects shown parenthetically. [www.hrblock.com]

ther, extraordinary events are not expected to recur, given the environment in which the company operates. Thus, losses from local transportation disruptions arising because of a major blizzard would not be extraordinary in Minnesota, but would in central Florida.

The most commonly reported extraordinary gains and losses are from retirements of debt. The FASB has mandated that all gains and losses from the retirement of debt, if material, must be reported as extraordinary, even though they do not conform to the normal criteria for such classification. Also, extraordinary gains or losses might stem from casualties, such as earthquakes or floods. Companies might sustain losses because of such casualties, or they might have gains resulting from insurance settlements exceeding the book value of property damaged. With the exception of debt retirements, few extraordinary gains and losses are found in company financial statements.

UNUSUAL GAINS AND LOSSES

Gains and losses that are either unusual or infrequently occurring, but do not meet both criteria for classification as extraordinary, are reported as a component of income from continuing operations. If material, they are reported as separate items. They are not adjusted for any income tax effects because tax effects are included in the company's reported income tax expense. Examples of these types of items include a loss from a major lawsuit settlement or a gain from the disposal of individual operating assets. Another example of this type of item is provided by Smith Corona Corporation, a major manufacturer of typewriters, which filed for bankruptcy in 1995. Investors who reviewed its income statement two years earlier should have been warned of the possible risk after the company reported restructuring costs of $16.5 million as a component of its operating loss.

WAS THAT AN EXTRAORDINARY OR ORDINARY FLOOD?

A chemical research company was located in Baltimore on the banks of Jones Falls, a stream running through the city. For three consecutive years, the amount of water flowing in Jones Falls increased dramatically in the spring and spread through the company's buildings, flooding some volatile chemicals that exploded on contact with water. The resulting damage was extensive and resulted in costly repairs. Management did not take any corrective action because the flooding was considered unusual and was not expected in future years. How would these losses affect your analysis of the company?

ACCOUNTING CHANGES

The consistency concept tells us that the accounting methods chosen by a company's management should be appropriate and used consistently from one period to the next. Consistency is important to decision makers because they depend on the financial statements to represent reality. If that picture is distorted by changes in the methods used to prepare the financial statements, decision makers will be unable to distinguish changes in economic reality from changes in the methods used to portray reality.

However, while accountants put considerable emphasis on consistency, accounting methods must be flexible enough to accommodate changing conditions. Thus, an entity might change its accounting procedures or the estimates used in preparing the statements as a result of improvements in reporting procedures, the introduction of new information, or changes in the entity itself.

Changes in Accounting Principles.   A change from one acceptable accounting method to another is considered a **change in accounting principle.** For example, changes in inventory costing methods, such as from FIFO to average cost, or changes in depreciation methods, such as from double-declining-balance to straight-line, are considered changes in accounting principles. When this type of change occurs, the new accounting method must be used for the entire annual reporting period and all future periods. In addition, a cumulative adjustment must be reported in the year of change at the bottom of the income statement between extraordinary items and net income, as shown in Exhibit 14–4. This cumulative adjustment is equal to the difference, net of tax, between the retained earnings at the beginning of the period as reported and what it would have been if the new method had always been used.

When a company makes a change in accounting principles, it generally does not restate prior-period financial statements included for comparative purposes. This leads to an inconsistency between financial statements of different periods and adversely affects comparability. To compensate, companies must describe any change in accounting principles and disclose both the effect of the change on the current period's income and what income would have been in all previous periods reported if the new method had been used during those periods. The figures reporting income "as if" the new method had always been used are referred to as **pro forma amounts.**

An exception to not restating the financial statements of prior periods occurs for several special types of changes and when a new authoritative standard specifies retroactive application. In these cases, no cumulative adjustment appears in the current financial statements. Instead, the cumulative adjustment is reported in the retained earnings statement, and prior-period financial statements included in current reports for comparative purposes are restated as if the company had always used the new accounting principle.

Financial statement users should be alert for changes in accounting principles so they can assess the effect on the company's reported income and determine how comparability with prior periods might be affected. Changes in accounting principles will be noted in the auditor's opinion, and they will be described in a note to the financial statements.

Changes in Accounting Estimates. Accounting numbers depend heavily on estimates. The amount of receivables expected to go bad, the lives and salvage values of fixed assets, and the percentage of completion of long-term contracts are all estimates that play crucial roles in accounting. By their nature, estimates are uncertain and subject to change over time. A **change in accounting estimate** is reflected in the current and future periods, but prior financial statements are not restated to reflect the new estimate. A new estimate is applied from the beginning of the year in which the change takes place, and it is used for all subsequent periods unless further changes in estimates are made. The effect of changes in estimates on income of the current period should be disclosed unless the estimates are made routinely each period, such as for uncollectible accounts.

PRIOR PERIOD ADJUSTMENTS

What happens if financial statements are issued and management later discovers they were incorrect? The past cannot be changed, and the books of prior periods cannot be reopened once they are closed. Instead, financial statements of prior periods are corrected in the current period through **prior period adjustments.**

Prior period adjustments are made with a correcting entry in the year in which the errors are discovered. If income was incorrect in previous years, an adjustment is made to retained earnings in the current year, because that is where the cumulative effect of the error is found. The correction is made as of the beginning of the current year, and operating results for the current year are reported as if no error had been made. In addition, any other accounts currently misstated are corrected. The current financial statements are issued based on corrected accounts, an adjustment is reported to beginning retained earnings for the amount by which retained earnings was misstated at the beginning of the year, and the prior years' financial statements included for comparative purposes are shown as corrected. A description of the error and its effect must be disclosed in the notes to the financial statements. The requirement to restate prior years' financial statements to eliminate the effects of the error permits decision makers to observe company trends undistorted by either errors or the correcting adjustments.

A CLOSER LOOK AT

A CORRECTION OF PRIOR PERIOD'S FINANCIAL STATEMENTS

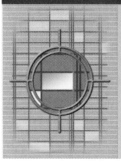

Tooly Company purchases a machine on January 1, 2001, for $800,000. The machine has a four-year life, no salvage value, and is to be depreciated using the straight-line method. Unfortunately, Kearny Botts, Tooly's bookkeeper, charges the entire cost of the equipment to Office Supplies Expense, and financial statements are issued with the error included. During the next year, Kearny notices that the company's 2001 Office Supplies Expense was almost as high as its Cost of Goods Sold, and he discovers and corrects his mistake. He determines that beginning retained earnings for 2002 is understated by the error in 2001's income:

Incorrectly reported Office Supplies Expense	$800,000
Depreciation Expense not reported ($800,000 ÷ 4)	200,000
Understatement of 2001 income and 2002 beginning Retained Earnings	$600,000

Kearny determines that he needs to increase Retained Earnings by $600,000, Equipment by $800,000, and Accumulated Depreciation by $200,000.

When financial statements are issued this year, last year's corrected statements will be included for comparative purposes. Last year's statements will be different from those originally issued as follows:

* Equipment will be $800,000 higher.

* Accumulated Depreciation will be $200,000 higher.

* Depreciation Expense will be $200,000 higher.

* Office Supplies Expense will be $800,000 lower.

* Net Income and ending Retained Earnings will be $600,000 higher.

Also, this year's retained earnings statement will have an adjustment to the beginning balance of Retained Earnings of $600,000 so readers can see the impact of the error and why last year's statements (included for comparative purposes) are different from those originally issued. Income taxes were ignored here for simplicity, but tax expense and taxes payable also would have to be corrected.

EARNINGS PER SHARE

Information for Decisions

Earnings per share is reported so investors can determine how much of a company's income will go to each share of common stock outstanding. Financial statement users need to be familiar with how this information is computed and reported so they can assess how they will share in the current and future earnings of the company and answer questions such as these: If a company has a policy of maintaining a fixed dividend payout ratio, what amount of dividends can I expect from the shares that I hold? Based on the historical price-earnings ratio, what is a reasonable selling price for the company's stock? To what extent might my share of the company's earnings be diluted if holders of other securities are able to convert them into common stock?

Understanding how a company's income is determined is crucial to evaluating the business. However, the most widely quoted measure of a business's success is its earnings per share. In general, a company's **earnings per share** indicates the amount of income for a given period of time that accrues to each share of its common stock. The amount of a company's net income provides decision makers with valuable information, but it does not indicate how it will be shared among those having a claim on it. Earnings per share, in a general sense, is the company's net income, minus preferred dividends, if any, divided by the number of common shares outstanding. It relates only to common shareholders and reflects how residual income is divided among them. Thus, the earnings of a company having many shares outstanding can be compared with earnings of a company having a small number of shares, if the earnings of both are stated on a per-share basis.

Earnings per share, its growth, and what it is projected to be in the future are often important factors in deciding whether to buy or sell a company's stock. Earnings per share is often used in estimating the price that an investor might pay for a company's stock by computing a measure called the price-earnings ratio (P/E), or earnings multiple. The **price-earnings ratio**, or P/E, is computed by dividing the price of a share of a company's common stock by its earnings per share. This resulting number can be compared with other companies in the industry. Conversely, if an average P/E or earnings multiple for the industry is known, the attractiveness of a company's stock price can be evaluated based on its earnings per share.

In Practice 14-6

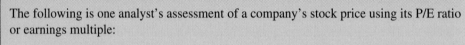

CASE'S PRICE-EARNINGS RATIO

The following is one analyst's assessment of a company's stock price using its P/E ratio or earnings multiple:

> *"It's a remarkable case of a company, poorly run and in terrible shape, that has really turned around," observes Barry Bannister of S. G. Warburg. Bannister . . . is talking about the ugly duckling of Tenneco's brood, the $4.3 billion-in-sales Case farm equipment division. Since Tenneco spun Case off in June 1994, Case shares have climbed from 19 to 25⅜.*
>
> *So if Wall Street thinks this ungainly duckling is now a swan, how come, based on projected per-share earnings of $3.63, up from $2.26 last year, Case is still dirt cheap? Its multiple on projected earnings is only seven, compared with Deere's 10 and Caterpillar's 10.7.[2]*

ANALYSIS

Deere and Caterpillar have similar P/Es, but Case's earnings multiple is lower because the market is not convinced that its poor past performance will not resurface. Those believing Case's troubles are over might be tempted to buy the stock with the expectation that its earnings multiple will eventually approach the industry average. [www.casecorp.com]

BASIC EARNINGS PER SHARE

All companies are required to report on the face of the income statement a basic earnings per share amount for each year reported. Basic earnings per share reflects the income accruing to the actual common shares outstanding. The computation of basic earnings per share involves dividing income by the number of common shares. If the number of shares changes during

[2]John F. Geer, Jr., "Swan Dreams: In Which a Notorious Binge Producer Learns Restraint," *Financial World* (July 4, 1995), p. 28.

the year, the income available to common shareholders should be divided by a weighted average of the number of common shares outstanding during the period.

When computing a weighted average, stock dividends and stock splits are not treated as the issuance of additional shares. Instead, all per-share amounts for the current and past years are restated to give effect to the stock dividend or split, as illustrated in Chapter 12. Restating all numbers to give effect to the split puts them on a comparable basis. Remember that a stock dividend or split does not change the relative ownership position of any stockholder.

A CLOSER LOOK AT

BASIC EARNINGS PER SHARE

Bigelow Company reported net income of $231,000 for the year. The company has no bonds or preferred stock outstanding. The company had 100,000 common shares outstanding for the first nine months of the year, and then issued 20,000 additional common shares, giving it 120,000 shares outstanding for the remaining three months of the year. The weighted average number of shares for computing earnings per share for the year is as follows:

$$
\begin{array}{rr}
100{,}000 \text{ shares} \times 9 \text{ months} = & 900{,}000 \\
120{,}000 \text{ shares} \times 3 \text{ months} = & \underline{360{,}000} \\
& 1{,}260{,}000 \\
\div & \underline{12} \\
& \underline{\underline{105{,}000}}
\end{array}
$$

Earnings per share is calculated as follows:

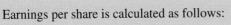

$231,000 \div 105,000 \text{ shares} = \$2.20 \text{ per share}$

DILUTED EARNINGS PER SHARE

The computation of earnings per share becomes more complex when convertible securities and stock options are considered. Convertible preferred stock and convertible bonds currently outstanding might someday be converted into common stock, and stock options might eventually be exercised. This means that an enterprise's income might have to be spread over more shares of common stock, an effect called **dilution of earnings per share.** Although the effects of future conversions and the exercise of options are unknown until such events occur, ignoring the potentially dilutive effect of convertible securities and options would provide decision makers with an unrealistic view of the degree to which existing stockholders will share in future earnings.

The FASB currently requires all companies to report basic earnings per share. In addition, for companies with convertible securities or stock options outstanding, a second figure called diluted earnings per share must be reported. Diluted earnings per share reflects what earnings per share would be if all dilutive securities were turned into common stock. In effect, the FASB requires reporting the best and worst cases with respect to earnings per share to help decision makers develop their own assessments of future earnings per share.

SUMMARY

A number of special situations require looking beyond the basic principles of revenue and income recognition presented in Chapter 5. Although revenues are generally recognized when the earnings process is complete and an exchange has taken place, some situations call for departures from this principle. For long-term contracts such as those found in the construction industry, recognizing income only when the contract is completed does not always provide the most useful information. Instead, the percentage-of-completion method, which recognizes income over time as the work is completed, often provides a more realistic view of a company's activities. This method can be used only when reliable estimates of expected revenues and costs and the percentage of completion are available.

In some cases, income is recognized at the completion of production, even though no exchange has taken place. This can occur only if all units of product are the same and an objectively determinable market price exists, such as with precious metals and agricultural commodities. If this approach is used, inventories are then valued at market or net realizable value.

Even when the realization and matching concepts are followed, complicating issues sometimes arise. The question of when a sale actually takes place is not always straightforward. If, for example, merchandise is in transit between seller and purchaser at the end of the period, a determination is needed as to whose inventory it is. The determination usually is based on the terms of the sale. When inventory is sold f.o.b. destination, it belongs to the seller until received by the purchaser; ownership of inventory sold f.o.b. shipping point is transferred when the goods are shipped.

Recognition of a sale does not always depend on the transfer of title to the goods. Title often remains with the seller or is transferred to a third party when the goods are used as collateral for a loan. Even though title may not transfer to the purchaser, a sale is recorded. Regardless of who holds title to such goods, the general test that is applied is, "Who loses if the goods are destroyed?"

Sometimes goods are shipped to other parties (consignees) to be sold by those parties on commission. Ownership of consigned inventory remains with the consignor until sold by the consignee. When the goods are sold by the consignee, the consignor recognizes the sale and the consignee recognizes commission income.

Several types of items are given special reporting treatment because they are unrelated to the long-run central operations of the business and separate reporting permits decision makers to focus on the entity's continuing activities. Gains and losses on the disposal of a business segment, along with profits and losses from operating the segment prior to sale, are reported in a separate section of the income statement, net of taxes, after income from continuing operations. Extraordinary gains and losses arise from events that are unusual and not expected to recur in the foreseeable future. They are reported, net of taxes, in a separate section of the income statement below gains and losses from the disposal of a segment.

Changes in accounting principles require application of the new principle from the beginning of the current period. In addition, a cumulative adjustment for the amount by which beginning retained earnings would have been different had the new principle always been used is reported in the income statement between extraordinary items and net income. For a few special changes, the cumulative adjustment is reported in the retained earnings statement and financial statements of prior periods are restated. This treatment also applies to corrections of prior periods' profits. Changes in accounting estimates do not require adjustment or restatement, simply application of the new estimate from the beginning of the current period.

Earnings per share is widely used as an indicator of the success of a business enterprise. It indicates the income accruing to each share of common stock and must be reported on the face of the income statement. Basic earnings per share is computed by dividing income available for common shareholders (net income minus preferred dividends) by a weighted average of the number of common shares outstanding during the period. For companies having dilutive securities outstanding, such as convertible bonds, convertible preferred stock, or stock options, a second figure, diluted earnings per share, may have to be reported. This figure is computed as if all of the dilutive securities are converted or exercised, and reflects the greatest possible dilution in the earnings accruing to each share of common stock.

LIST OF IMPORTANT TERMS

change in accounting estimate *(552)*

change in accounting principle *(551)*

completed-contract method *(541)*

consignment *(547)*

dilution of earnings per share *(555)*

discontinued operations *(548)*

earnings per share *(553)*

extraordinary gains and losses *(549)*

free on board *(545)*

percentage-of-completion method *(541)*

price–earnings ratio *(554)*

prior period adjustments *(552)*

pro forma amounts *(551)*

EXAMINING THE CONCEPTS

Q14-1 Why is an exchange transaction usually required before income is recognized?

Q14-2 What are some of the circumstances that might lead to a departure from the realization concept in recognizing income?

Q14-3 When is income recognized using the completed-contract method of accounting for long-term contracts? How is the amount of income to be recognized determined?

Q14-4 When is income recognized using the percentage-of-completion method of accounting for long-term contracts? How is the amount of income to be recognized determined?

Q14-5 Is the percentage-of-completion method or the completed-contract method of income recognition likely to report the greatest amount of income in the third year of a five-year contract? Explain why.

Q14-6 If you were evaluating a company's performance, and that company did most of its business under long-term construction-type contracts, which method of accounting for the contracts do you think would best inform you of the company's activities? Explain.

Q14-7 What conditions must exist for the percentage-of-completion method to be used?

Q14-8 Describe two methods of accounting for precious metals and agricultural commodities. Indicate the conditions that are important for income recognition under the two methods.

Q14-9 Compare the inventory valuation methods used for precious metals and expensive evening dresses. What attributes of precious metals provides support for the valuation method used?

Q14-10 Under normal sales conditions, what event or events must occur before a sale is recorded?

Q14-11 What does it mean to ship a product "f.o.b. destination"? How does this differ from shipping it "f.o.b. shipping point"? Which method would you prefer if you were the seller? Explain why.

Q14-12 What is the most general test of whether a sale has taken place?

Q14-13 Why might a party hold title to an asset when it is neither the purchaser nor seller of the asset? Explain the nature of such an arrangement.

Q14-14 Applebee Hardware has been offered a new line of unbreakable tools to be sold on consignment. What does it mean to carry products on consignment? How does this differ from the way in which inventory normally is acquired by retail stores? Who owns goods held on consignment?

Q14-15 What does it mean when a company reports a loss on discontinued operations? How is the amount of the reported gain or loss determined?

Q14-16 When must a company report income from continuing operations in its income statement? What types of adjustments to income from continuing operations might be added or deducted to arrive at net income? Give several examples.

Q14-17 From an accounting perspective, what is an extraordinary event? How does a company determine if an event is extraordinary? How are gains and losses from extraordinary events reported? Will all companies treat such events in the same manner? Explain why or why not.

Q14-18 How are the income tax effects of extraordinary gains and losses treated?

Q14-19 How do unusual gains and losses differ from extraordinary gains and losses? How are they reported? How are the income tax effects of unusual items treated in the financial statements?

Q14-20 Under what conditions might a company report a cumulative adjustment from a change in accounting principle? Give two examples of a change in accounting principle and explain how they would be reported.

Q14-21 What is meant by "pro forma" amounts? Give an example of when pro forma amounts must be reported.

Q14-22 What is meant by a change in accounting estimate? Give two examples of a change in accounting estimate. How are changes in accounting estimates reported?

Q14-23 What is meant by a prior period adjustment? When must prior period adjustments be made, and how are they reported? Give an example of a prior period adjustment.

Q14-24 What is "earnings per share" and why is it important? Where is earnings per share reported?

Q14-25 What amounts are used as the numerator and denominator in computing basic earnings per share?

Q14-26 Ace Company has convertible bonds outstanding. How might these be relevant to the computation of earnings per share?

Q14-27 What effect does convertible preferred stock outstanding have on the computation of basic and diluted earnings per share?

UNDERSTANDING ACCOUNTING INFORMATION

E14-1 Recognizing Income: A Key to Decision Making
In reviewing the financial statements of Global Corporation you discover that a number of special items were included in its income statements for the years ended December 31, 2000 and 2001. In 2000, Global reported a loss of $34 million from discontinued operations as a result of closing its facilities throughout Asia and a reduction of $7 million in reported income resulting from a change in accounting principles. During 2001, Global reported a gain of $21 million when land that was being held as a potential building site was purchased by the State of California under the right of eminent domain. In addition, a gain of $45 million resulted from an out-of-court settlement on a patent infringement lawsuit the company had filed several years earlier. Global's reported net income increased from $100 million in 2000 to $110 million in 2001, including all of the adjustments.

a. Why do generally accepted accounting principles require companies to report transactions such as those listed above as separate items in the income statement?
b. Based on the information provided, did Global Corporation's income from continuing operations increase or decrease in 2001?
c. Explain why an analysis of the impact of the special items in Global's income statements would be likely to cause an informed investor to arrive at a different evaluation of the future earnings potential of Global Corporation than one who relied solely on changes in the amount of reported net income.

E14-2 Special Income Recognition Issues The Broken Rock Mining Company is headquartered in Phoenix, Arizona, and has a series of gold and silver mines in the western United States and South America. It has in inventory at year-end 1,000 troy ounces of gold with a market price of $310 per ounce and 900,000 ounces of silver with a market price of 12 cents per troy ounce. Broken Rock's costs of producing the refined ore were $270 per troy ounce of gold and 9 cents per troy ounce of silver. In its income statement for the current period, Broken Rock Mining included income of $40,000 (1,000 ounces $\times$ $40) on the gold and $27,000 (900,000 ounces $\times$ $0.03) on the silver that was produced during the year but still held in inventory at year-end.

a. What unique characteristics of gold and silver make it possible for a mining company to recognize income on inventory that is not yet sold?
b. Why is Foghorn Motors not permitted to recognize the difference between the sticker price of $41,000 on a new sports utility vehicle it has just produced and its production and distribution costs of $32,000 as income at the time the SUV is produced?

c. If Broken Rock is confident that it will be able to extract an additional 300,000 ounces of gold from its largest mine at a cost of $270 per troy ounce, would it be appropriate for Broken Rock to recognize income of $12,000,000 [($310 − $270) $\times$ 300,000 ounces] in the current period? Explain.
d. The price of precious metals varies substantially from year to year. Is this likely to make reported income for mining companies more volatile than other types of companies? Explain.

E14-3 Special Sales Considerations Roadway Motor Homes manufactures an exclusive line of motor homes purchased primarily by corporate executives and country and western stars. Roadway sells its motor homes to dealers who then sell the units to customers. Because its motor homes are very expensive and its customers are quite demanding, Roadway offers all purchasers the right to return their motor homes within 30 days of delivery for a full refund. Of the 1,420 units sold last year, only 12 units were returned by customers and 8 of the customers purchased more expensive units. Explain your answers for each of the following:

a. Does the existence of the return privilege mean that Roadway should not record a sale until 30 days after delivery?
b. Should Roadway record a sale when the motor home is delivered to the dealer or when the dealer sells the motor home?
c. Roadway is considering extending the number of sales outlets by providing units to selected dealers on a consignment basis. How does the consignment process differ from that presently in use? At what point should Roadway recognize a sale for units placed on consignment?
d. Why is the time at which a sale is recognized of special importance in the financial reporting process?

E14-4 Special Income Events Booth Company's income statement for the current period included (1) a gain of $800,000 (net of tax) on the sale of one of its three major operating divisions, (2) an extraordinary loss of $320,000 (net of tax) on the retirement of bonds payable prior to maturity, and (3) an addition to income of $415,000 as a cumulative adjustment (net of tax) resulting from a change to straight-line depreciation from double-declining-balance depreciation on certain equipment.

a. Why are events such as these separately disclosed in the income statement?
b. What effect did the three events have on Booth's reported income for the current period?

c. What effect will each of the events have on reported net income in the following period?

d. What factors might cause an investor to view the gain of $800,000 on the sale of the operating division unfavorably?

E14-5 Earnings Per Share While Simple Corporation has only common stock outstanding, Complex Company has both preferred stock and common stock outstanding. Complex Company's preferred stock is convertible into common stock. Complex also has given its corporate officers the right to purchase a substantial number of common shares at a price that presently is well below the market price of the shares.

a. Why is the weighted average number of shares outstanding used in computing earnings per share rather than the number of shares actually outstanding at year-end?

b. If Simple Corporation sold 60,000 new shares of common stock to the public on April 30, what effect would the sale have on the weighted average shares outstanding used in computing earnings per share? What effect on the weighted average shares outstanding would occur if Simple issued 120,000 new shares of common stock as a stock dividend on October 31?

c. How does the computation of diluted earnings per share help investors gain a better basis of comparison between two companies such as Simple and Complex?

d. Should the fact that the officers of Complex Company can exercise their stock options at any point and purchase shares at less than current market price be taken into consideration in the computation of earnings per share? If included, would it be more appropriate to include the options in the computation of basic or diluted earnings per share, or both?

E14-6 Multiple Choice: Revenue Recognition Select the correct answer for each of the following:

1. When the percentage-of-completion method is used in accounting for a long-term contract:
   a. Income is reported before it is earned.
   b. Income is reported earlier than under the completed-contract method.
   c. More income is reported over the life of the project than under the completed-contract method.
   d. Income is reported as payments are received.

2. Which of the following companies is least likely to use the percentage-of-completion method of accounting?
   a. Textile manufacturer.
   b. Aircraft manufacturer.
   c. Office building contractor.
   d. Law firm doing title searches on all of the homes in Baylor County.

3. Gold typically is valued at:
   a. Lower of cost or market.
   b. Cost of mining and refining.

c. Selling price less remaining costs to sell.
d. Either a or c.

4. When merchandise is sold f.o.b. shipping point, it means:
   a. The price paid by the buyer includes the cost of transportation.
   b. Transfer of title takes place when the buyer orders the merchandise.
   c. Transfer of title takes place when the merchandise is received by the buyer.
   d. Transfer of title takes place when the merchandise is shipped.

5. When merchandise is sold f.o.b. destination:
   a. The carrier bears no responsibility for damage to the goods during shipping.
   b. Damage to merchandise in shipment is the responsibility of the buyer.
   c. Title does not pass until payment is made by the buyer.
   d. Title passes at the time the goods are received by the buyer.

6. When goods are sold on consignment:
   a. The consignor does not recognize income until the product is sold to a third party by the consignee.
   b. The consignee takes title to the product but does not need to pay for it until it is sold.
   c. The consignee must pay for the product at the time it is shipped to the consignee by the consignor.
   d. The consignor recognizes income at the time the product is shipped to the consignee.

E14-7 Multiple Choice: Special Items and Earnings Per Share Select the correct answer for each of the following:

1. Which of the following is an example of an extraordinary item?
   a. A building is destroyed by fire.
   b. The company president resigns to take a job with a larger company.
   c. Heavy frosts in the month of August kill the peanut crop in Georgia.
   d. Computing facilities become obsolete when a new type of computer is developed.

2. When a change in accounting principle is adopted during a period:
   a. A cumulative adjustment is included in net income in the period of the change and the new procedure is used for the entire year.
   b. Prior years' financial statements shown for comparative purposes are restated so they are consistent with the new principle.
   c. Current revenues and expenses are reported under the new procedure from the date of the change to the end of the year only.
   d. Revenues and expenses are reported under the new procedure at the start of the next year.

3. Pro forma figures are:
   a. Amounts that were actually reported .

b. Amounts that would have been reported if a different procedure or assumption had been used.

c. Amounts reported on specified government forms.

d. Incorrect amounts.

4. A change in an accounting estimate:

a. Requires a restatement of prior years' financial statements.

b. Should not recur again in the foreseeable future.

c. Is reflected in the current and future periods.

d. Results in a cumulative adjustment in the income statement in the period in which the change in estimate is made.

5. Basic earnings per share is based on:

a. Earnings available to common stockholders and the year-end number of common shares outstanding.

b. Earnings available to common stockholders and the weighted average number of common shares outstanding during the period.

c. Operating income and the year-end number of common shares outstanding.

d. Operating income and the number of common shares outstanding at the beginning of the period.

6. If convertible bonds are outstanding at the end of the accounting period, reported earnings per share will:

a. Include the dilutive effects of the bonds in both basic and diluted earnings per share.

b. Ignore the dilutive effects until the bonds are converted.

c. Include the dilutive effects of the bonds in diluted earnings per share, but not in basic earnings per share.

d. Be reported only in the notes to the financial statements.

E14-8 Construction Contracts Thompson Construction Company is involved in the construction of an electrical generating station for Whopper Electric Corp. The total project is expected to take 5 years to complete. The contract awarded to Thompson is $250,000,000, and the com-

pany expects the project to cost it $200,000,000. At the end of the first year of construction, Thompson has completed 20 percent of the total expected work, but based on costs incurred to date, it now expects its total cost for the project to be $215,000,000. At the end of the second year, 40 percent of the work has been completed, and Thompson estimates that its total costs under the contract will be $210,000,000.

a. What amount of income will Thompson report for each of the first 2 years of the contract if it uses the percentage-of-completion method of computing income?

b. What amount of income will Thompson report in each of the 2 years if the completed-contract method is used?

c. Which method provides better information for evaluating the activities of Thompson Construction? Explain why.

E14-9 Percentage-of-Completion Method Farnsworth Construction Company completed a 5-year construction project with total billings of $254 million and costs of $237 million in November 2000. Farnsworth uses the percentage-of-completion method in recognizing income on construction projects and reported a loss of $9 million for the year 2000 on this project due to unexpected costs associated with installing elevators and electrical service.

a. What amount of income would be reported in 2000 if Farnsworth had used the completed-contract method?

b. What amount of income did Farnsworth report on the project in the prior 4 years?

c. What amount of income would be reported by Farnsworth for 2000 if it had reported income of $12 million on the project in the prior 4 years?

E14-10 Recognizing Percentage-of-Completion Income The chief accountant of Hammer Construction Company developed the following spreadsheet format as a means of quickly determining the amount of income to be recognized using the percentage-of-completion method of income recognition on a major housing development:

Year	Dollar Amount of Contract	Total Estimated Cost	Total Estimated Profit	Total Percent Completed	Income Previously Recognized	Income to Be Recognized This Period
1	$1,200,000	$980,000	$220,000	15	$ —	$33,000
2	1,200,000	900,000		35		
3	1,200,000	940,000		50		
4	1,200,000	970,000		90		
5	1,200,000	961,000		100		

a. Complete the spreadsheet by inserting the appropriate amounts.

b. Compute the amount of income to be reported each year if the completed-contract method had been used.

E14-11 Commodities Inventory Barley Feed & Grain holds 450,000 bushels of #2 yellow corn. Barley purchased the corn from farmers at an average price of $2.20 per bushel during November and December 2000.

a. By December 31, 2000, corn prices rose to $2.35 per bushel. At what amount should Barley Feed and Gain value its inventory? Why?

b. On January 31, 2001, corn prices dropped to $2.19 per bushel. At what amount should Barley Feed and Grain value the inventory in its financial statements prepared at January 31, 2001? Why?

c. Why are commodities often adjusted to market price, while other types of inventories are not?

E14-12 Determining Point of Sale Florida Corporation has as a major customer, Portland Products, located in Portland, Oregon. Florida Corporation sells its products f.o.b. shipping point and mails a bill to each customer on the day the product is shipped. The following action was by taken Florida Corporation on the last three orders received in 2000 from Portland Products:

Order Number	Date Shipped	Date Delivered
#63	December 19, 2000	December 28, 2000
#64	December 29, 2000	January 4, 2001
#65	January 2, 2001	January 7, 2001

The bill for the first shipment was received by Portland Products prior to December 31, 2000. Bills for the other shipments were received in early 2001.

a. What does it mean to sell f.o.b. shipping point?

b. Which orders should Florida Corporation include in its 2000 sales?

c. Which orders should Portland Corporation include in its 2000 purchases?

d. How would the answers to parts b and c change if the products were shipped f.o.b. destination?

E14-13 Consignment Sales Bellweather Industries was interested in gaining a foothold in a number of western states. Bellweather offered several companies an opportunity to carry their line of scuba and diving gear on a consignment basis. For providing display space and local advertising, the consignee receives 25 percent of the sales price of all goods sold. On July 8, Bellweather shipped goods with a selling price of $89,000 to California Outfitters on consignment. The goods cost Bellweather $45,000 to manufacture. California Outfitters still had all of the goods on hand at the end of July, but sold goods for $65,000 in August that had cost Bellweather $33,000 to produce.

a. On July 31, will the goods shipped from Bellweather to California Outfitters appear on Bellweather's balance sheet or that of California Outfitters, or both? At what amount will the goods be reported?

b. With respect to the goods shipped to California Outfitters, what amount of profit should Bellweather recognize on the sale of those goods? How much revenue would be recognized in July and how much in August? What expenses should be recognized by Bellweather in connection with the sale, and when should they be reported in Bellweather's income statement?

c. How would California Outfitters' income from the sale of Bellweather's goods be reported in its income statement?

d. If either Bellweather Industries or California Outfitters were trying to get a bank loan using its inventory as collateral, what possible problems might arise given the consignment arrangement between them?

E14-14 Sale of Operating Division Fabric Corporation sold a major operating division in 2001 for $1,500,000. The book value of the division was $700,000 at the time of sale. Between the beginning of 2001 and the date of sale, the division reported an operating loss (before taxes) of $300,000. Fabric reported net income of $600,000 for 2001. The company's effective income tax rate is 30 percent.

a. Compute the amount of gain or loss reported by Fabric on the sale of the operating division.

b. Compute the amount of earnings from continuing operations reported by Fabric for 2001.

c. Present the portion of the income statement for Fabric that shows earnings from continuing operations and ends with net income.

E14-15 Change of Accounting Estimate Reliable Delivery Company purchased a fleet of delivery trucks with a newly developed fuel system that burns used textbooks. At the beginning of the third year of operating the trucks, the company concluded that the original estimated useful life of 6 years was overly conservative and a total useful life of 10 years was more appropriate. The total cost of the trucks was $260,000, and the estimated salvage value is $20,000. Reliable uses straight-line depreciation.

a. Compute the depreciation expense for years 2, 3, and 4.

b. Give all journal entries needed in the third year.

E14-16 Change in the Estimated Life of Goodwill Zalin Corporation purchased Amgren Company on January 1, 1998, and recorded goodwill of $5,600,000, which is amortized on a 10-year basis using straight-line write-off. On January 1, 2001, Zalin concluded the goodwill had a remaining life of 4 years.

a. What amount of unamortized goodwill should Zalin Corporation have reported at December 31, 2000?

b. What amount of amortization expense should Zalin record in 2001 and in each of the subsequent 3 years?

c. What amount of amortization expense would Zalin have recorded in each of the first 3 years if it had initially estimated the life of the goodwill to be 7 years?

E14-17 Change in Accounting Estimates Kinslow Company purchased a warehouse for $7,200,000 on January 1, 1989. The company uses straight-line depreciation and concluded it should depreciate the building over 30 years and use an estimated scrap value of $1,800,000. On January 1, 2001, Kinslow decided it needed to change the total estimated life of the building to 25 years and the estimated scrap value to $1,140,000.

a. What amount of depreciation expense should be recorded for 2000?
b. What should be the balance in accumulated depreciation at December 31, 2000?
c. What amount of depreciation expense should be recorded for 2001?
d. What is the impact of the changes in accounting estimate on reported net income for 2001?
e. What balance in accumulated depreciation should be reported at December 31, 2001?

E14-18 Change in Depreciation Method MTC Corporation paid $300,000 for equipment with an expected economic life of 10 years and scrap value of $25,000. For the first 2 years, MTC used double-declining-balance depreciation. On the first day of the third year of ownership, MTC elected to change to straight-line depreciation.

a. Determine the depreciation expense reported by MTC Corporation for each of the first 2 years and the balance in accumulated depreciation at the end of the second year.
b. Determine the amount of depreciation expense MTC Corporation would have recorded for each of the first 2 years using straight-line depreciation and the amount of accumulated depreciation that would that would have been reported at the end of the second year.
c. Determine the amount of the cumulative adjustment to be reported in the income statement for the third year as a result of the change in depreciation methods.
d. By what amount did the change in depreciation methods change reported net income for the third year?

E14-19 Recording Depletion Costs Smythe & Company developed an open-pit nickel mine containing an estimated 200,000 tons of ore. The total cost of purchasing the mine, opening it for operations, and the estimated cost of closing the mine was $84,000,000. Prior to January 1, 2000, Smythe mined 140,000 tons of ore. At that date, the company concluded that total production from the mine would be 250,000 tons of ore and the costs of closing the mine would increase from $4,000,000 to $8,500,000. During 2000, Smythe removed 35,000 tons of ore from the mine.

a. What amount of accumulated depletion should Smythe & Company have recorded by January 1, 2000?
b. What amount of depletion should Smythe & Company record for 2000?

E14-20 Change of Accounting Principle Purple Corporation has used a first-in-first-out (FIFO) inventory system since it was created. On December 31, 2001, Purple elected to change from the FIFO inventory method to the weighted-average method. Inventory purchases during 2001 totaled $350,000. The inventory balance reported by Purple on January 1, 2001, using FIFO was $60,000. A balance of $56,000 would have been reported under weighted average. The ending inventory balance would be reported as $120,000 under FIFO and $105,000 under weighted average.

a. What amount of cost of goods sold would be reported for 2001 if Purple continued using FIFO?
b. What amount will be reported for 2001 using the weighted average method?
c. What amount of cumulative adjustment will be reported in Purple's 2001 financial statements? Show how the amount of the adjustment is computed. Where will the cumulative adjustment be reported?

E14-21 Earnings Per Share Mega Corporation has 70,000 shares of $10-par common stock and 25,000 shares of $4-par preferred stock outstanding. The preferred stock pays a 10 percent annual dividend and is convertible into 20,000 shares of common stock. Mega Corporation reported 2000 net income of $180,000.

a. Compute the amount that should be reported as basic earnings per share for 2000.
b. What relevance does the convertibility of the preferred stock have for reporting earnings per share?

E14-22 Earnings Per Share with Treasury Stock Sly Corporation issued 400,000 shares of $1-par value common stock on January 1, 2000, and declared a 10 percent stock dividend on December 31, 2000. A total of 60,000 shares of common stock were purchased from a major stockholder on April 1, 2002, and are held as treasury shares on December 31, 2002. Sly reported net income of $695,000 and $742,000 in 2001 and 2002, respectively.

a. What amount should be reported as earnings per share for 2001?
b. What amount should be reported as earnings per share for 2002?

E14-23 Earnings Per Share with Convertible Preferred Stock Outstanding Burr Company has 500,000 shares of $4-par value preferred stock outstanding with a 6 percent cumulative annual dividend. Each share of preferred stock can be converted into one-half share of common stock at any time. Burr has 600,000 shares of common stock outstanding and reported net income of $750,000 for the current year.

a. What amount should be reported as basic earnings per share for the year?
b. What amount should be reported as diluted earnings per share for the year?

E14-24 Earnings Per Share with Convertible Bonds Outstanding Glowtec Corporation has 200,000 shares of $5-par value common stock outstanding. It also has $800,000 par value 8 percent bonds outstanding that were issued at par value on January 1, 1998, and mature on January 1, 2018. Each $1,000 par value bond can be converted into 50 shares of common stock at any time. Glowtec reported income from operations (before interest expense) of $480,000 for the year 2000.

a. What amount should Glowtec report as net income for 2000, ignoring income taxes?
b. What amount should be reported as basic earnings per share for 2000?
c. What amount should be reported as diluted earnings per share for 2000?

E14-25   Earnings Per Share with Convertible Bonds Issued During the Year   Timber Corporation has 200,000 shares of $5-par value common stock outstanding. On October 1, 2000, Timber issued $800,000 par value 8 percent bonds at par value. The bonds mature on October 1, 2020. Each $1,000 par value bond can be converted into 50 shares of common stock at any time. Timber reported income from operations (before interest expense) of $480,000 for the year 2000.

a. What amount should Timber report as net income for 2000?
b. What amount should be reported as basic earnings per share for 2000?
c. What amount should be reported as diluted earnings per share for 2000?

E14-26   Reporting Earnings Per Share   In 2000, Tallen Company reported earnings per share of $3.00. In 2001, the company reports net income of $400,000. Tallen had 100,000 common shares outstanding during 2000 and for much of 2001. However, toward the end of 2001, its common stock split 2 for 1.

a. What amount will Tallen report in its 2001 annual report as earnings per share for 2000 and 2001?
b. How does the treatment of stock splits differ from that of stock dividends in computing earnings per share?
c. Where in the annual report are earnings per share figures reported?

E14-27   Weighted-Average Shares   Ander Corporation has 60,000 shares of $5-par common stock outstanding at December 31, 2000. Of these shares, 10,000 were issued on April 1, 2000. Ander reported net income of $158,700 for 2000.

a. Compute the weighted-average number of common shares outstanding during 2000.
b. Compute Ander's earnings per share for 2000.

E14-28   Error in Recording Depreciation Expense   Beeline Bus Company purchased 3 buses at $300,000 each on January 1, 2000. On January 1, 2002, the company controller discovered that the estimated scrap value of $20,000 per bus had been ignored in recording straight-line depreciation in 2000 and 2001. The estimated economic lives of the buses remain at 10 years.

a. What amount of depreciation was recorded in 2000 and 2001?
b. What amount of depreciation expense should have been recorded in 2000 and 2001?
c. What amount of depreciation expense will Beeline report on the 3 buses in 2002?
d. How is the error in recording depreciation expense reported in 2002?

E14-29   Error in Reported Inventory Levels   Crown Company reported cost of goods sold of $495,000 and gross profit of $134,000 for 2000; however, the external auditor in performing the audit work discovered the company had incorrectly stated its inventory at January 1, 2000, at $32,000 rather than $48,000, and had incorrectly reported its inventory at December 31, 2000, at $52,000 rather than $41,000. Crown Company computes its cost of goods as follows:

$$
\begin{aligned}
&\text{Beginning inventory} \\
+\ &\underline{\text{Purchases}} \\
=\ &\text{Goods available for sale} \\
-\ &\underline{\text{Ending inventory}} \\
=\ &\text{Cost of goods sold}
\end{aligned}
$$

a. Assuming inventory purchases of $515,000 have been correctly recorded for the year, show the computation of cost of goods sold as reported by Crown Company for 2000. What amount should it have reported as cost of goods sold?
b. What amount should Crown Company have reported as gross profit for 2000?

P14-30   Error in Recording Revenue under Long-Term Construction Contract   Empire Builders uses the percentage-of-completion method of recording income under long-term construction contracts. On January 1, 2000, Empire entered into a 4-year contract with a total contract price of $30,000,000. The estimated total cost of the project at the end of each of the first 3 years and the actual cost at the end of the fourth year, the estimated percentage of completion, and the income recorded by Empire at the end of each year were as follows:

Contract Price	Cost of Project	Estimated Profit	Percentage of Completion	Income Recorded by Empire
$30,000,000	$24,000,000	$6,000,000	20%	$1,500,000
30,000,000	23,000,000	7,000,000	45	1,750,000
30,000,000	25,000,000	5,000,000	70	1,250,000
30,000,000	24,600,000	5,400,000	100	1,350,000

At the end of the fourth year, the controller reviewed the contract and discovered that the bookkeeper had incorrectly recorded one-fourth of the total estimated profit at the end of each year as income for the year.

a. Determine the amount that should be reported as income for each year using the percentage-of-completion method.
b. What was the amount of error in reported net income in each of the first 3 years under the contract?
c. What is the amount of the required correction to retained earnings as of January 1 of the fourth year?
d. What is the correct amount of income to be recognized in the fourth year of the project?

E14-31 Accounting Error In reviewing the account balances just before preparing financial statements for 2002, the financial vice president of Castaway Company discovered that $64,000 of equipment purchased on June 30, 2000, had been improperly charged to maintenance expense at the time of delivery. The equipment has an estimated useful life of 8 years with no residual value. Castaway Company uses straight-line depreciation. The balances reported for selected items for 2000, 2001, and 2002 are as follows:

	2000	**2001**	**2002**
Depreciation expense	$ 50,000	$ 60,000	$ 70,000
Maintenance expense	94,000	45,000	52,000
Net income	70,000	90,000	100,000
Retained earnings	240,000	280,000	340,000

Required:

a. For each of the items listed, show the corrected amount that would appear in the financial statements included in Castaway's 2002 annual report. Castaway includes financial statements for the current year and comparative statements for the 2 preceding years in its annual report. Ignore income taxes.
b. Give the journal entry that should be recorded on December 31, 2002, to correct Castaway's account balances.

E14-32 Accounting Changes The controller of Baldwin Corporation found an error in recording prepaid insurance in the previous year. A payment for a 5-year policy was charged to expense entirely in the year of payment. In addition, the controller decided to change in the current year from straight-line to double-declining-balance depreciation on equipment used in the general headquarters. He also has concluded that the general headquarters building should be depreciated over a 30-year life rather than the 40-year life currently being used.

a. Compare the accounting treatments used in connection with (1) the correction of an error, (2) a change from one generally accepted accounting principle to another, and (3) a change in accounting estimate.
b. Explain why different procedures are used.
c. What will be the impact of each of the 3 items on net income reported by Baldwin Corporation for the current year? Explain.

E14-33 Reporting Choices Indicate whether each of the following items should be reported as a part of income from continuing operations (IO), an extraordinary item (EI), a discontinued operation (DO), or excluded from the income statement (EX):

a. Sale of inventory at a loss.
b. Flood losses at time of annual spring thaw.
c. Cost of replacing an uninsured building destroyed when a passenger plane crashed into it.
d. Gain realized from sale of all operating assets of the European Products Division.
e. Write-off of a major account receivable.
f. Gain from selling land in Florida previously acquired for possible expansion.
g. Increase in value of land held in Maine.
h. Loss of computer equipment from power surge.
i. Theft of $10,000 by assistant controller.
j. Loss from operating Aerospace Division prior to its sale near the end of the year.

USING ACCOUNTING FOR DECISION MAKING

P14-34 Using   Percentage-of-Completion Evergreen Construction specializes in constructing golf courses. Currently, Evergreen has four golf courses under construction. Evergreen spends an average of 30 to 36 months in doing earth moving, building water hazards, constructing the club house, completing roads and cart paths, and related work. Another 6 to 12 months is spent sodding, planting, and doing other finish work. The president of Evergreen was especially pleased with reported profits in 2001. Three golf courses were finished and record profits were reported. The company uses the completed-contract method of income recognition.

The president is somewhat concerned about the profit picture for the future, however. One of the projects in progress is much larger than normal, with a total contract price of $6,000,000, and will not be completed until late in 2003. At the end of 2002, you are provided with the following data relating to the project and asked to assess its success thus far:

Year	Costs to Date	Expected Additional Cost	Total Expected Profit	% Completed
2000	$ —	$4,800,000	$1,200,000	0%
2001	1,200,000	3,400,000	1,400,000	20
2002	4,300,000	1,100,000	600,000	80

Evergreen's goal is to earn a profit of 20 percent on the base price of the contract. Because the completed-contract method is used, no income has been reported on this project.

a. Prepare a report that shows the president the amount of income that would have been recognized on the project by Evergreen in 2000, 2001, and 2002 if the percentage-of-completion method had been used.

b. What is your assessment of 2002 operations on this project?

c. What amount of cost savings would be needed in 2003 to meet the desired level of profit? What is your assessment of the prospects of attaining the desired level of profit on the project? Explain.

P14-35   Change in Shipping Procedures   Miracle Dust Corporation sells its super dust-free floor polish through wholesalers. Miracle Dust reported a $100,000 increase in sales in 2001. In reading the footnotes to the financial statements, you discover that Miracle Dust changed its terms of sale in 2001 from f.o.b. destination to f.o.b. shipping point. The following year-end sales were reported in 2000 and 2001:

Date Shipped to Customer	Date Received by Customer	Amount of Sale
Dec. 28, 2000	Jan. 2, 2001	$ 40,000
Dec. 30, 2000	Jan. 5, 2001	60,000
Dec. 28, 2001	Jan. 2, 2002	90,000
Dec. 30, 2001	Jan. 5, 2002	100,000

a. If Miracle Dust had not changed the terms of its sales, by what amount would reported sales have increased or decreased from 2000 to 2001?

b. Will the change in the way sales are recorded affect the way you evaluate the increase in sales reported for 2001? Explain.

c. What factors might have motivated Miracle Dust to make the change?

P14-36   Multiple Changes   Stumpville Products Corporation recently issued a press release stating that its net income for 2001 was $465,000 and earnings per share was $3.10. These amounts reflect a significant improvement from 2000 when reported net income was $300,000 and earnings per share was $2.00. Because you have thought of purchasing some shares of Stumpville, you read the remainder of the press release carefully and note the following:

1. In 2000, Stumpville correctly reported an extraordinary loss of $40,000 on the early retirement of bonds.

2. A $30,000 gain was recorded in 2001 as a result of a recovery from the insurance company for fire damage to buildings in 2000. A loss on the fire in the amount of $65,000 was reported in 2000.

3. Stumpville switched from double-declining-balance depreciation to straight-line depreciation on equipment at the beginning of 2001. A positive cumulative adjustment of $60,000 was recorded at the time of the switch. Depreciation expense was $10,000 less in 2001 using straight-line depreciation than if double-declining balance had still been used. Depreciation expense in 2000 would have been $14,000 less than reported if straight-line depreciation had been used then.

4. Stumpville charged to expense the full $60,000 premium on a 3-year liability insurance policy when purchased on January 1, 2000.

5. An extraordinary loss of $28,000 was reported in 2001 from earthquake damage to production facilities in central Ohio.

6. The president's salary was increased by $22,000 per year at the beginning of 2001.

Required:

a. Analyze each of the above items to determine the effect, if any, that each should have on 2000 and 2001 reported net income. Ignore any tax effects.

b. Compare the amounts of income reported for the 2 years and evaluate the accuracy of the press release. Did earnings really improve? By how much? What earnings figures are most useful to you as a potential investor? Explain. Make your comparison using these figures.

P14-37   Depletion Changes   HiTech Coal Mines has been operating a series of strip mines for nearly 60 years. At the time a coal mine is started, it is impossible to know exactly how much coal will be taken from a mine and the amount of reclamation costs that will be incurred after the mine closes. However, because these elements, as well as operating costs, are important in the planning process, HiTech periodically reviews each of its mines. One of its larger mines was opened at the beginning of 1997. At the beginning of 2001, potential production and reclamation costs were reviewed. Information relevant to operation of the mine is as follows:

1. The cost of opening the mine in 1997 was $4,000,000. At that time, total production from the mine was expected to be 2,500,000 tons, and the costs of reclamation and closing the mine were estimated at $1,500,000.

2. Production in the first 4 years was 100,000, 300,000, 500,000, and 400,000 tons, respectively.

3. Estimated coal remaining at January 1, 2001, was 1,800,000 tons. Due to new federal regulations, the estimated reclamation and closing costs were increased to $2,200,000.

4. Production in 2001 was 800,000 tons.

Required:

a. Prepare a report that shows the total amount of depletion costs for each of the first 4 years.
b. Describe how the changes in estimates listed are to be reported and how they will affect 2001 income. Compute total depletion and reclamation costs for 2001.
c. The price paid per ton of coal by one of HiTech's major customers is set on the basis of HiTech's cost per ton plus a profit of $2.00 per ton. The customer has just learned of the revised estimates by HiTech and is asking for a refund on the basis of being overcharged. What action should HiTech take? Justify your answer.

P14-38   Reporting Earnings Per Share   Memphis Metal Products (MMP) was started in 1994 with the sale of 200,000 shares of $10-par common stock at $12 per share. MMP has grown at a rapid rate and has needed additional funding. The following securities were issued:

1. On January 2, 1997, MMP issued 20,000 shares of 8 percent convertible preferred stock with a par value of $50.
2. On July 1, 2000, MMP sold an additional 50,000 shares of common stock at $32 per share.

MMP reported net income of $550,000 for 2000 and paid a common dividend of $1.00 per share in December. MMP has a 40 percent income tax rate.

a. Compute the amount to be reported as basic earnings per share by MMP for 2000.
b. In very general terms, how would the outstanding convertible preferred stock affect the reporting of earnings per share?
c. What is the likelihood of the preferred stock being voluntarily converted into common stock by the preferred shareholders? Explain.
d. Why is it useful to investors to have both the basic and diluted earnings per share amounts provided? In what way is basic earnings per share useful in evaluating MMP? In what way is diluted earnings per share useful?

P14-39   Other Income Statement Items   Bold Company has 3 major operating divisions and on May 31 decided to sell its Genetic Research Division to Anthrax Corporation for $1,200,000. Anthrax agreed to take all of the division's assets and liabilities. In the 3 months between the signing of the agreement and the actual transfer of ownership, the division reported revenues of $210,000 and total expenses of $170,000. The division had total assets of $1,590,000 and liabilities of $750,000 at the time of transfer on August 31. In the first 5 months of the year, the division reported revenues of $450,000 and expenses of $416,000. Bold Company spent $75,000 finding a purchaser and another $58,000 for the legal costs of completing the sale.

a. What, if any, income of the Genetic Research Division should be reported in Bold's income statement for the year? How should it be reported?
b. What amount of gain or loss on the sale of the division should be reported in Bold's income statement for the year?
c. This is the first time Bold has sold an operating division, and it does not intend to do so again in the foreseeable future. Should the gain or loss on the sale be reported as an extraordinary item? If not, how should it be reported?
d. Justify the reporting treatment of discontinued operations and the gain or loss on the sale of the Genetic Research Division from the perspective of a potential investor in Bold's common stock. What impact is the sale of the division likely to have on Bold's reported earnings for the following year?
e. What are some factors in addition to the division's net income or loss that should be taken into consideration when deciding whether or not to dispose of an operating division?
f. If Bold Company were to invest the money received from the sale of the division in a certificate of deposit, what rate of interest would Bold Company need to earn to equal the earnings it was making on the division that was sold? Is this likely to occur? Was the decision to sell the division wise or unwise? Explain.

EXPANDING YOUR HORIZONS

C14-40   Reporting Income from PepsiCo   The income statements for PepsiCo, Inc., and Subsidiaries for 1998 and 1997 contained the following information (stated in millions except per share amounts):

	1998	1997
Net Sales	$22,348	$20,917
Costs and Expenses, net		
Cost of sales	9,330	8,525
Selling, general and administrative expense	9,924	9,241
Amortization of intangible assets	222	199
Unusual impairment and other items	288	290
Operating Profit	2,584	2,662
Interest expense	(395)	(478)
Interest income	74	125
Income from Continuing Operations Before Income Taxes	2,263	2,309
Provision for Income Taxes	270	818
Income from Continuing Operations	1,993	1,491
Income from Discontinued Operations, net of tax	—	651
Net Income	$1,993	$2,142
Income Per Share—Basic		
Continuing operations	$ 1.35	$ 0.98
Discontinued operations	—	0.42
Net income	$ 1.35	$ 1.40
Average shares outstanding	1,480	1,528

Income Per Share—
   Assuming Dilution

Continuing operations	$ 1.31	$ 0.95
Discontinued operations	—	0.41
Net income	$ 1.31	$ 1.36
Average shares outstanding	1,519	1,570

a. PepsiCo's net income and earnings per share decreased from 1997 to 1998. What were the major factors causing the decline?

b. In projecting net income for 1999, would you anticipate net income and earnings per share will increase or continue to decrease? Explain.

c. In the notes to its financial statements, PepsiCo disclosed that in 1998 it recognized a tax benefit totaling $494 million as a result of a favorable settlement with the IRS and reduced its reported tax expense for 1998 by that amount. Does this additional information change your response to part b? In what way?

d. In 1997, PepsiCo reorganized and transferred ownership of three of its subsidiaries to a new company and then distributed ownership of the newly created company to its shareholders. The income from discontinued operations of $651 million in 1997 represents the income earned by the subsidiaries prior to the transfer of ownership. What were the names of the three companies that were transferred to the new company by PepsiCo? (Hint: Information of this type is reported in annual reports, Moody's Industrial Manual, SEC EDGAR files, company Web pages, and other investment sources).

C14-41 Analysis of MediaOne Group MediaOne Group was created by a transfer of operating divisions of U.S. West to the newly created company in 1996. The following information was presented in the Condensed Consolidated Statements of Operations for MediaOne Group for 1998 and 1997 (stated in millions, except per share amounts):

	1998	1997
Revenue:		
Domestic Cable and Broadband		
MediaOne	$ 2,467	$2,323
International Cable and Broadband	24	18
Corporate and Other	30	78
Current Operations	2,521	2,419
Domestic wireless	361	1,428
Total	$ 2,882	$3,847
Operating expenses	3,121	3,817
Income (loss) from operations	(239)	30
Interest expense	491	678
Equity losses in unconsolidated ventures	417	909
Gain on sale of domestic wireless		
investment	3,869	—
Other income (expense)—net	(84)	350
Income (loss) from continuing		
operations before income taxes	2,638	(1,207)
Income tax benefit (provision)	(1,208)	380

Income (loss) from continuing operations	1,430	(827)
Income from discontinued operations— net of income taxes	25,208	1,524
Extraordinary item net of tax—debt	(333)	—
Net income	26,305	697
Dividends and accretion on preferred stock	(55)	(52)
Loss on redemption of preferred securities	(53)	—
Earnings (loss) available for common stock	$26,197	$ 645
Earnings (loss) per common share		
Basic earnings (loss) from continuing operations	$ 2.18	$ (1.45)
Total basic earnings (loss)	$ 42.14	$ (0.88)
Diluted earnings (loss) from continuing operations	$ 2.10	$ (1.45)
Total diluted earnings (loss)	$ 39.29	$ (0.88)

a. By what amount did MediaOne's reported income (loss) from continuing operations increase or decrease in 1998 over 1997? Does the change in 1998 indicate that underlying operations of MediaOne have improved substantially? Explain your answer.

b. Net income for 1998 was significantly greater than in 1997. What were the major causes of the increase?

c. Does it appear that MediaOne had stock rights or convertible securities outstanding at December 31, 1997? December 31, 1998? How do you know?

d. What income statement items would the management of MediaOne be most likely to highlight to financial statement readers to encourage them to invest in MediaOne?

e. What income statement items would an investment analyst be most likely to point out in attempting to discourage an investor from purchasing shares of MediaOne?

 C14-42 Team Project: Special Income Items Using annual reports available through your library or by using an electronic database, find at least one company that reports the following:

a. *A change in accounting principle:* By reading the management discussion section and notes to the financial statements, determine the motivation of the company for the change. What was the impact on reported net income for the year of the change? What is the likely impact on future accounting periods? By how much would the previous year's income have been different if the new method had been used then? From the viewpoint of an investor or creditor, was this a wise change? Explain.

b. *An extraordinary item:* What event led to the extraordinary item? What impact did the amount reported have on income for the period in which it was reported? Does the company indicate any change in policy or future operating procedures as a result of the extraordinary item?

c. *Discontinued operations:* What appeared to be the primary motivation for disposing of the operations? Was a gain or loss reported? What was the impact on reported income for the period? What effect is the disposition likely to have on future operating results?

C14-43   Research Case: Reporting Income   Using the SEC EDGAR database, company home pages on the World Wide Web, or a similar database, do the following:

a. Accounting practices in the United States and Canada are similar, but there are a number of differences. For the securities of Canadian companies traded in the United States, a reconciliation of differences is usually found in the financial statements provided to U.S. security holders. Find two examples of Canadian companies following reporting or accounting practices that would not be acceptable in the United States. Focus first on the reporting of extraordinary gains and losses. What other differences did you find?

b. The chapter discussed revenue recognition and inventory valuation for precious metals such as gold. Examine the way in which several Canadian companies value their inventories of precious metals and compare that with the way in which similar U.S. companies value their inventories of precious metals. Do you find a general pattern?

c. Find three examples of U.S. companies with extraordinary gains or losses and describe the nature of the extraordinary items. Make sure that at least one of the extraordinary items you find is different from the others.

C14-44   Research Case: Disposal of a Segment   Using the SEC EDGAR database, company home pages on the World Wide Web, or a similiar database, do the following:

a. Find two companies that report the disposal of a segment. For each company, describe what is reported with respect to the discontinued segment. How are the tax effects associated with the segment reported? Has the discontinued segment generally been profitable? How can you tell?

b. For each company, determine what may have led to the disposal of the segment. This may be described in the notes to the financial statements, or you may have to search news articles for an analyst's assessment.

C14-45   Ethics and Income   The Bubble Company has been evaluating operating results for 2001. Things don't look very good. The company anticipates a small operating loss for the year for the first time in the last 10 years, and the stock price is sure to fall. If this occurs, the officers' stock options will lose their value, and no one is very happy. Now, the chief accountant reports that the company will have to change the way it records the costs of postemployment benefits for its employees, resulting in another big expense for the company. When the executive committee asks the accountant whether there will be any more such costs, the accountant reluctantly says that, because the economy is slowing, some of the equipment is not being fully utilized and may need to be sold. In addition, the company may have to increase its bad debt expense next year. Also, the experience with warranty costs seems to indicate that the estimated warranty expense may have to be increased next year.

After several hours of debating ways to make changes that would result in a positive return for 2001, the executive committee gives up, concluding that reporting a loss for the year will be inevitable. Now the committee reverses directions and tells the chief accountant to take all possible losses in 2001. Given that the company will have a loss for 2001 anyway, management wishes to increase the bad debt expense this year enough to cover a major portion of bad debt expense for next year. It also wishes to increase the warranty expense so the expense will be higher this year and lower next year and, if possible, to write off some of the old equipment and take the loss this year so there will be no depreciation expense or loss on it next year. In other words, if it is to be a loss year, let's "take a big bath" this year so we can look better during the next several years.

The proposals made by the executive committee seem to be following conservative accounting practices, recognizing all possible losses.

a. Are the proposals in accordance with generally accepted accounting principles?

b. Are the proposals ethical?

c. If you were the chief accountant, how would you respond?

d. From a potential investor's perspective, how do you view the proposed accounting practices? Explain.

Internet Exercises: Visit our Web site for additional exercises.

Annual Report Project Part 14

Refer to the Annual Report Project, Part 1, at the end of Chapter 1. Using the annual report of the company you have chosen, and any other available information, answer the following questions, providing sources and computations where appropriate.

a. Does your company disclose any special revenue recognition methods (e.g., percentage of completion)? If so, describe them.

b. Assess the trend in the company's earnings per share. For your company specifically, describe what might result in the potential dilution of the earnings per share.

c. In the past three years, has your company reported any extraordinary gains or losses? If so, describe what led to the gains or losses. Has your company reported any unusual or seldom recurring items (e.g., restructuring charges) that were not classified as extraordinary? If so, describe them.

d. During the past three years, did your company have any changes in the accounting and reporting methods it uses? If so, describe the changes.

Using Financial Statement Information

I've got to get straight about money. I need to look at my income and what I spend, what I've got and what I need, what I'm going to be getting and what I want. Trouble is, every time I start planning, I get all mixed up. I look at the little pieces, and then I miss the big picture. Sometimes I see the big picture, and it looks great, but then I lose track of the details. Long run, short run, big picture, details. How do you put all this stuff together?

"Like any statistic, ROE [return on equity] has its limitations. You need to be careful when weighing ROE for different industries.... In some cases accounting practices distort results and yield apple-and-orange comparisons."[1]

" . . . ratios are only helpful when one can draw comparisons across similar companies. 'After you lump financial services with the manufacturing operations, what companies is it comparable to?' asks [Dana Corp.'s Robert] Richter. 'What's the appropriate debt-to-equity ratio, or interest coverage? There aren't any answers because there aren't any comparables.' "[2]

[1]Richard S. Teitelbaum, "What's Driving Return on Equity," *Fortune* (April 28, 1996), p. 272.
[2]Dana Wechsler, "Mishmash Accounting," *Forbes* (November 27, 1989), p. 192.

Making financial decisions is complex, whether on the personal level or business level. At either level, knowing what decisions have to be made and determining what information is needed for making those decisions are key elements in achieving positive outcomes. As we have seen in earlier chapters, the proper identification, measurement, presentation, and interpretation of relevant information is important for effective decision making.

This chapter focuses on several aspects of financial reporting that make financial statements more useful for decision makers. First, we look at the role of the Securities and Exchange Commission in establishing financial reporting and disclosure standards and in improving reliability and comparability of financial statements. Next, we examine requirements regarding the level of financial statement disclosure because some decisions require information about a business enterprise as a whole, while others need more detailed information. The next topic deals with the timeliness of information and requirements regarding the frequency of reporting. We then examine financial statement disclosure briefly, followed by a comparative financial statement analysis using ratios and other forms of financial analysis presented in earlier chapters. Finally, in the second appendix to the chapter, we look at financial reporting for individuals. When you have completed this chapter, you should be able to:

1. Describe the importance of the Securities and Exchange Commission for users of financial information and provide a general overview of SEC reporting requirements.

2. Explain what is meant by consolidated financial statements, their advantages and limitations for decision makers, and the basic approach to preparing them.

3. Describe current requirements with respect to segment reporting and how such information can be useful for decision making.

4. Describe how interim financial reporting may help decision makers.

5. Identify the types of notes and supplemental information expected to be found in financial reports and link this information to decisions about enterprise activities.

6. Identify, describe, and use financial ratios to evaluate financial statements and identify specific characteristics of an enterprise.

7. Explain why understanding personal financial reporting is important, and how it differs from corporate financial reporting.

THE SECURITIES AND EXCHANGE COMMISSION

Information for Decisions

The Securities and Exchange Commission (SEC) is a government agency that is responsible for regulating financial reporting. Companies with securities that are publicly traded must file regular reports with the SEC. Knowledge of the SEC's requirements helps investors and creditors know what information is available to them and can provide them with a sense of confidence in that information. It can help them answer questions such as these: Will the SEC protect me from losses from investing in the stock of that new Internet company? How do I know that the company I am analyzing is not using an unacceptable accounting practice that will result in higher reported income? How do I know if some unusual special event, such as bankruptcy or reorganization, recently affected a company in which I am an investor? What is management's explanation as to why the company's income is higher this year than last?

One way that information is made more useful is by regulating it. The quality of information provided to decision makers can be improved by establishing standards to ensure its relevance, reliability, understandability, and comparability. The **Securities and Exchange Commission (SEC)** is a government agency having primary responsibility for regulating the financial reporting of companies with publicly traded securities. The SEC was established in 1934 to oversee the issuance and trading of securities by publicly held companies and to assure full and fair disclosure by those companies. The SEC was given authority over reporting and disclosure requirements.

As we have seen previously, accounting principles have developed through practice and from numerous pronouncements issued by authoritative bodies, such as the Financial Accounting Standards Board (FASB). The SEC, however, is particularly important because it is the only authoritative body mandated by law to regulate the reporting and disclosure practices of publicly held companies. Thus, we need to take a special look at the SEC and its requirements.

THE SEC AND DECISIONS

Managers, accountants, investors, creditors, and all parties preparing or interested in obtaining information about publicly held companies are affected by this powerful agency. Managers and accountants must make sure that they comply with SEC filing and reporting requirements. External decision makers must decide the extent to which they can rely on reported information. The SEC improves the reliability of reported information because it requires financial statements to be audited and will take action against companies violating its requirements. The SEC has also improved the information available for decision makers by specifying many types of information that must be reported and by requiring that information to be reported relatively frequently.

Regardless of the positive effect of the SEC on financial reporting, however, decision makers must keep in mind that the SEC regulates information provided by companies and not their activities. The SEC also does not guarantee the results of decisions made by information users. Each decision maker must judge the value and usefulness of information and how it should be incorporated into decisions.

AUTHORITY AND IMPACT OF THE SEC

Much of the formulation of major accounting standards has occurred in the private sector through the FASB and similar bodies. Although the SEC clearly has the power imparted by law, it has generally taken the position that it would prefer to see accounting standards established by the private sector. The SEC works closely with private-sector bodies such as the FASB so that outcomes are acceptable both to the private sector and the SEC. In some cases, the SEC has been more directive, making clear the desired outcome. If the FASB or other private-sector body issues a pronouncement with which the SEC disagrees, the SEC typically accepts the standard but requires companies to disclose in notes to the financial statements what the effects of using the SEC's preferred method would be.

Although the pronouncements of the FASB and other private-sector bodies do not directly have the force of law, the SEC has given them considerable authority. The SEC has said that financial statements filed with it that are not in conformity with pronouncements of the FASB and certain other private-sector bodies will be presumed to be misleading. Thus, indirectly, the FASB's pronouncements have the force of law behind them. When companies file financial statements with the SEC that are not in conformity with standards established by the private-sector authoritative bodies, the burden of proof is on the company to demonstrate that its financial statements are not misleading.

What can the SEC do if a company files misleading financial statements or other information? The SEC typically tries to negotiate with the company to change the information filed. If negotiations are unsuccessful, the SEC can go to court to have various civil or, as in the case of fraud, criminal penalties levied. However, one of the most powerful options the SEC has available is that it can stop all trading in a company's securities. Under the threat of being denied access to the capital markets and investors losing faith in the securities, companies usually adopt a spirit of cooperation with the SEC.

SEC FILING AND REPORTING REQUIREMENTS

The SEC has established numerous filing and reporting requirements for companies with securities that are to be sold to and traded by the public. These requirements are set forth in a series of regulations, pronouncements, and rulings that relate to financial statements, audit reports, and financial and nonfinancial disclosures to be filed with the SEC. Public companies are required to file a number of reports with the SEC, the most common of which are the following:

Registration statement—must be filed with the SEC before securities are issued. Registration statements require the inclusion of audited financial statements. Companies that register their securities with the SEC are referred to as **registrants.**

Form 10-K—must be filed annually and covers the last annual accounting period. It must include audited financial statements and other disclosures.

Form 10-Q—must be filed quarterly and covers the most recent three-month period. Less detailed than the 10-K, it must include financial statements, but the statements need not be audited.

Form 8-K—must be filed within fifteen days of the occurrence of an unscheduled material event, such as bankruptcy, change of auditor, or the disposal of a major segment of the business.

Filings with the SEC are publicly available information. The filings can be viewed in SEC offices or obtained on the Internet through the SEC's Web site (www.sec.gov). Companies will generally provide on request copies of their 10-K filings, and sometimes other filings, at no charge.

The information provided to the SEC by registrants is typically more extensive than that found in the annual report sent to stockholders, and it includes the following:

- A description of the business, its activities, and properties owned
- Audited comparative financial statements and related notes
- Quarterly financial statements, which need not be audited
- Selected financial data for a minimum of five years, including net sales, income or loss from continuing operations in total and on a per share basis, total assets, and long-term debt
- Management's discussion and analysis of operations and financial condition
- Information about common equity, including the markets in which the stock is traded, quarterly trading ranges for the stock over the past two years, approximate number of common shareholders, dividends paid during the past two years, and restrictions on the ability to pay dividends
- Other information, including major operating developments, line-of-business and foreign segment data, management background and compensation, major transactions between management and the company, and descriptions of major legal proceedings

To avoid duplication, many companies now include much of the information required by the SEC in their annual reports to stockholders and incorporate that information in SEC filings "by reference" to their annual reports. Thus, SEC requirements not only have led to more disclosure in SEC filings, but also have improved direct financial reporting to shareholders.

MANAGEMENT'S DISCUSSION AND ANALYSIS

One of the most important developments in financial reporting is the inclusion in annual reports of management's discussion and analysis of the company's financial condition and results of operations. The **management's discussion and analysis (MD&A)** section of the annual report presents management's detailed analysis of the company's position and operations, along with a line-by-line discussion of changes in the financial statements. In addition, it focuses on the company's liquidity, capital resources, matters expected to have a significant effect on the company, and the effects of inflation. This discussion permits statement users to gain a better perspective of the factors reflected in the current financial statements and those that will impact the company in the future. It helps provide decision makers with the "why" behind the numbers and, therefore, is invaluable in interpreting the information presented in the financial statements.

AMEREN CORPORATION'S MD&A

Item 7 of the SEC's Form 10-K, annual report pursuant to . . . the Securities Exchange Act of 1934, requires management's discussion and analysis of financial condition and results of operations. Under this section in its 1998 Form 10-K, Ameren stated the following:

> *Information required to be reported by this item is included on Pages 15 through 22 of the 1998 Annual Report and is incorporated herein by reference.*

Ameren Corporation is a holding company created in 1997 by a business combination involving Union Electric Company and CIPSCO Incorporated (Central Illinois Power). The company's annual report includes a detailed discussion by management of many aspects of the company's past and future business. The major subheadings of the analysis include, among others, the following:

> *Overview*
> *Results of Operations*
> *Liquidity and Capital Resources*
> *Dividends*
> *Rate Matters*
> *Contingencies*
> *Electric Industry Restructuring*
> *Effects of Inflation and Changing Prices*

ANALYSIS

Stockholders of Ameren would be particularly interested in management's discussion of this relatively new combined company. As do many companies, Ameren includes its MD&A in its annual report to stockholders and includes it in its Form 10-K by reference to the annual report. However, Ameren and most other companies also include the MD&A as an appendix to their 10-K report. Ameren's MD&A includes not only a discussion of the creation of the company and the results of its operations, but also information about its outlook for the future. [www.ameren.com]

LEVEL OF FINANCIAL STATEMENT DISCLOSURE

Information for Decisions

The information presented in financial statements is aimed at balancing the overall picture of a company's activities and condition with enough detail for financial statement users to make informed decisions. Financial statements combine the information from related companies but also present detailed information for different segments of the enterprise. Decision makers can then obtain an overall picture of the business and also assess how that overall picture is affected by the different segments of the enterprise. This permits decision makers to answer questions such as these: When I buy stock in this company, what is the overall enterprise in which I am investing, considering related companies? What is the overall debt position of the enterprise, regardless of how the debt is structured and which of the individual related companies issued the debt? How vulnerable is the company to sales reductions in different product, customer, or geographic markets?

One issue relating to the usefulness of information reported in financial statements that has been of particular concern to investors, creditors, managers, accountants, and the authoritative bodies is the level of disclosure about companies and their activities. The primary issue relates to what type of reporting best presents the overall picture of a company's activities and position and, at the same time, permits decision makers to grasp the details of the different aspects of the business enterprise. The general approach to resolving this issue has been for the authoritative bodies to require companies to present consolidated financial statements, along with additional disclosures relating to different business-line and geographic areas of the business.

CONSOLIDATED FINANCIAL STATEMENTS

Virtually every major business enterprise with which you are familiar actually involves a number of related companies. For example, while the financial statements of Gateway (in Appendix A) appear as those of a single company, they are actually the combined financial statements of more than a dozen related companies. Financial statements that report on the combined financial position and activities of one company and other companies that it controls are called **consolidated financial statements**.

Consolidated financial statements report the financial position and the activities of a parent company and one or more subsidiaries as if they were a single company. A **parent company** is one that controls another company, referred to as a **subsidiary.** Often, a group of affiliated companies is made up of a parent and tens or even hundreds of subsidiaries. Together the affiliated companies make up a consolidated entity. Although the parent and each of its subsidiaries are legal entities, the consolidated entity is not. Rather, the consolidated entity is considered to have economic reality and, accordingly, provides a basis for defining the reporting entity. A consolidated entity might appear as follows:

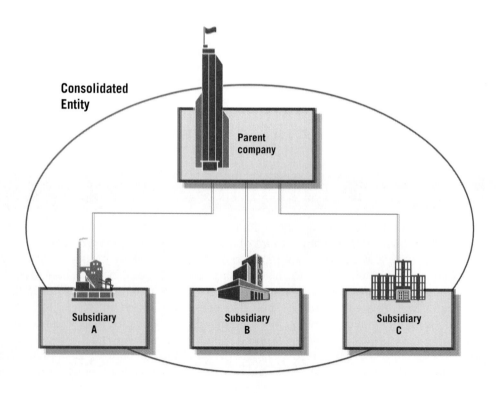

To say that a parent has **control** over a subsidiary means that it can direct subsidiary policies and can, in effect, use the subsidiary's assets as its own. Control is usually gained through ownership of a majority of a subsidiary's common stock, but control may be gained in other ways as well. For example, one company may control another with somewhat less than majority ownership if the remaining shares are widely held.

The parent company is referred to as having a **controlling interest** in a subsidiary. If the parent company does not own all of a subsidiary's capital stock, the portion owned by other stockholders is called the **noncontrolling interest** or the **minority interest.**

A business enterprise may operate through a group of related companies for a number of reasons. One reason is that, as we discussed in Chapter 1, each corporation is a separate legal entity. By isolating particular activities in separate subsidiaries, the liability of the overall group is limited. For example, losses from product liability suits against a subsidiary are limited to the assets of that subsidiary, thus shielding the assets of the parent and its other subsidiaries. In other cases, the use of subsidiaries may simply be a way of separating an enterprise's different activities.

In Practice 15-2

PRATT HOTEL CORPORATION AND ITS SUBSIDIARIES

Pratt Hotel Corporation formed special-purpose subsidiaries to acquire, develop, and operate a casino and hotel project in Atlantic City, New Jersey. The subsidiaries entered into an agreement with a subsidiary of Penthouse International, Ltd., for the acquisition and completion of the site. However, the project went awry, and Penthouse sold the site to Donald Trump. Subsequently, Penthouse sued and won a judgment against the Pratt subsidiaries.

ANALYSIS

Pratt Hotel Corporation and its other subsidiaries were protected because, regardless of the size of the judgment, the recovery from Pratt was limited to the relatively small amount of assets held by the special-purpose subsidiaries.

Consolidated Statements and Decision Making. Decision makers use consolidated financial statements to answer the same types of questions that we have discussed previously with respect to single-company financial statements. Consolidated financial statements bring together the financial statements of the parent and its subsidiaries and present an overall picture of the business enterprise as a whole. These statements are prepared primarily for those who have a long-run interest in the parent company, such as owners and long-term creditors, because ultimately the parent company is affected by the activities of its subsidiaries. The profits of the subsidiaries accrue to the parent, and the value of the parent's interests in its subsidiaries depends on how successful the subsidiaries are.

A decision maker attempting to analyze a company with many subsidiaries would find it virtually impossible to develop an overall picture by looking at the separate financial statements of each of the related companies. For that reason, decision makers generally find that consolidated financial statements provide an efficient means of looking at the enterprise as a whole.

Consolidated financial statements are widely used, but they do have some limitations. Those who are primarily interested in one of the subsidiaries, such as subsidiary creditors or noncontrolling shareholders, generally do not find consolidated financial statements useful because information about each subsidiary is combined with information about the parent and other subsidiaries. Although the creditors and stockholders of the parent have an indirect claim on the assets and profits of the subsidiaries, the claims of the creditors and noncontrolling stockholders of a subsidiary are limited to only that subsidiary. Accordingly, those having an interest primarily in a subsidiary are typically not well served by consolidated statements.

There is also a possibility for some confusion if the consolidated companies are dissimilar in nature. For example, suppose a manufacturing parent consolidates a savings bank subsidiary. The income statements and balance sheets of the two companies would differ significantly in structure and content if reported separately. When combined, traditional ratios, such as gross profit percentage, inventory turnover, times interest earned, and the debt-to-equity ratio, may not be meaningful.

In Practice 15-3

THE EFFECTS OF "MISHMASH ACCOUNTING" ON DANA CORP.

The FASB's standard requiring the consolidation of all subsidiaries regardless of the nature of their operations forced Dana Corp., the country's largest independent supplier of auto parts and systems, to consolidate its finance subsidiary. Although the company and its subsidiary themselves did not change, the financial reporting did. Thus, many of the ratios calculated from the financial statements changed, in some cases dramatically. In particular, the company's balance sheet reported $3.7 billion of liabilities after consolidation, even though Dana had a direct obligation for only $1.8 billion. The remaining $1.9 billion was debt of Dana's finance subsidiary, Diamond Financial Holdings, now included in the consolidated balance sheet.[3]

ANALYSIS

Although the overall business enterprise had not changed, the picture of Dana presented in the financial statements changed considerably with the implementation of the FASB's rule to consolidate all subsidiaries. Of particular concern to Dana and many companies was that finance subsidiary debt was now reported in the consolidated financial statements, where finance subsidiaries had not typically been consolidated previously. A major reason for the FASB's rule, however, was that many companies were hiding their debt by creating finance subsidiaries to borrow money for the parent. Not consolidating these subsidiaries permitted much "off-balance-sheet financing." [www.dana.com]

Another limitation of consolidated financial statements is that not all of the assets reported in the balance sheet are directly available for the parent's use. For example, the cash reported in the consolidated balance sheet is the sum of the cash held by the parent and all of its subsidiaries. Much of the cash reported is not immediately available to the parent and cannot be used, for example, to pay dividends.

[3]Dana Wechsler, "Mishmash Accounting," *Forbes* (November 27, 1989), p. 192.

Requirements for Consolidated Financial Statements.   Under generally accepted accounting principles, consolidated financial statements must be presented whenever general-purpose statements are issued to the public. The financial statements of all subsidiaries must be consolidated unless the parent's control over the subsidiary is temporary. Sometimes, parent-only financial statements are prepared for special purposes, such as bank loans. When parent-only financial statements are prepared, the parent's holdings of the capital stock of its subsidiaries are reported as long-term investments in the balance sheet.

Principles of Consolidated Financial Statements.   Consolidated financial statements for a combined entity are presented as if the related companies were actually a single company. The basic process of preparing consolidated statements is simple: all the like accounts of the affiliated companies are combined to get the consolidated totals. For example, if a parent company has cash of $1,000, and its subsidiaries A and B have cash of $300 and $500, respectively, the amount of cash reported in the consolidated balance sheet is the sum, $1,800.

However, the totals derived by adding together the like accounts of the individual companies will not all be the same as those that would be reported by a single company. An additional step is taken to remove the effects of transactions or relationships between the affiliated companies. All holdings or transactions entirely within the consolidated entity are removed or eliminated from the consolidated totals. The main items that are eliminated in preparing consolidated financial statements are as follows:

- *Parent's investment in subsidiary.* The parent's investment in the common stock of a subsidiary is carried in the parent's accounts as an investment. This account is eliminated when preparing consolidated statements so the consolidated entity does not appear to have an investment in itself.

- *Stockholders' equity.* The parent's stockholders' equity is considered to be the stockholders' equity of the consolidated entity. Most or all of the subsidiary stock is held within the consolidated entity and is eliminated. The claims of subsidiary stockholders other than the parent are shown in the consolidated balance sheet as "Noncontrolling Interest" or "Minority Interest."

- *Intercompany receivables/payables.* If one affiliate owes another affiliate money, this is reported as a receivable by one affiliate and a liability by the other. These amounts are eliminated to avoid appearing as if the consolidated entity owes itself money.

- *Intercompany sales and profits.* A company cannot sell to itself and recognize a sale and a profit. Because the consolidated entity is portrayed as if it were a single company, sales from one affiliate to another cannot be viewed as sales from a consolidated perspective and are eliminated. Similarly, any profit from intercompany sales cannot be recognized until it is confirmed through transactions with external parties.

The basic idea of consolidated financial statements might best be seen by keeping in mind the diagram of the consolidated entity on page 576. Holdings and transactions that are entirely within the boundaries of the consolidated entity are not reflected in the consolidated financial statements. On the other hand, transactions with unrelated parties cross the boundary of the consolidated entity and are properly reported in the consolidated statements.

SEGMENT DISCLOSURES

As we saw in the last section, much of the information in corporate financial statements is reported in aggregated, or combined, form. Although this often helps in making overall assessments, many decision makers also need greater detail. This is particularly true when a company operates in more than one industry or market. By analyzing a company's different activities, a decision maker is in a better position to assess a company's future and judge the economic impact of possible future events.

Companies are often reluctant to provide detailed information about their activities because they worry that such information might help competitors. However, the FASB has mandated that certain disaggregated information be included with corporate financial statements. These additional disclosures provide information about a company's different operating segments, the different geographic areas in which it operates, and major customers.

Segments, Products, and Geographic Region. Companies must report additional information for each significant operating segment. Similarly, if a company has significant revenues from the sale of its products in more than one global geographic region, it must report additional information by significant region.

The additional disclosures that companies must make for each segment include segment revenues and revenues by geographic location of the customers. In addition, the operating income of each segment must be reported, along with segment assets and capital expenditures. Other disclosures may also be required.

An example of the segment disclosures provided by Maytag Corporation can be seen in Exhibit 15–1, and its geographic disclosures are shown in Exhibit 15–2. Maytag indicates

EXHIBIT 15-1 MAYTAG'S SEGMENT INFORMATION

	Year Ended December 31		
In thousands	1998	1997	1996
Net sales			
Home appliances	$3,482,842	$3,035,593	$2,798,907
Commercial appliances	458,008	249,416	162,301
International appliances	128,440	122,902	40,448
Consolidated total	$4,069,290	$3,407,911	$3,001,656
Operating income			
Home appliances	$ 505,110	$ 351,665	$ 276,945
Commercial appliances	49,769	19,437	10,731
International appliances	5,939	11,605	3,802
Total for reportable segments	560,818	382,707	291,478
Corporate	(38,080)	(24,434)	(22,399)
Consolidated total	$ 522,738	$ 358,273	$ 269,079
Capital expenditures			
Home appliances	$ 126,019	$ 174,622	$ 216,321
Commercial appliances	9,044	7,412	2,694
International appliances	21,817	32,884	576
Total for reportable segments	156,880	214,918	219,591
Corporate	4,371	14,643	311
Consolidated total	$ 161,251	$ 229,561	$ 219,902
Depreciation and amortization			
Home appliances	$ 129,712	$ 125,125	$ 104,768
Commercial appliances	9,781	5,666	3,820
International appliances	7,533	6,410	1,412
Total for reportable segments	147,026	137,201	110,000
Corporate	1,528	962	1,279
Consolidated total	$ 148,554	$ 138,163	$ 111,279
Total assets			
Home appliances	$1,736,396	$1,753,109	$1,730,795
Commercial appliances	266,750	250,440	91,886
International appliances	255,361	220,089	189,362
Total for reportable segments	2,258,507	2,223,638	2,012,043
Corporate	329,156	290,516	317,897
Consolidated total	$2,587,663	$2,514,154	$2,329,940

MAYTAG'S GEOGRAPHIC INFORMATION

EXHIBIT 15-2

	Year Ended December 31		
In thousands	1998	1997	1996
Net sales			
United States	$3,601,790	$2,983,574	$2,674,127
China	128,440	122,902	40,448
Other foreign countries	339,060	301,435	287,081
Consolidated total	$4,069,290	$3,407,911	$3,001,656

	December 31		
In thousands	1998	1997	1996
Long-lived assets			
United States	$ 867,425	$ 866,316	$ 804,770
China	90,080	67,964	40,616
Other foreign countries	8,089	6,992	6,499
Consolidated total	$ 965,594	$ 941,272	$ 851,885

that its operating segments are (1) home appliances, (2) commercial appliances, and (3) international appliances, and it provides information for each segment relating to net sales, operating income, capital expenditures, depreciation and amortization, and total assets. It then provides geographic information on sales and long-lived assets, dividing its geographic operations into (1) the United States, (2) China, and (3) other foreign countries.

In Practice 15-4

MATTEL'S SIGNIFICANT CUSTOMERS

Mattel, Inc., a leading toy manufacturer, included the following disclosure in the notes to its financial statements for 1998, a year in which its total revenues were approximately $4.78 billion:

Customers accounting for more than 10% of the Company's consolidated net sales and related accounts receivable are as follows (in millions):

	1998	1997	1996
Worldwide sales for the year ended			
Toys "R" Us	$729.3	$859.5	$1,039.6
Wal-Mart	790.8	739.1	555.9
Accounts receivable as of December 31			
Toys "R" Us	$148.9	$260.7	$ 185.0
Wal-Mart	291.4	178.6	90.4

ANALYSIS

Both Toys "R" Us and Wal-Mart are important customers of Mattel. Together, they account for more than 30 percent of Mattel's business. Loss of either of these customers would cause a significant hardship for Mattel, and Mattel's investors and creditors need to be aware of this situation when evaluating the company. Similarly, financial statement users need to be aware that 45 percent of the company's receivables are from just two customers. Mattel chose to name its two most significant customers even though it is not required to disclose their names so long as it provides the required information about each.

Significant Customers. If a particular customer accounts for a significant portion of a company's sales, that fact must be disclosed. Some companies depend heavily on one or a few customers, and an awareness of such a relationship obviously is important for anyone analyzing the company. Many defense contractors, for example, suddenly fell on hard times when the U.S. Department of Defense significantly scaled back its acquisitions following the end of the Cold War. Although the importance of one or more significant customers must be disclosed, the names of these customers need not be provided. (See In Practice 15-4.)

INTERIM FINANCIAL REPORTING

Information for Decisions

All publicly traded companies file interim financial reports with the SEC quarterly. Although these reports are not audited, they provide timely information so decision makers can answer questions such as these: How does the company's performance so far this year compare with this time last year? Have any big surprises occurred this year that were not anticipated at the beginning of year? Are seasonal patterns in the current year consistent with those of prior periods?

Most of our discussion so far has focused on financial statements included in companies' annual reports. Recall, however, that in Chapter 4 we said that one of the qualities that makes information useful is its relevance, and one aspect of relevance is timeliness. Obviously, annual reports are issued only once each year, but decision makers often need information more frequently. **Interim financial reports,** issued between annual reports, help meet this need. All publicly traded companies are required to file interim reports quarterly with the SEC, and many companies also send interim reports to their stockholders. Interim reports are usually not audited because of the expense.

Companies may include as much information as they want in their interim reports, but most interim reports are very brief and include only summarized data. However, selected elements that often are crucial for decision makers are included. At a minimum, interim reports must include:

- Sales revenue, income tax expense, and net income
- Earnings per share for each period presented
- Disposal of a segment of the business, extraordinary items, unusual or infrequently occurring items, and accounting changes
- Significant changes in income taxes
- Contingent items
- Significant changes in financial position

In addition, companies having seasonal operations must disclose the seasonal nature of their activities. So statement users do not take the interim results as being indicative of the year as a whole, seasonal companies often supplement their interim reports with twelve-month data to the date of the report for the current and preceding years.

Interim reporting results in more timely information being available than does the annual report alone, but it also does more. Interim reports are presented in such a way as to help decision markers over the course of the year gradually build a picture of the entire annual reporting period. The aim is to avoid, as much as possible, big surprises in the annual report. In general, interim reporting follows the same principles as annual reporting.

In Practice 15-5

A.G. EDWARDS, INC.'S INTERIM FINANCIAL STATEMENTS

A.G.Edwards, Inc.

A.G. Edwards, Inc., presents an interim consolidated summary of earnings (unaudited), as follows:

	Three Months Ended		Twelve Months Ended
(*In thousands, except per share amounts*)	May 31, 1999	May 31, 1998	May 31, 1999
Operating Results			
Revenues	$651,136	$570,189	$2,321,746
Earnings before income taxes	136,873	123,896	483,764
Income taxes	52,330	47,890	183,110
Net earnings	84,543	76,006	300,654
Per Share Data			
Earnings			
Diluted	$ 0.88	$ 0.78	$ 3.10
Basic	$ 0.89	$ 0.79	$ 3.17
Average common and common equivalent shares outstanding (diluted)	96,134	97,944	96,854
Average common shares outstanding (basic)	94,655	95,883	94,945

The company also includes in its interim report a complete (unaudited) balance sheet. At the end, the report includes a statement that "The results of operations for the three months ended May 31, 1999, are not necessarily indicative of the results for the year ending February 29, 2000."

ANALYSIS

Income statement information is presented for the current quarter and for the same quarter of the previous year for comparative purposes. In addition, information for the twelve months to date is provided so that decision makers can see how results appear across all four quarters of the year to date. In spite of the company's statement that the quarter's results are not indicative of those for the year as a whole, the results of the most recent twelve-month period presented are little different from what might have been expected by projecting the first quarter's results last year over the following twelve months. [www.agedwards.com]

NOTES AND OTHER FINANCIAL STATEMENT INFORMATION

Information for Decisions

The notes to the financial statements are an integral part of the statements. They provide additional information so decision makers can answer questions such as these: How comparable are the company's accounting practices with those of other companies in the same industry? How will the company's lease obligations affect cash flows in each of the next few years? To what extent do current contingencies affect the riskiness of my investment in the company?

Although most of our discussion of useful accounting information for decision makers has focused on the financial statements, we also have referred frequently to other disclosures that accompany the financial statements. Now, before looking further at financial analysis, let's explore more fully the information found in the statement notes and other supplements.

All financial statements provide an indication of the importance of additional disclosures by stating "See accompanying notes to financial statements" or "The accompanying notes are an integral part of these financial statements." The **notes** are provided by management to supplement the numbers in the financial statements. Some forms of disclosure are mandated by generally accepted accounting principles, but management frequently has discretion in deciding whether to include certain details in the body of the financial statements or in the notes. For example, the allowance for uncollectible accounts receivable may be reported in the balance sheet as a reduction in accounts receivable or disclosed in the notes.

Because notes are designed to explain and expand on the information included in the body of the financial statements, they do not replace the information in the statements. With leases, for example, a decision maker assessing the effects of a company's reported lease obligations on future operating and financing activities will need information other than the amounts reported in the body of the statements. Information such as future lease payments for each of the next several years may be important, but it does not fit well in the body of the statements. Instead, it is provided in the notes.

You Decide 15-1

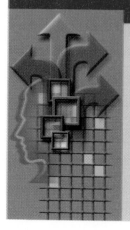

HOW MUCH DISCLOSURE IS REQUIRED?

In a recent court case, an investor sued a mineral development company and a major investment reporting service to recover her losses from an investment in the mineral development company. The investor's case is based on her reliance on the financial information given to her by her broker. The information had been copied from a financial information manual published by the investment reporting service. Although the manual included financial statements, it did not include notes. Of special importance was the omission of a note to the published financial statements that explained that most of the asset values of the development company were based on expected mineral discoveries. Without this note, the investor claimed to be unaware of the asset valuation bases. When minerals were not discovered, the development company declared bankruptcy. Who do you think will win the case? Why?

The content of some notes is specified by generally accepted accounting principles, while other notes are unique to the company and the activities in which it was involved during the year. Special activities, unusual events, and important changes should be described in the notes. Exhibit 15–3 summarizes the major required note disclosures that must accompany published financial statements. These required disclosures are quite extensive, but they are considered necessary to provide decision makers with a comprehensive picture of a company's activities and financial position. (See You Decide 15-1.)

SUMMARY OF REQUIRED NOTE DISCLOSURES

EXHIBIT 15-3

Accounts Receivable	• allowance for doubtful accounts
	• accounts pledged or assigned
Inventories	• valuation methods (e.g., lower of cost or market)
	• costing methods (e.g., FIFO, LIFO)
	• major categories of inventories
	• special inventory financing arrangements
Investments	• valuation methods
	• alternate valuations (e.g., market value)
Property, Plant, & Equipment	• depreciation methods
	• interest included in cost
	• accumulated depreciation
	• collateral arrangements, if any, for borrowings
Financial Instruments	• description, nature, and purpose
	• principal amounts and fair values
	• gains and losses from changes in fair values
Long-term Debt	• description of each type or issue of debt
	• maturities of debt by year
	• special terms or provisions
Pensions	• description of plans
	• amounts of all components used in computation of employers' cost and obligation
Other Postretirement Benefits (e.g., medical insurance)	• description of plans
	• amounts of all components used in computation of employers' cost and obligation
	• estimated effect of change in health care cost
Income Taxes	• amounts and classification of deferred taxes
	• reconciliation of reported income tax expense with taxes computed at the statutory rate
Stockholders' Equity	• par or stated value of stock
	• number of shares authorized, issued, outstanding
	• details of employee stock incentive plans
	• value of stock options granted
Contingencies	• description of unresolved events that could have a significant effect on the company in the future

SUMMARY OF SIGNIFICANT ACCOUNTING POLICIES

All companies are required to provide a **summary of significant accounting policies** used to prepare the financial statements. This permits decision makers to evaluate the information in the financial statements and assess how it compares with information provided by other companies. The description of some policies may be brief because more detail is provided in related notes. For example, depreciation policies might be described in more detail in a fixed assets note than in the summary of significant accounting policies. A summary of the most common accounting policy disclosures is shown in Exhibit 15–4.

| EXHIBIT 15-4 | CONTENT OF SUMMARY OF SIGNIFICANT ACCOUNTING POLICIES |

Consolidation Policy—a brief statement of which subsidiaries are consolidated and, if not all are consolidated, what the basis for exclusion is. Also, the treatment of intercompany transactions is described.

Cash and Cash Equivalents—a description of what securities are considered cash equivalents, as well as any policies that might affect the availability of cash.

Accounts Receivable—an explanation of any receivables that are special or that have nonroutine collection patterns.

Inventories—a description of inventory valuation methods used (e.g., cost, lower of cost or market) and inventory costing methods used (e.g., LIFO, FIFO). Special inventory valuation practices, such as for inventory being constructed under long-term contract, are described.

Other Current Assets—a description of content, if significant.

Investments—a description of investments and how they are valued.

Property, Plant, and Equipment—a brief statement about how fixed assets are valued and depreciated. Sometimes, the depreciation periods are disclosed. More detail is usually given in a subsequent note.

Liabilities—valuation and classification descriptions. This item may be omitted because liabilities are always discussed in detail in a separate note.

Owners' Equity—often omitted because policies relating to owners' equity are fairly standard. Computations for earnings per share may be described, as might the method of accounting for treasury stock, if any. Subsequent notes may describe stock options or special owners' equity transactions.

Revenue Recognition— a description of when revenues and other types of income are recognized.

Specialized Industry Practices—a description of recognition and measurement policies unique to the industry.

Other Items—an explanation of special accounting treatment accorded particular transactions or events, such as the adoption of a new accounting method.

Foreign Currency Translation—a description of the currencies used in the company's business and how they are restated to dollars.

Use of Estimates—a caveat explaining that accounting employs estimates that affect reported amounts and that estimates could differ from actual amounts.

Concentrations—when applicable, a description of the company's limited number of suppliers, customers, transportation channels, or similar factors that could adversely affect the company under certain conditions.

Reclassifications—a description of any amounts that have been reclassified from prior year financial statements to conform with current classification.

OTHER SUPPLEMENTAL INFORMATION

Most companies provide additional information beyond that shown in the financial statements and notes. This information is less directly related to explaining the financial statement information than it is to presenting and summarizing information thought useful to potential investors. Sometimes, the distinction between notes and other information is not clear, but both can be useful. Common types of supplemental information include quarterly financial information and five-year or ten-year financial summaries.

FINANCIAL ANALYSIS

Information for Decisions

Financial statement analysis often involves comparing reported information about a company over different time periods and between different companies during the same periods of time. With the many types of analysis available, decision makers can better assess a company's relative performance and financial position and answer questions such as these: Is the company's prof-itability improving or declining, and does this appear to be related to company-specific or industry-wide factors? How has the company's liquidity changed over the past several years, and does this have implications for extending credit to the company? Which of the companies I am analyzing is making better use of its assets and invested capital?

Throughout this book, we have discussed various financial ratios and other forms of financial analysis used to assist decision makers in understanding and analyzing the operations and financial structure of organizations. The purpose of this section is to bring together those summary measures and illustrate their use. To do this, a summary of key financial ratios is presented in Exhibit 15–5. Based on financial statement information from two computer companies, Gateway, Inc., and Dell Computer Corporation, we will look at how ratios and other analysis can be used to evaluate two companies in the same industry.

HORIZONTAL AND VERTICAL ANALYSIS

The analysis of financial statements often involves examining both the most recent statements and changes that have occurred over time. Two general forms of analysis are helpful.

Horizontal Analysis.   An analysis of financial statement data over a period of years is referred to as **horizontal analysis** or **trend analysis**. Typically, the amounts for the current period and one or more prior periods are compared to determine both the dollar amount and percentage change from period to period. Decision makers often select key variables and trace them over time. For example, key items in the income statement might be:

	2001	2000	Change Dollar	Change Percent
Net sales	$25,350	$23,120	$2,230	9.65%
Operating expenses	20,070	17,280	2,790	16.15
Net income	5,280	5,840	(560)	(9.59)

EXHIBIT 15-5	**SUMMARY OF KEY RATIOS**

1. Accounts receivable turnover: $\dfrac{\text{Net sales revenue}}{\text{Accounts receivable}}$

2. Asset turnover: $\dfrac{\text{Net sales revenue}}{\text{Total assets}}$

3. Cash flow per share: $\dfrac{\text{Cash provided by operations} - \text{preferred dividends}}{\text{Number of common shares outstanding}}$

4. Cash flow to current maturities of debt: $\dfrac{\text{Cash provided by operations}}{\text{Current maturities of debt}}$

5. Cash flow to total debt: $\dfrac{\text{Cash provided by operations}}{\text{Total debt}}$

6. Current ratio: $\dfrac{\text{Current assets}}{\text{Current liabilities}}$

7. Days sales in receivables: $\dfrac{\text{Accounts receivable}}{\text{Credit sales/365 days}}$

8. Days sales in inventory: $\dfrac{\text{Inventory}}{\text{Cost of goods sold/365 days}}$

9. Debt to equity: $\dfrac{\text{Long-term debt excluding deferred taxes}}{\text{Stockholders' equity}}$

10. Diluted earnings per share: $\dfrac{\text{Net income} - \text{preferred dividends} + \text{adjustment for conversion of securities}}{\text{Common shares outstanding} + \text{additional shares from potential conversion}}$

11. Dividend payout: $\dfrac{\text{Dividends paid}}{\text{Net income}}$

12. Dividend yield: $\dfrac{\text{Cash dividend per share}}{\text{Market price per share}}$

13. Dividends to operating cash flow: $\dfrac{\text{Dividends paid}}{\text{Cash provided by operations}}$

14. Earnings per share: $\dfrac{\text{Net income} - \text{preferred dividends}}{\text{Common shares outstanding}}$

15. Gross margin percentage: $\dfrac{\text{Net sales} - \text{cost of goods sold}}{\text{Net sales}}$

16. Inventory turnover: $\dfrac{\text{Cost of goods sold}}{\text{Inventory}}$

17. Long-term debt to total assets: $\dfrac{\text{Long-term debt}}{\text{Total assets}}$

18. Net income margin: $\dfrac{\text{Net income}}{\text{Net sales revenue}}$

SUMMARY OF KEY RATIOS (*Continued*)

EXHIBIT 15-5

19. Operating cycle: $\dfrac{\text{Accounts receivable}}{\text{Credit sales/365 days}} + \dfrac{\text{Inventory}}{\text{Cost ofgoods sold/365 days}}$

20. Price-earnings ratio: $\dfrac{\text{Market price per share of common stock}}{\text{Earnings per share}}$

21. Quick ratio: $\dfrac{\text{Quick assets*}}{\text{Current liabilities}}$

22. Return on assets: $\dfrac{\text{Net income}}{\text{Total assets}}$

23. Return on common equity: $\dfrac{\text{Net income} - \text{preferred dividends}}{\text{Stockholder's equity} - \text{preferred stock claims}}$

24. Return on total equity: $\dfrac{\text{Net income}}{\text{Stockholders' equity}}$

25. Times interest earned: $\dfrac{\text{Operating income}}{\text{Interest on long-term debt}}$

26. Times preferred dividends earned: $\dfrac{\text{Net income}}{\text{Preferred dividends}}$

*Normally consists of cash, short-term marketable securities, and accounts receivable

This analysis shows that income in 2001 decreased by $560 and was nearly 10 percent lower than in 2000. Although sales increased by almost 10 percent, operating expenses increased at a faster rate and resulted in a decrease in net income. The reasons for the decrease would most likely be found by analyzing cost of goods sold and other operating expenses.

Vertical Analysis. An analysis of the individual components of the financial statements is referred to as **vertical analysis.** In vertical analysis, the dollar amounts in the financial statement are restated as percentages to show their proportion of the totals. For example, if total assets were $200, cash of $10 would be presented as 5 percent. Vertical analysis is particularly useful in comparing companies of different sizes. Statements presented in percentages are called **common-size financial statements.** The following shows operating expenses and net income stated as a percent of sales:

	2001	**Common Size**	**2000**	**Common Size**
Net sales	$25,350	100.0	$23,120	100.0
Operating expenses	20,070	79.2	17,280	74.7
Net income	5,280	20.8	5,840	25.3

Vertical analysis can be used along with horizontal analysis to obtain a better picture of what has happened from one year to the next. In this case, costs and expenses make up a larger percentage of sales in 2001 than in 2000, and net income is a lower percentage. Exhibit 15–6 shows common-size financial statements for Gateway and Dell.

EXHIBIT 15-6 · **COMMON SIZE FINANCIAL STATEMENTS FOR GATEWAY AND DELL**

INCOME STATEMENTS

	Year Ended	
	12/31/98 **Gateway**	1/29/99 **Dell**
Net sales	100.0	100.0
Cost of goods sold	79.3	77.5
Gross profit	20.7	22.5
Selling, general and administrative expense	14.1	9.8
Other expense	—	1.5
Operating income	6.6	11.2
Financing and other income	.6	.2
Income before taxes	7.2	11.4
Provision for income taxes	2.6	3.4
Net income	4.6	8.0

BALANCE SHEETS

	Balance Sheet Date	
	12/31/98 **Gateway**	1/29/99 **Dell**
Assets		
Cash and cash equivalents	40.5	7.6
Marketable securities	5.5	38.7
Accounts receivable, net	19.3	30.4
Inventory	5.8	4.0
Other assets	6.0	11.5
Total current assets	77.1	92.2
Property, plant and equipment, net	18.4	7.6
Intangibles, net	2.3	—
Other assets	2.2	.2
Total assets	100.0	100.0
Liabilities and Stockholders' Equity		
Notes payable and current maturities of long-term debt	.4	—
Accounts payable	24.8	34.8
Accrued liabilities	14.4	18.9
Accrued royalties	5.8	—
Other current liabilities	4.1	—
Total current liabilities	49.5	53.7
Long-term debt	.1	7.4
Warranties and other liabilities	3.9	5.1
Total liabilities	53.5	66.2
Preferred stock	—	—
Common stock	.1	25.9
Additional paid-in capital	12.5	—
Retained earnings	34.0	8.8
Accumulated other comprehensive income	(.1)	(.9)
Total stockholders' equity	46.5	33.8
Total liabilities and stockholders' equity	100.0	100.0

RATIO ANALYSIS

Comparisons within financial statements and across time often are made with the help of summary measures and ratios, as discussed in earlier chapters. Use of the ratios and measures discussed in earlier chapters will be illustrated in the discussion that follows using financial statement information for Gateway, Inc. (previously named Gateway 2000, Inc.), and Dell Computer Corporation. The financial statements and summary measures are shown in Appendix 15–1. The companies will be analyzed with respect to liquidity, solvency, profitability, and return to investors.

Both Gateway and Dell manufacture and distribute computers for personal and business use. Gateway was founded in 1985. Its administrative headquarters is in San Diego, California, and its manufacturing headquarters is located in North Sioux City, South Dakota. It has operations in both Europe and Asia. Gateway shipped 3,541,000 PCs to customers throughout the world in 1998 and recorded total revenue of $7.47 billion. Gateway's fiscal year ends on December 31. Dell is the world's largest direct computer systems company, with revenue of $18.2 billion for the fiscal year ended January 29, 1999. Dell was incorporated in 1987, succeeding a predecessor corporation that was originally incorporated in 1984. The company is based in Round Rock, Texas, and also conducts operations worldwide. The manufacturing process of both companies is primarily the assembly of parts and subassemblies purchased from suppliers. Because they do not manufacture their own parts, neither company has a significant portion of its assets invested in property, plant, and equipment.

Liquidity.   Liquidity measures provide an indication of an entity's position with respect to cash and assets that may be converted into cash in the relatively near future. They indicate to what extent liquid resources will be available to meet near-term cash needs. Some liquidity measures for Gateway and Dell are as follows:

	(12/31/98) **Gateway**	**(1/29/99)** **Dell**
Current ratio	1.56	1.72
Quick ratio	1.32	1.43
Accounts receivable turnover	13.36	8.71
Days sales in receivables	27 days	42 days
Inventory turnover	35.26	51.78
Days sales in inventory	10 days	7 days
Operating cycle	37 days	49 days
Cash flow to current maturities of debt	79.51	n/a*

Although the current and quick ratios of Gateway and Dell are similar, Dell's ratios are slightly higher. Both companies hold a large portion of their assets in cash and marketable securities and have low inventory balances. This results in high current and quick ratios. Gateway's balance sheet, presented in Appendix 15–1, includes cash and marketable securities of $1,328,467,000. As Exhibit 15–6 shows, this represents 46 percent of Gateway's total assets. Dell's cash and marketable securities total $3,181,000,000, which also represents 46 percent of its total assets. Current assets represent a substantial portion of the total assets of both companies, with 77 percent for Gateway and 92 percent for Dell. As the current ratios indicate, current liabilities also make up nearly all of the liabilities of both companies, with 93 percent for Gateway and 81 percent for Dell. Both of these companies hold a much higher proportion of current assets and liabilities than do most other manufacturing companies, largely because they have no need for a heavy investment in manufacturing plant and equipment.

*n/a = not applicable

The operating cycle for Gateway is substantially shorter than for Dell. Accounts receivable are important to both companies. The number of days sales in receivables for Gateway is much lower than for Dell, indicating it collects its receivables more quickly. Neither company maintains a significant level of inventory relative to sales volume. The number-of-days-sales-in-inventory ratio is very low for both companies. In its annual Form 10-K filed with the SEC, Dell explains the low inventory level as the result of the company's build-to-order manufacturing process. The company can quickly produce customized computer systems with a process that permits reduced inventory levels and rapid inventory turnover. Gateway uses a similar process.

Because of the exceptionally high levels of liquidity and small amounts of long-term debt reported by both companies, the ratio of operating cash flow to current maturities of debt is not particularly meaningful.

Solvency.   Solvency measures help decisions makers evaluate an entity's ability to meet its obligations in a timely manner. Solvency measures for Gateway and Dell are as follows:

	(12/31/98) Gateway	(1/29/99) Dell
Long-term debt to total assets	.001	.07
Debt to equity	.002	.22
Times interest earned	531.43	78.69
Cash flow to total debt	.59	.54

The ratios show that both companies have small amounts of long-term debt relative to their total assets and owners' equity. Gateway is the more conservatively financed. Its long-term debt is less than .1 percent of total assets and less than .2 percent of owners' equity. Dell uses more long-term debt to finance its operations, with long-term debt equal to 7 percent of total assets and 22 percent of owners' equity. Both companies rely much more heavily on current liabilities than long-term debt. As shown in Exhibit 15–6, Gateway's total liabilities are equal to 54 percent of its total assets, and its current liabilities are equal to 50 percent of total assets. Dell's debt ratios are somewhat higher, with total liabilities representing 66 percent of total assets, and current liabilities representing 54 percent. When most of a company's assets are short-term, as is the case for Gateway and Dell, most of the liabilities are often short-term as well. The short-term assets are expected to be converted to cash in a timely fashion to pay the current liabilities.

Profitability.   Profitability measures provide indications of a company's operating success. For Gateway and Dell, some profitability measures are as follows:

	(12/31/98) Gateway	(1/29/99) Dell
Gross profit (margin) percentage	.21	.23
Net income margin (return on sales)	.05	.08
Return on common equity	.26	.63
Asset turnover	2.58	2.65
Return on assets	.12	.21

These ratios show that the companies have similar gross profits in relation to sales. This is often the case for companies in the same industry when the industry is relatively competitive. However, Dell has a far superior net income margin and return on common equity. What factors cause this difference? As shown in Exhibit 15–6, Dell's selling, general, and administrative expense represents 10 percent of sales, while the operating expenses of Gateway are more than 14 percent of sales. Dell's combination of a better gross profit percentage and a lower percentage of operating expenses results in a net income margin much higher than Gateway's. Further analysis would require an evaluation of financial statement data presented in Appendix 15–1 to see if the costs incurred by Gateway in 1998 were recurring or nonrecurring and whether these ratios have changed over time.

From an overall perspective, both Gateway and Dell are doing well. Although the return to common equity is quite high for both, Dell's return on common equity is substantially higher than Gateway's, as is its return on assets. One factor in Dell's higher return on common equity is that it uses more long-term debt relative to owners' equity than Gateway. This leverage increases the return on common equity when the company is operating profitably. The higher return on common equity and net assets is consistent with Dell's slightly higher asset turnover relative to sales and higher net income margin.

Return to Investors.   While profitability measures focus on the company, return measures are more direct indications of returns to investors. Return measures for Gateway and Dell are as follows:

	(12/31/98)	(1/29/99)
	Gateway	**Dell**
Earnings per share	2.33	.58
Diluted earning per share	2.18	.53
Dividend payout	-0-	-0-
Dividends to operating cash flow	-0-	-0-
Cash flow per share	5.80	.96

The most frequently used of these ratios is earnings per share. Typically, companies do not disclose sufficient information for decision makers to calculate these amounts independently. Nevertheless, participants in the securities markets tend to track earnings per share very closely. Stock prices often increase substantially when a projected earnings per share amount is exceeded and decline when it is not met. Over the past three years, Dell's earnings per share increased consistently from $0.18 in 1997 to $0.36 in 1998 and $0.58 in 1999. Gateway's earnings per share amount has been less consistent, falling from $1.64 in 1996 to $0.71 in 1997, and increasing to $2.23 in 1998. Although Gateway's return on common equity was lower than Dell's, Gateway's earnings per share for the last year was substantially higher than Dell's because Gateway has fewer shares of stock outstanding. Thus, each Gateway share earned a larger dollar return and, therefore, might be expected to sell in the market at a higher price.

Both companies have a significant number of outstanding stock options held by members of management, permitting them to acquire additional shares of stock at prices below current market prices. The dilutive effect of the options on earnings per share reduces Gateway's earnings per share from $2.33 to $2.18, a reduction of 6.4 percent, and Dell's earnings per share from $0.58 to $0.53, a reduction of 8.6 percent.

Dividend payout indicates the percentage of net income that is distributed in the form of dividends. Neither Gateway nor Dell pays a dividend, so the dividend payout is zero for both companies. The practice of not paying a dividend is not unusual in relatively new companies that are growing rapidly. These companies often tend to reinvest all of their earnings to expand their operations. Investors are willing to purchase shares in these companies in anticipation of dividends in the future and in expectation that share prices will rise sufficiently to provide them with an appropriate return at the time they sell their shares. In 1999, adjusting for stock splits, Dell's stock traded as high as $55 per share and Gateway's stock traded as high as $84 per share. The stock of both companies split 2 for 1 in 1999.

The final return measure listed is cash flow per share. This measure is substantially higher for Gateway, reflecting the lesser number of shares of stock outstanding. Both companies generated a significant amount of cash in excess of earnings, as shown by the cash flow per share. Cash flow per share is roughly double the earnings per share for both companies. Both companies used the cash received to increase their cash balances and marketable securities on hand at the end of the fiscal year. Gateway invested $235 million in property, plant, and equipment and other capital investments. Dell used $296 million for capital expenditures and $1,518 million to repurchase its own common stock. Dell also issued $494 million of long-term debt, which, when combined with the repurchase of common shares, significantly increased its leverage.

Overall Evaluation.   Both Gateway and Dell are structured so they can change their products quickly and efficiently. By focusing on assembling purchased parts and on marketing and distributing finished products, they can change quickly to keep ahead of a rapidly developing and changing computer market. Both companies have little long-term debt and large balances of marketable securities so they have the financial ability to move quickly into new products or new distribution patterns. Companies such as Gateway and Dell will succeed or fail based on their recognition and development of new ideas and their rapid incorporation of these ideas into their product lines.

Of the two companies, which is the best? Not surprisingly, the answer is, "It depends." First you must answer, "Best for whom?" Managers, employees, creditors, investors all have their own goals and decisions to make, so their decision criteria will differ. For example, short-term creditors may be interested only in liquidity. They expect to be paid in the near future, so what do they care about long-run profitability? On the other hand, long-term creditors and investors may focus more on long-term growth and profitability. Gateway and Dell are similar companies, but they present some differences in categories such as inventory and receivables management, the amount of financing with long-term debt, and return on common equity. Which company is best, therefore, will be in the eye of the decision maker.

Keep in mind, also, that the financial statements, and especially summary measures, present only a limited view for decision making. We can see in the financial statements the results of past decisions, but what will happen in the future? Will high-volume, low-cost computers continue to be popular? What effect will new developments in Internet connections have on the popularity of full-service PCs? What effect will the global economic environment have on computer sales and distribution patterns? Financial decisions often require a base of information from many sources, of which the financial statements are one.

SUMMARY

This chapter focuses on several issues that relate to the usefulness of financial statement information. They include the SEC's regulation of financial reporting, combining information from related companies into consolidated financial statements, the disaggregation of information by segments and geographic region, financial reporting between annual reports, financial statement analysis, and personal financial statements (in Appendix 15–2).

The Securities and Exchange Commission was established during the Great Depression to regulate the issuance and trading of securities and to assure full and fair disclosure by publicly traded companies. Although the SEC has permitted private-sector bodies, such as the FASB, to establish many reporting practices, the legal power rests with the SEC. The SEC requires that all companies with securities traded by the public file annual and quarterly reports with the SEC. In addition, reports must be filed when securities are being issued to the public and when significant events occur. SEC reporting requirements are quite extensive, and anyone analyzing a company should be familiar with the information filed with the SEC.

Consolidated financial statements present the financial position and results of operations for a parent company and one or more subsidiaries as if they were a single company. This permits financial statement users to gain an overall view of the business enterprise, encompassing all of its resources and activities. Because the consolidated entity is viewed as a single company, the effects of all intercompany holdings and

transactions are eliminated in preparing consolidated financial statements. Although consolidated statements are useful for those having a long-run interest in the entire entity, they do have some limitations. Consolidated statements may obscure information about the individual related companies included in the statements and may provide distorted or meaningless financial ratios when the consolidated affiliates are significantly different from one another in structure and activities.

Companies having different operating segments are required to provide information, such as sales and assets, about the segments of the business, and about different global regions in which their products and services are sold. This disaggregated information permits decision makers to gain a better understanding of the different parts of a business enterprise so they can assess how each impacts the company's overall results and how each will be affected by future economic events. Companies also are required to disclose when a significant portion of a company's sales are to a single party.

The SEC requires publicly traded companies to file quarterly reports, but many companies also send interim reports to their stockholders. Thus, decision makers can obtain financial information about companies on a more timely basis than waiting for annual reports. Interim reports aim at gradually building a picture of what will be reported in the annual financial statements. In general, the same principles and procedures are used in preparing interim statements as for annual statements.

Notes to the financial statements, and other supplemental disclosures, clarify and expand on the information in the financial statements. They are essential to fully understanding a business and its financial statements.

When analyzing financial statements, both horizontal analysis across time and a vertical analysis of the elements within a specific period's statements may be useful. Financial ratios and other summary measures may be used to indicate factors such as liquidity, solvency, profitability, and return to investors. The use of ratios is helpful in understanding relationships within the financial statements and helps decision makers see trends when used over time.

LIST OF IMPORTANT TERMS

common-size financial statements   (589)

consolidated financial statements   (576)

control   (577)

controlling interest   (577)

Form 8-K   (574)

Form 10-K   (574)

Form 10-Q   (574)

horizontal analysis   (587)

interim financial reports   (582)

management's discussion and analysis (MD&A)   (574)

minority interest   (577)

noncontrolling interest   (577)

notes   (584)

parent company   (576)

registrants   (574)

registration statement   (574)

Securities and Exchange Commission (SEC)   (572)

subsidiary   (576)

summary of significant accounting policies   (586)

trend analysis   (587)

vertical analysis   (589)

APPENDIX 15-1

COMPARATIVE FINANCIAL STATEMENTS AND RATIOS

GATEWAY, INC., COMPARATIVE RATIOS		
1998	**December 31**	
Computations (in thousands)	**1998**	**1997**
Current ratio	2,228,186/1,429,674	1.56	1.54
Quick ratio	1,887,318/1,429,674	1.32	1.14
Accounts receivable turnover	7,467,925/558,851	13.36	12.32
Days sales in receivables	558,851/(7,467,925/365)	27.3	29.6
Inventory turnover	5,921,651/167,924	35.26	20.93
Days sales in inventory	167,924/(5,921,651/365)	10.4	17.4
Operating cycle	27.3 days + 10.4 days	37.7	47.0
Cash flow to current maturities of debt	907,651/11,415	79.5	31.7
Long-term debt to total assets	3,360/2,890,380	.001	.004
Debt to equity	3,360/1,344,375	.002	.008
Times interest earned	494,227/930	531.4	246.4
Times preferred dividends earned	(no preferred stock)	N/A	N/A
Cash flow to total debt	907,651/1,546,005	.59	.40
Gross margin percentage	1,546,274/7,467,925	.21	.17
Net income margin	346,399/7,467,925	.046	.017
Return on common equity	346,399/1,344,375	.258	.118
Asset turnover	7,467,925/2,890,380	2.58	3.09
Return on assets	346,399/2,890,380	.120	.054
Earnings per share	(as reported)	2.23	.71
Diluted earnings per share	(as reported)	2.18	.70
Dividend payout	(no dividends)	N/A	N/A
Dividends to operating cash flow	(no dividends)	N/A	N/A
Cash flow per share	907,651/156,569	5.80	2.87

GATEWAY, INC., FINANCIAL STATEMENTS

CONSOLIDATED INCOME STATEMENTS

For the years ended December 31, 1996, 1997 and 1998

(in thousands, except per share amounts)

	1996	1997	1998
Net sales	$5,035,228	$6,293,680	$7,467,925
Cost of goods sold	4,099,073	5,217,239	5,921,651
Gross profit	936,155	1,076,441	1,546,274
Selling, general and administrative expenses	580,061	786,168	1,052,047
Nonrecurring expenses	—	113,842	—
Operating income	356,094	176,431	494,227
Other income, net	26,622	27,189	47,021
Income before income taxes	382,716	203,620	541,248
Provision for income taxes	132,037	93,823	194,849
Net income	$ 250,679	$ 109,797	$ 346,399
Net income per share:			
Basic	$ 1.64	$ .71	$ 2.23
Diluted	$ 1.60	$ .70	$ 2.18
Weighted average shares outstanding:			
Basic	152,745	153,840	155,542
Diluted	156,237	156,201	158,929

CONSOLIDATED BALANCE SHEETS

December 31, 1997 and 1998

(in thousands, except per share amounts)

	1997	1998
ASSETS		
Current assets:		
Cash and cash equivalents	$ 593,601	$1,169,810
Marketable securities	38,648	158,657
Accounts receivable, net	510,679	558,851
Inventory	249,224	167,924
Other	152,531	172,944
Total current assets	1,544,683	2,228,186
Property, plant and equipment, net	376,467	530,988
Intangibles, net	82,590	65,944
Other assets	35,531	65,262
	$2,039,271	$2,890,380
LIABILITIES AND STOCKHOLDERS' EQUITY		
Current liabilities:		
Notes payable and current maturities of long-term obligations	$ 13,969	$ 11,415
Accounts payable	488,717	718,071
Accrued liabilities	271,250	415,265
Accrued royalties	159,418	167,873
Other current liabilities	70,552	117,050
Total current liabilities	1,003,906	1,429,674
Long-term obligations, net of current maturities	7,240	3,360
Warranty and other liabilities	98,081	112,971
Total liabilities	1,109,227	1,546,005

Commitments and Contingencies (Notes 3 and 4)		
Stockholders' equity:		
Preferred stock, $.01 par value, 5,000 shares authorized; none issued and outstanding	—	—
Class A common stock, nonvoting, $.01 par value, 1,000 shares authorized; none issued and outstanding	—	—
Common stock, $.01 par value, 220,000 shares authorized; 154,128 shares and 156,569 shares issued and outstanding, respectively	1,541	1,566
Additional paid-in capital	299,483	365,986
Retained earnings	634,509	980,908
Accumulated other comprehensive loss	(5,489)	(4,085)
Total stockholders' equity	930,044	1,344,375
	$2,039,271	$2,890,380

Consolidated Statements of Cash Flows

For the years ended December 31, 1996, 1997 and 1998

(in thousands)

	1996	1997	1998
Cash flows from operating activities:			
Net income	$250,679	$109,797	$ 346,399
Adjustments to reconcile net income to net cash provided by operating activities:			
Depreciation and amortization	61,763	86,774	105,524
Provision for uncollectible accounts receivable	20,832	5,688	3,991
Deferred income taxes	(13,395)	(63,247)	(58,425)
Other, net	1,986	42	770
Nonrecurring expenses	—	113,842	—
Changes in operating assets and liabilities:			
Accounts receivable	(66,052)	(41,950)	(52,164)
Inventory	(54,261)	59,486	81,300
Other assets	(13,311)	(54,513)	451
Accounts payable	176,724	66,253	228,921
Accrued liabilities	51,390	48,405	144,899
Accrued royalties	1,885	34,148	8,455
Other current liabilities	43,057	35,816	76,278
Warranty and other liabilities	22,699	42,256	21,252
Net cash provided by operating activities	483,996	442,797	907,651
Cash flows from investing activities:			
Capital expenditures	(143,746)	(175,656)	(235,377)
Purchases of available-for-sale securities	—	(49,619)	(168,965)
Proceeds from maturities or sales of available-for-sale securities	3,030	10,985	48,924
Acquisitions, net of cash acquired	—	(142,320)	—
Other, net	2,667	(4,055)	(992)
Net cash used in investing activities	(138,049)	(360,665)	(356,410)

Cash flows from financing activities:

Proceeds from issuances of notes payable	10,000	10,000	—
Principal payments on long-term obligations and notes payable	(14,047)	(15,588)	(13,173)
Stock options exercised	9,520	5,741	36,159
Net cash provided by financing activities	5,473	153	22,986
Foreign exchange effect on cash and cash equivalents	(1,457)	(5,044)	1,982
Net increase in cash and cash equivalents	349,963	77,241	576,209
Cash and cash equivalents, beginning of year	166,397	516,360	593,601
Cash and cash equivalents, end of year	$516,360	$593,601	$1,169,810

DELL COMPUTER CORPORATION, COMPARATIVE RATIOS			
	Year Ended Jan. 29, 1999	**Jan. 29**	**Feb. 1**
	Computations (in millions)	**1999**	**1998**
Current ratio	6,339/3,695	1.72	1.45
Quick ratio	5,275/3,695	1.43	1.23
Accounts receivable turnover	18,243/2,094	8.71	8.30
Days sales in receivables	2,094/(18,243/365)	41.9	44.0
Inventory turnover	14,137/273	51.78	41.22
Days sales in inventory	273/(14,137/365)	7.0	8.9
Operating cycle	41.9 days + 7.0 days	48.9	52.9
Cash flow to current maturities of debt	(no current maturities)	N/A	N/A
Long-term debt to total assets	512/6,877	.074	.004
Debt to equity	512/2,321	.221	.013
Times interest earned	2,046/26	78.69	438.67
Times preferred dividends earned	(no preferred stock)	N/A	N/A
Cash flow to total debt	2,436/4,556	.54	.54
Gross margin percentage	4,106/18,243	.23	.22
Net income margin	1,460/18,243	.080	.077
Return on common equity	1,460/2,321	.629	.730
Asset turnover	18,243/6,877	2.65	2.89
Return on assets	1,460/6,877	.212	.221
Earnings per share	(as reported)	.58	.36
Diluted earnings per share	(as reported)	.53	.32
Dividend payout	(no dividends)	N/A	N/A
Dividends to operating cash flow	(no dividends)	N/A	N/A
Cash flow per share	2,436/2,543	.96	.62

DELL COMPUTER CORPORATION
CONSOLIDATED STATEMENT OF INCOME
(IN MILLIONS)

	Fiscal Year Ended		
	January 29, 1999	February 1, 1998	February 2, 1997
Net revenue	$18,243	$12,327	$7,759
Cost of revenue	14,137	9,605	6,093
Gross margin	4,106	2,722	1,666
Operating expenses:			
Selling, general and administrative	1,788	1,202	826
Research, development and engineering	272	204	126
Total operating expenses	2,060	1,406	952
Operating income	2,046	1,316	714
Financing and other	38	52	33
Income before income taxes and extraordinary loss	2,084	1,368	747
Provision for income taxes	624	424	216
Income before extraordinary loss	1,460	944	531
Extraordinary loss, net of taxes	—	—	(13)
Net income	$ 1,460	$ 944	$ 518
Basic earnings per common share (in whole dollars):			
Income before extraordinary loss	$ 0.58	$ 0.36	$ 0.19
Extraordinary loss, net of taxes	—	—	(0.01)
Earnings per common share	$ 0.58	$ 0.36	$ 0.18
Diluted earnings per common share (in whole dollars)	$ 0.53	$ 0.32	$ 0.17
Weighted average shares outstanding:			
Basic	2,531	2,631	2,838
Diluted	2,772	2,952	3,126

DELL COMPUTER CORPORATION
CONSOLIDATED STATEMENT OF FINANCIAL POSITION
(IN MILLIONS)

ASSETS

	January 29, 1999	February 1, 1998
Current assets:		
Cash	$ 520	$ 320
Marketable securities	2,661	1,524
Accounts receivable, net	2,094	1,486
Inventories	273	233
Other	791	349
Total current assets	6,339	3,912
Property, plant and equipment, net	523	342
Other	15	14
Total assets	$6,877	$4,268

LIABILITIES AND STOCKHOLDERS' EQUITY

Current liabilities:		
Accounts payable	$2,397	$1,643
Accrued and other	1,298	1,054
Total current liabilities	3,695	2,697
Long-term debt	512	17
Other	349	261
Commitments and contingent liabilities	—	—
Total liabilities	4,556	2,975
Stockholders' equity:		
Preferred stock and capital in excess of $.01 par value; shares issued and outstanding: none	—	—
Common stock and capital in excess of $.01 par value; shares issued and outstanding: 2,543 and 2,575, respectively	1,781	747
Retained earnings	606	607
Other	(66)	(61)
Total stockholders' equity	2,321	1,293
Total liabilities and stockholders' equity	$6,877	$4,268

DELL COMPUTER CORPORATION
CONSOLIDATED STATEMENT OF CASH FLOWS
(IN MILLIONS)

	Fiscal Year Ended		
	January 29, 1999	February 1, 1998	February 2, 1997
Cash flows from operating activities:			
Net income	$ 1,460	$ 944	$ 518
Adjustments to reconcile net income to net cash provided by operating activities:			
Depreciation and amortization	103	67	47
Tax benefits of employee stock plans	444	164	37
Other	11	24	29
Changes in:			
Operating working capital	367	365	622
Non-current assets and liabilities	51	28	109
Net cash provided by operating activities	2,436	1,592	1,362
Cash flows from investing activities:			
Marketable securities:			
Purchases	(16,459)	(12,305)	(9,538)
Maturities and sales	15,341	12,017	8,891
Capital expenditures	(296)	(187)	(114)
Net cash used in investing activities	(1,414)	(475)	(761)
Cash flows from financing activities:			
Purchase of common stock	(1,518)	(1,023)	(495)
Issuance of common stock under employee plans	212	88	57
Proceeds from issuance of long-term debt, net of issuance costs	494	—	—
Cash received from sale of equity options and other	—	37	—
Repurchase of 11% senior notes	—	—	(95)
Net cash used in financing activities	(812)	(898)	(533)
Effect of exchange rate changes on cash	(10)	(14)	(8)
Net increase in cash	200	205	60
Cash at beginning of period	320	115	55
Cash at end of period	$ 520	$ 320	$ 115

PERSONAL FINANCIAL REPORTING

Individuals are often called on to provide financial information to others. Such financial reporting may be very simple, as when you apply for a credit card. In other cases, more extensive information may be needed, including a complete set of personal financial statements. This may occur, for example, if an individual is seeking a large loan or is involved in a business venture where the participants' financial resources are important.

Decision makers using personal financial statements often use the information to answer some of the same types of questions that arise about businesses. Typical questions might include the following:

1. Will the individual be able to meet obligations as they come due? How liquid is the person's financial position? Does the individual's position provide an ample margin of safety against insolvency?

2. What are the individual's prospects for future cash inflows? What commitments does the person have that will lead to future cash outflows? How much can the individual borrow without impairing solvency?

Personal financial statements also are used for purposes such as reviewing the adequacy of resources accumulated for retirement, analysis of asset holdings, and estate planning.

The accrual basis of accounting is generally accepted for the preparation of personal financial statements. Considerable emphasis is placed on the individual's net worth, the difference between assets and liabilities. Two personal financial statements are generally prepared:

- Statement of financial condition (personal balance sheet)
- Statement of changes in net worth (personal income statement)

The statement of financial condition reports the individual's assets, liabilities, and net worth. The statement of changes in net worth reports changes in the individual's net asset position, with the changes increasing or decreasing the individual's net worth.

Although the personal balance sheet reports the individual's assets and liabilities, the valuation of these items differs from businesses. In general, assets are reported at their fair values, and liabilities are valued at the lower of the discounted future cash payments or the current cash settlement amount. In addition, an estimated income tax liability must be reported for the difference between the current fair values of the assets and liabilities and their tax bases. In other words, the balance sheet must report a liability for the estimated amount of tax that would have to be paid if the assets were sold on the balance sheet date for their fair values and the liabilities were paid. Assets are listed in the order of their liquidity, and liabilities are listed by maturity.

Changes in the values of the assets and liabilities are reported in the personal income statement, as is the change in the estimated income tax that would have to be paid on the changes. The personal income statement should distinguish between realized and unrealized changes in net worth. Realized changes result from converting assets into cash or settling liabilities. Unrealized changes result from changes in the value of assets while they are held or liabilities prior to settlement.

A CLOSER LOOK AT

PERSONAL FINANCIAL STATEMENTS

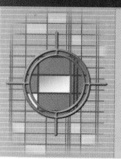

Mervyn Megabucks has applied for membership in the very exclusive Snob Ridge Country Club. Because membership is restricted to those of suitable financial means, he has been asked to submit personal financial statements so the membership committee can evaluate his suitability for membership. Mervyn submits a personal statement of financial condition, shown in Exhibit 15–7, and a personal statement of changes in net worth, shown in Exhibit 15–8.

Taking a closer look at the example, we can see from the personal statement of financial condition that Mervyn has a varied collection of assets. The cash is reported at the actual amount, and the cash surrender value of Mervyn's life insurance is reported at the amount stated in the policy. The receivable is reported at the present value of the amount expected to be collected. All other assets are reported at their current fair values. Liabilities are reported at the lower of their present values or current cash settlement amounts.

One of the most important points to remember about personal financial statements is that the valuation bases are not the same as for businesses. Specifically, the objectivity

EXHIBIT 15-7   PERSONAL STATEMENT OF FINANCIAL CONDITION

MERVYN MEGABUCKS	
STATEMENT OF FINANCIAL CONDITION	
DECEMBER 31, 2001	

Assets	
Cash	$ 6,500
Receivables from business associates	12,300
Cash surrender value of life insurance	400,000
Investments:	
Securities	2,340,700
Precious metals	205,000
Real estate	3,500,000
Copyrights	200,000
Personal residence	1,600,000
Personal property	920,000
Total Assets	$9,184,500
Liabilities and Net Worth	
Revolving charges	$ 5,300
Current estimated taxes payable	12,000
Bank loans	55,000
Note payable to employer	10,000
Mortgage payable on residence	982,000
Estimated taxes payable on increased value of assets	406,000
Net Worth	7,714,200
Total Liabilities and Net Worth	$9,184,500

PERSONAL STATEMENT OF CHANGES IN NET WORTH

EXHIBIT 15-8

MERVYN MEGABUCKS
STATEMENT OF CHANGES IN NET WORTH
2001

Realized Increases in Net Worth	
Salary	$ 600,000
Dividends and interest income	163,100
Rental income	81,500
Royalties	27,300
Gains on sales of investments	277,000
	$1,148,900
Realized Decreases in Net Worth	
Income taxes	$ 284,400
Property taxes	101,000
Interest expense	83,700
Personal expenditures	235,800
Uninsured casualty loss	46,000
	$ 750,900
Net Realized Increase in Net Worth	$ 398,000
Unrealized Increases in Net Worth	
Increase in value of investments	$ 323,000
Increase in cash surrender value of life insurance	21,000
Increase in value of residence	30,000
	$ 374,000
Unrealized Decreases in Net Worth	
Increase in estimated income taxes on increase in fair value of net assets	$ 92,000
Net Unrealized Increase in Net Worth	$ 282,000
Realized Increase in Net Worth	$ 398,000
Unrealized Increase in Net Worth	282,000
Net Worth at January 1, 2001	7,034,200
Net Worth at December 31, 2001	$7,714,200

concept, so important in accounting for businesses, plays a much reduced role in the financial statements of individuals. Thus, when evaluating personal financial statements, each item must be examined closely to determine whether it is valued reasonably and the degree of liquidity. For example, an investment in undeveloped real estate may be very difficult to value and even harder to sell. If important decisions are riding on information in personal financial statements, the information should be supported with recent appraisals, copies of loan agreements, and other supporting documents.

EXAMINING THE CONCEPTS

Q15-1 Why was the Securities and Exchange Commission established? What are the primary responsibilities of the SEC?

Q15-2 What approach has the SEC taken with regard to establishing generally accepted accounting principles and reporting practices?

Q15-3   What powers does the SEC have if it believes a company's financial statements or other filings are misleading?

Q15-4   When must a company file a registration statement with the SEC? What is the purpose of a registration statement filing?

Q15-5   When must a company file a Form 10-K report with the SEC? What is the purpose of a 10-K filing?

Q15-6   What type of information is included in an 8-K filing with the SEC? Why are 8-K filings required?

Q15-7   What information typically must be included in an annual report if it is to conform with information filed with the SEC?

Q15-8   What type of information is included in the management's discussion and analysis section of an annual report?

Q15-9   Why is management's discussion and analysis considered important for financial statement users?

Q15-10   What is meant by "incorporated by reference" in SEC filings? Is it legal?

Q15-11   When is a company considered to be a parent company? What means typically are used to become a parent company?

Q15-12   What is the purpose of consolidated financial statements? When must consolidated statements be prepared?

Q15-13   What is meant by a minority or noncontrolling interest? In what company is such an interest held?

Q15-14   Are consolidated financial statements prepared primarily for the benefit of the parent company shareholders, the noncontrolling shareholders, or for other parties? Explain.

Q15-15   Although the consolidated balance sheet for Heather Corporation shows a large cash balance, Heather is finding it difficult to pay its bills on time. Explain how this might occur.

Q15-16   How are the balances in the consolidated financial statements determined?

Q15-17   Why is a parent's investment in a subsidiary not reported in the consolidated financial statements?

Q15-18   How is the stockholders' equity of a subsidiary reported in the consolidated financial statements?

Q15-19   Why must all intercompany receivables/payables, sales, and profits be eliminated in preparing consolidated financial statements?

Q15-20   What types of segment information must companies disclose in the notes to their financial statements? Why might investors find segment information useful?

Q15-21   In what way might disclosures of information related to significant customers provide information useful in making credit and investment decisions?

Q15-22   What are interim financial statements? Why are interim statements needed? What characteristic of useful information implies a need for interim statements?

Q15-23   What information typically is included in interim financial statements?

Q15-24   The reported net income of Suntan Corporation for the second quarter of 2001 was 20 percent higher than for the first quarter. How would you determine if this was good news or bad news?

Q15-25   What basic accounting concepts are most important in assigning revenues and expenses to specific interim periods?

Q15-26   Distinguish between liquidity ratios and solvency ratios by identifying the type of decision that would be aided by each.

Q15-27A   In what way do the financial statements prepared for an individual typically differ from those of a corporation or other business enterprise?

Q15-28A   Why is a statement of changes in net worth rather than an income statement prepared for an individual? How does the statement of changes in net worth differ from an income statement?

Q15-29A   How does a statement of financial condition prepared for an individual differ from a statement of financial position prepared for a business enterprise?

UNDERSTANDING ACCOUNTING INFORMATION

E15-1   The Securities and Exchange Commission   The company you work for is growing rapidly and the owner is considering issuing stock to raise more equity capital. The owner is willing to hire professionals to help in the process but would like a general idea of the requirements that will need to be met when the company registers with the SEC.

You have been asked to provide information about each of the following:

a. The SEC forms that normally must be filed.
b. Which of the financial statements must be audited.
c. Nonfinancial information required in management's discussion and analysis.

d. Two examples of the types of information that must be provided in addition to the financial statements when an initial registration statement is filed.

E15-2   Level of Financial Statement Disclosure   Which of the following sections of the financial statements of Star Company are likely to contain the information needed to answer the questions provided below?

1. Consolidated financial statements
2. Industry segment reports
3. Significant geographical region reports
4. Disclosure of significant customers

a. The company has large defense contracts with the U.S. government in addition to its commercial operations. You are concerned about the effect on revenues if the company were to lose its defense contracts with the U.S. government.
b. A division of the company is a major supplier of air bags to the automobile industry. You are concerned about the impact on total revenue if auto sales were to decline significantly.
c. You know that your company has large operations in Brazil and you would like to know the value of assets held there so you can assess the potential for losses from a devaluation of the Brazilian real.
d. Your company controls a number of other companies and you know that some of the companies have large debts outstanding. You would like to know whether the combined liabilities of all the companies are excessive compared to the total assets controlled by the companies.

E15-3   Interim Financial Reporting   Your roommate just read that a local manufacturer of winter sporting goods reported income of $150,000 for the quarter ended March 31, 2001. This is a 25 percent reduction from the previous quarter. Your roommate has a summer internship arranged with the company and is concerned it might be canceled. How might the information contained in the company's interim financial report assist in answering the following questions?

a. Was the income of $150,000 more or less than the income reported for the same period last year?
b. Is the income of the company seasonal, and if so, was this a low season?
c. Was the income lower this quarter due to lower revenue or some special one-time expenses?

E15-4   Notes and Other Financial Statement Information   A classmate laments, "Why all the notes, significant accounting policies, and supplemental information? Why don't companies just tell us what the real income and assets are without all the extra complicated information?"

a. Why do companies use notes and supplemental information?
b. Identify an item that would be disclosed in the notes and an item that would be disclosed in supplemental information. Indicate why they would be important to a potential investor.

E15-5   Financial Analysis   Ratios computed from information provided in the financial statements of Histrionic Company for 2000 and 2001 and comparable industry ratios are as follows:

	Historic Company		Industry Average	
	2001	2000	2001	2000
Current ratio	2.15	2.85	2.76	2.55
Days sales in receivables	25	35	34	33
Debt to equity	1.69	1.40	1.16	1.18
Gross margin percentage	.37	.45	.42	.44
Net income margin	.09	.07	.06	.06
Return on assets	.15	.14	.12	.12
Dividend payout	.65	.61	.60	.58

Briefly discuss whether each of these ratios indicates that Histrionics is doing better or worse in the year 2001 than in 2000 and in comparison to industry averages.

E15-6   Multiple Choice: Consolidated Financial Statements   Select the correct answer for each of the following:
1. Consolidated financial statements must be prepared when:
   a. One company owns common stock of another.
   b. When one company owns bonds or preferred stock of another.
   c. When two or more companies own stock of a third company.
   d. When one company controls another company.
2. The primary purpose of preparing consolidated financial statements is to:
   a. Permit shareholders of subsidiary companies to know how much their companies have contributed to the profits of the consolidated entity.
   b. Make it possible for short-term creditors of the subsidiary to determine how much cash is available to pay their claims.
   c. Bring together the financial statements of two or more separate legal entities as if they were a single company.
   d. Bring together two or more separate operating divisions of a single company.
3. The minority or noncontrolling interest:
   a. Is excluded from consolidated statements.
   b. Is reported when the parent owns all of the subsidiary's capital stock.
   c. Is reported when the parent does not own all of the subsidiary's stock.
   d. Is reported whenever one company owns stock in another company.
4. Which of the following is likely to find consolidated statements to be of little value?
   a. Stockholders of the parent company.
   b. Creditors of a subsidiary.
   c. Long-term creditors of the parent company.
   d. Both b and c.

5. Which of the following is likely to find consolidated statements to be of value?
   a. Stockholders of the parent company.
   b. Creditors of a subsidiary.
   c. Long-term creditors of the parent company.
   d. Both a and c.

E15-7 Multiple Choice: Financial Reporting Select the correct answer for each of the following:

1. Which of the following are not reported in consolidated financial statements?
   a. Intercompany receivables and payables.
   b. The parent's investment in the subsidiary.
   c. The subsidiary's stockholders' equity accounts.
   d. All of the above are excluded.
2. Which of the following statements is correct?
   a. When consolidated financial statements are prepared, total liabilities will always equal the sum of the liabilities reported by the individual companies.
   b. The stockholders of a parent company are considered to be the primary owners of the consolidated entity.
   c. The claims of the minority or noncontrolling shareholders are eliminated when preparing consolidated financial statements and are not reported.
   d. All of the above.
3. When segment reports are presented:
   a. Operating income and segment assets must be reported for each segment.
   b. All costs of operating the company are assigned to the individual segments so that net income can be calculated accurately for each segment.
   c. Customers are given an opportunity to determine the cost of the products they are purchasing.
   d. Consolidated statements need not be prepared.
4. Interim financial statements:
   a. Are presented when a company has one or more major customers purchasing a significant part of the company's total output.
   b. Typically present only balance sheet information.
   c. Are necessary to provide greater detail when consolidated financial statements are prepared.
   d. Help build a picture of the annual reporting period.

E15-8 Multiple Choice: Special Reporting Issues Select the correct answer for each of the following:

1. Which of the following reports typically are not audited by external auditors?
   a. Interim financial statements.
   b. Consolidated financial statements.
   c. SEC 10-K filings.
   d. SEC registration filings.
2. The Securities and Exchange Commission:
   a. Is primarily interested in full and fair disclosure by companies with publicly traded securities.
   b. Prevents risky securities from being issued.
   c. Focuses primarily on developing new generally accepted accounting principles.

   d. Is the only governmental body that has issued common stock to the public and is publicly controlled.
3. Publicly held companies do not need to notify the Securities and Exchange Commission when:
   a. A major division is sold or another company acquired.
   b. The company declares bankruptcy.
   c. Sales fall more than 20 percent below budgeted amounts.
   d. The outside auditor is fired and a new audit firm is hired.
4. Companies must file a registration statement with the SEC when:
   a. The company loses a major customer.
   b. New securities are issued.
   c. A dividend is paid.
   d. All of the above.
5A Personal financial statements:
   a. Must be prepared in accordance with generally accepted accounting principles used for business enterprises.
   b. Report assets at historical cost.
   c. Exclude unrealized gains on marketable securities.
   d. Place emphasis on the net worth of the individual.

E15-9 Multiple Choice: Supplemental Information and Analysis Select the correct answer for each of the following:

1. Which of the following types of information about a company would you expect to find in its management's discussion and analysis?
   a. Expansion plans for subsequent years.
   b. An analysis of sales volume changes.
   c. An explanation of major changes in liquidity.
   d. All of the above.
2. Which of the following notes to the financial statements is required of all companies?
   a. A list of individual contingent liabilities and to whom payments may be required.
   b. Explanation of the products included in the major line of business.
   c. A summary of significant accounting policies.
   d. A discussion of major changes in sales revenue since last year.
3. You are analyzing a company's liquidity position to help make a decision whether or not to grant it credit. Which of the following is a liquidity ratio that might help in your decision?
   a. Net income margin.
   b. Asset turnover.
   c. Current ratio.
   d. All of the above.
4. Which of the following ratios would be included automatically in a vertical analysis of a full income statement?
   a. Net income as a percent of sales and the dividend payout ratio.
   b. The dividend payout ratio and the gross margin percentage.

c. The dividend payout ratio and earnings per share.

d. The gross margin percentage and net income as a percent of sales.

5. If a company's total revenues and gross margin percentage have declined and you were concerned about the level of sales and the profit margins in the countries in which the company operates, where would you look for more information?

   a. The notes and other supplemental information accompanying the financial statements.

   b. The management's discussion and analysis section of the annual report.

   c. The segment reporting section of the company's annual report.

   d. All of the above.

E15-10   Information Filed with the SEC   At the time Coldware Company decided to distribute its products nationally, it became clear the company would need to issue additional debt and become a publicly held company. As a result, Coldware filed two registration statements with the SEC on January 1, 2000, and issued both bonds and stock. A Form 10-K was filed with the SEC as of the end of 2000, and a Form 10-Q was filed with the SEC at the end of each quarter. In which of Coldware's filings with the SEC is a potential investor most likely to find the following information?

a. Operating results for the year 2000.

b. Sales for the months of April, May, and June.

c. A listing of the company's major manufacturing and distribution centers and their locations.

d. A history of the company and biographical information on the individuals serving on the board of directors.

e. A comparison of the operating results for the months of July, August, and September 2000 with those of 1999.

f. Audit opinion on the operating results for the year 2000.

g. Audit opinion on the operating results for the years 1998 and 1999.

h. Extraordinary loss on a warehouse destroyed by a tornado in September 2000.

i. Inventory balances at December 31, 2000.

E15-11   Using SEC Information   An investor has recently obtained Martel Corporation's annual report for the year ended December 31, 2000, a registration statement filed with the SEC on January 1, 2000, prior to issuing a new Series B Preferred Stock, the Forms 10-Q filed at the end of each quarter, and several Forms 8-K filed by Martel Corporation during 2000.

a. Which form is filed with the SEC to inform the public a company has fired its auditor? Why might it be very important that investors be informed within 15 days that the company has fired its auditor?

b. Which of the reports must be filed with the SEC before new securities can be issued? Why is the information contained in this filing much more comprehensive than in other filings with the SEC?

c. Which of the reports contains information on sales and operating profit for the first 3 months of 2000? Since only one-fourth of the year has passed, why is it important this information be made available?

d. Which of the above is expected to contain a discussion and analysis by management of the company's operating results and financial position? What does management's discussion and analysis provide that is not already evident by reading the financial statements?

E15-12   Critical Parties in the Financial Reporting Process   The FASB, SEC, external auditor, and individual companies with securities traded in our securities markets all play important roles in providing information to financial statement users.

a. Explain the role of each of these parties in the financial reporting process.

b. Which of the parties generally bears primary responsibility for the following?

   1. Choosing the depreciation method to be used for newly acquired assets.

   2. Providing assurance that the depreciation expense for the current period was computed using accounting procedures consistent with the prior year.

   3. Determining whether a new depreciation method should be considered to be generally accepted.

   4. Requiring a company to provide additional disclosures before being permitted to sell new securities.

   5. Making sure the accounting procedures used by the company are considered to be acceptable.

   6. Determining the useful lives of newly acquired assets.

   7. Deciding what information companies must disclose in addition to the information already included in the financial statements and notes to the financial statements.

   8. Gathering information from investors and financial analysts before deciding to permit a new depreciation method to be used.

E15-13   Gateway's Accounting Policies   The notes to the Gateway financial statements provide information on accounting choices and procedures used in preparing the financial statements. By looking at the summary of significant accounting policies in Gateway's 1998 financial statements presented in Appendix A, answer each of the following:

a. Which assets are considered to be cash equivalents for reporting purposes?

b. Gateway has invested in marketable securities that are classified as available-for-sale and reports them on its balance sheet at fair value. How are the net holding gains and losses on these securities reported in the financial statements?

c. What types of inventory does Gateway have on hand at December 31, 1998? How is the inventory valued?

d. How does the company account for the costs of purchased software after it has been capitalized?

e. Does Gateway recognize income f.o.b. shipping point or f.o.b. destination?

f. What was the weighted average number of common shares outstanding at December 31, 1998? How many additional shares of common stock were added to the weighted average number of common shares outstanding to arrive at the weighted average number of shares used in computing diluted earnings per share?

E15-14   Aggregated Financial Data   Rodisco Company purchased 90 percent of the stock of Mutual Company 4 years ago. When it prepares financial statements, Rodisco Corporation reports the amount it paid to acquire its ownership of Mutual Company as an investment in its balance sheet and it reports the amount of dividends received from Mutual Company during the year as dividend income. Since Mutual Company needs to generate cash to invest in new facilities, it has paid only a very small dividend each of the last 4 years. A shareholder of Rodisco recently read the report of a financial analyst and learned that Mutual Company had doubled its sales and its net income each of the last 4 years.

a. Why do the financial statements of Rodisco not appear to be prepared in accordance with generally accepted accounting principles?

b. What changes in Rodisco's income statement would appear if generally accepted accounting principles were applied?

c. What changes in Rodisco's balance sheet would appear if generally accepted accounting principles were applied?

d. Why is it important that Rodisco prepare its financial statements in accordance with generally accepted accounting principles in this case?

E15-15   Consolidated Statements   Hammel Corporation recently issued consolidated financial statements. The corporation has two major operating subsidiaries. Ima Pain holds Hammel stock in his retirement account and has carefully reviewed the consolidated statements. He has asked for your assistance in answering the following questions:

a. Although Hammel has two major subsidiaries, the consolidated balance sheet does not report an investment in either company in the Investments section. Has Hammel made a mistake in preparing the statements? Explain.

b. The ship-building subsidiary supposedly lost money last year, yet Hammel reports a satisfactory profit for the year, and there is no evidence of a loss. Has something been done to cover up the loss? Explain.

c. The claim of the minority interest of the manufacturing subsidiary is shown on the balance sheet, but the assets of the subsidiary are not identified anywhere. Has something been left out? Where are the assets?

d. Ima Pain thought the parent and both subsidiaries had issued additional stock during the year, but only the shares of the parent company are disclosed in the consolidated statements. Have all shares of the subsidiary been retired? Where are they?

E15-16   Transfers between Companies   Long Corporation produces and sells a broad line of recreational equipment. Each of the major equipment lines is produced by a separate wholly-owned subsidiary, and there are significant intercorporate sales. In 2001, sales reported by Long Corporation and its subsidiaries were as follows:

Selling Company	Total Sales	Amount Purchased by			
		Long Corp.	Tennis Corp.	Golf Corp.	Billiard Corp.
Long	$350,000	$	$70,000	$10,000	$25,000
Tennis	250,000	30,000		40,000	5,000
Golf	180,000	10,000	15,000		20,000
Billiard	240,000	20,000	30,000	25,000	

Required:

a. What is the total amount of sales by Tennis Corporation to unrelated parties?

b. What is the total amount of sales that would be reported in the consolidated income statement for Long Corporation and its subsidiaries?

c. Why is it important that intercorporate sales be eliminated when preparing a consolidated income statement?

d. What are some of the ratios that would be misstated if intercompany sales were not eliminated when preparing the consolidated income statement?

E15-17   Consolidated Balance Sheet   Down Corporation purchased 100 percent ownership of Topp Company for $80,000 and 100 percent ownership of Steady Company for $240,000 on January 1, 2000. Immediately after the purchases the companies reported the following amounts:

Company	Total Assets	Total Liabilities	Total Stockholders' Equity
Down Corp.	$950,000	$250,000	$700,000
Topp Co.	120,000	40,000	80,000
Steady Co.	370,000	130,000	240,000

If a consolidated balance sheet is prepared immediately after ownership of the two companies is purchased:

a. What amount of total assets will be reported?

b. What amount of total liabilities will be reported?

c. What amount of total stockholders' equity will be reported?

d. Why is it necessary to eliminate the balance in Down's investment account in each of the two companies when a consolidated balance sheet is prepared?

E15-18   Consolidated Amounts   Large Company owns all of the common stock of Small Company. Income statements for the companies for 2001 contained the following amounts:

	Large Co.	Small Co.
Sales Revenue	$600,000	$300,000
Cost of Goods Sold	(400,000)	(160,000)
Gross Profit	$200,000	$140,000
Income from Subsidiary	90,000	
Operating Expenses	(130,000)	(50,000)
Net Income	$160,000	$ 90,000

During 2001, Small Company purchased inventory for $10,000 and immediately sold it to Large Company at cost. In the consolidated income statement for 2001:

a. What amount will be reported as sales revenue?
b. What amount will be reported as cost of goods sold?
c. What amount will be reported as income from subsidiary?
d. What amount will be reported as operating expenses?
e. Why are some amounts reported in the consolidated income statement not equal to the sum of the amounts from the statements of the parent and subsidiary?

E15-19 Segment Information Broadline Company has 4 major product lines. In the United States, it produces refrigeration equipment and disk drives for computers. It also produces stereo equipment in Korea and electric appliance motors in Mexico. The electric motors used in its refrigeration equipment are purchased from the production facilities in Mexico.

a. Why would segment information for each of the 4 divisions be useful for decision makers in addition to the income statement and balance sheet of Broadline Company?
b. What information about the segments would you want if you were considering investing in the stock of Broadline?
c. Are there any special problems that might be encountered in evaluating the refrigeration division and the electric motor division?
d. While the sum of the segment earnings of the 4 operating divisions totaled $4,000,000, net income for the company as a whole was only $3,200,000. Explain why the totals are not the same.

E15-20 Segment Reporting Recycle Corporation has provided you with the following information about its operations for the past year:

1. The paper recycling division of Recycle Corporation reported operating revenues of $170,000 and operating costs of $348,000 during the past year. The operating loss was experienced because fewer people than expected were willing to separate their newspapers from other garbage so it could be picked up by Recycle's trucks.
2. During the past year, the plastics recycling division developed a new process for grinding plastic and using it to produce large tote bags used by other companies in shipping products to customers. The plastics division reported revenue of $630,000 and operating expenses of $410,000 for the year.

3. The glass recycling division was just started during the past year and had unexpectedly high operating costs because broken glass was puncturing truck tires. The glass recycling division had revenues of $62,000 and expenses of $81,000 for the year.
4. The City of Overconsumption in which Recycle Corporation operates has signed an agreement with the company to compensate the company for any losses on recycling newspapers if, at the end of 3 years, it is still operating at a loss in that part of its operations.

a. What amount will Recycle Corporation report as total revenues, total expenses, and operating income for the year?
b. Since Recycle Corporation is only involved in the business of recycling, should it prepare segment information? Explain.
c. In what ways might the disclosure of segment information for Recycle Corporation assist an investor in evaluating the company?
d. In what way should the existence of the contract with the city for potential reimbursement on losses incurred in recycling newspapers affect an investor's decision on whether to invest in Recycle Corporation?

E15-21 Segment Information Global Company reported net income for the current year of $850,000. Additional disclosures by Global Company indicated that it had substantial losses on its operations in Europe and South Korea and higher than normal profit on sales in the United States.

a. Discuss the importance of preparing segment information for a company such as Global.
b. Give at least 3 reasons why Global may have experienced a loss on its operations in foreign countries.
c. If Global reported a loss on the sale of discontinued foreign operations in South Korea in the fourth quarter, should investors be pleased or displeased? Explain why.
d. For Global Company, disclosure of assets invested and operating results by geographic region is important in properly valuing the company. What other types of disaggregated information might be useful to investors? Give an example of a company that might be expected to provide such information.

E15-22 Evaluating Interim Net Income Despite the fact that Pipper Company was able to reduce the per-unit cost of producing and selling its products, the company's second quarter net income was substantially below the amount reported for the first quarter. Briefly discuss how each of the following would impact your evaluation of operating results for the second quarter:

a. Industry sales data show that over the last 10 years there has been an average annual increase in sales of 10 percent. Pipper's sales in the first quarter increased by nearly 20 percent over the prior year.
b. The company sold its dental floss division during the second quarter and recorded a loss on the sale.
c. Management of Pipper failed to record depreciation expense on fixed assets during the first quarter and expensed

the proper amount for the first half of the year in the second quarter.

d. Unearned sales revenue increased substantially near the end of the second quarter. Pipper will recognize sales revenue as the products are delivered in the third quarter.

e. Pipper's sales are seasonal and it normally has 40 percent of its total annual sales in the second quarter.

E15-23 Examining Gateway's Segment Data The notes to Gateway's 1998 financial statements contain disclosures of sales and operating income reported by customer type and geographic region. Using the information provided in the notes to the financial statements, answer the following:

a. Were Gateway's 1998 sales to consumers or businesses greater? Was gross profit greater from its sales to consumers or businesses?

b. On the basis of the ratio of operating income to net sales, should Gateway place future emphasis on consumer or business sales? What other factors might Gateway wish to take into consideration before establishing its sales goals for the coming year?

c. What expenses does Gateway deduct in computing operating income for these segments? What costs are excluded in computing operating income for the segments?

d. What segments were used in Gateway's analysis by geographic region?

e. Which of these regions was the most profitable in 1998?

f. If Gateway wished to focus more heavily on sales outside the United States, on which geographic region should it place greatest effort? Explain.

E15-24 Quarterly Statements Net income for Standard Snowblower Corporation increased substantially in 2000 to $950,000 from only $278,000 a year earlier. Standard's income for each quarter in 2000 was $320,000, $80,000, $150,000, and $400,000, respectively.

a. How can decision making be improved by examining a company's quarterly financial statements?

b. Would you expect the quarterly earnings for Standard to be constant? What earnings pattern would you project for a company in this line of business? Explain.

c. Standard pays $8,000 rent each month on its main distribution center. Given the company's pattern of operations during the year, how should the total rent expense for the year be allocated to quarters to provide the most useful income statement information for decision makers? Explain.

d. Should management be given large performance bonuses for the improvement in profit in 2000? What factors might have contributed to the improvement?

E15-25 SEC Registration Thompson Tire and Crane recently provided the Securities and Exchange Commission with financial statements and other information in anticipation of issuing an additional 3,000,000 shares of convertible preferred stock. Management was quite shocked when the response from the SEC was to notify the company that the information was insufficient and that sale of the securities would be in violation of U.S. securities laws.

a. What type of filing must Thompson make with the SEC before issuing additional securities?

b. What authority does the SEC have with respect to regulating securities?

c. What basis does the SEC use when deciding whether to permit or deny requests to issue new securities?

d. What should Thompson's next action be?

E15-26 Financial Information Financial reports prepared in compliance with generally accepted accounting principles and SEC reporting requirements include full financial statements, notes, and management's discussion and analysis. Each of these parts of the financial reports tends to have specific types of information. Indicate where you would expect to find each of the following information items in a company's financial report. For each item, choose one or more of the following: financial statements (FS), notes and supplemental disclosures (NSD), management's discussion and analysis (MD&A), and none of these (None).

a. Segment reporting by major line of business.

b. Total dollar amount of inventory on hand.

c. Reasons for the decline in revenue this year.

d. The possible effect of international conflicts on the company's markets and overall revenue next year.

e. The amount of the allowance for doubtful accounts receivable for the past 2 years.

f. Total lease payments due in each of the next 5 years.

g. The number of shares and the par value of preferred stock outstanding.

h. Dividends declared for the past 2 years.

i. A reconciliation of reported income tax expense with federal tax rates.

j. A summary of significant accounting and reporting policies.

k. A list of employees.

l. The dollar amount of research and development expenditures, interest payments, and income tax payments.

E15-27 Selection of Ratios The controller of Oldtime Enterprises is concerned that the company has operated for too long using old production equipment and techniques and needs to modernize. Unfortunately, the company has no money on hand to purchase new machinery and equipment and would be forced to issue long-term debt to acquire the money needed for modernization. The controller is interested in analyzing Oldtime's financial position and operating activities and comparing its ratios with those of its most immediate competitors. Explain how each of the following ratios could provide information valuable in assessing Oldtime's financial position and operating results.

a. Long-term debt to total assets.

b. Debt to equity.

c. Gross margin percentage.

d. Operating cycle.

e. Times interest earned.

f. Return on assets.

E15-28 Selecting Appropriate Ratios Knight Owl Janitorial Services Company provides short-term cleaning and janitorial help for commercial buildings in downtown Lake Wobehere, Minnesota. Knight Owl Janitorial Services is owned by Marcy and Ken Knight who run the business from Marcy's home. Because demand fluctuates considerably from week to week and they have no place to store equipment or cleaning products, the company owns very little cleaning equipment or cleaning supplies. It rents most of the cleaning equipment it uses and purchases cleaning products a day or two in advance. Employees are hired on an hourly basis for each job. The owners do not receive salaries. Instead, they distribute money for living expenses as dividends on a monthly basis.

Indicate which of the following ratios would be useful in evaluating the financial position and operating results of Knight Owl Janitorial Services and which would not. Explain your reasoning for those that are not considered useful.

a. Accounts receivable turnover.

b. Asset turnover.

c. Cash flow per share.

d. Current ratio.

e. Days sales in receivables.

f. Days sales in inventory.

g. Earnings per share.

h. Inventory turnover.

i. Long-term debt to total assets.

j. Quick ratio.

k. Return on assets.

l. Return on common equity.

E15-29 Using Ratios to Analyze Liquidity You have received the following financial information of Morrow Company and Valley Enterprises:

	Morrow Company	Valley Enterprises
Cash	$ 60,000	$ 20,000
Accounts receivable	300,000	150,000
Inventory	360,000	100,000
Total current assets	$ 720,000	$ 270,000
Accounts payable	$ 110,000	$ 90,000
Wages payable	70,000	30,000
Other payables	30,000	10,000
Total current liabilities	$ 210,000	$ 130,000
Sales for year	$1,600,000	$1,000,000
Cost of goods sold for year	$1,200,000	$ 650,000

Before investing in either company, you have decided to use ratio analysis to assist in your evaluation.

a. Compute the current ratios for Morrow and Valley. Which company has the higher current ratio?

b. Compute the quick ratio for Morrow and Valley. Which company has the higher quick ratio?

c. Compute the days sales in receivables ratios for Morrow and Valley. Which company is better?

d. Compute the days sales in inventory ratios for Morrow and Valley. Which company is better?

e. What is the number of days in the operating cycle for Morrow and Valley?

f. On balance, which company appears to have the higher degree of liquidity? Does there appear to be a reason to be concerned about the liquidity position of either company? Explain.

E15-30 Using Ratios to Analyze Profitability You have received the following information on Tabor Company and Hill Corporation for the year 2000:

	Tabor Company	Hill Corporation
Sales	$1,600,000	$1,000,000
Cost of goods sold	1,200,000	400,000
Net income	250,000	320,000
Total assets, Dec. 31	1,300,000	1,080,000
Current liabilities, Dec. 31	210,000	130,000
Noncurrent liabilities, Dec. 31	500,000	100,000

Before investing in either company, you have decided to use ratio analysis to assist in your evaluation.

a. Compute the gross margin percentage for Tabor and Hill. Which company has the higher percentage?

b. Compute the net income margin for Tabor and Hill. Which company has the higher percentage?

c. Compute the return on assets for Tabor and Hill. Which company has the higher return?

d. What amount of stockholders' equity is reported by each company at December 31? Compute the return on common equity for Tabor and Hill. Which company has the higher return?

e. Why does the company with the higher net income margin and return on assets not also have the higher return on common equity?

E15-31 Using Ratios to Analyze Risk You have been given the following data on Mist Corporation and Binder Company:

	Mist Corporation	Binder Company
Total assets	$1,500,000	$900,000
Current assets	450,000	500,000
Current liabilities	300,000	180,000
Stockholders' equity	550,000	520,000
Net income for year completed	240,000	198,000

You have been asked to compute certain ratios and evaluate the relative desirability of investing in the companies.

a. Compute the return on assets for Mist and Binder. Which company earned the higher return?

b. Compute the return on common equity for Mist and Binder. Which company earned the higher return?

c. Compute the amount of long-term debt outstanding for each company and the debt-to-equity ratios for the companies. If an investor wished to avoid a company with a high level of debt, which company should be avoided?

d. How do the debt-to-equity ratios of the companies explain the fact that the company with the higher return on assets had a lower return on common equity than the other company?

E15-32 Using Ratios to Analyze Return to Investors
Using the following information on Pastor Company and Moss Corporation, answer the questions presented below:

	Pastor Company	Moss Corporation
Total par value of common shares outstanding ($5 par value per share)	$600,000	$1,000,000
Cash flow from operations	780,000	480,000
Net income	550,000	800,000
Total par value of preferred shares outstanding ($3 par value per share)	—	150,000
Preferred dividends paid per share	—	1.50
Common dividends paid	240,000	360,000

a. Compute the following ratios for Pastor Company and Moss Corporation:
  1. Earnings per share.
  2. Dividend payout.
  3. Cash flow per share.
  4. Dividends to operating cash flow.

b. Which company paid the higher dividend per share?

c. Which of the companies retained the larger proportion of its net income for possible reinvestment? How do you know?

d. Did either company potentially endanger future operations through its dividend policy? Explain.

E15-33 Using Ratios to Evaluate Ability to Repay Debt
Evans Manufacturing and Danville Plumbing and Heating are both considering applying to a regional bank for major loans to support anticipated expansion plans. The following information was included in the data presented to the bank lending officer:

	Evans Manufacturing	Danville Plumbing
Current assets	$500,000	$300,000
Land, buildings and equipment	350,000	300,000
Current liabilities	220,000	270,000
Long-term notes payable (8 percent interest paid annually)	450,000	100,000
Stockholders' equity	180,000	230,000
Cash flow from operations for past year	340,000	126,000
Operating income	380,000	74,000
Net income	190,000	86,000

a. In doing an analysis, the bank loan officer has asked you to calculate the following ratios for both companies:
  1. Current ratio.
  2. Long-term debt to total assets.
  3. Debt to equity.
  4. Times interest earned.
  5. Cash flow to total debt.

b. Which company has the greater ability to pay debt maturing shortly? Explain.

c. Which company appears to be a riskier investment? How do the ratios you calculated help in arriving at that judgment?

E15-34 Using Common-Size Financial Statements to Compare Operating Results
The following income statement data were presented by Trend Corporation and Malloway Company:

	Trend Corporation	Malloway Company
Sales	$780,000	$190,000
Cost of goods sold	430,000	130,000
Gross margin	$350,000	$ 60,000
Salaries and wages	$100,000	$ 20,000
Amortization of intangible assets	20,000	–
Interest expense	40,000	8,000
Income tax expense	70,000	10,000
Total operating expenses	$230,000	$ 38,000
Income before extraordinary items	$120,000	$ 22,000
Extraordinary items		14,000
Net income	$120,000	$ 36,000

a. Prepare common-size income statements for Trend and Malloway.

b. Which of the companies has the higher gross margin percentage?

c. Which of the companies has the smaller percent of operating expenses?

d. Which company is more profitable if extraordinary items are ignored?

e. Which company is more profitable if extraordinary items are taken into consideration?

f. How does the use of common-size income statements assist investors in making comparisons of the companies?

E15-35 Comparison of Annual Operating Results The following income statement data were presented by Wall-away Corporation for 2000 and 2001:

	2001	2000
Sales	$700,000	$650,000
Cost of goods sold	413,000	364,000
Gross margin	$287,000	$286,000
Salaries and wages	152,000	134,000
Amortization of intangible assets	10,000	13,000
Interest expense	40,000	22,000
Income tax expense	36,000	39,000
Total operating expenses	$238,000	$208,000
Income before discontinued operations and extraordinary items	$ 49,000	$ 78,000
Gain on sale of discontinued operations	42,000	
Extraordinary loss		(26,000)
Net income	$ 91,000	$ 52,000
Earnings per Share (based on 70,000 and 65,000 shares outstanding at December 31, 2001 and 2000, respectively)	$ 1.30	$ .80

a. Prepare common-size income statements for 2000 and 2001.

b. Has the gross margin percentage increased or decreased in 2001? By what amount?

c. Has income before discontinued operations and extraordinary items increased or decreased in relation to sales in 2001? By what amount?

d. Does the change in reported earnings per share agree with the results shown in the common-size data? Explain.

e. Based on your analysis, do you expect net income for the year 2002 to be higher or lower than for 2001? Explain.

E15-36 Using Common-Size Financial Statements to Analyze Financial Position Pratt Company and Tull Corporation reported the following balance sheet information:

	Pratt Company	Tull Corporation
Cash	$ 20,000	$ 60,000
Accounts receivable	30,000	200,000
Inventory	60,000	300,000
Property, plant, and equipment (net)	280,000	700,000
Goodwill	40,000	220,000
Total assets	$430,000	$1,480,000
Current liabilities	$ 68,000	$ 270,000
Bonds payable	100,000	550,000
Common stock	160,000	200,000
Retained earnings	102,000	460,000
Total Liabilities and owners' equity	$430,000	$1,480,000

a. Prepare common-size balance sheets for Pratt and Tull.

b. Which of the companies has the greater percentage of its assets invested in receivables?

c. Which of the companies has the greater percentage of its assets invested in property, plant, and equipment?

d. Which of the companies relies more heavily on debt financing?

e. Which company has received the greater portion of its financing from issuing common stock?

f. Which company has financed the larger proportionate share of its net assets through the retention of past earnings? How do you know?

g. How does the use of common-size financial statements assist in assessing the relative riskiness of the two companies?

E15-37 Comparison of Financial Position Zentil Corporation reported the following balance sheet amounts at January 1 and December 31, 2000:

	Dec. 31	Jan. 1
Cash	$ 20,000	$ 60,000
Accounts receivable	100,000	140,000
Inventory	175,000	100,000
Property, plant, and equipment (net)	625,000	400,000
Goodwill	60,000	70,000
Total assets	$980,000	$770,000
Current liabilities	$ 90,000	$110,000
Bonds payable	450,000	250,000
Common stock	120,000	120,000
Retained earnings	320,000	290,000
Total liabilities and owners' equity	$980,000	$770,000

a. Prepare common-size balance sheets for December 31 and January 1.

b. What were the major changes in asset composition during 2000?

c. How were the changes in assets financed?

d. Did Zentil's working capital balance increase or decrease in 2000? Did Zentil's current ratio increase or decrease in 2000?

e. Has Zentil become a more conservative company or a higher risk company during 2000? Explain.

E15-38 Balance Sheet Analysis Using Common-Size Comparisons The balance sheets of Mavis Corporation at January 1, 2000, and December 31, 2000, contained the following:

	Dec. 31	Jan. 1
Cash	$ 36,000	$ 9,000
Accounts receivable	171,000	102,000
Inventory	198,000	321,000
Buildings and equipment (net)	432,000	350,000
Patents and copyrights	63,000	68,000
Total assets	$900,000	$850,000
Accounts payable	$ 98,000	$ 78,000
Wages payable	80,000	151,000
Notes payable	380,000	300,000
Common stock	100,000	100,000
Retained earnings	242,000	221,000
Total liabilities and owners' equity	$900,000	$850,000

a. Prepare common-size balance sheets for December 31 and January 1.
b. Did the proportion of assets invested in current assets increase or decrease in 2000? By what amount?
c. What were the major changes in asset composition during 2000?
d. What were the major changes in the composition of liabilities and stockholders' equity in 2000?
e. Does it appear that Mavis Corporation gained in its ability to pay its current liabilities in 2000? Explain.

E15-39 Financial Statement Analysis Each of the following items describes decisions that managers, investors, or creditors may make about a business. In each case, identify a ratio or ratios that would help the decision maker in arriving at a decision or in identifying areas for further analysis:

a. Whether a decrease in net income is from:
   1. A decrease in sales or an increase in cost of goods sold.
   2. An increase in total operating expenses.
   3. An increase in an individual operating expense.
b. Does the company generate sufficient cash to pay dividends and pay the debts that come due without having to borrow additional money?
c. Is an increase in dividends associated with an increase in income or a higher payout of income?
d. Does the company rely more heavily on long-term debt financing than the industry as a whole?
e. Which of two companies has been more profitable in relation to invested capital?
f. Has the decline in the economic activity affected the company's ability to collect its accounts receivable?

g. Has the company been successful in reducing its investment in inventories as a result of installing a new ordering system and better production scheduling?
h. From among several companies, which one provides the greatest earnings for each share of stock? Do the companies generate enough cash to provide a margin of safety for stockholders?
i. How important are labor costs to the company's profitability?

E15-40A Personal Financial Statements Horace Pennypincher is nearing retirement age and wishes to prepare a statement of financial condition to see if it will be feasible for him to retire in January. He and his wife, Penelope, still live in the modest home they purchased when they were married. Although the Pennypinchers are very careful with their money, they have traveled and have purchased several pieces of antique furniture that are quite valuable. They also own several lots in southern California in a rapidly developing area; however, the U.S. Congress has just voted to establish a nuclear waste disposal site 3 miles south of the property. Horace has worked for 35 years for Tightwad Industries, which recently established a retirement plan that will pay Horace $600 per month until his death. Penelope did not work outside of the home during most of their married life because she was busy raising their 12 children. For the past several years, however, she has worked at a local store, but does not qualify for any retirement benefits. She expects to leave her job when Horace retires.

a. What basis should be used by Horace and Penelope in valuing each of their assets?
b. What other assets are Horace and Penelope likely to have that should be included in their statement of financial condition?
c. What types of liabilities might they have that should also be included?
d. How does the personal statement of financial condition differ from that of a business enterprise?

E15-41A Statement of Net Worth Horace and Penelope Pennypincher, of **E15-40A,** are interested in preparing a statement of changes in net worth for the past year. This past year they sold some of the stocks they owned that had appreciated substantially in value. They used the proceeds to purchase a new motor home for travel after retirement. The land they own in California is currently being rented out for truck farming operations. Keeping in mind the information in **E15-40A,** answer the following questions:

a. Why is a distinction made between realized and unrealized increases in net worth in the statement of changes in net worth?
b. What realized increases and decreases in net worth are likely to appear in the Pennypincher statement?
c. What unrealized increases and decreases in net worth are likely to appear in the Pennypincher statement?
d. How does the statement of changes in net worth differ from an income statement prepared for a business enterprise?

USING ACCOUNTING FOR DECISION MAKING

P15-42   Consolidated Balance Sheet Jennie's Plumbing and Heating recently purchased 100 percent of the stock of Ron's Repair Service. The balance sheets for the two companies immediately after the purchase of Ron's shares were:

	Jennie's Plumbing	Ron's Repair
Cash	$ 20,000	$ 8,000
Accounts receivable	50,000	30,000
Inventory	80,000	72,000
Investment in Ron's Repair	150,000	
Buildings and equipment	300,000	240,000
Less: Accumulated depreciation	(110,000)	(80,000)
Total assets	$490,000	$270,000
Accounts payable	$ 60,000	$ 75,000
Taxes payable	70,000	45,000
Common stock	200,000	100,000
Retained earnings	160,000	50,000
Total liabilities and equity	$490,000	$270,000

At the balance sheet date, Ron's Repair owes Jennie's Plumbing $15,000 on accounts payable.

a. Prepare a consolidated balance sheet for Jennie's Plumbing and its subsidiary.

b. Why are the stockholders' equity balances of Ron's Repair not included in the consolidated balance sheet?

c. Monona Wholesale Supply has extended credit of $10,000 to Jennie's Plumbing, and Winona Supply Company has extended credit of $10,000 to Ron's Repair. Which supplier has the stronger claim on the consolidated cash balance? Explain.

d. Jennie's Plumbing has applied to Fifth National Bank of Tuleville for a $75,000 short-term loan to open a showroom for bathroom and kitchen fixtures. Accounts receivable will be used as collateral, and Jennie's Plumbing has provided the bank with its consolidated balance sheet prepared immediately after the acquisition of Ron's Repair. From the bank's perspective, how would you rate the sufficiency of the collateral? Explain.

e. If Jennie's Plumbing had purchased only 80 percent of the stock of Ron's Repair, an item labeled "Noncontrolling Interest" would have been reported in the stockholders' equity section of the consolidated balance sheet. What does the amount assigned to the noncontrolling or minority interest in the consolidated balance sheet represent?

P15-43   Consolidated Income Statement Reich Manufacturing purchased all of the stock of Smith Supply Company on January 1, 1995. For the year ended December 31, 2000, the companies reported the following income statement data:

	Reich Mfg.	Smith Supply
Sales	$350,000	$200,000
Cost of goods sold	(200,000)	(120,000)
Gross profit margin	$150,000	$ 80,000
Interest income	7,000	
Interest expense		(5,000)
Other operating expenses	(23,000)	(25,000)
Income from subsidiary	50,000	
Net income	$184,000	$ 50,000

During 2000, Reich sold to Smith Supply at cost goods for which it had paid $60,000. Also, Smith Supply had borrowed money from Reich during the year; the full loan had been repaid by the end of the year, along with $4,000 of interest.

a. Prepare a consolidated income statement for Reich Manufacturing and its subsidiary for the year ended December 31, 2000.

b. Why must the effects of intercompany ownership and intercompany transactions be eliminated when preparing the consolidated income statement?

c. What would the gross profit and gross margin percentage have been if the effects of the intercompany sale were not eliminated? By how much do the gross profit and gross margin percentage change when the intercorporate sale of inventory is eliminated?

d. Compute the times interest earned ratio for the consolidated entity. How would this have been different if the appropriate eliminations were not made?

e. How useful are the consolidated financial statements to the creditors of Smith Supply Company? Explain. Would your answer be different if Reich agreed to guarantee Smith Supply's debt (pay the debt if Smith Supply defaults)? Why?

P15-44   Analyzing a Consolidated Balance Sheet Varwood Company is a subsidiary of Tabor Corporation. The balance sheets for Varwood Company and for the consolidated entity at December 31, 2000, contained the following balances:

	Varwood Company	Consolidated Amounts for Tabor Corp. and Subsidiary
Cash and receivables	$ 80,000	$120,000
Inventory	150,000	260,000
Land	70,000	200,000
Buildings and equipment	150,000	450,000
Less: Accum. depreciation	(70,000)	(210,000)
Total assets	$380,000	$820,000

Accounts payable	$ 40,000	$ 70,000
Notes payable	90,000	290,000
Common stock	50,000	100,000
Paid-in capital	30,000	80,000
Retained earnings	170,000	180,000
Noncontrolling interest		100,000
Total liabilities and equities	$380,000	$820,000

a. Does Tabor own 100 percent or less than 100 percent of Varwood's common stock? How do you know?

b. What percentage of Varwood's assets and liabilities are included in the consolidated balance sheet? Explain.

c. What is the amount of cash and accounts receivable reported by Tabor at December 31, 2000, if (1) there are no intercompany receivables and payables, and (2) Taber's accounts receivable contain a $20,000 receivable from Varwood?

d. Must Tabor share a portion of Varwood's net income with others? Explain. What portion of the income from Tabor's separate operations must be shared with the other stockholders of Varwood?

e. Which of the questions a through d could be answered if only the consolidated financial statements were available?

P15-45 Analyzing Segment Reports World Products Corporation has subsidiaries or major operating divisions in more than 30 countries. Each of its operating units produces one of three major product lines, and sales are made exclusively from the products produced by the World Products Corporation network. World Products disclosed the information (shown below) relating to operations in different geographic regions in its 2000 consolidated financial statements.

a. Compute the amounts to be reported in the 2000 consolidated income statement for World Products. Assume that cost of goods sold for a particular region is a constant percentage of sales.

b. What additional disaggregated information would World Products be expected to include with its financial statements? Explain how this information might be useful.

c. What difficulties might be associated with arriving at the amounts reported for each of the geographic areas?

d. If World Products Corporation were planning additional expansion, where would you recommend the expansion take place? Why?

P15-46 Quarterly Statements Ander Corporation prepares quarterly financial statements. During 2000, the following events occurred:

1. The company's total sales of $780,000 occurred by quarter, as follows: 20%, 40%, 15%, and 25%.
2. Quarterly cost of goods sold was $55,000, $170,000, $85,000, and $90,000, respectively.
3. Annual depreciation on the company's headquarters and sales facilities was $60,000.
4. The president's salary was $50,000.
5. Other operating costs totaled $90,000.
6. Income taxes of 40 percent must be paid on all income.
7. An extraordinary earthquake loss of $20,000 occurred in the third quarter.

Required:

a. Prepare an income statement for the year 2000 for Ander Corporation.

b. Prepare Ander's quarterly income statements for each quarter of 2000.

c. What information is provided by looking at the quarterly statements that might not be evident from the annual statements? Would the management of Ander be satisfied if one-half of the net income for 2000 was earned by June 30, 2000? Explain.

d. What basic concept of accounting suggests the need for financial reporting more frequently than once a year? Why might this be particularly important for Ander?

e. What types of comparisons with other companies are made possible through the presentation of quarterly earnings? What other comparisons might be important?

P15-47 Reporting to the SEC Bruse Company common shares are listed on the American Stock Exchange and are actively traded. In a recent article in one of the financial publications, you read about a number of interesting happenings at Bruse Company, and you want to learn more about the events before deciding whether to purchase shares for your retirement fund. For each item listed below, indicate which of the documents filed with the SEC would provide information about that item. When the item is found in the annual report, indicate where in the report it would be found.

1. Three members of the board of directors have resigned.
2. Bruse Company announced that shortly after the beginning of the next fiscal year it plans to sell 2 operating divisions and focus on its primary product line.

	Eastern Europe	Asia	South America	United States
Total sales	$300,000	$600,000	$200,000	$800,000
Cost of sales	(180,000)	(420,000)	(100,000)	(600,000)
Gross margin	$120,000	$180,000	$100,000	$200,000
Other identifiable costs	(70,000)	(100,000)	(30,000)	(50,000)
Segment earnings	$ 50,000	$ 80,000	$ 70,000	$150,000
Percentage of sales to related companies	10%	20%	25%	15%

3. Several new convertible securities were issued during the past year, and diluted earnings per share decreased sharply from last year's amount.
4. Sales in July through September were well below the previous year's levels.
5. The outside auditor resigned as a result of a disagreement with the company on several policy issues.
6. Depreciation expense for the most recent year was $280,000.
7. The board of directors voted to acquire Ohio Tile Corporation through an exchange of common stock.
8. An application to issue Bruse common shares to existing shareholders of Ohio Tile is submitted to the SEC.
9. A change in accounting procedures was adopted in October and resulted in a cumulative adjustment of $45,000 to net income.

P15-48 Budget Analysis   New England Ski Products recently established goals that it hopes to achieve with regard to asset and debt management. A summarized balance sheet and budgeted percentages at year-end are as follows:

	Actual	Budget
Current assets		
Cash and cash equivalents	$208,000	15%
Inventory	320,000	25
Other current assets	32,000	5
Noncurrent assets		
Buildings and equipment	200,000	35
Land	16,000	5
Other	24,000	15
Total	$800,000	100%
Current liabilities	$160,000	15%
Long-term debt	380,000	30
Common stock	120,000	15
Retained earnings	140,000	40
Total	$800,000	100%

Required:

a. At the balance sheet date, compute the actual balance sheet percentages for New England Ski Products.
b. Which of the current balance sheet amounts will require major adjustment to conform with the desired levels?
c. Discuss briefly what action can be taken to bring the actual amounts into agreement with the budgeted amounts.

P15-49   Developing Financial Ratios   You have obtained the financial statements of A-Tec and Bi-Sci, new companies in the high-tech industry. Both companies have just completed their second year of operations. You have acquired the following information for an analysis of the companies. All dollar amounts are stated in thousands.

	A-Tech		Bi-Sci	
	2002	2001	2002	2001
Cash and cash equivalents	$ 3	$ 2	$ 1	$ 1
Accounts receivable (net)	30	15	20	20
Inventory	40	20	30	30
Other current assets	5	1	3	1
Current liabilities	67	40	24	24
Property, plant & equip. (net)	310	170	115	104
Long-term debt	270	130	0	0
Sales (all credit sales)	950	675	600	600
Cost of goods sold	665	450	450	450
Net income	95	80	60	60
Owners' equity	51	38	145	132

a. Calculate the following ratios for the 2 companies for the 2 years:
   1. Current ratio.
   2. Working capital (dollar amount).
   3. Accounts receivable turnover.
   4. Inventory turnover.
   5. Asset turnover.
   6. Long-term debt to total assets.
   7. Debt to equity.
   8. Gross margin percentage.
   9. Net income margin.
   10. Return on assets.
b. Write a brief analysis of the companies based on the information given and the ratios computed. Be sure to touch on issues of liquidity, solvency, leverage, and profitability. Which company appears to be the better investment for a stockholder? Explain. Which company appears to be the better credit risk for a lender? Explain.

P15-50   Ameritech's Interim Statements   Ameritech's 1998 consolidated financial statements included the following note relating to its quarterly operating results:

15. Quarterly financial information (unaudited) (dollars in millions)

	Revenues	Operating Income	Net Income	Diluted Earnings per Share
1998				
1st Quarter	$ 4,133	$ 905	$ 492	$0.44
2nd Quarter	4,289	1,164	1,707	1.54
3rd Quarter	4,290	1,063	645	0.58
4th Quarter	4,442	1,061	762	0.68
Total	$17,154	$4,193	$3,606	$3.25
1997				
1st Quarter	$ 3,859	$ 912	$ 536	$0.48
2nd Quarter	3,986	1,041	537	0.49
3rd Quarter	4,006	962	613	0.56
4th Quarter	4,147	884	610	0.55
Total	$15,998	$3,799	$2,296	$2.08

The first quarter of 1998 includes a one-time pretax charge of $104 million ($64 million after-tax) for restructuring related to a cost containment program, as well as a one-time pretax charge of $54 million ($34 million after-tax) for a currency-related fair value adjustment in conjunction with our Tele Danmark investment. The second quarter of 1998 includes a one-time pretax gain of $1.5 billion ($1.0 billion after-tax) related to the sale of substantially all of our TCNZ shares. The fourth quarter of 1998 includes a one-time pretax charge of $38 million ($24 million after-tax) for the costs of early redemption of long-term debt, as well as a pretax gain of $170 million ($102 million after-tax) from the sale of certain telephone and directory assets to Century Telephone Enterprises, Inc.

The second quarter of 1997 includes a one-time after-tax charge of $87 million related to our share of the costs of a work force restructuring at Belgacom. The third quarter of 1997 includes a one-time pretax gain of $52 million ($37 million after-tax) resulting from the sale of our interest in Sky Network Television of New Zealand. Several other significant income and expense items were reported in the fourth quarter of 1997. However, the net result was not material to results for the quarter or year.

We calculated earnings per share on a quarter-by-quarter basis in accordance with GAAP. Quarterly EPS figures may not total EPS for the year due to fluctuations in the number of shares outstanding.

We have included all adjustments necessary for a fair statement of results for each period.

a. Compute the proportion of total revenue for the year that was reported in each quarter of 1997 and 1998. Do Ameritech sales appear to be seasonal?
b. Compute the proportion of operating income reported in each quarter of 1997 and 1998. Is the proportion of operating income for the year reported each quarter consistent with the proportion of total revenue reported?
c. Compute the proportion of net income for 1997 and 1998 earned in each quarter. Is the net income reported in each quarter consistent with the proportion of sales reported in the quarter?
d. The note contains information on a number of special charges and gains that were included in income during 1997 and 1998. Compute the amount that would have been reported as net income in each quarter of 1997 and 1998 if these special charges and gains (after tax) had not been reported.
e. With net income of $3,606 million reported in 1998 and $2,296 million reported in 1997, Ameritech has shown a sharp increase in net income in 1998. How does the analysis prepared in part d assist in evaluating the operating results between the 2 years?

P15-51 Evaluation of Geographic Segments Archer Daniels Midland's 1998 consolidated financial statements included the following note relating to its operations in the United States, Europe, and other foreign locations:

Note 11-Geographic Information

	1998	1997	1996
	(In millions)		
Net sales and other operating income:			
United States	$10,784	$ 9,773	$ 9,661
Europe	3,869	3,039	2,753
Other foreign	1,456	1,041	826
	$16,109	$13,853	$13,240
Sales or transfers between geographic areas:			
United States	$ 339	$ 354	$ 282
Europe	47	51	108
Other foreign	228	146	133
	$ 614	$ 551	$ 523
Earnings from operations:			
United States	$ 552	$ 550	$ 805
Europe	111	46	69
Other foreign	57	29	39
	$ 720	$ 625	$ 913
Identifiable assets:			
United States	$ 7,885	$ 6,663	$ 6,025
Europe	1,537	1,288	929
Other foreign	1,050	585	418
	$10,472	$ 8,536	$ 7,372

Earnings from operations represent earnings before other income (expense) and income taxes.

Sales or transfers between geographic areas are made at established transfer prices.

Identifiable assets exclude cash and cash equivalents, marketable securities and investments in and advances to affiliates. At June 30, 1998, approximately $1.4 billion of the Company's cash and cash equivalents, marketable securities and investments in affiliates were foreign assets, of which $681 million were in Europe.

a. What proportion of ADM's 1998 net sales and other operating income was generated by each geographic region?
b. What proportion of ADM's 1998 earnings from operations was generated by each geographic region? Did the contribution to earnings from operations of each region correspond to the net sales and other operating income for that region?
c. What proportion of ADM's identifiable assets were invested in each geographic region during 1998?
d. What was the return on identifiable assets of each geographic region for 1998? On the basis of return on identifiable assets, which is the most successful geographic region? Would you arrive at the same conclusion after analyzing the data for 1996?

P15-52A Personal Financial Statements Albert Jackson has applied for a personal loan. Cleveland State Bank has requested personal financial statements for Mr. Jackson, including a statement of financial condition and a statement of changes in net worth. The following is a listing of personal assets and liabilities:

1. A house was purchased for $150,000 in 1995. An 80 percent mortgage was taken out at the time of purchase and has been paid down to $90,000; however, interest rates have increased and the present value of the liability is estimated to be $80,000. The market value of the house is estimated in the range of $240,000 to $250,000. Brokerage commissions would be 6 percent if the house is sold through a broker.
2. A car was purchased last month for $18,500.
3. Cash and short-term certificates of deposit total $45,000.
4. A total of $140,000 is invested in stocks and $40,000 in bonds. The current market value of the stocks is $190,000, and the market value of the bonds is $34,000.

5. Mr. Jackson borrowed $39,000 to buy some of his stock, and one-third of it has been paid off.
6. Artworks costing $14,000 were purchased 15 years ago. Mr. Jackson thinks they are now worth $45,000. Current catalog listings indicate a value of approximately $22,000.
7. Four years ago, 3 lots were purchased for $75,000. The current mortgage is $50,000. An appraiser recently estimated the value of the lots at $120,000. A similar lot recently was sold for $30,000.

Mr. Jackson's income tax rate is 25 percent.

a. Prepare a statement of financial condition for Albert Jackson.
b. Mr. Jackson has requested a bank loan of $500,000 to purchase the net assets of Strong Moving and Storage Company. The company reports total assets of $300,000 and liabilities of $120,000. If you were the bank loan officer, would you approve the loan? Explain.

EXPANDING YOUR HORIZONS

C15-53 Segment Information for General Dynamics
The 1998 annual report of General Dynamics contained the following note to the financial statements (dollar amounts are stated in millions):

S. BUSINESS SEGMENT INFORMATION
The company's primary business is supplying sophisticated defense systems to the United States and its allies. Management has chosen to organize its business segments in accordance with several factors, including a combination of the nature of products and services offered, the nature of the production processes and the class of customer for the company's products. Operating segments are aggregated for reporting purposes consistent with these criteria. Management measures its segments' profit based primarily on operating earnings. As such, net interest and other income items have not been allocated to the company's segments. For a further description of the company's business segments, see Management's Discussion and Analysis of the Results of Operations and Financial Condition.

Summary financial information for each of the company's segments follows:

	Net Sales			Operating Earnings			Sales to U.S. Government		
	1998	1997	1996	1998	1997	1996	1998	1997	1996
Marine Systems	$2,666	$2,311	$2,332	$285	$234	$216	$2,645	$2,280	$2,316
Combat Systems	1,272	1,509	1,026	166	187	140	1,165	1,371	996
Information Systems & Technology	796	—	—	59	—	—	351	—	—
Other	236	242	223	32	25	(3)	—	—	—
	$4,970	$4,062	$3,581	$542	$446	$353	$4,161	$3,651	$3,312

	Identifiable Assets			Capital Expenditures			Depreciation, Depletion and Amortization		
	1998	1997	1996	1998	1997	1996	1998	1997	1996
Marine Systems	$1,421	$ 706	$ 806	$ 79	$28	$18	$ 40	$34	$40
Combat Systems	923	974	336	18	17	14	27	36	12
Information Systems & Technology	1,095	1,075	—	15	—	—	40	—	—
Other	406	371	388	16	19	12	15	17	12
Corporate*	727	965	1,769	30	19	31	4	4	3
	$4,572	$4,091	$3,299	$158	$83	$75	$126	$91	$67

Corporate identifiable assets include cash and equivalents and marketable securities, deferred taxes, real estate held for development and prepaid pension cost.

The company's 4 major business segments are (1) marine systems, (2) combat systems, (3) information systems and technology, and (4) other. Answer each of the following:

a. Which of the segments had the largest growth in net sales between 1996 and 1998?
b. Which segment had the largest increase in contribution to operating earnings between 1996 and 1998?
c. Compute the percent of net sales contributed by each segment for 1996, 1997, and 1998. What changes in the proportion of net sales contributed by each segment occurred during this period?
d. Compute the percent of operating earnings contributed by each segment for 1996, 1997, and 1998. What changes in the proportion of operating income contributed by each segment occurred during this period?

e. Compute the percent of sales to the U.S. government contributed by each segment during 1996, 1997, and 1998. What changes in the proportion of sales contributed by each segment occurred during this period?
f. Compute the return on identifiable assets (operating earnings/identifiable assets) earned by each segment for 1996, 1997, and 1998. What changes in the return on identifiable assets occurred over this period?
g. Based on the above analysis, which segment manager would you give the greatest reward at December 31, 1998? Explain why.

C15-54 **Operations at Toro** The comparative statements of earnings, balance sheets, and statements of cash flows for Toro Company follow:

CONSOLIDATED STATEMENTS OF EARNINGS
THE TORO COMPANY

(Dollars and shares in thousands, except per share data) Years ended October 31	1998	1997	1996
Net sales	$1,110,434	$1,051,204	$930,909
Cost of sales	726,118	663,167	589,186
Gross profit	384,316	388,037	341,723
Selling, general, and administrative expense	345,558	313,090	278,284
Restructuring and other unusual expense	15,042	2,600	—
Earnings from operations	23,716	72,347	63,439
Interest expense	(25,428)	(19,900)	(13,590)
Other income, net	8,473	7,897	10,331
Earnings before income taxes and extraordinary loss	6,761	60,344	60,180
Provision for income taxes	2,671	23,836	23,771
Net earnings before extraordinary loss	4,090	36,508	36,409
Extraordinary loss, net of income tax benefit of $1,087	—	1,663	—
Net earnings	$ 4,090	$ 34,845	$ 36,409
Basic net earnings per share of common stock			
before extraordinary loss	$ 0.32	$ 3.02	$ 3.00
Extraordinary loss per share, net of income tax benefit	—	0.14	—
Basic net earnings per share of common stock	$ 0.32	$ 2.88	$ 3.00
Weighted average number of common			
shares outstanding	12,794	12,095	12,141
Dilutive net earnings per share of common stock			
before extraordinary loss	$ 0.31	$ 2.93	$ 2.90
Extraordinary loss per share, net of income tax benefit	—	0.13	—
Dilutive net earnings per share of common stock	$ 0.31	$ 2.80	$ 2.90
Weighted average number of common and assumed			
conversion shares outstanding	13,198	12,466	12,555

The financial statements should be read in conjunction with the Notes to Consolidated Financial Statements.

CONSOLIDATED BALANCE SHEETS
THE TORO COMPANY

(Dollars in thousands, except share amounts) October 31	1998	1997
Assets		
Cash and cash equivalents	$ 90	$ 8
Receivables:		
Customers	246,504	255,318
Other	4,246	13,648
Subtotal	250,750	268,966
Less allowance for doubtful accounts	9,324	9,832
Total receivables	241,426	259,134
Inventories, net	184,306	160,122
Prepaid expenses and other current assets	14,618	10,454
Deferred income taxes	38,997	42,326
Total current assets	479,437	472,044
Property, plant, and equipment:		
Land and land improvements	12,130	9,334
Buildings and leasehold improvements	85,392	67,627
Equipment	233,017	220,880
Subtotal	330,539	297,841
Less accumulated depreciation	203,402	180,989
Total property, plant and equipment	127,137	116,852
Deferred income taxes	3,763	1,182
Goodwill and other assets	113,654	71,556
Total assets	$723,991	$661,634
Liabilities and Stockholders' Equity		
Current portion of long-term debt	$ 580	$ 365
Short-term borrowings	31,000	41,000
Accounts payable	65,273	58,397
Accrued warranties	46,344	40,792
Accrued marketing programs	28,946	22,691
Accrued compensation and benefit costs	36,344	32,552
Other accrued liabilities	49,723	42,036
Total current liabilities	258,210	237,833
Long-term debt, less current portion	196,844	177,650
Other long-term liabilities	5,538	4,988
Stockholders' equity:		
Stock, par value $1.00, authorized 35,000,000 shares; issued and outstanding 12,769,560 shares in 1998 (net of 738,495 treasury shares) and 12,189,244 shares in 1997 (net of 720,760 treasury shares)	12,770	12,189
Additional paid-in capital	56,546	31,371
Retained earnings	200,609	202,681
Foreign currency translation adjustment	(6,526)	(5,078)
Total stockholders' equity	263,399	241,163
Total liabilities and stockholders' equity	$723,991	$661,634

The financial statements should be read in conjunction with the Notes to Consolidated Financial Statements.

CONSOLIDATED STATEMENTS OF CASH FLOWS			
THE TORO COMPANY			
(Dollars in thousands) Years ended October 31	**1998**	**1997**	**1996**
Cash flows from operating activities:			
Net earnings	$ 4,090	$ 34,845	$36,409
Adjustments to reconcile net earnings to net cash provided by operating activities:			
Extraordinary loss on early extinguishment of debt	—	1,663	—
Provision for depreciation and amortization	38,240	30,878	18,170
Loss (gain) on disposal of property, plant, and equipment	789	573	(260)
Change in deferred income taxes	1,229	2,053	784
Tax benefits related to employee stock option transactions	491	2,611	1,490
Changes in operating assets and liabilities:			
Net receivables	26,391	15,067	(40,821)
Inventories	(12,755)	1,353	15,574
Prepaid expenses and other current assets	(3,629)	(6,595)	(1,131)
Accounts payable and accrued expenses	14,248	1,425	2,218
Net cash provided by operating activities	69,094	83,873	32,433
Cash flows from investing activities:			
Purchases of property, plant, and equipment	(33,893)	(37,023)	(21,389)
Proceeds from disposal of property, plant, and equipment	3,956	1,163	543
Increase in other assets	(929)	(12,784)	(857)
Acquisition of James Hardie Irrigation, net of cash acquired	—	(118,030)	—
Other acquisitions, net of cash acquired	(17,173)	—	—
Net cash used in investing activities	(48,039)	(166,674)	(21,703)
Cash flows from financing activities:			
Repayments of short-term borrowing	(10,000)	(2,627)	(550)
Proceeds from issuance of long-term debt	—	175,000	—
Repayments of long-term debt	(3,808)	(50,350)	(15,334)
Payments of debt issue costs and prepayment penalty	—	(5,770)	—
Decrease in other long-term liabilities	(50)	—	—
Net payments for termination of interest rate swap agreements	—	(23,650)	—
Proceeds from interest rate swap agreement	—	—	12,742
Proceeds from exercise of stock options	2,219	8,407	4,627
Purchases of common stock	(1,724)	(7,952)	(13,339)
Dividends on common stock	(6,162)	(5,794)	(5,834)
Net cash (used in) provided by financing activities	(19,525)	87,264	(17,688)
Foreign currency translation adjustment	(1,448)	(4,521)	(678)
Net increase (decrease) in cash and cash equivalents	82	(58)	(7,636)
Cash and cash equivalents at beginning of the fiscal year	8	66	7,702
Cash and cash equivalents at end of the fiscal year	$ 90	$ 8	$ 66
Supplemental disclosures of cash flow information:			
Cash paid during the fiscal year for:			
Interest	$24,363	$ 16,829	$15,335
Income taxes	3,345	25,459	20,447
Stock issued in connection with an acquisition	24,770	—	—
Debt issued in connection with an acquisition	15,761	—	—

The financial statements should be read in conjunction with the Notes to Consolidated Financial Statements.

a. Compute the following ratios for Toro for 1998 and 1997:
   1. Current ratio.
   2. Quick ratio.
   3. Days sales in receivables.
   4. Days sales in inventory.
   5. Operating cycle.
   6. Long-term debt to total assets.
   7. Debt to equity.
   8. Times interest earned.
   9. Cash flow to total debt (including accounts payable).
   10. Gross margin percentage.
   11. Net income margin.
   12. Return on common equity.
   13. Asset turnover.
   14. Return on assets.
   15. Basic earnings per share.
   16. Diluted earnings per share.
   17. Dividend payout.
   18. Dividends to operating cash flow.
   19. Cash flow per share.

b. What changes, if any, have occurred with respect to Toro's liquidity?

c. What changes, if any, have occurred with respect to Toro's solvency?

d. What changes, if any, have occurred with respect to Toro's profitability?

e. What changes, if any, have occurred with respect to Toro's return to investors?

f. Based on the financial statement information provided, would you feel secure in purchasing Toro bonds? Explain.

g. Based on the financial statement information provided, would you recommend purchasing Toro common shares?

C15-55 Evaluating Colgate–Palmolive's Operating Results The comparative statements of income, balance sheets, and statements of cash flows for Colgate–Palmolive Company follow:

CONSOLIDATED STATEMENTS OF INCOME

Dollars in Millions Except Per Share Amounts

	1998	1997	1996
Net sales	$8,971.6	$9,056.7	$8,749.0
Cost of sales	4,290.3	4,461.5	4,451.1
Gross profit	4,681.3	4,595.2	4,297.9
Selling, general and administrative expenses	3,197.1	3,237.0	3,052.1
Other expense, net	61.2	72.4	93.8
Interest expense, net	172.9	183.5	197.4
Income before income taxes	1,250.1	1,102.3	954.6
Provision for income taxes	401.5	361.9	319.6
Net income	$ 848.6	$ 740.4	$ 635.0
Earnings per common share, basic	$ 2.81	$ 2.44	$ 2.09
Earnings per common share, diluted	$ 2.61	$ 2.27	$ 1.96

CONSOLIDATED BALANCE SHEETS

Dollars in Millions Except Per Share Amounts

	1998	1997
Assets		
Current Assets		
Cash and cash equivalents	$ 181.7	$ 183.1
Marketable securities	12.8	22.2
Receivables (less allowances of $35.9 and $35.8, respectively)	1,085.6	1,037.4
Inventories	746.0	728.4
Other current assets	218.8	225.4
Total current assets	2,244.9	2,196.5
Property, plant and equipment, net	2,589.2	2,441.0
Goodwill and other intangibles, net	2,524.1	2,585.3
Other assets	327.0	315.9
	$7,685.2	$7,538.7
Liabilities and Shareholders' Equity		
Current Liabilities		
Notes and loans payable	$ 175.3	$ 158.4
Current portion of long-term debt	281.6	178.3
Accounts payable	726.1	716.9
Accrued income taxes	74.2	67.0
Other accruals	857.2	838.9
Total current liabilities	2,114.4	1,959.5
Long-term debt	2,300.6	2,340.3
Deferred income taxes	448.0	284.5
Other liabilities	736.6	775.8
Shareholders' Equity		
Preferred stock	376.2	385.3
Common stock, $1 par value (1,000,000,000 shares authorized, 366,426,590 shares issued)	366.4	366.4
Additional paid-in capital	1,191.1	1,027.4
Retained earnings	3,641.0	3,138.0
Cumulative translation adjustments	(799.8)	(693.7)
	4,774.9	4,223.4
Unearned compensation	(355.5)	(364.5)
Treasury stock, at cost	(2,333.8)	(1,680.3)
Total shareholders' equity	2,085.6	2,178.6
	$7,685.2	$7,538.7

CONSOLIDATED STATEMENTS OF CASH FLOWS

Dollars in Millions Except Per Share Amounts

	1998	1997	1996
Operating Activities			
Net income	$ 848.6	$ 740.4	$ 635.0
Adjustments to reconcile net income to net cash provided by operations:			
Restructured operations	(34.8)	(48.5)	(105.6)
Depreciation and amortization	330.3	319.9	316.3
Income taxes and other, net	60.7	18.5	13.2
Cash effects of changes in:			
Receivables	(15.2)	(61.6)	(15.4)
Inventories	(19.5)	(50.9)	(1.2)
Payables and accruals	8.7	180.0	75.1
Net cash provided by operations	1,178.8	1,097.8	917.4
Investing Activities			
Capital expenditures	(389.6)	(478.5)	(459.0)
Payment for acquisitions, net of cash acquired	(22.6)	(31.5)	(59.3)
Sale of non-core product lines	57.4	96.4	25.1
Sale of marketable securities and investments	18.7	68.5	1.2
Other	(15.8)	7.7	(12.0)
Net cash used for investing activities	(351.9)	(337.4)	(504.0)
Financing Activities			
Principal payments on debt	(677.5)	(670.7)	(1,164.6)
Proceeds from issuance of debt	762.9	350.4	1,077.4
Dividends paid	(345.6)	(333.4)	(296.2)
Purchase of common stock	(542.5)	(175.1)	(27.4)
Other	(27.3)	15.8	39.2
Net cash used for financing activities	(830.0)	(813.0)	(371.6)
Effect of exchange rate changes on cash and cash equivalents	1.7	(12.5)	(2.4)
Net (decrease) increase in cash and cash equivalents	(1.4)	(65.1)	39.4
Cash and cash equivalents at beginning of year	183.1	248.2	208.8
Cash and cash equivalents at end of year	$ 181.7	$ 183.1	$ 248.2
Supplemental Cash Flow Information			
Income taxes paid	$ 273.8	$ 261.3	$ 273.0
Interest paid	202.8	230.6	229.1
Principal payments on ESOP debt, guaranteed by the Company	6.1	5.5	5.0

Weighted average shares of common stock outstanding were 295.0 million and 295.3 million for 1998 and 1997, respectively. Dividends paid shown in the statement of cash flows include preferred dividends of $20.9 million and $21.1 million in 1998 and 1997, respectively.

a. Compute the following ratios for Colgate–Palmolive for 1998 and 1997:
   1. Gross margin percentage.
   2. Net income margin.
   3. Asset turnover.
   4. Return on assets.
   5. Return on common equity.
   6. Long-term debt to total assets.
   7. Debt to equity.
   8. Times interest earned.
   9. Cash flow to total debt (including accounts payable).
   10. Earnings per share.
   11. Dividend payout.
   12. Dividends to operating cash flow.
   13. Cash flow per share.

b. Which ratios are used in assessing Colgate–Palmolive's profitability? Did its profitability increase or decrease in 1998 over 1997? What return to common shareholders would have been earned in 1998 if the stockholders' equity balance had consisted of common stock only? What impact did the preferred shares outstanding have on the return earned by common shareholders in 1998?

c. Which ratios are used in assessing Colgate–Palmolive's solvency? Did its solvency improve or decline in 1998?

d. Which ratios are used in assessing Colgate–Palmolive's return to investors? Did its profitability increase or decrease in 1998? Why must preferred dividends be deducted in computing earnings per share and cash flow per share? Does this mean the common shareholders earned less than they would have if the preferred stock had not been outstanding? Explain.

C15-56 Inventory Estimation Based on Gross Profit Highlight Company reported sales of $600,000 in the first quarter of 2000. Because the company does not keep a running tally of the cost of inventory sold, the controller does not know how much inventory is actually on hand at the end of the quarter. The company, for the first time, is going to prepare quarterly financial reports to issue to its stockholders, but counting the inventory at the end of each quarter is too costly. Therefore, the controller decides to estimate how much inventory is on hand. By looking at the last annual balance sheet, the controller is able to determine that inventory on hand on January 1, 2000, was $250,000, and he knows that an additional $700,000 of inventory was purchased during the first quarter, providing a total $950,000 of goods available for sale. The company normally earns a 30 percent gross profit on sales. Based on this information, and using a well accepted method of inventory estimation called the gross profit method, the controller arrives at what he feels is a reasonable estimate of the cost of inventory on hand at the end of the first quarter of 2000.

a. What would you estimate as the cost of Highlight's inventory on hand at the end of the first quarter of 2000? Explain how you arrived at your estimate. Assume the company earned a consistent 30 percent gross margin on its $600,000 of sales.

b. If the gross profit method works reasonably well for interim estimates of inventory on hand, why not use it at year-end as well and avoid altogether the cost of an annual inventory count?

c. Under what conditions might this method of estimating inventory provide unreliable results?

d. Based on your estimate of Highlight's inventory at the end of the first quarter, what is your assessment of the company's inventory position? What factors might have contributed to it?

 C15-57   Team Assignment: Analyzing Financial Disclosures Using annual reports available through your library, or by using electronic databases, do the following:

a. Examine the financial statements of a gas or electric utility and a major retail company that issue consolidated financial statements. Determine the number of subsidiaries and the types of businesses in which they are involved.

b. Examine the quarterly earnings patterns of the 2 companies and compare them. Are the earnings patterns different? If so, in what way? What business and environmental factors would tend to lead to similar or different patterns?

c. Examine the disaggregated information (segment, product, or geographic) provided by the gas or electric utility and compare them to the disclosures provided by Gateway. What are the major differences in the type of information provided?

d. Do either the utility or retail company have any special reporting issues that are separately disclosed in the financial statements or notes? Attempt to identify one issue for each company and explain why it is important.

C15-58   Ethics and Quarterly Profits The management of the Forward Electronics Company has been proud of the company's record of growth over the past 5 years. Not only have sales and earnings been higher each year, but each quarter has been higher than the previous quarter for the past 20 quarters. The managers are happy because they have a good stock option plan and the stock price has been going up every quarter. However, operations in 2000 are a different story. There is more competition, and some new products are beginning to take Forward's market. Forward is developing a new sales strategy, but it will not go into effect until 2001.

In the middle of September, an emergency management meeting was called, and the accounting manager reported that unless something changed, third quarter sales and income would be much lower than last year. At the meeting, each manager was asked to do something to protect the growth record for one more quarter. Although it was not stated, everyone knew that a large number of stock options could be exercised and the shares sold in December. Continued growth would make these options much more valuable.

The sales manager proposed that they could add more sales and meet the original quota if the credit manager were to ease the credit limits a little and if the company relaxed its return policy so that more sales could be made that might eventually be returned. The credit manager agreed that the limits could be relaxed and some cash customers could be granted credit even though the uncollectible accounts would go up significantly. They all agreed to relax the company's return policy. The operations manager reported that he could provide enough merchandise for shipment this month to push sales over the quota if the sales department could get the orders. The shipping manager said that enough units could be shipped if he could hold the records open for just a day or two, maybe just over the weekend, at the end of the quarter so everything would go out the door. The accounting manager reluctantly agreed that as long as sales and shipping documents were dated before September 30, the sales would be included in revenue and earnings for the third quarter. A higher rate of sales returns and bad debts should be estimated for the quarter, but since none will be returned or actually go bad until later in the year, the increased allowances can wait.

The management committee met again on December 15, 2000. All of the actions proposed in the earlier meeting had been carried out. Forward maintained its growth record, stock prices continued to climb, and the stock options were well priced. Since the aggressive strategy worked, all the managers agreed to continue the practices at the end of the year so that the company's record of quarterly and annual growth would continue through all of 2001. This might also persuade the managers not to sell the stock acquired with the options until the year 2002. As a result of the agreement, the financial vice president drafted a management's discussion and analysis section for the annual report that said the growth record was intact and, with the new strategies, even better things were expected in 2001.

a. What do you think about the actions by each of the individual managers of Forward Electronics? Which, if any, are in violation of generally accepted accounting principles at the end of the quarter or the end of the year? Which, if any, are acceptable, but may not be ethical?

b. Even though Forward adopted a new sales strategy in 2001, it was not able to increase its sales. The structure of its market had changed. Management was able to sell its stock in early 2001 at good prices, but by April, revenues were down and Forward reported a loss for the first quarter. Sales returns and uncollectible accounts increased dramatically. Does this information affect your answers to the previous questions? Explain.

Internet Exercises: Visit our Web site for additional exercises.

Annual Report Project Part 15

Refer to the Annual Report Project, Part 1, at the end of Chapter 1. Using the annual report of the company you have chosen, and any other available information, answer the following questions, providing sources and computations where appropriate.

a. Does your company have any subsidiaries? How do you know? If it does have subsidiaries, list three. [*Note:* If the subsidiaries are not mentioned in the annual report to stockholders, a list of subsidiaries can normally be found toward the end of the Form 10-K filed with the SEC.]

b. What major topics are included in management's discussion and analysis for your company?

c. If your company has more than a single operating segment [see Part 4 of the Annual Report Project], what is the dollar amount of operating income from each segment?

d. Does your company disclose sales to a significant customer? If so, does it disclose that customer's name?

e. What is the current price of your company's stock? Was your investment strategy in Part 1 of the Annual Report Project successful? To what extent?

f. What do think the long-run prospects are for this company? Provide a brief analysis, focusing on those factors you think are most important for your company.

CHAPTER SIXTEEN

Financial Reporting in a Global Economy

REVIEW

The first fifteen chapters focused primarily on businesses operating in the United States following U.S. accounting practices.

WHERE THIS CHAPTER FITS

This last chapter considers some of the issues related to U.S. companies doing business abroad and having operations in other countries. In this chapter, we look at how companies report their global operations, and we consider some of the factors that affect the way accounting information influences decisions in the global environment.

My sister just got back from a trip to Japan. She says that, while she enjoyed Japanese food, every other day she ate at McDonald's or KFC where she could find familiar food. She says it seems unreal because the clerks are all Japanese and the menu is in Japanese. She had to point to pictures to order. KFC even served beer with the chicken, and you could get teriyaki sauce on your double cheeseburger at McDonald's. Someday I want to go to China. I wonder if I could open a McDonald's there. How much money would it take? I wonder how much the equipment would cost. Could I use dollars, or would it have to be in renminbi? Would I have to borrow money in China, or could it be borrowed from a U.S. bank? Would I have to report and pay taxes in China or the United States? This global business sounds complicated, but it would be interesting.

In 1999, McDonald's Corporation operated more than 25,000 stores in 115 different countries; over half of the stores were outside the United States. "Big Mac," the symbol of U.S. fast food, is really a global symbol. Each country that has a McDonald's franchise has its unique business problems: German law prohibits special promotions like "buy one, get one free"; in Denmark, some suppliers need special government permission to work on weekends; and in Poland, many customers want to bring their vodka to drink with their meals. McDonald's obtains supplies locally so it doesn't have to change currencies, but many of its U.S. suppliers set up operations in the countries McDonald's enters.[1]

[1]Based on Andrew E. Serwer, "McDonald's Conquers the World," *Fortune* (October 17, 1994), p. 108–115; and McDonald's Corporation news release.

We live in a global economy, and most major businesses operate in a global environment. Although in earlier chapters we did not focus on global factors, almost all of the company financial reports used for illustrations were affected by international sales, purchases, and operations. Japan-based Sony Corporation, for example, is an international company with extensive operations in the United States and around the world. Its primary currency is the yen, and its original financial statements are presented in yen and prepared in accordance with Japanese accounting principles. However, it also issues dollar-based financial statements for U.S. investors. Even though Nike is a U.S. company, it does more than one-third of its business internationally, mostly in Europe. Alberto-Culver, with its familiar personal care products, receives more than 25 percent of its revenue from outside the United States and holds more than 30 percent of its assets in foreign countries.

With companies operating in a global setting, their managers and employees, as well as investors and creditors, all must make financial decisions that involve international considerations. Accounting information used in these decisions must reflect the international setting of the operations. Unfortunately, different countries prepare accounting reports stated in different currencies and using different accounting methods. Although many of the accounting procedures are similar and techniques exist for putting financial statements from different countries on the same basis, accounting reports still reflect the economy and customs of each country.

In this chapter, we will focus on how the economic, political, and social differences of countries around the world are reflected in financial reports. This chapter will help you understand the financial reports of a global company so you can make more informed decisions about such considerations as a company's risks from foreign operations and how the rate of return earned on foreign investments differs from that earned in the United States. After reading this chapter, you should be able to:

1. Identify companies that are involved in global business and use this information to refine your decisions about those companies.

2. Explain how transactions involving two different currencies are reported, and identify the exchange risks that are present.

3. Describe how companies minimize their exposure to foreign currency exchange rate risks, why this is important, and what information is available in financial statements to help decision makers assess the rewards and risks of a company's international operations.

4. Explain how financial statements are translated into different currencies, and describe how a decision maker can determine what effect the translation has had on those statements.

5. Discuss the formulation of international accounting standards, explain the difficulties in achieving uniformity, and describe the effects of different standards on financial decisions.

6. Describe how financial ratios can provide useful information about a company's international operations.

DECISION MAKING IN A GLOBAL ECONOMY

Information for Decisions

When a company operates globally, financial decisions are affected by international regulations, customs, activities, and events. Different countries also use different currencies, and financial reporting is often based on different accounting principles. Understanding how financial reporting reflects these complexities helps financial statement users to better assess a company's operations and position and to answer questions such as the following: What effect will problems with China's economy have on the total revenues of this company? Can I rely on the dollar-based financial statements of this Japanese Company to be comparable with those of U.S. companies in the same industry? How is the company I'm evaluating affected by changes in the exchange rates of other currencies for U.S. dollars?

Most large corporations have an international business component and consider themselves to be global companies. For example, Gateway, a solid Midwestern U.S. company just over fifteen years old, indicates the global nature of its business by pointing out in its "Management's Discussion and Analysis of Financial Condition and Results of Operations" that it is sixth in computer sales worldwide; it also provides detailed information relating to its worldwide operations in Note 12 to its financial statements. Another U.S. company, Motorola, reports that well under half of its sales take place in the United States and more than a third of its assets are held in foreign countries.

As a manager, many of your financial decisions will be affected by international activities and events. Even as a consumer, your product selections and the prices you pay are affected by the international economy. Global business offers opportunities, but it also presents a variety of economic, tax, regulatory, and accounting issues. Understanding some of these issues can help managers and others make better decisions.

In Practice 16-1

NIKE, REEBOK, AND MATTEL

Nike, Inc., the well-known manufacturer and distributor of sporting goods, printed its letter to stockholders in its annual report a few years ago in English, French, German, Japanese, and Spanish, with excerpts shown in Exhibit 16–1. The company's 1998 annual report states that, although its total revenue increased slightly from the previous year, revenue from the United States was about 1 percent lower. Revenue from Europe increased by 17 percent, revenue from Asia/Pacific increased by about 1 percent, and revenue from Latin America/Canada and other areas increased by 21 percent.

Reebok, one of Nike's competitors, provides the following language choices on its home page under the category Investor Information: English, Chinese, French, German, Italian, Japanese, Korean, Portuguese, and Spanish. Mattel, Inc., a major toy manufacturer, included a letter to its stockholders in its 1998 annual report that was printed in several languages, as Nike had done previously; Mattel's report included French, German, Italian, Spanish, Japanese, and Chinese, in addition to English.

ANALYSIS

Nike, Reebok, and Mattel all indicate their status as international companies by providing information in a variety of languages. Nike's total revenues remained fairly stable in 1998 despite reduced revenue in the United States and the economic downturn in the Asia/Pacific region. However, Nike's 1998 operating income was almost 50 percent lower than in 1997, down from $1,295.2 million in 1997 to $653.0 million in 1998. Operating income in the Asia/Pacific region dropped from $175.0 million in 1997 to a $34.6 million loss in 1998. [www.nike.com] [www.reebok.com]

THE IMPACT OF GLOBAL FACTORS

Economic decisions and the information available to make those decisions depend on the economic, political, and legal characteristics that tend to be most pervasive. In a free-market economy, decision making is decentralized and is based on information about the wants and needs of members of society as captured in market prices. In well developed free-market economies, information is widely available at low cost and helps make the markets efficient.

Other economic factors may also affect types of decisions and related information. For example, in countries having high rates of inflation, decision makers must consider the changing purchasing power of money in all economic decisions. Information used in making those decisions may incorporate adjustments for inflation that are not included in the information used in countries with relatively stable currencies. In some cases, accounting information may

| EXHIBIT 16-1 | **NIKE: COMMUNICATING IN MANY LANGUAGES** |

THE TWO MAIN GOALS FOR THIS FISCAL YEAR ARE QUALITATIVE. First, we must get the whole international division positioned so it can resume faster growth once the underlying economies improve.

LES DEUX PRINCIPAUX OBJECTIFS DE CETTE ANNEE FISCALE SONT d'ordre qualitatif. D'abord nous devons positionner l'ensemble de la division internationale afin qu'elle puisse retrouver ses taux de croissance des dernières années dès que l'économie se rétablira.

DIE WICHTIGSTEN BEIDEN ZIELE FÜR DIESES BESCHÄFTSJAHR SIND qualitativer Natur. Erstens müssen wir die gesamten internationalen Niederlaussungen dahinbringen, daβ sie die Wachstrumsrate der vergangenen Jahre wieder erreichen. Das ist jedoch nur dann möglich,-wenn sich die wirtschaftlichen Rahmenbedingungen verbessert haben.

本会計年度の2つの主な目標は質的なものです。

　まず第一に、国際部門全体を適切に配置し、根本的な経済が改善したあかつには、過去数年の伸び率を取り戻さなければなりません。

　第二に、たとえ一桁の伸びであっても伸び続けて、米国内でのナイキ・ブランドを支えなければなりません。

LAS DOS METAS PRINCIPALES PARA ESTE AÑO FISCAL SON CUALITATIVAS. En primer lugar debemos organizar toda nuestra división internacional para asegurar que cuando las economías individuales de las que depende hayan mejorado, se puedan lograr otra vez las tasas de crecimiento de los últimos años.

be regulated to influence decisions that further national policies, such as some of the accounting methods used in several European countries to promote savings and investment.

In some countries, such as France, the main providers of capital are creditors, often with close ties to individual companies. Decision makers may have a more intimate knowledge of the companies with which they are dealing, and they may require less formal information than in countries where the suppliers of capital change frequently. Also, the emphasis for lenders tends to be more on preserving assets, while suppliers of equity capital tend to focus more on profitability.

Sometimes the information available for decision makers may be influenced by the legalistic orientation of the countries. Common law countries, such as the United States and Canada, tend to have more flexible accounting policies, often developed in the private sector, than countries that rely heavily on statutes and regulations, such as France and Germany. In some countries, tax policy is so important that accounting information must follow the tax laws, or at least is heavily influenced by them.

Further, cultural ties and geographic proximity may influence accounting information. The British Commonwealth countries, such as Canada and Australia, tend to follow similar accounting practices. Because many U.S. accountants came from England in the late 1800s and early 1900s, the British influence is strong in this country as well. On the other hand, countries having ties to continental Europe often follow accounting practices related to those in France and Germany. Also, the advent of regional alliances, such as the European Economic Union or the North American Free Trade Agreement, tends to promote more uniformity in accounting methods among members.

Because the world is made up of a patchwork of customs, laws and regulations, business practices, and accounting policies, decision making is particularly difficult in a global economy. Nevertheless, managers, investors, and creditors have no choice but to deal with the complexities of a global economy. Therefore, understanding how accounting information reflects these complexities is particularly important.

FINANCIAL REPORTING FOR GLOBAL BUSINESSES

Operating in a global environment presents several important financial reporting challenges. One question that arises is that if a domestic company has an operation in a foreign country that follows accounting principles different from those accepted in this country, how should that operation be reported in the company's financial statements?

A second issue of importance is how to report transactions that are denominated in a foreign currency. Almost every country (or group of countries) has its own currency, some of which are listed in Exhibit 16–2. Having such a wide variety of currencies complicates global transactions. When a company engages in a transaction with a party in a foreign country, the parties must agree on the currency to be used for payment. Suppose a U.S. company purchases a shipment of electronic components from a Japanese company and payment is to be made in yen. How is that transaction reported in the company's financial statements? How is financial reporting affected if the foreign currency changes in value between the time of the transaction and the time of payment?

A third issue arises when a company has a subsidiary or division located in a foreign country and that unit does business in the local (foreign) currency. It may also keep its records in the local currency. Because different currencies cannot simply be added together to prepare financial statements for the company as a whole, the issue of how to combine financial statements stated in foreign currency units with those stated in dollars must be resolved.

The first question is easily answered: Although a foreign operation may follow local (foreign) accounting principles for reporting in the foreign country, it must be reported using U.S. generally accepted accounting principles when included in the overall company's financial statements issued in this country. Therefore, if separate financial statements for the foreign operation are prepared for issuance in the foreign country, they must be changed to conform with accounting standards in this country before being included in the company's financial report.

The other two reporting issues are more complex and deserve closer examination. Let's look first at reporting transactions denominated in foreign currencies.

CURRENCIES OF COUNTRIES AROUND THE WORLD   EXHIBIT 16-2

Country	Currency
Brazil	Real
Canada	Dollar (Canadian)
China	Renminbi
Euro currency countries	Euro
France	Franc
Germany	Mark
Greece	Drachma
Hong Kong	Dollar (H.K.)
India	Rupee
Iran	Rial
Iraq	Dinar
Israel	Shekel
Italy	Lira
Japan	Yen
Mexico	Peso
Saudi Arabia	Riyal
South Africa	Rand
South Korea	Won
Thailand	Baht
United Kingdom	Pound Sterling
United States	Dollar (U.S.)

REPORTING TRANSACTIONS DENOMINATED IN FOREIGN CURRENCIES

Information for Decisions

When a U.S. company does business with foreign customers or suppliers, the transactions are reported in the company's financial statements in U.S. dollars. The dollar value of any receivables or payables denominated in foreign currencies arising from these transactions might change because of changing currency exchange rates. By understanding the accounting for foreign transactions and fluctuating exchange rates, decision makers can better understand a company's global operations and better assess the rewards and risks of doing business abroad. Decision makers are then in a better position to answer questions such as these: In which geographic areas of the world has the company had the greatest success and which show the greatest potential for future growth? If a company is operating in Brazil and the Brazilian real is devalued, how will that affect the company's income and the value of its assets and liabilities? How successful has the company been in avoiding the risks associated with doing business abroad?

Suppose you are visiting Tokyo and become homesick for a good, thick steak. After searching for a while, you find a restaurant that serves a large filet for 6,600 yen. Because you think in terms of U.S. dollars, this amount might be meaningless to you. Therefore, you must convert the amount from yen to dollars. To do that, you would need to know the **exchange rate,** or the rate at which one currency can be exchanged for another. If you found the exchange rate for converting yen into dollars was 110:1 (¥110 = $1), you would know that the steak dinner would cost you about $60 (¥6,600 ÷ 110), stated in U.S. currency. Companies buying or selling products in other countries must make the same type of currency conversions.

How are exchange rates determined, and how is one currency exchanged for another? Let's look briefly at currency exchange markets, and then at how transactions and currency fluctuations are reported.

FOREIGN EXCHANGE MARKETS

The current exchange rate between currencies of different countries is quoted daily in major newspapers such as *The Wall Street Journal*, as illustrated in Exhibit 16–3. For widely used currencies such as the Japanese yen and the British pound, future exchange rates are also quoted. The current exchange rate is known as the **spot rate.** The future exchange rate is referred to as the **forward rate** and is the rate currently agreed on for an exchange of currencies at a specified future date. Newspapers normally quote forward rates only up to 180 days, but longer contracts are available.

Exchange rates for currencies are determined in much the same way as any prices in a market economy, through supply and demand. For example, because many countries have imported more goods from Japan than they have exported to Japan, the value of the yen has risen against major currencies because importers must acquire yen to pay for their purchases.

For several decades after World War II, exchange rates between the major Western countries were fixed. That is, the rate at which one currency was exchanged for another tended to remain constant. Now, however, the exchange rates of most major countries "float" so that the rate can change from day to day or even hour to hour. For example, the exchange rate between the dollar and yen may sometimes change by two or three yen per

PUBLISHED CURRENCY EXCHANGE RATES*

EXHIBIT 16-3

CURRENCY TRADING

Thursday, January 20, 2000

EXCHANGE RATES

The New York foreign exchange mid-range rates below apply to trading among banks in amounts of $1 million and more, as quoted at 4 p.m. Eastern time by Reuters and other sources. Retail transactions provide fewer units of foreign currency per dollar. Rates for the 11 Euro currency countries are derived from the latest dollar-euro rate using the exchange ratios set 1/1/99.

Country	U.S. $ equiv. Thu	U.S. $ equiv. Wed	Currency per U.S. $ Thu	Currency per U.S. $ Wed
Argentina (Peso)	1.0002	1.0002	.9998	.9998
Australia (Dollar)	.6656	.6636	1.5023	1.5070
Austria (Schilling)	.07393	.07359	13.527	13.589
Bahrain (Dinar)	2.6525	2.6525	.3770	.3770
Belgium (Franc)	.0252	.0251	39.6558	39.8379
Brazil (Real)	.5609	.5583	1.7830	1.7910
Britain (Pound)	1.6549	1.6442	.6043	.6082
1-month forward	1.6548	1.6443	.6043	.6082
3-months forward	1.6547	1.6443	.6043	.6082
6-months forward	1.6543	1.6436	.6045	.6084
Canada (Dollar)	.6912	.6888	1.4468	1.4517
1-month forward	.6917	.6894	1.4457	1.4506
3-months forward	.6925	.6902	1.4440	1.4489
6-months forward	.6937	.6914	1.4416	1.4464
Chile (Peso) (d)	.001926	.001935	519.25	516.75
China (Renminbi)	.1208	.1208	8.2794	8.2797
Colombia (Peso)	.0005175	.0005148	1932.50	1942.50
Czech. Rep. (Koruna) ...				
Commercial rate	.02815	.02810	35.527	35.593
Denmark (Krone)	.1366	.1360	7.3200	7.3514
Ecuador (Sucre) ...				
Floating rate	.00004004	.00004004	24975.00	24975.00
Finland (Markka)	.1711	.1703	5.8449	5.8717
France (Franc)	.1551	.1544	6.4483	6.4779
1-month forward	.1554	.1547	6.4335	6.4623
3-months forward	.1561	.1555	6.4045	6.4322
6-months forward	.1572	.1564	6.3631	6.3924
Germany (Mark)	.5201	.5177	1.9227	1.9315
1-month forward	.5213	.5190	1.9182	1.9268
3-months forward	.5237	.5214	1.9096	1.9179
6-months forward	.5271	.5247	1.8973	1.9059
Greece (Drachma)	.003073	.003062	325.39	326.59
Hong Kong (Dollar)	.1286	.1285	7.7788	7.7793
Hungary (Forint)	.003985	.003971	250.96	251.85
India (Rupee)	.02296	.02297	43.550	43.540
Indonesia (Rupiah)	.0001370	.0001362	7300.00	7340.00
Ireland (Punt)	1.2917	1.2857	.7742	.7778
Israel (Shekel)	.2449	.2445	4.0828	4.0893
Italy (Lira)	.0005254	.0005230	1903.44	1912.18
Japan (Yen)	.009493	.009492	105.34	105.35
1-month forward	.009540	.009540	104.83	104.82

Country	U.S. $ equiv. Thu	U.S. $ equiv. Wed	Currency per U.S. $ Thu	Currency per U.S. $ Wed
3-months forward	.009634	.009633	103.79	103.80
6-months forward	.009784	.009784	102.21	102.21
Jordan (Dinar)	1.4075	1.4085	.7105	.7100
Kuwait (Dinar)	3.2841	3.2819	.3045	.3047
Lebanon (Pound)	.0006647	.0006634	1504.50	1507.50
Malaysia (Ringgit)	.2632	.2632	3.8001	3.8000
Malta (Lira)	2.4576	2.4480	.4069	.4085
Mexico (Peso) ...				
Floating rate	.1060	.1062	9.4330	9.4150
Netherland (Guilder)	.4616	.4595	2.1663	2.1763
New Zealand (Dollar)	.5140	.5149	1.9455	1.9421
Norway (Krone)	.1257	.1252	7.9583	7.9878
Pakistan (Rupee)	.01929	.01928	51.850	51.875
Peru (new Sol)	.2856	.2857	3.5020	3.5005
Philippines (Peso)	.02463	.02460	40.600	40.650
Poland (Zloty)	.2452	.2451	4.0775	4.0800
Portugal (Escudo)	.005074	.005051	197.08	197.99
Russia (Ruble) (a)	.03503	.03502	28.550	28.555
Saudi Arabia (Riyal)	.2666	.2666	3.7505	3.7505
Singapore (Dollar)	.5978	.5966	1.6728	1.6763
Slovak Rep. (Koruna)	.02405	.02393	41.587	41.788
South Africa (Rand)	.1640	.1636	6.0975	6.1135
South Korea (Won)	.0008885	.0008822	1125.50	1133.50
Spain (Peseta)	.006114	.006086	163.56	164.32
Sweden (Krona)	.1184	.1180	8.4478	8.4780
Switzerland (Franc)	.6314	.6272	1.5839	1.5943
1-month forward	.6336	.6296	1.5782	1.5883
3-months forward	.6381	.6342	1.5672	1.5767
6-months forward	.6445	.6405	1.5517	1.5612
Taiwan (Dollar)	.03248	.03249	30.785	30.775
Thailand (Baht)	.02684	.02676	37.255	37.375
Turkey (Lira)	.00000183	.00000183	547735.00	546755.00
United Arab (Dirham)	.2722	.2723	3.6731	3.6730
Uruguay (New Peso) ...				
Financial	.08571	.08574	11.668	11.663
Venezuela (Bolivar)	.001531	.001533	653.03	652.50
— — —				
SDR	1.3684	1.3661	.7308	.7320
Euro	1.0173	1.0126	.9830	.9876

Special Drawing Rights (SDR) are based on exchange rates for the U.S., German, British, French, and Japanese currencies. Source: International Monetary Fund.

a-Russian Central Bank rate. Trading band lowered on 8/17/98. b-Government rate. d-Floating rate; trading band suspended on 9/2/99.

The 3-month and 6-month forward rates for France, Germany, Japan and Switzerland appearing in the Foreign Exchange column were incorrectly calculated for the period beginning with August 13 and ending with October 7. Corrected data is available from Readers' Reference Service (413) 592-3600.

Key Currency Cross Rates Late New York Trading Jan. 20, 2000

	Dollar	Euro	Pound	SFranc	Guilder	Peso	Yen	Lira	D-Mark	FFranc	CdnDlr
Canada	1.4468	1.4718	2.3943	0.9134	.66787	.15338	.01373	.00076	.75248	.22437	....
France	6.4483	6.5599	10.6713	4.0712	2.9766	.68359	.06121	.00339	3.3538	....	4.4569
Germany	1.9227	1.9560	3.1819	1.2139	.88755	.20383	.01825	.00101	....	.29817	1.3289
Italy	1903.4	1936.3	3150.0	1201.7	878.65	201.78	18.069	....	989.97	295.18	1315.6
Japan	105.34	107.16	174.33	66.507	48.627	11.167	....	.05534	54.788	16.336	72.809
Mexico	9.4330	9.5962	15.611	5.9556	4.3544	....	.08955	.00496	4.9061	1.4629	6.5199
Netherlands	2.1663	2.2038	3.5850	1.3677	....	.22965	.02056	.00114	1.1267	.33595	1.4973
Switzerland	1.5839	1.6113	2.6212	....	.73115	.16791	.01504	.00083	.82379	.24563	1.0948
U.K.	.60430	.6147	....	.3815	.27894	.06406	.00574	.00032	.31428	.09371	.41766
Euro	.98300	....	1.6268	.62062	.45377	.10421	.00933	.00052	.51126	.15244	.67943
U.S.	....	1.0173	1.6549	.63135	.46162	.10601	.00949	.00053	.52010	.15508	.69118

Source: Reuters

*From *The Wall Street Journal* (January 21, 2000), p. C17.

dollar during a single day. This may not seem significant, but suppose you were holding a ¥100 million account receivable from the sale of construction equipment to a Japanese customer, with payment due in 30 days. If the exchange rate went from to ¥105 per dollar ($952,381) to ¥110 per dollar ($909,091) during the 30 days you held the receivable, you would suffer a loss of more than $40,000. This currency exchange loss might offset much of the profit from the sale.

U.S. companies engaged in transactions denominated in foreign currencies must deal with an exchange broker, such as a bank or other type of currency dealer, to convert to and from dollars. For example, once payment in yen is received from a Japanese customer, the yen have to be exchanged for dollars through a broker, unless the company needs yen. Similarly, if American Airlines purchased parts for its ATR aircraft from the French manufacturer, and the transaction was denominated in euros, the company would have to purchase for dollars the number of euros needed to pay for the parts. Quoted spot rates reflect the current demand for and supply of various currencies, while forward rates reflect assessments of what future demand and supply will be. Without currency dealers and the organized currency exchange markets, international commerce would be severely hindered.

FOREIGN TRANSACTIONS

If a U.S. company engages in foreign transactions, but those transactions are denominated in dollars, no special reporting problems are created. Sales and purchases denominated in dollars are recorded and reported in the normal manner regardless of where in the world the other parties are located. On the other hand, if the transactions are denominated in a foreign currency, special reporting considerations arise. Because the accounting records of domestic companies are stated in dollars, all transactions are recorded in dollars. Thus, if a sale or purchase is made and payment is in a foreign currency, the transaction is still recorded by the U.S. company in dollars. The amount of the sale or purchase is converted from the stated number of foreign currency units to dollars using the spot exchange rate at the date of the transaction. If, for example, a U.S. company purchased a shipment of cloth from a British manufacturer for £100,000 when the exchange rate was .65 British pound to $1, the company would record the purchase at $153,846 (£100,000 ÷ .65).

PAYMENT IN A FOREIGN CURRENCY

Most commercial transactions are on credit, and settlement does not take place for some period of time. Whenever a transaction involving borrowing or lending occurs between companies using two different currencies, the possibility of a gain or loss from currency fluctuations exists. For example, if a U.S. company sells merchandise to a customer in Mexico with the sale denominated in pesos and payment to be made in the future, the U.S. company is at risk because of the possibility of changes in the exchange rate of pesos for dollars. Similarly, if the U.S. company purchases merchandise on credit, with payment to be made in foreign currency units, the foreign currency units might either strengthen or weaken against the dollar, and the company might expend more or less dollars than if payment had been made immediately.

Companies that either hold foreign currency or receivables denominated in a foreign currency, or that owe amounts denominated in a foreign currency, are said to have exposed foreign currency positions. This means that they might have gains or losses from those foreign currency positions if the rate at which the foreign currency units can be converted to dollars changes. Such gains and losses are included in income in the period in which they occur.

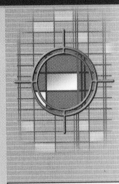

A CLOSER LOOK AT

PROFITS GONE UP IN SMOKE

Potbelly Heating Systems sold a large shipment of coal-burning stoves to a distributor in London for £250,000, payable in sixty days. Potbelly recorded a sale and a receivable of $400,000 based on a 1:1.60 exchange rate of pounds to dollars at the time of the sale. By the time the receivable came due and payment was made, the pound had weakened against the dollar, and the exchange rate was 1:1.55. Thus, when Potbelly collected the receivable and asked its bank to convert the pounds to dollars, the bank, using the current exchange rate of 1:1.55 at the time of collection, converted £250,000 into $387,500. The pounds would not buy as many dollars as they would have previously. Therefore, Potbelly incurred a loss from the currency fluctuation of $12,500 ($400,000 − $387,500), and this loss was recognized in its income statement.

Income Statement Effects	
Revenue	+ 400,000
Exchange Loss	+ 12,500
Net Income	+ 387,500

Balance Sheet Effects	
Assets	+ 400,000
Assets	− 12,500
Owners' Equity	+ 387,500

Journal Entries

Accounts Receivable	400,000	
Sales		400,000
Cash	387,500	
Foreign Currency Exchange Loss	12,500	
Accounts Receivable		400,000

The example reflects a loss from holding a receivable denominated in a currency that weakened against the dollar, but a U.S. company holding a receivable denominated in a currency that strengthened against the dollar would recognize a foreign exchange gain. If a company owed amounts payable in a foreign currency, the company would recognize a foreign exchange loss if the dollar were to weaken against the foreign currency and a gain if the dollar were to strengthen against the foreign currency.

You Decide 16-1

DO YOU WANT TO GO GLOBAL?

You have been working at Vanity Book Company as a part-time manager for the past year. Yesterday, you learned that the owner, Jean Daily, had received a standing order to ship fifty copies of the top ten new books each month to a distributor in Europe. The sales will be made at the current list price, plus a 20 percent charge for shipping and handling. Because you are really into accounting now, you know exactly what questions to ask. First, you ask whether the distributor will be paying in dollars. Then you ask whether payment will be made in advance. The answer from Jean is no to both questions. Payment will be made in euros within thirty days of the invoice date. A quick telephone call establishes that your local bank will change the euros into dollars for a 3 percent fee. Jean then asks, "Why are you frowning? It's a good deal, isn't it?" Do you think it is? What are the risks of participating in this plan?

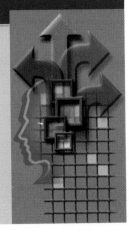

Companies having exposed foreign currency positions at the end of a fiscal period, holding either receivables or payables denominated in foreign currencies, must adjust their foreign-currency receivables and payables to the current dollar equivalent based on exchange rates at the balance sheet date. At the same time, gains or losses are recognized and reported in the income statement for the changes in the value of those receivables and payables because of changes in exchange rates. For example, if a U.S. company sold goods abroad for £100,000 at a time when the exchange rate was £1 to $1.50, it would recognize a sale and receivable for $150,000. If the company were still holding the receivable at the end of its fiscal year when the exchange rate was £1 to $1.54, the company would adjust the receivable to $154,000 (£100,000 × 1.54) to reflect the current exchange rate and recognize an exchange gain of $4,000.

REDUCING FOREIGN EXCHANGE RISK

Most companies are not in the business of trying to make money on changes in foreign currency exchange rates. They also do not want to be at risk when major exchange rate fluctuations occur because of the possibility of enormous losses. For example, Mexico devalued its peso by 50 percent in 1995, and assets denominated in pesos lost half of their value overnight. Thus, most companies try to avoid exposure to foreign exchange fluctuations.

One way of avoiding these risks is to denominate all international transactions in dollars, thus pushing the risk of currency fluctuations onto the other party. In many cases, however, this is not possible, and transactions must be denominated in the currency of the foreign country.

Another way of avoiding the risks associated with foreign exchange fluctuations is for a company with an exposed foreign currency position to offset, or **hedge,** that position. The most common type of hedge is to enter into a contract with a broker to buy or sell a fixed amount of foreign currency in the future at a price established now. This type of agreement is called a **forward exchange contract.** As an example, if you had to pay a Japanese supplier 750,000 yen six months from now, you could enter into an agreement with a broker to buy yen to be delivered in six months at a price set currently. Looking at Exhibit 16–3, you can see that the forward exchange rate for yen is listed in addition to the current exchange rate. This type of hedge fixes the purchase price of the yen to be used in paying the Japanese debt. When the time arrives to pay the debt, you pay the broker the agreed upon price in dollars and receive the yen, which are then used to pay the debt. Thus, even if the yen has increased in price by then, the amount you are required to pay remains unchanged. Whether a company pays more or less than the spot rate for a futures contract depends on the expected future change in the relative value of the currencies exchanged. Currency exchanges generally involve a small broker's commission, but the alternative is, in effect, to speculate on future currency fluctuations, and companies usually are eager to avoid this risk.

Companies can hedge both receivables and payables denominated in foreign currencies. While a foreign-currency liability is hedged by entering into a forward contract to purchase for dollars a foreign currency in the future at a price fixed currently, a foreign-currency receivable can be hedged by entering into a forward contract to sell for dollars a foreign currency in the future at a price fixed currently. As long as the forward contracts are strictly hedges by being for the same amounts and currencies as the foreign currency positions being covered, the gains or losses on the hedges are offset against the losses or gains on the covered positions, and no net gains or losses are recognized when exchange rates change. Gains and losses on speculative exchange agreements must be recognized in income currently.

Decision makers are interested in a company's policies with respect to hedging foreign currency positions because gains and losses from currency fluctuations can be substantial. Some companies have been very successful operating in the international arena, only to see their profits wiped out by unhedged foreign currency losses. Other companies have lost substantial amounts by speculating on possible future changes in exchange rates. Substantial gains or losses from currency fluctuations reported in a company's income statement indicate that either the company is not hedging exposed positions or it is speculating in the currency markets. In both cases, the risk is substantially higher than if the company avoided gains and losses from currency fluctuations. Decision makers should also examine the notes to the financial statements to determine company policies on hedging and speculation.

Gateway hedges its foreign currency transactions by using forward contracts. The company provides substantial disclosure regarding the hedging activities and related contracts in Note 1(p) to its financial statements, shown in Appendix A.

In Practice 16-2

HONEYWELL, INC.

Honeywell, a manufacturer of many types of control devices, does more than one-third of its business outside the United States. In its 1998 financial report, note 6 includes the following disclosure:

Honeywell has entered into various foreign currency exchange contracts designed to manage its exposure to exchange rate fluctuations on foreign currency transactions. Foreign exchange contracts reduce Honeywell's overall exposure to exchange rate movements, since the gains and losses on these contracts offset losses and gains on the assets, liabilities, and transactions being hedged. Honeywell hedges a significant portion of all known foreign exchange exposures, including non-functional currency receivables and payables and foreign currency imports and exports ... At December 31, 1998, these contracts generally have a term of less than one year and are primarily denominated in Belgian francs ($366.8), Deutsche marks ($253.3), Great Britain pounds ($129.9) and Canadian dollars ($89.3) [in millions].

ANALYSIS

Foreign exchange hedging contracts are an important business tool for Honeywell. The company does not want to take the risk of changing currency values, so rates are locked in with hedging contracts. [www.honeywell.com]

You Decide 16-2

WHAT IS A GOOD RETURN?

You want to invest the $10,000 your uncle gave you to get started when you graduate from college. Now that you are reading *The Wall Street Journal* regularly, you notice that Canadian government bonds due in five years pay 8½ percent interest, while U.S. government bonds for the same period are paying only 6½ percent. You know that a higher interest rate means more money, and you trust the Canadian government. How much more interest would you get from the Canadian bonds over the five-year period? If the current exchange rate is $.68 U.S. for 1 Canadian dollar , how much can the exchange rate go up or down during the next five years and still allow you to be ahead from investing in the Canadian bonds? Would you invest in the Canadian or U.S. bonds? Could you hedge your investment? Explain.

FINANCIAL STATEMENT TRANSLATION

Information for Decisions

When the financial statements of foreign subsidiaries or divisions are consolidated with those of the U.S. parent company, the accounting practices must be made consistent with those accepted in the United States and foreign currencies must be translated into U.S. dollars. Financial statement users need to understand the translation and reporting process so they can better assess the potential effects of global economic events on the companies they are examining and answer questions such as these: If a foreign subsidiary has an exposed asset position, what are the potential implications for future income and cash flows? What is implied by a large Cumulative Translation Adjustment reported in the balance sheet?

Not only do many U.S. companies engage in transactions with parties in other countries, but they often establish subsidiaries, divisions, or operating units abroad. Those foreign units frequently engage in transactions, maintain their records, and prepare financial statements all in the local currency. When the U.S. parent prepares its financial statements, however, U.S. accounting standards usually require that the financial statements of the company's foreign units be combined with those of the parent. These financial statements must all be combined and presented in U.S. dollars and using U.S. generally accepted accounting principles. Once the financial statements of foreign units are converted to U.S. accounting standards, they must then be translated from the foreign currency to U.S. dollars.

The currency of the primary operating environment in which a foreign unit spends and receives cash is referred to as its **functional currency.** For companies operating in the United States, the functional currency is the U.S. dollar. Gateway indicates that most of its international operations also use the dollar as the functional currency. The financial statements of those Gateway subsidiaries for which the local (foreign) currency is the functional currency must be translated into dollars to be combined with the financial statements of the parent.

In most cases, the financial statements of a foreign unit stated in its functional currency are translated into U.S. dollars using the **current rate method of translation.** Using this method, income statement amounts are translated at the exchange rates current at the date those elements were recognized. Because operating transactions occur frequently throughout the period, average exchange rates for the period are generally used for translating income statement amounts. Assets and liabilities are translated at the exchange rates current at the balance sheet date. Owners' equity accounts, except retained earnings, are translated at the rate that existed when the subsidiary or operating unit was created or when ownership was acquired. Retained earnings at the end of a period is computed by adding the translated net income to the retained earnings balance translated at the end of the last period and by deducting dividends for the period, translated at the date of declaration.

This translation process is relatively simple, but one complication arises. When this approach is used, the balance sheet will not balance. Because companies do not hold equal amounts of assets and liabilities, the translation process results in a net difference from changes in exchange rates. This difference is reported in the owners' equity section of the balance sheet as a **cumulative translation adjustment** (or accumulated other comprehensive income). The change in this accumulated translation adjustment from year to year is reported as an element of the company's other comprehensive income. This amount may be useful to decision makers in assessing the effects of changing exchange rates on the particular collection of foreign assets and liabilities held by the company.

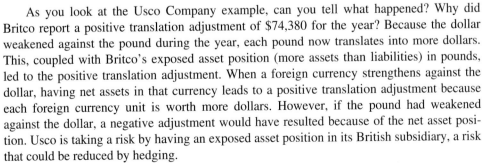

A CLOSER LOOK AT

FINANCIAL STATEMENT TRANSLATION

Assume that the following exchange rates existed between the British pound and the U.S. dollar at the dates indicated:

January 1, 1990	£1 = $1.80
January 1, 2001	1 = 1.60
December 31, 2001	1 = 1.64
Average for 2001	1 = 1.62

Usco Company is a U.S. corporation with a British subsidiary, Britco Company, which was established by Usco at the beginning of 1990. As of the beginning of 2001, Usco had a positive cumulative (over all prior periods) translation adjustment related to its British subsidiary of $67,300, and this amount was reported as an element of Usco's stockholders' equity in its December 31, 2000, balance sheet. In preparing consolidated financial statements for 2001, Usco must translate the financial statements of Britco to U.S. dollars. The translation of these statements using the current rate method is shown in Exhibit 16–4.

Britco's cumulative translation adjustment of $141,680, the amount needed to balance the translated balance sheet, has increased by $74,380 from the $67,300 reported in the December 31, 2000, balance sheet. This increase occurred because of the increase in the value of the pound during 2001. This positive adjustment is not included in net income, however. Instead, it is reported as an element of other comprehensive income, as shown in Britco's Statement of Comprehensive Income in Exhibit 16–4. The cumulative translation adjustment is reported in the balance sheet as an element of Britco's stockholders' equity.

As you look at the Usco Company example, can you tell what happened? Why did Britco report a positive translation adjustment of $74,380 for the year? Because the dollar weakened against the pound during the year, each pound now translates into more dollars. This, coupled with Britco's exposed asset position (more assets than liabilities) in pounds, led to the positive translation adjustment. When a foreign currency strengthens against the dollar, having net assets in that currency leads to a positive translation adjustment because each foreign currency unit is worth more dollars. However, if the pound had weakened against the dollar, a negative adjustment would have resulted because of the net asset position. Usco is taking a risk by having an exposed asset position in its British subsidiary, a risk that could be reduced by hedging.

Although Usco reported a positive translation adjustment in the example, many companies experience the opposite effect. For example, Baxter International reported a foreign currency translation loss of $75 million in 1998 and $202 million in 1997. These losses occurred because the company held foreign assets in excess of its foreign liabilities at a time when the dollar gained in strength.

EXHIBIT 16-4   **TRANSLATION OF FOREIGN-CURRENCY FINANCIAL STATEMENTS**

BRITCO COMPANY
INCOME STATEMENT
FOR THE YEAR ENDED DECEMBER 31, 2001

	Pounds	Exchange Rate	Dollars
Sales	£2,320,000	Average 1.62	$3,758,400
Cost of goods sold	(1,640,000)	1.62	(2,656,800)
Gross margin	£ 680,000		$1,101,600
Selling & administrative expenses	(310,000)	1.62	(502,200)
Interest expense	(84,500)	1.62	(136,890)
Net income	£ 285,500		$ 462,510

BRITCO COMPANY
STATEMENT OF COMPREHENSIVE INCOME
FOR THE YEAR ENDED DECEMBER 31, 2001

Net income	$462,510
Other comprehensive Income:	
Foreign currency translation adjustment	74,380
Comprehensive income	$536,890

BRITCO COMPANY
BALANCE SHEET
DECEMBER 31, 2001

	Pounds	Exchange Rate	Dollars
Assets:			
Cash	£ 131,000	12/31/01 1.64	$ 214,840
Accounts receivable	895,000	1.64	1,467,800
Inventory	1,250,000	1.64	2,050,000
Property and equipment (net)	3,419,000	1.64	5,607,160
Total assets	£5,695,000		$9,339,800
Liabilities:			
Accounts payable	£ 673,000	12/31/01 1.64	$1,103,720
Long-term debt	2,160,000	1.64	3,542,400
Total liabilities	£2,833,000		$4,646,120
Stockholders' equity:			
Common stock	£1,000,000	1/1/90 1.80	$1,800,000
Retained earnings	1,862,000	Computed	2,752,000
Cumulative translation adjustment		Balancing amount	141,680
Total equity	£2,862,000		$4,693,680
Total liabilities and equity	£5,695,000		$9,339,800

Operating in a global economy adds new levels of complexity to decision making. Not only must decision makers be concerned with foreign customs, laws, and regulations, but fluctuating currency exchange rates require close attention. Foreign holdings and transactions must always be evaluated in light of currency rate movements. When analyzing the information provided in companies' financial statements, questions such as "What is the exposed asset position?" and "How volatile is the currency?" have to be considered along with issues of liquidity, solvency, and profitability.

ARE THEY PAPER LOSSES?

During 2000, the Yankee Motor Bike Company invested more than $10 million in buildings and facilities in Poland so it could begin distributing motor bikes in Poland and other Eastern European countries. Capital for this venture was raised by borrowing dollars from U.S. banks and converting the dollars to Polish zlotys, which were then used in Poland to buy and build the distribution facilities. The Poland operation was established as a separate subsidiary, 80 percent owned by Yankee and 20 percent owned by the local government. The president of Yankee stated that the excellent opportunities for profits, as well as the chance to help out the Eastern European economies, more than offset the risks involved. Other than the risk that bikes cannot be sold at a profit in Poland, what risks does Yankee face? If the Polish zloty falls in value against the U.S. dollar during 2001, will Yankee show an exchange gain or loss in the consolidated financial statements? If a gain or loss related to changing exchange rates is included in the company's income for 2001, what is its source? If a cumulative gain or loss related to changing exchange rates is shown in Yankee's balance sheet, what is its source? Is it possible for Yankee to hedge its risks? How?

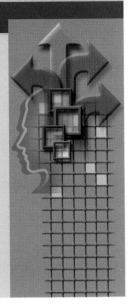

INTERNATIONAL ACCOUNTING STANDARDS

Information for Decisions

The lack of consistent accounting standards across different countries makes comparisons difficult for decision makers in a global economy. Because of the need for information useful in making decisions that extend beyond national boundaries, efforts are underway to develop and strengthen international accounting standards. An understanding of how accounting standards compare from country to country and the extent to which uniform international accounting standards are used helps decision makers more effectively employ the information available to them and answer questions such as these: To what extent is the net income of this foreign company comparable to a U.S. company in the same industry? Do the financial statements of the company reflect accounting standards aimed at full and fair disclosure or accounting standards that promote other goals, such as tax policy?

As the number of companies operating in a global environment has increased, the number of banks and financial institutions doing business in other countries, and the number of mutual funds and individual investors who hold ownership in foreign companies, has increased as well. With these changes, the demand for **international accounting standards** has become obvious. Decision makers need to be able to understand the financial reports of foreign companies and how they are prepared. They also need to be able to make meaningful comparisons between companies in different countries. However, the lack of consistency in accounting procedures from country to country hinders this process.

As an example, Japanese companies traditionally report low net income in their financial reports compared with equivalent companies in other countries, especially the United States. A primary reason is that Japanese law requires accounting income to equal taxable income. Therefore, Japanese companies tend to select accounting practices that result in the lowest possible reported income. Japanese companies commonly report the largest depreciation and inventory loss deductions possible, practices not followed in the United States. Thus, comparisons of financial reports between U.S. and Japanese companies can be misleading. Comparing cash flows might provide more meaningful information than accrual-basis income in this case.

Cultural differences also enter into the choice of accounting standards. In Germany, managers are less interested in short-term profitability than they are in continued long-term growth. Increased market share, development of new technology, and enterprise continuity are top priorities. On the other hand, the focus in the United States is on current operating results and earnings. It is not surprising that accounting procedures used in Germany are regarded as more conservative than those found in the United States.

Although comparisons between companies of different countries are difficult, and companies must often incur additional accounting and reporting costs when doing business in other countries, movement toward a solution has been slow. Why is international standardization difficult? As we saw earlier, accounting standards tend to follow the cultural and business practices of the country. Further, given nationalistic tendencies worldwide, no country wants "foreign" standards imposed on its accounting practices. Yet, most countries would welcome some type of compromise.

To help find that compromise, the **International Accounting Standards Committee (IASC)** was formed in 1973. Its membership consists of representatives from professional accounting bodies from more than a hundred countries, including the American Institute of CPAs. Although the IASC has no legal authority to enforce its standards, the professional groups in each country have pledged to support its efforts. The IASC has taken a diplomatic approach. It started by setting broad accounting principles and leaving the details of how the standards were to be applied to individual countries. The early IASC standards generally permitted several alternative treatments so that the practices of most major countries were encompassed within the standards. In the mid-1980s, the IASC began issuing new standards and amending existing standards to allow fewer alternatives. Its goal is to move, over time, to having common standards with few or no alternatives.

As an example of the IASC's approach, the original standards for valuing inventory included a wide range of methods, including LIFO, even though LIFO is used in few countries other than the United States. IASC's more recent standards permit a much narrower range of alternatives, and LIFO is permitted only if its effects on the income statement and balance sheet are disclosed. The disclosures of most U.S. companies now comply with the IASC inventory standards.

Although progress in establishing uniform international accounting standards has been slow, the stage is set for greater acceptance of international standards. The U.S. Securities and Exchange Commission (SEC) has agreed to accept standards developed by the IASC if certain conditions are met to ensure reliability and limiting of alternatives. The IASC is working actively to meet the conditions set by the SEC, and recent deliberations of the U.S. Financial Accounting Standards Board have included agreement with international standards as a key element. Further, regional trade groups, such as the European Union, are lowering trade and other barriers between the participating countries. As they do this, they are increasing the pressure for greater harmonization in accounting and financial reporting procedures.

More and more, decision makers are having to make decisions that involve U.S. companies operating abroad and foreign companies operating or raising capital in this country. A firm understanding of U.S. accounting practices, and how those of other countries differ, is essential when making comparisons across national boundaries.

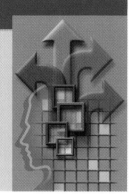

You Decide 16-4

WHAT HAPPENED TO NET INCOME?

An article in *The Wall Street Journal* described a computer model developed to demonstrate the effects of differing global accounting standards.[2] The model, created by two Rider College professors, used an imaginary company with gross revenues of $1.5 million. According to the article, the company would report net income of $34,000 in the United States, $260,600 in Britain, and $240,600 in Australia. As an investor looking for opportunities worldwide, which country would you choose? Why? If the differences are all the result of different accounting standards, is there one right choice? What kind of accounting standards could cause this much difference?

ANALYSIS OF GLOBAL BUSINESSES

Information for Decisions

Most global companies report key financial figures by geographic area. This information can help decision makers analyze the potential rewards and risks of a company's operations and answer questions such as these: In which geographic areas should the company expand its operations? How dependent is the company on operations in unstable regions of the world?

As we have seen previously, the use of standard financial ratios and comparisons can help in making decisions and in identifying areas that warrant closer examination. When analyzing global enterprises, an examination of international operations separate from domestic operations and in relation to overall operations is often important. Let's look at an example.

As you can see from Exhibit 16–5, McDonald's Corporation reports, in a note to its financial statements, revenues, income, and assets by geographic region. McDonald's had an overall operating income margin (operating income ÷ sales) of 22.2 percent in 1998 and 24.6 percent in both 1997 and 1996. These results reflect a respectable, but not spectacular, return on sales. Although sales are increasing, the operating margin trend is static to negative.

Because McDonald's is a truly global company, with restaurants in more than 115 countries, an examination of the company's operations by geographic region might prove useful.

[2]Lee Burton, "All Accountants Soon May Speak the Same Language," *The Wall Street Journal* (August 29, 1995), p. A15.

Based on the information in Exhibit 16–5, operating margins for the company's different geographic regions can be computed as follows:

	Operating Income Margin		
	1998	**1997**	**1996**
United States	21.4%	26.3%	24.9%
Europe	25.5	25.6	26.4
Asia/Pacific	21.5	24.2	27.9
Latin America	22.7	23.5	19.1
Other	18.5	18.1	19.2

What does this information imply for McDonald's future growth? Partly the answer depends on what happens to the worldwide economy. During much of 1997 and 1998, the U.S. economy was extremely strong, but the economies of countries in the rest of the world were weak, in some cases, seriously so. This weakness is especially reflected in the declining margins for the Asia/Pacific area, which reported margins between 30 percent and 40 percent in the early 1990s. Margins in the European segment held up well given the weak economies, but U.S. margins are disappointing in the midst of a record economy and reflect heavy competition in the fast-food business.

For McDonald's, this data with current economic forecasts might imply that McDonald's should focus on Europe and the Asia/Pacific areas. With the improving European

EXHIBIT 16-5

MCDONALD'S CORPORATION GEOGRAPHIC SEGMENT INFORMATION

Segment and geographic information

The Company operates exclusively in the food service industry. Substantially all revenues result from the sale of menu products at restaurants operated by the Company, franchisees or affiliates. The Company's reportable segments are based on geographic area. All intercompany revenues and expenses are eliminated in computing revenues and operating income. The Other segment includes Canada, Africa and the Middle East.

(In millions)	1998	1997	1996
U.S.	$ 4,868.1	$ 4,602.7	$ 4,590.3
Europe	4,466.7	3,931.5	3,613.8
Asia/Pacific	1,633.2	1,522.8	1,272.8
Latin America	814.7	709.2	595.7
Other	638.7	642.6	613.9
Total revenues	$12,421.4	$11,408.8	$10,686.5
U.S.	$ 1,043.9	$ 1,210.8	$ 1,144.0
Europe	1,139.8	1,007.2	953.8
Asia/Pacific	351.4	369.1	355.1
Latin America	184.7	166.5	113.7
Other	118.2	116.3	118.0
Corporate	(76.1)	(61.6)	(52.0)
Total operating income	$ 2,761.9	$ 2,808.3	$ 2,632.6
U.S.	$ 7,795.4	$ 7,753.4	$ 7,553.5
Europe	6,932.1	6,005.4	5,925.3
Asia/Pacific	2,659.7	2,125.6	2,111.8
Latin America	1,339.6	1,177.8	900.3
Other	678.7	661.6	622.8
Corporate	378.9	517.7	272.3
Total assets	$19,784.4	$18,241.5	$17,386.0

economies, the already relatively high margins might be increased. As the Asia/Pacific economies improve, the decrease in margins during the past several years may reverse just as dramatically. In fact, preliminary 1999 data show McDonald's sales and operating margins increasing significantly in Europe (excluding Russia) and the Asia/Pacific segments, and operating margins increasing in the United States despite lackluster sales increases.

You Decide 16-5

WHERE DO WE GO NEXT?

You have been asked to provide an analysis to help your company decide whether to expand its domestic or its international operations. Your company now conducts about 70 percent of its business in the United States and about 30 percent in Europe and in the Asia/Pacific region. You request a printout of operating results for the past two years and are given the information shown below. What is your recommendation with respect to where your company's expansion should take place? Explain.

		United States	Europe	Asia/Pacific
Revenue	2000	$200,000	$50,000	$20,000
	1999	200,000	30,000	10,000
Net Income	2000	$16,000	$5,000	$3,000
	1999	20,000	3,000	1,000
Assets	2000	$300,000	$75,000	$25,000
	1999	240,000	40,000	10,000

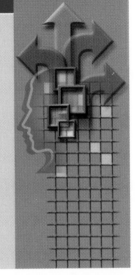

SUMMARY

Few businesses or individuals remain untouched today by the global economy. Most major businesses now operate internationally to expand their opportunities and increase their rate of return. For many companies, the return and growth rate is higher in countries outside the United States, and many major companies must be considered more multinational companies than domestic.

Although many rewards are found in international operations, additional risks are incurred as well. Customs, laws, regulations, and business practices all differ from country to country and add complexity to operating in a global economy.

One important factor affecting transactions across international boundaries is that different countries use different currencies. Companies engaging in transactions that are denominated in foreign currencies and that hold assets or liabilities denominated in foreign currencies are at risk for exchange gains and losses that arise when exchange rates change. These gains and losses are treated as a normal cost of doing business and must be reported in income as incurred. However, foreign-currency assets or liabilities that are exposed to this type of risk can be hedged by entering into forward contracts to buy or sell a specified number of foreign currency units in the future at a price determined currently. Gains and losses on hedge contracts are then offset against the losses and gains on foreign-currency asset or liability position so that no net gain or loss need be reported. Gains and losses from currency speculation must be reported in the period incurred. Notes to the financial statements usually provide important information about foreign currency exposure and the degree to which it is hedged.

When companies structure their foreign operations as separate divisions or subsidiaries, the financial statements of those units must be translated into U.S. dollars before being combined with statements reflecting U.S. operations. The foreign-currency financial statements are translated into dollars using the year-end exchange rate for assets and liabilities and the period's average exchange rate for income statement elements. Because exchange rates change over time, translation adjustments (gains and losses) occur. These translation adjustments are not included in net income, however. Instead, they are reported as other comprehensive income for the period and are included on a cumulative basis as a separate element of stockholders' equity.

One impediment to international trade and investing across national boundaries is that different countries have different accounting standards. Therefore, financial statements issued by a company in another country may not be comparable to those in the United States. The International Accounting Standards Committee has attempted to bring about uniformity of standards throughout the world, and it has had some limited success. Nevertheless, increased global trading and investing and the advent of regional alliances should lead to more widely followed global standards.

Because international operations are so important for many companies, financial statement analysis should include careful attention to a company's operations and holdings abroad. The types of analyses applied to the company as a whole should also be applied to its geographic segment information, where possible. In this way, decision makers can better assess the rewards and risks of international activities.

LIST OF IMPORTANT TERMS

cumulative translation adjustment
  (640)

current rate method of translation
  (640)

exchange rate *(634)*

forward exchange contract
  (638)

forward rate *(634)*

functional currency *(640)*

hedge *(638)*

international accounting standards
  (643)

International Accounting Standards
  Committee (IASC) *(644)*

spot rate *(634)*

EXAMINING THE CONCEPTS

Q16-1 How would you distinguish between doing business overseas and being a global company?

Q16-2 Identify two U.S. companies other than those mentioned in the chapter that do a significant proportion of their business in countries outside the United States. How do you know they are U.S. companies?

Q16-3 Would the existence of a fixed exchange rate between countries reduce the risk of entering into business transactions with companies in other countries? Explain.

Q16-4 What factors might cause currency exchange rates to fluctuate?

Q16-5 For companies doing business internationally, why is specification of the currency in which transactions are denominated important?

Q16-6 If you are holding a note receivable denominated in Canadian dollars and the exchange rate changes from $1.35 (Canadian) for $1 (U.S.) to $1.25 (Canadian) for $1 (U.S.) prior to collection, would you have a gain or loss?

Q16-7 If you have the choice of denominating a transaction with a French customer in U.S. dollars or in euros, which choice would eliminate the risk of exchange loss on the transaction? Explain why.

Q16-8 Why do companies become involved in transactions denominated in foreign currencies?

Q16-9 How are exchange gains and losses on receivables and payables denominated in foreign currencies reported?

Q16-10 When you are holding a receivable denominated in Japanese yen and the dollar weakens (it takes more dollars to buy yen), will you have an exchange gain or loss?

Q16-11 If you suspect that a country might devalue its currency, would you be better paying off loans denominated in that currency now or after the devaluation? Why?

Q16-12 Explain the statement, "Acme uses foreign currency exchange contracts to hedge underlying exposures such as nonfunctional currency receivables and payables. Company policy prohibits speculation in foreign currency contracts."

Q16-13 The *spot rate* is a term used to identify the current rate of exchange between two currencies. What term is used to identify the rate of exchange at some date in the future? How are contracts for future exchanges of currencies used by businesses?

Q16-14 What kind of transactions or what set of business decisions would lead to an exposed liability position in a foreign currency?

Q16-15 How are gains and losses from holding foreign currencies and from agreements for future exchanges of foreign currencies recognized?

Q16-16 What is a functional currency? When will a company choose U.S. dollars as its functional currency?

Q16-17 What is meant by financial statement translation? In very general terms, how is this process accomplished?

Q16-18 Explain how using the current rate method of currency translation can result in a gain or loss. How is this gain or loss reported?

Q16-19 If a company is based in Germany, but manufactures and sells products in the United States, would you expect its primary financial statements to be prepared in dollars or in euros? Explain.

Q16-20 What is a cumulative translation adjustment, and how is it reported in the financial statements?

Q16-21 How can you tell whether a company had a foreign currency translation gain or loss in the current year?

Q16-22 If a company discloses in its financial statements that it has an exposed asset position, what does this tell you about its foreign currency risks?

Q16-23 Why might a company use different depreciation methods in different countries?

Q16-24 What role does the International Accounting Standards Committee play in setting international accounting standards? What is IASC's goal?

Q16-25 Why is a single set of accounting standards not adopted by all countries?

Q16-26 How could management's decisions benefit from information about the net income margin earned in each country or region in which the company operates?

UNDERSTANDING ACCOUNTING INFORMATION

E16-1 Decisions Making in a Global Economy Your company has been manufacturing its products exclusively in the United States. Because of increased sales to Europe, you are considering establishing a plant in France. In what way might each of the following affect your decision on whether to build a manufacturing plant in France?

a. Stability of the currency in international markets.
b. Availability of capital through the sale of bonds or common stock.
c. Tax policies and procedures.
d. Tariffs and import restrictions.

E16-2 Financial Reporting for Global Businesses U.S. Company recently established a subsidiary in Japan to facilitate sales in that country. In analyzing the financial statements prepared by the subsidiary and consolidating its financial statements with those of the U.S. parent company, representatives of the U.S. Company have questioned whether the accounting standards used in Japan or the United States should be utilized. Explain your answers to each of the following:

a. Which accounting principles should be used by the subsidiary in recording its activities and in preparing financial statements to be provided to creditors in Japan?
b. Which accounting principles should be applied when computing income taxes payable in Japan?
c. Which accounting principles should be used in accounting for the subsidiary when its financial statements are consolidated with those of the parent company?
d. What would be the likely cause if, after a successful first year of operations in Japan, the value of the subsidiary's net assets included in the parent company's consolidated statements declined from the beginning of the year to the end of the year?

E16-3 Reporting Transactions Denominated in Foreign Currencies Downfield Corporation is U.S.-based and has substantial sales in the countries of Toyland and Barkland. Downfield's international sales are denominated in the currency of the country of the purchaser, and payment is received 120 days after delivery of the product. Explain your answers to each of the following:

a. Should Downfield Corporation record sales revenue at the time the products are delivered to its international customers or when payment is received?
b. During the last year, Downfield recorded a rather large foreign currency exchange gain on its accounts receivable from customers in the country of Toyland. Did the value of the currency of Toyland increase or decrease against the U.S. dollar during the year?
c. Although substantial sales were made in Barkland during the year and its currency decreased in value against the U.S. dollar, Downfield did not report a foreign currency exchange loss in its income statement for the year because it had hedged its receivable balances.
    1. What type of transaction did Downfield enter into to hedge its receivables?
    2. Does the fact that Downfield hedged its receivables mean that it did not record a loss on the value of its receivables?
    3. How did entering into a hedge transaction permit Downfield to avoid reporting a loss?

E16-4 Financial Statement Translation Americana Corporation established several foreign subsidiaries 20 years ago and the subsidiaries are included in the consolidated financial statements of Americana Corporation. In reviewing Americana's consolidated financial statements prepared at December 31, 2000, you are asked by a colleague to explain each of the following:

a. Why is a different exchange rate used in translating the amounts reported in the income statement and balance sheet?

b. Is a cumulative translation adjustment reported in the books of the subsidiary companies or only in the consolidated financial statements? Explain why.

c. Although Americana's subsidiaries reported a profit for 2000, the cumulative translation adjustment reported in the consolidated balance sheet decreased. How might this occur?

d. How does the amount by which the subsidiary's assets exceed its liabilities affect the change in the cumulative translation adjustment during the year when the value of its currency increases against the dollar?

E16-5 International Accounting Standards   The reporting practices used by companies in the country of Crossbow are more conservative than those used in the United States and typically result in lower reported income.

a. Why has progress been slow in developing uniform international accounting standards?

b. Which accounting body was been established to assist in developing greater uniformity in accounting standards between countries? What authority does this organization have?

c. Identify two accounting practices that might be used in the country of Crossbow that would result in more conservative financial statements than those produced in the United States.

d. What actions might investors take to compare a U.S. company and a Crossbow company?

E16-6 Multiple Choice: Exchange Transactions   Select the correct answer for each of the following:

1. When a company operates in a global environment, decisions about its operations may be influenced by:
   a. The currency in which transactions take place.
   b. Differences in the nature of economic activity between countries.
   c. The proportion of sales that take place in each country.
   d. All of the above factors.

2. A sale on credit from a U.S. company to a customer in a different country may involve an exchange gain or loss if:
   a. The exchange rate between the currencies remains fixed.
   b. The sale is denominated in U.S. dollars.
   c. The seller accepts the currency of the buyer as payment.
   d. The exchange transaction takes place after year-end.

3. If Ward Manufacturing, a U.S. company, sells heavy equipment to a customer in London and accepts a note receivable denominated in British pounds, due in 90 days, Ward could suffer an exchange loss when:
   a. The customer does not make full payment because of defects in the equipment.
   b. The value of the pound increases relative to the dollar (a pound buys more dollars) before the note is paid.

c. The value of the pound decreases relative to the dollar (a pound buys fewer dollars) before the note is paid.

d. The note requires that interest be paid in British pounds.

4. Jurgens Arts, a U.S. company, buys and sells art objects that it purchases from Southeast Asian countries. A recent shipment arrived from Indonesia. The bill is for 7 million rupiah, payable in 30 days. The current exchange rate is 7,000 rupiah for $1. Jurgens would record the transaction as:

a. Art Inventory	7,000,000	
Accounts Payable		7,000,000
b. Art Inventory	1,000	
Accounts Payable		1,000
c. Art Inventory	7,000	
Accounts Payable		1,000
Exchange Gain		6,000
d. Art Inventory	7,000	
Accounts Payable		7,000

E16-7 Multiple Choice: Exchange Rates   Select the correct answer for each of the following:

1. The Albert Company makes a $1,000,000 loan to its Swiss subsidiary when the spot rate is 1.50 Swiss francs for $1 and the 90-day forward rate is 1.45 francs for $1. At the time of the loan, the Swiss subsidiary will record in francs a liability of:
   a. 666,667 francs.
   b. 145,000 francs.
   c. 1,500,000 francs.
   d. 689,655 francs.

2. Beata Clothing Company buys on credit a shipment of winter coats from Poland at a cost of 410,000 zlotys. The spot rate is 4.10 zlotys to $1 at the time of the sale. If the rate is 4.00 zlotys to $1 when payment is made, Beata will have experienced an exchange:
   a. Gain of $2,500.
   b. Loss of $2,500.
   c. Gain of $4,100.
   d. Loss of $4,100

3. You have been sent by your company to buy $10,000 of leather goods in Mexico for a special promotion. You know that you will have to make the purchases in Mexican pesos, so you look up the exchange rates. You find that the spot rate is 9.50 pesos to $1 and the 30-day forward rate is 9.80 pesos to $1. When you exchange your dollars for pesos today, you can expect to receive:
   a. 98,000 pesos.
   b. 1,053 pesos.
   c. 1,020 pesos.
   d. 95,000 pesos.

4. When currency exchange rates are allowed to move freely:
   a. Rates will usually remain the same over a long period of time.

b. There is a risk of an exchange gain or loss on outstanding receivables denominated in a foreign currency.

c. The forward rate will be the same as the spot exchange rate.

d. All of the above.

E16-8 Multiple Choice: Hedging Select the correct answer for each of the following:

1. A company might use a hedge:
   a. When it has equal foreign currency asset and liability positions.
   b. To avoid paying a liability denominated in a foreign currency.
   c. When it has a large receivable denominated in U.S. dollars.
   d. When it has a large receivable denominated in a foreign currency.

2. When a company does not hedge an exposed asset position denominated in a foreign currency, it will:
   a. Realize an exchange loss if the assets decline in value.
   b. Realize an exchange gain if the foreign currency becomes weaker (more units in exchange for a dollar).
   c. Realize an exchange loss if the foreign currency becomes weaker (more units in exchange for a dollar).
   d. Both a and b are correct.

3. Your company buys much of its raw materials in the country of Bactar, and you have been following the country's economy. You believe that Bactar's currency, the bak, may lose some of its value relative to the dollar, and you want to use this information to help your company. If the bak declines in value (more baks are required per $1), you can expect the cost of your raw materials to:
   a. Increase because the dollar is now stronger.
   b. Decrease because the dollar is now stronger.
   c. Remain the same if you have been making the purchases in baks.
   d. Not be affected unless there is an exposed liability position.

4. Which of the following are risks that you might expect a company to hedge against?
   a. An exposed asset position in a foreign subsidiary.
   b. An exposed liability position in a foreign subsidiary.
   c. Purchase commitments denominated in a foreign currency.
   d. All of the above.

E16-9 Multiple Choice: Financial Statement Translation Select the correct answer for each of the following:

1. A U.S. company has subsidiaries in several different countries. The subsidiaries prepare their financial statements stated in the local currencies. The U.S. parent company:
   a. Cannot prepare consolidated financial statements.
   b. Must identify the functional currency of each subsidiary and prepare consolidated financial statements in that currency.

c. Must prepare consolidated financial statements in U.S. dollars and include the foreign subsidiaries.

d. Must require each of the subsidiaries to keep their records in U.S. dollars.

2. The current rate method of foreign currency translation converts:
   a. Income and inventory at the average exchange rate for the year and all other financial statement items at the year-end exchange rate.
   b. All of the asset and liability accounts at the average exchange rate.
   c. All of the income statement accounts at the average exchange rate for the year.
   d. Property, plant, and equipment at historical exchange rates.

3. When a company reports a cumulative translation adjustment in its balance sheet, the information can be used to help determine:
   a. Whether the company has subsidiaries or divisions that keep records stated in foreign currencies.
   b. Whether the company's foreign operations have been profitable.
   c. The length of time the subsidiary has been owned.
   d. The amount of sales to a foreign subsidiary.

4. The Avante Company's Italian subsidiary has completed 1 year of operation as a Western European distribution center. The financial statements for the year, in lira, have been sent to Avante's home office in New York for consolidation using the current rate method. You are surprised to find that the converted statements do not balance unless a significant positive cumulative translation adjustment (gain) is included. This gain may be the result of:
   a. A significant exposed asset position of the subsidiary and a decrease in the value of the lira during the year.
   b. A significant exposed liability position of the subsidiary and a decrease in the value of the lira during the year.
   c. An insufficient original investment in the subsidiary.
   d. None of the above.

E16-10 Multiple Choice: International Accounting and Analysis Select the correct answer for each of the following:

1. The current status of international accounting standards is that:
   a. International standards only apply to those companies that list their securities on U.S. stock exchanges.
   b. International standards require all companies to prepare their published financial statements in accordance with their national tax laws.
   c. Companies in all countries must adopt international accounting standards before their securities can be traded.
   d. The International Accounting Standards Committee has no legal authority to enforce the standards that it has adopted.

2. International accounting standards benefit decision makers by:
   a. Assuring that the income reported by a company in its financial statements is the same as the income used for computing taxes payable.
   b. Assuring that companies focus on long-term stability rather than on reporting high current income.
   c. Assisting in investment decisions that require comparisons between companies operating in different countries.
   d. Eliminating the risk of exchange gains or losses from fluctuations in currency exchange rates.

3. Standardization of international accounting has made progress, but each step is difficult because:
   a. Accounting standards often reflect each individual country's economic and cultural preferences.
   b. There is a natural reluctance for a country to adopt "foreign standards."
   c. The formal organizations that are working toward standardization do not have legal status in many countries.
   d. All of the above.

4. The Glenn Company makes 75 percent of its sales in the United States and 25 percent in Germany. The gross margin on sales in the United States is 20 percent, and it is 40 percent in Germany. If these gross margin rates remain unchanged, a $100,000 increase in sales in Germany would generate:
   a. Three-fourths as much gross margin as an equivalent increase in sales in the United States.
   b. Twice as much gross margin on sales as an equivalent increase in sales in the United States.
   c. Three times as much gross margin as an equivalent increase in sales in the United States.
   d. One-fourth as much gross margin as an equivalent increase in sales in the United States.

5. The Fantasy Company earned an 11 percent net income margin on all of its global operations in 2000. As an interested decision maker, you want to know whether Fantasy will increase this margin in 2001. You would be interested in:
   a. Whether the sales revenue generated in each country is expected to change.
   b. Whether the operating income margins in the individual countries are all equal.
   c. Whether Fantasy expects changes in production and general and administrative costs in the individual countries.
   d. All of the above.

E16-11 Foreign Currency Conversion You have been assigned to review the safety features in the information services department of each division of your company. To do this, you are planing a trip to 3 different countries in Europe. Your company has provided you with all the necessary travel tickets; however, you will have to pay your own daily expenses and be reimbursed later. You are scheduled to spend 4 days in France, 2 days in Belgium, and 5 days in Germany. You estimate that your expenses will be $400 per day. You want to be able to pay in local currency, so you call your bank and get the following exchange rates:

France (franc)	6.10 to $1
Belgium (franc)	37.57 to $1
Germany(mark)	1.82 to $1

How much of each currency will you need for your trip?

E16-12 Sales Denominated in Foreign Currency Swift Corporation sold products to a foreign company with the sales price stated in FCU (foreign currency units). The products were delivered on November 1, 2001, at an agreed-upon price of 400,000 FCU. Payment is to be received on March 1, 2002. Swift Corporation's year-end is December 31, 2001. Relevant exchange rates are as follows:

November 1, 2001	1 FCU = $3.00 U.S.
December 31, 2001	1 FCU = $3.08 U.S.
March 1, 2002	1 FCU = $3.02 U.S.

a. What sale price should Swift Corporation record at November 1, 2001?
b. What is the value of Swift's accounts receivable at December 31, 2001?
c. What amount of gain or loss on foreign currency transactions should Swift record at December 31, 2001?
d. What is the value of the payment received at March 1, 2002?
e. What amount of gain or loss on foreign currency transactions should Swift record at March 1, 2002?
f. Was Swift better off or worse off from having received payment on March 1, 2002, rather than on November 1, 2001? By what amount?

E16-13 Sales Denominated in Foreign Currency Trend Corporation sold products to a foreign company with the sales price stated in FCU (foreign currency units). The products were delivered on December 1, 2001, at an agreed-upon price of 250,000 FCU. Payment is to be received on February 1, 2002. Trend Corporation's year-end is December 31, 2001. Relevant exchange rates are as follows:

December 1, 2001	1 FCU = $4.10 U.S.
December 31, 2001	1 FCU = $3.82 U.S.
February 1, 2002	1 FCU = $4.07 U.S.

a. What sale price should Trend Corporation record at December 1, 2001?
b. What is the value of Trend's accounts receivable at December 31, 2001?

c. What amount of gain or loss on foreign currency transactions should Trend record at December 31, 2001?

d. What is the value of the payment received at February 1, 2002?

e. What amount of gain or loss on foreign currency transactions should Trend record at February 1, 2002?

f. Was Trend Corporation better off or worse off from having received payment on February 1, 2002, rather than on December 1, 2001? By what amount?

E16-14 Purchases Denominated in Foreign Currency
Superior Lighting Company purchased light fixtures from a foreign company with the purchase price stated in FCU (foreign currency units). The products were received on November 1, 2000, at an agreed-upon price of 400,000 FCU. Payment is to be made on March 1, 2001. Superior Lighting Corporation's year-end is December 31, 2000. Relevant exchange rates are as follows:

November 1, 2000	1 FCU = $3.00 U.S.
December 31, 2000	1 FCU = $3.08 U.S.
March 1, 2001	1 FCU = $3.02 U.S.

a. What amount should Superior Lighting record as the purchase price of the lighting fixtures at November 1, 2000?

b. What amount should Superior Lighting report as its accounts payable at December 31, 2000?

c. What amount of gain or loss on foreign currency transactions should Superior Lighting record at December 31, 2000?

d. What dollar amount should Superior Lighting report for its payment on March 1, 2001?

e. What amount of gain or loss on foreign currency transactions should Superior Lighting record at March 1, 2001?

f. Was Superior Lighting better off or worse off from having delayed payment on its account until March 1, 2001, rather than paying on November 1, 2000? By what amount?

E16-15 Purchases Denominated in Foreign Currency
Western Import Company purchased inventory items from a foreign company with the purchase price stated in FCU (foreign currency units). The inventory items were received on December 1, 2000, at an agreed-upon price of 250,000 FCU. Payment is to be made on February 1, 2001. Western Import's year-end is December 31, 2000. Relevant exchange rates are as follows:

December 1, 2000	1 FCU = $4.10 U.S.
December 31, 2000	1 FCU = $3.82 U.S.
February 1, 2001	1 FCU = $4.07 U.S.

a. What amount should Western Import record as the purchase price of the inventory items at December 1, 2000?

b. What amount should Western Import report as its accounts payable at December 31, 2000?

c. What amount of gain or loss on foreign currency transactions should Western Import record at December 31, 2000?

d. What dollar amount should Western Import report for its payment on February 1, 2001?

e. What amount of gain or loss on foreign currency transactions should Western Import record at February 1, 2001?

f. Was Western Import better off or worse off from having delayed payment on its account until February 1, 2001, rather than paying on December 1, 2000? By what amount?

E16-16 Exchange Transactions The Kraft Company, based in the United States, recently made a large sale to a new customer in Sweden. The sale totaled 2.2 million Swedish Krona, and payment is to be received in Krona in 90 days. If the spot rate of exchange is 8.389 Swedish Krona to $1 on the date of the sale and the 90-day forward rate is 8.295 to 1:

a. How much will Kraft Company report as sales revenue and accounts receivable on the date of the sale?

b. How much gain or loss will Kraft incur if the exchange rate is 8.280 when the receivable is collected and the company does not hedge?

c. How will the gain or loss in part b be reported?

E16-17 Exchange Transactions The Worldwide Company sent its catalog to several distributors in foreign countries this year, and, for the first time, it received orders from outside the United States. Thus far, all buyers have paid in U.S. dollars. However, next year Worldwide is considering accepting payment in other currencies. To demonstrate how payments in foreign currencies would affect the company, you agree to illustrate how some of this year's sales would have been reported in the financial statements if the payments had been received in other currencies. For each of the following sales transactions, show how the transaction was reported at the date of sale and the date of collection in dollars, and how the transaction would have been reported if the payment had been received in the foreign currency of the customer:

a. A sale of $53,000 to a German customer made on account to be paid in 30 days. The spot rate at the date of sale was 1.82 marks to $1. At the collection date, the rate was 1.84 marks to $1.

b. A sale of $87,000 to a French customer made on account to be paid in 60 days. The spot rate at the date of sale was 6.18 francs to $1. At the collection date, the rate was 6.15 francs to $1.

c. A sale of $21,000 to an Australian customer was collected in cash. The spot rate at the date of the sale was 1.53 Australian dollars to $1 (U.S.).

E16-18 Exchange Gains and Losses You are analyzing the financial statements of a distributing company that you know makes sales to customers in several foreign countries. You are also sure that the sales are not always stated in dollars, so there is the possibility that the company has had exchange gains or losses. However, when you look at the income statement, no gains or losses on foreign currency transactions appear.

a. Is it possible that the company had no gains or losses? Under what circumstances could this be the case?

b. If the company had exchange gains and losses, where are they most likely to be reported in the financial statements? Where would you look in the annual report to try to find out more about the company's foreign currency activities?

E16-19   Net Asset Position   Tropic Corporation discloses in its financial statements that it has an exposed asset position in a subsidiary located in another country:

a. What foreign currency risks has the company assumed as a result of its investment?

b. How can a decision maker assess the riskiness of a company's exposed asset position in another currency?

c. Why might the cumulative translation adjustment reported in Tropic's consolidated balance sheet not represent the amount Tropic would realize as a gain or loss if it sold its ownership of the subsidiary?

E16-20   Forward Contracts   Assume that each of the following transactions can be hedged by buying or selling Japanese yen in the forward market. The quoted yen to dollar exchange rates are:

Spot	¥120 = $1
30-day forward	¥110 = $1
60-day forward	¥114 = $1
180-day forward	¥112 = $1

If Spiller Company hedges each of the following transactions (except d), what dollar amount will the company receive or pay when the receivable or payable is settled?

a. Auto parts inventory is purchased for ¥2,400,000 payable in 60 days.

b. Photographic supplies are sold for ¥800,000, with payment to be received in 30 days.

c. Cartons and other fast-food supplies are sold for ¥4,000,000, with payment to be received in 180 days.

d. Artworks are purchased for ¥700,000 payable immediately in cash.

E16-21   Using Forward Contracts   The Moller Company is involved in global operations. A footnote in its 2000 financial report includes the following statement: "The Moller Company uses forward and option contracts to hedge its exposure to fluctuations in foreign currency rates. At year-end, contract commitments and balance sheet exposures were hedged with forward contracts."

a. Identify an example of a contract commitment that would have an exposure to fluctuating foreign currency rates.

b. Describe how a balance sheet asset exposure can be hedged with forward contracts.

c. What is the potential risk of a balance sheet liability exposure in a time of fluctuating exchange rates? Why would this exposure influence your evaluation of the company? Would the country in which the liability exists influence your decision?

E16-22   Hedging Other than Currency   Hedges are a way to fix the price of a currency or any other product, especially commodities. Other than for currencies, identify two industries in which hedging might be used. Describe specifically the products involved and how hedging might be used to benefit companies in those industries.

E16-23   Hedging Payables   Trade Corporation signed a contract to purchase electronic gauges from a foreign company with payment to be made in FCU (foreign currency units). A shipment costing 700,000 FCU was received on July 1 when the exchange rate was 20 FCU to $1. Trade Corporation paid for the gauges on September 1 when the exchange rate was 17 FCU to $1. Trade Corporation could have hedged its liability at the time it received the gauges by purchasing FCU for delivery on September 1 at a price of 19 FCU to $1.

a. What amount should Trade Corporation report as the purchase price of the gauges?

b. What was the actual amount paid by Trade Corporation on September 1, assuming it did not hedge its liability?

c. Trade Corporation considered entering into a contract with an exchange broker on July 1 to receive 700,000 FCU on September 1 as a hedge of its liability. The exchange broker would have charged a fee of $3,000 for entering into the contract. Would Trade Corporation have been better off or worse off by hedging its liability? By what amount?

E16-24   Financial Statement Translation   The following items will be included in Global Company's consolidated financial statements, which include several foreign subsidiaries. The current rate method is to be used in translating the financial statements of the foreign subsidiaries to dollars. Indicate which exchange rate or other amount will be used in translating each of the items: the current rate at the balance sheet date (CR), the average rate for the year (AR), or a computed amount (CA).

Cash	_____	Property, plant, & equipment	_____
Sales	_____	Retained earnings	_____
Inventory	_____	Cost of goods sold	_____
Net income	_____	Accounts receivable	_____
Common stock	_____	Selling expense	_____
Goodwill	_____	Prepaid expenses	_____
Bonds payable	_____	Current maturities of bonds	_____
Depreciation	_____	Translation adjustment	_____

E16-25 Financial Statement Translation The Overseas Company reported a cumulative translation adjustment gain of $357,000 on its balance sheet at the end of last year. You have been eagerly awaiting the balance sheet for this year because you know that the dollar has strengthened against most world currencies this year (each dollar buys more units of a foreign currency). You expect an even larger positive cumulative translation adjustment in the balance sheet at the end of this year. However, when the financial statements arrive, you are very disappointed to find that there is a $217,000 cumulative translation adjustment loss reported on the balance sheet.

a. What is the total amount of the cumulative translation loss for this year alone?
b. What might explain the negative cumulative translation adjustment in the balance sheet when the dollar had strengthened during the year?
c. Prepare an example to show what might have led to a negative cumulative translation adjustment in the current year after reporting a positive cumulative translation adjustment the year before.

E16-26 Financial Statement Translation Asian Opportunities wishes to include its wholly owned subsidiary in its consolidated financial statements. The financial statements of the subsidiary, stated in foreign currency units (FCU), are as follows:

Relevant exchange rates:

January 1, 2000	125 FCU to 1.00 dollar U.S.
Average rate for 2000	120 FCU to 1.00 dollar U.S.
December 31, 2000	115 FCU to 1.00 dollar U.S.
January 1, 1997	200 FCU to 1.00 dollar U.S.

The subsidiary was established on January 1, 1997, and Asian Opportunities acquired 100 percent of its common stock on that date for 3,000,000 FCU. The controller of Asian Opportunities has communicated with the company's external accountants and learned that the proper retained earnings balance in U.S. dollars at December 31, 2000, is $20,000.

a. Translate the subsidiary's financial statements into U.S. dollars.
b. If the subsidiary is liquidated at December 31, 2000, with all assets sold at book value and its liabilities paid, what dollar amount would Asian Opportunities receive if it immediately converted the FCU received into U.S. dollars?
c. If the exchange rate of the FCU had remained at 200 FCU per dollar, would the cumulative translation adjustment at December 31, 2000, be larger or smaller than the amount computed in part a above? Explain why.

FOREIGN SUBSIDIARY
INCOME STATEMENT
FOR THE YEAR ENDED DECEMBER 31, 2000

	FCU	Exchange Rate	Dollars
Sales	10,000,000		
Costs and expenses	8,000,000		
Net income	2,000,000		

FOREIGN SUBSIDIARY
BALANCE SHEET
DECEMBER 31, 2000

	FCU	Exchange Rate	Dollars
Assets:			
Current assets	3,000,000		
Plant & equipment (net)	9,000,000		
Total assets	12,000,000		
Liabilities:			
Current liabilities	1,500,000		
Long-term debt	3,000,000		
Total liabilities	4,500,000		
Owners' equity:			
Common stock	3,000,000		
Retained earnings	4,500,000		
Cumulative translation adjustment	—		
Total equity	7,500,000		
Total liabilities & equity	12,000,000		

E16-27 Financial Statement Translation World Company's Subsidiary A operates in Canada, and its financial statements are presented in Canadian dollars. The subsidiary was established on January 1, 2001, and had no retained earnings at that date. It paid no dividends in 2001. All revenues and expenses occurred uniformly throughout the year. World Company is located in the United States and must translate the subsidiary's financial statement into U.S. dollars before preparing consolidated financial statements. Subsidiary A's income statement and balance sheet appear as follows:

World Company—Subsidiary A
Balance Sheet
December 31, 2001

Assets

Current assets	C$ 55,000
Property, plant, and equipment (net)	285,000
Total assets	C$340,000

Liabilities and Equities

Current liabilities	C$ 20,000
Long-term notes payable	115,000
Common stock	100,000
Retained earnings	105,000
Total liabilities and equities	C$340,000

World Company—Subsidiary A
Income Statement
Year ended December 31, 2001

Sales	C$650,000
Cost of sales	(410,000)
Gross margin	C$240,000
Selling and administrative expenses	(135,000)
Net income	C$105,000

Some exchange rates for 2001 are as follows:

January 1, 2001	$1.30 Canadian to $1.00 U.S.
December 31, 2001	$1.40 Canadian to $1.00 U.S.
Average for 2001	$1.34 Canadian to $1.00 U.S.

Prepare Subsidiary A's income statement and balance sheet translated into U.S. dollars. Include the cumulative translation adjustment.

E16-28 Translation of Subsidiary Financial Statements Potter Corporation established Northland Company as a wholly owned subsidiary on January 1, 2000. The currency in the country of North where Northland Company is located is the NC. Balance sheets at January 1, 2000, and December 31, 2000, and the income statement for Northland Company for the year ended December 31, 2000, are as follows:

NORTHLAND COMPANY BALANCE SHEETS JANUARY 1 AND DECEMBER 31, 2000		
	Dec. 31, 2000	**Jan. 1, 2000**
Cash	NC 70,000	NC 50,000
Accounts receivable	100,000	90,000
Inventory	150,000	120,000
Buildings and equipment (net)	400,000	300,000
Total assets	NC 720,000	NC 560,000
Accounts payable	NC 60,000	NC 110,000
Bonds payable	400,000	250,000
Common stock	200,000	200,000
Retained earnings	60,000	—
Total liabilities and owners' equity	NC 720,000	NC 560,000

NORTHLAND COMPANY INCOME STATEMENT YEAR ENDED DECEMBER 31, 2000		
Sales		NC 800,000
Cost of goods sold		(520,000)
Gross margin		280,000
Salary and wages	NC 100,000	
Depreciation expense	30,000	
Other operating expenses	90,000	(220,000)
Net income		NC 60,000

Relevant exchange rates are as follows:

January 1, 2000	1 NC = $0.80 U.S.
December 31, 2000	1 NC = $0.90 U.S.
Average rate for year 2000	1 NC = $0.86 U.S.

a. Prepare a translated income statement for Northland Company for the year 2000.
b. Prepare translated balance sheets for Northland Company at January 1, 2000, and December 31, 2000.
c. Should the translation adjustment reported in the balance sheet at December 31, 2000, be positive or negative? Explain.
d. What dollar amount did Potter Corporation invest when it started Northland?
e. If Potter Corporation liquidated Northland Company at December 31, 2000, by selling Northland's assets at book value and immediately paying its liabilities, what dollar amount would Potter receive?

E16-29   Translation of Subsidiary Financial Statements
Assume that Potter Corporation created Northland Company as a wholly owned subsidiary on January 1, 2000, and that its operating results for 2000 and its balance sheets at January 1 and December 31, 2000, are as presented in **E16-28.** In this case, it is assumed the relevant exchange rates for 2000 declined as follows:

January 1, 2000	1 NC = $0.80 U.S.
December 31, 2000	1 NC = $0.72 U.S.
Average rate for year 2000	1 NC = $0.75 U.S.

a. Prepare a translated income statement for Northland Company for the year 2000.
b. Prepare translated balance sheets for Northland Company at January 1, 2000, and December 31, 2000.
c. Should the translation adjustment reported in the balance sheet at December 31, 2000, be positive or negative? Explain.

d. What dollar amount did Potter Corporation invest when it started Northland?
e. If Potter Corporation liquidated Northland Company at December 31, 2000, by selling Northland's assets at book value and immediately paying its liabilities, what dollar amount would Potter receive? Would Potter Corporation recognize a gain or a loss on the liquidation? What amount?

E16-30   International Accounting Standards   One of the international standards-setting organizations is the International Accounting Standards Committee (IASC).

a. Who are the members of the IASC? How are they selected?
b. Evaluate the authority of the IASC in comparison to a governmental agency such as the U.S. Securities and Exchange Commission.
c. Why would governmental agencies of a number of countries acting together have difficulty setting international accounting standards?
d. Would you expect the demand for international accounting standards to be increasing or decreasing? Why?

E16-31   Analysis of Global Business   You have gathered the following information about the revenues and operating income of JOL Company over the last 2 years:

Revenues (in millions)	**2001**	**2000**
U.S.	$257,150	$233,500
Europe	155,000	135,000
South America	70,000	60,000
Net Income (in millions)		
U.S.	$25,715	$23,350
Europe	12,600	13,500
South America	13,000	11,000

Compute the percent of sales revenue, the percent change in sales revenue in 2001, and the return on sales by geographic area. If the trends from 2000 to 2001 are expected to continue, which geographic area would you recommend that JOL consider for expansion? Explain why you chose that geographic area.

USING ACCOUNTING FOR DECISION MAKING

P16-32   Allocating Foreign Sales   Overdale Company has subsidiaries located in many countries. While each subsidiary produces a unique set of products, they all carry a full line of Overdale specialty products. Overdale has just completed an agreement to deliver $950,000 worth of products to a company in central Europe. Because of Overdale's broad geographic diversification, the products can be delivered by subsidiaries in any of three countries or by the parent company. The tax laws and financial reporting procedures are somewhat different in

each of the countries and the cost of delivering the products is also somewhat different from each country.

a. Why might Overdale consider giving a 2 percent discount if the product is shipped from the United States and the transaction is denominated in dollars?
b. What factors should Overdale take into consideration in deciding which of the subsidiaries should make the sale and receive payment?

c. If the exchange rate of the purchaser's country is very stable against the U.S. dollar, does it matter which subsidiary is used? Explain.

d. How might the percentage ownership of the foreign subsidiaries affect the decision as to which subsidiary to use?

P16-33   Analysis of Transactions   Kramer Corporation purchased pollution control devices from a foreign company with the purchase price stated in FCU (foreign currency units). At the time Kramer Corporation signed the contract in the amount of 600,000 FCU for delivery of the equipment, the exchange rate was 6.0 FCU for $1. At the time the equipment was received by Kramer Corporation, the rate was 5.6 FCU for $1. At the time payment was made by Kramer Corporation, the rate had increased to 6.4 FCU per $1.

a. At what amount should Kramer record the equipment?

b. In what way, if any, should Kramer account for the change in exchange rates between the signing of the contract and the delivery of the equipment?

c. In what way, if any, should Kramer account for the change in exchange rates between the date of delivery and payment?

d. Would Kramer have been wise to pay for the equipment at the time of delivery, or was it wise to wait? What dollar amount did the company gain or lose as a result of waiting?

e. In what ways might Kramer have eliminated the risk of currency fluctuations affecting the amount paid for the equipment? When should these actions have taken place?

P16-34   Receivables in Foreign Currency   Montana Corporation sold inventory costing $150,000 to a company in Atlantis for 900,000 atlans, the official currency of Atlantis. At the time the inventory was ordered, the exchange rate was 3.0 atlans for $1. At the time the inventory was shipped, the exchange rate was 2.5 atlans for $1. At the time payment was received, the rate had increased to 3.5 atlans to $1. Sales are made f.o.b. shipping point.

a. At what amount should Montana Corporation record the sale? What profit should Montana report on the sale?

b. In what way, if any, should Montana account for the change in exchange rates between the date the order is received and the shipment of the inventory?

c. In what way, if any, should Montana account for the change in exchange rates between the date of shipment and the receipt of payment?

d. Montana did not take any action to reduce the risk of currency fluctuations related to this transaction. Was that a wise decision? What actions might Montana have taken to reduce or eliminate the effects of currency fluctuations?

P16-35   Translation of Foreign Balance Sheets   The translated balance sheets of Lumpo Mining Company at January 1, 2000, and December 31, 2000, are as follows:

Lumpo Mining Company
Balance Sheets
January 1 and December 31, 2000

	Jan. 1, 2000	Dec. 31, 2000
Cash	$ 42,000	$ 90,000
Accounts receivable	108,000	198,000
Inventory	120,000	153,000
Buildings and equipment (net)	240,000	450,000
Total assets	$510,000	$891,000
Accounts payable	$ 30,000	$ 54,000
Bonds payable	90,000	180,000
Common stock	150,000	150,000
Retained earnings	140,000	200,000
Cumulative translation adjustment	100,000	307,000
Total liabilities and owners' equity	$510,000	$891,000

The burm (BR) is the currency for the country in which Lumpo Mining Company is located. Relevant exchange rates are as follows:

At date of establishment	1 BR = $.50 U.S.
January 1, 2000	1 BR = $.60 U.S.
December 31, 2000	1 BR = $.90 U.S.
Average rate for year 2000	1 BR = $.75 U.S.

a. What number of burms did Lumpo Mining have on hand at December 31, 2000?

b. Did the number of burms held by Lumpo Mining increase or decrease in 2000? By what amount?

c. What number of burms did Lumpo Mining receive on December 31, 2000, when it issued additional bonds?

d. What number of burms did Lumpo Mining receive when its stock was issued?

e. Assuming Lumpo paid no dividends in 2000, what was its net income for 2000 stated in U.S. dollars?

f. Assuming Lumpo paid no dividends in 2000, what was its net income for 2000 stated in burms?

P16-36   Translation of Foreign Income Statements   Domestic Corporation is a U.S. company that owns all of the common stock of External Corporation. The income statements of External Corporation for 2000 and 2001 are presented below. The currency for the country in which External Corporation is located is the eagle (EG).

External Corporation
Income Statements
Years Ended December 31

	2001	2000
Sales	EG 700,000	EG 650,000
Cost of Goods Sold	(460,000)	(400,000)
Gross Margin	EG 240,000	EG 250,000
Salary and Wages	EG 100,000	EG 60,000
Depreciation Expense	20,000	20,000
Other Operating Expenses	60,000	90,000
Total Operating and Other Expenses	EG(180,000)	EG(170,000)
Net Income	EG 60,000	EG 80,000

Relevant exchange rates are as follows:

Average rate for year 2000	1 EG = $.30 U.S.
Average rate for year 2001	1 EG = $.45 U.S.

a. Translate the income statements for 2000 and 2001 into U.S. dollars.
b. Which year had the higher gross margin stated in eagles? By what amount?
c. Which year had the higher gross margin translated into U.S. dollars? By what amount?
d. Which measure of gross margin is the more useful in measuring the return to Domestic Corporation? Which measure is the more useful in evaluating the operating activities of External Corporation?
e. Which year had the higher net income stated in eagles? By what amount?
f. Which year had the higher net income translated into U.S. dollars? By what amount?
g. Why is it important that the management of Domestic Corporation not base its evaluation of the management of External Corporation solely on the financial statements translated into U.S. dollars?

P16-37 Reporting Transactions Denominated in Foreign Currencies Western Corporation is a U.S. company with a sales representative in Brazil. To make travel possible, the company purchased an automobile for its representative on January 1, 1999, for 60,000 Brazilian reals. The purchase contract requires the company to pay 25 percent of the purchase price on January 1, 1999, and the remainder in three equal installments at the end of 30 days, 60 days, and 90 days. The exchange rates at the payment dates were:

January 1, 1999	$1.00 = R$1.20
January 31, 1999 (30 days)	$1.00 = R$1.80
March 2, 1999 (60 days)	$1.00 = R$2.10
April 1, 1999 (90 days)	$1.00 = R$1.70

Note: The real was significantly devalued during this time period and the above rates approximate the actual exchange rates.

a. What was the cost of the automobile in dollars?
b. What amount would Western Company report as accounts payable on January 1, 1999?
c. What amount of gain or loss on foreign currency fluctuations would Western record on January 31, 1999?
d. What balance in accounts payable would Western report on January 31, 1999, after the January payment is made?
e. What amount of gain or loss would Western record on March 2, 1999?
f. What balance in accounts payable would Western report on March 2, 1999, after the March payment is made?
g. What amount of gain or loss would Western record on April 1, 1999?
h. Was Western Corporation better off or worse off by choosing to pay for the automobile in 4 installments rather than making payment in full on January 1, 1999? By what amount?

P16-38 Analysis of Global Business US Corporation has investments in Indonesia and France. While the return on assets invested in Indonesia last year was 20 percent higher than the return on assets invested in the United States, the return on assets invested in France was 10 percent lower than in the United States.

a. What risks would you consider when deciding whether to invest more in Indonesia?
b. What other factors would you consider in deciding whether to invest more in Indonesia or in France?
c. Would the fact that US Corporation reports a cumulative translation loss on its investment in Indonesia and a cumulative translation gain on its investment in France influence your decision? In what way?
d. Assume that US Corporation decides to invest further in France. If it expects the franc to decline in value against the dollar, how might this affect the way in which the company chooses to finance the expansion?

P16-39 Exchange Transactions Tom Peatty, the purchasing agent of Blown Glass Company, has received a bid for a new special glassblowing machine manufactured in Denmark. The machine is priced at 5,765,000 Danish kroner. The terms of sale require payment in kroner within 60 days of shipment. In a separate letter, the supplier indicates that if Blown Glass wishes to pay in dollars, the price is $1,100,000 and, again, payment must be made within 60 days of shipment. Tom contacts the international desk of the company's bank and gets the following information.

1. The spot rate for kroner is 5.765 to $1.
2. The 60 day forward rate for kroner is 5.850 to $1.
3. The bank will charge 1 percent to change approximately $1,000,000 to kroner and prepare a cashier's check in kroner.
4. If the payment is in dollars, a regular company check can be used for the payment.

Required:

a. Prepare an analysis that identifies the factors that Tom should consider in choosing a method of payment. Recommend a method of payment and provide justification.
b. Assume that Tom chooses to pay in kroner. When should he purchase the kroner? Why?
c. At what amount should the machine be recorded? Explain how you determined the amount.

P16-40 Exchange Risk Stateside Company has an exposed asset position of approximately 1.85 billion foreign currency units (FCU) in its foreign subsidiary, and you want to convince the executive committee that there is a risk involved. Today's spot rate is 1,610 FCU to $1.

a. Calculate the potential gain or loss if the exchange rate changes to 1,500 FCU to $1, an increase in value, or if the FCU rate changes to 1,700 FCU to $1, a decrease in value. Which change should cause more concern? Why?
b. Would the risk of exchange rate fluctuations between the FCU and dollar be of any importance to Stateside Company if it plans to continue to invest additional money in the subsidiary and does not plan to transfer any of the assets of the subsidiary back to the United States in the foreseeable future? Explain.
c. Write a brief memo to the executive committee explaining the exchange risk associated with the foreign subsidiary and outline steps that might be taken to reduce the risk.

P16-41 International Accounting Standards The ROM Specialty Company is considering buying an interest in CD Limited, a foreign company operating in Europe. ROM has agreed to pay five times last year's net income for a 40 percent interest in CD Limited. However, while reviewing the financial statements, ROM discovers that CD Limited has not established an allowance for uncollectible accounts receivable and that CD Limited is using accelerated depreciation for its store fixtures. When ROM inquires, CD's management says that these accounting practices are required for both tax and financial statement reporting in their country.

a. What should ROM do with respect to these differences in accounting methods when calculating net income to be used in determining the price to pay for CD Limited? Explain.
b. Should ROM go ahead with the original price formula of five times last year's net income? Why?
c. ROM will hold less than a controlling interest in CD, so it will not consolidate the financial statements of CD with its own. Therefore, is there any point in translating CD's financial statements into U.S. dollars? Explain.

P16-42 Analysis of Global Business Kraul Corporation has major operating divisions located outside the United States. Your boss, the manager of international operations, has asked you to analyze the recent performance of the two divisions.

I. Selected income statement data for the divisions for 2000 and 2001, stated in U.S. dollars, are as follows:

	2000	2001
Division A		
Sales	$500,000	$800,000
Cost of goods sold	300,000	400,000
Net income	50,000	60,000
Division B		
Sales	700,000	800,000
Cost of goods sold	560,000	680,000
Net income	60,000	88,000

Required:

a. Calculate the gross margin and gross margin percentage for the two divisions for 2000 and 2001. On the basis of this information, which division has had the better overall performance? Which had the greater improvement? Explain.
b. Calculate the net income margin for the two divisions for 2000 and 2001. Which division had the better overall performance? Which had the greater improvement? Explain.
c. What other types of information would you take into consideration in evaluating the operating performance of the divisions?
d. To which division manager would you award the greater bonus for 2001? Explain why.

II. When you deliver your analysis of Divisions A and B to your manager, she asks you to look at the amount the company has invested in assets assigned to each of the divisions. You go back to the accounting department and receive the following information:

	2000	2001
Division A		
Total assets	$1,000,000	$1,000,000
Division B		
Total assets	700,000	1,200,000

Required:

a. Calculate the return on assets for each division for 2000 and 2001.
b. Which of the divisions has had the better overall performance? Which had the greater improvement? Explain.
c. Based on the information you developed relating to return on assets, to which division manager would you award the greater bonus for 2001? Explain why.
d. What other considerations might be relevant given that the divisions are located outside the United States?

EXPANDING YOUR HORIZONS

C16-43 Foreign Transactions and Decisions The Gilbert Company has received a bid from a Canadian supplier to furnish the raw materials the company uses in manufacturing one of its major product lines. The price quoted is 16.50 Canadian dollars per unit. Gilbert currently purchases the raw materials from a U.S. supplier and pays only $12.50 per unit.

a. If the exchange rate between the United States and Canadian dollars is C$1.36 to $1, is the raw material cheaper if purchased in the United States or in Canada? By what amount?

b. Would your answer change if you discovered that the 180-day forward rate for Canadian dollars is C$1.40 to $1? Why?

c. Having generated a numerical answer to the question of where to buy raw materials, are there other factors that should be considered in making this decision? What are the implications of purchasing raw materials in a foreign country and importing them into the United States? Identify as many factors as you can. How do these factors affect your decision? What would be the impact of moving the manufacturing process to Canada?

d. What are the possible implications of political unrest in Canada? What would happen if your supplier is in Quebec and the province votes in favor of the separation of Quebec from Canada? Would political unrest change the currency exchange rate? Would you benefit or lose?

 C16-44 Team Project: Operating Globally Identify three companies operating in the same industry. Obtain the financial statements of these companies directly from the companies, their home pages on the World Wide Web, the SEC EDGAR database, or other sources. Assign a team member or subgroup to each company to analyze its global operations. The analysis should include as much of the following information as possible:

1. Major product lines in the United States and in other countries.

2. Revenues in total and by country or geographic area for at least 2 years.

3. Income in total and by country or geographic area for the same periods.

4. Asset investment in total and by country or geographic area for the same periods.

Required:

a. Complete a financial analysis that will allow comparisons of the companies using financial ratios such as return on sales, return on assets, and other appropriate measures.

b. Prepare an analysis comparing the success of each company's global operations in relation to its U.S. operations. Which of the companies is most successful internationally?

c. Can you tell how long each company has been operating globally? Which of the companies, if any, would you recommend place greater emphasis on global expansion? Explain.

C16-45 Carnival's Foreign Currency Transactions The following are excerpts from the notes to the financial statements of Carnival Corporation for the year ending November 30, 1998:

INFORMATION TAKEN FROM NOTE 7:

Foreign Currency Contracts

The Company enters into forward foreign currency contracts to reduce its exposures relating to rate changes in foreign currency. These contracts are subject to gain or loss from changes in foreign currency rates. However, any realized gain or loss will be offset by gains or losses on the underlying hedged foreign currency transactions. Certain exposures to credit losses related to counterparty nonperformance exist, but the Company does not anticipate nonperformance by the counterparties, as they are large, well-established financial institutions. The fair values of the Company's forward hedging instruments discussed below are estimated based on prices quoted by financial institutions for these or similar instruments, adjusted for maturity differences.

Several of the Company's contracts for the construction of cruise vessels are denominated in Italian lira. The Company entered into forward foreign currency contracts with notional amounts of $745 million and $834 million at November 30, 1998 and 1997, respectively, to fix the price of these vessels into U.S. dollars (see Note 9). At November 30, 1998 and 1997, these forward contracts had an estimated fair value of approximately $815 million and $876 million, resulting in gains of $70 million and $41 million, respectively.

NOTE 9—COMMITMENTS AND CONTINGENCIES

Capital Expenditures

A description of ships under contract for construction at November 30, 1998, is as follows (in millions, except passenger capacity data):

Vessel	Expected Service Date (1)	Shipyard	Passenger Capacity (2)	Estimated Total Cost (3)	Remaining Cost to Be Paid
Carnival:					
Carnival Triumph	7/99	Fincantieri (4)	2,758	$ 410	$ 299
Carnival Victory	8/00	Fincantieri	2,758	440	434
Newbuild	4/01	Masa-Yards	2,100	375	357
Carnival Conquest	12/02	Fincantieri	2,758	450	429
Carnival Glory	8/03	Fincantieri	2,758	450	429
Total Carnival			13,132	2,125	1,948
Holland America:					
Volendam	8/99	Fincantieri (4)	1,440	300	240
Zaandam	3/00	Fincantieri (4)	1,440	300	256
Newbuild	11/00	Fincantieri	1,380	300	55
Total Holland America			4,260	900	551
Total			17,392	$3,025	$2,499

(1) The expected service date is the date the vessel is expected to begin revenue generating activities.

(2) In accordance with cruise industry practice, passenger capacity is calculated based on two passengers per cabin even though some cabins can accommodate three or four passengers.

(3) Estimated total cost is the total cost of the completed vessel and includes the contract price with the shipyard, design and engineering fees, estimated capitalized interest, various owner supplied items and construction oversight costs.

(4) These construction contracts are denominated in Italian Lira and have been fixed into U.S. dollars through the utilization of forward foreign currency contracts (see Note 7).

In connection with the vessels under construction, the Company has paid $526 million through November 30, 1998 and anticipates paying approximately $680 million during fiscal 1999 and approximately $1.8 billion thereafter.

Required:

a. Does the information in Note 9 reflect foreign currency transactions or foreign currency translation? Explain.

b. State in your own words, without going into detail, generally what Carnival has done as described in the notes.

c. What is the nature of the arrangements described in Note 7?

d. On which ships listed in the table is there a risk of a foreign currency gain or loss for Carnival? Why? Has Carnival done anything to avoid or reduce this risk? Explain.

e. Describe how, in relation to the ships under construction for Carnival, a foreign currency change in relation to the dollar will affect Carnival's financial statements in the current and future periods.

C16-46 Ethics, Made in the USA The All Purpose Sporting Goods Company has provided a variety of sporting goods and clothing to Speed Mart, a major discount chain, for more than 20 years. Speed Mart recently has been subject to adverse publicity for selling products manufactured in countries with significant human rights abuses. The bad publicity, including pickets at some store locations, has led Speed Mart to establish a policy that at least 75 percent of its merchandise must be produced by U.S. manufacturers.

All Purpose has just received a letter from Speed Mart indicating that at least 75 percent of Speed Mart's future purchases from All Purpose must have been manufactured in the United States. The letter also indicates that Speed Mart recognizes it may be more expensive to purchase goods manufactured in the United States and it is willing to permit up to a 10 percent cost increase in the first year. However, All Purpose has a problem: an analysis of its sales to Speed Mart last year shows that 85 percent of the sales were of products manufactured outside the United States. Because of the relative costs, only a few special items are still manufactured in the United States. Prior studies indicated that the cost of manufacturing the products in the United States would be at least 25 percent higher than it now costs in foreign plants.

When you deliver these reports to All Purpose's vice president of operations, he is not nearly as upset as you had anticipated. However, you are surprised and a little dismayed by the analysis he requests next. He asks you to determine how much it would cost to continue to have products manufactured overseas but shipped to the United States partly assembled, with the final assembly done in All Purpose's U.S.

plant. Deliveries to Speed Mart would then be made from All Purpose's U.S. manufacturing plant.

Identify any ethical issues that are involved with the vice president's proposal. Should All Purpose label its prod-ucts "manufactured in the USA"? How do you think the company would fare if it were to include a label stating "assembled in the USA" on its products? What other alternatives can you suggest to All Purpose?

www.wiley.com/college/king

Internet Exercises: Visit our Web site for additional exercises.

Annual Report Project Part 16

Refer to the Annual Report Project, Part 1, at the end of Chapter 1. Using the annual report of the company you have chosen, and any other available information, answer the following questions, providing sources and computations where appropriate.

a. Does your company have any foreign subsidiaries that are consolidated in the company's financial statements? In what countries are those subsidiaries located? Does your company report in its financial statements any adjustments from translating foreign-currency financial statements of subsidiaries into dollars? If so, in which financial statement(s) are they reported, and what is the amount?

b. Does your company engage in any transactions that are denominated in a foreign currency? [*Note:* Examine the notes to the financial statements for a discussion of foreign-currency transactions.] If so, did it report any gains or losses from exchange-rate fluctuations? Explain.

c. Does your company do business abroad? If so, in what geographic regions does it operate, and what percentage of total sales is reported for each region?

Gateway Annual Report

Gateway (NYSE: GTW), a *Fortune* 500 company founded in 1985, provides complete computing solutions for clients worldwide. The company employs more than 19,000 people around the globe.

Gateway shipped 3,541,000 PCs to customers throughout the world in 1998, generating total revenue of $7.47 billion.

Our administrative headquarters is in San Diego, California. Manufacturing headquarters is located in North Sioux City, South Dakota, along with sales and client support operations. Gateway Business headquarters is in Irvine, California.

Gateway also has a manufacturing and phone center in Hampton, Virginia, and a manufacturing center in Salt Lake City, Utah. Additional U.S. sales and customer support facilities are located in Sioux Falls, South Dakota, and Kansas City, Missouri, with customer support phone centers in Vermillion, South Dakota, Colorado Springs, Colorado, and Rio Rancho, New Mexico. Our Information Technology headquarters is in Lakewood, Colorado.

European operations are based in Dublin, Ireland. Active European markets now include the United Kingdom, Ireland, France, Germany, Belgium, Luxembourg, Switzerland, Austria, Sweden and the Netherlands. Along the Pacific Rim, the company has sales and support operations in Japan, Australia, Hong Kong and Malaysia, manufacturing facilities in Malaysia and operations in Cyprus.

Management's Discussion and Analysis of Financial Condition and Results of Operations

This Report includes forward-looking statements made based on current management expectations pursuant to the safe harbor provisions of the Private Securities Litigation Reform Act of 1995. These statements are not guarantees of future performance and actual outcomes may differ materially from what is expressed or forecasted. Factors that could cause future results to differ from the Company's expectations include the following: competitive market conditions; infrastructure requirements; financial instruments; suppliers; short product cycles; access to technology; international operations; credit risk; e-commerce issues; risks of acquisition; inventory risks; customer or geographic sales mix; loss of key managers; and the Year 2000 transition. For a discussion of these factors, see "Item 1 Business - Factors that May Affect Gateway's Business and Future Results" in the Company's Annual Report on Form 10-K.

Results of Operations

The following table sets forth, for the periods indicated, certain data derived from the Company's consolidated income statements:

	1996	Increase (Decrease)	1997	Increase	1998
			(dollars in thousands)		
Net sales	$ 5,035,228	25%	$ 6,293,680	19%	$ 7,467,925
Gross profit	$ 936,155	15%	$ 1,076,441	44%	$ 1,546,274
Percentage of net sales	18.6%		17.1%		20.7%
Selling, general and administrative expenses	$ 580,061	36%	$ 786,168	34%	$ 1,052,047
Percentage of net sales	11.5%		12.5%		14.1%
Nonrecurring expenses	—		$ 113,842		—
Percentage of net sales	—		1.8%		—
Operating income	$ 356,094	(50%)	$ 176,431	180%	$ 494,227
Percentage of net sales	7.1%		2.8%		6.6%
Net income	$ 250,679	(56%)	$ 109,797	215%	$ 346,399

Sales. Gateway added over $1.1 billion in sales in 1998 compared to 1997, achieving annual sales of $7.47 billion. This represents an increase of 19% over 1997. Sales to the consumer segment represented 53% of total sales while business segment sales were 47% of total sales. Sales were driven by continued strong unit growth of 37% in 1998 compared to unit growth of 35% in 1997. The Company's unit growth outpaced the worldwide market in 1998 by approximately three times the market growth rate, leading to continued gains in market share. Based on shipments in the fourth quarter, Gateway improved its ranking to number 3 in the U.S. PC market and was number 6 worldwide. These market share gains were driven by several top line initiatives including the development and execution of a new advertising strategy; the Your:)Ware℠ marketing program; and significant expansion of Gateway Country Stores. The new marketing strategy focuses on reaching an expanded customer base through a new branding campaign and the use of broader advertising media such as television and newspapers. The Your:)Ware℠ program offers customers internet access, financing options, software bundles, and provides for trade-in options. As a result of these initiatives, Gateway was able to reach a broader cross section of customers in 1998. Partially offsetting strong unit growth, the Company's average unit prices (AUPs) were approximately 14% lower in 1998 compared to an 8% decline in 1997. AUPs continued to decline in 1998 due to component cost decreases and significant growth in the sub $1,000 PC market. The Company expects the industry trend of declining AUPs to continue and intends to mitigate this by diversifying its revenue stream with software bundles, internet service, financing and other service offerings.

The following table summarizes the Company's net sales, for the periods indicated, by geographic region:

	1996	Increase	1997	Increase (Decrease)	1998
			(dollars in thousands)		
Net sales:					
United States	$ 4,246,047	25%	$ 5,303,828	21%	$ 6,412,405
Europe	552,671	15%	634,616	(10%)	570,191
Asia Pacific	236,510	50%	355,236	37%	485,329
Consolidated	$ 5,035,228	25%	$ 6,293,680	19%	$ 7,467,925

In the United States unit shipments rose 39% in 1998 and 35% in 1997 due to the factors discussed above. The Asia Pacific region ("APAC") continued to achieve significant increases in unit shipments with growth of 63% in 1998 and 84% in 1997. Unit shipments in the European region ("EMEA") increased 5% in 1998 down from 20% in 1997. The Company has put new management in place in EMEA and is focusing on the top line initiatives previously discussed to address the declining unit shipment growth.

Gross Profit. Gross profit in 1998 rose to $1.55 billion, an increase of approximately 44% from 1997. Gross profit for the consumer and business segments for 1998 was $760.8 million and $783.3 million, respectively. Approximately 40% of the gross profit increase was the result of sales growth, while approximately 60% resulted from margin productivity. Margin productivity was driven by the diversified revenue stream with Your:)Ware℠ bundles, effective pricing initiatives, aggressive supplier management and decreasing component costs. As a percentage of sales, gross profit for 1998 increased to 20.7% from 17.1% in 1997, improving sequentially every quarter during 1998. For additional quarterly financial information, see Note 13 of the notes to the consolidated financial statements. The increase over 1997 is partially attributable to the adverse effects of excess inventories experienced in the third quarter of 1997.

Selling, General and Administrative Expenses. To support its significant growth during 1998, the Company made investments in infrastructure, personnel, marketing and internet development which contributed to an increase of 34% in selling, general and administrative expenses over 1997. Gateway opened a new manufacturing and sales facility in Salt Lake City, an administrative headquarters in San Diego and a new Information Technology and Support facility in Lakewood, Colorado. In addition, the Company made a significant investment in new employees, including the expansion of its executive management team. As a result, personnel costs increased 35% in 1998 compared to 1997. The Company expects selling, general and administrative expenses to continue to increase in support of its anticipated growth, but at a rate below that of anticipated revenue growth.

Operating Income. Strong unit growth and gross margin efficiencies contributed to a 180% increase in operating income for 1998. In addition, the increase is attributable to the nonrecurring pre-tax charges recorded in the third quarter of 1997. Operating income improved to 6.6% in 1998 from 2.8% in 1997. Operating income in 1998 for the consumer and business segments were $461.4 million and $600.8 million, respectively, while operating expenses in 1998 not allocated to a segment were $568.0 million. Operating income for the consumer and business segments includes selling, general and administrative expenses and other overhead charges directly attributable to the segment and excludes certain expenses managed outside the reportable segments. Costs excluded from the consumer and business segments primarily consist of corporate marketing costs and other general and administrative expenses that are separately managed.

Other Income. Other income, net includes other income net of expenses, such as interest income and expense and foreign exchange transaction gains and losses. Other income, net increased to $47.0 million in 1998 from $27.2 million in 1997, primarily due to the additional interest income generated by increases in cash balances and marketable securities.

Income Taxes. The Company's annualized effective tax rate decreased to 36% for 1998 from the 46.1% recorded in 1997. The effective tax rate for 1997 was impacted unfavorably by the nonrecurring expenses relating to the write-off of in-process research and development arising in connection with the acquisitions of ALR and certain assets of Amiga Technologies which were nondeductible for income taxes.

Liquidity and Capital Resources

The following table presents selected financial statistics and information for the periods indicated:

	1996	1997	1998
	(dollars in thousands)		
Cash and marketable securities	$ 516,360	$ 632,249	$ 1,328,467
Days of sales in accounts receivable	26	23	22
Inventory turnover	21	21	40
Days in accounts payable	29	27	36

At December 31, 1998, the Company had cash and cash equivalents of $1.17 billion, marketable securities of $158.7 million and an unsecured committed credit facility with certain banks aggregating $225 million, consisting of a revolving line of credit facility and a sub-facility for letters of credit. At December 31, 1998, no amounts were outstanding under the revolving line of credit. Approximately $2.0 million was committed to support outstanding standby letters of credit. Management believes the Company's current sources of working capital, including amounts available under existing credit facilities, will provide adequate flexibility for the Company's financial needs for at least the next 12 months.

The Company generated $907.7 million in cash from operations during the year, including $398.3 million of net income adjusted for non-cash items. Other significant factors increasing available cash include a decrease in inventory levels of $81.3 million and an increase in accounts payable and other accrued liabilities of $479.8 million, partially offset by an increase in accounts receivable. The decrease in inventory levels, decrease in days sales in accounts receivable and increase in days purchases in accounts payable is attributable to the Company's increased focus on working capital management. The Company used approximately $235.4 million for the construction of new facilities, information systems and equipment and $120.0 million to purchase investments in marketable securities, net of proceeds of securities sold. As discussed previously, the Company continued to expand the retail Gateway Country stores with 107 new stores added in 1998, bringing the total number of stores to 144 as of December 31, 1998.

At December 31, 1998, the Company had long-term indebtedness and capital lease obligations of approximately $14.8 million. These obligations relate to the Company's investments in equipment and facilities. The Company anticipates that it will retain all earnings in the foreseeable future for development of its business and will not distribute earnings to its stockholders as dividends.

As of February 28, 1999, the Company has made a commitment to purchase approximately $290 million of consumer finance receivables used to purchase the Company's products which were originated by a financial institution on behalf of Gateway.

New Accounting Pronouncements

In June of 1998, the Financial Accounting Standards Board issued SFAS No. 133, "Accounting for Derivative Instruments and Hedging Activities" which is effective for fiscal years beginning after June 15, 1999. The objective of the statement is to establish accounting and reporting standards for derivative instruments and hedging activities. The Company uses foreign currency forward contracts, a derivative instrument, to hedge foreign currency transactions and anticipated foreign currency transactions. The adoption of this new accounting pronouncement is not expected to be material to the Company's consolidated financial position or results of operations.

In 1998, the Accounting Standards Executive Committee (AcSEC) issued Statement of Accounting Position ("SOP") No. 98-1, "Accounting for the Costs of Computer Software Developed or Obtained for Internal Use," which is effective for fiscal years beginning after December 15, 1998. The SOP provides guidance on when costs incurred for internal-use computer software are and are not to be capitalized, and on the accounting for such software that is marketed to customers. The adoption of this SOP is not expected to have a material impact on the Company's consolidated financial position or results of operations.

Year 2000

The "Year 2000" issue has arisen because many existing computer programs and chip-based embedded technology systems use only the last two digits to refer to a year, and therefore, do not properly recognize a year that begins with "20" instead of the familiar "19." If not corrected, many computer applications could fail or create erroneous results.

State of Readiness: The Company has adopted a seven-step process toward Year 2000 readiness consisting of the following: (i) awareness: fostering an understanding of and commitment to the problem and its potential risks; (ii) inventory: identifying and locating systems and technology components that may be affected; (iii) assessment: reviewing these components for Year 2000 compliance and assessing the scope of potential Year 2000 issues; (iv) planning: defining the technical solutions, labor and work plans necessary for each affected system; (v) remediation/replacement: completing the programming to upgrade or replace the problem software or hardware; (vi) testing and compliance validation: conducting testing followed by independent validation by a separate internal verification team; and (vii) implementation: placing the corrected systems and technology back into the business environment with a management monitoring system to ensure ongoing compliance.

The Company has grouped its internal systems and technology into the following three categories for purposes of Year 2000 compliance: (i) information resource applications and technology consisting of enterprise-wide systems supported by the Company's centralized information technology organization (IT); (ii) business processes consisting of hardware, software, and associated computer chips as well as external vendors used in the operation of the Company's core business functions; and (iii) building systems consisting of non-IT equipment that use embedded computer chips such as elevators, automated room key systems and HVAC equipment. The Company is prioritizing its efforts based on the severity with which non compliance would affect service, core business processes or revenues, and whether there are viable, non-automated fallback procedures (Mission Criticality).

As of the end of the fourth quarter, the Company believes the Awareness and Inventory phases are complete for both IT systems and building systems and 50% complete for business processes. For IT systems, the Company believes the assessment, planning and remediation/replacement phases are over 65% complete with testing and compliance validation complete for 20% of the inventory. For business processes and building systems, the Company believes the assessment and planning phases are over 40% complete with a substantial amount of work in process. The progress level for remediation/replacement and testing and compliance validation is currently at 20%. The Company plans to complete the remediation/replacement and testing phases for its mission critical IT systems by the end of the second quarter of 1999 with the remaining half of 1999 reserved for unplanned contingencies and compliance validation and quality assurance. For mission critical business processes and building systems, the same level of completion is targeted for October 1999.

The Company has also initiated Year 2000 compliance communications with its significant third party suppliers, vendors and business partners. The Company is focusing its efforts on the business interfaces most critical to its customer service, core business processes and revenues, including those third parties that support the most critical enterprise-wide IT systems, the Company's primary suppliers of non-IT products, or provide the most critical payment processing functions. Responses have been received from a majority of the third parties that comprise this group.

Costs: During 1998, the Company expensed incremental costs of approximately $3.3 million related to the Year 2000 remediation efforts, and has expensed $3.6 million on a life-to-date basis. The current total estimated cost to complete the Year 2000 remediation efforts is from $14 to $16 million, exclusive of upgrades to existing applications and implementation of new systems. Internal and external costs specifically associated with modifying internal-use software for the Year 2000 will be charged to expense as incurred. All of these costs are being funded through operating cash flows.

Year 2000 Contingency Plans: The Company is reviewing its existing contingency plans for potential modification to address specific Year 2000 issues as they arise and expects to continue this process during the next four fiscal quarters.

Company Products: With respect to PC products sold to customers, for all the Company hardware based on the Intel(r) family of Pentium processors (Pentium(r), Pentium(r) Pro, Pentium II(r), Pentium(r)II Xeon(tm) and Celeron(tm) processors) and using an operating system provided by the Company, the Company warrants to customers that such systems sold after January 1, 1997, will process dates correctly before, during and after January 1, 2000. This warranty applies to desktop, portable, Destination(r), and server products, and it is governed by the terms and conditions outlined in the original system warranty. It does not include application software, or non-Company branded external hardware peripherals such as printers, scanners and joysticks. Because the Company does not control the design of these products, it cannot ensure how they access or calculate date information in the computer. Certain hardware sold before January 1, 1997 will require remediation or replacement to become Year 2000 compliant. The Company may experience increased customer claims for Year 2000 failures for these products and for failures resulting from software or non-Company branded external hardware peripherals. Additional information concerning the Year 2000 issue and the Company's compliance program is available on the Company's website at www.gateway.com/.

Risks of the Company's Year 2000 Issues: Based on current information, the Company believes that the Year 2000 problem will not have a material adverse effect on the Company, its consolidated financial position, results of operations or cash flows. However, there are no assurances that Year 2000 remediation by the Company or third parties will be properly and timely completed, and failure to do so could have a material adverse effect on the Company, its business and its financial condition. The Company cannot predict the effects that Year 2000 non-compliance would have on it, which would ultimately depend on numerous uncertainties such as: (i) whether significant third parties properly and timely address the Year 2000 issue; (ii) whether broad-based or systemic economic failures may occur, and the severity and duration of such failures, including loss of utility and/or telecommunications services, and errors or failures in financial transactions or payment processing systems such as credit cards; and (iii) whether the Company becomes the subject of litigation or other proceedings regarding any Year 2000-related events and the outcome of any such litigation or proceedings.

Quantitative and Qualitative Disclosures About Market Risk

The results of the Company's foreign operations are affected by changes in exchange rates between certain foreign currencies and the United States dollar. The functional currency for most of the Company's foreign operations is the U.S. dollar. The functional currency for the remaining operations is the local currency in which the subsidiaries operate. Sales made in foreign currencies translate into higher or lower sales in U.S. dollars as the U.S. dollar strengthens or weakens against other currencies. Therefore, changes in exchange rates may negatively affect the Company's consolidated net sales (as expressed in U.S. dollars) and gross margins from foreign operations. The majority of the Company's component purchases are denominated in U.S. dollars.

The Company uses foreign currency forward contracts to hedge foreign currency transactions and probable anticipated foreign currency transactions. These forward contracts are designated as a hedge of international sales by U.S. dollar functional currency entities and intercompany purchases by certain foreign subsidiaries. The principal currencies hedged are the British Pound, Japanese Yen, French Franc, Australian Dollar, Singapore Dollar, and the Deutsche Mark over periods ranging from one to six months. Forward contracts are accounted for on a mark-to-market basis, with realized and unrealized gains or losses recognized currently. Gains or losses arising from forward contracts that are effective as a hedge are included in the basis of the designated transactions. Fluctuations in U.S. dollar currency exchange rates did not have a significant impact on the Company's consolidated financial position, results of operations or cash flows in any given reporting period. Forward contracts designated to hedge foreign currency transaction exposure of $257,051,000 and $266,471,000 were outstanding at December 31, 1997 and 1998, respectively. The estimated fair value of these forward contracts at December 31, 1997 and 1998 was $253,519,000 and $271,573,000, respectively, based on quoted market prices.

Foreign currency exchange contracts are sensitive to changes in foreign currency exchange rates. At December 31, 1998, a hypothetical 10% adverse change in foreign currency exchange rates underlying the Company's open forward contracts would result in an unrealized loss of approximately $29.1 million. Unrealized gains/losses in foreign currency exchange contracts represent the difference between the hypothetical rates and the current market exchange rates. Consistent with the nature of an economic hedge any unrealized gains or losses would be offset by corresponding decreases or increases, respectively, of the underlying transaction being hedged.

The Company is not subject to material market risk with respect to its investment in marketable securities.

Report of Independent Accountants

To the Stockholders and Board of Directors of Gateway 2000, Inc.

In our opinion, the accompanying consolidated balance sheets and the related consolidated statements of income, cash flows and changes in stockholders' equity and comprehensive income presents fairly, in all material respects, the consolidated financial position of Gateway 2000, Inc. at December 31, 1997 and 1998, and the consolidated results of its operations and its cash flows for each of the three years in the period ended December 31, 1998, in conformity with generally accepted accounting principles. These financial statements are the responsibility of the Company's management; our responsibility is to express an opinion on these financial statements based on our audits. We conducted our audits of these statements in accordance with generally accepted auditing standards which require that we plan and perform the audit to obtain reasonable assurance about whether the financial statements are free of material misstatement. An audit includes examining, on a test basis, evidence supporting amounts and disclosures in the financial statements, assessing the accounting principles used and significant estimates made by management, and evaluating the overall financial statement presentation. We believe that our audits provide a reasonable basis for the opinion expressed above.

PricewaterhouseCoopers LLP

San Diego, California
January 21, 1999

CONSOLIDATED INCOME STATEMENTS

For the years ended December 31, 1996, 1997 and 1998

(in thousands, except per share amounts)

	1996	1997	1998
Net sales	$ 5,035,228	$ 6,293,680	$ 7,467,925
Cost of goods sold	4,099,073	5,217,239	5,921,651
Gross profit	936,155	1,076,441	1,546,274
Selling, general and administrative expenses	580,061	786,168	1,052,047
Nonrecurring expenses	–	113,842	–
Operating income	356,094	176,431	494,227
Other income, net	26,622	27,189	47,021
Income before income taxes	382,716	203,620	541,248
Provision for income taxes	132,037	93,823	194,849
Net income	$ 250,679	$ 109,797	$ 346,399
Net income per share:			
Basic	$ 1.64	$ .71	$ 2.23
Diluted	$ 1.60	$ .70	$ 2.18
Weighted average shares outstanding:			
Basic	152,745	153,840	155,542
Diluted	156,237	156,201	158,929

The accompanying notes are an integral part of the consolidated financial statements.

CONSOLIDATED BALANCE SHEETS

December 31, 1997 and 1998

(in thousands, except per share amounts)

	1997	1998
ASSETS		
Current assets:		
Cash and cash equivalents	$ 593,601	$ 1,169,810
Marketable securities	38,648	158,657
Accounts receivable, net	510,679	558,851
Inventory	249,224	167,924
Other	152,531	172,944
Total current assets	1,544,683	2,228,186
Property, plant and equipment, net	376,467	530,988
Intangibles, net	82,590	65,944
Other assets	35,531	65,262
	$ 2,039,271	$ 2,890,380
LIABILITIES AND STOCKHOLDERS' EQUITY		
Current liabilities:		
Notes payable and current maturities of long-term		
obligations	$ 13,969	$ 11,415
Accounts payable	488,717	718,071
Accrued liabilities	271,250	415,265
Accrued royalties	159,418	167,873
Othe~~The accompanying notes are an integral part of the consolidated financial statements.~~		50
Total current liabilities	1,003,906	1,429,674
Long-term obligations, net of current maturities	7,240	3,360
Warranty and other liabilities	98,081	112,971
Total liabilities	1,109,227	1,546,005
Commitments and Contingencies (Notes 3 and 4)		
Stockholders' equity:		
Preferred stock, $.01 par value, 5,000 shares		
authorized; none issued and outstanding	—	—
Class A common stock, nonvoting, $.01 par value,		
1,000 shares authorized; none issued and		
outstanding	—	—
Common stock, $.01 par value, 220,000 shares		
authorized; 154,128 shares and 156,569 shares		
issued and outstanding, respectively	1,541	1,566
Additional paid-in capital	299,483	365,986
Retained earnings	634,509	980,908
Accumulated other comprehensive loss	(5,489)	(4,085)
Total stockholders' equity	930,044	1,344,375
	$ 2,039,271	$ 2,890,380

The accompanying notes are an integral part of the consolidated financial statements.

CONSOLIDATED STATEMENTS OF CASH FLOWS
For the years ended December 31, 1996, 1997 and 1998
(in thousands)

	1996	1997	1998
Cash flows from operating activities:			
Net income	$ 250,679	$ 109,797	$ 346,399
Adjustments to reconcile net income to net cash provided by operating activities:			
Depreciation and amortization	61,763	86,774	105,524
Provision for uncollectible accounts receivable	20,832	5,688	3,991
Deferred income taxes	(13,395)	(63,247)	(58,425)
Other, net	1,986	42	770
Nonrecurring expenses	—	113,842	—
Changes in operating assets and liabilities:			
Accounts receivable	(66,052)	(41,950)	(52,164)
Inventory	(54,261)	59,486	81,300
Other assets	(13,311)	(54,513)	451
Accounts payable	176,724	66,253	228,921
Accrued liabilities	51,390	48,405	144,899
Accrued royalties	1,885	34,148	8,455
Other current liabilities	43,057	35,816	76,278
Warranty and other liabilities	22,699	42,256	21,252
Net cash provided by operating activities	483,996	442,797	907,651
Cash flows from investing activities:			
Capital expenditures	(143,746)	(175,656)	(235,377)
Purchases of available-for-sale securities	—	(49,619)	(168,965)
Proceeds from maturities or sales of available-for-sale securities	3,030	10,985	48,924
Acquisitions, net of cash acquired	—	(142,320)	—
Other, net	2,667	(4,055)	(992)
Net cash used in investing activities	(138,049)	(360,665)	(356,410)
Cash flows from financing activities:			
Proceeds from issuances of notes payable	10,000	10,000	—
Principal payments on long-term obligations and notes payable	(14,047)	(15,588)	(13,173)
Stock options exercised	9,520	5,741	36,159
Net cash provided by financing activities	5,473	153	22,986
Foreign exchange effect on cash and cash equivalents	(1,457)	(5,044)	1,982
Net increase in cash and cash equivalents	349,963	77,241	576,209
Cash and cash equivalents, beginning of year	166,397	516,360	593,601
Cash and cash equivalents, end of year	$ 516,360	$ 593,601	$ 1,169,810

The accompanying notes are an integral part of the consolidated financial statements.

CONSOLIDATED STATEMENTS OF CHANGES IN STOCKHOLDERS' EQUITY AND COMPREHENSIVE INCOME

For the years ended December 31, 1996, 1997 and 1998

(in thousands)

	Common Stock Shares	Common Stock Amount	Additional Paid-in Capital	Retained Earnings	Accumulated Other Comprehensive Income (Loss)	Total
Balances at December 31, 1995	149,106	$ 1,492	$ 279,701	$ 274,033	$ 293	$ 555,519
Comprehensive income:						
Net income	—	—	—	250,679	—	250,679
Other comprehensive income:						
Foreign currency translation	—	—	—	—	225	225
Unrealized gain on available-for-sale securities	—	—	—	—	31	31
Comprehensive income						250,935
Stock issuances under employee plans, including tax benefit of $30,451	6,545	66	39,905	—	—	39,971
Stock retirement	(2,139)	(22)	(30,862)	—	—	(30,884)
Balances at December 31, 1996	153,512	1,536	288,744	524,712	549	815,541
Comprehensive income:						
Net income	—	—	—	109,797	—	109,797
Other comprehensive income:						
Foreign currency translation	—	—	—	—	(6,053)	(6,053)
Unrealized gain on available-for-sale securities	—	—	—	—	15	15
Comprehensive income						103,759
Stock issuances under employee plans, including tax benefit of $5,003	616	5	10,739	—	—	10,744
Balances at December 31, 1997	154,128	1,541	299,483	634,509	(5,489)	930,044
Comprehensive income:						
Net income	—	—	—	346,399	—	346,399
Other comprehensive income:						
Foreign currency translation	—	—	—	—	1,549	1,549
Unrealized loss on available-for-sale securities	—	—	—	—	(145)	(145)
Comprehensive income						347,803
Stock issuances under employee plans, including tax benefit of $29,769	2,423	24	65,904	—	—	65,928
Stock issued to officer	18	1	599	—	—	600
Balances at December 31, 1998	156,569	$ 1,566	$ 365,986	$ 980,908	$ (4,085)	$ 1,344,375

The accompanying notes are an integral part of the consolidated financial statements.

1. Summary of Significant Accounting Policies:

Gateway 2000, Inc. (the "Company") is a direct marketer of personal computers ("PCs") and PC-related products. The Company develops, manufactures, markets and supports a broad line of desktop and portable PCs, digital media (convergence) PCs, servers, workstations and PC-related products used by individuals, families, businesses, government agencies and educational institutions.

The significant accounting policies used in the preparation of the consolidated financial statements of the Company are as follows:

(a) Principles of Consolidation:

The consolidated financial statements include the accounts of the Company and its wholly-owned subsidiaries. All significant intercompany accounts and transactions have been eliminated.

(b) Use of Estimates and Certain Concentrations:

The preparation of financial statements in conformity with generally accepted accounting principles requires management to make estimates and assumptions that affect the reported amounts of assets and liabilities and disclosure of contingent assets and liabilities at the date of the financial statements and the reported amounts of revenues and expenses during the reporting period. Actual results could differ from those estimates.

Certain components used by the Company in manufacturing of PC systems are purchased from a limited number of suppliers. An industry shortage or other constraints of any key component could result in delayed shipments and a possible loss of sales, which could affect operating results adversely.

(c) Cash and Cash Equivalents:

The Company considers all highly liquid debt instruments and money market funds with an original maturity of three months or less to be cash equivalents. The carrying amount approximates fair value because of the short maturities of these instruments.

(d) Marketable Securities:

The carrying amounts of marketable securities used in computing unrealized and realized gains and losses are determined by specific identification. Fair values are determined using quoted market prices. For available-for-sale securities, which are carried at fair value at the balance sheet dates, net unrealized holding gains and losses are reported in accumulated other comprehensive income (loss). Held-to-maturity securities are recorded at amortized cost. Amortization of related discounts or premiums is included in the determination of net income.

Marketable securities at December 31, 1998 consisted of available-for-sale mutual funds, commercial paper and debt securities, with a market value of $158,657,000 and an amortized cost of $158,788,000, with variable maturities through 1999. Realized and unrealized gains and losses are not material for any of the periods presented.

(e) Inventory:

Inventory, which is comprised of component parts, subassemblies and finished goods, is valued at the lower of first-in, first-out (FIFO) cost or market. On a quarterly basis, the Company compares on a part by part basis, the amount of the inventory on hand and under commitment with its latest forecasted requirements to determine whether write-downs for excess or obsolete inventory are required.

(f) Property, Plant and Equipment:

Property, plant and equipment are stated at cost. Depreciation is provided using straight-line and accelerated methods over the assets' estimated useful lives, ranging from four to forty years. Amortization of leasehold improvements is computed using the shorter of the lease term or the estimated useful life of the underlying asset. Upon sale or retirement of property, plant and equipment, the related costs and accumulated depreciation or amortization are removed from the accounts and any gain or loss is included in the determination of net income.

The Company capitalizes costs of purchased software and, once technological feasibility has been established, costs incurred in developing software for internal use. Amortization of software costs begins when the software is placed in service and is computed on a straight-line basis over the estimated useful life of the software, generally from three to five years.

(g) Intangible Assets:

Intangible assets principally consist of technology, a customer base and distribution network, an assembled work force and trade name obtained through acquisition. The cost of intangible assets is amortized on a straight-line basis over the estimated periods benefited, ranging from three to ten years.

(h) Long-lived Assets:

The Company reviews for the impairment of long-lived assets whenever events or changes in circumstances indicate that the carrying amount of an asset may not be recoverable. An impairment loss would be recognized when the sum of the expected undiscounted future net cash flows expected to result from the use of the asset and its eventual disposition is less than its carrying amount.

(i) Royalties:

The Company has royalty-bearing license agreements that allow the Company to sell certain hardware and software which is protected by patent, copyright or license. Royalty costs are accrued and included in cost of goods sold when products are shipped or amortized over the period of benefit when the license terms are not specifically related to the units shipped.

(j) Warranty and Other Post-sales Support Programs:

The Company provides currently for the estimated costs that may be incurred under its warranty and other post-sales support programs.

(k) Comprehensive Income:

Effective January 1, 1998, the Company adopted Statement of Financial Accounting Standards (SFAS) No. 130, "Reporting Comprehensive Income." SFAS 130 establishes new rules for the reporting of comprehensive income and its components; however the adoption of this statement had no impact on the Company's current or previously reported net income or stockholders' equity. SFAS 130 requires the display and reporting of comprehensive income, which includes all changes in stockholders' equity with the exception of additional investments by stockholders or distributions to stockholders. Comprehensive income for the Company includes net income, foreign currency translation effects and unrealized gains or losses on available-for-sale securities which are charged or credited to the accumulated other comprehensive income (loss) account within stockholders' equity.

(l) Revenue Recognition:

Sales are recorded when products are shipped. A provision for estimated sales returns is recorded in the period in which related sales are recognized. Revenue from separately priced extended warranty programs is deferred and recognized over the extended warranty period on a straight-line basis.

(m) Income Taxes:

The provision for income taxes is computed using the liability method, under which deferred tax assets and liabilities are recognized for the expected future tax consequences of temporary differences between the financial reporting and tax bases of assets and liabilities. Deferred tax assets are reduced by a valuation allowance when it is more likely than not that some portion or all of the deferred tax assets will not be realized.

(n) Net Income Per Share:

Basic earnings per common share is computed using the weighted average number of common shares outstanding during the period. Diluted earnings per common share is computed using the combination of dilutive common stock equivalents and the weighted average number of common shares outstanding during the period.

The following table sets forth a reconciliation of shares used in the computation of basic and diluted earnings per share.

	1996	1997	1998
		(in thousands)	
Net income for basic and diluted earnings per share	$ 250,679	$ 109,797	$ 346,399
Weighted average shares for basic earnings per share	152,745	153,840	155,542
Dilutive effect of stock options	3,492	2,361	3,387
Weighted average shares for diluted earnings per share	156,237	156,201	158,929

All references in the financial statements to number of common shares and per share amounts have been retroactively restated to reflect a two-for-one common stock split effective in June 1997.

(o) Stock-based Compensation:

The Company measures compensation expense for its employee stock-based compensation using the intrinsic value method. Compensation charges related to non-employee stock-based compensation are measured using fair value methods.

(p) Foreign Currency:

The Company uses the U.S. dollar as its functional currency for the majority of its international operations. For subsidiaries where the local currency is the functional currency, the assets and liabilities are translated into U.S. dollars at exchange rates in effect at the balance sheet date. Income and expense items are translated at the average exchange rates prevailing during the period. Gains and losses from translation are included in accumulated other comprehensive income (loss). Gains and losses resulting from remeasuring monetary asset and liability accounts that are denominated in currencies other than a subsidiary's functional currency are included in "Other income, net".

The Company uses foreign currency forward contracts to hedge foreign currency transactions and probable anticipated foreign currency transactions. These forward contracts are designated as a hedge of international sales by U.S. dollar functional currency entities and intercompany purchases by certain foreign subsidiaries. The principal currencies hedged are the British Pound, Japanese Yen, French Franc, Australian Dollar, Singapore Dollar and the Deutsche Mark over periods ranging from one to six months. Forward contracts are accounted for on a mark-to-market basis, with realized and unrealized gains or losses recognized currently. Gains or losses arising from forward contracts which are effective as a hedge are included in the basis of the designated transactions. The related receivable or liability with counterparties to the forward contracts is recorded in the consolidated balance sheet. Cash flows from settlements of forward contracts are included in operating activities in the consolidated statements of cash flows. Aggregate transaction gains and losses included in the determination of net income are not material for any period presented. Forward contracts designated to hedge foreign currency transaction exposure of $257,051,000 and $266,471,000 were outstanding at December 31, 1997 and 1998, respectively. The estimated fair value of these forward contracts at December 31, 1997 and 1998 was $253,519,000 and $271,573,000, respectively, based on quoted market prices.

The Company continually monitors its positions with, and the credit quality of, the major international financial institutions which are counterparties to its foreign currency forward contracts, and does not anticipate nonperformance by any of these counterparties.

(q) Segment Data:

During 1998, the Company adopted SFAS No. 131, "Disclosures about Segments of an Enterprise and Related Information." SFAS No. 131 supercedes SFAS No. 14, "Financial Reporting for Segments of a Business Enterprise", replacing the "industry segment" approach with the "management" approach. The management approach designates the internal reporting that is used by management for making operating decisions and assessing performance as the source of the Company's reportable segments. SFAS 131 also requires disclosures about products and services, geographic areas and major customers. The adoption of SFAS 131 did not affect the consolidated financial position or results of operations of the Company but did affect its disclosure of segment information (Note 12).

(r) New Accounting Pronouncements:

In June of 1998, the Financial Accounting Standards Board issued SFAS No. 133, "Accounting for Derivative Instruments and Hedging Activities" which is effective for fiscal years beginning after June 15, 1999. The objective of the statement is to establish accounting and reporting standards for derivative instruments and hedging activities. The Company uses foreign currency forward contracts, a derivative instrument, to hedge foreign currency transactions and anticipated foreign currency transactions. The adoption of this new accounting pronouncement is not expected to be material to the Company's consolidated financial position or results of operations.

In 1998, the Accounting Standards Executive Committee (AcSEC) issued Statement of Accounting Position ("SOP") No. 98-1, "Accounting for the Costs of Computer Software Developed or Obtained for Internal Use," which is effective for fiscal years beginning after December 15, 1998. The SOP provides guidance on when costs incurred for internal-use computer software are and are not to be capitalized, and on the accounting for such software that is marketed to customers. The adoption of this SOP is not expected to have a material impact on the Company's consolidated financial position or results of operations.

2. Financing Arrangements:

(a) Credit Agreement:

The Company is party to an unsecured bank credit agreement (the "Agreement"), totaling $225 million. The Agreement consists of (1) a revolving line of credit facility for committed loans and bid loans; and (2) a sub-facility for letters of credit. Borrowings under the agreement bear interest at the banks' base rate or, at the Company's option, borrowing rates based on a fixed spread over the London Interbank Offered Rate (LIBOR). The Agreement requires the Company to maintain a minimum tangible net worth and maximum debt leverage ratio, as well as minimum fixed charge coverage. There were no borrowings outstanding at the end of 1997 and 1998.

At December 31, 1997 and 1998, approximately $3,515,000 and $2,000,000, respectively, was committed to support outstanding standby letters of credit.

(b) Long-term Obligations:

The carrying amount of the Company's long-term obligations approximates fair value, which is estimated based on current rates offered to the Company for obligations of the same remaining maturities. Long-term obligations consist of the following:

	December 31,	
	1997	**1998**
	(in thousands)	
Notes payable through 2001 with interest rates ranging from zero to 7.03%	$ 20,568	$ 14,408
Obligations under capital leases, payable in monthly installments at fixed rates ranging from 3.28% to 15.33% through 2002 (Note 3)	641	367
	21,209	14,775
Less current maturities	13,969	11,415
	$ 7,240	$ 3,360

The long-term obligations, excluding obligations under capital leases, have the following maturities as of December 31, 1998:

	(in thousands)
1999	$ 11,085
2000	2,841
2001	482
2002	—
2003	—
	$ 14,408

3. Commitments:

The Company leases certain operating facilities and equipment under noncancelable operating leases expiring at various dates through 2013. Rent expense was approximately $11,873,000, $16,105,000, and $25,713,000 for 1996, 1997 and 1998, respectively.

Future minimum lease payments under terms of these leases as of December 31, 1998 are as follows:

	Capital Leases	**Operating Leases**
	(in thousands)	
1999	$ 330	$ 39,400
2000	38	39,695
2001	12	38,794
2002	1	36,256
2003	—	26,523
Thereafter	—	25,910
Total minimum lease payments	$ 381	$ 206,578
Less amount representing interest	14	
Present value of net minimum lease payments	$ 367	

The Company has entered into licensing and royalty agreements which allow it to use certain hardware and software intellectual properties in its products. Minimum royalty payments due under these agreements for the period 1999 through 2002 total approximately $350,000,000. Total royalty expense is expected to be greater than this minimum amount for these periods.

4. Contingencies:

The Company is a party to various lawsuits and administrative proceedings arising in the ordinary course of its business. The Company evaluates such lawsuits and proceedings on a case-by-case basis, and its policy is to vigorously contest any such claims which it believes are without merit. The Company's management believes that the ultimate resolution of such pending matters will not materially adversely affect the Company's business, financial position, results of operations or cash flows.

5. Income Taxes:

The components of the provision for income taxes are as follows:

	1996	**1997**	**1998**
		For the year ended December 31,	
		(in thousands)	
Current:			
United States	$ 140,451	$ 154,049	$ 244,076
Foreign	4,981	3,021	9,198
Deferred:			
United States	(1,727)	(49,564)	(40,055)
Foreign	(11,668)	(13,683)	(18,370)
	$ 132,037	$ 93,823	$ 194,849

Income before income taxes included approximately $2,400,000, ($24,000,000) and ($13,100,000) related to foreign operations for the years ended December 31, 1996, 1997 and 1998, respectively.

A reconciliation of the provision for income taxes and the amount computed by applying the federal statutory income tax rate to income before income taxes is as follows:

	1996	**1997**	**1998**
		(in thousands)	
Federal income tax at statutory rate	$ 133,951	$ 71,267	$ 189,437
Nondeductible purchased research and development costs	—	20,704	—
Other, net	(1,914)	1,852	5,412
Provision for income taxes	$ 132,037	$ 93,823	$ 194,849

Deferred tax assets and deferred tax liabilities result from temporary differences in the following accounts:

	1997	**1998**
		December 31,
		(in thousands)
U.S. deferred tax assets:		
Inventory	$ 20,572	$ 17,721
Accounts receivable	6,775	5,206
Accrued liabilities	35,793	52,143
Other liabilities	36,912	60,539
Other	3,612	8,048
Total U.S.	103,664	143,657
Foreign deferred tax assets:		
Operating loss carryforwards	17,832	33,454
Other	2,459	5,207
Total foreign	20,291	38,661
Total deferred tax assets	123,955	182,318
U.S. deferred tax liabilities:		
Intangible assets	34,006	29,440
Property, plant & equipment	2,668	4,104
Other	3,439	6,507
Total deferred tax liabilities	40,113	40,051
Net deferred tax assets	$ 83,842	$ 142,267

The Company has foreign net operating loss carryforwards of $67,600,000. Of this amount, $10,500,000 expires in the year 2000, $27,400,000 in the year 2002, $14,300,000 in the year 2006 and $7,100,000 in the year 2008. The remaining $8,300,000 can be carried forward indefinitely. The Company has assessed its forecast of future taxable income and the expiration of carryforwards and has determined that is it more likely than not that the deferred tax asset relating to foreign net operating loss carryforwards will be realized.

6. Stock Option Plans:

The Company maintains various stock option plans for its employees. Employee options are generally granted at the fair market value of the related common stock at the date of grant. These options generally vest over a four-year period from the date of grant or the employee's initial date of employment. In addition, these options expire, if not exercised, ten years from the date of grant. The Company also maintains option plans for non-employee directors. Option grants to non-employee directors generally have an exercise price equal to the fair market value of the related common stock on the date of grant. These options generally vest over one to three-year periods and expire, if not exercised, ten years from the date of grant.

For all of the Company's stock option plans, options for 1,283,000, 2,582,000 and 2,728,000 shares of common stock were exercisable at December 31, 1996, 1997 and 1998 with a weighted average exercise price of $4.28, $9.86 and $17.42, respectively. In addition, options for 672,000, 556,000 and 280,000 shares of Class A common stock were exercisable at December 31, 1996, 1997 and 1998 with a weighted average exercise price of $2.06, $2.01 and $1.93, respectively. Class A common stock may be converted into an equal number of shares of common stock at any time. There were 12,309,000, 8,328,000 and 11,265,000 shares of common stock available for grant under the plans at December 31, 1996, 1997 and 1998, respectively.

The following table summarizes activity under the stock option plans for 1996, 1997 and 1998 (in thousands, except per share amounts):

	Common Stock	Weighted-Average Price	Class A Common Stock	Weighted-Average Price
Outstanding, December 31, 1995	8,739	$ 3.16	962	$ 2.14
Granted	3,260	15.75	—	—
Exercised	(6,305)	1.43	(241)	2.13
Forfeited	(254)	14.15	(8)	3.25
Outstanding, December 31, 1996	5,440	12.20	713	2.12
Granted	5,253	36.08	—	—
Exercised	(463)	11.56	(153)	2.50
Forfeited	(775)	23.69	—	—
Outstanding, December 31, 1997	9,455	22.98	560	2.02
Granted	6,118	45.17	—	—
Exercised	(2,143)	16.59	(280)	2.10
Forfeited	(1,103)	32.76	—	—
Outstanding, December 31, 1998	12,327	$ 34.19	280	$ 1.93

The following table summarizes information about the Company's Common Stock options outstanding at December 31, 1998 (in thousands, except per share amounts):

	Options Outstanding			Options Exercisable	
Range of Exercise Prices	Number Outstanding at 12/31/98	Weighted-Average Remaining Contractual Life	Weighted-Average Price	Number Exercisable at 12/31/98	Weighted-Average Price
$ 1.19 -13.38	1,928	5.57	$ 9.01	1,259	$ 6.76
13.44 -29.07	2,287	7.65	22.93	939	20.01
29.31 -33.75	2,405	8.87	33.06	267	32.35
34.00 -44.75	2,811	8.94	39.55	262	43.88
45.06 -62.50	2,896	9.68	55.56	1	61.75

The weighted average fair value per share of options granted during 1996, 1997 and 1998 was $9.65, $21.61 and $27.33, respectively. The fair value of these options was estimated on the date of grant using the Black-Scholes option pricing model with the following weighted-average assumptions used for all grants in 1996, 1997 and 1998: dividend yield of zero percent; expected volatility of 60 percent; risk-free interest rates ranging from 4.7 to 7.2 percent; and expected lives of the options of three and one-half years from the date of vesting.

Since all stock options have been granted with exercise prices equal to the fair market value of the related common stock at the date of grant, no compensation expense has been recognized under the Company's stock option plans. Had compensation cost under the plans been determined based on the estimated fair value of the stock options granted in 1996, 1997 and 1998, net income and net income per share would have been reduced to the pro forma amounts indicated below:

	1996	1997	1998
	(in thousands, except per share amounts)		
Net income - as reported	$ 250,679	$ 109,797	$ 346,399
Net income - pro forma	$ 241,729	$ 85,804	$ 297,470
Net income per share - as reported			
Basic	$ 1.64	$ .71	$ 2.23
Diluted	$ 1.60	$ .70	$ 2.18
Net income per share - pro forma			
Basic	$ 1.58	$ .56	$ 1.91
Diluted	$ 1.55	$ .55	$ 1.87

The pro forma effect on net income for 1996, 1997 and 1998 is not fully representative of the pro forma effect on net income in future years because it does not take into consideration pro forma compensation expense related to the vesting of grants made prior to 1995.

7.   Retirement Savings Plan:

The Company has a 401(k) defined contribution plan which covers employees who have attained 18 years of age and have been employed by the Company for at least six months. Participants may contribute up to 20% of their compensation in any plan year and receive a 50% matching employer contribution of up to 6% of their annual eligible compensation. The Company contributed $871,000, $2,068,000, and $4,730,000 to the Plan during 1996, 1997 and 1998, respectively.

8.   Acquisition:

During the third quarter of 1997, the Company acquired substantially all of the outstanding shares of common stock of Advanced Logic Research, Inc. (ALR), a manufacturer of network servers and personal computers, for a cash purchase price of approximately $196,400,000. The operating results of ALR were not material for all periods presented.

9.   Nonrecurring Expenses:

The Company recorded several nonrecurring pretax charges during the third quarter of 1997 totaling approximately $113,800,000. Of the nonrecurring charges, approximately $59,700,000 was for the write-off of in-process research and development acquired in the purchase of ALR and certain assets of Amiga Technologies. Also included in the nonrecurring charges was a non-cash write-off of approximately $45,200,000 resulting from the abandonment of a capitalized internal use software project and certain computer equipment. In addition, approximately $8,600,000 was recorded for severance of employees and the closing of a foreign office.

10.   Selected Balance Sheet Information:

	December 31,	
	1997	**1998**
	(in thousands)	
Accounts receivable, net:		
Accounts receivable	$ 530,743	$ 573,799
Allowance for uncollectible accounts	(20,064)	(14,948)
	$ 510,679	$ 558,851
Inventory:		
Components and subassemblies	$ 215,318	$ 155,746
Finished goods	33,906	12,178
	$ 249,224	$ 167,924
Property, plant and equipment, net:		
Land	$ 21,431	$ 21,784
Leasehold improvements	21,666	57,118
Buildings	162,318	186,361
Construction in progress	15,448	74,105
Internal use software	81,412	94,306
Office and production equipment	186,281	249,924
Furniture and fixtures	42,055	66,578
Vehicles	4,105	15,402
	534,716	765,578
Accumulated depreciation and amortization	(158,249)	(234,590)
	$ 376,467	$ 530,988

11.   Supplemental Statements of Cash Flows Information:

	Year ended December 31,		
	1996	**1997**	**1998**
	(in thousands)		
Supplemental disclosure of cash flow information:			
Cash paid during the year for interest	$ 665	$ 716	$ 930
Cash paid during the year for income taxes	$ 101,774	$ 163,710	$ 200,839
Supplemental schedule of noncash investing and financing activities:			
Capital lease obligations incurred for the purchase of new equipment	$ 3,126	$ 4,593	$ 6,741
Acquisitions			
Fair value of assets acquired		$ 271,189	
Less: Liabilities assumed		70,773	
Cash acquired		58,096	
Acquisitions, net of cash acquired		$ 142,320	

12.   Segment Data:

Prior to 1998, the Company managed its business segments principally on a geographic basis. The reportable segments were comprised of the United States; Europe, Middle East and Africa ("EMEA"); and Asia Pacific ("APAC"). During 1998, the Company began to manage its business activities primarily in two customer focused segments: consumer and business. The accounting policies of the various segments are the same as those described in the "Summary of Significant Accounting Policies" in Note 1. The Company evaluates the performance of its consumer and business segments based on segment sales, gross profit and operating income and does not include segment assets or other income and expense items for management reporting purposes. Operating income for these segments includes selling, general, and administrative expenses and other overhead charges directly attributable to the segment and excludes certain expenses managed outside the reportable segments. Costs excluded from the consumer and business segments primarily consist of corporate marketing costs and other general and administrative expenses that are separately managed. Prior periods' segment information has not been restated to reflect the consumer and business segments as it is impractical to do so.

The following table sets forth summary information by segment:

	Consumer	**Business**	**Non-segment**	**Consolidated**
		(in thousands)		
1998:				
Net sales	$ 3,945,071	$ 3,522,854	$ —	$ 7,467,925
Gross profit	760,816	783,262	2,196	1,546,274
Operating income (loss)	$ 461,351	$ 600,844	$ (567,968)	$ 494,227

The following table sets forth information about the Company's operations by geographic area:

	United States	EMEA	APAC	Inter-segment Eliminations	Consolidated
			(in thousands)		
1998:					
Net sales to external customers	$ 6,412,405	$ 570,191	$ 485,329	$ —	$ 7,467,925
Net sales between geographic segments	53,073	22,298	11,358	(86,729)	—
Operating income (loss)	500,881	(6,685)	1,233	(1,202)	494,227
Segment assets	2,473,627	209,820	206,933	—	2,890,380
Long-lived assets	522,972	57,548	30,184	—	610,704
Other income, net	44,524	1,380	2,041	(924)	47,021
Income taxes	205,129	(3,048)	(7,232)	—	194,849
Depreciation and amortization	84,378	9,820	12,318	(992)	105,524
1997:					
Net sales to external customers	$ 5,303,828	$ 634,616	$ 355,236	$ —	$ 6,293,680
Net sales between geographic segments	56,922	16,163	21,071	(94,156)	—
Operating income (loss)	198,638	(11,566)	(9,733)	(908)	176,431
Non-recurring expenses	111,394	1,100	1,348	—	113,842
Segment assets	1,701,654	187,215	150,402	—	2,039,271
Long-lived assets	380,757	59,261	34,278	—	474,296
Other income, net	25,223	2,946	(798)	(182)	27,189
Income taxes	104,552	568	(11,297)	—	93,823
Depreciation and amortization	67,895	6,695	12,292	(108)	86,774
1996:					
Net sales to external customers	$ 4,246,047	$ 552,671	$ 236,510	$ —	$ 5,035,228
Net sales between geographic segments	30,208	23,538	4,087	(57,833)	—
Operating income (loss)	347,348	19,930	(9,946)	(1,238)	356,094
Segment assets	1,349,781	178,988	144,642	—	1,673,411
Long-lived assets	248,272	48,025	44,815	—	341,112
Other income, net	24,533	2,108	(19)	—	26,622
Income taxes	138,724	1,572	(8,259)	—	132,037
Depreciation and amortization	46,688	4,236	10,839	—	61,763

Net sales between geographic segments are recorded using internal transfer prices set by the Company. The United Sates operating income is net of corporate expenses. Export sales from the United States to unaffiliated customers are not material for any period presented.

13.   Selected Quarterly Financial Data (Unaudited):

The following tables contain selected unaudited consolidated quarterly financial data for the Company:

	1st Quarter	2nd Quarter	3rd Quarter	4th Quarter
		(in thousands, except per share amounts)		
1998:				
Net sales	$1,727,927	$1,618,909	$1,815,516	$ 2,305,573
Gross profit	336,494	333,688	377,807	498,285
Operating income	109,201	83,989	113,355	187,682
Net income	75,871	60,740	80,645	129,143
Net income per share:				
Basic	$.49	$.39	$.52	$.83
Diluted	$.48	$.38	$.51	$.81
Weighted average shares outstanding:				
Basic	154,548	155,427	155,849	156,324
Diluted	157,575	158,887	159,518	159,567
Stock sales price per share:				
High	$48.25	$58.81	$67.13	$61.63
Low	$32.50	$42.56	$46.44	$41.50
1997:				
Net sales	$1,419,336	$1,392,658	$1,504,851	$ 1,976,835
Gross profit	265,793	260,358	195,250	355,040
Nonrecurring expenses	—	—	113,842	—
Operating income (loss)	94,878	79,851	(137,850)	139,551
Net income (loss)	67,516	56,483	(107,113)	92,910
Net income (loss) per share:				
Basic	$ .44	$ .37	$ (.70)	$ .60
Diluted	$ .43	$ .36	$ (.68)	$ .59
Weighted average shares outstanding:				
Basic	153,557	153,740	153,980	153,840
Diluted	157,291	156,231	156,875	156,526
Stock sales price per share:				
High	$ 32.63	$ 37.38	$ 44.75	$ 36.13
Low	$ 23.81	$ 26.19	$ 31.50	$ 25.13

14.   Subsequent Event (Unaudited):

As of February 28, 1999, the Company has made a commitment to purchase approximately $290 million of consumer finance receivables used to purchase the Company's products which were originated by a financial institution on behalf of Gateway. These receivables have terms of two to four years and earn interest at rates ranging from 14.9% to 26.99%.

Common Stock

The Company's Common Stock is traded on the New York Stock Exchange under the symbol GTW. For information on market prices of Gateway's Common Stock, please refer to note 13 above. There were 4,226 stockholders of record as of March 25, 1999.

Present Value and Future Value Tables

TABLE 1

FUTURE AMOUNT OF 1 (FUTURE AMOUNT OF A SINGLE SUM)

(n) Periods	½%	¾%	1%	1½%	2%	3%	4%	5%
1	1.00500	1.00750	1.01000	1.01500	1.02000	1.03000	1.04000	1.05000
2	1.01003	1.01506	1.02010	1.03023	1.04040	1.06090	1.08160	1.10250
3	1.01508	1.02267	1.03030	1.04568	1.06121	1.09273	1.12486	1.15763
4	1.02015	1.03034	1.04060	1.06136	1.08243	1.12551	1.16986	1.21551
5	1.02525	1.03807	1.05101	1.07728	1.10408	1.15927	1.21665	1.27628
6	1.03038	1.04585	1.06152	1.09344	1.12616	1.19405	1.26532	1.34010
7	1.03553	1.05370	1.07214	1.10984	1.14869	1.22987	1.31593	1.40710
8	1.04071	1.06160	1.08286	1.12649	1.17166	1.26677	1.36857	1.47746
9	1.04591	1.06956	1.09369	1.14339	1.19509	1.30477	1.42331	1.55133
10	1.05114	1.07758	1.10462	1.16054	1.21899	1.34392	1.48024	1.62889
11	1.05640	1.08566	1.11567	1.17795	1.24337	1.38423	1.53945	1.71034
12	1.06168	1.09381	1.12683	1.19562	1.26824	1.42576	1.60103	1.79586
13	1.06699	1.10201	1.13809	1.21355	1.29361	1.46853	1.66507	1.88565
14	1.07232	1.11028	1.14947	1.23176	1.31948	1.51259	1.73168	1.97993
15	1.07768	1.11860	1.16097	1.25023	1.34587	1.55797	1.80094	2.07893
16	1.08307	1.12699	1.17258	1.26899	1.37279	1.60471	1.87298	2.18287
17	1.08849	1.13544	1.18430	1.28802	1.40024	1.65285	1.94790	2.29202
18	1.09393	1.14396	1.19615	1.30734	1.42825	1.70243	2.02582	2.40662
19	1.09940	1.15254	1.20811	1.32695	1.45681	1.75351	2.10685	2.52695
20	1.10490	1.16118	1.22019	1.34686	1.48595	1.80611	2.19112	2.65330
21	1.11042	1.16989	1.23239	1.36706	1.51567	1.86029	2.27877	2.78596
22	1.11597	1.17867	1.24472	1.38756	1.54598	1.91610	2.36992	2.92526
23	1.12155	1.18751	1.25716	1.40838	1.57690	1.97359	2.46472	3.07152
24	1.12716	1.19641	1.26973	1.42950	1.60844	2.03279	2.56330	3.22510
25	1.13280	1.20539	1.28243	1.45095	1.64061	2.09378	2.66584	3.38635
26	1.13846	1.21443	1.29526	1.47271	1.67342	2.15659	2.77247	3.55567
27	1.14415	1.22354	1.30821	1.49480	1.70689	2.22129	2.88337	3.73346
28	1.14987	1.23271	1.32129	1.51722	1.74102	2.28793	2.99870	3.92013
29	1.15562	1.24196	1.33450	1.53998	1.77584	2.35657	3.11865	4.11614
30	1.16140	1.25127	1.34785	1.56308	1.81136	2.42726	3.24340	4.32194
31	1.16721	1.26066	1.36133	1.58653	1.84759	2.50008	3.37313	4.53804
32	1.17304	1.27011	1.37494	1.61032	1.88454	2.57508	3.50806	4.76494
33	1.17891	1.27964	1.38869	1.63448	1.92223	2.65234	3.64838	5.00319
34	1.18480	1.28923	1.40258	1.65900	1.96068	2.73191	3.79432	5.25335
35	1.19073	1.29890	1.41660	1.68388	1.99989	2.81386	3.94609	5.51602
36	1.19668	1.30865	1.43077	1.70914	2.03989	2.89828	4.10393	5.79182
37	1.20266	1.31846	1.44508	1.73478	2.08069	2.98523	4.26809	6.08141
38	1.20868	1.32835	1.45953	1.76080	2.12230	3.07478	4.43881	6.38548
39	1.21472	1.33831	1.47412	1.78721	2.16474	3.16703	4.61637	6.70475
40	1.22079	1.34835	1.48886	1.81402	2.20804	3.26204	4.80102	7.03999
48	1.27049	1.43141	1.61223	2.04348	2.58707	4.13225	6.57053	10.40127
60	1.34885	1.56568	1.81670	2.44322	3.28103	5.89160	10.51963	18.67919

6%	7%	8%	9%	10%	11%	12%	15%	(n) Periods
1.06000	1.07000	1.08000	1.09000	1.10000	1.11000	1.12000	1.15000	1
1.12360	1.14490	1.16640	1.18810	1.21000	1.23210	1.25440	1.32250	2
1.19102	1.22504	1.25971	1.29503	1.33100	1.36763	1.40493	1.52088	3
1.26248	1.31080	1.36049	1.41158	1.46410	1.51807	1.57352	1.74901	4
1.33823	1.40255	1.46933	1.53862	1.61051	1.68506	1.76234	2.01136	5
1.41852	1.50073	1.58687	1.67710	1.77156	1.87041	1.97382	2.31306	6
1.50363	1.60578	1.71382	1.82804	1.94872	2.07616	2.21068	2.66002	7
1.59385	1.71819	1.85093	1.99256	2.14359	2.30454	2.47596	3.05902	8
1.68948	1.83846	1.99900	2.17189	2.35795	2.55803	2.77308	3.51788	9
1.79085	1.96715	2.15892	2.36736	2.59374	2.83942	3.10585	4.04556	10
1.89830	2.10485	2.33164	2.58043	2.85312	3.15176	3.47855	4.65239	11
2.01220	2.25219	2.51817	2.81267	3.13843	3.49845	3.89598	5.35025	12
2.13293	2.40985	2.71962	3.06581	3.45227	3.88328	4.36349	6.15279	13
2.26090	2.57853	2.93719	3.34173	3.79750	4.31044	4.88711	7.07571	14
2.39656	2.75903	3.17217	3.64248	4.17725	4.78459	5.47357	8.13706	15
2.54035	2.95216	3.42594	3.97031	4.59497	5.31089	6.13039	9.35762	16
2.69277	3.15882	3.70002	4.32763	5.05447	5.89509	6.86604	10.76126	17
2.85434	3.37993	3.99602	4.71712	5.55992	6.54355	7.68997	12.37545	18
3.02560	3.61653	4.31570	5.14166	6.11591	7.26334	8.61276	14.23177	19
3.20714	3.86968	4.66096	5.60441	6.72750	8.06231	9.64629	16.36654	20
3.39956	4.14056	5.03383	6.10881	7.40025	8.94917	10.80385	18.82152	21
3.60354	4.43040	5.43654	6.65860	8.14028	9.93357	12.10031	21.64475	22
3.81975	4.74053	5.87146	7.25787	8.95430	11.02627	13.55235	24.89146	23
4.04893	5.07237	6.34118	7.91108	9.84973	12.23916	15.17863	28.62518	24
4.29187	5.42743	6.84847	8.62308	10.83471	13.58546	17.00000	32.91895	25
4.54938	5.80735	7.39635	9.39916	11.91818	15.07986	19.04007	37.85680	26
4.82235	6.21387	7.98806	10.24508	13.10999	16.73865	21.32488	43.53532	27
5.11169	6.64884	8.62711	11.16714	14.42099	18.57990	23.88387	50.06561	28
5.41839	7.11426	9.31727	12.17218	15.86309	20.62369	26.74993	57.57545	29
5.74349	7.61226	10.06266	13.26768	17.44940	22.89230	29.95992	66.21177	30
6.08810	8.14511	10.86767	14.46177	19.19434	25.41045	33.55511	76.14354	31
6.45339	8.71527	11.73708	15.76333	21.11378	28.20560	37.58173	87.56507	32
6.84059	9.32534	12.67605	17.18203	23.22515	31.30821	42.09153	100.69983	33
7.25103	9.97811	13.69013	18.72841	25.54767	34.75212	47.14252	115.80480	34
7.68609	10.67658	14.78534	20.41397	28.10244	38.57485	52.79962	133.17552	35
8.14725	11.42394	15.96817	22.25123	30.91268	42.81808	59.13557	153.15185	36
8.63609	12.22362	17.24563	24.25384	34.00395	47.52807	66.23184	176.12463	37
9.15425	13.07927	18.62528	26.43668	37.40434	52.75616	74.17966	202.54332	38
9.70351	13.99482	20.11530	28.81598	41.14479	58.55934	83.08122	232.92482	39
10.28572	14.97446	21.72452	31.40942	45.25926	65.00087	93.05097	267.86355	40
16.39387	25.72891	40.21057	62.58524	97.01723	149.79695	230.39078	819.40071	48
32.98769	57.94643	101.25706	176.03129	304.48164	524.05724	897.59693	4383.99875	60

TABLE 2

PRESENT VALUE OF 1 (PRESENT VALUE OF A SINGLE SUM)

(n) Periods	½%	¾%	1%	1½%	2%	3%	4%	5%
1	.99502	.99256	.99010	.98522	.98039	.97087	.96154	.95238
2	.99007	.98517	.98030	.97066	.96117	.94260	.92456	.90703
3	.98515	.97783	.97059	.95632	.94232	.91514	.88900	.86384
4	.98025	.97055	.96098	.94218	.92385	.88849	.85480	.82270
5	.97537	.96333	.95147	.92826	.90573	.86261	.82193	.78353
6	.97052	.95616	.94205	.91454	.88797	.83748	.79031	.74622
7	.96569	.94904	.93272	.90103	.87056	.81309	.75992	.71068
8	.96089	.94198	.92348	.88771	.85349	.78941	.73069	.67684
9	.95610	.93496	.91434	.87459	.83676	.76642	.70259	.64461
10	.95135	.92800	.90529	.86167	.82035	.74409	.67556	.61391
11	.94661	.92109	.89632	.84893	.80426	.72242	.64958	.58468
12	.94191	.91424	.88745	.83639	.78849	.70138	.62460	.55684
13	.93722	.90743	.87866	.82403	.77303	.68095	.60057	.53032
14	.93256	.90068	.86996	.81185	.75788	.66112	.57748	.50507
15	.92792	.89397	.86135	.79985	.74301	.64186	.55526	.48102
16	.92330	.88732	.85282	.78803	.72845	.62317	.53391	.45811
17	.91871	.88071	.84438	.77639	.71416	.60502	.51337	.43630
18	.91414	.87416	.83602	.76491	.70016	.58739	.49363	.41552
19	.90959	.86765	.82774	.75361	.68643	.57029	.47464	.39573
20	.90506	.86119	.81954	.74247	.67297	.55368	.45639	.37689
21	.90056	.85478	.81143	.73150	.65978	.53755	.43883	.35894
22	.89608	.84842	.80340	.72069	.64684	.52189	.42196	.34185
23	.89162	.84210	.79544	.71004	.63416	.50669	.40573	.32557
24	.88719	.83583	.78757	.69954	.62172	.49193	.39012	.31007
25	.88277	.82961	.77977	.68921	.60953	.47761	.37512	.29530
26	.87838	.82343	.77205	.67902	.59758	.46369	.36069	.28124
27	.87401	.81730	.76440	.66899	.58586	.45019	.34682	.26785
28	.86966	.81122	.75684	.65910	.57437	.43708	.33348	.25509
29	.86533	.80518	.74934	.64936	.56311	.42435	.32065	.24295
30	.86103	.79919	.74192	.63976	.55207	.41199	.30832	.23138
31	.85675	.79324	.73458	.63031	.54125	.39999	.29646	.22036
32	.85248	.78733	.72730	.62099	.53063	.38834	.28506	.20987
33	.84824	.78147	.72010	.61182	.52023	.37703	.27409	.19987
34	.84402	.77565	.71297	.60277	.51003	.36604	.26355	.19035
35	.83982	.76988	.70591	.59387	.50003	.35538	.25342	.18129
36	.83564	.76415	.69892	.58509	.49022	.34503	.24367	.17266
37	.83149	.75846	.69200	.57644	.48061	.33498	.23430	.16444
38	.82735	.75281	.68515	.56792	.47119	.32523	.22529	.15661
39	.82323	.74721	.67837	.55953	.46195	.31575	.21662	.14915
40	.81914	.74165	.67165	.55126	.45289	.30656	.20829	.14205
48	.78710	.69861	.62026	.48936	.38654	.24200	.15219	.09614
60	.74137	.63870	.55045	.40930	.30478	.16973	.09506	.05354

6%	7%	8%	9%	10%	11%	12%	15%	(n) Periods
.94340	.93458	.92593	.91743	.90909	.90090	.89286	.86957	1
.89000	.87344	.85734	.84168	.82645	.81162	.79719	.75614	2
.83962	.81630	.79383	.77218	.75132	.73119	.71178	.65752	3
.79209	.76290	.73503	.70843	.68301	.65873	.63552	.57175	4
.74726	.71299	.68058	.64993	.62092	.59345	.56743	.49718	5
.70496	.66634	.63017	.59627	.56447	.53464	.50663	.43233	6
.66506	.62275	.58349	.54703	.51316	.48166	.45235	.37594	7
.62741	.58201	.54027	.50187	.46651	.43393	.40388	.32690	8
.59190	.54393	.50025	.46043	.42410	.39092	.36061	.28426	9
.55839	.50835	.46319	.42241	.38554	.35218	.32197	.24719	10
.52679	.47509	.42888	.38753	.35049	.31728	.28748	.21494	11
.49697	.44401	.39711	.35554	.31863	.28584	.25668	.18691	12
.46884	.41496	.36770	.32618	.28966	.25751	.22917	.16253	13
.44230	.38782	.34046	.29925	.26333	.23199	.20462	.14133	14
.41727	.36245	.31524	.27454	.23939	.20900	.18270	.12289	15
.39365	.33873	.29189	.25187	.21763	.18829	.16312	.10687	16
.37136	.31657	.27027	.23107	.19785	.16963	.14564	.09293	17
.35034	.29586	.25025	.21199	.17986	.15282	.13004	.08081	18
.33051	.27651	.23171	.19449	.16351	.13768	.11611	.07027	19
.31180	.25842	.21455	.17843	.14864	.12403	.10367	.06110	20
.29416	.24151	.19866	.16370	.13513	.11174	.09256	.05313	21
.27751	.22571	.18394	.15018	.12285	.10067	.08264	.04620	22
.26180	.21095	.17032	.13778	.11168	.09069	.07379	.04017	23
.24698	.19715	.15770	.12641	.10153	.08170	.06588	.03493	24
.23300	.18425	.14602	.11597	.09230	.07361	.05882	.03038	25
.21981	.17220	.13520	.10639	.08391	.06631	.05252	.02642	26
.20737	.16093	.12519	.09761	.07628	.05974	.04689	.02297	27
.19563	.15040	.11591	.08955	.06934	.05382	.04187	.01997	28
.18456	.14056	.10733	.08216	.06304	.04849	.03738	.01737	29
.17411	.13137	.09938	.07537	.05731	.04368	.03338	.01510	30
.16425	.12277	.09202	.06915	.05210	.03935	.02980	.01313	31
.15496	.11474	.08520	.06344	.04736	.03545	.02661	.01142	32
.14619	.10723	.07889	.05820	.04306	.03194	.02376	.00993	33
.13791	.10022	.07305	.05340	.03914	.02878	.02121	.00864	34
.13011	.09366	.06763	.04899	.03558	.02592	.01894	.00751	35
.12274	.08754	.06262	.04494	.03235	.02335	.01691	.00653	36
.11579	.08181	.05799	.04123	.02941	.02104	.01510	.00568	37
.10924	.07646	.05369	.03783	.02674	.01896	.01348	.00494	38
.10306	.07146	.04971	.03470	.02430	.01708	.01204	.00429	39
.09722	.06678	.04603	.03184	.02210	.01538	.01075	.00373	40
.06100	.03887	.02487	.01598	.01031	.00668	.00434	.00122	48
.03031	.01726	.00988	.00568	.00328	.00191	.00111	.00023	60

TABLE 3

FUTURE AMOUNT OF AN ORDINARY ANNUITY OF 1

(n) Periods	½%	¾%	1%	1½%	2%	3%	4%	5%
1	1.00000	1.00000	1.00000	1.00000	1.00000	1.00000	1.00000	1.00000
2	2.00500	2.00750	2.01000	2.01500	2.02000	2.03000	2.04000	2.05000
3	3.01502	3.02256	3.03010	3.04522	3.06040	3.09090	3.12160	3.15250
4	4.03010	4.04523	4.06040	4.09090	4.12161	4.18363	4.24646	4.31013
5	5.05025	5.07556	5.10101	5.15227	5.20404	5.30914	5.41632	5.52563
6	6.07550	6.11363	6.15202	6.22955	6.30812	6.46841	6.63298	6.80191
7	7.10588	7.15948	7.21354	7.32299	7.43428	7.66246	7.89829	8.14201
8	8.14141	8.21318	8.28567	8.43284	8.58297	8.89234	9.21423	9.54911
9	9.18212	9.27478	9.36853	9.55933	9.75463	10.15911	10.58280	11.02656
10	10.22803	10.34434	10.46221	10.70272	10.94972	11.46338	12.00611	12.57789
11	11.27917	11.42192	11.56683	11.86326	12.16872	12.80780	13.48635	14.20679
12	12.33556	12.50759	12.68250	13.04121	13.41209	14.19203	15.02581	15.91713
13	13.39724	13.60139	13.80933	14.23683	14.68033	15.61779	16.62684	17.71298
14	14.46423	14.70340	14.94742	15.45038	15.97394	17.08632	18.29191	19.59863
15	15.53655	15.81368	16.09690	16.68214	17.29342	18.59891	20.02359	21.57856
16	16.61423	16.93228	17.25786	17.93237	18.63929	20.15688	21.82453	23.65749
17	17.69730	18.05927	18.43044	19.20136	20.01207	21.76159	23.69751	25.84037
18	18.78579	19.19472	19.61475	20.48938	21.41231	23.41444	25.64541	28.13238
19	19.87972	20.33868	20.81090	21.79672	22.84056	25.11687	27.67123	30.53900
20	20.97912	21.49122	22.01900	23.12367	24.29737	26.87037	29.77808	33.06595
21	22.08401	22.65240	23.23919	24.47052	25.78332	28.67649	31.96920	35.71925
22	23.19443	23.82230	24.47159	25.83758	27.29898	30.53678	34.24797	38.50521
23	24.31040	25.00096	25.71630	27.22514	28.84496	32.45288	36.61789	41.43048
24	25.43196	26.18847	26.97346	28.63352	30.42186	34.42647	39.08260	44.50200
25	26.55912	27.38488	28.24320	30.06302	32.03030	36.45926	41.64591	47.72710
26	27.69191	28.59027	29.52563	31.51397	33.67091	38.55304	44.31174	51.11345
27	28.83037	29.80470	30.82089	32.98668	35.34432	40.70963	47.08421	54.66913
28	29.97452	31.02823	32.12910	34.48148	37.05121	42.93092	49.96758	58.40258
29	31.12439	32.26094	33.45039	35.99870	38.79223	45.21885	52.96629	62.32271
30	32.28002	33.50290	34.78489	37.53868	40.56808	47.57542	56.08494	66.43885
31	33.44142	34.75417	36.13274	39.10176	42.37944	50.00268	59.32834	70.76079
32	34.60862	36.01483	37.49407	40.66829	44.22703	52.50276	62.70147	75.29883
33	35.78167	37.28494	38.86901	42.29861	46.11157	55.07784	66.20953	80.06377
34	36.96058	38.56458	40.25770	43.93309	48.03380	57.73018	69.85791	85.06696
35	38.14538	39.85381	41.66028	45.59209	49.99448	60.46208	73.65222	90.32031
36	39.33610	41.15272	43.07688	47.27597	51.99437	63.27594	77.59831	95.83632
37	40.53279	42.46136	44.50765	48.98511	54.03425	66.17422	81.70225	101.62814
38	41.73545	43.77982	45.95272	50.71989	56.11494	69.15945	85.97034	107.70955
39	42.94413	45.10817	47.41225	52.48068	58.23724	72.23423	90.40915	114.09502
40	44.15885	46.44648	48.88637	54.26789	60.40198	75.40126	95.02552	120.79977
48	54.09783	57.52071	61.22261	69.56522	79.35352	104.40840	139.26321	188.02539
60	69.77003	75.42414	81.66967	96.21465	114.05154	163.05344	237.99069	353.58372

6%	7%	8%	9%	10%	11%	12%	15%	(n) Periods
1.00000	1.00000	1.00000	1.00000	1.00000	1.00000	1.00000	1.00000	1
2.06000	2.07000	2.08000	2.09000	2.10000	2.11000	2.12000	2.15000	2
3.18360	3.21490	3.24640	3.27810	3.31000	3.34210	3.37440	3.47250	3
4.37462	4.43994	4.50611	4.57313	4.64100	4.70973	4.77933	4.99338	4
5.63709	5.75074	5.86660	5.98471	6.10510	6.22780	6.35285	6.74238	5
6.97532	7.15329	7.33592	7.52334	7.71561	7.91286	8.11519	8.75374	6
8.39384	8.65402	8.92280	9.20044	9.48717	9.78327	10.08901	11.06680	7
9.89747	10.25980	10.63663	11.02847	11.43589	11.85943	12.29969	13.72682	8
11.49132	11.97799	12.48756	13.02104	13.57948	14.16397	14.77566	16.78584	9
13.18079	13.81645	14.48656	15.19293	15.93743	16.72201	17.54874	20.30372	10
14.97164	15.78360	16.64549	17.56029	18.53117	19.56143	20.65458	24.34928	11
16.86994	17.88845	18.97713	20.14072	21.38428	22.71319	24.13313	29.00167	12
18.88214	20.14064	21.49530	22.95339	24.52271	26.21164	28.02911	34.35192	13
21.01507	22.55049	24.21492	26.01919	27.97498	30.09492	32.39260	40.50471	14
23.27597	25.12902	27.15211	29.36092	31.77248	34.40536	37.27972	47.58041	15
25.67253	27.88805	30.32428	33.00340	35.94973	39.18995	42.75328	55.71747	16
28.21288	30.84022	33.75023	36.97371	40.54470	44.50084	48.88367	65.07509	17
30.90565	33.99903	37.45024	41.30134	45.59917	50.39593	55.74972	75.83636	18
33.75999	37.37896	41.44626	46.01846	51.15909	56.93949	63.43968	88.21181	19
36.78559	40.99549	45.76196	51.16012	57.27500	64.20283	72.05244	102.44358	20
39.99273	44.86518	50.42292	56.76453	64.00250	72.26514	81.69874	118.81012	21
43.39229	49.00574	55.45676	62.87334	71.40275	81.21431	92.50258	137.63164	22
46.99583	53.43614	60.89330	69.53194	79.54302	91.14788	104.60289	159.27638	23
50.81558	58.17667	66.76476	76.78981	88.49733	102.17415	118.15524	184.16784	24
54.86451	63.24904	73.10594	84.70090	98.34706	114.41331	133.33387	212.79302	25
59.15638	68.67647	79.95442	93.32398	109.18177	127.99877	150.33393	245.71197	26
63.70577	74.48382	87.35077	102.72314	121.09994	143.07864	169.37401	283.56877	27
68.52811	80.69769	95.33883	112.96822	134.20994	159.81729	190.69889	327.10408	28
73.63980	87.34653	103.96594	124.13536	148.63093	178.39719	214.58275	377.16969	29
79.05819	94.46079	113.28321	136.30754	164.49402	199.02088	241.33268	434.74515	30
84.80168	102.07304	123.34587	149.57522	181.94343	221.91317	271.29261	500.95692	31
90.88978	110.21815	134.21354	164.03699	201.13777	247.32362	304.84772	577.10046	32
97.34316	118.93343	145.95062	179.80032	222.25154	275.52922	342.42945	644.66553	33
104.18376	128.25876	158.62667	196.98234	245.47670	306.83744	384.52098	765.36535	34
111.43478	138.23688	172.31680	215.71076	271.02437	341.58955	431.66350	881.17016	35
119.12087	148.91346	187.10215	236.12472	299.12681	380.16441	484.46312	1014.34568	36
127.26812	160.33740	203.07032	258.37595	330.03949	422.98249	543.59869	1167.49753	37
135.90421	172.56102	220.31595	282.62978	364.04343	470.51056	609.83053	1343.62216	38
145.05846	185.64029	238.94122	309.06646	401.44778	523.26673	684.01020	1546.16549	39
154.76197	199.63511	259.05652	337.88245	442.59256	581.82607	767.09142	1779.09031	40
256.56453	353.27009	490.13216	684.28041	960.17234	1352.69958	1911.58980	5456.00475	48
533.12818	813.52038	1253.21330	1944.79213	3034.81640	4755.06584	7471.64111	29219.99164	60

TABLE 4

PRESENT VALUE OF AN ORDINARY ANNUITY OF 1

(n) Periods	½%	¾%	1%	1½%	2%	3%	4%	5%
1	.99502	.99256	.99010	.98522	.98039	.97087	.96154	.95238
2	1.98510	1.97772	1.97040	1.95588	1.94156	1.91347	1.88609	1.85941
3	2.97025	2.95556	2.94099	2.91220	2.88388	2.82861	2.77509	2.72325
4	3.95050	3.92611	3.90197	3.85438	3.80773	3.71710	3.62990	3.54595
5	4.92587	4.88944	4.85343	4.78264	4.71346	4.57971	4.45182	4.32948
6	5.89638	5.84560	5.79548	5.69719	5.60143	5.41719	5.24214	5.07569
7	6.86207	6.79464	6.72819	6.59821	6.47199	6.23028	6.00205	5.78637
8	7.82296	7.73661	7.65168	7.48593	7.32548	7.01969	6.73274	6.46321
9	8.77906	8.67158	8.56602	8.36052	8.16224	7.78611	7.43533	7.10782
10	9.73041	9.59958	9.47130	9.22218	8.98259	8.53020	8.11090	7.72173
11	10.67703	10.52067	10.36763	10.07112	9.78685	9.25262	8.76048	8.30641
12	11.61893	11.43491	11.25508	10.90751	10.57534	9.95400	9.38507	8.86325
13	12.44615	12.34235	12.13374	11.73153	11.34837	10.63496	9.98565	9.39357
14	13.48871	13.24302	13.00370	12.54338	12.10625	11.29607	10.56312	9.89864
15	14.41662	14.13699	13.86505	13.34323	12.84926	11.93794	11.11839	10.37966
16	15.33993	15.02431	14.71787	14.13126	13.57771	12.56110	11.65230	10.83777
17	16.25863	15.90502	15.56225	14.90765	14.29187	13.16612	12.16567	11.27407
18	17.17277	16.77918	16.39827	15.67256	14.99203	13.75351	12.65930	11.68959
19	18.08236	17.64683	17.22601	16.42617	15.67846	14.32380	13.13394	12.08532
20	18.98742	18.50802	18.04555	17.16864	16.35143	14.87747	13.59033	12.46221
21	19.88798	19.36280	18.85698	17.90014	17.01121	15.41502	14.02916	12.82115
22	20.78406	20.21121	19.66038	18.62082	17.65805	15.93692	14.45112	13.16300
23	21.67568	21.05331	20.45582	19.33086	18.29220	16.44361	14.85684	13.48857
24	22.56287	21.88915	21.24339	20.03041	18.91393	16.93554	15.24696	13.79864
25	23.44564	22.71876	22.02316	20.71961	19.52346	17.41315	15.62208	14.09394
26	24.32402	23.54219	22.79520	21.39863	20.12104	17.87684	15.98277	14.37519
27	25.19803	24.35949	23.55961	22.06762	20.70690	18.32703	16.32959	14.64303
28	26.06769	25.17071	24.31644	22.72672	21.28127	18.76411	16.66306	14.89813
29	26.93302	25.97589	25.06579	23.37608	21.84438	19.18845	16.98371	15.14107
30	27.79405	26.77508	25.80771	24.01584	22.39646	19.60044	17.29203	15.37245
31	28.65080	27.56832	26.54229	24.64615	22.93770	20.00043	17.58849	15.59281
32	29.50328	28.35565	27.26959	25.26714	23.46833	20.38877	17.87355	15.80268
33	30.35153	29.13712	27.98969	25.87895	23.98856	20.76579	18.14765	16.00255
34	31.19555	29.91278	28.70267	26.48173	24.49859	21.13184	18.41120	16.19290
35	32.03537	30.68266	29.40858	27.07559	24.99862	21.48722	18.66461	16.37419
36	32.87102	31.44681	30.10751	27.66068	25.48884	21.83225	18.90828	16.54685
37	33.70250	32.20527	30.79951	28.23713	25.96945	22.16724	19.14258	16.71129
38	34.52985	32.95808	31.48466	28.80505	26.44064	22.49246	19.36786	16.86789
39	35.35309	33.70529	32.16303	29.36458	26.90259	22.80822	19.58448	17.01704
40	36.17223	34.44694	32.83469	29.91585	27.35548	23.11477	19.79277	17.15909
48	42.58032	40.18478	37.97396	34.04255	30.67312	25.26671	21.19513	18.07716
60	51.72556	48.17337	44.95504	39.38027	34.76089	27.67556	22.62349	18.92929

6%	7%	8%	9%	10%	11%	12%	15%	(n) Periods
.94340	.93458	.92593	.91743	.90909	.90090	.89286	.86957	1
1.83339	1.80802	1.78326	1.75911	1.73554	1.71252	1.69005	1.62571	2
2.67301	2.62432	2.57710	2.53130	2.48685	2.44371	2.40183	2.28323	3
3.46511	3.38721	3.31213	3.23972	3.16986	3.10245	3.03735	2.85498	4
4.21236	4.10020	3.99271	3.88965	3.79079	3.69590	3.60478	3.35216	5
4.91732	4.76654	4.62288	4.48592	4.35526	4.23054	4.11141	3.78448	6
5.58238	5.38929	5.20637	5.03295	4.86842	4.71220	4.56376	4.16042	7
6.20979	5.97130	5.74664	5.53482	5.33493	5.14612	4.96764	4.48732	8
6.80169	6.51523	6.24689	5.99525	5.75902	5.53705	5.32825	4.77158	9
7.36009	7.02358	6.71008	6.41766	6.14457	5.88923	5.65022	5.01877	10
7.88687	7.49867	7.13896	6.80519	6.49506	6.20652	5.93770	5.23371	11
8.38384	7.94269	7.53608	7.16073	6.81369	6.49236	6.19437	5.42062	12
8.85268	8.35765	7.90378	7.48690	7.10336	6.74987	6.42355	5.58315	13
9.29498	8.74547	8.24424	7.78615	7.36669	6.98187	6.62817	5.72448	14
9.71225	9.10791	8.55948	8.06069	7.60608	7.19087	6.81086	5.84737	15
10.10590	9.44665	8.85137	8.31256	7.82371	7.37916	6.97399	5.95424	16
10.47726	9.76322	9.12164	8.54363	8.02155	7.54879	7.11963	6.04716	17
10.82760	10.05909	9.37189	8.75563	8.20141	7.70162	7.24967	6.12797	18
11.15812	10.33560	9.60360	8.95012	8.36492	7.83929	7.36578	6.19823	19
11.46992	10.59401	9.81815	9.12855	8.51356	7.96333	7.46944	6.25933	20
11.76408	10.83553	10.01680	9.29224	8.64869	8.07507	7.56200	6.31246	21
12.04158	11.06124	10.20074	9.44243	8.77154	8.17574	7.64465	6.35866	22
12.30338	11.27219	10.37106	9.58021	8.88322	8.26643	7.71843	6.39884	23
12.55036	11.46933	10.52876	9.70661	8.98474	8.34814	7.78432	6.43377	24
12.78336	11.65358	10.67478	9.82258	9.07704	8.42174	7.84314	6.46415	25
13.00317	11.82578	10.80998	9.92897	9.16095	8.48806	7.89566	6.49056	26
13.21053	11.98671	10.93516	10.02658	9.23722	8.54780	7.94255	6.51353	27
13.40616	12.13711	11.05108	10.11613	9.30657	8.60162	7.98442	6.53351	28
13.59072	12.27767	11.15841	10.19828	9.36961	8.65011	8.02181	6.55088	29
13.76483	12.40904	11.25778	10.27365	9.42691	8.69379	8.05518	6.56598	30
13.92909	12.53181	11.34980	10.34280	9.47901	8.73315	8.08499	6.57911	31
14.08404	12.64656	11.43500	10.40624	9.52638	8.76860	8.11159	6.59053	32
14.23023	12.75379	11.51389	10.46444	9.56943	8.80054	8.13535	6.60046	33
14.36814	12.85401	11.58693	10.51784	9.60858	8.82932	8.15656	6.60910	34
14.49825	12.94767	11.65457	10.56682	9.64416	8.85524	8.17550	6.61661	35
14.62099	13.03521	11.71719	10.61176	9.67651	8.87859	8.19241	6.62314	36
14.73678	13.11702	11.77518	10.65299	9.70592	8.89963	8.20751	6.62882	37
14.84602	13.19347	11.82887	10.69082	9.73265	8.91859	8.22099	6.63375	38
14.94907	13.26493	11.87858	10.72552	9.75697	8.93567	8.23303	6.63805	39
15.04630	13.33171	11.92461	10.75736	9.77905	8.95105	8.24378	6.64178	40
15.65003	13.73047	12.18914	10.93358	9.89693	9.03022	8.29716	6.65853	48
16.16143	14.03918	12.37655	11.04799	9.96716	9.07356	8.32405	6.66515	60

Glossary

accelerated depreciation any method of depreciation that systematically allocates more of an asset's cost to expense in the earlier years of the asset's life and less in later years, such as the declining-balance method.

accounting the process of identifying, measuring, classifying and accumulating, summarizing, and communicating information about economic entities that is primarily quantitative and is useful to decision makers.

accounting cycle the series of steps needed to record, accumulate, process, and report financial information.

accounting entity the organizational unit for which financial statements are prepared.

accounting equation the fundamental relationship of financial statement elements to one another, stated as: Assets = Liabilities + Owners' Equity.

accounts payable amounts due to vendors or suppliers, arising in the normal course of business and, hence, one type of trade payable; reported as a liability in the balance sheet.

accounts receivable amounts due from customers, arising in the normal course of business and, hence, one type of trade receivable; reported as an asset in the balance sheet.

accounts receivable turnover an indicator of efficiency relating to normal trade receivables, computed as net sales revenue divided by accounts receivable.

accrual accounting the system consisting of generally accepted accounting principles used in the preparation of financial statements and relying on recognition and measurement rules for the reporting of revenues and expenses rather than on cash flows.

accrue to grow over time, as when an expense (e.g., rent) accrues during a period.

accrued expenses expenses that increase over time and are reported because the associated benefits are received and an obligation is incurred, although payment is not yet made.

accrued income income that increases over time and is earned and reported before the related cash is received; gives rise to a receivable (e.g., interest receivable).

accumulated depreciation the amount of all depreciation previously recorded on reported plant and equipment since acquisition; recorded in a permanent contra-asset account and deducted from the related assets for financial reporting in the balance sheet.

additional paid-in (or contributed) capital stockholders' equity amounts paid in or contributed to the corporation over and above the amount assigned to capital stock; reported in the balance sheet.

adjusting entries entries made in the accounting records periodically to modify account balances so they are fairly presented in the financial statements.

adverse opinion a type of auditor's report indicating that, in the auditor's opinion, the financial statements are not fairly presented in accordance with generally accepted accounting principles.

aging of accounts an approach to estimating the appropriate balance to report in the allowance for uncollectible accounts, based on the percentage in each of several time-outstanding categories of accounts expected to be uncollected.

allowance for uncollectible accounts a contra-asset account reflecting the amount of accounts receivable not expected to be collected; treated as a deduction from accounts receivable so the balance sheet reports the anticipated amount of cash to be collected on account.

allowance method the generally accepted method used to account for anticipated uncollectible accounts so that the cost of bad debts is matched against the related revenue recognized and accounts receivable are valued at the net amount expected to be collected.

amortization the systematic allocation of an amount to different periods; with respect to intangible assets, the allocation of their cost to the periods benefiting from their use.

annual report a report issued by entities to owners or other interested parties; usually includes financial statements, additional financial data, an auditor's report, and other information about the entity.

annuity a series of equal payments made at equal intervals over time.

articles of copartnership an agreement between partners specifying the rights and responsibilities of all owners in a partnership.

articulation a characteristic of financial statements, that the relationship among the statements is such that they fit together to form a meaningful whole, and a change in one financial statement often results in a change in another.

assets things of value owned or controlled by an entity as a result of past transactions that are expected to provide future benefits; reported in the balance sheet.

asset turnover sales revenue (from operations) divided by (average) total assets; a measure of the effectiveness with which assets are used.

assigning accounts a means of borrowing money by using specific accounts receivable as collateral.

audit an examination of an entity's financial reports, financial records, and accounting system aimed at ensuring the reliability and fairness of reported information.

audit report an auditor's statement indicating the work performed, the responsibility assumed, and an opinion about the fairness of the accompanying financial statements.

auditor an individual who performs audits and who either works within the entity being audited (internal auditor) or is external (independent auditor).

average cost a method of computing the cost of inventory held and sold, determined by dividing the inventory cost by the number of inventory units available during the period, assigning the same cost to all units.

bad debt expense the estimated cost of uncollectible accounts related to the current period's sales; reported as an expense in the income statement.

balance sheet a basic financial statement that reports an entity's financial position at a specific point in time and includes the amounts of its assets, liabilities, and owners' equity.

bank reconciliation an internal document prepared to compare the cash balance from an entity's financial records with the balance reported by the bank; used to reveal discrepancies that might have resulted from errors or dishonesty.

basic earnings per share the amount of earnings for the period accruing to each share of common stock, based on the weighted average number of shares outstanding during the period.

bond a formal financial instrument that reflects an obligation to pay a specified amount of money in the future; usually has a maturity of at least five years.

bond discount the amount by which the par or maturity value of a bond exceeds the issue price at date of issue or book value after issue.

bond indenture the formal agreement between a bond issuer and the bondholders specifying all terms of the bond issue.

bond premium the amount by which the issue price of a bond at date of issue, or book value after issue, exceeds the par or maturity value.

books the formal, permanent financial records of an entity consisting of the journals and ledgers.

book value the amount at which an item is reported in the financial statements, including adjustment for any associated valuation accounts: for a depreciable asset, cost minus accumulated depreciation; for a liability, par or face value minus any discount or plus any premium; for common stock, total stockholders' equity minus the claims of preferred stockholders.

business enterprise an entity or organization that exists to earn a profit by selling goods and/or services.

callable with respect to stock or a bond, able to be retired by the issuer at the issuer's option.

capital the financial resources needed to operate a business enterprise.

capitalized recorded as an asset, usually indicating that it is noncurrent.

capital leases long-term noncancellable rental agreements that transfer most of the rewards and risks of ownership from the lessor (owner) to the lessee.

capital markets a mechanism that facilitates the exchange of cash and other financial resources.

capital stock a security that provides evidence of an ownership interest in a corporation; reported in the stockholders' equity section of the balance sheet.

carrying amount book value.

cash coins, currency, and unrestricted bank deposits; reported as an asset in the balance sheet.

cash cycle the amount of time between the expenditure of cash to acquire resources and the receipt of cash from revenues generated; the operating cycle.

cash discounts a price reduction given for making payment within a specified time.

cash equivalents very short-term marketable securities that can easily be converted to cash; reported as assets in the balance sheet.

cash flow per share cash provided by operations, less preferred dividends, with the difference divided by the number of common shares outstanding; particularly useful as an indicator of a company's ability to pay dividends.

cash flows an organization's cash receipts (cash inflows) or cash payments (cash outflows).

cash flows from operations the amount of cash generated by or used in an organization's normal operating activities; reported in the cash flow statement.

cash flows related to financing cash inflows from borrowing (other than normal trade credit) and from issuing stock and cash outflows to owners and to repay debt; reported in the cash flow statement.

cash flows related to investing cash outflows for the acquisition of property, plant, equipment, and long-term securities and cash inflows from selling such assets; reported in the cash flow statement.

cash flow to current maturities of debt cash provided by operations divided by debt maturing in the near future, excluding normal trade payables; an indicator of the ability to meet current debt obligations.

cash flow to total assets cash flow from operations divided by (average) total assets; used as an indicator of return.

cash flow to total debt cash flow from operations divided by total liabilities; an indicator of the ability to meet debt obligations over the long run.

cash forecasts projections of future cash inflows and outflows.

certified internal auditor (CIA) an accountant who has passed the Certified Internal Auditor Examination and met the education and experience certification requirements established by the Institute of Internal Auditors; internal auditors conduct financial and operational audits of the companies that employ them.

certified management accountant (CMA) an accountant who has passed the Certificate in Management Accounting Examination and met the education and experience certification requirements established by the Institute of Management Accountants; management accountants engage in a full range of accounting and financial activities within an entity.

certified public accountant (CPA) an accountant who has passed the Uniform Certified Public Accountant Examination and met state education and experience certification requirements; CPAs often offer their services to the public and serve as independent external auditors.

change in accounting estimate a change in the estimates made regarding future occurrences that are used in determining the numbers reported in the financial statements.

change in accounting principle a change in the accounting methods used in the preparation of financial statements; a cumulative adjustment for the effects of such changes on retained earnings is reported in the income statement or, in a few special cases, in the retained earnings statement.

chart of accounts a listing (often accompanied by a description) of all of an organization's ledger accounts.

checks outstanding   checks that have been issued but have not cleared the bank of the issuer.

closing entries   accounting entries used to transfer the balances of temporary accounts to retained earnings and to clear the temporary accounts so they can be used to accumulate information for the next accounting period.

common stock   a type of capital stock that represents the true residual ownership of a corporation; usually has the right to vote, has no fixed dividend, and reflects a claim on the assets that ranks lower than the claims of creditors and preferred stockholders; reported in the stockholders' equity section of the balance sheet.

common-size financial statements   financial statements stated in percentages rather than currency units.

comparable   indicating that information is more useful because it is prepared on the same basis as other information to which it might be compared.

comparative financial statements   financial statements for the same entity for different periods, presented together so they can be compared.

compensating balances   cash amounts that must be maintained in bank accounts, usually earning little or no interest, as a requirement for a bank loan; a means by which banks increase the effective interest rate on loans.

completed-contract method   a method of accounting for long-term contracts, such as construction contracts, that recognizes all of the revenue and income upon completion of the contract.

compounding   the earning of interest on principal and previously earned interest.

compound interest   interest that is computed on both principal and previously earned interest.

comprehensive income   an accounting measure of a company's periodic performance equal to the sum of the company's *net income* and its *other comprehensive income*.

conservatism   a concept of accounting that, under certain conditions, discourages recognizing gains and increases in asset values but encourages recognizing losses and decreases in asset values.

consignment   an arrangement in which the owner of merchandise transfers possession but not ownership to another party so the other party may attempt to sell the goods and earn a commission.

consistency   a characteristic of information that makes it more useful because the methods used in its preparation do not change over time.

consolidated financial statements   financial statements of a company (parent) and the other companies (subsidiaries) it controls, presented as if they all were a single company.

contingent liability   a possible future obligation arising from a past event but dependent on future occurrences.

contra account   a valuation account that reduces another account balance.

contra-asset account   a valuation account that offsets (is deducted from) an asset account in the balance sheet.

contra-liability   a valuation account that offsets (is deducted from) a liability account in the balance sheet.

contributed capital   owners' initial and subsequent investment in a corporation; reported in the stockholders' equity section of the balance sheet.

control   the ability to dictate policies; with respect to a corporation, control is usually gained through majority ownership of the outstanding common stock.

controlling interest   in a corporation, those parties able to dictate policies, usually because they hold majority ownership.

convertible bonds   bonds that may be exchanged for the issuer's common stock at the option of the bondholder.

corporation   a form of organization that is a separate legal entity.

cost flow assumptions   with respect to inventory, assumptions made about how the cost of inventory purchased is assigned to units of inventory sold and units of inventory remaining on hand; used when the number of inventory units is so large that identifying the actual cost with specific units is not feasible.

cost of goods sold   the cost of inventory sold during the period; reported as an expense in the income statement.

cost of sales   *cost of goods sold.*

costs   economic sacrifices.

credit   an accounting term referring to an entry on the right side of a ledger account or an entry that increases revenues, liabilities, and owners' equity elements and decreases expenses and assets.

cumulative adjustment from a change in accounting principle   the total effect on a company's retained earnings of changing accounting methods; reported at the bottom of the income statement.

cumulative preferred stock   preferred stock that has the right to any missed dividends before any dividends can be paid to common stockholders; reported in the stockholders' equity section of the balance sheet.

cumulative translation adjustment   an amount that arises from the translation of financial statements stated in a foreign currency into the domestic currency (dollars); reported as an element of owners' equity in the balance sheet.

current assets   cash and those assets expected to be sold, converted into cash, or consumed within one year or the operating cycle of the firm, whichever is longer; an asset category included in a classified balance sheet.

current liabilities   obligations expected to be satisfied within one year or the operating cycle of the firm, whichever is longer, by using current assets or incurring other current liabilities; a liability category included in a classified balance sheet.

current rate method of translation   a method of translating financial statements stated in foreign currency units into the domestic currency using exchange rates for revenues and expenses current when transactions took place and for assets and liabilities, rates current at the balance sheet date.

current ratio   current assets divided by current liabilities; an indicator of liquidity.

debentures   unsecured bonds backed only by an organization's promise to pay; reported as a liability in the balance sheet.

debit   an accounting term referring to an entry on the left side of a ledger account or an entry that increases expenses and assets and decreases revenues, liabilities, and owners' equity elements.

debt-to-equity ratio   a measure of solvency usually computed as the ratio of long-term debt (excluding deferred taxes) to stockholders' equity.

decision a choice from among two or more alternatives.

declaration date the date that a corporation's board of directors votes to pay a specific dividend to holders of a stated class of stock.

declining-balance depreciation a depreciation method in which a fixed percentage is applied to the remaining book value of an asset each period to calculate that period's depreciation expense; the percentage is usually double the straight-line rate.

deferred charges primarily long-term prepaid expenses; reported in the balance sheet.

deferred income taxes differences between the amount of income tax owed to taxing authorities based on taxable income and the amount reported as an expense in the income statement, arising because of differences in when revenues or expenses are recognized for tax reporting and financial reporting.

defined benefit plan a type of pension or other postretirement benefit plan in which the benefits to be received by the retiree are specified.

defined contribution plan a type of pension or other postretirement benefit plan in which contributions to the plan by the employer are specified but benefits depend on, among other things, how successfully contributions are invested.

depletion the allocation of the cost of natural-resource-bearing land that expires because of the removal of the resources.

deposits in transit bank deposits recorded by the depositor but not yet by the bank.

depreciation the systematic allocation of the cost of a tangible operating (fixed) asset to the periods benefiting from its use.

diluted earnings per share the amount of earnings for the period that would accrue to each share of common stock if all outstanding securities convertible into common stock were converted.

dilution of earnings per share the reduction in the amount of earnings accruing to each share of common stock because of the issuance of additional shares.

direct approach an approach to presenting the computation of cash generated from operations in the cash flow statement that starts with cash collections from customers, adds operating cash inflows, and subtracts operating cash outflows; preferred over the indirect approach by the Financial Accounting Standards Board but used by a relatively small number of companies.

disclaimer a statement that the auditor is unable to render an audit opinion because of unusual uncertainties, poor records, or limitations of the scope of the audit.

disclosures information provided by a company to the public; usually refers to information in addition to the elements of the financial statements and includes notes to the financial statements and parenthetical presentations in the body of the financial statements.

discontinued operations a major business activity in which the enterprise will no longer engage.

discount with respect to bonds or stock, the amount by which the par or stated value exceeds the issue price.

discounting the process of determining the present value of some future cash payment(s).

discount rate the interest rate that equates a future cash payment or stream of future cash payments to the present value; expresses a time value of money.

dividend a distribution of income from a corporation to its owners.

dividend payout the portion of a company's net income that it distributes to the owners.

dividends to operating cash flow the ratio of current dividends to cash generated from operations; an indication of how secure the dividends are.

dividend yield the cash dividend per share of stock divided by the price per share.

double-declining-balance depreciation declining-balance depreciation using a rate that is twice the straight-line rate.

double-entry bookkeeping the type of accounting system employed by most organizations that recognizes that each transaction has at least two effects and, therefore, records each transaction in at least two accounts; the dual effect also permits a regular check on the functioning of the system.

drawing rights the right to withdraw cash from a business, generally used with respect to a partnership.

earnings per share the amount of net income accruing to each share of common stock; reported on the face of the income statement.

effective interest method the accounting method of amortizing the discount or premium associated with a financial instrument that recognizes interest each period based on the yield of the instrument at issuance applied to the book value of the instrument.

effective rate the actual interest rate, including compounding; the yield.

Electronic Data Gathering, Analysis, and Retrieval (EDGAR) system a database containing submissions of financial and other reports by companies required to file forms with the U.S. Securities and Exchange Commission.

entering recording a transaction in the accounting records, or more specifically, in the journal.

entity in accounting, the organization or enterprise for which accounting reports are presented.

equities owners' claims against the assets of a business enterprise; reported in the balance sheet.

exchange rate with respect to currencies, the rate at which one currency can be changed into units of another.

exchange transaction an economic event in which one party gives something of value to another and receives something of value in return.

ex-dividend date the first date that a share of stock trades without the right to the latest dividend.

expenses the cost of goods and services used up in conducting a business's central operations; reported in the income statement.

expired costs costs not expected to provide future benefits.

extraordinary gains and losses gains and losses that are both unusual and infrequently recurring; reported in a separate section of the income statement.

extraordinary items *extraordinary gains and loses.*

face amount   the stated amount of a note or bond that must be paid at maturity; par value.

financial accounting   the area of accounting dealing with providing financial information to decision makers that are external to the reporting entity.

financial audit   the process of gathering information about an entity to form an opinion on the fairness of its financial statements.

financial statement elements   the individual revenue, expense, gain, loss, asset, liability, and owners' equity items reported in the financial statements.

financial statements   accounting reports that provide financial information about an entity's operations, financial position, cash flows, and changes in equity.

Financial Accounting Standards Board (FASB)   the primary private-sector body responsible for developing financial accounting and reporting standards for nongovernmental entities.

financing cash flows   see *cash flows related to financing.*

finished goods   manufactured inventories that are completed and ready for sale to customers; reported as an asset in the balance sheet.

first-in, first-out (FIFO)   an inventory cost-flow assumption that the first inventory costs incurred are the first expensed when goods are sold.

fiscal year   the twelve-month period chosen for financial reporting.

fixed asset turnover   a measure of operating efficiency, calculated as operating revenues divided by fixed assets.

fixed assets   *property, plant, and equipment.*

fixed costs   costs that do not vary with changes in the level of operating activity.

footnotes   *notes to the financial statements.*

Form 8-K   a report describing any unscheduled material event, required to be filed with the Securities and Exchange Commission by all companies with publicly traded securities within fifteen days of the occurrence of the event.

Form 10-K   a report required to be filed annually with the Securities and Exchange Commission by all companies with publicly traded securities; it includes audited financial statements and other disclosures.

Form 10-Q   a report required to be filed quarterly with the Securities and Exchange Commission by all companies with publicly traded securities; it includes unaudited financial statements.

forward exchange contract   an agreement for the exchange of currencies at a specified time in the future using an exchange rate established at the time of the agreement.

forward rate   the rate set currently for the exchange of currencies at a specified future time.

free cash flow   the amount of cash generated from operations after maintaining productive capacity.

free on board (f.o.b.)   terms of trade, indicating whether the seller or purchaser pays the freight charges on goods shipped.

freight-in   shipping charges on goods purchased.

functional currency   the primary currency used in operating activities; relevant when translating the financial statements of foreign subsidiaries or divisions.

future value   a cash amount at a specified time in the future.

gains   increases in net assets from peripheral or incidental transactions or events.

general journal entry form   accounting notation used to record transactions in handwritten systems, with all accounts and amounts to be debited on top and to the left and all accounts to be credited on the bottom and to the right.

general ledger   the set of accounting records in which information is accumulated by individual financial statement element.

generally accepted accounting principles (GAAP)   the body of concepts, practices, and procedures that serves as the basis for financial reporting to external parties; developed through historical usage and pronouncements of authoritative bodies.

going-concern concept   a basic concept of accounting stating that, in the absence of evidence to the contrary, the reporting entity should be viewed as continuing in operation indefinitely, and its assets and liabilities should be valued accordingly.

goodwill   an intangible asset reflecting the combination of those factors that increase the earning power of an enterprise so that its value as a whole is greater than the value of its net assets; reported in the balance sheet.

gross margin   net sales revenue minus cost of goods sold; shown in a multi-step income statement.

gross profit   *gross margin.*

gross profit (margin) percentage   gross profit divided by net sales revenue.

hedge   with respect to foreign currencies, a means of avoiding the risks of currency fluctuations, usually by entering into an exchange agreement to offset an exposed position.

historical cost   original sacrifice; the exchange price when an asset was acquired or a liability incurred.

horizontal analysis   *trend analysis.*

implicit interest   interest included in the face amount of a financial instrument without it being stated explicitly.

income statement   a basic financial statement that reports the results of a business enterprise's operations and includes the amounts of revenues, expenses, gains, losses, and net income for the fiscal period.

indirect approach   an approach to presenting the computation of cash generated from operations in the cash flow statement that starts with net income and adjusts for items that affect income differently from cash flows; used by most companies.

intangible assets   noncurrent assets, other than financial instruments, that lack physical existence; reported in the balance sheet.

interest-bearing notes   written promises to pay that include explicitly stated interest.

interim financial reports   financial reports issued between annual reports, usually quarterly.

internal control   the set of policies and procedures established within an entity aimed at safeguarding the entity's resources, ensuring compliance with the entity's policies, and providing for the reliability of information.

international accounting standards   policies and procedures for external financial reporting that are not specific to an individual country but are meant to have applicability to financial reporting in many countries.

International Accounting Standards Committee (IASC) a committee with representation from many countries having the purpose of establishing international accounting standards.

inventory goods held for sale to customers, or parts, materials, and supplies to be used in producing goods to sell to customers.

inventory turnover a measure of efficiency related to inventory, calculated as cost of goods sold divided by the (average) inventory balance.

investing cash flows see *cash flows related to investing.*

investments an asset category on the balance sheet that includes long-term holdings of stocks, bonds, notes of other companies, government securities, and real estate and other items held for appreciation in value rather than to be used in operations.

journal the set of accounting records in which transactions are initially entered and are included in their entirety in chronological order; the books of original entry.

journalizing the act of making or recording an entry in the journal.

last-in, first-out (LIFO) an inventory cost-flow assumption that the last inventory costs incurred are the first expensed when goods are sold.

ledger accounts devices within the general ledger used to accumulate information about individual financial statement elements.

legal capital an amount defined by state law as not being available for distribution to owners; usually the par or stated value of the capital stock issued.

lessee a party having the right to use the property of another (lessor) through an agreement that provides for a specified payment in exchange.

lessor a party allowing the use of owned property by another (lessee) through an agreement that provides for a specified payment in exchange.

leverage the use of long-term debt for financing an enterprise's operations; usually measured by comparing the amount of a company's debt with its equity.

liabilities present obligations for probable future sacrifices of economic benefits; reported in the balance sheet.

limited liability a legal characteristic of a corporation by which claims against the corporation normally are limited to the corporation's assets; thus, potential losses by owners of a corporation are limited to the amount they have invested in the corporation.

liquidity the availability of cash.

long-term liabilities those liabilities not classified as current; typically those obligations that are not expected to be satisfied within one year, or the operating cycle of the firm, whichever is longer.

losses decreases in net assets from peripheral or incidental transactions or events.

lower-of-cost-or-market rule a general rule for reporting most inventories requiring that they be reported at their original cost or current market value, whichever is lower.

management's discussion and analysis (MD&A) a section of the Securities and Exchange Commission's required 10-K filing, also included in many companies' annual reports, providing management's analysis of the company's activities and position and detailing why changes occurred from the previous year.

managerial accounting the area of accounting dealing with providing financial information to decision makers within an entity.

margin on sales net income divided by net sales revenue.

market economy an economy in which individual decision makers decide how much to produce, how much to buy, and when to engage in exchange transactions; thus, market forces determine prices and the assortment and quantities of goods and services provided.

marketable securities financial instruments that can be sold readily in organized markets; reported as assets in the balance sheet.

matching concept a basic concept of accounting stating that costs should be recognized in the same period as the associated benefits.

materiality the level of significance of an item of information for a decision; amounts too small to have an effect on a decision are considered immaterial.

minority interest the noncontrolling ownership of a corporation (subsidiary) in which another corporation (parent) holds a controlling interest.

Modified Accelerated Cost Recovery System (MACRS) an accelerated method of depreciation acceptable for federal income tax reporting.

net after subtracting or offsetting another amount.

net assets assets minus liabilities; equal to owners' equity.

net earnings *net income.*

net income revenues and gains minus expenses and losses; the bottom line reported in the income statement.

net loss negative net income, occurring when expenses and losses exceed revenues and gains.

net sales sales revenue less sales returns and allowances.

net worth the difference between assets and liabilities.

nominal interest rate the stated interest rate, typically used to compute cash interest payments.

nonbusiness entity an organization engaged in activities not aimed at earning profits; governmental and not-for-profit entities.

noncontrolling interest see *minority interest.*

noncurrent assets those assets not classified as current; noncurrent categories on the balance sheet typically include Investments, Plant and Equipment, and Intangibles.

noninterest-bearing notes written promises to pay that do not include explicitly stated interest; interest typically is implicit in the face amount of the note.

no-par stock capital stock having no assigned par value; it may have a stated value.

notes payable a written promise to pay cash to another party; reported as a liability in the balance sheet.

notes receivable a written claim to receive cash from another party, usually a customer unless indicated otherwise; reported as an asset in the balance sheet.

notes to the financial statements the additional disclosures included with the financial statements to provide explanations or greater detail.

number of times interest is earned a measure of the ability to service debt, calculated as operating income divided by interest on long-term debt.

objectivity a basic concept of accounting stating that information reported in financial statements should be reliable and subject to verification.

operating cash flows see *cash flows from operations.*

operating cycle the average time needed to complete one full set of transactions, going from cash to inventory (if any), to receivables, back to cash.

operating income revenues less operating expenses; frequently excludes interest.

operating leases a rental agreement under which most of the rewards and risks of ownership are retained by the property owner.

opportunity cost the sacrifice made by not undertaking the next best alternative.

organization costs costs associated with starting a new business; reported as an intangible asset on the balance sheet.

other comprehensive income an element of *comprehensive income* that includes (1) unrealized gains and losses on available-for-sale investments in securities, (2) certain pension adjustments, and (3) foreign-currency translation adjustments.

owners' equity the owners' claim on the assets of the business entity, generally equal to amounts contributed by the owners and undistributed profits; reported in the balance sheet.

parent company a corporation that holds a controlling interest in another corporation.

participating preferred stock preferred stock that shares in dividends with the common stock on a basis stated in the preferred stock agreement.

partnership an association of two or more individuals or entities to engage in business activities for a profit.

par value the maturity value of a bond, or an arbitrary amount assigned by the issuer to a share of capital stock.

payment date with respect to dividends, the date that dividend checks are mailed to stockholders.

percentage-of-completion method a method of accounting for long-term contracts under which income is recognized as the project progresses rather than when it is completed.

periodic inventory system a method of accounting for inventory costs under which current balances for inventory and cost of goods sold are not maintained but are determined at the end of the accounting period after counting the remaining inventory on hand.

periodicity a basic concept of accounting stating that financial information is most useful if it is provided to decision makers periodically and that such information is tentative because it requires that accounting allocations be made between past, present, and future periods.

permanent accounts ledger accounts that are not closed to retained earnings at the end of each period but carry their balances over from period to period; reported on the balance sheet.

perpetual inventory system a method of accounting for inventory costs under which current balances for inventory and cost of goods sold are maintained during the accounting period.

planned economy a type of economy in which key decisions relating to prices and the allocation of resources are made by a central planning authority.

posting the process of transferring amounts entered in the journal to the appropriate ledger accounts.

postretirement benefits benefits provided by a company to its retirees, including pensions and health-care benefits.

preemptive right the right of current stockholders to maintain their proportionate ownership in a corporation by purchasing new shares of stock before the shares are offered to others.

preferred stock a type of capital stock that has a higher claim on assets and dividends than common stock; typically has a fixed dividend and liquidation value and lacks the right to vote; reported in the stockholders' equity section of the balance sheet.

premium with respect to bonds or stock, the amount by which the issue price exceeds the par or stated value.

prepaid expenses amounts paid in advance for operating expenses that will benefit future periods; reported as assets in the balance sheet.

present value an amount today equivalent to a future cash payment or stream of future cash payments given a specific time value of money.

price-earnings ratio the ratio of the per share price of a company's common stock to its earnings per common share; often viewed as an indicator of the stock market's assessment of the company's future earnings potential.

prior period adjustments corrections of errors in previously issued financial statements.

profit net income.

pro forma amounts amounts computed "as if" a specified event had occurred.

property, plant, and equipment long-lived tangible operating assets; a balance sheet category.

qualified opinion a type of auditor's report indicating that the financial statements overall are fairly presented, but a specific item or set of items within the statements is not in accordance with generally accepted accounting principles or the disclosure is inadequate.

quality of earnings an attribute of reported earnings related to the extent to which accounting methods have affected the amount reported; conservative accounting methods are viewed as resulting in higher quality earnings.

quick ratio quick assets (cash, short-term marketable securities, current receivables) divided by current liabilities; a stringent measure of liquidity.

raw materials a type of inventory representing one of the basic inputs to the manufacturing process; reported as an asset on the balance sheet.

realizable value the amount of cash expected to be received from an asset.

realization the process of converting noncash assets into cash or claims to cash.

realization concept a basic concept of accounting indicating that revenues normally are recognized when they are earned and an exchange has taken place.

recognition the process of recording an item in the financial records of an entity so that it is reported in the financial statements.

record date with respect to dividends declared, the date on which a company compiles a list of stockholders from its current records to receive its latest dividend.

recourse the right to require payment, as against the seller of a receivable if the debtor does not pay.

registrants organizations filing registration statements with the Securities and Exchange Commission.

registration statement a report required to be filed with the Securities and Exchange Commission before securities can be issued to the public; must include audited financial statements.

relevant with respect to information, pertaining to the decision at hand by having feedback or predictive value and being timely.

reliable with respect to information, providing confidence to users that the information represents what it purports to represent by being representationally faithful, neutral, and verifiable.

replacement cost the cost of replacing an asset currently.

research and development costs costs of developing new products or processes.

residual claims claims that are satisfied after those of others having priority; said of owners' claims because those of creditors must be satisfied first.

retained earnings the undistributed past net income of a corporation since its inception; reported in the stockholders' equity section of the balance sheet.

retained earnings statement a financial statement reporting the changes in a corporation's retained earnings during a fiscal period.

return on assets a measure of the profitability of a company's assets, in its simplest form computed as net income divided by (average) total assets; more correctly computed as net income before financing costs (that is, with the after-tax effect of interest added back) divided by average total assets.

return on common equity a measure of success in employing the capital of common stockholders, computed as the ratio of net income minus preferred dividends to (average) total stockholders' equity minus the claims of preferred stockholders.

return on investment a term used in a number of different ways to indicate the profit from invested money, stated as a percentage of the amount invested.

return on net assets a measure of profitability computed as net income divided by (average) net assets (assets minus liabilities); *return on owners' equity*.

return on owners' equity a measure of profitability computed as net income divided by (average) owners equity; *return on net assets*.

revenues amounts generated from the sale of a company's products or services to customers.

sales returns and allowances the amount of refunds granted to customers for returned or unsatisfactory merchandise.

salvage value the residual value of an operating asset at the end of its useful life to the owner.

secured debt debt backed by collateral on which the creditor has a direct claim in the event of default.

securities financial instruments providing evidence of a claim, usually that of an owner or creditor.

Securities and Exchange Commission (SEC) the federal agency that regulates the public issuance and trading of securities and is charged with assuring full and fair disclosure of information by companies with securities held by the public.

serial bonds bonds that mature in installments.

service-hours method of depreciation a depreciation method that assigns an equal portion of the cost (less salvage value) of an operating asset to each hour the asset is used.

simple interest interest computed without considering the effects of compounding.

sole proprietorship a business enterprise owned by a single person.

solvency the ability of an entity to meet its obligations as they come due.

specific identification a method of assigning cost to units of inventory under which the actual cost of a given unit of inventory is assigned to that unit.

spot rate the current rate at which one currency can be exchanged for another.

stated (nominal) rate the explicit interest rate specified in a borrowing agreement, used to calculate cash interest payments.

stated value an arbitrary amount assigned by the issuer to a share of capital stock, usually indicating legal capital in the absence of a par value.

statement of cash flows a basic financial statement that lists the sources and uses of cash during the fiscal period.

statement of financial position a basic financial statement that reports an entity's financial condition at a specific point in time and includes the amounts of its assets, liabilities, and owners' equity; *balance sheet*.

statement of changes in owners' equity a financial statement that reports the changes during the fiscal period in each of the individual owners' equity accounts.

statement of changes in stockholders' equity a statement of changes in owners' equity for a corporation; reports the changes during the fiscal period in each of the individual stockholders' equity accounts.

stock dividends dividends that are paid in shares of the company's own stock rather than in cash.

stockholders' equity the owners' claim on the assets of a corporation; a category in the balance sheet.

stock options rights to purchase stock, usually at a fixed price.

stock split the replacement of each share of a company's stock with multiple shares (e.g., 2 for 1, 3 for 1), leaving each stockholder with the same proportionate interest as before but evidenced by more shares.

stock warrants financial instruments providing evidence of the owner's right to buy stock at a given price.

straight-line amortization a method that allocates an equal amount (e.g., of intangible-asset cost, bond discount or premium) to each of a number of periods.

straight-line depreciation a depreciation method that assigns an equal portion of the cost (less salvage value) of an operating asset to each period during which the asset is used.

subsidiary a corporation that is controlled by another corporation (parent) through a majority ownership of its common stock.

summary of significant accounting policies a required disclosure that must accompany financial statements issued to the public that briefly describes the accounting methods used in preparing the financial statements; usually included as the first note to the financial statements.

supporting documents papers that provide evidence and details of each transaction or event entered into an entity's accounting records.

T-account a ledger account, especially one that is formatted in the shape of a T.

tangible assets assets having physical existence.

temporary accounts accounts that are used to accumulate information about financial statement elements for one fiscal period at a time and are closed out (their balances are transferred) to retained earnings (or other equity account for noncorporate or nonbusiness entities) at the end of each period; included for a business enterprise are all income statement elements and dividends.

temporary differences differences in income arising from using different recognition methods for financial reporting and tax reporting, leading to events being reported in the financial statements in one period and in the tax return in a different period.

term bonds bonds that mature all at one time.

time value of money the preference for having cash sooner rather than later because money held currently can be used to earn additional money in the future.

timeliness a characteristic of the relevance of information that relates to the information being received by decision makers when it is needed.

times preferred dividends earned a measure of the safety of preferred dividends, calculated as net income divided by the amount of the preferred dividend requirement.

trade payables accounts or notes payable to vendors or suppliers, arising in the normal course of business.

trade receivables accounts or notes receivable from customers, arising in the normal course of business.

treasury stock shares of a company's own stock that had previously been outstanding, were repurchased by the company, and are being held in its treasury for possible redistribution.

trend analysis the examination of a variable or factor over time to determine a pattern.

trial balance a listing of all of an entity's accounts and their balances at a specific point in time.

true no-par stock stock having neither an assigned par nor stated value.

uncollectible accounts accounts receivable that cannot be collected.

understandability a quality of useful information relating to whether decision makers will know what reported information means based on their general knowledge of business and a basic knowledge of accounting.

unearned income an obligation to provide goods or services to another party in the future because cash payment for the goods or services has been received; reported as a liability in the balance sheet.

unexpired costs costs expected to provide future benefits; generally reported as assets in the balance sheet.

units-of-production method of depreciation a depreciation method that assigns an equal portion of the cost (less salvage value) of an operating asset to each unit of inventory the asset is used to produce.

unqualified opinion a type of auditor's report indicating that the financial statements overall are fairly presented in accordance with generally accepted accounting principles.

valuation account an account that modifies the balance of another account by either being added to or deducted from the other balance.

variable costs costs that vary in direct proportion to the level of activity.

vendor a party from which the company purchases goods or services; a supplier.

verifiable with respect to information, capable of being reconstructed by parties other than those who developed the information originally.

vertical analysis an analysis of the individual components of the financial statements in relation to one another.

working capital current assets minus current liabilities.

work-in-process partially completed units of inventory held by a manufacturing company; reported as an asset in the balance sheet.

yield with respect to a debt security (obligation or investment), the actual rate of return; *effective rate.*

zero-coupon bond a bond that makes no cash interest payments (i.e., has a stated interest rate of zero).

Subject Index

Company Index